THE EMC MASTERPIECE SERIES

LITERATURE AND THE LANGUAGE ARTS

The American Tradition

EMC/Paradigm Publishing
St. Paul, Minnesota

Staff Credits:

For **EMC/Paradigm Publishing**, St. Paul, Minnesota

Eileen Slater
Editor

Christine Gensmer
Associate Editor

For **Penobscot School Publishing, Inc.**, Danvers, Massachusetts

Robert D. Shepherd
Executive Editor

Kimberly M. Leahy
Managing Editor

Sara Hyry
Christina Kolb
Associate Editors

Camilla Ayers
Sybil Fetter
Sheila Neylon
Copyeditors

Charles Q. Bent
Production Manager

Sara Day
Art Director

Heath P. O'Leary
Compositor

ISBN 0-8219-1270-4

Published by EMC/Paradigm Publishing
300 York Avenue
St. Paul, Minnesota 55101

Printed in the United States of America.
10 9 8 7 6 5 4 3   XXX 01 00 99 98 97 96

Acknowledgments:

Alfred A. Knopf, Inc.
From OF PLYMOUTH PLANTATION 1620–1647 by William Bradford, edit., Samuel Eliot Morison. Copyright 1952 by Samuel Eliot Morison and renewed 1980 by Emily M Beck. Reprinted by permission of Alfred A Knopf Inc. "The Negro Speaks of Rivers" From SELECTED POEMS by Langston Hughes. Copyright 1926 by Alfred A Knopf Inc and renewed 1954 by Langston Hughes. Reprinted by permission of the publisher. "Disillusionment of Ten O'Clock," "The Snow Man," "Anecdote of the Jar," and "Thirteen Ways of Looking at a Blackbird," From COLLECTED POEMS by Wallace Stevens. Copyright 1923 and renewed 1951 by Wallace Stevens. Reprinted by permission of Alfred A Knopf Inc. "Bells for John Whiteside's Daughter" From SELECTED POEMS by John Crowe Ransom. Copyright 1924 by Alfred A Knopf Inc and renewed 1952 by John Crowe Ransom. Reprinted by permission of the publisher.

The Archives of Claude McKay
"The Tropics in New York" by Claude McKay. Used by permission of The Archives of Claude McKay, Carl Cowl, Administrator.

Bantam Doubleday Dell Publishing Group, Inc.
"Pride and the Proudhammers", from TELL ME HOW LONG THE TRAIN'S BEEN GONE by James Baldwin. Copyright © 1968 by James Baldwin. Used by permission of Doubleday, a division of Bantam Doubleday Dell Publishing Group, Inc. "An Occurrence at Owl Creek Bridge" from *The Complete Stories of Ambrose Bierce*, published by Doubleday & Company, Inc. "I Stand Here Ironing", copyright © 1956, 1957, 1960, 1961 by Tillie Olsen. From TELL ME A RIDDLE by Tillie Olsen. Introduction by John Leonard. Used by permission of Delacorte Press/Seymour Lawrence, a division of Bantam Doubleday Dell Publishing Group, Inc. "The Geranium," copyright 1963 by Beatrice Roethke, Administratrix of the Estate of Theodore Roethke. From THE COLLECTED POEMS OF THEODORE ROETHKE by Theodore Roethke. Used by permission of Doubleday, a division of Bantam Doubleday Dell Publishing Group, Inc.

(continued on page 1083)

LITERATURE AND THE LANGUAGE ARTS

MAPLE LEVEL
THE BRITISH TRADITION

PINE LEVEL
THE AMERICAN TRADITION

WILLOW LEVEL
UNDERSTANDING LITERATURE

BIRCH LEVEL
EXPERIENCING LITERATURE

Consultants and Writers

Edmund J. Farrell, Ph.D.
Emeritus Professor of English
  Education
University of Texas at Austin

Roger Dick
Teacher of English and Humanities
Brooklyn Center High School
Brooklyn Center, Minnesota

David England, Ph.D.
Associate Dean for Teacher
  Education
Louisiana State University

Ellen Gabin
Consultant, Hispanic Literature
Rockport, Massachusetts

Donald Gray, Ph.D.
Professor of English
Indiana University

Susan Gubar, Ph.D.
Professor of English
Indiana University

Dael Angelico-Hart
Director of Language Arts
Danvers Public Schools
Danvers, Massachusetts

Gail Ross Hatcher
English Department Chairperson
T. Wingate Andrews High School
High Point, North Carolina

Jim O'Laughlin
Lecturer
University College
Northwestern University

Jane S. Shoaf, Ph.D.
Instructional Specialist for
  Communication Skills (retired)
North Carolina Department of
  Public Instruction

Kendra Sisserson
Language Arts Curriculum
  Facilitator
Academy for Aerospace Technology
Cocoa, Florida

Donald L. Stephan
English Department Chair
Sidney High School
Sidney, Ohio

James W. Swanson
English Instructor
Robbinsdale Armstrong High
  School
Plymouth, Minnesota

Jill Triplett
Special Collections Assistant
Wellesley College

Hope Vasholz
Teacher of English
Hammond High School
Columbia, Maryland

Arlette Ingram Willis, Ph.D.
Assistant Professor in the
  Department of Curriculum and
  Instruction
University of Illinois at Urbana-
  Champaign

Contents

To the Student

Reading Literature

Have you ever become so wrapped up in a movie that when the credits started to roll and the lights came up, you felt a kind of shock? One moment you were in the world on the screen, perhaps identifying with some hero and feeling her joys and sorrows. The next moment you were back in your own world again. The art of the filmmaker transported you from your time and place into another and back again.

When you read a good story, poem, or play, the same sort of transport should take place. The key to reading literature is to use your imagination to take the journey planned for you by the writer. This willingness to extend yourself imaginatively is the most important characteristic that you can have as a reader. Suppose, for example, that you read the following passage in a story:

> Three lions, a male and two females, lay sunning beside what remained of a kill—an eland, perhaps. We approached in the Range Rover. They ignored us. Chico stopped about fifty meters away, and we both took out binoculars for a closer look. The lions lay heavily, dreamily, sated, self-satisfied. A slight breeze ruffled their fur, yellow-brown like the savannah grass in this season between the rains. It was Chico who noticed that the kill wasn't an eland at all, for attached to part of it was, unmistakably, a large black boot.

It is possible to read that passage and comprehend it, intellectually, without having experienced it. However, reading literature is all about having experiences. To read the passage well, you need to picture three lions, to imagine what it might be like to approach them, to see in your mind's eye the yellow grass, to feel the slight breeze, to notice the boot. If you have done that—if you have imagined the scene vividly—then it will have an impact on you. That impact will be its significance—its meaning for you.

Imagine that you have taken a journey. You have hiked up a mountainside in Peru or have wandered though the Valley of the Kings in Egypt. You have gone shopping in the Ginza district of Tokyo or have bounced in a spacesuit over the surface of the moon. After such an experience, you return home a different person. You think about the experience and what it meant to you.

A work of literature is an opportunity to take just such an exotic journey. Using your imagination, you take the writer's trip. You have an experience. Then you reflect on the experience that you had. You think about what you thought and felt, about what the experience meant to you. That reflection is called **reader response.**

When you sit down to read a literary work, remember that your task, at that moment, is not to prepare for a quiz or to get ready for a class discussion. Your task is to use your imagination to have the experience that the writer has prepared for you. Think of the writer as a tour guide to interesting times and places. In those times and places, you will meet fascinating people and have powerful, moving experiences, ones that will enrich your life immeasurably.

Sharing Your Responses with Others

No two people are exactly alike. Because of this wonderful fact, the experience that you have when reading a particular story, poem, or play will be different from the experience had by the student who sits next to you. That's what makes discussing literature with other students interesting. You can share your experiences with others and learn from them. In this course you will have many opportunities to share responses in class discussion and in collaborative projects.

Educating Your Imagination

You might naturally ask, at the beginning of a course such as this, what you stand to gain from it. Two answers to that question have already been suggested: First, reading literature will provide you with many fascinating imaginative experiences. Second, discussing that literature and doing collaborative projects will provide opportunities for sharing with others. A third answer is implicit in the first two: Reading literature and sharing responses with others will educate your imagination. It will train you to think and feel in new ways.

Life is short, opportunities for real-life experience are limited, and events often happen only once, without your having had the chance to practice, first, how you might react to them. Reading literature is a way around all those difficulties. Through reading, you can find out what it might be like to sail around the globe, to march into battle, to fall in love, to lose a friend, to win a great prize, to live in the rain forest, to be faced with a moral dilemma, to confront your greatest fear, to travel backward in time or forward into the future. Writers write because they want to share interesting, valuable experiences with you—the reader. In the process of reading literary works and thinking about your own and others' responses to them, you will exercise your imaginative faculties and grow in ways that might otherwise have been impossible.

Using this Text

This text is first and foremost a literature anthology. The selections in units 1–12 have been chosen both for their historical importance and for their current relevance to the interests of students like you. To assist you in understanding the selections, the authors and editors have created activities that appear before and after the selections. These activities will also help you to develop your abilities in many language arts areas. Most of these activities ask you to refer to the section at the back of the book called the Language Arts Survey. Before doing the activity, you will read a section of the Survey, which will introduce you to some key concepts. Then you will apply what you have learned from the Survey when doing the activity.

Part One

UNDERSTANDING LITERATURE

UNIT 1 GENRES AND TECHNIQUES OF LITERATURE

In the Morning. *Winslow Homer*

'T is the good reader that makes the good book.

—Ralph Waldo Emerson
"Success"

The Oral Tradition

Are there favorite stories that people in your family like to tell? When you were a child, did people tell you bedtime stories? Did you learn rhymes and jingles and songs from your friends? Have you ever sat around a campfire and told ghost stories? Have you ever heard a minister, priest, rabbi, or teacher tell a story to make a point? If so, then you have experienced the oral tradition.

One pretty good definition of human beings is that we are storytelling creatures. Long before people invented writing, they were telling stories about their gods and heroes and experiences. The best of these stories were passed by word-of-mouth from generation to generation to form the basis of the literature that we know today. Some early stories were told in the form of poems. Some were in the form of songs. Others were in the form of what we would now call prose tales.

The passing of stories, poems, and songs by word-of-mouth from person to person is called oral transmission. The body of work created in this way in a particular culture is called that culture's oral tradition.

The United States is blessed with an enormous diversity in its people. No other country in the world has citizens from so many different races and ethnic backgrounds. The United States cannot, therefore, be said to have a single oral tradition. Rather, it has hundreds of oral traditions with origins in Native American culture and in Europe, Africa, Asia, and other parts of the globe. From the trickster tales of the Plains Indians to Yiddish tales told by European Jewish immigrants, from work songs and spirituals with roots in Africa to Scots-Irish ballads and western tall tales—America offers a feast for the professional folklorist, for students of literature, and for ordinary readers of the many collections of American folk literature.

The following are some common types of oral literature found in the United States:

Myths are stories about heroes and gods. Often myths explain where things came from or how the world took the shape that it has today.

Tall tales are stories with wildly exaggerated elements. Washington Irving's "The Legend of Sleepy Hollow" (Unit 4) is a literary version of a tall tale. Other examples would be the common childhood stories of Pecos Bill, Paul Bunyan, and Annie Oakley.

Legends are stories about famous people. Some are true; others are not. An example of a legend is the story of George Washington chopping down the cherry tree.

Ballads are poems or songs that tell stories. Examples of American ballads include "John Henry" and "Casey Jones."

Spirituals are religious songs from the African-American folk tradition. Examples of spirituals include "Follow the Drinking Gourd" (Unit 1) and "Swing Low, Sweet Chariot" (Unit 6).

Other works commonly found in the oral tradition include **parables, fables, fairy tales, epics,** and **proverbs.** For definitions of these, see the Handbook of Literary Terms.

The Lord Is My Shepherd. Eastman Johnson. National Museum of American Art, Washington DC/Art Resource, NY

"Follow the Drinking Gourd"[1]

ANONYMOUS AFRICAN-AMERICAN SONG OF THE UNDERGROUND RAILROAD

When the sun comes back and the first quail calls,
   Follow the drinking gourd,
For the old man is a-waiting for to carry you to freedom
   If you follow the drinking gourd.

Chorus

5   Follow the drinking gourd,
   Follow the drinking gourd,
For the old man is a-waiting for to carry you to freedom
   If you follow the drinking gourd.

The river bank will make a very good road,
10   The dead trees show you the way,
Left foot, peg foot[2] traveling on
   Follow the drinking gourd.

Repeat Chorus

The river ends between two hills,
   Follow the drinking gourd.
15 There's another river on the other side,
   Follow the drinking gourd.

Repeat Chorus

Where the little river meets the great big river,
   Follow the drinking gourd.
The old man is a-waiting for to carry you to freedom
20   If you follow the drinking gourd. ∎

---

1. **Drinking Gourd.** Dried, hollowed-out shell of a fruit (a melon or pumpkin, for example) used for dipping water to drink. In this selection, the speaker is using *drinking gourd* as code words for the Big Dipper, a constellation that served as a guide for escaping slaves.

2. **peg foot.** Wooden foot (replacement for a person's foot)

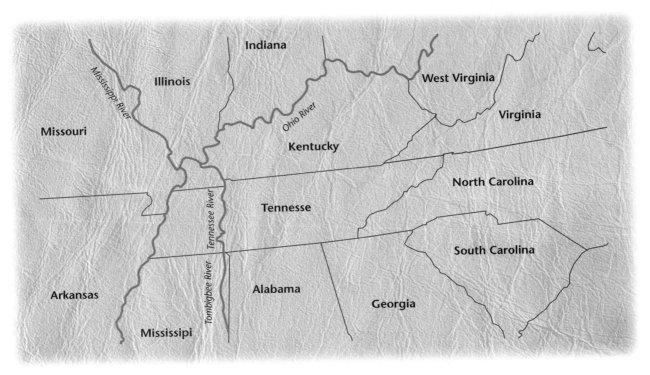

When the sun comes back and the first quail calls,— fol-low—— the drink-ing gourd, For the old man is a-wait-ing for to car-ry you to free-dom if you fol-low the drink-ing gourd.

Fol-low—— the drink-ing gourd, Fol-low—— the drink-ing gourd. For the old man is a-wait-ing for to car-ry you to free-dom if you fol-low the drink-ing gourd.

Responding to the Selection

What do you think it would be like to run for your life and for your freedom? How might communicating through songs help you cope with the stresses of your journey? Conversely, how might the need to communicate in code, for example by calling the guiding Big Dipper a "drinking gourd," burden you?

Reviewing the Selection

1. Who is singing this song? Where are they going and why? When are the travelers supposed to journey?

2. Who waits for the travelers?

3. How can the travelers use natural elements to help them find the way? What element recurs to guide them?

4. Where do the rivers lead the travelers?

5. What overriding image is used to guide the travelers toward their destination? Why is this signpost not openly identified? What time of year might be suggested by these natural events?

6. How will the person who waits help the travelers? Who might he be?

7. What forces influence the journey of the travelers? Why must they keep "traveling on"?

8. What might "the other side" refer to? What might the "great big river" be?

9. What can you infer about the challenges facing escaping slaves from your reading of "Follow the Drinking Gourd"?

10. How does the map accompanying the selection help you visualize the path taken by the travelers? In what ways do you think seeing the "drinking gourd" in the sky helped the travelers visualize their path to freedom?

Understanding Literature (Questions for Discussion)

1. **Theme.** A **theme** is a central idea in a literary work. What do you think is the theme of "Follow the Drinking Gourd"?

2. **Repetition. Repetition** is the use, again, of a sound, word, phrase, sentence, or other element. Through repetition writers return to or focus on their main points. What phrase is repeated again and again in "Follow the Drinking Gourd"?

3. **Spiritual.** A **spiritual** is a song, often but not always religious in context. The style originated in the South, among slaves who needed to express their sorrow and frustration in a nonthreatening forum. Like many ballads, spirituals may tell a story or contain a message. "Follow the Drinking Gourd" is no exception. Taught to slaves by a one-legged sailor named Peg Leg Joe, the song had a message for freedom hidden in its words. What is the message of "Follow the Drinking Gourd"?

4. **Refrain.** A **refrain,** or **chorus,** is a line or group of lines repeated in a poem or song. A refrain may emphasize an important idea. What is the refrain in "Follow the Drinking Gourd"? In what two ways is it used throughout the song?

The Process of Writing: Prewriting

A Personal Essay. A **personal essay** is a short work of nonfictional prose on a single topic related to the life or interests of the writer. Personal essays are characterized by an intimate and informal style and tone. They often, but not always, are written in the first person. There is no set, standard form for the personal essay. There are, however, some forms that are quite common. Here are a few:

ORGANIZATIONAL SCHEMES FOR PERSONAL ESSAYS

1. The author tells a story from his or her life and then draws some conclusion from it. The conclusion is usually a lesson that the author believes to have general applicability.

2. The author tells a brief anecdote from his or her life, draws some point or conclusion from it, and then applies that point or conclusion to other instances in life or in the world.

3. The author chooses some activity that he or she feels strongly about and describes that activity from a subjective, emotional point of view. The essay might take a narrative form, in which the author relates the history of his or her involvement in the activity, or it might divide the subject into two or three different parts or aspects and discuss each of these in turn.

4. The author begins by stating a position on some issue and then offers examples from his or her personal life to support or refute that position.

Try your hand at writing a personal essay following one of the forms described above. Before you begin, you might want to read E. B. White's "Walden," on page 769, which is widely believed to be a superb example of the personal essay. You should also read the Language Arts Survey, 1.1–1.34, to get a general overview of the writing process. Then follow these steps to plan your essay:

STEP 1 Reread the Language Arts Survey, 1.5, "Choosing and Focusing a Topic." To come up with a topic, try freewriting and thinking about experiences that you have had that were significant to you.

STEP 2 Look over the chart above and decide which of the types of personal essay you would like to write.

STEP 3 Use some combination of the prewriting techniques discussed in the Language Arts Survey, 1.10–1.29, to gather ideas for your personal essay. Particularly effective techniques for personal essays include recalling, freewriting, questioning, analyzing, clustering, and making a time line.

STEP 4 Make a rough outline of your essay, following the guidelines in the Language Arts Survey, 1.32, "Making a Rough Outline."

STEP 5 Save your prewriting notes and outline for reference in a later writing assignment.

Poetry

Recognizing a poem when you read one is a lot easier than describing what a poem is. That's because poetry comes in a wide variety of forms. Some poems rhyme and have regular rhythmical patterns. Others do not. Some poems fill one or more whole books. Others are only one or two lines long. Many poems depend on special devices of sound such as onomatopoeia and alliteration, and many use special techniques of meaning such as metaphor and symbolism, but some are simply designs or word pictures, like this concrete poem:

```
                    O   O
      B A L L           N
```

One thing that all poems have in common is that they use language in special ways to communicate thoughts or feelings. That's a useful definition, but not a particularly interesting one. Here are some interesting definitions of poetry put forward by important literary figures from the past:

Some Famous Definitions of Poetry

Poetry is . . .

"the spontaneous overflow of powerful feelings."
—William Wordsworth

"the best words in the best order."
—Samuel Taylor Coleridge

"the record of the best and happiest moments of the happiest and best minds."
—Percy Bysshe Shelley

"[language that] strike[s] the reader as a wording of his own highest thoughts, and appear[s] almost a remembrance."
—John Keats

"musical thought."
—Thomas Carlyle

"conceived and composed in the soul."
—Matthew Arnold

"a mixture of common sense, which not all have, with an uncommon sense, which very few have."
—John Masefield

"the supreme fiction."
—Wallace Stevens

"what gets lost in translation."
—Robert Frost

"not an assertion of truth, but the making of that truth more fully real to us."
—T. S. Eliot

The United States has produced many fine poets, including Phillis Wheatley, Henry Wadsworth Longfellow, Ralph Waldo Emerson, Walt Whitman, Edgar Lee Masters, Edwin Arlington Robinson, Robert Frost, Wallace Stevens, William Carlos Williams, Amy Lowell, Ezra Pound, Marianne Moore, Edna St. Vincent Millay, T. S. Eliot, E. E. Cummings, Langston Hughes, Gwendolyn Brooks, Elizabeth Bishop, and many others. Here's how one of the greatest of the American poets defined her craft:

"If I read a book and it makes my whole body so cold no fire can ever warm me, I know that it is poetry. If I feel physically as if the top of my head were taken off, I know that it is poetry. Is there any other way?"

—Emily Dickinson

The Hilltop. Frank Weston Benson, 1905. Malden Public Library

Elements of Poetry

Narrative Poetry. A **narrative poem** is a verse that tells a story. Examples of narrative poems include Edgar Allan Poe's "The Raven" (Unit 5), and Edwin Arlington Robinson's "Mr. Flood's Party" (Unit 8).

Dramatic Poetry. A **dramatic poem** is a verse that relies heavily on dramatic elements such as **monologue** (speech by a single character) or **dialogue** (conversation involving two or more characters). Often dramatic poems are narratives as well. In other words, they often tell stories. A **dramatic monologue** is a poem that presents the speech of a single character in a dramatic situation, often a moment of crisis or self-revelation. The speech is one side of an imagined conversation. See Edgar Lee Masters's "Lucinda Matlock" (Unit 8), Edwin Arlington Robinson's "Mr. Flood's Party" (Unit 8), and Robert Frost's "Home Burial" (Unit 8).

Lyric Poetry. A **lyric poem** is a highly musical verse that expresses the emotions of a speaker. There are many types of lyric poems. Among the most common types are the following:

Sonnet. A **sonnet** is a fourteen-line poem that follows one of a number of different rhyme schemes. Many sonnets deal with the subject of love. See Edna St. Vincent Millay's "Sonnet XXX" (Unit 1).

Ode. An **ode** is a lofty lyric poem on a serious theme. William Cullen Bryant's "Thanatopsis" (Unit 5) is an ode.

Free Verse Lyric. **Free verse**, or *vers libre*, is poetry that avoids use of regular rhyme, rhythm, meter, or division into stanzas. The first great writer of free verse in the United States was Walt Whitman. See his "Song of Myself" (Unit 7). See also T. S. Eliot's "The Love Song of J. Alfred Prufrock" (Unit 8), Langston Hughes's "The Negro Speaks of Rivers" (Unit 8), and Li-Young Lee's "A Story" (Unit 12).

Elegiac Lyric. An **elegiac lyric** expresses a speaker's feelings of loss, often because of the death of a loved one or friend. See Walt Whitman's "When Lilacs Last in the Dooryard Bloom'd" (Unit 6) and John Crowe Ransom's "Bells for John Whiteside's Daughter" (Unit 8).

Imagist Poem. An **imagist poem** is a lyric that presents a single vivid picture in words. See Ezra Pound's "In a Station of the Metro" (Unit 8), William Carlos Williams's "The Red Wheelbarrow" (Unit 8), and Amy Lowell's "A Lover" (Unit 8).

Techniques of Poetry: Meter and Stanza Form

Metrical verse follows a set rhythmical pattern. **Free verse,** or *vers libre,* does not. Instead, it follows the rhythms of ordinary speech.

Meter. The **meter** of a poem is its rhythmical pattern. English verse usually is described as being made up of rhythmical units called **feet.** A **foot** consists of some combination of **weakly stressed** (˘) and **strongly stressed** (/) syllables, as follows:

TYPE OF FOOT	PATTERN	EXAMPLE
iamb, or **iambic foot**	˘ /	˘ / afraid
trochee, or **trochaic foot**	/ ˘	/ ˘ freedom
anapest, or **anapestic foot**	˘ ˘ /	˘ ˘ / in a flash
dactyl, or **dactylic foot**	/ ˘ ˘	/ ˘ ˘ feverish
spondee, or **spondaic foot**	/ /	/ / baseball

Some writers on meter also use the term **pyrrhee,** or **pyrrhic foot,** to describe a foot with two weak stresses, as follows:

```
      anapest        pyrrhee
    ˘    ˘    /   |   ˘    ˘
    un   re   li  |   a   ble
```

The following terms are used to describe the number of feet in a line of poetry:

TERM	NUMBER OF FEET	EXAMPLE
monometer	one foot	Toˇday ˊ Weˇ play ˊ
dimeter	two feet	Following | closely Through the | forest
trimeter	three feet	God shed | His light | on thee
tetrameter	four feet	In the | greenest | of our | valleys
pentameter	five feet	A vast | re pub | lic famed| through ev | ry clime
hexameter or Alexandrine	six feet	In o | ther's eyes | we see | ourselves | the truth | to tell

   A complete description of the meter of a line includes both the term for the type of foot that predominates in the line and the term for the number of feet in the line. The most common meters in English are **iambic tetrameter** and **iambic pentameter**.

Stanza Form. A **stanza** is a group of lines in a poem. The following are some common types of stanza:

COUPLET
(*two lines*)

We dance round in a ring and suppose,
But the Secret sits in the middle and knows.

> —Robert Frost, "The Secret Sits"

TRIPLET OR
TERCET
(*three lines*)

Children picking up our bones
Will never know that these were once
As quick as foxes on the hill;

> —Wallace Stevens, "A Postcard from the Volcano"

QUATRAIN
(four lines)

By the rude bridge that arched the flood,
    Their flag to April's breeze unfurl'd,
Here once the embattled farmers stood,
    And fired the shot heard round the world.

             —Ralph Waldo Emerson, "Hymn Sung
              at the Completion of the Concord
              Monument, April 19, 1836"

QUINTAIN
(five lines)

    Gaunt the shadow on your green,
        Shenandoah!
The cut is on the crown
    (Lo, John Brown),
And the stabs shall heal no more.

             —Herman Melville, "The Portent"

SESTET
(six lines)

Once upon a midnight dreary, while I pondered, weak and weary,
Over many a quaint and curious volume of forgotten lore,
While I nodded, nearly napping, suddenly there came a tapping,
As of someone gently rapping, rapping at my chamber door.
"'Tis some visitor," I muttered, "tapping at my chamber door—
                    Only this, and nothing more."

        —Edgar Allan Poe, "The Raven"

HEPTASTICH
(seven lines)

In Heaven a spirit doth dwell
    "Whose heart-strings are a lute;"
None sing so wildly well
As the angel Israfel,
And the giddy stars (so legends tell)
Ceasing their hymns, attend the spell
    Of his voice, all mute.

           —Edgar Allan Poe, "Israfel"

OCTAVE
(eight lines)

The God who made New Hampshire
Taunted the lofty land
With little men;—
Small bat and wren
House in the oak:—
If earth-fire cleave
The upheaved land, and bury the folk,
The southern crocodile would grieve.

         —Ralph Waldo Emerson, "Ode, Inscribed to
          W. H. Channing"

Techniques of Poetry: Sound*

Rhythm. The **rhythm** is the pattern of beats or stresses in a line of verse or prose. A regular rhythmic pattern is called a **meter.**

Rhyme. Rhyme is the repetition of sounds at the ends of words. The following are some types of rhyme:

> **End Rhyme. End rhyme** is rhyme that occurs at the ends of lines.
>
> **Internal Rhyme. Internal rhyme** is the use of rhyming words within lines.
>
> **Slant Rhyme.** A **slant rhyme**, half rhyme, near rhyme, or off rhyme is the substitution of assonance or consonance for true rhyme. The pairs *world/boiled* and *bear/bore* are examples.

Alliteration. Alliteration is the repetition of initial consonant sounds. Edgar Allan Poe's "The Raven" contains the following example of alliteration: "And the silken sad uncertain rustling of each purple curtain."

Assonance. Assonance is the repetition of vowel sounds in stressed syllables that end with different consonant sounds, as in "weak and weary," also in "The Raven."

Consonance. Consonance is the repetition of a consonant sound preceded by a different vowel sound, as in *wind* and *sound.* This technique is also known as **slant rhyme.**

Onomatopoeia. Onomatopoeia is the use of words or phrases that sound like the things to which they refer. Examples include the words *pow, caw, clink,* and *murmur.*

Techniques of Poetry: Meaning*

Image. An **image** is a word or phrase that names something that can be seen, heard, touched, tasted, or smelled. A group of images that together create a given emotion in a reader or listener is called, in a phrase coined by T. S. Eliot, an **objective correlative.**

Figures of Speech. Figures of speech, or **tropes,** are expressions that have more than a literal meaning. The following are examples of common figures of speech:

> **Hyperbole.** A **hyperbole** is an exaggeration made for rhetorical effect.
>
> **Metaphor.** A **metaphor** is a figure of speech in which one thing is spoken or written about as if it were another. This figure of speech invites the reader to make a comparison between the two things: the writer's actual subject, the **tenor** of the metaphor, and another thing to which the subject is likened, the **vehicle** of the metaphor. In

*Note: These techniques are used commonly, but not exclusively, in poetry.

Emily Dickinson's metaphor "'Hope' is the thing with feathers—/That perches in the soul" the tenor is hope. The vehicle is a bird. **Personification** and **simile** are types of metaphor.

Metonymy. Metonymy is the naming of an object associated with a thing in place of the name of the thing itself. Speaking of *the White House* when one means *the president of the United States* is an example.

Personification. Personification is a figure of speech in which an idea, animal, or thing is described as if it were a person. *Night embraces us* is an example.

Simile. A **simile** is a comparison using *like* or *as*. T. S. Eliot's description of evening "spread out against the sky/Like a patient etherised upon a table" is an example.

Synaesthesia. Synaesthesia is a figure of speech that combines in a single expression images related to two or more different senses. Archibald MacLeish's line "Dumb/As old medallions to the thumb," which combines the senses of sound and touch, is an example of synaesthesia.

Synechdoche. A **synechdoche** is a figure of speech in which the name of part of something is used in place of the name of the whole, or vice versa. The use of *hired hands* for *laborers* is an example.

Understatement. An **understatement** is an ironic expression in which something of importance is emphasized by being spoken of as though it were not important.

Rhetorical Techniques. A **rhetorical technique** is an extraordinary but literal use of language to achieve a particular effect. The following rhetorical techniques are commonly used in poetry:

Antithesis. Antithesis is a rhetorical technique in which words, phrases, or ideas are strongly contrasted, often by means of repetition of grammatical structures. An example is Ralph Waldo Emerson's description of the taunting of "<u>lofty land</u>/With <u>little men</u>."

Chiasmus. A **chiasmus** is a rhetorical technique in which the order of occurrence of words or phrases is reversed, as in the traditional line "We can weather changes, but we can't change the weather."

Parallelism. Parallelism is a rhetorical technique in which a writer emphasizes the equal value or weight of two or more ideas by expressing them in the same grammatical form, as in Abraham Lincoln's phrase "of the people, by the people, for the people."

Repetition. Repetition is the use, again, of a sound, word, phrase, sentence, or other element. Walt Whitman used repetition in the line "I celebrate myself, and sing myself,/And what I assume, you shall assume."

Rhetorical Question. A **rhetorical question** is one asked for effect but not meant to be answered because the answer is clear from the context, as in Walt Whitman's "Has any one supposed it lucky to be born?"

"Sonnet XXX"

EDNA ST. VINCENT MILLAY

Love is not all: it is not meat nor drink
Nor slumber nor a roof against the rain;
Nor yet a floating spar[1] to men that sink
And rise and sink and rise and sink and sink again;
5 Love can not fill the thickened lung with breath,
Nor clean the blood, nor set the fractured bone;
Yet many a man is making friends with death
Even as I speak, for lack of love alone.
It well may be that in a difficult hour,
10 Pinned down by pain and moaning for release,
Or nagged by want[2] past resolution's power,
I might be driven to sell your love for peace,
Or trade the memory of this night for food.
It well may be. I do not think I would. ∎

---

1. **spar.** Any pole supporting or extending the sail of a ship; here, the parts of a ship that can be used to keep sailors afloat after the ship has wrecked
2. **want.** Physical need

Edna St. Vincent Millay

WORDS FOR EVERYDAY USE: res • o • lu • tion (rez´ə lōō´ shən) *n.,* determined state of mind; faithfulness to some person or idea

Responding to the Selection

Do you believe that love is as important as food for a hungry person or release for a person in pain? Discuss this question with your classmates.

Reviewing the Selection

RECALLING

1. In lines 1–4, what does the speaker say that love is not?

2. According to lines 5 and 6, what can love not do?

3. According to lines 7 and 8, what are many men doing?

4. According to lines 9–13, what might move the speaker to sell his or her love for peace? to trade the memory of that love for food?

INTERPRETING

5. According to lines 1 and 2, what other things does a person need besides love? In what ways do people, in the course of their lives, "rise and sink and rise and sink and sink again"?

6. What do the circumstances mentioned in lines 5 and 6 have in common? What needs do people sometimes have that cannot be met by love?

7. According to line 8, what might drive a person to make friends with death?

8. What question does the speaker consider in lines 9–14 of the poem? How does he or she answer that question?

SYNTHESIZING

9. Does the speaker believe that love is a fundamental need? Support your answer with evidence from the poem.

10. What do you think are people's most basic needs? Make a list of these. Is your list the same as the speaker's? How does it differ?

Understanding Literature (Questions for Discussion)

1. **Sonnet.** A **sonnet** is a fourteen-line poem that follows one of a number of different rhyme schemes. The **English, Elizabethan,** or **Shakespearean sonnet** can be divided into four parts: three quatrains, or four-line sections, and a final couplet, or two-line section. What is the subject of the first quatrain of "Sonnet XXX"? of the second quatrain? of the third quatrain? of the concluding couplet? Paraphrase each of these sections of the poem by stating its main idea in your own words.

2. **Rhyme Scheme.** A **rhyme scheme** is a pattern of rhymes in a poem. To determine the rhyme scheme of a poem, assign letters of the alphabet to each of the sounds that appear at the ends of lines. The end rhymes of the first four lines of "Sonnet XXX" have the rhyme scheme *abab,* as follows:

drink	*a*
rain	*b*
sink	*a*
again	*b*

   What is the rhyme scheme of the rest of the poem?

3. **Parallelism. Parallelism** is a rhetorical technique in which a writer emphasizes the equal value or weight of two or more ideas by expressing them in the same grammatical form. Find three examples of parallelism in "Sonnet XXX." What ideas of equal value are expressed in each example?

4. **Personification. Personification** is a figure of speech in which an idea, animal, or thing is described as if it were a person. What does Millay personify in line 7 of her poem? in line 11?

5. **Symbol.** A **symbol** is a thing that stands for or represents both itself and something else. Common symbols include doves for peace, roses for love or beauty, the color green for jealousy, the color red for anger, spring for youth, and winter or fall for age. In most people's lives, there are good times and bad times, times when their spirits rise and times when they sink. Lines 3 and 4 of this poem can be read as presenting a symbol of such a rise and fall of personal fortunes. If so, what is the speaker saying about the role of love in life? Does the speaker believe that love can be counted on to balance out good and bad fortune? Do you agree with the speaker?

6. **Theme.** A **theme** is a central idea in a literary work. What is the theme, or main idea, of "Sonnet XXX"?

The Process of Writing: Drafting

Drafting. Read the Language Arts Survey, 1.35–1.42, on drafting. Pay particular attention to section 1.42, "Organizing a Composition." Using the notes you created in the prewriting lesson in this unit, write a draft of your personal essay. Save your draft for later revision.

Language Lab

Coordinating Conjunctions. After reading the Language Arts Survey, 2.25, "Coordinating Conjunctions," rewrite the sentences below, adding coordinating conjunctions to link the sentence parts.

1. Edna St. Vincent Millay was born _____ raised in Maine in a family with a great interest in literature.

2. She enjoyed reading _____ , while still quite young, wrote poetry for a magazine called *St. Nicholas*.

3. Millay did not expect to attend college, _____ a family friend sponsored her studies at Barnard _____ Vassar.

4. Although she struggled with poverty, Millay also achieved literary _____ popular recognition with her second book, *A Few Figs from Thistles*.

5. Do you remember her best for winning the Pulitzer Prize _____ for her poetic figure of speech about burning the candle at both ends?

ABOUT THE AUTHOR

Edna St. Vincent Millay (1892–1950) was born in Rockland, Maine, and began to write poetry at an early age. In 1912, her poem "Renascence" was published in a collection called *The Lyric Year.* After attending Barnard and Vassar, she published a book of verse, *Renascence and Other Poems,* and moved to Greenwich Village in New York City. There she refined her poetic talents and worked as both an actor and playwright for the Provincetown Players, which produced her plays *The Princess Marries the Page, Aria da Capo,* and *Two Slatterns and a King.* Millay became a master of the sonnet, one of the most difficult of English poetic forms, and her poetry reached a large and enthusiastic audience. In 1923, she received a Pulitzer Prize for *The Ballad of the Harp-Weaver.* In that same year she married and bought a farm in upstate New York, where she continued her writing, including a sonnet cycle, or group of related sonnets, called *Fatal Interview.* Many of her later works dealt with social and political issues. Works by Millay include *Collected Sonnets* (1941), *Collected Lyrics* (1943), and *Collected Poems* (1953).

Fiction

The term *fiction* comes from the Latin *fictio,* meaning "something invented." Thus fiction is any prose writing that tells an invented or imaginary story. Some fiction, the historical novel, for example, is based on fact, while other forms, such as the fantasy tale, are highly unrealistic. Fictional works also vary in structure and length, from the newly recognized **short short** (a very brief short story) to the book-length **novel.** Other forms include the traditional **short story** and the **novella,** a fictional work of intermediate length.

The Development of Fiction

The oldest fictions are the prose stories told in the oral tradition, which include myths, legends, and fables. Early written prose fictions include Petronius's *Satyricon* and Apuleius's *The Golden Ass,* written by Romans in the first and second centuries. The first novel, *The Tale of Genji,* was written by a Japanese woman, Lady Murasaki Shikibu, in the eleventh century. Early fictions from Europe include Boccaccio's *Decameron,* a collection of short prose tales written in the mid-fourteenth century, and Cervantes's *Don Quixote,* a satire of medieval romance tales written in the early seventeenth century.

The Novel

The novel developed from various kinds of nonfictional writing, including autobiographies, biographies, travel sketches, journals, and letters. Arguably the first full-fledged novel in English was Aphra Behn's *Oroonoko,* published in 1688. Other early novels in English include Daniel Defoe's *Robinson Crusoe* (1719) and *Moll Flanders* (1722), and Samuel Richardson's *Pamela* (1740) and *Clarissa* (1747–1748). By the mid-1800s, the novel had become a popular form in the United States. Important American novelists include Nathaniel Hawthorne (1804–1864), Herman Melville (1819–1891), Mark Twain (1835–1910), Henry James (1843–1916), Kate Chopin (1850–1904), Edith Wharton (1862–1937), Stephen Crane (1871–1945), Theodore Dreiser (1871–1945), Willa Cather (1873–1947), Sherwood Anderson (1876–1941), Katherine Anne Porter (1890–1980), Zora Neale Hurston (1891–1960), F. Scott Fitzgerald (1896–1940), William Faulkner (1897–1962), Ernest Hemingway (1899–1961), Richard Wright (1908–1960), John Steinbeck (1902–1968), Eudora Welty (1909–   ), Saul Bellow (1915–   ), James Baldwin (1924–   ), Philip Roth (1933–   ), and Alice Walker (1944–   ).

The Short Story

The short story genre, or type, originated in the United States. Important American figures in the development of the short story include Washington Irving (1783–1859), Nathaniel Hawthorne, and Edgar Allan Poe (1809–1849). Poe was instrumental in defining the genre, which he described as a short work that creates a single dominant impression or effect on the reader. According to Poe, every detail in a short story should contribute to creating that overall impression or effect.

The Poor Man's Store. John Frederick Peto. 1885. Courtesy of Museum of Fine Arts, Boston. Gift of Maxim Karolik to the M. and M. Karolik Collection of American Paintings, 1815–1865

Elements of Fiction

CHARACTER

A **character** is a person (or sometimes an animal or even a personified thing) who figures in the action of a story. The following are some useful terms for describing characters:

A **protagonist**, or **main character**, is the central figure in a story.

An **antagonist** is a character who is pitted against a protagonist.

A **major character** is one with a significant role in the action of a story. A **minor character** is one who plays a lesser role. Because of limitations of length and focus, most short stories have, at most, one or two major characters.

A **one-dimensional character, flat character,** or **caricature** is one who exhibits a single dominant quality, or **character trait.**

A **three-dimensional, full,** or **rounded character** is one who exhibits the complexity of traits associated with actual human beings.

A **static character** is one who does not change during the course of the story.

A **dynamic character** is one who does change during the course of the story.

A **stock character** is one found again and again in different literary works. Examples of stock characters include the mad scientist and the absent-minded professor.

Motivation is the needs or desires felt by a character, impelling him or her to act or think in certain ways. For example, a character may be **motivated** by greed, love, or friendship. The particular reasons or causes behind a character's actions are his or her **motives.**

CHARACTERIZATION

Characterization is the use of literary techniques to create a character. Three major techniques of characterization used by fiction writers include the following: 1. direct description by a narrator or character, 2. portrayal of a character's words and behavior, and 3. representations of a character's internal states.

Direct description of a character includes what other characters say or think about that character. Skillful writers are able to create characterizations through a few well-chosen, significant details.

SETTING AND MOOD

The **setting** is the time and place in which a story occurs, together with all the details used to create a sense of a particular time and place. The **mood** is the emotion created in the reader by descriptions of the setting, of characters, and of events. In fiction, setting is most often revealed by means of description of such elements as landscape, scenery, buildings, furniture, clothing, weather, and seasons. It also can be revealed by how characters talk and behave. In its widest sense, setting includes the general social, political, moral, and psychological conditions in which characters find themselves. Many American novels and short stories deal with particular regions of the country (New York City, the western frontier, small towns in the South or Midwest, and so on). Writing in which particular settings play an important role is called **regional fiction.** The details used to create a particular regional setting are called **local color.**

CONFLICT

A **conflict** is a struggle between two forces in a literary work. A plot involves the introduction, development, and, often, the resolution, or ending, of a conflict. One side of the central conflict in a work of fiction usually is taken by the main character. That character may struggle against another character, against the forces of nature, against society or social norms, against fate, or against some element within himself or herself. A struggle that takes place between a character and some outside force is called an **external conflict.** A struggle that takes place within a character is called an **internal conflict.**

PLOT

A **plot** is a series of causally connected events in a literary work. The English novelist E. M. Forster explained, famously, that if the king dies and then the queen dies, that is a story, but if the king dies and then the queen dies of grief, that is a plot. A typical plot involves the following elements:

The **exposition,** or **introduction,** sets the tone and mood, introduces the characters and the setting, and provides necessary background information.

The **inciting incident** is the event that introduces the central conflict.

The **rising action,** or **complication,** develops the conflict to a high point of intensity.

The **climax** is the high point of interest or suspense.

The **crisis,** or **turning point,** often the same event as the climax, is the point in the plot where something decisive happens to determine the future course of events and the eventual working out of the conflict.

The **falling action** is all the events that follow the climax.

The **resolution** is the point at which the central conflict is ended, or resolved.

The **dénouement** is any material that follows the resolution and that ties up loose ends.

Plots are often illustrated using the following diagram, known as Freytag's Pyramid for its creator, Gustav Freytag:

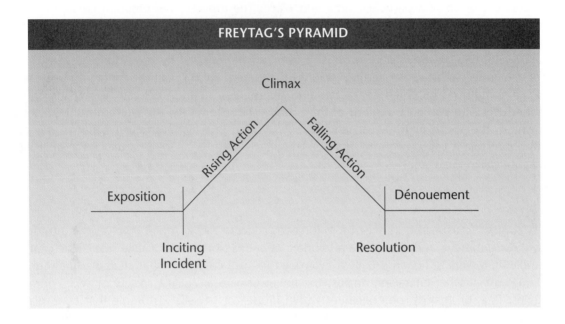

THEME

A **theme** is a central idea in a literary work. A long work such as a novel may deal with several interrelated themes.

> "[The short story writer] having conceived with deliberate care a certain unique or single effect to be wrought out . . . then invents . . . as may best aid him in establishing his preconceived effects. . . . In the whole composition there should be no word written, of which the tendency, direct or indirect, is not to the one pre-established design."
>
> —Edgar Allan Poe

"The Magic Barrel"

Bernard Malamud

Not long ago there lived in uptown New York, in a small, almost <u>meager</u> room, though crowded with books, Leo Finkle, a rabbinical student at the Yeshiva University.[1] Finkle, after six years of study, was to be <u>ordained</u> in June and had been advised by an acquaintance that he might find it easier to win himself a congregation if he were married. Since he had no present prospects of marriage, after two tormented days of turning it over in his mind, he called in Pinye Salzman, a marriage broker whose two-line advertisement he had read in the *Forward*.[2]

The matchmaker appeared one night out of the dark fourth-floor hallway of the graystone rooming house where Finkle lived, grasping a black, strapped portfolio that had been worn thin with use. Salzman, who had been long in the business, was of slight but dignified build, wearing an old hat, and an overcoat too short and tight for him. He smelled frankly of fish, which he loved to eat, and although he was missing a few teeth, his presence was not displeasing, because of an amiable manner curiously contrasted with mournful eyes. His voice, his lips, his wisp of beard, his bony fingers were animated, but give him a moment of repose and his mild blue eyes revealed a depth of sadness, a characteristic that put Leo a little at ease although the situation, for him, was <u>inherently</u> tense.

He at once informed Salzman why he had asked him to come, explaining that his home was in Cleveland, and that but for his parents, who had married comparatively late in life, he was alone in the world. He had for six years devoted himself almost entirely to his studies, as a result of which, understandably, he had found himself without time for a social life and the company of young women. Therefore he thought it the better part of trial and error—of embarrassing fumbling—to call in an experienced person to advise him on these matters. He remarked in passing that the function of the marriage broker was ancient and honorable, highly approved in the Jewish community, because it made practical the necessary without hindering joy. Moreover, his own parents had been brought together by a matchmaker. They had made, if not a financially profitable marriage—since neither had possessed any worldly goods to speak of—at least a successful one in the sense of their everlasting devotion to each other. Salzman listened

---

1. **Yeshiva University.** University in New York City offering both theological and secular courses
2. **Forward.** *The Jewish Daily Forward*, New York City newspaper written in the Yiddish language

in embarrassed surprise, sensing a sort of apology. Later, however, he experienced a glow of pride in his work, an emotion that had left him years ago, and he heartily approved of Finkle.

The two went to their business. Leo had led Salzman to the only clear place in the room, a table near a window that overlooked the lamp-lit city. He seated himself at the matchmaker's side but facing him, attempting by an act of will to suppress the unpleasant tickle in his throat. Salzman eagerly unstrapped his portfolio and removed a loose rubber band from a thin packet of much-handled cards. As he flipped through them, a gesture and sound that physically hurt Leo, the student pretended not to see and gazed steadfastly out the window. Although it was still February, winter was on its last legs, signs of which he had for the first time in years begun to notice. He now observed the round white moon, moving high in the sky through a cloud <u>menagerie</u>, and watched with half-open mouth as it penetrated a huge hen, and dropped out of her like an egg laying itself. Salzman, though pretending through eyeglasses he had just slipped on, to be engaged in scanning the writing on the cards, stole occasional glances at the young man's distinguished face, noting with pleasure the long, severe scholar's nose, brown eyes heavy with learning, sensitive yet <u>ascetic</u> lips, and a certain, almost hollow quality of the dark cheeks. He gazed around at shelves upon shelves of books and let out a soft, contented sigh.

When Leo's eyes fell upon the cards, he counted six spread out in Salzman's hand.

"So few?" he asked in disappointment.

"You wouldn't believe me how much cards I got in my office," Salzman replied. "The drawers are already filled to the top, so I keep them now in a barrel, but is every girl good for a new rabbi?"

Leo blushed at this, regretting all he had revealed of himself in a curriculum vitae[3] he had sent to Salzman. He had thought it best to acquaint him with his strict standards and specifications, but in having done so, he felt he had told the marriage broker more than was absolutely necessary.

He hesitantly inquired, "Do you keep photographs of your clients on file?"

"First comes family, amount of dowry, also what kind promises," Salzman replied, unbuttoning his tight coat and settling himself in the chair. "After come pictures, rabbi."

"Call me Mr. Finkle. I'm not yet a rabbi."

Salzman said he would, but instead called him doctor, which he changed to rabbi when Leo was not listening too attentively.

Salzman adjusted his horn-rimmed spectacles, gently cleared his throat and read in an eager voice the contents of the top card:

"Sophie P. Twenty four years. Widow one year. No children. Educated high school and two years college. Father promises eight thousand dollars. Has wonderful wholesale business. Also real estate. On the mother's side comes teach-

---

3. **curriculum vitae.** Summary of one's personal history and professional qualifications

---

W

WORDS FOR
EVERYDAY USE:

me • nag • er • ie (mə naj´ ər ē) *n.*, collection of wild or exotic animals

as • cet • ic (ə set´ik) *adj.*, self-denying; austere

ers, also one actor. Well known on Second Avenue."

Leo gazed up in surprise. "Did you say a widow?"

"A widow don't mean spoiled, rabbi. She lived with her husband maybe four months. He was a sick boy she made a mistake to marry him."

"Marrying a widow has never entered my mind."

"This is because you have no experience. A widow, especially if she is young and healthy like this girl, is a wonderful person to marry. She will be thankful to you the rest of her life. Believe me, if I was looking now for a bride, I would marry a widow."

Leo reflected, then shook his head.

Salzman hunched his shoulders in an almost <u>imperceptible</u> gesture of disappointment. He placed the card down on the wooden table and began to read another:

"Lily H. High school teacher. Regular. Not a substitute. Has savings and new Dodge car. Lived in Paris one year. Father is successful dentist thirty-five years. Interested in professional man. Well Americanized family. Wonderful opportunity."

"I knew her personally," said Salzman. "I wish you could see this girl. She is a doll. Also very intelligent. All day you could talk to her about books and theater and what not. She also knows current events."

"I don't believe you mentioned her age?"

"Her age?" Salzman said, raising his brows. "Her age is thirty-two years."

Leo said after a while, "I'm afraid that seems a little too old."

Salzman let out a laugh. "So how old are you, rabbi?"

"Twenty-seven."

"So what is the difference, tell me, between twenty-seven and thirty-two? My own wife is seven years older than me. So what did I suffer?—Nothing. If Rothschild's[4] daughter wants to marry you, would you say on account her age, no?"

"Yes," Leo said dryly.

Salzman shook off the no in the yes. "Five years don't mean a thing. I give you my word that when you will live with her for one week you will forget her age. What does it mean five years—that she lived more and knows more than somebody who is younger? On this girl, God bless her, years are not wasted. Each one that it comes makes better the bargain."

"What subjects does she teach in high school?"

"Languages. If you heard the way she speaks French, you will think it is music. I am in the business twenty-five years, and I recommend her with my whole heart. Believe me, I know what I'm talking, rabbi."

"What's on the next card?" Leo said abruptly.

Salzman reluctantly turned up the third card:

"Ruth K. Nineteen years. Honor student. Father offers thirteen thousand cash to the right bridegroom. He is a medical doctor. Stomach specialist with marvelous

---

4. **Rothschild's.** The Rothschilds were once a very wealthy Jewish family of international bankers and business leaders.

WORDS FOR EVERYDAY USE:

im • per • cep • ti • ble (im´ pər sep´ tə bəl) *adj.,* not able to be detected by the senses or the mind

practice. Brother in law owns own garment business. Particular people."

Salzman looked as if he had read his trump card.

"Did you say nineteen?" Leo asked with interest.

"On the dot."

"Is she attractive?" He blushed. "Pretty?"

Salzman kissed his finger tips. "A little doll. On this I give you my word. Let me call the father tonight and you will see what means pretty."

But Leo was troubled. "You're sure she's that young?"

"This I am positive. The father will show you the birth certificate."

"Are you positive there isn't something wrong with her?" Leo insisted.

"Who says there is wrong?"

"I don't understand why an American girl her age should go to a marriage broker."

A smile spread over Salzman's face.

"So for the same reason you went, she comes."

Leo flushed. "I am pressed for time."

Salzman, realizing he had been tactless, quickly explained. "The father came, not her. He wants she should have the best, so he looks around himself. When we will locate the right boy he will introduce him and encourage. This makes a better marriage than if a young girl without experience takes for herself. I don't have to tell you this."

"But don't you think this young girl believes in love?" Leo spoke uneasily.

Salzman was about to guffaw but caught himself and said soberly, "Love comes with the right person, not before."

Leo parted dry lips but did not speak. Noticing that Salzman had snatched a glance at the next card, he cleverly asked, "How is her health?"

"Perfect," Salzman said, breathing with difficulty. "Of course, she is a little lame on her right foot from an auto accident that it happened to her when she was twelve years, but nobody notices on account she is so brilliant and also beautiful."

Leo got up heavily and went to the window. He felt curiously bitter and upbraided himself for having called in the marriage broker. Finally, he shook his head.

"Why not?" Salzman persisted, the pitch of his voice rising.

"Because I detest stomach specialists."

"So what do you care what is his business? After you marry her do you need him? Who says he must come every Friday night in your house?"

Ashamed of the way the talk was going, Leo dismissed Salzman, who went home with heavy, melancholy eyes.

Though he had felt only relief at the marriage broker's departure, Leo was in low spirits the next day. He explained it as arising from Salzman's failure to produce a suitable bride for him. He did not care for his type of clientele. But when Leo found himself hesitating whether to seek out another matchmaker, one more polished than Pinye, he wondered if it could be—his protestations to the contrary, and although he honored his father and mother—that he did not, in essence, care for the match-making institution? This thought he quickly put out of mind yet found himself still upset. All day he ran around in the woods—missed an important appointment, forgot to give out his laundry, walked out of a Broadway cafeteria without paying and had to run back with the ticket in his hand; had even not recognized his landlady in the street when she passed with a friend and courteously called out, "A good evening to you, Doctor Finkle." By nightfall, however, he had regained sufficient calm to sink his nose into a book and there found peace from his thoughts.

Almost at once there came a knock on the door. Before Leo could say enter, Salzman, commercial cupid, was standing in the room. His face was gray and meager, his expression hungry, and he looked as if he would expire on his feet. Yet the marriage broker managed, by some trick of the muscles, to display a broad smile.

"So good evening. I am invited?"

Leo nodded, disturbed to see him again, yet unwilling to ask the man to leave.

Beaming still, Salzman laid his portfolio on the table. "Rabbi, I got for you tonight good news."

"I've asked you not to call me rabbi. I'm still a student."

"Your worries are finished. I have for you a first-class bride."

"Leave me in peace concerning this subject," Leo pretended lack of interest.

"The world will dance at your wedding."

"Please, Mr. Salzman, no more."

"But first must come back my strength," Salzman said weakly. He fumbled with the portfolio straps and took out of the leather case an oily paper bag, from which he extracted a hard, seeded roll and a small, smoked white fish. With a quick motion of his hand he stripped the fish out of its skin and began <u>ravenously</u> to chew. "All day in a rush," he muttered.

Leo watched him eat.

"A sliced tomato you have maybe?" Salzman hesitantly inquired.

"No."

The marriage broker shut his eyes and ate. When he had finished he carefully cleaned up the crumbs and rolled up the remains of the fish, in the paper bag. His spectacled eyes roamed the room until he

---

WORDS FOR EVERYDAY USE: **rav • e • nous • ly** (rav´ ə nəs lē) *adv.*, in a greedy or wildly hungry manner

discovered, amid some piles of books, a one-burner gas stove. Lifting his hat he humbly asked, "A glass tea you got, rabbi?"

Conscience-stricken, Leo rose and brewed the tea. He served it with a chunk of lemon and two cubes of lump sugar, delighting Salzman.

After he had drunk his tea, Salzman's strength and good spirits were restored.

"So tell me, rabbi," he said amiably, "you considered some more the three clients I mentioned yesterday?"

"There was no need to consider."

"Why not?"

"None of them suits me."

"What then suits you?"

Leo let it pass because he could give only a confused answer.

Without waiting for a reply, Salzman asked, "You remember this girl I talked to you—the high school teacher?"

"Age thirty-two?"

But, surprisingly, Salzman's face lit in a smile. "Age twenty-nine."

Leo shot him a look. "Reduced from thirty-two?"

"A mistake," Salzman avowed. "I talked today with the dentist. He took me to his safety deposit box and showed me the birth certificate. She was twenty-nine years last August. They made her a party in the mountains where she went for her vacation. When her father spoke to me the first time I forgot to write the age and I told you thirty-two, but now I remember this was a different client, a widow."

"The same one you told me about? I thought she was twenty-four?"

"A different. Am I responsible that the world is filled with widows?"

"No, but I'm not interested in them, nor for that matter, in school teachers."

Salzman pulled his clasped hands to his breast. Looking at the ceiling he devoutly exclaimed, "Yiddishe kinder,[5] what can I say to somebody that he is not interested in high school teachers? So what then you are interested?"

Leo flushed but controlled himself.

"In what else will you be interested," Salzman went on, "if you not interested in this fine girl that she speaks four languages and has personally in the bank ten thousand dollars? Also her father guarantees further twelve thousand. Also she has a new car, wonderful clothes, talks on all subjects, and she will give you a first-class home and children. How near do we come in our life to paradise?"

"If she's so wonderful, why wasn't she married ten years ago?"

"Why?" said Salzman with a heavy laugh. "—Why? Because she is *partikiler*.[6] This is why. She wants the *best*."

Leo was silent, amused at how he had entangled himself. But Salzman had aroused his interest in Lily H., and he began seriously to consider calling on her. When the marriage broker observed how intently Leo's mind was at work on the facts he had supplied, he felt certain they would soon come to an agreement.

---

5. **Yiddishe kinder.** Jewish children (Yiddish); Salzman is both calling Leo a child and lamenting the loss of the more traditional values Leo's parents' generation held.
6. **partikiler.** Particular; having high standards

WORDS FOR EVERYDAY USE: **a • vow** (ə vou´) *vt.*, admit frankly

Late Saturday afternoon, conscious of Salzman, Leo Finkle walked with Lily Hirschorn along Riverside Drive. He walked briskly and erectly, wearing with distinction the black fedora he had that morning taken with <u>trepidation</u> out of the dusty hat box on his closet shelf, and the heavy black Saturday coat he had thoroughly whisked clean. Leo also owned a walking stick, a present from a distant relative, but quickly put temptation aside and did not use it. Lily, petite and not unpretty, had on something signifying the approach of spring. She was au courant,[7] animatedly, with all sorts of subjects, and he weighed her words and found her surprisingly sound—score another for Salzman, whom he uneasily sensed to be somewhere around, hiding perhaps high in a tree along the street, flashing the lady signals with a pocket mirror; or perhaps a cloven-hoofed Pan,[8] piping <u>nuptial</u> ditties as he danced his invisible way before them, strewing wild buds on the walk and purple grapes in their path, symbolizing fruit of a union, though there was of course still none.

Lily startled Leo by remarking, "I was thinking of Mr. Salzman, a curious figure, wouldn't you say?"

Not certain what to answer, he nodded.

She bravely went on, blushing, "I for one am grateful for his introducing us. Aren't you?"

He courteously replied, "I am."

"I mean," she said with a little laugh—and it was all in good taste, or at least gave the effect of being not in bad—"do you mind that we came together so?"

He was not displeased with her honesty, recognizing that she meant to set the relationship aright, and understanding that it took a certain amount of experience in life, and courage, to want to do it quite that way. One had to have some sort of past to make that kind of beginning.

He said that he did not mind. Salzman's function was traditional and honorable—valuable for what it might achieve, which, he pointed out, was frequently nothing.

Lily agreed with a sigh. They walked on for a while and she said after a long silence, again with a nervous laugh, "Would you mind if I asked you something a little bit personal? Frankly, I find the subject fascinating." Although Leo shrugged, she went on half embarrassedly, "How was it that you came to your calling? I mean was it a sudden passionate inspiration?"

Leo, after a time, slowly replied, "I was always interested in the Law."

"You saw revealed in it the presence of the Highest?"

He nodded and changed the subject. "I understand that you spent a little time in Paris, Miss Hirschorn?"

"Oh, did Mr. Salzman tell you, Rabbi Finkle?" Leo winced but she went on, "It was ages ago and almost forgotten. I remember I had to return for my sister's wedding."

And Lily would not be put off. "When," she asked in a trembly voice, "did you become enamored of God?"

---

7. **au courant.** In keeping with the times; up-to-date (French)

8. **Pan.** Greek god of fields, forests, wild animals, flocks, and shepherds, represented as a man with the legs of a goat who plays a flutelike instrument

WORDS FOR EVERYDAY USE:

trep • i • da • tion (trep´ ə dā´ shən) *n.,* anxiety; nervousness

nup • tial (nup´ shəl) *adj.,* concerning marriage or a wedding

He stared at her. Then it came to him that she was talking not about Leo Finkle, but of a total stranger, some mystical figure, perhaps even passionate prophet that Salzman had dreamed up for her—no relation to the living or dead. Leo trembled with rage and weakness. The trickster had obviously sold her a bill of goods, just as he had him, who'd expected to become acquainted with a young lady of twenty-nine, only to behold, the moment he laid eyes upon her strained and anxious face, a woman past thirty-five and aging rapidly. Only his self control had kept him this long in her presence.

"I am not," he said gravely, "a talented religious person," and in seeking words to go on, found himself possessed by shame and fear. "I think," he said in a strained manner, "that I came to God not because I loved Him, but because I did not."

This confession he spoke harshly because its unexpectedness shook him.

Lily wilted. Leo saw a <u>profusion</u> of loaves of bread go flying like ducks high over his head, not unlike the winged loaves by which he had counted himself to sleep last night. Mercifully, then, it snowed, which he would not put past Salzman's <u>machinations</u>.

He was infuriated with the marriage broker and swore he would throw him out of the room the minute he reappeared. But Salzman did not come that night, and when Leo's anger had subsided, an unaccountable despair grew in its place. At first he thought this was caused by his disappointment in Lily, but before long it became evident that he had involved himself with Salzman without a true knowledge of his own intent. He gradually realized—with an emptiness that seized him with six hands—that he had called in the broker to find him a bride because he was incapable of doing it himself. This terrifying insight he had derived as a result of his meeting and conversation with Lily Hirschorn. Her probing questions had somehow irritated him into revealing—to himself more than her—the true nature of his relationship to God, and from that it had come upon him, with shocking force, that apart from his parents, he had never loved anyone. Or perhaps it went the other way, that he did not love God so well as he might, because he had not loved man. It seemed to Leo that his whole life stood starkly revealed and he saw himself for the first time as he truly was—unloved and loveless. This bitter but somehow not fully unexpected revelation brought him to a point of panic, controlled only by extraordinary effort. He covered his face with his hands and cried.

The week that followed was the worst of his life. He did not eat and lost weight. His beard darkened and grew ragged. He stopped attending seminars and almost never opened a book. He seriously considering leaving the Yeshiva, although he was deeply troubled at the thought of the loss of all his years of study—saw them like pages torn from a book, strewn over the city—and at the devastating effect of this decision upon

COMPLICATION AND THEME

Most of the plot of the story is taken up by the complication—the development of the central conflict. This revelation by Finkle deepens the conflict for we learn that in religious matters, as in choosing a mate, Finkle has not acted from love but from a sense of duty.

Most stories present some learning or growth on the part of the protagonist. The necessity of this growth is often the story's main idea, or theme.

WORDS FOR EVERYDAY USE:

pro • fu • sion (prō fyoo ´ zhən) *n.,* large number; abundance

mach • i • na • tion (mak ə nā´ shən) *n.,* clever plot or scheme

his parents. But he had lived without knowledge of himself, and never in the Five Books[9] and all the Commentaries—mea culpa[10]—had the truth been revealed to him. He did not know where to turn, and in all this desolating loneliness there was no *to whom*, although he often thought of Lily but not once could bring himself to go downstairs and make the call. He became touchy and irritable, especially with his landlady, who asked him all manner of personal questions; on the other hand, sensing his own disagreeableness, he waylaid her on the stairs and apologized <u>abjectly</u>, until mortified, she ran from him. Out of this, however, he drew the consolation that he was a Jew and that a Jew suffered. But gradually, as the long and terrible week drew to a close, he regained his composure and some idea of purpose in life: to go on as planned. Although he was imperfect, the ideal was not. As for his quest of a bride, the thought of continuing afflicted him with anxiety and heartburn, yet perhaps with this new knowledge of himself he would be more successful than in the past. Perhaps love would now come to him and a bride to that love. And for this sanctified seeking who needed a Salzman?

The marriage broker, a skeleton with haunted eyes, returned that very night. He looked, withal, the picture of frustrated expectancy—as if he had steadfastly waited the week at Miss Lily Hirschorn's side for a telephone call that never came.

Casually coughing, Salzman came immediately to the point: "So how did you like her?

Leo's anger rose and he could not refrain from chiding the matchmaker: "Why did you lie to me, Salzman?"

Salzman's pale face went dead white, the world had snowed on him.

"Did you not state that she was twenty-nine?" Leo insisted.

"I gave you my word—"

"She was thirty-five, if a day. *At least* thirty-five."

"Of this don't be too sure. Her father told me—"

"Never mind. The worst of it was that you lied to her."

"How did I lie to her, tell me?"

"You told her things about me that weren't true. You made me out to be more, consequently less than I am. She had in mind a totally different person, a sort of semimystical Wonder Rabbi."

"All I said, you was a religious man."

"I can imagine."

Salzman sighed. "This is my weakness that I have," he confessed. "My wife says to me I shouldn't be a salesman, but when I have two fine people that they would be wonderful to be married, I am so happy that I talk too much." He smiled wanly. "This is why Salzman is a poor man."

Leo's anger left him. "Well, Salzman, I'm afraid that's all."

The marriage broker fastened hungry eyes on him.

"You don't want any more a bride?"

"I do," said Leo, "but I have decided to seek her in a different way. I am no longer

9. **Five Books.** The Pentateuch, or Five Books of Moses, consists of Genesis, Exodus, Leviticus, Numbers, and Deuteronomy.
10. **mea culpa.** I am to blame' (Latin).

WORDS FOR EVERYDAY USE: ab • ject • ly (ab´jekt´ lē) *adv.*, *miserably*; in a manner that suggests a lack of self-respect

interested in an arranged marriage. To be frank, I now admit the necessity of pre-marital love. That is, I want to be in love with the one I marry."

"Love?" said Salzman, astounded. After a moment he remarked, "For us, our love is our life, not for the ladies. In the ghetto they—"

"I know, I know," said Leo. "I've thought of it often. Love, I have said to myself, should be a by-product of living and worship rather than its own end. Yet for myself I find it necessary to establish the level of my need and fulfill it."

Salzman shrugged but answered, "Listen, rabbi, if you want love, this I can find for you also. I have such beautiful clients that you will love them the minute your eyes will see them."

Leo smiled unhappily. "I'm afraid you don't understand."

But Salzman hastily unstrapped his portfolio and withdrew a manila packet from it.

"Pictures," he said, quickly laying the envelope on the table.

Leo called after him to take the pictures away, but as if on the wings of the wind, Salzman had disappeared.

March came. Leo had returned to his regular routine. Although he felt not quite himself yet—lacked energy—he was making plans for a more active social life. Of course it would cost something, but he was an expert in cutting corners; and when there were no corners left he would make circles rounder. All the while Salzman's pictures had lain on the table, gathering dust. Occasionally as Leo sat studying, or enjoying a cup of tea, his eyes fell on the manila envelope, but he never opened it.

The days went by and no social life to speak of developed with a member of the opposite sex—it was difficult, given the circumstances of his situation. One morning Leo toiled up the stairs to his room and stared out the window at the city. Although the day was bright his view of it was dark. For some time he watched people in the street below hurrying along and then turned with a heavy heart to his little room. On the table was the packet. With a sudden <u>relentless</u> gesture he tore it open. For a half-hour he stood by the table in a state of excitement, examining the photographs of the ladies Salzman had included. Finally, with a deep sigh he put them down. There were six, of varying degrees of attractiveness, but look at them long enough and they all became Lily Hirschorn: all past their prime, all starved behind bright smiles, not a true personality in the lot. Life, despite their frantic yoohooings, had passed them by; they were pictures in a briefcase that stank of fish. After a while, however, as Leo attempted to return the photographs into the envelope, he found in it another, a snapshot of the type taken by a machine for a quarter. He gazed at it a moment and let out a cry.

Her face deeply moved him. Why, he could at first not say. It gave him the impression of youth—spring flowers, yet age—a sense of having been used to the bone, wasted; this came from the eyes, which were hauntingly familiar yet absolutely strange. He had a vivid impression that he had met her before,

WORDS FOR EVERYDAY USE: re • lent • less (ri lent´ lis) *adj.*, harsh; pitiless but try as he might he could not place her although he could almost recall her name, as if he had read it in her own handwriting. No, this couldn't be; he would have remembered her. It was not, he affirmed, that she had an extraordinary beauty—no, though her face was attractive enough; it was that *something* about her moved him. Feature for feature, even some of the ladies of the photographs could do better; but she leaped forth to his heart—had *lived*, or wanted to—more than just wanted, perhaps regretted how she had lived—had somehow deeply suffered: it could be seen in the depths of those reluctant eyes, and from the way the light enclosed and shone from her, and within her, opening realms of possibility: this was her own. Her he desired. His head ached and eyes narrowed with the intensity of his gazing, then as if an obscure fog had blown up in the mind, he experienced fear of her and was aware that he had received an impression, somehow, of evil. He shuddered, saying softly, it is thus with us all. Leo brewed some tea in a small pot and sat sipping it without sugar, to calm himself. But before he had finished drinking, again with excitement he examined the face and found it good: good for Leo Finkle. Only such a one could understand him and help him seek whatever he was seeking. She might, perhaps, love him. How she had happened to be among the discards in Salzman's barrel he could never guess, but he knew he must urgently go find her.

Leo rushed downstairs, grabbed up the Bronx telephone book, and searched for Salzman's home address. He was not listed, nor was his office. Neither was he in the Manhattan book. But Leo remembered having written down the address on a slip of paper after he had read Salzman's advertisement in the "personals" column of the *Forward*. He ran up to his room and tore through his papers, without luck. It was <u>exasperating</u>. Just when he needed the matchmaker he was nowhere to be found. Fortunately Leo remembered to look in his wallet. There on a card he found his name written and a Bronx address. No phone number was listed, the reason—Leo now recalled—he had originally communicated with Salzman by letter. He got on his coat, put a hat on over his skull cap and hurried to the subway station. All the way to the far end of the Bronx he sat on the edge of his seat. He was more than once tempted to take out the picture and see if the girl's face was as he remembered it, but he <u>refrained</u>, allowing the snapshot to remain in his inside coat pocket, content to have her so close. When the train pulled into the station he was waiting at the door and bolted out. He quickly located the street Salzman had advertised.

The building he sought was less than a block from the subway, but it was not an office building, nor even a loft, nor a store in which one could rent office space. It was a very old tenement house. Leo found Salzman's name in pencil on a soiled tag under the bell and climbed three dark flights to his apartment. When he knocked, the door was opened by a thin, asthmatic, gray-haired woman, in felt slippers.

WORDS FOR EVERYDAY USE:

ex • as • per • a • ting (eg zas´pər āt iŋ) *part.*, irritating, annoying

re • frain (ri frān´) *vi.*, hold back; keep oneself from doing something

"Yes?" she said, expecting nothing. She listened without listening. He could have sworn he had seen her, too, before but knew it was an illusion.

"Salzman—does he live here? Pinye Salzman," he said, "the matchmaker?"

She stared at him a long minute. "Of course."

He felt embarrassed. "Is he in?"

"No." Her mouth, though left open, offered nothing more.

"The matter is urgent. Can you tell me where his office is?"

"In the air." She pointed upward.

"You mean he has no office?" Leo asked.

"In his socks."

He peered into the apartment. It was sunless and dingy, one large room divided by a half-open curtain, beyond which he could see a sagging metal bed. The near side of a room was crowded with rickety chairs, old bureaus, a three-legged table, racks of cooking utensils, and all the <u>apparatus</u> of a kitchen. But there was no sign of Salzman or his magic barrel, probably also a figment of the imagination. An odor of frying fish made Leo weak to the knees.

"Where is he?" he insisted. "I've got to see your husband."

At length she answered, "So who knows where he is? Every time he thinks a new thought he runs to a different place. Go home, he will find you."

"Tell him Leo Finkle."

She gave no sign she had heard.

He walked downstairs, depressed.

But Salzman, breathless, stood waiting at his door.

Leo was astounded and overjoyed. "How did you get here before me?"

"I rushed."

"Come inside."

They entered. Leo fixed tea, and a sardine sandwich for Salzman. As they were drinking he reached behind him for the packet of pictures and handed them to the marriage broker.

Salzman put down his glass and said expectantly, "You found somebody you like?"

"Not among these."

The marriage broker turned away.

"Here is the one I want." Leo held forth the snapshot.

Salzman slipped on his glasses and took the picture into his trembling hand. He turned ghastly and let out a groan.

"What's the matter?" cried Leo.

"Excuse me. Was an accident this picture. She isn't for you."

Salzman frantically shoved the manila packet into his portfolio. He thrust the snapshot into his pocket and fled down the stairs.

Leo, after momentary paralysis, gave chase and cornered the marriage broker in the <u>vestibule</u>. The landlady made hysterical outcries but neither of them listened.

"Give me back the picture, Salzman."

"No." The pain in his eyes was terrible.

"Tell me who she is then."

"This I can't tell you. Excuse me."

He made to depart, but Leo, forgetting himself, seized the matchmaker by his tight coat and shook him frenziedly.

"Please," sighed Salzman. "*Please*."

Leo ashamedly let him go. "Tell me

AMBIGUITY

An ambiguity is an intentional double meaning. Of whom besides Salzman might it be said that his office is "In the air" and "who knows where he is? . . . he will find you"?

CLIMAX

The climax is the high point of interest or suspense in a story. At this point, Finkle, having finally discovered the match that he wants, learns that he might not be able to have that match.

WORDS FOR EVERYDAY USE:

ap • pa • ra • tus (ap´ ə rat´ əs) *n.*, materials and tools needed for a specific purpose

ves • ti • bule (ves´ tə byo͞ol´) *n.*, hallway or small room at the entrance of a building

who she is," he begged. "It's very important for me to know."

"She is not for you. She is a wild one—wild, without shame. This is not a bride for a rabbi."

"What do you mean wild?"

"Like an animal. Like a dog. For her to be poor was a sin. This is why to me she is dead now."

"In God's name, what do you mean?"

"Her I can't introduce to you," Salzman said.

"Why are you so excited?"

"Why, he asks," Salzman said, bursting into tears. "This is my baby, my Stella, she should burn in hell."

Leo hurried up to bed and hid under the covers. Under the covers he thought his life through. Although he soon fell asleep he could not sleep her out of his mind. He woke, beating his breast. Though he prayed to be rid of her, his prayers went unanswered. Through days of torment he endlessly struggled not to love her; fearing success, he escaped it. He then concluded to convert her to goodness, himself to God. The idea alternately nauseated and exalted him.

He perhaps did not know that he had come to a final decision until he encountered Salzman in a Broadway cafeteria. He was sitting alone at a rear table, sucking the bony remains of a fish. The marriage broker appeared <u>haggard</u>, and transparent to the point of vanishing.

Salzman looked up at first without recognizing him. Leo had grown a pointed beard and his eyes were weighted with wisdom.

"Salzman," he said, "love has at last come to my heart."

"Who can love from a picture?" mocked the marriage broker.

"It is not impossible."

"If you can love her, then you can love anybody. Let me show you some new clients that they just sent me their photographs. One is a little doll."

"Just her I want," Leo murmured.

"Don't be a fool, doctor. Don't bother with her."

"Put me in touch with her, Salzman," Leo said humbly. "Perhaps I can be of service."

Salzman had stopped eating and Leo understood with emotion that it was now arranged.

Leaving the cafeteria, he was, however, afflicted by a tormenting suspicion that Salzman had planned it all to happen this way.

Leo was informed by letter that she would meet him on a certain corner, and she was there one spring night, waiting under a street lamp. He appeared, carrying a small bouquet of violets and rosebuds. Stella stood by the lamppost, smoking. She wore white with red shoes, which fitted his expectations, although in a troubled moment he had imagined the dress red, and only the shoes white. She waited uneasily and shyly. From afar he saw that her eyes—clearly her father's—were filled with desperate innocence. He pictured, in her, his own redemption. Violins and lit candles revolved in the sky. Leo ran forward with flowers outthrust.

Around the corner, Salzman, leaning against a wall, chanted prayers for the dead. ■

WORDS FOR EVERYDAY USE: **hag • gard** (hag´ərd) *adj.*, having a wasted or exhausted look

Responding to the Selection

How do you think love and marriage should be related? What is your reaction to Leo Finkle's use of a marriage broker? How did you feel when he rejected the idea and pursued a love based on instinct instead? Explain your thinking.

Reviewing the Selection

RECALLING

1. What kind of services does Pinye Salzman sell? What is the nature of Leo Finkle's business with Pinye Salzman?

2. Who are the women Salzman initially suggests as potential brides? What characteristics do they have?

3. When Pinye Salzman reappears at Finkle's apartment after Leo's meeting with Lily Hirschorn, how does Leo react? What does Salzman do?

4. What does Leo find in the photographs Salzman leaves behind? How does he behave after his discovery?

INTERPRETING

5. Why does Leo Finkle want to buy Pinye Salzman's help? On what important reason has he based his decision to contact Salzman?

6. Why does Leo reject the first batch of women? How does he feel about the matchmaking process now?

7. How do you explain Leo's actions at this meeting? In what ways do they suggest the change in his feelings about the marriage process?

8. The photograph Leo finds touches important emotions inside him. What are these feelings? What elements in the photograph contribute to the effect?

SYNTHESIZING

9. What suspicion torments Leo at the end of the story? What would this interpretation of the events suggest about Pinye Salzman's character?

10. What inference does Salzman invite through his description of Stella? Identify some clues to support your answer.

Understanding Literature (Questions for Discussion)

1. **Motivation.** A **motivation** is a force that moves a character to think, feel, or behave in a certain way. Think about Leo Finkle's actions throughout "The Magic Barrel." How do you think his motivations change as the story progresses?

2. **Background Information.** Often part of the exposition or introduction to a literary work, **background information** orients readers to important details about major characters. These details might include family background, opinions, physical traits, strengths and weaknesses, or anything the writer feels readers must know in order to understand the story. Find three facts from "The Magic Barrel" that provide background information.

3. **Characterization. Characterization** is the use of literary techniques to create a character. These techniques may include description of the character's appearance, insight into the character's thinking processes, and observation of the character's actions. What techniques does Bernard Malamud use to portray Leo Finkle and Pinye Salzman?

4. **Dialect. Dialect** is a version of a language spoken by the people of a particular place, time, or social group. The use of dialect helps writers create vivid characters by placing those characters in a social, temporal, or geographic context. Find some examples of dialect in "The Magic Barrel." From what context do they originate? What do they tell you about the characters in the story?

5. **Figurative Language. Figurative language** is language that suggests something more than the literal meanings of the words. For example, "winter was on its last legs," suggests that winter is almost dead, or over. What other examples of figurative language can you find in "The Magic Barrel"? How do they affect your experience as a reader of the story?

The Process of Writing: Evaluating and Revising

Evaluation and Revision. Read the Language Arts Survey, 1.43–1.45, on various methods for evaluating and revising. Using the writing assignment you began on page 9, exchange papers with a classmate for peer evaluation. Then consider your peer's comments as you complete a self-evaluation. Employ the four types of revision—adding or expanding, deleting, replacing, and moving—in response to both evaluations.

Drama

Drama is literature enacted in front of an audience by people who play the parts of the characters. No one knows for certain how drama originated, but we do know that ritual performances have been held by people around the globe since long before the beginning of recorded history.

The first literary dramas were created long ago in ancient Greece and may have developed from reenactments of ritual sacrifices. In fact, the ancient Greek word *tragōidia,* from which our word *tragedy* derives, meant "song of the goats." According to one theory, people in ancient Greece would come together to sacrifice an animal to win a god's favor. Eventually, that sacrifice developed into an elaborate show involving an actor, a priest, and a chorus with whom the priest interacted. In the fifth century BC, the Greek playwright Aeschylus added a second actor, and drama as we know it was born.

Types of Stages

In classical times, dramas were performed in open-air amphitheaters, or **arena stages.** In the Middle Ages, plays were often produced on the backs of wagons in the courtyards of inns. From these developed the **thrust stage** used in Elizabethan England, a platform that jutted into an area open to the sky. In the nineteenth and twentieth centuries, the **proscenium stage,** or **picture stage,** became common. Such a stage is a box-like area with three walls (or curtains) and a removed "fourth wall" through which the audience views the action.

Types of Drama

Most dramas can be classified as either comedies or tragedies. A **comedy,** in its original sense, was any work with a happy ending. The term is widely used today to refer to any humorous work, especially one prepared for the stage or the screen. A **tragedy** initially was a drama that told the story of the fall of a person of high status, though in recent years the word has been used to describe any play about the downfall of a central character, or protagonist, who wins the audience's sympathies in some way.

Drama in the United States

The United States has produced many of the world's finest dramatists. Important figures in the history of American drama include Eugene O'Neill (1888–1953), Elmer Rice (1892–1967), Thornton Wilder (1897–1975), Lillian Hellman (1905–1984), Tennessee Williams (1911–1983), Arthur Miller (1915–), Edward Albee (1928–), Lanford Wilson (1937–), August Wilson (1945–), David Mamet (1947–), and Beth Henley (1952–).

The earliest American theatrical productions were vaudeville shows and **melodramas,** plays with exaggerated characters, scenes, and situations. From the 1920s through the 1950s, American **Realist theater** blossomed in the work of O'Neill, Hellman, and Miller. Williams and Albee introduced to American theater many experimental elements, extending and enriching the Realist tradition.

The trial of two "witches" at Salem, Massachusetts, in 1692.
Illustration by Howard Pyle.
The Granger Collection, New York

Elements of Drama

THE PLAYWRIGHT AND THE SCRIPT

Playwright. The author of a play is the **playwright.** The relationship between a playwright and the play is more tenuous that that of an ordinary author to his or her text. A novelist or poet has enormous control over the form in which his or her work will be presented to its audience, the reader. A playwright, in contrast, must depend upon the interpretations given his or her work by producers, directors, set designers, actors, and other persons involved in producing the work for the stage. The playwright's art is collaborative.

Script. A **script** is the written work from which a drama is produced. It contains stage directions and dialogue and may be divided into acts and scenes.

> **Stage Directions. Stage directions** are notes provided by the playwright to describe how something should be presented or performed on the stage. Stage directions often describe elements of the **spectacle,** such as lighting, music, sound effects, costumes, properties, and set design. They also may describe entrances and exits, the movements of characters, facial expressions, gestures, body language, tone of voice, or other elements related to the acting of the play. Sometimes, especially in reading versions of plays, stage directions provide historical or background information. Stage directions usually are printed in italics and enclosed in brackets or parentheses. In stage directions, the parts of the stage are often described using the terms *up, down, right, left,* and *center,* which describe stage areas from the point of view of the actors.

Stage Areas

Up Right	Up Center	Up Left
Right Center	Center	Left Center
Down Right	Down Center	Down Left

> **Dialogue. Dialogue** is the term used to describe the speech of actors in a play. The dialogue usually consists of the characters' names and the words and other utterances to be spoken by the actors. The dialogue of a play may contain many **monologues,** or long speeches given by actors. A speech given by a lone character on stage is called a **soliloquy.** A statement intended to be heard by the audience or by a single other character but not by other characters on the stage is called an **aside.**

Acts and Scenes. An **act** is a major division of a drama. The plays of ancient Rome and of Elizabethan England were typically divided into **five acts.** In the Modern Era, **three-act** and **one-act plays** are quite common. The acts may be divided into scenes. Typically, a **scene** begins with the entrance of one or more characters and ends with the exit of one or more characters. The time and place of acts or scenes may change from one to the next.

THE SPECTACLE

Spectacle. The **spectacle** is all the elements of the drama presented to the senses of the audience—the lights, sets, curtains, costumes, makeup, music, sound effects, properties, and movements of the actors, including any special movement such as pantomime or dance. Spectacle is one major feature that differentiates dramatic from nondramatic works. The following chart describes common parts of the spectacle.

ELEMENT OF SPECTACLE	DESCRIPTION
Stage	This is the area in which the action is performed. An **arena stage,** or **theater in the round,** is one in which the audience stands or sits around a circular or semicircular open space. A **thrust stage** is one that extends into the audience, which is situated on three sides of the playing area. A **proscenium,** or **picture stage,** is one that has an arch around an opening that acts as a removed "fourth wall."
Set	The set is everything placed upon the stage to give the impression of a particular setting, or time and place. Sets often include walls, furnishings, and painted backdrops.
Properties	Properties are items that can be carried on and off the stage by actors or manipulated by actors during scenes. Examples of properties include books, fans, gavels, and walking sticks.
Sound Effects	These are sounds introduced to create mood or to indicate the presence of something. Common sound effects include thunder, ringing telephones, and police sirens.
Blocking	This is the act of determining how actors will move on a stage. Blocking is almost always done by the director of the play.

FROM

The Crucible

ARTHUR MILLER

Background Note: In 1692, a series of trials was held in Salem, Massachusetts, of persons accused of witchcraft. Many people in the community and in surrounding areas had developed a disease resembling epilepsy, and suspicions arose that the afflictions might be the work of witches. The governor of the colony of Massachusetts, Sir William Phips, instituted court proceedings. The proceedings were inflamed by accusations made by the daughters of a Salem minister named Parris. These daughters, including Abigail Parris, pretended to be possessed by spirits and made spectacles in the courtroom during examinations of the accused witches. In all, nineteen persons were hanged as a result of the trials, and one person was pressed to death. Many others were imprisoned and tortured.

Arthur Miller became interested in the Salem witch trials during the McCarthy Era of the 1950s, a time when a similar "witch hunt" occurred in the United States, this one for suspected communists and other radicals in public office and the entertainment industry. Miller's play explores the psychology of mob hysteria and guilt by association. In this scene from the play, John Proctor, whose wife, Elizabeth, has been arrested as a witch, has brought to the court Mary Warren, who has evidence that Abigail and the other afflicted girls have been pretending. As the scene opens, Abigail interrupts an interrogation of John Proctor by the prosecutor, Danforth.

STAGE DIRECTIONS

Stage directions are notes that tell about the movements and ways of speaking of characters, about the setting, or about such elements of the spectacle as lighting, costumes, properties, and sound effects.

▶ *Abigail, with a weird, wild, chilling cry, screams up to the ceiling.*

ABIGAIL. You will not! Begone! Begone, I say!

DANFORTH. What is it, child? (*But Abigail, pointing with fear, is now raising up her frightened eyes, her awed face, toward the ceiling—the girls are doing the same—and now Hawthorne, Haler, Putnam, Cheever, Herrick, and Danforth do the same.*) What's there? (*He lowers his eyes from the ceiling, and now he is frightened; there is real tension in his voice.*) Child! (*She is transfixed—with all the girls, she is whimpering open-mouthed, agape at the ceiling.*) Girls! Why do you—?

MERCY LEWIS. (*pointing*) It's on the beam! Behind the rafter!

DANFORTH. (*looking up*) Where!

ABIGAIL. Why—? (*She gulps.*) Why do you come, yellow bird?

PROCTOR. Where's a bird? I see no bird!

ABIGAIL. (*to the ceiling*) My face? My face?

PROCTOR. Mr. Hale—

DANFORTH. Be quiet!

PROCTOR. (*to Hale*) Do you see a bird?

DANFORTH. Be quiet!!

ABIGAIL. (*to the ceiling, in a genuine conversation with the "bird," as though trying to talk* *it out of attacking her*) But God made my face; you cannot want to tear my face. Envy is a deadly sin, Mary.

MARY WARREN. (*on her feet with a spring, and horrified, pleading*) Abby!

ABIGAIL. (*unperturbed, continuing to the "bird"*) Oh, Mary, this is a black art[1] to change your shape. No, I cannot, I cannot stop my mouth; it's God's work I do.

MARY WARREN. Abbey, I'm *here!*

PROCTOR. (*frantically*) They're pretending, Mr. Danforth!

ABIGAIL. (*Now she takes a backward step, as though in fear the bird will swoop down momentarily.*) Oh, please, Mary! Don't come down.

SUSANNA WALCOTT. Her claws, she's stretching her claws!

PROCTOR. Lies, lies.

ABIGAIL. (*backing further, eyes still fixed above*) Mary, please don't hurt me!

MARY WARREN. (*to Danforth*) I'm not hurting her!

DANFORTH. (*to Mary Warren*) Why does she see this vision?

MARY WARREN. She sees nothin'!

ABIGAIL. (*now staring full front as though hypnotized, and mimicking the exact tone of Mary Warren's cry*) She sees nothin'!

MARY WARREN. (*pleading*) Abby, you mustn't!

ABIGAIL AND ALL THE GIRLS. (*all transfixed*) Abby, you mustn't!

MARY WARREN. (*to all the girls*) I'm here, I'm here!

GIRLS. I'm here, I'm here!

DANFORTH. (*horrified*) Mary Warren! Draw back your spirit out of them!

MARY WARREN. Mr. Danforth!

GIRLS. (*cutting her off*) Mr. Danforth!

DANFORTH. Have you compacted with the devil? Have you?

MARY WARREN. Never, never!

GIRLS. Never, never!

DANFORTH. (*growing hysterical*) Why can they only repeat you?

PROCTOR. Give me a whip—I'll stop it!

MARY WARREN. They're sporting, They—!

GIRLS. They're sporting!

MARY WARREN. (*turning on them all hysterically and stamping her feet*) Abby, stop it!

GIRLS. (*stamping their feet*) Abby, stop it!

MARY WARREN. Stop it!

GIRLS. Stop it!

MARY WARREN. (*screaming it out at the top of her lungs, and raising her fists*) Stop it!!

GIRLS. (*raising their fists*) Stop it!!

Mary Warren, utterly <u>confounded</u>, and becoming overwhelmed by Abigail's—and the girls'—utter conviction, starts to whimper, hands half raised, powerless, and all the girls begin whimpering exactly as she does.

DANFORTH. A little while ago you were afflicted. Now it seems you afflict others; where did you find this power?

MARY WARREN. (*staring at Abigail*) I— have no power.

GIRLS. I have no power.

PROCTOR. They're <u>gulling</u> you, Mister!

---

1. **black art.** Evil magic

WORDS FOR EVERYDAY USE:

con • found (kən found´) *vt.,* confuse, bewilder

gull (gul) *vt.,* trick; dupe

DANFORTH. Why did you turn about this past two weeks? You have seen the Devil, have you not?

HALE. (*indicating Abigail and the girls*) You cannot believe them!

MARY WARREN. I—

PROCTOR. (*sensing her weakening*) Mary, God damns all liars!

DANFORTH. (*pounding it into her*) You have seen the Devil, you have made compact with Lucifer,[2] have you not?

Mary utters something unintelligible, staring at Abigail, who keeps watching the "bird" above.

PROCTOR. God damns liars, Mary!

DANFORTH. I cannot hear you. What do you say? (*Mary utters again unintelligibly.*) You will confess yourself or you will hang! (*He turns her roughly to face him.*) Do you know who I am? I say you will hang if you do not open with me!

PROCTOR. Mary, remember the angel Raphael—do that which is good and—

ABIGAIL. (*pointing upward*) The wings! Her wings are spreading! Mary, please, don't, don't—!

HALE. I see nothing, Your Honor!

DANFORTH. Do you confess this power! (*He is an inch from her face.*) Speak!

ABIGAIL. She's going to come down! She's walking the beam!

DANFORTH. Will you speak!

MARY WARRREN. (*staring in horror*) I cannot!

GIRLS. I cannot!

PARRIS. Cast the Devil out! Look him in the face! Trample him! We'll save you, Mary, only stand fast against him and—

ABIGAIL. (*looking up*) Look out! She's coming down!

She and all the girls run to one wall, shielding their eyes. And now, as though cornered, they let out a gigantic scream, and Mary, as though infected, opens her mouth and screams with them. Gradually Abigail and the girls leave off, until only Mary is left there, staring up at the "bird," screaming madly. All watch her, horrified by this evident fit. Proctor strides to her.

PROCTOR. Mary, tell the Governor what they— (*He has hardly got a word out, when seeing him coming for her, she rushes out of his reach, screaming in horror.*)

MARY WARREN. Don't touch me—don't touch me! (*At which the girls halt at the door.*)

PROCTOR. (*astonished*) Mary!

MARY WARREN. (*pointing at Proctor*) You're the Devil's man!

He is stopped in his tracks.

PARRIS. Praise God!

GIRLS. Praise God!

PROCTOR. (*numbed*) Mary, how—?

MARY WARREN. I'll not hang with you! I love God, I love God.

DANFORTH. (*to Mary*) He bid you do the Devil's work?

MARY WARREN. (*hysterically, indicating Proctor*) He come at me by night and every day to sign, to sign, to—

DANFORTH. Sign what?

PARRIS. The Devil's book? He come with a book?

MARY WARREN. (*hysterically, pointing at Proctor, fearful of him*) My name, he want my name. "I'll murder you," he says, "if my wife hangs! We must go and overthrow the court," he says!

Danforth's head jerks toward Proctor, shock and horror in his face.

PROCTOR. (*turning, appealing to Hale*) Mr. Hale!

---

2. **Lucifer.** Name for the devil

MARY WARREN. (*her sobs beginning*) He wake me every night, his eyes were like coals and his fingers claw my neck, and I sign, I sign . . .

HALE. Excellency, this child's gone wild!

PROCTOR (*as Danforth's wide eyes pour on him*) Mary, Mary!

MARY WARREN, (*screaming at him*) No, I love God; I go your way no more. I love God, I bless God. (*Sobbing, she rushes to Abigail.*) Abby, Abby, I'll never hurt you more! (*They all watch, as Abigail, out of her infinite charity, reaches out and draws the sobbing Mary to her, and then looks up to Danforth.*) ■

Responding to the Selection

Why does Mary Warren turn on Proctor and make an accusation against him? What pressures lead her to do this? Discuss social pressure with your classmates. Why is it important to stand up for what you believe in the face of such pressure?

Reviewing the Selection

RECALLING

1. What does Abigail claim to see on the beam, behind the rafter? What does Abigail say is "a deadly sin"?

2. What question does Danforth ask Mary after she says, "I'm not hurting her"?

3. What does Mary mean when she says that the girls are "sporting"?

4. Of what does Mary accuse Proctor? To whom does Mary rush at the end of the selection?

INTERPRETING

5. According to Abigail, who is making the bird appear? What is the bird?

6. What pressure does Danforth's question put on Mary? What might happen to Mary if the court believes Abigail and the girls?

7. Does Mary see the bird? What explanation for the bird does she offer at first?

8. Why does Mary change her mind and accuse Proctor?

9. In Puritan New England, debate raged over the admissibility in court of "spectral evidence," the evidence of spirits seen by some people but not by others. What example of such "spectral evidence" appears in this selection? Why isn't such evidence now admissible in courts of law?

10. What pressures are put on Mary to denounce Proctor? Is what Mary does understandable? excusable? moral? Why, or why not?

Understanding Literature (Questions for Discussion)

1. **Stage Directions. Stage directions** are notes included in a play in addition to the dialogue for the purpose of describing how something should be performed on stage. Stage directions describe movements and ways of speaking of characters, the setting, and such elements of the spectacle as lighting, costumes, properties, and sound effects. Find examples in this scene of stage directions that indicate parts of the setting and stage directions that indicate how characters are to speak or move.

2. **Character. Characters** are the people (or sometimes animals) who figure in the action of a literary work. In a play, the names of characters are given before the words that they speak. Who are the major characters in this scene from *The Crucible*? Who are the minor characters? Briefly describe the personalities of the major characters, based on their words and actions in this scene. Which characters do you admire? Which do you not admire? Why?

3. **Dialogue. Dialogue** is conversation involving two or more characters. In a play, dialogue appears after the characters' names and is not placed in quotation marks, as it would be in a novel or short story. Find examples in this scene of dialogue that would probably not be spoken by characters in a modern setting but that is appropriate to Miller's setting of the play in colonial New England.

4. **Set and Properties.** In a drama, the **set** is the physical area of the stage, along with any backdrops, curtains, walls, or fixed pieces of scenery or furniture. **Properties** are small objects that can be carried on and off the stage. If you were designing a set for this scene from *The Crucible,* what elements would you have to include? What properties might you have the actors use?

5. **Blocking. Blocking** is the process of planning the movements of actors on a stage. What movements described in the stage directions for this scene would have to be taken into account by the person, such as the director, who was planning the blocking of the scene?

6. **Theme.** A **theme** is a central idea in a literary work. What do you think is the theme of this scene from the play? What does the scene reveal about the forces that cause people to give in to mob hysteria? Why do some people foresake their convictions in situations like the one described in this scene?

The Process of Writing: Proofreading

Proofreading. Read the Language Arts Survey, 1.47, "Proofreading Checklist," and 1.48, "Preparing Your Manuscript." Proofread the personal essay that you revised for the revision lesson on page 41. Then prepare a clean, final copy of your essay and proofread it once more. When preparing your final copy, follow proper manuscript form as described in the Language Arts Survey or by your teacher.

Language Lab

The Parts of Speech. Review the Language Arts Survey, 2.3–2.31, "The Parts of Speech." Then identify the part of speech of each italicized word in the paragraph below.

[1] *Joseph Raymond McCarthy* entered the United States Senate in 1946. [2] *After* two undistinguished years in the Senate, [3] *he* gained national recognition in 1950 by charging that over two hundred Communists [4] *had infiltrated* the State Department, that part of the government that oversees foreign relations. At the time, the United States was at war with the Communist government in North Korea, and many citizens of the country were [5] *deeply* fearful about Communist advances in Europe and China. McCarthy's charges struck a chord with the people, and for several years thereafter, [6] *innocent* people were hounded from their jobs in government and in the entertainment industry because of "suspected" Communist activities and "associations" with Communists. Targets [7] *of* McCarthyism included such well-known literary figures as Ring Lardner, Jr., and Lillian Hellman. McCarthy went too far, however, when he made accusations against such popular figures as President Dwight D. Eisenhower. In 1954, the Senate formally voted to condemn McCarthy for his [8] *conduct,* and the McCarthy Era came to an end. Did anything positive come out of the McCarthy Era? [9] *Yes,* this period in American history gave people a new understanding of the dangers of character assassination, guilt by association, [10] *and* mass hysteria. It also gave us Arthur Miller's fine play, The Crucible.

Arthur Miller (1915–) was born in New York City. During his youth, his father's business failed as part of the general economic downturn known as the Great Depression. This failure had a permanent impact on Miller, who went on to write great plays on themes related to social and political justice. After graduating from high school, Miller worked and raised money to attend the University of Michigan. There he began writing plays. His most famous work, *Death of a Salesman* (1949), tells the story of the tragic downfall of its title character, partially as a result of his willingness to do anything for the "almighty dollar." Miller's play is a classic exposé of the consequences of hypocrisy and greed. When Miller was called before the House Un-American Activities Committee and asked to name suspected communists whom he had met ten years before at a writer's meeting, he refused to do so. He was cited for contempt but overturned the citation on appeal. Miller's other plays included *The Crucible* (1953) and *A View from the Bridge* (1955). In addition to his plays for the stage, Miller wrote screenplays, including the script for *The Misfits,* a film that starred his second wife, Marilyn Monroe.

Nonfiction

Nonfiction writing, unlike the other types of literature considered so far, explores actual people, places, things, events, and ideas. Types of nonfiction writing include the following:

Histories, such as the selections from Imamu Baraka's *Blues People* (Unit 1), Bartolomé de las Casas's *The Very Brief Relation of the Devastation of the Indies* (Unit 2), John Smith's *The General History of Virginia, New England, and the Summer Isles* (Unit 2), William Bradford's *Of Plymouth Plantation* (Unit 2), and W. E. B. Du Bois's *The Souls of Black Folk* (Unit 7), provide accounts of past events.

Of importance to historians in preparing their works are many types of public records, such as **speeches, sermons, contracts, deeds, constitutions, laws,** and **political tracts.** Examples in this text include the selection from the Iroquois Constitution (Unit 2), Jonathan Edwards's "Sinners in the Hands of an Angry God" (Unit 2), Patrick Henry's Speech in the Virginia Convention (Unit 3), Thomas Paine's *Crisis No. 1* (Unit 3), the Declaration of Independence (Unit 3), Abraham Lincoln's "A House Divided" (Unit 6), and Gettysburg Address (Unit 6), Robert E. Lee's "Farewell to His Army" (Unit 6), Chief Joseph's "I Will Fight No More Forever" (Unit 7), Cochise's "I Am Alone" (Unit 7), William Faulkner's Address upon Receiving the Nobel Prize Acceptance Speech (Unit 11), and John F. Kennedy's Inaugural Address (Unit 12).

Other types of nonfiction, closely related to histories, are **biographies** and **autobiographies,** which can be thought of as histories of individual people. A biography is the story of a person's life. An autobiography is the story of a person's life, written by that person. John Smith's *The General History of Virginia, New England, and the Summer Isles* is an interesting example of an autobiography because, although it is the history of his own life, Smith chose to write from the third-person point of view, typical of the biography. Other examples of autobiographies in this text include the selections from *The Autobiography of Benjamin Franklin* (Unit 3), *Narrative of the Life of Frederick Douglass, an American Slave, Written by Himself* (Unit 6), and Booker T. Washington's *Up from Slavery* (Unit 6).

Biographers often work from the **letters, diaries,** and **journals** of their subjects. Examples of letters in this text are Abigail Adams's Letter to John Adams, May 7, 1776 (Unit 3), and Abraham Lincoln's Letter to Mrs. Bixby (Unit 6). Henry David Thoreau's *Walden* (Unit 4) and Ralph Waldo Emerson's *Self-Reliance* (Unit 4), were developed from journals or diaries kept by their authors.

Emerson's *Self-Reliance* and the chapters in Thoreau's *Walden* are examples of a form of nonfiction known as the **essay.** The word *essay* originally meant a "trial or attempt." In an essay, a writer does not attempt an exhaustive treatment of a topic but rather presents a single main idea, or thesis, about the topic.

Share Croppers. Robert Gwathmey, 1941, 17 3/4" × 12 3/4", watercolor. Courtesy of San Diego Museum of Art. Museum purchase with funds provided by Mrs. Leon D. Bonnet.

Purpose and Mode in Nonfiction

Purpose. A writer's **purpose,** or **aim,** is what he or she wants a work to accomplish. Nonfiction writing generally is produced with some overall purpose in mind. The following chart classifies types of writing by purpose.

TYPE OF WRITING	PURPOSE
Expressive Writing	The writer expresses himself or herself, describing personal feelings, attitudes, ideas, values, or beliefs.
Expository or Informative Writing	The writer attempts to inform others about a subject.
Persuasive Writing	The writer attempts to persuade others to adopt some belief or to take some course of action.
Literary Writing	The writer creates an imaginary world to entertain and, sometimes, to instruct.

This classification system derives from the work of James Kinneavy, who, in *A Theory of Discourse,* bases his classification of writing on an analysis of the standard "communication model." According to this model, a sender encodes a message about some subject in a set of symbols and then transmits that message to a recipient. In **expressive writing,** the emphasis is on the sender of the message, the writer. The major purpose is to express the writer's state of mind. In **expository writing,** the emphasis is on the subject. The major purpose is to provide information about that subject. In **persuasive writing,** the emphasis is on the recipient. The major purpose is to change the recipient's mind or to move the recipient to action. In **literary writing,** the emphasis is on the symbols—the words themselves and the form into which they are organized. The major purpose is to create an imaginary world by which to entertain or instruct.

Mode. Another common classification system divides various types of writing according to the method of treatment of the subject. The following chart describes methods of treating subjects, or **modes** of writing, that are commonly used in nonfiction.

MODE OF WRITING	DESCRIPTION
Narration	Writing in this mode describes events. Histories, biographies, autobiographies, and news reports all make extensive use of narration.
Dialogue	Writing in this mode presents words as they were actually spoken by people.
Description	Writing in this mode portrays in words how things look, sound, smell, taste, or feel.
Exposition	Writing in this mode presents facts or opinions in an organized manner.

Types of Exposition. There are many modes of expository writing used in nonfiction works. The following chart describes some of the most common.

MODE OF EXPOSITION	DESCRIPTION
Analysis	Writing in this mode breaks something into its parts and shows how the parts are related.
Classification	Writing in this mode places subjects into categories, or classes, according to their properties or characteristics.
Comparison and Contrast	Writing in this mode presents similarities and differences.
Process/How to	Writing in this mode presents the steps in a process.

FROM

Blues People

IMAMU AMIRI BARAKA

Since most Negroes before and after slavery were agricultural laborers, the corn songs and arwhoolies,[1] the shouts and hollers, issued from one kind of work. Some of the work songs, for instance, use as their measure[2] the grunt of a man pushing a heavy weight or the blow of a hammer against a stone to provide the <u>metrical</u> precision and rhythmical <u>impetus</u> behind the singer. ("Take this hammer, uh,/Take it to the captain, uh,/Take it to the captain, uh,/Tell him I'm gone.") Contemporary work songs, for example, songs recorded by Negro convicts working in the South—laying railroad ties, felling trees, breaking rocks, take their impetus from the work being done, and the form of the singing itself is dictated by the work. These workers for the most part do not sing blues. The labor is central to the song: not only is the recurring grunt or moan of these work songs some kind of metrical and rhythmical insistence,[3] it is the very <u>catalyst</u> for the song. On one recent record, the Louisiana Folklore Society's, *Prison Worksongs* recorded in Angola, Louisiana, at the Louisiana State Penitentiary there, one song listed as *Take This Hammer* begins as that song, but lasts as that for only about three "bars" (three strokes of the hammer) and then wanders irresolutely[4] into *Alberta,*

Berta, several blues verses, and a few lines from a spiritual. The point is that the primitive blues was at once a more formal music since the three-line, twelve-bar song became rapidly standardized, and was also a more liberated music since there was literally *more* to sing about. In one's leisure one can begin to <u>formalize</u> a method of singing as well as find new things to sing about. (It is an interesting thought that perhaps all the music that Negroes in America have made might have been quite different if the work that they were brought here to do had been different. Suppose Negroes had been brought to this country to make vases or play basketball. How might the blues have developed then from the impetus of work songs geared to those occupations?)

Work songs and shouts were, of course, almost always *a capella*.[5] It would have been extremely difficult for a man to pick cotton or shuck corn and play an instrument at the same time. For this reason pre-blues secular singing[6] did not have

---

1. **arwhoolies.** Field hollers
2. **as their measure.** As a way of marking the regular pattern of rhythm
3. **insistence.** Demand
4. **irresolutely.** Hesitantly
5. **a capella.** Without instrumental accompaniment
6. **secular singing.** Singing not related to religious practice

---

WORDS FOR EVERYDAY USE:

met • ri • cal (me´ tri kəl) *adj.,* related to the number of beats in each line of a verse or song

im • pe • tus (im´pə təs) *n.,* driving force behind an activity

cat • a • lyst (kat´ ə list´) *n.,* something that stimulates or hastens a result

for • mal • ize (fôr´ mə līz´) *vt.,* give definite form to

the discipline or strict formality that a kind of singing employing instruments must have. But it is obvious from the very earliest form of the blues that instrumental accompaniment was beginning to be taken into consideration. The twelve-bar blues[7]—the more or less final form of blues—is constructed so that each verse is of three lines, each line about four bars long. The words of the song usually occupy about one-half of each line, leaving a space of two bars for either a sung answer or an instrumental response.

It may seem strange that the formal blues should evolve *after* slavery, after so many years of bondage and exposure by the slaves to the larger Western cultural unit,[8] into a form that is patently non-Western;[9] the three-line verse form of the blues springs from no readily apparent Western source. But the use of instruments on a large scale was also something that happened after the Emancipation;[10] the very possession of instruments, except those few made from African models, was rare in the early days of slavery. The stereotyped pictures that many of the apologists[11] for the Southern way of life used as flyleaves for their numerous novels after the Civil War, depicting a happy-go-lucky black existentialist[12] strumming merrily on his banjo while sitting on a bale of cotton, were, I'm sure, more romantic fiction than fact. The slave would hardly have had the time to sit on his master's bale of cotton during the work day, and the only instruments that were in common usage among the slaves were drums, rattles, tambourines,

Folksinger. Charles White. Collection of Harry Belafonte. Courtesy Heritage Gallery, Los Angeles, CA

scrapers (the jawbone of a horse over which a piece of wood was scraped), and the like; even such an African instrument as the banjo was very scarce. The guitar was not commonly played by Negroes until much after the Civil War. An instrument like the harmonica grew in popularity among a great many Negroes simply because it took up almost no space and was so easy to carry around. But even the harmonica did not come into common use until after slavery, and certainly the possession and mastery[13] of European instruments did not occur until much later.

7. **twelve-bar blues.** Music in which each verse consists of twelve units, marked by twelve accented beats

8. **Western cultural unit.** Customs and values of the West, mainly of European Americans who controlled the lives of African-American slaves for four hundred years

9. **patently non-Western.** Uniquely and definitely outside the Western tradition

10. **the Emancipation.** President Abraham Lincoln signed the Emancipation Proclamation in 1862, legally freeing all African Americans from slavery.

11. **apologists.** People who try to rationalize or explain an unpopular political position, such as the idea that slavery was good for the slaves

12. **existentialist.** Someone who takes the philosophical point of view that actuality is better than possibility

13. **mastery.** Ability to use properly

When primitive or country blues did begin to be influenced by instruments, it was the guitar that had the most effect on the singers. And when the great masses of Negroes were just beginning to learn the instrument, the relatively simple chords of the country blues were probably what they learned. Conceivably, this also brought about another change: blues, a vocal music, was made to conform to an instrument's range. But, of course, the blues widened the range of the instrument, too. Blues guitar was not the same as classical or "legitimate"[14] guitar: the strings had to make vocal sounds, to imitate the human voice and its eerie cacophonies.[15] Perhaps the reason why the guitar was at once so popular was not only because it was much like the African instrument, the banjo (or *banjor*), but because it was an instrument that still permitted the performer to *sing*.

When the Negro finally did take up the brass instruments for strictly instrumental blues or jazz, the players still persisted in singing in the "breaks."[16] This could be done easily in the blues tradition with the call-and-response form of blues. Even much later in the jazz tradition, not only were instruments made to sound like the human voice but a great many of the predominantly instrumental songs were still partially sung. The first great soloist of jazz, Louis Armstrong,[17] was a formidable blues singer, as was the great jazz pianist Jelly Roll Morton.[18] Both men sang blues almost as beautifully as they played their instruments.

The primitive blues was still very much a vocal music; the singers relied on the unpredictability and mobility of the human voice for their imaginative catalysts. But the growing use of European instruments such as brass and reeds almost precluded song, except as accompaniment or as an interlude.[19] When Negroes began to master more and more "European" instruments and began to think musically in terms of their timbres,[20] as opposed to, or in conjunction with, the voice, blues began to change, and the era of jazz was at hand. ■

14. **legitimate.** Conventional
15. **cacophonies.** Loud, unharmonious sounds
16. **breaks.** Pauses in the music, for example, in the two-bar, half-line break in each line of twelve-bar blues
17. **Louis Armstrong.** (1900–1971) Jazz musician famous for his singing voice
18. **Jelly Roll Morton.** (1885–1941) Famed for his trumpet playing and his distinctive scat, or improvisational, singing style
19. **precluded . . . interlude.** Replaced song except as a break in the vocal music
20. **timbres.** Tonal quality of sounds

ORGANIZATION

Though various organization strategies are used by Baraka throughout this piece, the overall pattern is chronological, in order of the occurrence of events in time.

CLASSIFICATION

Classification divides a subject or subjects into categories according to particular features. While not rigidly structured, Baraka's discussion of African-American music looks at three musical styles: work songs, blues, and jazz.

Responding to the Selection

In general, do you enjoy reading historical analysis? Did you find this selection from *Blues People* interesting? What, if any, topics from the selection would you like to learn more about?

WORDS FOR EVERYDAY USE:

con • ceiv • a • bly (kən sēv′ə blē) *adv.,* in a manner that can be understood or imagined

ee • rie (ir′ē) *adj.,* mysterious; weird

pre • dom • i • nant • ly (prē däm′ə nənt lē) *adv.,* mostly; prevailingly

for • mi • da • ble (fôr′mə də bəl) *adj.,* strikingly impressive

con • junc • tion (kən juŋk′shən) *n.,* association; combination

Reviewing the Selection

RECALLING

1. What kinds of songs are central to early African-American music?

2. In what current circumstances do work songs still appear?

3. From what musical source did the sounds of early African-American work songs primarily come?

4. When did formal blues music evolve? What instrument had the most effect on blues singers?

INTERPRETING

5. What situation led to the creation of African-American music?

6. How are work songs related to their source?

7. Why were most work songs primarily vocal?

8. What additional element influenced the development of formal blues? Which instrument fit the blues singers' goals?

SYNTHESIZING

9. How was African-American music changed by musicians' growing expertise with "European" instruments?

10. How would you characterize the relationship between African-American music and the expanding opportunity and skills of its musicians?

Understanding Literature (Questions for Discussion)

1. **Anecdote.** An **anecdote** is a brief story, usually one that serves a specific purpose of the author. Find an example of an anecdote in the selection from *Blues People*. What purpose does it serve?

2. **Special Vocabulary. Special vocabulary** includes words from other languages and/or from particular fields, such as science or the arts. Find an example of special vocabulary in this selection. Use a dictionary to learn the meaning and origins of the term. Why do you think Baraka chose to use this word in his writing? How does it enrich his exposition?

The Process of Writing: Proofreading and Publishing

Proofreading and Publishing. Proofread the most recent draft of the personal essay you have been writing for this unit. Refer to the Language Arts Survey, 1.47, "Proofreading Checklist," as you work. Share a clean, final copy of your manuscript with your peers.

ELEMENTS OF NONFICTION / FROM BLUES PEOPLE **59**

UNIT REVIEW

Genres and Techniques of Literature

VOCABULARY FROM THE SELECTIONS

abjectly, 35
apparatus, 38
ascetic, 28
avow, 32
catalyst, 56
conceivably, 58
confound, 47
conjunction, 58

eerie, 58
exasperating, 37
formalize, 56
formidable, 58
gull, 47
haggard, 39
imperceptible, 29
impetus, 56

inherently, 27
machination, 34
meager, 27
menagerie, 28
metrical, 56
nuptial, 33
ordain, 27
predominantly, 58

profusion, 34
ravenously, 31
refrain, 37
relentless, 36
resolution, 18
trepidation, 33
vestibule, 38

LITERARY TERMS

anecdote, 59
background
    information, 41
blocking, 50
character, 50
characterization, 41
dialect, 41

dialogue, 50
figurative
    language, 41
motivation, 41
parallelism, 20
personification, 20
properties, 50

refrain, 8
repetition, 8
rhyme scheme, 20
sonnet, 19
set, 50
special
    vocabulary, 59

spiritual, 8
stage directions, 50
symbol, 20
theme, 8, 20, 50

SYNTHESIS: QUESTIONS FOR WRITING, RESEARCH, OR DISCUSSION

THE ORAL TRADITION

1. **Spirituals and the Oral Tradition.** Why were the spirituals transmitted orally instead of being written down? What special historical circumstance made oral transmission of the spirituals necessary? What messages did the spirituals convey?

POETRY

2. **Lyric Poetry.** How do lyric poems differ from narrative and dramatic ones? What special poetic devices, including devices of sound and rhetorical techniques, are used in "Sonnet XXX"? What characteristics make this poem a sonnet?

FICTION

3. **Short Story Structure.** Into what parts is a typical plot divided? What events in "The Magic Barrel" correspond to these parts?

DRAMA

4. **The Spectacle in Drama.** Imagine that you will be directing a production of the scene from *The Crucible* given in this unit. Make a complete list, with descriptions, of the following elements of the spectacle in your production: the stage set, the lighting, the properties, and the costumes.

NONFICTION

5. **Purpose and Organization in Nonfiction.** What is the main purpose of the selection in this unit from *Blues People*? What method of organization does the selection use?

LANGUAGE LAB   THE PARTS OF SPEECH

Thousands of years ago in ancient India, grammarians developed a method for classifying words in categories or types. These types are known as the **parts of speech.** The eight parts of speech are shown on the following chart.

	THE EIGHT PARTS OF SPEECH
1	A **noun** is the name of a person, place, thing, or idea. *Tennessee Williams, Laura, Africa, New York City, barrel, people, poetry, sadness*
2	A **pronoun** is a word that stands for or refers to a noun. *she, it, them, anything, someone, which, that, whose*
3	A **verb** is a word that describes an action or a state of being. *tell, disappoint, were singing, drink, is, are, were, be, appear, grow*
4	An **adjective** is a word that modifies a noun or a pronoun. *magic, shy, pale, confused, resourceful, courageous*
5	An **adverb** is a word that modifies a verb, an adjective, or another adverb. *quietly, insistently, extremely, very, only, later*
6	A **preposition** is a word that shows a relationship between a noun or a pronoun and some other word in a sentence. *about, against, around, as, between, down, for, from, in, of, off, outside, through, under*
7	A **conjunction** is a word that is used to join words, groups of words, or complete sentences. *and, or, nor, for, but, so, yet, because, since, unless, when, but also*
8	An **interjection** is a word used to express an emotion or to indicate a pause in speech or writing. *wow, oh, yes, yikes, well, hey, oh my, hi*

SENTENCE MODEL

INT	ADV	ADJ	N	V	ADJ	CONJ	ADJ	PREP	PRO	N
Oh,	painfully	shy	Laura	feels	rejected	and	humiliated	by	her	caller.

LANGUAGE ARTS SURVEY

For additional help, see the Language Arts Survey, 2.3–2.31.

Exercise A   Identifying the Parts of Speech

Identify the part of speech of each italicized word in the following paragraph. Use *n.* for noun, *pro.* for pronoun, *v.* for verb, *adj.* for adjective, *adv.* for adverb, *prep.* for preposition, *conj.* for conjunction, and *int.* for interjection.

>   *v.*   *conj.*
>
> EXAMPLE: Tennessee Williams *enjoyed* a long *and* productive career.

Williams revised some of [1] *his* one-act plays and short stories to create many of his full-length plays. Was <u>The Glass Menagerie</u> a [2] *revision* of an earlier work? [3] *Yes,* says a scholar who has traced its origins. Before it came to Broadway in 1945, <u>The Glass Menagerie</u> had been through [4] *several* revisions. Sometime before 1943, Williams wrote "Portrait of a Girl in Glass," a short story that he had also adapted [5] *into* a one-act play. While working for MGM studios in 1943, Williams [6] *wrote* a movie treatment for the story, entitled "The Gentleman Caller." Working with the script [7] *later* that year, he expanded the play to seven scenes, [8] *and* it is this version that appears in most literary anthologies. During rehearsals for the play, [9] *Williams* revised the script once more, adding an eighth scene; this version of the play is the one that [10] *usually* is performed.

Exercise B Using the Parts of Speech in Writing

Many words in English can be used as more than one part of speech. Identify the part of speech of each italicized word below. Then, write a new sentence using each word as the part of speech given in parentheses.

LANGUAGE ARTS SURVEY

For additional help, see the Language Arts Survey, 2.30–2.31.

v.

EXAMPLE: The gentleman caller, Jim, will *call* on Laura in the next scene. (Use as a noun.)

n.

The director has announced a casting call for the part of Laura.

1. The main *character* in Bernard Malamud's "The Magic Barrel" is Leo Finkle. (Use as an adjective.)

2. Although he is best known for his poetry, Imamu Amiri Baraka also has written essays, short stories, *plays,* a novel, and an autobiography. (Use as a verb.)

3. Williams built his reputation on the plays he wrote between 1945 and 1961; his *later* plays received less favorable reviews. (Use as an adverb.)

4. "*Wow,* that was a powerful production of <u>The Glass Menagerie!</u>" exclaimed one of the theatergoers. (Use as a verb.)

5. The drinking gourd has been worn smooth from *age* and use. (Use as a verb.)

6. We attended the cast party *after* we saw the play's final performance. (Use as a preposition.)

7. While living in Greenwich Village in the late 1950s, Baraka associated with such *Beat* poets as Allen Ginsberg and Frank O'Hara. (Use as a verb.)

8. Laura's unicorn is made of *glass.* (Use as an adjective.)

9. Bernard Malamud's stories often *blend* reality with fantasy. (Use as a noun.)

10. Some people transmit stories of the *past* orally. (Use as a preposition.)

Part Two

THE AMERICAN TRADITION

Quaker Meeting. Courtesy of Museum of Fine Arts, Boston. Bequest of Maxim Karolik

ere individuals of all nations are melted into a
new race . . . whose labors and posterity will
one day cause great changes in the world.

—J. Hector St. Jean de Crèvecoeur,
"What Is an American?"

THE FIRST AMERICANS

Long before the first Europeans set foot on American soil, peoples from Asia came to the Americas, crossing a land bridge now submerged beneath the Bering Strait. The date of the arrival of the first humans in America is unknown, with estimates ranging from twenty thousand to fifty thousand years ago. Other people may have arrived in South America via sea routes from the South Pacific, though that theory remains controversial.

THE PRE-COLUMBIAN CULTURES OF NORTH AMERICA

Descendants of the first Americans populated North, Central, and South America, creating an extraordinary variety of cultures. When Europeans arrived in the late fifteenth century, there were perhaps 240 distinct Native American cultures in North America alone and a population variously estimated at between one million and two million people. Historians, archaeologists, and anthropologists divide these cultures into eight major groups, those of the Northwest Coast, California, the Northern Plateau, the Great Basin, the Southwest, the Plains, the Eastern Woodlands, and the Southeast. Although these cultures varied widely in their social customs, modes of government, economic systems, dress, religions, architecture, and languages, they shared a common reverence for and connection with the natural world. Europeans, in contrast, tended to see the natural world as something to be subdued, owned, and turned to human ends.

Buffalo Bull's Back Fat, head chief, Blood Tribe (Blackfoot). George Catlin, 1832. National Museum of American Art, Washington, DC/Art Resource, NY

LITERARY EVENTS

► = American Events

1517. Martin Luther posts his 95 Theses, beginning the Protestant Reformation

1516. Ludovico Ariosto's *Orlando Furioso* published

1515. Sir Thomas More's *Utopia* published

1513. Niccolo Machiavelli writes *The Prince*

1510. *Everyman,* English morality play, performed

1475	1500	1525

►1492. Christopher Columbus crosses the Atlantic and lands in the Bahamas

►1502. Amerigo Vespucci returns from the New World; his account of the voyage led to his name being given to the New World

►1521. Aztec capital of Tenochtitlán falls to Hernando Cortés of Spain

HISTORICAL EVENTS

THE ARRIVAL OF THE EUROPEANS

Historians today believe that the first Europeans to arrive in North America were Norse sailors. In 1001, **Leif Ericsson** established a very brief settlement in Labrador, which he called **Vinland,** or "Land of Wine." However, the Norse soon withdrew from the Americas, and it was almost five hundred years before Europeans returned. They did so as the result of a misguided attempt by the Italian sailor **Christopher Columbus** to find a route from Europe via the Atlantic to Japan and China. Funded by the king and queen of Spain, Columbus's expedition set sail on August 3, 1492. After months of fear and upset among the crew, the sailors arrived on October 12 at an island in the present-day Bahamas that Columbus named San Salvador. Thinking that he had reached India, Columbus called the natives whom he met "Indians." Although he made two subsequent voyages across the

Reconstructions of Columbus's ships, the Nina, Pinta, and Santa Maria

Atlantic Ocean, Columbus died without realizing that he had "discovered" two continents. These continents were called by Europeans **"the Americas"** because of a mistake made by a German mapmaker who believed, erroneously, that the continents had been discovered by the Portuguese explorer Amerigo Vespucci.

After Columbus's initial voyage, European powers competed with one another to seize the opportunity that they imagined the "New World" offered them. Throughout the next two hundred years, many European explorers set sail for the Americas, including Juan Ponce de León, Vasco Nuñez de Balboa, Ferdinand Magellan, Hernando Cortés, Francisco Pizarro, Hernando de Soto, Cabeza de Vaca, Giovanni da Verrazano, Jacques Cartier, Samuel de Champlain, Father Jacques Marquette, Louis Joliet, Robert de La Salle, John Cabot, Francis Drake, Humphrey Gilbert, Walter Ralegh, Martin Frobisher, and Henry Hudson. The Spanish, Dutch, French, and English all established colonies in North America.

1591. William Shakespeare's *The Comedy of Errors* produced

1578. Holinshed's *Chronicles of English History to 1575* published

1550	1575	1600

1534. Henry VIII breaks with the Church of Rome, founds the Church of England

►1541. Hernando de Soto discovers the Mississippi River

►1558. Queen Elizabeth crowned

1565. Spanish found first permanent North American settlement in St. Augustine, Florida

►1584. Sir Walter Ralegh founds the colony at Roanoke

1588. England defeats the Spanish Armada

For the native population of the Americas, the arrival of Europeans spelled disaster. Millions of Native Americans in North, Central, and South America died as a result of European diseases, to which they had no natural immunities. Millions more were enslaved or driven from their ancestral lands. An account of the devastation of the first Native Americans to come in contact with Europeans is given in the selection from **Bartolomé de las Casas** in this unit.

JAMESTOWN AND THE ORIGINS OF THE PLANTATION SYSTEM

In 1587, a group of 117 English settlers led by **Sir Walter Ralegh** and **John White** founded a colony on **Roanoke Island,** off the coast of what is now North Carolina. After going back to England for supplies, John White returned to Roanoke in 1590 to find no trace of the colony that he left behind. The fate of the Roanoke colonists remains a mystery.

Settled in 1607, **Jamestown, Virginia,** was the first English colony to survive. The colonists hoped to establish a self-sustaining community, but because they knew little of the new land, they were not successful at first. They endured uncertainty and almost unimaginable hardship, facing fierce weather with little food and, for the most part, hastily fashioned holes in the ground for shelter. The numbers tell the grim story: of the 104 Jamestown colonists who survived the ocean voyage, only 38 lived through the first winter. In the face of such conditions, and with a community made up mostly of upper-class men unaccustomed to manual labor, **John Smith,** a natural leader among the colonists, was forced to proclaim that "he who does not work shall not eat," and to institute a rigorous, organized schedule of planting and working. In his *General History of Virginia, New England, and the Summer Isles,* an excerpt from which appears in this unit, Smith tells the story of being captured by Native Americans and rescued by the young daughter of **Powhatan,** their chief. The story of Smith's rescue by this girl, whose nickname was **Pocahantas,** may or may not be true, but it has captured the imaginations of Americans and contains, at least, a symbolic truth: only with the assistance of native peoples were the colonists able to survive. Native Americans taught the colonists how to build adequate shelters and how to cultivate crops such as corn and tobacco for food and export.

LITERARY EVENTS

► = American Events

►1624. John Smith's *The General History of Virginia* published
1623. Shakespeare's First Folio is published posthumously
1615. Miguel de Cervantes's *Don Quixote* published

1668. John Dryden becomes first English poet laureate

1655. Molière's first play performed

►1650. Anne Bradstreet's *The Tenth Muse Lately Sprung Up* published

►1638. The Bay Psalm Book becomes the first printed in New England

1625	1650	1675

1603. Elizabeth I dies; James VII of Scotland crowned James I
►1607. Jamestown settlement founded by Virginia company
1608. French found Quebec

1642. Civil War in England

►1643. The New England Confederation formed of Massachusetts, Plymouth, Connecticut, and New Haven colonies

HISTORICAL EVENTS

►1625. Dutch found New Amsterdam settlement (later New York) on Manhattan Island
►1620. Pilgrims establish Plymouth settlement; Mayflower Compact
►1621. Pilgrims and Native Americans celebrate first Thanksgiving

1648. Oliver Cromwell and the Roundheads defeat the royalists

1660. English Civil War ends

Jamestown did not develop into a community of small family farms, like those soon to be established in New England. Instead, it turned tobacco into a profitable export crop, creating large plantations and importing slaves to do the work. Thus developed the plantation system and the slave trade that would have a dramatic effect on the subsequent course of North American history.

Belle Grove Plantation, Virginia

NEW ENGLAND COLONIZATION AND THE PURITAN ERA

Two other settlements begun in the early colonial years played a decisive role in North American history and literature. The **Plymouth Colony,** founded in 1620, and **The Massachusetts Bay Colony,** founded in 1630, were Puritan settlements. The New England colonists, like the Jamestown settlers, endured great difficulties and depended for their survival on the assistance of Native Americans. The core group of the Plymouth colonists, often referred to as the **Pilgrims,** were **Separatist Puritans,** so called because they had separated from the Church of England after giving up hope of "purifying" that church of what they considered to be Popish, or Catholic, tendencies. After moving from England to Holland to escape religious persecution, the Pilgrims set sail for North America on the *Mayflower* in 1620. They landed on Cape Cod and established their colony by means of the **Mayflower Compact** in what is now the town of Plymouth, Massachusetts. After a difficult winter, the colonists learned from native peoples, particularly **Squanto,** a member of the **Wampanoag** group, how to plant native crops. Under the direction of governor **William Bradford,** the colony flourished.

In 1691, Plymouth incorporated with a much larger settlement of Puritans, the Massachusetts Bay Colony. This group was made up of Congregationalist Puritans who did not separate entirely from the Church of England, believing it could be reformed from within.

►1704. America's first newspaper, the *News-Letter,* appears in Boston

►1702. Cotton Mather's *Magnolia Christi Americana* published

►1693. Cotton Mather's *The Wonders of the Invisible World* published

►1688. Aphra Behn writes *Oroonoko,* the first novel in English

►1683. William Penn's *A General Description of Pennsylvania* published

1678. John Bunyan's *Pilgrim's Progress* published

►1741. Jonathan Edwards delivers "Sinners in the Hands of an Angry God"

►1731. Benjamin Franklin founds first public library company in Philadelphia

►1729. Benjamin Franklin purchases *The Pennsylvania Gazette*

1700   **1725**   **1750**

►1682. William Penn founds Philadelphia; Louisiana territory and the Mississippi Valley claimed by the Sieur de La Salle for the French

1685. James II succeeds Charles II

1688. Willam and Mary of Orange assume throne

►1692. Salem Witch Trials begin

1702. Anne succeeds William
1714. George I succeeds Anne
1715. Louis XIV dies in France after a seventy-two year reign

1727. George I succeeded by George II

►1737. First city-paid police force founded by Benjamin Franklin in Philadelphia

►1739. French explorers Pierre and Paul Mallet become first Europeans to view the Rocky Mountains

►1744. King George's War with France breaks out in North America and the Caribbean

They found inspiration for their early struggles in America in the belief that their actions were divinely guided. Their governor, **John Winthrop,** would write in his *A Model of Christian Charity* that they were about the business of building, as described in the New Testament, a "city upon a hill" in the new land.

PURITAN BELIEFS

The first Puritans in these settlements shared several basic religious and social beliefs. First, they had a remarkably strong belief in the importance of the community as a whole. Their belief that they were on a grand historical and religious mission formed a common purpose and sense of support, and they imagined the destiny of the community as everyone's responsibility. Various consent agreements or compacts, such as the Mayflower Compact mentioned previously, reflected and formalized this communal orientation. John Winthrop envisioned the Puritans bound together in a selfless, harmonious community directed by God. Second, the Puritans believed in **original sin,** the idea that because of the transgression of Adam and Eve, all people were born sinful and could be saved only by divine grace. Third, although they thought they were a chosen people, they did not believe that all souls among them were chosen. They adopted the French theologian **John Calvin's** theory of **predestination,** holding that God has chosen in advance which souls are to be saved and which are not. They understood this to mean they could not change their individual fates directly, by force of will. Since none could be sure of having been saved, however, they maintained a steady and humble watch over their lives for proof that they were among the **elect,** those chosen for salvation by God at the beginning of time. Finally, the Puritans shared a belief in hard work, thinking that material and social successes were signs of God's providence and that such work, though it could not win salvation, was nonetheless a sign of salvation. This complex belief in strict moral propriety, community service, and hard work is today referred to as the **Puritan Ethic.**

POLITICS, SOCIETY, AND THE PROBLEM OF ORTHODOXY

Despite these shared beliefs, a notable though subdued tension existed in Puritan society and politics between its official, orthodox beliefs and the beliefs of some colonists. Puritan communities functioned as **theocracies,** societies guided by religious law, and early Puritan leaders were largely intolerant of any opposition, religious or political. When **Roger Williams** voiced his objections in 1635 about what he saw as the Puritans' arrogant intolerance of diversity and about the taking of lands from the Native Americans, he was banished from Massachusetts. He went on to found the colony of Rhode Island and to espouse principles of religious freedom. In 1637, when **Anne Hutchinson** bypassed the official church and began teaching her own theories in home Bible classes with other women and their husbands, she was accused of threatening the religion and of being more a "husband than a wife." She was banished from Massachusetts as well. Although advanced among colonies of the time in supporting education for women, Massachusetts was not necessarily interested in being educated by women on matters of church doctrine. Its leaders retained an Old Testament model of patriarchal authority.

Even though pressures from progressive elements led in 1662 to the **Half-Way Covenant,** which relaxed old rules and allowed more people direct membership in the church, tensions remained. Some saw the relaxing of orthodoxy as a sign of weakness, and their concerns surfaced dramatically in the belief that Satan had infiltrated the town of Salem and nearby

A witch trial at Salem, Massachusetts, in 1692. The Granger Collection, NY

communities. The **Salem Witch Trials,** begun in 1692, resulted in the execution of twenty people and the imprisonment and torture of many more. Followed by embarrassment and recanting, the trials further diminished the Puritan hold on New England. In 1692, a new Massachusetts charter changed the colony's government from a theocratic one to a secular one in which voting was no longer restricted by religious requirements.

RELIGION AND ALLEGORY IN EARLY PURITAN WRITING

Religion was a dominant influence and presence in the works of early Puritan writers. In sermons, colonial histories, personal diaries, and devotional poetry, Puritan writers often explored the story of spiritual struggles in personal and public life, interpreting or portraying events as emblems, or **allegories,** of the progress of souls or of God's design. In diaries, writers would record their thoughts from day to day and chart their individual spiritual development, often reading seemingly trivial everyday events or conflicts as signs of God's will working itself out in the world. Puritan writers of history sought to find Biblical precedents in current events and in the various travails of their communities as a whole.

Puritan literature was not entirely an expression of official views and beliefs, however, and in it we can find examples of the struggle with orthodoxy and conformity mentioned earlier. For example, in her "Prologue," the poet **Anne Bradstreet** asserted that her male critics' judgment was distorted by their views of women: "For such despite they cast on female wits:/If what I do prove well, it won't advance,/They'll say it's stol'n, or else it was by chance."

Although not all Puritans in seventeenth-century New England were educated, they nonetheless valued and promoted education and reading. They founded **Harvard College** in 1636 and began the first colonial printing press two years later. Writers of this era were influenced by their European counterparts, and some of their works, including the poems of Bradstreet, reveal a familiarity with the styles, themes, and figures of the newly available literature of classical Greece and Rome.

THE EUROPEAN ENLIGHTENMENT AND THE GREAT AWAKENING

The emergence in mid-seventeenth-century England of scientific and empirical thinking, legitimated and encouraged by the formation in 1660 of a science academy called **The Royal Society,** was to have a significant effect on later Puritan intellectuals such as **Cotton Mather** and **Jonathan Edwards.** English Enlightenment thinkers such as **John Locke** and **Isaac Newton** believed that **empirical inquiry**, the study of human experience and the natural world, was the proper approach for achieving true knowledge. In opposition to medieval theories of innate knowledge derived from God, Locke held that people begin life as blank slates and must slowly build up their knowledge from sense impressions. Similarly for Newton, the proper focus of study was nature, the analysis of which, he believed, supported religious belief by revealing the orderly plan of God's design.

In the preachings and writings of Jonathan Edwards, this Enlightenment emphasis on empirical evidence and human experience gave rise to the claim that one needed to feel or experience God, not just intuit his existence from one's belief or from the Bible. Such experiences, or **awakenings,** as they came to be called, formed the basis for a religious revival, called the **Great Awakening,** which from its beginnings in 1734 in Edwards's Northampton congregation quickly spread to Boston and then throughout the colonies. Edwards's eventual call for a return to stricter church membership requirements and his demand for proof of an awakening and conversion were ultimately unpopular, however, and he was removed from his pulpit in 1750.

Echoes:

Origins of the American Tradition

"Where today are the Pequot? Where are the Narragansett, the Mohican, the Pokanoket, and many other once powerful tribes of our people? They have vanished . . . as snow before a summer sun."

> —Tecumseh, Shawnee chief, on the destruction of Native American peoples and ways of life

"The earth receives my body . . .
Each in its own turn so that
The circle of life is never broken."

> —Anonymous Taos Pueblo saying on the interconnectedness of people and nature

"He shall make us a praise and glory that men shall say of succeeding plantations, 'the lord make it like that of NEW ENGLAND.' For we must consider that we shall be as a city upon a hill. The eyes of all people are upon us, so that if we shall deal falsely with our God in this work we have undertaken, and so cause Him to withdraw His present help from us, we shall be made a story and a by-word through the world."

> —John Winthrop on the creation of the Massachusetts Bay Colony

"I will fear GOD, and honor the KING.
I will honor my Father & Mother.
I will Obey my Superiors.
I will Submit to my Elders.
I will Love my Friends.
I will hate no Man.
I will forgive my Enemies, and pray to God for them.
I will as much as in me lies keen all God's Holy Commandments."

> —"The Dutiful Child's Promises," from *The New England Primer*

"I am obnoxious to each carping tongue
Who says my hand a needle better fits,
A poet's pen all scorn I should thus wrong,
For such despite they cast on female wits:
If what I do prove well, it won't advance,
They'll say it's stol'n, or else it was by chance.

> —Anne Bradstreet on men's responses to women writers in the Puritan Era

"Unclean, unclean: my Lord, undone, all vile,
    Yea, all defiled: what shall Thy servant do?
Unfit for Thee: not fit for holy soil,
    Nor for communion of saints below.
    A bag of botches, lump of loathsomeness:
    Defiled by touch, by issue: Leproused flesh."

> —Edward Taylor, Puritan minister, on the unredeemed state of humankind

from the Iroquois Constitution

ABOUT THE SELECTION

The **Iroquois Constitution,** dating from the fifteenth or sixteenth century, joined together several peoples who lived on the shores of the Great Lakes into the Iroquois League, or Iroquois Confederacy. Initially, the Iroquois League included the Mohawk, Oneida, Onondaga, Cayuga, and Seneca. In the 1700s, however, the Tuscarora joined the Confederacy, making it the League of Six Nations. Tradition holds that the league was begun by Dekanawidah, a Huron whose words open the constitution, and by Hiawatha, an Onondaga who lived among the Mohawks. Each brought to the league his own special talents. Dekanawidah was a diplomat who envisioned the many branches of the Iroquois people united under his Tree of Great Peace. Hiawatha brought this message of unity—the Great Law of Peace—to the Iroquois people as he traveled the country.

The Iroquois lived by hunting, trading, and raising crops such as corn, beans, and squash. For shelter, they built magnificent long houses, covered with elm bark, that housed several families. Kinship groups, or clans, many named after totem, or symbolic, animals such as the beaver or hawk, were united into half tribes, or moieties. These were united into tribes, and the tribes into the league. Decisions of the league were made in great council meetings. Each member of the league had one vote, and all member nations had to agree before any action was taken. The league was ruled by fifty male peace chiefs, or sachems, who were chosen by the Iroquois women. The political system of the Iroquois was well known to the Founding Fathers of the United States, including Benjamin Franklin, who saw in the Iroquois Constitution a model for representative government.

After the coming of Europeans, many Native American populations were decimated by epidemics of diseases such as smallpox. During the Colonial Period, the total Iroquois population numbered only about twelve thousand, and the total number of Iroquois warriors at any time numbered only a little over two thousand. Despite these small numbers, the Iroquois waged successful war against neighboring groups and held both British and French invaders at bay. Particularly impressive was the ability of the Iroquois to battle successfully against the French, who were allied with the the Huron. During the American Revolution, two Iroquois groups sided with the colonists. The rest, led by Chief Joseph Brant, sided with the British, leading George Washington to send troops in retaliation to destroy Iroquois settlements, fields, and stores of food. Later treaties set aside reservation lands for the Onondaga, Seneca, and Tuscarora in New York. The Mohawks and Cayuga settled in Canada, and the Oneida in Wisconsin.

READER'S JOURNAL

What do you consider to be the ideal form of government? If you were going to design a constitution for a new country, what elements would that constitution have? Write about these questions in your journal.

LANGUAGE SKILLS

Read the Language Arts Survey, 2.118, "Organizations and Institutions," and 2.125, "Sacred Beings and Writings." As you read the following selection, find examples of each type of capitalization and copy them into your journal. Also see if you can find in the selection an example of the capitalization of the name of a legal work.

FROM THE

Iroquois Constitution

I am Dekanawidah and with the Five Nations[1] confederate lords I plant the Tree of the Great Peace. I name the tree the Tree of the Great Long Leaves. Under the shade of this Tree of the Great Peace we spread the soft white feathery down of the globe thistle as seats for you, Adodarhoh, and your cousin lords.

We place you upon those seats, spread soft with the feathery down of the globe thistle, there beneath the shade of the spreading branches of the Tree of Peace. There shall you sit and watch the council fire of the <u>confederacy</u> of the Five Nations, and all the affairs of the Five Nations shall be transacted at this place before you.

Roots have spread out from the Tree of the Great Peace, one to the north, one to the east, one to the south, and one to the west. The name of these roots is the Great White Roots and their nature is peace and strength.

If any man or any nation outside the Five Nations shall obey the laws of the Great Peace and make known their <u>disposition</u> to the lords of the confederacy, they may trace the roots to the tree and if their minds are clean and they are obedient and promise to obey the wishes of the confederate council, they shall be welcomed[2] to take shelter beneath the Tree of the Long Leaves.

We place at the top of the Tree of the Long Leaves an eagle who is able to see afar.

If he sees in the distance any evil approaching or any danger threatening he will at once warn the people of the confederacy.

On what terms would someone outside the Five Nations gain acceptance?

---

1. **Five Nations.** The Mohawk, Oneida, Onondaga, Cayuga, and Seneca tribes. These tribes formed the Iroquois Confederacy.
2. **they shall be welcomed.** The Tuscarora tribe joined the Confederacy in 1722.

WORDS FOR EVERYDAY USE:

con • fed • er • a • cy (kən fed´ ər ə sē) *n.,* people or groups united for common purpose

dis • po • si • tion (dis´ pə zish´ ən¯) *n.,* state of mind; general nature

that serve as food and give their pelts for clothing, to the great winds and the lesser winds, to the thunderers, to the sun, the mighty warrior, to the moon, to the messengers of the Creator who reveal his wishes and to the Great Creator who dwells in the heavens above, who gives all the things useful to men, and who is the source and the ruler of health and life.

Then shall the Onondaga lords declare the council open. . . .

All lords of the Five Nations' Confederacy must be honest in all things. . . . It shall be a serious wrong for anyone to lead a lord into trivial affairs, for the people must ever hold their lords high in <u>estimation</u> out of respect to their honorable positions.

When a candidate lord is to be installed he shall <u>furnish</u> four strings of shells (or wampum)[3] one span in length bound together at one end. Such will constitute the evidence of his pledge to the confederate lords that he will live according to the constitution of the Great Peace and exercise justice in all affairs.

When the pledge is furnished the speaker of the council must hold the shell strings in his hand and address the opposite side of the council fire and he shall commence his address saying: "Now behold him. He has now become a confederate lord. See how splendid he looks." An address may then follow. At the end of it he shall send the bunch of shell strings to the opposite side and they shall be received as evidence of the pledge. Then shall the opposite side say:

---

3. **wampum.** Small beads made of shell, usually white or dark purple in color

What acknow-
ledgments
occurred at the
opening of a
council meeting?

The smoke of the confederate council fire shall ever ascend and pierce the sky so that other nations who may be allies may see the council fire of the Great Peace. . . .

Whenever the confederate lords shall assemble for the purpose of holding a council, the Onondaga lords shall open it by expressing their gratitude to their cousin lords and greeting them, and they shall make an address and offer thanks to the earth where men dwell, to the streams of water, the pools, the springs and the lakes, to the maize and the fruits, to the medicinal herbs and trees, to the forest trees for their usefulness, to the animals

WORDS FOR
EVERYDAY USE:

es • ti • ma • tion (es´ tə mā´ shən) *n.,* respect; value
fur • nish (fur´ nish) *vt.,* supply or provide

"We now do crown you with the sacred emblem of the deer's antlers, the emblem of your lordship. You shall now become a mentor of the people of the Five Nations. The thickness of your skin shall be seven spans—which is to say that you shall be proof against anger, offensive actions and criticism. Your heart shall be filled with peace and good will and your mind filled with a yearning for the welfare of the people of the confederacy. With endless patience you shall carry out your duty and your firmness shall be tempered with tenderness for your people. Neither anger nor fury shall find lodgement in your mind and all your words and actions shall be marked with calm deliberation. In all of your deliberations in the confederate council, in your efforts at law making, in all your official acts, self-interest shall be cast into oblivion. Cast not over your shoulder behind you the warnings of the nephews and nieces should they chide you for any error or wrong you may do, but return to the way of the Great Law which is just and right. Look and listen for the welfare of the whole people and have always in view not only the present but also the coming generations, even those whose faces are yet beneath the surface of the ground—the unborn of the future nation." ∎

Illustration by Helen Abraham

What view should a lord take?

Responding to the Selection

Think about the way in which the Iroquois began their council meetings. To whom or what did they offer thanks before proceeding? What is the relationship between these nations and the land? Are people today as connected to the natural environment? Discuss these questions with your classmates.

Reviewing the Selection

1. Who plants and names the Tree of the Great Peace with Dekanawidah?

2. To whom is Dekanawidah speaking? Who do you think Adodarhoh is?

3. What rituals begin each Iroquois council meeting?

4. How does a candidate lord show his pledge to the council? What does his offering symbolize?

▶▶ 5. What is the purpose of the meeting at which Dekanawidah speaks? Why do you think oratory skills were prized by the Iroquois?

▶▶ 6. Why do you think Dekanawidah refers to the assembled lords as "cousins"? Are they literally related to one another?

▶▶ 7. What relationship exists between the Iroquois and the natural environment?

▶▶ 8. According to the constitution, what qualities should a leader have? What qualities should a leader put aside?

9. In what ways is framing a constitution like planting a tree? In what ways are the spreadout roots of a tree like a confederacy of nations?

10. What special ceremony did the Iroquois hold for the installation of a new "confederate lord"? In what ways is this ceremony similar to and different from the inauguration of a United States president or the swearing in of a United States senator or representative?

Understanding Literature (Questions for Discussion)

Symbol. A **symbol** is a thing that stands for or represents both itself and something else. The chart below lists some common symbols used in literary works. In the Iroquois Constitution, what does the tree symbolize? its roots? What does it mean to take shelter under the leaves of this tree? What does the eagle perched in the top of the tree symbolize?

SYMBOL	CONVENTIONAL INTERPRETATION
wind	change, inspiration
rainbow	hope
rose	beauty, love
moon	fickleness, inconstancy
roads, paths	the journey through life
spring	youth
	CONTINUED

fall, winter	age
woods, darkness	spiritual or moral confusion
storm	trouble, confusion, anger
thorns	trouble, pain, suffering
stars	unchangeableness, constancy
mirror	vanity, introspection
snake	evil, duplicity
owl	wisdom
fox	craftiness

Responding in Writing

Speech. According to the Iroquois Constitution, a newly accepted candidate lord may make an address to his fellow council lords. Imagine you are such a lord and write the text of your acceptance speech. Try to use the speaking style exemplified by the selection. Refer to the Language Arts Survey, 1.7, "Choosing and Analyzing an Audience."

Writing Skills

Venn Diagram. Read the Language Arts Survey, 1.24, "Venn Diagrams." Then consider the goals and overall structure of the Iroquois form of government as described on page 68 and in the selection. How is that form of government similar to and different from the government of the United States? To organize your thoughts, create a Venn diagram similar to the one shown here:

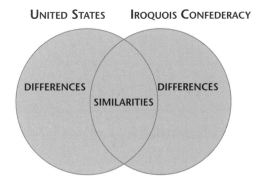

UNITED STATES   IROQUOIS CONFEDERACY

DIFFERENCES   DIFFERENCES

SIMILARITIES

Use the information in your diagram to write a brief comparison-contrast paragraph explaining your ideas. Refer to the Language Arts Survey, 1.9, "Modes of Writing," and 1.38–1.40, "Drafting: Paragraphs."

Language Lab

Using Precise Nouns. Read the Language Arts Survey, 2.32, "Using Precise Nouns." Then rewrite the sentences below using precise nouns. Don't worry about whether your new sentences are factually correct.

1. Hiawatha, who may have lived in the fifteenth century, is a famous figure in Iroquois legend.

2. The name Hiawatha, in a Native American language, means "He Makes Rivers."

3. According to tradition, Hiawatha helped to form a political body and became a chief of a Native American group.

4. Legend holds that it was another respected chief who convinced Hiawatha of the importance of establishing peace among the nations.

5. One of the most famous works of the American poet Henry Wadsworth Longfellow is his "Song of Hiawatha," written in 1855.

PROJECT

Constitution. Imagine that you and your classmates win a trip to the South Seas. On the way there, you are shipwrecked on an island with no means of contacting the outside world. On the island, you find plenty of natural shelter, fruit to eat, and other necessities of life. After living on the island for some time, you decide that you need to create a constitution for your new island government. Work with other students to write such a constitution establishing the basic laws and political structure of your new country. Do not refer to any existing constitutions as you are writing yours. When you are finished, you may wish to compare your constitution to actual constitutions such as that of the United States of America.

FROM "The Song of Hiawatha"

You shall hear how Hiawatha
Prayed and fasted in the forest,
Not for greater skill in hunting,
Not for greater craft in fishing,
Not for triumphs in the battle,
And renown among the warriors,
But for profit of the people,
For advantage of the nations.

Henry Wadsworth Longfellow

"Song of the Sky Loom"
Tewa Tribal Song

ABOUT THE SELECTION

The language of **"Song of the Sky Loom"** is taken directly from weaving. The Tewa, a Pueblo people of the Southwest, are accomplished weavers. They, in their turn, passed the art on to the Navajo, now renowned weavers of blankets and rugs. In addition to weaving, the Tewa make intricately decorated pottery and elaborate baskets. They live in multilevel, multiunit adobe structures often built into the hard mesas of the Southwest. Like other Pueblo peoples, the Tewa have a vital interdependence with nature, performing various rituals and ceremonies related to nature, especially to bringing much-needed rain.

Elk-Foot of the Taos Tribe. *Eanger Irving Couse, circa 1909. National Museum of American Art, Washington, DC/Art Resource, NY*

READER'S JOURNAL

Think of an art form to describe yourself. Are you a painting? a sculpture? a musical work? a ceramic pot? a patchwork quilt? Write a short paragraph in your journal identifying the art form and explaining why you chose it.

SPEAKING AND LISTENING SKILLS

"Song of the Sky Loom" can be experienced more fully as a spoken work of literature. Read the Language Arts Survey, 3.4, "Active Listening." Then listen as a classmate reads the poem aloud.

"Song of the Sky Loom"

TEWA TRIBAL SONG

Who is addressed in this song?

O our Mother the Earth, O our Father the Sky,
Your children are we, and with tired backs
We bring you the gifts you love.
Then weave for us a garment of brightness;
5   May the warp[1] be the white light of morning,
May the weft[2] be the red light of evening,
May the fringes be the falling rain,
May the border be the standing rainbow.
Thus weave for us a garment of brightness,
10   That we may walk fittingly where birds sing,
That we may walk fittingly where grass is green,
O our Mother the Earth, O our Father the Sky. ■

Of what will the garment be woven?

---

1. **warp.** Threads in a loom that run lengthwise
2. **weft.** Horizontal threads in a loom. The weft crosses the warp to make a woven fabric.

Responding to the Selection

How does "Song of the Sky Loom" make you feel? What images does it create in your mind?

Reviewing the Selection

RECALLING

1. To whom is "Song of the Sky Loom" addressed? How do the speakers name themselves?

2. What elements of nature are described in the poem?

INTERPRETING

3. What is the speakers' message? What do "we" offer, and what do "we" ask in return?

4. What role does each element of nature play in the tapestry woven by Mother Earth and Father Sky? How are the elements linked to one another?

SYNTHESIZING

5. What is the central comparison in "Song of the Sky Loom"? What relationship does the poem suggest exists between humans and the divine?

Understanding Literature (Questions for Discussion)

1. **Parallelism. Parallelism** is a rhetorical technique in which a writer emphasizes the equal value or weight of two or more ideas by expressing them in the same grammatical form. What examples of parallelism can you identify in "Song of the Sky Loom"? What is the common link between the several ideas named? (Refer to the Language Arts Survey, 2.57, "Achieving Parallelism.")

2. **Metaphor.** A **metaphor** is a figure of speech in which one thing is spoken or written about as if it were another, thus encouraging a comparison between features of the two things. The writer's, or speaker's, actual subject is called the *tenor* of the metaphor, while the thing to which it is likened is called the *vehicle*. What are the tenor and vehicle of the central metaphor the "Song of the Sky Loom"? What is the "garment of brightness"?

3. **Myth.** A **myth** is a story that explains objects or events in the natural world as resulting from the action of some supernatural force or entity. Every early culture around the globe has produced its own myths, or supernatural explanations of natural phenomena. What mythical elements appear in "Song of the Sky Loom"? What can you infer about Tewa religious beliefs and practices based on this poem?

4. Tone. Tone is the emotional attitude toward the reader or toward the subject implied by a literary work. What attitude toward the natural world does this poem express? What adjectives could you use to name this tone?

Responding in Writing

Hymn. A **hymn** is a song of praise or thanksgiving. Imagine that you have been invited to speak at an Earth Day celebration in your community. Write a brief hymn praising or offering thanks for some aspect of the natural world. If you wish to do so, you can model your hymn on "Song of the Sky Loom," using parallelism and unrhymed lines to express your thoughts and feelings. To gather ideas for writing, try creating a cluster chart or sensory detail chart. Refer to the Language Arts Survey, 1.17, "Clustering," and 1.18, "Sensory Detail Charts."

Language Lab

Grammar. Answer the following questions, referring to "Song of Sky Loom" and to the parts of the Language Arts Survey indicated in parentheses.

1. What interjections are used in the first and last lines of this poem? (See the Language Arts Survey, 2.29, "Interjections.")

2. In what line of this poem does the subject come before the main verb? (See the Language Arts Survey, 2.64, "Inverting Sentences for Emphasis," and 2.40, "Simple Sentences: SUB + LV + SUB or ADJ.")

3. What linking verb is used in each line from line 5 through line 8? What auxiliary verb is used in each line? (See the Language Arts Survey, 2.13, "Linking Verbs," and 2.14, "Auxiliary Verbs.")

4. In what lines of this poem is the usual order of subject + auxiliary verb + main verb varied so that the auxiliary verb comes first? How would the meanings of these lines change if the subject came first? (See the Language Arts Survey, 2.64, "Inverting Sentences for Emphasis.")

5. Are the words *falling* and *standing,* in lines 7 and 8, gerunds or participles? What about the word *fittingly,* in lines 10 and 11? Explain your answer. (See the Language Arts Survey, 2.16, "Verbals: Participles," and 2.17, "Verbals: Gerunds.")

Language Skills

Formal English, Informal English, and Register. Read the Language Arts Survey, 2.147, "Formal and Informal English," and 2.148, "Register." Is the language of "Song of the Sky Loom" formal or informal? Explain. What is the register of the language used in the poem? For what sort of occasion would such language be appropriate? Many people associate formal language with big words and complicated sentence structures. Can language be formal without being complicated or stuffy? Explain.

PROJECT

Early Native American Art and Architecture. The hundreds of different Native American cultures that existed before the coming of the Europeans created a wide variety of exquisite types of art and architecture. Working in a small group, research the early Native American art and architecture of one of the following cultural groups of North, Central, or South America:

the Penobscot, Algonquin, Iroquois, Ojibway, or Delaware (eastern North America)

the Cherokee, Creek, Chickasaw, Alabama, Choctaw, Apalachee, Timucua, or Catawba (southeastern United States)

the Blackfoot, Crow, Sioux, Cheyenne, Pawnee, Arapaho, Kiowa, or Comanche (western plains of North America)

the Anasazi, Hopi, Navaho, Apache, Zuni, or Pima (southwestern North America)

the Coast Salish or Wenatchee (northwestern coast of North America)

the Olmec, Aztec, or Maya (Central America)

the Inca, Chimú, or Nazca (South America)

Refer to the Language Arts Survey, 4.20–4.27, for information on conducting research. Present the results of your research in an oral report to your classmates. Use visual aids such as maps and pictures from books to make your report vivid and interesting.

from *The Very Brief Relation of the Devastation of the Indies*
by Bartolomé de las Casas

ABOUT THE AUTHOR

Bartolomé de las Casas (1474–1566) first voyaged to the Caribbean in 1502 with his father. He soon found himself taking part in Spanish attacks on the Taino people in response to a rebellion. Such attacks were common and exceedingly brutal. De las Casas was rewarded with a group of Native American slaves for his work in the attacks. He continued to receive such benefits even after becoming a priest in 1512 or 1513.

In 1515 de las Casas realized the cruelty and inhumanity that surrounded him and in which he participated. De las Casas became a spokesperson for rights of the native peoples of the New World. He gave up all of his slaves and urged other slaveholders to do the same. Returning to Spain to plead his case, he was appointed protector of the indigenous peoples. With the permission of the Spanish government, de las Casas began a colony on the coast of Venezuela. The peaceful settlement did not last long because the Spanish continued to raid the coast for slaves, rousing the anger of the native Cumaná.

Despite the growing existence of slavery and the lack of success of his colony, de las Casas continued to strive for the end of enslavement, working both in the colonies and in Europe. He used oral arguments, writings including *The Very Brief Relation of the Devastation of the Indies,* and his own example to argue his case. In the 1530s, laws were passed that banned further enslavement and gave native people the protection of the courts. De las Casas tried to enforce the laws in Mexico where he was serving as bishop, but firm resistance by the colonists led to the repeal of the laws.

ABOUT THE SELECTION

The Very Brief Relation of the Devastation of the Indies, or the *Relation,* as it is sometimes called, exposed the grievous behavior of Spanish explorers in the New World. The excerpt included here focuses on Spanish actions at Hispaniola. Hispaniola, an island in the Caribbean Sea, is thought to be one of Christopher Columbus's first landing sites. Certainly, it is where he began his first colonies. The island, which is now divided between the countries of Haiti and the Dominican Republic, was occupied by the Arawak. While the first exchanges between Columbus and the Arawak were relatively friendly, this situation soon changed. Columbus's later voyages, and the voyages of the explorers who followed him over the years, produced savage treatment of the native people. In combination with European diseases against which the native people had no resistance, Spanish cruelty killed most of the native people of the Caribbean Islands. There are no pure Arawaks living in the Caribbean today.

READER'S JOURNAL

Why do you think human beings so often mistreat those over whom they have power? Think about situations you know from history or your own experience. Then write a brief paragraph in your journal that attempts to explain this unfortunate part of human nature.

LANGUAGE SKILLS

Read the Language Arts Survey, 2.12, "Action Verbs." Then identify some action verbs from the selection. Group the verbs into physical and mental actions.

FROM

The Very Brief Relation of the Devastation of the Indies

BARTOLOMÉ DE LAS CASAS

From *Hispaniola*

This was the first land in the New World to be destroyed and <u>depopulated</u> by the Christians, and here they began their <u>subjection</u> of the women and children, taking them away from the Indians to use them and ill use them, eating the food they provided with their sweat and toil. The Spaniards did not content themselves with what the Indians gave them of their own free will, according to their ability, which was always too little to satisfy enormous appetites, for a Christian eats and consumes in one day an amount of food that would <u>suffice</u> to feed three houses inhabited by ten Indians for one month. And they committed other acts of force and violence and <u>oppression</u> which made the Indians realize that these men had not come from Heaven.[1] And some of the Indians concealed their foods while others concealed their wives and children and still others fled to the mountains to avoid the terrible transactions of the Christians.

And the Christians attacked them with <u>buffets</u> and beatings, until finally they laid hands on the nobles of the villages. . . . From that time onward the Indians began to seek ways to throw the Christians out of their lands. They took up arms, but their weapons were very weak and of little service

According to de las Casas, how much did Christians eat?

What did the native people begin to seek?

---

1. **realize . . . Heaven.** Columbus and other early European voyagers reported that the natives took them to be gods who had come from the heavens.

WORDS FOR EVERYDAY USE:

de • pop • u • late (dē päp´yə lāt´) *vt.,* reduce the population of, especially by violence or disease

sub • jec • tion (sub jek´shən) *n.,* bringing under control or dominion

suf • fice (sə fīs´) *vi.,* be enough

op • pres • sion (ə presh´ən) *n.,* keeping down by cruel or unjust use of authority

buf • fet (buf´it) *n.,* blow with the hand or fist

in offense and still less in defense. (Because of this, the wars of the Indians against each other are little more than games played by children.) And the Christians, with their horses and swords and pikes began to carry out massacres and strange cruelties against them. . . .

And because all the people who could do so fled to the mountains to escape these <u>inhuman</u>, ruthless, and ferocious acts, the Spanish captains, enemies of the human race, pursued them with the fierce dogs they kept which attacked the Indians, tearing them to pieces and devouring them. And because on few and far between occasions, the Indians justifiably killed some Christians, the Spaniards made a rule among themselves that for every Christian slain by the Indians, they would slay a hundred Indians.

From *The Coast of Pearls, Paria, and the Island of Trinidad*

[The Spaniards] have brought to the island of Hispaniola and the island of San Juan[2] more than two million souls taken captive, and have sent them to do hard labor in the mines, labors that caused many of them to die. And it is a great sorrow and heartbreak to see this coastal land which was so <u>flourishing</u>, now a depopulated desert.

This is truth that can be verified, for no more do they bring ships loaded with Indians that have been thus attacked and captured as I have related. No more do they cast overboard into the sea the third part of the numerous Indians they stow on their vessels, these dead being added to those they have killed in their native lands, the captives crowded into the holds of their ships, without food or water, or with very little, so as not to deprive the Spanish tyrants who call themselves ship owners and who carry enough food for themselves on their voyages of attack. And for the pitiful Indians who died of hunger and thirst, there is no remedy but to cast them into the sea. And verily, as a Spaniard told me, their ships in these regions could voyage without compass or chart, merely by following for the distance between the Lucayos Islands[3] and Hispaniola, which is sixty or seventy leagues,[4] the trace of those Indian corpses floating in the sea, corpses that had been cast overboard by earlier ships.

Afterward, when they disembark on the island of Hispaniola, it is heartbreaking to see those naked Indians, heartbreaking for anyone with a <u>vestige</u> of piety, the famished state they are in, fainting and falling down, weak from hunger, men, women, old people, and children.

Then, like sheep, they are sorted out into flocks of ten or twenty persons, separating fathers from sons, wives from husbands, and the Spaniards draw lots, the ship owners carrying off their share, the best flock, to compensate them for the moneys they have invested in their fleet of two or three ships, the <u>ruffian</u> tyrants getting their share of captives who will be house slaves, and when in this "*repartimiento*"[5] a tyrant gets an old person or an invalid, he says, "Why do you give me this

In what way did the Spaniards say they would retaliate for each Christian slain?

What condition were the native people in when they arrived at Hispaniola?

2. **San Juan.** Puerto Rico
3. **Lucayos Islands.** The Bahamas
4. **leagues.** Linear unit of measure that varies in different periods of time; usually equal to about three miles
5. **repartimiento.** Distribution (Spanish). A royal decree in 1503 ordered masters of native persons to try to convert them to Christianity and hold their property. In reality it was a system of slavery.

WORDS FOR EVERYDAY USE:

in • hu • man (in hyōō´mən) *adj.*, unfeeling; cruel; barbarous
flour • ish (flʉr´ish) *vi.*, grow vigorously; thrive; prosper
ves • tige (ves´tij) *n.*, trace; bit
ruf • fi • an (ruf´ē ən) *adj.*, brutal; violent; lawless

THE CARIBBEAN

one? To bury him? And this sick one, do you give him to me to make him well?" See by such remarks in what esteem the Spaniards hold the Indians and judge if they are accomplishing the divine concepts of love for our fellow man, as laid down by the prophets.

The tyranny exercised by the Spaniards against the Indians in the work of pearl fishing is one of the most cruel that can be imagined. There is no life as infernal and desperate in this century that can be compared with it, although the mining of gold is a dangerous and burdensome way of life. The pearl fishers dive into the sea at a depth of five fathoms, and do this from sunrise to sunset, and remain for many minutes without breathing, tearing the oysters out of their rocky beds where the pearls are formed. They come to the surface with a netted bag of these oysters where a Spanish torturer is waiting in a canoe or skiff, and if the pearl diver shows signs of wanting to rest, he is showered with blows, his hair is pulled, and he is thrown back into the water, obliged to continue the hard work of tearing out the oysters and bringing them again to the surface.

The food given the pearl divers is codfish, not very nourishing, and the bread made of maize, the bread of the Indies. At night the pearl divers are chained so they cannot escape.

Often a pearl diver does not return to the surface, for these waters are <u>infested</u> with man-eating sharks of two kinds, both vicious marine animals that can kill, eat, and swallow a whole man.

In this harvesting of pearls let us again consider whether the Spaniards preserve the divine concepts of love for their fellow men, when they place the bodies of the Indians in such mortal danger, and their

What happened if a pearl diver wanted to rest?

WORDS FOR EVERYDAY USE: **in • fest** (in fest´) *vt.*, overrun or inhabit in large numbers

souls, too, for these pearl divers perish without the holy sacraments.[6] And it is solely because of the Spaniards' greed for gold that they force the Indians to lead such a life, often a brief life, for it is impossible to continue for long diving into the cold water and holding the breath for minutes at a time, repeating this hour after hour, day after day; the continual cold penetrates them, constricts the chest, and they die spitting blood, or weakened by diarrhea.

The hair of these pearl divers, naturally black, is as if <u>burnished</u> by the saltpeter in the water, and hangs down their backs making them look like sea dogs or monsters of another species. And in this extraordinary labor, or, better put, in this infernal labor, the Lucayan Indians are finally consumed, as are captive Indians from other provinces. And all of them were publicly sold for one hundred and fifty castellanos,[7] these Indians who had lived happily on their islands until the Spaniards came, although such a thing was against the law. But the unjust judges did nothing to stop it. For all the Indians of these islands are known to be great swimmers.[8] ■

Why didn't the judges stop the enslavement and mistreatment of the native population?

---

6. **sacraments.** Certain rites believed to be means of grace: baptism, confirmation, the Eucharist, penance, holy orders, matrimony, and Anointing of the Sick in Roman and Eastern Orthodox churches; baptism and the Lord's Supper in Protestant churches

7. **castellanos.** Spanish gold coin bearing the arms of Castile

8. **But the unjust . . . great swimmers.** Spanish judges ignored the mistreatment of the native peoples because their abilities at pearl diving were impressive.

Responding to the Selection

How do you think Bartolomé de las Casas felt when he witnessed his own people behaving so abominably? How would you feel if you saw a friend behave cruelly? What might you do or say in response?

WORDS FOR EVERYDAY USE: **bur • nish** (bʉr′nish) *vt.,* make shiny by rubbing

Reviewing the Selection

1. What did the Spaniards make native women and children do?

2. How did the Spanish react to native efforts at self-defense?

3. How were pearl divers treated by the Spaniards?

4. Did the judges stop the illegal sale of natives?

5. Why, according to de las Casas, did the Spaniards want so much food?

6. Why did they punish the natives so severely?

7. What was the inevitable fate of the pearl divers? What word does de las Casas use to describe their labor?

8. Why didn't the judges stop the sale of natives? What motivated the Spaniards in their relations with the natives?

9. Why do you think Bartolomé de las Casas risked everything, even incurring a charge of treason against Spain, to write the *Relation*?

10. Why do you think the natives continued to resist, hiding in the mountains and sometimes killing Christians?

Understanding Literature (Questions for Discussion)

1. **Mood. Mood,** or **atmosphere,** is the emotion created in the reader by part or all of a literary work. Whether sadness, suspense, or humor, mood provides writers with an important tool to engage the reader's attention. Describe the mood of the *Relation.* Find four examples of concrete details that you feel support that mood.

2. **Point of View. Point of view** is the vantage point from which a story, whether fiction or nonfiction, is told. A story may be told by one of the participants, who uses *I* to refer to himself or herself or by an outsider who avoids the use of *I*. From what point of view is the *Relation* told? How can you tell?

from *The General History of Virginia, New England, and the Summer Isles*

by John Smith

ABOUT THE AUTHOR

John Smith (1580–1631) was born in Willoughby, England. As a youth, he worked on his father's farm and was apprenticed to a shopkeeper. At the age of twenty, he went to Hungary to fight against the Turks, was taken captive, escaped to Russia, and then returned to England. In 1606, he joined a group of about one hundred people and set sail for the New World. There, on the Chesapeake Bay, he helped to found the first permanent English colony in America, Jamestown. Smith explored Virginia, making maps of the land and its waterways. In 1607, he was captured by Powhatan, chief of one of the native peoples of Chesapeake Bay. In later writings, he claimed to have been saved from execution by the chief's young daughter, known to history by her nickname, Pocahontas. Smith served as governor of the Jamestown Colony from 1608 to 1609, at which time he returned to England. Smith returned to America in 1614, this time to a part of the continent that he called New England. There he made maps of the coastline. In 1615, Smith was captured by pirates but managed to escape. Smith published several maps and accounts of his explorations, including *Map of Virginia* (1612), *A Description of New England* (1616), and *The True Travels, Adventures, and Observations of Captain John Smith in Europe, Asia, Africa, and America* (1630).

ABOUT THE SELECTION

In *The General History of Virginia, New England, and the Summer Isles*, John Smith presents a detailed and often exciting account of the events in the early years of the Virginia Colony from 1607, the year of its founding at Jamestown, to 1609, the year when Smith departed Virginia never to return. *The General History of Virginia* was completed in 1624, fifteen years after Smith's return to England. The book includes writings by other colonists as well as by Smith and covers events in both British colonies in America at that time— Plymouth Plantation in New England and the Jamestown Colony in Virginia. In this part of the account, Smith describes how he was saved from death by Pocahontas, the sixteen-year-old daughter of Chief Powhatan.

READER'S JOURNAL

Before you begin to read John Smith's history, think for a moment about stories you may have heard about the early colonial period in North America. In what way are the colonists typically presented? the Native Americans? To what extent do you believe the portrayals of colonists and Native Americans, given that most accounts came from the colonial perspective?

LANGUAGE SKILLS

Read the Language Arts Survey, 2.56, "Using the Active Voice." As you read the selection, make two lists of verbs that are used—active voice and passive voice. Which type of verb is used more often?

FROM

The General History of Virginia...

JOHN SMITH

What Happened Till the First Supply

Being thus left to our fortunes, it fortuned[1] that within ten days, scarce ten amongst us could either go[2] or well stand, such extreme weakness and sickness oppressed us. And thereat none need marvel if they consider the cause and reason, which was this: While the ships stayed, our allowance was somewhat bettered by a daily proportion of biscuit which the sailors would <u>pilfer</u> to sell, give, or exchange with us for money, sassafras,[3] or furs. But when they departed, there remained neither tavern, beer house, nor place of relief but the common kettle.[4] Had we been as free from all sins as <u>gluttony</u> and drunkenness we might have been <u>canonized</u> for saints, but our President[5] would never have been admitted for engrossing to his private,[6] oatmeal, sack,[7] oil, aqua vitae,[8] beef, eggs, or what not but the kettle: that indeed he allowed equally to be distributed, and that was half a pint of wheat and as much barley boiled with water for a man a day, and this, having fried some twenty-six weeks in the ship's hold, contained as many worms as grains so that we might truly call it rather so much bran than corn; our drink was water, our lodgings castles in the air.

---

1. **fortuned.** Happened
2. **go.** Go about; walk
3. **sassafras.** Tree with aromatic bark, the root bark of which was valued for its supposed medicinal qualities
4. **common kettle.** Public or general cooking pot
5. **President.** Edward Maria Wingfield (*circa* 1560–1613), first president of Virginia colony
6. **private.** Private or personal stock
7. **sack.** Dry, Spanish white wine, popular in England during the sixteenth and seventeenth centuries
8. **aqua vitae.** Brandy

Why might the colonists have been canonized as saints? Why wouldn't the president have been included as a saint?

WORDS FOR EVERYDAY USE:	**pil • fer** (pil′fər) *vt.*, steal **glut • ton • y** (glut′'n ē) *n.*, habit or act of eating too much **can • on • ize** (kan′ən īz′) *vt.*, declare a deceased person a saint in formal church procedure

What did the speaker feel about the difficulties the colonists had undergone?

With this lodging and diet, our extreme toil in bearing and planting palisades[9] so strained and bruised us and our continual labor in the extremity of the heat had so weakened us, as were cause sufficient to have made us as miserable in our native country or any other place in the world.

From May to September, those that escaped lived upon sturgeon[10] and sea crabs. Fifty in this time we buried: the rest seeing the President's projects to escape these miseries in our pinnace[11] by flight (who all this time had neither felt want nor sickness) so moved our dead spirits as we deposed him and established Ratcliffe in his place . . .

What type of person was Captain Smith? Does the fact that the author described himself in this passage influence your description?

But now was all our provision spent, the sturgeon gone, all helps abandoned, each hour expecting the fury of the savages; when God, the patron of all good endeavors, in that desperate <u>extremity</u> so changed the hearts of the savages that they brought such plenty of their fruits and provision as no man wanted.

And now where some affirmed it was ill done of the Council[12] to send forth men so badly provided, this incontradictable reason will show them plainly they are too ill advised to nourish such ill <u>conceits</u>: First, the fault of our going was our own: what could be thought fitting or necessary we had, but what we should find, or want, or where we should be, we were all ignorant and supposing to make our passage in two months, with victual to live and the advantage of the spring to work; we were at sea five months where we both spent our victual and lost the opportunity of the time and season to plant, by the unskillful <u>presumption</u> of our ignorant transporters that understood not at all what they undertook.

Such actions have ever since the world's beginning been subject to such accidents, and everything of worth is found full of difficulties, but nothing so difficult as to establish a commonwealth so far remote from men and means and where men's minds are so untoward[13] as neither do well themselves nor suffer others. But to proceed.

The new President and Martin, being little beloved, of weak judgment in dangers, and less industry in peace, committed the managing of all things abroad[14] to Captain Smith, who, by his own example, good words, and fair promises set some to mow, others to bind thatch, some to build houses, others to thatch them, himself always bearing the greatest task for his own share, so that in short time he provided most of them lodgings, neglecting any for himself . . .

Leading an expedition on the Chickahominy River, Captain Smith and his men are attacked by Indians, and Smith is taken prisoner.

When this news came to Jamestown, much was their sorrow for his loss, few expecting what <u>ensued</u>.

Six or seven weeks those barbarians kept him prisoner, many strange triumphs and

---

9. **palisades.** Pointed stakes set in the ground to form a fence for fortification or defense
10. **sturgeon.** Large, edible, bony fish
11. **pinnace.** Small sailing ship
12. **Council.** Group in charge of the Virginia experiment
13. **untoward.** Stubborn
14. **abroad.** Outside of the enclosed camp

WORDS FOR EVERYDAY USE:

ex • trem • i • ty (ek strem´ə tē) *n.*, state of extreme necessity, danger, etc.

con • ceit (kən sēt´) *n.*, idea, thought; personal opinion

pre • sump • tion (prē zump´shən) *n.*, overstepping of proper bounds or the taking of something for granted

en • sue (en sōō) *vi.*, come afterward; follow immediately

<u>conjurations</u> they made of him, yet he so demeaned himself amongst them, as he not only diverted them from surprising the fort, but procured his own liberty, and got himself and his company such estimation amongst them, that those savages admired him.

The manner how they used and delivered him is as followeth:

The savages having drawn from George Cassen whither Captain Smith was gone, prosecuting[15] that opportunity they followed him with three hundred bowmen, conducted by the King of Pamunkee, who in divisions searching the turnings of the river found Robinson and Emry by the fireside; those they shot full of arrows and slew. Then finding the Captain, as is said, that used the savage that was his guide as his shield (three of them being slain and divers[16] others so galled),[17] all the rest would not come near him. Thinking thus to have returned to his boat, regarding them, as he marched, more than his way, slipped up to the middle in an oozy creek and his savage with him; yet dared they not come to him till being near dead with cold he threw away his arms. Then according to their composition[18] they drew him forth and led him to the fire where his men were slain. Diligently they chafed his benumbed limbs.

---

15. **prosecuting.** Following up or pursuing
16. **divers.** Several
17. **galled.** Wounded
18. **composition.** Habits; customary manners

WORDS FOR EVERYDAY USE:

con • jur • a • tion (kän´joo rā´shən) *n.*, magic; sorcery

What did Smith give to Opechancanough?

What did Smith say he demonstrated with the compass?

What happened to Smith despite his demonstration? Who saved him? How did this person save him?

He demanding for their captain, they showed him Opechancanough, King of Pamunkee, to whom he gave a round ivory double compass dial. Much they marveled at the playing of the fly and needle,[19] which they could see so plainly and yet not touch it because of the glass that covered them. But when he demonstrated by that globe-like jewel the roundness of the earth and skies, the sphere of the sun, moon, and stars, and how the sun did chase the night round about the world continually, the greatness of the land and sea, the <u>diversity</u> of nations, variety of complexions, and how we were to them antipodes[20] and many other such like matters, they all stood as amazed with admiration.

Notwithstanding, within an hour after, they tied him to a tree, and as many as could stand about him prepared to shoot him, but the King holding up the compass in his hand, they all laid down their bows and arrows and in a triumphant manner led him to Orapaks where he was after their manner kindly feasted and well used. . . .

At last they brought him to Werowocomoco, where was Powhatan, their Emperor. Here more than two hundred of those grim courtiers stood wondering at him, as he had been a monster, till Powhatan and his train had put themselves in their greatest braveries. Before a fire upon a seat like a bedstead, he sat covered with a great robe made of raccoon skins and all the tails hanging by. On either hand did sit a young wench of sixteen or eighteen years and along on each side the house, two rows of men and behind them as many women, with all their heads and shoulders painted red, many of their heads bedecked with the white down of birds, but every one with something, and a great chain of white beads about their necks.

At his entrance before the King, all the people gave a great shout. The Queen of Appomattoc was appointed to bring him water to wash his hands, and another brought him a bunch of feathers, instead of a towel, to dry them; having feasted him after their best barbarous manner they could, a long consultation was held, but the conclusion was, two great stones were brought before Powhatan; then as many as could, laid hands on him, dragged him to them, and thereon laid his head and being ready with their clubs to beat out his brains, Pocahontas, the King's dearest daughter, when no <u>entreaty</u> could prevail, got his head in her arms and laid her own upon his to save him from death; whereat the Emperor was contented he should live to make him hatchets, and her bells, beads, and copper, for they thought him as well of all occupations as themselves.[21] For the King himself will make his own robes, shoes, bows, arrows, pots; plant, hunt, or do anything so well as the rest.

Two days after, Powhatan, having disguised himself in the most fearfulest manner he could, caused Captain Smith to be brought forth to a great house in the woods and there upon a mat by the fire to be left alone. Not long after, from behind a mat that divided the house, was made

---

19. **fly and needle.** Parts of a compass
20. **antipodes.** On opposite sides of the earth
21. **him as well . . . as themselves.** He had as much

WORDS FOR EVERYDAY USE:

di • ver • si • ty (də vʉr´sə tē) *n.,* variety
en • treat • y (en trēt´ē) *n.,* earnest request

the most <u>dolefulest</u> noise he ever heard; then Powhatan more like a devil than a man, with some two hundred more as black as himself, came unto him and told him now they were friends, and presently he should go to Jamestown to send him two great guns and a grindstone for which he would give him the country of Capahowasic and forever esteem him as his son Nantaquond.

So to Jamestown with twelve guides Powhatan sent him. That night they quartered in the woods, he still expecting (as he had done all this long time of his imprisonment) every hour to be put to one death or other, for all their feasting. But almighty God (by His divine providence) had <u>mollified</u> the hearts of those stern barbarians with compassion. The next morning betimes[22] they came to the fort, where Smith having used the savages with what kindness he could, he showed Rawhunt, Powhatan's trusty servant, two demiculverins[23] and a millstone to carry Powhatan: they found them somewhat too heavy, but when they did see him discharge them, being loaded with stones, among the boughs of a great tree loaded with icicles, the ice and branches came so tumbling down that the poor savages ran away half dead with fear. But at last we regained some conference with them and gave them such toys and sent to Powhatan, his women, and children such presents as gave them in general full content.

Now in Jamestown they were all in combustion, the strongest preparing once more to run away with the pinnace; which, with the hazard of his life, with saker falcon[24] and musket shot, Smith forced now the third time to stay or sink.

Some, no better than they should be, had plotted with the President the next day to have him put to death by the Levitical law,[25] for the lives of Robinson and Emry; pretending the fault was his that had led them to their ends; but he quickly took such order with such lawyers that he laid them by their heels till he sent some of them prisoners for England.

Now every once in four or five days, Pocahontas with her attendants brought him so much provision that saved many of their lives, that else for all this had starved with hunger.

His relation of the plenty he had seen, especially at Werowocomoco, and of the state and bounty of Powhatan (which till that time was unknown), so revived their dead spirits (especially the love of Pocahontas) as all men's fear was abandoned.

Thus you may see what difficulties still crossed any good endeavor; and the good success of the business being thus oft brought to the very period of destruction: yet you see by what strange means God hath still delivered it.   ■

What did some of the colonists wish to do with Smith? Why did they wish to do this?

Who saved the colonists?

---

22. **betimes.** Early
23. **demiculverins.** Large cannons
24. **saker falcon.** Small cannon
25. **Levitical law.** Biblical law from the Old Testament that states "He that killeth man shall surely be put to death" (Leviticus 24:17).

WORDS FOR EVERYDAY USE: dole • ful (dōl´fəl) *adj.*, full of or causing sorrow or sadness
mol • li • fy (mäl´ə fī´) *vt.*, soothe the temper of

Responding to the Selection

Entering a foreign or unfamiliar culture can be both fascinating and frightening. If you had been in Smith's place in Powhatan's village, what emotions might you have been feeling? Would you ever like to visit a place where the customs are different from your own? Where would you like to go?

Reviewing the Selection

RECALLING

1. Describe the people present at the event that Smith relates. What people are there, and what do they look like?

2. Who orders Smith's execution? Who saves Smith from death? How does she save him?

3. What does Pocahontas bring to Smith and his fellow colonists regularly after the rescue? How do her gifts help the colonists?

4. What effect does the knowledge of Powhatan's wealth, power, and plenty have upon the colonists?

INTERPRETING

5. Why do you think Powhatan dresses himself in his "greatest braveries" to speak with John Smith? Why does Smith feel that the courtiers treat him "as if he had been a monster"? Explain why this is a natural reaction to Smith's presence in the village.

6. Smith's account explains very little about Pocahontas. Therefore, the reader is free to build a story around the bare facts that Smith presents. Why do you think Pocahontas saves Smith's life?

7. Why is the meeting with Powhatan crucial to the survival of the colony of Jamestown?

8. Why does the knowledge that Powhatan has all the food and goods that he needs encourage the colonists? How do you think they expect to benefit from his good fortune?

SYNTHESIZING

9. It is possible that Smith was never in danger from Powhatan at all, that he misunderstood a custom of Powhatan's people and mistakenly assumed he was in mortal danger. Why do you think Smith told this story over and over again and included it in his history fifteen years later? Do you think Smith believed his interpretation of the events fifteen years later, or might he have had other reasons for telling the story?

10. What qualities did it take to be an early colonist in America? What qualities of character did Powhatan and Pocahontas show in their first meeting with a European?

PREREADING

from *Of Plymouth Plantation*
by William Bradford

ABOUT THE AUTHOR

William Bradford (1590–1657) was born in Austerfield in Yorkshire, England, and was educated in the arts of farming. Bradford joined the community of Separatists, Puritans who had left the Church of England. To escape persecution, the Separatists fled to Holland, where Bradford joined them in 1609. The group was later granted land in the New World and sailed across the Atlantic on the *Mayflower*, landing in Plymouth, Massachusetts, in 1620. Despite initial hardships, the colonists survived and they elected Bradford their governor, a position he held for over thirty years. Bradford wrote a history of the founding of Plymouth Colony, including the history of the Puritan and Separatist movements. Bradford's descriptions of the voyage of the *Mayflower*, the writing of the Mayflower Compact, and the Pilgrims' and Native Americans' celebration of Thanksgiving have become a vital part of American culture as an example of freedom won through courage and determination.

ABOUT THE SELECTION

William Bradford began writing *Of Plymouth Plantation* in 1630, ten years after the settlement of the colony. He continued this work until 1650, covering events through 1646. The manuscript was in two parts, the first part of which was copied into the Plymouth church records by the time of the American Revolution. After the revolution, the manuscript disappeared, and the second part was lost for almost a century. Then the entire manuscript was discovered in the residence of the bishop of London and was published, finally, in 1856. In 1897, the manuscript was returned to America to be kept in the State House in Boston.

READER'S JOURNAL

What would make you leave your home and travel to a strange, unsettled land? profit? hopes for better lives for your children? How do you think the Pilgrims must have felt on leaving Europe? What fears might they have had? what hopes and dreams?

THINKING SKILLS

Read the Language Arts Survey, 4.13, "Making Hypotheses." Then, as you read this selection, decide what hypotheses William Bradford presents to explain the causes of the events he reports.

FROM

Of Plymouth Plantation

William Bradford

Book I, Chapter IX. Of Their Voyage and How They Passed the Sea; and of Their Safe Arrival at Cape Cod

What does the haughty young man want to do? What happens to him during the trip?

September 6. These troubles[1] being blown over, and now all being compact together in one ship, they put to sea again with a <u>prosperous</u> wind, which continued divers days together, which was some encouragement unto them; yet, according to the usual manner, many were afflicted with seasickness. And I may not omit here a special work of God's providence. There was a proud and very <u>profane</u> young man, one of the seamen, of a lusty,[2] able body, which made him the more haughty; he would always be condemning the poor people in their sickness and cursing them daily with grievous execrations;[3] and did not let[4] to tell them that he hoped to help to cast half of them overboard before they came to their journey's end, and to make merry with what they had; and if he were by any gently <u>reproved</u>, he would curse and swear most bitterly. But it pleased God before they came half seas over, to smite this young man with a grievous disease, of which he died in a desperate manner, and so was himself the first that was thrown overboard. Thus his curses <u>light</u> on his own head, and it was an astonishment to all his fellows for they noted it to be the just hand of God upon him.

After they had enjoyed fair winds and weather for a season, they were encountered

---

1. **troubles.** Another vessel, the *Speedwell*, had proved unseaworthy and everything was transferred to the *Mayflower*.
2. **lusty.** Strong; energetic
3. **execrations.** Curses
4. **let.** Hesitate

Words for Everyday Use:

pros • per • ous (präs´ pər əs) *adj.*, conducive to success; favorable

pro • fane (prō fān´) *adj.*, showing disrespect for sacred things

re • prove (ri proov´) *vt.*, speak to in disapproval

light (līt) *vi.*, fall or strike suddenly

The Beginning of New England: after the painting by Clyde O. Deland. *The Granger Collection, NY*

many times with cross winds and met with many fierce storms with which the ship was shroudly[5] shaken, and her upper works made very leaky; and one of the main beams in the midships was bowed and cracked, which put them in some fear that the ship could not be able to perform the voyage. So some of the chief of the company, perceiving the mariners to fear the sufficiency of the ship as appeared by their mutterings, they entered into serious <u>consultation</u> with the master and other officers of the ship, to consider in time of the danger, and rather to return than to cast themselves into a desperate and <u>inevitable</u> peril. And truly there was great distraction and difference of opinion amongst the mariners themselves; fain[6] would they do what could be done for their wages' sake (being now near half the seas over) and on the other hand they were <u>loath</u> to hazard their lives too des-

perately. But in examining of all opinions, the master and others affirmed they knew the ship to be strong and firm under water; and for the buckling of the main beam, there was a great iron screw the passengers brought out of Holland, which would raise the beam into his place; the which being done, the carpenter and master affirmed that with a post put under it, set firm in the lower deck and otherways bound, he would make it sufficient. And as for the decks and upper works, they would caulk them as well as they could, and though with the working of the ship they would not long keep staunch,[7] yet there would otherwise be no great danger, if they did not overpress her with sails. So they committed themselves to the will of God and resolved to proceed.

What made the people on the ship worry about their voyage?

Why did the people decide to continue with their voyage?

---

5. **shroudly.** Shrewdly, meaning wickedly
6. **fain.** Gladly
7. **staunch.** Watertight

WORDS FOR EVERYDAY USE:

con • sul • ta • tion (kän′səl tā′shən) *n.,* meeting to discuss, decide, or plan something

in • ev • i • ta • ble (in ev′ i tə bəl) *adj.,* that cannot be avoided or evaded

loath (lōth) *adj.,* unwilling, reluctant

In <u>sundry</u> of these storms the winds were so fierce and the seas so high, as they could not bear a knot of sail, but were forced to hull[8] for divers days together. And in one of them, as they thus lay at hull in a mighty storm, a lusty young man called John Howland, coming upon some occasion above the gratings was, with a seele[9] of the ship, thrown into sea; but it pleased God that he caught hold of the topsail halyards[10] which hung overboard and ran out at length. Yet he held his hold (though he was sundry fathoms under water) till he was hauled up by the same rope to the brim of the water, and then with a boat hook and other means got into the ship again and his life saved. And though he was something ill with it, yet he lived many years after and became a profitable member both in church and commonwealth. In all this voyage there died but one of the passengers, which was William Butten, a youth, servant to Samuel Fuller, when they drew near the coast.

But to omit other things (that I may be brief) after long beating at sea they fell with that land which is called Cape Cod; the which being made and certainly known to be it, they were not a little joyful. After some <u>deliberation</u> had amongst themselves and with the master of the ship, they tacked[11] about and resolved to stand for the southward (the wind and weather being fair) to find some place about Hudson's River for their habitation. But after they had sailed that course about half the day, they fell amongst dangerous shoals and roaring breakers, and they were so far entangled therewith as they conceived themselves in great danger; and the

What reasons led to the creation of the Mayflower Compact?

wind shrinking upon them withal, they resolved to bear up again for the Cape and thought themselves happy to get out of those dangers before night overtook them, as by God's good providence they did. And the next day they got into Cape Harbor[12] where they rid in safety.

From *Book II, Chapter XI. The Remainder of Anno 1620*

THE MAYFLOWER COMPACT

I shall a little return back, and begin with a combination[13] made by them before they came ashore; being the first foundation of their government in this place. Occasioned partly by the discontented and <u>mutinous</u> speeches that some of the strangers[14] amongst them had let fall from them in the ship: That when they came ashore they would use their own liberty, for none had power to command them, the patent[15] they had being for Virginia and not for New England, which belonged to another government, with which the Virginia Company had nothing to do. And partly that such an act by them done, this their condition considered, might be as firm as any patent, and in some respects more sure.

---

8. **hull.** Drift with the wind with short sails
9. **seele.** Roll
10. **halyards.** Rope for raising and lowering a sail
11. **tacked.** Change course against the wind
12. **Cape Harbor.** The ship arrived in Cape Harbor, now known as Provincetown Harbor, on November 11, 1620, sixty-five days after leaving England.
13. **combination.** Union
14. **strangers.** Those outside the Puritan church
15. **patent.** Document granting a right or privilege

WORDS FOR EVERYDAY USE:

sun • dry (sun′drē) *adj.*, various; miscellaneous

de • lib • er • a • tion (di lib′ər ā′shən) *n.*, discussion; consideration of alternatives

mu • ti • nous (myo͞ot′′n əs) *adj.*, inclined to revolt against authority

The form was as followeth:
IN THE NAME OF GOD, AMEN.

We whose names are underwritten, the loyal subjects of our dread Sovereign Lord King James, by the Grace of God of Great Britain, France, and Ireland King, Defender of the Faith, etc.

Having undertaken, for the Glory of God and advancement of the Christian Faith and Honor of our King and Country, a Voyage to plant the First Colony in the Northern Parts of Virginia, do by these presents solemnly and mutually in the presence of God and one of another, Covenant and Combine ourselves together into a Civil Body Politic, for our better ordering and preservation and furtherance of the ends aforesaid; and by virtue hereof to enact, constitute and frame such just and equal Laws, Ordinances, Acts, Constitutions and Offices, from time to time, as shall be thought most meet[16] and convenient for the general good of the Colony, unto which we promise all due submission and obedience. In witness whereof we have hereunder subscribed our names at Cape Cod, the 11th of November, in the year of the reign of our Sovereign Lord King James, of England, France and Ireland the eighteenth, and of Scotland the fifty-fourth. Anno Domini 1620.

THE STARVING TIME

But that which was most sad and lamentable was, that in two or three months' time half of their company died, especially in January and February, being the depth of winter, and wanting houses and other comforts; being infected with the scurvy[17] and other diseases which this long voyage and their inaccommodate[18] condition had brought upon them. So as there died some times two or three of a day in the foresaid time, that of 100 and odd persons, scarce fifty remained. And of these, in the time of most distress, there was but six or seven persons who to their great commendations, be it spoken, spared no pains night nor day, but with abundance of toil and hazard of their own health, fetched them wood, made them fires, dressed them meat, made their beds, washed their loathsome clothes, clothed and unclothed them. In a word, did all the homely[19] and necessary offices for them which dainty and queasy stomachs cannot endure to hear named; and all this willingly and cheerfully, without any grudging in the least, showing herein their true love unto their friends and brethren; a rare example and worthy to be remembered. Two of these seven were Mr. William Brewster, their reverend Elder, and Myles Standish, their Captain and military commander, unto whom myself and many others were much beholden in our low and sick condition. And yet the Lord so upheld these persons as in this general calamity they were not at all infected either with sickness or lameness. And what I have said of these I may say of many others who died in this general visitation, and others yet living; that whilst they had health, yea, or

---

16. **meet.** Suitable, fit
17. **scurvy.** Disease characterized by weakness and bleeding gums
18. **inaccommodate.** Lacking adequate housing
19. **homely.** Intimate

For what purpose is the Civil Body Politic formed? For what does the compact provide?

How many people died? Why was the death rate so high?

any strength continuing, they were not wanting[20] to any they had need of them. And I doubt not but their <u>recompense</u> is with the Lord.

From *Book II, Chapter XII. Anno 1621*

FIRST THANKSGIVING

Q *What reports were made to people in England?*

They began now to gather in the small harvest they had, and to fit up their houses and dwellings against winter, being all well recovered in health and strength and had all things in good plenty. For as some were thus employed in affairs abroad, others were exercised in fishing, about cod and bass and other fish, of which they took good store, of which every family had their portion. All the summer there was no want; and now began to come in store of fowl,[21] as winter approached, of which this place did abound when they came first (but afterward decreased by degrees). And besides waterfowl there was great store of wild turkeys, of which they took many, besides venison, etc. Besides they had about a peck a meal a week to a person, or now since harvest, Indian corn to that proportion. Which made many afterwards write so largely of their plenty here to their friends in England, which were not <u>feigned</u> but true reports. ∎

20. **wanting.** Lacking in attention
21. **fowl.** Birds

Responding to the Selection

After reading about the Pilgrims' troubles, would you have been willing to join the expedition? Why, or why not?

Reviewing the Selection

RECALLING

1. When the Pilgrims' ship began to look unseaworthy, why were the sailors reluctant to turn around and go back to England?

2. How many of the passengers died during the trip?

3. What did the "strangers" aboard ship threaten to do when they went ashore?

4. Compare the events of January and February 1621 with the events of the fall of 1621.

INTERPRETING

5. Bradford does not explicitly record the Pilgrims' response to the news that the ship might lack seaworthiness. How willing do you suppose they were to return to Europe? Why might they have resisted that possibility?

6. Why did the Pilgrims stop their travels near Cape Cod rather than go farther south, where their charter gave them permission to land? Do you think they were right to do so?

7. Why did the leaders of the Pilgrims insist that every man who was going ashore first sign the Mayflower Compact? How would the compact help the Pilgrims?

8. What were some of the indications that the Pilgrims formed a close, sharing community, where everyone depended on everyone else?

SYNTHESIZING

9. Bradford does not mention the "discontented and mutinous" strangers in his reports of what happened after everyone went ashore. Do you suppose they gave no further trouble? What do you suppose they were doing by the end of the first year in America?

10. In what ways were Bradford and the other Pilgrims sustained by their religious faith? Why was this faith particularly important to them in the New World?

Understanding Literature (Questions for Discussion)

1. **Chronological Order.** Chronological order is the arrangement of details in order of their occurrence. Why does chronological order suit Bradford's purpose? Make a time line of the events related in this selection.

2. **Irony.** Irony is a difference between appearance and reality. In *irony of situation* an event occurs that violates the expectations of the characters, the reader, or the audience. What did the haughty young man expect at the beginning of the selection? What was ironic about his demise?

Responding in Writing

Lyric Poem or Memoir. In *Of Plymouth Plantation,* Bradford describes the first Thanksgiving, which occurred in the fall of 1621. The first Thanksgiving was a three-day feast held by the Pilgrims to celebrate the bounty of the autumn harvest, the survival of the colony, and the aid given the Pilgrims by neighboring Native Americans. By the mid-nineteenth century, Thanksgiving Day had become a traditional holiday in New England, and it was proclaimed an official national holiday in 1863 by President Abraham Lincoln. Write a lyric poem of thanksgiving appropriate for reading on Thanksgiving Day. Your poem can be about the first Thanksgiving or about something for which you personally are thankful. If you prefer to do so, write a brief memoir, or autobiographical account, describing a Thanksgiving celebration in which you participated. Whether you decide to write a lyric poem or a memoir, use concrete sensory details to make your subject vivid for your readers. If you decide to write a lyric poem, you may wish to do some library research on the first Thanksgiving or some freewriting about things for which you are thankful. If you decide to write a memoir, begin by making a time line listing the events that occurred on the day that you will be describing. Refer to the Language Arts Survey, 1.12, "Freewriting"; 1.19, "Time Lines"; and 4.20–4.28, on research techniques.

PREREADING

from *The New England Primer*
Anonymous

ABOUT THE SELECTION

The New England Primer was the first textbook produced in America to teach reading. Evidence places publication of the first edition between 1687 and 1690. Since the New England colonies were founded for religious reasons, it was only natural that religion formed the basis of all education and therefore dominated the book. Its contents included the Lord's Prayer and the Apostles' Creed, a series of moral and instructive sentences from the Bible, and an illustrated alphabet. The *Primer* was popular throughout the English colonies and was sold in the United States until the nineteenth century. The excerpt here is the alphabet from the 1727 edition of the *Primer*.

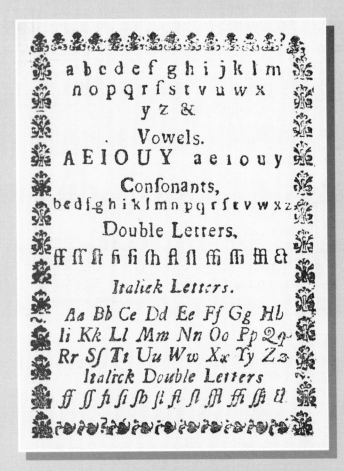

Double Letters.
ff fi ſh fl ſl ffi fſ

Italick Letters.
Ce Dd Ee Ff G
Ll Mm Nn Oo
Tt Uu Ww Xx
ick Double Lett
G ſh ſi fl ſl fſ

READER'S JOURNAL
You have probably seen illustrated alphabet books published in recent years. Perhaps you even remember some of the pictures or rhymes in these books. What makes this approach to learning the alphabet more enjoyable than mere memorization? Jot down your ideas in your journal.

LANGUAGE SKILLS
Read the Language Arts Survey, 2.134, "Proofreading for Spelling Errors." Then examine this selection for words whose spelling has changed since publication of the *Primer*. List the words as they are spelled in the text and as they are spelled today.

FROM

The New England Primer

ANONYMOUS

Why should a student pay close attention to this book?

What might the description "No man of blood" mean?

A — In *Adam's* Fall
We finned[1] all.

B — Thy Life to mend
This *Book* attend.

C — The *Cat* doth play
And after flay.

D — A *Dog* will bite
A Thief at Night.

E — An *Eagles* Flight
Is out of Sight.

F — An idle *Fool*
Is whipt at School.

G — As runs the *Glaſs*
Man's life doth paſs.

H — My *Book* and *Heart*
Shall never part.

J — *Job* feels the Rod
Yet bleſſes GOD.

K — Our *K I N G* the
good
No man of blood.

L — The *Lion* bold
The *Lamb* doth hold.

M — The *Moon* gives light
In time of night.

---

1. **finned.** Sinned. The letter *s* often appears as an *f* in the early print style of the *Primer*.

N — Nightingales fing
In Time of Spring.

O — The *Royal Oak*
it was the Tree
That fav'd His
Royal Majeftie.

P — *Peter* denies
His Lord and cries

Q — Queen *Efther* comes
in Royal State
To Save the Jews
from difmal Fate

R — *Rachol* doth mourn
For her firft born.

S — *Samuel* anoints
Whom God appoints:

T — *Time* cuts down all
Both great and fmall.

U — *Uriah's* beauteous Wife
Made *David* feek his
Life.

W — *Whales* in the Sea
God's Voice obey.

X — *Xerxes* the great did
die,
And fo muft you & I.

Y — *Youth* forward flips
Death fooneft nips.

Z — *Zacheus* he
Did climb the Tree
His Lord to Fee.

What attitude toward death is expressed in this passage?

Responding to the Selection

Which—if any—of the rhymes in this alphabet might appear in a modern alphabet book? Why would others among these rhymes be unsuitable for a modern American book? How have ideas about child rearing changed since the Puritan Era?

Reviewing the Selection

RECALLING

1. What animals appear in the rhyme for the letter *L*?

2. Which letters have rhymes that might refer to the *Primer* itself?

3. During an era of political chaos and revolution in seventeenth-century England, the king saved himself from enemies by hiding in a tree. Which letter has a rhyme referring to this incident?

4. To what kind of glass does the rhyme for the letter *G* refer?

INTERPRETING

5. What two qualities might the animals referred to in the rhyme for the letter *L* represent?

6. Explain the couplet for the letter *B*. To what book does it refer?

7. Which couplet tells how New Englanders felt about the king during the seventeenth century?

8. What does the rhyme for the letter *F* tell about the treatment of school children during the time the *Primer* was in use?

9. At least three rhymes warn of age and death. Identify the letters with these rhymes. Do you think that these are appropriate rhymes for children? Why, or why not?

10. After reading the selection, what can you tell about the differences between education and culture in the 1600s and 1700s and education and culture today?

Understanding Literature (Questions for Discussion)

1. **Aim.** A writer's **aim** is the primary purpose that his or her work is meant to achieve. The aim of the *Primer* was education, but education in what? What characteristics of the alphabet support your answer?

2. **Allusion.** An **allusion** is a figure of speech in which a reference is made to a person, event, object, or work from history or literature. Identify three allusions in this alphabet to the Bible.

3. **Couplet.** A **couplet** is a pair of rhyming lines that express a complete thought. Which letter is given a verse that is not a couplet? How would you describe that particular verse? Several of the couplets are written in four lines of type simply because the width of the page limits the number of characters on a line. Identify one of those couplets, writing it in couplet form.

Responding in Writing

1. **Annotations.** An **annotation** for a literary work is an explanatory note for some part of that work. For example, annotations often explain difficult vocabulary and obscure references. If you are unfamiliar with the references in this selection, do some research to familiarize yourself with them. Write two annotations for the section of the alphabet from *O* through *S*.

2. **Children's Lesson Story.** Write a lesson story for an audience of young children, with the aim not merely of entertaining your audience but also of educating the children about good behavior. Choose a behavior you wish to promote. Then write a short story that demonstrates why this behavior is desired. You may wish to demonstrate rewards for following the behavior and punishments for deviating from such behavior. Refer to the Language Arts Survey, 2.148, "Register."

3. **Curriculum.** A **curriculum** consists of the courses provided by a school. What courses would you need to understand all the historical and biblical references in the *Primer* alphabet? Write a curriculum for your studies, with a short description of each course.

Language Lab

Linking Verbs. Read the Language Arts Survey, 2.13, "Linking Verbs." On a separate sheet of paper, write each verb from the following sentences. Underline each linking verb.

1. Some modern people feel ignorant when they read Puritan writings.

2. Although the language looks familiar, its meaning is sometimes obscure because of historical and religious references with which modern-day people are often unfamiliar.

3. Footnotes are one means of providing information about obscure references in literary works and other written materials.

4. Religion was the central force within the Puritan community, and all aspects of life felt its influence.

5. That is why Puritan writings were full of religious references.

Thinking Skills

Classifying. Read the Language Arts Survey, 4.7, "Classifying." Then create a system for classifying the verses in this selection. Identify each class, and list the letters whose verses share the characteristics of that class.

PROJECTS

1. **Pop Culture Alphabet Book.** With a small group, create an original alphabet book in which you associate the letters with elements of pop culture (Example: *R* is for rap). Begin with a brainstorming session during which all suggestions are listed. Next, vote on the best word for each letter, and decide what form to use—phrases, couplets, or another form. Divide the alphabet among the group members, and write the entries. Illustrate them as your group chooses. Finally, assemble the pages, and add a title page and cover.

2. **Memory Bee.** Try playing the game known as a Memory Bee. Two teams are needed. After no more than five minutes of memorizing the *Primer* alphabet, each team chooses a representative to run the contest. The leaders make out a card for each letter of the alphabet and mix the cards. Then they take turns drawing letters and challenging the opposing team with them, spelling-bee style. If a team member can name the person or thing associated with the letter, the team gets one point. If the member can recite the entire couplet, the team gets three points. The team with the most points after twelve turns wins.

"To My Dear and Loving Husband"

by Anne Bradstreet

ABOUT THE AUTHOR

Anne Bradstreet (*circa* 1612–1672) had the advantage of an education unusual for women of her time and began writing poetry as a child. She married Simon Bradstreet, a graduate of Cambridge University and an associate of her father, when she was only sixteen. A year after marriage to Anne, Simon was appointed to assist in the preparations of the Massachusetts Bay Company, and the Bradstreets sailed to the New World. Life in the new world was hard, especially for Anne, who had been weakened by a childhood illness. When her husband became governor of the Bay Colony, Anne's duties increased as well. Despite her many obligations, Bradstreet found time to continue writing poetry, as she had when she was a young girl. Unknown to Anne, her brother-in-law had a collection of her poetry printed in London in 1650—the first published volume of poems by a New World resident.

ABOUT THE SELECTION

The date of composition of **"To My Dear and Loving Husband,"** like most of Anne Bradstreet's work, is unknown. Originally, she distributed her writings only among family and friends, but after publication of some poems, she then decided to put out a second, authorized edition. That second edition did not appear until after her death, being published in Boston in 1678. "To My Dear and Loving Husband" appeared in the second edition. The poem remains a noble expression of the sustaining and transforming power of love.

"To My Dear and Loving Husband"

ANNE BRADSTREET

If ever two were one, then surely we.
If ever man were loved by wife, then thee;
If ever wife was happy in a man,
Compare with me, ye women, if you can.
5   I prize thy love more than whole mines of gold
Or all the riches that the East doth hold.
My love is such that rivers cannot quench,
Nor ought but love from thee, give <u>recompense</u>.
Thy love is such I can no way repay,
10   The heavens reward thee <u>manifold</u>, I pray.
Then while we live, in love let's so <u>persevere</u>
That when we live no more, we may live ever. ■

How much does the speaker prize her husband's love?

If the couple persevere in their love, what will be the consequences?

Responding to the Selection

What is special about the marriage that Anne Bradstreet describes? What must happen for people to develop the sort of relationship indicated by this poem? Discuss these questions with your classmates.

WORDS FOR
EVERYDAY USE:

rec • om • pense (rek´əm pens´) *n.,* reward; compensation, payment
man • i • fold (man´ə fōld´) *adv.,* in many forms or ways
per • se • vere (pʉr´sə vir´) *vi.,* continue in spite of difficulty; persist

Elizabeth Freake and Baby Mary. *Artist unknown, circa 1671–74. Worcester Art Museum, Worcester, MA. Gift of Mr. and Mrs. Albert W. Rice.*

Reviewing the Selection

RECALLING

1. Both lines 1 and 2 consist of elliptical sentences—that is, not all the words are provided; some are understood. Write out the complete sentences, supplying the understood words. (If you like, use *you* instead of *thee*.)

2. What is the sense, or meaning, of *prize* in line 5?

3. *Recompense* means "payment." What is the one thing that can be recompense for the speaker's love?

4. According to lines 11 and 12, what will help the speaker and her beloved to live forever?

INTERPRETING

5. Why did Bradstreet use elliptical sentences? What effect do they have on the poem?

6. Complete the comparison suggested in line 7 by the use of the word *quenched:* My love is like _____.

7. Restate line 10 in your own words.

8. What sorts of difficulties might these people or any married people face? Why is it important to any relationship to be willing to persevere in spite of difficulties?

9. In your own words, how would you describe the relationship between the speaker and her husband?

10. In lines 11 and 12, the speaker suggests that if the two persevere in their love while living, they will live forever. What does the speaker believe about the afterlife? about the consequences of being, in this life, someone who perseveres in love despite its difficulties?

Understanding Literature (Questions for Discussion)

1. **Hyperbole**. A **hyperbole** is an exaggeration made for rhetorical effect. Find an instance of hyperbole in this poem.

2. **Oxymoron**. An **oxymoron** is a statement that contradicts itself. What oxymoron appears in the final lines of this poem? Why do you suppose the poet chose to use this technique? What is its effect?

3. **Sight rhyme**. **Sight rhyme**, or **eye rhyme**, is a pair of words, generally at the ends of lines of verse, that are spelled similarly but pronounced differently. In which lines of the selection is sight rhyme used?

Language Lab

Inverting Sentences for Emphasis. Read the Language Arts Survey, 2.64, "Inverting Sentences for Emphasis." Then rewrite these lines in usual word order, that is, *subject-verb-object*.

1. My love I have not confessed.
2. Not to keep secrets, it's best.
3. Thy love I cannot repay.
4. The heavens reward thee, I pray.
5. My future in your hands I rest.

Study and Research Skills

Formal Note-taking. Read the Language Arts Survey, 4.32, "Formal Note-taking." Then look up Anne Bradstreet in two library reference books. Take one or more notes from each reference book, using the note form recommended in the Language Arts Survey.

from "Sinners in the Hands of an Angry God"
by Jonathan Edwards

ABOUT THE AUTHOR

Jonathan Edwards (1703–1758) was born in East Windsor, Connecticut. He was a dedicated scholar even as a child and was admitted to Yale College when he was only thirteen. Edwards flourished in the rigorous academic setting and devoted himself to the study of theology. Edwards came from a line of noteworthy ministers and was determined to carry on his family's tradition. Edwards moved to Northampton, Massachusetts, where he succeeded his grandfather as minister of the local church, married, and raised a family. Edwards's goal as a minister was not only to heighten his followers' commitment to religion, but to enrich their religious experience. Known for his vivid and fiery sermons, Edwards sought to make religion so moving and real that it was almost a physical experience. Edwards's religious views gained great popularity and began the Great Awakening, a religious revival that swept across the colonies in the 1730s. When he decided, however, to actually name prestigious members of the clergy who were not expressing the proper devotion and reinstate the rite of communion, he was dismissed from his church. Edwards then served as a missionary to the Housatonic Indians and was elected president of the College of New Jersey (now Princeton).

ABOUT THE SELECTION

The following excerpt is from **"Sinners in the Hands of an Angry God,"** a sermon Edwards delivered in Enfield, Connecticut, on Sunday, July 8, 1741. Another minister who was present reported that Edwards spoke with calm dignity, yet the effect was highly emotional, with "such a breathing of distress, and weeping, that the preacher was obliged to speak to the people and desire silence, that he might be heard." The text of the sermon was published over eighty years later, in 1829–1830, in a multivolume edition of Edwards's works.

FROM

"Sinners in the Hands of an Angry God"

JONATHAN EDWARDS

You probably are not sensible[1] of this; you find you are kept out of hell, but do not see the hand of God in it; but look at other things, as the good state of your bodily <u>constitution</u>, your care of your own life, and the means you use for your own preservation. But indeed these things are nothing; if God should withdraw His hand, they would <u>avail</u> no more to keep you from falling, than the thin air to hold up a person that is suspended in it.

Your wickedness makes you as it were heavy as lead, and to tend downwards with great weight and pressure towards hell; and if God should let you go, you would immediately sink and swiftly descend and plunge into the bottomless <u>gulf</u>, and your healthy constitution, and your own care and prudence, and best <u>contrivance</u>, and all your righteousness, would have no more influence to uphold you and keep you out of hell, than a spider's web would have to stop a fallen rock. Were it not for the <u>sovereign</u> pleasure of God, the earth would not bear you one moment; for you are a burden to it; the creation groans with you; the creature is made subject to the bondage of your corruption, not willingly; the sun does not willingly shine upon you to give you light to serve sin and Satan; the earth does not willingly yield her increase[2] to satisfy your lusts; nor is it willingly a stage for your wickedness to be acted upon; the air does not willingly

According to Edwards, what would happen to people if God withdrew his hand? What would fail to save them?

To what are people a burden, according to Edwards?

---

1. **sensible.** Aware
2. **increase.** Harvest

---

serve you for breath to maintain the flame of life in your vitals,[3] while you spend your life in the service of God's enemies. God's creatures are good, and were made for men to serve God with, and do not willingly subserve to any other purpose, and groan when they are abused to purposes so directly contrary to their nature and end. And the world would spew[4] you out, were it not for the sovereign hand of Him who hath subjected it in hope. There are black clouds of God's wrath now hanging directly over your heads, full of the dreadful storm, and big with thunder; and were it not for the restraining hand of God, it would immediately burst forth upon you. The sovereign pleasure of God, for the present, stays His rough wind; otherwise it would come with fury, and your destruction would come like a whirlwind, and you would be like the chaff of the summer threshing floor. . . .[5]

The bow of God's wrath is bent, and the arrow made ready on the string, and justice bends the arrow at your heart, and strains the bow, and it is nothing but the mere pleasure of God, and that of an angry God, without any promise or obligation at all, that keeps the arrow one moment from being made drunk with your blood. Thus all you that never passed under a great change of heart, by the mighty power of the Spirit of God upon your souls, all you that were never born again, and made new creatures, and raised from being dead in sin, to a state of new, and before altogether unexperienced light and life, are in the hands of an angry God. However you may have reformed your life in many things,

and may have had religious affections,[6] and may keep up a form of religion in your families and closets,[7] and in the house of God, it is nothing but His mere pleasure that keeps you from being this moment swallowed up in everlasting destruction. However unconvinced you may now be of the truth of what you hear, by and by you will be fully convinced of it. Those that are gone from being in the like circumstances with you see that it was so with them; for destruction came suddenly upon most of them; when they expected nothing of it and while they were saying, peace and safety: now they see that those things on which they depended for peace and safety, were nothing but thin air and empty shadows.

The God that holds you over the pit of hell, much as one holds a spider or some loathsome insect over the fire, abhors you, and is dreadfully provoked: His wrath towards you burns like fire; He looks upon you as worthy of nothing else but to be cast into the fire; He is of purer eyes than to bear to have you in His sight; you are ten thousand times more abominable in His eyes than the most hateful venomous serpent is in ours. You have offended Him infinitely more than ever a stubborn rebel did his prince; and yet it is nothing but His hand that holds you from falling into the fire every moment. It is to be ascribed to nothing else, that you did not go to hell the last night; that you was suffered to

What is hanging directly over the heads of people?

How does Edwards address those who may doubt his words?

Which people are in the hands of an angry God?

---

3. **vitals.** Necessary organs
4. **spew.** Throw up; eject
5. **chaff . . . threshing floor.** *Chaff*—husks of wheat that are left behind; *threshing floor*—place where grain is separated from its husks
6. **affections.** Feelings
7. **closets.** Studies; meditations

WORDS FOR EVERYDAY USE:

sub • serve (səb sʉrv´) vt., be useful or helpful; serve

loath • some (lōth´səm) adj., disgusting

ab • hor (ab hôr´) vt., shrink from in disgust

pro • voke (prō vōk´) vt., anger, irritate, annoy

as • cribe (ə skrīb´) vt., assign; attribute

The Sermon. *Gari Melchers, 1886. National Museum of American Art, Washington, DC/Art Resource*

awake again in this world, after you closed your eyes to sleep. And there is no other reason to be given, why you have not dropped into hell since you arose in the morning, but that God's hand has held you up. There is no other reason to be given why you have not gone to hell, since you have sat here in the house of God, provoking His pure eyes by your sinful wicked manner of attending His solemn worship. Yea, there is nothing else that is to be given as a reason why you do not this very moment drop down into hell.

O sinner! Consider the fearful danger you are in: it is a great furnace of wrath, a wide and bottomless pit, full of the fire of wrath, that you are held over in the hand of that God, whose wrath is provoked and <u>incensed</u> as much against you, as against many of the damned in hell. You hang by a slender thread, with the flames of divine wrath flashing about it, and ready every moment to singe it, and burn it asunder; and you have no interest in any Mediator, and nothing to lay hold of to save yourself, nothing to keep off the flames of wrath, nothing of your own, nothing that you have done, nothing that you can do, to <u>induce</u> God to spare you one moment. ∎

According to Edwards, how much control do people who are sinful in the eyes of God have over their destinies?

Responding to the Selection

Can you sympathize with the members of Edwards's congregation who reacted to this sermon with weeping? What two emotions might be involved? Which emotion do you think this sermon appeals to most?

Reviewing the Selection

RECALLING

1. According to Edwards, what does the average person think keeps him or her alive? To what does Edwards give complete credit?

2. What are some of the elements of creation that Edwards lists as "not willingly" serving the sinner?

3. What does Edwards claim is required to take a person out of the sinner classification?

4. Paragraphs 4 and 5 both build up the same image. What is this image?

INTERPRETING

5. In paragraph 2, Edwards compares the sinner first with a fallen rock and later with chaff on a threshing floor. What does he mean by each of these similes?

6. Which elements of nature does Edwards use in paragraph 2 to represent God's anger? What qualities do these elements have in common with anger?

7. What abstract ideal is personified—described as a person—in paragraph 3? In what action is this personified ideal occupied? Why is this comparison frightening?

8. In paragraph 4, Edwards traces the threat to the sinner's continued existence from the previous night, through rising in the morning, to sitting in church as Edwards speaks. Why might this progression be particularly effective in arousing fear?

SYNTHESIZING

9. Which of the images in this sermon is the most memorable? Why?

10. Do you think that this sermon could be influential, on a short-term basis, in inspiring listeners to throw themselves on the mercy of an angry God? What would you expect would be its long-term impact? Why?

Understanding Literature (Questions for Discussion)

1. **Effect.** The **effect** of a literary work is the general impression or emotional impact that it achieves. Describe the effect of this sermon.

2. **Emphasis. Emphasis** is the importance placed on an element in a literary work. Repetition and elaboration are two of the techniques used to produce emphasis. Identify a paragraph in which Edwards uses both techniques to emphasize an important concept. State the concept being emphasized. Then identify the repeated words or phrases, and list some additions or changes that elaborate on the original statement.

Responding in Writing

Comparison and Contrast. Read the following speech from William Shakespeare's play *The Merchant of Venice.* Write a brief essay comparing and contrasting the view of God presented in this speech with that presented in Edwards's sermon.

> PORTIA: The quality of mercy is not strain'd,
> It droppeth as the gentle rain from heaven
> Upon the place beneath. It is twice blessed:
> It blesseth him that gives and him that takes.
> 'Tis mightiest in the mightiest, it becomes
> The throned monarch better than his crown.
> His scepter shows the force of temporal power,
> The attribute to awe and majesty,
> Wherein doth sit the dread and fear of kings;
> But mercy is above this sceptered sway,
> It is enthroned in the hearts of kings,
> It is an attribute to God himself;
> And earthly power doth then show likest God's
> When mercy seasons justice.
>
> —act IV, scene i, *The Merchant of Venice*

Language Lab

Concrete and Abstract Nouns. Read the Language Arts Survey, 2.4, "Concrete and Abstract Nouns." On a separate sheet of paper, write each of the nouns in these sentences. Underline the concrete nouns once. Underline the abstract ones twice.

1. Jonathan Edwards was the last great spokesperson for Puritanism.

2. His concept of the omnipotence of God and the unworthiness of humans was uncompromising.

3. He wrote and spoke with such power that congregations reacted with barely controllable emotion.

4. For years, his words inspired an era of belief called "The Great Awakening."

5. Eventually, however, his inability to compromise ended in his downfall.

Speaking and Listening Skills

A Communication Model. Read the Language Arts Survey, 3.1, "A Communication Model." What are some of the nonverbal signs that a speaker such as Edwards might employ in delivering a sermon? Describe these signs.

PROJECT

Exploring the Protestant Reformation and the Puritan Movement. In small groups, do library research on the life and work of Martin Luther, John Calvin, and John Knox. One person from each group might represent Luther, Calvin, Knox, and Edwards in a discussion of their religious goals.

"Upon the Burning of Our House"
by Anne Bradstreet

In silent night when rest I took
For sorrow near I did not look
I wakened was with thund'ring noise
And piteous shrieks of dreadful voice.
5 That fearful sound of "Fire!" and "Fire!"
Let no man know is my desire.
I, starting up, the light did spy,
And to my God my heart did cry
To strengthen me in my distress
10 And not to leave me succorless.[1]
Then, coming out, beheld a space
The flame consume my dwelling place.
And when I could no longer look,
I blest His name that gave and took,
15 That laid my goods now in the dust.
Yea, so it was, and so 'twas just.
It was His own, it was not mine,
Far be it that I should repine;[2]
He might of all justly bereft
20 But yet sufficient for us left.
When by the ruins oft I past
My sorrowing eyes aside did cast,
And here and there the places spy
Where oft I sat and long did lie:
25 Here stood that trunk, and there that chest,
There lay that store I counted best.
My pleasant things in ashes lie,
And them behold no more shall I.
Under thy roof no guest shall sit,
30 Nor at thy table eat a bit.
No pleasant tale shall e'er be told,
Nor things recounted done of old.
No candle e'er shall shine in thee,
Nor bridegroom's voice e'er heard shall be.
35 In silence ever shall thou lie,
Adieu,[3] Adieu, all's vanity.
Then straight I 'gin my heart to chide,[4]
And did thy wealth on earth abide?[5]

Didst fix thy hope on mold'ring dust?
40 The arm of flesh didst make thy trust?
Raise up thy thoughts above the sky
That dunghill mists away may fly.
Thou hast an house on high erect,
Framed by that mighty Architect,
45 With glory richly furnished,
Stands permanent though this be fled.
It's purchased and paid for too
By Him who hath enough to do.
A price so vast as is unknown
50 Yet by His gift is made thine own;
There's wealth enough, I need no more,
Farewell, my pelf,[6] farewell my store.
The world no longer let me love,
My hope and treasure lies above.

"Huswifery"[7] by Edward Taylor

Make me, O Lord, Thy Spinning Wheel complete.
    Thy Holy Word my Distaff[8] make for me.
Make mine Affections Thy Swift Flyers[9] neat
    And make my Soul thy holy Spool[10] to be.
5   My conversation make to be Thy Reel[11]
    And reel the yarn thereon spun of Thy Wheel.

Make me Thy Loom then, knit therein this Twine:
    And make Thy Holy Spirit, Lord, wind quills:
Then weave the Web Thyself. The yarn is fine.
10   Thine Ordinances make my Fulling Mills.[12]
    Then dye the same in Heavenly Colors Choice,
    All pinked[13] with Varnished Flowers of Paradise.

Then clothe therewith mine Understanding, Will,
    Affections, Judgment, Conscience, Memory,
15 My Words, and Actions, that their shine may fill
    My ways with glory and Thee glorify.
    Then mine apparel shall display before Ye
    That I am Clothed in Holy robes for glory.

---

1. **succorless.** Helpless
2. **repine.** Complain; worry
3. **adieu.** Farewell (French)
4. **chide.** Scold
5. **abide.** Stay; remain
6. **pelf.** Money or wealth regarded with contempt

---

7. **Huswifery.** Housekeeping, here specifically weaving
8. **Distaff.** Tool that holds the raw wool
9. **Flyers.** Parts that regulate the spinning
10. **Spool.** Part on which yarn is wound
11. **Reel.** Part that takes up the finished thread
12. **Fulling Mills.** Where cloth is beaten and cleansed
13. **pinked.** Adorned

from *The Wonders of the Invisible World*
by Cotton Mather

But I shall no longer detain my reader from his expected entertainment, in a brief account of the trials which have passed upon some of the malefactors[1] lately executed at Salem, for the witchcrafts whereof they stood convicted. For my own part, I was not present at any of them; nor ever had I any personal prejudice at the persons thus brought upon the stage; much less at the surviving relations of those persons, with and for whom I would be as hearty a mourner as any man living in the world: The Lord comfort them! But having received a command[2] so to do, I can do no other than shortly relate the chief matters of fact, which occurred in the trials of some that were executed, in an abridgment collected out of the court papers on this occasion put into my hands. You are to take the truth, just as it was; and the truth will hurt no good man. There might have been more of these, if my book would not thereby have swollen too big; and if some other worthy hands did not perhaps intend something further in these collections; for which cause I have only singled out four or five, which may serve to illustrate the way of dealing, wherein witchcrafts use to be concerned; and I report matters not as an advocate, but as an historian.

The Trial of Martha Carrier
AT THE COURT OF OYER AND TERMINER,[3] HELD BY ADJOURNMENT AT SALEM, AUGUST 2, 1692.

I. Martha Carrier was indicted for the bewitching certain persons, according to the form usual in such cases, pleading not guilty to her indictment; there were first brought in a considerable number of the bewitched persons who not only made the court sensible[4] of an horrid witchcraft committed upon them, but also deposed that it was Martha Carrier, or her shape, that grievously tormented them, by biting, pricking, pinching and choking of them. It was further deposed that while this Carrier was on her examination before the magistrates, the poor people were so tortured that every one expected their death upon the very spot, but that upon the binding of Carrier they were eased. Moreover the look of Carrier then laid the afflicted people for dead; and her touch, if her eye at the same time were off them, raised them again: which things were also now seen upon her trial. And it was testified that upon the mention of some having their necks twisted almost round, by the shape of this Carrier, she replied, "It's no matter though their necks had been twisted quite off."

II. Before the trial of this prisoner, several of her own children had frankly and fully confessed not only that they were witches themselves, but that this their mother had made them so. This confession they made with great shows of repentance, and with much demonstration of truth. They related place, time, occasion; they gave an account of journeys, meetings and mischiefs by them performed, and were very credible in what they said. Nevertheless, this evidence was not produced against the prisoner at the bar,[5] inasmuch as there was other evidence enough to proceed upon.

III. Benjamin Abbot gave his testimony that last March was a twelvemonth, this Carrier was very angry with him, upon laying out some land near her husband's: her expressions in this anger were that she would stick as close to Abbot as the bark stuck to the tree; and that he should repent of it afore seven years came to an end, so as Doctor Prescot should never cure him. These words were heard by others besides Abbot himself; who also heard her say, she would hold his nose as close to the grindstone as ever it was held since his name was Abbot. Presently after this, he was taken with a swelling in his foot, and then with a pain in his side, and exceedingly tormented. It bred into a sore, which was lanced[6] by Doctor Prescot, and several gallons of corruption[7] ran out of it. For six weeks it continued very bad, and then another sore bred in the groin, which was also lanced by Doctor Prescot. Another sore then bred in his groin which was likewise cut, and put him to very great misery: he was brought unto death's door, and so remained until Carrier was taken, and carried away by the constable from which very day he began to mend, and so grew better every day, and is well ever since.

Sarah Abbot also, his wife, testified that her husband was not only all this while afflicted in his body, but also that strange, extraordinary and unaccountable calamities befell his cattle; their death being such as they could guess at no natural reason for.

IV. Allin Toothaker testified that Richard, the son of Martha Carrier, having some difference with him, pulled him down by the hair of the head. When he rose again he was going to strike at Richard Carrier but fell down flat on his back to the ground and had not power to stir hand or foot, until he told Carrier he yielded; and then he saw the shape of Martha Carrier go off his breast.

This Toothaker had received a wound in the wars; and he now testified that Martha Carrier told him he should

---

1. **malefactors.** Wrongdoers
2. **command.** Request by the judges to explain the sentencing of those convicted in the Salem witch trials
3. **of oyer and terminer.** To hear and determine
4. **sensible.** Aware
5. **bar.** Court
6. **lanced.** Cut open
7. **corruption.** Infected fluid

never be cured. Just afore the apprehending of Carrier, he could thrust a knitting needle into his wound four inches deep; but presently after her being seized, he was thoroughly healed.

He further testified that when Carrier and he some times were at variance she would clap her hands at him, and say he should get nothing by it; whereupon he several times lost his cattle, by strange deaths, whereof no natural causes could be given.

V. John Rogger also testified that upon the threatening words of this malicious Carrier, his cattle would be strangely bewitched; as was more particularly then described.

VI. Samuel Preston testified that about two years ago, having some difference with Martha Carrier, he lost a cow in a strange, preternatural,[1] unusual manner; and about a month after this, the said Carrier, having again some difference with him she told him he had lately lost a cow, and it should not be long before he lost another; which accordingly came to pass, for he had a thriving and well-kept cow, which without any known cause quickly fell down and died.

VII. Phebe Chandler testified that about a fortnight before the apprehension of Martha Carrier, on a Lordsday, while the Psalm was singing in the Church this Carrier then took her by the shoulder and shaking her, asked her, where she lived: she made her no answer, although as Carrier, who lived next door to her father's house, could not in reason but know who she was. Quickly after this, as she was at several times crossing the fields, she heard a voice, that she took to be Martha Carrier's, and it seemed as if it was over her head. The voice told her she should within two or three days be poisoned. Accordingly, within such a little time, one half of her right hand became greatly swollen and very painful; as also part of her face: whereof she can give no account how it came. It continued very bad for some days; and several times since she has had a great pain in her breast; and been so seized on her legs that she has hardly been able to go. She added that lately, going well

to the house of God, Richard, the son of Martha Carrier, looked very earnestly upon her, and immediately her hand, which had formerly been poisoned, as is abovesaid, began to pain her greatly, and she had a strange burning at her stomach; but was then struck deaf, so that she could not hear any of the prayer, or singing, till the two or three last words of the Psalm.

VIII. One Foster, who confessed her own share in the witchcraft for which the prisoner stood indicted, affirmed that she had seen the prisoner at some of their witch-meetings, and that it was this Carrier, who persuaded her to be a witch. She confessed that the devil carried them on a pole to a witch-meeting; but the pole broke, and she hanging about Carrier's neck, they both fell down, and she then received an hurt by the fall, whereof she was not at this very time recovered.

IX. One Lacy, who likewise confessed her share in this witchcraft, now testified, that she and the prisoner were once bodily present at a witch-meeting in Salem Village; and that she knew the prisoner to be a witch, and to have been at a diabolical sacrament, and that the prisoner was the undoing of her and her children by enticing them into the snare of the devil.

X. Another Lacy, who also confessed her share in this witchcraft, now testified, that the prisoner was at the witch-meeting, in Salem Village, where they had bread and wine administered unto them.

XI. In the time of this prisoner's trial, one Susanna Sheldon in open court had her hands unaccountably tied together with a wheel-band so fast that without cutting, it could not be loosed: it was done by a specter; and the sufferer affirmed it was the prisoner's.

Memorandum. This rampant hag, Martha Carrier, was the person of whom the confessions of the witches, and of her own children among the rest, agreed that the devil had promised her she should be Queen of Hebrews.

---

1. **preternatural.** Abnormal

UNIT REVIEW

Origins of the American Tradition

VOCABULARY FROM THE SELECTIONS

abhor, 120
ascribe, 120
avail, 119
buffet, 89
burnish, 92
calamity, 105
canonize, 95
commendation, 105
conceit, 96
confederacy, 77
conjuration, 97
constitution, 119
consultation, 103
contrivance, 119
deliberation, 104

depopulate, 89
disposition, 77
diversity, 98
doleful, 99
ensue, 96
entreaty, 98
estimation, 78
extremity, 96
feign, 106
flourish, 90
furnish, 78
gluttony, 95
gulf, 119
incense, 121
induce, 121

inevitable, 103
infest, 91
inhuman, 90
light, 102
loath, 103
loathsome, 120
manifold, 115
mollify, 99
mutinous, 104
oppression, 89
ordinance, 105
persevere, 115
pilfer, 95
presumption, 96
profane, 102

prosperous, 102
provoke, 120
recompense, 106,
    115
reprove, 102
ruffian, 90
sovereign, 119
subjection, 89
subserve, 120
suffice, 89
sundry, 104
vestige, 90

LITERARY TERMS

aim, 112
allusion, 112
chronological order,
    108
couplet, 112

effect, 123
emphasis, 123
hyperbole, 117
irony, 108
metaphor, 85

mood, 93
myth, 85
oxymoron, 117
parallelism, 85
point of view, 93

sight rhyme, 117
symbol, 80
tone, 86

SYNTHESIS: QUESTIONS FOR WRITING, RESEARCH, OR DISCUSSION

GENRE STUDIES

1. **Poetry.** Bradstreet's poem "To My Dear and Loving Husband" is built on couplets. A couplet is a pair of rhyming lines expressing a complete thought. Each couplet expands her notion of love. Examine each couplet and give its central thought.

THEMATIC STUDIES

2. **Order, Harmony, and Judgment.** Edwards, the Tewa, and the framers of the Iroquois Constitution use extended metaphors to express their themes. What theme does each selection convey? How does the metaphor in each fit the theme? Refer to the definition of *extended metaphor* in the Handbook of Literary Terms.

HISTORICAL/BIOGRAPHICAL STUDIES

3. **Political Thought and Education.** *The New England Primer* was a vehicle for evolving political thought. What view of the English king is evident in the selection printed in this text? Research subsequent editions of the *Primer* and see how this view changed as the colonists headed toward revolution.

4. **Settlers' Goals.** Compare the goals of the settlers of Virginia with the goals of the Puritan settlers of Massachusetts. Refer to the introduction to this unit and to the writings of Smith, Bradford, and Edwards.

LANGUAGE LAB   THE SENTENCE

A **sentence** contains a subject and a verb and expresses a complete idea. A group of words that does not contain both a subject and a verb and that does not express a complete idea is a **sentence fragment**.

LANGUAGE ARTS SURVEY

For additional help, see the Language Arts Survey, 2.61.

CORRECTING SENTENCE FRAGMENTS
SENTENCE FRAGMENT: Among friends. (*does not express a complete idea*)
COMPLETE SENTENCE: Anne Bradstreet often distributed her work among friends.
SENTENCE FRAGMENT: Wrote poetry as a child. (*does not contain a subject*)
COMPLETE SENTENCE: Bradstreet wrote poetry as a child.
SENTENCE FRAGMENT: In 1650, a collection of Bradstreet's poetry. (*does not contain a verb*)
COMPLETE SENTENCE: In 1650, a collection of Bradstreet's poetry was published.

When two sentences are run together without proper punctuation or conjunctions, they are called a **run-on.** The following chart shows ways to correct run-ons.

LANGUAGE ARTS SURVEY

For additional help, see the Language Arts Survey, 2.62.

CORRECTING RUN-ONS	
RUN-ON:	The Five Nations of the Iroquois Confederation agreed to keep peace among themselves, they made war on enemy nations.
CORRECTED USING A COMMA AND A COORDINATING CONJUNCTION:	The Five Nations of the Iroquois Confederation agreed to keep peace among themselves, but they made war on enemy nations.
CORRECTED BY TURNING ONE SENTENCE INTO A SUBORDINATE CLAUSE:	Although the Five Nations of the Iroquois Confederation agreed to keep peace among themselves, they made war on enemy nations.
CORRECTED BY ADDING A SEMICOLON AND A CONJUNCTIVE ADVERB:	The Five Nations of the Iroquois Confederation agreed to keep peace among themselves; however, they made war on enemy nations.

To add variety, interest, and clarity to your writing, combine sentences by adding words, phrases, and clauses. Use the methods described in the following chart.

Exercise Correcting Fragments and Run-ons

Rewrite the following paragraph, correcting all sentence fragments and run-ons.

EXAMPLE: Many native peoples lost their lands to Europeans, the nations of the Iroquois Confederation kept their territory for almost two hundred years.

> While many native peoples lost their lands to Europeans, the nations of the Iroquois Confederation kept their territory for almost two hundred years.

LANGUAGE ARTS SURVEY

For additional help, see the Language Arts Survey, 2.61–2.62.

Around 1570, the Mohawk, Oneida, Onondaga, Cayuga, and Seneca peoples. Formed the Iroquois Confederation, or Five Nations. Before this time, the five groups often had warred against each other, their agreement to keep peace among themselves strengthened them. Against their enemies who included other Native Americans and, later, Europeans. Their Algonquian-speaking enemies called them Iroquois, or "real adders," the Iroquois called themselves We Who Are of the Extended Lodge. Representatives from each nation formed a governing council, the women of the respective groups elected men to serve on the council. In 1715, the Tuscarora joined the confederation. Which was then known as the Six Nations.

Midnight Ride of Paul Revere. *Grant Wood, 1931. The Metropolitan Museum of Art.*
Arthur Hoppock Hearn Fund, 1950. (50.117)

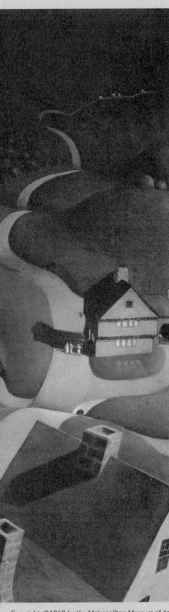

To secure these rights, governments are instituted among men, deriving their just powers from the consent of the governed.

—Thomas Jefferson
Declaration of Independence

133

The Emergence of American Diversity

Portrait of Benjamin Franklin. Robert Feke, *circa 1746. Harvard University, Portrait Collection. Bequest of Dr. John Collins Warren, 1856*

During the Colonial Period, New England remained relatively homogenous, populated primarily by Puritans of British descent. However, the Mid-Atlantic and the South saw rapid growth and an influx of different peoples, religions, and ways of life. Indeed, by the time of the **American Revolution**, the colonies had achieved a great deal of the social diversity that we now think of as distinctively American.

In the colony of Pennsylvania, **Quakers** of English and Welsh descent established a community based on equality for all citizens and tolerance of religious diversity, for the Quakers believed people to have within them a divine spark that could be demonstrated through love for "all in God's world." In the 1680s, the Quakers became the first group in America to advocate the abolition of slavery, and, unlike the Puritans, they allowed women a voice in religious affairs. As a result of tolerant Quaker attitudes, Pennsylvania by the 1750s had attracted people from a wide variety of ethnic and religious groups, including Native Americans and free persons of African descent. It had also become a center for progressive thinking. **Benjamin Franklin** himself, though he had earlier mocked Quaker meetings in his writings, adopted the Quaker rhetoric of equality and went on to play important roles in the American Revolution, which included helping to establish the terms of the **Treaty of Paris** that ended the war.

In other parts of the Mid-Atlantic such as New York, New Jersey, and Delaware, which saw new arrivals of Jewish, German, and Irish immigrants, the communal social and economic relations practiced by the Puritans and the Quakers were supplanted by an emerging **Capitalist** ethic of individual profit-making. One result was that in these places land came to be viewed more as a commodity than as part of a homestead or as a source of a community's sustenance. Many middle-sized farms emerged on which owners used wage-laborers, indentured servants, and slaves.

LITERARY EVENTS

► = American Events

1760. Laurence Sterne's *The Life and Opinions of Tristram Shandy* published

1759. Voltaire's *Candide* published

►1755. Samuel Johnson's *A Dictionary of the English Language* published

►1755. Benjamin Franklin's "Observations Concerning the Increase of Mankind" published

►1752. George Berkeley's *On the Prospect of Planting Arts and Learning in America* published

1751. Denis Diderot's *Encyclopedie* published

1750	1755	1760

HISTORICAL EVENTS

1750. British pass the Iron Act, prohibiting colonies from producing iron products

►1751. Benjamin Franklin experiments with electricity

►1752. Philadelphia's Liberty Bell is cast

►1754. The French and Indian War begins

1759. British win decisive victory over French outside Quebec City

1760. George III succeeds George II

By the mid-eighteenth century the economies of the Southern colonies were centered primarily on commercial agriculture, particularly on the cultivation of cotton and tobacco. The heavy reliance of commercial **plantations** on slave labor had a number of social consequences of concern during and after the revolutionary period, not the least of which was that in many areas (and in some entire states such as South Carolina), the majority of the population consisted of enslaved African Americans.

The overall sense of dynamism and opportunity that the colonies, rural and urban, were coming to represent can perhaps be seen best in the growth of the population itself. In 1650, the total population of the colonies was almost 60,000; by the 1790s, it was 3,500,000. Infant mortality rates were down, fertility rates were up, and many more children were surviving into adulthood. The young country had a young populace; in 1776, the year of independence from Britain, roughly half of the people were twenty-one or younger. Benjamin Franklin and others extolled abroad the virtues of America's healthy environment, as well as the many opportunities that the colonies offered for economic advancement through hard work. Europeans, increasingly non-English ones, heeded the call, often fleeing economic hardship and overcrowding at home.

REBELLION AGAINST GREAT BRITAIN

The diverse and growing population of the colonies, bound to provide supplies and soldiers for English wars and to help pay for those wars afterward, found subservience to distant England increasingly irksome. In 1763, after the **French and Indian War,** England imposed, through the Stamp Act, the first in a series of heavy taxes that would prove unpopular in the colonies and serve as a focal point of colonial resentment. The colonists began boycotting British goods, leading the British to repeal the Stamp Act. Then, in March 1770, British soldiers and colonial citizens skirmished in Boston, resulting in the deaths of five colonists. Among the colonists killed in this so-called **Boston Massacre** was **Crispus Attucks,** the first African American to die in the Revolutionary cause. In 1773, when England imposed a new tax on tea, colonial patriots held what is known as the **Boston Tea Party,** dumping tea from British ships into Boston Harbor. The British

▶1774. Benjamin Franklin's "On the Rise of Progress of the Differences between Great Britain and the American Colonies and Johann von Goethe's *The Sorrows of Young Werther* published

▶1773. Phillis Wheatley publishes volume of poetry

▶1772. Philip Morin Freneau and Hugh Henry Breckinridge publish *The Rising Glory of America*

▶1770. *The Massachusetts Spy,* anti-British Whig newspaper begins publication

▶1767. John Dickinson's *Letters from a Farmer in Pennsylvania* published

1762. Jean Jacques Rousseau publishes *The Social Contract* and *Emile*

1765	**1770**	**1775**

1763. Treaty of Paris cedes Canada to Great Britain

▶1765. British pass Quartering Act and Stamp Act

▶1765. Sons of Liberty clubs formed to resist Stamp Act

▶1766. Stamp Act repealed; Declatory Acts passed

▶1767. British pass Townshend Revere Acts

▶1770. Boston Massacre; British kill colonists

▶1773. Daniel Boone leads settlers into Kentucky against George's edict; Tea Act; Boston Tea Party

▶1774. First Continental Congress

▶1775. American Revolution begins; Battles of Lexington and Concord; George Washington appointed commander in chief of the Continental Army

George Washington

Parliament responded with severe restrictions on the self-government of Massachusetts, known as the **Intolerable Acts.** In counterresponse, representatives from the colonies met in Philadelphia in 1774 for the **First Continental Congress.** There they vented their outrage in letters of protest to King George, asked citizens to boycott British goods, and called for the organization of militia, or armed citizens, to defend against British aggression throughout the colonies.

In April 1775, British General Thomas Gage moved troops toward Concord, Massachusetts, with the aim of capturing rebel arms and leaders, but the rebels had been forewarned, thanks to **Paul Revere, William Dawes,** and **Samuel Prescott.** On Concord Bridge, on the morning of April 19, thirty-five militiamen blocked the path of seven hundred British troops. After a brief standoff, a shot was fired, and the American Revolution had begun. That day, fighting between British troops and colonial militiamen in Concord and Lexington left almost three hundred British soldiers and one hundred colonials dead or wounded.

The **Second Continental Congress,** meeting in Philadelphia in May 1775, organized an army under **General George Washington.** In June, after the **Battle of Bunker Hill,** near Boston, King George officially declared the colonies in rebellion against the crown. Early in 1776, Thomas Paine, recently arrived in America from Great Britain, published his pamphlet *Common Sense,* the first work to call for the colonies' independence. In June of that year, acting on resolutions introduced by Richard Henry Lee, a delegate from Virginia, the Continental Congress voted in favor of independence and appointed a committee, which included **Thomas Jefferson,** Benjamin Franklin, and **John Adams,** to draft a **Declaration of Independence.** Jefferson wrote a draft of that declaration which, with some changes, was adopted on July 4, thereafter known in the United States as **Independence Day.**

LITERARY EVENTS

► = American Events

► 1787. James Madison and Alexander Hamilton publish *The Federalist Papers*

► 1783. Noah Webster's *Spelling Book* published

1782. J. Hector St. Jean de Crèvecoeur's *Letters from an American Farmer* published

1781. L. Immanuel Kant's *Critique of Pure Reason*

1778. Fanny Burney's *Evelina* introduces the novel of manners

► 1776. Declaration of Independence; Thomas Paine publishes *Common Sense* and *Crisis*

1780	1785	1790

► 1778. France recognizes America's independence

1779. Spain declares war on Britain

► 1781. General Cornwallis of Britain surrenders at Yorktown

► 1789. French Revolution; George Washington becomes the first president

HISTORICAL EVENTS

► 1783. Treaty of Paris recognizes independence of the thirteen colonies

► 1787. Constitutional Convention

► 1788. U.S. Constitution ratified

The Philosophical Background of the Revolution

The Declaration of Independence was a bold document, for it declared that "all men are created equal," that people have certain "inalienable rights" that cannot be taken from them, that governments derive their right to rule from the consent of the governed, and that when a government fails to protect the natural rights of its citizens, those citizens have not only a right but a duty to rebel. The theories that informed the Declaration of Independence had their origins in the European **Enlightenment,** or **Age of Reason,** and in European **Romanticism.** Thinkers of the Enlightenment, encouraged by discoveries in the natural sciences such as those made by **Sir Isaac Newton,** believed that through reason people could discover principles that would guarantee social and political harmony. The English philosopher **Thomas Hobbes,** though a monarchist, argued that certain natural rights existed that no individual could turn over to a sovereign. Another English philosopher, **John Locke,** reasoned that to ensure the preservation of their natural rights, a people should balance the power of the sovereign against the power of Parliament and retain the right to rebel against oppression. The French philosopher **Jean-Jacques Rousseau** argued that governments are instituted as a **social contract** made by the people for their mutual benefit. Rousseau was one of the foremost thinkers of the **Romantic Movement,** which began in the eighteenth century and continued into the nineteenth century. Among other goals, this movement championed democratic ideals and the rights of the individual, rights that were to be enshrined in the **Bill of Rights**—the first ten Amendments to the United States Constitution.

Paul Revere. *John Singleton Copley*

1798. Samuel Taylor Coleridge and William Wordsworth publish *Lyrical Ballads;* Thomas Robert Malthus publishes "Essay on the Principles of Population"

▶1798. Charles Brookden Brown's *Alcuin: A Dialogue on the Rights of Women* and *Wieland, or the Transformation*

▶1793. Joel Barlow's *Advice to the Privileged Orders* published

1792. Mary Wollstonecraft's *Vindication of the Rights of Women* published

1790	1795	1800

▶1791. The Bill of Rights becomes U.S. law

1793. Reign of Terror begins; Louis XVI and Marie Antoinette guillotined

▶1793. Fugitive Slave Act passed

▶1799. Napoleon Bonaparte becomes first consul of France; Rosetta Stone

1795. Napoleon Bonaparte named commander of the Armée d'Interieur

▶1796. John Adams becomes president, Thomas Jefferson vice president

THE NEW NATION

Phillis Wheatley

In 1777, Congress adopted the **Articles of Confederation,** which created a weak central government and left most power to the former colonies, now sovereign states. In 1781, the British, under General George Cornwallis, suffered a decisive defeat at Yorktown, Virginia, effectively ending the war, despite sporadic fighting over the next one and a half years. In 1783, the American Revolution officially ended with the signing of the Treaty of Paris, in which Great Britain gave up its claims on the colonies. In 1787, delegates in Philadelphia adopted a new Constitution, beginning with these stirring words:

> We, the people of the United States, in order to form a more perfect Union, establish justice, insure domestic tranquility, provide for the common defense, promote the general welfare, and secure the blessings of liberty to ourselves and our posterity do ordain and establish this Constitution for the United States of America.

The task of establishing "a more perfect union" from the diverse peoples of the United States would prove challenging in years to come, but the very diversity that would create tensions in the young country would also be its greatest strength. By the time of the Revolution, America had already produced the first of its great African-American poets in the person of **Phillis Wheatley.** In the years since, its diversity has made American literature one of the finest the world has ever seen.

A NATION OF READERS

As the population of the young country grew and standards of living climbed, literacy increased dramatically. By the end of the eighteenth century, most of the white population could read, and literacy was blossoming among free African Americans in the North. This burst of literacy created a demand for more and more literature of various kinds, a demand met by technological developments in printing that brought into full flower the "reading revolution." One critical factor underlying the increased demand for printed works was the heightened value that "print culture" (as opposed to spoken or oral culture) was coming to play in shaping the ideals of the emerging nation. Print came to be seen not merely as a means of transmitting information but as a new way of conducting public discourse on important issues. People were beginning to associate print with public debate held without regard to distinctions of status or person. Through the printed word, one might present arguments, as Thomas Paine did in *Common Sense,* and have those arguments stand or fall solely on their merit. Print became, therefore, a vehicle for the new nation's democratic identity and principles.

Echoes:
The American Revolution

"In reality there is perhaps no one of our natural Passions so hard to subdue as *Pride*. . . . For even if I could conceive that I had completely overcome it, I should probably be proud of my Humility."

—Benjamin Franklin, on pride

"Here [in America] individuals of all nations are melted into a new race of men, whose labors and posterity will one day cause great changes in the world."

—J. Hector St. Jean de Crèvecoeur, on American diversity

"Strange order of things! Oh, Nature, where are thou?—Are not these blacks thy children as well as we?"

—J. Hector St. Jean de Crèvecoeur, on slavery

"These are the times that try men's souls. The summer soldier and the sunshine patriot will, in this crisis, shrink from the service of their country; but he that stands it now, deserves the love and thanks of man and woman."

—Thomas Paine, in *Crisis, No. 1,* on the American Revolution

"A little rebellion now and then is a good thing."

—Thomas Jefferson, writing about Shay's Rebellion in a letter to James Madison

"The tree of liberty must be refreshed from time to time with the blood of patriots and tyrants."

—Thomas Jefferson, in a letter to W. S. Smith

"In framing a government which is to be administered by men over men, the great difficulty lies in this: you must first enable the government to control the governed; and in the next place oblige it to control itself."

—James Madison, *The Federalist Papers, No. 51,* on control of government

from *The Autobiography of Benjamin Franklin*
from "Remarks Concerning the Natives of North America"
by Benjamin Franklin

ABOUT THE AUTHOR

Benjamin Franklin (1706–1790) was a writer, scientist, inventor, and diplomat. Born the tenth child in a large Boston family, he left school to work for his father, a maker of soap and candles. Unsatisfied with his father's profession, Franklin entered the printing trade as his brother's apprentice and had his first essay published under the name "Silence Dogood." At the age of sixteen, Franklin undertook the responsibility of running his brother's paper while his brother was imprisoned for an article he printed. At seventeen, Franklin moved to Philadelphia where he started a printing shop that produced paper currency for the Pennsylvania colony as well as a newspaper, the *Pennsylvania Gazette*. His *Poor Richard's Almanac,* known for its witty sayings and practical good sense, was enormously successful and was published annually for twenty-five years. These enterprises helped to make Franklin quite wealthy. A man of many talents with a keen intelligence and a passion for science, Franklin experimented with electricity and invented both a cookstove and bifocal glasses. He also started a library and was instrumental in the founding of the University of Pennsylvania. Respected for his insight and wisdom, Franklin represented the colonies in England, served on the committee that drafted the Declaration of Independence, signed the treaty that ended the American Revolution, and was a delegate to the Constitutional Convention.

ABOUT THE SELECTIONS

Benjamin Franklin wrote *The Autobiography of Benjamin Franklin* over a period of twenty years. It covers his life only until 1758, before his career as a diplomat. He began writing in 1771 and wrote the last two sections between 1788 and 1790, when illness forced him to put the work aside. Although the first part of the book was published in 1791, the entire work was not published until 1868. Franklin's writing style was developed, he noted, by imitation of great models, primarily of such Neoclassical masters as Joseph Addison. (The Neoclassicists of the eighteenth century valued reason and sought to discover orderly principles, or natural laws, by which the life of an individual or of a nation could be conducted in order to achieve relative harmony and tranquility. For more information on Neoclassicism, see the introduction to this unit and the entry on *Neoclassicism* in the Handbook of Literary Terms.)

During his stay in France from 1776 to 1785 as the United States' ambassador, Franklin had his own press with which he printed several pamphlets, mostly on light topics. The selection from **"Remarks Concerning the Natives of North America"** comes from one of the essays he produced at that time. The essay was published in 1784.

READER'S JOURNAL

In the following selection, Franklin discusses a time in his youth when he was first establishing himself as a writer and printer. As you will see from the selection, Franklin had tremendous drive and worked hard to achieve his goals. What goals do you want to achieve in your youth? What do you hope to accomplish by the time you are twenty-five? Write about these questions in your journal.

LANGUAGE SKILLS

Read the Language Arts Survey, 2.17, "Verbals: Gerunds." Then examine the selection to find examples of gerunds. Note each gerund and how it is used, for example, as subject or object of a verb (identify the verb), or object of a preposition (identify the preposition).

FROM

The Autobiography of Benjamin Franklin

Benjamin Franklin

My Brother had in 1720 or '21, begun to print a Newspaper. It was the second that appeared in America and was called the *New England Courant.*[1] The only one before it was *The Boston News Letter.* I remember his being dissuaded by some of his Friends from the Undertaking, as not likely to succeed, one Newspaper being in their Judgment enough for America. At this time (1771) there are not less than five-and-twenty. He went on, however, with the Undertaking, and after having worked in composing the Types and printing off the Sheets, I was employed to carry the Papers through the Streets to the Customers. He had some <u>ingenious</u> Men among his Friends who amused themselves by writing little Pieces for this Paper, which gained it Credit and made it more in Demand, and these Gentlemen often visited us. Hearing their Conversations and their Accounts of the Approbation[2] their Papers were received with, I was excited to try my Hand among them. But being still a Boy, and suspecting that my Brother would object to printing any Thing of mine in his Paper if he knew it to be mine, I contrived to disguise my Hand, and writing an anonymous Paper, I put it

What was Benjamin Franklin excited to try? Why was he excited? What was his one worry?

---

1. **It was . . . New England Courant.** James Franklin's paper was actually the fifth American paper.
2. **Approbation.** Approval or commendation

Words for Everyday Use:
in • gen • ious (in jēn´yəs) *adj.*, having great mental ability

in at Night under the Door of the Printing-House.

It was found in the Morning and communicated to his Writing Friends when they called in as Usual. They read it, commented on it in my Hearing, and I had the exquisite Pleasure of finding it met with their Approbation, and that, in their different Guesses at the Author, none were named but Men of some Character among us for Learning and Ingenuity. I suppose now that I was rather lucky in my Judges, and that perhaps they were not really so very good ones as I then esteemed them. Encouraged however by this, I wrote and conveyed in the same Way to the Press several more Papers, which were equally approved, and I kept my Secret till my small Fund of Sense for such Performances was pretty well exhausted, and then I discovered[3] it, when I began to be considered a little more by my Brother's Acquaintance, and in a manner that did not quite please him, as he thought, probably with reason, that it tended to make me too vain. And perhaps this might be one Occasion of the Differences that we began to have about this Time. Though a Brother, he considered himself as my Master, and me as his Apprentice,[4] and accordingly expected the same Services from me as he would from another; while I thought he demeaned me too much in some he required of me, who from a Brother expected more <u>Indulgence</u>. Our Disputes were often brought before our Father, and I fancy I was either generally in the right or else a better Pleader, because the Judgment was generally in my favor. But my Brother was passionate and had often beaten me, which I took extremely amiss; and, thinking

Why was James Franklin imprisoned?

What was one cause of the differences between Franklin and his brother?

my Apprenticeship very tedious, I was continually wishing for some Opportunity of shortening it, which at length offered in a manner unexpected.

One of the Pieces in our Newspaper, on some political Point which I have now forgotten, gave Offense to the Assembly. He was taken up, censured, and imprisoned[5] for a Month by the Speaker's Warrant. I suppose because he would not discover his Author. I too was taken up and examined before the Council; but though I did not give them any Satisfaction, they contented themselves with <u>admonishing</u> me, and dismissed me, considering me perhaps as an Apprentice who was bound to keep his Master's Secrets. During my Brother's Confinement, which I resented a good deal, notwithstanding our private Differences, I had the Management of the Paper, and I made bold to give our Rulers some Rubs[6] in it, which my Brother took very kindly, while others began to consider me in an unfavorable Light, as a young Genius that had a Turn for Libeling and Satire.[7] My Brother's Discharge was accompanied with an Order of the House (a very odd one) "that James Franklin should no longer print the paper called the *New England Courant*." There was a <u>Consultation</u> held in our Printing-House among his Friends what he should do in this Case. Some pro-

---

3. **discovered.** Revealed
4. **Apprentice.** Person under legal agreement to work a specified length of time for a master craftsman in return for instruction and, formerly, support
5. **imprisoned.** James Franklin was charged with libel in 1722 because his paper linked local officials to pirates who were raiding outside Boston Harbor.
6. **Rubs.** Insults
7. **Libeling and Satire.** *Libeling*—making false public accusation; *satire*—humorous but critical portrayal

WORDS FOR EVERYDAY USE:

in • dul • gence (in dul´jəns) *n.*, favor or privilege

ad • mon • ish (ad män´ish) *vt.*, caution against specific faults

con • sul • ta • tion (kän´səl tā´shən) *n.*, meeting to discuss, decide, or plan something

posed to <u>evade</u> the Order by changing the Name of the Paper; but my Brother seeing Inconveniences in that, it was finally concluded on as a better Way to let it be printed for the future under the Name of Benjamin Franklin. And to avoid the Censure of the Assembly that might fall on him as still printing it by his Apprentice, the Contrivance was that my old Indenture[8] should be returned to me with a full Discharge on the Back[9] of it, to be shown on Occasion; but to secure to him the Benefit of my Service, I was to sign new Indentures for the Remainder of the Term, which were to be kept private. A very flimsy Scheme it was; but however, it was immediately executed, and the Paper went on accordingly under my Name for several Months.[10] At length a fresh Difference arising beween my Brother and me, I took upon me to assert my Freedom, presuming that he would not <u>venture</u> to produce the new Indentures. It was not fair in me to take this Advantage, and this I therefore reckon one of the first Errata[11] of my Life; but the Unfairness of it weighed little with me, when under the Impressions of Resentment, for the Blows his Passion too often urged him to bestow upon me. Though he was otherwise not an ill-natured Man: perhaps I was too saucy and provoking. ∎

How did the newspaper come to be published under Franklin's name?

In what way did Franklin take advantage of his brother? Why might the "Unfairness of it" weigh little with him?

---

8. **Indenture.** Contract binding a person to work for another for a given length of time
9. **Discharge on the Back.** Release of the remainder
10. **Paper . . . several Months.** Actually, the paper remained in Franklin's name until 1726, nearly three years after he left Boston.
11. **Errata.** Printer's term for errors

Responding to the Selection

If you had a chance to read more of the *Autobiography,* what would attract you to do so? curiosity about the adventures in which Franklin was involved? appreciation for his humor? interest in the character of the man himself? What do you find most appealing about this work?

WORDS FOR EVERYDAY USE:

e • vade (ē vād´) vt., avoid or escape from by deceit or cleverness

ven • ture (ven´chər) vt., undertake the risk of

Reviewing the Selection

1. What tasks did Benjamin Franklin perform for his brother as his apprentice?

2. How did Franklin trick his brother into publishing his writing?

3. How did James Franklin offend the Assembly? What was his punishment for the offense?

4. What finally led to Franklin's leaving the newspaper and his job as apprentice?

▶▶ 5. Franklin and his brother often had disagreements. Explain why Franklin often felt misused and wished to end the apprenticeship.

▶▶ 6. Why did Franklin resort to trickery in order to get his work printed? Why did he finally reveal that he was the author?

▶▶ 7. How did Franklin benefit from the Assembly's restrictions on his brother's printing?

▶▶ 8. How did Franklin feel about abandoning his apprenticeship at the time he left? How had his attitude concerning the incident and his actions changed by the time he wrote his autobiography? Why had it changed?

9. Franklin had signed the new indenture that secretly made him his brother's apprentice for the remainder of the previously agreed-upon term, but he eventually left the job knowing his brother could not publicly prosecute him. Do you think Franklin acted fairly? Was he justified in leaving his brother? Explain why, or why not.

10. Franklin published the newspaper by himself during his brother's absence. What do you think he might have learned about himself and the newspaper business during that time? How do you think that experience affected his decision to leave his brother later?

Understanding Literature (Questions for Discussion)

1. **Style. Style** is the manner in which something is said or written. Any recurring feature that distinguishes one writer's work from another can be said to be part of that writer's style. Franklin's style includes many of the qualities of Neoclassicism. (See the definition of Neoclassicism in the Handbook of Literary Terms.) What characteristics of the *Autobiography* do you notice that set off Franklin's work from that of other prose writers you have read?

2. **Persona.** A **persona** consists of the qualities of a person or character that are shown through speech or actions. What qualities does Franklin wish the reader to perceive in

him? How does he show these qualities in his account? How accurately do you suppose the persona in his work reflects Franklin's character?

3. **Autobiography.** An **autobiography** is the story of a person's life, written by that person. Name some advantages that an autobiography has over a biography—that is, an account of a person's life written by someone else. Name some advantages a biography has over an autobiography. From this excerpt, do you feel you can trust Franklin's account? Why, or why not?

4. **Proverb, or Aphorism.** A **proverb,** or **aphorism,** is a short saying or pointed statement. The following is a list of aphorisms from the writings of Benjamin Franklin. Many come from Franklin's *Poor Richard's Almanac,* which he edited under the pseudonym of Richard Saunders. Discuss the meanings of these aphorisms with your classmates. Paraphrase them, and identify those that offer advice about living a good life. Discuss how this advice might be applied to your own lives.

Aphorisms from *Poor Richard's Almanac* and Other Writings by Benjamin Franklin

"A learned blockhead is a greater blockhead than an ignorant one."

"A penny saved is a penny earned."

"A plowman on his legs is higher than a gentleman on his knees."

"A word to the wise is enough and many words won't fill a bushel."

"At the workingman's house hunger looks in, but dares not enter."

"Beware of little expenses; a small leak will sink a great ship."

"Creditors have better memories than debtors."

"Early to bed, and early to rise, makes a man healthy, wealthy, and wise."

"Experience keeps a dear school, but fools will learn in no other, and scarce in that."

"God heals, and the doctor takes the fee."

"God helps them that help themselves."

"Have you somewhat to do tomorrow, do it today."

"He that falls in love with himself, will have no rivals."

"He that goes a-borrowing goes a-sorrowing."

"I should have no objection to a repetition of the same life from its beginning, only asking the advantages authors have in a second edition to correct some faults of the first."

"If you will not hear reason, she'll surely rap your knuckles."

"If you would like to know the value of money, go and try to borrow some."

"If you would not be forgotten as soon as you are dead, either write things worth reading or do things worth writing."

"In this world nothing can be said to be certain except death and taxes."

"Keep your eyes wide open before marriage and half-shut afterwards."

"Little strokes fell great oaks."

"Lost time is never found again."

"Necessity never made a good bargain."

"Plow deep, while sluggards sleep, and you shall have corn to sell and to keep."

"snug/as a bug/in a rug"

"The early bird catches the worm."

"There never was a good war, or a bad peace."

"Time is money."

"We must indeed all hang together, or, most assuredly, we shall all hang separately."

"What maintains one vice would bring up two children."

Language Lab

Verbals. Read the Language Arts Survey, 2.16, "Verbals: Participles," and 2.17, "Verbals: Gerunds." Then find the gerunds and participles in these sentences. Identify each gerund with a single underscore and each participle with a double underscore.

1. To young Franklin, publishing was a challenging and rewarding career.

2. Even though annoying disagreements with his brother drove him into running away to Philadelphia, the printing skills he acquired gave him valuable experience.

3. Joining his abilities in writing and publishing with keen business sense, Franklin gained success quickly.

4. Then he enjoyed experimenting with electricity and inventing useful tools, such as the bifocals used by many people today.

5. Retired from business at age forty-two, Franklin spent most of the rest of his life as a diplomat, serving his country as ambassador to France.

> *The body of*
> *Benjamin Franklin, printer,*
> *(Like the cover of an old book,*
> *Its contents worn out,*
> *And stript of its lettering and gilding)*
> *Lies here, food for worms!*
> *Yet the work itself shall not be lost,*
> *For it will, as he believed, appear once more*
> *In a new*
> *And more beautiful edition,*
> *Corrected and amended*
> *By its Author!*

READER'S JOURNAL

Imagine that you have been asked to come up with a plan for the ideal education for a young person in your society. What would your plan be? What do you think young people should learn? What subjects should they study? What skills should they develop? Write about these questions in your journal.

THINKING SKILLS

Read the Language Arts Survey, 4.8, "Comparing and Contrasting." Then, as you read the selection, make a chart to compare and contrast the colonists' and the Native Americans' ideas about education.

FROM

"Remarks Concerning the Natives of North America"

Benjamin Franklin

Savages we call them, because their manners differ from ours, which we think the perfection of <u>civility</u>; they think the same of theirs.

Perhaps, if we could examine the manners of different nations with <u>impartiality</u>, we should find no people so rude, as to be without any rules of politeness; nor any so polite, as not to have some remains of rudeness.

The Indian men, when young, are hunters and warriors; when old, counselors; for all their government is by counsel of the sages;[1] there is no force, there are no prisons, no officers to compel obedience, or inflict punishment. Hence they generally study <u>oratory</u>, the best speaker having the most influence. The Indian women till the ground, dress the food, nurse and bring up the children, and preserve and hand down to <u>posterity</u> the memory of public transactions. These employments of men and women are accounted natural and honorable. Having few artificial wants, they have abundance of leisure for improvement by conversation. Our laborious manner of life, compared with theirs, they esteem[2] slavish and base; and the learning, on which we value ourselves, they regard as frivolous and useless. An instance of this occurred at the Treaty of Lancaster, in Pennsylvania, *anno* 1744, between the government of Virginia and the Six Nations.[3] After the

How do the Native Americans regard the white people's learning?

---

1. **sages.** Very wise people, widely respected for their wisdom, experience, and judgment
2. **esteem.** Consider; hold to be
3. **Six Nations.** Confederation of Iroquoian peoples, comprising the Mohawk, Oneida, Onondaga, Cayuga, Seneca, and Tuscarora

---

WORDS FOR EVERYDAY USE:

ci • vil • i • ty (sə vil´ə tē) *n.,* politeness

im • par • ti • al • i • ty (im pär´shē al´ i tē) *n.,* free of bias

or • a • to • ry (ôr´ə tôr´ē) *n.,* art of public speaking

pos • ter • i • ty (päs ter´ə tē) *n.,* all of a person's descendants

The Twin, Wife of Bloody Hand. George Catlin, 1832. National Museum of American Art, Washington, DC/Art Resource, NY

What offers do the commissioners make to the Native Americans?

What does the speaker for the Six Nations say about different nations' conceptions of things?

principal business was settled, the commissioners from Virginia acquainted the Indians by a speech, that there was at Williamsburg a college, with a fund for educating Indian youth; and that, if the Six Nations would send down half a dozen of their young lads to that college, the government would take care that they should be well provided for, and instructed in all the learning of the white people. It is one of the Indian rules of politeness not to answer a public proposition the same day that it is made; they think it would be treating it as a light matter, and that they show it respect by taking time to consider it, as of a matter important. They therefore deferred their answer till the day following; when their speaker began, by expressing their deep sense of the kindness of the Virginia government, in making them that offer; "for we know," says he, "that you highly esteem the kind of learning taught in those Colleges, and that the maintenance of our young men, while with you, would be very expensive to you. We are convinced, therefore, that you mean to do us good by your proposal; and we thank you <u>heartily</u>. But you, who are wise, must know that different nations have different conceptions of things; and you will therefore not take it amiss, if our ideas of this kind of education happen not to be the same with yours. We have had some experience of it; several of our young people were formerly brought up at the colleges of the northern provinces; they

WORDS FOR EVERYDAY USE: heart • i • ly (härt´l ē) *adv.,* in a friendly, sincere, way

were instructed in all your sciences; but, when they came back to us, they were bad runners, ignorant of every means of living in the woods, unable to bear either cold or hunger, knew neither how to build a cabin, take a deer, or kill an enemy, spoke our language imperfectly, were therefore neither fit for hunters, warriors, nor counselors; they were totally good for nothing. We are however not the less obliged by your kind offer, though we decline accepting it; and, to show our grateful sense of it, if the gentlemen of Virginia will send us a dozen of their sons, we will take great care of their education, instruct them in all we know, and make *men* of them." ∎

Q What reasons does the speaker give for declining the offer?

Q What offer does the speaker make in return?

Responding to the Selection

The Native Americans and the colonists in this selection have very different ideas about an appropriate education for a young person. What are those ideas? What do they reveal about the cultures of these people? If you could redesign the curriculum, or program of study, at your school, what changes would you make? What do you think young people should study today? Discuss these questions with your classmates.

Reviewing the Selection

RECALLING

1. According to Franklin, how did the colonists often refer to the natives of North America? Why did the colonists call them that?

2. Explain the offer the commissioners of Virginia made to the Six Nations.

3. What were the Native Americans' reasons for refusing the offer?

4. What counteroffer did the speaker for the Six Nations make in response to the commissioners' offer?

INTERPRETING

▶▶ 5. What is the definition of the word *savage?* Why could the term be considered negative and insulting? What does the term suggest about the self-image of the people who use the term?

▶▶ 6. How do you think the commissioners expected their offer to be received? What response do you think they expected from the Native Americans?

▶▶ 7. Summarize the reasons why the representatives of the Six Nations thought that their college-educated sons were "good for nothing."

▶▶ 8. Do you think the Six Nations' offer was well received? Based on what you know about relations between the white people and the natives of North America, what might have been the reaction of the commissioners to the speaker's suggestion?

9. In your opinion, what are the best methods by which two cultures can learn about each other? What attitudes must both cultures demonstrate in order to get along?

10. Read the Six Nations' speaker's words carefully. From this speech, how would you describe the relationship between the tribes he represented and colonial society at that time?

Understanding Literature (Questions for Discussion)

1. **Chiasmus.** A **chiasmus** is a rhetorical technique in which the order of occurrence of words or phrases is reversed, as in the line "We can weather changes, but we can't change the weather." Identify an example of chiasmus within the first third of this excerpt. Which words (in slightly varied forms) are reversed?

2. **Neoclassicism. Neoclassicism** is the term used to describe the revival during the English Enlightenment or Restoration Era of ideals of art and literature derived from the Greek and Roman classics. Critical among these ideals were reason and civility; the Neoclassicists cherished in art and life such characteristics as balance, proportion, restraint, and wit. How do these ideals influence Franklin's remarks? Point out passages in which Franklin balances ideas or phrases, where he points out uncivil or irrational attitudes, where he recommends restraint, and/or where he is witty or shows an appreciation for wit.

3. **Stereotype.** A **stereotype** is an uncritically accepted fixed or conventional idea, particularly such an idea held about whole groups of people. Against what stereotype does Franklin's essay present an argument? Why might the Native Americans have been justified in considering the colonists savages? Why might people think that a civilization is savage or uncivilized simply because it is very different from their own? Why is it so difficult for people from very different cultures to accept one another's ways of life as equally advanced, despite the differences?

Responding in Writing

1. **Agenda.** An **agenda** is a list of the topics or items of business to be discussed in a meeting. Write an agenda for a meeting of Ambassador Franklin with representatives of King Louis XVI of France to raise support for the United States in its war with Britain. List specific topics that either side might want to consider. (Refer to the Language Arts Survey, 3.6, "Discussion.")

2. **Cartoon.** Draw a one- to four-panel cartoon, with speech balloons or captions, that points out the ridiculousness of a widely accepted belief or practice, just as "Remarks Concerning the Natives of North America" challenges the white person's assumption that college learning would benefit eighteenth-century Native Americans.

Language Lab

Words as Other Parts of Speech. Read the Language Arts Survey, 2.30–2.31, "Words as Other Parts of Speech I and II." Then find the single word used as two different parts of speech in each pair of sentences below. Copy the word and identify the part of speech it is used as in each sentence.

1. Did his apprentice's departure cause James Franklin's newspaper to go under?

    No; in fact, for three more years the paper was printed under Benjamin Franklin's name.

2. Franklin achieved great business success in Philadelphia, Pennsylvania.

    With part of the money that he earned from his business, Franklin funded public works.

3. One of Franklin's most famous inventions, a free-standing stove, successfully countered the drafts that usually chilled colonists in their poorly insulated homes.

    Franklin helped draft the Declaration of Independence, and he was one of its signers.

4. Franklin made more than one trip across the Atlantic Ocean.

    As ambassador, he rarely tripped in his dealings with the French court.

5. While in France, Franklin frequently appeared at great events wearing a fur cap.

    Franklin's participation in the Constitutional Convention capped a long career of public service.

PROJECTS

1. **Pamphlet.** Try your hand at some Franklinesque writing and printing. Choose a topic that is light and entertaining, such as silly dog tricks or outdated clothing styles. Write an essay on the topic in a style imitating Benjamin Franklin's. Type your essay, or input it on a computer, and lay it out in the form of a four-page pamphlet. Print or duplicate several copies for distribution.

2. **Invention.** Review the inventions credited to Benjamin Franklin. Then, with one or more classmates, brainstorm ideas for a new invention. Begin by choosing some currently unmet need, such as organizing all the papers for your classes or keeping your textbooks from becoming worn and tattered. Then brainstorm possible solutions to that problem. Select the best approach and refine it. Then draw plans for, or make a model of, your invention. Be sure to provide captions or notes to indicate how the invention might work.

3. **Humor Calendar.** With several co-editors, collect jokes and funny anecdotes from your friends. Then create a calendar with a joke or story for each week of the year.

PREREADING

Speech in the Virginia Convention
by Patrick Henry

ABOUT THE AUTHOR

Patrick Henry (1736–1799) was a distinguished statesman and orator during the American Revolution. Born in Hanover County, Virginia, Henry's public schooling was brief, for his education was taken over by his father, a well-educated gentleman. Henry first tried his hand as a storekeeper but proved to be a poor businessman. He then turned to law and received his license in 1760. Gaining fame as an orator, he was elected to the Virginia House of Burgesses, where he became a leader. His speech against the Stamp Act in 1765 is considered one of his finest, and who can forget the words he uttered in the Virginia Convention on March 23, 1775: "I know not what course others may take, but as for me, give me liberty or give me death!" He served as governor of Virginia, became a conservative member of the Federalist party, and declined membership in the Constitutional Convention and the U.S. Senate. He refused George Washington's offers of appointment as secretary of state and chief justice of the Supreme Court. He was chiefly responsible for the drafting of the Bill of Rights. In 1796, Henry was elected governor of Virginia for the sixth time but refused to take office. His last campaign was for the office of representative in the Virginia state legislature. He won the election but died before taking office.

ABOUT THE SELECTION

The **Speech in the Virginia Convention**, probably Patrick Henry's best-known oration, was not written down until years after its delivery on March 23, 1775. It had so captured the attention of its listeners that they were able to recall it for Henry's biographer, William Wirt. The speech was delivered to the Virginia Convention during a time of growing political unrest. Over a year before, on December 16, 1773, disguised men had defied the British Parliament by dumping imported tea into Boston Harbor to avoid paying the taxes on it. In retaliation, Parliament had passed harsh measures in 1774 that became known as the Intolerable Acts. British soldiers were sent to the colonies to enforce the acts and were lodged in Massachusetts homes. Despite the British presence, colonists in Massachusetts, as in other colonies, were stockpiling arms and ammunition, and their militia—the Minutemen—were drilling in anticipation of clashes with the soldiers. Henry referred to these preparations in his line "Our brethren are already in the field!" Less than a month after Henry's speech, his prediction of open battle in the North was fulfilled in the opening skirmishes of the American Revolution at Lexington and Concord on April 19, 1775.

READER'S JOURNAL

Recall what you know of the events that led to the American Revolution. Try to put yourself in those times, unable to predict the outcome of a war, knowing only that the forces of England were much larger than those of the colonies. If you had been a colonist, would you have favored war or tried to settle the differences peacefully? In your journal, write about the stand you would have taken, and why.

LANGUAGE SKILLS

Read the Language Arts Survey, 2.25, "Coordinating Conjunctions." Then examine this selection for examples of coordinating conjunctions between words, phrases, and clauses. List at least three examples.

Speech in the Virginia Convention

PATRICK HENRY

Mr. President:[1] No man thinks more highly than I do of the patriotism, as well as abilities, of the very worthy gentlemen who have just addressed the house. But different men often see the same subject in different lights: and, therefore, I hope it will not be thought disrespectful to those gentlemen, if, entertaining, as I do, opinions of a character very opposite to theirs, I shall speak forth my sentiments freely and without reserve. This is no time for ceremony. The question before the house is one of awful moment to this country. For my own part, I consider it as nothing less than a question of freedom or slavery. And in proportion to the magnitude of the subject ought to be the freedom of the debate. It is only in this way that we can hope to arrive at truth, and fulfill the great responsibility which we hold to God and our country. Should I keep back my opinions at such a time, through fear of giving offense, I should consider myself as guilty of treason toward my country, and of an act of disloyalty toward the Majesty of Heaven, which I revere above all earthly kings.

Mr. President, it is natural to man to indulge in the illusions of hope. We are apt to shut our eyes against a painful truth, and listen to the song of that siren till she transforms us into beasts. Is this the part of wise men, engaged in a great and arduous struggle for liberty? Are we disposed to be of the number of those who having eyes see not, and having ears hear not, the things which so nearly concern their <u>temporal</u> salvation? For my part, whatever anguish of spirit it may cost, I am willing to know the whole truth; to know the worst and to provide for it.

1. **Mr. President.** President of the Virginia Convention

WORDS FOR EVERYDAY USE:

tem • po • ral (tem′pə rəl) *adj.,* lasting only for a time; temporary

Patrick Henry speaking against the Stamp Act in the Virginia House of Burgesses in 1765. Nineteenth-century colored engraving. The Granger Collection, NY

our petition <u>comports</u> with those warlike preparations which cover our waters and darken our land. Are fleets and armies necessary to a work of love and reconciliation? Have we shown ourselves so unwilling to be reconciled that force must be called in to win back our love? Let us not deceive ourselves, sir. These are the implements of war and <u>subjugation</u>—the last arguments to which kings resort.

I ask gentlemen, sir, what means this <u>martial</u> array,[3] if its purpose be not to force us to <u>submission</u>? Can gentlemen assign any other possible motive for it? Has Great Britain any enemy in this quarter of the world, to call for all this accumulation of navies and armies? No, sir, she has none. They are meant for us: they can be meant for no other. They are sent over to bind and rivet upon us those chains which the British ministry have been so long forging.

And what have we to oppose to them? Shall we try argument? Sir, we have been trying that for the last ten years. Have we anything new to offer upon the subject? Nothing. We have held the subject up in every light of which it is capable; but it has been all in vain. Shall we resort to entreaty and humble supplication? What terms shall we find which have not been already exhausted? Let us not, I beseech[4] you, sir, deceive ourselves longer.

Sir, we have done everything that could be done to <u>avert</u> the storm which is now coming on. We have petitioned; we have

What guides the speaker?

I have but one lamp by which my feet are guided, and that is the lamp of experience. I know of no way of judging of the future but by the past. And judging by the past, I wish to know what there has been in the conduct of the British ministry for the last ten years to justify those hopes with which gentlemen have been pleased to <u>solace</u> themselves and the house? Is it that <u>insidious</u> smile with which our petition[2] has been lately received? Trust it not, sir: it will prove a snare to your feet. Suffer not yourselves to be betrayed with a kiss. Ask yourselves how this gracious reception of

How have the colonists responded to British threats?

2. **petition.** "Olive Branch Petition," in which the king was asked to intercede between Parliament and the colonies

3. **array.** Display; assembly

4. **beseech.** Beg; plead

WORDS FOR EVERYDAY USE:

so • lace (säl´is) *vt.*, comfort, relieve
in • sid • i • ous (in sid´ē əs) *adj.*, sly; crafty
com • port (kəm pôrt´) *vi.*, agree; go along
sub • ju • ga • tion (sub´jə gā´shen) *n.*, takeover; enslavement

mar • tial (mär´shəl) *adj.*, warlike; of the military
sub • mis • sion (sub mish´ən) *n.*, act of yielding; surrendering
a • vert (ə vurt´) *vt.*, prevent

remonstrated; we have supplicated; we have prostrated ourselves before the throne, and have implored its interposition[5] to arrest the tyrannical hands of the ministry and Parliament. Our petitions have been slighted; our remonstrances have produced additional violence and insult; our supplications have been disregarded; and we have been spurned with contempt from the foot of the throne! In vain, after these things, may we indulge the fond[6] hope of peace and reconciliation. There is no longer any room for hope. If we wish to be free, if we mean to preserve inviolate those inestimable privileges for which we have been so long contending, if we mean not basely to abandon the noble struggle in which we have been so long engaged, and which we have pledged ourselves never to abandon until the glorious object of our contest shall be obtained— we must fight! I repeat it, sir, we must fight! An appeal to arms and to the God of Hosts is all that is left us!

They tell us, sir, that we are weak— unable to cope with so formidable an adversary. But when shall we be stronger? Will it be the next week, or the next year? Will it be when we are totally disarmed, and when a British guard shall be stationed in every house? Shall we gather strength by irresolution and inaction? Shall we acquire the means of effectual resistance by lying supinely on our backs and hugging the delusive phantom of hope until our enemies shall have bound us hand and foot? Sir, we are not weak, if we make a proper use of those means which the God of nature hath placed in our power. Three millions of people, armed in the holy cause of liberty, and in such a country as that which we possess, are invincible by any force which our enemy can send against us. Besides, sir, we shall not fight our battles alone. There is a just God who presides over the destinies of nations and who will raise up friends to fight our battles for us. The battle, sir, is not to the strong alone; it is to the vigilant, the active, the brave. Besides, sir, we have no election.[7] If we were base enough to desire it, it is now too late to retire from the contest. There is no retreat but in submission and slavery! Our chains are forged! Their clanging may be heard on the plains of Boston! The war is inevitable—and let it come! I repeat it, sir, let it come![8]

It is in vain, sir, to extenuate the matter. Gentlemen may cry, "Peace, peace"—but there is no peace. The war is actually begun! The next gale that sweeps from the north will bring to our ears the clash of resounding arms! Our brethren are already in the field! Why stand we here idle? What is it that gentlemen wish? What would they have? Is life so dear, or peace so sweet, as to be purchased at the price of chains and slavery? Forbid it, Almighty God! I know not what course others may take; but as for me, give me liberty or give me death! ■

Who is favored in battle?

---

5. **interposition.** Intervention
6. **fond.** Foolish
7. **election.** Choice
8. **The war . . . come.** Boston had recently been occupied by British troops under the leadership of General Howe.

WORDS FOR EVERYDAY USE:

re • mon • strate (ri män´strāt´) vt., demonstrate

pros • trate (präs´trāt´) vt., bow down

in • vi • o • late (in vī´ə lit) adj., sacred

in • es • ti • ma • ble (in es´tə mə bəl) adj., too great to be measured

for • mi • da • ble (fôr´mə de bəl) adj., overwhelming

ef • fec • tu • al (e fek´chōō əl) adj., effective

su • pine • ly (sōō´pīn´lə) adv., passively

Responding to the Selection

You are probably familiar with the final sentence of this speech. Why can it be quoted outside of this speech? Was it more meaningful to you in the context of the speech?

Reviewing the Selection

RECALLING

1. According to Henry, what is the only way to arrive at truth?

2. What evidence suggests strongly to Henry that Britain means to wage war "to force us to submission"?

3. What efforts have the colonists made to maintain peace? How have their efforts been received by the British government?

4. What is Henry's response to the possibility that war may break out soon?

INTERPRETING

5. Why does Henry feel he must speak out in opposition to the previous speakers who urged moderation and the maintenance of a peaceful attitude toward Britain?

6. Why does Henry distrust the "insidious smile with which our petition has been lately received"?

7. Henry argues that peaceful options have been exhausted and that war will come sooner or later. Summarize the argument Henry makes for fighting now instead of waiting.

8. What does Henry see as the alternative to war? Why is that alternative so unthinkable?

SYNTHESIZING

9. If you had been a representative to the Virginia Convention, would Henry's words have persuaded you to take up arms against Britain? In your opinion, which of his arguments are most convincing?

10. Describe the probable reaction of the Massachusetts colonists to Henry's speech. Describe the probable reaction of the British government to his speech.

Understanding Literature (Questions for Discussion)

1. **Rhetorical Question.** A **rhetorical question** is one asked for effect but not meant to be answered because the answer is clear from the context. Paragraph 2 contains this example: "Are we disposed to be of the number of those who having eyes see not, and

having ears hear not, the things which so nearly concern their temporal salvation?" Identify three more passages in which the speaker poses rhetorical questions.

2. **Enlightenment.** The **Enlightenment** was an eighteenth-century philosophical movement characterized by belief in reason, the scientific method, and the perfectibility of people and society. Look for indications in this speech that Patrick Henry participated in this movement. (a) Where does he support the importance of using reason as a guide to action? (b) The scientific method calls for hypothesizing and predicting, experimenting to test the hypothesis, and basing further action on the results of the experiments. What hypothesis have the previous speakers presented with regard to the political situation? What "experimental results" does Henry report? What prediction does he make based on observable phenomena? (c) Does Henry accept the idea that people and society are perfectible—or, at least, that they can be improved? What passages support your answer?

3. **Parallelism. Parallelism** is a rhetorical technique in which a writer emphasizes the equal value or weight of two or more ideas by expressing them in the same grammatical form. For example, in the phrase "freedom or slavery" (paragraph 1, sentence 5), Henry balances two nouns; in "the magnitude of the subject" and "the freedom of the debate" (paragraph 1, sentence 6), he balances two noun phrases; and in "Should I keep back my opinions" and "I should consider myself as guilty of treason" (paragraph 1, sentence 8), he equates two predicates. Find at least four other instances of parallelism. For each, identify the grammatical form used.

Responding in Writing

1. **Nomination Speech.** Select a character from a book, play, or movie to run for election to your state legislature. Write a brief nomination speech, presenting the character's credentials and calling on your audience to support the nomination. Use rhetorical techniques, such as those in Henry's speech to the Virginia Convention to excite your audience about your candidate.

2. **Minutes.** In the minutes of a meeting, the secretary of an organization summarizes the discussion on each item of business and records formal movements and decisions. Imagine that you are the secretary for the Virginia Convention. Write a brief passage for the minutes, covering Patrick Henry's speech.

3. **Petition.** Patrick Henry referred to the petitions that his countrymen had sent to the king of England, seeking what they perceived as their rights as English citizens. Consider your various roles, as family member, student, citizen, and so on. What rights do you feel belong to a role, but have not been open to you? Who might be able to improve this situation? Write a petition to the authority figure you choose, identifying the rights that you seek and explaining why you deserve them.

Language Lab

Functions of Sentences. Read the Language Arts Survey, 2.36, "The Functions of Sentences." Then identify the functions of each of the following sentences from Patrick Henry's speech.

1. Let us not deceive ourselves, sir.

2. This is no time for ceremony.

3. And what have we to oppose to them?

4. There is no retreat but in submission and slavery!

5. Sir, we are not weak, if we make a proper use of those means which the God of nature hath placed in our power.

Speaking and Listening Skills

Public Speaking. Read the Language Arts Survey, 3.7, "Public Speaking." Then join with a small group of classmates. Take two to three minutes to brainstorm topics for extemporaneous speeches explaining, supporting, or attacking objects, practices, or ideas. Then each group member should write two topics on a slip of paper. After the slips are mixed up in a container, each member should draw one, choose one of the two suggested topics, and give an extemporaneous one- to two-minute speech on the topic.

PROJECTS

1. **Royal Television Commercial.** King George III needs to make his case to the American colonists. Write a television commercial to arouse support for him. Write the text and describe the audiovisual techniques to be used, including still photographs, animated sequences, and music.

2. **Pre-Revolutionary Twenty Questions.** Each person in the class should select a known or anonymous person from pre-Revolutionary America, for example, George Washington or one of the accusers in the Salem witch trials, and do any necessary research to represent that person. Then the class should play a game of Twenty Questions. Each player takes a turn representing his or her selected person, and the rest of the class may ask up to twenty questions to determine the person's identity. All questions must have yes or no answers.

from *Crisis, No. 1*
by Thomas Paine

ABOUT THE AUTHOR

Thomas Paine (1737–1809) was born in the village of Thetford, in Norfolk, England, the son of a Quaker father and an Anglican mother. He received little formal education. He attended grammar school until he was thirteen and then worked as an apprentice in the shop belonging to his father, a corset maker. Benjamin Franklin, who met Paine in London, recognized the younger man's potential and supplied him with letters of introduction when he sailed for Philadelphia. There Paine became a spokesperson against slavery and the author of a pamphlet entitled *Common Sense,* the first published work in the colonies to call for independence from Great Britain. Paine helped to raise money for weapons to be used by the American revolutionaries, and wrote sixteen pamphlets, the *Crisis* papers, to lift the morale of the troops. While he received numerous political appointments, he found public office confining. He returned to England, where his *Rights of Man,* a condemnation of hereditary monarchy, led to charges of treason. He fled to France where, ironically for this supporter of both the American and the French Revolutions, he was arrested for expressing the view that the French king should be exiled instead of executed. With the help of the American ambassador, Paine won release from prison, left France, and returned to America. On his return, he wrote *The Age of Reason,* the title of which is often taken to describe the entire period of the eighteenth century in Europe. During the last part of his life, Paine lived on land granted to him by the state of New York for his service during the Revolution. Unfortunately, few people remembered Paine's important contributions, and many disliked him because of his unorthodox religious views. This champion of freedom, whose words helped to forge the American experiment in democracy, spent his last years in poverty and obscurity.

ABOUT THE SELECTION

The following selection is from the first of a series of sixteen pamphlets published from 1776 to 1783 entitled *Crisis.* In December 1776, when the first pamphlet appeared, the American cause was at low ebb. Washington and his troops had just retreated to Trenton, and support for the revolution was wavering. The rebels welcomed Paine's words of encouragement and inspiration; in fact, Washington immediately read them to his troops to lift their morale. Paine tried to conceal his identity by signing his pamphlets "Common Sense" instead of using his own name because the sentiments he expressed in them were clearly treasonous, but the identity of the author was soon common knowledge.

READER'S JOURNAL

In colonial days and the early days of the American Revolution, pamphlets and newspapers were the only ways to spread ideas among the colonies. Today, television is the medium through which many people air their views. Have you ever seen a television show in which someone presented a strongly held point of view? Freewrite in your journal about such a person whom you have seen on TV and explain the cause he or she was supporting. Was the speaker convincing enough to change your mind?

THINKING SKILLS

Read the Language Arts Survey, 4.8, "Comparing and Contrasting." Then, as you read Paine's essay, identify the part in which he compares the actions of the colonists to those of a person defending his or her house against an intruder. Consider these questions: Why does Paine make this comparison? What point does he wish to make by means of this comparison? Is the comparison effective? Why, or why not?

FROM

Crisis, No. 1

THOMAS PAINE

Who may fail to respond to the needs of the country?

These are the times that try men's souls. The summer soldier and the sunshine patriot will, in this crisis, shrink from the service of their country, but he that stands it now, deserves the love and thanks of man and woman. Tyranny, like hell, is not easily conquered; yet we have this <u>consolation</u> with us, that the harder the conflict, the more glorious the triumph. What we obtain too cheap, we esteem too lightly: it is dearness only that gives everything its value. Heaven knows how to put a proper price upon its goods; and it would be strange indeed if so celestial an article as freedom should not be highly rated. Britain, with an army to enforce her tyranny, has declared that she has a right (not only to tax) but "to bind us in all cases whatsoever," and if being bound in that manner is not slavery, then is there not such a thing as slavery upon earth. Even the expression is <u>impious</u>; for so unlimited a power can belong only to God.

Whether the independence of the continent was declared too soon, or delayed too long, I will not now enter into as an argument; my own simple opinion is, that had it been eight months earlier, it would have been much better. We did not make a proper use of last winter, neither could we, while we were in a dependent state. However, the fault, if it were one, was all our own;[1] we have none to blame but

---

1. **own.** Paine wanted an immediate declaration of independence uniting the colonies.

WORDS FOR EVERYDAY USE:

con • so • la • tion (kän′sə lā′shən) *n.*, comfort

im • pi • ous (im′pē əs) *adj.*, lacking reverence for God

ourselves. But no great deal is lost yet. All that Howe[2] has been doing for this month past is rather a ravage than a conquest, which the spirit of the Jerseys,[3] a year ago, would have quickly <u>repulsed</u>, and which time and a little <u>resolution</u> will soon recover.

I have as little superstition in me as any man living, but my secret opinion has ever been, and still is, that God Almighty will not give up a people to military destruction, or leave them unsupportedly to perish, who have so earnestly and so repeatedly sought to avoid the <u>calamities</u> of war, by every decent method which wisdom could invent. Neither have I so much of the infidel[4] in me as to suppose that He has relinquished the government of the world, and given us up to the care of devils; and as I do not, I cannot see on what grounds the King of Britain can look up to heaven for help against us: a common murderer, a highwayman, or a housebreaker has as good a pretense as he.

'Tis surprising to see how rapidly a panic will sometimes run through a country. All nations and ages have been subject to them: Britain has trembled like an ague[5] at the report of a French fleet of flat-bottomed boats, and in the fourteenth century[6] the whole English army, after ravaging the kingdom of France, was driven back like men petrified with fear;

and this brave exploit was performed by a few broken forces collected and headed by a woman, Joan of Arc. Would that heaven might inspire some Jersey maid to spirit up her countrymen, and save her fair fellow sufferers from ravage and ravishment! Yet panics, in some cases, have their uses; they produce as much good as hurt. Their <u>duration</u> is always short; the mind soon grows through them, and acquires a firmer habit than before. But their peculiar advantage is that they are the touchstones[7] of sincerity and <u>hypocrisy</u>, and bring things and men to light, which might otherwise have lain forever undiscovered. In fact, they have the same effect on secret traitors, which an imaginary apparition would have upon a private murderer. They sift out the hidden thoughts of man, and hold them up in public to the world. Many a disguised tory[8] has lately shown his head, that shall <u>penitentially</u> solemnize with curses the day on which Howe arrived upon the Delaware. . . .

The far and the near, the home counties and the back,[9] the rich and poor will suffer or rejoice alike. The heart that feels not now is dead: the blood of his children will curse his cowardice who shrinks back at a time when a little might have saved the whole, and made them happy. I love the man that can smile in trouble, that can gather strength from distress, and grow

What benefits arise from panic?

Whom does Paine admire?

---

2. **Howe.** Lord William Howe was commander of the British Army in America from 1775 to 1778.

3. **Jerseys.** East and West Jersey were separate colonies.

4. **infidel.** Person who does not accept some particular theory, belief, etc.; used derogatorily

5. **ague.** Chill; fit of shivering

6. **fourteenth century.** Actually the fifteenth; Joan of

Arc triumphed over the English in 1429.

7. **touchstones.** Types of stone formerly used to test the purity of gold or silver; hence, any test for determining genuineness or value

8. **tory.** Supporter of continued allegiance to Great Britain

9. **back.** Backwoods

WORDS FOR EVERYDAY USE:

re • pulse (ri puls´) vt., drive back
res • o • lu • tion (rez´ə loo´shən) n., determination
ca • lam • i • ty (kə lam´ə tē) n., deep trouble or misery
du • ra • tion (doo rā´shən) n., continuance in time

hy • poc • ri • sy (hi päk´rə sē) n., pretending to be what one is not, or to feel what one does not feel
pen • i • ten • tial • ly (pen´i ten´shəl lē) adv., in a manner suggesting regret for wrongdoing

brave by <u>reflection</u>. 'Tis the business of little minds to shrink; but he whose heart is firm, and whose conscience approves his conduct, will pursue his principles unto death. My own line of reasoning is to myself as straight and clear as a ray of light. Not all the treasures of the world, so far as I believe, could have <u>induced</u> me to support an <u>offensive</u> war, for I think it murder; but if a thief breaks into my house, burns and destroys my property, and kills or threatens to kill me, or those that are in it, and to "bind me in all cases whatsoever"[10] to his absolute will, am I to suffer it? What signifies it to me, whether he who does it is a king or a common man; my countryman or not my countryman; whether it be done by an individual villain, or an army of them? If we reason to the root of things we shall find no difference; neither can any just cause be assigned why we should punish in the one case and pardon in the other. Let them call me rebel, and welcome, I feel no concern from it; but I should suffer the misery of devils were I to make a whore of my soul by swearing allegiance to one whose character is that of a <u>sottish</u>, stupid, stubborn, worthless, brutish man. I conceive likewise a horrid idea in receiving mercy from a being, who at the last day shall be shrieking to the rocks and mountains to cover him, and fleeing with terror from the orphan, the widow, and the slain of America. ∎

---

10. **"bind me . . . whatsoever."** On February 24, 1776, the Declaratory Act of Parliament established British authority over the American colonies.

Responding to the Selection

If you had been an American soldier at this time, would *Crisis, No. 1* have inspired you to carry on? What phrases or sentences do you find most effective and memorable? Which arguments do you find most persuasive?

Reviewing the Selection

RECALLING

1. How does Paine describe the time in which his pamphlet is written? What does he fear some supporters of the revolution might do?

2. According to Paine, God will help and protect the Americans. Why is God on the revolutionary side? Why would God not support the king of Britain?

3. What example of panic from history does Paine cite? What happened as a result of panic? Is panic always harmful?

4. Why would Paine refuse to support what he calls an offensive war?

INTERPRETING

▶▶ 5. Why does Paine entitle his pamphlet *Crisis?* Restate in your own words what is meant by the phrase "The summer soldier and the sunshine patriot."

▶▶ 6. Why does Paine mention God in this essay? How do you think Paine's assurance of God's endorsement of the American Revolution affected the pamphlet's American readers?

▶▶ 7. Why are panics sometimes useful? How has the present panic helped the revolution?

▶▶ 8. Does Paine consider the American Revolution to be an offensive war? What is his justification for waging war against England?

SYNTHESIZING

9. Why does Paine find the phrase "to bind [us or me] in all cases whatsoever" so objectionable? Find the two places where he uses the phrase. How does it contribute to his argument with the king of England?

10. Paine's demand for independence from the English monarchy was considered treasonous by the English. Imagine if Paine were alive today and criticizing the United States government the way he criticized the English government. How do you think his opinions would be received in modern America if they were so openly antigovernment? Would he be protected by freedom of speech or would he be in trouble? In your opinion, should his freedom of speech be protected?

Understanding Literature (Questions for Discussion)

1. **Argumentation. Argumentation** presents reasons or arguments for accepting a position or for adopting a course of action. Summarize the arguments Paine gives for continuing to wage war against England.

2. **Assonance. Assonance** is the repetition of vowel sounds in stressed syllables that end with different consonant sounds. Read these lines from the opening paragraph: "These are the times that try men's souls. The sunshine soldier and the summer patriot will, in this crisis, shrink from the service of their country." What vowel sound is repeated in the first sentence? in the second sentence? Notice how the repetition of sounds makes the lines more memorable.

3. **Rhetorical Question.** A **rhetorical question** is one asked for effect but not meant to be answered because the answer is clear from context. Find a rhetorical question in *Crisis, No. 1*. What answer does the author make clear?

Language Lab

Agreement of Pronouns and Antecedents. Read the Language Arts Survey, 2.82, "Agreement of Pronouns and Antecedents." Rewrite each sentence below to make every italicized pronoun agree with its antecedent. Circle the antecedent.

1. The summer soldier will, in this crisis, shrink from the service of *their* country.

2. God will not give up a people to military destruction, or leave *her* to perish.

3. Would that heaven might inspire some Jersey maid to spirit up *his* countrymen.

4. Many a disguised tory has lately shown *their* head.

5. The man whose heart is firm, and whose conscience approves his conduct, will pursue *their* principles unto death.

Thinking Skills

Propaganda. Read the Language Arts Survey, 4.15, "Understanding Propaganda Techniques." Identify propaganda techniques that are used in *Crisis, No.1*. Do you believe that propaganda is justifiable depending on why it is used, or do you feel that it is unfair under any circumstances? Explain your answer.

"To S. M., a Young African Painter, on Seeing His Works"
by Phillis Wheatley

ABOUT THE AUTHOR

Phillis Wheatley (*circa* 1753–1784) was born in West Africa, captured as a child, and brought on a slave ship to Boston in 1761. There John Wheatley, a Boston tailor, purchased the girl to work for his wife, Susannah, who provided an education for Wheatley. A child prodigy, Wheatley rapidly learned to read both English and Latin. By the age of fourteen, she was writing poetry. She achieved fame early for a poem that she wrote about an evangelical preacher named George Whitefield. In 1773, she went to London with the Wheatleys' son, Nathaniel, partly to seek support for her first book, *Poems on Various Subjects, Religions and Morals.* She returned to Boston before the publication of her work, having received news that Susannah Wheatley was dying. Before Susannah's death in 1774, the family released Wheatley from slavery. In 1776, the year in which America declared its independence from Britain, Wheatley met General George Washington after she had written a poem dedicated to him. In 1778, Wheatley married John Peters, a freedman. Her later life was one of grief as she endured poverty and the loss of two children. Her third child, ill when Phillis Wheatley died, passed away shortly afterward and was buried with her in an unmarked grave. Rediscovered in the 1830s, Wheatley's poetry shows her to have been an eloquent spokesperson for her faith, for American independence, and for the abolition of slavery.

ABOUT THE SELECTION

Phillis Wheatley wrote **"To S. M., a Young African Painter, on Seeing His Works"** in praise of the work of Scipio Moorhead, a servant to the Reverend John Moorhead of Boston. It was published in her volume of 1773.

READER'S JOURNAL

Think about a painting or other work of art that you find particularly moving or interesting. If you cannot think of one, look through this textbook until you find one that you like. In your journal, freewrite about the work, explaining what attracts you to it.

LANGUAGE SKILLS

Read the Language Arts Survey, 2.18, "Verbals: Infinitives." Then look for examples of infinitives as you read the selection.

"To S. M.,[1] a Young African Painter, on Seeing His Works"

PHILLIS WHEATLEY

To show the laboring bosom's deep intent,
And thought in living characters to paint,
When first thy pencil did those beauties give,
And breathing figures learnt from thee to live,
5 How did those prospects give my soul delight,
A new creation rushing on my sight?
Still, wond'rous youth! each noble path pursue,
On deathless glories fix thine <u>ardent</u> view:
Still may the painter's and the poet's fire
10 To aid thy pencil, and thy verse conspire!
And may the charms of each seraphic[2] theme
Conduct thy footsteps to immortal fame!
High to the blissful wonders of the skies
<u>Elate</u> thy soul, and raise thy wishful eyes.
15 Thrice[3] happy, when exalted to survey
That splendid city, crowned with endless day,

> What does the speaker hope for the subject of the poem?

---

1. **S. M.** Scipio Moorhead, servant to a Boston minister
2. **seraphic.** Angelic
3. **Thrice.** Triple (extremely)

WORDS FOR EVERYDAY USE:
ar • dent (ärd´ 'nt) adj., intensely enthusiastic or devoted
e • late (ē lāt´) vt., raise the spirits of

Whose twice six gates[4] on radiant hinges ring:
Celestial Salem[5] blooms in endless spring.

Calm and serene thy moments glide along,
20   And may the muse[6] inspire each future song!
Still, with the sweets of <u>contemplation</u> blest,
May peace with <u>balmy</u> wings your soul invest!
But when these shades of time are chased away,
And darkness ends in everlasting day,
25   On what seraphic pinions[7] shall we move,
And view the landscape in the realms above?
There shall thy tongue in heavenly murmurs flow,
And there my muse with heavenly <u>transport</u> glow:
No more to tell of Damon's[8] tender sighs,
30   Or rising radiance of Aurora's[9] eyes,
For nobler themes demand a nobler strain,
And purer language on the <u>ethereal</u> plain.
Cease, gentle muse! the solemn gloom of night
Now seals the fair creation from my sight. ■

What words are used to describe the artist's movements? Who inspires him?

What event does the speaker describe in the last lines of the poem? Why, in the last line, is she unable to see the creation?

---

4. **twice six gates.** Twelve gates to heaven
5. **Salem.** Jerusalem
6. **muse.** Any of the nine goddesses who preside over literature and the arts in Greek mythology

7. **pinions.** Wings
8. **Damon.** Mythical hero and loyal friend (to Pythias)
9. **Aurora.** Mythical goddess of dawn

Responding to the Selection

Wheatley advises the young painter as follows: "High to the blissful wonders of the skies/Elate thy soul, and raise thy wishful eyes." What conditions at the time of the writing of this poem would have made it difficult for an African-American artist or writer to have such a positive vision? What makes Wheatley's optimism and positive spirit so remarkable?

WORDS FOR EVERYDAY USE:

con • tem • pla • tion (kän´ təm plā´ shən) *n.*, thoughtful inspection, study, or meditation
balm • y (bäm´ ē) *adj.*, soothing, mild, or pleasant

trans • port (trans´ pôrt) *n.*, strong emotion; rapture
e • the • re • al (ē thir´ ē əl) *adj.*, not earthly; heavenly; celestial

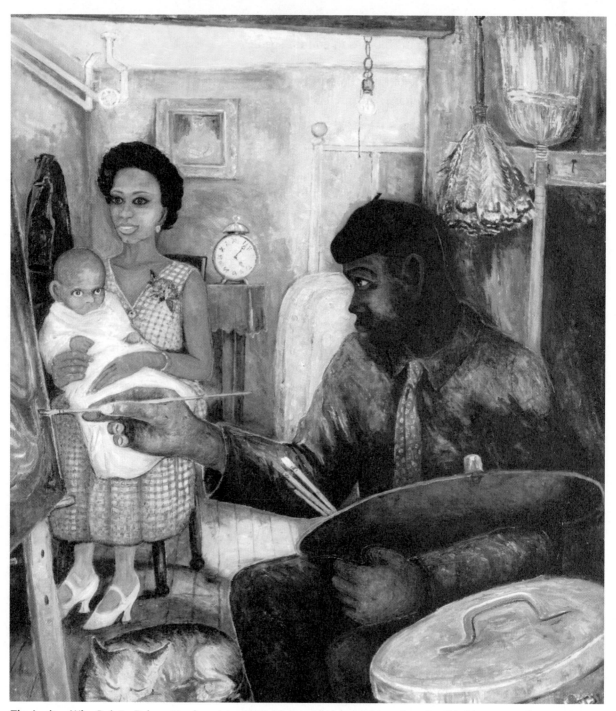

The Janitor Who Paints. *Palmer Hayden, circa 1937. National Museum of American Art, Washington, DC/Art Resource*

Reviewing the Selection

1. What is the speaker's emotional response to the painter's work?

2. What advice does the speaker give the painter for selecting subjects and themes for his paintings?

3. What does the speaker hope will aid the painter in the creation of his work?

4. The speaker refers to the time of death as "when these shades of time are chased away,/And darkness ends in everlasting day." What does the speaker picture as happening to the artist after death?

5. What does the speaker mean when she says that the painter creates "breathing figures"? What does she mean by "A new creation"?

6. Why might the speaker suggest that the painter try different themes for his work? What does she suggest may be his reward for painting "each seraphic theme"?

7. What might the speaker mean by the phrase: "Still may the painter's and the poet's fire/To aid thy pencil, and thy verse conspire"?

8. How should the poet's and the painter's work change after they die and "view the landscape in the realms above"?

9. The speaker wishes the painter peace and the blessing of "sweets of contemplation." Why is time for contemplation necessary for artists such as painters and writers?

10. Why do you think Wheatley responded to the young man's painting with a poem instead of a letter of encouragement? What message could a poem send that a letter might not communicate?

Understanding Literature (Questions for Discussion)

1. **Heroic Couplet.** A **heroic couplet** is a pair of rhyming iambic pentameter lines. An iambic foot contains one weakly stressed syllable followed by a strongly stressed syllable. A pentameter line has five iambic feet. Which pairs of lines in this poem are heroic couplets?

2. **Allusion.** An **allusion** is a rhetorical technique in which reference is made to a person, event, object, or work from history or literature. Identify two or three allusions in this poem, and explain their meanings.

Responding in Writing

1. **Abstract.** An **abstract** is a brief account of the main ideas or arguments presented in a work. Write an abstract of the Wheatley poem or of another selection in this unit.
2. **Captions.** Collect prints or other copies of about six pieces of art or fine photography by African Americans. Write an imaginative caption for each, to explain its origins or to highlight its features.

Language Lab

Common and Proper Nouns. Read the Language Arts Survey, 2.3, "Common and Proper Nouns." Then make two lists of the nouns in the sentences below, one headed *Common Nouns* and the other *Proper Nouns.*

1. The origins of Phillis Wheatley are still a mystery.
2. Records of the time suggest that the ship that brought her to North America came from an area called Senegambia, near the west coast of Africa.
3. Today the nations of Senegal and Gambia occupy much of that territory.
4. That Phillis was given an education was extraordinary, even for a white woman of the time.
5. Wheatley became a firm advocate of freedom for the colonies, a fact that may be related to her own lack of personal freedom.

Applied English/Tech Prep Skills

Writing Memoranda. Read the Language Arts Survey, 5.6, "Writing Memoranda." Imagine that you are the president of a Fortune 500 company called American Amalgamated Motors. Your board of directors has approved a donation of $1,250,000 to the Emerson Institute of American Arts and Crafts to begin a collection of works by famous African-American artists, to be called the "Scipio Moorhead Collection" in honor of the artist to whom Wheatley's poem is addressed. Write a memo to Ms. Paula Palette, director of the museum, announcing your company's decision. Follow proper memo form.

PROJECT

Multimedia Show. Work with a group to develop a multimedia show about elements of modern American culture that are products of African or African-American artists and performers. Your show can include live demonstrations, as of dance or poetry; audiotapes, as of jazz or popular music; videotapes, as of political speeches or dramatic performances; and such visual media as sculpture, painting, and photography. Your show must include commentary and transitional material that holds the elements together.

Declaration of Independence
by Thomas Jefferson

ABOUT THE AUTHOR

Thomas Jefferson (1743–1826) was a man of many talents and achievements. Born in 1743 in Albemarle County, Virginia, Jefferson attended William and Mary College in Williamsburg, studied law, and was admitted to the bar. He kept up his studies, mastering law, political philosophy, architecture, and a number of foreign languages.

Jefferson's political career began after college when he was elected to the Virginia House of Burgesses. In 1774, he wrote a pamphlet denying British authority over America. In 1775, he was sent as a delegate to the Second Continental Congress, where he drafted, with input from Benjamin Franklin, John Adams, and others, the Declaration of Independence. Jefferson then returned to the Virginia legislature, and drafted a statute guaranteeing religious freedom. In 1779, he became governor of Virginia. In 1789, he became the first secretary of state under the new Constitution. During that time, he became embroiled in a controversy with Alexander Hamilton that resulted in the formation of the American two-party political system.

In 1779, Jefferson became vice president under John Adams. Then, in 1800, he was elected president. As president, he more than doubled the size of the country through the Louisiana Purchase, an acquisition of North American lands owned by France. After his retirement from public life, Jefferson devoted himself to planning the buildings and curriculum of the new University of Virginia, believing that education was key to the survival of democratic ideals. The Library of Congress was founded with some ten thousand volumes from Jefferson's private library. He died a few hours before John Adams on the fourth of July, fifty years after the signing of the Declaration of Independence.

ABOUT THE SELECTION

In June of 1776, Richard Lee, a delegate from Virginia, brought before the Continental Congress two resolutions, one calling for separation from Great Britain and the other calling for formation of a new government. After much debate, Congress decided to accept the resolutions and set up a committee to draft a declaration of independence. Jefferson drafted the document, adding a strong statement against slavery that was deleted from the version adopted on July 4, 1776. The **Declaration of Independence** is unique in its insistence on inalienable rights, rights that cannot be taken away from the people, and on the notion that government derives its legitimacy from the consent of the governed. The Declaration of Independence is divided into three parts: the basic argument of the Declaration, a list of grievances against Great Britain, and the formal declaration of independence and nationhood. The original document is on display at the National Archives in Washington, DC.

READER'S JOURNAL

Do you believe that people have basic rights that should not be taken away from them by any government? If so, what do you think that these rights are? Write about these questions in your journal.

STUDY AND RESEARCH SKILLS

Read the Language Arts Survey, 4.18, "Reading Actively," and 4.10, "Analyzing." Then, as you read the Declaration of Independence, analyze it, making notes of key points, or main ideas, in each of its three major sections.

Declaration of Independence

THOMAS JEFFERSON

IN CONGRESS, JULY 4, 1776

What is the reason for the drafting of the Declaration as stated in its opening paragraph?

When in the course of human events, it becomes necessary for one people to dissolve the political bands which have connected them with another, and to assume, among the powers of the earth, the separate and equal station to which the laws of nature and of nature's God entitle them, a decent respect to the opinions of mankind requires that they should declare the causes which impel them to the separation.

We hold these truths to be self-evident: —that all men are created equal; that they are endowed by their Creator with certain <u>unalienable</u> rights; that among these are life, liberty, and the pursuit of happiness. That, to secure these rights, governments are instituted among men, deriving their just powers from the consent of the governed; that, whenever any form of government becomes destructive of these ends, it is the right of the people to alter or to abolish it, and to institute a new government, laying its foundation on such principles, and organizing its powers in such form, as to them shall seem most likely to effect their safety and happiness. Prudence, indeed, will dictate that governments long established should not be changed for light and <u>transient</u> causes; and, accordingly, all experience hath shown that mankind are more disposed to suffer, while evils are sufferable, than to right themselves by abolishing the forms to which they are accustomed. But, when a long train of abuses and <u>usurpations</u>, pursuing invariably the same object, <u>evinces</u> a design to reduce them under absolute despotism,[1] it is their right, it is their duty, to throw off such government,

---

1. **despotism.** Government by a tyrant

WORDS FOR EVERYDAY USE:

un • al • ien • a • ble (un āl´ yən ə bəl) *adj.,* that which may not be taken away

tran • si • ent (tran´ sē ənt) *adj.,* not permanent; temporary

u • sur • pa • tion (yōō zər pā´ shən) *n.,* unlawful or violent taking of power

e • vince (ē vins´) *vt.,* show plainly

IN CONGRESS, JULY 4, 1776.

A DECLARATION

BY THE REPRESENTATIVES OF THE

UNITED STATES OF AMERICA,

IN GENERAL CONGRESS ASSEMBLED.

and to provide new guards for their future security. Such has been the patient <u>sufferance</u> of these colonies; and such is now the necessity that constrains them to alter their former systems of government. The history of the present King of Great Britain[2] is a history of repeated injuries and usurpations, all having, in direct object, the establishment of an absolute tyranny over these States. To prove this, let facts be submitted to a candid world.

He has refused his <u>assent</u> to laws the most wholesome and necessary for the public good.

He has forbidden his Governors to pass laws of immediate and pressing impor-tance, unless suspended in their operation till his assent should be obtained; and when so suspended, he has utterly neglected to attend to them.

He has refused to pass other laws for the accommodation of large districts of people, unless these people would relinquish the right of representation in the legisla-ture—a right <u>inestimable</u> to them, and formidable to tyrants only.

He has called together legislative bodies at places unusual, uncomfortable, and dis-tant from the depository of their public

What had the king asked the people to relinquish? What did this right mean to them? Why is such a right formidable to tyrants?

---

2. **present King of Great Britain.** King George III (1760–1820)

WORDS FOR EVERYDAY USE:

suf • fer • ance (suf´ ər əns) *n.,* power to tolerate pain
as • sent (ə sent´) *n.,* agreement

in • es • ti • ma • ble (in es´ tə mə bəl) *adj.,* that which cannot be measured

records, for the sole purpose of fatiguing them into <u>compliance</u> with his measure.

He has dissolved representative houses repeatedly, for opposing, with manly firmness, his invasions on the rights of the people.

What has the king dissolved? What effect has this had on the people?

He has refused, for a long time after such dissolutions, to cause others to be elected; whereby the legislative powers, incapable of annihilation, have returned to the people at large for their exercise; the State remaining, in the meantime, exposed to all dangers of invasion from without, and <u>convulsions</u> within.

He has endeavored to prevent the population of these States; for that purpose obstructing the laws for the <u>naturalization</u> of foreigners; refusing to pass others to encourage their migration hither, and raising the conditions of new appropriations of lands.

He has obstructed the administration of justice, by refusing his assent to laws for establishing judiciary powers.

He has made judges dependent on his will alone for the <u>tenure</u> of their offices, and the amount and payment of their salaries.

He has erected a multitude of new offices, and sent hither swarms of officers to harass our people and eat out their substance.

What has the king declared? What destructive things has he done?

He has kept among us in times of peace, standing armies, without the consent of our legislatures.

He has affected to render the military independent of, and superior to, the civil power.

He has combined with others to subject us to a jurisdiction foreign to our constitutions, and unacknowledged by our laws; giving his assent to their acts of pretended legislation:

For quartering large bodies of armed troops among us;

For protecting them, by a mock trial, from punishment for any murders which they should commit on the inhabitants of these States;

For cutting off our trade with all parts of the world;

For imposing taxes on us without our consent;

For depriving us, in many cases, of the benefits of trial by jury;

For transporting us beyond the seas, to be tried for pretended offences;

For abolishing the free system of English laws in a neighboring province, establishing there an arbitrary government, and enlarging its boundaries, so as to render it at once an example and fit instrument for introducing the same absolute rule into these colonies;

For taking away our charters, abolishing our most valuable laws, and altering, fundamentally, the forms of our governments;

For suspending our own legislatures, and declaring themselves invested with power to legislate for us in all cases whatsoever.

He has <u>abdicated</u> government here, by declaring us out of his protection, and waging war against us.

He has plundered our seas, ravaged our coasts, burnt our towns, and destroyed the lives of our people.

He is at this time transporting large armies of foreign mercenaries[3] to complete the works of death, desolation, and tyranny,

---

3. **mercenaries.** Hired soldiers

WORDS FOR EVERYDAY USE:

com • pli • ance (kəm plī´əns) *n.*, act of giving in to wishes or demands

con • vul • sion (kən vul´shən) *n.*, sudden, violent disturbance

nat • u • ral • i • za • tion (nach´ər əl iz´ā shən) *n.*, bestowal of the rights of citizenship

ten • ure (ten´yər) *n.*, right to hold a position permanently

ab • di • cate (ab´ di kāt´) *vt.*, give up a right or a responsibility

already begun with circumstances of cruelty and perfidy[4] scarcely paralleled in the most barbarous ages, and totally unworthy the head of a civilized nation.

He has constrained our fellow-citizens, taken captive on the high seas, to bear arms against their country, to become the executioners of their friends and brethren, or to fall themselves by their hands.

He has excited domestic insurrection amongst us, and has endeavored to bring on the inhabitants of our frontiers the merciless Indian savages, whose known rule of warfare is an undistinguished destruction of all ages, sexes, and conditions.

In every state of these oppressions we have petitioned for redress, in the most humble terms; our repeated petitions have been answered only by repeated injury. A prince whose character is thus marked by every act which may define a tyrant is unfit to be the ruler of a free people.

Nor have we been wanting in our attentions to our British brethren. We have warned them, from time to time, of attempts by their legislature to extend an unwarrantable jurisdiction over us. We have reminded them of the circumstances of our emigration and settlement here. We have appealed to their native justice and magnanimity; and we have conjured them, by the ties of our common kindred, to disavow these usurpations, which would inevitably interrupt our connections and correspondence. They, too, have been deaf to the voice of justice and of consanguinity.[5] We must, therefore, acquiesce in the necessity which denounces our separation; and hold them, as we hold the rest of mankind, enemies in war, in peace friends.

WE, THEREFORE, THE REPRESENTATIVES OF THE UNITED STATES OF AMERICA, in General Congress assembled, appealing to the Supreme Judge of the world for the rectitude of our intentions, do, in the name and by the authority of the good people of these colonies, solemnly publish and declare, That these United Colonies are, and of right ought to be, FREE AND INDEPENDENT STATES; that they are absolved from all allegiance to the British crown, and that all political connection between them and the state of Great Britain is, and ought to be, totally dissolved; and that, as free and independent states, they have full power to levy war, conclude peace, contract alliances, establish commerce, and to do all other acts and things which independent states may of right do. And, for the support of this declaration, with a firm reliance on the protection of Divine Providence, we mutually pledge to each other our lives, our fortunes, and our sacred honor. ∎

What powers do the united colonies have?

---

4. **perfidy.** Betrayal of trust
5. **consanguinity.** Close connection; relatedness

WORDS FOR EVERYDAY USE:

in • sur • rec • tion (in´sə rek´shən) n., uprising
re • dress (rē´dres´) n., compensation
mag • na • nim • i • ty (mag´nə nim´ə tē) n., state of being above pettiness
ac • qui • esce (ak´wē es´) vi., agree without protest
rec • ti • tude (rek´tə tood´) n., correctness

Responding to the Selection

What do you think Jefferson meant when he wrote that "all men are created equal"? when he wrote of the rights to "life, liberty, and the pursuit of happiness"? Discuss these questions with your classmates.

Reviewing the Selection

RECALLING

1. In what state, according to Jefferson, are all men created?

2. What is an "unalienable" right? What rights does Jefferson list as being unalienable?

3. What specific grievances did the colonists have against the British monarch?

4. What does the last paragraph of the selection "solemnly publish and declare"?

INTERPRETING

5. In what sense are all people "equal"? What is the difference between equality and identity?

6. According to the Declaration, why are governments "instituted among" people? What right does a people have when its government "becomes destructive" of the ends of securing the rights to "life, liberty, and the pursuit of happiness"?

7. Which of the offenses attributed to the British crown do you find most offensive? Why?

8. What could the colonies do on their own after declaring independence that they could not do on their own before making that declaration?

SYNTHESIZING

9. The eighteenth-century English philosopher John Locke held that people are born with "natural rights" that cannot be taken from them. The eighteenth-century French philosopher Jean-Jacques Rousseau believed that government is a social contract entered into by the people for their mutual protection and well-being. In what ways are these ideas reflected in the Declaration of Independence?

10. The Declaration ends with a personal statement made by its signers: "[F]or the support of this declaration, . . . we mutually pledge to each other our lives, our fortunes, and our sacred honor." What risks were the signers of the Declaration taking upon themselves? In what way does their willingness to take on this risk show their commitment to liberty?

Understanding Literature (Questions for Discussion)

1. **Alliteration. Alliteration** is the repetition of initial consonant sounds. In addition to his many other talents, Thomas Jefferson was known as a great prose stylist. Reread the sentence that begins with the words "We hold these truths to be self-evident." What makes this sentence so memorable? What examples of alliteration can you find in the sentence?

2. **Parallelism. Parallelism** is a rhetorical technique in which a writer emphasizes the equal value or weight of two or more ideas by expressing them in the same grammatical form. How does Jefferson use parallelism in his presentation of the grievances against King George?

Responding in Writing

Credo. Thomas Jefferson was a great defender of individual liberty, of the rights of people to speak their minds freely and openly, to express their beliefs without fear. Take advantage of this freedom to write your own credo, or statement of belief, expressing your own most strongly held opinions and values. Follow Jefferson's model and use parallelism to express your beliefs effectively. Refer to the Language Arts Survey, 2.57, "Achieving Parallelism."

PROJECT

Analyzing the Bill of Rights. The first ten amendments to the Constitution of the United States, ratified in 1791 and known collectively as the Bill of Rights, are printed on the next page. Working with other students in a small group, paraphrase each of these amendments (that is, put them into your own words). Then discuss situations to which the amendments, which have the force of law, might be applied.

The Bill of Rights

Amendment 1

Congress shall make no law respecting an establishment of religion, or prohibiting the free exercise thereof; or abridging the freedom of speech, or of the press; or the right of the people peaceably to assemble, and to petition the Government for a redress of grievances.

Amendment 2

A well-regulated militia, being necessary to the security of a free State, the right of the people to keep and bear arms shall not be infringed.

Amendment 3

No soldier shall, in time of peace, be quartered in any house, without the consent of the owner, nor in time of war, but in a manner to be prescribed by law.

Amendment 4

The right of the people to be secure in their persons, houses, papers, and effects, against unreasonable searches and seizures, shall not be violated, and no warrants shall issue, but upon probable cause, supported by oath or affirmation, and particularly describing the place to be searched, and the persons or things to be seized.

Amendment 5

No person shall be held to answer for a capital, or otherwise infamous crime, unless on a presentment or indictment of a Grand Jury, except in cases arising in the land or naval forces, or in the militia, when in actual service in time of war or public danger; nor shall any person be subject for the same offense to be twice put in jeopardy of life or limb; nor shall be compelled in any criminal case to be a witness against himself, nor be deprived of life, liberty, or property, without due process of law; nor shall private property be taken for public use without just compensation.

Amendment 6

In all criminal prosecutions, the accused shall enjoy the right to a speedy and public trial, by an impartial jury of the State and district wherein the crime shall have been committed, which district shall have been previously ascertained by law, and to be informed of the nature and cause of the accusation; to be confronted with the witnesses against him; to have compulsory process for obtaining witnesses in his favor, and to have the assistance of counsel for his defense.

Amendment 7

In suits at common law, where the value in controversy shall exceed twenty dollars, the right of trial by jury shall be preserved, and no fact tried by a jury shall be otherwise reexamined in any court of the United States, than according to the rules of the common law.

Amendment 8

Excessive bail shall not be required, nor excessive fines imposed, nor cruel and unusual punishments inflicted.

Amendment 9

The enumeration in the Constitution, of certain rights, shall not be construed to deny or disparage others retained by the people.

Amendment 10

The powers not delegated to the United States by the Constitution, nor prohibited by it to the States, are reserved to the States respectively, or to the people.

Letter to John Adams, May 7, 1776
by Abigail Adams

ABOUT THE AUTHOR

Abigail Adams (1744–1818) was born in Weymouth, Massachusetts, the daughter of a minister. At the age of twenty, she married John Adams, a Boston lawyer who played important roles in the founding and governing of the United States. An ardent supporter of the American Revolution, Adams began a remarkable correspondence with her husband when, in 1774, he became a delegate to the First Continental Congress (a federal parliamentary body established by the British colonies in America). From 1774 to 1783 (the year in which a peace treaty was signed with England), John Adams was often away from home, involved in work that included the drafting of the Declaration of Independence, the conduct of the American Revolution and the formation of the new nation. During this time, Adams kept up a lively, fascinating correspondence with him. This correspondence offers many insights into the revolution and into daily life during the period. In her letters, Adams proved to be one of the first American champions of women's rights. She was particularly interested in expanding educational opportunities for women, which at that time were few. Adams was also an ardent opponent of slavery. After the American Revolution, John Adams served as a diplomat in Europe, and she traveled with him, living at various times in Paris, The Hague, and London. John Adams served as the first vice president of the new nation and then as its second president, and during this period, Adams divided her time between the family residence in Massachusetts and the temporary capital in Philadelphia. In 1800, Adams became the first First Lady to live in the new White House in Washington, DC. Her son John Quincy Adams became the sixth president of the United States.

ABOUT THE SELECTION

Abigail Adams wrote the following letter to her husband, John, then a delegate to the First Continental Congress. The letter was written shortly before the drafting of the Declaration of Independence, at a time when members of the Congress were debating whether to declare the colonies' independence from Britain.

Letter to John Adams, May 7, 1776

ABIGAIL ADAMS

Braintree[1]

How many are the solitary hours I spend, <u>ruminating</u> upon the past and anticipating the future whilst you, overwhelmed with the cares of state, have but few moments you can devote to any individual. All domestic pleasures and enjoyments are absorbed in the great and important duty you owe your country "for our country is, as it were, a secondary god and the first and greatest parent. It is to be preferred to parents, wives, children, friends and all things; the gods only excepted. For if our country perishes, it is as impossible to save an individual as to preserve one of the fingers of a mortified hand." Thus do I suppress every wish and silence every murmur, acquiescing in a painful separation from the companion of my youth and the friend of my heart.

I believe it is near ten days since I wrote you a line. I have not felt in a humor to entertain you. If I had taken up my pen, perhaps some unbecoming invective might have fallen from it; the eyes of our rulers have been closed and a lethargy has seized almost every member. I fear a fatal security has taken possession of them. Whilst the building is in flame, they tremble at the expense of water to quench it. In short, two months have elapsed since the evacuation of Boston and very little has been done in that time to secure it or the harbor from future invasion until the people are all in a flame, and no one among us that I have heard of even mentions expense. They think universally that there has been an amazing neglect somewhere. Many have turned out as volunteers to work upon

Why must the good of the country come before the needs of individuals?

---

1. **Braintree.** Town south of Boston

WORDS FOR EVERYDAY USE:

ru • mi • nate (roo͞′mə nāt′) *vt.,* turn over in one's mind

Nodles Island, and many more would go upon Nantasket if it was once set on foot. "It is a maxim of state that power and liberty are like heat and moisture; where they are well mixed everything prospers; where they are single, they are destructive."

A government of more stability is much wanted in this colony, and they are ready to receive it from the hands of the Congress, and since I have begun with maxims of state, I will add another: A people may let a king fall, yet still remain a people, but if a king lets his people slip from him, he is no longer a king. And as this is most certainly our case, why not proclaim to the world in decisive terms your own importance?

Shall we not be despised by foreign powers for hesitating so long at a word?

I cannot say that I think you very generous to the ladies, for whilst you are proclaiming peace and good will to men, emancipating all nations, you insist upon retaining an absolute power over wives. But you must remember that arbitrary power is like most other things which are very hard, very liable to be broken—and notwithstanding all your wise laws and maxims, we have it in our power not only to free ourselves but to subdue our masters, and without violence throw both your natural and legal authority at our feet—

Charm by accepting, by submitting sway
Yet have our humor most when we obey.

I thank you for several letters which I have received since I wrote last. They alleviate a tedious absence, and I long earnestly for a Saturday evening and experience a similar pleasure to that which I used to find in the return of my friend

John Adams. Gilbert Stuart, 1826. National Museum of American Art, Washington DC/Art Resource, NY

upon that day after a week's absence. The idea of a year dissolves all my philosophy.

Our little ones, whom you so often recommend to my care and instruction, shall not be deficient in virtue or probity[2] if the precepts of a mother have their desired effect, but they would be doubly enforced could they be indulged with the example of a father constantly before them; I often point them to their sire

Engaged in a corrupted state
Wrestling with vice and faction. ■

2. **probity.** Integrity

If people lose faith in their leader, what happens?

Responding to the Selection

In her letter, Abigail Adams shows a sense of high moral purpose. Discuss with your classmates the issues that Adams raises: the relative importance of personal and political duties, the need for stable government, the duties owed by a king to his subjects, equality of political rights for women, and the moral education of children. What are Adams's views on these issues? What are your own?

Reviewing the Selection

RECALLING

1. According to the opening of the letter, how does Adams spend her time? With what duties is her husband "overwhelmed"?

2. According to Adams, whose "eyes . . . have been closed"? Who is suffering from a "fatal security"?

3. According to Adams, when is a king no longer a king?

4. To whom, according to Adams, have her husband and the other delegates proclaimed "peace and good will"? To whom have they failed to give just consideration?

INTERPRETING

5. Does Adams resent her husband's absence? Why, or why not?

6. What metaphor does Adams use in the second paragraph of her letter to describe the reluctance of some members of the Congress to take the necessary actions to create an army and to petition for independence?

7. For centuries, most British subjects believed that kings were divinely appointed, that their will was supreme and beyond any earthly challenge. Does Adams subscribe to such a view? Under what circumstances, according to Adams, are people justified in saying that their king is no longer their king?

8. What might Adams have wanted her husband and the other delegates to do with regard to women?

9. The United States was the first country in the world founded on the principle that government derives its rights from "the consent of the governed" and is justified in exercising those rights only as long as the governed continue in their consent. Why might this have seemed like an extremely radical idea at the time? What passages in Adams's letter show that she believes government not consented to by the governed to be illegitimate?

10. The seventeenth-century philosopher Thomas Hobbes argued that life in the "state of nature" is "solitary, poor, nasty, brutish, and short" and that a strong central authority, a sovereign or king, is necessary to maintain order and ensure self-preservation. In what respect would Adams have agreed with Hobbes? In what respect would she have disagreed?

Understanding Literature (Questions for Discussion)

Aim. A writer's **aim** is the primary purpose that his or her work is meant to accomplish. Reread paragraph 5 of Adams's letter. What might have been her purpose for including this paragraph in the letter? What might she have hoped that her husband and the other delegates might do?

Thinking Skills

Paraphrase. Read the Language Arts Survey, 4.30, "Paraphrasing and Summarizing." Then paraphrase, or put into your own words, paragraph 5 of Adams's letter.

Responding in Writing

Letter. Choose some political issue of interest to you and write a letter to a political figure, such as your town's mayor, your congressperson, or one of your senators, regarding that issue. Refer to the Language Arts Survey, 5.3, "The Form of a Business Letter," and write your letter in proper business letter form. (Note: A reference librarian in your community will be able to help you to identify the names and titles of political figures at the local, state, and national levels.)

from *Letters from an American Farmer*
by J. Hector St. Jean de Crèvecoeur

I wish I could be acquainted with the feelings and thoughts which must agitate the heart and present themselves to the mind of an enlightened[1] Englishman, when he first lands on this continent. He must greatly rejoice that he lived at a time to see this fair country discovered and settled; he must necessarily feel a share of national pride, when he views the chain of settlements which embellishes these extended shores. When he says to himself, this is the work of my countrymen, who, when convulsed by factions,[2] afflicted by a variety of miseries and wants, restless and impatient, took refuge here. They brought along with them their national genius, to which they principally owe what liberty they enjoy, and what substance they possess. Here he sees the industry of his native country displayed in a new manner, and traces in their works the embryos of all the arts, sciences, and ingenuity which flourish in Europe. Here he beholds fair cities, substantial villages, extensive fields, an immense country filled with decent houses, good roads, orchards, meadows, and bridges, where an hundred years ago all was wild, woody, and uncultivated! What a train of pleasing ideas this fair spectacle must suggest; it is a prospect which must inspire a good citizen with the most heartfelt pleasure. The difficulty consists in the manner of viewing so extensive a scene. He is arrived on a new continent; a modern society offers itself to his contemplation, different from what he had hitherto seen. It is not composed, as in Europe, of great lords who possess everything, and of a herd of people who have nothing. Here are no aristocratical families, no courts, no kings, no bishops, no ecclesiastical dominion,[3] no invisible power giving to a few a very visible one; no great manufacturers employing thousands, no great refinements of luxury. The rich and the poor are not so far removed from each other as they are in Europe. Some few towns excepted, we are all tillers of the earth, from Nova Scotia to West Florida. We are a people of cultivators, scattered over an immense territory, communicating with each other by means of good roads and navigable rivers, united by the silken bands of mild government, all respecting the laws, without dreading their power, because they are equitable. We are all animated with the spirit of an industry which is unfettered and unrestrained, because each person works for himself. If he travels through our rural districts he views not the hostile castle, and the haughty mansion, contrasted with the clay-built hut and miserable cabin, where cattle and men help to keep each other warm, and dwell in meanness, smoke, and indigence.[4] A pleasing uniformity of decent competence appears throughout our habitations. The meanest of our log-houses is a dry and comfortable habitation. Lawyer or merchant are the fairest titles our towns afford; that of a farmer is the only appellation of the rural inhabitants of our country. It must take some time ere he can reconcile himself to our dictionary, which is but short in words of dignity, and names of honor. There, on a Sunday, he sees a congregation of respectable farmers and their wives, all clad in neat homespun, well mounted, or riding in their own humble wagons. There is not among them an esquire, saving the unlettered[5] magistrate. There he sees a parson as simple as his flock, a farmer who does not riot on the labor of others. We have no princes, for whom we toil, starve, and bleed; we are the most perfect society now existing in the world. Here man is free as he ought to be; nor is this pleasing equality so transitory as many others are. Many ages will not see the shores of our great lakes replenished with inland nations, nor the unknown bounds of North America entirely peopled. Who can tell how far it extends? Who can tell the millions of men whom it will feed and contain? for no European foot has as yet traveled half the extent of this mighty continent!

The next wish of this traveler will be to know whence[6] came all these people? They are a mixture of English, Scotch, Irish, French, Dutch, Germans and Swedes. From this promiscuous breed, that race now called Americans have arisen. The eastern provinces must indeed be excepted,[7] as being the unmixed descendants of Englishmen. I have heard many wish that they had been more intermixed also: for my part, I am no wisher, and think it much better as it has happened. They exhibit a most conspicuous figure in this great and variegated picture; they too enter for a great share in the pleasing perspective displayed in these thirteen provinces.[8] I know it is fashionable to reflect on them, but respect them for what they have done; for the accuracy and wisdom with which they have settled their territory; for the decency of their manners; for their early love of letters; their ancient college,[9] the first in this hemisphere; for their industry, which to me who am but a farmer is the criterion of everything. There never was a people, situated as they are, who with so ungrateful a soil have done more in so short a time.

---

1. **enlightened.** Knowledgeable; full of understanding
2. **convulsed by factions.** Upset by disagreement among groups of citizens
3. **ecclesiastical dominion.** Religious authority over a state
4. **indigence.** Poverty
5. **unlettered.** Uneducated

6. **whence.** From where
7. **excepted.** Excluded
8. **provinces.** Colonies
9. **college.** Harvard College (founded in 1636) in Cambridge, Massachusetts

"To the Right Honorable William, Earl of Dartmouth"
by Phillis Wheatley

Hail, happy day, when, smiling like the morn,
Fair *Freedom* rose *New-England* to adorn:
The northern clime[1] beneath her genial[2] ray,
Dartmouth, congratulates thy blissful sway:
5   Elate with hope her race no longer mourns,
Each soul expands, each grateful bosom burns,
While in thine hand with pleasure we behold
The silken reins, and *Freedom's* charms unfold.
Long lost to realms beneath the northern skies
10 She shines supreme, while hated *faction* dies:
Soon as appear'd the *Goddess* long desir'd;
Sick at the view, she languish'd and expir'd;[3]
Thus from the splendors of the morning light
The owl in sadness seeks the caves of night.

15   No more, *America*, in mournful strain
Of wrongs, and grievance unredress'd complain,
No longer shalt thou dread the iron chain,
Which wanton *Tyranny* with lawless hand
Had made, and with it meant t' enslave the land.

20   Should you, my lord, while you peruse my song,
Wonder from whence my love of *Freedom* sprung,
Whence flow these wishes for the common good,
By feeling hearts alone best understood,
I, young in life, by seeming cruel fate
25 Was snatch'd from *Afric's* fancy'd happy seat:
What pangs excruciating must molest,
What sorrows labor in my parent's breast?
Steel'd was that soul and by no misery mov'd
That from a father seiz'd his babe belov'd:
30 Such, such my case. And can I then but pray
Others may never feel tyrannic sway?

        For favors past, great Sir, our thanks are due,
And thee we ask thy favors to renew,
Since in thy pow'r, as in thy will before,
35 To sooth the griefs, which thou did'st once deplore.
May heav'nly grace the sacred sanction give
To all thy works, and thou forever live
Not only on the wings of fleeting *Fame*,
Though praise immortal crowns the patriot's name,
40 But to conduct to heav'ns refulgent fane,[4]
May fiery coursers sweep th' ethereal plain,

And bear thee upwards to that blest abode,
Where, like the prophet, thou shalt find thy God.

from *Common Sense*
by Thomas Paine

From III. Thoughts on the Present State of American Affairs

In the following pages I offer nothing more than simple facts, plain arguments, and common sense: and have no other preliminaries to settle with the reader, than that he will divest himself of prejudice and prepossession, and suffer his reason and his feelings to determine for themselves: that he will put on, or rather that he will not put off, the true character of a man, and generously enlarge his views beyond the present day.

Volumes have been written on the subject of the struggle between England and America. Men of all ranks have embarked in the controversy, from different motives, and with various designs; but all have been ineffectual, and the period of debate is closed. Arms as the last resource decide the contest; the appeal was the choice of the King, and the continent has accepted the challenge.

◆   ◆   ◆

A government of our own is our natural right: and when a man seriously reflects on the precariousness of human affairs, he will become convinced that it is infinitely wiser and safer to form a constitution of our own in a cool deliberate manner, while we have it in our power, than to trust such an interesting event to time and chance. If we omit it now, some Massanello[5] may hereafter arise, who, laying hold of popular disquietudes, may collect together the desperate and the discontented, and by assuming to themselves the powers of government, finally sweep away the liberties of the continent like a deluge. Should the government of America return again into the hands of Britain, the tottering situation of things will be a temptation for some desperate adventurer to try his fortune; and in such a case, what relief can Britain give? Ere she could hear the news, the fatal business might be done; and ourselves suffering like the wretched Britons under the oppression of the conqueror. Ye that oppose independence now, ye know not what ye do: ye are opening a door to eternal tyranny by keeping vacant the seat of government. There are thousands and tens of thousands, who would think it glorious to expel from the continent that barbarous and hellish power.

---

1. **clime.** Region
2. **genial.** Warm and friendly
5. **languish'd and expir'd.** Suffered and died
4. **refulgent fane.** Radiant, glowing temple or church

---

5. **Massanello.** Thomas Anello, or Massanello, a fisherman, became king for a day after inciting a revolt against the Spanish who were occupying his city of Naples.

UNIT REVIEW

The American Revolution

VOCABULARY FROM THE SELECTIONS

abdicate, 174
acquiesce, 175
admonish, 142
ardent, 166
assent, 173
avert, 154
balmy, 167
calamity, 161
civility, 147
compliance, 174
comport, 154
consolation, 160
consultation, 142
contemplation, 167
convulsion, 174
duration, 161

effectual, 155
elate, 166
ethereal, 167
evade, 143
evince, 172
formidable, 155
heartily, 148
hypocrisy, 161
impartiality, 147
impious, 160
induce, 162
indulgence, 142
inestimable, 155, 173
ingenious, 141
insidious, 154

insurrection, 175
inviolate, 155
magnanimity, 175
martial, 154
naturalization, 174
offensive, 162
oratory, 147
penitentially, 161
posterity, 147
prostrate, 155
rectitude, 175
redress, 175
reflection, 162
remonstrate, 155
repulse, 161
resolution, 161

ruminate, 180
solace, 154
sottish, 162
subjugation, 154
submission, 154
sufferance, 173
supinely, 155
temporal, 153
tenure, 174
transient, 172
transport, 167
unalienable, 172
usurpation, 172
venture, 143

LITERARY TERMS

aim, 183
alliteration, 177
allusion, 169
aphorism, 145
argumentation, 164

assonance, 164
autobiography, 145
chiasmus, 150
Enlightenment, 157
heroic couplet, 169

Neoclassicism, 150
parallelism, 157, 177
persona, 144

proverb, 145
rhetorical question, 156, 164
stereotype, 150
style, 144

SYNTHESIS: QUESTIONS FOR WRITING, RESEARCH, OR DISCUSSION

GENRE STUDIES

1. **Poetry.** Interestingly, Phillis Wheatley achieves with her poem what the subject of her poem achieves with his painting. In some ways her poem is a treatise on what an artist or poet can do. Discuss Wheatley's view of art and what an artist does.

THEMATIC STUDIES

2. **The Search for Freedom.** Examine the writings of Henry, Paine, and Jefferson. Their words were important tools in the American Revolution. Each makes a clear statement of case followed by a rallying cry. How does each define freedom? What price is it sometimes necessary to pay for freedom? Which expressions from their works would have had an emotional impact: Discuss their statements of situation, their concept of the nature of freedom, and the power of their language.

3. **Future Rebellions.** Even as most of America moved toward independence, some groups were overlooked. Examine Franklin's "Remarks Concerning the Natives of North America" and Adams's letter to her husband. What seeds of future conflict do you find? What appeals by the representatives of the two minorities are given? How would you characterize their presentations?

HISTORICAL/BIOGRAPHICAL STUDIES

4. **The Emerging Nation.** Economic factors play an important role in history and politics. What economic factors in the Mid-Atlantic and Southern colonies made independence feasible? What other growth factors strengthened the colonies?

5. **European Roots.** The Declaration of Independence can trace its roots to the European Age of Reason and Romanticism. Name three or four philosophers, writers, or scientists whose work in Europe had influence on the colonists. Briefly describe their work and explain how it is related to the thinking of the colonists.

LANGUAGE LAB   EDITING FOR ERRORS IN VERBS

During the editing or proofreading stage of the writing process, check your work to make sure that it is free of errors in the use of verbs. The following chart describes common errors in verb usage.

COMMON ERRORS IN VERB USAGE

Improper Shifts in Verb Tense. Throughout a passage, the tenses, or times, of verbs should be consistent.

IMPROPER SHIFT FROM
PAST TO PRESENT TENSE: As the young country grew, literacy increases dramatically.
CORRECTED SENTENCE: As the young country grew, literacy increased dramatically.

Misuse of Irregular Verb Forms. Many verbs, such as *swim, go, bring, bite, buy, fight,* and *see,* have irregular past tense forms. Make sure to use the proper verb form in the past tense. If you are unsure about the proper form, check a dictionary.

MISUSE OF IRREGULAR VERB FORM: Franklin had went to Philadelphia to start a printing shop.
CORRECTED SENTENCE: Franklin had gone to Philadelphia to start a printing shop.

Split Infinitives. An **infinitive** is a verb form made up of the word *to* and the base form of the verb, as in *to play* or *to suggest.* In formal speech and writing, try to avoid placing a modifier between *to* and the verb.

SPLIT INFINITIVE: Paine had to quickly flee to France.
CORRECTED SENTENCE: Paine had to flee quickly to France.

Agreement of Subject and Verb. A verb should agree in number with its subject. If the subject is a compound joined by *and,* the verb should be plural. If the subject is a compound joined by *or, either . . . or,* or *neither . . . nor,* the verb should agree with the nearer subject.

AGREEMENT ERROR: Phillis Wheatley and Nathaniel was seeking support for publishing Wheatley's poems.
CORRECTED SENTENCE: Phillis Wheatley and Nathaniel were seeking support for publishing Wheatley's poems.
AGREEMENT ERROR: Neither Thomas Jefferson nor the other delegates was sure how successful their efforts would be.
CORRECTED SENTENCE: Neither Thomas Jefferson nor the other delegates were sure how successful their efforts would be.

LANGUAGE ARTS SURVEY

For additional help, see the Language Arts Survey, 2.65.

LANGUAGE ARTS SURVEY

For additional help, see the Language Arts Survey, 2.66–2.67.

LANGUAGE ARTS SURVEY

For additional help, see the Language Arts Survey, 2.68.

LANGUAGE ARTS SURVEY

For additional help, see the Language Arts Survey, 2.70.

EXERCISE A Correcting Errors in Verb Usage

Rewrite the following sentences, correcting the errors in verb usage.

EXAMPLE: America was to quite rapidly become a nation of readers.
America was to become quite rapidly a nation of readers.

LANGUAGE ARTS SURVEY

For additional help, see the Language Arts Survey, 2.65–2.75.

1. Print became a vehicle to indelibly forge the nation's identity.
2. Franklin enters the printing trade and had his first essay published.
3. Neither Franklin nor his family members was above disputes.
4. People neither remembered nor like Paine in his later years.
5. Adams believed that to foolishly suffer from false security was unwise.

EXERCISE B Revising for Errors in Verb Usage

Rewrite the following paragraphs, correcting the errors in verb usage.

EXAMPLE: Phillis was buyed by John and Susannah Wheatley.
Phillis was bought by John and Susannah Wheatley.

A.   [1] Phillis Wheatley is born in West Africa and was captured as a child. [2] John and Susannah Wheatley provides the young slave girl with an education. [3] Wheatley had to abruptly return home from London when she heard of Susannah's death. [4] Wheatley meets George Washington after having dedicated a poem to him.

B.   [1] Neither Paine nor the other revolutionists is properly respected today for their courageous stand against tyranny. [2] They chose to decisively act for the good of the people despite great potential danger to themselves. [3] They could have been throwed into prison or executed for treason against Great Britain. [4] They fighted for freedom, knowing that by so doing they make their own lives precarious. [5] Americans and other citizens of democratic states around the world owes the revolutionists a great debt of thanks.

Watson and the Shark. John Singleton Copley. Courtesy of Museum of Fine Arts, Boston.
Gift of Mr. George von Lengerke Meyer

But oh! shipmates! on the starboard hand of every woe, there is a sure delight; and higher the top of that delight, than the bottom of the woe is deep.

—Herman Melville
Moby-Dick

THE NEW ENGLAND RENAISSANCE (1800–1860)

SOCIAL EXPANSION AND DEMOCRATIZATION

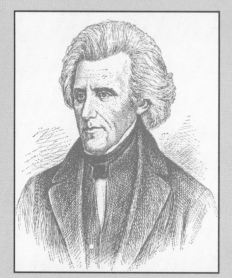

Andrew Jackson

After the **Louisiana Purchase** of 1803, which doubled the size of the country, the United States expanded rapidly across the continent. By 1836, the original thirteen colonies had grown into twenty-five states, stretching as far west as Arkansas. Two important technological developments helped to make that expansion seem less daunting. The invention of the telegraph by **Samuel Morse** in 1838 made it possible to communicate across distances instantly. The introduction of the steam locomotive by **John Stephens** in 1825 made possible the development of a railway system to connect towns and cities across the vast country. By the 1850s, the East Coast was connected to Chicago by rail and beyond that to the western side of the Mississippi. Still, while industrial transformation was well underway in various part of the East, the rest of the country remained predominantly agricultural, with many new farms springing up in the new territories.

The 1820s, culminating in the presidency of **Andrew Jackson**, saw an ideological shift to the "common people." In many states, voting rights, which the wealthy property owners who framed the Constitution had not granted, were extended to all free men. This shift was also felt in an emerging local and national interest in the public's cultural and educational life. In the mid-1830s, **Horace Mann** of Massachusetts undertook studies that would eventually lead to more systematic methods for public education throughout the North. Many states, beginning with Massachusetts, began to offer free public education at the primary and secondary levels; by 1850, free education was widespread in the North. In addition, the **Lyceum Movement** emerged. Begun in 1826, lyceums were institutions that offered educational and inspirational lectures, debates, and entertainments in large public halls. These presentations covered a wide range of subject matters, from philosophy to anthropology to the questions of slavery and women's rights. By 1860, there were more than 3000 lyceums in the United States serving as focal points for the transmission of ideas and culture.

ROMANTICISM AND TRANSCENDENTALISM

In Europe, the cultural and political era of the Enlightenment was superseded by **Romanticism.** Enlightenment thinkers of the eighteenth century had stressed objectivity and the power of reason to discover the laws of the universe in an objective, scientific, systematic fashion. To the young writers of the Romantic Period, the Enlightenment emphasis on reason undervalued private, subjective experience, including human emotions and the creative imagination. The English poet and essayist Samuel Taylor Coleridge, building on his reading of German writers such as Immanuel Kant, argued that there was a higher form of reason, to be distinguished from the ordinary "understanding" by which we know things in the physical world of sense perception. This higher reason was an intuitive capacity to grasp "metaphysical" truths in the physical world, to see in nature more than the mere operation of regu-

Horace Mann

larity and laws, and to see in life more than the practical advancement of social systems of organization. Nature was a repository of and stimulus for such intuitions, which might transform the individual by granting him or her access to higher truths than ordinary experience and social interaction could afford. British writers of the **Romantic Era,** including Coleridge; William Wordsworth; John Keats; Percy Shelley; Mary Shelley; and George Gordon, Lord Byron, praised the natural over the artificial, emotion over reason, and the individual conscience over all types of authority and external control.

European Romanticism had a profound impact on American literature. By the first decades of the nineteenth century, its influence could already be seen in the works of the American "Knickerbocker" writers such as **Washington Irving.** Centered around New York City, these writers had begun to turn their attention toward nature and to critique the ethic of material

1811. Jane Austen's *Sense and Sensibility* published

▶1814. Francis Scott Key's "Star Spangled Banner" published

1816. Georg Hegel completes third volume of philosophy

▶1817. William Cullen Bryant's "Thanatopsis" published

1818. Mary Shelley's *Frankenstein* published

1819. Arthur Schopenhauer's *The World as Will and Idea* published

▶1820. Washington Irving's *The Sketch Book* published

▶1826. James Fenimore Cooper's *The Last of the Mohicans* published

▶1827. *The Freeman's Journal*, first African-American newspaper

▶1828. Noah Webster's *An American Dictionary of the English Language* published

▶1830. Oliver Wendell Holmes's "Old Ironsides" published

1815   **1820**   **1825**   **1830**

▶1812. War of 1812 against Britain
▶1812. James Madison reelected
▶1814. Bombing of Fort McHenry
▶1814. Treaty of Ghent ends War of 1812
▶1815. Battle of New Orleans; United States defeats Britain, both armies unaware of the Treaty of Ghent
1815. Battle of Waterloo; Napolean defeated
▶1816. James Monroe elected president
▶1817. First Seminole War

1819. Florida purchased from Spain
▶1820. James Monroe reelected
▶1820. Missouri Compromise

▶1823. The Monroe Doctrine

▶ 1825. John Quincy Adams elected president
1825. Decembrist Revolution quelled in Russia

▶1828. Andrew Jackson elected president

▶1830. President Jackson signs Indian Removal Act

Washington Irving

success and social advancement espoused by writers like Benjamin Franklin in the post-Revolutionary years.

The real flowering of Romanticism in American literature came in the New England literary movement called **Transcendentalism,** which gave its own distinctive inflection and variation to European Romanticism and put the United States on the world literary map to stay. At the core of Transcendentalism was a belief in a realm of spiritual or transcendent truths beyond sense perception and material existence. These truths could be intuited by humans in heightened moments of contemplation or under the influence of natural environs. Though quite abstract, the Transcendentalist philosophy had a number of quite practical implications. The Transcendentalists valued spiritual over material success, and so opposed the materialism, or desire for increased wealth, that was present in the American psyche since the time of the Puritans and that was elevated to an ideal in the writings of Benjamin Franklin. Contrast, for example, the Transcendentalist Ralph Waldo Emerson's "Things are in the saddle/And ride mankind" with Benjamin Franklin's "Get what you can, and what you get hold; 'Tis the stone that will turn all your lead into gold." Because they believed each person capable of intuiting truths directly, the Transcendentalists also dismissed tradition and social convention— any authority beyond that of the individual conscience. Emerson wrote, for example, that "Nothing is at last sacred but the integrity of our own mind. . . . The only right is what is after my constitution, the only wrong what is against it." Emerson's friend **Henry David Thoreau** carried out an experiment in self-reliance, in keeping with Transcendentalist philosophy, building for himself a small cabin in the woods near Walden Pond in order to live simply and in closer contact with nature. Thoreau's *Walden,* a record of this experience, tells us, "If a man does not keep pace with his companions, perhaps it is because he hears a different drummer. Let him step to the music which he hears, however measured or far away." Thoreau's keen observations of nature have made his book a source of inspiration to environmentalists around the world, in addition to being one of the definitive statements of American individualism.

LITERARY EVENTS

► = American Events

►1831. William Lloyd Garrison's *The Liberator* published

►1831. John Greenleaf Whittier's *Legends of New England in Prose and Verse* published

►1835. Alexis de Tocqueville's *Democracy in America* published

►1837. Ralph Waldo Emerson's "The American Scholar" and "Concord Hymn" published

►1837. Nathaniel Hawthorne's *Twice-Told Tales* published

►1839. Edgar Allan Poe's "The Fall of the House of Usher" published

►1841. Ralph Waldo Emerson's *Self-Reliance* published

►1841. Henry Wadsworth Longfellow's *Ballads and Other Poems* published

►1842. Edgar Allan Poe's "The Raven" published

1843. Søren Kierkegaard's *Either-Or* published

►1843. Edgar Allan Poe's "The Pit and the Pendulum" published

1843. Charles Dickens's *A Christmas Carol* published

1835   **1840**   **1845**

HISTORICAL EVENTS

►1831. Nat Turner's rebellion

►1832. Andrew Jackson reelected

►1835. Second Seminole War

►1835. Texas secedes from Mexico

►1836. Texas wins independence, becomes a republic

►1836. Martin Van Buren elected president

1837. Queen Victoria becomes monarch in Britain

►1838. Underground Railroad begins

►1838. Trail of Tears; Cherokee forced to march; thousands die

►1840. William Henry Harrison elected president

►1841. President Harrison dies; John Tyler succeeds

►1843. Dorothea Dix begins humanitarian reforms

►1844. James Knox Polk elected president

1845. Potato famine in Ireland; immigration to United States increases

Emerson was an eternal optimist in his view of nature's goodness; in the midst of the 1837 economic panic and subsequent nationwide depression, he could blithely remark that "on the bosom of this vast (natural) plenty the blight of trade & manufacture seems to me a momentary mischance." Thoreau was capable of similar optimism, though he generally was much more socially reclusive and skeptical of his peers.

Several other major writers of the period, though influenced by Transcendentalism, did not take so sanguine a view of nature. In short stories such as "Rappaccini's Daughter" and in the brilliant allegorical novel *The Scarlet Letter,* **Nathaniel Hawthorne** dealt with the darker aspects of human nature, specifically with sin and the ways in which humans deal with temptation and guilt. Hawthorne joined a Boston-area Transcendentalist utopian community called **Brook Farm** in 1840, but left a year later in disgust, and wrote a satire about it called *The Blithedale Romance.* **Herman Melville** explored the forces of evil and obsession in his masterpiece, *Moby-Dick.* **Edgar Allan Poe** brought the horror story to its zenith, exploring the psychology of madness and terror in such works as "The Pit and the

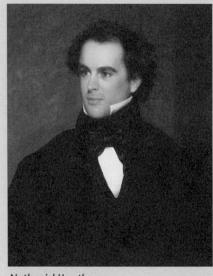

Nathaniel Hawthorne.
Peabody Essex Museum

Pendulum" and "The Fall of the House of Usher." Irving, Hawthorne, and Poe were collectively responsible for the development of the modern short story, a form that Poe defined as a brief fictional work designed to create in the reader a single dominant impression or effect.

THE WRITING PROFESSION AND SOCIAL PURPOSE

Despite their recognition by some important figures abroad, the Transcendentalists were not popular writers. Of the seven hundred copies of Thoreau's *Walden* printed in the first edition, most were eventually returned to him, unsold, by the publisher. Thoreau eventually filled orders himself by mail. It remained for later generations to recognize the quintessentially American genius that informed Transcendentalism.

▶1846. Henry Wadsworth Longfellow's *The Belfry of Bruges and Other Poems* published
1847. Charlotte Brontë's *Jane Eyre* published
1847. Emily Brontë's *Wuthering Heights* published
▶1854. Henry David Thoreau's *Walden* published
1848. William Makepeace Thackeray's *Vanity Fair*
▶1855. Walt Whitman's *Leaves of Grass* published
▶1850. Nathaniel Hawthorne's *The Scarlet Letter*
▶1851. Herman Melville's *Moby-Dick* published
1857. Gustave Flaubert's *Madame Bovary*
▶1851. Nathaniel Hawthorne's *The House of the Seven Gables*
▶1852. Harriet Beecher Stowe's *Uncle Tom's Cabin* published
1859. Charles Dickens's *A Tale of Two Cities* published

1850   **1855**   **1860**

▶1846. Mexican War; United States annexes New Mexico
▶1854. Kansas-Nebraska Act repeals Missouri Compromise
▶1848. Zachary Taylor elected president
▶1849. First gold rush
▶1856. James Buchanan elected president
▶1849. Harriet Tubman escapes from slavery
▶1850. President Taylor dies; Millard Fillmore succeeds
▶1856. "Bleeding Kansas"
▶1852. Franklin Pierce elected president
▶1857. Dred Scott decision

Some American writers were popular, however, and there were American bestsellers in this era, notably the historical novels of **James Fenimore Cooper** and Herman Melville's tales of seafaring adventure such as *Typee* and *Omoo.* The economics of publication, however, did not yet favor writing as a source of income, even if a work was popular. It was not yet possible to make a living in America as a professional writer because, though United States Copyright laws were enacted in the states in 1841, there was no international copyright protection until 1891. American books could be sold legally in England without paying royalties to the American author, and English books could be sold in America without paying royalties to the English author. The cost of publishing a book from abroad was therefore less than the cost of publishing a work by an American. To get their books published under such circumstances, American writers usually had to sell their books without any claim to royalties.

Why, then, did these individuals write? One answer is that they were committed to effecting change and believed in the power of literature to shape society. Thoreau's *Walden,* for example, is a kind of guide for living a simple life characterized by a fundamental relation to the natural world. Emerson, too, sought to change how people live and think, to teach people how to trust their own better natures.

NEW ENGLAND RENAISSANCE POETRY

Other writers of the period also had social purpose in their writing; for example, **Henry Wadsworth Longfellow**, **James Russell Lowell**, **John Greenleaf Whittier**, and **Oliver Wendell Holmes** wrote poems on various social and political issues of the time such as slavery. These men were not social rebels, however; they were models of the respectable citizen-poet, and their poetry was highly popular. They were part of a group now known alternately as the **Fireside**, or **Schoolroom, Poets** because their work was quite popular among families reading in the evening around the fire and because their work came to be recited and memorized widely in American schoolrooms. Their most popular poems were songlike, containing regular rhythms and rhymes that made the poems easy to recite and remember. These poets offered mostly idealized, romantic, morally uplifting views of the nation and its past, in lyric and narrative verse. Though the work of the Fireside Poets has often been denigrated by twentieth-century critics as unchallenging, their works helped to create greater popular interest in poetry and to elevate the status of the poet in the national imagination; indeed, Longfellow's seventy-fifth birthday was an occasion for a national celebration. The work of another poet of this era, **Edgar Allan Poe**, was similarly straightforward in its rhymes and rhythms but explored elements of the gothic, the macabre, and the mysterious.

Completely different from the Fireside or Schoolroom Poetry in almost every respect was the poetry of **Emily Dickinson**, which is generally more highly regarded by critics today. Dickinson called her poems her "letter to the world," but of the hundreds that she wrote, only a handful were read by the world in her lifetime; the rest were discovered in a storage trunk by her sister and later published by a friend. Dickinson's poetry does not follow the regular rhythmic patterns of the Schoolroom poets; it is full of interrupted thoughts and sudden bursts of awareness, often jarring the reader through irony and paradox into a wholly different, more unsettling view of the world. Dickinson often treats not an idealized past but a vivid present or an uncertain future, addressing time, isolation, and death from a surprising number of perspectives. Though she seems not to have directly registered the social issues of the day in her poetry, her work does reflect an awareness of some issues being treated by her contemporaries.

Echoes:

New England Renaissance Prose

Quotations from Ralph Waldo Emerson

On accomplishment: "If a man write a better book, preach a better sermon, or make a better mouse-trap than his neighbor, tho' he build his house in the woods, the world will make a beaten path to his door."

On ambition: "Hitch your wagon to a star."

On consistency: "A foolish consistency is the hobgoblin of little minds."

On enthusiasm: "Nothing great was ever achieved without enthusiasm."

On history: "There is properly no history, only biography."

On individuality: "Whoso would be a man must be a nonconformist."

On individuality: "To believe your own thought, to believe that what is true for you in your private heart is true for all men,—that is genius."

On rewards for actions: "The reward of a thing well done, is to have done it."

On society: "Society everywhere is in conspiracy against the manhood of every one of its members."

On the histories of words: "Language is fossil poetry."

On writing: "The art of writing consists in putting two things together that are unlike and that belong together like a horse & cart."

Quotations from Henry David Thoreau

On economics: "For more than five years I maintained myself thus solely by the labor of my hands, and I found, that by working about six weeks in a year, I could meet all the expenses of living."

On government: "I heartily accept the motto, 'That government is best which governs least.' "

On individuality: "If a man does not keep pace with his companions, perhaps it is because he hears a different drummer. Let him step to the music which he hears, however measured or far away."

On nature: "I frequently tramped eight or ten miles through the deepest snow to keep an appointment with a beech-tree, or a yellow birch, or an old acquaintance among the pines."

On nature: "I once had a sparrow alight on my shoulder for a moment while I was hoeing in a village garden, and I felt that I was more distinguished by that circumstance than I should have been by any epaulet I could have worn."

On solitude: "I never found the companion that was so companionable as solitude."

On technology: "Men have become the tools of their tools."

On the failure to follow one's dreams: "The mass of men live lives of quiet desperation."

On travel: "I have traveled a good deal in Concord."

"Rappaccini's Daughter"
by Nathaniel Hawthorne

ABOUT THE AUTHOR

Nathaniel Hawthorne (1804–1864) was born in Salem, Massachusetts. His ancestors took part in the Salem witch trials and the Quaker persecution. He studied at Bowdoin College where he met Franklin Pierce and Henry Wadsworth Longfellow. For over a decade after graduation, he studied the Puritans and wrote, anonymously publishing his first novel, *Fanshawe*. Then he directed his efforts to short stories and published *Twice-Told Tales*. His next collection, *Mosses from an Old Manse*, received a glowing review by Herman Melville. After leaving employment as a surveyor at the Salem Customs House, Hawthorne published *The Scarlet Letter*. From 1850 on, Hawthorne concentrated on writing for children, notably *The House of Seven Gables* and *The Blithedale Romance*. Hawthorne was named American consul at Liverpool and Manchester, England (1853–1855) by President Franklin Pierce. When he left this post, he traveled through Europe and published *The Marble Faun*. When he died, he left several unfinished works.

ABOUT THE SELECTION

In 1842, Nathaniel Hawthorne and his wife moved to Emerson's former home, The Old Manse, in Concord, Massachusetts. During the following four years, Hawthorne produced many of his finest stories, publishing them individually in magazines or in the collections *Twice-Told Tales* and *Mosses from an Old Manse*. **"Rappaccini's Daughter"** was first published in December 1844, in the *Democratic Review,* with a mock-autobiographical introduction. The story shows many of Hawthorne's characteristic traits, including strong use of symbolism, a psychological approach, and a focus on the Puritan preoccupation with evil.

READER'S JOURNAL

Have you ever had a friend who was a bad influence on you or who eventually proved to be hurtful? Have you disliked or feared someone and later learned that this person had helped you? Think of friends and acquaintances who seemed to be one way but turned out to be quite different. Freewrite in your journal about the difficulty of recognizing a person's true nature.

LANGUAGE SKILLS

Read the Language Arts Survey, 2.27, "Subordinating Conjunctions," and 2.50, "Adding Subordinate Clauses." Then list several subordinate clauses you find in "Rappaccini's Daughter." Briefly identify how each clause adds to the meaning of the sentence (for example, "describes the stranger") or how it is used in the sentence (for example, "the object of the verb *recollected*").

"Rappaccini's Daughter"

NATHANIEL HAWTHORNE

A young man, named Giovanni Guasconti, came, very long ago, from the more southern region of Italy, to pursue his studies at the University of Padua. Giovanni, who had but a scanty supply of gold ducats in his pocket, took lodgings in a high and gloomy chamber of an old edifice,[1] which looked not unworthy to have been the palace of a Paduan[2] noble, and which, in fact, exhibited over its entrance the armorial bearings of a family long since extinct. The young stranger, who was not unstudied in the great poem of his country, recollected that one of the ancestors of this family, and perhaps an occupant of this very mansion, had been pictured by Dante as a partaker of the immortal agonies of his Inferno.[3] These <u>reminiscences</u> and associations, together with the tendency to heartbreak natural to a young man for the first time out of his native sphere, caused Giovanni to sigh heavily, as he looked around the desolate and ill-furnished apartment.

"Holy Virgin, signor,[4]" cried old dame Lisabetta, who, won by the youth's remarkable beauty of person, was kindly endeavoring to give the chamber a habitable air, "what a sigh was that to come out of a young man's heart! Do you find this old mansion gloomy? For the love of heaven, then, put your head out of the window, and you will see as bright sunshine as you have left in Naples."

What causes Giovanni to sigh?

---

1. **edifice.** Building
2. **Paduan.** From Padua, Italy
3. **Dante . . . his Inferno.** Dante Alighieri (1265–1321), Italian poet who wrote *The Divine Comedy;* "Inferno" is that section of *The Divine Comedy* which describes hell and the suffering of the damned.
4. **signor.** Sir (Italian)

WORDS FOR EVERYDAY USE: rem • i • nis • cence (rəm´ə nis´əns) *n.,* memory or something remembered

Guasconti mechanically did as the old woman advised, but could not quite agree with her that the Lombard[5] sunshine was as cheerful as that of southern Italy. Such as it was, however, it fell upon a garden beneath the window, and expended its fostering influences on a variety of plants, which seemed to have been cultivated with exceeding care.

"Does this garden belong to the house?" asked Giovanni.

"Heaven forbid, signor!—unless it were fruitful of better pot-herbs than any that grow there now," answered old Lisabetta. "No: that garden is cultivated by the own hands of Signor Giacomo Rappaccini, the famous Doctor, who, I warrant him, has been heard of as far as Naples. It is said he distils these plants into medicines that are as potent as a charm. Oftentimes you may see the signor Doctor at work, and perchance the signora[6] his daughter, too, gathering the strange flowers that grow in the garden."

The old woman had now done what she could for the aspect of the chamber, and, commending the young man to the protection of the saints, took her departure.

Giovanni still found no better occupation than to look down into the garden beneath his window. From its appearance, he judged it to be one of those botanic gardens, which were of earlier date in Padua than elsewhere in Italy, or in the world. Or, not improbably, it might once have been the pleasure place of an opulent family; for there was the ruin of a marble fountain in the center, sculptured with rare art, but so woefully shattered that it was impossible to trace the original design from the chaos of remaining fragments. The water, however, continued to gush and sparkle into the sunbeams as cheerfully as ever. A little gurgling sound ascended to the young man's window, and made him feel as if the fountain were an immortal spirit, that sung its song unceasingly, and without heeding the vicissitudes[7] around it; while one century embodied it in marble, and another scattered the garniture[8] on the soil. All about the pool into which the water subsided, grew various plants, that seemed to require a plentiful supply of moisture for the nourishment of gigantic leaves, and, in some instances, flowers gorgeously magnificent. There was one shrub in particular, set in a marble vase in the midst of the pool, that bore a profusion of purple blossoms, each of which had the luster and richness of a gem; and the whole together made a show so resplendent that it seemed enough to illuminate the garden, even had there been no sunshine. Every portion of the soil was peopled with plants and herbs, which, if less beautiful, still bore tokens of assiduous[9] care; as if all had their individual virtues, known to the scientific mind that fostered them. Some were placed in urns, rich with old carving, and others in common garden-pots; some crept serpent-like along the ground, or climbed on high, using whatever means of ascent was offered them. One plant had wreathed itself round

What does Giovanni find particularly eye-catching in the garden?

---

5. **Lombard.** Lombardy, region of northern Italy on the border of Switzerland
6. **signora.** Mrs., Madam; Italian title of respect
7. **vicissitudes.** Changes
8. **garniture.** Decoration, ornament
9. **assiduous.** Done with constant and careful attention

WORDS FOR EVERYDAY USE:

as • pect (as´pekt´) n., appearance

op • u • lent (äp´yoo lənt) adj., very wealthy or rich

re • splend • ent (ri splen´dənt) adj., shining brightly

a statue of Vertumnus,[10] which was thus quite veiled and shrouded in a drapery of hanging foliage, so happily arranged that it might have served a sculptor for a study.

While Giovanni stood at the window, he heard a rustling behind a screen of leaves, and became aware that a person was at work in the garden. His figure soon emerged into view, and showed itself to be that of no common laborer, but a tall, emaciated, sallow, and sickly looking man, dressed in a scholar's garb[11] of black. He was beyond the middle term of life, with grey hair, a thin grey beard, and a face singularly marked with intellect and cultivation, but which could never, even in his more youthful days, have expressed much warmth of heart.

Nothing could exceed the intentness with which this scientific gardener examined every shrub which grew in his path; it seemed as if he was looking into their inmost nature, making observations in regard to their creative essence, and discovering why one leaf grew in this shape, and another in that, and wherefore such and such flowers differed among themselves in hue and perfume. Nevertheless, in spite of the deep intelligence on his part, there was no approach to intimacy between himself and these vegetable existences. On the contrary, he avoided their actual touch, or the direct inhaling of their odors, with a caution that impressed Giovanni most disagreeably; for the man's <u>demeanor</u> was that of one walking among <u>malignant</u> influences, such as savage beasts, or deadly snakes, or evil spirits, which, should he allow them one moment of license, would wreak upon him some

terrible fatality. It was strangely frightful to the young man's imagination, to see this air of insecurity in a person cultivating a garden, that most simple and innocent of human toils, and which had been alike the joy and labor of the unfallen parents of the race. Was this garden, then, the Eden of the present world?—and this man, with such a perception of harm in what his own hands caused to grow, was he the Adam?[12]

To what is the garden compared? the gardener?

The distrustful gardener, while plucking away the dead leaves or pruning the too luxuriant growth of the shrubs, defended his hands with a pair of thick gloves. Nor were these his only armor. When, in his walk through the garden, he came to the magnificent plant that hung its purple gems beside the marble fountain, he placed a kind of mask over his mouth and nostrils, as if all this beauty did but conceal a deadlier malice. But finding his task still too dangerous, he drew back, removed the mask, and called loudly, but in the infirm voice of a person affected with inward disease:

What does the gardener do when examining the plant that Giovanni noticed?

"Beatrice!—Beatrice!"

"Here am I, my father! What would you?" cried a rich and youthful voice from the window of the opposite house; a voice as rich as a tropical sunset, and which made Giovanni, though he knew not why, think of deep hues of purple or crimson, and of perfumes heavily delectable.— "Are you in the garden?"

"Yes, Beatrice," answered the gardener, "and I need your help."

What images does the voice suggest to Giovanni?

---

10. **Vertumnus.** Roman god of the changing seasons
11. **garb.** Attire; manner of dress
12. **Adam.** Name of the first man created, according to the book of Genesis in the Bible

WORDS FOR EVERYDAY USE:

de • mean • or (di mēn´ər) *n.*, way of behaving; manner

ma • lig • nant (mə lig´nənt) *adj.*, wishing evil

Soon there emerged from under a sculptured portal the figure of a young girl, arrayed with as much richness of taste as the most splendid of the flowers, beautiful as the day, and with a bloom so deep and vivid that one shade more would have been too much. She looked redundant[13] with life, health, and energy; all of which attributes were bound down and compressed, as it were, and girdled tensely, in their luxuriance, by her virgin zone. Yet Giovanni's fancy must have grown morbid, while he looked down into the garden; for the impression which the fair stranger made upon him was as if here were another flower, the human sister of those vegetable ones, as beautiful as they—more beautiful than the richest of them—but still to be touched only with a glove, nor to be approached without a mask. As Beatrice came down the garden path, it was observable that she handled and inhaled the odor of several of the plants, which her father had most sedulously[14] avoided.

What does Giovanni dream?

What does Beatrice do that her father does not?

"Here, Beatrice," said the latter,—"see how many needful offices require to be done to our chief treasure. Yet, shattered as I am, my life might pay the penalty of approaching it so closely as circumstances demand. Henceforth, I fear, this plant must be consigned to your sole charge."

"And gladly will I undertake it," cried again the rich tones of the young lady, as she bent toward the magnificent plant, and opened her arms as if to embrace it. "Yes, my sister, my splendor, it shall be Beatrice's task to nurse and serve thee; and thou shalt reward her with thy kisses and perfumed breath, which to her is as the breath of life!"

Then, with all the tenderness in her manner that was so strikingly expressed in her words, she busied herself with such attentions as the plant seemed to require; and Giovanni, at his lofty window, rubbed his eyes, and almost doubted whether it were a girl tending her favorite flower, or one sister performing the duties of affection to another. The scene soon <u>terminated</u>. Whether Doctor Rappaccini had finished his labors in the garden, or that his watchful eye had caught the stranger's face, he now took his daughter's arm and retired. Night was already closing in; oppressive exhalations seemed to proceed from the plants, and steal upward past the open window; and Giovanni, closing the lattice, went to his couch, and dreamed of a rich flower and beautiful girl. Flower and maiden were different and yet the same, and fraught[15] with some strange peril in either shape.

But there is an influence in the light of morning that tends to rectify whatever errors of fancy, or even of judgment, we may have incurred during the sun's decline, or among the shadows of the night, or in the less wholesome glow of moonshine. Giovanni's first movement on starting from sleep, was to throw open the window, and gaze down into the garden which his dreams had made so fertile of mysteries. He was surprised, and a little ashamed, to find how real and matter-of-fact an affair it proved to be, in the first rays of the sun, which gilded the dewdrops that hung upon

---

13. **redundant.** Overfull, as though having more than one's share of life
14. **sedulously.** Diligently; persistently
15. **fraught.** Filled

WORDS FOR EVERYDAY USE:

ter • mi • nate (tʉr′ mə nāt′) vi., end, stop, cease

leaf and blossom, and, while giving a brighter beauty to each rare flower, brought everything within the limits of ordinary experience. The young man rejoiced, that, in the heart of the barren city, he had the privilege of overlooking this spot of lovely and luxuriant vegetation. It would serve, he said to himself, as a symbolic language, to keep him in communion with nature. Neither the sickly and thought-worn Doctor Giocomo Rappaccini, it is true, nor his brilliant daughter were now visible; so that Giovanni could not determine how much of the singularity which he attributed to both, was due to their own qualities, and how much to his wonder-working fancy. But he was inclined to take a most rational view of the whole matter.

In the course of the day, he paid his respects to Signor Pietro Baglioni, professor of medicine in the University, a physician of eminent repute, to whom Giovanni had brought a letter of introduction. The professor was an elderly personage, apparently of genial nature, and habits that might almost be called jovial; he kept the young man to dinner, and made himself very agreeable by the freedom and liveliness of his conversation, especially when warmed by a flask or two of Tuscan wine. Giovanni, conceiving that men of science, inhabitants of the same city, must needs be on familiar terms with one another, took an opportunity to mention the name of Dr. Rappaccini. But the professor did not respond with so much <u>cordiality</u> as he had anticipated.

"Ill would it become a teacher of the divine art of medicine," said Professor Pietro Baglioni, in answer to a question of Giovanni, "to withhold due and well-considered praise of a physician so eminently skilled as Rappaccini. But, on the other hand, I should answer it but scantily to my conscience, were I to permit a worthy youth like yourself, Signor Giovanni, the son of an ancient friend, to imbibe <u>erroneous</u> ideas respecting a man who might hereafter chance to hold your life and death in his hands. The truth is, our worshipful Doctor Rappaccini has as much science as any member of the faculty—with perhaps one single exception—in Padua, or all Italy. But there are certain grave objections to his professional character."

"And what are they?" asked the young man.

"Has my friend Giovanni any disease of body or heart, that he is so inquisitive about physicians?" said the Professor, with a smile. "But as for Rappaccini, it is said of him—and I, who know the man well, can answer for its truth—that he cares infinitely more for science than for mankind. His patients are interesting to him only as subjects for some new experiment. He would sacrifice human life, his own among the rest, or whatever else was dearest to him, for the sake of adding so much as a grain of mustard-seed to the great heap of his accumulated knowledge."

"Methinks he is an awful[16] man, indeed," remarked Guasconti, mentally recalling the cold and purely intellectual aspect of Rappaccini. "And yet, worshipful Professor, is it not a noble spirit? Are there many men capable of so spiritual a love of science?"

16. **awful.** Awe-inspiring

What does Baglioni find objectionable about Rappaccini?

"God forbid," answered the Professor, somewhat <u>testily</u>—"at least, unless they take sounder views of the healing art than those adopted by Rappaccini. It is his theory, that all medicinal virtues are comprised within those substances which we term vegetable poisons. These he cultivates with his own hands, and is said even to have produced new varieties of poison, more horribly <u>deleterious</u> than Nature, without the assistance of this learned person, would ever have plagued the world with. That the signor Doctor does less mischief than might be expected, with such dangerous substances, is undeniable. Now and then, it must be owned, he has effected—or seemed to effect—a marvelous cure. But, to tell you my private mind, Signor Giovanni, he should receive little credit for such instances of success—they being probably the work of chance—but should be held strictly accountable for his failures, which may justly be considered his own work."

The youth might have taken Baglioni's opinions with many grains of allowance, had he known that there was a professional warfare of long continuance between him and Doctor Rappaccini, in which the latter was generally thought to have gained the advantage. If the reader be inclined to judge for himself, we refer him to certain black-letter tracts on both sides, preserved in the medical department of the University of Padua.

"I know not, most learned Professor," returned Giovanni, after musing on what had been said of Rappaccini's exclusive zeal for science—"I know not how dearly this physician may love his art; but surely there is one object more dear to him. He has a daughter."

"Aha!" cries the Professor with a laugh. "So now our friend Giovanni's secret is out. You have heard of this daughter, whom all the young men in Padua are wild about, though not half a dozen have ever had the good hap to see her face. I know little of the Signora Beatrice, save that Rappaccini is said to have instructed her deeply in his science, and that, young and beautiful as fame reports her, she is already qualified to fill a professor's chair. Perchance her father destines her for mine! Other absurd rumors there be, not worth talking about, or listening to. So now, Signor Giovanni, drink off your glass of Lacryma."

Guasconti returned to his lodgings somewhat heated with the wine he had quaffed,[17] and which caused his brain to swim with strange fantasies in reference to Doctor Rappaccini and the beautiful Beatrice. On his way, happening to pass by a florist's, he bought a fresh bouquet of flowers.

Ascending to his chamber, he seated himself near the window, but within the shadow thrown by the depth of the wall, so that he could look down into the garden with little risk of being discovered. All beneath his eye was a solitude. The strange plants were basking in the sunshine, and now and then nodding gently to one another, as if in acknowledgment of sympathy and kindred. In the midst, by the shattered fountain, grew the magnificent shrub, with its purple gems clustering

What is Rappaccini's particular interest?

Why might Baglioni have a motivation to lie about Rappaccini?

---

17. **quaffed.** Drunk

WORDS FOR EVERYDAY USE:

tes • ti • ly (tes´tə lē) *adv.,* in an irritable manner

del • e • te • ri • ous (del´ə tir´ē əs) *adj.,* harmful to health or well-being

all over it; they glowed in the air, and gleamed back again out of the depths of the pool, which thus seemed to overflow with colored radiance from the rich reflection that was steeped in it. At first, as we have said, the garden was a solitude. Soon, however,—as Giovanni had half-hoped, half-feared, would be the case,—a figure appeared beneath the antique sculptured <u>portal</u>, and came down between the rows of plants, inhaling their various perfumes, as if she were one of those beings of old classic fable, that lived upon sweet odors. On again beholding Beatrice, the young man was even startled to perceive how much her beauty exceeded his recollection of it; so brilliant, so vivid in its character, that she glowed amid the sunlight, and, as Giovanni whispered to himself, positively illuminated the more shadowy intervals of the garden path. Her face being now more revealed than on the former occasion, he was struck by its expression of simplicity and sweetness; qualities that had not entered into his idea of her character, and which made him ask anew, what manner of mortal she might be. Nor did he fail again to observe, or imagine, an <u>analogy</u> between the beautiful girl and the gorgeous shrub that hung its gem-like flowers over the fountain; a resemblance which Beatrice seemed to have indulged a fantastic humor in heightening, both by the arrangement of her dress and the selection of its hues.

Approaching the shrub, she threw open her arms, as with a passionate ardor, and drew its branches into an intimate embrace; so intimate, that her features were hidden in its leafy bosom, and her glistening ringlets all intermingled with the flowers.

"Give me thy breath, my sister," exclaimed Beatrice; "for I am faint with common air! And give me this flower of thine, which I separate with gentlest fingers from the stem, and place it close beside my heart."

With these words, the beautiful daughter of Rappaccini plucked one of the richest blossoms of the shrub, and was about to fasten it in her bosom. But now, unless Giovanni's draughts of wine had bewildered his senses, a singular incident occurred. A small orange-colored reptile of the lizard or chameleon species, chanced to be creeping along the path, just at the feet of Beatrice. It appeared to Giovanni—but, at the distance from which he gazed, he could scarcely have seen anything so minute—it appeared to him, however, that a drop or two of moisture from the broken stem of the flower descended upon the lizard's head. For an instant, the reptile contorted itself violently, and then lay motionless in the sunshine. Beatrice observed this remarkable <u>phenomenon</u>, and crossed herself, sadly, but without surprise; nor did she therefore hesitate to arrange the fatal flower in her bosom. There it blushed, and almost glimmered with the dazzling effect of a precious stone, adding to her dress and aspect the one appropriate charm, which nothing else in the world could have supplied. But Giovanni, out of the shadow of his window bent forward and shrank back, and murmured and trembled.

What shocking incident occurs?

WORDS FOR EVERYDAY USE:

por • tal (pôrt ´l) *n.,* doorway, gate, or entrance
a • nal • o • gy (ə nal´ə jē) *n.,* similarity in some respects between things otherwise unlike
phe • nom • e • non (fə näm´ə nən´) *n.,* extremely unusual or extraordinary thing or occurrence

"Am I awake? Have I my senses?" said he to himself. "What is this being?—beautiful, shall I call her?—or inexpressibly terrible?"

Beatrice now strayed carelessly through the garden, approaching closer beneath Giovanni's window, so that he was compelled to thrust his head quite out of its concealment in order to gratify the intense and painful curiosity which she excited. At this moment, there came a beautiful insect over the garden wall; it had perhaps wandered through the city and found no flowers nor verdure among those antique haunts of men, until the heavy perfumes of Doctor Rappaccini's shrubs had lured it from afar. Without alighting on the flowers, this winged brightness seemed to be attracted by Beatrice, and lingered in the air and fluttered about her head. Now here it could not be but that Giovanni Guasconti's eyes deceived him. Be that as it might, he fancied that while Beatrice was gazing at the insect with childish delight, it grew faint and fell at her feet!—its bright wings shivered! it was dead!—from no cause that he could discern, unless it were the atmosphere of her breath. Again Beatrice crossed herself and sighed heavily, as she bent over the dead insect.

An impulsive movement of Giovanni drew her eyes to the window. There she beheld the beautiful head of the young man—rather a Grecian than an Italian head, with fair, regular features, and a glistening of gold among his ringlets—gazing down upon her like a being that hovered in mid-air. Scarcely knowing what he did, Giovanni threw down the bouquet which he had hitherto held in his hand.

What does Beatrice say she would like to give Giovanni in return? Why doesn't she?

What happens to the bouquet Giovanni gives to Beatrice?

"Signora," said he, "there are pure and healthful flowers. Wear them for the sake of Giovanni Guasconti!"

"Thanks, Signor," replied Beatrice, with her rich voice, that came forth as it were like a gush of music; and with a mirthful expression half childish and half womanlike. "I accept your gift, and would fain[18] recompense it with this precious purple flower; but if I toss it into the air, it will not reach you. So Signor Guasconti must even content himself with my thanks."

She lifted the bouquet from the ground, and then as if inwardly ashamed at having stepped aside from her maidenly reserve to respond to a stranger's greeting, passed swiftly homeward through the garden. But, few as the moments were, it seemed to Giovanni when she was on the point of vanishing beneath the sculptured portal, that his beautiful bouquet was already beginning to wither in her grasp. It was an idle thought; there could be no possibility of distinguishing a faded flower from a fresh one at so great a distance.

For many days after the incident, the young man avoided the window that looked into Doctor Rappaccini's garden, as if something ugly and monstrous would have blasted his eyesight, had he been betrayed into a glance. He felt conscious of having put himself, to a certain extent, within the influence of an unintelligible power, by the communication which he had opened with Beatrice. The wisest course would have been, if his heart were in any real danger, to quit his lodgings and Padua itself, at once; the next wiser, to

---

18. **fain.** With eagerness; gladly

WORDS FOR EVERYDAY USE:

ver • dure (vʊr´jər) n., green growing plants and trees

rec • om • pense (rek´ əm pens´) vt., repay; reward

un • in • tel • li • gi • ble (un in tel´i jə bəl) adj., that cannot be understood

Carnival Evening. Henri Rousseau, 1886. Philadelphia Museum of Art, Louis E. Stern Collection

have accustomed himself, as far as possible, to the familiar and day-light view of Beatrice; thus bringing her rigidly and systematically within the limits of ordinary experience. Least of all, while avoiding her sight, should Giovanni have remained so near this extraordinary being, that the proximity and possibility even of intercourse, should give a kind of substance and reality to the wild <u>vagaries</u> which his imagination ran riot continually in producing. Guasconti had not a deep heart—or at all events, its depths were not sounded now—but he had a quick fancy, and an ardent southern temperament, which rose every instant to a higher fever-pitch. Whether or no Beatrice possessed those terrible attributes—that fatal breath—the <u>affinity</u> with those so beautiful and deadly flowers—which were indicated by what Giovanni had witnessed, she had at least instilled a fierce and subtle poison into his system. It was not love, although her rich beauty was a madness to him; nor horror, even while he fancied her spirit to be imbued with the same <u>baneful</u> essence that seemed to pervade her physical frame; but a wild offspring of both love and horror that had each parent in it, and burned like one and shivered like the other. Giovanni knew not what to dread; still less did he know

What poison has Beatrice unwittingly instilled in Giovanni?

what to hope; *hope* and *dread* kept a continual warfare in his breast, alternately vanquishing one another and starting up afresh to renew the contest. Blessed are all simple emotions, be they dark or bright! It is the <u>lurid</u> intermixture of the two that produces the illuminating blaze of the infernal regions.

Sometimes he endeavored to <u>assuage</u> the fever of his spirit by a rapid walk through the streets of Padua, or beyond its gates; his footsteps kept time with the throbbings of his brain, so that the walk was apt to accelerate itself to a race. One day, he found himself arrested; his arm was seized by a portly personage who had turned back on recognizing the young man, and expended much breath in overtaking him.

"Signor Giovanni!—stay, my young friend!" cried he. "Have you forgotten me? That might well be the case, if I were as much altered as yourself."

It was Baglioni, whom Giovanni had avoided, ever since their first meeting, from a doubt that the professor's sagacity would look too deeply into his secrets. Endeavoring to recover himself, he stared forth wildly from his inner world into the outer one, and spoke like a man in a dream.

"Yes; I am Giovanni Guasconti. You are Professor Pietro Baglioni. Now let me pass!"

"Not yet—not yet, Signor Giovanni Guasconti," said the Professor, smiling, but at the same time scrutinizing the youth with an earnest glance.—"What; did I grow up side by side with your father, and shall his son pass me like a stranger, in these old streets of Padua? Stand still, Signor Giovanni; for we must have a word or two, before we part."

"Speedily, then, most worshipful Professor, speedily!" said Giovanni, with feverish impatience. "Does not your worship see that I am in haste?"

Now, while he was speaking, there came a man in black along the street, stooping and moving feebly, like a person in inferior health. His face was all overspread with a most sickly and sallow hue, but yet so pervaded with an expression of piercing and active intellect, that an observer might easily have overlooked the merely physical attributes, and have seen only this wonderful energy. As he passed, this person exchanged a cold and distant salutation with Baglioni, but fixed his eyes upon Giovanni with an intentness that seemed to bring out whatever was within him worthy of notice. Nevertheless, there was a peculiar quietness in the look, as if taking merely a <u>speculative</u>, not a human interest, in the young man.

"It is Doctor Rappaccini!" whispered the Professor, when the stranger had passed.—"Has he ever seen your face before?"

"Not that I know," answered Giovanni starting at the name.

"He *has* seen you!—he must have seen you!" said Baglioni, hastily. "For some purpose or other, this man of science is making a study of you. I know that look of his! It is the same that coldly illuminates his face, as he bends over a bird, a mouse, or a butterfly, which, in pursuance of some experiment, he has killed by the perfume of a flower;—a look as deep as nature

What sort of look does Rappaccini give Giovanni?

What warning does Baglioni give Giovanni?

WORDS FOR EVERYDAY USE:

lu • rid (loor´id) *adj.*, vivid in a harsh or shocking way

as • suage (ə swāj´) *vt.*, lessen; calm; pacify

spec • u • la • tive (spek´ yoō lāt´ iv) *adj.*, theoretical

itself, but without nature's warmth of love. Signor Giovanni, I will stake my life upon it, you are the subject of one of Rappaccini's experiments!"

"Will you make a fool of me?" cried Giovanni, passionately. "*That*, Signor Professor, were an <u>untoward</u> experiment."

"Patience, patience!" replied the <u>imperturbable</u> Professor.—"I tell thee, my poor Giovanni, that Rappaccini has a scientific interest in thee. Thou hast fallen into fearful hands! And the Signora Beatrice? What part does she act in this mystery?"

But Guasconti, finding Baglioni's <u>pertinacity</u> intolerable, here broke away and was gone before the Professor could again seize his arm. He looked after the young man intently, and shook his head.

"This must not be," said Baglioni to himself. "The youth is the son of my old friend, and should not come to any harm from which the arcana[19] of medical science can preserve him. Besides, it is too insufferable an impertinence in Rappaccini, thus to snatch the bud out of my own hands, as I may say, and make use of him for his infernal experiments. This daughter of his! It shall be looked to. Perchance, most learned Rappaccini, I may foil you where you little dream of it!"

Meanwhile, Giovanni had pursued a circuitous route, and at length found himself at the door of his lodgings. As he crossed the threshold, he was met by old Lisabetta, who smirked and smiled, and was evidently desirous to attract his attention; vainly, however, as the <u>ebullition</u> of his feelings had momentarily subsided into a cold and dull <u>vacuity</u>. He turned his eyes full upon the withered face that was puckering itself into a smile, but seemed to behold it not. The old dame, therefore, laid her grasp upon his cloak.

"Signor!—Signor!" whispered she, still with a smile over the whole breadth of her visage, so that it looked not unlike a grotesque carving in wood, darkened by centuries—"Listen, Signor! There is a private entrance into the garden!"

"What do you say?" exclaimed Giovanni, turning quickly about, as if an inanimate thing should start into feverish life.—"A private entrance into Doctor Rappaccini's garden!"

"Hush! hush!—not so loud!" whispered Lisabetta, putting her hand over his mouth. "Yes; into the worshipful Doctor's garden, where you may see all his fine shrubbery. Many a young man in Padua would give gold to be admitted among those flowers."

Giovanni put a piece of gold into her hand.

"Show me the way," said he.

A surmise, probably excited by his conversation with Baglioni, crossed his mind, that this interposition of old Lisabetta might perchance be connected with the intrigue, whatever were its nature, in which the Professor seemed to suppose that Doctor Rappaccini was involving him. But such a suspicion, though it disturbed Giovanni, was inadequate to restrain him. The instant he was aware of the possibility of approaching Beatrice, it seemed an absolute necessity of his existence to do so. It mattered not whether she were angel or demon; he was irrevocably within her sphere, and must obey the law that whirled

19. **arcana.** Secrets or mysteries

Q *What possibility does Giovanni consider?*

WORDS FOR
EVERYDAY USE:

un • to • ward (un tō´ərd) *adj.,* improper, unseemly; not favorable
im • per • turb • a • ble (im´pər tʉr´ bə bəl) *adj.,* that cannot be disconnected or disturbed
per • ti • nac • i • ty (pʉr´tə nas´ə tē) *n.,* stubborn persistence; obstinacy
eb • ul • li • tion (eb´ə lish´ən) *n.,* boiling or bubbling up
va • cu • i • ty (va kōō´ə tē) *n.,* empty space, void, or vacuum

him onward, in ever lessening circles, towards a result which he did not attempt to foreshadow. And yet, strange to say, there came across him a sudden doubt, whether this intense interest on his part were not <u>delusory</u>— whether it were really of so deep and positive a nature as to justify him in now thrusting himself into an incalculable position—whether it were not merely the fantasy of a young man's brain, only slightly, or not at all, connected with his heart!

He paused—hesitated—turned half about—but again went on. His withered guide led him along several obscure passages, and finally undid a door, through which, as it was opened, there came the sight and sound of rustling leaves, with the broken sunshine glimmering among them. Giovanni stepped forth, and forcing himself through the entanglement of a shrub that wreathed its tendrils over the hidden entrance, he stood beneath his own window, in the open area of Doctor Rappaccini's garden.

How often is it the case, that, when impossibilities have come to pass, and dreams have condensed their misty substance into tangible realities, we find ourselves calm, and even coldly self-possessed, amid circumstances which it would have been a delirium of joy or agony to anticipate! Fate delights to thwart us thus. Passion will choose his own time to rush upon the scene, and lingers sluggishly behind, when an appropriate adjustment of events would seem to summon his appearance. So was it now with Giovanni. Day after day, his pulses had throbbed with feverish blood, at the improbable idea of an interview with Beatrice, and of standing with her, face to face, in this very garden, basking in the oriental sunshine of her beauty, and snatching from her full gaze the mystery which he deemed the riddle of his own existence. But now there was a singular and untimely <u>equanimity</u> within his breast. He threw a glance around the garden to discover if Beatrice or her father were present, and perceiving that he was alone, began a critical observation of the plants.

The aspect of one and all of them dissatisfied him; their gorgeousness seemed fierce, passionate, and even unnatural. There was hardly an individual shrub which a wanderer, straying by himself through a forest, would not have been startled to find growing wild, as if an unearthly face had glared at him out of the thicket. Several, also, would have shocked a delicate instinct by an appearance of artificialness, indicating that there had been such commixture, and, as it were, adultery of various vegetable species, that the production was no longer of God's making, but the monstrous offspring of man's <u>depraved</u> fancy, glowing with only an evil mockery of beauty. They were probably the result of experiment, which, in one or two cases, had succeeded in mingling plants individually lovely into a compound possessing the questionable and ominous character that distinguished the whole growth of the garden. In fine, Giovanni recognized but two or three plants in the collection, and those of a kind that he well knew to be poisonous. While busy with these contemplations, he

WORDS FOR EVERYDAY USE:

de • lu • so • ry (di loo´sə rē) *adj.,* quality of seeming unreal

e • qua • nim • i • ty (ek´wə nim´ ə tē) *n.,* evenness of mind or temper

de • praved (dē prāvd´) *adj.,* morally bad; corrupt

heard the rustling of a silken garment, and turning, beheld Beatrice emerging from beneath the sculptured portal.

Giovanni had not considered with himself what should be his deportment; whether he should apologize for his intrusion into the garden, or assume that he was there with the privity, at least, if not the desire of Doctor Rappaccini or his daughter. But Beatrice's manner placed him at his ease, though leaving him still in doubt by what agency he had gained admittance. She came lightly along the path, and met him near the broken fountain. There was surprise in her face, but brightened by a simple and kind expression of pleasure.

"You are a connoisseur in flowers, Signor," said Beatrice with a smile, alluding to the bouquet which he had flung her from the window. "It is no marvel, therefore, if the sight of my father's rare collection has tempted you to take a nearer view. If he were here, he could tell you many strange and interesting facts as to the nature and habits of these shrubs, for he has spent a lifetime in such studies, and this garden is his world."

"And yourself, lady"—observed Giovanni—"if fame says true—you, likewise, are deeply skilled in the virtues indicated by these rich blossoms, and these spicy perfumes. Would you deign[20] to be my instructress, I should prove an apter scholar than under Signor Rappaccini himself."

"Are there such idle rumors?" asked Beatrice, with the music of a pleasant laugh. "Do people say that I am skilled in my father's science of plants? What a jest is there! No; though I have grown up among these flowers, I know no more of them than their hues and perfume; and sometimes, methinks I would fain rid myself of even that small knowledge. There are many flowers here, and those not the least brilliant, that shock and offend me, when they meet my eye. But, pray, Signor, do not believe these stories about my science. Believe nothing of me save what you see with your own eyes."

What does Beatrice ask Giovanni to do?

"And must I believe all that I have seen with my own eyes?" asked Giovanni pointedly, while the recollection of former scenes made him shrink. "No, Signora, you demand too little of me. Bid me believe nothing, save what comes from your own lips."

It would appear that Beatrice understood him. There came a deep flush to her cheek; but she looked full into Giovanni's eyes, and responded to his gaze of uneasy suspicion with a queen-like haughtiness.

Why does Beatrice blush?

"I do so bid you, Signor!" she replied. "Forget whatever you may have fancied in regard to me. If true to the outward senses, still it may be false in its essence. But the words of Beatrice Rappaccini's lips are true from the heart outward. Those you may believe!"

A fervor glowed in her whole aspect, and beamed upon Giovanni's consciousness like the light of truth itself. But while she spoke, there was a fragrance in the atmosphere around her, rich and delightful, though evanescent, yet which the young man, from an indefinable reluctance, scarcely dared to draw into his

---

20. **deign.** Condescend to do something slightly beneath one's dignity

| WORDS FOR EVERYDAY USE: | **de • port • ment** (dē pôrt´mənt) *n.,* manner of conducting or bearing oneself | **fer • vor** (fûr´vər) *n.,* great warmth or emotion |
| | **con • nois • seur** (kän´ə sûr´) *n.,* person who has expert knowledge in some field | **ev • a • nes • cent** (ev´ə nes´ənt) *adj.,* tending to fade; vanishing |

lungs. It might be the odor of the flowers. Could it be Beatrice's breath, which thus embalmed her words with a strange richness, as if by steeping them in her heart? A faintness passed like a shadow over Giovanni, and flitted away; he seemed to gaze through the beautiful girl's eyes into her transparent soul, and felt no more doubt or fear.

The tinge of passion that had colored Beatrice's manner vanished; she became gay, and appeared to derive a pure delight from her communion with the youth, not unlike what the maiden of a lonely island might have felt, conversing with a voyager from the civilized world. Evidently her experience of life had been confined within the limits of that garden. She talked now about matters as simple as the daylight or summer clouds, and now asked questions in reference to the city, or Giovanni's distant home, his friends, his mother, and his sisters; questions indicating such seclusion, and such lack of familiarity with modes and forms, that Giovanni responded as if to an infant. Her spirit gushed out before him like a fresh rill,[21] that was just catching its first glimpse of the sunlight, and wondering at the reflections of earth and sky which were flung into its bosom. There came thoughts, too, from a deep source, and fantasies of a gem-like brilliancy, as if diamonds and rubies sparkled upward among the bubbles of the fountain. Ever and anon, there gleamed across the young man's mind a sense of wonder, that he should be walking side by side with the being who had so wrought upon his imagination—whom he had idealized in such hues of terror—in whom he had positively witnessed such manifestations of dreadful attributes—that he should be conversing with Beatrice like a brother, and should find her so human and so maiden-like. But such reflections were only momentary; the effect of her character was too real, not to make itself familiar at once.

In this free intercourse, they had strayed through the garden, and now, after many turns among its avenues, were come to the shattered fountain, beside which grew the magnificent shrub with its treasury of glowing blossoms. A fragrance was diffused from it, which Giovanni recognized as identical with that which he had attributed to Beatrice's breath, but incomparably more powerful. As her eyes fell upon it, Giovanni beheld her press her hand to her bosom, as if her heart were throbbing suddenly and painfully.

"For the first time in my life," murmured she, addressing the shrub, "I had forgotten thee!"

"I remember, Signora," said Giovanni, "that you once promised to reward me with one of these living gems for the bouquet, which I had the happy boldness to fling to your feet. Permit me now to pluck it as a memorial of this interview."

He made a step towards the shrub, with extended hand. But Beatrice darted forward, uttering a shriek that went through his heart like a dagger. She caught his hand, and drew it back with the whole force of her slender figure. Giovanni felt her touch thrilling through his fibres.

"Touch it not!" exclaimed she, in a voice of agony. "Not for thy life! It is fatal!"

Then, hiding her face, she fled from him, and vanished beneath the sculptured portal. As Giovanni followed her with his

---

21. **rill.** Little brook or stream

What has Beatrice forgotten for the first time in her life?

What does Giovanni do that frightens Beatrice?

eyes, he beheld the <u>emaciated</u> figure and pale intelligence of Doctor Rappaccini, who had been watching the scene, he knew not how long, within the shadow of the entrance.

No sooner was Guasconti alone in his chamber, than the image of Beatrice came back to his passionate musings, invested with all the witchery that had been gathering around it ever since his first glimpse of her, and now likewise imbued with a tender warmth of girlish womanhood. She was human: her nature was endowed with all gentle and feminine qualities; she was worthiest to be worshiped; she was capable, surely, on her part, of the height and heroism of love. Those tokens, which he had hitherto considered as proofs of a frightful peculiarity in her physical and moral system, were now either forgotten, or, by the subtle <u>sophistry</u> of passion, <u>transmuted</u> into a golden crown of enchantment, rendering Beatrice the more admirable, by so much as she was the more unique. Whatever had looked ugly, was now beautiful; or, if incapable of such a change, it stole away and hid itself among those shapeless half-ideas, which throng the dim region beyond the daylight of our perfect consciousness. Thus did Giovanni spend the night, nor fell asleep, until the dawn had begun to awake the slumbering flowers in Doctor Rappaccini's garden, whither his dreams doubtless led him. Up rose the sun in his due season, and flinging his beams upon the young man's eyelids, awoke him to a sense of pain. When thoroughly aroused, he became sensible of a burning and tingling agony in his hand—in his right hand—the very hand which

Beatrice had grasped in her own, when he was on the point of plucking one of the gem-like flowers. On the back of that hand there was now a purple print, like that of four small fingers, and the likeness of a slender thumb upon his wrist.

Oh, how stubbornly does love—or even that cunning semblance of love which flourishes in the imagination, but strikes no depth of root into the heart—how stubbornly does it hold its faith, until the moment come, when it is doomed to vanish into thin mist! Giovanni wrapt a handkerchief about his hand, and wondered what evil thing had stung him, and soon forgot his pain in a <u>reverie</u> of Beatrice.

After the first interview, a second was in the inevitable course of what we call fate. A third; a fourth; and a meeting with Beatrice in the garden was no longer an incident in Giovanni's daily life, but the whole space in which he might be said to live; for the anticipation and memory of that ecstatic hour made up the remainder. Nor was it otherwise with the daughter of Rappaccini. She watched for the youth's appearance, and flew to his side with confidence as unreserved as if they had been playmates from early infancy—as if they were such playmates still. If, by any unwonted[22] chance, he failed to come at the appointed moment, she stood beneath the window, and sent up the rich sweetness of her tones to float around him in his chamber, and echo and reverberate throughout his heart— "Giovanni! Giovanni! Why tarriest thou? Come

What has happened to Giovanni's hand?

How do Giovanni and Beatrice feel about each other?

---

22. **unwonted.** Not common or usual

WORDS FOR EVERYDAY USE:

e • ma • ci • at • ed (ē mā´shē āt əd) *part.*, abnormally thin

soph • ist • ry (säf´is trē) *n.*, unsound or misleading but clever, plausible, and subtle

argument or reasoning

trans • mute (trans myo͞ot´) *vt.*, change from one form, species, or condition into another

rev • er • ie (rev´ər ē) *n.*, dreamy thinking

down!"—And down he hastened into that Eden of poisonous flowers.

But, with all this intimate familiarity, there was still a reserve in Beatrice's demeanor, so rigidly and invariably sustained, that the idea of <u>infringing</u> it scarcely occurred to his imagination. By all appreciable signs, they loved; they had looked love, with eyes that conveyed the holy secret from the depths of one soul into the depths of the other, as if it were too sacred to be whispered by the way; they had even spoken love, in those gushes of passion when their spirits darted forth in <u>articulated</u> breath, like tongues of long-hidden flame; and yet there had been no seal of lips, no clasp of hands, nor any slightest caress, such as love claims and hallows. He had never touched one of the gleaming ringlets of her hair; her garment—so marked was the physical barrier between them—had never been waved against him by a breeze. On the few occasions when Giovanni had seemed tempted to overstep the limit, Beatrice grew so sad, so stern, and withal wore such a look of desolate separation, shuddering at itself, that not a spoken word was requisite to repel him. At such times, he was startled at the horrible suspicions that rose, monster-like, out of the caverns of his heart, and stared him in the face; his love grew thin and faint as the morning mist; his doubts alone had substance. But when Beatrice's face brightened again, after the momentary shadow, she was transformed at once from the mysterious, questionable being, whom he had watched with so much awe and horror; she was now the beautiful and unsophisticated girl, whom

What happens in the classic book Baglioni has been reading? Why does he relate this story to Giovanni?

he felt that his spirit knew with a certainty beyond all other knowledge.

A considerable time had now passed since Giovanni's last meeting with Baglioni. One morning, however, he was disagreeably surprised by a visit from the Professor, whom he had scarcely thought of for whole weeks, and would willingly have forgotten still longer. Given up, as he had long been, to a pervading excitement, he could tolerate no companions, except upon condition of their perfect sympathy with his present state of feeling. Such sympathy was not to be expected from Professor Baglioni.

The visitor chatted carelessly, for a few moments, about the gossip of the city and the University, and then took up another topic.

"I have been reading an old classic author lately," said he, "and met with a story that strangely interested me. Possibly you may remember it. It is of an Indian prince, who sent a beautiful woman as a present to Alexander the Great. She was as lovely as the dawn, and gorgeous as the sunset; but what especially distinguished her was a certain rich perfume in her breath—richer than a garden of Persian roses. Alexander, as was natural to a youthful conqueror, fell in love at first sight with this magnificent stranger. But a certain sage physician, happening to be present, discovered a terrible secret in regard to her."

"And what was that?" asked Giovanni, turning his eyes downward to avoid those of the Professor.

"That this lovely woman," continued Baglioni, with emphasis, "had been nour-

WORDS FOR **E**VERYDAY **U**SE:	**in • fring • ing** (in frinj´ iŋ) *part.*, violating; trespassing **ar • tic • u • lat • ed** (ar tik´ yo͞o lāt´əd) *adj.*, made up of distinct syllables or words, as human speech

ished with poisons from her birth upward, until her whole nature was so imbued with them, that she herself had become the deadliest poison in existence. Poison was her element of life. With that rich perfume of her breath, she blasted the very air. Her love would have been poison!—her embrace death! Is not this a marvelous tale?"

"A childish fable," answered Giovanni, nervously starting from his chair. "I marvel how your worship finds time to read such nonsense, among your graver studies."

"By the by," said the Professor, looking uneasily about him, "what singular fragrance is this in your apartment? Is it the perfume of your gloves? It is faint, but delicious, and yet, after all, by no means agreeable. Were I to breathe it long, methinks it would make me ill. It is like the breath of a flower—but I see no flowers in the chamber."

"Nor are there any," replied Giovanni, who had turned pale as the Professor spoke; "nor, I think, is there any fragrance, except in your worship's imagination. Odors, being a sort of element combined of the sensual and the spiritual, are apt to deceive us in this manner. The recollection of a perfume—the bare idea of it—may easily be mistaken for a present reality."

"Aye; but my sober imagination does not often play such tricks," said Baglioni; "and were I to fancy any kind of odor, it would be that of some vile apothecary[23] drug, wherewith my fingers are likely enough to be imbued. Our worshipful friend Rappaccini, as I have heard, tinctures his medicaments with odors richer than those of Araby. Doubtless, likewise, the fair and learned Signora Beatrice would minister to her patients with draughts as sweet as a maiden's breath. But woe to him that sips them!"

Giovanni's face evinced many contending emotions. The tone in which the Professor alluded to the pure and lovely daughter of Rappaccini was a torture to his soul; and yet, the intimation of a view of her character, opposite to his own, gave instantaneous distinctness to a thousand dim suspicions, which now grinned at him like so many demons. But he strove hard to quell them, and to respond to Baglioni with a true lover's perfect faith.

"Signor Professor," said he, "you were my father's friend—perchance, too, it is your purpose to act a friendly part towards his son. I would fain feel nothing towards you, save respect and deference. But I pray you to observe, Signor, that there is one subject on which we must not speak. You know not the Signora Beatrice. You cannot, therefore, estimate the wrong—the blasphemy, I may even say—that is offered to her character by a light or injurious word."

"Giovanni!—my poor Giovanni!" answered the Professor, with a calm expression of pity "I know this wretched girl far better than yourself. You shall hear the truth in respect to the poisoner Rappaccini, and his poisonous daughter. Yes; poisonous as she is beautiful! Listen; for even should you do violence to my gray hairs, it shall not silence me. That old fable of the Indian

---

23. **apothecary.** Druggist or pharmacist

How does Giovanni respond to Baglioni's tale? Which of his actions reveal that he believes the professor's story?

WORDS FOR EVERYDAY USE:

im • bue (im byoo´) vt., fill; saturate

e • vince (ē vins´) vt., show plainly; indicate

woman has become a truth, by the deep and deadly science of Rappaccini, and in the person of the lovely Beatrice!"

Giovanni groaned and hid his face.

"Her father," continued Baglioni, "was not restrained by natural affection from offering up his child, in this horrible manner, as the victim of his insane zeal for science. For—let us do him justice—he is as true a man of science as ever distilled his own heart in an alembic.[24] What, then, will be your fate? Beyond a doubt, you are selected as the material of some new experiment. Perhaps the result is to be death—perhaps a fate more awful still! Rappaccini, with what he calls the interest of science before his eyes, will hesitate at nothing."

"It is a dream!" muttered Giovanni to himself, "surely it is a dream!"

"But," resumed the professor, "be of good cheer, son of my friend! It is not yet too late for the rescue. Possibly, we may even succeed in bringing back this miserable child within the limits of ordinary nature, from which her father's madness has estranged her. Behold this little silver vase! It was wrought by the hands of the renowned Benvenuto Cellini,[25] and is well worthy to be a lovegift to the fairest dame in Italy. But its contents are invaluable. One little sip of this antidote would have rendered the most virulent poisons of the Borgias[26] innocuous. Doubt not that it will be as <u>efficacious</u> against those of Rappaccini. Bestow the vase, and the precious liquid within it, on your Beatrice, and hopefully await the result."

Baglioni laid a small, exquisitely wrought silver phial[27] on the table, and withdrew, leaving what he had said to produce its effect upon the young man's mind.

"We will thwart Rappaccini yet!" thought he, chuckling to himself, as he descended the stairs. "But, let us confess the truth of him, he is a wonderful man!—a wonderful man indeed! A vile empiric,[28] however, in his practice, and therefore not to be tolerated by those who respect the good old rules of the medical profession!"

Throughout Giovanni's whole acquaintance with Beatrice, he had occasionally, as we have said, been haunted by dark <u>surmises</u> as to her character. Yet, so thoroughly had she made herself felt by him as a simple, natural, most affectionate and guileless creature, that the image now held up by Professor Baglioni, looked as strange and incredible, as if it were not in accordance with his own original conception. True, there were ugly recollections connected with his first glimpses of the beautiful girl; he could not quite forget the bouquet that withered in her grasp, and the insect that perished amid the sunny air, by no ostensible agency, save the fragrance of her breath. These incidents, however, dissolving in the pure light of her character, had no longer the efficacy of facts, but were acknowledged as mistaken fantasies, by whatever testimony of the senses they might appear to be substantiated. There is

24. **alembic.** Apparatus used for distilling
25. **Benvenuto Cellini.** (1500–1578) Italian goldsmith and sculptor
26. **Borgias.** Italian family, religiously and politically influential during the Renaissance, but also known for cruelty
27. **phial.** Small bottle
28. **empiric.** Person who relies on practical experiences rather than on scientific principles

What does Baglioni give to Giovanni? What is it supposed to do?

WORDS FOR EVERYDAY USE:

ef • fi • ca • cious (ef´i kā´shəs) *adj.*, producing or capable of producing the desired effect

sur • mise (sər mīz´) *n.*, conjecture; guess

something truer and more real, than what we can see with the eyes, and touch with the finger. On such better evidence, had Giovanni founded his confidence in Beatrice, though rather by the necessary force of her high attributes, than by any deep and generous faith, on his part. But, now, his spirit was incapable of sustaining itself at the height to which the early enthusiasm of passion had exalted it; he fell down, grovelling among earthly doubts, and defiled therewith the pure whiteness of Beatrice's image. Not that he gave her up; he did but distrust. He resolved to institute some decisive test that should satisfy him, once for all, whether there were those dreadful peculiarities in her physical nature, which could not be supposed to exist without some corresponding monstrosity of soul. His eyes, gazing down afar, might have deceived him as to the lizard, the insect, and the flowers. But if he could witness, at the distance of a few paces, the sudden blight of one fresh and healthful flower in Beatrice's hand, there would be room for no further question. With this idea, he hastened to the florist's, and purchased a bouquet that was still gemmed with the morning dewdrops.

It was now the customary hour of his daily interview with Beatrice. Before descending into the garden, Giovanni failed not to look at his figure in the mirror; a vanity to be expected in a beautiful young man, yet, as displaying itself at that troubled and feverish moment, the token of a certain shallowness of feeling and insincerity of character. He did gaze, however, and said to himself, that his features had never before possessed so rich a grace, nor his eyes such vivacity, nor his cheeks so warm a hue of superabundant life.

"At least," thought he, "her poison has not yet <u>insinuated</u> itself into my system. I am no flower to perish in her grasp!"

With that thought, he turned his eyes on the bouquet, which he had never once laid aside from his hand. A thrill of indefinable horror shot through his frame, on perceiving that those dewy flowers were already beginning to droop; they wore the aspect of things that had been fresh and lovely, yesterday. Giovanni grew white as marble, and stood motionless before the mirror, staring at his own reflection there, as at the likeness of something frightful. He remembered Baglioni's remark about the fragrance that seemed to pervade the chamber. It must have been the poison in his breath! Then he shuddered—shuddered at himself! Recovering from his stupor, he began to watch, with curious eye, a spider that was busily at work, hanging its web from the antique cornice of the apartment, crossing and recrossing the artful system of interwoven lines, as vigorous and active a spider as ever dangled from an old ceiling. Giovanni bent towards the insect, and emitted a deep, long breath. The spider suddenly ceased its toil; the web vibrated with a tremor originating in the body of the small artisan. Again Giovanni sent forth a breath, deeper, longer, and imbued with a venomous feeling out of his heart; he knew not whether he were wicked or only desperate. The spider made a convulsive gripe with his limbs, and hung dead across the window.

What does Giovanni assume about Beatrice's outer and inner nature?

What does Giovanni realize about himself?

WORDS FOR EVERYDAY USE:
in • sin • u • ate (in sin′yo͞o āt´) vt., introduce or work into gradually

"Accursed! Accursed!" muttered Giovanni, addressing himself. "Hast thou grown so poisonous, that this deadly insect perishes by the breath?"

At that moment, a rich, sweet voice came floating up from the garden:—

"Giovanni! Giovanni! It is past the hour! Why tarriest thou! Come down!"

"Yes," muttered Giovanni again. "She is the only being whom my breath may not slay! Would that it might!"

He rushed down, and in an instant, was standing before the bright and loving eyes of Beatrice. A moment ago, his wrath and despair had been so fierce that he could have desired nothing so much as to wither her by a glance. But, with her actual presence, there came influences which had too real an existence to be at once shaken off; recollections of the delicate and benign power of her feminine nature, which had so often enveloped him in a religious calm; recollections of many a holy and passionate outgush of her heart, when the pure fountain had been unsealed from its depths, and made visible in its transparency to his mental eye; recollections which, had Giovanni known how to estimate them, would have assured him that all this ugly mystery was but an earthly illusion, and that, whatever mist of evil might seem to have gathered over her, the real Beatrice was a heavenly angel. Incapable as he was of such high faith, still her presence had not utterly lost its magic. Giovanni's rage was quelled into an aspect of sullen insensibility. Beatrice, with a quick spiritual sense, immediately felt that there was a gulf of blackness between them, which neither he nor she could pass. They walked on together, sad and silent, and came thus to the marble fountain, and to its pool of water on the ground, in the midst of which grew the shrub that bore gem-like blossoms. Giovanni was affrighted at the eager enjoyment—the appetite, as it were—with which he found himself inhaling the fragrance of the flowers.

"Beatrice," asked he abruptly, "whence came this shrub?"

"My father created it," answered she, with simplicity.

"Created it! created it!" repeated Giovanni. "What mean you, Beatrice?"

"He is a man fearfully acquainted with the secrets of nature," replied Beatrice; "and, at the hour when I first drew breath, this plant sprang from the soil, the off-spring of his science, of his intellect, while I was but his earthly child. "Approach it not!" continued she, observing with terror that Giovanni was drawing nearer to the shrub. "It has qualities that you little dream of. But I, dearest Giovanni,—I grew up and blossomed with the plant, and was nourished with its breath. It was my sister, and I loved it with a human affection: for—alas! hast thou not suspected it? there was an awful doom."

Here Giovanni frowned so darkly upon her that Beatrice paused and trembled. But her faith in his tenderness reassured her, and made her blush that she had doubted for an instant.

"There was an awful doom," she continued,—"the effect of my father's fatal love of science—which estranged me from all society of any kind. Until Heaven sent thee, dearest Giovanni, Oh! how lonely was thy poor Beatrice!"

"Was it a hard doom?" asked Giovanni, fixing his eyes upon her.

"Only of late have I known how hard it was," answered she tenderly. "Oh, yes; but my heart was torpid,[29] and therefore quiet."

---

29. **torpid.** Dormant; sluggish

How did the plant come into being? What is its relation to Beatrice?

Why is Giovanni incapable of seeing Beatrice's true nature?

Giovanni's rage broke forth from his sullen gloom like a lightning flash out of a dark cloud.

"Accursed one!" cried he, with venomous scorn and anger. "And finding thy solitude wearisome, thou hast severed me, likewise, from all the warmth of life, and enticed me into thy region of unspeakable horror!"

"Giovanni!" exclaimed Beatrice, turning her large bright eyes upon his face. The force of his words had not found its way into her mind; she was merely wonder-struck.

"Yes, poisonous thing!" repeated Giovanni, beside himself with passion. "Thou has done it! Thou has blasted me! Thou hast filled my veins with poison! Thou hast made me as hateful, as ugly, as loathsome and deadly a creature as thyself,—a world's wonder of hideous monstrosity! Now—if our breath be happily as fatal to ourselves as to all others—let us join our lips in one kiss of unutterable hatred, and so die!"

"What has befallen me?" murmured Beatrice, with a low moan out of her heart. "Holy Virgin pity me, a poor heartbroken child!"

"Thou! Dost thou pray?" cried Giovanni, still with the same fiendish scorn. "Thy very prayers, as they come from thy lips, taint the atmosphere with death. Yes, yes; let us pray! Let us to church, and dip our fingers in the holy water at the portal! They that come after us will perish as by a pestilence. Let us sign crosses in the air! It will be scattering curses abroad in the likeness of holy symbols!"

"Giovanni," said Beatrice calmly, for her grief was beyond passion, "why dost thou join thyself with me thus in those terrible words? I, it is true, am the horrible thing thou namest me. But thou!—what hast thou to do, save with one other shudder at my hideous misery, to go forth out of the garden and mingle with thy race, and forget that there ever crawled on earth such a monster as poor Beatrice?"

"Dost thou pretend ignorance?" asked Giovanni, scowling upon her. "Behold! This power have I gained from the pure daughter of Rappaccini!"

There was a swarm of summer-insects flitting through the air, in search of the food promised by the flower-odors of the fatal garden. They circled round Giovanni's head, and were evidently attracted towards him by the same influence which had drawn them, for an instant, within the sphere of several of the shrubs. He sent forth a breath among them, and smiled bitterly at Beatrice, as at least a score of the insects fell dead upon the ground.

"I see it! I see it!" shrieked Beatrice. "It is my father's fatal science! No, no, Giovanni; it was not I! Never, never! I dreamed only to love thee, and be with thee a little time, and so to let thee pass away, leaving but thine image in mine heart. For, Giovanni—believe it—though my body be nourished with poison, my spirit is God's creature, and craves love as its daily food. But my father!—he has united us in this fearful sympathy. Yes; spurn me!—tread upon me!—kill me! Oh, what is death, after such words as thine? But it was not I! Not for a world of bliss would I have done it!"

Giovanni's passion had exhausted itself in its outburst from his lips. There now came across a sense, mournful, and not without tenderness, of the intimate and peculiar relationship between Beatrice and himself. They stood, as it were, in an utter solitude, which would be made none the less solitary by the densest throng of human life. Ought not, then, the desert of humanity around them to press this insulated pair close together? If they should be cruel to one

How does Giovanni behave toward Beatrice?

What does Beatrice say her intentions were? Does she resemble in any way the woman Giovanni has accused her of being?

another, who was there to be kind to them? Besides, thought Giovanni, might there not still be a hope of his returning within the limits of ordinary nature, and leading Beatrice—the redeemed Beatrice—by the hand? Oh, weak, and selfish, and unworthy spirit, that could dream of an earthly union and earthly happiness as possible, after such deep love had been so bitterly wronged as was Beatrice's love by Giovanni's blighting words! No, no; there could be no such hope. She must pass heavily, with that broken heart, across the borders—she must bathe her hurts in some fount of Paradise, and forget her grief in the light of immortality—and *there* be well!

But Giovanni did not know it.

"Dear Beatrice," said he, approaching her, while she shrank away, as always at his approach, but now with a different impulse—"dearest Beatrice, our fate is not yet so desperate. Behold! There is a medicine, potent, as a wise physician has assured me, and almost divine in its efficacy. It is composed of ingredients the most opposite to those by which thy awful father has brought this calamity upon thee and me. It is distilled of blessed herbs. Shall we not quaff it together and thus be purified from evil?"

"Give it me!" said Beatrice, extending her hand to receive the little silver phial which Giovanni took from his bosom. She added, with a peculiar emphasis; "I will drink—but do thou await the result."

She put Baglioni's antidote to her lips; and, at the same moment, the figure of Rappaccini emerged from the portal, and came slowly towards the marble fountain. As he drew near, the pale man of science seemed to gaze with a triumphant expression at the beautiful youth and maiden, as might an artist who should spend his life in achieving a picture or a group of statuary, and finally be satisfied with his success. He paused—his bent form grew erect with conscious power, he spread out his hand over them, in the attitude of a father imploring a blessing upon his children. But those were the same hands that had thrown poison into the stream of their lives! Giovanni trembled. Beatrice shuddered nervously, and pressed her hand upon her heart.

"My daughter," said Rappaccini, "thou art no longer lonely in the world! Pluck one of those precious gems from thy sister shrub, and bid thy bridegroom wear it in his bosom. It will not harm him now! My science, and the sympathy between thee and him, have so wrought within his system, that he now stands apart from common men, as thou dost, daughter of my pride and triumph, from ordinary women. Pass on, then, through the world, most dear to one another, and dreadful to all besides!"

"My father," said Beatrice, feebly—and still, as she spoke, she kept her hand upon her heart—"wherefore didst thou inflict this miserable doom upon thy child?"

"Miserable!" exclaimed Rappaccini. "What mean you, foolish girl? Dost thou deem it misery to be endowed with[30] marvelous gifts, against which no power nor strength could avail an enemy? Misery, to be able to quell the mightiest with a breath? Misery, to be as terrible as thou art beautiful? Wouldst thou, then, have preferred the condition of a weak woman, exposed to all evil, and capable of none?"

"I would fain have been loved, not feared," murmured Beatrice, sinking down upon the ground.—"But now it matters not; I am going, father, where the evil, which thou hast striven to mingle with my being, will pass away like a dream—like the fragrance of these poisonous flowers,

---

30. **endowed with.** Given

What does Giovanni realize? Why is it too late?

Why is Beatrice shrinking from Giovanni now?

which will no longer taint my breath among the flowers of Eden. Farewell, Giovanni! Thy words of hatred are like lead within my heart—but they, too, will fall away as I ascend. Oh, was there not, from the first, more poison in thy nature than in mine?"

To Beatrice—so radically had her earthly part been wrought upon by Rappaccini's skill—as poison had been life, so the powerful antidote was death. And thus the poor victim of man's ingenuity and of thwarted nature, and of the fatality that attends all such efforts of perverted wisdom, perished there, at the feet of her father and Giovanni. Just at that moment, Professor Pietro Baglioni looked forth from the window, and called loudly, in a tone of triumph mixed with horror, to the thunderstricken man of science:

"Rappaccini! Rappaccini! And is *this* the upshot of your experiment?" ∎

What does Beatrice ask Giovanni?

Responding to the Selection

How do you think Rappaccini felt at the end of the story? Do you suppose he blamed himself for what happened? or Giovanni? or Baglioni? Which of the three would you hold responsible for Beatrice's death? Why?

Reviewing the Selection

RECALLING

1. When and in what city does the story take place? How does Giovanni Guasconti happen to be on the scene?

2. What color links the spectacular shrub in the garden with Beatrice? Name at least one other characteristic common to the two.

3. Who is Baglioni? What is his relationship with Rappaccini?

4. Before Giovanni meets Beatrice, what does he see, or think he sees, that makes him fear her? After he meets her, what makes him ignore his fears until Baglioni's visit?

INTERPRETING

▶▶ 5. Giovanni suspects that Rappaccini has arranged for him to visit the garden. Why does he think so? What might be Rappaccini's reasons for allowing a man to visit Beatrice? for choosing Giovanni to be that man?

▶▶ 6. During their first meeting in the garden, why does Beatrice stop Giovanni from plucking a blossom from her "sister" plant? What causes her to hide her face and run away?

▶▶ 7. Could Giovanni trust Baglioni's opinion of Rappaccini? Why, or why not? At the tale's end, why does Baglioni's voice suggest triumph as well as horror?

▶▶ 8. When Giovanni suggests that both he and Beatrice drink Baglioni's antidote, why does she say, "I will drink—but do thou await the result"?

9. Is Giovanni truly in love with Beatrice? Is she truly in love with him? Give reasons for your answers.

10. Giovanni called Beatrice a "poisonous thing"; she claimed that there was more poison in his nature than in hers. With whom do you agree?

Understanding Literature (Questions for Discussion)

1. **Fantasy.** A **fantasy** is a literary work that contains highly unrealistic elements. Identify some of the fantastic elements in "Rappaccini's Daughter."

2. **Symbol.** A **symbol** is a thing that stands for or represents both itself and something else. For example, the lush, poisonous foliage in Rappaccini's garden probably represents temptation or evil. If so, what does the fountain that flows "cheerfully" into the garden pool symbolize? Does Beatrice also represent evil, or something more complex? What might Rappaccini himself symbolize?

3. **Allusion.** An **allusion** is a figure of speech in which a reference is made to a person, event, object, or work from history or literature. According to the Bible, God declared that "It is not good for man to be alone" and therefore created Eve to be Adam's partner in the Garden of Eden. In the final scene of "Rappaccini's Daughter," set in the poisonous garden, Rappaccini tells Beatrice that, due to his science, Giovanni is a fit partner and "thou art no longer lonely." How does this allusion to the Biblical story of creation demonstrate Rappaccini's pride? What light does it throw on the nature of the evil in Rappaccini and his garden?

Responding in Writing

1. **Recommendations.** Frequently, students and job-seekers must submit recommendations from teachers, former employers, or others who can attest to their abilities and habits. What sort of recommendation might Baglioni write for Giovanni on the basis of their first meeting? Which of Giovanni's qualities—both good and bad—would seem important to him and worth mentioning? Would Rappaccini's opinion at the time Giovanni began to visit Beatrice be similar, or would he emphasize different qualities in the young man? Take the role of each of these learned men; for each, write a short recommendation for Giovanni for admission to graduate school.

2. **Diary Entries.** In his conversations with Beatrice, Giovanni discovered that she had little, if any, experience with the world outside her father's garden. What topics, then, might she discuss in her diary? Write three diary entries in Beatrice's style of speaking: the first preceding Giovanni's moving in next door, the second following his first words to her from the upper-floor window, and the third about his visits to the garden.

3. **News Story.** Write one of these news stories about Beatrice Rappaccini: (1) a factual, objective report on her death and the coroner's decision blaming it on natural causes; (2) a sensational, tabloid-style report on her ability to kill small animals with her breath, and humans with her kiss.

Language Lab

Subordinate Clauses. Read the material about subordinate clauses and their introductory words in the Language Arts Survey, 2.11, "Relative Pronouns," and 2.27, "Subordinating Conjunctions." Then find the subordinate clause or clauses in each of these sentences. Write out each subordinate clause, draw one line under any relative pronoun that connects the clause, and draw two lines under any introductory subordinating conjunction.

1. Nathaniel Hawthorne, who died over a century ago, still ranks as one of the greatest of American authors.

2. His most important work, *The Scarlet Letter*, examines the effects on a sinner of guilt that is hidden.

3. The setting of this novel, like that of many other tales by Hawthorne, is Puritan New England, where one of Hawthorne's ancestors served as a judge in witch trials.

4. Although Nathaniel Hawthorne did not accept the optimism of the Transcendentalists, he befriended many members of the movement, including Ralph Waldo Emerson and Henry Thoreau, with whom he enjoyed conversations and ice-skating.

5. Another activity that Hawthorne enjoyed was gardening, as readers will discover when they read his introduction to *Mosses from an Old Manse,* a collection of short stories that Hawthorne wrote while he lived in the house named in the title.

Thinking Skills

Decision Making. Read the Language Arts Survey, 4.3, "Strategies for Decision Making." Then think about Giovanni's predicament when he discovers that his breath is poisonous. Develop at least two different approaches to resolving the problem, besides confronting and accusing Beatrice. Apply either of the strategies described in the survey to select the best approach—one that, if possible, will avoid Beatrice's death.

PROJECTS

1. **Fantasy Garden Catalog.** Work with a partner to create a two- to four-page catalog advertising fantastic plants such as those in Rappaccini's garden. Brainstorm possible variations on existing plants, or combinations of two or more species. Use your imagination to produce frightening, mysterious, or comical plants. Develop illustrations of the plants by drawing, using computer art programs, or splicing together pieces of pictures of real plants. Write a description of each plant, keeping a consistent tone, which may be academic, attention-getting, or tongue-in-cheek. Lay out the pages, pasting art and text in place.

2. **Paraphrasing.** Work with a small group of students to translate some of the dialogue in "Rappaccini's Daughter" into modern English, either formal or informal. Refer to the Language Arts Survey, 2.147, "Formal and Informal English." Take turns reading the speeches aloud and restating the ideas in language more natural to your group. Try not to change the thoughts as you change words or word order. (Of course, any translation will necessarily change the meaning somewhat. Robert Frost once wrote that "Poetry is what gets lost in the translation." You may find it interesting to discuss with your classmates the differences between some of the "translations" and the original passages.)

"The Pit and the Pendulum"
by Edgar Allan Poe

ABOUT THE AUTHOR

Edgar Allan Poe (1809–1849) led a short, troubled life but managed in his forty years to make major contributions to literary form and to criticism. Considered to be one of the two creators of the modern short story (the other being Nathaniel Hawthorne), Poe also invented detective fiction, wrote lyric poetry, and pioneered the psychological horror story. Poe's major innovation in the last of these literary forms was to use a technique of double meaning, whereby a tale could be read as being either about the supernatural or about the imaginings of a madman. Few writers have had such enduring popularity and influence as Poe. As a critic, Poe offered a superb definition of the short story, which he thought of as a brief fictional work, the details of which are carefully chosen to create in the reader a single dominant impression.

Poe's father deserted the family when Edgar was a year old. His mother died at the age of twenty-four, and Poe, two years old, was taken in by John Allan, a prosperous Richmond, Virginia, merchant. Poe attended the University of Virginia and did well in his studies. He joined the army after writing *Tamerlane and Other Poems* and was appointed to West Point, but poor class attendance led to his expulsion from the academy. Poe later held various editorial jobs, reviewed literary works, and wrote one novel, *The Narrative of Arthur Gordon Pym,* in addition to producing numerous short stories and poems. Briefly famous and successful after the publication of his poem "The Raven" (Unit 5), Poe nonetheless spent most of his adult life in poverty, losing one job after another due to drinking and quarrelsomeness. After his death, he was hailed as a genius, particularly in France, where he greatly influenced the Symbolist poets Paul Valéry and Charles Baudelaire.

ABOUT THE SELECTION

"**The Pit and the Pendulum**" is a tale of terror, a short story nightmare. The Spanish Inquisition, which lasted from the 1400s to the 1800s, provides a fitting setting for this story of a man who finds himself imprisoned for reasons he cannot understand and becomes the helpless victim of unknowable and cruel torturers. The Inquisition began as an attempt by the Catholic Church to identify and punish heretics, those who refused to believe in the church's teachings. However, it degenerated into an excuse for those in power to persecute their enemies, as was the case with the prisoner in this tale. Poe's stories often were set in foreign locales, rarely in familiar American locations. Removed from familiar settings, the stories take on romantic, exotic overtones that add to their overall mood of strangeness and suspense.

"The Pit and the Pendulum"

Edgar Allan Poe

I was sick—sick unto death with that long agony; and when they at length unbound me, and I was permitted to sit, I felt that my senses were leaving me. The sentence—the dread sentence of death—was the last of distinct <u>accentuation</u> which reached my ears. After that, the sound of the <u>inquisitorial</u> voices seemed merged in one dreamy <u>indeterminate</u> hum. It conveyed to my soul the idea of *revolution*—perhaps from its association in fancy with the burr of a mill wheel. This only for a brief period; for presently I heard no more. Yet, for a while, I saw; but with how terrible an exaggeration! I saw the lips of the black-robed judges. They appeared to me white—whiter than the sheet upon which I trace these words—and thin even to grotesqueness; thin with the intensity of their expression of firmness—of immovable resolution—of stern contempt of human torture. I saw that the decrees of what to me was Fate were still issuing from those lips. I saw them <u>writhe</u> with a deadly <u>locution</u>. I saw them fashion the syllables of my name; and I shuddered because no sound succeeded. I saw, too, for a few moments of delirious horror, the soft and nearly imperceptible waving of the sable draperies which enwrapped the walls of the apartment. And then my vision fell upon the seven tall candles upon the table. At first they wore the aspect of charity, and seemed white slender angels who would save me; but then, all at once, there came a most deadly nausea over my spirit, and I felt every fiber in my frame thrill as if I had touched the wire of a galvanic[1] battery, while the angel forms became meaningless specters, with heads of flame, and I saw that from them there would be no help. And then there

What exaggerations does the prisoner see?

---

1. **galvanic.** Producing an electric current

WORDS FOR EVERYDAY USE:

ac • cen • tu • a • tion (ak sen´choo ā´ shən) *n.*, emphasis; clear pronunciation

in • quis • i • to • ri • al (in kwiz´ə tôr´ē əl) *adj.*, prying

in • de • ter • mi • nate (in´dē tʉr´mi' nit) *adj.*, unspecific; unsettled

writhe (rīth) *vt.*, make twisting movements

lo • cu • tion (lō kyoo´shən) *n.*, word; phrase

stole into my fancy, like a rich musical note, the thought of what sweet rest there must be in the grave. The thought came gently and stealthily, and it seemed long before it attained full appreciation; but just as my spirit came at length properly to feel and entertain it, the figures of the judges vanished, as if magically, from before me; the tall candles sank into nothingness; their flames went out utterly; the blackness of darkness <u>supervened</u>; all sensations appeared swallowed up in a mad rushing descent as of the soul into Hades.[2] Then silence, and stillness, and night were the universe.

I had swooned; but still will not say that all of consciousness was lost. What of it there remained I will not attempt to define, or even to describe; yet all was not lost. In the deepest slumber—no! In delirium—no! In a swoon—no! In death—no! even in the grave all is *not* lost. Else there is no immortality for man. Arousing from the most profound of slumbers, we break the gossamer web of *some* dream. Yet in a second afterward (so frail may that web have been), we remember not that we have dreamed. In the return to life from the swoon there are two stages; first, that of the sense of mental or spiritual; secondly, that of the sense of physical, existence. It seems probable that if, upon reaching the second stage, we could recall the impressions of the first, we should find these impressions eloquent in memories of the gulf beyond. And that gulf is—what? How at least shall we distinguish its shadows from those of the tomb? But if the impressions of what I have termed the first stage, are not, at will, recalled, yet, after long interval, do they not come unbidden, while we marvel whence they come? He who has never swooned is not he who finds strange palaces and wildly familiar faces in coals that glow; is not he who beholds floating in midair the sad visions that the many may not view; is not he who ponders over the perfume of some novel flower—is not he whose brain grows bewildered with the meaning of some musical <u>cadence</u> which has never before arrested his attention.

Amid frequent and thoughtful endeavors to remember; amid <u>earnest</u> struggles to regather some token of the state of seeming nothingness into which my soul had lapsed, there have been moments when I have dreamed of success; there have been brief, very brief periods when I have <u>conjured</u> up remembrances which the lucid reason of a later epoch assures me could have had reference only to that condition of seeming unconsciousness. These shadows of memory tell, indistinctly, of tall figures that lifted and bore me in silence down—down—still down—till a hideous dizziness oppressed me at the mere idea of the <u>interminableness</u> of the descent. They tell also of a vague horror at my heart, on account of that heart's unnatural stillness. Then comes a sense of sudden motionlessness throughout all things; as if those who bore me (a ghastly train!) had outrun, in their descent, the limits of the limitless, and paused from the wearisomeness of their toil. After this I call to mind flatness and dampness; and then all is madness—the madness of a

What sorts of visions has the prisoner experienced?

---

2. **Hades.** In Greek mythology, home of the dead; underground

WORDS FOR EVERYDAY USE:

su • per • vene (soo̅′pər vēn´) *vi.*, happen unexpectedly

ca • dence (cād´ʼns) *n.*, rhythmic flow of sound or tone

ear • nest (ʉr′nist) *adj.*, serious; intense

con • jure (kun´jər) *vt.*, call

in • ter • mi • na • ble (in tʉr′mi nə bəl) *adj.*, without, or seemingly without, end

memory which busies itself among forbidden things.

Very suddenly there came back to my soul motion and sound—the tumultuous motion of the heart, and, in my ears, the sound of its beating. Then a pause in which all is blank. Then again sound, and motion, and touch—a tingling sensation pervading my frame. Then the mere consciousness of existence, without thought—a condition which lasted long. Then, very suddenly, *thought*, and shuddering terror, and earnest endeavor to comprehend my true state. Then a strong desire to lapse into insensibility. Then a rushing revival of soul and a successful effort to move. And now a full memory of the trial, of the judges, of the sable draperies, of the sentence, of the sickness, of the swoon. Then entire forgetfulness of all that followed; of all that a later day and much earnestness of endeavor have enabled me vaguely to recall.

So far, I had not opened my eyes. I felt that I lay upon my back, unbound. I reached out my hand, and it fell heavily upon something damp and hard. There I suffered it to remain for many minutes, while I strove to imagine where and *what* I could be. I longed, yet dared not to employ my vision. I dreaded the first glance at objects around me. It was not that I feared to look upon things horrible, but that I grew aghast lest there should be *nothing* to see. At length, with a wild desperation at heart, I quickly unclosed my eyes. My worst thoughts, then, were confirmed. The blackness of eternal night <u>encompassed</u> me. I struggled for breath. The intensity of the darkness seemed to oppress and stifle me. The atmosphere was intolerably close. I

Where does the prisoner fear he is?

still lay quietly, and made effort to exercise my reason. I brought to mind the inquisitorial proceedings, and attempted from that point to deduce my real condition. The sentence had passed; and it appeared to me that a very long interval of time had since elapsed. Yet not for a moment did I suppose myself actually dead. Such a supposition, notwithstanding what we read in fiction, is altogether inconsistent with real existence;—but where and in what state was I? The condemned to death, I knew, perished usually at the autos-da-fe,[3] and one of these had been held on the very night of the day of my trial. Had I been remanded to my dungeon, to await the next sacrifice, which would not take place for many months? This I at once saw could not be. Victims had been in immediate demand. Moreover, my dungeon, as well as all the condemned cells at Toledo,[4] had stone floors, and light was not altogether excluded.

A fearful idea now suddenly drove the blood in torrents upon my heart, and for a brief period, I once more relapsed into insensibility. Upon recovering, I at once started to my feet, trembling convulsively in every fiber. I thrust my arms wildly above and around me in all directions. I felt nothing; yet dreaded to move a step, lest I should be <u>impeded</u> by the walls of a *tomb*. Perspiration burst from every pore, and stood in cold big beads upon my forehead. The agony of suspense grew at length intolerable, and I cautiously moved

---

3. **autos-da-fe.** Public ceremonies in which the inquisitors pronounced judgment and passed sentences on heretics
4. **Toledo.** Spanish city

WORDS FOR EVERYDAY USE:

en • com • pass (en kum´pəs) *vt.*, surround

im • pede (im pēd´) *vt.*, obstruct; hinder

forward, with my arms extended, and my eyes straining from their sockets, in the hope of catching some faint ray of light. I proceeded for many paces; but still all was blackness and vacancy. I breathed more freely. It seemed evident that mine was not, at least, the most hideous of fates.

And now, as I still continued to step cautiously onward, there came thronging upon my recollection, a thousand vague rumors of the horrors of Toledo. Of the dungeons there had been strange things narrated—fables I had always deemed them—but yet strange, and too ghastly to repeat, save in a whisper. Was I left to perish of starvation in this subterranean world of darkness; or what fate, perhaps even more fearful, awaited me? That the result would be death, and a death of more than customary bitterness, I knew too well the character of my judges to doubt. The mode and the hour were all that occupied or distracted me.

My outstretched hands at length encountered some solid obstruction. It was a wall, seemingly of stone masonry—very smooth, slimy, and cold. I followed it up; stepping with all the careful distrust with which certain antique narratives had inspired me. This process, however, afforded me no means of ascertaining the dimensions of my dungeon; as I might make its circuit, and return to the point whence I set out, without being aware of the fact; so perfectly uniform seemed the wall. I therefore sought the knife which had been in my pocket, when led into the inquisitorial chamber; but it was gone; my clothes had been exchanged for a wrapper of coarse serge.[5] I had thought of forcing the blade in some minute crevice of the masonry, so as to identify my point of departure. The difficulty, nevertheless, was but trivial; although, in the disorder of my fancy, it seemed at first <u>insuperable</u>. I tore a part of the hem from the robe and placed the fragment at full length, and at right angles to the wall. In groping my way around the prison, I could not fail to encounter this rag upon completing the circuit. So, at least I thought; but I had not counted upon the extent of the dungeon, or upon my own weakness. The ground was moist and slippery. I staggered onward for some time, when I stumbled and fell. My excessive fatigue induced me to remain prostrate; and sleep soon overtook me as I lay.

Upon awaking, and stretching forth an arm, I found beside me a loaf and a pitcher with water. I was too much exhausted to reflect upon this circumstance, but ate and drank with <u>avidity</u>. Shortly afterward, I resumed my tour around the prison, and with much toil, came at last upon the fragment of the serge. Up to the period when I fell I had counted fifty-two paces, and upon resuming my walk, I had counted forty-eight more;—when I arrived at the rag. There were in all, then, a hundred paces; and, admitting two paces to the yard, I presumed the dungeon to be fifty yards in circuit. I had met, however, with many angles in the wall, and thus I could form no guess at the shape of the vault; for vault I could not help supposing it to be.

I had little object—certainly no hope—in these researches; but a vague curiosity

What were the rumors about Toledo?

How does the prisoner measure his cell?

---

5. **serge.** Sturdy fabric

WORDS FOR EVERYDAY USE:

in • su • per• a • ble (in sōō´pər ə bəl) *adj.,* insurmountable

a • vid • i • ty (ə vid´ə tē) *n.,* eagerness; enthusiasm

prompted me to continue them. Quitting the wall, I resolved to cross the area of the enclosure. At first I proceeded with extreme caution, for the floor, although seemingly of solid material, was treacherous with slime. At length, however, I took courage, and did not hesitate to step firmly; endeavoring to cross in as direct a line as possible. I had advanced some ten or twelve paces in this manner, when the remnant of the torn hem of my robe became entangled between my legs. I stepped on it, and fell violently on my face.

How does the prisoner discover the pit?

In the confusion attending my fall, I did not immediately apprehend a somewhat startling circumstance, which yet, in a few seconds afterward, and while I still lay prostrate, arrested my attention. It was this—my chin rested upon the floor of the prison, but my lips and the upper portion of my head, although seemingly at a less elevation than the chin, touched nothing. At the same time my forehead seemed bathed in a clammy vapor, and the peculiar smell of decayed fungus arose to my nostrils. I put forward my arm, and shuddered to find that I had fallen at the very brink of a circular pit, whose extent, of course, I had no means of ascertaining at the moment. Groping about the masonry just below the margin, I succeeded in dislodging a small fragment, and let it fall into the <u>abyss</u>. For many seconds I hearkened to its reverberations as it dashed against the sides of the chasm in its descent; at length there was a sullen plunge into water, succeeded by loud echoes. At the same moment there came a sound resembling the quick opening, and as rapid closing of a door overhead, while a faint gleam of light flashed suddenly through the gloom, and as suddenly faded away.

What condition follows the prisoner's quenching his thirst?

I saw clearly the doom which had been prepared for me, and congratulated myself upon the timely accident by which I had escaped. Another step before my fall, and the world had seen me no more. And the death just avoided, was of that very character which I had regarded as fabulous and frivolous in the tales respecting the Inquisition. To the victims of its tyranny, there was the choice of death with its direst physical agonies, or death with its most hideous moral horrors. I had been reserved for the latter. By long suffering my nerves had been unstrung, until I trembled at the sound of my own voice, and had become in every respect a fitting subject for the species of torture which awaited me.

Shaking in every limb, I groped my way back to the wall; resolving there to perish rather than risk the terrors of the wells, of which my imagination now pictured many in various positions about the dungeon. In other conditions of mind I might have had courage to end my misery at once by a plunge into one of these abysses; but now I was the veriest of cowards. Neither could I forget what I had read of these pits—that the *sudden* extinction of life formed no part of their most horrible plan.

Agitation of spirit kept me awake for many long hours; but at length I again slumbered. Upon arousing, I found by my side, as before, a loaf and a pitcher of water. A burning thirst consumed me, and I emptied the vessel at a draught. It must have been drugged; for scarcely had I drunk, before I became irresistibly drowsy.

WORDS FOR EVERYDAY USE:

a • byss (ə bis´) *n.,* bottomless hole

A deep sleep fell upon me—a sleep like that of death. How long it lasted of course, I know not; but when, once again, I unclosed my eyes, the objects around me were visible. By a wild sulphurous[6] luster, the origin of which I could not at first determine, I was enabled to see the extent and aspect of the prison.

In its size I had been greatly mistaken. The whole circuit of its walls did not exceed twenty-five yards. For some minutes this fact occasioned me a world of vain trouble; vain indeed! for what could be of less importance, under the terrible circumstances which environed me, than the mere dimensions of my dungeon? But my soul took a wild interest in trifles, and I busied myself in endeavors to account for the error I had committed in my measurement. The truth at length flashed upon me. In my first attempt at exploration I had counted fifty-two paces, up to the period when I fell; I must then have been within a pace or two of the fragment of serge; in fact, I had nearly performed the circuit of the vault. I then slept, and upon awaking, I must have returned upon my steps—thus supposing the circuit nearly double what it actually was. My confusion of mind prevented me from observing that I began my tour with the wall to the left; and ended it with the wall to the right.

I had been deceived, too, in respect to the shape of the enclosure. In feeling my way I had found many angles, and thus deduced an idea of great irregularity; so potent is the effect of total darkness upon one arousing from lethargy or sleep! The angles were simply those of a few slight depressions, or niches, at odd intervals. The general shape of the prison was square. What I had taken for masonry seemed now to be iron, or some other metal, in huge plates, whose sutures or joints occasioned the depression. The entire surface of this metallic enclosure was rudely daubed in all the hideous and repulsive devices to which the charnel[7] superstition of the monks has given rise. The figures of fiends in aspects of menace, with skeleton forms, and other more really fearful images, overspread and disfigured the walls. I observed that the outlines of these monstrosities were sufficiently distinct, but that the colors seemed faded and blurred, as if from the effects of a damp atmosphere. I now noticed the floor, too, which was of stone. In the center yawned the circular pit from whose jaws I had escaped; but it was the only one in the dungeon.

What absorbs the prisoner's interest?

All this I saw indistinctly and by much effort: for my personal condition had been greatly changed during slumber. I now lay upon my back, and at full length, on a species of low framework of wood. To this I was securely bound by a long strap resembling a surcingle.[8] It passed in many <u>convolutions</u> about my limbs and body, leaving at liberty only my head, and my left arm to such extent that I could, by dint of much exertion, supply myself with food from an earthen dish which lay by my side on the floor. I saw, to my horror, that the pitcher had been removed. I say

What change has taken place?

6. **sulphurous.** Similar to the color of burning sulphur, suggesting the fires of hell
7. **charnel.** Building where bodies and bones are placed
8. **surcingle.** Strap passed around a horse's body to hold on a saddle

---

WORDS FOR EVERYDAY USE: con • vo • lu • tion (kän´və lōō´ shən) *n.*, twist, coil, fold

to my horror, for I was consumed with intolerable thirst. This thirst it appeared to be the design of my persecutors to stimulate, for the food in the dish was meat <u>pungently</u> seasoned.

What is most frightening about the pendulum?

Looking upward, I surveyed the ceiling of my prison. It was some thirty or forty feet overhead, and constructed much as the side walls. In one of its panels a very singular figure riveted my whole attention. It was the painted figure of Time as he is commonly represented, save that, in lieu of a scythe, he held what, at a casual glance, I supposed to be the pictured image of a huge pendulum such as we see on antique clocks. There was something, however, in the appearance of this machine which caused me to regard it more attentively. While I gazed directly upward at it (for its position was immediately over my own) I fancied that I saw it in motion. In an instant afterward the fancy was confirmed. Its sweep was brief, and of course slow. I watched it for some minutes, somewhat in fear, but more in wonder. Wearied at length with observing its dull movement, I turned my eyes upon the other objects in the cell.

What attracts the rats?

A slight noise attracted my notice, and, looking to the floor, I saw several enormous rats traversing it. They had issued from the well, which lay just within view to my right. Even then, while I gazed, they came up in troops, hurriedly, with ravenous eyes, allured by the scent of the meat. From this it required much effort and attention to scare them away.

It might have been half an hour, perhaps even an hour (for I could take but imperfect note of time), before I again cast my eyes upward. What I then saw confounded and amazed me. The sweep of the pendulum had increased in extent by nearly a yard. As a natural consequence, its velocity was also much greater. But what mainly disturbed me was the idea that it had perceptibly *descended*. I now observed—with what horror it is needless to say—that its nether extremity was formed of a crescent of glittering steel, about a foot in length from horn to horn; the horns upward, and the under edge evidently as keen as that of a razor. Like a razor also, it seemed massy and heavy, tapering from the edge into a solid and broad structure above. It was appended to a weighty rod of brass, and the whole *hissed* as it swung through the air.

I could no longer doubt the doom prepared for me by monkish <u>ingenuity</u> in torture. My <u>cognizance</u> of the pit had become known to the inquisitorial agents—*the pit*, whose horrors had been destined for so bold a recusant[9] as myself—*the pit*, typical of hell, and regarded by rumor as the Ultima Thule[10] of all their punishments. The plunge into this pit I had avoided by the merest of accidents, and I knew that surprise, or entrapment into torment, formed an important portion of all the grotesquerie of these dungeon deaths. Having failed to fall, it was no part of the demon plan to hurl me into the abyss; and thus (there being no alternative) a different and a milder destruction awaited me. Milder! I half smiled in my agony as I thought of such application of such a term.

---

9. **recusant.** Person who refuses to obey an established authority
10. **Ultima Thule.** Farthest limit

WORDS FOR EVERYDAY USE:

pun • gent • ly (pun´jənt lē) *adv.,* sharply, strongly

in • ge • nu • i • ty (in´jə no͞o´ə tē) *n.,* cleverness

cog • ni • zance (käg´nə zəns) *n.,* knowledge

What boots it[11] to tell of the long, long hours of horror more than mortal, during which I counted the rushing oscillations of the steel! Inch by inch—line by line—with a descent only appreciable at intervals that seemed ages—down and still down it came! Days passed—it might have been that many days passed—ere it swept so closely over me as to fan me with its acrid breath. The odor of the sharp steel forced itself into my nostrils. I prayed—I wearied heaven with my prayer for its more speedy descent. I grew frantically mad, and struggled to force myself upward against the sweep of the fearful scimitar.[12] And then I fell suddenly calm, and lay smiling at the glittering death, as a child at some rare bauble.

There was another interval of utter insensibility; it was brief; for, upon again lapsing into life there had been no perceptible descent in the pendulum. But it might have been long; for I knew there were demons who took note of my swoon, and who could have arrested the vibration at pleasure. Upon my recovery, too, I felt very—oh, inexpressibly sick and weak, as if through long <u>inanition</u>. Even amid the

For what does the prisoner pray?

---

11. **What boots it.** What good is it
12. **scimitar.** Curved sword

WORDS FOR EVERYDAY USE: in • a • ni • tion (in´ə nish´ ən) *n.*, lack of strength due to lack of food

agonies of that period, the human nature craved food. With painful effort I outstretched my left arm as far as my bonds permitted, and took possession of the small remnant which had been spared me by the rats. As I put a portion of it within my lips, there rushed to my mind a half-formed thought of joy—of hope. Yet what business had *I* with hope? It was, as I say, a half-formed thought—man has many such which are never completed. I felt that it was of joy—of hope; but I felt also that it had perished in its formation. In vain I struggled to perfect—to regain it. Long suffering had nearly annihilated all my ordinary powers of mind. I was an imbecile—an idiot.

The vibration of the pendulum was at right angles to my length. I saw that the crescent was designed to cross the region of the heart. It would fray the serge of my robe—it would return and repeat its operations—again—and again. Notwithstanding its terrifically wide sweep (some thirty feet or more) and the hissing vigor of its descent sufficient to sunder these very walls of iron, still the fraying of my robe would be all that, for several minutes, it would accomplish. And at this thought I paused. I dared not go further than this reflection. I dwelt upon it with a <u>pertinacity</u> of attention—as if, in so dwelling, I could arrest *here* the descent of the steel. I forced myself to ponder upon the sound of the crescent as it should pass across the garment—upon the peculiar thrilling sensation which friction of cloth produces on the nerves. I pondered upon all this frivolity until my teeth were on edge.

Down—steadily down it crept. I took a frenzied pleasure in contrasting its downward with its lateral velocity. To the right—to the left—far and wide—with the shriek of a damned spirit; to my heart with the stealthy pace of the tiger! I alternately laughed and howled as the one or the other idea grew predominant.

Down—certainly, relentlessly down! It vibrated within three inches of my bosom! I struggled violently, furiously, to free my left arm. This was free only from the elbow to the hand. I could reach the latter, from the platter beside me, to my mouth, with great effort, but no farther. Could I have broken the fastenings above the elbow I would have seized and attempted to arrest the pendulum. I might as well have attempted to arrest an avalanche!

Down—still unceasingly—still inevitably down! I gasped and struggled at each vibration. I shrunk convulsively at its every sweep. My eyes followed its outward or upward whirls with the eagerness of the most unmeaning despair; they closed themselves spasmodically at the descent, although death would have been a relief, oh! how unspeakable! Still I quivered in every nerve to think how slight a sinking of the machinery would precipitate that keen, glistening ax upon my bosom. It was *hope* that prompted the nerve to quiver—the frame to shrink. It was *hope*—the hope that triumphs on the rack—that whispers to the death-condemned even in the dungeons of the Inquisition.

I saw that some ten or twelve vibrations would bring the steel in actual contact with my robe, and with this observation there suddenly came over my spirit all the keen, collected calmness of despair. For the first time during many hours—or perhaps

WORDS FOR EVERYDAY USE:

per • ti • nac • i • ty (pʉr′tə nas′ ə tē) *n.*, stubbornness days—I *thought*. It now occurred to me that the bandage, or surcingle, which enveloped me, was *unique*. I was tied by no separate cord. The first stroke of the razorlike crescent athwart any portion of the band, would so detach it that it might be unwound from my person by means of my left hand. But how fearful, in that case, the proximity of the steel! the result of the slightest struggle, how deadly! Was it likely, moreover, that the minions of the torturer had not foreseen and provided for this possibility? Was it probable that the bandage crossed my bosom in the track of the pendulum? Dreading to find my faint, and, as it seemed, my last hope frustrated, I so far elevated my head as to obtain a distinct view of my breast. The surcingle enveloped my limbs and body close in all directions—*save in the path of the destroying crescent.*

Scarcely had I dropped my head back into its original position, when there flashed upon my mind what I cannot better describe than as the unformed half of that idea of deliverance to which I have previously alluded, and of which a moiety only floated indeterminately through my brain when I raised food to my burning lips. The whole thought was now present—feeble, scarcely sane, scarcely definite—but still entire. I proceeded at once, with the nervous energy of despair, to attempt its execution.

For many hours the immediate vicinity of the low framework upon which I lay, had been literally swarming with rats. They were wild, bold, ravenous; their red eyes glaring upon me as if they waited but for motionlessness on my part to make me their prey. "To what food," I thought, "have they been accustomed in the well?"

They had devoured, in spite of all my efforts to prevent them, all but a small remnant of the contents of the dish. I had fallen into an habitual seesaw, or wave of the hand about the platter; and, at length, the unconscious uniformity of the movement deprived it of effect. In their voracity the vermin frequently fastened their sharp fangs in my fingers. With the particles of the oily and spicy viand which now remained, I thoroughly rubbed the bandage wherever I could reach it; then, raising my hand from the floor, I lay breathlessly still.

At first the ravenous animals were startled and terrified at the change—at the cessation of movement. They shrank alarmedly back; many sought the well. But this was only for a moment. I had not counted in vain upon their voracity. Observing that I remained without motion, one or two of the boldest leaped upon the framework and smelt at the surcingle. This seemed the signal for a general rush. Forth from the well they hurried in fresh troops. They clung to the wood—they overran it, and leaped in hundreds upon my person. The measured movement of the pendulum disturbed them not at all. Avoiding its strokes, they busied themselves with the anointed bandage. They pressed—they swarmed upon me in ever accumulating heaps. They writhed upon my throat; their cold lips sought my own; I was half stifled by their

What actions are part of the prisoner's plan?

What do the rats do?

| WORDS FOR EVERYDAY USE: | **moi • e • ty** (moi ə tē) *n.,* half
 ver • min (vur´mən) *n.,* small animals regarded as pests
 vi • and (vī´ənd) *n.,* article of food | **ces • sa • tion** (se sā´shən) *n.,* ceasing or stopping
 vo • rac • i • ty (vô ras´ə tē) *n.,* greediness
 a • noint • ed (ə noint´əd) *part.,* rubbed with the oil from the meat |

thronging pressure; disgust, for which the world has no name, swelled my bosom and chilled, with a heavy clamminess, my heart. Yet one minute, and I felt that the struggle would be over. Plainly I perceived the loosening of the bandage. I knew that in more than one place it must be already severed. With a more than human resolution I lay *still.*

Nor had I erred in my calculations—nor had I endured in vain. I at length felt that I was *free.* The surcingle hung in <u>ribands</u> from my body. But the stroke of the pendulum already pressed upon my bosom. It had divided the serge of the robe. It had cut through the linen beneath. Twice again it swung, and a sharp sense of pain shot through every nerve. But the moment of escape had arrived. At a wave of my hand my deliverers hurried tumultuously away. With a steady movement—cautious, sidelong, shrinking, and slow—I slid from the embrace of the bandage and beyond the reach of the scimitar. For the moment, at least, *I was free.*

Free!—and in the grasp of the Inquisition! I had scarcely stepped from my wooden bed of horror upon the stone floor of the prison, when the motion of the hellish machine ceased and I beheld it drawn up, by some invisible force, through the ceiling. This was a lesson which I took desperately to heart. My every motion was undoubtedly watched. Free!—I had but escaped death in one form of agony, to be delivered unto worse than death in some other. With that thought I rolled my eyes nervously around on the barriers of iron that hemmed me in. Something unusual—some change which, at first, I could not appreciate distinctly—it was obvious, had taken place in the apartment. For many minutes of a dreamy and trembling <u>abstraction</u>, I busied myself in vain, unconnected <u>conjecture</u>. During this period, I became aware, for the first time, of the origin of the sulphurous light which <u>illuminated</u> the cell. It proceeded from a <u>fissure</u>, about half an inch in width, extending entirely around the prison at the base of the walls, which thus appeared, and were, completely separated from the floor. I endeavored, but of course in vain, to look through the <u>aperture</u>.

As I arose from the attempt, the mystery of the alteration in the chamber broke at once upon my understanding. I have observed that, although the outlines of the figures upon the walls were sufficiently distinct, yet the colors seemed blurred and indefinite. These colors had now assumed, and were momentarily assuming, a startling and most intense brilliancy, that gave to the spectral and fiendish portraitures an aspect that might have thrilled even firmer nerves than my own. Demon eyes, of a wild and ghastly vivacity, glared upon me in a thousand directions where none had been visible before, and gleamed with the lurid luster of a fire that I could not force my imagination to regard as unreal.

Unreal!—Even while I breathed there came to my nostrils the breath of the vapor of the heated iron! A suffocating odor pervaded the prison! A deeper glow settled each moment in the eyes that glared at my agonies! A richer tint of crimson <u>diffused</u> itself over the pictured horrors of blood. I panted! I gasped for breath! There could

Why is the prisoner free but not free?

WORDS FOR EVERYDAY USE:

rib • and (rib´ənd) n., ribbon

ab • strac • tion (ab strak´shən) n., mental withdrawal; absent-mindedness

con • jec • ture (kən jek´chər) n., speculation

il • lu • mi • nate (i lo͞o´mə nāt´) vt., light up

fis • sure (fish´ər) n., deep crack

ap • er • ture (ap´ər cher) n., opening; hole

dif • fuse (di fyo͞os´) vt., spread out; pour out

be no doubt of the design of my tormentors—oh! most unrelenting! oh! most demoniac of men! I shrank from the glowing metal to the center of the cell. Amid the thought of the fiery destruction that <u>impended</u>, the idea of the coolness of the well came over my soul like <u>balm</u>. I rushed to its deadly brink. I threw my straining vision below. The glare from the enkindled roof illumined its inmost recesses. Yet, for a wild moment, did my spirit refuse to comprehend the meaning of what I saw. At length it forced—it wrestled its way into my soul—it burned itself in upon my shuddering reason.—Oh! for a voice to speak!—oh! horror!—oh! any horror but this! With a shriek, I rushed from the margin, and buried my face in my hands—weeping bitterly.

The heat rapidly increased, and once again I looked up, shuddering as with a fit of the <u>ague</u>. There had been a second change in the cell—and now the change was obviously in the *form*. As before, it was in vain that I, at first, endeavored to appreciate or understand what was taking place. But not long was I left in doubt. The inquisitorial <u>vengeance</u> had been hurried by my twofold escape, and there was to be no more <u>dallying</u> with the King of Terrors. The room had been square. I saw that two of its iron angles were now acute—two, consequently, obtuse. The fearful difference quickly increased with a low rumbling or moaning sound. In an instant the apartment had shifted its form into that of a <u>lozenge</u>. But the alteration stopped not here—I neither hoped nor desired it to stop. I could have clasped the red walls to my bosom as a garment of eternal peace. "Death," I said, "any death but that of the pit!" Fool! might I have not known that *into the pit* it was the object of the burning iron to urge me? Could I resist its glow? or, if even that, could I withstand its pressure? And now, flatter and flatter grew the lozenge, with a rapidity that left me no time for contemplation. Its center, and of course, its greatest width, came just over the yawning gulf. I shrank back—but the closing walls pressed me resistlessly onward. At length for my seared and writhing body there was no longer an inch of foothold on the firm floor of the prison. I struggled no more, but the agony of my soul found vent in one loud, long, and final scream of despair. I felt that I tottered upon the brink—I <u>averted</u> my eyes—.

There was a <u>discordant</u> hum of human voices! There was a loud blast as of many trumpets! There was a harsh grating as of a thousand thunders! The fiery walls rushed back! An outstretched arm caught my own as I fell, fainting, into the abyss. It was that of General Lasalle. The French army had entered Toledo. The Inquisition was in the hands of its enemies. ∎

What form does the rescue take?

WORDS FOR EVERYDAY USE:

im • pend (im pend´) *vi.*, be about to happen
balm (bäm) *n.*, anything healing or soothing
a • gue (a´gyoo) *n.*, fever with chills
venge • ance (ven´jəns) *n.*, revenge

dal • ly (dal´ē) *vi.*, waste time
loz • enge (läz´ənj) *n.*, diamond shape
a • vert (ə vʉrt´) *vt.*, turn away
dis • cord • ant (dis kôrd´nt) *adj.*, disagreeing; conflicting

Responding to the Selection

The main character in this tale escapes death three times. Of the three methods of death, which would have been most terrifying to you? Why? Answer these questions in your journal.

Reviewing the Selection

RECALLING

1. What causes the prisoner to be confined to his cell? What does he remember about the reason why he is imprisoned?

2. Describe the cell where the prisoner is kept.

3. How does the prisoner escape the descending pendulum?

4. How is the prisoner saved at the end of the story?

INTERPRETING

5. What could account for the speaker's fuzzy memory of the events that led to his imprisonment?

6. Why is there a pit in the center of the cell? Why wasn't the prisoner executed immediately?

7. What does the prisoner's plan for escape tell you about his character? Why did it take so long for him to devise his plan for escape from the swinging blade?

8. When does the prisoner scream out in despair? How does he feel when he hears the voices and feels the arm catching his arm?

SYNTHESIZING

9. What does the reader understand about why the prisoner is arrested and condemned? Why do you think the writer is ambiguous about this information?

10. Tales of terror, or horror stories, force readers to confront their deepest fears. Why do you think that stories such as this one are still popular with modern readers?

Understanding Literature (Questions for Discussion)

1. **Point of View. Point of view** is the vantage point from which a story is told. This story is written from a first-person point of view, in which the narrator uses words such as *I* and *me.* The point of view is also classified as limited, meaning that the narrator can reveal only his private, internal thoughts. How does the first-person limited point of view add to the suspense in the story?

2. **Romance.** In the nineteenth century, fictional adventures that took place in exotic locations and involved extraordinary or mysterious events and characters were called **romances**. What is the location in which this story takes place? Can the story be categorized as an adventure? Do you think that the setting and the plot are exotic enough to consider this story a romance? Why, or why not?

3. **Mood. Mood**, or **atmosphere**, is the emotion created in the reader by part or all of a literary work. How would you describe the mood of "The Pit and the Pendulum"? What details does Poe use to create the mood?

Responding in Writing

1. **Press Release.** The lifesaving event at the end of the story, the conquest of the tormentors by the French army, and the release of the prisoner would be covered as a major news story if it happened today. Write a press release describing the events leading up to the prisoner's rescue from his cell. The press release should offer facts and should avoid opinion.

2. **Storyboard.** When writers and directors imagine a play or movie, they often describe and picture the major events of the story in a **storyboard**. Decide on the major events of "The Pit and the Pendulum." Then make a storyboard with descriptions of scenes accompanied by drawings of the main character in the settings where he finds himself.

3. **Gothic Tale.** A **Gothic tale** is a story containing elements of horror, suspense, mystery, and magic. Try your hand at writing a Gothic tale. Choose characters, settings, and plot events that evoke terror or suspense. Include details that add to the dark, brooding feeling.

Language Lab

Using Context Clues. Read the Language Arts Survey, 2.138, "Using Context Clues I." Then read each of the following sentences. Write the definition of each underlined word, using context clues to deduce its meaning.

1. The prisoner searched frantically for a <u>crevice</u> in the masonry but could find no such crack or opening.

2. He had been <u>remanded</u>, or sent back, to his dungeon after the sentence was passed.

3. Pictures of <u>monstrosities</u> such as fiends, leering skeletons, and evil spirits covered the wall.

4. The prisoner was horrified to see several rats <u>traversing</u>, or traveling across, the floor.

5. The prisoner went through a period of <u>insensibility</u> and remembered nothing that happened during this time of unconsciousness.

Study and Research Skills

Informal Note-taking. Read the Language Arts Survey, 4.31, "Informal Note-taking." Then look up the Spanish Inquisition in an encyclopedia and take notes for a brief oral report on it.

PROJECTS

1. **Role Playing a Trial.** After doing research on the Inquisition, role play an Inquisition trial. Try to imagine what the inquisitors might ask and how the defendant might respond. Enact the trial from the reading of the charges through the defense and the prosecution to the eventual sentencing.

2. **Taking a Survey.** Many people enjoy tales of horror and suspense while others find them distasteful. Take a survey of various groups of people concerning their reaction to horror stories. The results of the survey will be more interesting if you categorize your interviewees by age, sex, or some other criterion. Publish the results of your survey in a graph or chart.

NOVEL

from *Moby-Dick*
"The Whiteness of the Whale"
by Herman Melville

ABOUT THE AUTHOR

Herman Melville (1819–1891) was born into a relatively wealthy family, whose fortune declined. Melville had a variety of jobs until he sailed on a whaler for the South Seas. Jumping ship in the Marquesas, he lived with a tribe of natives, was picked up by an Australian whaler, took part in a mutiny, and was imprisoned. He was twenty-five when he returned home and began writing *Typee,* a story about his South Sea adventures. Published in 1846, *Typee* was a tremendous success and was soon followed by other popular stories of the seafaring life, including *Omoo* (1847), *Mardi* (1849), *Redburn* (1849), and *White-Jacket* (1850). Melville's greatest book, *Moby-Dick* (1851), was unfortunately poorly received. His reputation tarnished, Melville wrote anonymous short stories for magazines and sought political appointments. Before his death, a revival of his fame began, leaving Melville with the hope that his reputation as a writer would be reestablished. Today, that reputation rests largely on his masterwork, *Moby-Dick,* a work of genius little understood until the twentieth century.

ABOUT THE SELECTION

Although not well received at the time it was published and almost forgotten by the public at the time of Melville's death, **Moby-Dick** is today seen as one of the greatest American novels. It begins as a narrative about a whaling expedition and turns into a metaphorical study of the nature of good, evil, and reality. It includes detailed descriptions of the adventure and drudgery of whaling, varied and sharp characterization, and philosophical discussions on God, man, and the universe. The narrator is a sailor, Ishmael. The main character is his ship's captain, Ahab, who sees the great white whale, Moby-Dick, as a symbol of all that challenges his being and who pursues the beast with a single-minded intensity that eventually destroys his entire ship and crew, save Ishmael. In the chapter "**The Whiteness of the Whale,**" the narrator ponders the question of what makes this whale so threatening, not only to the mad Ahab but even to a fairly reasonable person like himself.

When *Moby-Dick* was published in 1851, most of Melville's audience, hoping for more of the straightforward adventure and romantic settings of his earliest books, *Typee* and *Omoo,* did not appreciate the book, and the reviews were derogatory. In the 1920s, the book received critical acclaim as a masterpiece.

FROM

Moby-Dick

Herman Melville

CHAPTER XXXII
"The Whiteness of the Whale"

In what things does whiteness add to beauty?

What the white whale was to Ahab, has been hinted; what, at times, he was to me, as yet remains unsaid.

Aside from those more obvious considerations touching Moby Dick, which could not but occasionally awaken in any man's soul some alarm, there was another thought, or rather vague, nameless horror concerning him, which at times by its intensity completely overpowered all the rest; and yet so mystical and well nigh <u>ineffable</u> was it, that I almost despair of putting it in a comprehensible form. It was the whiteness of the whale that above all things appalled me. But how can I hope to explain myself here; and yet, in some

What was the most appalling thing about the whale?

dim, random way, explain myself I must, else all these chapters might be naught.

Though in many natural objects, whiteness refiningly enhances beauty, as if imparting some special virtue of its own, as in marbles, japonicas,[1] and pearls; and though various nations have in some way recognized a certain royal pre-eminence in this hue, even the barbaric, grand old king of Pegu[2] placing the title "Lord of the White Elephants" above all their other magniloquent ascriptions of dominion; and the modern kings of Siam[3] unfurling the same snow-white quadruped

---

1. **japonicas.** Any of various trees, shrubs, or plants associated with the Far East
2. **Pegu.** City in southern Mayanmar, formerly Burma, for centuries the capital of Burma but now a shadow of its former splendor
3. **Siam.** Former name of Thailand

Words for Everyday Use:
in • ef • fa • ble (in ef´ə bəl) *adj.,* too overwhelming to be expressed in words; awesome

in the royal standard; and the Hanoverian flag bearing the one figure of a snow-white charger; and the great Austrian Empire, Cæsarian, heir to overlording Rome, having for the imperial color the same imperial hue; . . . and though, besides, all this, whiteness has been even made significant of gladness, for among the Romans a white stone marked a joyful day; and though in other mortal sympathies and symbolizings, this same hue is made the emblem of many touching, noble things—the innocence of brides, the <u>benignity</u> of age; though among the native people of America the giving of the white belt of wampum was the deepest pledge of honor; though in many climes, whiteness typifies the majesty of Justice in the ermine[4] of the Judge, and contributes to the daily state of kings and queens drawn by milk-white steeds; though even in the higher mysteries of the most <u>august</u> religions it has been made the symbol of the divine spotlessness and power; by the Persian fire worshippers, the white forked flame being held the holiest on the altar; and in the Greek mythologies, Great Jove himself being made incarnate in a snow-white bull; and though to the noble Iroquois, the midwinter sacrifice of the sacred White Dog was by far the holiest festival of their theology, that spotless, faithful creature being held the purest <u>envoy</u> they could send to the Great Spirit with the annual tidings of their own fidelity; and though directly from the Latin word for white, all Christian priests derive the name of one part of their sacred vesture, the alb or tunic, worn beneath the cassock;[5] and though among the holy pomps[6] of the Romish faith, white is specially employed in the celebration of the Passion of our Lord; though in the Vision of St. John, white robes are given to the redeemed, and the four-and-twenty elders stand clothed in white before the great white throne, and the Holy One that sitteth there white like wool; yet for all these accumulated associations, with whatever is sweet, and honorable, and <u>sublime</u>, there yet lurks an elusive something in the innermost idea of this hue, which strikes more of panic to the soul than that redness which affrights in blood.

This elusive quality it is, which causes the thought of whiteness, when divorced from more kindly associations, and coupled with any object terrible in itself, to heighten that terror to the furthest bounds. Witness the white bear of the poles, and the white shark of the tropics; what but their smooth, flaky whiteness makes them the <u>transcendent</u> horrors they are? That ghastly whiteness it is which imparts such an abhorrent mildness, even more loathsome than terrific, to the dumb gloating of their aspect. So that not the fierce-fanged tiger in his heraldic coat can so stagger courage as the white-shrouded bear or shark.

Bethink thee of the albatross,[7] whence come those clouds of spiritual wonderment and pale dread, in which that white

What are some of the symbols of honor associated with the color white?

What other emotion does the color white arouse? What animals impart this feeling?

---

4. **ermine.** Weasel that turns white in winter; has highly prized fur

5. **alb . . . cassock.** *Alb* (from Latin *alba,* "white")—white linen garment worn by priests. *Cassock*—outer garment, generally black

6. **pomps.** Religious pageants

7. **albatross.** Large white bird found chiefly in the South Seas; used as a symbol of guilt in a poem by Samuel Taylor Coleridge

WORDS FOR EVERYDAY USE:	be • nig • ni • ty (bi nig´nə tē) *n.,* kindliness au • gust (ô gust´) *adj.,* magnificent; worthy of respect en • voy (än´voi) *n.,* messenger; agent	sub • lime (sə blīm´) *adj.,* noble; majestic tran • scend • ent (tran sen´dənt) *adj.,* beyond the limits of knowledge or experience

What two feelings did the White Steed evoke?

phantom sails in all imaginations? Not Coleridge first threw that spell; but God's great, unflattering laureate,[8] Nature.

Most famous in our Western annals and Indian traditions is that of the White Steed of the Prairies; a magnificent milk-white charger, large-eyed, small-headed, bluff-chested, and with the dignity of a thousand monarchs in his lofty, overscorning carriage. He was the elected Xerxes[9] of vast herds of wild horses, whose pastures in those days were only fenced by the Rocky Mountains and the Alleghanies. At their flaming head he westward trooped it like that chosen star which every evening leads on the hosts of light. The flashing cascade of his mane, the curving comet of his tail, invested him with housings more resplendent than gold and silver-beaters could have furnished him. A most imperial and archangelical apparition of that unfallen, western world, which to the eyes of the old trappers and hunters revived the glories of those primeval times when Adam walked majestic as a god, bluff-browed and fearless as this mighty steed. Whether marching amid his aides and marshals in the van of countless cohorts that endlessly streamed it over the plains, like an Ohio; or whether with his circumambient[10] subjects browsing all around at the horizon, the White Steed gallopingly reviewed them with warm nostrils reddening through his cool milkiness; in whatever aspect he presented himself, always to the bravest Indians he was the object of trembling reverence and awe. Nor can it be questioned from what stands on legendary record of this noble horse, that it was his spiritual whiteness

In what two ways is the color white related to death?

chiefly, which so clothed him with divineness; and that this divineness had that in it which, though commanding worship, at the same time enforced a certain nameless terror.

But there are other instances where this whiteness loses all that accessory and strange glory which invests it in the White Steed and Albatross. . . .

Nor, in quite other aspects, does Nature in her least palpable but not the less malicious agencies, fail to enlist among her forces this crowning attribute of the terrible. From its snowy aspect, the gauntleted ghost of the Southern Seas has been denominated the White Squall. Nor, in some historic instances, has the art of human malice omitted so potent an auxiliary. How wildly it heightens the effect of that passage in Froissart,[11] when, masked in the snowy symbol of their faction, the desperate White Hoods of Ghent murder their bailiff in the market-place!

Nor, in some things, does the common, hereditary experience of all mankind fail to bear witness to the supernaturalism of this hue. It cannot well be doubted, that the one visible quality in the aspect of the dead which most appals the gazer, is the marble pallor lingering there; as if indeed that pallor were as much like the badge of consternation in the other world, as of mortal trepidation here. And from that pallor of the dead, we borrow the expressive hue of the shroud in which we wrap them. Nor even in our superstitions do we

---

8. **laureate.** One to whom honor is given
9. **Xerxes.** (*circa* 519–465 BC) King of Persia
10. **circumambient.** Extending all around
11. **Froissart.** Jean Froissart (*circa* 1337–1410), French chronicler and poet

---

Words for Everyday Use:

pri • me • val (prī mē´vəl) *adj.*, of the earliest times or ages

gaunt • let • ed (gônt´lit id) *adj.*, wearing a gauntlet, or glove; figuratively, combative

con • ster • na • tion (kän´stər nā´shən) *n.*, dismay; great fear

trep • i • da • tion (trep´ə dā´shən) *n.*, fearful uncertainty

fail to throw the same snowy mantle round our phantoms; all ghosts rising in a milk-white fog—Yea, while these terrors seize us, let us add, that even the king of terrors, when personified by the evangelists, rides on his pallid horse.[12]

Therefore, in his other moods, symbolize whatever grand or gracious thing he will by whiteness, no man can deny that in its profoundest idealized significance it calls up a peculiar apparition to the soul.

But though without dissent this point be fixed, how is mortal man to account for it? To analyze it, would seem impossible. Can we, then, by the citation of some of those instances wherein this thing of whiteness—though for the time either wholly or in great part stripped of all direct associations calculated to import to it aught fearful, but nevertheless, is found to exert over us the same sorcery, however modified;—can we thus hope to light upon some chance clue to conduct us to the hidden cause we seek ?

Let us try. But in a matter like this, subtlety appeals to subtlety; and without imagination no man can follow another into these halls. And though, doubtless, some at least of the imaginative impressions about to be presented may have been shared by most men, yet few perhaps were entirely conscious of them at the time, and therefore may not be able to recall them now.

Why to the man of untutored ideality, who happens to be but loosely acquainted with the peculiar character of the day, does the bare mention of Whitsuntide[13] marshal in the fancy such long, dreary, speechless processions of slow-pacing pilgrims, down-cast and hooded with newfallen snow? Or to the unread, unsophisticated Protestant of the Middle American States, why does the passing mention of a White Friar or a White Nun, evoke such an eyeless statue in the soul?

Or what is there apart from the traditions of dungeoned warriors and kings (which will not wholly account for it) that makes the White Tower of London tell so much more strongly on the imagination of an untravelled American, than those other storied structures, its neighbors—the Byward Tower, or even the Bloody? And those sublimer towers, the White Mountains of New Hampshire, whence, in peculiar moods, comes that gigantic ghostliness over the soul at the bare mention of that name, while the thought of Virginia's Blue Ridge is full of a soft, dewy, distant dreaminess? Or why, <u>irrespective</u> of all latitudes and longitudes, does the name of the White Sea exert such a spectralness over the fancy, while that of the Yellow Sea lulls us with mortal thoughts of long lacquered mild afternoons on the waves, followed by the <u>gaudiest</u> and yet sleepiest of sunsets? Or, to choose a wholly unsubstantial instance, purely addressed to the fancy, why, in reading the old fairy tales of Central Europe, does "the tall pale man" of the Hartz forests, whose changeless pallor unrustlingly glides through the green of the groves—why is this phantom

What does the color white call up?

What natural things are noted for their whiteness? How do they differ from things named with different colors?

---

12. **king . . . horse.** Death is depicted in the Bible as riding on a pale horse.

13. **Whitsuntide.** Week beginning with Whitsunday (White Sunday) on Pentecost (seventh Sunday after Easter), marked by ceremonies and processions

WORDS FOR EVERYDAY USE:

ir • re • spec • tive (ir´ri spek´tiv) *adj.,* regardless

gaud • i • est (gôd´ē əst) *adj.,* brightest and showiest, but lacking good taste

The Whale Fishery, The Sperm Whale in a Flurry. *Lithograph by Currier & Ives. The Granger Collection, NY*

more terrible than all the whooping imps of the Blocksburg?

Nor is it, altogether, the remembrance of her cathedral-toppling earthquakes; nor the stampedoes of her frantic seas; nor the tearlessness of arid skies that never rain; nor the sight of her wide field of leaning spires, wrenched cope-stones,[14] and crosses all adroop (like canted yards[15] of anchored fleets); and her suburban avenues of housewalls lying over upon each other, as a tossed pack of cards;—it is not these things alone which make tearless Lima, the strangest, saddest city thou can'st see. For Lima has taken the white veil; and there is a higher horror in this whiteness of her woe. Old as Pizarro,[16] this whiteness keeps her ruins for ever new; admits not the cheerful greenness of complete decay; spreads over her broken ramparts the rigid pallor of an apoplexy[17] that fixes its own distortions.

I know that, to the common apprehension, this phenomenon of whiteness is not confessed to be the prime agent in exaggerating the terror of objects otherwise terrible; nor to the unimaginative mind is there aught of terror in those appearances whose awfulness to another mind almost solely consists in this one phenomenon, especially when exhibited under any form at all approaching to muteness or universality. What I mean by these two

What makes Lima the saddest city you can see?

___

14. **cope-stones.** Uppermost stone in a structure
15. **canted yards.** Tilted masts on a ship
16. **Pizarro.** Francisco Pizarro (*circa* 1474–1541), Spanish conqueror of Peru
17. **apoplexy.** Loss of the power to feel, think, or move

statements may perhaps be respectively elucidated by the following examples.

First: The mariner, when drawing nigh the coasts of foreign lands, if by night he hear the roar of breakers, starts to vigilance, and feels just enough of trepidation to sharpen all his faculties; but under precisely similar circumstances, let him be called from his hammock to view his ship sailing through a midnight sea of milky whiteness—as if from encircling headlands[18] shoals of combed white bears were swimming round him, then he feels a silent, superstitious dread; the shrouded phantom of the whitened waters is horrible to him as a real ghost; in vain the lead assures him he is still off soundings;[19] heart and helm they both go down; he never rests till blue water is under him again. Yet where is the mariner who will tell thee, "Sir, it was not so much the fear of striking hidden rocks, as the fear of that hideous whiteness that so stirred me?"

Second: To the native Indian of Peru, the continual sight of the snow-howdahed Andes conveys naught of dread, except, perhaps, in the mere fancying of the eternal frosted desolateness reigning at such vast altitudes, and the natural conceit of what a fearfulness it would be to lose oneself in such inhuman solitude. Much the same is it with the backwoodsman of the West, who with comparative indifference views an unbound prairie sheeted with driven snow, no shadow of tree or twig to break the fixed trance of whiteness. Not so the sailor, beholding the scenery of the Antarctic seas; where at times, by some infernal trick of legerdemain[20] in the powers of frost and air, he shivering and half shipwrecked, instead of rainbows speaking hope and solace to his misery, views what seems a boundless churchyard grinning upon him with its lean ice monuments and splintered crosses.

But thou sayest, methinks this white-lead chapter about whiteness is but a white flag hung out from a craven soul; thou surrenderest to a hypo,[21] Ishmael.

Tell me, why this strong young colt, foaled in some peaceful valley of Vermont, far removed from all beasts of prey—why is it that upon the sunniest day, if you but shake a fresh buffalo robe behind him, so that he cannot even see it, but only smells its wild animal muskiness—why will he start, snort, and with bursting eyes paw the ground in phrensies of affright? There is no remembrance in him of any gorings of wild creatures in his green northern home, so that the strange muskiness he smells cannot recall to him anything associated with the experience of former perils; for what knows he, this New England colt, of the black bisons of distant Oregon?

No; but here thou beholdest even in a dumb brute, the instinct of the knowledge of the demonism in the world. Though thousands of miles from Oregon, still when he smells that savage musk, the rending, goring bison herds are as present as to the deserted wild foal of the prairies, which this instant they may be trampling into dust.

What frightens the colt? Why?

What is more horrible to the sailor than the dangerous rocks?

---

18. **headlands.** Points of land reaching out into the water
19. **lead . . . soundings.** A weight attached to a line and tossed over the side of the ship is used to determine depth. Here the depth is still greater than the length of the sounding line.
20. **legerdemain.** Sleight of hand, deception; trickery
21. **hypo.** Morbid depression of spirits

WORDS FOR EVERYDAY USE:

e • lu • ci • date (ə loo´sə dāt´) *vt.*, make clear

cra • ven (krā´vən) *adj.*, very cowardly

What words are used to describe the sea, the mountains, and the prairies? To what are all of these things compared?

Thus, then, the muffled rollings of a milky-sea; the bleak rustlings of the <u>festooned</u> frosts of mountains; the desolate shiftings of the windrowed snows of prairies; all these, to Ishmael, are as the shaking of that buffalo robe to the frightened colt!

Though neither knows where lie the nameless things of which the mystic sign gives forth such hints; yet with me, as with the colt, somewhere those things must exist. Though in many of its aspects this visible world seems formed in love, the invisible spheres were formed in fright.

But not yet have we solved the <u>incantation</u> of this whiteness, and learned why it appeals with such power to the soul; and more strange and far more <u>portentous</u>— why, as we have seen, it is at once the most meaning symbol of spiritual things, nay, the very veil of the Christian's Deity; and yet should be as it is, the intensifying agent in things the most appalling to mankind.

What questions does the narrator ask about whiteness? What explanations might there be for fear or horror caused by whiteness?

Is it that by its indefiniteness it shadows forth the heartless voids and immensities of the universe, and thus stabs us from behind with the thought of annihilation, when beholding the white depths of the milky way? Or is it, that as in essence whiteness is not so much a color as the visible absence of color; and at the same time the concrete of all colors; is it for these reasons that there is such a dumb blankness, full of meaning, in a wide landscape of snows—a colorless, all-color of atheism from which we shrink? And when we consider that other theory of the natural philosophers, that all other earthly hues—every stately or lovely emblazoning—the sweet tinges of sunset skies and woods; yea, and the gilded velvets of butterflies, and the butterfly cheeks of young girls; all these are but subtle deceits, not actually inherent in substances, but only laid on from without; so that all deified Nature absolutely paints like the harlot, whose allurements cover nothing but the charnel-house[22] within; and when we proceed further, and consider that the mystical cosmetic which produces every one of her hues, the great principle of light, for ever remains white or colorless in itself, and if operating without medium upon matter, would touch all objects, even tulips and roses, with its own blank tinge—pondering all this, the <u>palsied</u> universe lies before us a leper;[23] and like wilful travellers in Lapland,[24] who refuse to wear colored and coloring glasses upon their eyes, so the wretched infidel gazes himself blind at the monumental white shroud that wraps all the prospect around him. And of all these things Albino whale was the symbol. Wonder ye then at the fiery hunt? ∎

---

22. **charnel-house.** Place where corpses or bones are deposited
23. **leper.** One suffering from leprosy, a disease that attacks the skin and nerves causing white scaly scabs, deformities, and loss of sensation
24. **Lapland.** Extreme northern region of Europe

WORDS FOR EVERYDAY USE:

fes • tooned (fes tōōnd´) *part.*, adorned with curving decorations

in • can • ta • tion (in´kan tā´shən) *n.*, chanting of magical words; spell

por • ten • tous (pôr ten´təs) *adj.*, ominous; warning of evil

pal • sied (pôl´ zēd) *part.*, paralyzed

Responding to the Selection

Did the narrator convince you that there is something threatening in the whiteness of the whale? With which of his statements about white being a scary color did you agree?

Reviewing the Selection

RECALLING

1. Early in the excerpt, the narrator notes many situations in which whiteness is associated with respected and honorable people, events, and ideas. List three of these situations.

2. The narrator claims that some animals automatically become more impressive and feared because of their whiteness. Name three of them.

3. What is the attitude of a sailor when approaching an unknown coast in the darkness of night? What is a sailor's attitude approaching such a coast in the whiteness of fog?

4. What does the narrator say can scare a Vermont-bred colt? Why is it so remarkable that this object has an effect on the colt?

INTERPRETING

5. Find the fifth sentence of the chapter, beginning with the words "Though in many natural objects." With which words does the sentence end? Summarize the main idea of the sentence in your own words.

6. According to the narrator, in what ways is whiteness associated with death?

7. Does the typical sailor admit that he fears the whiteness of fog? What point is the narrator making by mentioning this?

8. According to the narrator, how is he like the frightened colt?

SYNTHESIZING

9. The narrator claims, "Though in many of its aspects this visible world seems formed in love, the invisible spheres were formed in fright." What does this observation have to do with whiteness?

10. Do you suppose that the complete novel *Moby-Dick* gives a more specific statement of what the whiteness of the whale represents? Give a reason for your answer.

Understanding Literature (Questions for Discussion)

1. **Allusion.** An **allusion** is a rhetorical technique in which reference is made to a person, event, object, or work from history or literature. The narrator alludes to historical events, religious practices, and other practices and writings to support his arguments that white is revered but too complex to be trusted. List at least five allusions in the selection to people or events outside the novel.

2. **Elaboration. Elaboration,** or **amplification**, is a writing technique in which a subject is introduced and then expanded upon by means of repetition with slight changes, the addition of details, or similar devices. An example of this device is found in the fifth sentence of this selection. Find another example of this device in the selection.

3. **Onomatopoeia. Onomatopoeia** is the use of words or phrases that sound like the things to which they refer. Here is an example of onomatopoeia found in the selection: "why . . . does 'the tall pale man' of the Hartz forests, whose changeless pallor unrustlingly glides through the green of the groves—why is this phantom more terrible than all the whooping imps of the Blocksburg?" Which sounds suggest gliding? Which suggest "whooping" or, at least, excited noisemaking?

Responding in Writing

1. **Descriptive Paragraph.** Think of a situation that always makes your adrenaline rise and your heart beat faster, as the shaking of the buffalo robe frightened the colt. Describe the situation so as to suggest what aspects of it, harmless as they may seem, panic you.

2. **Obituary.** Write two obituaries for Herman Melville—the first presenting the attitude toward the writer that existed at the time of his death, and the second presenting the attitude that came into being in the 1920s. The selection of facts should vary between the two obituaries, reflecting the opinions of each time.

3. **Slogan.** The main ideas of many ad campaigns and political movements have been popularized by short, stirring, and easy-to-remember slogans. Examples are "Taxation without representation is tyranny," "Remember the Alamo," and "We shall overcome." Come up with a slogan that summarizes this excerpt's attitude toward whiteness.

Language Lab

Comparison of Adjectives and Adverbs. Read the Language Arts Survey, 2.86, "Comparison of Adjectives and Adverbs." Then use that information to correct the following sentences.

1. What could be more friendlier than the color green?

2. Of all the seasons of the year, spring is the more encouraging, and I believe strongliest that this effect is due to the arrival of green leaves.

3. Even the most rainiest of spring days is enjoyabler than a temperate winter day.

4. Nature skillfulliest uses an extraordinarily rich palette of greens to paint the grasses, trees, bushes, and other plants that appear at this most welcomest time of year.

5. Of course, I admit that green is also most unfortunate the color of many molds that grow in my refrigerator abundantlier than flowers in my garden.

Speaking and Listening Skills

Discussion. Read the Language Arts Survey, 3.6, "Discussion." Then join a small group of classmates to discuss whether any colors have inherent meanings for all people. Report your conclusions to the class.

PROJECTS

1. **Background Report.** Many of the allusions in the chapter "The Whiteness of the Whale" are obscure and confusing. Work with a group to develop a background report that clarifies as many of these allusions as possible. Each member of the group is to select one or more of the allusions and research them, producing short explanations and illustrations, where possible. Together, assemble the individual reports on a bulletin board or poster or as separate pages of a book. As the heading for each report, use the quotation from the chapter that includes the allusion.

2. **Collage.** Collect scraps of white materials having different tints and textures. Combine them in a flat or three-dimensional collage that brings out the contrasts in shade and feel.

3. **A Focused Thesaurus.** Develop a thesaurus that lists nouns and adjectives related to the concept of whiteness. Begin by identifying all the words in the excerpt from *Moby-Dick* that touch on this concept, such as *pallid, milk,* and *snowy,* and add as many as you can. Indicate how the meaning of each word is differentiated from the others. Refer to the Language Arts Survey, 4.25, "Using Thesauruses."

NONFICTION

from *Self-Reliance*
by Ralph Waldo Emerson

ABOUT THE AUTHOR

Ralph Waldo Emerson (1803–1882) grew up in Boston and became the greatest American thinker of his day. At the age of fourteen, he entered Harvard, graduating with honors in 1821. Thereafter, he taught school and then studied for the ministry. In 1829, he was ordained as junior pastor of Boston's Second Church, and in the same year, he married Ellen Tucker, who died sixteen months later of tuberculosis. With literary friends from Boston, Emerson founded a magazine, *The Dial,* which became an important vehicle for the **Transcendentalist Movement,** of which Emerson was a leader. The Transcendentalist, like the English Romantics, believed in a deep spiritual connection between people and nature. Emerson also believed that by attending closely to one's innermost thoughts and feelings, one could glimpse the great spirit of the universe, what Emerson called the "Over-Soul." Such beliefs led Emerson to a radical individualism that helped to shape the American spirit. The finest expression of this individualism is, perhaps, his essay "Self-Reliance." Emerson traveled in Europe and, on returning, moved to Concord, Massachusetts and married Lydia Jackson, with whom he had four children. During their fifty years of marriage, the Emersons entertained at home many of the leading intellectuals of the day, including their neighbors the Alcotts and Henry David Thoreau. Today, Emerson's house in Concord remains a place of literary pilgrimage in America. Emerson himself has become a symbol of American optimism and independent thinking.

ABOUT THE SELECTION

Self-Reliance was first published in 1841 as part of the book *Essays.* It is a combination of different ideas from a journal in which Emerson recorded his thoughts for years. Emerson used his journal as a source of ideas for his frequent lectures. He would test and perfect his style and wording before audiences, noting their reactions. He would then condense his ideas into essay form, as he does here in *Self-Reliance,* for a wider audience to read and reread.

READER'S JOURNAL

Have you ever been in a situation where you had to choose between what you thought was the right course of action and the course that others thought you should take? What was your final decision? Did you think for yourself or were you swayed by the opinions of others? Were you satisfied with the outcome? Freewrite in your journal about such an incident.

READING SKILLS

Read the Language Arts Survey, 4.16, "Reading Rates: Slow and Careful Reading." As you read, take a few moments to think about the ideas in Emerson's essay and how they apply to situations in your own life.

FROM

Self-Reliance

RALPH WALDO EMERSON

There is a time in every man's education when he arrives at the conviction that envy is ignorance; that imitation is suicide; that he must take himself for better, for worse, as his portion; that though the wide universe is full of good, no kernel of nourishing corn can come to him but through his toil bestowed on that plot of ground which is given to him to till.

♦ ♦ ♦

Trust thyself: every heart vibrates to that iron string. Accept the place the divine Providence has found for you; the society of your contemporaries, the connexion of events. Great men have always done so and confided themselves childlike to the genius of their age, betraying their perception that the Eternal was stirring at their heart, working through their hands, predominating in all their being.

♦ ♦ ♦

Society everywhere is in conspiracy against the manhood of every one of its members. Society is a joint-stock company[1] in which the members agree for the better securing of his bread to each shareholder, to surrender the liberty and culture of the eater. The virtue in most

Whom should you trust? What should you accept?

---

1. **joint-stock company.** Company in which joint owners hold the capital

WORDS FOR
EVERYDAY USE: pre • dom • i • nate (prē däm´ə nāt´) vi., have authority or influence over others

request is conformity. Self-reliance is its <u>aversion</u>. It loves not realities and creators, but names and customs.

Whoso would be a man must be a nonconformist. He who would gather immortal palms must not be hindered by the name of goodness, but must explore if it be goodness. Nothing is at last sacred but the integrity of our own mind.

What evidence does the speaker offer to suggest that being misunderstood is not bad?

◆　◆　◆

What I must do, is all that concerns me, not what the people think. This rule, equally <u>arduous</u> in actual and in intellectual life, may serve for the whole distinction between greatness and meanness. It is the harder, because you will always find those who think they know what is your duty better than you know it. It is easy in the world to live after the world's opinion; it is easy in solitude to live after our own; but the great man is he who in the midst of the crowd keeps with perfect sweetness the independence of solitude.

By what opinion is it easy to live? Whose opinion should you follow?

◆　◆　◆

A foolish consistency is the hobgoblin of little minds, adored by little statesmen and philosophers and divines. With consistency a great soul has simply nothing to do. He may as well concern himself with his shadow on the wall. Out upon your guarded lips! Sew them up with packthread, do. Else, if you would be a man, speak what you think today in words as hard as cannon balls, and tomorrow speak what tomorrow thinks in hard words again, though it contradict every thing you said today. Ah, then, exclaim the aged ladies, you shall be sure to be misunderstood. Misunderstood! It is a right fool's word. Is it so bad then to be misunderstood? Pythagoras was misunderstood, and Socrates, and Jesus, and Luther, and Copernicus, and Galileo, and Newton, and every pure and wise spirit that ever took flesh. To be great is to be misunderstood.

◆　◆　◆

I hope in these days we have heard the last of conformity and consistency. Let the words be gazetted and ridiculous henceforward.[2] Instead of the gong for dinner, let us hear a whistle from the Spartan fife.[3] Let us bow and apologize never more. A great man is coming to eat at my house. I do not wish to please him: I wish that he should wish to please me. I will stand here for humanity, and though I would make it kind, I would made it true. Let us affront and reprimand the smooth mediocrity and <u>squalid</u> contentment of the times, and hurl in the face of custom, and trade, and office, the fact which is the upshot of all history, that there is a great responsible Thinker and Actor moving wherever moves a man; that a true man belongs to no other time or place, but is the center of things. Where he is, there is nature. . . . Every true man is a cause, a country, and an age; requires infinite spaces and numbers and time fully to accomplish his thought;—and posterity seem to follow his steps as a procession. A

---

2. **gazetted and ridiculous henceforward.** Labeled and not used from now on

3. **gong . . . fife.** The gong stands for ease and leisure, and the fife represents disciplined, alert life.

WORDS FOR EVERYDAY USE:	**a • ver • sion** (ə vur′zhən) *n.*, definite dislike
	ar • du • ous (är′jōō əs) *adj.*, difficult
	squal • id (skwäl′id) *adj.*, wretched, miserable

man Cæsar is born, and for ages after, we have a Roman Empire. Christ is born, and millions of minds so grow and cleave[4] to his genius, that he is confounded with virtue and the possible of man. An institution is the lengthened shadow of one man; as, the Reformation, of Luther; Quakerism, of Fox; Methodism, of Wesley; Abolition, of Clarkson.[5] Scipio,[6] Milton called, "the height of Rome;" and all history resolves itself very easily into the biography of a few stout and earnest persons. ■

---

4. **cleave.** Cling; adhere
5. **Reformation . . . Clarkson.** Martin Luther (1483–1546), founder of the Reformation; George Fox (1624–1691), founder of Quakerism; John Wesley (1703–1791), founder of Methodism; and Thomas Clarkson (1760–1846), abolitionist
6. **Scipio.** (237-183 BC) Roman conqueror of Carthage, a city-state of ancient Africa

Responding to the Selection

Choose a quote from *Self-Reliance* that you agree with strongly. Why did you choose that one? What about it makes sense to you? Why is it important to remember that idea? Discuss with your classmates the quote you chose and your response to it.

Reviewing the Selection

RECALLING

1. According to Emerson, what does each person come to realize at a certain point in education?

2. What is the virtue that society asks of each person? Does Emerson believe that people should fulfill that request? If not, what should people strive for instead?

3. Emerson says that it is easy to live your life doing what other people think is appropriate and it is also easy to act on your own beliefs when you are alone. What type of behavior does he say is difficult but essential for greatness?

4. Name some of the people Emerson says were misunderstood in their time. What qualities do these people have in common?

INTERPRETING

5. Why does Emerson say that "imitation is suicide"? What is the alternative to imitation that Emerson recommends?

6. Why does Emerson advocate nonconformity? What does he mean by nonconformity?

7. What does Emerson mean by the phrase "the independence of solitude"? Why is it something for which to strive?

8. Why might great people sometimes be inconsistent? Why does Emerson feel that consistency is unimportant?

9. What are some of the benefits of relying on yourself rather than upon others for your values and your principles?

10. In your opinion, if society values conformity over individualism, why do nonconformists seem to have the greatest impact on society? Why can nonconformists change society so radically, as Cæsar, Jesus, and Martin Luther did?

Understanding Literature (Questions for Discussion)

1. **Essay and Theme.** An **essay** is a brief work of prose nonfiction. A good essay develops a single idea. A **theme** is a central idea in a literary work. Identify at least one theme that runs through *Self-Reliance.*

2. **Aphorism.** An **aphorism** is a short saying or pointed statement. An aphorism that gains currency and is passed from generation to generation is called a proverb or adage. Select two quotations from Emerson that could be considered to be aphorisms and that you believe have the potential of becoming proverbs. Explain why you chose them and why you think they will speak to many generations.

3. **Metaphor.** A **metaphor** is a figure of speech in which one thing is spoken or written about as if it were another. In the metaphor "Society is a joint-stock company," how are society and a company similar?

Responding in Writing

1. **Biography.** A **biography** is the story of a person's life, told by someone other than that person. Read about the life of one of the people that Emerson mentions in his essay: Scipio, Pythagoras, Socrates, Jesus, Luther, Copernicus, Galileo, Newton, Cæsar, Fox, Wesley, Clarkson. Write a brief biography about that person, including the most memorable events in his life.

2. **Advice Column.** Imagine that Emerson were the writer of an advice column. What kinds of questions might he be asked? What might his advice be? Compose an appropriate question to pose to Emerson and then write an answer in the style of Emerson.

3. **Billboard Ad.** Emerson often gave lectures to groups to supplement his income. Create a billboard advertising an upcoming lecture. Include what his topics would be. Give the potential audience good reasons for paying to see and hear him.

Language Lab

Correcting Run-ons. Read the Language Arts Survey, 2.62, "Correcting Run-ons." Then read each of the following sentences. If it is a run-on, rewrite it correctly.

1. Emerson trained to be a minister for years when he began his ministry he found that it had lost its meaning.

2. After visiting Europe, Emerson's spirits were revived, and he was inspired to write his first book.

3. Emerson lectured on many topics he always included a discussion of the moral principles that underlay his thinking.

4. Believing that slavery was an abomination, Emerson delivered lectures against it even when he was emotionally involved with his subject he kept his dignity.

5. Emerson's optimism is obvious in most of his works he believed that people have within themselves everything they need to know about the meaning of their own existence.

Study and Research Skills

Paraphrasing and Summarizing. Read the Language Arts Survey, 4.30, "Paraphrasing and Summarizing." Then choose two of the passages from *Self-Reliance* and rewrite them in your own words.

PROJECTS

1. **Advice Booklet.** Everyone has been given advice from his or her parents, relatives, and friends while growing up. Have everyone in your class ask friends and family for advice or rules by which to live that he or she was given as a child. Assemble and organize all the advice in a booklet, perhaps even including illustrations.

2. **Proverb Charades.** Write proverbs on slips of paper, one to a slip. You may wish to include aphorisms from writers such as Emerson, Henry David Thoreau, or Benjamin Franklin. Divide your class into two teams and have team members take turns selecting proverbs and pantomiming them for the rest of the team. See how long it takes each team to guess the proverb that is written on the sheet.

NONFICTION

from *Walden*
by Henry David Thoreau

ABOUT THE AUTHOR

Henry David Thoreau (1817–1862) lived in Concord, Massachusetts, most of his life. He won his place in American literature by, as he put it, traveling a good deal in Concord. He made numerous trips to Maine, Cape Cod, and New Hampshire, and also traveled to Quebec, Canada, and Minnesota in an unsuccessful attempt to strengthen his tubercular lungs. Thoreau never married. He read widely and wrote constantly in his journals, using them as sources for lectures, essays, and his books *A Week on the Concord and Merrimack Rivers* (1849) and *Walden* (1854). His neighbors knew him as an educated man without an occupation. He worked as a school teacher, a handyman at Ralph Waldo Emerson's house, and a tutor. Thoreau lived for two years in a cabin he built on Emerson's property at Walden Pond. During that time, he also surveyed property, wrote magazine articles, and worked in his father's pencil factory. Sections of his books *The Maine Woods* and *Cape Cod* were published after his death. His most popular books during his lifetime were *Slavery in Massachusetts* and *A Plea for Captain John Brown*. A naturalist and social philosopher, he was forty-four when he died at his mother's house in Concord.

ABOUT THE SELECTION

One of the two books that Thoreau published during his lifetime, **Walden** is drawn from the journals he kept before, during, and after his stay on Emerson's property at Walden Pond from July 4, 1845, to September 6, 1847. His first book, *A Week on the Concord and Merrimack Rivers,* was published in 1849 but did not sell well. The unpopularity of his first book caused Thoreau to hold back his *Walden* manuscript for five years. During that time he revised and reworked the text numerous times, enriching and perfecting the work. The book firmly established his reputation as a writer as well an an outspoken individualist.

FROM

Walden

HENRY DAVID THOREAU

FROM "ECONOMY"

The mass of men lead lives of quiet desperation. What is called <u>resignation</u> is confirmed desperation. From the desperate city you go into the desperate country, and have to console yourself with the bravery of minks and muskrats. A stereotyped but unconscious despair is concealed even under what are called the games and amusements of mankind. There is no play in them, for this comes after work. But it is a characteristic of wisdom not to do desperate things.

When we consider what, to use the words of the catechism, is the chief end of man,[1] and what are the true necessaries and means of life, it appears as if men had deliberately chosen the common mode of living because they preferred it to any other. Yet they honestly think there is no choice left. But alert and healthy natures remember that the sun rose clear. It is never too late to give up our prejudices. No way of thinking or doing, however ancient, can be trusted without proof. What every body echoes or in silence passes by as true today may turn out to be falsehood tomorrow, mere smoke of opinion, which some had trusted for a cloud that would sprinkle fertilizing rain on their fields. What old people say you cannot do you try and find that you can. Old deeds for old people, and new deeds for new. Old people did not know enough once, perchance, to fetch fresh fuel to keep the fire a-going; new people put a little dry wood under a pot, and are whirled

What kind of lives do most people lead? What does Thoreau call resignation?

What happens to things people believe to be true?

---

1. **When . . . man.** Refers to a line from the shorter Catechism in the *New England Primer,* "What is the chief end of man? Man's chief end is to glorify God and enjoy him forever."

WORDS FOR EVERYDAY USE: res • ig • na • tion (rez´ig nā´shən) *n.,* submission, patient acceptance

Does Thoreau believe in the wisdom of old age? Why, or why not?

round the globe with the speed of birds, in a way to kill old people, as the phrase is. Age is no better, hardly so well, qualified for an instructor as youth, for it has not profited so much as it has lost. One may almost doubt if the wisest man has learned any thing of absolute value by living. Practically, the old have no very important advice to give the young, their own experience has been so partial, and their lives have been such miserable failures, for private reasons, as they must believe; and it may be that they have some faith left which belies that experience, and they are only less young than they were. I have lived some thirty years on this planet and I have yet to hear the first syllable of valuable or even <u>earnest</u> advice from my seniors. They have told me nothing, and probably cannot tell me any thing, to the purpose. Here is life, an experiment to a great extent untried by me; but it does not avail me that they have tried it. If I have any experience which I think valuable, I am sure to reflect that this my Mentors[2] said nothing about.

◆ ◆ ◆

To what does Thoreau compare the condition of humans?

Near the end of March, 1845, I borrowed an axe and went down to the woods by Walden Pond, nearest to where I intended to build my house, and began to cut down some tall arrowy white pines, still in their youth, for timber. It is difficult to begin without borrowing, but perhaps it is the most generous course thus to permit your fellow-men to have an interest in your enterprise. The owner of the axe, as he released his hold on it, said

that it was the apple of his eye; but I returned it sharper than I received it. It was a pleasant hillside where I worked, covered with pine woods, through which I looked out on the pond, and a small open field in the woods where pines and hickories were springing up. The ice in the pond was not yet dissolved, though there were some open spaces, and it was all dark colored and <u>saturated</u> with water. There were some slight flurries of snow during the days that I worked there, but for the most part when I came out on to the railroad, on my way home, its yellow sand heap stretched away gleaming in the hazy atmosphere, and the rails shone in the spring sun, and I heard the lark and pewee and other birds already come to commence another year with us. They were pleasant spring days, in which the winter of man's discontent was thawing as well as the earth, and the life that had lain torpid began to stretch itself. One day, when my axe had come off and I had cut a green hickory for a wedge, driving it with a stone and had placed the whole to soak in a pond hole in order to swell the wood, I saw a striped snake run into the water, and he lay on the bottom, apparently without inconvenience, as long as I staid there, or more than a quarter of an hour; perhaps because he had not yet fairly come out of the torpid state. It appeared to me that for a like reason men remain in their present low and primitive condition; but if they should feel the influence of the spring of springs arousing them, they would of necessity rise to a higher and

---

2. **Mentors.** Wise advisors; from Mentor, the friend of Odysseus in Homer's *Odyssey* who educated his son

W

WORDS FOR
EVERYDAY USE:

ear • nest (ɜr´nist) *adj.,* serious; sincere

sat • u • rat • ed (sach´ə rāt´əd) *adj.,* thoroughly soaked

more _ethereal_ life. I had previously seen the snakes in frosty mornings in my path with portions of their bodies still numb and inflexible, waiting for the sun to thaw them. On the 1st of April it rained and melted the ice, and in the early part of the day, which was very foggy, I heard a stray goose groping about over the pond and cackling as if lost, or like the spirit of the fog.

So I went on for some days cutting and hewing timber, and also studs and rafters, all with my narrow axe, not having many communicable or scholarlike thoughts, singing to myself,—

> Men say they know many things;
> But lo! they have taken wings,—
> The arts and sciences
> And a thousand appliances
> The wind that blows
> Is all that any body knows.

I hewed the main timbers six inches square, most of the studs on two sides only, and the rafters and floor timbers on one side, leaving the rest of the bark on, so that they were just as straight and much stronger than sawed ones. Each stick was carefully mortised or tenoned[3] by its stump, for I had borrowed other tools by this time. My days in the woods were not very long ones, yet I usually carried my dinner of bread and butter, and read the newspaper in which it was wrapped, at noon, sitting amid the green pine boughs which I had cut off, and to my bread was imparted some of their fragrance, for my hands were covered with a thick coat of pitch. Before I had done I was more the friend than the foe of the pine tree, though I had cut down some of them, having become better acquainted with it. Sometimes a rambler in the wood was attracted by the sound of my axe, and we chatted pleasantly over the chips which I had made.

By the middle of April, for I made no haste in my work, but rather made the most of it, my house was framed and ready for the raising. I had already bought the shanty of James Collins, an Irishman who worked on the Fitchburg Railroad, for boards. James Collins' shanty was considered an uncommonly fine one. When I called to see it he was not at home. I walked about the outside, at first unobserved from within, the window was so deep and high. It was of small dimensions, with a peaked cottage roof, and not much else to be seen, the dirt being raised five feet all around as if it were a compost heap. The roof was the soundest part, though a good deal warped and made brittle by the sun. Door-sill there was none, but a _perennial_ passage for the hens under the door board. Mrs. C. came to the door and asked me to view it from the inside. The hens were driven in by my approach. It was dark, and had a dirt floor for the most part, dank, clammy, and aguish, only here a board and there a board which would not bear removal. She lighted a lamp to show me the inside of the roof and the walls, and also that the board floor extended under the bed, warning me not to step into the cellar, a sort of dust hole two feet deep. In her own words, they

What is the shanty like?

---

3. **mortised or tenoned.** Joined or fastened

Who watches
Thoreau? What
effect does the
spectator have on
the occasion?

Why is the cellar
of a house so
important?

were "good boards overhead, good boards all around, and a good window,"—of two whole squares originally, only the cat had passed out that way lately. There was a stove, a bed, and a place to sit, an infant in the house where it was born, a silk parasol, gilt-framed looking-glass, and a patent new coffee mill nailed to an oak sapling, all told. The bargain was soon concluded, for James had in the mean while returned. I to pay four dollars and twenty-five cents tonight, he to vacate at five tomorrow morning, selling to nobody else meanwhile: I to take possession at six. It were well, he said, to be there early, and anticipate certain indistinct but wholly unjust claims on the score of ground rent and fuel. This he assured me was the only <u>encumbrance</u>. At six I passed him and his family on the road. One large bundle held their all,— bed, coffee-mill, looking-glass, hens, all but the cat, she took to the woods and became a wild cat, and, as I learned afterward, trod in a trap set for woodchucks, and so became a dead cat at last.

I took down this dwelling the same morning, drawing the nails, and removed it to the pond side by small cartloads, spreading the boards on the grass there to bleach and warp back again in the sun. One early thrush gave me a note or two as I drove along the woodland path. I was informed treacherously by a young Patrick that neighbor Seeley, an Irishman, in the intervals of the carting, transferred the still tolerable, straight, and drivable nails, staples, and spikes to his pocket, and then stood when I came back to pass the time of day, and look freshly up, unconcerned, with spring thoughts, at the devastation;

there being a dearth[4] of work, as he said. He was there to represent spectatordom, and help make this seemingly insignificant event one with the removal of the gods of Troy. [5]

I dug my cellar in the side of a hill sloping to the south, where a woodchuck had formerly dug his burrow, down through sumach and blackberry roots, and the lowest stain of vegetation, six feet square by seven deep, to a fine sand where potatoes would not freeze in any winter. The sides were left shelving, and not stoned; but the sun having never shone on them, the sand still keeps its place. It was but two hours' work. I took particular pleasure in this breaking of ground, for in almost all latitudes men dig into the earth for an equable temperature. Under the most splendid house in the city is still to be found the cellar where they store their roots as of old, and long after the superstructure has disappeared <u>posterity</u> remark its dent in the earth. The house is still but a sort of porch at the entrance of a burrow.

At length, in the beginning of May, with the help of some of my acquaintances, rather to improve so good an occasion for neighborliness than from any necessity, I set up the frame of my house. No man was ever more honored in the character of his raisers than I. They are destined, I trust, to assist at the raising of loftier structures one day. I began to occupy my house on the 4th of July, as soon as it was boarded and roofed, for the boards were carefully feather-edged and lapped, so that

---

4. **dearth.** Scarcity
5. **gods of Troy.** Reference to Virgil's *Aeneid* in which Aeneas escapes with his household gods

WORDS FOR
EVERYDAY USE:

en • cum • brance (en kum′brəns) *n.,* hindrance

pos • ter • i • ty (päs ter′ə tē) *n.,* succeeding generations

it was perfectly impervious to rain;[6] but before boarding I laid the foundation of a chimney at one end, bringing two cartloads of stones up the hill from the pond in my arms. I built the chimney after my hoeing in the fall, before a fire became necessary for warmth, doing my cooking in the mean while out of doors on the ground, early in the morning: which mode I still think is in some respects more convenient and agreeable than the usual one. When it stormed before my bread was baked, I fixed a few boards over the fire, and sat under them to watch my loaf, and passed some pleasant hours in that way. In those days, when my hands were much employed, I read but little, but the least scraps of paper which lay on the ground, my holder, or table-cloth, afforded me as much entertainment, in fact answered the same purpose as the Iliad.[7]

◆ ◆ ◆

FROM "WHERE I LIVED AND WHAT I LIVED FOR"

Every morning was a cheerful invitation to make my life of equal simplicity, and I may say innocence, with Nature herself. I have been as sincere a worshipper of Aurora[8] as the Greeks. I got up early and bathed in the pond; that was a religious exercise, and one of the best things which I did. They say that characters were engraven on the bathing tub of king Tching-thang to this effect: "Renew thyself completely each day; do it again, and again, and forever again."[9] I can understand that. Morning brings back the heroic ages. I was as much affected by the faint hum of a mosquito making its invisible and unimaginable tour through my apartment at earliest dawn, when I was sitting with door and windows open, as I could be by any trumpet that ever sang of fame. It was Homer's requiem; itself an Iliad and Odyssey in the air, singing its own wrath and wanderings. There was something cosmical about it, a standing advertisement, till forbidden,[10] of the everlasting vigor and fertility of the world. The morning, which is the most memorable season of the day, is the awakening hour. Then there is least somnolence in us; and for an hour, at least, some part of us awakes which slumbers all the rest of the day and night. Little is to be expected of that day, if it can be called a day, to which we are not awakened by our Genius, but by the mechanical nudgings of some servitor, are not awakened by our own newly-acquired force and aspirations from within, accompanied by the undulations of celestial music, instead of factory bells and a fragrance filling the air—to a higher life than we fell asleep from; and thus the darkness bear its fruit, and prove itself to be good, no less than the light. That man who does not believe that each day contains an earlier, more sacred, and auroral hour than he has yet profaned, has despaired of life, and is pursuing a descending and darkening way. After a

---

6. **feather-edged . . . rain.** The boards' thin edges overlapped, making the roof watertight.

7. **Iliad.** Greek epic by Homer

8. **Aurora.** Goddess of dawn

9. **"Renew . . . again."** From Confucius, Chinese philosopher

10. **standing . . . forbidden.** Advertisement that was to be run "till forbidden" or stopped by the advertiser

---

WORDS FOR EVERYDAY USE:

as • pi • ra • tion (as´pə rā´shən) n., strong ambition

un • du • la • tion (un´dyoo lā´shən) n., act of moving in waves

What is the "highest of arts"?

Why did Thoreau go to the woods?

What meaning does Thoreau give to the word awake?

partial <u>cessation</u> of his sensuous life, the soul of man, or its organs rather, are reinvigorated each day, and his Genius tries again what noble life it can make. All memorable events, I should say, transpire in morning time and in a morning atmosphere. The Vedas[11] say, "All intelligences awake with the morning." Poetry and art, and the fairest and most memorable of the actions of men, date from such an hour. All poets and heroes, like Memnon,[12] are the children of Aurora, and emit their music at sunrise. To him whose elastic and vigorous thought keeps pace with the sun, the day is a perpetual morning. It matters not what the clocks say or the attitudes and labors of men. Morning is when I am awake and there is a dawn in me. Moral reform is the effort to throw off sleep. Why is it that men give so poor an account of their day if they have not been slumbering? They are not such poor calculators. If they had not been overcome with drowsiness they would have performed something. The millions are awake enough for physical labor; but only one in a million is awake enough for effective intellectual exertion, only one in a hundred millions to a poetic or divine life. To be awake is to be alive. I have never yet met a man who was quite awake. How could I have looked him in the face?

We must learn to reawaken and keep ourselves awake, not by mechanical aids, but by an infinite expectation of the dawn, which does not forsake us in our soundest sleep. I know of no more encouraging fact than the unquestionable ability of man to elevate his life by a conscious <u>endeavor</u>. It is something to be able to paint a particular picture, or to carve a statue, and so to make a few objects beautiful; but it is far more glorious to carve and paint the very atmosphere and medium through which we look, which morally we can do. To affect the quality of the day, that is the highest of arts. Every man is tasked to make his life, even in its details, worthy of the contemplation of his most elevated and critical hour. If we refused, or rather used up, such <u>paltry</u> information as we get, the oracles[13] would distinctly inform us how this might be done.

I went to the woods because I wished to live deliberately, to front only the essential facts of life, and see if I could not learn what it had to teach, and not, when I came to die, discover that I had not lived. I did not wish to live what was not life, living is so dear; nor did I wish to practice resignation, unless it was quite necessary. I wanted to live deep and suck out all the marrow of life, to live so sturdily and Spartan-like[14] as to put to rout all that was not life, to cut a broad swath and shave close, to drive life into a corner, and reduce it to its lowest terms, and, if it proved to be mean, why then to get the whole and genuine meanness of it, and publish its meanness to the world; or if it were sublime, to know it by experience, and be able to give a true account of it in my next excursion. For most men, it appears to me, are in a strange uncertainty about it, whether it is of the devil or of God, and have somewhat hastily concluded

---

11. **Vedas.** Hindu scriptures
12. **Memnon.** King killed by Achilles in the Trojan War
13. **oracles.** People in communication with the gods
14. **Spartan-like.** Without excess comforts

WORDS FOR EVERYDAY USE:

ces • sa • tion (se sā´shən) *n.*, stopping

en • deav • or (en dev´ər) *n.*, effort, attempt

pal • try (pôl´trē) *adj.*, insignificant

Walden Pond. *Concord, Massachusetts*

that it is the chief end of man here to "glorify God and enjoy him forever."[15]

Still we live meanly, like ants; though the fable tells us that we were long ago changed into men;[16] like pygmies we fight with cranes; it is error upon error, and clout upon clout, and our best virtue has for its occasion a <u>superfluous</u> and evitable wretchedness. Our life is frittered away by detail. An honest man has hardly need to count more than his ten fingers, or in extreme cases he may add his ten toes, and lump the rest. Simplicity, simplicity, simplicity! I say, let your affairs be as two or three, and not a hundred or a thousand; instead of a million count half a dozen, and keep your accounts on your thumb nail. In the midst of this chopping sea of civilized life, such are the clouds and storms and quicksands and thousand-and-one items to be allowed for, that a man has to live, if he would not founder and go to the bottom and not make his port at all, by dead reckoning, and he must be a great calculator indeed who succeeds. Simplify, simplify. Instead of three

What does Thoreau recommend?

---

15. **"glorify . . . forever."** Reference to the *New England Primer*
16. **fable . . . men.** Refers to a Greek fable in which Zeus turns ants into men

WORDS FOR EVERYDAY USE:　　**su • per • flu • ous** (sə pʉr´flo͞o əs) *adj.,* excessive

meals a day, if it be necessary eat but one, instead of a hundred dishes, five; and reduce other things in proportion. Our life is like a German Confederacy, made up of petty states, with its boundary forever <u>fluctuating</u>, so that even a German cannot tell you how it is bounded at any moment. The nation itself, with all its so called internal improvements, which, by the way, are all external and superficial, is just such an <u>unwieldy</u> and overgrown establishment, cluttered with furniture and tripped up by its own traps, ruined by luxury and heedless expense, by want of calculation and a worthy aim, as the million households in the land; and the only cure for it as for them is in a rigid economy, a stern and more than Spartan simplicity of life and elevation of purpose. It lives too fast. Men think that it is essential that the Nation have commerce, and export ice, and talk through a telegraph, and ride thirty miles an hour, without a doubt, whether they do or not; but whether we should live like baboons or like men, is a little uncertain. If we do not get out sleepers,[17] and forge rails, and devote days and nights to the work, but go to tinkering upon our lives to improve them, who will build railroads? And if railroads are not built, how shall we get to heaven in season? But if we stay at home and mind our business, who will want railroads? We do not ride on the railroad; it rides upon us. Did you ever think what those sleepers are that underlie the railroad? Each one is a man, an Irish-man, or a Yankee man. The rails are laid on them, and they are covered with sand, and the cars run smoothly over them. They are sound sleepers, I

assure you. And every few years a new lot is laid down and run over; so that, if some have the pleasure of riding on a rail, others have the misfortune to be ridden upon. And when they run over a man that is walking in his sleep, a supernumerary[18] sleeper in the wrong position, and wake him up, they suddenly stop the cars, and make a hue and cry about it, as if this were an exception. I am glad to know that it takes a gang of men for every five miles to keep the sleepers down and level in their beds as it is, for this is a sign that they may sometime get up again.

Why should we live with such hurry and waste of life? We are determined to be starved before we are hungry. Men say that a stitch in time saves nine, and so they take a thousand stitches today to save nine tomorrow. As for work, we haven't any of any consequence. We have the Saint Vitus' dance[19] and cannot possibly keep our heads still. If I should only give a few pulls at the parish bell-rope, as for a fire, that is, without setting the bell, there is hardly a man on his farm in the outskirts of Concord, notwithstanding that press of engagements which was his excuse so many times this morning, nor a boy, nor a woman, I might almost say, but would forsake all and follow that sound, not mainly to save property from the flames, but, if we will confess the truth, much more to see it burn, since burn it must, and we, be it known, did not set it on fire,—or to see it put out, and have a hand in it, if that is

---

17. **sleepers.** Railroad ties
18. **supernumerary.** Extra
19. **Saint Vitus' dance.** Refers to a nervous disorder with symptoms of jerky motions

---

WORDS FOR
EVERYDAY USE:

fluc • tu • ate (fluk´chōō āt´) *vi.*, change or vary continuously

un • wield • y (un wēl´dē) *adj.*, hard to manage

done as handsomely; yes, even if it were the parish church itself. Hardly a man takes a half hour's nap after dinner, but when he wakes he holds up his head and asks "What's the news?" as if the rest of mankind had stood his sentinels. Some give directions to be waked every half hour, doubtless for no other purpose; and then, to pay for it, they tell what they have dreamed. After a night's sleep the news is as indispensable as the breakfast. "Pray tell me any thing new that has happened to a man any where on this globe",—and he reads it over his coffee and rolls, that a man had had his eyes gouged out this morning on the Wachito River; never dreaming the while that he lives in the dark unfathomed mammoth cave of this world, and has but the rudiment of an eye himself.[20]

♦ ♦ ♦

I left the woods for as good a reason as I went there. Perhaps it seemed to me that I had several more lives to live, and could not spare any more time for that one. It is remarkable how easily and insensibly we fall into a particular route, and make a beaten track for ourselves. I had not lived there a week before my feet wore a path from my door to the pond-side; and though it is five or six years since I trod it, it is still quite distinct. It is true, I fear that others may have fallen into it, and so helped to keep it open. The surface of the earth is soft and impressible by the feet of men; and so with the paths which the mind travels. How worn and dusty, then, must be the highways of the world, how deep the ruts of tradition and conformity! I did not wish to take a cabin passage, but rather to go before the mast and on the deck of the world, for there I could best see the moonlight amid the mountains. I do not wish to go below now.

I learned this, at least, by my experiment; that if one advances confidently in the direction of his dreams, and endeavors to live the life which he has imagined, he will meet with a success unexpected in common hours. He will put some things behind, will pass an invisible boundary; new, universal, and more liberal laws will begin to establish themselves around and within him; or old laws be expanded, and interpreted in his favor in a more liberal sense, and he will live with the license of a higher order of beings. In proportion as he simplifies his life, the laws of the universe will appear less complex, and solitude will not be solitude, nor poverty poverty, nor weakness weakness. If you have built castles in the air, your work need not be lost; that is where they should be. Now put the foundations under them.

It is a ridiculous demand which England and America make, that you shall speak so that they can understand you. Neither men nor toadstools grow so. As if that were important, and there were not enough to understand you without them. As if Nature could support but one order of understandings, could not sustain birds as well as quadrupeds, flying as well as creeping things, and *hush* and *who*, which Bright[21] can understand, were the best English. As if there were safety in stupidity alone. I fear chiefly lest my expression may not be *extra-vagant* enough, may not wander far enough beyond the narrow limits of my daily experience, so as to be adequate to the truth of which I have been convinced. *Extra vagance!* it depends on how you are yarded. The migrating buffalo, which seeks new pastures in another latitude, is not extravagant like the cow which kicks over the pail, leaps the cow-yard

What did Thoreau learn?

Why did Thoreau leave the woods? What easily happens to people?

---

20. **dark . . . himself.** Reference to sightless fish found in Mammoth Cave
21. **Bright.** Name for an ox

fence, and runs after her calf, in milking time. I desire to speak somewhere *without* bounds; like a man in a waking moment, to men in their waking moments; for I am convinced that I cannot exaggerate enough even to lay the foundation of a true expression. Who that has heard a strain of music feared then lest he should speak extravagantly any more forever? In view of the future or possible, we should live quite laxly and undefined in front, our outlines dim and misty on that side; as our shadows reveal an insensible perspiration toward the sun. The volatile truth of our words should continually betray the inadequacy of the residual statement. Their truth is instantly *translated*; its literal monument alone remains. The words which express our faith and piety are not definite; yet they are significant and fragrant like frankincense[22] to superior natures.

Why level downward to our dullest perception always, and praise that as common sense? The commonest sense is the sense of men asleep, which they express by snoring. Sometimes we are inclined to class those who are once-and-a-half witted with the half-witted, because we appreciate only a third part of their wit. Some would find fault with the morning-red, if they ever got up early enough. "They pretend," as I hear, "that the verses of Kabir have four different senses; illusion, spirit, intellect, and the exoteric doctrine of the Vedas;" but in this part of the world it is considered a ground for complaint if a man's writings admit of more than one interpretation. While England endeavors to cure the potato-rot, will not any endeavor to cure the brain-rot, which prevails so much more widely and fatally?

I do not suppose that I have attained to obscurity, but I should be proud if no more fatal fault were found with my pages on this score than was found with the Walden ice. Southern customers objected to its blue color, which is the evidence of its purity, as if it were muddy, and preferred the Cambridge ice, which is white, but tastes of weeds. The purity men love is like the mists which envelop the earth, and not like the azure ether beyond.

Some are dinning in our ears that we Americans, and moderns generally, are intellectual dwarfs compared with the ancients, or even the Elizabethan[23] men. But what is that to the purpose? A living dog is better than a dead lion.[24] Shall a man go and hang himself because he belongs to the race of pygmies, and not be the biggest pygmy that he can? Let every one mind his own business, and endeavor to be what he was made.

Why should we be in such desperate haste to succeed, and in such desperate enterprises? If a man does not keep pace with his companions, perhaps it is because he hears a different drummer. Let him step to the music which he hears, however measured or far away. It is not important that he should mature as soon as an apple-tree or an oak. Shall he turn his spring into summer? If the condition of things which we were made for is not yet, what were any reality which we can substi-

22. **frankincense.** Type of incense
23. **Elizabethan.** From the time of Queen Elizabeth I (1533–1603)
24. **A living . . . lion.** Ecclesiastes 9:4

Does Thoreau advocate conformity?

WORDS FOR EVERYDAY USE:

lax • ly (laks´lē) *adv.*, loosely, not strictly

vol • a • tile (väl´ə təl) *adj.*, unstable; fleeting

tute? We will not be shipwrecked on a vain reality. Shall we with pains erect a heaven of blue glass over ourselves, though when it is done we shall be sure to gaze still at the true ethereal heaven far above, as if the former were not? ■

Responding to the Selection

Basing your answer on what you learned of Thoreau in this excerpt, do you think you would get along with the author? Give reasons.

Reviewing the Selection

RECALLING

1. According to Thoreau, age alone does not qualify people to be teachers of the young. Why not?

2. Describe the area in which Thoreau built his home.

3. Why did Thoreau decide to live in the woods for a while? What did he hope to learn from his experience?

4. Name one thing Thoreau learned from his experiment of life in the woods.

INTERPRETING

▶▶ 5. Explain why Thoreau encourages us to examine our assumptions and "to give up our prejudices." Describe his attitudes toward what older people consider to be conventional wisdom.

▶▶ 6. What evidence suggests that Thoreau was not interested in expending a lot of money or time in building a home that others would admire?

▶▶ 7. What does Thoreau mean when he urges us to "Simplify, simplify"?

▶▶ 8. Do you believe that Thoreau "heard a different drummer"? Explain your answer.

9. If you wanted to withdraw from modern society for a while, where would you go? What would you do? Does stepping back from normal life seem like a good idea? Why, or why not?

10. Choose a passage or paragraph that strikes a chord in you. Explain why you agree with the sentiments Thoreau has expressed in that passage.

Understanding Literature (Questions for Discussion)

1. **Allusion.** An **allusion** is a rhetorical technique in which a reference is made to a person, event, object, or work from history or literature. In the second paragraph of the excerpt is an allusion to Mentor, a character in Homer's *Odyssey* who taught Odysseus's son. (Today the proper noun *Mentor* has become the common noun *mentor,* meaning *guide.*) Find at least two other references to Greek mythology or literature in the selection.

2. **Aphorism.** An **aphorism** is a short saying or pointed statement. This excerpt begins with a famous aphorism, "The mass of men lead lives of quiet desperation." The final paragraph includes what may be Thoreau's best-known statement, "If a man does not keep pace with his companions, perhaps it is because he hears a different drummer." Select one of these aphorisms and suggest an explanation for its popularity.

3. **Tone. Tone** is the emotional attitude toward the reader or toward the subject implied by a literary work. Consider such statements in this excerpt as these: "I have lived some thirty years on this planet, and I have yet to hear the first syllable of valuable or even earnest advice from my seniors"; "I have never yet met a man who was quite awake"; "Our life is frittered away by detail." How would you describe the attitude toward the reader implied in these statements? Whom does Thoreau expect to be his reader? How does he expect his reader to react to these statements?

Responding in Writing

1. **Real Estate Ad.** Thoreau has "left the woods" and wants to sell his small house there. Write a newspaper ad accurately describing the building and highlighting its advantages.

2. **Blues.** The **blues** are a style of music that expresses sadness; a song or composition in this style has melancholy words. Write a blues song in response to Thoreau's statement that "The mass of men lead lives of quiet desperation."

3. **Epitaph.** An **epitaph** is an inscription on a tomb or gravestone in memory of the person buried there. Write an epitaph for Henry David Thoreau.

Language Lab

Editing Sentences. Read the Language Arts Survey, 2.58, "Deleting Repeated or Unnecessary Ideas." Then revise these sentences, following Thoreau's edict to "Simplify, simplify."

1. The usual picture we get from *Walden* is that Thoreau lived a rather solitary life by himself.

2. However, many sequences show how the neighbors who lived around Walden Pond were an important part of the writer's life.

3. For example, one neighbor lent Thoreau an axe, and he was careful to sharpen that axe before he returned the tool when he was finished with it.

4. Thoreau also notes that he had pleasant chats when he talked with people who were taking walks in his woods.

5. The passage about his contract with James Collins, in which he made a bargain with Collins to buy the boards of the Irishman's shanty, is amusing and makes the reader laugh.

Thinking Skills

Problem Solving. Read the Language Arts Survey, 4.1, "Strategies for Problem Solving I." Then analyze the selection as an example of problem solving as outlined in the diagram. If going into the woods was the action, what was the problem? What did Thoreau expect to gain from the action? How did he evaluate and apply the results?

PROJECT

Nature Study. While at Walden, Thoreau observed nature closely, taking notes on the activities of ants as well as the beauty of the scenery. Create a display on topics of nature of interest to you. Try to select items that work together to develop a theme, or an appreciation of some particular aspect of nature. Possible highlights could include audiotapes of bird songs, photographs of trees, weather charts, videotapes of tornadoes, or even an ant colony. Each item should have both a label and a short essay explaining its presence in the display.

"The Legend of Sleepy Hollow"
by Washington Irving

(Found among the Papers of the Late Diedrich Knickerbocker)

A pleasing land of drowsy head it was,
Of dreams that wave before the half-shut eye;
And of gay castles in the clouds that pass,
Forever flushing round a summer sky.
—*Castle of Indolence*[1]

In the bosom of one of the spacious coves which indent the eastern shore of the Hudson, at that broad expansion of the river denominated by the ancient Dutch navigators the Tappaan Zee, and where they always prudently shortened sail, and implored the protection of St. Nicholas when they crossed, there lies a small market town or rural port, which by some is called Greensburgh, but which is more universally and properly known by the name of Tarry Town. This name was given it, we are told, in former days, by the good housewives of the adjacent country, from the inveterate propensity of their husbands to linger about the village tavern on market days. Be that as it may, I do not vouch for the fact, but merely advert to it, for the sake of being precise and authentic. Not far from this village, perhaps about three miles, there is a little valley, or rather lap of land among high hills, which is one of the quietest places in the whole world. A small brook glides through it, with just murmur enough to lull you to repose, and the occasional whistle of a quail, or tapping of a woodpecker, is almost the only sound that ever breaks in upon the uniform tranquillity.

I recollect that when a stripling, my first exploit in squirrel shooting was in a grove of tall walnut trees that shades one side of the valley. I had wandered into it at noon time, when all nature is peculiarly quiet, and was startled by the roar of my own gun, as it broke the sabbath stillness around, and was prolonged and reverberated by the angry echoes. If ever I should wish for a retreat, whither I might steal from the world and its distractions, and dream quietly away the remnant of a troubled life, I know of none more promising than this little valley.

From the listless repose of the place, and the peculiar character of its inhabitants, who are descendants from the original Dutch settlers, this sequestered glen has long been known by the name of SLEEPY HOLLOW, and its rustic lads are called the Sleepy Hollow Boys throughout all the neighboring country. A drowsy, dreamy influence seems to hang over the land, and pervade the very atmosphere. Some say that the place was bewitched by a high German[2] doctor during the early days of the settlement; others, that an old Indian chief, the prophet or wizard of his tribe, held his powwows there before the country was discovered by Master Hendrick Hudson.[3] Certain it is, the place still continues under the sway of some witching power, that holds a spell over the minds of the good people, causing them to walk in a continual reverie. They are given to all kinds of marvelous beliefs; have trances and visions, and see strange sights, and hear music and voices in the air. The whole neighborhood abounds with local tales, haunted spots, and twilight superstitions; stars shoot and meteors glare oftener across the valley than in any other part of the country, and the night-mare, with her whole nine fold,[4] seems to make it the favorite scene of her gambols.

The dominant spirit, however, that haunts this enchanted region, and seems to be commander of all the powers of the air, is the apparition of a figure on horseback without a head. It is said by some to be the ghost of a Hessian trooper,[5] whose head had been carried away by a cannon-ball, in some nameless battle during the revolutionary war, and who is ever and anon seen by various of the country people, hurrying along in the gloom of night, as if on the wings of the wind. His haunts are not confined to the valley, but extend at times to the adjacent roads, and especially to the vicinity of a church that is at no great distance. Indeed, certain of the most authentic historians of those parts, who have been careful in collecting and collating the floating facts concerning this specter, allege, that the body of the trooper having been buried in the churchyard, the ghost rides forth to the scene of battle in nightly quest of his head, and the rushing speed with which he sometimes passes along the hollow, like a midnight blast, is owing to his being belated, and in a hurry to get back to the churchyard before daybreak.

Such is the general purport of this legendary superstition, which has furnished materials for many a wild story in that region of shadows; and the specter is known, at all the country firesides, by the name of The Headless Horseman of Sleepy Hollow.

It is remarkable that the visionary turn I have mentioned is not confined to the native inhabitants of the valley, but is imperceptibly acquired by every one who resides there for a time. However wide awake they may have been before they entered that sleepy region, they are sure, in a little time, to imbibe the witching influence of the air, and begin to grow

---

1. **Castle of Indolence.** Poem by James Thomson (1700–1748)
2. **high German.** From southern Germany
3. **Hendrick Hudson.** English navigator who worked for the Dutch

4. **night-mare, . . . fold.** Demon and her nine offspring who tormented sleepers
5. **Hessian trooper.** German mercenary soldier hired by the British to fight in the American Revolution

imaginative—to dream dreams, and see apparitions.

I mention this peaceful spot with all possible laud; for it is in such little retired Dutch valleys, found here and there embosomed in the great state of New York, that populations, manners, and customs, remained fixed, while the great torrent of emigration and improvement, which is making such incessant changes in other parts of this restless country, sweeps by them unobserved. They are like those little nooks of still water, which border a rapid stream, where we may see the straw and bubble riding quietly at anchor, or slowly revolving in their mimic harbor, undisturbed by the rushing of the passing current. Though many years have elapsed since I trod the drowsy shades of Sleepy Hollow, yet I question whether I should not still find the same trees and the same families vegetating in its sheltered bosom.

In this by-place of nature there abode, in a remote period of American history, that is to say, some thirty years since, a worthy wight[1] of the name of Ichabod Crane, who sojourned, or, as he expressed it, "tarried," in Sleepy Hollow, for the purpose of instructing the children of the vicinity. He was a native of Connecticut, a state which supplies the Union with pioneers for the mind as well as the forest, and sends forth yearly its legions of frontier woodmen and country schoolmasters. The cognomen[2] of Crane was not inapplicable to his person. He was tall, but exceedingly lank, with narrow shoulders, long arms and legs, hands that dangled a mile out of his sleeves, feet that might have served for shovels, and his whole frame most loosely hung together. His head was small, and flat at top, with huge ears, large green glassy eyes, and a long snipe nose, so that it might have been mistaken for a weathercock perched upon his spindle neck, to tell which way the wind blew. To see him striding along the profile of a hill on a windy day, with his clothes bagging and fluttering about him, one might have mistaken him for the genius[3] of famine descending upon the earth, or some scarecrow eloped from a cornfield.

His schoolhouse was a low building of one large room rudely constructed of logs; the windows partly glazed, and partly patched with leaves of old copy books. It was most ingeniously secured at vacant hours, by a withe[4] twisted in the handle of the door, and stakes set against the window shutters; so that though a thief might get in with perfect ease, he would find some embarrassment in getting out; an idea most probably borrowed by the architect, Yost Van Houten, from the mystery of an eelpot. The school-house stood in rather a lonely but a pleasant situation, just at the foot of a woody hill, with a brook running close by, and a formidable birch tree growing at one end of it. From hence the low murmur of his pupils' voices conning over their lessons, might be heard of a drowsy summer's day, like the hum of a bee-hive; interrupted now and then by the authoritative voice of the master, giving menace or command, or, peradventure, the appalling sound of the birch, as he urged some tardy loiterer along the flowery path of knowledge. Truth to say, he was a conscientious man, that ever bore in mind the golden maxim, "spare the rod and spoil the child."—Ichabod Crane's scholars certainly were not spoiled.

I would not have it imagined, however, that he was one of those cruel potentates of the school, who joy in the smart[5] of their subjects, on the contrary, he administered justice with discrimination rather than severity; taking the burthen off the backs of the weak, and laying it on those of the strong. Your mere puny stripling, that winced at the least flourish of the rod, was passed by with indulgence; but the claims of justice were satisfied, by giving a double portion to some little, tough, wrong-headed, broad-skirted Dutch urchin, who sulked and swelled and grew dogged and sullen beneath the birch. All this he called "doing his duty by their parents;" and he never inflicted a chastisement without following it by the assurance, so consolatory to the smarting urchin, that he would remember it and thank him for it the longest day he had to live.

When school hours were over, he was even the companion and playmate of his larger boys; and would convoy some of the smaller ones home of a holyday, who happened to have pretty sisters, or good housewives for mothers, noted for the comforts of the cupboard. Indeed, it behooved him to keep on good terms with his pupils. The revenue arising from his school was small, and would have been scarcely sufficient to furnish him with daily bread, for he was a huge feeder, and though lank, had the dilating powers of an Anaconda; but to help out his maintenance, he was, according to country custom in those parts, boarded and lodged at the houses of the farmers, whose children he instructed. With these he lived alternately a week at a time, thus going the rounds of the neighborhood, with all his worldly effects tied up in a cotton handkerchief.

That all this might not be too onerous on the purses of his rustic patrons, who are apt to consider the costs of schooling a grievous burthen, and schoolmasters mere drones, he had various ways of rendering himself both useful and agreeable. He assisted the farmers occasionally in the light labors of their farms, helped to make hay, mended the fences, took the horses to water, drove the cows from pasture, and cut wood for the winter fire. He laid aside, too, all the dominant dignity and absolute sway, with which he lorded it in his little empire, the school, and became wonderfully gentle and ingratiating. He found favor in the eyes of the mothers, by petting the children, particularly the youngest, and like the lion bold, which whilome[6] so magnanimously the lamb did hold,[7] he would sit with a child on one knee, and rock a cradle with his foot, for whole hours together.

In addition to his other vocations, he was the singing-master of the neighborhood, and picked up many

---

1. **wight.** Person
2. **cognomen.** Last name
3. **genius.** Image
4. **withe.** Flexible branch used as a rope
5. **smart.** Pain
6. **whilome.** Formerly
7. **lion . . . hold.** Reference to the *New England Primer* in which the verse for *L* is "The lion bold/The lamb doth hold."

bright shillings by instructing the young folks in psalmody.[1] It was a matter of no little vanity to him on Sundays, to take his station in front of the church gallery, with a band of chosen singers; where, in his own mind, he completely carried away the palm from the parson. Certain it is, his voice resounded far above all the rest of the congregation, and there are peculiar quavers still to be heard in that church, and which may even be heard half-a-mile off, quite to the opposite side of the mill-pond, of a still Sunday morning, which are said to be legitimately descended from the nose of Ichabod Crane. Thus, by diverse little make shifts, in that ingenious way which is commonly denominated "by hook and by crook," the worthy pedagogue got on tolerably enough, and was thought, by all those who understood nothing of the labor of headwork, to have a wonderful easy life of it.

The schoolmaster is generally a man of some importance in the female circle of a rural neighborhood, being considered a kind of idle gentlemanlike personage, of vastly superior taste and accomplishments to the rough country swains, and, indeed, inferior in learning only to the parson. His appearance, therefore, is apt to occasion some little stir at the tea-table of a farmhouse, and the addition of a supernumerary dish of cakes or sweetmeats, or, peradventure, the parade of a silver tea-pot. Our man of letters, therefore, was peculiarly happy in the smiles of all the country damsels. How he would figure among them in the churchyard, between services on Sundays; gathering grapes for them from the wild vines that overrun the surrounding trees; reciting for them all the epitaphs on the tombstones, or sauntering, with a whole bevy of them, along the banks of the adjacent mill-pond; while the more bashful country bumpkins hung sheepishly back, envying his superior elegance and address.

From his half itinerant life, also he was a kind of traveling gazette, carrying the whole budget of local gossip from house to house; so that his appearance was always greeted with satisfaction. He was, moreover, esteemed by the women as a man of great erudition, for he had read several books quite through, and was a perfect master of Cotton Mather's History of New-England Witchcraft, in which, by the way, he most firmly and potently believed.

He was, in fact, an odd mixture of small shrewdness and simple credulity. His appetite for the marvelous, and his powers of digesting it, were equally extraordinary; and both had been increased by his residence in this spell-bound region. No tale was too gross or monstrous for his capacious swallow. It was often his delight, after his school was dismissed of an afternoon, to stretch himself on the rich bed of clover, bordering the little brook that whimpered past his schoolhouse, and there con over old Mather's direful tales, until the gathering dusk of evening made the printed page a mere mist before his eyes. Then, as he wended his way, by swamp and stream and awful[2] woodland, to the farmhouse where he happened to be quartered, every sound of nature, at that witching hour, fluttered his excited imagination: the

moan of the whip-poor-will from the hillside; the boding cry of the tree-toad, that harbinger of storm; the dreary hooting of the screech-owl; or the sudden rustling in the thicket, of birds frightened from their roost. The fire-flies, too, which sparkled most vividly in the darkest places, now and then startled him, as one of uncommon brightness would stream across his path; and if, by chance, a huge blockhead of a beetle came winging his blundering flight against him, the poor varlet was ready to give up the ghost, with the idea that he was struck with a witch's token. His only resource on such occasions, either to drown thought, or drive away evil spirits, was to sing psalm tunes;—and the good people of Sleepy Hollow, as they sat by their doors of an evening, were often filled with awe, at hearing his nasal melody, "in linked sweetness long drawn out," floating from the distant hill, or along the dusky road.

Another of his sources of fearful pleasure was, to pass long winter evenings with the old Dutch wives, as they sat spinning by the fire, with a row of apples roasting and sputtering along the hearth, and listen to their marvelous tales of ghosts and goblins, and haunted fields and haunted brooks, and haunted bridges and haunted houses, and particularly of the headless horseman, or galloping Hessian of the Hollow, as they sometimes called him. He would delight them equally by his anecdotes of witchcraft, and of the direful omens and portentous sights and sounds in the air, which prevailed in the earlier times of Connecticut; and would frighten them woefully with speculations upon comets and shooting stars, and with the alarming fact that the world did absolutely turn round, and that they were half the time topsy-turvy!

But if there was a pleasure in all this, while snugly cuddling in the chimney corner of a chamber that was all of a ruddy glow from the crackling wood fire, and where, of course, no specter dare to show its face, it was dearly purchased by the terrors of his subsequent walk homewards. What fearful shapes and shadows beset his path, amidst the dim and ghostly glare of a snowy night!—With what wistful look did he eye every trembling ray of light streaming across the waste fields from some distant window!—How often was he appalled by some shrub covered with snow, which like sheeted specter beset his very path!—How often did he shrink with curdling awe at the sound of his own steps on the frosty crust beneath his feet; and dread to look over his shoulder, lest he should behold some uncouth being tramping close behind him!—and how often was he thrown into complete dismay by some rushing blast, howling among the trees, in the idea that it was the galloping Hessian on one of his nightly scourings.

All these, however, were mere terrors of the night, phantoms of the mind, that walk in darkness; and though he had seen many specters in his time, and been more than once beset by Satan in diverse shapes, in his lonely perambula-

---

1. **psalmody.** Singing versions of the psalms
2. **awful.** Terrifying

tions, yet daylight put an end to all these evils; and he would have passed a pleasant life of it, in despite of the Devil and all his works, if his path had not been crossed by a being that causes more perplexity to mortal man, than ghosts, goblins, and the whole race of witches put together, and that was—a woman.

Among the musical disciples who assembled, one evening in each week, to receive his instructions in psalmody, was Katrina Van Tassel, the daughter and only child of a substantial Dutch farmer. She was a blooming lass of fresh eighteen; plump as a partridge; ripe and melting and rosy-cheeked as one of her father's peaches, and universally famed, not merely for her beauty, but her vast expectations. She was withal a little of a coquette, as might be perceived even in her dress, which was a mixture of ancient and modern fashions, as most suited to set off her charms. She wore the ornaments of pure yellow gold, which her great-great-grandmother had brought over from Saardam;[1] the tempting stomacher[2] of the olden time, and withal a provokingly short petticoat, to display the prettiest foot and ankle in the country round.

Ichabod Crane had a soft and foolish heart toward the sex; and it is not to be wondered at, that so tempting a morsel soon found favor in his eyes, more especially after he had visited her in her paternal mansion. Old Baltus Van Tassel was a perfect picture of a thriving, contented, liberal-hearted farmer. He seldom, it is true, sent either his eyes or his thoughts beyond the boundaries of his own farm; but within those every thing was snug, happy, and well-conditioned. He was satisfied with his wealth, but not proud of it, and piqued himself upon the hearty abundance, rather than the style in which he lived. His strong hold was situated on the banks of the Hudson, in one of those green, sheltered, fertile nooks, into which the Dutch farmers are so fond of nestling. A great elm tree spread its broad branches over it, at the foot of which bubbled up a spring of the softest and sweetest water, in a little kind of well, formed of a barrel, and then stole sparkling away through the grass, to a neighboring brook, that babbled along among elders and dwarf willows. Hard by the farmhouse was a vast barn, that might have served for a church; every window and crevice of which seemed bursting forth with the treasures of the farm; the flail was busily resounding within it; swallows and martins skimmed twittering about the eaves, and rows of pigeons, some with one eye turned up, as if watching the weather, some with their heads under their wings, or buried in their bosoms, and others, swelling, and cooing, and bowing about their dames, were enjoying the sunshine on the roof. Sleek unwieldy porkers were grunting in the repose and abundance of their pens, from whence sallied forth, now and then, troops of sucking pigs, as if to snuff the air. A stately squadron of snowy geese were riding in an adjoining pond, convoying whole fleets of ducks; regiments of turkeys were gobbling about the farm yard, and guinea fowls fretting like ill-tempered housewives, with their peevish discontented cry. Before the barn door strutted the gallant cock, that pattern of a husband, a warrior, and a fine gentleman, clapping his burnished wings, and crowing in the pride and gladness of his heart—sometimes tearing up the earth with his feet, and then generously calling his ever-hungry family of wives and children to enjoy the rich morsel he had discovered.

The pedagogue's mouth watered, as he looked upon this sumptuous promise of luxurious winter fare. In his devouring mind's eye, he pictured to himself every roasting pig running about with a pudding in its belly, and an apple in its mouth; the pigeons were snugly put to bed in a comfortable pie, and tucked in with a coverlet of crust; the geese were swimming in their own gravy; and the ducks pairing cosily in dishes, like snug married couples, with a decent competency of onion sauce; in the porkers he saw carved out the future sleek side of bacon, and juicy relishing ham; not a turkey, but he beheld daintily trussed up, with its gizzard under its wing, and, peradventure, a necklace of savory sausages; and even bright chanticleer[3] himself lay sprawling on his back, in a side dish, with uplifted claws, as if craving that quarter, which his chivalrous spirit disdained to ask while living.

As the enraptured Ichabod fancied all this, and as he rolled his great green eyes over the fat meadow lands, the rich fields of wheat, of rye, of buckwheat, and Indian corn and the orchards burthened with rudely fruit, which surrounded the warm tenement[4] of Van Tassel, his heart yearned after the damsel who was to inherit these domains, and his imagination expanded with the idea, how they might be readily turned into cash, and the money invested in immense tracts of wild land, and shingle palaces in the wilderness. Nay, his busy fancy already put him in possession of his hopes, and presented to him the blooming Katrina, with a whole family of children, mounted on the top of a wagon loaded with household trumpery, with pots and kettles dangling beneath; and he beheld himself bestriding a pacing mare, with a colt at her heels, setting out for Kentucky, Tennessee, or the Lord knows where!

When he entered the house, the conquest of his heart was complete. It was one of those spacious farm houses, with high-ridged, but lowly-sloping roofs, built in the style handed down from the first Dutch settlers. The low, projecting eaves formed a piazza along the front, capable of being closed up in bad weather. Under this were hung flails, harness, various utensils of husbandry, and nets for fishing in the neighboring river. Benches were built along the sides for summer use; and a great spinning wheel at one end, and a churn at the other, showed the various uses to which this important porch might be devoted. From this piazza the wondering Ichabod entered the hall, which formed the center of the mansion, and the place of usual residence. Here,

---

1. **Saardam.** Now Zaandam, a city near Amsterdam
2. **stomacher.** Decorative waistband worn over a dress
3. **chanticleer.** Rooster
4. **tenement.** Residence

rows of resplendent pewter, ranged on a long dresser, dazzled his eyes. In one corner stood a huge bag of wool ready to be spun; in another a quantity of linsey-woolsey just from the loom; ears of Indian corn, and strings of dried apples and peaches, hung in gay festoons along the walls, mingled with the gaud of red peppers; and a door left ajar, gave him a peep into the best parlor, where the claw-footed chairs, and dark mahogany tables, shone like mirrors; andirons, with their accompanying shovel and tongs, glistened from their covert of asparagus tops; mock oranges and conch shells decorated the mantlepiece; strings of various colored birds' eggs were suspended above it; a great ostrich egg was hung from the center of the room, and a corner cupboard, knowingly left open, displayed immense treasures of old silver and well-mended china.

From the moment Ichabod laid his eyes upon these regions of delight, the peace of his mind was at an end, and his only study was how to gain the affections of the peerless daughter of Van Tassel. In this enterprise, however, he had more real difficulties than generally fell to the lot of a knight-errant of yore, who seldom had any thing but giants, enchanters, fiery dragons, and such like easily conquered adversaries, to contend with; and had to make his way merely through gates of iron and brass, and walls of adamant,[1] to the castle keep, where the lady of his heart was confined; all which he achieved as easily as a man would carve his way to the center of a Christmas pie, and then the lady gave him her hand as a matter of course. Ichabod, on the contrary, had to win his way to the heart of a country coquette, beset with a labyrinth of whims and caprices, which were for ever presenting new difficulties and impediments, and he had to encounter a host of fearful adversaries of real flesh and blood, the numerous rustic admirers, who beset every portal to her heart, keeping a watchful and angry eye upon each other, but ready to fly out in the common cause against any new competitor.

Among these, the most formidable, was a burley, roaring, roystering blade, of the name of Abraham, or, according to the Dutch abbreviation, Brom Van Brunt, the hero of the country round, which rung with his feats of strength and hardihood. He was broad shouldered and double jointed, with short curly black hair, and a bluff, but not unpleasant countenance, having a mingled air of fun and arrogance. From his Herculean frame and great powers of limb, he had received the nick-name of BROM BONES, by which he was universally known. He was famed for great knowledge and skill in horsemanship, being as dexterous on horseback as a Tartar. He was foremost at all races and cockfights, and with the ascendancy which bodily strength always acquires in rustic life, was the umpire in all disputes, setting his hat on one side, and giving his decisions with an air and tone that admitted of no gainsay or appeal. He was always ready for either a fight or a frolick; had more mischief than ill-will in his composition; and with all his overbearing roughness, there was a strong dash of waggish good humor at bottom. He had three or four boon companions of his own stamp,

who regarded him as their model, and at the head of whom he scoured the country, attending every scene of feud or merriment for miles round. In cold weather he was distinguished by a fur cap, surmounted with a flaunting fox's tail, and when the folks at a country gathering descried this well-known crest at a distance, whisking about among a squad of hard riders, they always stood by for a squall. Sometimes his crew would be heard dashing along past the farm-houses at midnight, with whoop and halloo, like a troop of Don Cossacks,[2] and the old dames, startled out of their sleep, would listen for a moment till the hurry scurry had clattered by, and then exclaim, "aye, there goes Brom Bones and his gang!" The neighbors looked upon him with a mixture of awe, admiration, and good-will; and when any mad-cap prank, or rustic brawl, occurred in the vicinity, always shook their heads, and warranted Brom Bones was at the bottom of it.

This rantipole[3] hero had for some time singled out the blooming Katrina for the object of his uncouth gallantries, and though his amorous toyings were something like the gentle caresses and endearments of a bear, yet it was whispered that she did not altogether discourage his hopes. Certain it is, his advances were signals for rival candidates to retire, who felt no inclination to cross a lion in his amours; insomuch, that when his horse was seen tied to Van Tassel's paling,[4] of a Sunday night, (a sure sign that his master was courting, or, as it is termed, "sparking," within,) all other suitors passed by in despair, and carried the war into other quarters.

Such was the formidable rival with whom Ichabod Crane had to contend and, considering all things, a stouter man than he would have shrunk from the competition, and a wiser man would have despaired. He had, however, a happy mixture of pliability and perseverance in his nature; he was in form and spirit like a supple jack—yielding, but tough; though he bent, he never broke; and though he bowed beneath the slightest pressure, yet, the moment it was away—jerk!—he was as erect, and carried his head as high as ever.

To have taken the field openly against his rival, would have been madness; for he was not a man to be thwarted in his amours, any more than that stormy lover, Achilles.[5] Ichabod, therefore, made his advances in a quiet and gently-insinuating manner. Under cover of his character of singing master, he made frequent visits at the farm-house; not that he had any thing to apprehend from the meddlesome interference of parents, which is so often a stumbling block in the path of lovers. Balt Van Tassel was an easy indulgent soul; he loved his daughter better even than his pipe, and like a reasonable man, and an excellent father, let her have her way in every thing. His notable little wife too, had enough to do to attend

---

1. **adamant.** Impenetrable stone of fable and legend
2. **Don Cossacks.** Russian Cavalry
3. **rantipole.** Unruly
4. **paling.** Fence
5. **Achilles.** Legendary warrior Achilles sulks over a lost love until he is roused to fight in anger.

to her housekeeping and manage the poultry, for, as she sagely observed, ducks and geese are foolish things, and must be looked after, but girls can take care of themselves. Thus while the busy dame bustled about the house, or plied her spinning wheel at one end of the piazza, honest Balt would sit smoking his evening pipe at the other, watching the achievements of a little wooden warrior, who, armed with a sword in each hand, was most valiantly fighting the wind on the pinnacle of the barn. In the mean time, Ichabod would carry on his suit with the daughter by the side of the spring under the great elm, or sauntering along in the twilight, that hour so favorable to the lover's eloquence.

I profess not to know how women's hearts are wooed and won. To me they have always been matters of riddle and admiration. Some seem to have but one vulnerable point, or door of access; while others have a thousand avenues, and may be captured a thousand different ways. It is a great triumph of skill to gain the former, but a still greater proof of generalship to maintain possession of the latter, for a man must battle for his fortress at every door and window. He that wins a thousand common hearts, is therefore entitled to some renown; but he who keeps undisputed sway over the heart of a coquette, is indeed a hero. Certain it is, this was not the case with the redoutable Brom Bones; and from the moment Ichabod Crane made his advances, the interests of the former evidently declined; his horse was no longer seen tied at the palings on Sunday nights, and a deadly feud gradually arose between him and the preceptor of Sleepy Hollow.

Brom, who had a degree of rough chivalry in his nature, would fain have carried matters to open warfare, and settled their pretensions to the lady, according to the mode of those most concise and simple reasoners, the knights-errant of yore—by single combat: but Ichabod was too conscious of the superior might of his adversary to enter the lists against him; he had overheard the boast of Bones, that he would "double the schoolmaster up, and put him on a shelf;" and he was too wary to give him an opportunity. There was something extremely provoking in this obstinately pacific system; it left Brom no alternative but to draw upon the funds of rustic waggery in his disposition, and play off boorish practical jokes upon his rival. Ichabod became the object of whimsical persecution to Bones, and his gang of rough riders. They harried his hitherto peaceful domains; smoked out his singing school, by stopping up the chimney; broke into the school-house at night, in spite of its formidable fastenings of withe and window stakes, and turned every thing topsy-turvy, so that the poor schoolmaster began to think all the witches in the country held their meetings there. But what was still more annoying, Brom took all opportunities of turning him into ridicule in presence of his mistress, and had a scoundrel dog, whom he taught to whine in the most ludicrous manner, and introduced as a rival of Ichabod's, to instruct her in psalmody.

In this way, matters went on for some time, without producing any material effect on the relative situations of the contending powers. On a fine autumnal afternoon, Ichabod, in pensive mood, sat enthroned on the lofty stool from whence he usually watched all the concerns of his little literary realm. In his hand he swayed a ferule, that scepter of despotic power; the birch of justice reposed on three nails, behind the throne a constant terror to evil doers; while on the desk before him might be seen sundry contraband articles and prohibited weapons, detected upon the persons of idle urchins, such as half-munched apples, popguns, whirligigs, fly-cages, and whole legions of rampant little paper game cocks. Apparently there had been some appalling act of justice recently inflicted, for his scholars were all busily intent upon their books, or slyly whispering behind them with one eye kept upon the master; and a kind of buzzing stillness reigned throughout the school-room. It was suddenly interrupted by the appearance of a negro in tow-cloth jacket and trousers, a round crowned fragment of a hat, like the cap of Mercury,[1] and mounted on the back of a ragged, wild, half-broken colt, which he managed with a rope by way of halter. He came clattering up to the school door with an invitation to Ichabod to attend a merry-making, or "quilting frolick," to be held that evening at Mynheer Van Tassel's, and having delivered his message with that air of importance, and effort at fine language, which a negro is apt to display on petty embassies of the kind, he dashed over the brook, and was seen scampering away up the hollow, full of the importance and hurry of his mission.

All was now bustle and hubbub in the late quiet school room. The scholars were hurried through their lessons, without stopping at trifles; those who were nimble, skipped over half with impunity, and those who were tardy, had a smart application now and then in the rear, to quicken their speed, or help them over a tall word. Books were flung aside, without being put away on the shelves; inkstands were overturned, benches thrown down, and the whole school turned loose an hour before the usual time; bursting forth like a legion of young imps, yelping and racketing about the green, in joy at their early emancipation.

The gallant Ichabod now spent at least an extra half hour at his toilet, brushing and furbishing up his best, and indeed only suit of rusty black, and arranging his looks by a bit of broken looking glass, that hung up in the school house. That he might make his appearance before his mistress in the true style of a cavalier, he borrowed a horse from the farmer with whom he was domiciliated, a choleric old Dutchman, of the name of Hans Van Ripper, and thus gallantly mounted, issued forth like a knight-errant in quest of adventures. But it is meet I should, in the true spirit of romantic story, give some account of the looks and equipments of my hero and his steed. The animal he bestrode was a broken-down plough horse, that had outlived almost every thing but his viciousness. He was gaunt and shagged, with a ewe neck and hammer head; his rusty mane and tail were tangled and knotted

---

1. **cap of Mercury.** Winged cap like that worn by Mercury, the messenger of the gods

with burrs, one eye had lost its pupil, and was glaring and spectral, but the other had the gleam of a genuine devil in it. Still he must have had fire and mettle in his day, if we may judge from his name, which was Gunpowder. He had, in fact, been a favorite steed of his master's, the choleric Van Ripper, who was a furious rider, and had infused, very probably, some of his own spirit into the animal, for, old and broken-down as he looked, there was more lurking deviltry in him than in any young filly in the country.

Ichabod was a suitable figure for such a steed. He rode with short stirrups, which brought his knees nearly up to the pommel of the saddle; his sharp elbows stuck out like grasshoppers'; he carried his whip perpendicularly in his hand, like a scepter, and as the horse jogged on, the motion of his arms was not unlike the flapping of a pair of wings. A small wool hat rested on the top of his nose, for so his scanty strip of forehead might be called, and the skirts of his black coat fluttered out almost to the horse's tail. Such was the appearance of Ichabod and his steed, as they shambled out of the gate of Hans Van Ripper, and it was altogether such an apparition as is seldom to be met with in broad day light.

It was, as I have said, a fine autumnal day, the sky was clear and serene, and nature wore that rich and golden livery which we always associate with the idea of abundance. The forests had put on their sober brown and yellow, while some trees of the tenderer kind had been nipped by the frosts into brilliant dyes of orange, purple, and scarlet. Streaming files of wild ducks began to make their appearance high in the air; the bark of the squirrel might be heard from the groves of beech and hickory nuts, and the pensive whistle of the quail at intervals from the neighboring stubble field.

The small birds were taking their farewell banquets. In the fullness of their revelry, they fluttered, chirping and frolicking, from bush to bush, and tree to tree, capricious from the very profusion and variety around them. There was the honest cock-robin, the favorite game of stripling sportsmen, with its loud querulous note; and the twittering blackbirds flying in sable clouds; and the golden winged woodpecker, with his crimson crest, his broad black gorget, and splendid plumage; and the cedar bird, with its red tipt wings and yellow tipt tail, and its little monteiro cap[1] of feathers; and the blue jay, that noisy coxcomb, in his gay light blue coat and white under clothes, screaming and chattering, nodding, and bobbing, and bowing, and pretending to be on good terms with every songster of the grove.

As Ichabod jogged slowly on his way, his eye, ever open to every symptom of culinary abundance, ranged with delight over the treasures of jolly autumn. On all sides he beheld vast store of apples, some hanging in oppressive opulence on the trees, some gathered into baskets and barrels for the market, others heaped up in rich piles for the cider-press. Further on he beheld great fields of Indian corn, with its golden ears peeping from their leafy coverts, and holding out the promise of cakes and hasty pudding; and the yellow pumpkins lying beneath them, turning up their fair round bellies to the sun, and giving ample prospects of the most luxurious

of pies; and anon he passed the fragrant buckwheat fields, breathing the odor of the bee-hive, and as he beheld them, soft anticipations stole over his mind of dainty slap-jacks, well buttered, and garnished with honey or treacle,[2] by the delicate little dimpled hand of Katrina Van Tassel.

Thus feeding his mind with many sweet thoughts and "sugared suppositions," he journeyed along the sides of a range of hills which look out upon some of the goodliest scenes of the mighty Hudson. The sun gradually wheeled his broad disk down into the west. The wide bosom of the Tappaan Zee lay motionless and glassy, excepting that here and there a gentle undulation waved and prolonged the blue shadow of the distant mountain: a few amber clouds floated in the sky, without a breath of air to move them. The horizon was of a fine golden tint, changing gradually into a pure apple green, and from that into a deep blue of the mid-heaven. A slanting ray lingered on the woody crests of the precipices that overhung some parts of the river, giving greater depth to the dark grey and purple of their rocky sides. A sloop was loitering in the distance, dropping slowly down with the tide, her sail hanging uselessly against the mast, and as the reflection of the sky gleamed along the still water, it seemed as if the vessel was suspended in the air.

It was toward evening that Ichabod arrived at the castle of the Heer Van Tassel, which he found thronged with the pride and flower of the adjacent country. Old farmers, a spare, leathern-faced race, in homespun coats and small clothes, blue stockings, huge shoes and magnificent pewter buckles. Their brisk withered little dames in close crimped caps, long waisted short gowns, homespun petticoats, with scissors and pincushions, and gay calico pockets, hanging on the outside. Buxom lasses, almost as antiquated as their mothers, excepting where a straw hat, a fine riband, or perhaps a white frock, gave symptoms of city innovations. The sons, in short square-skirted coats with rows of stupendous brass buttons, and their hair generally queued in the fashion of the times, especially if they could procure an eel-skin for the purpose, it being esteemed throughout the country as a potent nourisher and strengthener of the hair.

Brom Bones, however, was the hero of the scene, having come to the gathering on his favorite steed Daredevil, a creature, like himself, full of mettle and mischief, and which no one but himself could manage. He was in fact noted for preferring vicious animals, given to all kinds of tricks, which kept the rider in constant risk of his neck, and held a tractable well-broken horse as unworthy a lad of spirit.

Fain would I pause to dwell upon the world of charms that burst upon the enraptured gaze of my hero, as he entered the state parlor of Van Tassel's mansion. Not those of the bevy of buxom lasses, with their luxurious display of red and white: but the ample charms of a genuine Dutch country tea-table, in the sumptuous time of autumn. Such heaped up platters of cakes of various and almost indescrib-

---

1. **monteiro cap.** Hunting cap
2. **treacle.** Molasses

able kinds, known only to experienced Dutch housewives. There was the doughty dough-nut, the tenderer oly koek,[1] and the crisp and crumbling cruller; sweet cakes and short cakes, ginger cakes and honey cakes, and the whole family of cakes. And then there were apple pies and peach pies and pumpkin pies; not to mention slices of ham and smoked beef, together with broiled shad and roasted chickens; besides delectable dishes of preserved plums, and peaches, and pears, and quinces; with bowls of milk and cream, all mingled higgledy-piggledy, pretty much as I have enumerated them, with the motherly tea-pot sending up its clouds of vapor from the midst—Heaven bless the mark! I want breath and time to discuss this banquet as it deserves, and am too eager to get on with my story. Happily, Ichabod Crane was not in so great a hurry as his historian, but did ample justice to every dainty.

He was a kind and thankful toad, whose heart dilated in proportion as his skin was filled with good cheer, and whose spirits rose with eating, as some men's do with drink. He could not help, too, rolling his large eyes round him as he eat, and chuckling with the possibility that he might one day be lord of all this scene of almost unimaginable luxury and splendor. Then, he thought, how soon he'd turn his back upon the old school house; snap his fingers in the face of Hans Van Ripper, and every other niggardly patron, and kick any itinerant pedagogue out of doors that dared to call him comrade!

Old Baltus Van Tassel moved about among his guests with a face dilated with content and good humour, round and jolly as the harvest moon. His hospitable attentions were brief, but expressive, being confined to a shake of the hand, a slap on the shoulder, a loud laugh, and a pressing invitation to "reach to, and help themselves."

And now the sound of the music from the common room or hall, summoned to the dance. The musician was an old grey-headed negro, who had been the itinerant orchestra of the neighborhood for more than half a century. His instrument was as old and battered as himself. The greater part of the time he scraped away on two or three strings, accompanying every movement of the bow with a motion of the head; bowing almost to the ground, and stamping with his foot whenever a fresh couple were to start.

Ichabod prided himself upon his dancing as much as upon his vocal powers. Not a limb, not a fibre about him was idle, and to have seen his loosely hung frame in full motion, and clattering about the room, you would have thought Saint Vitus[2] himself, that blessed patron of the dance, was figuring before you in person. He was the admiration of all the negroes, who, having gathered, of all ages and sizes, from the farm and the neighborhood, stood forming a pyramid of shining black faces at every door and window, gazing with delight at the scene, rolling their white eye-balls, and showing grinning rows of ivory from ear to ear. How could the flogger of urchins be otherwise than animated and joyous; the lady of his heart was his partner in the dance; she smiled graciously in reply to all his amorous oglings, while Brom Bones, sorely smitten with love and jealousy, sat brooding by himself in one corner.

When the dance was at an end, Ichabod was attracted to a knot of the sager folks, who, with old Van Tassel, sat smoking at one end of the piazza, gossiping over former times, and drawling out long stories about the war.

This neighborhood, at the time of which I am speaking, was one of those highly favored places which abound with chronicle and great men. The British and American line had run near it during the war; it had, therefore, been the scene of marauding, and been infested with refugees, cow boys,[3] and all kind of border chivalry. Just sufficient time had elapsed to enable each story teller to dress up his tale with a little becoming fiction, and in the indistinctness of his recollection, to make himself the hero of every exploit.

There was the story of Doffue Martling, a large, blue-bearded Dutchman, who had nearly taken a British frigate with an old iron nine-pounder from a mud breastwork,[4] only that his gun burst at the sixth discharge. And there was an old gentleman who shall be nameless, being too rich a mynheer to be lightly mentioned, who in the battle of Whiteplains, being an excellent master of defense, parried a musket ball with a small sword, insomuch that he absolutely felt it whiz round the blade, and glance off at the hilt: in proof of which, he was ready at any time to show the sword, with the hilt a little bent. There were several more who had been equally great in the field, not one of whom but was persuaded that he had a considerable hand in bringing the war to a happy termination.

But all these were nothing to the tales of ghosts and apparitions that succeeded. The neighborhood is rich in legendary treasures of the kind. Local tales and superstitions thrive best in these sheltered, long settled retreats; but they are trampled under foot, by the shifting throng that forms the population of most of our country places. Besides, there is no encouragement for ghosts in the generality of our villages, for they have scarce had time to take their first nap, and turn themselves in their graves, before their surviving friends have traveled away from the neighborhood, so that when they turn out of a night to walk the rounds, they have no acquaintance left to call upon. This is perhaps the reason why we so seldom hear of ghosts excepting in our long-established Dutch communities.

The immediate cause, however, of the prevalence of supernatural stories in these parts, was doubtless owing to the vicinity of Sleepy Hollow. There was a contagion in the very air that blew from that haunted region; it breathed forth an atmosphere of dreams and fancies infecting all the land. Several of the Sleepy Hollow people were present at Van Tassel's, and, as usual, were doling out their wild and

---

1. **oly koek.** Type of doughnut
2. **Saint Vitus.** Christian martyr prayed to by Catholics for relief from nervous disorders
3. **cow boys.** Tory, or British, supporting raiders
4. **breastwork.** Fortification

wonderful legends. Many dismal tales were told about funeral trains, and mournful cries and wailings heard and seen about the great tree where the unfortunate Major André[1] was taken, and which stood in the neighborhood. Some mention was made also of the woman in white, that haunted the dark glen at Raven Rock, and was often heard to shriek on winter nights before a storm, having perished there in the snow. The chief part of the stories, however, turned upon the favorite specter of Sleepy Hollow, the headless horseman, who had been heard several times of late, patroling the country; and it was said, tethered his horse nightly among the graves in the churchyard.

The sequestered situation of this church seems always to have made it a favorite haunt of troubled spirits. It stands on a knoll, surrounded by locust trees and lofty elms, from among which its decent, whitewashed walls shine modestly forth, like Christian purity, beaming through the shades of retirement. A gentle slope descends from it to a silver sheet of water, bordered by high trees, between which, peeps may be caught at the blue hills of the Hudson. To look upon its grass-grown yard, where the sunbeams seem to sleep so quietly, one would think that here at least the dead might rest in peace. On one side of the church extends a wide woody dell, along which raves a large brook among broken rocks and trunks of fallen trees. Over a deep black part of the stream, not far from the church, was formerly thrown a wooden bridge; the road that led to it, and the bridge itself, were thickly shaded by overhanging trees, which cast a gloom about it, even in the day time; but occasioned a fearful darkness at night. Such was one of the favorite haunts of the headless horseman, and the place where he was most frequently encountered. The tale was told of old Brouwer, a most heretical disbeliever in ghosts, that he met the horseman returning from his foray into Sleepy Hollow, and was obliged to get up behind him; that they galloped over bush and brake, over hill and swamp, until they reached the bridge, when the horseman suddenly turned into a skeleton, threw old Brouwer into the brook, and sprang away over the treetops with a clap of thunder.

This story was immediately matched by a thrice marvelous adventure of Brom Bones, who made light of the galloping Hessian as an errant jockey. He affirmed, that on returning one night from the neighborhood village of Sing-Sing, he had been overtaken by this midnight trooper; that he had offered to race with him for a bowl of punch, and would have won it too, for Daredevil beat the goblin horse all hollow, but just as they came to the church bridge, the Hessian bolted, and vanished in a flash of fire.

All these tales, told in that drowsy under tone with which men talk in the dark, the countenances of the listeners only now and then receiving a casual gleam from the glare of a pipe, sunk deep in the mind of Ichabod. He repaid them in kind with large extracts from his invaluable author, Cotton Mather, and added many very marvellous events that had taken place in his native state of Connecticut, and fearful sights which he had seen in his nightly walks about Sleepy Hollow.

The revel now gradually broke up. The old farmers gathered together their families in their wagons, and were heard for some time rattling along the hollow roads, and over the distant hills. Some of the damsels, mounted on pillions[2] behind their favorite swains, and their light-hearted laughter mingling with the clatter of hoofs, echoed along the silent woodlands, sounding fainter and fainter until they gradually died away—and the late scene of noise and frolic was all silent and deserted. Ichabod only lingered behind, according to the custom of country lovers, to have a tête-a-tête[3] with the heiress; fully convinced that he was now on the high road to success. What passed at this interview I will not pretend to say, for in fact I do not know. Something, however, I fear me, must have gone wrong, for he certainly sallied forth, after no very great interval, with an air quite desolate and chopfallen—Oh these women! these women! Could that girl have been playing off any of her coquettish tricks?—Was her encouragement of the poor pedagogue all a mere sham to secure her conquest of his rival?—Heaven only knows, not I!—Let it suffice to say, Ichabod stole forth with the air of one who had been sacking a hen roost, rather than a fair lady's heart. Without looking to the right or left to notice the scene of rural wealth, on which he had so often gloated, he went straight to the stable, and with several hearty cuffs and kicks, roused his steed most uncourteously from the comfortable quarters in which he was soundly sleeping, dreaming of mountains of corn and oats, and whole valleys of timothy and clover.

It was the very witching time of night that Ichabod, heavyhearted and bedrooped, pursued his travel homewards, along the sides of the lofty hills which rise above Tarry Town, and which he had traversed so cheerily in the afternoon. The hour was as dismal as himself. Far below him the Tappaan Zee spread its dusky and indistinct waste of waters, with here and there the tall mast of a sloop, riding quietly at anchor under the land. In the dead hush of midnight, he could even hear the barking of the watch-dog from the opposite shore of the Hudson; but it was so vague and faint as only to give an idea of his distance from this faithful companion of man. Now and then, too, the long-drawn crowing of a cock, accidentally awakened, would sound far, far off, from some farm house away among the hills—but it was like a dreaming sound in his ear. No signs of life occurred near him, but occasionally the melancholy chirp of a cricket, or perhaps the gutteral twang of a bullfrog, from a neighboring marsh, as if sleeping uncomfortably and turning suddenly in his bed.

All the stories of ghosts and goblins that Ichabod had heard in the afternoon, now came crowding upon his recollection. The night grew darker and darker; the stars seemed to sink deeper in the sky, and driving clouds occasionally hid them from his sight. He had never felt so lonely and dismal. He was, more-

---

1. **Major André.** British spy arrested in Tarrytown
2. **pillions.** Pads that allow a second rider to sit behind a saddled rider
3. **tête-a-tête.** French for "head-to-head," meaning a private conversation

over, approaching the very place where many of the scenes of the ghost stories had been laid. In the center of the road stood an enormous tulip tree, which towered like a giant above all the other trees of the neighborhood, and formed a kind of landmark. Its limbs were vast, gnarled, and fantastic, twisting down almost to the earth, and rising again into the air, and they would have formed trunks for ordinary trees. It was connected with the tragical story of the unfortunate André, who had been taken prisoner hard by it, and it was universally known by the name of Major André's tree. The common people regarded it with a mixture of respect and superstition, partly out of sympathy for the memory of its ill-starred namesake, and partly from the tales, strange sights, and doleful lamentations, told concerning it.

As Ichabod approached this fearful tree, he began to whistle; he thought his whistle was answered: it was but a blast sweeping sharply through the dry branches. As he approached a little nearer, he thought he saw something white, hanging in the midst of the tree: he paused and ceased whistling; but on looking more narrowly, perceived that it was a place where the tree had been scathed by lightning, and the white wood laid bare. Suddenly he heard a groan—his teeth chattered, and his knees smote against the saddle: it was but the rubbing of one huge bough upon another, as they were swayed about by the breeze. He passed the tree in safety, but new perils lay still before him.

About two hundred yards from the tree, a small brook crossed the road, and ran into a marshy and thickly wooded glen, known by the name of Wiley's Swamp. A few rough logs, laid side by side, served for a bridge over this stream. On that side of the road where the brook entered the wood, a group of oaks and chestnuts, matted thick with wild grape vines, threw a cavernous gloom over it. To pass this bridge, was the severest trial. It was at this identical spot that the unfortunate André was captured, and under the covert of those chestnuts and vines were the sturdy yeomen concealed who surprised him. This has ever since been considered a haunted stream, and fearful are the feelings of the schoolboy who has to pass it alone after dark.

As he approached the stream, his heart began to thump; he, however, summoned up all his resolution, gave his horse half a score of kicks in the ribs, and attempted to dash briskly across the bridge; but instead of starting forward, the perverse old animal made a lateral movement, and ran broadside against the fence. Ichabod, whose fears increased with the delay, jerked the reins on the other side, and kicked lustily with the contrary foot: it was all in vain; his steed started, it is true, but it was only to plunge to the opposite side of the road into a thicket of brambles and alder bushes. The schoolmaster now bestowed both whip and heel upon the starvelling ribs of old Gunpowder, who dashed forward, snuffling and snorting, but came to a stand just by the bridge with a suddenness that had nearly sent his rider sprawling over his head. Just at this moment a plashy tramp by the side of the bridge caught the sensitive ear of Ichabod. In the dark shadow of the grove, on the margin of the brook, he beheld something huge, misshapen, black and towering. It stirred not, but seemed gathered up in the gloom, like some gigantic monster ready to spring upon the traveler.

The hair of the affrighted pedagogue rose upon his head with terror. What was to be done? To turn and fly was now too late; and besides, what chance was there of escaping ghost or goblin, if such it was, which can ride upon the wings of the wind? Summoning up, therefore, a show of courage, he demanded in stammering accents—"who are you?" He received no reply. He repeated his demand in a still more agitated voice.—Still there was no answer. Once more he cudgelled the sides of the inflexible Gunpowder, and shuttering his eyes, broke forth with involuntary fervor into a psalm tune. Just then the shadowy object of alarm put itself in motion, and with a scramble and a bound, stood at once in the middle of the road. Though the night was dark and dismal, yet the form of the unknown might now in some degree be ascertained. He appeared to be a horseman of large dimensions, and mounted on a black horse of powerful frame. He made no offer of molestation or sociability, but kept aloof on one side of the road, jogging along on the blind side of old Gunpowder, who had now got over his fright and waywardness.

Ichabod, who had no relish for this strange midnight companion, and bethought himself of the adventure of Brom Bones with the galloping Hessian, now quickened his steed, in hopes of leaving him behind. The stranger, however, quickened his horse to an equal pace; Ichabod pulled up, and fell into a walk, thinking to lag behind—the other did the same. His heart began to sink within him; he endeavored to resume his psalm tune, but his parched tongue clove to the roof of his mouth, and he could not utter a stave.[1] There was something in the moody and dogged silence of this pertinacious companion, that was mysterious and appalling. It was soon fearfully accounted for. On mounting a rising ground, which brought the figure of his fellow traveller in relief against the sky, gigantic in height, and muffled in a cloak, Ichabod was horror-struck, on perceiving that he was headless! but his horror was still more increased, on observing, that the head, which should have rested on his shoulders, was carried before him on the pommel of the saddle! His terror rose to desperation; he rained a shower of kicks and blows upon Gunpowder, hoping, by a sudden movement, to give his companion the slip—but the specter started full jump with him. Away, then, they dashed, through thick and thin; stones flying, and sparks flashing, at every bound. Ichabod's flimsy garments fluttered in the air, as he stretched his long lank body away over his horse's head, in the eagerness of his flight.

They had now reached the road which turns off to Sleepy Hollow; but Gunpowder, who seemed possessed with a demon, instead of keeping up it, made an opposite turn, and plunged headlong down hill to the left. This road leads through a sandy hollow shaded by trees for about a quarter of a mile, where it crosses the bridge famous in goblin story,

---

1. **stave.** Line or verse

and just beyond swells the green knoll on which stands the whitewashed church.

As yet the panic of the steed had given his unskillful rider an apparent advantage in the chase, but just as he had got half way through the hollow, the girths of the saddle gave way, and he felt it slipping from under him; he seized it by the pommel, and endeavored to hold it firm, but in vain; and had just time to save himself by clasping old Gunpowder round the neck, when the saddle fell to the earth, and he heard it trampled under foot by his pursuer. For a moment of terror of Hans Van Ripper's wrath passed across his mind—for it was his Sunday saddle; but this was no time for petty fears: the goblin was hard on his haunches; and, unskillful rider that he was! he had much-ado to maintain his seat; sometimes slipping on one side, sometimes on another, and sometimes jolted on the high ridge of his horse's back bone, with a violence that he verily feared would cleave him asunder.

An opening in the trees now cheered him with the hopes that the Church Bridge was at hand. The wavering reflection of a silver star in the bosom of the brook told him that he was not mistaken. He saw the walls of the church dimly glaring under the trees beyond. He recollected the place where Brom Bones's ghostly competitor had disappeared. "If I can but reach that bridge," thought Ichabod, "I am safe."[1] Just then he heard the black steed panting and blowing close behind him; he fancied he felt his hot breath. Another convulsive kick in the ribs, and old Gunpowder sprung upon the bridge; he thundered over the resounding planks; he gained the opposite side, and now Ichabod cast a look behind to see if his pursuer should vanish, according to rule, in a flash of fire and brimstone. Just then he saw the goblin rising in his stirrups, and in the very act of hurling his head at him. Ichabod endeavored to dodge the horrible missile, but too late. It encountered his cranium with a tremendous crash—he was tumbled headlong into the dust, and Gunpowder, the black steed, and the goblin rider, passed by like a whirlwind—

The next morning the old horse was found without his saddle, and the bridle under his feet, soberly cropping the grass at his master's gate. Ichabod did not make his appearance at breakfast—dinner-hour came, but no Ichabod. The boys assembled at the schoolhouse, and strolled idly about the banks of the brook; but no schoolmaster. Hans Van Ripper now began to feel some uneasiness about the fate of poor Ichabod, and his saddle. An inquiry was set on foot, and after diligent investigation they came upon his traces. In one part of the road leading to the church, was found the saddle trampled in the dirt; the tracks of horses' hoofs deeply dented in the road, and evidently at furious speed, were traced to the bridge, beyond which, on the bank of a broad part of the brook, where the water ran deep and black, was found the hat of the unfortunate Ichabod, and close beside it a shattered pumpkin.

The brook was searched, but the body of the schoolmaster was not to be discovered. Hans Van Ripper, as executor of his estate, examined the bundle which contained all his worldly effects. They consisted of two old shirts and a half; two stocks for the neck; a pair of worsted stockings with holes in them; an old pair of corduroy small-clothes; a book of psalm tunes full of dog's ears; a pitch pipe out of order; a rusty razor; a small pot of bear's grease for the hair, and a cast-iron comb. As to the books and furniture of the schoolhouse, they belonged to the community, excepting Cotton Mather's History of Witchcraft, a New-England Almanac, and a book of dreams and fortune telling, in which last was a sheet of foolscap much scribbled and blotted by several fruitless attempts to make a copy of verses in honor of the heiress of Van Tassel. These magic books and the poetic scrawl were forthwith consigned to the flames by Hans Van Ripper, who from that time forward determined to send his children no more to school, observing, that he never knew any good come of this same reading and writing. Whatever money the schoolmaster possessed, and he had received his quarter's pay but a day or two before, he must have had about his person at the time of his disappearance.

The mysterious event caused much speculation at the Church on the following Sunday. Knots of gazers and gossips were collected in the church-yard at the bridge, and at the spot where the hat and pumpkin had been found. The stories of Brouwer, of Bones, and a whole budget of others, were called to mind; and when they had diligently considered them all, and compared them with the symptoms of the present case, they shook their heads, and came to the conclusion, that Ichabod had been carried off by the galloping Hessian. As he was a bachelor, and in nobody's debt, nobody troubled his head any more about him, the school was removed to a different quarter of the hollow, and another pedagogue reigned in his stead.

It is true, an old farmer, who had been down to New York on a visit several years after, and from whom this account of the ghostly adventure was received, brought home the intelligence that Ichabod Crane was still alive; that he had left the neighborhood partly through fear of the goblin and Hans Van Ripper, and partly in mortification at having been suddenly dismissed by the heiress; that he had changed his quarters to a distant part of the country; had kept school and studied law at the same time; had been admitted to the bar, turned politician, electioneered, written for the newspapers, and finally had been made a Justice of the Ten Pound Court.[2] Brom Bones too, who, shortly after his rival's disappearance, conducted the blooming Katrina in triumph to the altar, was observed to look exceedingly knowing whenever the story of Ichabod was related, and always burst into a hearty laugh at the mention of the pumpkin; which led some to suspect that he knew more about the matter than he chose to tell.

The old country wives, however, who are the best judges

---

1. **I am safe.** Crane believed the superstition that spirits could not cross water.

2. **Ten Pound Court.** Small-claims court

of these matters maintain to this day, that Ichabod was spirited away by supernatural means; and it is a favorite story often told about the neighborhood round the winter evening fire. The bridge became more than ever an object of superstitious awe, and that may be the reason why the road has been altered of late years, so as to approach the church by the border of the millpond. The schoolhouse being deserted, soon fell to decay, and was reported to be haunted by the ghost of the unfortunate pedagogue; and the plough boy, loitering homeward of a still summer evening, has often fancied his voice at a distance, chanting a melancholy psalm tune among the tranquil solitudes of Sleepy Hollow.

POSTSCRIPT, FOUND IN THE HANDWRITTING OF MR. KNICKERBOCKER

The preceding Tale is given, almost in the precise words in which I heard it related at the corporation meeting of the ancient city of the Manhattoes, at which were present many of its sagest and most illustrious burghers. The narrator was a pleasant, shabby, gentlemanly old fellow, in pepper and salt clothes, with a sadly humorous face, and one whom I strongly suspected of being poor, he made such efforts to be entertaining. When his story was concluded, there was much laughter and approbation, particularly from two or three deputy aldermen, who had been asleep the greater part of the time. There was, however, one tall, dry-looking old gentleman, with beetling eyebrows, who maintained a grave and rather severe face throughout; now and then folding his arms, inclining his head, and looking down upon the floor, as if turning a doubt over in his mind. He was one of your wary men, who never laugh but upon good grounds—when they have reason and the law on their side. When the mirth of the rest of the company had subsided, and silence was restored, he leaned one arm on the elbow of his chair, and sticking the other a-kimbo, demanded, with a slight, but exceedingly sage motion of the head, and contraction of the brow, what was the moral of the story, and what it went to prove.

The story-teller, who was just putting a glass of wine to his lips, as a refreshment after his toils, paused for a moment, looked at his inquirer with an air of infinite deference, and lowering the glass slowly to the table, observed, that the story was intended most logically to prove,

"That there is no situation in life but has its advantages and pleasures, provided we will but take a joke as we find it:

"That, therefore, he that runs races with goblin troopers, is likely to have rough riding of it:

"Ergo, for a country schoolmaster to be refused the hand of a Dutch heiress, is a certain step to high preferment in the state."

The cautious old gentleman knit his brows tenfold closer after this explanation, being sorely puzzled by the ratiocination of the syllogism; while me thought the one in pepper and salt eyed him with something of a triumphant leer. At length he observed, that all this was very well, but still he thought the story a little on the extravagant—there were one or two points on which he had his doubts.

"Faith, sir," replied the story-teller, "as to that matter, I don't believe one half of it myself."

from "The Fall of the House of Usher"
by Edgar Allan Poe

During the whole of a dull, dark, and soundless day in the autumn of the year, when the clouds hung oppressively low in the heavens, I had been passing alone, on horseback, through a singularly dreary tract of country; and at length found myself, as the shades of the evening drew on, within view of the melancholy House of Usher. I know not how it was—but, with the first glimpse of the building, a sense of insufferable gloom pervaded my spirit. I say insufferable; for the feeling was unrelieved by any of that half-pleasurable, because poetic, sentiment, with which the mind usually receives even the sternest natural images of the desolate or terrible. I looked upon the scene before me—upon the mere house, and the simple landscape features of the domain—upon the bleak walls—upon the vacant eye-like windows—upon a few rank sedges—and upon a few white trunks of decayed trees—with an utter depression of soul which I can compare to no earthly sensation more properly than to the after-dream of the reveler upon opium—the bitter lapse into common life—the hideous dropping off of the veil. There was an iciness, a sinking, a sickening of the heart—an unredeemed dreariness of thought which no goading of the imagination could torture into aught of the sublime. What was it—I paused to think—what was it that so unnerved me in the contemplation of the House of Usher? It was a mystery all insoluble; nor could I grapple with the shadowy fancies that crowded upon me as I pondered. I was forced to fall back upon the unsatisfactory conclusion, that while, beyond doubt, there *are* combinations of very simple natural objects which have the power of thus affecting us, still the reason, and the analysis, of this power, lie among considerations beyond our depth. It was possible, I reflected, that a mere different arrangement of the particulars of the scene, of the details of this picture, would be sufficient to modify, or perhaps to annihilate its capacity for sorrowful impression; and, acting upon this idea, I reined my horse to the precipitous brink of a black and lurid tarn[1] that lay in unruffled luster by the dwelling, and gazed down—but with a shudder even more thrilling than before—upon the remodeled and inverted images of the gray sedge, and the ghastly tree-stems, and the vacant and eye-like windows.

---

1. **tarn.** Small lake

New England Renaissance Prose

VOCABULARY FROM THE SELECTIONS

abstraction, 236
abyss, 230
accentuation, 226
affinity, 207
ague, 237
analogy, 205
anointed, 235
aperture, 236
arduous, 254
aspect, 200
aspiration, 263
assuage, 208
august, 243
aversion, 254
avert, 237
avidity, 229
balm, 237
baneful, 207
benignity, 243
cadence, 227
cessation, 235, 264
cognizance, 232
conjecture, 236
conjure, 227
connoisseur, 211
consternation, 244
convolution, 231
cordiality, 203

craven, 247
dally, 237
deleterious, 204
delusory, 210
demeanor, 201
depraved, 210
diffuse, 236
discordant, 237
earnest, 260
ebullition, 209
elucidate, 247
emaciated, 213
encompass, 228
encumbrance, 262
endeavor, 264
envoy, 243
ethereal, 261
evanescent, 211
fervor, 211
festooned, 248
fissure, 236
fluctuate, 266
gaudiest, 245
gauntleted, 244
illuminate, 236
imbue, 215
impede, 228
impend, 237

inanition, 233
incantation, 248
indeterminate, 226
ineffable, 242
ingenuity, 232
inquisitorial, 226
insinuate, 217
insuperable, 229
interminable, 227
irrespective, 245
laxly, 268
locution, 226
lozenge, 237
lurid, 208
malignant, 201
moiety, 235
palsied, 248
paltry, 264
perennial, 261
pertinacity, 209,
234
phenomenon, 205
portal, 205
portentous, 248
posterity, 262
predominate, 253
primeval, 244
pungently, 232

recompense, 206
reminiscence, 199
resignation, 259
resplendent, 200
reverie, 213
riband, 236
saturated, 260
speculative, 208
squalid, 254
sublime, 243
superfluous, 265
supervene, 227
surmise, 216
terminate, 202
testily, 204
transcendent, 243
trepidation, 244
undulation, 263
unintelligible, 206
untoward, 209
unwieldy, 266
vengeance, 237
verdure, 206
vermin, 235
viand, 235
volatile, 268
voracity, 235
writhe, 226

allusion, 222, 250, 270
aphorism, 256, 270
elaboration, 250
essay, 256
fantasy, 222
metaphor, 256
mood, 239

onomatopoeia, 250
point of view, 238
romance, 239
symbol, 222
theme, 256
tone, 270

SYNTHESIS: QUESTIONS FOR WRITING, RESEARCH, OR DISCUSSION

GENRE STUDIES

1. **Short Story.** The work of Washington Irving, Nathaniel Hawthorne, and Edgar Allan Poe contributed to the development of the short story as a literary form. From Poe came the definition that all aspects of the short story combine to create one dominant impression. Examine two short stories from this unit. What dominant impression is created in each one? What details create this impression?

THEMATIC STUDIES

2. **Appearance and Reality.** Sometimes a fine line separates the credible from the incredible. Examine this theme in the excerpt from *Moby-Dick* and in one short story in the unit.

3. **Transcendentalism.** Transcendentalism in New England was an outgrowth of the Romantic Era in Europe. Review the definition of Transcendentalism in the unit introduction and select passages from Emerson and Thoreau that illustrate Transcendental philosophy.

HISTORICAL/BIOGRAPHICAL STUDIES

4. **Copyright Laws.** The lack of an international copyright law until 1891 meant many writers could not support themselves by their writing. Yet, they continued to write and to create. Discuss the creative process, the impulse to write, regardless of monetary gain.

LANGUAGE LAB EDITING FOR ERRORS IN PRONOUNS

Case is the form that a noun or a pronoun takes to indicate its use in a sentence: nominative, objective, or possessive. The nominative case is used for the subject of a verb or for a predicate nominative. The objective case is used for a direct object, an indirect object, or the object of a preposition. The possessive case is used to show possession. For additional help, see the Language Arts Survey, 2.76–2.77. The following chart lists common errors in pronoun usage.

PRONOUN USAGE

Who and Whom. The pronoun *who* is referred to as an interrogative pronoun when it is used to form a question. When it is used to introduce a subordinate clause, it is referred to as a relative pronoun. In both cases, the nominative is *who,* the objective is *whom,* and the possessive is *whose.*

SUBJECT:	*Who* designed Monticello?
DIRECT OBJECT:	*Whom* did Jefferson hire to construct his home?
OBJECT OF PREPOSITION:	To *whom* did Jefferson give the plans?

Pronouns in Comparisons. The ends of sentences that compare people or things are often left unexpressed. Pronouns in such sentences should be the same case as they would have been if the sentence had been completed.

EXAMPLE:	Referring to Thomas Jefferson, the guide said that no revolutionary had done as much to shape the United States as *he* [had done].

Agreement of Pronouns and Antecedents. Check the pronouns in your writing to be sure they agree in **number, person,** and **gender** with their antecedents.

INCORRECT NUMBER:	The guide spoke about several architectural landmarks on the campus and *its* historical significance.
CORRECT NUMBER:	The guide spoke about several architectural landmarks on the campus and *their* historical significance.

Reference of Pronouns to Antecedents. Avoid weak, ambiguous, indefinite, and general references between pronouns and antecedents.

WEAK REFERENCE:	During the prospective-students tour, they asked many questions.
CLEAR ANTECEDENT:	During their tour, the prospective students asked many questions.
AMBIGUOUS REFERENCE:	As the tour guide spoke of Jefferson, he seemed to come to life.
CLEAR REFERENCE:	As the tour guide spoke of him, Jefferson seemed to come to life.
INDEFINITE REFERENCE:	Since Jefferson's death, they have grouped his writings into four categories.
PRONOUN ELIMINATED:	Since Jefferson's death, scholars have grouped his writings into four categories.
GENERAL REFERENCE:	In the informational brochure, it had a complete biography of Jefferson.
SENTENCE REWORDED:	The informational brochure had a complete biography of Jefferson.

EXERCISE A Avoiding Errors in Pronoun Usage

In each sentence below, choose the correct word from within the parentheses.

EXAMPLE: The writer of the New England Renaissance (who, whom) I most admire is Ralph Waldo Emerson.
whom

LANGUAGE ARTS SURVEY

For additional help, see the Language Arts Survey, 2.78–2.82.

1. The scholar believed that no one had researched the life of Nathaniel Hawthorne more thoroughly than (her, she).

2. Melville's early writings were well received by (his, their) audience.

3. Tina thinks that the short stories of Poe are the best ever written and none can compare to (them, they).

4. (Who, whom) wrote "The Legend of Sleepy Hollow"?

5. Both Thoreau and Emerson printed works based on (his, their) journals.

6. To (who, whom) did you lend my copy of *Moby-Dick?*

7. Emerson said that people must be nonconformists and that nothing is sacred but the integrity of (our, their) minds.

8. Did the end of "The Pit and the Pendulum" surprise you as much as it did (I, me)?

9. Dr. Heideigger offered his friends water from the fountain of youth, and he watched the effects on (him, them).

10. Thoreau's advice to "simplify, simplify" is difficult for Alana to follow but nobody needs to simplify as much as (her, she).

Exercise B Correcting Errors in Pronoun Usage

Rewrite the following sentences, correcting the errors in pronoun usage.

EXAMPLE: The University of Virginia seal says that it was founded in 1819.
The University of Virginia seal reads, "Founded 1819."

LANGUAGE ARTS SURVEY

For additional help, see the Language Arts Survey, 2.83 and 2.84.

1. Thomas Jefferson founded the University of Virginia. He considered this one of his three greatest accomplishments.

2. As the whale watch began, they read a segment from *Moby-Dick.*

3. In *Poor Richard's Almanack,* they convey Franklin's common-sense philosophy.

4. Tony, a fan of Thoreau, went to visit Walden Pond because he had lived there.

5. When Patrick Henry delivered speeches, it often created an impassioned response from his audience.

Still Life with Copper Tankard. William M. Harnett

Ur day of dependence, our long apprenticeship to the learning of other lands, draws to a close. . . . Events, actions arise, that must be sung, that will sing themselves. Who can doubt that poetry will revive and lead in a new age?

—Ralph Waldo Emerson
"The American Scholar"

PREREADING

"Thanatopsis"
by William Cullen Bryant

ABOUT THE AUTHOR

William Cullen Bryant (1794–1878), born in rural Cummington, Massachusetts, had an abiding love for nature. He briefly attended Williams College in 1810 but dropped out, hoping to go to Yale. Because his father could not afford that expense, Bryant read for the law and was admitted to practice in 1815. Heavily influenced by the English Romantic poets Thomas Gray and William Wordsworth, Bryant began to write poetry at a young age but realized that he could not afford to pursue a full-time career as a poet. Appointed justice of the peace in Great Barrington in 1820, the following year Bryant married Frances Fairchild and published a volume entitled *Poems.* The Bryants moved to New York City, where he worked as an editor of the *New York Review* and *Atheneum Magazine.* Thereafter, he became editor-in-chief and part owner of the *Evening Post,* a position that brought him wealth, fame, and influence. Bryant championed humanitarian causes, including the abolition of slavery and of debtors' prisons. He also became a key figure in American political life, helping to form the Republican Party and to get both Andrew Jackson and Abraham Lincoln elected president. He traveled widely in Europe and in the Middle East and published letters about his experiences. Bryant continued writing into his seventies, translating Homer's epics, *The Odyssey* and *The Iliad,* and writing poems.

ABOUT THE SELECTION

Bryant probably began **"Thanatopsis"** in 1811, when he was only sixteen years old. The subject and moral outlook of the poem owe much to Thomas Gray's "Elegy Written in a Country Churchyard." The first version of the poem consisted of the present poem's lines 18–66. Bryant's father submitted this poem and another on the subject of death to the *North American Review* in 1817, and the two were mistakenly published as a single work. In 1821, Bryant completed "Thanatopsis," framing the original lines with an introduction (lines 1–17) and a conclusion (lines 66–82). In the earlier version, the central lines had been in the poet's own voice; in the later version, the speaker is a romanticized and personified Nature. The ideas in the three parts of the poem betray the changes in the poet's thinking over the ten years of its composition. Nevertheless, the beauty of the poem's language and the grandeur of its images immediately established Bryant's literary reputation and helped to create pride in the ability of Americans to match the literary creations of the British Romantic school.

READER'S JOURNAL

Some people perceive nature as violent and cruel, while others see it as beautiful and inspirational. Write briefly in your journal about your attitude toward nature. Support your opinion with specific observations.

LANGUAGE SKILLS

Read about particular uses of capitalization in the Language Arts Survey, 2.120–2.122, "Personal Names," "Place Names," and "Poetry." Then find examples in the poem of all three types of capitalization.

"Thanatopsis[1]"

WILLIAM CULLEN BRYANT

To him who in the love of Nature holds
<u>Communion</u> with her visible forms, she speaks
A various language; for his gayer hours
She has a voice of gladness, and a smile
5   And eloquence of beauty, and she glides
Into his darker musings, with a mild
And gentle sympathy, that steals away
Their sharpness, ere he is aware. When thoughts
Of the last bitter hour come like a <u>blight</u>
10   Over thy spirit, and sad images
Of the stern agony, and shroud, and pall,
And breathless darkness, and the narrow house,[2]
Make thee to shudder, and grow sick at heart,—
Go forth under the open sky, and list[3]
15   To Nature's teachings, while from all around—
Earth and her waters, and the depths of air,—
Comes a still voice—Yet a few days, and thee
The all-beholding sun shall see no more

What effect can thoughts of death have?

Where should the reader seek comfort?

---

1. **Thanatopsis.** This word, coined by Bryant, means "views and thoughts on death."
2. **shroud . . . narrow house.** *Shroud*—cloth used to wrap a corpse for burial; *pall*—cloth draped over a coffin; *narrow house*—grave
3. **list.** Listen

WORDS FOR EVERYDAY USE:

com • mun • ion (kə myo͞on´yən) *n.,* act of sharing thoughts and actions

blight (blīt) *n.,* anything that destroys or prevents growth

Among the Sierra Nevada Mountains, California. *Albert Bierstadt, 1868. National Museum of American Art, Washington, DC/Art Resource, NY*

In all his course; nor yet in the cold ground,
20   Where thy pale form was laid, with many tears,
Nor in the embrace of ocean shall exist
Thy image. Earth, that nourished thee, shall claim
Thy growth, to be resolv'd to earth again;
And, lost each human trace, surrend'ring up
25   Thine individual being, shalt thou go
To mix forever with the elements,
To be a brother to th' <u>insensible</u> rock
And to the sluggish <u>clod</u>, which the rude swain
Turns with his share,[4] and treads upon. The oak
30   Shall send his roots abroad, and pierce thy mould.[5]
Yet not to thy eternal resting place
Shalt thou retire alone—nor couldst thou wish

---

4. **share.** Plough
5. **mould.** Form or body

WORDS FOR EVERYDAY USE:

in • sen • si • ble (in sen´sə bəl) *adj.,* lacking sensation; unaware
clod (kläd) *n.,* lump, such as lump of earth or clay

Couch more magnificent. Thou shalt lie down
With <u>patriarchs</u> of the infant world—with kings

35 The powerful of the earth—the wise, the good,
Fair forms, and <u>hoary</u> seers of ages past,
All in one mighty <u>sepulcher</u>.—The hills
Rock-ribb'd and ancient as the sun,—the vales
Stretching in <u>pensive</u> quietness between;

40 The <u>venerable</u> woods—rivers that move
In majesty, and the complaining brooks
That make the meadows green; and pour'd round all,
Old ocean's grey and melancholy waste,—
Are but the solemn decorations all

45 Of the great tomb of man. The golden sun,
The planets, all the infinite host of heaven,
Are shining on the sad abodes of death,
Through the still <u>lapse</u> of ages. All that tread
The globe are but a handful to the tribes

50 That slumber in its bosom.—Take the wings
Of morning—and the Barcan desert[6] pierce,
Or lose thyself in the continuous woods
Where rolls the Oregan,[7] and hears no sound,
Save his own dashings—yet—the dead are there,

55 And millions in those solitudes, since first
The flight of years begin, have laid them down
In their last sleep—the dead reign there alone.—
So shalt thou rest—and what if thou shalt fall
Unnoticed by the living—and no friend

60 Take note of thy departure? All that breathe
Will share thy destiny. The gay will laugh
When thou art gone, the solemn brood of care
Plod on, and each one as before will chase
His favorite phantom; yet all these shall leave

65 Their mirth and their employments, and shall come,
And make their bed with thee. As the long train
Of ages glide away, the sons of men,
The youth in life's green spring, and he who goes
In the full strength of years, matron, and maid,

70 The bow'd with age, the infant in the smiles

---

6. **Barcan desert.** Desert in northeast Libya
7. **Oregan.** Early spelling of Oregon

With whom will the reader share the grave?

What is the ratio of living to deceased?

What happens after a single death?

WORDS FOR EVERYDAY USE:

pa • tri • arch (pā´trē ärk´) *n.*, father, ruler; founder
hoar • y (hôr´ē) *adj.*, having white or gray hair
sep • ul • cher (sep´əl kər) *n.*, vault for burial
pen • sive (pen´siv) *adj.*, expressing deep
thoughtfulness, often with some sadness
ven • er • a • ble (ven´ər ə bəl) *adj.*, worthy of respect by reason of age and dignity
lapse (laps) *n.*, gliding or passing away

And beauty of its innocent age cut off,—
Shall one by one be gathered to thy side,
By those, who in their turn shall follow them.
So live, that when thy summons comes to join

75   The innumerable caravan, that moves
To the pale realms of shade, where each shall take
His chamber in the silent halls of death,
Thou go not, like the quarry-slave at night,
Scourged to his dungeon, but sustain'd and sooth'd

80   By an unfaltering trust, approach thy grave,
Like one who wraps the drapery of his couch
About him, and lies down to pleasant dreams. ■

What should be the reader's attitude approaching the grave?

Responding to the Selection

How does thinking about the earth as one great, common grave make you feel? Is the fact that you share this fate with all humanity comforting? Do you agree that the poem's attitude gives death dignity?

Reviewing the Selection

RECALLING

1. The introduction (lines 1–17) describes various moods of a person. Identify two of these moods, which draw different responses from Nature.

2. Who is the speaker up to line 17 of the poem? Who begins to speak in line 17?

3. Who are some of the people the speaker lists as lying down in "one mighty sepulcher"?

4. How does the speaker advise the listener to go to the grave?

INTERPRETING

▶▶ 5. In your own words, explain each of the "sad images" of lines 11 and 12: the "stern agony," the "shroud," the "pall," the "breathless darkness," and the "narrow house."

▶▶ 6. In what way will every human become "a brother to th' insensible rock" (line 27)?

▶▶ 7. Does the speaker feel that a dignified funeral is important? Cite lines of the poem that support your answer.

▶▶ 8. The speaker does not explicitly identify in whom or what the listener is to place an "unfaltering trust" (line 80). What or whom do you suppose the speaker had in mind?

9. In this poem, is Nature the same as the planet Earth? If not, how would you describe it?

10. If this poem were published today, do you think it would become as popular as it did with the people of 175 years ago? Why, or why not?

Understanding Literature (Questions for Discussion)

1. **Blank Verse. Blank verse** is unrhymed poetry written in iambic pentameter. (An iambic pentameter line consists of five feet, each containing two syllables, the first weakly stressed and the second strongly stressed.) Copy the first five lines of "Thanatopsis" and mark the strongly stressed syllables with accent marks. Which line is least regular?

2. **Elaboration. Elaboration**, or **amplification**, is a writing technique in which a subject is introduced and then expanded upon by means of repetition with slight changes, the addition of details, or similar devices. How does this poem make use of the technique of elaboration? What is the idea that is elaborated?

Language Lab

Prepositions. Read the Language Arts Survey, 2.24, "Prepositions." Then write out these sentences. Underline each prepositional phrase with a single underscore and each preposition with a double underscore.

1. "Thanatopsis," the best-known poem by William Cullen Bryant, draws its title from the Greek language.

2. In Greek, *thanatopsis* means "view of death"; no one could object to this phrase as a summary of the poem.

3. Despite Bryant's upbringing in the Calvinistic tradition, the poem reflects toward its topic a Wordsworthian pantheism, or nature worship.

4. Bryant seems to have been strongly impressed by the ideas of several English poets grouped by the title "graveyard school."

5. Clearly, however, the major influence on Bryant was William Wordsworth, one of the greatest English Romantic poets, who wrote about Nature as a loving friend to humanity.

"The Chambered Nautilus"

by Oliver Wendell Holmes

ABOUT THE AUTHOR

Oliver Wendell Holmes (1809–1894) was born in Cambridge, Massachusetts, and was class poet at Harvard in 1829. After first studying law, he then went to Paris to study medicine. He was awarded his M.D. degree from Harvard in 1836, the year his *Poems* was published. After serving as professor of anatomy at Dartmouth from 1839 to 1840, he moved to Boston, where he wrote medical treatises. He married Amelia Lee Jackson in 1840, and the couple raised three children, the first of whom, Oliver Wendell Holmes, Jr., became a famous Supreme Court justice. From 1847 until 1882, Holmes was a professor of anatomy at Harvard, writing several important scientific papers, including one that demonstrated that childhood fevers, a common cause of death, were spread by contact with infected persons. He became known as an essayist and poet in the late 1850s when the *Atlantic Monthly,* which he helped found, serialized his humorous essays and printed his poems, including "The Chambered Nautilus" and "The Deacon's Masterpiece." Of his four volumes of essays, the most famous is *The Autocrat at the Breakfast Table,* which presents the reflections of an imaginary cultured man who lives in a boarding house and entertains other guests with his lively conversation. Holmes also wrote three novels—"medicated novels" was his term for them—that dealt with genetic and psychological determinism. (Determinism is the belief that people's ideas, thoughts, feelings, and actions are caused by outside hereditary and environmental forces. From the 1860s through the 1880s, Holmes published volumes of poems and essays, as well as a biography of Ralph Waldo Emerson. Holmes was the most famous after-dinner speaker of his time, a leading figure in literary circles, and a witty writer of occasional verse.

ABOUT THE SELECTION

"**The Chambered Nautilus**" was published in the February 1858 issue of the *Atlantic Monthly* in one of Holmes's *Autocrat of the Breakfast Table* essays. The creature of the title is a mollusk, related to clams and octopi, that gradually builds a spiral shell with a series of air-filled chambers. The creature acquired the name *nautilus,* from the Greek word for "sailor," because of the belief that it had a membrane that served as a sail, by means of which it navigated the waters of the Indian and Pacific oceans. Triton, referred to in line 26, was a Greek god of the sea, often pictured as blowing a horn made of a spiral, twisted seashell. Holmes may have conceived the idea for the poem when reading the essay "Compensation," by Ralph Waldo Emerson, which compares human development to that of a shellfish.

READER'S JOURNAL

Have you ever put a curving seashell to your ear to hear the ocean's roar? What do people like about the look and feel of shells? Think about how shells affect your senses. Write about what makes handling seashells so satisfying.

THINKING SKILLS

Read the Language Arts Survey, 4.8, "Comparing and Contrasting." Then, as you read the poem, think about the two things that are being compared in it and what they have in common.

"The Chambered Nautilus"

OLIVER WENDELL HOLMES

This is the ship of pearl, which, poets feign,
    Sails the unshadowed main,—
    The venturous bark that flings
On the sweet summer wind its purpled wings
5   In gulfs enchanted, where the siren sings,
      And coral reefs lie bare,
Where the cold sea-maids rise to sun their streaming hair.

Its webs of living gauze no more unfurl;
    Wrecked is the ship of pearl!
10   And every chambered cell,
Where its dim dreaming life was wont to dwell,
As the frail tenant shaped his growing shell,
    Before thee lies revealed,—
Its irised ceiling rent, its sunless crypt unsealed!

15   Year after year beheld the silent toil
    That spread his lustrous coil;
    Still, as the spiral grew,
He left the past year's dwelling for the new,
Stole with soft step its shining archway through,
20   Built up its idle door,
Stretched in his last-found home, and knew the old no more.

> Why is the "ship of pearl" described as "Wrecked"?

Illustration by Rodney Busch

> Thanks for the heavenly message brought by thee,
>   Child of the wandering sea,
>   Cast from her lap, forlorn!
> 25 From thy dead lips a clearer note is born
> Than ever Triton blew from wreathéd horn!
>   While on mine ear it rings,
> Through the deep caves of thought I hear a voice that sings:—
>
> Build thee more stately mansions, O my soul,
> 30   As the swift seasons roll!
>   Leave thy low-vaulted past!
> Let each new temple, nobler than the last,
> Shut thee from heaven with a dome more vast,
>   Till thou at length art free,
> 35 Leaving thine outgrown shell by life's unresting sea!   ∎

What is the message the nautilus brings to the speaker?

Responding to the Selection

Did the poet's link between the development of a shell and that of a person seem natural to you? How does referring to a picture of the shell aid in understanding and appreciating the poem?

Reviewing the Selection

RECALLING

1. What fantastic details does the speaker provide about the life of the nautilus?

2. Review lines 10–14. What do they tell you about the present physical condition of the shell that is being described?

3. To whom are stanzas 1–3 addressed? stanza 4? stanza 5?

4. What does the singing voice of stanza 4 tell its listener to build? What might these structures represent?

INTERPRETING

5. Remember that Holmes was a scientific person, a trained physician. Why do you suppose the speaker in Holmes's poem introduces the shellfish with imagined details instead of using a scientifically accurate description?

6. In the first three stanzas, how does the speaker give the shellfish a personality? What are some of the details that make the audience more sympathetic toward it?

7. In stanza 4, the speaker credits the nautilus for bringing a message, but whose voice is singing?

8. From what do the soul's mansions, temples, and domes separate the soul? When does the separation end?

SYNTHESIZING

9. Which do you think was more important to Holmes in choosing this particular shellfish— its name and related myth of being able to sail the waters, or its compartmented shape and pearly walls? How would the message of the poem be affected if either of these sets of characteristics was lacking?

10. Review the poem for instances of alliteration, assonance, or other sound effects. Which phrases seemed most melodious or striking to you? Explain why.

Understanding Literature (Questions for Discussion)

1. **Stanza.** A **stanza** is a recurring pattern of grouped lines in a poem. How many stanzas are in this poem? How many lines are in each stanza? What rhyme pattern do you find in each stanza?

2. **Apostrophe.** An **apostrophe** is a rhetorical technique in which an object or person is directly addressed. Identify an example of apostrophe in the fourth stanza. Who or what is being addressed? The apostrophe signals a development in the content of the poem. How do the lines that follow the apostrophe differ from those before it?

3. **Euphony. Euphony** is pleasing sound. Listen carefully to the sounds in the first half of stanza 5. How does the repeated sound of *l* suggest a steady forward movement at the same time as it contributes strongly to the euphony of the lines?

Language Lab

Pronouns and Antecedents. Read the Language Arts Survey, 2.82, "Agreement of Pronouns and Antecedents." Then rewrite these sentences, using pronouns correctly.

1. Long ago, people really believed in myths, but today we see it simply as literature.

2. Still, mythology says something about human nature that makes him more than just old stories.

3. In the Greek myths, sirens are "cold sea-maids," as the poem says, but to us she stands for all sorts of temptations, such as the temptation to seek dangerous adventure or to act in a greedy manner in order to become wealthy.

4. Everybody knows that they can blame Pandora for the world's problems, for according to Greek myth, she was the one who let all the evils of the world out of a box.

5. Though different cultures call their gods of war by different names, he represents the same weaknesses in all of us, distrust and hostility toward people who are not like ourselves.

Study and Research Skills

Reference Works. Read the material about specialized encyclopedias in the Language Arts Survey, 4.23, "Using Reference Works." Then investigate a library to find out which encyclopedias of literature, mythology, literary terms, authors, and the like are available in the reference department. List the title and the particular focus of each. Look up Triton in two of these encyclopedias and compare the amount and type of information provided.

PREREADING

"Stanzas on Freedom"

by James Russell Lowell

ABOUT THE AUTHOR

James Russell Lowell (1819–1891) was born in Cambridge, Massachusetts, and educated at Harvard. He studied law, but never practiced it, choosing a literary and academic life instead. Lowell was an idealist who devoted himself to a number of causes, including women's rights; temperance, or abstinence from alcohol; and abolition. In 1844, he married Maria White, also a writer and dedicated abolitionist. Lowell contributed to antislavery papers, including the *National Anti-Slavery Standard* and the *Pennsylvania Freeman*. He became recognized nationally in 1848 upon the publication of *Second Series, A Fable for Critics,* the first series of *The Bigelow Papers,* and *The Vision of Sir Launfal.* After the death of three of his children and his wife, a distraught Lowell continued to publish his work in magazines. In 1855 he became professor of modern languages at Harvard. He turned his writing mainly to criticism and essays. In 1857, he became the editor of the *Atlantic Monthly,* and later became coeditor of the *North American Review.* He used his magazines to promote the Union cause during the Civil War in which he lost many friends and family members. He served as United States ambassador to Spain from 1877 to 1880 and as ambassador to England from 1880 to 1885. Some of Lowell's poems remain popular, but his main literary influence was as a critic and an editor.

ABOUT THE SELECTION

Before the Civil War, a strong abolitionist movement flourished among the writers of New England. An ardent abolitionist himself, Lowell wrote a number of poems and prose selections in support of his views. He contributed regularly to abolitionist publications, including the *National Anti-Slavery Standard,* which he also edited. In **"Stanzas on Freedom,"** Lowell pleads with his fellow citizens to recognize the horrors of slavery and the necessity of eradicating it.

READER'S JOURNAL

Is there any social problem you feel strongly about, such as gang conflicts, drug abuse, or discrimination based on race or gender? What would be an effective way to make your point of view known? Freewrite in your journal about how you could advertise your stand on one major social issue; then explain your point of view regarding the problem and your thoughts on how to work toward its solution.

WRITING SKILLS

Read the Language Arts Survey, 1.7, "Choosing and Analyzing an Audience." Then, as you read the poem, decide who the intended audience for this poem is and what the speaker wants to convince that audience to think and do.

"Stanzas on Freedom"

JAMES RUSSELL LOWELL

According to Lowell, why are people not "truly free and brave"?

Men! whose boast it is that ye
Come of fathers brave and free,
If there breathe on earth a slave,
Are ye truly free and brave?
5   If ye do not feel the chain,
When it works a brother's pain,
Are ye not base slaves indeed,
Slaves unworthy to be freed?

Women! who shall one day bear
10   Sons to breathe New England air,
If ye hear, without blush,
Deeds to make the roused blood rush
Like red lava through your veins,
For your sisters now in chains—
15   Answer! are ye fit to be
Mothers of the brave and free?

Is true freedom but to break
<u>Fetters</u> for our own dear sake,
And, with leathern[1] hearts, forget

---

1. **leathern.** Like leather; tough, hard

WORDS FOR EVERYDAY USE:

fet • ter (fet´ər) *n.,* shackle or chain for the feet

Last Sale of Slaves on the Courthouse Steps. T. Satterwhite Noble, 1860. Missouri Historical Society

What is true
freedom?

20   That we owe mankind a debt?
        No! true freedom is to share
        All the chains our brothers wear,
        And, with heart and hand, to be
        <u>Earnest</u> to make others free!

25   They are slaves who fear to speak
        For the fallen and the weak;
        They are slaves who will not choose
        Hatred, scoffing, and abuse,
        Rather than in silence shrink
30   From the truth they needs must think;
        They are slaves who dare not be
        In the right with two or three.   ∎

WORDS FOR   ear • nest (ʉr´nist) *adj.*, zealous and sincere
EVERYDAY USE:

Responding to the Selection

The speaker maintains that those who tolerate injustice and cruelty to others are not free themselves. Do you agree with the speaker? Explain why, or why not.

Reviewing the Selection

1. According to the speaker, what social injustice prevents people from being truly free and brave?

2. What question does the speaker ask the women of New England? Is this question the same as the one that he asks the men? If not, how is it different?

3. According to the speaker, what is true freedom? What does he say true freedom is not?

4. What does the speaker call those who "fear to speak/For the fallen and the weak"? What does he recommend that they do?

5. In what sense did the existence of slavery diminish the freedom and courage of everyone?

6. What does the speaker mean when he asks women if they can hear about injustice "without blush"?

7. What is the debt all people owe humanity? Why is simply taking care of one's own problems not enough to pay the debt?

8. Why does the speaker scold those who believe slavery is wrong and yet choose not to speak out about it? Explain some reasons why someone might choose not to act on his or her principles.

9. How might an abolitionist react to this poem? On the other hand, how might a slaveholder react? Describe the probable effect of such a poem on relations between the North and the South.

10. The speaker has slightly different messages for the men and the women. Why do you think he varied his message for each gender? What might a modern woman find objectionable in Lowell's approach?

Understanding Literature (Questions for Discussion)

1. **Stanza.** A **stanza** is a recurring pattern of grouped lines in a poem. How many stanzas are there in this poem? To whom is the first stanza addressed? the second?

2. **Couplet.** A **couplet** is a pair of rhyming lines that expresses a complete thought. Identify five examples of couplets from the poem. Couplets are often easy to memorize. Why would ease of recall make couplets an appropriate choice for use in a poem such as this?

3. **Apostrophe.** An **apostrophe** is a rhetorical technique in which an object or person is directly addressed. Whom does the speaker address in "Stanzas on Freedom"? Considering the poet's purpose in writing, why do you think he speaks so directly to his audience?

4. **Rhetorical Question.** A **rhetorical question** is one asked for effect but not meant to be answered because the answer is clear from the context. What rhetorical questions does the speaker ask in this poem? What point does the speaker wish to make by means of each of these rhetorical questions?

Language Lab

Double Negatives. Read the Language Arts Survey, 2.88, "Double Negatives." Then read each of the following sentences. If you find a double negative, rewrite the sentence correctly.

1. If you allow others to be enslaved, you cannot hardly be called free yourself.

2. Women who don't care not at all for the suffering of their sisters are not fit to be the mothers of the free and brave.

3. If you don't work for the freedom of all, you aren't fulfilling your responsibility to mankind.

4. You can't scarcely in good conscience feel like a decent person when you ignore your responsibilities.

5. You are a slave if you can't never think for yourself and you let others control your actions.

Study and Research Skills

Using Searching Tools. Read the Language Arts Survey, 4.21, "Using Searching Tools." Visit your school or local library and search the card catalog or the computerized catalog for materials relating to slavery. Record the title, author, and call number of five books that you turn up in your search.

"The Village Blacksmith"
by Henry Wadsworth Longfellow

ABOUT THE AUTHOR

Henry Wadsworth Longfellow (1807–1882) was the most popular of the so-called "Fireside Poets," a group that included Ralph Waldo Emerson, John Greenleaf Whittier, James Russell Lowell, and Oliver Wendell Holmes. The name of the group derived from the fact that people often entertained one another in the evening by reading aloud by the fireside. Longfellow was born in Portland, Maine, and attended Bowdoin College there. Following graduation and language study in Europe, Longfellow taught foreign languages first at Bowdoin and then at Harvard. Well-known works by Longfellow include "A Psalm of Life," "The Wreck of the Hesperus," "Excelsior," "The Arsenal at Springfield," *Evangeline, Song of Hiawatha,* "The Children's Hour," *The Courtship of Miles Standish,* and "Paul Revere's Ride" (one of the *Tales of a Wayside Inn*). Longfellow also edited an important anthology, *The Poets and Poetry of Europe.* As famous in Britain as in the United States, he received honorary degrees from Oxford and Cambridge and was given a private audience with Queen Victoria. After his death, a bust of Longfellow was installed in the Poet's Corner of Westminster Abbey, making him the only American poet to be so honored.

ABOUT THE SELECTION

"The Village Blacksmith" was first published in an 1841 collection called *Ballads and Other Poems.* At the time of the poem's publication, Longfellow was a professor at Harvard. His poetry collections had begun to make him famous, not only in America but also in England. Sweet, romantic, didactic, and occasionally gripping in their retellings of stories from history or legend, Longfellow's poems appealed greatly to the tastes of the day. This poem focuses on a common man, honest and hard-working, whose strength and positive attitude matched the popular notion of the ideal citizen of the young, unsophisticated country.

READER'S JOURNAL

Every day you see workers performing their jobs with dedication. Think about a worker whom you admire. Picture him or her on the job, and then freewrite in your journal about what that person might do on a typical day.

LANGUAGE SKILLS

Read the Language Arts Survey, 2.19, "Adjectives and Articles." As you read "The Village Blacksmith," make a running list of the adjectives you encounter. Which of these questions do most of the adjectives answer: What kind? Which ones? How many?

"The Village Blacksmith"

HENRY WADSWORTH LONGFELLOW

Under a spreading chestnut tree
   The village smithy[1] stands:
The smith, a mighty man is he,
   With large and <u>sinewy</u> hands,
5   And the muscles of his brawny arms
   Are strong as iron bands.

His hair is crisp,[2] and black, and long,
   His face is like the tan;
His brow is wet with honest sweat,
10   He earns whate'er he can,
And looks the whole world in the face,
   For he owes not any man.

Week in, week out, from morn till night,
   You can hear his bellows[3] blow,
15   You can hear him swing his heavy sledge,
   With measured beat and slow,
Like a sexton[4] ringing the village bell,
   When the evening sun is low.

What words are used to describe the strength of the smith?

To what is the smith swinging his sledge compared?

---

1. **smithy.** Blacksmith shop
2. **crisp.** Curly and wiry
3. **bellows.** Fan for keeping a fire going
4. **sexton.** Church official who rings the bells

WORDS FOR EVERYDAY USE:
   sin • ew • y (sin´yo͞o ē) *adj.*, muscular; strong

Pat Lyon at the Forge. John Neagle, 1826–1827. Courtesy of the Museum of Fine Arts, Boston. Herman and Zoe Oliver Sherman Fund, 1975

And children coming home from school
20   Look in at the open door;
They love to see the flaming forge,
    And hear the bellows roar,
And catch the burning sparks that fly
    Like chaff[5] from a threshing floor.

25 He goes on Sunday to the church,
    And sits among his boys;
He hears the parson pray and preach,
    He hears his daughter's voice
Singing in the village choir,
30   And it makes his heart rejoice.

It sounds to him like her mother's voice,
    Singing in Paradise!
He needs must think of her once more,
    How in the grave she lies;
35 And with his hard, rough hand he wipes
    A tear out of his eyes.

Toiling—rejoicing—sorrowing,
    Onward through life he goes;
Each morning sees some task begin,
40   Each evening sees it close;
Something attempted, something done,
    Has earned a night's repose.

Thanks, thanks to thee, my worthy friend.
    For the lesson thou hast taught!
45 Thus at the flaming forge of life
    Our fortunes must be <u>wrought</u>;
Thus on its sounding anvil shaped
    Each burning deed and thought.   ■

---

5. **chaff.** Husks of grain separated during threshing

What does the smith do on Sundays? What does he hear? How does he feel?

Of what does the smith's daughter's voice remind him? What effect does it have on him?

WORDS FOR EVERYDAY USE: **wrought** (rôt) *alt. pp. of* work, worked; made

Responding to the Selection

The blacksmith is probably not a wealthy man. What gifts that are more important than money does life offer him? Which aspects of his life, if any, seem attractive to you? With which aspects of his life, if any, would you have difficulty coping?

Reviewing the Selection

RECALLING

1. What does the village blacksmith look like?

2. What evidence does the poem provide that the blacksmith is hardworking?

3. What has happened to the blacksmith's wife? What details show you how he feels about this?

4. According to the speaker, what lesson can be learned from the life of the blacksmith?

INTERPRETING

5. How would you describe the character of the blacksmith? Cite details from the poem that support your answer.

6. Do you think that the blacksmith's job gives him high prestige in the village? Compare his job with a modern job, such as car mechanic or truck driver. How are they similar or different?

7. What is the blacksmith's relationship with his children? How do you know?

8. Restate the lesson the blacksmith teaches in your own words. How does his life teach that lesson?

SYNTHESIZING

9. What qualities made the blacksmith a popular character in American culture in the nineteenth century? Are those qualities still considered desirable in the United States today? If not, what other qualities are now more important?

10. Some critics think that this poem is overly sentimental and preachy. Tell why you agree or disagree with their point of view.

Understanding Literature (Questions for Discussion)

1. **Image.** An **image** is a word or phrase that names something that can be seen, heard, touched, tasted, or smelled. What images does Longfellow use to describe the blacksmith?

2. **Alliteration. Alliteration** is the repetition of initial consonant sounds. Find two examples of alliteration in the poem.

3. **Narrative Poem.** A **narrative poem** is a verse that tells a story. Do you think that "The Village Blacksmith" is a narrative poem? Why, or why not?

Responding in Writing

Character Sketch. Read the Language Arts Survey, 1.17, "Clustering." Then make a cluster chart about a person you know well. Circle your topic in the center of the page and connect associated ideas to the topic and to each other. Include details about how the person looks, sounds, and acts. Use the information in your chart to write a brief description, or character sketch, of your subject.

Language Lab

Adding Prepositional Phrases. Read the Language Arts Survey, 2.47, "Adding Prepositional Phrases." Then read each sentence below. Underline each prepositional phrase and circle the word it modifies. Draw an arrow connecting the word and its modifying phrase. Finally, tell whether the phrase is adjectival or adverbial.

1. Under the spreading chestnut tree the village smithy stands.

2. The smith is a mighty man with large and sinewy hands.

3. On Sunday, he goes to church and sits among his boys.

4. The mother of his children is now dead and he remembers her with sadness.

5. Each deed and thought must be shaped on the sounding anvil.

"Telling the Bees"
by John Greenleaf Whittier

ABOUT THE AUTHOR

John Greenleaf Whittier (1807–1892), one of the so-called schoolroom or fireside poets, is known for his simple, lovely poems about life in rural New England, such as "Telling the Bees" and *Snow-Bound,* and for such politically oriented verse as "Barbara Fritchie" and "Icabod." Whittier was raised a Quaker in Massachusetts. His early religious training, with its emphasis on the brotherhood of all people, deeply influenced the course of his life and of his work. His poems were also strongly influenced by the work of Robert Burns, the pre-Romantic Scottish poet who wrote in rural dialect about rustic subjects. Whittier published his first poems in the newspaper published by William Lloyd Garrison, *The Abolitionist Leader.* Because of his religious beliefs and the influence of Garrison, Whittier himself became a strong advocate of abolition, speaking at antislavery meetings, editing antislavery newspapers, and writing both prose and verse in opposition to slavery. Whittier also served as a Massachusetts state legislator. Works by Whittier include *Legends of New-England in Prose and Verse* (1829), *Poems Written During the Progress of the Abolition Question* (1835), *Voices of Freedom* (1846), *Home Ballads, Poems and Lyrics* (1860), and *Snow-Bound* (1866).

ABOUT THE SELECTION

A year after the death of his mother, Whittier wrote this simple poem about the death of a loved one, **"Telling the Bees."** Whittier was deeply affected by his mother's death; he had never married and had supported his mother and two sisters most of his life. To explain his poem, Whittier wrote this note when he submitted it for publication in the *Atlantic Monthly* magazine (which he cofounded with Oliver Wendell Holmes): "A remarkable custom, brought from the Old Country, formerly prevailed in the rural district of New England. On the death of a member of the family, the bees were at once informed of the event, and their hives dressed in mourning. This ceremonial was supposed to be necessary to prevent the swarms from leaving their hives and seeking a new home."

READER'S JOURNAL

Have you ever had an experience that was so clear and vibrant that you can remember it perfectly, even years later? Perhaps it was a time of great happiness, excitement, or sadness. Freewrite about such a memorable experience in your journal.

LANGUAGE SKILLS

Read the Language Arts Survey, 2.66, "Irregular Verbs I." Then choose ten verbs from the poem. Make a chart presenting the base form, the past, and the past participle of each verb. Identify each verb as regular or irregular.

"Telling the Bees"

JOHN GREENLEAF WHITTIER

Here is the place; right over the hill
    Runs the path I took;
You can see the gap in the old wall still,
    And the steppingstones in the shallow brook.

5   There is the house, with the gate red-barred,
    And the poplars[1] tall;
And the barn's brown length, and the cattle yard,
    And the white horns tossing above the wall.

There are the beehives ranged in the sun;
10   And down by the <u>brink</u>
Of the brook are her poor flowers, weed-o'errun,[2]
    Pansy and daffodil, rose and pink.

A year has gone, as the tortoise goes,
    Heavy and slow;
15 And the same rose blows, and the same sun glows,
    And the same brook sings of a year ago.

What has the year been like according to the speaker? What do you think the speaker means by making this comparison?

---

1. **poplars.** Trees of the willow family with soft wood, rapid growth, and spikes of flowers without petals
2. **weed-o'errun.** Taken over by weeds

WORDS FOR EVERYDAY USE: **brink** (briŋk) *n.*, edge, especially at the top of a steep place

Stone City Iowa. *Grant Wood. Joslyn Art Museum, Omaha, NE*

There's the same sweet clover smell in the breeze;
    And the June sun warm
Tangles his wings of fire in the trees,
20   Setting, as then, over Fernside farm.

I mind me how with a lover's care
    From my Sunday coat
I brushed off the burrs,[3] and smoothed my hair,
    And cooled at the brookside my brow and throat.

25   Since we parted, a month had passed,—
    To love, a year;
Down through the beeches[4] I looked at last
    On the little red gate and the well sweep[5] near.

What did the speaker do "with a lover's care"?

What other sign of love is used?

---

3. **burrs.** Rough, prickly seedcases of certain plants
4. **beeches.** Trees with smooth, gray bark; hard wood; dark green leaves; and edible nuts; classical symbol of romantic couple
5. **sweep.** Long pole mounted on a pivot with a bucket at one end; used for raising water

I can see it all now,—the slantwise rain
30   Of light through the leaves,
The sundown's blaze on her windowpane,
        The bloom of her roses under the eaves.

Just the same as a month before,—
        The house and the trees,
35   The barn's brown gable, the vine by the door,—
        Nothing changed but the hives of bees.

Before them, under the garden wall,
        Forward and back,
Went drearily singing the chore-girl small,
40   Draping each hive with a shred of black.

To what journey does the speaker refer? What was the chore-girl telling the bees?

Trembling, I listened: the summer sun
        Had the chill of snow;
For I knew she was telling the bees of one
        Gone on the journey all must go!

45   Then I said to myself, "My Mary weeps
        For the dead today:
Haply[6] her blind old grandsire sleeps
        The fret and the pain of his age away."

But her dog whined low; on the doorway sill,
50   With his cane to his chin,
The old man sat; and the chore-girl still
        Sung to the bees stealing out and in.

And the song she was singing ever since
        In my ear sounds on:—

What does the speaker learn from the chore-girl's song?

55   "Stay at home, pretty bees, fly not hence!
        Mistress Mary is dead and gone!"   ■

_____

6. **Haply.** Perhaps

Responding to the Selection

The speaker in the poem looks back on this experience with a combination of sadness and peace. How do people usually respond to the death of a loved one? What stages of feeling do they go through? Does the speaker's response in this poem seem like a realistic, reasonable response to the death of a loved one? Do you imagine it would be similar to your response a year after the death of someone close to you?

Reviewing the Selection

RECALLING

1. The speaker in the poem seems to be walking with a friend and describing a past event. How long has it been since the event the speaker is describing?

2. Whom was the speaker expecting to see at the house? What was his relationship with that person?

3. Who did the speaker first think had died?

4. How did the speaker discover who had really died?

INTERPRETING

5. Describe the speaker's mood for the past year.

6. Why did the speaker brush the burrs from his coat and smooth his hair? Why was he dressed in a "Sunday suit"?

7. Why did the summer sun suddenly have "the chill of snow" when the speaker saw the chore-girl draping the hives in black?

8. The speaker still hears the song the chore-girl sang on that day. What does his persistent memory of the song suggest about the importance of the event?

SYNTHESIZING

9. The speaker seems to be talking to someone as the poem opens. Why do you think he has brought someone to the house he visited one year ago? Why might he share the story of that day?

10. The speaker mentions all the things that are the same as they were last year. Why does he emphasize the permanence of the country setting?

Understanding Literature (Questions for Discussion)

1. **Point of View. Point of view** is the vantage point from which a story is told. Identify the point of view—first-person or third-person—from which this story of this poem is told. Why is this point of view especially effective in such a personal poem?

2. **Tone. Tone** is the emotional attitude toward the reader or toward the subject implied by a literary work. Would you describe the tone of this poem as conversational or dramatic? Explain your choice.

3. **Mood. Mood** is the emotion created in the reader by part or all of a literary work. How would you describe the mood of this poem? Explain your answer.

Responding in Writing

1. **Obituary.** An **obituary** is a brief description of someone who died, meant to be printed publicly to inform readers of a death. Using what you know about Mary in the poem, write an obituary for her. You may add details that are not mentioned in the poem.

2. **Diary Entry.** Write a diary entry for the speaker telling how he reacted to the news of his loved one's death. What did he do, say, and think on that day after he heard the bad news?

Language Lab

Shifts in Verb Tense. Read the Language Arts Survey, 2.65, "Improper Shifts in Verb Tense." Rewrite the following sentences, correcting the verb tense shift in each.

1. I showed my companion the path over the hill that I take last year.

2. I brushed the burrs off my Sunday coat and smooth my hair.

3. After we parted, a month passed before I return.

4. The brook still sings and the sun glowed the same as before.

5. The chore-girl sang a song and is draping black mourning cloth on the hives.

Thinking Skills

Making Hypotheses. Read the Language Arts Survey, 4.13, "Making Hypotheses." What hypothesis did the speaker in this poem make when he saw the chore-girl draping black on the bee hives? Was it a logical hypothesis? Why, or why not? What discovery disproved the hypothesis?

PROJECTS

1. **Customs and Superstitions.** Together with other members of the class, survey friends and family about their customs and superstitions. Assemble the information you gather into a classroom booklet. You may wish to categorize your findings in some way, such as by country of origin, purpose, or occasion for use.

2. **Cemetery Visit.** Visit a cemetery and read some of the tombstones there. If possible, find tombstones from the nineteenth century and record what was written on them. How are those tombstones and their inscriptions different from modern ones? Present your findings to the class.

"Concord Hymn"
"The Rhodora"

by Ralph Waldo Emerson

ABOUT THE AUTHOR

A biography of **Ralph Waldo Emerson** appears on page 252.

ABOUT THE SELECTIONS

On April 18, 1775, British soldiers marched out of Boston, intent on destroying colonial supplies of powder and guns in nearby Lexington and Concord. The next morning, the soldiers met opposition from American volunteer militia, or Minutemen, who confronted them by the bridge over the Concord River. After a brief exchange of gunfire that resulted in casualties on both sides, the British were turned back and the American Revolution began in earnest. Sixty-two years later, grateful citizens erected a monument to commemorate the heroism of the Americans on that day. Emerson, a local resident, contributed his **"Concord Hymn"** as part of the celebration. On July 4, 1837, at the dedication of the monument, celebrants first read aloud Emerson's "Concord Hymn" and then sang it to the tune of a traditional church hymn, "Old Hundred." Today, stanza 1 of this poem is engraved on the base of the statue of a Minuteman that stands at the site of the historic confrontation.

The ideas presented in **"The Rhodora"** are extensions of thoughts expressed in the long essay *Nature,* Emerson's first published book. In *Nature,* published in 1836, Emerson maintains that all natural forms, such as "a leaf, sunbeam, a landscape, the ocean," are harmonious and always beautiful. They work together to express a universal beauty and truth that transcend the beauty and truth of the natural world. Humans can understand absolute, or universal, beauty and truth only through what can be experienced through our senses. "The Rhodora," written in 1847, is an eloquent statement of Emerson's belief in the value of each of nature's creations, including every individual.

READER'S JOURNAL

Has anyone ever done something for which you are grateful? How has that person's kindness, intelligence, or courage affected your life? In your journal, freewrite about a situation in which someone's actions benefited you and how you feel toward that person now.

THINKING SKILLS

Read the Language Arts Survey, 3.2, "Elements of Verbal Communication." Then, as you read the poem, imagine how it would have sounded when it was read aloud the first time. Practice reading it aloud yourself, following the guidelines in the Language Arts Survey.

"Concord Hymn"

RALPH WALDO EMERSON

Sung at the Completion of the
Battle Monument, April 19, 1836

By the rude bridge that arched[1] the flood,
    Their flag to April's breeze unfurled,
Here once the embattled farmers stood,
    And fired the shot heard round the world.

5   The foe[2] long since in silence slept;
    Alike the conqueror silent sleeps;
And Time the ruined bridge has swept
    Down the dark stream which seaward creeps.

On this green bank, by this soft stream,
10   We set today a votive[3] stone;
That memory may their deed redeem,
    When, like our sires,[4] our sons are gone.

Spirit, that made those heroes dare
    To die, and leave their children free,
15   Bid Time and Nature gently spare
    The shaft we raise to them and thee. ∎

What happened to the bridge that was the site of the battle?

For what did they fight?

---

1. **rude . . . arched.** Lexington–Concord Bridge; stone bridge across the Concord River
2. **foe.** England
3. **votive.** Expressing thanks or devotion
4. **sires.** Fathers

Responding to the Selection

How does the speaker feel toward the colonists who fought for independence? What are your feelings toward them? What would you say to these people if you could speak to them today? Write about these questions in your journal.

Reviewing the Selection

RECALLING

1. Who fired "the shot heard round the world"?

2. What happened at the Concord Bridge in 1775?

3. How is the historic event being commemorated?

4. How long does the speaker hope the memory of the battle will last?

INTERPRETING

5. Why does the speaker call the first shot fired at Concord "the shot heard round the world"? What is the significance of this shot?

6. Why did the heroes risk their lives? What was their goal?

7. What is the purpose of the monument at the Concord Bridge?

8. Find clues that make clear how the speaker feels about the event that took place here.

SYNTHESIZING

9. Do you think that this poem was well-received at the dedication ceremony? If the dedication were held today, why would modern listeners like or dislike the poem?

10. Why do people erect monuments? What feelings are monuments meant to produce? Do you believe that monuments are worthwhile? Why, or why not?

Understanding Literature (Questions for Discussion)

1. **Meter.** The **meter** of a poem is its rhythmical pattern. A line of poetry can be described as being made up of rhythmical units called *feet*. A foot is a unit of rhythm consisting of strongly and weakly stressed syllables. How many feet are there in this line?

    And fired | the shot | heard round | the world.

    Now read the poem again. This time count the number of feet in each line. Is the number of feet consistent throughout the poem? Why is that pattern appropriate for a hymn?

2. **Apostrophe.** An **apostrophe** is a rhetorical technique in which an object or person is directly addressed. Identify the use of apostrophe in the poem. Whom or what does the speaker address? What does the speaker ask of that person or thing?

3. **Alliteration.** **Alliteration** is the repetition of initial consonant sounds. Find examples of alliteration in stanzas 2 and 3 of this poem.

Language Lab

Semicolons. Read the Language Arts Survey, 2.97, "Semicolons." Then correctly add semicolons to the sentences below.

1. The American farmers decided to take a stand against what they considered to be British tyranny they would not retreat from the oncoming battle.

2. The heroes of Concord had passed away years ago however, their deeds were recalled with gratitude by their descendants.

3. They read the poem, loudly and with emotion they sang the song, replacing the traditional lyrics with new words and they dedicated the monument, hoping that the heroes would be remembered for generations.

4. The setting is deceptively peaceful yet, sixty years ago upon this site a historic battle was fought.

5. The statue of the Minuteman still stands beside the Concord Bridge it commemorates the courage of the men who fought there in 1775.

READER'S JOURNAL

For many people, experiences in nature are particularly satisfying and uplifting. Have you ever experienced a special moment in nature, for example, when you were hiking or bicycling? Try to recreate that moment in your mind, and jot down in your journal a few notes about the sights you saw, the sounds you heard, and the emotions you felt.

THINKING SKILLS

Read the Language Arts Survey, 2.64, "Inverting Sentences for Emphasis." Find at least two instances in this poem in which the usual order of subject + verb + predicate has been changed. Rewrite the sentences in the usual order.

"The Rhodora[1]"

RALPH WALDO EMERSON

On Being Asked, Whence[2] Is the Flower?

In May, when sea-winds pierced our solitudes,
I found the fresh Rhodora in the woods,
Spreading its leafless blooms in a damp nook,
To please the desert and the sluggish brook.
5   The purple petals, fallen in the pool,
Made the black water with their beauty gay;
Here might the red-bird come his plumes to cool,
And court the flower that cheapens his array.
Rhodora! if the sages[3] ask thee why
10   This charm is wasted on the earth and sky,
Tell them, dear, that if eyes were made for seeing,
Then Beauty is its own excuse for being:
Why thou wert there,[4] O rival of the rose!
I never thought to ask, I never knew;
15   But, in my simple ignorance, suppose
The self-same Power that brought me there brought you. ■

Who enjoys what the flower offers?

---

1. **Rhodora.** Deciduous plant, native to northeastern
United States, that bears pink flowers in spring
2. **Whence.** From where
3. **sages.** Wise older people
4. **thou wert there.** You were there

Responding to the Selection

The speaker in this poem focuses on a flower that holds special meaning for him. What natural objects found in the woods, on the mountains, at the beach, or in the meadow do you find particularly beautiful or affecting? Choose two of these objects and explain why you chose them.

Reviewing the Selection

RECALLING

1. At what time of year does the speaker find the rhodora in the woods?

2. Where is the rhodora growing? What is the rhodora's effect on the area in which it is blooming?

3. What might "sages" ask the rhodora? According to the speaker, how can the rhodora justify its blooming alone in the woods when usually no one sees it?

4. What brought the speaker to the same place as the rhodora?

INTERPRETING

5. Why is the rhodora especially beautiful at this time of year? Why do you think the speaker compares the rhodora to a rose?

6. Does the speaker believe that any other person besides himself has appreciated the rhodora's beauty? Why is the isolated location of the rhodora significant to the speaker?

7. Does the speaker really believe that the sages are wise? Explain why, or why not.

8. Do you think that the speaker is glad that he happened upon the rhodora in the woods? What do you think he gained through this encounter?

SYNTHESIZING

9. Winter in New England is long and cold, and spring is always welcome. Why does the sight of the rhodora delight the speaker so? What springtime sight gives you the most pleasure?

10. Which flower do you think the speaker would find more pleasing—the rhodora blooming alone in the woods or the pampered orchid blooming in a greenhouse? Would the speaker find them equally pleasing? Explain your answer.

Understanding Literature (Questions for Discussion)

1. **Rhyme. Rhyme** is the repetition of sounds at the ends of words. Identify the rhyme scheme of "The Rhodora," labeling the sound at the end of each line with a letter of the alphabet. If the sound is the same as one that came before, label it with the same letter. If it is a different sound, assign it a new letter. When you are done, look for the pattern or rhyme scheme.

2. **Romanticism. Romanticism** was a literary and artistic movement of the eighteenth and nineteenth centuries that placed value on emotion or imagination over realism, and on nature and wildness over human works. Explain why this poem may be categorized as Romantic.

Responding in Writing

1. **Stream of Consciousness. Stream-of-consciousness writing** attempts to render the flow of feelings, thoughts, and impressions within the minds of characters. Imagine that you are walking in the woods on that May day with the speaker. Write a long paragraph that describes what you would be experiencing and thinking as you hike along. Include your thoughts on finding the rhodora by the stream.

2. **Editorial.** Write an editorial in which you state your point of view on the desirability of preserving wilderness areas in the United States. Begin by explaining the issue you will be discussing; then give at least three reasons why you feel as you do. Conclude with a recommendation about what you believe is the correct course of action.

Language Lab

Correcting Modifiers. Read the Language Arts Survey, 2.63, "Correcting Dangling or Misplaced Modifiers." Then correctly rewrite each sentence below.

1. While blooming by a quiet stream, the speaker discovered a hidden rhodora.

2. Fallen into the water, the river washed the petals downstream.

3. Cooling his plumes at the brook, the rhodora's purple petals contrasted with the bird's red feathers.

4. The Transcendentalists had a lasting effect on American literature who believed that through intuition humans can know truth.

5. Even more useful than the teachings of organized religion, Emerson believed that the most direct way to enlightenment was an openness to nature.

"This is my letter to the World"
"The Soul selects her own Society—"
"Because I could not stop for Death—"
"I heard a Fly buzz—when I died—"

by Emily Dickinson

ABOUT THE AUTHOR

Emily Dickinson (1830–1886) lived a private life, rarely venturing beyond her home and her close circle of family and friends, but she lived that life intensely, in vivid moments of observation and reflection captured in astonishingly original verse. Considered by many critics and writers to be the greatest of American lyric poets, she did not seek fame, for which she had considerable contempt, but rather kept her writing to herself, sharing small portions of it with her intimates. Only seven of her poems were published during her lifetime, all anonymously and without her full consent. The first volumes of her poetry, published after her death, mangled the work by "correcting" her unconventional punctuation and her purposeful deviations from grammatical propriety. Only in 1955, with the publication of *The Poems of Emily Dickinson,* edited by T. H. Johnson, did the full extent of her achievement become known.

At her death, which occurred in the house in Amherst, Massachusetts, where she was born, Dickinson had produced well over one thousand lyrics. These explored a tremendous range of subjects in language remarkable for its wit, inventiveness, and economy of expression. Taken as a whole, her verses, most of them quite brief, present a complex self-portrait, a sort of spiritual autobiography. Her voice is alternately humble and proud, intimate and aloof, ecstatic and sorrowful, but always questioning, reflective, and intensely alive. She was a keen observer of particulars—capable of sudden, breathtaking generalizations that synthesized these particulars into truths.

Much nonsense has been made of the few details known of her life, which because of its outward meagerness has invited much speculation. This speculation has centered on her various male friends and on her famed reclusiveness. She was born to a prominent Amherst family. Her closest friends were her brother, William Austin, and her sister, Lavinia. Neither Emily nor Lavinia married. Emily seldom left Amherst, although she did spend one year at Mt. Holyoke Female Seminary, ten miles away, and took a trip to Washington and Philadelphia with her father. Her grandfather was one of the founders of Amherst College. Her father, Edward, served as treasurer of Amherst College, a state representative, and a state senator.

Dickinson attended Amherst Academy before spending her year at Mt. Holyoke. At home again, she delighted in reading books that might "joggle the Mind." She read a few books very deeply, especially the Bible, the plays of Shakespeare, and the works of such contemporary writers as Emerson, Keats, Tennyson, and George Eliot. Early on, she was befriended by Benjamin Newton, a law student who encouraged her writing. His early death led to a period of spiritual crisis during which she turned for advice to a well-known minister from Philadelphia, Charles Wadsworth, who became a close friend. In the late 1850s, she wrote drafts of love letters to an unknown person identified in the letters as "Master," and some of her poems of the period reflect the frustrations and tensions of thwarted romantic feeling.

She corresponded with the critic Thomas Wentworth Higginson, who encouraged but failed to understand her work, and she was courted by a family friend, Judge Otis P. Lord. Perhaps because of physical problems, her last twenty-five years were spent in seclusion from all but the closest of friends and family members.

ABOUT THE SELECTIONS

When T. H. Johnson numbered all Dickinson's known poems for his three-volume edition of *The Poems of Emily Dickinson* (1955), he used such clues as handwriting differences to infer the order of composition. **"This is my letter to the World"** was assigned number 441. It was written in the early 1860s, probably in 1862, when Dickinson was most prolific, averaging a poem a day.

In **"The Soul selects her own Society—,"** written in about 1862, Dickinson might be speaking about herself. Contemporary scholars have offered various explanations for Dickinson's withdrawal from society, including thwarted love and physical disabilities. The poems themselves support the theory that her reclusiveness was the determined, willful act of someone who wished to encounter life on her own terms. This view is supported, for example, by the affirmation in "The Soul selects her own Society" of an individual's freedom to choose associates.

Most critics agree that **"Because I could not stop for Death—"** is one of Dickinson's best poems. The writer and critic Allen Tate has written that it is "one of the greatest in the English language; it is flawless to the last detail. . . . Every image is precise and . . . fused with the central idea." The poem was written in 1863 and published in 1890 in the first collection of Dickinson's work.

As a member of a solid New England family, Emily Dickinson was immersed in the Puritan tradition, and for many years she attended church services twice each Sunday. Many of her poems deal with religious subjects, often with questions about the relationship of the individual soul to God and about immortality and the afterlife. In **"I heard a Fly buzz—when I died—,"** the speaker imagines her own death, expressing with brilliant irony her fears about the transition from this life to the next.

READER'S JOURNAL

If you were to write a "letter to the world" that would be read by others after your death, what would that letter say? Write such a letter, to be placed in a time capsule to be opened sometime late in the next century.

RESEARCH SKILLS

Read the Language Arts Survey, 4.29, "Bibliographies and Bibliography Cards." Then use the card catalog in a library to find at least four books with information about Emily Dickinson and her work. Make bibliography cards for these books, following proper form as described in the Language Arts Survey.

"This is my letter to the World"

EMILY DICKINSON

Where does the poet find her subject matter?

This is my letter to the World
That never wrote to Me—
The simple News that Nature told—
With tender Majesty

5   Her Message is committed
To Hands I cannot see—
For love of Her—Sweet—countrymen—
Judge tenderly—of Me   ■

Responding to the Selection

What does the speaker of this poem ask of you, her reader? What reason does the speaker give for judging her work tenderly? Do you find this reason persuasive? Why, or why not?

Reviewing the Selection

1. What does the speaker call her poem, or her poetry in general?

2. Which line of stanza 1 describes the content of the speaker's "letter"?

3. Which lines of the poem describe those to whom the speaker's work "is committed"?

4. Whom or what is referred to by the word "Her" in line 7?

5. Why does the speaker say that her writing is intended for others who "never wrote to Me"?

6. Is the poet being sincere or ironic—or both—in describing nature's "News" as "simple"?

7. Which word in stanza 2 suggests that a poem is incomplete without a reader?

8. What benefit does the speaker suggest is possible for the reader who judges her work "tenderly"? What information or understanding might the reader gain?

9. Why does the poet request that she be judged "tenderly"? What fears might she have about her audience?

10. During her lifetime, Dickinson intentionally kept her poetry from being published. What light does this poem shed on her motives? Is it likely that she meant never to share her work with an audience?

Understanding Literature (Questions for Discussion)

1. **Personification. Personification** is a figure of speech in which an idea, animal, or thing is described as if it were a person. What force is personified in this poem? What qualities of humans are given to the force?

2. **Apology.** An **apology** is a literary defense. Explain how this poem can be seen as an apology. What does it defend?

3. **Meter.** The **meter** of a poem is its rhythmical pattern. How many feet, or beats, are used in most of the lines of this poem? The even-numbered lines are the most regular. Describe these lines completely, telling both the type of foot (for example, iambic or trochaic) and the number of feet per line. Refer to the section on *meter* in the Handbook of Literary Terms.

Responding in Writing

Original Lyric Poem. Choose a scene in nature or a particularly meaningful moment for you, and write an original lyric poem about your topic. Use short lines and verses, in the style of Emily Dickinson. Be sure to focus on a single image or moment.

Language Lab

Semicolons and Dashes. Read the Language Arts Survey, 2.97, "Semicolons," and 2.98, "Dashes." Then rewrite the following sentences, inserting semicolons or dashes where they are needed.

1. I toured New England recently did I tell you that I visited three very old graveyards?

2. There's a big difference between the old tombstones and modern ones the old ones have much more personality.

3. On many old stones, the writing has worn off however, the pictures are still visible.

4. The old stones have carvings of skulls, skeletons, and grieving mourners our ancestors faced death more directly, I think.

5. I made several rubbings of the old tombstones here are two of them.

Applied English/Tech Prep Skills

Personal Letters. Read the Language Arts Survey, 5.2, "The Form of a Personal Letter." Choose a writer, either living or past, whose work you enjoy. Write a letter to that writer, discussing such topics as the writer's works, attitudes or experiences that you and the writer share, and ideas for new works by either the writer or you. Follow the correct form for a personal letter.

READER'S JOURNAL

Who are your closest friends? Did you choose them, or have you just been thrown together by chance? Do you expect them to be close friends two years from now? Why, or why not? Write about how friendships form—and about how you believe they *should* form.

LANGUAGE SKILLS

Review the guidelines for using capitalization in the Language Arts Survey, 2.107–2.133. As you read the poem, note the places where Dickinson uses irregular capitalization. Consider why she might have chosen to emphasize these particular words by capitalizing them.

"The Soul selects her own Society—"

EMILY DICKINSON

The Soul selects her own Society—
Then—shuts the Door—
To her divine Majority—
Present no more—

5   Unmoved—she notes the Chariots—pausing—
At her low Gate—
Unmoved—an Emperor be kneeling
Upon her Mat—

I've known her—from an ample nation—
10   Choose One—
Then—close the Valves of her attention—
Like Stone—   ■

Responding to the Selection

Does a person have a right to choose his or her own friends and acquaintances? Is your own experience of choosing friends and acquaintances similar to or different from the experience of the speaker in the poem? Discuss these questions with your classmates.

Reviewing the Selection

RECALLING

1. What three verbs appear in stanza 1? If you were to write stanza 1 using commas, periods, or no punctuation in place of the dashes, where would you place a sentence break?

2. Who or what is "her divine Majority"?

3. Identify two attractions that fail to tempt the interest of the soul.

4. In the final stanza, how does the soul block off access by anyone or anything other than the one she has chosen?

INTERPRETING

5. Which of the three verbs in stanza 1 expresses a command? Explain the command.

6. Before the creation of such democracies as the United States, where the vote of the majority rules, kings were thought to rule by divine right. When the poet substitutes the words "divine Majority" for the phrase "divine Majesty," what attitude toward groups of people, or majorities, does she suggest?

7. What real-life attractions might be symbolized by the "Chariots" and the "Emperor"?

8. Do you suppose that the phrase "ample nation" in the final stanza refers to the United States, another country, or simply to a large number of people? Explain your answer.

SYNTHESIZING

9. Until the final stanza, every line of the poem has four or more syllables. The second and final lines of the last stanza, however, have only two syllables each. How does this abruptness contribute to the meaning of the stanza?

10. What good qualities or advantages do you see in this description of an individual's selection of friends? What possible drawbacks might the speaker's actions have?

Understanding Literature (Questions for Discussion)

1. **Sight Rhyme.** A **sight rhyme**, or **eye rhyme**, is a pair of words, generally at the ends of lines of verse, that are spelled similarly but pronounced differently. Find an example of sight rhyme in this poem.

2. **Slant Rhyme.** A **slant rhyme** is one in which the rhyming sounds are similar but not exact. Identify examples of slant rhyme in this poem.

3. **Repetition.** **Repetition** is the use, again, of a sound, word, phrase, sentence, or other element. Where is repetition of a word used in this poem? What is its effect? Where is the strongest use of repetition of a sound? For what purpose?

Language Lab

Voice and Mood. Read the Language Arts Survey, 2.69, "Voice and Mood," on the subjunctive mood and the past subjunctive. Then write these sentences and underline each verb that is used in the subjunctive mood.

1. To understand Dickinson's work, it is important that the reader remember the pressures on women of her day.

2. Society required that a single woman marry in order to be respected.

3. Certainly, friends would suggest that a girl accept almost any proposal, no matter how undesirable.

4. Were I a woman in Dickinson's era, I would not have been able to plan a career of my own.

5. Can you imagine Dickinson's surprise and pleasure if she were to see the great number of modern women, both single and married, with important careers in business, science, and the arts?

Study and Research Skills

Etymology. Read the information about etymologies in the Language Arts Survey, 4.24, "Using Dictionaries." The word *majority* comes from the Latin word *maior*, meaning "greater." The Latin word for "great" is *magnus*. Using a dictionary that gives etymologies, identify at least four other English words that are drawn from either *maior* or *magnus*.

"Because I could not stop for Death—"

EMILY DICKINSON

Because I could not stop for Death—
He kindly stopped for me—
The Carriage held but just Ourselves—
And Immortality.

5   We slowly drove—He knew no haste
And I had put away
My labor and my leisure too,
For His <u>Civility</u>—

We passed the School, where Children strove
10   At recess—in the Ring—
We passed the Fields of Gazing Grain—
We passed the Setting Sun—

Or rather—He passed Us—
The Dews drew quivering and Chill—
15   For only Gossamer, my Gown—
My Tippet[1]—only Tulle[2]—

What three things does the carriage pass?

---

1. **Tippet.** Short cape worn over the shoulders
2. **Tulle.** Thin netting

WORDS FOR
EVERYDAY USE:
    ci • vil • i • ty (sə vil´ə tē) *n.*, gentleness; a civilized manner

Winter Sunday in Norway, Maine. *Artist unknown,* circa *1860. New York State Historical Association, Cooperstown, NY*

We paused before a House that seemed
A Swelling of the Ground—
The Roof was scarcely visible—
20   The Cornice[3]—in the Ground

What is this house?

Since then—'tis Centuries—and yet
Feels shorter than the Day
I first surmised the Horses Heads
Were toward Eternity—   ■

3. **Cornice.** Molded projection at the top of a building

Responding to the Selection

What sort of attitude toward death is reflected in this poem? How is Death portrayed? Do you share the speaker's conception of death? Why, or why not?

Reviewing the Selection

1. How does stanza 1 picture Death?

2. Identify the three visual images the speaker notes during the carriage ride.

3. To which sense does most of stanza 4 relate? How does this stanza make you feel?

4. What do you learn in stanza 6 about the speaker?

▶▶ 5. Why do you think that the speaker could not stop for death?

▶▶ 6. In what way do the three images reflect stages of life? What is the speaker saying about the presence of Death as a factor in all of a person's life?

▶▶ 7. What "House" is described in stanza 5?

▶▶ 8. What is the speaker's attitude toward Death?

9. Review the poem for references to time. Do these references present a single concept or a development in the speaker's understanding of time? Discuss your findings.

10. Do you suppose the speaker is dead at the beginning of the poem or passes from life to death at some point during the journey? Give a reason for your answer.

Understanding Literature (Questions for Discussion)

1. **Stanza.** A **stanza** is a recurring pattern of grouped lines in a poem. How many stanzas form this poem? Describe the development of the poem's story, stanza by stanza.

2. **Extended Metaphor.** An **extended metaphor** is a point-by-point presentation of one thing as though it were another. For what is the carriage ride in this poem an extended metaphor? Explain several of the points it mentions.

3. **Assonance. Assonance** is the repetition of vowel sounds in stressed syllables that end with different consonant sounds. Find at least two examples of assonance in this poem.

4. **Irony. Irony** is a contradiction between appearance and reality. What makes the speaker's comments about Death in stanza 1 of the poem witty and ironic? How do the speaker's feelings about Death progress throughout the poem?

5. **Point of View. Point of view** is the vantage point from which a literary work is told. This poem is told from the first-person point of view by a speaker who uses the words *I, me,* and *ourselves.* What is unusual about this speaker? From what perspective does she view the events that she relates? What might account for the calmness and humor of her description of her experience of Death?

READER'S JOURNAL

Have you ever tried to meditate? Is it easy to concentrate on a single thought? How can you eliminate distractions? Set aside a quiet time of ten to twenty minutes to try to limit your thoughts to a topic meaningful to you. Slow your breathing, assume a comfortable position, and close your eyes. Then rate how successful you were. Record difficulties you encountered.

WRITING SKILLS

Review the nature and purpose of sensory details by reading the Language Arts Survey, 1.40, "Elaboration: Types of Supporting Details." Then find at least three sensory details in this poem. Be ready to discuss which sense(s) each detail appeals to.

"I heard a Fly buzz— when I died—"

EMILY DICKINSON

I heard a Fly buzz—when I died—
The Stillness in the Room
Was like the Stillness in the Air—
Between the Heaves of Storm—

5   The Eyes around—had wrung them dry—
and Breaths were gathering firm
For that last Onset—when the King
Be witnessed—in the Room

I willed my Keepsakes[1]—Signed away
10   What portion of me be
Assignable—and then it was
There interposed[2] a Fly—

With Blue—uncertain stumbling Buzz—
Between the light—and me—
15   And then the Windows failed—and then
I could not see to see—   ■

Who else is in the room besides the speaker?

---

1. **Keepsakes.** Personal items that are treasured
2. **interposed.** Appeared suddenly

Responding to the Selection

Did the deathbed scene pictured in this poem seem believable to you? Did it surprise you? Did it sadden or frighten you? Why, or why not?

Reviewing the Selection

RECALLING

1. In your own words, describe the scene at the beginning of the poem.

2. What sensory details tell you that the speaker's death is not sudden or unexpected?

3. All the sentences and clauses in the poem except one follow the subject-verb pattern. Identify the clause that breaks away from that pattern. What pattern does it use?

4. What does the speaker notice about the fly? What does she notice about the rest of the room after the fly enters?

INTERPRETING

5. How does stanza 1 suggest that something momentous is about to happen?

6. Who is the "King" whose arrival is expected? What will his arrival signify?

7. Why did the poet vary the sentence pattern in the single clause? What effect does the unusual word order produce?

8. At what moment does the action stop? What is the speaker's mood at that point? Why?

SYNTHESIZING

9. What fear(s) about death—and life—does this poem explore?

10. What is surprising about the ending of this poem? How does the speaker's actual experience contradict the expectations of the people gathered around her deathbed?

Understanding Literature (Questions for Discussion)

1. **Synaesthesia.** Synaesthesia is a figure of speech that combines in a single expression images related to two or more different senses. Find an example of synaesthesia in stanza 4. To what two senses does the expression relate?

2. **Onomatopoeia. Onomatopoeia** is the use of words or phrases that sound like the things to which they refer. Read line 13 aloud. What is described? What repeated sounds in the words suggest the thing described?

3. **Symbol.** A **symbol** is a thing that stands for or represents both itself and something else. For example, a dove is a traditional symbol of peace. Of what is light a traditional symbol? (Think, for example, of conventional expressions such as "a sudden illumination" and "to shed light on a problem.") What literal interpretation might be given to the light in the last stanza? What symbolic interpretation might it be given? In the Middle Ages, one of the demons of hell was considered to be Beelzebub, the so-called "Lord of the Flies." What literal interpretation might be given to what the speaker sees at the end of the stanza? What symbolic interpretation might it be given? What various interpretations might be given of the speaker's inability to see at the end of the poem?

Responding in Writing

Description. Read the Language Arts Survey, 1.18, "Sensory Detail Charts," paying particular attention to the sample sensory detail chart. Then select an object or room with which you are familiar, and create a sensory detail chart for that subject. List at least two details in each column, in other words, for each sense. Use the information in your chart to write a description of the object or room.

PROJECTS

1. **Assembling an Anthology.** With a small group of students who enjoy writing poetry, work together to assemble an anthology of original poems. Begin by sharing poems all of you have written and selecting a reasonable number to represent each member of the group. Split up the tasks of designing the cover and any artwork, typing or inputting the manuscript, laying out pages, and duplicating and assembling pages. Use desktop publishing methods, if possible. Make your anthology available to classmates, teachers, and parents.

2. **Community Survey.** Work with a large group, such as your whole class, to collect data for a community survey concerning the arts. Draw up a small number of specific questions concerning community attitudes toward the arts, artists, and/or community resources in the arts (museums, theaters, libraries, etc.). After every group member has interviewed three or more different community members, tabulate your results. Look for generalizations you can justifiably draw from the results. Announce your findings through a classroom display, letter to the editor of the local paper, or some other means.

3. **Historical Research/Women's Studies.** Do independent research on the roles and rights of women in the United States in the mid-1800s. If you like, focus on individuals whose unusual accomplishments throw the usual lot of women into stronger contrast. Present your findings in a paper or multimedia presentation.

"The Raven"

by Edgar Allan Poe

ABOUT THE AUTHOR

A biography of **Edgar Allan Poe** appears on page 225.

ABOUT THE SELECTION

"The Raven" was Edgar Allan Poe's first international success. When it was published in 1845 in the *New York Evening Mirror*, the editor warned readers that "it would stick to the memory of everybody who reads it." It seems that this prophecy came true, because soon after the poem's publication, "The Raven" was read and reread by critics, poets, and students all over the world. To this day, "The Raven" is included in many anthologies; it has become a staple in the education of many American students. Poe himself considered it to be one of his finest works. In 1846, he claimed that "future generations will be able to sift the gold from the dross, and 'The Raven' will be beheld, shining above them all as a diamond of purest water."

"The Raven"

EDGAR ALLAN POE

Once upon a midnight dreary, while I pondered, weak and weary,
Over many a quaint and curious volume of forgotten lore,
While I nodded, nearly napping, suddenly there came a tapping,
As of some one gently rapping, rapping at my chamber door.
5   " 'Tis some visiter," I muttered, "tapping at my chamber door—
                           Only this, and nothing more."

Ah, distinctly I remember it was in the bleak December,
And each separate dying ember wrought its ghost upon the floor.
Eagerly I wished the morrow;—vainly I had tried to borrow
10   From my books <u>surcease</u> of sorrow—sorrow for the lost Lenore—
For the rare and radiant maiden whom the angels name Lenore—
                           Nameless here for evermore.

What is the cause of the speaker's sorrow?

And the silken sad uncertain rustling of each purple curtain
Thrilled me—filled me with fantastic terrors never felt before;
15   So that now, to still the beating of my heart, I stood repeating
" 'Tis some visiter <u>entreating</u> entrance at my chamber door—
Some late visiter entreating entrance at my chamber door;—
                           This it is, and nothing more."

Presently my soul grew stronger; hesitating then no longer,
20   "Sir," said I, "or Madam, truly your forgiveness I implore;

WORDS FOR EVERYDAY USE:
sur • cease (sʉr sēs´) *n.*, respite; end
en • treat (en trēt´) *vt.*, beg; implore; ask earnestly

But the fact is I was napping, and so gently you came rapping,
And so faintly you came tapping, tapping at my chamber door,
That I scarce was sure I heard you"—here I opened wide the door,—
                                    Darkness there, and nothing more.

25 Deep into that darkness peering, long I stood there wondering, fearing,
Doubting dreaming dreams no mortal ever dared to dream before;
But the silence was unbroken, and the darkness gave no token,
And the only word there spoken was the whispered word, "Lenore!"
This *I* whispered, and an echo murmured back the word, "Lenore!"
30   Merely this, and nothing more.

Then into the chamber turning, all my soul within me burning,
Soon I heard again a tapping somewhat louder than before.
"Surely," said I, "surely that is something at my window lattice;
Let me see, then, what thereat is, and this mystery explore—
35 Let my heart be still a moment and this mystery explore;—
                                    'Tis the wind, and nothing more!"

What enters through the open window?

Open here I flung the shutter, when, with many a flirt and flutter,
In there stepped a stately raven of the saintly days of yore;
Not the least obeisance made he; not an instant stopped or stayed he;
40 But, with mien of lord or lady, perched above my chamber door—
Perched upon a bust of Pallas[1] just above my chamber door—
                                    Perched, and sat, and nothing more.

Where does the visitor sit?

Then this ebony bird beguiling my sad fancy into smiling,
By the grave and stern decorum of the countenance it wore,
45 "Though thy crest be shorn and shaven, thou," I said, "art sure no craven,
Ghastly grim and ancient raven wandering from the Nightly shore—
Tell me what thy lordly name is on the Night's Plutonian[2] shore!"
                                    Quoth the raven, "Nevermore."

Does the speaker find the visitor's response meaningful?

50 Much I marvelled this ungainly fowl to hear discourse so plainly,
Though its answer little meaning—little relevancy bore;
For we cannot help agreeing that no sublunary[3] being
Ever yet was blessed with seeing bird above his chamber door—
Bird or beast upon the sculptured bust above his chamber door,
                                    With such name as "Nevermore."

----

1. **Pallas.** Greek goddess of wisdom
2. **Plutonian.** Black; relating to the underworld
3. **sublunary.** Earthly

WORDS FOR
EVERYDAY USE:

lat • tice (lat´is) *n.,* shutter; openwork structure used as a screen
o • bei • sance (ō bā´səns) *n.,* gesture of respect
mien (mēn) *n.,* manner; appearance
cra • ven (krā´vən) *n.,* coward

55 But the raven, sitting lonely on the placid bust, spoke only
   That one word, as if his soul in that one word he did outpour.
   Nothing farther then he uttered—not a feather then he fluttered—
   Till I scarcely more than muttered, "Other friends have flown before—
   On the <u>morrow</u> *he* will leave me, as my hopes have flown before."
60   Quoth the raven, "Nevermore."

   Wondering at the stillness broken by reply so aptly spoken,
   "Doubtless," said I, "what it utters is its only stock and store,
   Caught from some unhappy master whom unmerciful Disaster
   Followed fast and followed faster—so, when Hope he would <u>adjure</u>,
65 Stern Despair returned, instead of the sweet Hope he dared adjure—
                 That sad answer, "Nevermore!"

WORDS FOR
EVERYDAY USE:
 mor • row (mär´ō) *n.,* next day
 ad • jure (ə jer´) *vt.,* urge; beg

Where does the speaker sit?

But the raven still <u>beguiling</u> all my sad soul into smiling,
Straight I wheeled a cushioned seat in front of bird, and bust, and door;
Then upon the velvet sinking, I betook myself to linking
70   Fancy unto fancy thinking what this <u>ominous</u> bird of yore—

What this grim, ungainly, ghastly, gaunt, and ominous bird of yore
                    Meant in croaking "Nevermore."

This I sat engaged in guessing, but no syllable expressing
To the fowl whose fiery eyes now burned into my bosom's core;
75   This and more I sat divining, with my head at ease reclining

Of whom is the speaker thinking?

On the cushion's velvet lining that the lamplight gloated o'er,
But whose velvet violet lining with the lamplight gloating o'er,
                    She shall press, ah, nevermore!

Then, methought, the air grew denser, perfumed from an unseen <u>censer</u>
80   Swung by angels whose faint foot-falls tinkled on the tufted floor.
"Wretch," I cried, "thy God hath lent thee—by these angels he hath sent thee
Respite—respite and Nepenthe[4] from thy memories of Lenore!
Let me <u>quaff</u> this kind Nepenthe and forget this lost Lenore!"
                    Quoth the raven, "Nevermore."

85   "Prophet!" said I, "thing of evil!—prophet still, if bird or devil!—
Whether Tempter sent, or whether <u>tempest</u> tossed thee here ashore,
Desolate, yet all <u>undaunted</u>, on this desert land enchanted—
On this home by Horror haunted—tell me truly, I implore—
Is there—*is* there balm in Gilead?[5]—tell me—tell me, I implore!"
90   Quoth the raven, "Nevermore."

How has the speaker's attitude toward the raven's answers changed?

"Prophet!" said I, "thing of evil!—prophet still, if bird or devil!
By that Heaven that bends above us—by that God we both adore—
Tell this soul with sorrow laden if, within the distant Aidenn,[6]
It shall clasp a sainted maiden whom the angels name Lenore—
95   Clasp a rare and radiant maiden whom the angels name Lenore."
                    Quoth the raven, "Nevermore."

---

4. **Nepenthe.** Potion used to induce forgetfulness of pain or sorrow

5. **balm in Gilead.** Gilead is a mountainous area in the Middle East where evergreens provide medicinal resins.

The question echoes Jeremiah 8:22, "Is there no balm in Gilead?"

6. **Aidenn.** Name created by Poe to suggest Eden

WORDS FOR EVERYDAY USE:

be • guil • ing (bē gīlʹiŋ) *part.*, charming; leading by deception

om • i • nous (ämʹə nəs) *adj.*, forewarning evil

cen • ser (senʹsər) *n.*, container for burning incense

quaff (kwäf) *vi.*, drink deeply

tem • pest (temʹpəst) *n.*, violent storm

un • daunt • ed (ən dôntʹəd) *adj.*, resolute in the face of danger

"Be that word our sign of parting, bird or fiend!" I shrieked, upstarting—
Get thee back into the tempest and the Night's Plutonian shore!
Leave no black <u>plume</u> as a token of that lie thy soul hath spoken!
100   Leave my loneliness unbroken—quit the bust above my door!
Take thy beak from out my heart, and take thy form from off my door!"
                         Quoth the raven, "Nevermore."

And the raven, never flitting, still is sitting, still is sitting
On the pallid bust of Pallas just above my chamber door;
105   And his eyes have all the seeming of a demon that is dreaming,
And the lamp-light o'er him streaming throws his shadow on the floor;
And my soul from out that shadow that lies floating on the floor
                         Shall be lifted—nevermore! ■

Responding to the Selection

How does the appearance of the raven affect the speaker's mood? Do you think that the raven is real or is it simply imagined by the speaker? If imagined, what does the raven reveal about the speaker's frame of mind? Answer these questions in your journal.

Reviewing the Selection

RECALLING

1. What is the speaker doing when he first hears the rapping at his door?

2. Who or what enters the room through the open window?

3. What is the raven's single-word answer to every question?

4. How does the raven react to the speaker's anger?

INTERPRETING

5. Why does the speaker hesitate before answering the door?

6. Describe the raven. How is it different from normal birds? What is the speaker's reaction to it?

7. The speaker soon knows how the raven will respond to his questions and commands. Why does he continue to talk to it and ask it questions?

8. Why does the speaker become so angry at the raven that he orders it to leave his room?

WORDS FOR EVERYDAY USE: **plume** (plüm) *n.,* feather

9. Other birds, such as the parrot, also can be trained to speak. Why do you think Poe chose the raven to visit the despondent speaker? What other animal could he have chosen? How would a different animal have changed the poem?

10. What feelings does the word *nevermore* create in you? Why is it such a sorrowful word?

Understanding Literature (Questions for Discussion)

1. **Rhyme. Rhyme** is the repetition of sounds at the ends of words. A particular kind of rhyme called *internal rhyme*, in which rhyming words appear within lines of verse, can be found in "The Raven," for example, "Wondering at the stillness <u>broken</u> by reply so aptly <u>spoken</u>." Find at least five other examples of internal rhyme in the poem. Does the internal rhyme add to your enjoyment of the poem? Why, or why not?

2. **Alliteration. Alliteration** is the repetition of initial consonant sounds. Find examples of the use of alliteration in stanzas 3, 5, and 12. Find at least one other example of alliteration in another stanza.

3. **Run-on Line.** A **run-on line** is a line of verse in which the sense or the grammatical structure does not end with the end of the line but rather is continued on one or more subsequent lines. Find two examples of run-on lines in "The Raven." Then identify two examples of the opposite of run-on lines, that is, **end-stopped lines** in which both the sense and the grammar are complete at the end of the line. What is the effect of including a variety of lines in a poem rather than only one or the other?

Responding in Writing

1. **Comic Strip.** The intense emotions and strange events of "The Raven" could make an interesting comic strip. Draw a comic strip telling the story of "The Raven." Include details about the changing appearance and emotions of the speaker, as well as details about the setting, such as the speaker's lonely, gloomy room.

2. **Fantasy.** Talking animals have appeared in folk tales, myths, children's stories, and fantasies for centuries. Write an original fantasy in which an animal that repeats a word or phrase plays a major role. First, decide on the characters and setting and make preliminary notes. Then map out the story events. Finally, write the story, including dialect from all characters.

Language Lab

Quotation Marks. Read the Language Arts Survey, 2.104, "Quotation Marks I." For each quotation below, add the correct punctuation.

1. It is a visitor tapping at my door I said.

2. Nevermore said the enigmatic raven.

3. I said that others had left me and that the raven would soon leave, too.

4. I pleaded Tell me if I shall ever escape from my memories of Lenore.

5. Take thy beak from out my heart, and take thy form from off my door I shrieked.

Study and Research Skills

Reference Works. Read the Language Arts Survey, 4.23, "Using Reference Works." Find at least two types of references that contain information about Edgar Allan Poe. List the names of the sources in which you found the information you were seeking.

PROJECTS

1. **Interview.** After researching Edgar Allan Poe, choose a critical point in his life and stage an interview with him. Work with a partner; one person should play Poe, and the other the interviewer. Have significant people from Poe's life appear with him on stage and review their relationships. Discuss the major events in Poe's life and his plans for the future.

2. **1840s Diorama.** In "The Raven," Poe refers to his chamber, in particular to its doorway, its shutters, and its furnishings. Find out how a typical parlor or bedroom of the 1840s would have been arranged and furnished. Construct a diorama, or model, of the room in which the events of the poem could have taken place.

"Old Ironsides"[1]
by Oliver Wendell Holmes

Ay, tear her tattered ensign[2] down!
    Long has it waved on high,
And many an eye has danced to see
    That banner in the sky;
5 Beneath it rung the battle shout,
    And burst the cannon's roar;—
The meteor of the ocean air
    Shall sweep the clouds no more!

Her deck, once red with heroes' blood
10   Where knelt the vanquished foe,
When winds were hurrying o'er the flood
    And waves were white below,
No more shall feel the victor's tread,
    Or know the conquered knee;—
15 The harpies[3] of the shore shall pluck
    The eagle of the sea!

O better that her shattered hulk
    Should sink beneath the wave;
Her thunders shook the mighty deep
20   And there should be her grave;
Nail to the mast her holy flag,
    Set every thread-bare sail,
And give her to the god of storms,—
    The lightning and the gale!

"Each and All"
by Ralph Waldo Emerson

Little thinks, in the field, yon red-cloaked clown,[4]
Of thee from the hill-top looking down;
The heifer that lows in the upland farm,
Far-heard, lows not thine ear to charm;
5 The sexton, tolling his bell at noon,
Deems not that great Napoleon
Stops his horse, and lists with delight,
Whilst his files sweep round yon Alpine height;
Nor knowest thou what argument
10 Thy life to thy neighbor's creed has lent.
All are needed by each one;
Nothing is fair or good alone.
I thought the sparrow's note from heaven,
Singing at dawn on the alder bough;
15 I brought him home, in his nest, at even;

He sings the song, but it cheers not now,
For I did not bring home the river and sky;—
He sang to my ear,—they sang to my eye.
The delicate shells lay on the shore;
20 The bubbles of the latest wave
Fresh pearls to their enamel gave;
And the bellowing of the savage sea
Greeted their safe escape to me.
I wiped away the weeds and foam,
25 I fetched my sea-born treasures home;
But the poor, unsightly, noisome things
Had left their beauty on the shore,
With the sun, and the sand, and the wild uproar.
The lover watched his graceful maid,
30 As 'mid the virgin train she strayed,
Nor knew her beauty's best attire
Was woven still by the snow-white choir.
At last she came to his hermitage,
Like the bird from the woodlands to the cage;—
35 The gay enchantment was undone,
A gentle wife, but fairy none.
Then I said, "I covet truth;
Beauty is unripe childhood's cheat;
I leave it behind with the games of youth."—
40 As I spoke, beneath my feet
The ground-pine curled its pretty wreath,
Running over the club-moss burrs;
I inhaled the violet's breath;
Around me stood the oaks and firs;
45 Pine-cones and acorns lay on the ground,
Over me soared the eternal sky,
Full of light and of deity;
Again I saw, again I heard,
The rolling river, the morning bird;—
50 Beauty through my senses stole;
I yielded myself to the perfect whole.

"Brahma"[5]
by Ralph Waldo Emerson

If the red slayer think he slays,
    Or if the slain think he is slain,
They know not well the subtle ways
    I keep, and pass, and turn again.

---

1. **Old Ironsides.** USS *Constitution*, oldest warship in U.S. Navy
2. **ensign.** Flag
3. **harpies.** In Greek mythology, harpies were voracious monsters.
4. **clown.** Peasant
5. **Brahma.** Supreme spirit of the universe in the Hindu religion

5 Far or forgot to me is near;
    Shadow and sunlight are the same;
The vanished gods to me appear;
    And one to me are shame and fame.

They reckon ill who leave me out;
10   When me they fly, I am the wings;
I am the doubter and the doubt,
    And I the hymn the Brahmin[1] sings.

The strong gods pine for my abode,
    And pine in vain the sacred Seven;[2]
15 But thou, meek lover of the good!
    Find me, and turn thy back on heaven.

"There's a certain Slant of light—"
by Emily Dickinson

There's a certain Slant of light,
Winter Afternoons—
That oppresses, like the Heft
Of Cathedral Tunes—

5 Heavenly Hurt, it gives us—
We can find no scar,
But internal difference,
Where the Meanings, are—

None may teach it—Any—
10 'Tis the Seal Despair—
An imperial affliction
Sent us of the Air—

When it comes, the Landscape listens—
Shadows—hold their breath—
15 When it goes, 'tis like the Distance
On the look of Death—

"I never saw a Moor—"
by Emily Dickinson

I never saw a Moor—
I never saw the Sea—
Yet know I how the heather looks
And what a Billow be.

5 I never spoke with God
Nor visited in Heaven—
Yet certain am I of the spot
As if the Checks[3] were given—

"'Hope' is the thing with feathers—"
by Emily Dickinson

"Hope" is the thing with feathers—
That perches in the soul—
And sings the tune without the words—
And never stops—at all—

5 And sweetest—in the Gale—is heard—
And sore must be the storm—
That could abash the little Bird
That kept so many warm—

I've heard it in the chilliest land—
10 And on the strangest Sea—
Yet, never, in Extremity,
It asked a crumb—of Me.

"Much Madness is divinest Sense—"
by Emily Dickinson

Much Madness is divinest Sense—
To a discerning Eye—
Much Sense—the starkest Madness—
'Tis the Majority
5 In this, as All, prevail—
Assent—and you are sane—
Demur—you're straightway dangerous—
And handled with a Chain—

"If you were coming in the Fall"
by Emily Dickinson

If you were coming in the Fall,
I'd brush the Summer by
With half a smile and half a spurn,
As Housewives do, a Fly.

5 If I could see you in a year,
I'd wind the months in balls—
And put them each in separate Drawers,
For fear the numbers fuse—

If only Centuries, delayed,
10 I'd count them in my Hand,

---

  1. **Brahmin.** Hindu priest
  2. **sacred Seven.** Most sacred of the Hindu saints
  3. **Checks.** Tickets on seats to mark the destination of passengers whose tickets have been collected

Subtracting, till my fingers dropped
Into Van Diemen's land.[1]

If certain, when this life was out—
That yours and mine, should be
15 I'd toss it yonder, like a Rind,
And take Eternity—

But, now, uncertain of the length
Of this, that is between,
It goads me, like the Goblin Bee—
20 That will not state—its sting.

"After great pain, a formal feeling comes—"
by Emily Dickinson

After great pain, a formal feeling comes—
The Nerves sit ceremonious, like Tombs—
The stiff Heart questions was it He, that bore,
And Yesterday, or Centuries before?

5 The Feet, mechanical, go round—
Of Ground, or Air, or Ought—
A Wooden way
Regardless grown,
A Quartz contentment, like a stone—

10 This is the Hour of Lead—
Remembered, if outlived,
As Freezing persons, recollect the Snow—
First—Chill—then Stupor—then the letting go—

"Alone"
by Edgar Allan Poe

From childhood's hour I have not been
As others were—I have not seen
As others saw—I could not bring
My passions from a common spring—
5 From the same source I have not taken
My sorrow—I could not awaken
My heart to joy at the same tone—
And all I lov'd—I lov'd alone—
Then—in my childhood—in the dawn
10 Of a most stormy life—was drawn
From ev'ry depth of good and ill
The mystery which binds me still—
From the torrent, or the fountain—
From the red cliff of the mountain—

15 From the sun that round me roll'd
In its autumn tint of gold—
From the lightning in the sky
As it pass'd me flying by—
From the thunder, and the storm—
20 And the cloud that took the form
(When the rest of Heaven was blue)
Of a demon in my view—

"To Helen"
by Edgar Allan Poe

Helen, thy beauty is to me
Like those Nicéan barks[2] of yore,
That gently, o'er a perfumed sea,
The weary, way-worn wanderer bore
5 To his own native shore.

On desperate seas long wont to roam,
Thy hyacinth hair, thy classic face,
Thy Naiad[3] airs have brought me home
To the glory that was Greece,
10 And the grandeur that was Rome.

Lo! in yon brilliant window-niche
How statue-like I see thee stand,
The agate lamp within thy hand!
Ah, Psyche,[4] from the regions which
15 Are Holy-Land!

"Annabel Lee"
by Edgar Allan Poe

It was many and many a year ago,
In a kingdom by the sea
That a maiden there lived whom you may know,
By the name of ANNABEL LEE;
5 And this maiden she lived with no other thought
Than to love and be loved by me.

I was a child and she was a child,
In this kingdom by the sea;
But we loved with a love that was more than love—
10 I and my ANNABEL LEE—
With a love that the wingèd seraphs[5] of heaven
Coveted her and me.

---

1. **Van Diemen's land.** Tasmania; island south of Australia discovered by the Dutch; once named for Van Diemen, the Dutch governor
2. **Nicéan barks.** Boats of Nice, France
3. **Naiad.** Fairylike
4. **Psyche.** Goddess of the soul
5. **seraphs.** Highest order of angels

And this was the reason that, long ago,
　　In this kingdom by the sea,
15 A wind blew out of a cloud, chilling
　　　My beautiful ANNABEL LEE;
So that her highborn kinsmen came
　　And bore her away from me,
To shut her up in a sepulchre
20 　　In this kingdom by the sea.

The angels, not half so happy in heaven,
　　Went envying her and me—
Yes!—that was the reason (as all men know,
　　In this kingdom by the sea)
25 That the wind came out of the cloud by night,
　　Chilling and killing my ANNABEL LEE.

But our love it was stronger by far than the love
　　Of those who were older than we—
　　Of many far wiser than we—
30 And neither the angels in heaven above,
　　Nor the demons down under the sea,
Can ever dissever my soul from the soul
　　Of the beautiful ANNABEL LEE:

For the moon never beams, without bringing me
　　dreams
35 　Of the beautiful ANNABEL LEE;
And the stars never rise, but I feel the bright eyes
　　Of the beautiful ANNABEL LEE:
And so, all the night tide, I lie down by the side
Of my darling—my darling—my life and my bride,
40 　In her sepulchre there by the sea—
　　In her tomb by the sounding sea.

"The Arsenal at Springfield"
by Henry Wadsworth Longfellow

This is the Arsenal. From floor to ceiling,
　　Like a huge organ, rise the burnished arms:
But from their silent pipes no anthem pealing
　　Startles the villages with strange alarms.

5 Ah! what a sound will rise, how wild and dreary,
　　When the death angel touches those swift keys!
What loud lament and dismal Miserere[1]
　　Will mingle with their awful symphonies!

I hear even now the infinite fierce chorus,
10 　The cries of agony, the endless groan,
Which, through the ages that have gone before us,
　　In long reverberations reach our own.

On helm and harness rings the Saxon hammer,
　　Through Cimbric[2] forest roars the Norseman's song,
15 And loud, amid the universal clamor,

O'er distant deserts sounds the Tartar[3] gong.
I hear the Florentine, who from his palace
　　Wheels out his battle bell with dreadful din,
And Aztec priests upon their teocallis[4]
20 　Beat the wild war drums made of serpent's skin;

The tumult of each sacked and burning village;
　　The shout that every prayer for mercy drowns;
The soldiers' revels in the midst of pillage;
　　The wail of famine in beleaguered towns;

25 The bursting shell, the gateway wrenched asunder,
　　The rattling musketry, the clashing blade;
And ever and anon, in tones of thunder
　　The diapason[5] of the cannonade,

Is it, O man, with such discordant noises,
30 　With such accursed instruments as these,
Thou drownest Nature's sweet and kindly voices,
　　And jarrest the celestial harmonies?

Were half the power that fills the world with terror,
　　Were half the wealth bestowed on camps and courts,
35 Given to redeem the human mind from error;
　　There were no need of arsenals or forts:

The warrior's name would be a name abhorred!
　　And every nation, that should lift again
Its hand against a brother, on its forehead
40 　Would wear forevermore the curse of Cain![6]

Down the dark future, through long generations,
　　The echoing sounds grow fainter and then cease:
And like a bell, with solemn, sweet vibrations,
　　I hear once more the voice of Christ say, "Peace!"

45 Peace! and no longer from its brazen portals
　　The blast of War's great organ shakes the skies!
But beautiful as songs of the immortals,
　　The holy melodies of love arise.

---

　1. **Miserere.** Biblical reference to Psalm 51, which begins "Have mercy upon me, O God."
　2. **Cimbric.** Of a Germanic people from central Europe
　3. **Tartar.** The Tartars ruled parts of Asia and Eastern Europe in the fourteenth and fifteenth centuries.
　4. **teocallis.** Temples erected by the Aztecs in Mexico and Central America
　5. **diapason.** Entire range of an activity
　6. **Cain.** According to the Bible, Cain was the first murderer.

"A Psalm of Life"
by Henry Wadsworth Longfellow

"Life that shall send
A challenge to its end,
And when it comes, say, 'Welcome, friend.'"

What the Heart of the Young Man Said to the Psalmist

I
Tell me not, in mournful numbers,
    Life is but an empty dream!
For the soul is dead that slumbers,
    And things are not what they seem.

II
Life is real—life is earnest—
    And the grave is not its goal:
Dust thou art, to dust returnest,
    Was not spoken of the soul.

III
Not enjoyment, and not sorrow,
    Is our destin'd end or way;
But to act, that each to-morrow
    Find us farther than to-day.

IV
Art is long, and time is fleeting,
    And our hearts, though stout and brave,
Still, like muffled drums, are beating
    Funeral marches to the grave.

V
In the world's broad field of battle,
    In the bivouac of Life,
Be not like dumb, driven cattle!
    Be a hero in the strife!

VI
Trust not Future, howe'er pleasant!
    Let the dead Past bury its dead!
Act—act in the glorious Present!
    Heart within, and God o'er head!

VII
Lives of great men all remind us
    We can make our lives sublime,
And, departing, leave behind us
    Footsteps on the sands of time.

VIII
Footsteps, that, perhaps another,
    Sailing o'er life's solemn main,
A forlorn and shipwreck'd brother,
    Seeing, shall take heart again.

IX
Let us then be up and doing,
    With a heart for any fate;
Still achieving, still pursuing,
    Learn to labor and to wait.

"Ichabod!"[1]
by John Greenleaf Whittier

So fallen! so lost! the light withdrawn
    Which once he wore!
The glory from his gray hairs gone
    Forevermore!

5 Revile him not—the Tempter hath
    A snare for all;
And pitying tears, not scorn and wrath,
    Befit his fall!

Oh! dumb be passion's stormy rage,
10   When he who might
Have lighted up and led his age,
    Falls back in night.

Scorn! would the angels laugh, to mark
    A bright soul driven,
15 Fiend-goaded, down the endless dark,
    From hope and heaven!

Let not the land, once proud of him,
    Insult him now,
Nor brand with deeper shame his dim,
20   Dishonored brow.

But let its humbled sons, instead,
    From sea to lake,
A long lament, as for the dead,
    In sadness make.

25 Of all we loved and honored, nought
    Save power remains—
A fallen angel's pride of thought,
    Still strong in chains.

All else is gone; from those great eyes
30   The soul has fled:
When faith is lost, when honor dies,
    The man is dead!

Then, pay the reverence of old days
    To his dead fame;
35 Walk backward, with averted gaze,
    And hide the shame!

---

1. **Icabod!** The title of the poem refers to 1 Samuel 4:21, which reads, "And she named the child Ichabod, saying, The glory is departed from Israel." Icabod here refers to Daniel Webster, Senator from Massachusetts, whose support of the Fugitive Slave Act led Whittier, a staunch abolitionist, to write this work.

from *Snow-Bound: A Winter Idyl*
by John Greenleaf Whittier

The sun that brief December day
Rose cheerless over hills of gray,
And, darkly circled, gave at noon
A sadder light than waning moon
5 Slow tracing down the thickening sky
Its mute and ominous prophecy,
A portent seeming less than threat,
It sank from sight before it set.
A chill no coat, however stout,
10 Of homespun stuff could quite shut out,
A hard, dull bitterness of cold,
That checked, mid-vein, the circling race
Of life-blood in the sharpened face,
The coming of the snow-storm told.

15 The wind blew east: we heard the roar
Of Ocean on his wintry shore,
And felt the strong pulse throbbing there
Beat with low rhythm our inland air.

Meanwhile we did our nightly chores,—
20 Brought in the wood from out of doors,
Littered the stalls, and from the mows
Raked down the herd's-grass for the cows;
Heard the horse whinnying for his corn;
And, sharply clashing horn on horn,
25 Impatient down the stanchion rows
The cattle shake their walnut bows;
While, peering from his early perch
Upon the scaffold's pole of birch,
The cock his crested helmet bent
30 And down his querulous challenge sent.

Unwarmed by any sunset light
The gray day darkened into night,
A night made hoary with the swarm
And whirl-dance of the blinding storm,
35 As zigzag wavering to and fro
Crossed and recrossed the winged snow:
And ere the early bed-time came
The white drift piled the window-frame,
And through the glass the clothes-line posts
40 Looked in like tall and sheeted ghosts.
So all night long the storm roared on:
The morning broke without a sun;

In tiny spherule traced with lines
Of Nature's geometric signs,
45 In starry flake, and pellicle,
All day the hoary meteor fell;
And, when the second morning shone,
We looked upon a world unknown,
On nothing we could call our own.
50 Around the glistening wonder bent
The blue walls of the firmament,
No cloud above, no earth below,—
A universe of sky and snow!
The old familiar sights of ours
55 Took marvellous shapes, strange domes and towers
Rose up where sty or corn-crib stood,
Or garden wall, or belt of wood;
A smooth white mound the brush-pile showed,
A fenceless drift what once was road;
60 The bridle-post an old man sat
With loose-flung coat and high cocked hat;
The well-curb had a Chinese roof
And even the long sweep, high aloof,
In its slant splendor, seemed to tell
65 Of Pisa's leaning miracle.

◆ ◆ ◆

740 Yet, haply, in some lull of life,
Some Truce of God which breaks its strife,
The worldling's eyes shall gather dew,
Dreaming in throngful city ways
Of winter joys his boyhood knew
745 And dear and early friends—the few
Who yet remain—shall pause to view
These Flemish pictures of old days;
Sit with me by the homestead hearth,
And stretch the hands of memory forth
750 To warm them at the wood-fire's blaze!
And thanks untraced to lips unknown
Shall greet me like the odors blown
From unseen meadows newly mown,
Or lilies floating in some pond,
755 Wood-fringed, the wayside gaze beyond;
The traveller owns the grateful sense
Of sweetness near, he knows not whence,
And, pausing, takes with forehead bare
The benediction of the air.

UNIT REVIEW

New England Renaissance Poetry

VOCABULARY FROM THE SELECTIONS

adjure, 341
beguiling, 342
blight, 291
brink, 312
censer, 342
civility, 332
clod, 292
communion, 291
craven, 340
earnest, 303
entreat, 339

fetter, 302
hoary, 293
insensible, 292
lapse, 293
lattice, 340
mien, 340
morrow, 341
obeisance, 340
ominous, 342
patriarch, 293
pensive, 293

plume, 343
quaff, 342
sepulcher, 293
sinewy, 307
surcease, 339
tempest, 342
undaunted, 342
venerable, 293
wrought, 308

LITERARY TERMS

alliteration, 310, 320, 344
apology, 327
apostrophe, 300, 305, 320
assonance, 334
blank verse, 295
couplet, 305
elaboration, 295
euphony, 300
extended metaphor, 334
image, 310

irony, 334
meter, 319, 327
mood, 315
narrative poem, 310
onomatopoeia, 337
personification, 327
point of view, 315, 334
repetition, 331
rhetorical question, 305
rhyme, 323, 344

Romanticism, 323
run-on line, 344
sight rhyme, 331
slant rhyme, 331
stanza, 300, 305, 334
symbol, 337
synaesthesia, 336
tone, 315

SYNTHESIS: QUESTIONS FOR WRITING, RESEARCH, OR DISCUSSION

GENRE STUDIES

1. Romantic Poetry. Romantic poetry celebrates the value of the common person, individual liberty, the common bonds of all people, emotion over reason, and the connection of human beings to the natural world. Think about these poems: "Thanatopsis," by William Cullen Bryant; "Stanzas on Freedom," by James Russell Lowell; "The Village Blacksmith," by Henry Wadsworth Longfellow; ""Telling the Bees" and "Snow-Bound: A Winter Idyl," by John Greenleaf Whittier; and "The Raven," "Alone," and "Annabel Lee," by Edgar Allan Poe. What makes each of these a fine example of a Romantic poem?

2. Didacticism. A work of **didactic literature** has as its primary purpose teaching a moral lesson. In the nineteenth century, didactic literature was quite popular. What qualities make "Thanatopsis," by Bryant; "The Chambered Nautilus," by Holmes; "The Village Blacksmith" and "A Psalm of Life," by Longfellow; and "The Rhodora" and "Each and All," by Emerson, examples of didactic poetry? What lesson does each of these poems teach?

THEMATIC STUDIES

3. Individualism. Much of American literature celebrates the values of individualism and self-reliance. How is the theme of individualism treated in "The Soul selects her own Society—" and "This is my letter to the World," by Dickinson? in "Alone," by Poe?

HISTORICAL/BIOGRAPHICAL STUDIES

4. Occasional Verse. Occasional verse is poetry written for a specific occasion. What occasions prompted the writing of Emerson's "Concord Hymn," Whittier's "Icabod!," and Holmes's "Old Ironsides"? Do some research on these occasions and describe each occasion and the poet's response to it.

5. Slavery. Many of the poets of the New England Renaissance were vehemently opposed to the institution of slavery. What abolitionist sentiments are expressed in Whittier's "Icabod!" and Lowell's "Stanzas on Freedom"? What message does each poet have for the proponents of slavery?

LANGUAGE LAB ### EDITING FOR ERRORS IN MODIFIERS

A **modifier** is a word that modifies—that is, changes or explains—the meaning of another word. When editing your writing, you should watch carefully for these errors in modifier usage.

<table>
<tr><th colspan="2">MODIFIER USAGE</th></tr>
</table>

Modifiers with Action and Linking Verbs

To modify the subject of a **linking verb,** use an **adjective.** To modify an **action verb,** use an **adverb.**

LINKING VERB AND ADJECTIVE: By the 1820s, Washington Irving's reputation *was established* both in the United States and in Europe.

ACTION VERB AND ADVERB: Throughout his early adulthood, Irving *lived mostly* in England.

Comparison of Adjectives and Adverbs

Each modifier has three forms of comparison: **positive, comparative,** and **superlative.** Most one-syllable modifiers and some two-syllable modifiers form the comparative and superlative degrees by adding *–er* and *–est.* Other two-syllable modifiers, and all modifiers of more than two syllables, use *more* and *most* to form these degrees. To show a decrease in the quality of any modifier, form the comparative and superlative degrees by using *less* and *least.*

EXAMPLES: *sturdy, sturdier, sturdiest*
popular, more popular, most popular
successful, less successful, least successful

Illogical and Double Comparisons

An **illogical comparison** occurs when one member of a group is compared with the group of which it is a part. Clarify an illogical comparison by including the word *other* or *else* in the sentence. A **double comparison** occurs when two comparative forms or two superlative forms are used to modify the same word. Correct a double comparison by editing out one of the comparative or superlative forms.

ILLOGICAL: Ralph Waldo Emerson embodied Transcendentalism more than nineteenth-century American writers.

LOGICAL: Ralph Waldo Emerson embodied Transcendentalism more than any other nineteenth-century American writer.

DOUBLE COMPARISON: From his most youngest days, William Cullen Bryant wanted to be a poet.

SINGLE COMPARISON: From his youngest days, William Cullen Bryant wanted to be a poet.

Double Negatives

A **double negative** is a construction in which two negative words are used instead of one. Do not use more than one negative word, such as *no, none, not* (and its contraction, *–n't*), *nothing, barely, hardly,* or *scarcely,* in the same sentence.

DOUBLE NEGATIVE: Transcendentalists didn't adhere to none of the laws of eighteenth-century philosophy.

SINGLE NEGATIVE: Transcendentalists didn't adhere to the laws of eighteenth-century philosophy.

LANGUAGE ARTS SURVEY

For additional help, see the Language Arts Survey, 2.85.

LANGUAGE ARTS SURVEY

For additional help, see the Language Arts Survey, 2.86.

LANGUAGE ARTS SURVEY

For additional help, see the Language Arts Survey, 2.87.

LANGUAGE ARTS SURVEY

For additional help, see the Language Arts Survey, 2.88.

LANGUAGE ARTS
SURVEY

For additional help,
see the Language
Arts Survey, 2.89.

Other Problems with Modifiers

Distinguish between the following modifiers: *this* and *these, that* and *those, those* and *them, bad* and *badly,* and *good* and *well.*

Exercise A Correcting Errors in Modifier Usage

Rewrite the following sentences, correcting the errors in modifier usage.

EXAMPLE: William Cullen Bryant held steady to his Unitarian beliefs.
William Cullen Bryant held steadily to his Unitarian beliefs.

LANGUAGE ARTS

For additional help,
see the Language
Arts Survey,
2.85–2.89.

1. Captain Ahab can't think of nothing but the White Whale.

2. Emerson's hymn commemorates the many soldiers who died heroic at the battles of Lexington and Concord.

3. Rappaccini's daughter felt herself growing more weaker.

4. Before her death, the woman willed them keepsakes to her relatives.

5. The fly sounded more louder than anything in the room.

6. The prisoner edged careful away from the deep pit.

7. Thoreau's experiment at Walden Pond went good.

8. The young student felt badly for the poisoned girl and tried to cure her.

9. Emily Dickinson seems to have thought good of death.

10. I was so frightened by them scenes of suspense that I couldn't hardly finish "The Pit and the Pendulum."

Exercise B Avoiding Errors in Modifier Usage

In each sentence below, choose the correct word from within the parentheses.

EXAMPLE: After they worked in the garden, a dip in Walden Pond felt (good, well).
good

LANGUAGE ARTS
SURVEY

For additional help,
see the Language
Arts Survey,
2.85–2.89.

1. After many battles, the *Constitution,* nicknamed *Old Ironsides,* was damaged (bad, badly) and scheduled for destruction.

2. Oliver Wendell Holmes (could, couldn't) hardly believe the news of the *Constitution's* fate.

3. Holmes wrote (eloquent, eloquently) in the ship's defense in his poem "Old Ironsides."

4. Holmes's poem received such a (good, well) response that the destruction plans were canceled and the ship was rebuilt.

5. Today, the reconstructed *Constitution* stands (majestic, majestically) on exhibit in Charlestown, Massachusetts.

Rainy Day in Camp. *Winslow Homer, 1871. The Metropolitan Museum of Art. Gift of Mrs. William F. Milton, 1923 (23.77.1)*

We here highly resolve that these dead shall not have died in vain, that this nation, under God, shall have a new birth of freedom.

—Abraham Lincoln
The Gettysburg Address

A House Divided

Farm, Massanutten Mountains

In the early years of the nineteenth century, the new nation developed in two different directions. The North became a center for industrial manufacturing and the export of finished goods. The South, in contrast, was almost entirely agricultural, producing rice, tobacco, cotton, and sugar and exporting many of these goods to Great Britain. To protect its export business, the North favored high tariffs on imported goods. The South, which depended on imports for finished products, naturally opposed high tariffs. The economic differences between the North and the South created enormous tensions, exacerbated by fundamental differences in lifestyle. Many people in the North lived in cities and towns and worked in factories, in mills, or on small farms. Most of the people in the South worked the land, some on small farms and some on large rice, tobacco, cotton, and sugar plantations.

The Issue of Slavery

At the very inception of the United States, differences arose between Northerners and Southerners over the issue of slavery. Thomas Jefferson had included a strong antislavery statement in his draft of the Declaration of Independence, but pressure from Southern delegates led to its deletion from the declaration in its final form. As the **plantation system** developed, the South began to depend more and more on imported slaves to carry out the work of its large "factory farms." While some Southerners opposed slavery, most saw it as a necessary part of the Southern economy. The slave trade was ended by law in 1808, but smuggling of slaves into the United States continued until the outbreak of the Civil War in 1860. By 1830, there were approximately three million slaves of African descent in the United States. About 2,500,000 of these people were forced agricultural laborers. By 1860, the number of enslaved blacks in the country had reached almost four million.

Apologists for slavery in America have often argued that the institution was benign because owners treated their "valuable property" well; however, the truth is slavery was brutal. Slaves typically worked hard, from sunup to sundown. They were fed meagerly; lived in squalid, flea-infested shacks; were often whipped for minor "offenses" by cruel overseers; were forbidden by law to learn to read and write; were sold away from their wives, husbands, or children; and suffered the basic indignity of continual subservience to others. Thousands of slaves ran away to freedom or to find family members from whom they had been separated, and hundreds revolted against their owners. In 1800, the Virginia militia put down a revolt of over a thousand slaves near Richmond. In 1822, a free black organizer named **Denmark Vesey** was hanged for attempting to organize a slave revolt in Charleston. In 1831, **Nat Turner** succeeded in organizing a revolt that led to bloody fighting and the deaths of 160 people.

Illustration from abolitionist literature

In the North, a strong movement emerged for the abolition, or ending by law, of slavery. The leader of the Northern abolitionists was **William Lloyd Garrison,** whose newspaper, *The Liberator,* called for an immediate end to the South's "peculiar institution." Other important antislavery publications included the first black-owned newspaper, **John Russwurm** and **Samuel Cornish's** *Freedom's Journal,* and **Frederick Douglass's** *The North Star.* The New England Anti-Slavery Society, based in Massachusetts, and the Free African Society of Philadelphia became important voices in the antislavery movement. Some abolitionists, such as **Elijah P. Lovejoy** and **Charles T. Torrey,** both Protestant ministers, died for the cause. Other abolitionists organized what became known as the **Underground Railroad**, a system of safe houses and guides for leading runaways from slave states in the South to free states in the North. The most famous conductor on the Underground Railroad was **Harriet Tubman**, herself a runaway slave.

Robert E. Lee

Ulysses S. Grant

By the 1850s, a great deal of national energy, both political and literary, was focused on the question of slavery. At the center of concern were two issues: fugitive slave laws and the status of slavery in new territories. The **Fugitive Slave Act** of 1850 established that "good citizens" in free states could be deputized to assist federal marshals in the capture of runaway slaves. The act also imposed heavy fines for anyone assisting a runaway, a provision that greatly heightened tensions in the North, where many prominent people were involved directly or indirectly in the abolitionist movement and in the Underground Railroad. One such Northerner, **Henry David Thoreau,** in a speech called "Slavery in Massachusetts," spoke out publicly after a famous local case about the enforcement of the act, asserting that he had "lost his country." In 1852, **Harriet Beecher Stowe's** antislavery novel *Uncle Tom's Cabin* became a bestseller, helping to turn the tide of opinion in the North against slavery.

In the years preceding the Civil War, the country debated the question of whether slavery would be allowed in newly added territories such as California, New Mexico, Utah, Kansas, and Nebraska. The **Missouri Compromise** of 1820 allowed slavery only south of the 36°30' parallel. A second compromise, put forward by Senator **Henry Clay** of Kentucky in 1850, called for California to be a free state, for new territories to decide on their own whether to be free or slave, and provided protections for slavery as it already existed in the South. This compromise was supported by **Daniel Webster** of Massachusetts, who believed it necessary in order to preserve the Union. In 1854, after much debate, the **Kansas-Nebraska Act** was passed, allowing voters in these new states to decide the issue of slavery for themselves. There followed bitter, bloody fighting in Kansas between proslavery and antislavery forces. Among the latter was a fiery militant named **John Brown.** In 1857, the Supreme Court's **Dred Scott decision** upheld the right of a slave owner to continue to own a slave, even if he moved into free territory. In the presidential election of 1857 and in the debates between senatorial candidates **Stephen Douglas** and **Abraham Lincoln** in 1858, the issue of slavery in new territories and states was paramount. Then, in 1859, John Brown led a raid on the government arsenal at **Harpers Ferry,** Virginia, hoping to capture weapons and to turn those over to slaves, thus beginning a slave revolt throughout the South. Brown was hanged and became a martyr to the antislavery cause, celebrated in "The Battle Hymn of the Republic."

SECESSION AND CIVIL WAR

When Abraham Lincoln became president in 1860, seven states—South Carolina, Mississippi, Florida, Alabama, Georgia, Louisiana, and Texas—had already voted to secede from the Union. In 1861, delegates from throughout the South met in Montgomery, Alabama, and formed the **Confederate States of America,** choosing **Jefferson Davis** of Mississippi as their new president. On April 12, 1861, Confederate troops fired on the federal stronghold at **Fort Sumter,** on Charleston Harbor, thus beginning the most troubled period in American history. Lincoln offered to put Virginian **Robert E. Lee** in charge of the Union

Ulysses S. Grant

army, but Lee, who was initially opposed to secession, declined, not wishing to fight against the people of his own state. When Virginia seceded from the Union, Lee took command of the Grand Army of the Confederacy.

Many people on both sides expected the **Civil War** to be over in a month, but it lasted five years. Union troops lost the first major campaign of the war, suffering defeat at the First Battle of Bull Run by troops under **Stonewall Jackson** and **P. G. T. Beauregard.** That defeat moved the Union to action. The Grand Army of the Potomac was organized under **George B. McClellan.** In the fighting that followed at Shiloh, New Orleans, Bull Run, Antietam, Fredericksburg, Chancellorsville, Gettysburg, Vicksburg, and Petersburg, among other places, 360,000 Union soldiers and 329,000 Confederate soldiers lost their lives, many more from disease than from battle. Union forces were at first plagued by poor leadership, but eventually, under the able direction of **Ulysses S. Grant,** the hero of the Battle of Vicksburg, they were able to bring the war to an end, invading the Confederate capital of Richmond, Virginia, in April 1865. General Robert E. Lee surrendered to Grant at **Appomattox Court House** in Virginia on April 9.

THE LITERATURE OF ABOLITION AND PROTEST

Well before the war there was a large and substantial body of abolitionist writing, including the work of several of the writers of the New England Renaissance such as Emerson, Thoreau, Whittier, and Lowell. Abolitionist societies, like the New England Anti-Slavery Society, sprang up as networks for support; by 1850 there were about two thousand of these. Publishers such as William Lloyd Garrison and Frederick Douglass made important contributions to the cause, as did novelists such as Harriet Beecher Stowe.

Though some of this literature was written by Northern whites, especially women, who were attempting in part to appeal to the family concerns of their Southern female counterparts, African Americans in the South developed two original forms of literature that played an important role in the abolitionist movement. First was the **spiritual**, which combined

Walt Whitman

African and European music and a poetic text using religious images from the Bible to create dramatic symbols of the suffering of slaves and their hopes for deliverance. Second was the **slave narrative,** an autobiographical account of the life of a former slave, chronicling the extraordinary conditions under which he or she had lived. Ranging in length from a few pages to an entire book, hundreds of slave narratives were published in the decades before the war. These narratives were remarkable for a number of reasons, not least of which was that most of their authors had come from Southern states that by law prohibited teaching blacks to read or write. They deployed various literary strategies designed to gain sympathy without offending their primarily white audiences, many of whom were unschooled in the gorier details and horrors of slavery and not anxious to see evil in their Southern Christian counterparts. For example, Frederick Douglass's narrative, excerpted in this unit, tries repeatedly to put blame on the institution of slavery rather than on individual owners; of one owner's wife Douglass noted, "When I went there, she was a pious, warm, and tender-hearted woman. . . . Slavery soon proved its ability to divest her of these heavenly qualities."

THE LITERATURE OF THE WAR

Much of the literature during and immediately after the war addressed itself to a concern with restoring a national identity, hoping to find threads of unity amid the horrific bloodletting, and often doing this by appealing to and honoring the courage and heroism of those who had fought. Lincoln, in the speeches excerpted in this unit, Lee, and **Walt Whitman,** in his elegy to Lincoln, honor the efforts of those in the war while insisting in various ways on a national identity and on reconciliation. As Whitman expressed it in one poem, "For my enemy is dead, a man divine as myself is dead."

In the first decades after the war, writings about the war became vehicles for achieving that reconciliation and reshaping the nation's self-image or identity. Much of this writing romanticized the war and the contributions of those who participated in it, glorifying the United States itself in the process; however, there also emerged a contrary voice in the works of **Ambrose Bierce** and **Stephen Crane.** These writers explored the darker aspects of the war, portraying courage and heroism as myths, seeing actions as the result of accident or panic under environmental pressures rather than as reflections of human strength and triumph.

Echoes:
Slavery and the Civil War

"'A house divided against itself cannot stand.' I believe this government cannot endure, permanently half slave and half free."

—Abraham Lincoln, in a speech delivered in 1858

"In thinking of America, I sometimes find myself admiring her bright blue sky—her grand old woods—her fertile fields—her beautiful rivers—her mighty lakes and star-crowned mountains. But my rapture is soon checked when I remember that all is cursed with the infernal spirit of slave-holding and wrong; When I remember that with the waters of her noblest rivers, the tears of my brethren are borne to the ocean, disregarded and forgotten; That her most fertile fields drink daily of the warm blood of my outraged sisters, I am filled with unutterable loathing."

—Frederick Douglass, former slave, editor of *The North Star,* and crusader against slavery

"I can anticipate no greater calamity for the country than a dissolution of the Union. It would be an accumulation of all the evils we complain of, and I am willing to sacrifice everything but honor for its preservation. . . . Secession is nothing but revolution."

—Robert E. Lee, later leader of the Confederate forces, writing about secession in a letter to his son dated January 1861

"My paramount object in this struggle is to save the Union. . . . If I could save the Union without freeing any slave, I would do it; and if I could save it by freeing all the slaves, I would do it; and if I could save it by freeing some and leaving others alone, I would also do that. . . . I have here stated my purpose according to my views of official duty and I intend no modification of my oft-expressed personal wish that all men everywhere could be free."

—Abraham Lincoln, in a letter to Horace Greeley, dated August 22, 1862

from *Narrative of the Life of Frederick Douglass, an American Slave, Written by Himself*

by Frederick Douglass

ABOUT THE AUTHOR

Frederick Douglass (1818–1895) was an eloquent speaker, a tireless campaigner against slavery, and a champion of civil rights for women and for persons of African descent. Born a slave in Maryland, Douglass was taught to read and write in violation of a Maryland state law prohibiting the education of African Americans. After escaping to Massachusetts in 1838, he associated with such prominent abolitionists as William Lloyd Garrison, J. G. Birney, and John Brown, and he became an influential force in the fight to end slavery. In 1845, he published the first of three autobiographies, *Narrative of the Life of Frederick Douglass, an American Slave*, in which he told of his childhood, his youth, and his escape to freedom. After traveling in Britain and Ireland, where he lectured for the abolitionist cause, Douglass returned to America. Friends helped him to buy his freedom, and he moved to Rochester, New York, where he began publishing an abolitionist newspaper, *The North Star*, later called *Frederick Douglass's Weekly* and *Frederick Douglass's Monthly*. In 1855, he published an expanded, updated version of his autobiography, *My Bondage and My Freedom,* which was followed in 1881 by a final autobiographical volume, *The Life and Times of Frederick Douglass*. Unjustly implicated in John Brown's attack on the arsenal at Harpers Ferry, West Virginia, which Brown had hoped would instigate a slave revolt, Douglass fled to Canada and England before the Civil War. During the war, he returned to the United States where he helped to organize regiments of African-American soldiers to fight for the Northern cause, and he personally called on Abraham Lincoln, sixteenth president of the United States, to secure fair compensation for those soldiers. He also worked as a conductor on the Underground Railroad. After the war, Douglass held a number of political offices, including United States marshall and recorder of deeds for the District of Columbia, minister to Haiti, and chargé d'affaires to Santo Domingo. He also continued his political activities, lobbying for legislation to prevent discrimination of all kinds.

ABOUT THE SELECTION

Frederick Douglass had already established himself as an orator of exceptional ability when he determined to commit the heart of his speeches, that is, his experiences under slavery, to writing in *Narrative of the Life of Frederick Douglass, an American Slave, Written by Himself*. Knowing that publication of the book would reveal his identity and make him a target for slave-catchers, he went to England until money could be raised to buy his freedom.

READER'S JOURNAL

What is your favorite song? What feelings do you usually have when you hear it or sing it? Write in your journal about how music makes you feel and about how your feelings affect your choices of music.

WRITING SKILLS

Read the Language Arts Survey, 1.6, "Choosing a Purpose or Aim." Then identify the mode of Douglass's writing and the reasons it was so well suited for his purpose.

FROM

Narrative of the Life of Frederick Douglass, an American Slave, Written by Himself

FREDERICK DOUGLASS

Colonel Lloyd[1] kept from three to four hundred slaves on his home plantation, and owned a large number more on the neighboring farms belonging to him. The names of the farms nearest to the home plantation were Wye Town and New Design. Wye Town was under the overseership of a man named Noah Willis. New Design was under the overseership of a Mr. Townsend. The overseers of these, and all the rest of the farms, numbering over twenty, received advice and direction from the managers of the home plantation. This was the great business place. It was the seat of government for the whole twenty farms.[2] All disputes among the overseers were settled here. . . .

Here, too, the slaves of all the other farms received their monthly allowance of food, and their yearly clothing. The men and women slaves received, as their monthly allowance of food, eight pounds of pork, or its equivalent in fish, and one bushel of corn meal. Their yearly clothing consisted of two coarse linen shirts, one pair of linen trousers, like the shirts, one jacket, one pair of trousers for winter, made of coarse negro cloth, one pair of stockings, and one pair of shoes; the whole of which could not have cost more

How many slaves did Colonel Lloyd own?

What happened at the "home plantation"?

---

1. **Colonel Lloyd.** Owner of the large plantation in Maryland where Douglass was born
2. **twenty farms.** Lloyd family papers indicate only thirteen farms.

When was Douglass separated from his mother? What happened to children who were separated from their mothers in this way?

than seven dollars. The allowance of the slave children was given to their mothers, or the old women having the care of them. My mother and I were separated when I was but an infant—before I knew her as my mother. It is a common custom, in the part of Maryland from which I ran away, to part children from their mothers at a very early age. Frequently, before the child has reached its twelfth month, its mother is taken from it, and hired out on some farm a considerable distance off, and the child is placed under the care of an old woman, too old for field labor. The children unable to work in the field had neither shoes, stockings, jackets, nor trousers, given to them; their clothing consisted of two coarse linen shirts per year. When these failed them, they went naked until the next allowance-day. Children from seven to ten years old, of both sexes, almost naked, might be seen at all seasons of the year.

The home plantation of Colonel Lloyd wore the appearance of a country village. All the mechanical operations for all the farms were performed here. The shoemaking and mending, the blacksmithing, cartwrighting, coopering,[3] weaving, and grain-grinding, were all performed by the slaves on the home plantation. The whole place wore a businesslike aspect very unlike the neighboring farms. The number of houses, too, conspired to give it advantage over the neighboring farms. It was called by the slaves the *Great House Farm*. Few privileges were esteemed higher, by the slaves of the out-farms, than that of being selected to do errands at the Great House Farm. It was associated in their

How did some slaves feel about doing errands at the Great House Farm? Why?

minds with greatness. A representative could not be prouder of his election to a seat in the American Congress, than a slave on one of the out-farms would be of his election to do errands at the Great House Farm. They regarded it as evidence of great confidence reposed in them by their overseers; and it was on this account, as well as a constant desire to be out of the field from under the driver's lash, that they esteemed it a high privilege, one worth careful living for. He was called the smartest and most trusty fellow, who had this honor conferred upon him the most frequently. The competitors for this office sought as <u>diligently</u> to please their overseers, as the office-seekers in the political parties seek to please and deceive the people. The same traits of character might be seen in Colonel Lloyd's slaves, as are seen in the slaves of the political parties.

The slaves selected to go to the Great House Farm, for the monthly allowance for themselves and their fellow slaves, were peculiarly enthusiastic. While on their way, they would make the dense old woods, for miles around, reverberate with their wild songs, revealing at once the highest joy and the deepest sadness. They would compose and sing as they went along, consulting neither time nor tune. The thought that came up, came out—if not in the word, in the sound—and as frequently in the one as in the other. They would sometimes sing the most pathetic sentiment in the most <u>rapturous</u> tone, and the most rapturous sentiment in the most pathetic tone. Into all of their songs they

---

3. **cartwrighting, coopering.** *Cartwrighting*—building carts; *coopering*—making barrels

---

WORDS FOR EVERYDAY USE:

dil • i • gent • ly (dil´ə jənt lē) *adv.* painstakingly, industriously

rap • tur • ous (rap´ chər əs) *adj.* full of joy or pleasure

would manage to weave something of the Great House Farm. Especially would they do this when leaving home. They would then sing most exultingly the following words:

> I am going away to the Great House Farm!
> O, yea! O, yea! O!

This they would sing, as a chorus, to words which to many would seem unmeaning jargon, but which, nevertheless, were full of meaning to themselves. I have sometimes thought that the mere hearing of those songs would do more to impress some minds with the horrible character of slavery, than the reading of whole volumes of philosophy on the subject could do.

I did not, when a slave, understand the deep meaning of those rude and apparently incoherent songs. I was myself within the circle; so that I neither saw nor heard as those without might see and hear. They told a tale of woe which was then altogether beyond my feeble comprehension; they were tones loud, long, and deep; they breathed the prayer and complaint of souls boiling over with the bitterest anguish. Every tone was a testimony against slavery, and a prayer to God for deliverance from chains. The hearing of those wild notes always depressed my spirit, and filled me with ineffable sadness. I have frequently found myself in tears while hearing them. The mere recurrence to those songs, even now, afflicts me; and while I am writing these lines, an expression of feeling has already found its way down my cheek.

To those songs I trace my first glimmering conception of the dehumanizing character of slavery. I can never get rid of that conception. Those songs still follow me, to deepen my hatred of slavery, and quicken my sympathies for my brethren in bonds. If any one wishes to be impressed with the soul-killing effects of slavery, let him go to Colonel Lloyd's plantation, and, on allowance-day, place himself in the deep pine woods; and there let him, in silence, analyze the sounds that shall pass through the chambers of his soul, and if he is not thus impressed, it will only be because "there is no flesh in his obdurate heart."

I have often been utterly astonished, since I came to the north, to find persons who could speak of the singing, among slaves, as evidence of their contentment and happiness. It is impossible to conceive of a greater mistake. Slaves sing most when they are most unhappy. The songs of the slave represent the sorrows of his heart; and he is relieved by them, only as an aching heart is relieved by its tears. At least, such is my experience. I have often sung to drown my sorrow, but seldom to express my happiness. Crying for joy, and singing for joy, were alike uncommon to me while in the jaws of slavery. The singing of a man cast away upon a desolate island might be as appropriately considered as evidence of contentment and happiness, as the singing of a slave; the songs of the one and of the other are prompted by the same emotion. ∎

According to Douglass, what might some songs by slaves tell people about the character of slavery?

What astonished Douglass? According to him, when did slaves sing? What did their songs represent?

WORDS FOR EVERYDAY USE:

ob • dur • ate (äb´door it) adj., unsympathetic; hardened

The Slave Narrative

Narrative of the Life of Frederick Douglass, an American Slave, was perhaps the greatest of a series of autobiographical accounts by escaped slaves that helped to turn the tide of opinion against the institution of slavery. Other important slave narratives include the following:

A Narrative of the Uncommon Sufferings and Surprising Deliverance of Briton Hammon, a Negro Man (1760)

A Narrative of the Lord's Wonderful Dealings with J. Murrant, a Black, Taken Down from His Own Relation (1784)

The Interesting Narrative of Olaudah Equiano, or Gustavus Vassa, the African (1789)

Scenes in the Life of Harriet Tubman (1869)

Responding to the Selection

What did you learn from this selection? Had you ever thought of music in this way before? Do you think this will affect the way you listen to some songs in the future?

Reviewing the Selection

RECALLING

1. Approximately how many slaves did Colonel Lloyd own?

2. What were the lives of slave children like?

3. With what group outside of slavery does Douglass compare the slaves chosen to run errands to the Great House Farm?

4. Describe the "songs" sung by the slaves sent for supplies on allowance-day.

INTERPRETING

5. How did Colonel Lloyd coordinate the management of his many farms?

6. What effect would you expect the separation of children from their mothers to have on family relationships? Why would this effect be desirable to the slaveholder?

7. Why do you suppose Douglass had such a low opinion of many politicians?

8. How could listening to slaves' singing, rather than seeing them being sold, beaten, or otherwise mistreated, teach most clearly the "dehumanizing character" and "soul-killing effects" of slavery?

9. In what ways is the music we now call the blues similar to the singing Douglass describes?

10. Why do you suppose some people of the time chose to interpret the slaves' singing as a sign of happiness? What was wrong with this interpretation?

Understanding Literature (Questions for Discussion)

1. **Tone**. **Tone** is the emotional attitude toward the idea or toward the subject implied by a literary work. It may be expressed by word choice, imagery, and other techniques. What is Douglass's attitude toward slavery? toward enslaved people? How does his word choice express his tone? Find specific examples from the text to support your answer.

2. **Thesis**. A **thesis** is a main idea that is supported in a work of nonfictional prose. From what you have read in this excerpt, state a thesis of Douglass's autobiography as a whole.

3. **Stereotype**. A **stereotype** is an uncritically accepted fixed or conventional idea, particularly such an idea held about whole groups of people. Against what stereotype did Douglass argue in this excerpt? What was his nonstereotypical interpretation of the situation under discussion? How did his analogy with "a man cast away upon a desolate island" reinforce his interpretation?

Language Lab

Appositives. Read the Language Arts Survey, 2.48, "Adding Appositives and Appositive Phrases." Then revise these sentences, adding to each a word or phrase in apposition to the italicized word(s). Use the information provided in parentheses following each sentence.

1. *Frederick Douglass* worked to free slaves by speaking, writing, and serving as a conductor on the Underground Railroad. (Douglass was a famous autobiographer, speaker, and newspaper publisher.)

2. *Harriet Tubman* chose another route. (Tubman was known as the Moses of her people.)

3. After escaping from a Maryland plantation in 1849, Tubman worked with the *Underground Railroad*. (The Underground Railroad was a series of safe houses between slave states and free states.)

4. Acting as a *conductor*, Tubman was responsible for liberating about three hundred people from slavery. (A conductor was a guide.)

5. After the war, both Tubman and Douglass strongly supported the civil rights struggle and the *women's suffrage movement*. (The women's suffrage movement was an attempt to secure voting rights for women.)

"Swing Low, Sweet Chariot"
Anonymous African-American Spiritual

ABOUT THE SELECTION

By the middle of the nineteenth century, there were more than four million slaves in the United States. Most came from the west coast of Africa. As explained in Imamu Amiri Baraka's *Blues People*, an excerpt from which appears on page 56, West Africans lived in closely knit communities and often engaged in communal labor accompanied by song. In America, such traditional songs developed into the work songs and calls of laborers on plantations. These work songs typically contained repeated lines or phrases and were sung in unison by the workers or in an answer-response format.

Kept from practicing their traditional religions, many African Americans adopted Christianity. Slave owners actively encouraged the Christianizing of the slaves, some because of concern for their slaves' immortal souls, but many more out of hope that people who look for rewards in the next life might be happier with a terrible lot in this one. Combining elements of traditional African music, work songs, and Christian hymns, African Americans created a new kind of music known as the spiritual, a forerunner of many modern musical styles, including gospel and blues. Spirituals such as **"Swing Low, Sweet Chariot"** had Christian themes. They often retold stories from the Bible or dealt with subjects such as salvation and the afterlife. Their form was that of the traditional folk hymn, with repeated elements of the kind found in work songs. They were often sung by groups, with rhythmical accompaniments like those found in African music. Interestingly, many of the spirituals, such as "Swing Low, Sweet Chariot," were intentionally ambiguous, or allegorical, dealing on one level with deliverance from earthly toil into a pleasant afterlife in heaven and on another level with deliverance from slavery.

"Swing Low, Sweet Chariot"

ANONYMOUS AFRICAN-AMERICAN SPIRITUAL

Swing low, sweet chariot,
Coming for to carry me home,
Swing low, sweet chariot,
Coming for to carry me home.

5   I looked over Jordan[1] and what did I see
Coming for to carry me home,
A band of angels coming after me,
Coming for to carry me home.

If you get there before I do,
10   Coming for to carry me home,
Tell all my friends I'm coming too,
Coming for to carry me home.

Swing low, sweet chariot,
Coming for to carry me home,
15   Swing low, sweet chariot,
Coming for to carry me home. ∎

Where does the speaker want to go?

What does the speaker want his or her friends to know?

---

1. **Jordan.** According to a biblical story, the Israelites in exile had to cross the Jordan River to reach the Promised Land of Canaan.

Responding to the Selection

How does this singer feel about being taken away to another place? Why might this song be comforting? Do you have any favorite songs or stories that help you to "escape" temporarily and relax?

Reviewing the Selection

RECALLING

1. What is coming to carry the singer home?

2. Over what river does the singer look? What does the singer see?

3. Who, according to stanza 3, is being addressed by the singer?

4. Toward what does the singer feel that he or she is bound?

INTERPRETING

5. If this song is interpreted as being about escape from slavery, what might the "sweet chariot" be? (Hint: See the introduction to this unit.)

6. If this song deals with slavery, what actual river in the United States might be represented?

7. If this song deals with slavery, whom might the singer be addressing in stanza 3? What plan is shared by the singer and the person being addressed?

8. If this song deals with slavery, what might be the "home" referred to throughout the song?

SYNTHESIZING

9. Why might this song have been comforting to the person singing it? What feelings does the song express?

10. "Swing Low, Sweet Chariot" is written in a kind of code. What intention does it reveal? Under what circumstances did it acquire such a meaning? What reason might a singer have had to express his or her real intention symbolically rather than explicitly?

Understanding Literature (Questions for Discussion)

1. **Theme.** A **theme** is a central idea in a literary work. What is the theme of "Swing Low, Sweet Chariot"?

2. **Allusion.** An **allusion** is a reference in a literary work to another literary work or to some other part of history or culture. In II Kings 2:11, the prophet Elijah is described as being carried into heaven after the appearance of a fiery chariot:

   > And it came to pass, as they still went on, and talked, that, behold, there appeared a chariot of fire, and horses of fire, and parted them both asunder; and Elijah went up by a whirlwind into heaven.

   See footnote 1 on page 371, which describes the Jordan River. Then explain the two biblical allusions in the song and how they are related to escape from slavery.

3. **Spiritual.** A **spiritual** is a type of religious song that originated in the African-American folk tradition. Many spirituals are ambiguous (in other words, they have double meanings). The spiritual "Go Down, Moses," for example, describes the captivity of the Israelites in Egypt, but it can also be read as describing the captivity of the slaves in America:

   > When Israel was in Egypt land
   > Let my people go
   > Oppressed so hard they could not stand
   > Let my people go.

   What is the symbolic interpretation of "Swing Low, Sweet Chariot"?

4. **Refrain.** A **refrain** is a repeated line or group of words in a song or poem. Often spirituals were sung by a lone singer, with a group of people joining in for the refrain. What is the refrain in "Swing Low, Sweet Chariot"? To what does the word "home" in this refrain refer?

The Gettysburg Address
by Abraham Lincoln

ABOUT THE AUTHOR

Abraham Lincoln (1809–1865), known to history as the Great Emancipator and responsible for preserving the Union during the Civil War, rose from obscurity to a place of reverence in the annals of American history. Born to frontier parents in a backwoods cabin in Kentucky, he nonetheless managed to school himself through voracious reading. In fact, the figure of the young Lincoln reading by candlelight in the evening has become a part of American legend. Lincoln's mother died when he was nine. His father remarried a woman who singled out Abraham for special attention and was later referred to by him as his "angel mother." A strong, lanky youth, Lincoln split rails to fence in the family farm when they moved to Illinois, and then held a succession of jobs as a flatboatman, storekeeper, postmaster, and surveyor. He served as a captain in the Black Hawk War and decided to prepare himself for a career in law. Again, he schooled himself, reading law books and passing the bar exam in 1836. Moving to the Illinois capital of Springfield, he was elected to the state legislature, where he served four terms. His romance with Ann Rutledge was cut short by her death at age nineteen, and he married Mary Todd in 1842. In 1858, Lincoln entered the state senatorial race against Stephen A. Douglas. Lincoln lost that election, but the Lincoln-Douglas Debates showed the losing candidate to be a brilliant speaker, combining learned references with homespun witticisms and steeltrap logic. In 1860, running as the candidate of the newly formed Republican party, Lincoln was elected the sixteenth president of the United States. Perhaps no other president has faced such a crisis on taking office, for immediately he was embroiled in the Civil War, brought about by the succession of Southern states from the Union to form the Confederacy. After many false starts and mistakes, Lincoln finally installed the proper leadership to lead his Union troops to victory. During the war, Lincoln issued the Emancipation Proclamation, freeing slaves in states then in rebellion. After the war he worked for passage of the Thirteenth Amendment, which ended slavery in the United States once and for all. In April 1865, shortly after being reelected for a second term as president, Lincoln was assassinated while watching a play at Ford's Theater in Washington.

On November 19, 1863, Lincoln delivered his famous address at the dedication of the national cemetery at Gettysburg. Gettysburg had been the site of one of the bloodiest battles in the Civil War; in July 1863, Union and Confederate troops fought for a grueling three days on the usually peaceful farmlands of Pennsylvania. Many historians feel that this battle signified the turning point of the Civil War. However, at the time that Lincoln gave his speech, the war was still unfinished. In light of the bitterness of the conflict, one of the most remarkable aspects of **The Gettysburg Address** is its avoidance of angry or inflammatory rhetoric that would incite listeners to further hostility against the enemy. Instead, the speech focuses on the sacrifice of the participants in the battle and the need for rededication to the principles of the nation's founders. There was a sharp contrast between this simple three-paragraph speech and the two-hour address by well-known orator Edward Everett that preceded it. In fact, Lincoln's speech was considered unimportant at the time of its delivery.

The Wit and Wisdom of Abraham Lincoln

On a book: "People who like this sort of thing will find this the sort of thing they like."

On being asked to replace a general: "It is best not to swap horses while crossing the river."

On charity toward one's enemies: "Am I not destroying my enemies when I make friends of them?"

On deception: "You can fool all the people some of the time, and some of the people all the time, but you cannot fool all the people all of the time."

On economy in speech: "He can compress the most words into the smallest ideas, of any man I ever met."

On government: "No man is good enough to govern another man without that other's consent."

On justice: "He reminds me of the man who murdered both his parents, and then, when sentence was about to be pronounced, pleaded for mercy on the grounds that he was an orphan."

On personal appearance: "The Lord prefers common-looking people. That is the reason He makes so many of them."

On slavery: "I intend no modification of my oft-expressed personal wish that all men everywhere should be free."

On slavery: "In giving freedom to the slave, we assure freedom to the free,—honorable alike in what we give and what we preserve."

On slavery: "Slavery is founded on the selfishness of man's nature—opposition to it on his love of justice."

On the conduct of the war: "Now, gentlemen, we have got our harpoon into the monster, but we must still take uncommon care, or else by a single flop of his tail he will send us all into eternity."

On the Union: "A house divided against itself cannot stand. I believe this government cannot endure permanently, half slave and half free."

On voting: "The ballot is stronger than the bullet."

To Harriet Beecher Stowe, author of the popular antislavery novel *Uncle Tom's Cabin*: "So you're the little woman who wrote the book that made this great war!"

READER'S JOURNAL

Imagine you are a leader responsible for encouraging a discouraged group. Perhaps you are the coach of a football team that is losing at halftime, or the head of an environmental organization that has just learned about a major oil spill on a nearby beach. How would you inspire your subordinates? What arguments might induce your listeners to continue their struggle? In your journal, write the words and methods you might use to inspire your listeners.

LANGUAGE SKILLS

Read the Language Arts Survey, 2.15, "Transitive and Intransitive Verbs." Find five transitive and five intransitive verbs in The Gettysburg Address. For each transitive verb, identify the direct object.

The Gettysburg Address

ABRAHAM LINCOLN

What event is taking place at the time this speech is delivered? What is being tested by this event?

What should people do to honor the dead?

Four score and seven years ago our fathers brought forth on this continent, a new nation, conceived in Liberty, and dedicated to the proposition that all men are created equal.

Now we are engaged in a great civil war, testing whether that nation, or any nation so conceived and so dedicated, can long endure. We are met on a great battlefield of that war. We have come to dedicate a portion of that field, as a final resting place for those who here gave their lives that that nation might live. It is altogether fitting and proper that we should do this.

But, in a larger sense, we can not dedicate—we can not consecrate—we can not hallow—this ground. The brave men, living and dead, who struggled here, have consecrated it, far above our poor power to add or detract. The world will little note, nor long remember what we say here, but it can never forget what they did here. It is for us the living, rather, to be dedicated here to the unfinished work which they who fought here have thus far so nobly advanced. It is rather for us to be here dedicated to the great task remaining before us—that from these honored dead we take increased devotion to that cause for which they gave the last full measure of devotion—that we here highly resolve that these dead shall not have died in vain—that this nation, under God, shall have a new birth of freedom—and that government of the people, by the people, for the people, shall not perish from the earth. ■

WORDS FOR EVERYDAY USE:
score (skôr) *n.*, set of twenty
con • se • crate (kan´si krāt´) *vt.*, make or declare sacred

Responding to the Selection

Audience members were probably expecting a long speech from the president. How might they have reacted to this short address? How would you have responded to this speech? Do you think it should have been longer? Why, or why not?

Reviewing the Selection

RECALLING

1. Lincoln refers to an event "Four score and seven years ago." To what date and event is he referring?

2. Lincoln uses the word "dedicate" six times in the course of this brief speech. Look up the word and decide which of its meanings were intended by Lincoln.

3. Why does Lincoln say that, in a larger sense, he cannot consecrate the cemetery? Who has consecrated it better than he can?

4. To what cause does Lincoln ask that his listeners dedicate themselves?

INTERPRETING

5. Why does Lincoln begin by referring to the principles of the founders of the United States? What emotions does he hope to evoke in his listeners?

6. Keeping in mind that the Emancipation Proclamation was issued in January 1863, why do you think Lincoln emphasized that the nation was "dedicated to the proposition that all men are created equal"?

7. What does Lincoln mean by the phrase, "the last full measure of devotion"? How did the soldiers show this devotion? To what were they devoted?

8. Under what circumstances would the dead be considered to have died in vain? What can the listeners do to ensure that the deaths were not futile?

9. Lincoln said, "The world will little note, nor long remember what we say here." However, this speech has been repeated for over one hundred years, and has even been memorized by admirers and students during that time. Why do you think this speech has touched Americans so deeply since 1863? What qualities make it memorable?

10. Why is this simple speech so appropriate to the dedication of a cemetery in which thousands of people have been buried? Why do you think Lincoln chose to speak simply and avoided long sentences and fancy phrases at this time?

Understanding Literature (Questions for Discussion)

1. **Parallelism. Parallelism** is a rhetorical technique in which a writer emphasizes the equal value or weight of two or more ideas by expressing them in the same grammatical form. Lincoln uses parallelism extensively in the final sentence of this selection. Notice, for example, that the sentence contains a number of clauses beginning with the word *that*. (A **clause** is a group of words containing a subject and a verb.) Paraphrase each of these clauses. Then examine the series of phrases *of the people, by the people, for the people* near the end of the speech. Identify the parts of speech used in this series of phrases. (Refer to the Language Arts Survey, 2.3, "Common and Proper Nouns"; 2.24, "Prepositions"; and 2.47, "Adding Prepositional Phrases.") Then explain the difference in meaning of each phrase. Which phrase describes all governments? Which describes all governments that have the people's welfare at heart? Which describes only democratic governments?

2. **Antithesis. Antithesis** is a rhetorical technique in which words, phrases, or ideas are strongly contrasted, often by means of a repetition of grammatical structure. Find an example of the use of antithesis in The Gettysburg Address. What is the effect of this use of antithesis? How does it strengthen the speech?

3. **Syntax. Syntax** is the pattern of arrangement of words in a statement. Many people enjoy the unusual syntax that Lincoln uses in The Gettysburg Address. Choose one of the ten sentences in this speech and reword it in a more normal, everyday kind of language, paying special attention to changing the order of the words whenever possible. Then decide which sentence you like better—Lincoln's or your own. Explain your choice.

Responding in Writing

News Story. Imagine that you were a member of the audience at the dedication of the national cemetery at Gettysburg. How might you have reported the proceedings? Write a short news article in which you describe the scene and review Lincoln's speech.

Language Lab

Achieving Parallelism. Read the Language Arts Survey, 2.57, "Achieving Parallelism." Then rewrite each of the following sentences below to achieve parallelism.

1. Our ancestors brought forth a new nation conceived in liberty and it was also being dedicated to the principle of equality for all people.

2. It is fitting and proper to dedicate the cemetery and setting aside a portion of the cemetery to the fallen soldiers.

3. The brave men who were fighting and died here consecrated the ground better than we can.

4. The world does not note nor will it remember what we say here.

5. We must resolve that these dead shall not have died in vain and to dedicate ourselves to the preservation of the nation.

Thinking Skills

Memorizing. Read the Language Arts Survey, 4.4, "Memorizing." Then choose and practice a method for memorizing items in a series, such as the last ten presidents of the United States or the names of important battles in the Civil War. Be ready to display your memorization skills and explain which method of memorization you used.

PROJECTS

1. **Report on the Battle of Gettysburg.** The Battle of Gettysburg is a rich topic for study and analysis. Research the events and strategies of the battle and write a report that describes some of its major skirmishes, efforts, and errors.

2. **Choral Reading.** Work with a group to research speeches, sayings, and jokes attributed to Abraham Lincoln. Practice reading these works aloud, and then present them to an audience. Works may be read by individuals or by groups of two or three taking turns or speaking in unison.

"An Occurrence at Owl Creek Bridge"
by Ambrose Bierce

ABOUT THE AUTHOR

Ambrose Bierce (1842–*circa* 1914), known as "Bitter Bierce," was a cynical, unhappy man with a sharp, satirical wit. Born in Ohio, he grew up in a large, poor family. An unhappy childhood followed by exposure to unimaginable brutality during the Civil War combined to create in Bierce the pessimism that became the dominant trait of his character and his fiction. After spending a year at a military academy, Bierce joined the Union army, rising to the rank of lieutenant. He was a distinguished soldier and participated in a number of major battles. His war experiences provided material for some of his best stories, including "An Occurrence at Owl Creek Bridge" and "Chickamauga." After the war he moved to San Francisco and worked as a journalist, establishing himself through witty, satirical columns as a major literary figure in that rough-and-tumble frontier city. There Bierce counted among his friends such major writers as Mark Twain and Bret Harte. In 1872 he married, moving with his wife to England, where he continued his journalistic work. The relationship with Mrs. Bierce was not a happy one. In *The Cynic's Word Book* (1906), later retitled as *The Devil's Dictionary,* Bierce defined love as "a temporary insanity, curable by marriage." Returning to San Francisco, Bierce worked for many years for *The San Francisco Examiner*, published by William Randolph Hearst. Disaster plagued him: his marriage ended in divorce, one son was killed in a fight, and another son died of alcoholism. In 1913, Bierce traveled to Mexico, which was then in the throes of a civil war. There he disappeared without a trace. His greatest legacy, besides his humorous, if grotesque, *The Devil's Dictionary,* was a handful of stories acclaimed today for their suspensefulness and their psychological realism.

ABOUT THE SELECTION

Bierce, a Civil War veteran who had served with distinction, uses details about military customs and regulations to lend authenticity to this strange tale. In its use of authentic, precisely observed details, the story is a fine early example of American Realism. The story is also an early example of Naturalism, a type of writing that reveals the forces beyond people's control that determine not only their circumstances and fate but also their characters, personalities, and subjective experiences. Unlike traditional straightforward narratives that present plot events chronologically, this story relies on flashbacks and journeys into the mind of the main character. Bierce's stories paved the way for much modern fiction with portrayals of the private psychological states of characters. Although Bierce is often remembered for his bitter and caustic wit, in **"An Occurrence at Owl Creek Bridge"** he concentrates on telling a good story with enough twists and turns to keep the reader guessing until the last sentence.

"An Occurrence at Owl Creek Bridge"

Ambrose Bierce

I

A man stood upon a railroad bridge in northern Alabama, looking down into the swift water twenty feet below. The man's hands were behind his back, the wrists bound with a cord. A rope closely encircled his neck. It was attached to a stout cross timber above his head and the slack fell to the level of his knees. Some loose boards laid upon the sleepers[1] supporting the metals of the railway supplied a footing for him and his executioners—two private soldiers of the Federal army, directed by a sergeant who in civil life may have been a deputy sheriff. At a short remove upon the same temporary platform was an officer in the uniform of his rank, armed. He was a captain. A sentinel at each end of the bridge stood with his rifle in the position known as "support," that is to say, vertical in front of the left shoulder, the hammer resting on the forearm thrown straight across the chest—a formal and unnatural position, enforcing an erect carriage of the body. It did not appear to be the duty of these two men to know what was occurring at the center of the bridge; they merely blockaded the two ends of the foot planking that traversed it.

Beyond one of the sentinels nobody was in sight; the railroad ran straight away into a forest for a hundred yards, then, curving, was lost to view. Doubtless there was

What is about to happen to the man?

---

1. **sleepers.** Ties that support railroad tracks

WORDS FOR EVERYDAY USE: sen • ti • nel (sen´ti nəl) *n.*, person acting as a guard

an outpost farther along. The other bank of the stream was open ground—a gentle <u>acclivity</u> topped with a stockade of vertical tree trunks, loopholed for rifles with a single <u>embrasure</u> through which protruded the muzzle of a brass cannon commanding the bridge. Midway of the slope between bridge and fort were the spectators—a single company of infantry in line, at "parade rest," the butts of the rifles on the ground, the barrels inclining slightly backward against the right shoulder, the hands crossed upon the stock. A lieutenant stood at the right of the line, the point of his sword upon the ground, his left hand resting upon his right. Excepting the group of four at the center of the bridge, not a man moved. The company faced the bridge, staring stonily, motionless. The sentinels, facing the banks of the stream, might have been statues to adorn the bridge. The captain stood with folded arms, silent, observing the work of his subordinates, but making no sign. Death is a dignitary who when he comes announced is to be received with formal manifestations of respect, even by those most familiar with him. In the code of military etiquette silence and fixity are forms of deference.

The man who was engaged in being hanged was apparently about thirty-five years of age. He was a civilian, if one might judge from his habit, which was that of a planter. His features were good—a straight nose, firm mouth, broad forehead, from which his long, dark hair was combed straight back, falling behind his ears to the collar of his well-fitting frock coat. He wore a mustache and pointed beard, but no whiskers; his eyes were large and dark gray, and had a kindly expression which one would hardly have expected in one whose neck was in the hemp.[2] Evidently this was no vulgar assassin. The liberal military code makes provision for hanging many kinds of persons, and gentlemen are not excluded.

The preparations being complete, the two private soldiers stepped aside and each drew away the plank upon which he had been standing. The sergeant turned to the captain, saluted and placed himself immediately behind that officer, who in turn moved apart one pace. These movements left the condemned man and the sergeant standing on the two ends of the same plank, which spanned three of the crossties of the bridge. The end upon which the civilian stood almost, but not quite, reached a fourth. This plank had been held in place by the weight of the captain; it was now held by that of the sergeant. At a signal from the former the latter would step aside, the plank would tilt and the condemned man go down between two ties. The arrangement commended itself to his judgment as simple and effective. His face had not been covered nor his eyes bandaged. He looked a moment at his "unsteadfast footing," then let his gaze wander to the swirling water of the stream racing madly beneath his feet. A piece of dancing driftwood caught his attention and his eyes followed it down the current. How slowly it appeared to move! What a sluggish stream!

He closed his eyes in order to fix his last thoughts upon his wife and children. The

---

2. **hemp.** Rope made of hemp

What is Death? How should Death be received?

What does the man who is about to be hanged look like? What do his clothes reveal about him? What aspect of his appearance is surprising?

WORDS FOR EVERYDAY USE:

ac • cliv • i • ty (ə kliv′ə tē) *n.*, upward slope

em • bra • sure (em brā′zhər) *n.*, slanted opening in a wall that increases the firing angle of a gun

water, touched to gold by the early sun, the brooding mists under the banks at some distance down the stream, the fort, the soldiers, the piece of drift—all had distracted him. And now he became conscious of a new disturbance. Striking through the thought of his dear ones was a sound which he could neither ignore nor understand, a sharp, distinct, metallic percussion like the stroke of a blacksmith's hammer upon the anvil; it had the same ringing quality. He wondered what it was, and whether immeasurably distant or near by—it seemed both. Its recurrence was regular, but as slow as the tolling of a death knell. He awaited each stroke with impatience and—he knew not why—apprehension. The intervals of silence grew progressively longer; the delays became maddening. With their greater infrequency the sounds increased in strength and sharpness. They hurt his ear like the thrust of a knife; he feared he would shriek. What he heard was the ticking of his watch.

He unclosed his eyes and saw again the water below him. "If I could free my hands," he thought, "I might throw off the noose and spring into the stream. By diving I could evade the bullets and, swimming vigorously, reach the bank, take to the woods and get away home. My home, thank God, is as yet outside their lines; my wife and little ones are still beyond the invader's farthest advance."

As these thoughts, which have here to be set down in words, were flashed into the doomed man's brain rather than evolved from it the captain nodded to the sergeant. The sergeant stepped aside.

II

Peyton Farquhar was a well-to-do planter, of an old and highly respected Alabama family. Being a slave owner and like other slave owners a politician he was naturally an original secessionist and ardently devoted to the Southern cause. Circumstances of an imperious nature, which it is unnecessary to relate here, had prevented him from taking service with the gallant army that had fought the disastrous campaigns ending with the fall of Corinth, and he chafed under the inglorious restraint, longing for the release of his energies, the larger life of the soldier, the opportunity for distinction. That opportunity, he felt, would come, as it comes to all in war time. Meanwhile he did what he could. No service was too humble for him to perform in aid of the South, no adventure too perilous for him to undertake if consistent with the character of a civilian who was at heart a soldier, and who in good faith and without too much qualification assented to at least a part of the frankly villainous dictum that all is fair in love and war.

One evening while Farquhar and his wife were sitting on a rustic bench near the entrance to his grounds, a gray-clad soldier rode up to the gate and asked for a drink of water. Mrs. Farquhar was only too happy to serve him with her own white hands. While she was fetching the water her husband approached the dusty horseman and inquired eagerly for news from the front.

"The Yanks are repairing the railroads," said the man, "and are getting ready for another advance. They have reached the Owl Creek bridge, put it in order and built a stockade on the north bank. The commandant has issued an order, which is posted everywhere, declaring that any civilian caught interfering with the railroad, its bridges, tunnels or trains will be summarily hanged. I saw the order."

"How far is it to the Owl Creek bridge?" Farquhar asked.

What was the man unable to do? What did he long to do?

What sound did the man seem to hear? What effect did the sound have on him? What was he actually hearing?

"About thirty miles."

"Is there no force on this side the creek?"

"Only a picket post[3] half a mile out, on the railroad, and a single sentinel at this end of the bridge."

What does Farquhar have in mind?

"Suppose a man—a civilian and student of hanging—should elude the picket post and perhaps get the better of the sentinel," said Farquhar, smiling, "what could he accomplish?"

The soldier reflected. "I was there a month ago," he replied. "I observed that the flood of last winter had lodged a great quantity of driftwood against the wooden pier at this end of the bridge. It is now dry and would burn like tow."[4]

The lady had now brought the water, which the soldier drank. He thanked her ceremoniously, bowed to her husband and rode away. An hour later, after nightfall, he repassed the plantation, going northward in the direction from which he had come. He was a Federal scout.

Who is the soldier in the gray uniform? What is the importance of the revelation of his identity?

III

As Peyton Farquhar fell straight downward through the bridge he lost consciousness and was as one already dead. From this state he was awakened—ages later, it seemed to him—by the pain of a sharp pressure upon his throat, followed by a sense of suffocation. Keen, poignant agonies seemed to shoot from his neck downward through every fiber of his body and limbs. These pains appeared to flash along well defined lines of ramification and to beat with an inconceivably rapid periodicity. They seemed like streams of pulsating fire heating him to an intolerable temperature. As to his head, he was conscious of nothing but a feeling of fullness—of congestion. These sensations were unaccompanied by thought. The intellectual part of his nature was already <u>effaced</u>; he had power only to feel, and feeling was torment. He was conscious of motion. Encompassed in a luminous cloud, of which he was now merely the fiery heart, without material substance, he swung through unthinkable arcs of <u>oscillation</u>, like a vast pendulum. Then all at once, with terrible suddenness, the light about him shot upward with the noise of a loud splash; a frightful roaring was in his ears, and all was cold and dark. The power of thought was restored; he knew that the rope had broken and he had fallen into the stream. There was no additional strangulation; the noose about his neck was already suffocating him and kept the water from his lungs. To die of hanging at the bottom of a river!—the idea seemed to him <u>ludicrous</u>. He opened his eyes in the darkness and saw above him a gleam of light, but how distant, how inaccessible! He was still sinking, for the light became fainter and fainter until it was a mere glimmer. Then it began to grow and brighten, and he knew that he was rising toward the surface—knew it with reluctance, for he was now very comfortable. "To be hanged and drowned," he thought, "that is not so bad; but I do not wish to be shot. No; I will not be shot; that is not fair."

What thought does Farquhar have as he rises to the surface of the water?

---

3. **picket post.** Troops that protect an army from a surprise attack
4. **tow.** Flammable fibers of hemp or flax

WORDS FOR EVERYDAY USE:

ef • face (ə fās´) *vt.,* erase, wipe out

os • cil • la • tion (äs´ə lā´shən) *n.,* act of swinging back and forth

lu • di • crous (lōō´di krəs) *adj.,* absurd, ridiculous

He was not conscious of an effort, but a sharp pain in his wrist apprised him that he was trying to free his hands. He gave the struggle his attention, as an idler might observe the feat of a juggler, without interest in the outcome. What splendid effort!—what magnificent, what superhuman strength! Ah, that was a fine endeavor! Bravo! The cord fell away; his arms parted and floated upward, the hands dimly seen on each side in the growing light. He watched them with a new interest as first one and then the other pounced upon the noose at his neck. They tore it away and thrust it fiercely aside, its undulations resembling those of a watersnake. "Put it back, put it back!" He thought he shouted these words to his hands, for the undoing of the noose had been succeeded by the direst pang that he had yet experienced. His neck ached horribly; his brain was on fire; his heart, which had been fluttering faintly, gave a great leap, trying to force itself out at his mouth. His whole body was racked and wrenched with an insupportable anguish! But his disobedient hands gave no heed to the command. They beat the water vigorously with quick, downward strokes, forcing him to the surface. He felt his head emerge; his eyes were blinded by the sunlight; his chest expanded convulsively, and with a supreme and crowning agony his lungs engulfed a great draft of air, which instantly he expelled in a shriek!

He was now in full possession of his physical senses. They were, indeed, preternaturally keen and alert. Something in the awful disturbance of his organic system had so exalted and refined them that they made record of things never before perceived. He felt the ripples upon his face and heard their separate sounds as they struck. He looked at the forest on the bank of the stream, saw the individual trees, the leaves and the veining of each leaf—saw the very insects upon them: the locusts, the brilliant-bodied flies, the gray spiders stretching their webs from twig to twig. He noted the prismatic colors in all the dewdrops upon a million blades of grass. The humming of the gnats that danced above the eddies of the stream, the beating of the dragonflies' wings, the strokes of the water spiders' legs, like oars which had lifted their boat—all these made audible music. A fish slid along beneath his eyes and he heard the rush of its body parting the water.

He had come to the surface facing down the stream; in a moment the visible world seemed to wheel slowly round, himself the pivotal point, and he saw the bridge, the fort, the soldiers upon the bridge, the captain, the sergeant, the two privates, his executioners. They were in silhouette against the blue sky. They shouted and <u>gesticulated</u>, pointing at him. The captain had drawn his pistol, but did not fire; the others were unarmed. Their movements were grotesque and horrible, their forms gigantic.

Suddenly he heard a sharp report and something struck the water smartly within a few inches of his head, spattering his face with spray. He heard a second report, and saw one of the sentinels with his rifle at his shoulder, a light cloud of blue smoke rising from the muzzle. The man in the water saw the eye of the man on the

In what state are Farquhar's senses? What sensory details does he notice?

WORDS FOR EVERYDAY USE: ges • tic • u • late (jes tik´yōo lāt´) vi., make gestures with hands or arms

What does Farquhar notice about the marksman? What does he fear this means? Is the superstition he had heard true?

What sound does Farquhar hear? What does he take it to mean?

bridge gazing into his own through the sights of the rifle. He observed that it was a gray eye and remembered having read that gray eyes were keenest, and that all famous marksmen had them. Nevertheless, this one had missed.

A counterswirl had caught Farquhar and turned him half round; he was again looking into the forest on the bank opposite the fort. The sound of a clear, high voice in a monotonous singsong now rang out behind him and came across the water with a distinctness that pierced and subdued all other sounds, even the beating of the ripples in his ears. Although no soldier, he had frequented camps enough to know the dread significance of that deliberate, drawling, <u>aspirated</u> chant; the lieutenant on shore was taking a part in the morning's work. How coldly and pitilessly—with what an even, calm intonation, presaging, and enforcing tranquillity in the men—with what accurately measured intervals fell those cruel words:

"Attention, company! . . . Shoulder arms! . . . Ready! . . . Aim! . . . fire!"

Farquhar dived—dived as deeply as he could. The water roared in his ears like the voice of Niagara, yet he heard the dulled thunder of the volley and, rising again toward the surface, met shining bits of metal, singularly flattened, oscillating slowly downward. Some of them touched him on the face and hands, then fell away, continuing their descent. One lodged between his collar and neck; it was uncomfortably warm and he snatched it out.

As he rose to the surface, gasping for breath, he saw that he had been a long time under water; he was perceptibly farther down stream—nearer to safety. The soldiers had almost finished reloading; the metal ramrods flashed all at once in the sunshine as they were drawn from the barrels, turned in the air, and thrust into their sockets. The two sentinels fired again, independently and ineffectually.

The hunted man saw all this over his shoulder; he was now swimming vigorously with the current. His brain was as energetic as his arms and legs; he thought with the rapidity of lightning.

"The officer," he reasoned, "will not make that martinet's[5] error a second time. It is as easy to dodge a volley as a single shot. He has probably already given the command to fire at will. God help me, I cannot dodge them all!"

An appalling splash within two yards of him was followed by a loud, rushing sound, *diminuendo*,[6] which seemed to travel back through the air to the fort and died in an explosion which stirred the very river to its deeps! A rising sheet of water curved over him, fell down upon him, blinded him, strangled him! The cannon had taken a hand in the game. As he shook his head free from the commotion of the smitten water he heard the deflected shot humming through the air ahead, and in an instant it was cracking and smashing the branches in the forest beyond.

"They will not do that again," he thought; "the next time they will use a charge of grape.[7] I must keep my eye

---

5. **martinet's.** Of a strict disciplinarian
6. **diminuendo.** Musical term meaning a reduction in volume
7. **grape.** Cluster of small iron balls fired from a cannon

---

WORDS FOR EVERYDAY USE: **as • pi • rat • ed** (as´pə rāt´əd) *adj.*, articulated with a puff of breath before or after

upon the gun; the smoke will apprise me—the report arrives too late; it lags behind the missile. That is a good gun."

Suddenly he felt himself whirled round and round—spinning like a top. The water, the banks, the forests, the now distant bridge, fort and men—all were commingled and blurred. Objects were represented by their colors only; circular horizontal streaks of color—that was all he saw. He had been caught in a vortex and was being whirled on with a velocity of advance and gyration that made him giddy and sick. In a few moments he was flung upon the gravel at the foot of the left bank of the stream—the southern bank—and behind a projecting point which concealed him from his enemies. The sudden arrest of his motion, the abrasion of one of his hands on the gravel, restored him, and he wept with delight. He dug his fingers into the sand, threw it over himself in handfuls and audibly blessed it. It looked like diamonds, rubies, emeralds; he could think of nothing beautiful which it did not resemble. The trees upon the bank were giant garden plants; he noted a definite order in their arrangement, inhaled the fragrance of their blooms. A strange, roseate light shone through the spaces among their trunks and the wind made in their branches the music of aeolian harps.[8] He had no wish to perfect his escape—was content to remain in that enchanting spot until retaken.

A whiz and rattle of grapeshot among the branches high above his head roused him from his dream. The baffled cannoneer had fired him a random farewell. He sprang to his feet, rushed up the sloping bank, and plunged into the forest.

All that day he traveled, laying his course by the rounding sun. The forest

Photograph: Ken Pelka

Young Soldier. *Separate study of a soldier giving water to a wounded companion. Winslow Homer, 1861. Cooper-Hewitt, National Design Museum, Smithsonian Inst./Art Resource, NY*

seemed interminable; nowhere did he discover a break in it, not even a woodman's road. He had not known that he lived in so wild a region. There was something uncanny in the revelation.

What causes Farquhar's delight and contentment?

---

8. **aeolian harps.** Harps that produce music when air blows over the strings

By night fall he was fatigued, footsore, famishing. The thought of his wife and children urged him on. At last he found a road which led him in what he knew to be the right direction. It was as wide and straight as a city street, yet it seemed untraveled. No fields bordered it, no dwelling anywhere. Not so much as the barking of a dog suggested human habitation. The black bodies of the trees formed a straight wall on both sides, terminating on the horizon in a point, like a diagram in a lesson in perspective. Overhead, as he looked up through this rift in the wood, shone great golden stars looking unfamiliar and grouped in strange constellations. He was sure they were arranged in some order which had a secret and <u>malign</u> significance. The wood on either side was full of singular noises, among which— once, twice, and again, he distinctly heard whispers in an unknown tongue.

His neck was in pain and lifting his hand to it he found it horribly swollen. He knew that it had a circle of black where the rope had bruised it. His eyes felt congested; he could no longer close them. His tongue was swollen with thirst; he relieved its fever by thrusting it forward from between his teeth into the cold air. How softly the turf had carpeted the untraveled avenue—he could no longer feel the roadway beneath his feet!

Doubtless, despite his suffering, he had fallen asleep while walking, for now he sees another scene—perhaps he has merely recovered from a delirium. He stands at the gate of his own home. All is as he left it, and all bright and beautiful in the morning sunshine. He must have traveled the entire night. As he pushes open the gate and passes up the wide white walk, he sees a flutter of female garments; his wife, looking fresh and cool and sweet, steps down from the veranda to meet him. At the bottom of the steps she stands waiting, with a smile of ineffable joy, an attitude of matchless grace and dignity. Ah, how beautiful she is! He springs forward with extended arms. As he is about to clasp her he feels a stunning blow upon the back of the neck; a blinding white light blazes all about him with a sound like the shock of a cannon—then all is darkness and silence!

Peyton Farquhar was dead; his body, with a broken neck, swung gently from side to side beneath the timbers of the Owl Creek bridge. ∎

What description is given of Farquhar? What image does this description bring to mind?

What is revealed in the last paragraph about Farquhar's actions?

Responding to the Selection

At what point did you begin to suspect that things were not as they seemed in this story? Did the imaginary or dream sequence remind you of other stories you have read or seen enacted at the movies or on television? How were those other stories similar to this one?

WORDS FOR EVERYDAY USE: **ma • lign** (mə līn´) *adj.*, malicious, evil

Reviewing the Selection

RECALLING

1. Describe the man on the railroad bridge and explain his situation. What is about to happen to him? How do you know?

2. What does the gray-clad soldier tell Farquhar and his wife when he stops by their home?

3. What prevents Farquhar from being killed by hanging? How does he escape the soldiers?

4. What happens to Farquhar at the end of the story?

INTERPRETING

5. How did the man get into this predicament? What was his crime and who is punishing him?

6. What details suggest that Farquhar might attempt to destroy the railroad bridge?

7. As Farquhar continues his escape, he begins to experience strange occurrences. Which sights and experiences seem strange to you?

8. How could Farquhar have dreamed or thought all these experiences so quickly? Does this story seem plausible to you?

SYNTHESIZING

9. Do you agree that "all is fair in love and war," as Farquhar believes? Do you feel that Farquhar's punishment was deserved and justified because it was an act of war?

10. Do you enjoy stories in which the characters are really dreaming or imagining much of the action? Give reasons why, or why not.

Understanding Literature (Questions for Discussion)

1. **Flashback.** A **flashback** is a section of a literary work that presents an event or series of events that occurred earlier than the current time in the work. How does the flashback in this story advance the story's plot? What necessary information does the flashback provide?

2. **Psychological Fiction. Psychological fiction** is fiction that emphasizes the interior, subjective experiences of its characters, and especially such fiction when it deals with emotional or mental disturbance or anguish. What parts of the story qualify it as psychological fiction?

3. **Naturalism. Naturalism** was a literary movement of the late nineteenth and early twentieth centuries that portrayed the lives of characters as being determined, or caused, by outside events beyond their control. What elements of this story make it an example of Naturalism?

4. **Climax.** The **climax** is the point of highest interest and suspense in a literary work. The term is sometimes also used to describe the turning point of the action in a story or play, the point at which the rising action ends and the falling action begins. See the Handbook of Literary Terms for more information on these elements of plot. Identify the climax in this story. Then describe the falling action.

Responding in Writing

1. **Directions.** Bierce gives specific details about the way each soldier is standing and holding his rifle. His description is so exact that a reader could duplicate the position of the rifle after a careful reading. Write directions for a simple action that you know well. Include specific details so the reader can carry out your instructions after a careful reading. Refer to the Language Arts Survey, 1.40, "Elaboration: Types of Supporting Details."

2. **Daydream.** Everyone daydreams occasionally. Like the main character in "An Occurrence at Owl Creek Bridge," you can feel as if you were somewhere else when you daydream. Write a descriptive paragraph about a daydream you had or that you could have. Let your imagination go.

Language Lab

Auxiliary Verbs. Read the Language Arts Survey, 2.14, "Auxiliary Verbs." Underline the auxiliary verbs in the following sentences.

1. It did not appear to be the duty of these two men to know what was occurring at the center of the bridge.

2. The sentinels, facing the banks of the stream, might have been statues to adorn the bridge.

3. This plank had been held in place by the weight of the captain.

4. "The Yanks are repairing the railroads," said the man, "and are getting ready for another advance."

5. The captain had drawn his pistol, but did not fire.

Thinking Skills

Remembering and Visualizing. Read the Language Arts Survey, 4.5, "Remembering and Visualizing." Then take a few moments to remember and visualize an incident in which your senses came alive, for example, when you jumped into cold water, when you descended into a damp basement, or when you sat by a roaring bonfire. Jot down some notes on what your senses experienced at that time.

"A Mystery of Heroism"
"Do not weep, maiden, for war is kind"
by Stephen Crane

ABOUT THE AUTHOR

Stephen Crane (1871–1900) lived only twenty-eight years, but in that time he established himself as a great American fiction writer and poet. A literary pioneer, Crane applied to fiction his belief that human beings are pawns, moved by forces beyond their control to take actions beyond their understanding. This idea that nature—the forces of heredity and environment—causes humans to think, believe, feel, and act as they do is known in philosophy as Determinism and in literary theory as Naturalism. To the Determinist or Naturalist, free will is an illusion, because the decisions that people believe they are making freely are in fact the inevitable consequences of the forces acting upon them.

Crane was born in Newark, New Jersey, the youngest of fourteen children. His father, a Methodist minister, died when Crane was nine years old. Crane attended Syracuse University but left after one semester. In 1893, Crane finished revising his novel *Maggie: A Girl of the Streets,* the draft of which he had finished while at Syracuse. Shocked by the novel's grim realism, publishers rejected the book, and Crane was forced to pay for its publication. In 1894, Crane's masterful novel about the Civil War, *The Red Badge of Courage,* was published serially in a magazine, and Crane began work as a reporter. In 1895, the novel was released in book form, and Crane's reputation was established. That same year, Crane issued the first volume of his experimental free verse, *The Black Rider.* This was followed by another volume of poetry, *War Is Kind,* in 1899. Crane's experiences as a reporter in Mexico, the American West, and Florida provided material for a number of short stories, including "The Blue Hotel" and "The Open Boat." As a reporter, Crane covered the Greco-Turkish War and the Spanish-American War, seeing firsthand, the cruelties of battle about which he had written so eloquently. Before his death, Crane spent some time in England, where he met many famous writers, including H. G. Wells, Joseph Conrad, and Henry James. By that time, he was severely ill with tuberculosis. He died at a health spa in Badenweiler, Germany.

ABOUT THE SELECTIONS

Readers of *The Red Badge of Courage* and the other war stories and poems of Stephen Crane are often surprised to learn that Crane did not experience the Civil War firsthand. The astonishingly realistic details of these works are tributes to what a writer can do through careful, exhaustive research. **"A Mystery of Heroism"** is a definitive example of both Realism and Naturalism in American fiction. **"Do not weep, maiden, for war is kind"** illustrates typical characteristics of Crane's poetry—irony, realistic details, and a conversational tone, all expressed in free verse void of traditional patterns of rhyme, rhythm, and stanza form.

READER'S JOURNAL

Have you ever done something and later wondered why you did it? Have you ever felt swept along by events and not really in control of what was happening? Write about such an experience in your journal.

LANGUAGE SKILLS

"A Mystery of Heroism" contains some examples of dialect spoken by soldiers during the time of the Civil War. Read the Language Arts Survey, 2.150, "Dialects of English." Then, as you read the story, copy three examples of dialect into your journal and translate them into contemporary English of the kind spoken in your community.

"A Mystery of Heroism"

STEPHEN CRANE

The dark uniforms of the men were so coated with dust from the <u>incessant</u> wrestling of the two armies that the regiment almost seemed a part of the clay bank which shielded them from the shells. On the top of the hill a battery[1] was arguing in tremendous roars with some other guns, and to the eye of the infantry the artillerymen, the guns, the caissons,[2] the horses, were distinctly outlined upon the blue sky. When a piece was fired, a red streak as round as a log flashed low in the heavens, like a monstrous bolt of lightning. The men of the battery wore white duck trousers, which somehow emphasized their legs; and when they ran and crowded in little groups at the bidding of the shouting officers, it was more impressive than usual to the infantry.

Fred Collins, of A Company, was saying, "Thunder! I wisht I had a drink. Ain't

What happens to the bugler?

there any water round here?" Then somebody yelled, "There goes th' bugler!"

As the eyes of half the regiment swept in one machine-like movement, there was an instant's picture of a horse in a great <u>convulsive</u> leap of a death-wound and a rider leaning back with a crooked arm and spread fingers before his face. On the ground was the crimson terror of an exploding shell, with fibers of flame that seemed like lances.[3] A glittering bugle swung clear of the rider's back as fell headlong the horse and the man. In the air was an odor as from a conflagration.

Sometimes they of the infantry looked down at a fair little meadow which spread at their feet. Its long green grass was

---

1. **battery.** Place equipped with heavy guns
2. **caissons.** Two-wheeled carts for carrying ammunition and supplies
3. **lances.** Long, sharp weapons

WORDS FOR EVERYDAY USE:

in • ces • sant (in ses´ənt) *adj.,* not ceasing or stopping
con • vul • sive (kən vul´siv) *adj.,* marked by violent contractions or spasms

---

rippling gently in a breeze. Beyond it was the gray form of a house half torn to pieces by shells and by the busy axes of soldiers who had pursued firewood. The line of an old fence was now dimly marked by long weeds and by an occasional post. A shell had blown the well-house to fragments. Little lines of gray smoke ribboning upward from some embers indicated the place where had stood the barn.

From beyond a curtain of green woods there came the sound of some stupendous scuffle, as if two animals of the size of islands were fighting. At a distance there were occasional appearances of swift-moving men, horses, batteries, flags; and with the crashing of infantry volleys were heard, often, wild and frenzied cheers. In the midst of it all Smith and Ferguson, two privates of A Company, were engaged in a heated discussion which involved the greatest questions of the national existence.

The battery on the hill presently engaged in a frightful duel. The white legs of the gunners scampered this way and that way, and the officers redoubled their shouts. The guns, with their demeanors of <u>stolidity</u> and courage, were typical of something infinitely self-possessed in this clamor of death that swirled around the hill.

One of a "swing" team[4] was suddenly smitten quivering to the ground, and his maddened brethren dragged his torn body in their struggle to escape from this turmoil and danger. A young soldier astride one of the leaders swore and fumed in his saddle and furiously jerked at the bridle. An officer screamed out an order so violently that his voice broke and ended the sentence in a falsetto shriek. The leading company of the infantry regiment was somewhat exposed, and the colonel ordered it moved more fully under the shelter of the hill. There was the clank of steel against steel.

A lieutenant of the battery rode down and passed them, holding his right arm carefully in his left hand. And it was as if this arm was not at all a part of him, but belonged to another man. His sober and reflective charger[5] went slowly. The officer's face was grimy and perspiring, and his uniform was tousled as if he had been in direct grapple with an enemy. He smiled grimly when the men stared at him. He turned his horse toward the meadow.

Collins, of A Company, said, "I wisht I had a drink. I bet there's water in that there ol' well yonder!"

"Yes; but how you goin' to git it?"

For the little meadow which intervened was now suffering a terrible onslaught of shells. Its green and beautiful calm had vanished utterly. Brown earth was being flung in monstrous handfuls. And there was a massacre of the young blades of grass. They were being torn, burned, <u>obliterated</u>. Some curious fortune of the battle had made this gentle little meadow the object of the red hate of the shells, and each one as it exploded seemed like an <u>imprecation</u> in the face of a maiden.

The wounded officer who was riding across this expanse said to himself: "Why, they couldn't shoot any harder if the whole army was massed here!"

A shell struck the gray ruins of the house, and as, after the roar, the shattered

In what ways does the description of the guns differ from the description of the soldiers?

---

4. **"swing" team.** Middle team of a group of six soldiers on horseback
5. **charger.** War horse

WORDS FOR EVERYDAY USE:

sto • lid • i • ty (stə lid´ə tē´) n., display of little or no emotion

ob • lit • er • ate (ə blit´ər āt´) vt., do away with entirely, leaving no trace

im • pre • ca • tion (im´pri kā´shən) n., curse

wall fell in fragments, there was a noise which resembled the flapping of shutters during a wild gale of winter. Indeed, the infantry paused in the shelter of the bank appeared as men standing upon a shore contemplating a madness of the sea. The angel of calamity had under its glance the battery upon the hill. Fewer white-legged men labored about the guns. A shell had smitten one of the pieces, and after the flare, the smoke, the dust, the wrath of this blow were gone, it was possible to see white legs stretched horizontally upon the ground. And at that interval to the rear where it is the business of battery horses to stand with their noses to the fight, awaiting the command to drag their guns out of the destruction, or into it, or wheresoever these incomprehensible humans demanded with whip and spur—in this line of passive and dumb spectators, whose fluttering hearts yet would not let them forget the iron laws of man's control of them—in this rank of brute-soldiers there had been relentless and hideous carnage. From the ruck[6] of bleeding and prostrate horses, the men of the infantry could see one animal raising its stricken body with its forelegs and turning its nose with mystic and profound eloquence toward the sky.

Some comrades joked Collins about his thirst. "Well, if yeh want a drink so bad, why don't yeh go git it?"

"Well, I will in a minnet, if yeh don't shut up!"

A lieutenant of artillery floundered his horse straight down the hill with as little concern as if it were level ground. As he galloped past the colonel of the infantry, he threw up his hand in swift salute. "We've got to get out of that," he roared angrily. He was a black-bearded officer, and his eyes, which resembled beads, sparkled like those of an insane man. His jumping horse sped along the column of infantry.

The fat major, standing carelessly with his sword held horizontally behind him and with his legs far apart, looked after the receding horseman and laughed. "He wants to get back with orders pretty quick, or there'll be no batt'ry left," he observed.

The wise young captain of the second company hazarded to the lieutenant-colonel that the enemy's infantry would probably soon attack the hill, and the lieutenant-colonel snubbed him.

A private in one of the rear companies looked out over the meadow, and then turned to a companion and said, "Look there, Jim!" It was the wounded officer from the battery, who some time before had started to ride across the meadow, supporting his right arm carefully with his left hand. This man had encountered a shell, apparently, at a time when no one perceived him, and he could now be seen lying face downward with a stirruped foot stretched across the body of his dead horse. A leg of the charger extended slantingly upward, precisely as stiff as a stake. Around this motionless pair the shells still howled.

There was a quarrel in A Company. Collins was shaking his fist in the faces of some laughing comrades. "Dern yeh! I ain't afraid t' go. If yeh say much, I will go!"

"Of course, yeh will! You'll run through that there medder, won't yeh?"

Collins said, in a terrible voice: "You see now!"

At this ominous threat his comrades broke into renewed jeers.

Collins gave them a dark scowl, and went to find his captain. The latter was conversing with the colonel of the regiment.

"Captain," said Collins, saluting and standing at attention—in those days all trousers bagged at the knees—"Captain, I

---

6. **ruck.** Mass, collection, heap

want t' get permission to go git some water from that there well over yonder!"

The colonel and the captain swung about simultaneously and stared across the meadow. The captain laughed. "You must be pretty thirsty, Collins?"

"Yes, sir, I am."

"Well—ah," said the captain. After a moment, he asked, "Can't you wait?"

"No, sir."

The colonel was watching Collins's face. "Look here, my lad," he said, in a pious sort of voice—"Look here, my lad"—Collins was not a lad—"don't you think that's taking pretty big risks for a little drink of water?"

"I dunno," said Collins uncomfortably. Some of the resentment toward his companions, which perhaps had forced him into this affair, was beginning to fade. "I dunno w'ether 'tis."

The colonel and the captain contemplated him for a time.

"Well," said the captain finally.

"Well," said the colonel, "if you want to go, why, go."

Collins saluted. "Much obliged t' yeh."

As he moved away the colonel called after him. "Take some of the other boys' canteens[7] with you, an' hurry back, now."

"Yes, sir, I will."

The colonel and the captain looked at each other then, for it had suddenly occurred that they could not for the life of them tell whether Collins wanted to go or whether he did not.

They turned to regard Collins, and as they perceived him surrounded by <u>gesticulating</u> comrades, the colonel said, "Well, by thunder! I guess he's going."

Collins appeared as a man dreaming. In the midst of the questions, the advice, the warnings, all the excited talk of his company mates, he maintained a curious silence.

They were very busy in preparing him for his ordeal. When they inspected him carefully, it was somewhat like the examination that grooms give a horse before a race; and they were amazed, staggered, by the whole affair. Their astonishment found vent in strange repetitions.

"Are yeh sure a-goin'?" they demanded again and again.

"Certainly I am," cried Collins at last, furiously.

He strode sullenly away from them. He was swinging five or six canteens by their cords. It seemed that his cap would not remain firmly on his head, and often he reached and pulled it down over his brow.

There was a general movement in the compact column. The long animal-like thing moved slightly. Its four hundred eyes were turned upon the figure of Collins.

"Well, sir, if that ain't th' derndest thing! I never thought Fred Collins had the blood in him for that kind of business."

"What's he goin' to do, anyhow?"

"He's goin' to that well there after water."

"We ain't dyin' of thirst, are we? That's foolishness."

"Well, somebody put him up to it, an' he's doin' it."

"Say, he must be a desperate cuss."

When Collins faced the meadow and walked away from the regiment, he was

Why might Collins be silent?

Why might the colonel and the captain be unsure whether Collins wants to cross the meadow?

---

7. **canteens.** Containers for holding water

WORDS FOR EVERYDAY USE: ges • tic • u • lat • ing (jes tik´yoō lāt´iŋ) *part.*, making gestures

Does Collins want to go to the well? Why, or why not?

Does Collins feel like a hero? Why, or why not?

vaguely conscious that a chasm, the deep valley of all prides, was suddenly between him and his comrades. It was <u>provisional</u>, but the provision was that he return as a victor. He had blindly been led by quaint emotions, and laid himself under an obligation to walk squarely up to the face of death.

But he was not sure that he wished to make a retraction, even if he could do so without shame. As a matter of truth, he was sure of very little. He was mainly surprised.

It seemed to him supernaturally strange that he had allowed his mind to maneuver his body into such a situation. He understood that it might be called dramatically great.

However, he had no full appreciation of anything, excepting that he was actually conscious of being dazed. He could feel his dulled mind groping after the form and color of this incident. He wondered why he did not feel some keen agony of fear cutting his sense like a knife. He wondered at this, because human expression had said loudly for centuries that men should feel afraid of certain things, and that all men who did not feel this fear were phenomena—heroes.

He was, then, a hero. He suffered that disappointment which we would all have if we discovered that we were ourselves capable of those deeds which we most admire in history and legend. This, then, was a hero. After all, heroes were not much.

No, it could not be true. He was not a hero. Heroes had no shames in their lives, and, as for him, he remembered borrow-ing fifteen dollars from a friend and promising to pay it back the next day, and then avoiding that friend for ten months. When, at home, his mother had aroused him for the early labor of his life on the farm, it had often been his fashion to be irritable, childish, diabolical; and his mother had died since he had come to the war.

He saw that, in this matter of the well, the canteens, the shells, he was an intruder in the land of fine deeds.

He was now about thirty paces from his comrades. The regiment had just turned its many faces toward him.

From the forest of terrific noises there suddenly emerged a little uneven line of men. They fired fiercely and rapidly at distant foliage on which appeared little puffs of white smoke. The spatter of skirmish firing was added to the thunder of the guns on the hill. The little line of men ran forward. A color-sergeant fell flat with his flag as if he had slipped on ice. There was hoarse cheering from this distant field.

Collins suddenly felt that two demon fingers were pressed into his ears. He could see nothing but flying arrows, flaming red. He lurched from the shock of this explosion, but he made a mad rush for the house, which he viewed as a man submerged to the neck in a boiling surf might view the shore. In the air little pieces of shell howled, and the earthquake explosions drove him insane with the menace of their roar. As he ran the canteens knocked together with a rhythmical tinkling.

As he neared the house, each detail of the scene became vivid to him. He was

---

WORDS FOR EVERYDAY USE:

pro • vi • sion • al (prō vizh´ə nəl) *adj.*, lasting for a short while, not permanent

aware of some bricks of the vanished chimney lying on the sod. There was a door which hung by one hinge.

Rifle bullets called forth by the insistent skirmishers came from the far-off bank of foliage. They mingled with the shells and the pieces of shells until the air was torn in all directions by hootings, yells, howls. The sky was full of fiends who directed all their wild rage at his head.

When he came to the well, he flung himself face downward and peered into its darkness. There were <u>furtive</u> silver glintings some feet from the surface. He grabbled one of the canteens and, unfastening its cap, swung it down by the cord. The water flowed slowly in with an <u>indolent</u> gurgle.

And now, as he lay with his face turned away, he was suddenly smitten with the terror. It came upon his heart like the grasp of claws. All the power faded from his muscles. For an instant he was no more than a dead man.

The canteen filled with a maddening slowness, in the manner of all bottles. Presently he recovered his strength and addressed a screaming oath to it. He leaned over until it seemed as if he intended to try to push water into it with his hands.

What does Collins begin to feel as he fills the canteen?

His eyes as he gazed down into the well shone like two pieces of metal, and in their expression was a great appeal and a great curse. The stupid water derided him.

There was the blaring thunder of a shell. Crimson light shone through the swift-boiling smoke, and made a pink reflection on part of the wall of the well. Collins jerked out his arm and canteen with the same motion that a man would use in withdrawing his head from a furnace.

He scrambled erect and glared and hesitated. On the ground near him lay the old well bucket, with a length of rusty chain. He lowered it swiftly into the well. The bucket struck the water and then, turning lazily over, sank. When, with hand reaching tremblingly over hand, he hauled it out, it knocked often against the walls of the well and spilled some of its contents.

In running with a filled bucket, a man can adopt but one kind of gait. So, through this terrible field over which screamed practical angels of death, Collins ran in the manner of a farmer chased out of a dairy by a bull.

His face went staring white with anticipating—anticipation of a blow that would whirl him around and down. He would fall as he had seen other men fall, the life knocked out of them so suddenly that their knees were no more quick to touch the ground than their heads. He saw the long blue line of the regiment, but his comrades were standing looking at him from the edge of an impossible star. He was aware of some deep wheel ruts and hoofprints in the sod beneath his feet.

The artillery officer who had fallen in this meadow had been making groans in the teeth of the tempest of sound. These futile cries, wrenched from him by his agony, were heard only by shells, bullets. When wild-eyed Collins came running, this officer raised himself. His face contorted and blanched from pain, he was about to utter some great beseeching cry. But suddenly his face straightened, and he called: "Say, young man, give me a drink of water, will you?"

Collins had no room amid his emotions for surprise. He was mad from the threats of destruction.

"I can't!" he screamed, and in his reply was a full description of his quaking apprehension. His cap was gone and his hair was riotous. His clothes made it appear that he had been dragged over the ground by the heels. He ran on.

The officer's head sank down, and one elbow crooked. His foot in its brass-bound stirrup still stretched over the body of his horse and the other leg was under the steed.

But Collins turned. He came dashing back. His face had now turned gray, and in his eyes was all terror. "Here it is! here it is!"

The officer was as a man gone in drink. His arm bent like a twig. His head drooped as if his neck were of willow. He was sinking to the ground, to lie face downward.

Collins grabbed him by the shoulder. "Here it is. Here's your drink. Turn over. Turn over, man, for God's sake!"

With Collins hauling at his shoulder, the officer twisted his body and fell with his face turned toward that region where lived the unspeakable noises of the swirling missiles. There was the faintest shadow of a smile on his lips as he looked at Collins. He gave a sigh, a little primitive breath like that from a child.

Collins tried to hold the bucket steadily, but his shaking hands caused the water to splash all over the face of the dying man. Then he jerked it away and ran on.

The regiment gave him a welcoming roar. The grimed faces were wrinkled in laughter.

Why might Collins change his mind and return to the dying soldier?

His captain waved the bucket away. "Give it to the men!"

The two genial, skylarking young lieutenants were the first to gain possession of it. They played over it in their fashion.

When one tried to drink, the other teasingly knocked his elbow. "Don't Billie! You'll make me spill it," said the one. The other laughed.

Suddenly there was an oath, the thud of wood on the ground, and a swift murmur of astonishment among the ranks. The two lieutenants glared at each other. The bucket lay on the ground, empty. ■

What happens to the water Collins brings from the well?

Responding to the Selection

Do you think that the actions of the main character, or protagonist, in this story are heroic? Does the character think that his own actions are heroic? Why, or why not? Did reading this story give you any insights into what sometimes causes people to act heroically? Discuss these questions with your classmates.

Reviewing the Selection

RECALLING

1. Of what does Collins complain at the beginning of the story? Why do the other members of the regiment taunt him?

2. What does Collins decide to do?

3. What does Collins decide that he is as he heads toward the well?

4. Who stops Collins as he is returning from the well with the bucket? What does this person request? What is Collins's initial reaction? What does he then decide to do?

INTERPRETING

5. How does Collins feel as a result of the other soldiers' taunts?

6. What makes going to the well a very dangerous action to undertake? Why does Collins decide to go?

7. How would you describe Collins's state of mind as he heads toward the well? Does he act as the result of a conscious, free decision? What discovery does Collins make about heroism as he considers his own actions?

8. What makes it dangerous for Collins to bring the dying soldier a drink of water? Why does Collins do this despite the danger?

9. On the way to the well, Collins thinks, "This, then, was a hero. After all, heroes were not much." Why does he think this? Do you agree with Collins? Why, or why not?

10. When Collins returns with the water, how do the men react to him? What happens to the bucket of water? What purpose has Collins's heroism served? What point do you think the author is making about heroism by ending the story in this way?

Understanding Literature (Questions for Discussion)

1. **Psychological Fiction. Psychological fiction** is fiction that emphasizes the interior, subjective experiences of its characters, and especially such fiction when it deals with emotional or mental disturbance or anguish. What feelings cause Collins to decide to go to the well? What makes this a "desperate" thing to do? What feelings does Collins note in himself as he makes his perilous walk?

2. **Naturalism. Naturalism** was a literary movement of the late nineteenth and early twentieth centuries that saw actions and events as resulting inevitably from biological or natural forces or from forces in the environment. Does Collins in this story act heroically as a result of a free, conscious, well-thought-out decision? How would you paraphrase this thought of Collins's: "It seemed to him supernaturally strange that he had allowed his mind to maneuver his body into such a situation"? What do you think the author is saying about the forces that impel people to heroic actions? Explain.

3. **Theme.** A **theme** is a central idea in a work of literature. Which is the more heroic act, going for the water or bringing the water to the dying man? Why?

4. **Simile and Metaphor.** A **simile** is a comparison using *like* or *as*. A **metaphor** is a description of one thing as if it were another. The description invites the reader to make a comparison between two things. Read the following similes and metaphors from the story. Explain what things are being compared in each case and what these two things have in common.

   • "When a piece was fired, a red streak as round as a log flashed low in the heavens, like a monstrous bolt of lightning."

   • "From beyond a curtain of green woods there came the sound of some stupendous scuffle, as if two animals of the size of islands were fighting."

   • ". . . the red hate of the shells . . ."

   • "A leg of the charger extended slantingly upward, precisely as stiff as a stake."

   • ". . . the shells still howled."

   • "There was a general movement in the compact column. The long animal-like thing moved slightly. Its four hundred eyes were turned upon the figure of Collins."

   • ". . . he was vaguely conscious that a chasm, the deep valley of all prides, was suddenly between him and his comrades."

- ". . . some keen agony of fear cutting his sense like a knife."
- ". . . he made a mad rush for the house, which he viewed as a man submerged to the neck in a boiling surf might view the shore."
- "The sky was full of fiends who directed all their wild rage at his head."
- ". . . his comrades were standing looking at him from the edge of an impossible star."
- "His arm bent like a twig. His head drooped as if his neck were of willow."

Responding in Writing

Citation for Bravery. Imagine that you are one of the commanders in charge of Collins's regiment. Write a brief statement commending him for his actions during the battle.

PROJECT

Battles of the Civil War. Working with other students in a small group, choose a famous battle of the Civil War, research that battle, and report on it to your class. Possible battles to consider include the following:

Fort Sumter	Shiloh	Vicksburg	Petersburg
Bull Run	New Orleans	Fort Wagner	The *Merrimack* and
Fredericksburg	Sharpsburg	Gettysburg	the *Monitor*
Chancellorsville	Antietam	Chickamauga	

Death of Reynolds Gettysburg

READER'S JOURNAL

What can one possibly say to the parent or spouse of a person who dies in battle? If you were given the task of comforting someone who had lost a loved one in a war, what words would you choose? What would be your message? Write a few of your ideas in your journal.

SPEAKING AND LISTENING SKILLS

Read the Language Arts Survey, 3.2, "Elements of Verbal Communication." Then after you read the poem, practice presenting the poem with another reader. One person should read aloud stanzas 1, 3, and 5, and the other should read aloud stanzas 2 and 4.

"Do not weep, maiden, for war is kind"

STEPHEN CRANE

What happens to the lover?

Do not weep, maiden, for war is kind.
Because your lover threw wild hands toward the sky
And the affrighted steed ran on alone,
Do not weep.
5   War is kind.

Hoarse, booming drums of the regiment,
Little souls who thirst for fight,
These men were born to drill and die.
The unexplained glory flies above them,
10   Great is the Battle-God, great, and his Kingdom—
A field where a thousand corpses lie.

Do not weep, babe, for war is kind.
Because your father tumbled in the yellow trenches,
Raged at his breast, gulped and died,
15   Do not weep.
War is kind.

Does the speaker believe in the "virtue of slaughter" and the "excellence of killing"? What makes you think so?

Swift blazing flag of the regiment,
Eagle with crest of red and gold,
These men were born to drill and die.
20   Point for them the virtue of slaughter,
Make plain to them the excellence of killing
And a field where a thousand corpses lie.

Mother whose heart hung humble as a button
On the bright splendid shroud of your son,
25   Do not weep.
War is kind.

Responding to the Selection

In what ways is war not kind? Discuss this question with your classmates.

Reviewing the Selection

RECALLING

1. What three people are addressed by the speaker of the poem? What does the speaker say to each of these people?

2. What happens to the lover, the father, and the son?

INTERPRETING

3. Does the speaker mean literally what he says to the three people he addresses? Explain.

4. What emotional effect does the description of what happens to the lover, the father, and the son have on the reader?

SYNTHESIZING

5. This poem is written in mock heroic language. What phrases in the two indented stanzas of the poem suggest that the speaker does not, in fact, believe that war is kind?

Understanding Literature (Questions for Discussion)

1. **Irony. Irony** is a difference between appearance and reality. In **verbal irony,** something is said that implies its opposite. What examples of verbal irony can you find in this poem?

2. **Free Verse. Free verse** is poetry that does not employ traditional patterns of rhyme, rhythm, or stanza form. Free verse tends to sound a lot more like ordinary speech than traditional verse does. What elements in this poem show that it is intended as speech, or one side of an imaginary conversation?

   When writing free verse, poets often invent their own unique structures, or organizational patterns, to replace traditional rhyming stanzas. What is the structure of this poem? Into how many stanzas is it divided? What do stanzas 1, 3, and 5 have in common? What kind of language is being mocked in stanzas 2 and 4? Why might stanzas 2 and 4 be more traditional in their use of poetic devices, such as a regular meter and rhyme, than stanzas 1, 3, and 5?

3. **Parallelism and Alliteration. Parallelism** is a rhetorical technique in which a writer emphasizes the equal value or weight of two or more ideas by expressing them in the same grammatical form. **Alliteration** is the repetition of initial consonant sounds. When writing free verse, poets often make use of devices such as parallelism and alliteration, in place of traditional rhymes, to give their work a poetic quality. What examples of parallelism and alliteration can you find in the poem?

from "A House Divided"
by Abraham Lincoln

SPEECH DELIVERED AT SPRINGFIELD, ILLINOIS,
AT THE CLOSE OF THE REPUBLICAN STATE
CONVENTION. JUNE 16, 1858

If we could first know *where* we are, and *whither* we are tending, we could better judge *what* to do, and *how* to do it.

We are now far into the *fifth* year, since a policy was initiated, with the *avowed* object, and *confident* promise, of putting an end to slavery agitation.

Under the operation of that policy, that agitation has not only, *not ceased*, but has *constantly augmented.*

In my opinion, it *will* not cease, until a *crisis* shall have been reached, and passed—

"A house divided against itself cannot stand."[1]

I believe this government cannot endure, permanently half *slave* and half *free.*

I do not expect the Union to be *dissolved*—I do not expect the house to *fall*—but I *do* expect it will cease to be divided.

It will become *all* one thing, or *all* the other.

Either the *opponents* of slavery, will arrest the further spread of it, and place it where the public mind shall rest in the belief that it is in course of ultimate extinction; or its *advocates* will push it forward, till it shall become alike lawful in *all* the States, *old* as well as *new—North* as well as *South.*

Letter to Mrs. Bixby
by Abraham Lincoln

Executive Mansion, Washington,
November 21, 1864

Mrs. Bixby, Boston, Massachusetts:

Dear Madam:

I have been shown in the files of the War Department a statement of the Adjutant–General of Massachusetts that you are the mother of five sons who have died gloriously on the field of battle. I feel how weak and fruitless must be any words of mine which should attempt to beguile you from the grief of a loss so overwhelming. But I cannot refrain from tendering to you the consolation that may be found in the thanks of the Republic they died to save. I pray that our Heavenly Father may assuage the anguish of your bereavement, and leave you only the cherished memory of the loved and lost, and the solemn pride that must be yours to have laid so costly a sacrifice upon the altar of freedom.

Yours very sincerely and respectfully,

Abraham Lincoln

from the Second Inaugural Address
by Abraham Lincoln

On the occasion corresponding to this four years ago, all thoughts were anxiously directed to an impending civil war. All dreaded it—all sought to avert it. While the inaugural address was being delivered from this place, devoted altogether to *saving* the Union without war, insurgent agents were in the city seeking to *destroy* it without war—seeking to dissol[v]e the Union, and divide effects, by negotiation. Both parties deprecated war; but one of them would *make* war rather than let the nation survive; and the other would *accept* war rather than let it perish. And the war came.

One eighth of the whole population were colored slaves, not distributed generally over the Union, but localized in the Southern part of it. These slaves constituted a peculiar and powerful interest. All knew that this interest was, somehow, the cause of the war. To strengthen, perpetuate, and extend this interest was the object for which the insurgents would rend the Union, even by war; while the government claimed no right to do more than to restrict the territorial enlargement of it. Neither party expected for the war, the magnitude, or the duration, which it has already attained. Neither anticipated that the *cause* of the conflict might cease with, or even before, the conflict itself should cease. Each looked for an easier triumph, and a result less fundamental and astounding. Both read the same Bible, and pray to the same God; and each invokes His aid against the other. It may seem strange that any men should dare to ask a just God's assistance in wringing their bread from the sweat of other men's faces; but let us judge not that we be not judged. The prayers of both could not be answered; that

---

1. **"A house . . . stand."** Biblical reference to Mark 3:25, "If a house be divided against itself, that house cannot stand."

of neither has been answered fully. The Almighty has his own purposes. "Woe unto the world because of offenses! for it must needs be that offenses come; but woe to that man by whom the offense cometh!" If we shall suppose that American Slavery is one of those offenses which, in the providence of God, must needs come, but which, having continued through His appointed time, He now wills to remove, and that He gives to both North and South, this terrible war, as the woe due to those by whom the offense came, shall we discern therein any departure from those divine attributes which the believers in a Living God always ascribe to Him? Fondly do we hope—fervently do we pray—that this mighty scourge of war may speedily pass away. Yet, if God wills that it continue, until all the wealth piled by the bond-man's two hundred and fifty years of unrequited toil[1] shall be sunk, and until every drop of blood drawn with the lash, shall be paid by another drawn with the sword, as was said three thousand years ago, so still it must be said "the judgments of the Lord, are true and righteous altogether."

With malice toward none; with charity for all; with firmness in the right, as God gives us to see the right, let us strive on to finish the work we are in; to bind up the nation's wounds; to care for him who shall have borne the battle, and for his widow, and his orphan—to do all which may achieve and cherish a just and lasting peace, among ourselves, and with all nations.

"Farewell to His Army"
by Robert E. Lee

Headquarters, Army Northern Virginia,
April 10, 1865

After four years of arduous service, marked by unsurpassed courage and fortitude, the Army of Northern Virginia has been compelled to yield to overwhelming numbers and resources. I need not tell the survivors of so many hard-fought battles, who have remained steadfast to the last, that I have consented to this result from no distrust of them; but, feeling that valor and devotion could accomplish nothing that could compensate for the loss that would have attended the continuation of the contest, I have determined to avoid the useless sacrifice of those whose past services have endeared them to their countrymen. By the terms of the agreement, officers and men can return to their homes, and remain there until exchanged.[2]

You will take with you *the satisfaction that proceeds from the consciousness of duty faithfully performed*; and I earnestly pray that a merciful God will extend to you his blessing and protection. With an unceasing admiration of your constancy and devotion to your country, and a grateful remembrance of your kind and generous consideration of myself, I bid you an affectionate farewell.

"O Captain! My Captain!"
by Walt Whitman

O Captain! my Captain! our fearful trip is done,
The ship has weather'd every rack,[3] the prize we
    sought is won,
The port is near, the bells I hear, the people all
    exulting,
While follow eyes the steady keel,[4] the vessel grim
    and daring;
5   But O heart! heart! heart!
      O the bleeding drops of red,
        Where on the deck my Captain lies,
        Fallen cold and dead.

O Captain! my Captain! rise up and hear the bells;
10 Rise up—for you the flag is flung—for you the bugle
    trills,
For you bouquets and ribbon'd wreaths—for you the
    shores a-crowding,
For you they call, the swaying mass, their eager faces
    turning;
    Here Captain! dear father!
      This arm beneath your head!
15   It is some dream that on the deck,
        You've fallen cold and dead.

My Captain does not answer, his lips are pale and still,
My father does not feel my arm, he has no pulse nor
    will,
The ship is anchor'd safe and sound, its voyage
    closed and done,
20 From fearful trip the victor ship comes in with object
    won;
    Exult O shores, and ring O bells!
      But I with mournful tread,
        Walk the deck my Captain lies,
        Fallen cold and dead.

---

1. **bond-man's . . . toil.** Refers to the period of slavery in which the slaves were not requited or paid for their labor
2. **exchanged.** Discharged from military service
3. **rack.** Upheaval; torment
4. **keel.** Beam along the bottom of a boat that supports the frame

from "When Lilacs Last in the Dooryard Bloom'd" by Walt Whitman

1

When lilacs last in the dooryard bloom'd,
And the great star[1] early droop'd in the western sky
    in the night,
I mourn'd, and yet shall mourn with ever-returning
    spring.
Ever-returning spring, trinity sure to me you bring,
5 Lilac blooming perennial and drooping star in the
    west,
And thought of him I love.

2

O powerful western fallen star!
O shades of night—O moody, tearful night!
O great star disappear'd—O the black murk that
    hides the star!
10 O cruel hands that hold me powerless—O helpless
    soul of me!
O harsh surrounding cloud that will not free my
    soul.

6

Coffin that passes through lanes and streets,
Through day and night with the great cloud
    darkening the land,
35 With the pomp of the inloop'd flags with the cities
    draped in black,
With the show of the States themselves as of crape-
    veil'd women standing,
With processions long and winding and the
    flambeaus[2] of the night,
With the countless torches lit, with the silent sea of
    faces and the unbared heads,
With the waiting depot, the arriving coffin, and the
    sombre faces,
40 With dirges through the night, with the thousand
    voices rising strong and solemn,
With all the mournful voices of the dirges pour'd
    around the coffin,
The dim-lit churches and the shuddering organs—
    where amid these you journey,
With the tolling tolling bells' perpetual clang,
Here, coffin that slowly passes,
45 I give you my sprig of lilac.

7

(Nor for you, for one alone,
Blossoms and branches green to coffins all I bring,
For fresh as the morning, thus would I chant a song
    for you O sane and sacred death.

All over bouquets of roses,
50 O death, I cover you over with roses and early lilies,
But mostly and now the lilac that blooms the first,
Copious I break, I break the sprigs from the bushes,
With loaded arms I come, pouring for you,
For you and the coffins all of you O death.)

from *Up from Slavery*
by Booker T. Washington

After the coming of freedom there were two points upon which practically all the people on our place were agreed, and I find that this was generally true throughout the South: that they must change their names, and that they must leave the old plantation for at least a few days or weeks in order that they might really feel sure that they were free.

In some way a feeling got among the colored people that it was far from proper for them to bear the surname of their former owners, and a great many of them took other surnames. This was one of the first signs of freedom. When they were slaves, a colored person was simply called "John" or "Susan." There was seldom occasion for more than the use of one name. If "John" or "Susan" belonged to a white man by the name of "Hatcher," sometimes he was called "John Hatcher," or as often "Hatcher's John." But there was a feeling that "John Hatcher" or "Hatcher's John" was not the proper title by which to denote a freeman; and so in many cases "John Hatcher" was changed to "John S. Lincoln" or "John S. Sherman," the initial "S" standing for no name, it being simply a part of what the colored man proudly called his "entitles."[3]

As I have stated, most of the colored people left the old plantation for a short while at least, so as to be sure, it seemed, that they could leave and try their freedom on to see how it felt. After they had remained away for a time, many of the older slaves, especially, returned to their old homes and made some kind of contract with their former owners by which they remained on the estate.

My mother's husband, who was the stepfather of my brother John and myself, did not belong to the same owners as did my mother. In fact, he seldom came to our plantation. I remember seeing him there perhaps once a

---

1. **great star.** Refers to Venus but comes to be associated with Lincoln
2. **flambeaus.** Torches
3. **"entitles."** That to which one has a right; also implies giving a title or name to oneself

year, that being about Christmas time. In some way, during the war, by running away and following the Federal soldiers, it seems, he found his way into the new state of West Virginia.[1] As soon as freedom was declared, he sent for my mother to come to the Kanawha Valley, in West Virginia. At that time a journey from Virginia over the mountains to West Virginia was rather a tedious and in some cases a painful undertaking. What little clothing and few household goods we had were placed in a cart, but the children walked the greater portion of the distance, which was several hundred miles.

I do not think any of us had been very far from the plantation, and the taking of a long journey into another state was quite an event. The parting from our former owners and the members of our own race on the plantation was a serious occasion. From the time of our parting till their death we kept up a correspondence with the older members of the family, and in later years we have kept in touch with those who were the younger members. We were several weeks making the trip, and most of the time we slept in the open air and did our cooking over a log fire out of doors. One night I recall that we camped near an abandoned log cabin, and my mother decided to build a fire in that for cooking, and afterward to make a "pallet"[2] on the floor for our sleeping. Just as the fire had gotten well started a large black snake fully a yard and a half long dropped down the chimney and ran out on the floor. Of course we at once abandoned that cabin. Finally we reached our destination—a little town called Malden, which is about five miles from Charleston, the present capital of the state.

At that time salt-mining was the great industry in that part of West Virginia, and the little town of Malden was right in the middle of the salt-furnaces. My stepfather had already secured a job at a salt-furnace, and he had also secured a little cabin for us to live in. Our new house was no better than the one we had left on the old plantation in Virginia. In fact, in one respect it was worse. Notwithstanding the poor condition of our plantation cabin, we were at all times sure of pure air. Our new home was in the midst of a cluster of cabins crowded closely together, and as there were no sanitary regulations, the filth about the cabins was often intolerable. Some of our neighbors were colored people, and some were the poorest and most ignorant and degraded white people. It was a motley mixture. Drinking, gambling, quarrels, fights, and shockingly immoral practices were frequent. All who lived in the little town were in one way or another connected with the salt business. Though I was a mere child, my stepfather put me and my brother at work in one of the furnaces. Often I began work as early as four o'clock in the morning.

The first thing I ever learned in the way of book knowledge was while working in this salt-furnace. Each salt-packer had his barrels marked with a certain number. The number allotted to my stepfather was "18." At the close of the day's work the boss of the packers would come around and put "18" on each of our barrels, and I soon learned to recognize that figure wherever I saw it, and after a while got to the point where I could make that figure, though I knew nothing about any other figures or letters.

From the time that I can remember having any thoughts about anything, I recall that I had an intense longing to learn to read. I determined, when quite a small child, that, if I accomplished nothing else in life, I would in some way get enough education to enable me to read common books and newspapers. Soon after we got settled in some manner in our new cabin in West Virginia, I induced my mother to get hold of a book for me. How or where she got it I do not know, but in some way she procured an old copy of Webster's "blue-back" spelling-book, which contained the alphabet, followed by such meaningless words as "ab," "ba," "ca," "da." I began at once to devour this book, and I think that it was the first one I ever had in my hands. I had learned from somebody that the way to begin to read was to learn the alphabet, so I tried in all the ways I could think of to learn it—all of course without a teacher, for I could find no one to teach me. At that time there was not a single member of my race anywhere near us who could read, and I was too timid to approach any of the white people. In some way, within a few weeks, I mastered the greater portion of the alphabet. In all my efforts to learn to read my mother shared fully my ambition, and sympathized with me and aided me in every way that she could. Though she was totally ignorant, so far as mere book knowledge was concerned, she had high ambitions for her children, and a large fund of good, hard, common sense which seemed to enable her to meet and master every situation. If I have done anything in life worth attention, I feel sure that I inherited the disposition from my mother.

In the midst of my struggles and longing for an education, a young colored boy who had learned to read in the state of Ohio came to Malden. As soon as the colored people found out that he could read, a newspaper was secured, and at the close of nearly every day's work this young man would be surrounded by a group of men and women who were anxious to hear him read the news contained in the papers. How I used to envy this man! He seemed to me to be the one young man in all the world who ought to be satisfied with his attainments.

About this time the question of having some kind of a school opened for the colored children in the village began to be discussed by members of the race. As it would be the first school for Negro children that had

---

1. **new state of West Virginia.** West Virginia became a state in 1863.

2. **"pallet."** Small bed or a pad filled with straw and used directly on the floor

ever been opened in that part of Virginia, it was, of course, to be a great event, and the discussion excited the widest interest. The most perplexing question was where to find a teacher. The young man from Ohio who had learned to read the papers was considered, but his age was against him. In the midst of the discussion about a teacher, another young colored man from Ohio, who had been a soldier, in some way found his way into town. It was soon learned that he possessed considerable education, and he was engaged by the colored people to teach their first school. As yet no free schools[1] had been started for colored people in that section, hence each family agreed to pay a certain amount per month, with the understanding that the teacher was to "board 'round"—that is, spend a day with each family. This was not bad for the teacher, for each family tried to provide the very best on the day the teacher was to be its guest. I recall that I looked forward with an anxious appetite to the "teacher's day" at our little cabin.

This experience of a whole race beginning to go to school for the first time, presents one of the most interesting studies that has ever occurred in connection with the development of any race. Few people who were not right in the midst of the scenes can form any exact idea of the intense desire which the people of my race showed for an education. As I have stated, it was a whole race trying to go to school. Few were too young, and none too old, to make the attempt to learn. As fast as any kind of teachers could be secured, not only were day-schools filled, but night-schools as well. The great ambition of the older people was to try to learn to read the Bible before they died. With this end in view, men and women who were fifty or seventy-five years old would often be found in the night-school. Sunday-schools were formed soon after freedom, but the principal book studied in the Sunday- school was the spelling-book. Day-school, night-school, Sunday-school, were always crowded, and often many had to be turned away for want of room.

The opening of the school in the Kanawha Valley, however, brought to me one of the keenest disappointments that I ever experienced. I had been working in a salt-furnace for several months, and my stepfather had discovered that I had a financial value, and so, when the school opened, he decided that he could not spare me from my work. This decision seemed to cloud my every ambition. The disappointment was made all the more severe by reason of the fact that my place of work was where I could see the happy children passing to and from school, mornings and afternoons. Despite this disappointment, however, I determined that I would learn something, anyway. I applied myself with greater earnestness than ever to the mastering of what was in the "blue-back" speller.

My mother sympathized with me in my disappointment, and sought to comfort me in all the ways she could, and to help me find a way to learn. After a while I

succeeded in making arrangements with the teacher to give me some lessons at night, after the day's work was done. These night lessons were so welcome that I think I learned more at night than the other children did during the day. My own experiences in the night-school gave me faith in the night-school idea, with which, in after years, I had to do both at Hampton and Tuskegee. But my boyish heart was still set upon going to the day-school, and I let no opportunity slip to push my ease. Finally I won, and was permitted to go to the school in the day for a few months, with the understanding that I was to rise early in the morning and work in the furnace till nine o'clock, and return immediately after school closed in the afternoon for at least two more hours of work.

The schoolhouse was some distance from the furnace, and as I had to work till nine o'clock, and the school opened at nine, I found myself in a difficulty. School would always be begun before I reached it, and sometimes my class had recited. To get around this difficulty I yielded to a temptation for which most people, I suppose, will condemn me; but since it is a fact, I might as well state it. I have great faith in the power and influence of facts. It is seldom that anything is permanently gained by holding back a fact. There was a large clock in a little office in the furnace. This clock, of course, all the hundred or more workmen depended upon to regulate their hours of beginning and ending the day's work. I got the idea that the way for me to reach school on time was to move the clock hands from half-past eight up to the nine o'clock mark. This I found myself doing morning after morning till the furnace "boss" discovered that something was wrong, and locked the clock in a case. I did not mean to inconvenience any body. I simply meant to reach that schoolhouse in time.

When, however, I found myself at the school for the first time, I also found myself confronted with two other difficulties. In the first place, I found that all of the other children wore hats or caps on their heads, and I had neither hat nor cap. In fact, I do not remember that up to the time of going to school I had ever worn any kind of covering upon my head, nor do I recall that either I or anybody else had even thought anything about the need of covering for my head. But, of course, when I saw how all the other boys were dressed, I began to feel quite uncomfortable. As usual, I put the case before my mother, and she explained to me that she had no money with which to buy a "store hat," which was a rather new institution at that time among the members of my race and was considered quite the thing for young and old to own, but that she would find a way to help me out of the difficulty. She accordingly got two pieces of "homespun"[2]

---

1. **free schools.** Schools set up and supervised by the Freedmen's Bureau, an agency set up after the Civil War to aid African Americans in transition from slavery to freedom
2. **homespun.** Coarse, loosely woven cloth spun at home

and sewed them together, and I was soon the proud possessor of my first cap.

The lesson that my mother taught me in this has always remained with me, and I have tried as best I could to teach it to others. I have always felt proud, whenever I think of the incident, that my mother had strength of character enough not to be led into the temptation of seeming to be that which she was not—of trying to impress my schoolmates and others with the fact that she was able to buy me a "store hat" when she was not. I have always felt proud that she refused to go into debt for that which she did not have the money to pay for. Since that time I have owned many kinds of caps and hats, but never one of which I have felt so proud as of the cap made of the two pieces of cloth sewed together by my mother. I have noted the fact, but without satisfaction, I need not add, that several of the boys who began their careers with "store hats" and who were my schoolmates and used to join in the sport that was made of me because I had only a "homespun" cap, have ended their careers in the penitentiary, while others are not able now buy any kind of hat.

My second difficulty was with regard to my name, or rather *a* name. From the time when I could remember anything, I had been called simply "Booker." Before going to school it had never occurred to me that it was needful or appropriate to have an additional name. When I heard the school-roll called, I noticed that all of the children had at least two names, and some of them indulged in what seemed to me the extravagance of having three. I was in deep perplexity, because I knew that the teacher would demand of me at least two names, and I had only one. By the time the occasion came for the enrolling of my name, an idea occurred to me which I thought would make me equal to the situation; and so, when the teacher asked me what my full name was, I calmly told him "Booker Washington,"[1] as if I had been called by that name all my life; and by that name I have since been known. Later in life I found that my mother had given me the name of "Booker Taliaferro" soon after I was born, but in some way that part of my name seemed to disappear, and for a long while was forgotten, but as soon as I found out about it I revived it, and made my full name "Booker Taliaferro Washington." I think there are not many men in our country who have had the privilege of naming themselves in the way that I have.

More than once I have tried to picture myself in the position of a boy or man with an honored and distinguished ancestry which I could trace back through a period of hundreds of years, and who had not only inherited a name, but fortune and a proud family homestead; and yet I have sometimes had the feeling that if I had inherited these, and had been a member of a more popular race, I should have been inclined to yield to the temptation of depending upon my ancestry and my color to do that for me which I should do for myself. Years ago I resolved that because I had no ancestry myself I would leave a record of which my children would be proud, and which might encourage them to still higher effort.

The world should not pass judgment upon the Negro, and especially the Negro youth, too quickly or too harshly. The Negro boy has obstacles, discouragements, and temptations to battle with that are little known to those not situated as he is. When a white boy undertakes a task, it is taken for granted that he will succeed. On the other hand, people are usually surprised if the Negro boy does not fail. In a word, the Negro youth starts out with the presumption against him.

The influence of ancestry, however, is important in helping forward any individual or race, if too much reliance is not placed upon it. Those who constantly direct attention to the Negro youth's moral weaknesses, and compare his advancement with that of white youths, do not consider the influence of the memories which cling about the old family homesteads. I have no idea, as I have stated elsewhere, who my grandmother was. I have, or have had, uncles and aunts and cousins, but I have no knowledge as to what most of them are. My case will illustrate that of hundreds of thousands of black people in every part of our country. The very fact that the white boy is conscious that, if he fails in life, he will disgrace the whole family record, extending back through many generations, is of tremendous value in helping him to resist temptations. The fact that the individual has behind and surrounding him proud family history and connection serves as a stimulus to help him to overcome obstacles when striving for success.

The time that I was permitted to attend school during the day was short, and my attendance was irregular. It was not long before I had to stop attending day-school altogether, and devote all of my time again to work. I resorted to the night-school again. In fact, the greater part of the education I secured in my boyhood was gathered through the night-school after my day's work was done. I had difficulty often in securing a satisfactory teacher. Sometimes, after I had secured some one to teach me at night, I would find, much to my disappointment, that the teacher knew but little more than I did. Often I would have to walk several miles at night in order to recite my night-school lessons. There was never a time in my youth, no matter how dark and discouraging the days might be, when one resolve did not continually remain with me, and that was a determination to secure an education at any cost.

Soon after we moved to West Virginia, my mother adopted into our family, notwithstanding our poverty, an orphan boy, to whom afterward we gave the name of James B. Washington. He has ever since remained a member of the family.

---

1. **Booker Washington.** Washington was his stepfather's first name.

After I had worked in the salt-furnace for some time, work was secured for me in a coal mine which was operated mainly for the purpose of securing fuel for the salt-furnace. Work in the coal mine I always dreaded. One reason for this was that any one who worked in a coal mine was always unclean, at least while at work, and it was a very hard job to get one's skin clean after the day's work was over. Then it was fully a mile from the opening of the coal mine to the face of the coal, and all, of course, was in the blackest darkness. I do not believe that one ever experiences anywhere else such darkness as he does in a coal mine. The mine was divided into a large number of different "rooms" or departments, and, as I never was able to learn the location of all these "rooms," I many times found myself lost in the mine. To add to the horror of being lost, sometimes my light would go out, and then, if I did not happen to have a match, I would wander about in the darkness until by chance I found some one to give me a light. The work was not only hard, but it was dangerous. There was always the danger of being blown to pieces by a premature explosion of powder, or of being crushed by falling slate.[1] Accidents from one or the other of these causes were frequently occurring, and this kept me in constant fear. Many children of the tenderest years were compelled then, as is now true I fear, in most coal mining districts, to spend a large part of their lives in these coal mines, with little opportunity to get an education; and, what is worse, I have often noted that, as a rule, young boys who begin life in a coal mine are often physically and mentally dwarfed. They soon lose ambition to do anything else than to continue as a coal miner.

In those days, and later as a young man, I used to try to picture in my imagination the feelings and ambitions of a white boy with absolutely no limit placed upon his aspirations and activities. I used to envy the white boy who had no obstacles placed in the way of his becoming a Congressman, Governor, Bishop, or President by reason of the accident of his birth or race. I used to picture the way that I would act under such circumstances; how I would begin at the bottom and keep rising until I reached the highest round of success.

In later years, I confess that I do not envy the white boy as I once did. I have learned that success is to be measured not so much by the position that one has reached in life as by the obstacles which he has overcome while trying to succeed. Looked at from this standpoint, I almost reach the conclusion that often the Negro boy's birth and connection with an unpopular race is an advantage, so far as real life is concerned. With few exceptions, the Negro youth must work harder and must perform his task even better than a white youth in order to secure recognition. But out of the hard and unusual struggle which he is compelled to pass, he gets a strength, a confidence, that one misses whose pathway is comparatively smooth by reason of birth and race.

From any point of view, I had rather be what I am, a member of the Negro race, than be able to claim membership with the most favored of any other race. I have always been made sad when I have heard members of any race claiming rights and privileges, or certain badges of distinction, on the ground simply that they were members of this or that race, regardless of their own individual worth or attainments. I have been made to feel sad for such persons because I am conscious of the fact that mere connection with what is known as a superior race will not permanently carry an individual forward unless he has individual worth, and mere connection with what is regarded as an inferior race will not finally hold an individual back if he possesses intrinsic, individual merit. Every persecuted individual and race should get much consolation out of the great human law, which is universal and eternal, that merit, no matter under what skin found, is in the long run, recognized and rewarded. This I have said here, not to call attention to myself as an individual, but to the race to which I am proud to belong.

ABOLITIONIST VOICES

from *An Appeal in Favor of That Class of Americans Called Africans*
by Lydia Maria Child

We first debase the nature of man by making him a slave, and then very coolly tell him that he must always remain a slave because he does not know how to use freedom. We first crush people to the earth, and then claim the right of trampling on them forever, because they are prostrate. Truly, human selfishness never invented a rule which worked out so charmingly both ways!

from *Freedom Journal* March 16, 1827
by John B. Russwurm

Education being an object of the highest importance to the welfare of society, we shall endeavor to present just and adequate views of it, and to urge upon our brethren the necessity and expediency of training their children . . . It is surely time that we should awake from this lethargy of years, and make a concentrated effort for the education of our youth. We form a spoke in the human wheel, and it is necessary that we should understand our dependence on the different parts, and their on us, in order to perform our part with propriety.

1.**slate.** Hard, fine-grained rock

The interesting fact that there are *five hundred thousand* free persons of color, one half of whom might peruse, and the whole benefitted by the publication of the Journal; that no publication, as yet, has been devoted exclusively to their improvement—that many selections from approved standard authors, which are within the reach of few, may occasionally be made—and more important still, that this large body of our citizens have no public channel—all serve to prove the real necessity, at present, for the appearance of the FREEDOM'S JOURNAL.

from Editorial in *The Liberator*, January 1, 1831
by William Lloyd Garrison

I am aware that many object to the severity of my language, but is there not cause for severity? I will be harsh as truth, and as uncompromising as justice. On this subject, I do not wish to think, or speak, or write, with moderation. No! No! Tell a man whose house in on fire to sound a moderate alarm . . . but urge me not to use moderation in cause like the present . . .

I am in earnest—I will not equivocate—I will not excuse—I will not retreat a single inch—AND I WILL BE HEARD.

from "Appeal to the Christian Women of the Southern States"
by Angelina Grimké

Man, who was created in the image of his Maker, never can properly be termed a thing, though the laws of the Slave States do call him a "chattel personal"[1]; Man, I assert, never was put under the feet of men by the first charter of human rights which was given by God . . . It has been justly remarked that "God never made a slave," he made man upright, his back was not made to carry burdens, nor his neck to wear a yoke, and the man must be crushed within him, before his back can be fitted to the burden of perpetual slavery; and that his back is not fitted to it, is manifest by the insurrections that so often disturb the peace and security of slaveholding countries . . . Slavery always has, and always will produce insurrections wherever it exists, because it is a violation of the natural order of things, and no human power can much longer perpetuate it.

from *Slavery*
by William Ellery Channing

I come now to what is to my own mind the great argument against seizing and using a man as property. He cannot be property in the sight of God and justice, because his a Rational, Moral, Immortal Being; because created in God's image, and therefore in the highest sense his child; because created to unfold godlike faculties, and to govern himself by a Divine Law written on his heart, and republished in God's Word. His whole nature forbids that he should be seized as property. From his very nature it follows, that so to seize him is to offer an insult to his Maker, and to inflict aggravated social wrong. . . .

No man, who seriously considers what human nature is, and what it was made for, can think of setting up a claim to a fellow-creature. What! own a spiritual being, a being made to know and adore God, and who is to outlive the sun and stars? What! chain to our lowest uses a being made for truth and virtue? convert into a brute instrument that intelligent nature, on which the idea of Duty has dawned, and which is a nobler type of God than all outward creation! Should we not deem it a wrong which no punishment could expiate, were one of our children seized as property, and driven by the ship to toil? And shall God's child, dearer to him than an only son to a human parent, be thus degraded?

from Argument before the Supreme Court in the Case of Wharton Jones v. John Vanzandt, 1846
by Salmon P. Chase

The law of the Creator, which invests every human being with an inalienable title to freedom, cannot be repealed by any inferior law, which asserts that man is property. Such a law may be enforced by power; but the exercise of the power must be confined within the jurisdiction of the state, which establishes the law. It cannot be enforced—it can have no operation whatever—in any other jurisdiction. The very moment a slave passes beyond the jurisdiction of the state, in which he is held as such, he ceases to be a slave; not because any law or regulation of the state which he enters confers freedom upon him, but because he continues to be a man and leaves behind him the law of force, which made him a slave.

---

1. **"chattel personal."** Movable item of personal property

UNIT REVIEW

Slavery and the Civil War

VOCABULARY FROM THE SELECTIONS

acclivity, 382
aspirated, 386
consecrate, 376
convulsive, 392
diligently, 366
efface, 384
embrasure, 382
furtive, 397
gesticulate, 385
gesticulating, 395
imprecation, 393
incessant, 392

indolent, 397
ludicrous, 384
malign, 388
obdurate, 367
obliterate, 393
oscillation, 384
provisional, 396
rapturous, 366
score, 376
sentinel, 381
stolidity, 393

LITERARY TERMS

alliteration, 403
allusion, 373
antithesis, 378
climax, 390
flashback, 389
free verse, 403
irony, 403
metaphor, 400
Naturalism, 389, 400
parallelism, 378, 403

psychological fiction, 389, 400
refrain, 373
simile, 400
spiritual, 361, 373
stereotype, 369
syntax, 378
theme, 373, 400
thesis, 369
tone, 369

SYNTHESIS: QUESTIONS FOR WRITING, RESEARCH, OR DISCUSSION

GENRE STUDIES

1. **Speeches.** A good speech is written in simple, direct language that appeals to the emotions and interests of its audience. With these criteria in mind, answer the following question: What qualities make The Gettysburg Address, "A House Divided," Lincoln's Second Inaugural Address, and Lee's "Farewell to His Army" excellent speeches? Why are these speeches so often remembered and quoted?

2. **Spirituals.** Many spirituals were ambiguous. Explain what ambiguity is. Then explain how and why ambiguity was used in spirituals such as "Swing Low, Sweet Chariot" in this unit and "Follow the Drinking Gourd" in Unit 1.

THEMATIC STUDIES

3. **Naturalism.** Naturalism is the philosophical belief that people's actions, thoughts, feelings, and values result not from the free action of the will but rather are caused, or determined, by external forces or by heredity. What makes Ambrose Bierce's "An Occurrence at Owl Creek Bridge" and Stephen Crane's "A Mystery of Heroism" examples of Naturalism?

HISTORICAL/BIOGRAPHICAL STUDIES

4. **Abraham Lincoln.** Study the selections by Lincoln in this unit, the quotations from Lincoln on the "Echoes" page at the end of the unit introduction, and the two poems about Lincoln by Whitman ("O Captain! My Captain!" and "When Lilacs Last in the Dooryard Bloom'd"). What sort of person do you think Lincoln was, based on these materials? What were his concerns, both moral and political? Why is Lincoln so greatly revered today?

5. **Slavery and Its Aftermath.** Based on the unit introduction, the selection from Douglass's *Narrative*, and the spiritual "Swing Low, Sweet Chariot," answer the following questions: What was the institution of slavery like for the enslaved? What hardships did it impose? How did enslaved people feel about the institution of slavery? Why was it important for ex-slaves to become educated? What difficulties did ex-slaves encounter?

LANGUAGE LAB   EDITING FOR ERRORS IN USAGE

There are some words that are often misused. When editing your writing, you should watch carefully for these usage problems.

LANGUAGE ARTS SURVEY

For additional help, see the Language Arts Survey, 2.90.

LANGUAGE ARTS SURVEY

For additional help, see the Language Arts Survey, 2.91.

LANGUAGE ARTS SURVEY

For additional help, see the Language Arts Survey, 2.92.

COMMON USAGE ERRORS

adapt, adopt. *Adapt* means to modify something to fit a specific use or situation. *Adopt* means to make something one's own.

EXAMPLES: Some soldiers could not *adapt* to the harsh realities of war.

Some soldiers *adopted* an attitude of bravado to survive their experiences.

affect, effect. If you wish to use a verb meaning "have an effect on," use *affect.* If you wish to use a noun meaning "the result of an action," use *effect.*

EXAMPLES: The Civil War *affected* the entire country.

The *effects* of the war would be felt by generations to come.

imply, infer. *Imply* means "to express indirectly rather than openly." *Infer* means "to arrive at a conclusion by reasoning from evidence."

EXAMPLES: Your silence *implies* that you were very moved by Whitman's poem.

What can you *infer* from the poem about the emotional scars left by the Civil War?

like, as, as if. *Like* is a preposition, not a conjunction, and should not be used in place of *as* or *as if* in your writing.

EXAMPLE: The lilacs returned *as if* they had no knowledge of death and suffering.

literally. Use *literally* in the sense "actually," not in the sense "not actually, but in effect, or for all practical purposes."

EXAMPLE: A successful and accomplished orator, Frederick Douglass would *literally* speak for hours.

Douglass was a *virtually* tireless speaker.

of. The preposition *of* should not be used in place of *have* after verbs such as *could, should, would, might, must,* and *ought.*

EXAMPLE: Abraham Lincoln must *have* experienced an enormous amount of stress as president.

than, then. Use *than* as a conjunction in comparisons. Use *then* as an adverb that tells when something occurred.

EXAMPLES: Stephen Crane wrote more in his short life *than* other writers write in a lifetime.

Crane wrote *The Red Badge of Courage,* and *then* got his first view of war as a correspondent in Greece.

Exercise A Avoiding Usage Problems

In each sentence below, choose the correct word from within the parentheses.

EXAMPLE: I enjoy Stephen Crane's fiction more (than, then) his poetry.
than

1. The title of Booker T. Washington's autobiography, *Up from Slavery*, (implies, infers) the struggles and triumphs of Washington's life.

2. Lincoln wrote more (than, then) one version of The Gettysburg Address; he penned one at the White House, revised it on the train, and (than, then) delivered a slightly different version at the ceremony.

3. Many spirituals were (adapted, adopted) from Methodist hymns.

4. In "An Occurrence at Owl Creek Bridge," it seems (as if, like) the spy is making a daring escape from his executors.

5. The reader can (imply, infer) Whitman's sorrow over Lincoln's death from "When Lilacs Last in the Dooryard Bloom'd."

6. The news of Stephen Crane's early death from tuberculosis must (have, of) been shocking and saddening.

7. During his accomplished lifetime, Booker T. Washington served (as, like) an educator and lecturer.

8. More (than, then) 214,900 men, both Union and Confederate, died in Civil War battles.

9. The rhyme and meter of "Oh Captain! My Captain!" have a highly emotional (affect, effect).

10. Who could (have, of) predicted Lincoln's assassination?

Exercise B Proofreading for Usage Errors

Proofread the following paragraph for usage errors and correct any improperly used words.

In the twentieth century, Abraham Lincoln's Gettysburg Address is more revered then almost any other speech in United States history. However, it had a quite different affect when Lincoln first delivered it. The main speaker at the Gettysburg Cemetery dedication ceremony was not Lincoln, but well-known orator Edward Everett. To an audience that had just listened to Everett's two-hour speech, it must of seemed like Lincoln spoke for only a brief moment. In fact, Lincoln's speech was virtually just ten sentences long. Unused to such brevity, some people thought Lincoln's speech should of been longer and more grandiose; perhaps they believed that length and complexity inferred greatness. However, Everett's recognition of the speech's impact can be implied in his comment to Lincoln: "I should be glad if I could flatter myself that I came as near to the central idea of the occasion in two hours as you did in two minutes."

LANGUAGE ARTS SURVEY

For additional help, see the Language Arts Survey, 2.90–2.92.

LANGUAGE ARTS SURVEY

For additional help, see the Language Arts Survey, 2.90–2.92.

American Gothic. Grant Wood, American, 1891–1942. Oil on beaver board, 1930, 74.3 x 62.4 cm. Friends of the American Art Collection, 1930.934

Every part of this soil is sacred in the estimation of my people. Every hillside, every valley, every plain and grove, has been hallowed by some sad or happy event in days long vanished. Even the rocks, which seem to be dumb and dead as they swelter in the sun along the silent shore, thrill with memories of stirring events connected with the lives of my people, and the very dust upon which you now stand responds more lovingly to their footsteps than to yours.

—Chief Seattle of the
Suquamish and Duwamish

417

Wagon train

AN EXPANDING NATION

Without doubt, the Civil War was the most costly event in the history of the United States. Fought on American soil between Americans, it wrought destruction throughout the South, cost the federal government more than fifteen billion dollars, and resulted in an estimated 618,000 deaths of Union and Confederate soldiers. In five years' time, the country lost an entire generation of its male youth. After the war, an exhausted nation set about the painful business of **Reconstruction**, setting the conditions under which rebellious states would be readmitted to the Union.

Many Civil War veterans, having traveled away from home for the first time in their lives, developed a taste for freewheeling adventure, a willingness to strike out for places unknown. Some headed west to homestead or to seek their fortunes. They were joined by thousands of settlers moving from lands along the Mississippi River and by recent European immigrants who, finding little hope in the increasingly crowded cities of the East, looked to the frontier for a better life. In a few decades, people of European descent had established homes across the American West, from the prairie lands of Nebraska to the coasts of California. In the course of this **Westward Expansion**, Americans developed a self-reliance that gave substance to what might otherwise have been a merely theoretical belief in freedom and democracy. By the end of the century, most of the United States territories from the Atlantic to the Pacific had become states with the exceptions of Oklahoma, New Mexico, and Arizona.

LITERARY EVENTS

► = American Events

►1870. Ralph Waldo Emerson's "Civilization" published

►1869. Louisa May Alcott's *Little Women* and Bret Harte's "The Outcasts of Poker Flat" published

►1868. Bret Harte's "The Luck of Roaring Camp" published

►1866. Walt Whitman's "O Captain! My Captain!" published

1866. Feodor Dostoyevsky's *Crime and Punishment* published

1860	1865	1870

HISTORICAL EVENTS

►1860. Navajos attack Fort Defiance, New Mexico; Pony Express begins

►1861. Kansas enters Union

►1862. Cochise leads Apaches in raids; Sioux uprising under Little Crow; Homestead Act; Congress funds construction of transcontinental railroads

►1863. Nez Percé forced to sign treaty and give up land; Kit Carson resettles Navajos and Apaches

►1864. Navajos set off on "long walk" to Bosque Redondo concentration camp; Cheyenne, Arapahoe, Apache, Comanche, and Kiawa massacred at Sand Creek

►1866. Reconstruction begins in South

►1867. Alaska purchased, Nebraska admitted to Union

►1868. Attempt to impeach President Johnson; Ulysses S. Grant elected president

►1869. Union Pacific and Central Pacific Railroads link

►1870. First African-American legislators take seats at Washington, DC

PIONEERS, PROSPECTORS, AND RANCHERS

The Westward Expansion, begun early in the century, was encouraged by the **Homestead Act** of 1862, which, for a fee of ten dollars, granted 160 acres of federal land in the Western Territories to anyone who would live on that land for five years. This expansion was a continuation of efforts begun in the 1820s by adventurous settlers following the routes carved out by traders and trappers. Throughout the period from the 1820s to the 1870s, pioneers loaded their belongings and their dreams onto covered wagons and headed west along the Mormon, Oregon, California, Santa Fe, and Old Spanish trails. By the 1840s, many Americans had come to believe that it was their **"Manifest Destiny,"** in the words of one newspaperman, to cover the continent from coast to coast. The expansion was fueled, as well, by dreams of striking it rich prospecting for gold and silver. The discovery of gold in 1848 at Sutter's Mill, on California's Sacramento River, was the first of many **"gold rushes"** that led to the building of boom towns—Sacramento, San Francisco, Boise, Silver City, Virginia City, Carson City, Denver, Pueblo, Tuscon, Tombstone, Custer City, and Deadwood. These towns became legendary for their rough-and-tumble lawlessness, giving rise to the legends of the **"Wild West,"** with its gamblers, gunfighters, prospectors, and other colorful characters, including Calamity Jane, Deadwood Dick, Wild Bill Hickock, Annie Oakley, Billy the Kid, and Jesse James.

Jesse James

Cattle ranching, begun in Texas, became a big business throughout the Western Plains. Ranchers would herd their cattle together and drive them over great distances to new railway stops that would take the cattle back east, to Chicago, the center of the developing stockyard and meatpacking industry. The ranch owner and the cowboy drover were added to the West's long list of colorful stock characters. Ellsworth, Dodge City, and Abilene were among the greatest of the western cattle towns.

▶1883. James Whitcomb Riley's *The Old Swimmin' Hole and 'Leven More Poems* published

▶1881. Helen Maria Fiske Hunt Jackson's *A Century of Dishonor* published

1879. Henrik Ibsen's *A Doll's House* published

▶1879. Henry James's *Daisy Miller* published

1877. Leo Tolstoy's *Anna Karenina* published

▶1876. Mark Twain's *Tom Sawyer* published

1872. George Eliot's *Middlemarch* published

1885. Émile Zola's *Germinal* published

▶ 1884. Mark Twain's *The Adventures of Huckleberry Finn* published

1875	1880	1885

▶1871. Indian Appropriation Act makes Native Americans wards of the federal government; Cochise forced to surrender; Chicago fire

▶1872. Ulysses S. Grant reelected president; Victoria Woodhull runs for president; Susan B. Anthony arrested for trying to vote

▶1875. Comanche chief Quanah Parker ends his resistance; Tennessee enacts first "Jim Crow" law

▶1876. Colorado admitted to Union; Chiricahua leader Geronimo terrorizes white settlers; Battle of Little Big Horn

▶1877. Electoral commission appoints Rutherford B. Hayes president; Nez Percé captured fleeing to Canada

▶1880. James Abram Garfield elected president

▶1881. Garfield assassinated; Chester Alan Arthur succeeds as president

▶1882. Chinese Exclusion Act; first immigration restrictions

▶1884. Grover Cleveland elected president

THE DISPLACEMENT OF NATIVE AMERICANS

Four Young Ilte Indians

While the nineteenth century was one of new frontiers for settlers of European descent, it was one of heartbreak and trial for Native Americans, who were forced from their ancestral lands, killed in numerous "Indian Wars," and confined to reservations, often undesirable sections of the country far from their original homes. The **Indian Removal Act** passed by Congress in 1830 gave the president of the United States the power to require that all native peoples east of the Mississippi move west. This power was used by President Andrew Jackson, over the objections of the Supreme Court, to remove Cherokee peoples from Georgia and Tennessee to the newly established Indian Territory in what is now Oklahoma. Escorted by federal troops, thirteen thousand Cherokee were put on a forced march, now known as the **"Trail of Tears"** because of the deaths of some four thousand of their number en route. The Cherokee were one of many peoples who had either to fight or to submit to being moved to reservations.

The building of railroads led to widespread slaughter of the herds of Great Plains buffalo that provided sustenance to the Native Americans of that region. As new settlers moved westward, they continually revised their ideas about what lands would belong to Native Americans "for as long as the waters run," breaking numerous treaties and promises. Some Native American groups fought back. The 1860s and 1870s saw warfare between United States troops and native groups throughout the West, with much brutality and carnage on both sides. In 1864, a massacre of over four hundred Cheyenne men, women, and children led to all-out war between the United States government and the combined forces of the Cheyenne, the Sioux, and other Plains peoples. In 1876, the Sioux defeated Lieutenant George Armstrong Custer at the **Battle of Little Big Horn,** killing the 264 men in his company. In 1886, federal troops overpowered and captured **Geronimo**, the leader of the Chiricahua Apaches, who had fought

LITERARY EVENTS

► = American Events

►1891. Ambrose Bierce's *Tales of Soldiers and Civilians* published
1891. Thomas Hardy's *Tess of the d'Urbervilles*, and Oscar Wilde's *The Picture of Dorian Gray* published

►1890. *Poems by Emily Dickinson* published posthumously

►1886. William Dean Howells's *Indian Summer* published
1886. Robert Louis Stevenson's *The Strange Case of Dr. Jekyll and Mr. Hyde* published

►1896. Sarah Orne Jewett's "Country of the Pointed Firs" published

►1895. Stephen Crane's *The Red Badge of Courage* published

►1899. Kate Chopin's *The Awakening* published

►1894. Mark Twain's *Pudd'nhead Wilson* published

►1893. Frederick Jackson Turner's "The Significance of the Frontier in American History" published

1890	1895	1900

HISTORICAL EVENTS

►1886. Haymarket riots; Geronimo captured

►1889. North Dakota, South Dakota, Montana, and Washington admitted to Union

►1890. Battle of Wounded Knee ends Native American resistance; Sherman Anti-Trust Act

►1892. Grover Cleveland elected

►1893. Hawaii annexationists overthrow Queen Liliuokalani

►1895. Booker T. Washington's Atlanta Compromise

►1896. Utah admitted to Union; William McKinley elected president

►1897. United States annexes Hawaii

►1898. Spanish-American War; Louisiana adopts "grandfather clause," restricting African-American voters

1899. Great Britain begins the Boer War; Philippine insurrection

Wagons approach a challenging crossing.

long and successfully against the invaders of his people's land in the Southwest. In 1887, they captured **Chief Joseph** of the Nez Percé after his people's long flight, punctuated by fighting. That same year, Congress passed the **Dawes Act**, which granted citizenship to Native Americans after twenty-five years but took away Native American reservation lands for use by settlers, offering in exchange small plots for heads of families. In 1889, in another of a string of broken promises, the United States Congress opened up much of Indian Territory to new settlement. In a single day, the entire territory was settled. In 1890, at **Wounded Knee,** South Dakota, federal troops massacred over two hundred mostly unarmed Sioux in what was to be the last action of the Indian Wars.

IMMIGRATION, THE GROWTH OF CITIES, AND INDUSTRIALISM

The last forty years of the nineteenth century was a time of unprecedented change in American cities. Between 1880 and 1900, nine million immigrants arrived in the United States from Europe. Previous immigration had been made up for the most part of northern Europeans. The new wave of immigration brought southern and eastern Europeans, as well as Asians, thus greatly diversifying the United States population. This trend would continue and expand in the first two decades of the next century.

Another important trend during these years was the growth of cities. By 1900, fully 40 percent of the United States population lived in urban centers. Many of these people were recent immigrants, many were newly free African Americans from rural areas of the South, and many more were white citizens moving from farms to find jobs in America's booming industrial centers. American industry had benefited from technological developments made during the Civil War era, and a class of millionaire industrialists had emerged with monopolistic control of meatpacking, railroads, and the production of oil and steel. The fabulous wealth

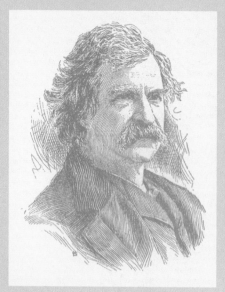

Mark Twain

of these often unscrupulous industrialists, satirized in Mark Twain's *The Gilded Age,* which he coauthored with Charles Dudley Warner, stood in sharp contrast with the poverty and terrible working conditions of the average laborer. At the turn of the century, the so-called "**muckraker**" journalists Ida Tarbell and Lincoln Steffans would make careers of exposing unscrupulous practices among business people and corrupt political officials.

THE EXPANDING LITERARY FRONTIER

The literature of the early nineteenth century in America was dominated by Romanticism and concentrated in New England. The great authors of the period were primarily scholarly, moralistic gentlemen, and public tastes ran to the sentimental and nostalgic. Expansion across the frontier in the late nineteenth century was accompanied by an equally dramatic expansion of literary frontiers. Significant writers appeared across the breadth of the nation, in the Midwest, the South, and the West. Many of these writers were women, such as **Sarah Orne Jewett**, **Kate Chopin**, and **Mary Wilkins Freeman.** Many were journalists and adventurers, such as **Mark Twain**, **Bret Harte**, **Ambrose Bierce**, and **Stephen Crane.** One of the greatest writers of the period, **Henry James**, spent much of his life in Europe, chronicling the lives of newly wealthy Americans living abroad. The characters in the fiction of the day became correspondingly diverse, including gunfighters and ranchers, runaway slaves and Civil War soldiers, steamboat captains and con artists, Cajuns and Creoles, pioneer women and children, millionaire tycoons and the desperate urban poor. The literature of the period fulfilled the vision of Walt Whitman: "I hear America singing, the varied carols I hear."

REGIONALISM AND LOCAL COLOR

One outgrowth of this diversity was **Regionalism,** or **local color** writing. The mostly female readers of the many new magazines in the East developed an intense interest in the lives and lifestyles of persons living in such faraway, exotic parts of the country as the Louisiana bayou, the Mississippi River valley, and the western boom towns. Journalists and others rushed to fill the demand. Soon, most regions of the country were represented by local colorists who created often humorous pieces about the odd characters scattered across the newly conquered continent. One of the first of these local color writers was Bret Harte, who wrote stories from San Francisco such as "The Luck of Roaring Camp" and "The Outcasts of Poker Flat," beginning a fascination with the West in American popular culture. **Samuel Clemens,** who took the pseudonym Mark Twain, traveled widely throughout the country, posting short stories and humorous sketches about peoples and places as diverse as the con artists, steamboat captains, and riverboat gamblers of the Mississippi River, the natives and missionaries of the Sandwich Islands (later Hawaii), and the denizens of western mining camps, as in his tall tale "The Notorious Jumping Frog of Calaveras County." Kate Chopin and **George Washington Cable** wrote of the people of the Louisiana bayou country. **Joel Chandler Harris** wrote dialectical pieces based on the oral traditions of African Americans in the South. **Edward Eggleston** and **James Whitcomb Riley** wrote of the Hoosiers of backwoods Indiana. Sarah Orne Jewett and Mary Wilkins Freeman wrote of backwoods New England.

Original wagon wheel from Oregon Trail carriage

THE EMERGENCE OF REALISM

The presentation in fiction of local dialect and varied, unsavory characters were two expressions of a new and dominant mode in American fiction of the late nineteenth century—**Realism.** The early nineteenth-century Romantics of New England had tended to present idealized materials designed to inspire lofty emotions. The Realists, in contrast, drew portraits from life, often shocking more sensitive readers with their grim depictions of realities, as the country itself had been shocked by the grim realities of the Civil War. Ambrose Bierce wrote devastatingly bitter, unsentimental portrayals of the horrors of the war, including such masterful short stories as "Chickamauga" and "An Occurrence at Owl Creek Bridge." Twain, widely known for his satirical humor, often involving exaggerated, colorful characters, also showed elements of Realism. Because of its realistic use of a variety of dialects and its quintessentially American theme of the individual's quest for freedom, Twain's *The Adventures of Huckleberry Finn* is often considered the greatest of American novels. Ernest Hemingway wrote, for example, that "All modern American literature comes from one book by Mark Twain called *Huckleberry Finn*." The great champion of Realism was the novelist **William Dean Howells,** who, as editor of *Harper's Weekly, Harper's Monthly,* and the *North American Review,* promoted the works of Twain and James. In novels such as *The Rise of Silas Lapham, Annie Kilburn, A Hazard of New Fortunes,* and *Quality of Mercy,* Howells presented the breakdown of traditional values and the misery of the poor that he observed in urban America. Several authors applied the penetrating accuracy of Realism to the interior lives of their characters, pioneering what became known as **Psychological Realism.** Among these, though very different in attitude, experience, style, and subject matter, are Ambrose Bierce in stories such as "An Occurrence at Owl Creek Bridge," Kate Chopin in works such as "The

Jack London

Story of an Hour" and *The Awakening,* **Charlotte Perkins Gilman** in her feminist horror tale "The Yellow Wallpaper," and **Henry James** in novels such as *Portrait of a Lady* and *The Turn of the Screw.*

THE RISE OF NATURALISM

Naturalism was an extension and refinement of Realism, based on the theories of the French novelist **Émile Zola.** Inspired by nineteenth-century naturalists such as Charles Darwin and Thomas Huxley, Zola held that people's actions and beliefs resulted not from free will but from the arbitrary, outside forces of heredity and environment. He believed that, like a naturalist studying the causes of behavior in animals, the novelist could write "scientific" fiction that demonstrated the exact causes of human behavior. In the United States, Naturalism found its champion in Stephen Crane. In novels like *The Red Badge of Courage* and stories like "The Open Boat," "The Blue Hotel," and "A Mystery of Heroism," Crane showed human beings to be pawns manipulated by the cruel, indifferent forces of nature and society, a philosophy expressed succinctly in his poem "A Man Said to the Universe." Crane's Naturalism, however, was tempered by his belief that in such an indifferent universe, people must stick together with acts of kindness and compassion to counter the terrible forces to which they are subjected. At the turn of the century, Naturalism was to become a dominant mode in American fiction, realized in the works of such writers as **Frank Norris,** author of *McTeague* and *The Octopus;* **Jack London,** author of "To Build a Fire" and *The Call of the Wild,* and **Theodore Dreiser,** author of *Sister Carrie* and *An American Tragedy.*

Echoes:

Frontiers

Quotations from Mark Twain

On flattery: "I can live for two months on a good compliment."

On golf: "Golf is good walk spoiled."

On grief and joy: "Grief can take care of itself, but to get the full value from joy you must have somebody to divide it with."

On his own writing: "You don't know about me without you have read a book by the name of *The Adventures of Tom Sawyer;* but that ain't no matter. That book was made by Mr. Mark Twain, and he told the truth, mainly."

On humans: "Man is the only animal that blushes. Or needs to."

On the desire to teach others to be good: "To be good is noble, but to teach others how to be good is nobler—and less trouble."

On obedience: "Of all God's creatures there is only one that cannot be made the slave of the lash. That one is the cat. If man could be crossed with the cat it would improve man, but it would deteriorate the cat."

On parents: "When I was a boy of fourteen, my father was so ignorant I could hardly stand to have the old man around. But when I got to be twenty-one, I was astonished at how much he had learned in seven years."

On politeness: "Good breeding consists in concealing how much we think of ourselves and how little we think of the other person."

On school: "I have never let my schooling interfere with my education."

On success: "All you need in this life is ignorance and confidence, and then success is sure."

"The Outcasts of Poker Flat"
by Bret Harte

ABOUT THE AUTHOR

Bret Harte (1836–1902) was the pen name of Francis Brett Harte, who gave many Easterners their first glimpse of the Old West in his amusing stories, full of local color and characterized by unusual juxtapositions of characters and surprise endings. Though associated with the West, Harte was born in Albany, New York. After his father died, he moved in 1854 to California, where he married and gathered the material he would later use in his stories, riding shotgun on Wells Fargo stagecoaches and prospecting like so many other Californians in those days of the Gold Rush. Settling in San Francisco, he worked as a typesetter and then as a writer for the *Californian.* In 1861, he took a job as editor of the *Overland Monthly,* in which he published the work that would make him famous, including the stories "The Luck of Roaring Camp" and "The Outcasts of Poker Flat" and the poem "Plain Language from Truthful James." Becoming well known in literary circles, he socialized with such San Francisco luminaries as Ambrose Bierce and Mark Twain. Harte's regionalism met with an eager audience back East, so eager that the *Atlantic Monthly* in Boston offered him the then astronomical sum of ten thousand dollars to write twelve pieces for the magazine. Harte left for Boston, but the pieces that he produced under his contract were mediocre, and his fame subsided. Thereafter, Harte produced several collections of stories, two novels, and two plays, but none equaled his earlier work. He served as a United States diplomat in Prussia and in Scotland and then settled in London, England, where he lived for the rest of his life.

ABOUT THE SELECTION

"**The Outcasts of Poker Flat**" is an example of nineteenth-century regional literature. Regional writers portray what is special about a particular part of the country. They write about the specific landscape, people, values, and modes of life of a region. Regionalists explore issues that are common to all human beings, but they do so only by way of writing about a particular time and place. Harte is known for his stories about life on America's Western frontier, especially his amusing explorations of the people and the landscape of northern California's High Sierras, the Gold Rush region. In "The Outcasts of Poker Flat," Harte treats the conflict between a society and its "outcasts," those people whose behavior is unacceptable to the moral values that the majority at least pretend to uphold. Harte explores this timeless conflict, however, by describing the fate of some typical characters from the American frontier. Today these characters are familiar to anyone who watches Western movies, but in the nineteenth century they were still new, and Harte was one of the first to describe them.

"The Outcasts of Poker Flat"

Bret Harte

As Mr. John Oakhurst, gambler, stepped into the main street of Poker Flat on the morning of the twenty-third of November, 1850, he was conscious of a change in its moral atmosphere from the preceding night. Two or three men, conversing earnestly together, ceased as he approached, and exchanged significant glances. There was a Sabbath lull in the air, which, in a settlement unused to Sabbath influences, looked <u>ominous</u>.

Mr. Oakhurst's calm, handsome face betrayed small concern of these indications. Whether he was conscious of any <u>predisposing</u> cause, was another question. "I reckon they're after somebody," he reflected; "likely it's me." He returned to his pocket the handkerchief with which he had been whipping away the red dust of Poker Flat from his neat boots, and quietly discharged his mind of any further <u>conjecture</u>.

In point of fact, Poker Flat was "after somebody." It had lately suffered the loss of several thousand dollars, two valuable horses, and a prominent citizen. It was experiencing a spasm of virtuous reaction, quite as lawless and ungovernable as any of the acts that had provoked it. A secret committee[1] had determined to rid the town of all improper persons. This was done permanently in regard of two men who were then hanging from the boughs of a sycamore in the gulch, and temporarily in the banishment of certain other objectionable characters. I regret to say that some of these were ladies. It is but due

To what are the citizens of Poker Flat reacting?

---

1. **secret committee.** Vigilance committee; group that helps maintain order and punish crime when processes of law are not effective

to the sex, however, to state that their impropriety was professional, and it was only in such easily established standards of evil that Poker Flat ventured to sit in judgment.

Why do vigilantes resent Oakhurst?

Mr. Oakhurst was right in supposing that he was included in this category. A few of the committee had urged hanging him as a possible example, and a sure method of reimbursing themselves from his pockets of the sums he had won from them. "It's agin justice," said Jim Wheeler, "to let this yer young man from Roaring Camp—an entire stranger—carry away our money." But a crude sentiment of equity residing in the breasts of those who had been fortunate enough to win from Mr. Oakhurst, overruled this narrower local prejudice.

Mr. Oakhurst received his sentence with philosophic calmness, none the less coolly, that he was aware of the hesitation of his judges. He was too much of a gambler not to accept Fate. With him life was at best an uncertain game, and he recognized the usual percentage in favor of the dealer.

A body of armed men accompanied the deported wickedness of Poker Flat to the outskirts of the settlement. Besides Mr. Oakhurst, who was known to be a coolly desperate man, and for whose intimidation the armed escort was intended, the <u>expatriated</u> party consisted of a young woman familiarly known as "The Duchess"; another, who had gained the <u>infelicitous</u> title of "Mother Shipton,"[2] and "Uncle Billy," a suspected sluice[3] robber and confirmed drunkard. The <u>cavalcade</u> provoked no comments from the spectators, nor was any word uttered by

Who are the other deportees?

the escort. Only when the gulch which marked the uttermost limit of Poker Flat was reached, the leader spoke briefly and to the point. The exiles were forbidden to return at the peril of their lives.

As the escort disappeared, their pent-up feelings found vent in a few hysterical tears from "The Duchess," some bad language from Mother Shipton, and a Partheian[4] volley of expletives from Uncle Billy. The philosophic Oakhurst alone remained silent. He listened calmly to Mother Shipton's desire to cut somebody's heart out, to the repeated statements of "The Duchess" that she would die in the road, and to the alarming oaths that seemed to be bumped out of Uncle Billy as he rode forward. With the easy good-humor characteristic of his class, he insisted upon exchanging his own riding-horse, "Five Spot," for the sorry mule which the Duchess rode. But even this act did not draw the party into any closer sympathy. The young woman readjusted her somewhat draggled plumes with a feeble, faded <u>coquetry</u>; Mother Shipton eyed the possessor of "Five Spot" with malevolence, and Uncle Billy included the whole party in one sweeping <u>anathema</u>.

The road to Sandy Bar—a camp that not having as yet experienced the regenerating influences of Poker Flat, consequently seemed to offer some invitation to the emigrants—lay over a steep mountain

---

2. **Mother Shipton.** (1488–1560) Known as a witch and believed to have been taken by the devil and to have born him an imp

3. **sluice.** Trough used to separate gold from other materials

4. **Partheian.** Like the Partheians, an ancient people from Asia known for firing shots while in retreat

---

Words for Everyday Use:		
ex • pa • tri • at • ed (eks pā´trē āt´id) *part.*, driven from one's land	**cav • al • cade** (kav´əl kād´) *n.*, procession (of horses)	
in • fe • lic • i • tous (in fə lis´ə təs) *adj.*, unfortunate, unsuitable	**co • quet • ry** (kō´kə trē) *n.*, flirting	
	a • nath • e • ma (ə nath´ə mə) *n.*, curse	

range. It was distant a day's severe journey. In that advanced season, the party soon passed out of the moist, temperate regions of the foot-hills, into the dry, cold, bracing air of the Sierras.[5] The trail was narrow and difficult. At noon the Duchess, rolling out of her saddle upon the ground, declared her intention of going no further, and the party halted.

The spot was singularly wild and impressive. A wooded amphitheater, surrounded on three sides by <u>precipitous</u> cliffs of naked granite, sloped gently toward the crest of another precipice that overlooked the valley. It was undoubtedly the most suitable spot for a camp, had camping been advisable. But Mr. Oakhurst knew that scarcely half the journey to Sandy Bar was accomplished, and the party were not equipped or provisioned for delay. This fact he pointed out to his companions curtly, with a philosophic commentary on the folly of "throwing up their hand before the game was played out." But they were furnished with liquor, which in this emergency stood them in place of food, fuel, rest and prescience. In spite of his <u>remonstrances</u>, it was not long before they were more or less under its influence. Uncle Billy passed rapidly from a <u>bellicose</u> state into one of stupor, the Duchess became maudlin, and Mother Shipton snored. Mr. Oakhurst alone remained erect, leaning against a rock, calmly surveying them.

Mr. Oakhurst did not drink. It interfered with a profession which required coolness, impassiveness and presence of mind, and, in his own language, he "couldn't afford it." As he gazed at his recumbent fellow-exiles, the loneliness begotten of his pariah-trade,[6] his habits of life, his very vices, for the first time seriously oppressed him. He bestirred himself in dusting his black clothes, washing his hands and face, and other acts characteristic of his studiously neat habits, and for a moment forgot his annoyance. The thought of deserting his weaker and more pitiable companions never perhaps occurred to him. Yet he could not help feeling the want of that excitement, which singularly enough was most conducive to that calm <u>equanimity</u> for which he was notorious. He looked at the gloomy walls that rose a thousand feet sheer above the circling pines around him; at the sky, ominously clouded; at the valley below, already deepening into shadow. And doing so, suddenly he heard his own name called.

A horseman slowly ascended the trail. In the fresh, open face of the newcomer, Mr. Oakhurst recognized Tom Simson, otherwise known as "The Innocent" of Sandy Bar. He had met him some months before over a "little game," and had, with perfect equanimity, won the entire fortune— amounting to some forty dollars—of that <u>guileless</u> youth. After the game was finished, Mr. Oakhurst drew the youthful speculator behind the door and thus addressed him: "Tommy, you're a good little man, but you can't gamble worth a cent. Don't try it over again." He then handed him his money back, pushed him gently from the room, and so made a devoted slave of Tom Simson.

---

5. **Sierras.** Mountains in California
6. **pariah-trade.** Profession scorned by others

Why is it unwise to halt the journey?

Why does Oakhurst not drink?

WORDS FOR EVERYDAY USE:

pre • cip • i • tous (prē sip´ə təs) *adj.,* steep
re • mon • strance (ri män strəns´) *n.,* protest, objection
bel • li • cose (bel´i kōs) *adj.,* hostile, eager to fight

e • qua • nim • i • ty (ek´wə nim´ə tē) *n.,* evenness of temper; quality of remaining calm
guile • less (gīl´lis) *adj.,* without deceit

There was a remembrance of this in his boyish and enthusiastic greeting of Mr. Oakhurst. He had started, he said, to go to Poker Flat to seek his fortune. "Alone?" No, not exactly alone; in fact—a giggle—he had run away with Piney Woods. Didn't Mr. Oakhurst remember Piney? She that used to wait on the table at the Temperance House? They had been engaged a long time, but old Jake Woods had objected, and so they had run away, and were going to Poker Flat to be married, and here they were. And they were tired out, and how lucky it was they had found a place to camp and company. All this The Innocent delivered rapidly, while Piney—a stout, comely damsel of fifteen—emerged from behind the pine tree, where she had been blushing unseen, and rode to the side of her lover.

Mr. Oakhurst seldom troubled himself with sentiment. Still less with propriety. But he had a vague idea that the situation was not felicitous. He retained, however, his presence of mind sufficiently to kick Uncle Billy, who was about to say something, and Uncle Billy was sober enough to recognize in Mr. Oakhurst's kick a superior power that would not bear trifling. He then endeavored to <u>dissuade</u> Tom Simson from delaying further, but in vain. He even pointed out the fact that there was no provision, nor means of making a camp. But, unluckily, "The Innocent" met this objection by assuring the party that he was provided with an extra mule loaded with provisions, and by the discovery of a rude attempt at a log-house near the trail. "Piney can stay with Mrs. Oakhurst," said The Innocent,

pointing to the Duchess, "and I can shift for myself."

Nothing but Mr. Oakhurst's admonishing foot saved Uncle Billy from bursting into a roar of laughter. As it was, he felt compelled to retire up the canyon until he could recover his gravity. There he confided the joke to the tall pine trees, with many slaps of his leg, <u>contortions</u> of his face, and the usual profanity. But when he returned to the party, he found them seated by a fire—for the air had grown strangely chill and the sky overcast—in apparently amicable conversation. Piney was actually talking in an impulsive, girlish fashion to the Duchess, who was listening with an interest and animation she had not shown for many days. The Innocent was holding forth, apparently with equal effect, to Mr. Oakhurst and Mother Shipton, who was actually relaxing into amiability. "Is this yer a d——d picnic?" said Uncle Billy, with inward scorn, as he surveyed the sylvan group, the glancing fire-light and the tethered animals in the foreground. Suddenly an idea mingled with the alcoholic fumes that disturbed his brain. It was apparently of a <u>jocular</u> nature, for he felt impelled to slap his leg again and cram his fist into his mouth.

As the shadows crept slowly up the mountain, a slight breeze rocked the tops of the pine trees, and moaned through their long and gloomy aisles. The ruined cabin, patched and covered with pine boughs, was set apart for the ladies. As the lovers parted, they unaffectedly exchanged a parting kiss, so honest and sincere that it might have been heard above the swaying pines. The frail Duchess and the malevolent Mother

Where are Tom Simson and Piney Woods going?

Why does Oakhurst urge Simson not to delay?

WORDS FOR EVERYDAY USE:

dis • suade (di swād´) *vt.*, talk out of
con • tor • tion (kən tôr´shən) *n.*, twisting out of shape

joc • u • lar (jäk´yoo lər) *adj.*, humorous

Shipton were probably too stunned to remark upon this last evidence of simplicity, and so turned without a word to the hut. The fire was replenished, the men lay down before the door, and in a few minutes were asleep.

Mr. Oakhurst was a light sleeper. Toward morning he awoke benumbed and cold. As he stirred the dying fire, the wind, which was now blowing strongly, brought to his cheek that which caused the blood to leave it—snow!

He started to his feet with the intention of awakening the sleepers, for there was no time to lose. But turning to where Uncle Billy had been lying he found him gone. A suspicion leaped to his brain and a curse to his lips. He ran to the spot where the mules had been tethered; they were no longer there. The tracks were already rapidly disappearing in the snow.

The momentary excitement brought Mr. Oakhurst back to the fire with his usual calm. He did not waken the sleepers. The Innocent slumbered peacefully, with a smile on his good-humored, freckled face; the virgin Piney slept beside her frailer sisters as sweetly as though attended by celestial guardians, and Mr. Oakhurst, drawing his blanket over his shoulders, stroked his mustachios and waited for the dawn. It came slowly in a whirling mist of snowflakes, that dazzled and confused the eye. What could be seen of the landscape appeared magically changed. He looked over the valley, and summed up the present and future in two words—"Snowed in!"

A careful inventory of the provisions, which, fortunately for the party, had been stored within the hut, and so escaped the <u>felonious</u> fingers of Uncle Billy, disclosed the fact that with care and prudence they might last ten days longer. "That is," said Mr. Oakhurst, *sotto voce*[7] to The Innocent, "if you're willing to board us. If you ain't—and perhaps you'd better not—you can wait till Uncle Billy gets back with provisions." For some occult reason, Mr. Oakhurst could not bring himself to disclose Uncle Billy's rascality, and so offered the hypothesis that he had wandered from the camp and had accidentally stampeded the animals. He dropped a warning to the Duchess and Mother Shipton, who of course knew the facts of their associate's defection. "They'll find out the truth about us all, when they find out anything," he added, significantly, "and there's no good frightening them now."

Tom Simson not only put all his worldly store at the disposal of Mr. Oakhurst, but seemed to enjoy the prospect of their enforced seclusion. "We'll have a good camp for a week, and then the snow'll melt, and we'll all go back together." The cheerful gayety of the young man and Mr. Oakhurst's calm infected the others. The Innocent, with the aid of pine boughs, <u>extemporized</u> a thatch for the roofless cabin, and the Duchess directed Piney in the rearrangement of the interior with a taste and tact that opened the blue eyes of that provincial maiden to their fullest extent. "I reckon now you're used to fine things at Poker Flat," said Piney. The Duchess turned away sharply to conceal something that reddened her cheeks

7. **sotto voce.** In an undertone, so as not to be overheard

Who departs from the camp? What does he take?

What kind of outlook does Simson have?

WORDS FOR EVERYDAY USE:

fe • lo • ni • ous (fə lō′nē əs) *adj.,* of a criminal

ex • tem • po • rize (eks tem′pə rīz′) *vt.,* contrive in a makeshift way to meet a pressing need

through its professional tint, and Mother Shipton requested Piney not to "chatter." But when Mr. Oakhurst returned from a weary search for the trail, he heard the sound of happy laughter echoed from the rocks. He stopped in some alarm, and his thoughts first naturally reverted to the whiskey—which he had prudently *cachéd*.[8] "And yet it don't somehow sound like whiskey," said the gambler. It was not until he caught sight of the blazing fire through the still blinding storm, and the group around it, that he settled to the conviction that it was "square fun."

Whether Mr. Oakhurst had *cachéd* his cards with the whiskey as something debarred the free access of the community, I cannot say. It was certain that, in Mother Shipton's words, he "didn't say cards once" during that evening. Haply the time was beguiled by an accordion, produced somewhat <u>ostentatiously</u> by Tom Simson, from his pack. Notwithstanding some difficulties attending the manipulation of this instrument, Piney Woods managed to pluck several reluctant melodies from its keys, to an accompaniment by The Innocent on a pair of bone castanets. But the crowning festivity of the evening was reached in a rude camp-meeting hymn, which the lovers, joining hands, sang with great earnestness and <u>vociferation</u>. I fear that a certain defiant tone and Covenanter's swing[9] to its chorus, rather than any devotional quality, caused it to speedily infect the others, who at last joined in the refrain:

"I'm proud to live in the service of the Lord

And I'm bound to die in His army."[10]

How do the snowbound campers pass the time?

The pines rocked, the storm eddied and whirled above the miserable group, and the flames of their altar leaped heavenward, as if in token of the vow.

At midnight the storm abated, the rolling clouds parted, and the stars glittered keenly above the sleeping camp. Mr. Oakhurst, whose professional habits had enabled him to live on the smallest possible amount of sleep, in dividing the watch with Tom Simson, somehow managed to take upon himself the greater part of that duty. He excused himself to The Innocent, by saying that he had "often been a week without sleep." "Doing what?" asked Tom. "Poker!" replied Oakhurst, sententiously; "when a man gets a streak of luck—he don't get tired. The luck gives in first. Luck," continued the gambler, reflectively, "is a mighty queer thing. All you know about it for certain is that it's bound to change. And it's finding out when it's going to change that makes you. We've had a streak of bad luck since we left Poker Flat—you come along and slap you get into it, too. If you can hold your cards right along you're all right. For," added the gambler, with cheerful irrelevance,

"I'm proud to live in the service of the Lord,

And I'm bound to die in His army."

The third day came, and the sun, looking through the white-curtained valley,

---

8. **cachéd.** Hidden
9. **Covenanter's swing.** Sung with a vigorous rhythm with a martial beat, as done by the covenanters, a group of Scottish Presbyterians who wished to separate from the Church of England
10. **"I'm proud . . . His army."** Refrain of the early American spiritual "Service of the Lord"

WORDS FOR EVERYDAY USE:

os • ten • ta • tious • ly (äs ten tā´shəs lē) *adv.,* so as to attract attention

vo • cif • er • a • tion (vō sif´ər ā´shən) *n.,* shouting

saw the outcasts divide their slowly decreasing store of provisions for the morning meal. It was one of the peculiarities of that mountain climate that its rays diffused a kindly warmth over the wintry landscape, as if in regretful commiseration of the past. But it revealed drift on drift of snow piled high around the hut; a hopeless, uncharted, trackless sea of white lying below the rocky shores to which the castaways still clung. Through the marvelously clear air, the smoke of the pastoral village of Poker Flat rose miles away. Mother Shipton saw it, and from a remote pinnacle of her rocky fastness, hurled in that direction a final malediction. It was her last <u>vituperative</u> attempt, and perhaps for that reason was invested with a certain degree of sublimity. It did her good, she privately informed the Duchess. "Just you go out there and cuss, and see." She then set herself to the task of amusing "the child," as she and the Duchess were pleased to call Piney. Piney was no chicken, but it was a soothing and ingenious theory of the pair to thus account for the fact that she didn't swear and wasn't improper.

When night crept up again through the gorges, the reedy notes of the accordion rose and fell in fitful spasms and long-drawn gasps by the flickering campfire. But music failed to fill entirely the aching void left by insufficient food, and a new diversion was proposed by Piney—story-telling. Neither Mr. Oakhurst nor his female companions caring to relate their personal experiences, this plan would have failed, too, but for The Innocent. Some months before he had chanced upon a stray copy of Mr. Pope's[11] ingenious translation of the Iliad. He now proposed to narrate the principal incidents of that poem—having thoroughly mastered the argument and fairly forgotten the words—in the current vernacular of Sandy Bar. And so for the rest of that night the Homeric demi-gods again walked the earth. Trojan bully and wily Greek wrestled in the winds, and the great pines in the canyon seemed to bow to the wrath of the son of Peleus.[12] Mr. Oakhurst listened with quiet satisfaction. Most especially was he interested in the fate of "Ash-heels,"[13] as The Innocent persisted in denominating the "swift-footed Achilles."

So with small food and much of Homer and the accordion, a week passed over the heads of the outcasts. The sun again forsook them, and again from leaden skies the snow-flakes were sifted over the land. Day by day closer around them drew the snowy circle, until at last they looked from their prison over drifted walls of dazzling white, that towered twenty feet above their heads. It became more and more difficult to replenish their fires, even from the fallen trees beside them, now half-hidden in the drifts. And yet no one complained. The lovers turned from the dreary prospect and looked into each other's eyes, and were happy. Mr. Oakhurst settled himself coolly to the losing game before him. The Duchess, more

How does Simson distract the outcasts' attention?

What do the outcasts need?

---

11. **Mr. Pope's.** (1688–1744) English poet Alexander Pope. His translation of Homer's *Iliad* was written in heroic couplets.
12. **son of Peleus.** Achilles, chief hero on the Greek side of the Trojan War
13. **Ash-heels.** The speaker means Achilles (ak il´ēz), whose only vulnerable spot was his heel, a fact emphasized by the mispronunciation

WORDS FOR EVERYDAY USE: vi • tu • per • a • tive (vī tōō´ pə rā´tiv) *adj.,* abusive; viciously fault-finding

cheerful than she had been, assumed the care of Piney. Only Mother Shipton—once the strongest of the party—seemed to sicken and fade. At midnight on the tenth day she called Oakhurst to her side. "I'm going," she said, in a voice of <u>querulous</u> weakness, "but don't say anything about it. Don't waken the kids. Take the bundle from under my head and open it." Mr. Oakhurst did so. It contained Mother Shipton's rations for the last week, untouched. "Give 'em to the child," she said, pointing to the sleeping Piney. "You've starved yourself," said the gambler. "That's what they call it," said the woman querulously, as she lay down again, and turning her face to the wall, passed quietly away.

The accordion and the bones were put aside that day, and Homer was forgotten. When the body of Mother Shipton had been committed to the snow, Mr. Oakhurst took The Innocent aside, and showed him a pair of snow-shoes, which he had fashioned from the old pack-saddle. "There's one chance in a hundred to save her yet," he said, pointing to Piney; "but it's there," he added pointing toward Poker Flat. "If you can reach there in two days she's safe." "And you?" asked Tom Simson. "I'll stay here," was the curt reply.

The lovers parted with a long embrace. "You are not going, too," said the Duchess, as she saw Mr. Oakhurst apparently waiting to accompany him. "As far as the canyon." he replied. He turned suddenly, and kissed the Duchess, leaving her pallid face aflame, and her trembling limbs rigid with amazement.

Night came, but not Mr. Oakhurst. It brought the storm again and the whirling snow. Then the Duchess, feeding the fire,

What is happening to Mother Shipton? What has she been doing?

WORDS FOR EVERYDAY USE: quer • u • lous (kwer´yo͞o ləs) adj., full of complaint

found that some one had quietly piled beside the hut enough fuel to last a few days longer. The tears rose to her eyes, but she hid them from Piney.

The women slept but little. In the morning, looking into each other's faces, they read their fate. Neither spoke; but Piney, accepting the position of the stronger, drew near and placed her arm around the Duchess's waist. They kept this attitude for the rest of the day. That night the storm reached its greatest fury, and rending asunder the protecting pines, invaded the very hut.

Toward morning they found themselves unable to feed the fire, which gradually died away. As the embers slowly blackened, the Duchess crept closer to Piney, and broke the silence of many hours: "Piney, can you pray?" "No, dear," said Piney, simply. The Duchess, without knowing exactly why, felt relieved, and putting her head upon Piney's shoulder, spoke no more. And so reclining, the younger and purer pillowing the head of her soiled sister upon her virgin breast, they fell asleep.

The wind lulled as if it feared to waken them. Feathery drifts of snow, shaken from the long pine boughs, flew like white-winged birds, and settled about them as they slept. The moon through the rifted clouds looked down upon what had been the camp. But all human stain, all trace of earthly travail, was hidden beneath the spotless mantle mercifully flung from above.

They slept all that day and the next, nor did they waken when voices and footsteps broke the silence of the camp. And when pitying fingers brushed the snow from their wan faces, you could scarcely have told from the equal peace that dwelt upon them, which was she that had sinned. Even the Law of Poker Flat recognized this, and turned away, leaving them still locked in each other's arms.

But at the head of the gulch, on one of the largest pine trees, they found the deuce of clubs pinned to the bark with a bowie knife. It bore the following, written in pencil, in a firm hand:

†

BENEATH THIS TREE
LIES THE BODY
OF

JOHN OAKHURST,
WHO STRUCK A STREAK OF BAD LUCK
ON THE 23^D OF NOVEMBER, 1850,
AND
HANDED IN HIS CHECKS
ON THE 7TH DECEMBER, 1850

†

And pulseless and cold, with a Derringer[14] by his side and a bullet in his heart, though still calm as in life, beneath the snow, lay he who was at once the strongest and yet the weakest of the outcasts of Poker Flat. ∎

What do Piney and the Duchess understand?

What has Oakhurst done?

---

14. **Derringer.** Short-barreled pocket pistol, invented by Henry Derringer

Responding to the Selection

In Harte's story there are three main groups of characters: the townspeople of Poker Flat, the outcasts, and the two young people from Sandy Bar. With whom do you sympathize most, the people who want to rid their town of immoral and suspicious characters, the outcasts, or the young couple? Why?

Reviewing the Selection

RECALLING

1. Why are the outcasts thrown out of Poker Flat?

2. Who do the outcasts meet on the road to Sandy Bar? What do the names of these two people tell the reader about them?

3. What does Oakhurst discover has happened in the middle of the night?

4. How do the young people sing the hymn around the campfire? What does this tell us about them? Why do the outcasts join in the singing?

INTERPRETING

5. Do you believe that the people of Poker Flat are justified in throwing out some of the community's members? Why, or why not?

6. Why are the two young people traveling to Poker Flat? What kind of town is Poker Flat? Is the elopement of the young people wise or unwise?

7. Why does Oakhurst lie to the young people about Uncle Billy's theft? Why might the truth frighten the young people?

8. The narrator says that Oakhurst is "at once the strongest and yet the weakest of the outcasts of Poker Flat." In what way is he strong, and in what way is he weak?

SYNTHESIZING

9. When they find Piney and the Duchess dead, the people of Poker Flat can't tell the difference between the two. The "human stain" of the Duchess is "hidden beneath the spotless mantle" of snow, and the narrator says that "you could scarcely have told from the equal peace that dwelt upon them, which was she that had sinned." What comment is the narrator making here about outcasts and ordinary people?

10. How do the various characters in the story respond to their streak of bad luck? In your opinion, which characters are the most admirable?

Understanding Literature (Questions for Discussion)

1. **Stereotype or Stock Character.** A **stereotypical,** or **stock, character** is one who does not deviate from conventional expectations of such a character. Who are the stock characters in Bret Harte's story about the American frontier? In what ways is their behavior predictable? In what ways is their behavior unpredictable? What are some other stock characters in stories of the American West? How do we expect them to behave?

2. **Sentimentality. Sentimentality** is an excessive expression of emotion. What one generation of readers thinks of as a normal amount of emotion in a story, another generation of readers finds excessive. Do you think Bret Harte's story is sentimental? What are the moments in the story when the reader is meant to feel the greatest emotion? What makes those moments emotional? What are some of the most sentimental moments in other stories you have read in books or seen at the movies? Do you like sentimental stories or not? Why?

Responding in Writing

Parody. A **parody** is a literary work that imitates another work for humorous, often satirical, purposes. Work with other students to plan a parody of a piece of Western fiction. Begin by coming up with a list of stock characters from Westerns, such as the straight-shooting, straight-talking, fearless lawman; the sharp-shooting, reckless young gunfighter; the kindly, honest owner of the general store; the discontented Eastern lady transplanted to the lawless, uncomfortable frontier; the sunburned old prospector certain that he will hit the mother lode any day, and so on. After creating a list of such characters, make up humorous names, dress, and habits for them. Then work on creating a setting. Name the town in which these people live. Draw a map of Main Street. Name the businesses and other places there. Again, strive to create names that are humorous. Next, create a plot by thinking of a conflict, or struggle, that might arise in the town. Here are some possibilities:

1. A mysterious Man in Black arrives in town, walks into the local watering hole, and challenges any and all comers to a pea-shooting contest

2. The cattlemen of the town become angry when a flamingo rancher starts buying up range land and fencing it in to create preserves for his birds

3. The Jones Brothers—five strapping sons of a local rancher whose collective I.Q. equals that of a cabbage—all fall in love with the lovely Miss Elvira Hornswaggle

Finally, brainstorm a list of events involving your characters that show the conflict being introduced, developed, and resolved. See if you can come up with a humorous, surprise ending for your story.

"A White Heron"
by Sarah Orne Jewett

ABOUT THE AUTHOR

Sarah Orne Jewett (1849–1909) was born in South Berwick, Maine, the daughter of a small-town country doctor. When she was young she often traveled with her father when he made house calls to his patients in the country. Inspired by the work of Harriet Beecher Stowe, as a teenager she published her first short story in the *Atlantic Monthly*, a well-known national magazine. In the fiction she wrote when she grew older, she described and celebrated rural Maine and its people. Her novel *A Country Doctor* tells of a young woman from New England who takes the then unheard-of step of refusing to marry to pursue a career in medicine. Jewett is best known for her collections of short stories, including *Deephaven* (1877), *A White Heron* (1886), *The King of Folly Island* (1888), *A Native of Winby* (1893), and her finest work, *The County of the Pointed Firs* (1896).

ABOUT THE SELECTION

"**A White Heron,**" which appeared in a collection by the same name, is an example of regional literature. The nineteenth-century regionalists wrote at a time when the United States was being rapidly industrialized, when the production of material goods was being taken from people in their homes and transferred to machines in factories. Industrialization was accompanied by the movement of large numbers of people from the country to the city, where they could find work. Ancient, old-growth forests were being cut down to plant farms to feed city dwellers, and the wild animals that inhabited these places were losing their natural habitats. Like much regional literature, "A White Heron" can be seen as a protest against these events. It encourages the reader to develop an intimate relationship with a place. Above all, it describes a conflict felt during frontier days by people who lived off the land: the conflict between a desire to conquer the natural world and the need to relate to it on its own terms. This conflict is still being worked out in our own time.

READER'S JOURNAL

Have you ever known something that somebody else wanted to know? Did you keep it a secret, or did you tell someone? Why, or why not? If you don't mind telling it, what was the secret? If you did tell the secret, to whom did you tell it? Why? Were you happy that you told the secret? Why, or why not?

LANGUAGE SKILLS

Read the Language Arts Survey, 2.150, "Dialects of English." Then find a sentence in the selection in which a character speaks in a regional dialect. Rewrite the sentence in standard English. What differences does the sentence that you chose show between the regional dialect and standard English?

"A White Heron"

Sarah Orne Jewett

I

The woods were already filled with shadows one June evening, just before eight o'clock, though a bright sunset still glimmered faintly among the trunks of the trees. A little girl was driving home her cow, a plodding, <u>dilatory</u>, provoking creature in her behavior, but a valued companion for all that. They were going away from whatever light there was, and striking deep into the woods, but their feet were familiar with the path, and it was no matter whether their eyes could see it or not.

There was hardly a night the summer through when the old cow could be found waiting at the pasture bars; on the contrary, it was her greatest pleasure to hide herself away among the high huckleberry bushes, and though she wore a loud bell she had made the discovery that if one stood perfectly still it would not ring. So Sylvia had to hunt for her until she found her, and call Co'! Co'! with never an answering Moo, until her childish patience was quite spent. If the creature had not given good milk and plenty of it, the case would have seemed very different to her owners. Besides, Sylvia had all the time there was, and very little use to make of it. Sometimes in pleasant weather it was a consolation to look upon the cow's pranks as an intelligent attempt to play hide and seek, and as the child had no playmates she lent herself to this amusement with a good deal of zest. Though this chase had been so long that the wary animal herself had given an unusual signal of her whereabouts, Sylvia had only laughed when she came upon Mistress Moolly at the swamp-side, and urged her affectionately homeward with a twig of birch leaves. The old cow was not inclined to wander farther, she even turned in the

Why might Sylvia look upon the cow as a playmate?

WORDS FOR EVERYDAY USE:

dil • a • to • ry (dil´ə tôr´ē) *adj.*, causing delay

right direction for once as they left the pasture, and stepped along the road at a good pace. She was quite ready to be milked now, and seldom stopped to browse. Sylvia wondered what her grandmother would say because they were so late. It was a great while since she had left home at half past five o'clock, but everybody knew the difficulty of making this errand a short one. Mrs. Tilley had chased the hornéd torment[1] too many summer evenings herself to blame anyone else for lingering, and was only thankful as she waited that she had Sylvia, nowadays, to give such valuable assistance. The good woman suspected that Sylvia loitered occasionally on her own account; there never was such a child for straying about out-of-doors since the world was made! Everybody said that it was a good change for a little maid who had tried to grow for eight years in a crowded manufacturing town, but, as for Sylvia herself, it seemed as if she never had been alive at all before she came to live at the farm. She thought often with wistful compassion of a wretched geranium that belonged to a town neighbor.

"'Afraid of folks,'" old Mrs. Tilley said to herself, with a smile, after she had made the unlikely choice of Sylvia from her daughter's houseful of children, and was returning to the farm. "'Afraid of folks,' they said! I guess she won't be troubled no great with 'em up to the old place!" When they reached the door of the lonely house and stopped to unlock it, and the cat came to purr loudly, and rub against them, a deserted pussy, indeed, but fat with young robins, Sylvia whispered that this was a beautiful place to live in, and she never should wish to go home.

The companions followed the shady woodroad, the cow taking slow steps, and the child very fast ones. The cow stopped long at the brook to drink, as if the pasture were not half a swamp, and Sylvia stood still and waited, letting her bare feet cool themselves in the shoal water, while the great twilight moths struck softly against her. She waded on through the brook as the cow moved away, and listened to the thrushes with a heart that beat fast with pleasure. There was a stirring in the great boughs overhead. They were full of little birds and beasts that seemed to be wide awake, and going about their world, or else saying good-night to each other in sleepy twitters. Sylvia herself felt sleepy as she walked along. However, it was not much farther to the house, and the air was soft and sweet. She was not often in the woods so late as this, and it made her feel as if she were a part of the gray shadows and the moving leaves. She was just thinking how long it seemed since she first came to the farm a year ago, and wondering if everything went on in the noisy town just the same as when she was there; the thought of the great red-faced boy who used to chase and frighten her made her hurry along the path to escape from the shadow of the trees.

Suddenly this little woods-girl is horror-stricken to hear a clear whistle not very far away. Not a bird's whistle, which would have a sort of friendliness, but a boy's whistle, determined, and somewhat

---

1. **hornéd torment.** Exasperating cow

WORDS FOR EVERYDAY USE:

wretch • ed (rech´id) *adj.,* miserable

shoal (shōl) *adj.,* shallow

aggressive. Sylvia left the cow to whatever sad fate might await her, and stepped discreetly aside into the bushes, but she was just too late. The enemy had discovered her, and called out in a very cheerful and persuasive tone, "Halloa, little girl, how far is it to the road?" and trembling Sylvia answered almost <u>inaudibly</u>, "A good ways."

She did not dare to look boldly at the tall young man, who carried a gun over his shoulder, but she came out of her bush and again followed the cow, while he walked alongside.

"I have been hunting for some birds," the stranger said kindly, "and I have lost my way, and need a friend very much. Don't be afraid," he added <u>gallantly</u>. "Speak up and tell me what your name is, and whether you think I can spend the night at your house, and go out gunning early in the morning."

Sylvia was more alarmed than before. Would not her grandmother consider her much to blame? But who could have foreseen such an accident as this? It did not seem to be her fault, and she hung her head as if the stem of it were broken, but managed to answer "Sylvy," with much effort when her companion again asked her name.

Mrs. Tilley was standing in the doorway when the trio came into view. The cow gave a loud moo by way of explanation.

"Yes, you'd better speak up for yourself, you old trial! Where'd she tucked herself away this time, Sylvy?" But Sylvia kept an awed silence; she knew by instinct that her grandmother did not comprehend the <u>gravity</u> of the situation. She must be mis-

taking the stranger for one of the farmer-lads of the region.

The young man stood his gun beside the door, and dropped a lumpy gamebag beside it; then he bade Mrs. Tilley good-evening, and repeated his wayfarer's story, and asked if he could have a night's lodging

"Put me anywhere you like," he said. "I must be off early in the morning, before day; but I am very hungry, indeed. You can give me some milk at any rate, that's plain."

"Dear sakes, yes," responded the hostess, whose long slumbering hospitality seemed to be easily awakened. "You might fare better if you went out to the main road a mile or so, but you're welcome to what we've got. I'll milk right off, and you make yourself at home. You can sleep on husks or feathers," she <u>proffered</u> graciously. "I raised them all myself. There's good pasturing for geese just below here towards the ma'sh. Now step round and set a plate for the gentleman, Sylvy!" And Sylvia promptly stepped. She was glad to have something to do, and she was hungry herself.

It was a surprise to find so clean and comfortable a little dwelling in this New England wilderness. The young man had known the horrors of its most primitive housekeeping, and the dreary <u>squalor</u> of that level of society which does not rebel at the companionship of hens. This was the best thrift of an old-fashioned farmstead, though on such a small scale that it seemed like a <u>hermitage</u>. He listened eagerly to the old woman's quaint talk, he watched Sylvia's pale face and shining gray

Why might Sylvia be alarmed?

In what is the guest interested?

eyes with ever growing enthusiasm, and insisted that this was the best supper he had eaten for a month, and afterward the new-made friends sat down in the doorway together while the moon came up.

Soon it would be berry-time, and Sylvia was a great help at picking. The cow was a good milker, though a plaguy thing to keep track of, the hostess gossiped frankly, adding presently that she had buried four children, so Sylvia's mother, and a son (who might be dead) in California were all the children she had left. "Dan, my boy, was a great hand to go gunning," she explained sadly. "I never wanted for pa'tridges or gray squer'ls while he was to home. He's been a great wand'rer, I expect, and he's no hand to write letters. There, I don't blame him, I'd ha' seen the world myself if it had been so I could.

Why has the young man come in Sylvia's direction?

"Sylvia takes after him," the grandmother continued affectionately, after a minute's pause. "There ain't a foot o' ground she don't know her way over, and the wild creaturs counts her one o' themselves. Squer'ls she'll tame to come an' feed right out o' her hands, and all sorts o' birds. Last winter she got the jay-birds to bange-ing[2] here, and I believe she'd 'a' scanted herself[3] of her own meals to have plenty to throw out amongst 'em, if I hadn't kep' watch. Anything but crows, I tell her, I'm willin' to help support—though Dan he had a tamed one o' them that did seem to have reason same as folks. It was round here a good spell after he went away. Dan an' his father they didn't hitch,—but he never held up his head ag'in after Dan had dared him an' gone off."

The guest did not notice this hint of family sorrows in his eager interest in something else.

"So Sylvy knows all about birds, does she?" he exclaimed, as he looked round at the little girl who sat, very demure but increasingly sleepy, in the moonlight. "I am making a collection of birds myself. I have been at it ever since I was a boy." (Mrs. Tilley smiled.) "There are two or three very rare ones I have been hunting for these five years. I mean to get them on my own ground if they can be found."

"Do you cage 'em up?" asked Mrs. Tilley doubtfully, in response to this enthusiastic announcement.

"Oh, no, they're stuffed and preserved, dozens and dozens of them," said the ornithologist, "and I have shot or snared every one myself. I caught a glimpse of a white heron three miles from here on Saturday, and I have followed it in this direction. They have never been found in this district at all. The little white heron, it is," and he turned again to look at Sylvia with the hope of discovering that the rare bird was one of her acquaintances.

But Sylvia was watching a hop-toad in the narrow footpath.

"You would know the heron if you saw it," the stranger continued eagerly. "A queer tall white bird with soft feathers and long thin legs. And it would have a nest perhaps in the top of a high tree, made of sticks, something like a hawk's nest."

Sylvia's heart gave a wild beat; she knew that strange white bird, and had once stolen softly near where it stood in some

---

2. **bangeing.** Hanging around
3. **'a' scanted herself.** Would have deprived herself

WORDS FOR EVERYDAY USE:

de • mure (di myoor´) *adj.*, modest; shy

or • ni • thol • o • gist (ôr´nə thäl´ə jist) *n.*, one who studies birds

bright green swamp grass, away over at the other side of the woods. There was an open place where the sunshine always seemed strangely yellow and hot, where tall, nodding rushes grew, and her grandmother had warned her that she might sink in the soft black mud underneath and never be heard of more. Not far beyond were the salt marshes just this side the sea itself, which Sylvia wondered and dreamed about, but never had seen, whose great voice could sometimes be heard above the noise of the woods on stormy nights.

"I can't think of anything I should like so much as to find that heron's nest," the handsome stranger was saying. "I would give ten dollars to anybody who could show it to me," he added desperately, "and I mean to spend my whole vacation hunting for it if need be. Perhaps it was only migrating, or had been chased out of its own region by some bird of prey."

Mrs. Tilley gave amazed attention to all this, but Sylvia still watched the toad, not divining, as she might have done at some calmer time, that the creature wished to get to its hole under the doorstep, and was much hindered by the unusual spectators at that hour of the evening. No amount of thought, that night, could decide how many wished-for treasures the ten dollars, so lightly spoken of, would buy.

The next day the young sportsman hovered about the woods, and Sylvia kept him company, having lost her first fear of the friendly lad, who proved to be most kind and sympathetic. He told her many things about the birds and what they knew and

Louisiana Heron. *Rodney Busch. Private collection*

where they lived and what they did with themselves. And he gave her a jackknife, which she thought as great a treasure as if she were a desert-islander. All day long he did not once make her troubled or afraid except when he brought down some unsuspecting singing creature from its bough. Sylvia would have liked him vastly better without his gun; she could not understand why he killed the very birds he seemed to like so much. But as the day waned, Sylvia still watched the young man with loving admiration. She had never seen anybody so charming and delightful; the woman's heart, asleep in the child, was vaguely thrilled by a dream of love. Some <u>premonition</u> of that great power stirred and swayed these young creatures who traversed the solemn woodlands with soft-footed silent care. They stopped to listen to a

How does Sylvia feel about the young man killing birds?

bird's song; they pressed forward again eagerly, parting the branches,—speaking to each other rarely and in whispers; the young man going first and Sylvia following, fascinated, a few steps behind, with her gray eyes dark with excitement.

Is Sylvia hoping to help find the white heron?

She grieved because the longed-for white heron was elusive, but she did not lead the guest, she only followed, and there was no such thing as speaking first. The sound of her own unquestioned voice would have terrified her,—it was hard enough to answer yes or no when there was need of that. At last evening began to fall, and they drove the cow home together, and Sylvia smiled with pleasure when they came to the place where she heard the whistle and was afraid only the night before.

What keeps Sylvia awake?

II

Half a mile from home, at the farther edge of the woods, where the land was highest, a great pine tree stood, the last of its generation. Whether it was left for a boundary mark, or for what reason, no one could say; the woodchoppers who had felled its mates were dead and gone long ago, and a whole forest of sturdy trees, pines and oaks and maples, had grown again. But the stately head of this old pine towered above them all and made a landmark for sea and shore miles and miles away. Sylvia knew it well. She had always believed that whoever climbed to the top of it could see the ocean; and the little girl had often laid her hand on the great rough trunk and looked up wistfully at those dark boughs that the wind always stirred, no matter how hot and still the air might be below. Now she thought of the tree with a new excitement, for why, if one climbed it at break of day, could not one see all the world, and easily discover from whence the white heron flew, and mark the place, and find the hidden nest?

What a spirit of adventure, what wild ambition! What fancied triumph and delight and glory for the later morning when she could make known the secret! It was almost too real and too great for the childish heart to bear.

All night the door of the little house stood open and the whippoorwills came and sang upon the very step. The young sportsman and his old hostess were sound asleep, but Sylvia's great design kept her broad awake and watching. She forgot to think of sleep. The short summer night seemed as long as the winter darkness, and at last when the whippoorwills ceased, and she was afraid the morning would after all come too soon, she stole out of the house and followed the pasture path through the woods, hastening toward the open ground beyond, listening with a sense of comfort and companionship to the drowsy twitter of a half-awakened bird, whose perch she had jarred in passing. Alas, if the great wave of human interest which flooded for the first time this dull little life should sweep away the satisfactions of an existence heart to heart with nature and the dumb life of the forest!

There was the huge tree asleep yet in the paling moonlight, and small and silly Sylvia began with utmost bravery to mount to the top of it, with tingling, eager blood coursing the channels of her whole frame, with her bare feet and fingers, that pinched and held like bird's claws to the

WORDS FOR EVERYDAY USE:

course (kôrs) *vi.,* move swiftly; flow through

monstrous ladder reaching up, up, almost to the sky itself. First she must mount the white oak tree that grew alongside, where she was almost lost among the dark branches and the green leaves heavy and wet with dew; a bird fluttered off its nest, and a red squirrel ran to and fro and scolded pettishly at the harmless house-breaker. Sylvia felt her way easily. She had often climbed there, and knew that higher still one of the oak's upper branches chafed against the pine trunk, just where its lower boughs were set close together. There, when she made the dangerous pass from one tree to the other, the great enterprise would really begin.

She crept out along the swaying oak limb at last, and took the daring step across into the old pine tree. The way was harder than she thought; she must reach far and hold fast, the sharp dry twigs caught and held her and scratched her like angry talons, the pitch made her thin little fingers clumsy and stiff as she went round and round the tree's great stem, higher and higher upward. The sparrows and robins in the woods below were beginning to wake and twitter to the dawn, yet it seemed much lighter there aloft in the pine tree, and the child knew that she must hurry if her project were to be of any use.

The tree seemed to lengthen itself out as she went up, and to reach farther and farther upward. It was like a great main-mast to the voyaging earth; it must truly have been amazed that morning through all its <u>ponderous</u> frame as it felt this determined spark of human spirit winding its way from higher branch to branch. Who knows how steadily the least twigs held themselves to advantage this light, weak creature on her way! The old pine must have loved his new dependent. More than all the hawks, and bats, and moths, and even the sweet-voiced thrushes, was the brave, beating heart of the solitary gray-eyed child. And the tree stood still and frowned away the winds that June morning while the dawn grew bright in the east.

Sylvia's face was like a pale star, if one had seen it from the ground, when the last thorny bough was past, and she stood trembling and tired but wholly tri-umphant, high in the treetop. Yes, there was the sea with the dawning sun making a golden dazzle over it, and toward that glorious east flew two hawks with slow-moving <u>pinions</u>. How low they looked in the air from that height when one had only seen them before far up, and dark against the blue sky. Their gray feathers were as soft as moths; they seemed only a little way from the tree, and Sylvia felt as if she too could go flying away among the clouds. Westward, the woodlands and farms reached miles and miles into the distance; here and there were church steeples, and white villages; truly it was a vast and awesome world!

The birds sang louder and louder. At last the sun came up bewilderingly bright. Sylvia could see the white sails of ships out at sea, and the clouds that were purple and rose-colored and yellow at first began to fade away. Where was the white heron's nest in the sea of green branches, and was this wonderful sight and pageant of the world the only reward for having climbed

WORDS FOR EVERYDAY USE:

pon • der • ous (pän´dər əs) *adj.,* very heavy

pin • ion (pin´yən) *n.,* part of a bird's wing

What "day's pleasure" is the young man anticipating?

to such a giddy height? Now look down again, Sylvia, where the green marsh is set among the shining birches and dark hemlocks; there where you saw the white heron once you will see him again; look, look! a white spot of him like a single floating feather comes up from the dead hemlock and grows larger, and rises, and comes close at last, and goes by the landmark pine with steady sweep of wing and outstretched slender neck and crested head. And wait! wait! do not move a foot or a finger, little girl, do not send an arrow of light and consciousness from your two eager eyes, for the heron has perched on a pine bough not far beyond yours, and cries back to his mate on the nest, and plumes his feathers for the new day!

The child gives a long sigh a minute later when a company of shouting catbirds comes also to the tree, and <u>vexed</u> by their fluttering and lawlessness the solemn heron goes away. She knows his secret now, the wild, light, slender bird that floats and wavers, and goes back like an arrow presently to his home in the green world beneath. Then Sylvia, well satisfied, makes her perilous way down again, not daring to look far below the branch she stands on, ready to cry sometimes because her fingers ache and her lamed feet slip. Wondering over and over again what the stranger would say to her, and what he would think when she told him how to find his way straight to the heron's nest.

Does Sylvia tell the location of the white heron's nest? Why, or why not?

"Sylvy, Sylvy!" called the busy old grandmother again and again, but nobody answered, and the small husk bed was empty and Sylvia had disappeared.

The guest waked from a dream, and remembering his day's pleasure hurried to dress himself that might it sooner begin. He was sure from the way the shy little girl looked once or twice yesterday that she had at least seen the white heron, and now she must really be made to tell. Here she comes now, paler than ever, and her worn old frock is torn and tattered, and smeared with pine pitch. The grandmother and the sportsman stand in the door together and question her, and the splendid moment has come to speak of the dead hemlock tree by the green marsh.

But Sylvia does not speak after all, though the old grandmother fretfully <u>rebukes</u> her, and the young man's kind, appealing eyes are looking straight in her own. He can make them rich with money; he has promised it, and they are poor now. He is so well worth making happy, and he waits to hear the story she can tell.

No, she must keep silence! What is it that suddenly forbids her and makes her dumb? Has she been nine years growing and now, when the great world for the first time puts out a hand to her, must she thrust it aside for a bird's sake? The murmur of the pine's green branches is in her ears, she remembers how the white heron came flying through the golden air and how they watched the sea and the morning together, and Sylvia cannot speak; she cannot tell the heron's secret and give its life away.

Dear loyalty, that suffered a sharp pang as the guest went away disappointed later in the day, that could have served and followed him and loved him as a dog loves!

WORDS FOR EVERYDAY USE:

vex (veks) *vt.*, annoy

re • buke (ri byōōk´) *vt.*, blame or scold in a sharp way

Many a night Sylvia heard the echo of his whistle haunting the pasture path as she came home with the loitering cow. She forgot even her sorrow at the sharp report of his gun and the sight of thrushes and sparrows dropping silent to the ground, their songs hushed and their pretty feathers stained and wet with blood. Were the birds better friends than their hunter might have been,—who can tell? Whatever treasures were lost to her, woodlands and summertime, remember! Bring your gifts and graces and tell your secrets to this lonely country child! ■

Responding to the Selection

At the end of the story, Sylvia does not tell the young man where the white heron nests. Were you glad that she did not tell, or did you think she should have told him? Why?

Reviewing the Selection

RECALLING

1. Why is Sylvia usually late in getting home when she goes to fetch the cow from the pasture? How is the cow similar to Sylvia?

2. Why does Sylvia's grandmother, Mrs. Tilley, bring Sylvia rather than one of Sylvia's brothers or sisters to the farm?

3. Whom does Sylvia meet on the way home? What is he doing on the road?

4. Why is Sylvia at first afraid of the young man? How does Sylvia's attitude toward him change in the course of the story?

INTERPRETING

5. What does the young man want to know about the white heron? Why does he want to know it? What does he offer Sylvia in return for this knowledge?

6. Why does Sylvia want the money that the young man offers in return for knowledge of where the white heron nests?

7. What does Sylvia do to find out what the young man wants to know?

8. Why does Sylvia decide not to tell the young man the secret?

9. At one point in the story, Mrs. Tilley says to the young wanderer, "I'd ha' seen the world myself if it had been so I could." Why is it that Mrs. Tilley cannot go and see the world? How do the men in the story, the young man and Mrs. Tilley's son, Dan, differ from the women? The narrator of "A White Heron" calls the young man by many different names. What are these names? Why is he called by them? What does the fact that he has so many names tell us about him? How is he similar to Mrs. Tilley's son, Dan?

10. When the story begins, Sylvia is a shy country girl, a companion to all the creatures in the natural world. With the arrival of the strange young man, however, she begins to take an interest in people. "The great wave of human interest," the narrator says, "flooded for the first time this dull little life." How does Sylvia resolve this conflict between her love for nature and her interest in the young man? Besides the money he was going to give her, what does Sylvia lose by not telling the young man about the heron? Is this a great loss? What are the "gifts," "graces," and "secrets" that the narrator asks the woodlands to give her in return?

Understanding Literature (Questions for Discussion)

1. **Motif.** A **motif** is any element that recurs in one or more works of literature. Each time the motif occurs it means something slightly different because it occurs in different moments in the story. In "A White Heron," for example, images of birds occur repeatedly. Find all the moments in the story in which birds are mentioned. What does each occurrence of this motif teach us about Sylvia's or the young man's relationship to birds? What does each one teach us about their relationship to nature?

2. **Conflict.** A **conflict** is a struggle between two forces in a literary work. In "A White Heron," the central conflict is **internal.** It occurs within Sylvia, who is the main character, or **protagonist.** Sylvia's love of the creatures in the woods conflicts with her desire to help the young man find the heron. What are examples of Sylvia's close relationship with the animals? Why does she want to help the young man find the heron? What are some other conflicts or struggles within the story? What is the relation between these minor conflicts and the main conflict?

Responding in Writing

Character Sketch. Choose a character from the story: the grandmother, Sylvia, or the young man. Write a character sketch of this person. A **character sketch** is a description of a person that reveals such details as the person's appearance, habits, occupation, background, beliefs, values, attitudes, and personality. You can write a character sketch by answering the following questions:

1. What does the character look like? What does the character wear?

2. What does the character do for work and for play?

3. How does the character speak? Use examples from the story.

4. What are the major personality traits of the character? The character, for instance, might be shy, playful, aggressive, simple-minded, or serious. For each trait, provide an illustration from the story.

5. How do the other characters in the story view the character you have chosen?

6. What is a quotation from the character that illustrates his or her personality or beliefs? Write it down and describe what it illustrates about the character.

7. How is your character different from the other characters in the story?

8. Do you like the character? Why, or why not?

9. If you were the character, what would you want out of life? What plans or goals would you have for the future?

10. If you had to compare the character to an animal, which animal would you choose. Why?

Language Lab

Correcting Run-ons. Read the Language Arts Survey, 2.62, "Correcting Run-ons." Then rewrite the following run-ons. Correct each one either by making it into two or three separate sentences or by adding a comma and a coordinating conjunction. If the sentence is not a run-on, copy it as it is.

1. Regional writers write about a particular part of the country they write about what makes the region special.

2. Sarah Orne Jewett wrote about rural Maine, she was brought up in the area.

3. The story "A White Heron" is about a shy young country girl who loves the creatures in the woods because they are the companions with whom she plays, these creatures bring her great happiness.

4. The young man in "A White Heron" treats the creatures of the woods as something to study, Sylvia treats them as companions.

5. Sarah Orne Jewett was a nineteenth-century "feminist" writer, other nineteenth-century feminists include Kate Chopin and Mary E. Wilkins Freeman.

"The Story of an Hour"
by Kate Chopin

ABOUT THE AUTHOR

Kate Chopin (1851–1904), born Kate O'Flaherty, was raised in St. Louis. When she was four years old, her father died in a train wreck. She was brought up by her French-speaking Creole mother, her grandmother, and her great-grandmother, who was a fine storyteller. Until the age of seventeen, she attended a Catholic school called the St. Louis Academy of the Sacred Heart. At eighteen, she met a twenty-five-year-old banker named Oscar Chopin, whom she married. The Chopins moved to New Orleans, her husband's hometown, and before she was thirty years old, Kate Chopin gave birth to six children. When her husband's cotton business failed, the couple moved to Cloutierville in Natchitoches Parish, Louisiana. Her family physician in St. Louis recognized the quality of the writing in Chopin's letters from Louisiana and urged her to write as an outlet for her emotions. Many of the stories that Chopin was to write in later years dealt with the lives of the Creoles and Cajuns whom she came to know in Louisiana. When her husband suddenly died of swamp fever, Chopin moved back to St. Louis and began her literary career. She wrote two novels, over one hundred short stories, poetry, book reviews, and literary criticism, all while raising her six children. Chopin's second novel, *The Awakening* (1899), met with much censorship in its time but is today considered a masterpiece, having received renewed critical attention in the twentieth century because of its strong feminist message.

ABOUT THE SELECTION

Kate Chopin began her career as a regional writer, like Bret Harte and Sarah Orne Jewett. In her fiction, she carefully portrayed the landscape of the Gulf Islands and the people of Louisiana—the French Creoles of New Orleans and the rural Cajuns of Natchitoches. Besides being a regionalist, however, Kate Chopin was a pioneering feminist writer. Her most famous novel, *The Awakening*, tells the story of the intellectual and emotional development of a young woman. The novel scandalized Chopin's contemporaries, partially because it depicts the woman's rebellion against her husband's authority. **"The Story of an Hour"** is another fine example of Chopin's feminist fiction.

"The Story of an Hour"

KATE CHOPIN

Knowing that Mrs. Mallard was afflicted with a heart trouble, great care was taken to break to her as gently as possible the news of her husband's death.

It was her sister Josephine who told her, in broken sentences; veiled hints that revealed in half concealing. Her husband's friend Richards was there, too, near her. It was he who had been in the newspaper office when intelligence of the railroad disaster was received, with Brently Mallard's name leading the list of "killed." He had only taken the time to assure himself of its truth by a second telegram, and had hastened to forestall any less careful, less tender friend in bearing the sad message.

She did not hear the story as many women have heard the same, with a paralyzed inability to accept its significance. She wept at once, with sudden, wild abandonment, in her sister's arms. When the storm of grief had spent itself she went away to her room alone. She would have no one follow her.

There stood, facing the open window, a comfortable, roomy armchair. Into this she sank, pressed down by a physical exhaustion that haunted her body and seemed to reach into her soul.

She could see in the open square before her house the tops of trees that were all aquiver with the new spring life. The delicious breath of rain was in the air. In the street below a peddler was crying his wares. The notes of a distant song which someone was singing reached her faintly, and countless sparrows were twittering in the eaves.

There were patches of blue sky showing here and there through the clouds that had met and piled one above the other in the west facing her window.

She sat with her head thrown back upon the cushion of the chair, quite motionless except when a sob came up into her throat and shook her, as a child who has cried itself, to sleep continues to sob in its dreams.

She was young, with a fair, calm face, whose lines bespoke repression and even a certain strength. But now there was a dull stare in her eyes, whose gaze was fixed away off yonder on one of those patches

What is Mrs. Mallard's immediate reaction to news of her husband's death?

of blue sky. It was not a glance of reflection but rather indicated a suspension of intelligent thought.

There was something coming to her and she was waiting for it, fearfully. What was it? She did not know; it was too subtle and elusive to name. But she felt it, creeping out of the sky, reaching toward her through the sounds, the scents, the color that filled the air.

Now her bosom rose and fell <u>tumultuously</u>. She was beginning to recognize this thing that was approaching to possess her, and she was striving to beat it back with her will—as powerless as her two white slender hands would have been.

When she abandoned herself, a little whispered word escaped her slightly parted lips. She said it over and over under her breath: "free, free, free! The vacant stare and the look of terror that had followed it went from her eyes. They stayed keen and bright. Her pulses beat fast, and the coursing blood warmed and relaxed every inch of her body.

She did not stop to ask if it were or were not a monstrous joy that held her. A clear and exalted perception enabled her to dismiss the suggestion as trivial.

She knew that she would weep again when she saw the kind, tender hands folded in death; the face that had never looked save with love upon her, fixed and gray and dead. But she saw beyond that bitter moment a long procession of years to come that would belong to her absolutely. And she opened and spread her arms out to them in welcome.

There would be no one to live for her during those coming years; she would live

What is the thought that possesses her?

for herself. There would be no powerful will bending hers in that blind persistence with which men and women believe they have a right to impose a private will upon a fellow creature. A kind intention or a cruel intention made the act seem no less a crime as she looked upon it in that brief moment of illumination.

And yet she had loved him—sometimes. Often she had not. What did it matter! What could love, the unsolved mystery, count for in face of this possession of self-assertion which she suddenly recognized as the strongest impulse of her being!

"Free! Body and soul free!" she kept whispering.

Josephine was kneeling before the closed door with her lips to the keyhole, imploring for admission. "Louise, open the door! I beg; open the door—you will make yourself ill. What are you doing, Louise? For heaven's sake open the door."

"Go away. I am not making myself ill." No; she was drinking in a very elixir of life[1] through that open window.

Her fancy was running riot along those days ahead of her. Spring days, and summer days, and all sorts of days that would be her own. She breathed a quick prayer that life might be long. It was only yesterday she had thought with a shudder that life might be long.

She arose at length and opened the door to her sister's <u>importunities</u>. There was a feverish triumph in her eyes, and she carried herself unwittingly like a goddess of Victory. She clasped her sister's waist, and

---

1. **elixir of life.** Substance sought by medieval alchemists to prolong life indefinitely

WORDS FOR EVERYDAY USE:

tu • mul • tu • ous • ly (tōō mulʹ chōō əs lē) *adv.*, wildly

im • por • tu • ni • ty (imʹpor tōōnʹ i tē) *n.*, persistent demand

together they descended the stairs. Richards stood waiting for them at the bottom.

Someone was opening the front door with a latchkey. It was Brently Mallard who entered, a little travel-stained, composedly carrying his gripsack[2] and umbrella. He had been far from the scene of accident, and did not know there had been one. He stood amazed at Josephine's piercing cry; at Richards's quick motion to screen him from the view of his wife.

But Richards was too late.

When the doctors came they said she had died of heart disease—of joy that kills. ■

Is it really joy that kills Mrs. Mallard?

---

2. **gripsack.** Small bag for traveling clothes

Responding to the Selection

Do you approve or disapprove of Mrs. Mallard's response to her husband's "death"? Why?

Reviewing the Selection

RECALLING

1. What does Mrs. Mallard learn from her sister Josephine at the beginning of the story? Why does Josephine have to break this news gently?

2. What does Mrs. Mallard do when she hears the news? What appears to be Mrs. Mallard's reaction to the news?

3. What is Mrs. Mallard's second response to the news?

4. Who enters the house just as Josephine and Mrs. Mallard are descending the stairs? What happens to Mrs. Mallard?

INTERPRETING

5. How well does Mr. Mallard's friend Richards check the truth of the news? Why does he want to be the first person to break the news to Mrs. Mallard?

6. What sights and smells does Mrs. Mallard experience at the open window in her room? What do these sights and smells represent to her?

7. How did Mr. Mallard treat Mrs. Mallard in their marriage? What are Mrs. Mallard's feelings about Mr. Mallard?

8. How does Mrs. Mallard appear as she walks down the stairs? What does her appearance reveal?

SYNTHESIZING

9. Why is the story called "The Story of an Hour"? What hour does the story describe? Is this a happy and fulfilling hour, a disappointing hour, or both? Explain.

10. To what does Mrs. Mallard look forward? What happens to her at the end of the story? Why?

Understanding Literature (Questions for Discussion)

1. **Reversal**. A **reversal** is a dramatic change in the direction of events in a narrative, especially a change in the fortunes of the protagonist. There are two major reversals in "The Story of an Hour." The first occurs when Mrs. Mallard's sadness about her husband's death turns to joy at the freedom she feels. The second occurs when her husband opens the door and everyone learns that he has not died. Does your response to Mrs. Mallard change when her sadness turns to joy? How do you feel when you learn that Mrs. Mallard's husband is dead?

2. **Irony**. **Irony** is a difference between appearance and reality. **Dramatic irony** occurs when a situation appears one way to the reader of the story and another way to the characters in the story. At the end of the selection, the doctors say that Mrs. Mallard died of "joy that kills." How is this an example of dramatic irony? What do the doctors believe to be the cause of Mrs. Mallard's death? What actually caused her death? How does it feel to realize that you know the truth and the doctors in the story do not?

Responding in Writing

1. **Paragraph**. A **paragraph** is a group of sentences that develops one main idea or that serves a single purpose. A paragraph often consists of a topic sentence that states the main idea and several sentences that explain and support the main idea with specific details. Choose one of the following topic sentences. Then write a paragraph in support of that sentence using details from the story.
   • Kate Chopin's short story, "The Story of an Hour," has a surprising plot.
   • Mrs. Mallard, the main character of "The Story of an Hour," has a love-hate relationship with her husband.
   • "The Story of an Hour" is a feminist story.

2. **Diary Entry.** Imagine that you are Mrs. Mallard and that you are sitting in the room alone, thinking about the death of your husband and about your future life. Write a diary entry that she might have written at that time.

Language Lab

Combining Sentences. Read the Language Arts Survey, 2.51–2.53, on combining sentences. Then combine the following pairs of sentences using single words, phrases, or clauses.

1. She sank into the armchair. She was pressed down by a physical exhaustion that haunted her body and seemed to reach into her soul.

2. She sat with her head thrown back upon the cushion of the chair. She was quite motionless.

3. There was something coming to her. She was waiting for it.

4. Her pulse beat fast. The coursing blood warmed and relaxed every inch of her body.

"The Notorious Jumping Frog of Calaveras County"
by Mark Twain

ABOUT THE AUTHOR

Mark Twain (1835–1910) was the pseudonym of Samuel Langhorne Clemens. Clemens took the name from a term for "the second mark," referring to water that was two fathoms deep, or a safe depth for a boat, a term that he encountered as a riverboat pilot. Born in Florida, Missouri, Twain grew up in the nearby river town of Hannibal. At the age of twenty-one, he headed to New Orleans to depart for a trip to the Amazon. The plan fell apart, but Twain found a position as an apprentice riverboat pilot, a prestigious job that fulfilled a childhood dream. Before the Civil War, a lucrative trade was done on the Mississippi. When the war interrupted that trade, and Twain was forced to find another job, he went west and took a job as a reporter for the *Sacramento Union.* He began to write his most famous books in 1870. *The Adventures of Tom Sawyer* (1876), *Life on the Mississippi* (1883), and *The Adventures of Huckleberry Finn* (1883) all draw from his experiences on the Mississippi River. *Huckleberry Finn,* often referred to as the great American novel, tells the story of a boy named Huck who, together with an escaped slave named Jim, travels down the Mississippi on a raft. Alternately funny and serious, the book is an implicit indictment of racism, showing that beneath outward differences, people have similar feelings and dreams. In the 1890s, Twain suffered a series of misfortunes, including the death of a daughter, the illness of another daughter and of his wife, and monetary loss due to failed speculative investments. The writings of Twain's last years contain a great deal of bitterness directed at the hypocrisies of his fellow human beings. Twain's severest criticisms, included in *The War Prayer* and *Letters from Earth*, were not published until long after his death. Born on the day of the appearance of Halley's comet, Twain died on the day of its reappearance seventy-two years later.

ABOUT THE SELECTION

"The Notorious Jumping Frog of Calaveras County" is Twain's retelling of a popular nineteenth-century tall tale. A **tall tale** is a lighthearted and humorous story that contains highly exaggerated, unrealistic events. Twain first became known nationally when the story was published in the *Saturday Press* in 1865. The story is also an outstanding example of regional writing. It portrays the entertainments of simple, uneducated men living in a frontier mining camp. The setting is a perfect arena for Twain to display his gift for capturing regional dialects.

"The Notorious Jumping Frog of Calaveras County"

MARK TWAIN

Why does the narrator visit Simon Wheeler?

In compliance with the request of a friend of mine, who wrote me from the East, I called on good-natured, <u>garrulous</u> old Simon Wheeler, and inquired after my friend's friend, Leonidas W. Smiley, as requested to do, and I hereunto <u>append</u> the result. I have a lurking suspicion that *Leonidas W.* Smiley is a myth; that my friend never knew such a personage; and that he only <u>conjectured</u> that if I asked old Wheeler about him, it would remind him of his infamous *Jim* Smiley, and he would go to work and bore me to death with some exasperating reminiscence of him as long and as tedious as it should be useless to me. If that was the design, it succeeded.

What does the narrator suspect about Leonidas W. Smiley?

I found Simon Wheeler dozing comfortably by the barroom stove of the <u>dilapidated</u> tavern in the decayed mining camp of Angel's, and I noticed that he was fat and bald-headed, and had an expression of winning gentleness and simplicity upon his tranquil countenance. He roused up, and gave me good-day. I told him a friend of mine had commissioned me to make some inquiries about a cherished companion of his boyhood named *Leonidas* W. Smiley—*Rev. Leonidas W.* Smiley, a young minister of the Gospel, who he had heard was at one time a resident of Angel's Camp. I added that if Mr. Wheeler could tell me anything about this

WORDS FOR EVERYDAY USE:

gar • ru • lous (gar´ə ləs) *adj.,* talking much or too much

ap • pend (ə pend´) *vt.,* attach or affix

con • jec • ture (kən jek´chər) *vi.,* guess

di • lap • i • dat • ed (də lap´ə dāt id) *adj.,* falling to pieces or into disrepair

Rev. Leonidas W. Smiley, I would feel under many obligations to him.

Simon Wheeler backed me into a corner and blockaded me there with his chair, and then sat down and reeled off the monotonous narrative which follows this paragraph. He never smiled, he never frowned, he never changed his voice from the gentle-flowing key to which he tuned his initial sentence, he never betrayed the slightest suspicion of enthusiasm; but all through the <u>interminable</u> narrative there ran a vein of impressive earnestness and sincerity, which showed me plainly that, so far from his imagining that there was anything ridiculous or funny about his story, he regarded it as a really important matter, and admired its two heroes as men of transcendent genius in *finesse*.[1] I let him go on in his own way, and never interrupted him once.

Rev. Leonidas W. H'm, Reverend Le— well, there was a feller here once by the name of *Jim* Smiley, in the winter of '49— or maybe it was the spring of '50—I don't recollect exactly, somehow, though what makes me think it was one or the other is because I remember the big flume[2] warn't finished when he first come to the camp; but any way, he was the curiousest man about always betting on anything that turned up you ever see, if he could get anybody to bet on the other side; and if he couldn't he'd change sides. Any way that suited the other man would suit *him*—any way just so's he got a bet, *he* was satisfied. But still he was lucky, uncommon lucky; he most always come out winner. He was always ready and laying for a chance; there couldn't be no solit'ry thing mentioned but that feller'd offer to bet on it, and take ary side you please, as I was just telling you. If there was a horse-race, you'd find him flush[3] or you'd find him busted[4] at the end of it; if there was a dog-fight, he'd bet on it; if there was a cat-fight, he'd bet on it; if there was a chicken-fight, he'd bet on it; why, if there was two birds setting on a fence, he would bet you which one would fly first, or if there was a camp-meeting,[5] he would be there reg'lar to bet on Parson Walker, which he judged to be the best <u>exhorter</u> about here, and so he was too, and a good man. If he even see a straddle-bug[6] start to go anywheres, he would bet you how long it would take him to get to—to wherever he was going to, and if you took him up, he would foller that straddle-bug to Mexico but what he would find out where he was bound for and how long he was on the road. Lots of the boys here has seen that Smiley, and can tell you about him. Why, it never made no difference to *him*—he'd bet on *any* thing—the dangdest feller. Parson Walker's wife laid very sick once, for a good while, and it seemed as if they warn't going to save her; but one morning he come in, and Smiley up and asked him how she was, and he said she was considable better—thank the Lord for his inf'nite mercy—and coming on so smart that with the blessing of Prov'dence she'd

What is curious about Jim Smiley?

1. **transcendent . . . finesse.** Extraordinary skill, cunning, or artfulness
2. **flume.** Artificial channel for carrying water to furnish power or transport objects
3. **flush.** Well supplied with money
4. **busted.** Penniless
5. **camp-meeting.** Religious gathering at the camp, or mining community
6. **straddle-bug.** Long-legged insect

WORDS FOR EVERYDAY USE:

in • ter • mi • na • ble (in tʉr´mi nə bel) *adj.*, without, or apparently without, end

ex • hor • ter (eg zôrt´ər) *n.*, one who urges earnestly, by advice or warning

get well yet; and Smiley, before he thought says, "Well, I'll resk two-and-a-half she don't anyway."

Thish-yer Smiley had a mare—the boys called her the fifteen-minute nag, but that was only in fun, you know, because of course she was faster than that—and he used to win money on that horse, for all she was so slow and always had the asthma, or the distemper, or the consumption, or something of that kind. They used to give her two or three hundred yards start, and then pass her under way; but always at the fag end[7] of the race she'd get excited and desperate-like, and come <u>cavorting</u> and straddling up, and scattering her legs around limber, sometimes in the air, and sometimes out to one side among the fences, and kicking up m-o-r-e dust and raising m-o-r-e racket with her coughing and sneezing and blowing her nose—and *always* fetch up at the stand just about a neck ahead, as near as you could cipher it down.

And he had a little small bull-pup, that to look at him you'd think he warn't worth a cent but to set around and look <u>ornery</u> and lay for a chance to steal something. But as soon as money was up on him he was a different dog; his underjaw'd begin to stick out like the fo'castle[8] of a steamboat, and his teeth would uncover and shine like the furnaces. And a dog might tackle him and bully-rag him, and bite him, and throw him over his shoulder two or three times, and Andrew Jackson—which was the name of the pup—Andrew Jackson would never let on but what *he* was satisfied, and hadn't expected nothing else—and the bets being doubled and doubled on the other side all the time, till the money was all up; and then all of a sudden he would grab that other dog jest by the j'int of his hind leg and freeze to it—not chaw, you understand, but only just grip and hang on till they throwed up the sponge, if it was a year. Smiley always come out winner on that pup, till he harnessed a dog once that didn't have no hind legs, because they'd been sawed off in a circular saw, and when the thing had gone along far enough, and the money was all up, and he come to make a snatch for his pet holt[9] he see in a minute how he's been imposed on, and how the other dog had him in the door, so to speak, and he 'peared surprised, and then he looked sorter discouraged-like, and didn't try no more to win the fight, and so he got shucked out bad. He give Smiley a look, as much as to say his heart was broke, and it was *his* fault, for putting up a dog that hadn't no hind legs for him to take holt of, which was his main dependence in a fight, and then he limped off a piece and laid down and died. It was a good pup, was that Andrew Jackson, and would have made a name for hisself if he'd lived, for the stuff was in him and he had genius—I know it, because he hadn't no opportunities to speak of, and it don't stand to reason that a dog could make such a fight as he could under them circumstances if he hadn't no talent. It always makes me feel sorry when I think of that last fight of his'n, and the way it turned out.

In what way does the dog without hind legs have an advantage over Andrew Jackson?

---

7. **fag end.** Last part
8. **fo'castle.** Upper deck of a boat; part of a bow that protrudes
9. **pet holt.** Favorite hold

WORDS FOR EVERYDAY USE:

ca • vort (kə vôrt´) *vi.,* leap about, prance

or • ner • y (ôr´nər ē) *adj.,* having an ugly or mean disposition

Well, thish-yer Smiley had rat-terriers[10] and chicken cocks,[11] and tomcats and all them kind of things, till you couldn't rest, and you couldn't fetch nothing for him to bet on but he'd match you. He ketched a frog one day, and took him home, and said he cal'lated to educate him; and so he never done nothing for three months but set in his back yard and learn that frog to jump. And you bet you he *did* learn him, too. He'd give him a little punch behind, and the next minute you'd see that frog whirling in the air like a doughnut—see him turn one summerset, or maybe a couple, if he got a good start, and come down flat-footed and all right, like a cat. He got him up so in the matter of ketching flies, and kep' him in practice so constant, that he'd nail a fly every time as fur as he could see him. Smiley said all a frog wanted was education, and he could do 'most anything—and I believe him. Why, I've seen him set Dan'l Webster down here on this floor—Dan'l Webster was the name of the frog—and sing out, "Flies, Dan'l, flies!" and quicker'n you could wink he'd spring straight up and snake a fly off'n the counter there, and flop down on the floor ag'in as solid as a gob of mud, and fall to scratching the side of his head with his hind foot as indifferent as if he hadn't no idea he'd been doin' any more'n any frog might do. You never see a frog so modest and straightfor'ard as he was, for all he was so gifted. And when it come to fair and square jumping on a dead level, he could get over more ground at one straddle than any animal of his breed you ever see. Jumping on a dead level was his strong suit, you understand; and when it come to that, Smiley would ante up money on him as long as he had a red.[12] Smiley was monstrous proud of his frog, and well he might be, for fellers that had traveled and been everywheres all said he laid over any frog that ever *they* see.

Well, Smiley kep' the beast in a little lattice box, and he used to fetch him down-town sometimes and lay for a bet. One day a feller—a stranger in the camp, he was—come acrost him with his box, and says:

"What might it be that you've got in the box?"

And Smiley says, sorter indifferent-like. "It might be a parrot, or it might be a canary, maybe, but it ain't—it's only just a frog."

And the feller took it, and looked at it careful, and turned it round this way and that, and says. "H'm—so 'tis. Well, what's *he* good for?"

"Well," Smiley says, easy and careless, "he's good enough for *one* thing, I should judge—he can outjump any frog in Calaveras county."

The feller took the box again, and took another long, particular look, and give it back to Smiley, and says, very deliberate, "Well," he says, "I don't see no p'ints about that frog that's any better'n any other frog."

"Maybe you don't," Smiley says. "Maybe you understand frogs and maybe you don't understand em; maybe you've had experience, and maybe you ain't only a amature, as it were. Anyways, I've got *my* opinion, and I'll resk forty dollars that he can outjump any frog in Calaveras county."

And the feller studied a minute, and then says, kinder sad like, "Well, I'm only a stranger here, and I ain't got no frog; but if I had a frog, I'd bet you."

And then Smiley says. "That's all right—that's all right—if you'll hold my box a

What is amusing or ironic about calling a frog modest?

10. **rat-terriers.** Small, aggressive dogs
11. **chicken cocks.** Roosters trained to fight each other
12. **red.** Red cent; a very small amount of money

minute, I'll go and get you a frog." And so the feller took the box. and put up his forty dollars along with Smiley's, and set down to wait.

So he set there a good while thinking and thinking to hisself, and then he got the frog out and prized his mouth open and took a teaspoon and filled him full of quailshot[13]—filled him pretty near up to his chin—and set him on the floor. Smiley he went to the swamp and slopped around in the mud for a long time, and finally he ketched a frog, and fetched him in, and give him to this feller, and says:

"Now, if you're ready, set him alongside of Dan'l, with his forepaws just even with Dan'l's, and I'll give the word." Then he says, "One—two—three—*git!*" and him and the feller touched up the frogs from behind, and the new frog hopped off lively, but Dan'l give a heave, and hysted up his shoulders—so—like a Frenchman, but it warn't no use—he couldn't budge; he was planted as solid as a church, and he couldn't no more stir than if he was anchored out. Smiley was a good deal surprised, and he was disgusted too, but he didn't have no idea what the matter was, of course.

The feller took the money and started away; and when he was going out at the door, he sorter jerked his thumb over his shoulder—so—at Dan'l, and says, again very deliberate, "Well," he says, "*I* don't see no p'ints about that frog that's any better'n any other frog."

Smiley he stood scratching his head and looking down at Dan'l a long time, and at last he says, "I do wonder what in the nation that frog throw'd off for—I wonder if there ain't something the matter with him—he 'pears to look mighty baggy, somehow." And he ketched Dan'l by the nap of the neck, and hefted him, and says, "Why blame my cats if he don't weigh five pound!" and turned him upside down and he belched out a double handful of shot. And then he see how it was, and he was the maddest man—he set the frog down and took out after that feller, but he never ketched him. And—"

Here Simon Wheeler heard his name called from the front yard, and got up to see what was wanted. And turning to me as he moved away, he said: "Just set where you are, stranger, and rest easy—I ain't going to be gone a second."

But, by your leave, I did not think that a continuation of the history of the enterprising <u>vagabond</u> *Jim* Smiley would be likely to afford me much information concerning the *Rev. Leonidas W.* Smiley, and so I started away.

At the door I met the sociable Wheeler returning, and he button-holed[14] me and recommenced;

"Well, thish-yer Smiley had a yaller one-eyed cow that didn't have no tail, only jest a short stump like a bannanner, and—"

However, lacking both time and inclination, I did not wait to hear about the <u>afflicted</u> cow, but took my leave. ∎

---

13. **quailshot.** Lead pellets used for hunting quail
14. **button-holed.** Made a person listen to one, as if by grabbing his or her coat by a buttonhole

Words for Everyday Use:

vag • a • bond (vag´ ə bänd´) *n.*, wandering, idle, disreputable, or shiftless person
af • flic • ted (ə flikt´ əd) *part.*, having a physical condition, usually painful or distressing

Responding to the Selection

Do you find Simon Wheeler's story as boring, tedious, and monotonous as the narrator finds it, or do you find it as interesting as Simon finds it?

Reviewing the Selection

RECALLING

1. Where does the story take place?

2. Why does the narrator go to see Simon Wheeler? About whom does Simon Wheeler tell his story?

3. What two animals besides the frog does Jim Smiley use for gambling?

4. What does Smiley bet the stranger?

INTERPRETING

5. Think about what the men at the camp do. Why is it funny that this place is called Angel's Camp?

6. What is the narrator's response to Wheeler's story? Why might the narrator have this response?

7. Why do Smiley's animals always win?

8. Which frog wins the contest? Why?

SYNTHESIZING

9. The tale ends when Wheeler tries to trap the narrator into listening to another story about one of Jim Smiley's animals, "a yaller one-eyed cow that didn't have no tail, only jest a short stump like a bannanner." How does the narrator respond when Wheeler starts to tell the second story? What makes this response humorous?

10. Throughout his story of "The Notorious Jumping Frog of Calaveras County," Twain draws a contrast between things that are lowly and uneducated and things that are lofty and educated. What are some examples of this contrast?

Understanding Literature (Questions for Discussion)

1. **Dialect.** A **dialect** is a version of a language spoken by the people of a particular place, time, or social group. In "The Notorious Jumping Frog of Calaveras County," Simon Wheeler speaks an uneducated Western dialect, and the narrator speaks an educated Eastern dialect. What are the differences between the narrator's language and Simon Wheeler's language? Use particular examples from the selection to show how they differ.

2. **Frame Tale.** A **frame tale** is a story that itself provides a vehicle for the telling of other stories. In "The Notorious Jumping Frog of Calaveras County," the frame tale is the narrator's story of his visit to Simon Wheeler. It is a vehicle for another story, Simon Wheeler's tale of Jim Smiley's frog. What is Simon Wheeler's attitude toward his story about Jim Smiley? What is the frame narrator's attitude toward Wheeler's story? What do you think is Twain's attitude toward Jim Smiley's story?

Responding in Writing

1. **Tall Tale.** A **tall tale** is a story, often lighthearted or humorous, that contains highly exaggerated, unrealistic events. Write a tall tale modeled on Simon Wheeler's story of Jim Smiley's frog in "The Notorious Jumping Frog of Calaveras County." First choose an animal, perhaps a pet dog, cat, or rabbit. Give the animal a name and some extraordinary talent or ability. Begin by describing the animal and its history: where your narrator acquired it, how it was trained, and how it became famous. Tell some anecdotes that illustrate its uniqueness. End the tale by telling the story of the animal's final performance or the story of its death or retirement. Feel free to exaggerate when describing the animal's good or bad qualities and when relating the incidents of its past.

2. **Essay.** An **essay** is a brief work of prose nonfiction. Write a five-paragraph essay in support of one of the following theses about "The Notorious Jumping Frog of Calaveras County." Your essay should include an introduction to the thesis, three paragraphs that support the thesis, and a conclusion. To aid you in your writing, each of the following theses includes an italicized plural noun. This noun can be elaborated into three main ideas that can be developed into the body of your essay. For example, if you choose to support the first thesis, each paragraph in the body of your essay could describe and illustrate a different technique that Twain used to make his story funny.

   1. In "The Notorious Jumping Frog of Calaveras County," Twain uses three main *techniques* to make the story humorous.

   2. There are at least three major *differences* between the narrator's language and the language of Simon Wheeler.

   3. In "The Notorious Jumping Frog of Calaveras County," Twain makes use of three *types* of exaggeration.

   4. In Mark Twain's "The Notorious Jumping Frog of Calaveras County," Simon Wheeler, the narrator of the story within the story, displays three primary character *traits.*

Language Lab

Varieties of English. Read the Language Arts Survey, 2.147–2.150, on the varieties of English. Then rewrite the following sentences in standard, formal English.

1. He most always come out a winner.

2. There couldn't be no solit'ry thing mentioned but that feller'd offer to bet on it, and take ary side you please.

3. Smiley always come out a winner on that pup, till he harnessed a dog once that didn't have no hind legs.

4. He give Smiley a look, as much as to say his heart was broke, and it was his fault, for putting up a dog that hadn't no hind legs for him to take holt of.

5. So he set there a good while thinking and thinking to hisself.

PROJECTS

1. **Oral Interpretation.** Find a recording or videotape of actor Hal Holbrook's brilliant one-person stage show *Mark Twain Tonight* and listen to or view it with your class. After doing this, discuss with your classmates which of Holbrook's selections from Twain's writing you most enjoyed and how Holbrook's acting contributed to making those selections come alive. Refer to the Language Arts Survey, 3.8, "Oral Interpetation."

2. **Telling a Tall Tale.** Here's a very short tall tale that has been part of the American oral tradition for years:

> A fellow was camping up in Maine during mosquito season. One night as he was getting ready to bed down, he saw against the outside of his tent, illuminated by a lantern he'd left sitting outside, the shadows of two mosquitoes. From the size of their shadows, the mosquitoes appeared to be six, maybe seven feet tall. These were Maine mosquitoes, after all. The man lay still, listening as one of them whispered to the other, "Well, shall we eat 'im here, or carry 'im back to camp?" The other mosquito answered, "I say we eat 'im here. If we carry 'im back, the big ones are liable to steal 'im from us."

Think up your own brief tall tale. Then sit with some other students and tell your tales. Try to outdo one another in your use of wild exaggerations, or hyperboles. Why do you think that telling such stories was a popular entertainment in the Old West?

"I Will Fight No More Forever"
by In-mut-too-yah-lat-lat, Chief Joseph of the Nez Percé

ABOUT THE AUTHOR

In-mut-too-yah-lat-lat (*circa* 1840–1904), or Thunder Traveling over the Mountains, known in English as **Chief Joseph,** is remembered as a valiant leader who attempted to preserve the way of life of his people, the Nez Percé, in the face of overwhelming odds. He was born in Wallowa Valley, the ancestral home of the Nez Percé, in what the United States government then called Oregon Territory. His father, a Nez Percé chief, had been converted to Christianity, and Joseph himself attended a school run by missionaries. In the first part of the nineteenth century, relations between the Nez Percé and the persons of European descent in their midst were fairly good. However, relations became strained with increasing white settlement. At that time, the United States government negotiated treaties with some Nez Percé to obtain land rights for the settlers, but the Nez Percé did not consider the negotiators to be their legitimate representatives. In 1877, Chief Joseph was preparing to move with his people to a reservation in Idaho when he learned of an attack that had been made by three Native Americans on some settlers. Fearing reprisals, Joseph decided to flee with his people to Canada. Pursued by troops of the United States Army, this group of men, women, and children traveled over a thousand miles, often meeting and defeating their pursuers in combat. Surrounded by United States troops and recognizing that his weakened, small band had the means neither to escape nor to continue fighting, Chief Joseph surrendered in October of 1877, only forty miles from the Canadian border and freedom. The Nez Percé under Chief Joseph were further decimated by sickness after their removal to a temporary reservation in what is now Oklahoma. In 1885, those who remained were sent to the Colville Indian Reservation in Washington State.

ABOUT THE SELECTION

"I Will Fight No More Forever" is the surrender speech of In-mut-too-yah-lat-lat, known to persons of European descent as Chief Joseph. In-mut-too-yah-lat-lat was chief of the Wal-lam-wat-kin band of the Chute-pa-lu. To the French who first encountered them, the Chute-pa-lu were known as the "Nez Percé," a name that refers to the custom of piercing the nose for personal adornment. The speech was delivered on October 5, 1877, when Chief Joseph surrendered to General Nelson Miles. Chief Joseph was told that, after the surrender, his people would be returned to their homeland. That promise, like so many others made to Native Americans, was not kept.

"I Will Fight No More Forever"

CHIEF JOSEPH

Tell General Howard[1] I know his heart. What he told me before, I have in my heart. I am tired of fighting. Our chiefs are killed. Looking Glass is dead. Toohoolhoolzote[2] is dead. The old men are all dead. It is the young men who say yes and no. He who led on the young men is dead. It is cold and we have no blankets. The little children are freezing to death. My people, some of them, have run away to the hills and have no blankets, no food; no one knows where they are— perhaps freezing to death. I want to have time to look for my children and see how many I can find. Maybe I shall find them among the dead. Hear me, my chiefs. I am tired; my heart is sick and sad. From where the sun now stands I will fight no more forever. ∎

What does Chief Joseph want time to do? What does he expect to find?

---

1. **General Howard.** Oliver Howard (1830–1909), who conducted the operation against Chief Joseph and the Nez Percé (1877)
2. **Looking Glass . . . Toohoolhoolzote.** Two Nez Percé leaders

Postscript

In April of 1879, Chief Joseph provided the following account of his attempt to achieve justice for his people by political means: "At last I was granted permission to come to Washington. . . . I am glad we came. I have shaken hands with a great many friends, but there are some things I want to know which no one seems able to explain. . . . I cannot understand why so many chiefs are allowed to talk in so many different ways, and promise so many different

(cont.)

things. I have seen the Great Father Chief, the next Great Chief, the Commissioner Chief, the Law Chief, and many other law chiefs,[1] and they all say they are my friends and that I shall have justice; but while their mouths all talk right, I do not understand why nothing is done for my people. I have heard talk and talk, but nothing is done. Good words do not last long unless they amount to something. Words do not pay for my dead people. They do not pay for my country, now overrun by white men. They do not protect my father's grave. They do not pay for all my horses and cattle. Good words will not give me back my children. . . . It makes my heart sick when I remember all the good words and all the broken promises. . . . All men were made by the same Great Spirit Chief. They are all brothers. The earth is the mother of all people, and all people should have equal rights upon it." ∎

---

1. **Great Father Chief . . . other law chiefs.** President Theodore Roosevelt, various members of his administration, and various members of Congress

Responding to the Selection

How did reading Chief Joseph's speech make you feel? Why might this speech be quoted often? What qualities make it moving and memorable?

Reviewing the Selection

RECALLING

1. How does Chief Joseph feel at the time of his surrender?

2. What has happened to all of the peoples' leaders, the chiefs and the old men? Who has taken their place?

3. What is the condition of the children?

4. Where have some of Chief Joseph's people run to after the defeat? What might be their condition?

INTERPRETING

5. Why does Chief Joseph surrender?

6. What is dangerous about having the chiefs dead and the young men in charge?

7. What might happen to the people if all the children die?

8. What does Chief Joseph want time to do? What does he fear?

9. To whom does Chief Joseph address his surrender speech? What does he ask of this person? What does he pledge to him? Why?

10. The most famous line from Chief Joseph's surrender speech is the last: "From where the sun now stands I will fight no more forever." What does this sentence mean? What does it mean for him to say that he will fight "no more forever"? How does that differ from simply saying that he will fight "no more"? What does the position of the sun mark? Why does he say that he will not fight "From where the sun now stands"?

Understanding Literature (Questions for Discussion)

Oral Tradition. The body of work passed down by word-of-mouth from generation to generation within a culture is known as that culture's **oral tradition.** To appreciate fully the words of Chief Joseph, it helps to remember that his was an oral society. The knowledge, laws, history, and customs of his people were passed down orally rather than in writing. Simplicity, directness, and honesty in speech are prized in many oral societies, for these qualities ensure that the speech will be remembered and can be trusted. What puzzled Chief Joseph about his dealings with politicians on the subject of an appropriate homeland for his people?

Responding in Writing

Comparison. Reread the concluding lines of the Postscript to Chief Joseph's surrender speech. Then read the opening lines of the Declaration of Independence in Unit Three. Write a paragraph comparing the ideas expressed in these two documents. What similarity exists between Chief Joseph's beliefs and those expressed by Thomas Jefferson in the Declaration?

POETRY

"A Man Said to the Universe"
by Stephen Crane

ABOUT THE AUTHOR

See the biography of **Stephen Crane** on page 391.

ABOUT THE SELECTION

The poetry of Stephen Crane was influenced by late nineteenth- and early twentieth-century **Naturalism**, a philosophical perspective and literary movement that viewed human action as strictly determined by biological and environmental forces. In **"A Man Said to the Universe,"** Crane presents an imaginary dialogue that perfectly illustrates the world view of the Naturalists. The universe is not so much antagonistic as indifferent to human endeavor. Much of Crane's work emphasizes that in a world governed by natural laws indifferent to human life, compassion and solidarity are of the utmost importance.

READER'S JOURNAL

Think of a time when the environment in which you found yourself was particularly indifferent to your comfort and well-being. For instance, you might have been caught in a rainstorm or a blizzard, or you might have had to endure a seemingly unbearable heat wave or cold spell. In your journal, describe the situation. How did you respond to it?

LANGUAGE SKILLS

Read the Language Arts Survey, 2.104–2.105, "Quotation Marks I and II." Then read 2.93, "End Marks," paying particular attention to the discussion of the exclamation point. Using the correct form for quotation marks, write a dialogue between two people in which the first person exclaims something and the second answers the exclamation calmly.

"A Man Said to the Universe"

STEPHEN CRANE

A man said to the universe,
"Sir, I exist!"
"However," replied the universe,
"The fact has not created in me
A sense of obligation." ∎

Responding to the Selection

How do you feel about the man's exclamation to the universe? If you were the man, how would you respond in turn to the universe's reply? What else might the man say to the universe? What are some other ways that the universe might respond to the man's exclamation?

Reviewing the Selection

1. Who are the two participants in the dialogue?

2. What does each participant say to the other?

3. Under what circumstance might a person proclaim his or her existence so passionately? What can you infer about the life of the man who speaks in this poem?

4. What attitude is expressed by the universe in its reply to the man?

5. According to this poem, what relationship exists between the universe and human beings?

Understanding Literature (Questions for Discussion)

1. **Personification. Personification** is a figure of speech in which an idea, animal, or thing is described as if it were a person. Crane personifies the universe by having the man address it as "Sir" and by imagining that the universe can speak. What other human attributes might we give to Crane's universe? What human traits, both physical and emotional, would you ascribe to the universe?

2. **Irony. Irony** is a difference between appearance and reality. What attitude does the universe in this poem have toward the man? What statement is being made about the universe? Given this statement, why is it ironic that Crane has personified the universe in the poem?

3. **Dialogue.** A **dialogue** is a conversation involving two or more people or characters. What is the topic of the conversation between the man and the universe? What other topics of conversation might arise between a person and the universe? What is the tone of the conversation in this poem—serious or idle? playful or angry? polite or impolite? What would the conversation be like if it continued? About what might the man and the universe argue? What questions might the universe put to the man? What questions might the man put to the universe? On what points would they disagree? On what would they agree? What would it be like if there were other characters involved? Who would the other characters be, and what would they say?

Responding in Writing

Dialogue. Write a continuation of the dialogue between the man and the universe begun by Crane. See question 3 in the Understanding Literature section for ideas.

POETRY

from "Song of Myself"
by Walt Whitman

ABOUT THE AUTHOR

Walt Whitman (1819–1892) was the son of a Long Island farmer who turned carpenter and moved his family to Brooklyn in 1823. Whitman left school at age eleven, became an office boy in a law firm, then worked for a doctor. By twelve he was working in the printing office of a newspaper. By fifteen he was on his own. In his midteens he contributed pieces to a Manhattan newspaper and attended debating societies. After working as a journeyman printer for a time, Whitman returned home where he taught school and continued to work on newspapers. Later in his life, Whitman held various newspaper positions in Manhattan and Brooklyn, including reviewer of books, musicals, and theater events. He attended many operas and claimed that they inspired him to write *Leaves of Grass*. Sometime in 1851 or 1852 he became a house builder, making friends with the working class as well as the upper class. Always self-taught, Whitman began to write full time, later combining that career with his job as a clerk in the attorney general's office. Whitman's rise to fame was slow and at times his poetry drew harsh criticism. He suffered a paralytic stroke in 1873 and lost his job but continued writing. Of all American writers of his period, Whitman was the best example of fidelity to his art.

ABOUT THE SELECTION

Whitman writes within the tradition of **Romanticism,** a literary and artistic movement of the eighteenth and nineteenth centuries that placed value on emotion and imagination rather than reason. The Romantics elevated the individual over society, nature over human works, country life over city life, common people over aristocrats, and freedom over control or authority. **"Song of Myself"** is the first poem of *Leaves of Grass*, a single volume that Whitman spent his life writing. The poem is Whitman's effort to describe his personality, or as he put it: "one man's—the author's—identity, ardors, observations, faiths, and thoughts." The selection that follows exemplifies all the themes for which Whitman is best known: his belief that small, insignificant, lowly subjects are in fact worthy of poetry; his democratic celebration of the common people; and his love of natural and animal pleasure. All of these themes are summed up in the grass, the symbol central to his life work. Like all the poems in *Leaves of Grass*, "Song of Myself" is written in **free verse**: the poem does not fit into any planned form, and it has no regular pattern of rhyme, meter, or stanza length. To Whitman, a poem is like an acorn that grows into an oak. It has a life of its own. The poet provides the energy necessary to its growth, but it develops spontaneously, in largely unpredictable ways.

READER'S JOURNAL

Think of some person, place, or thing that people in general consider lowly, common, insignificant, or unworthy of attention but that you find fascinating. What is interesting about it? Why is it important? What makes it wonderful in your eyes? Write an entry in your journal celebrating it.

LANGUAGE SKILLS

Read the Language Arts Survey, 2.13, "Linking Verbs." Then make a three-columned chart using sentences from the selection that use linking verbs. In the columns of your chart, list (1) the noun; (2) the noun, pronoun, or adjective that describes or identifies the first noun; and (3) the linking verb that connects the two.

FROM
"Song of Myself"

WALT WHITMAN

1

What does the speaker celebrate? In what way is the speaker connected to the reader?

I celebrate myself, and sing myself,
And what I assume you shall assume,
For every atom belonging to me as good belongs to you.

I loafe and invite my soul,
5   I lean and loafe at my ease observing a spear of summer
        grass.

My tongue, every atom of my blood, form'd from this soil,
        this air,
Born here of parents born here from parents the same, and
        their parents the same,
I, now thirty-seven years old in perfect health begin,
Hoping to cease not till death.

10 Creeds and schools in abeyance,
Retiring back a while sufficed at what they are, but never
        forgotten,
I harbor for good or bad, I permit to speak at every hazard,

WORDS FOR EVERYDAY USE:

creed (krēd) *n.*, statement of belief, principles, or opinions on any subject

a • bey • ance (ə bā´əns) *n.*, temporary suspension, as of an activity or function

suf • fice (sə fīs´) *vt.*, be enough; be sufficient or adequate

har • bor (här´bər) *vt.*, serve as, or provide, a place of protection

Nature without check with original energy.
Looks down, is erect, or bends an arm on an <u>impalpable</u>
    certain rest,

15   Looking with side-curved head curious what will come next,
Both in and out of the game and watching and wondering at
    it.

Backward I see in my own days where I sweated through fog
    with <u>linguists</u> and <u>contenders</u>,
I have no mockings or arguments, I witness and wait.

                   ◆   ◆   ◆

6

A child said *What is the grass?* fetching it to me with full
    hands;

20   How could I answer the child? I do not know what it is any
    more than he.

I guess it must be the flag of my <u>disposition</u>, out of hopeful
    green stuff woven.

Or I guess it is the handkerchief of the Lord,
A scented gift and remembrancer designedly dropt,
Bearing the owner's name someway in the corners, that we
    may see and remark, and say *Whose?*

25   Or I guess the grass is itself a child, the produced babe of
    the vegetation.

Or I guess it is a uniform hieroglyphic,[1]
And it means, Sprouting alike in broad zones and narrow
    zones,
Growing among black folks as among white,

---

1. **hieroglyphic.** Picture or symbol representing a word,
syllable, or sound, used by the ancient Egyptians and others instead of alphabetical letters

What question does the child ask? What is the speaker's first response?

What does the speaker say the grass is?

WORDS FOR EVERYDAY USE:

im • pal • pa • ble (im pal´pə bəl) *adj.,* that which cannot be felt by touching

lin • guist (liŋ´gwist) *n.,* specialist in the science of language

con • tend • er (kən ten´dər) *n.,* one who strives or fights in competition

dis • po • si • tion (dis´pə zis´hən) *n.,* one's customary frame of mind

Kanuck, Tuckahoe, Congressman, Cuff,[2] I give them the
    same, I receive them the same.

30   And now it seems to me the beautiful uncut hair of graves.

Tenderly will I use you curling grass,
It may be you transpire from the breasts of young men,
It may be if I had known them I would have loved them,
It may be you are from old people, or from offspring taken
    soon out of their mothers' laps,
35   And here you are the mothers' laps.

This grass is very dark to be from the white heads of old
    mothers,
Darker than the colorless beards of old men,
Dark to come from under the faint red roofs of mouths.

O I perceive after all so many uttering tongues,
40   And I perceive they do not come from the roofs of mouths
    for nothing.

I wish I could translate the hints about the dead young men
    and women,
And the hints about old men and mothers, and the offspring
    taken soon out of their laps.

What do you think has become of the young and old men?
And what do you think has become of the women and
    children?

45   They are alive and well somewhere,
The smallest sprout shows there is really no death,
And if ever there was it led forward life, and does not wait at
    the end to arrest it,
And ceas'd the moment life appear'd.

All goes onward and outward, nothing collapses,
50   And to die is different from what any one supposed, and
    luckier.

◆   ◆   ◆

*What does the
speaker hear?
What hints does
the speaker not
understand?*

*What does the
smallest sprout
show?*

---

2. **Kanuck, Tuckahoe, Congressman, Cuff.** *Kanuck*—
French Canadian; *Tuckahoe*— Virginian; *Cuff*—from the
African word *cuffee*, refers to African Americans.

7

Has any one supposed it lucky to be born?
I hasten to inform him or her it is just as lucky to die, and I
    know it.

I pass death with the dying and birth with the new-wash'd
    babe, and am not contain'd between my hat and boots,

And peruse manifold objects, no two alike and every one
    good,
55   The earth good and the stars good, and their adjuncts all
    good.

I am not an earth nor an adjunct of an earth,
I am the mate and companion of people, all just as immortal
    and fathomless as myself,
(They do not know how immortal, but I know.)

Every kind for itself and its own, for me mine male and
    female,
60   For me those that have been boys and that love women,
For me the man that is proud and feels how it stings to be
    slighted,
For me the sweet-heart and the old maid, for me mothers
    and the mothers of mothers,
For me lips that have smiled, eyes that have shed tears,
For me children and the begetters of children.

65   Undrape! you are not guilty to me, nor stale nor discarded,
I see through the broadcloth and gingham[3] whether or no,
And am around, tenacious, acquisitive, tireless, and cannot
    be shaken away.

◆ ◆ ◆

31

I believe a leaf of grass is no less than the journey-work of
    the stars,
And the pismire[4] is equally perfect, and a grain of sand, and
    the egg of the wren,

---

3. **broadcloth and gingham.** *Broadcloth*—fine wool;
gingham—cotton cloth that is woven in checks or plaids
4. **pismire.** Ant

What attitude does the speaker have toward death? Why might the speaker feel this way?

What does the speaker say he is not? What does the speaker claim to be?

70   And the tree-toad is a chief-d'oeuvre[5] for the highest,
             And the running blackberry would adorn the parlors of heaven,
             And the narrowest hinge in my hand puts to scorn all machinery,
             And the cow crunching with depress'd head surpasses any statue,
             And a mouse is miracle enough to stagger sextillions[6] of <u>infidels</u>.

75   I find I incorporate gneiss,[7] coal, long-threaded moss, fruits,
                 grains, <u>esculent</u> roots,
             And am stucco'd with <u>quadrupeds</u> and birds all over,
             And have distanced what is behind me for good reasons,
             But call any thing back again when I desire it.

             In vain the speeding or shyness,
80   In vain the plutonic rocks[8] send their old heat against my
                 approach,
             In vain the mastodon retreats beneath its own powder'd bones,
             In vain objects stand leagues off and assume manifold shapes,
             In vain the ocean settling in hollows and the great monsters lying
                 low,

---

5. **chief-d'oeuvre.** Master or culminating work
6. **sextillions.** Number represented by one followed by twenty-one zeros
7. **gneiss.** Metamorphic rock with minerals arranged in layers
8. **plutonic rocks.** Rocks formed far below the surface of the earth

WORDS FOR EVERYDAY USE:

in • fi • del (in´fə del´) *n.,* person who does not believe in a particular religion

es • cu • lent (es´kyo͞o lənt) *adj.,* fit for food, edible

quad • ru • ped (kwä´dro͞o ped´) *n.,* animal, especially a mammal, with four feet

In vain the buzzard houses herself with the sky,
85 In vain the snake slides through the creepers and logs,
In vain the elk takes to the inner passes of the woods,
In vain the razor-bill'd auk[9] sails far north to Labrador,[10]
I follow quickly, I ascend to the nest in the <u>fissure</u> of the cliff.

◆ ◆ ◆

32

I think I could turn and live with animals, they are so placid
   and self-contain'd,
90 I stand and look at them long and long.

They do not sweat and whine about their condition,
They do not lie awake in the dark and weep for their sins,
They do not make me sick discussing their duty to God,
Not one is dissatisfied, not one is demented with the mania of
   owning things,
95 Not one kneels to another, nor to his kind that lived thousands
   of years ago,
Not one is respectable or unhappy over the whole earth.

◆ ◆ ◆

Why would the speaker like to live with the animals? In what ways are they different from humans?

52

The spotted hawk swoops by and accuses me, he complains of
   my gab and my <u>loitering</u>.

I too am not a bit tamed, I too am untranslatable,
I sound my <u>barbaric</u> yawp[11] over the roofs of the world.

100 The last scud of day holds back for me,
It flings my likeness after the rest and true as any on the
   shadow'd wilds,
It coaxes me to the vapor and the dusk.

I depart as air, I shake my white locks at the runaway sun,
I effuse my flesh in eddies, and drift it in lacy <u>jags</u>.

---

9. **auk.** Shore bird of northern seas with a heavy body, a
short tail, and short wings used as paddles
10. **Labrador.** Region along the Atlantic coast of northeastern Canada
11. **yawp.** Loud, harsh cry or call

105   I bequeath myself to the dirt to grow from the grass I love,
         If you want me again look for me under your boot-soles.

         You will hardly know who I am or what I mean,
         But I shall be good health to you nevertheless,
         And filter and fibre your blood.·

110   Failing to fetch me at first keep encouraged,
         Missing me one place search another,
         I stop somewhere waiting for you.   ■

Where should you look to see the speaker? What will the speaker do for the people he is addressing?

Responding to the Selection

In "Song of Myself," Whitman views death as a force that unites him with both nature and other human beings. How do you feel about Whitman's views? Do you find Whitman's views comforting and hopeful or unrealistic and unsatisfying?

Reviewing the Selection

RECALLING

1. What answer does Whitman give in response to the question "What is the grass?"

2. What does Whitman say about dying in sections 6 and 7?

3. What are the small, commonplace, and insignificant things that Whitman describes in section 31? To what does he compare each of these "lowly" things?

4. What are the lives of animals like according to Whitman in section 32?

INTERPRETING

5. Why does he want to treat the grass tenderly? According to Whitman, what does a sprout of vegetation prove about life and death?

6. What reasons does Whitman give for that view of death? Why might he feel that way?

7. What do Whitman's comparisons indicate about his feelings for commonplace things?

8. Why could Whitman "turn and live with" the animals? What view does he express about humans in contrast to animals?

9. Why is the free verse form a good vehicle for Whitman's message?

10. In this poem Whitman both sounds his "barbaric yawp," proclaiming his existence, and reconciles himself to death. In what way is examining death an affirmation of life for Whitman?

Understanding Literature (Questions for Discussion)

1. **Elaboration. Elaboration**, or **amplification**, is a writing technique in which a subject is introduced and then expanded upon by means of repetition with slight changes, the addition of details, or similar devices. For instance, in section 6 the child asks, "What is the grass?" The speaker responds with a series of possibilities, each of which begins with the same phrase: "I guess . . ." Find other examples of elaboration in the selection. What is its effect in each case? What is its effect in general?

2. **Symbol.** A **symbol** is a thing that stands for or represents both itself and something else. In Whitman's poem, the grass is both a conventional symbol, one with widely recognized associations, and an idiosyncratic symbol, one that assumes secondary meanings because of the special uses to which it is put by the writer. Find all the passages in which the symbol of the grass occurs. What does the grass symbolize in each of these instances?

3. **Parallelism. Parallelism** is a rhetorical technique in which a writer emphasizes the equal value or weight of two or more ideas by expressing them in the same grammatical form. Find examples of parallelism in "Song of Myself." What ideas are being emphasized by the speaker?

4. **Catalog.** A **catalog** is a list of people or things. What is cataloged in this poem? Why do you think Whitman used this list? What else might he have included?

Responding in Writing

1. **Free Verse. Free verse** is poetry that avoids the use of regular rhyme, rhythm, meter, or division into stanzas. Write a free verse poem using section 6 of Whitman's "Song of Myself" as a model. For the symbol of the grass, however, substitute some other natural object: a river, mountain, bird, or rock. Begin the poem with a line similar to Whitman's: "A child said *What is the . . . ?*" Write the rest of the poem by elaborating upon the answer in the way Whitman does. Begin each stanza with the phrase, "I guess it is . . ."

2. **Wanted Poster.** Whitman celebrated behavior that was "lawless as snowflakes." His disregard for conventional poetic subjects and forms made him unacceptable to genteel society in his day. Create a wanted poster for Walt Whitman. Include a picture, a description of his appearance, and a list of the crimes for which the authorities want to imprison him.

POETRY

"We Wear the Mask"
by Paul Laurence Dunbar

ABOUT THE AUTHOR

Paul Laurence Dunbar (1872–1906) was born in Dayton, Ohio, the son of former slaves. His father, Joshua, was a United States Army soldier and plasterer, and his mother, Matilda, was a laundry worker. His mother had no formal education but taught Dunbar to read when he was four. He reported that both his parents were "fond of books" and read aloud to the family in the evenings as they sat around the fire. This poet, novelist, and short story writer said that he made his first attempt at rhyming when he was about six and found a poem by Wordsworth. He thought it had been written by a man in Dayton of the same name. The idea that someone he knew wrote poetry impressed his young mind and, "after that I rhymed continually," he said. He was encouraged in his writing aspirations by a high school teacher and by a classmate named Orville Wright who was later to become a pioneer of aviation. He was the only African American in his class, which served, he said, to spur his ambitions. After graduating with honors from high school, he held a series of manual labor jobs. He wrote in his free time, began submitting poems to local newspapers, and in 1893, printed *Oak and Ivy*. He gained national recognition in 1896 with the publication of *Lyrics of Lowly Life* and a full-page, enthusiastic review of *Majors and Minors* (1895) in *Harper's Weekly*. That launched him as a reader on the lecture circuit in the United States and in Europe and eventually landed him a series of jobs at the Library of Congress, where he worked until sickness forced him to leave. His works include *Majors and Minors* (1895), *The Uncalled* (novel, 1896), *Lyrics of the Hearthside* (1899), *The Love of Landry* (novel, 1900), *Uncle Eph's Christmas* (one-act musical, 1900), *The Fanatics* (novel, 1901), *The Sport of the Gods* (novel, 1902), *Lyrics of Love and Laughter* (1903), and *Lyrics of Sunshine and Shadow* (1905).

ABOUT THE SELECTION

While Dunbar's reputation rests on his poems and short stories written in African-American dialect, Dunbar himself considered his nondialectical work to be his best. At the time Dunbar wrote his poems, including **"We Wear the Mask,"** the use of dialect was very popular; consequently and regrettably, many of Dunbar's poems not written in dialect were neglected. In its formal language and use of rhyme, the selection shows the influence of poets Robert Burns and James Whitcomb Riley, both of whom Dunbar admired.

Mask. *Sargend Claude Johnson.
National Museum of American Art,
Washington, DC/Art Resource*

READER'S JOURNAL

Have you ever hidden your feelings from someone? Have you ever put on a "happy face" when you were feeling sadness or pain? Why did you wear an emotional mask? What did it feel like to wear such a mask? How did others respond to you? Write about the experience in your journal.

LANGUAGE SKILLS

Read the Language Arts Survey, 2.147, "Formal and Informal English." Then identify some formal words in the selection and note what mood or tone they lend to the poem.

"We Wear the Mask"

PAUL LAURENCE DUNBAR

We wear the mask that grins and lies,
It hides our cheeks and shades our eyes—
This debt we pay to human guile;[1]
With torn and bleeding hearts we smile,
5   And mouth with myriad[2] subtleties.

Why should the world be otherwise,
In counting all our tears and sighs?
Nay, let them only see us, while
      We wear the mask.

10   We smile, but, O great Christ, our cries
To thee from tortured souls arise.
We sing, but oh the clay is vile[3]
Beneath our feet, and long the mile;
But let the world dream otherwise,
15   We wear the mask! ∎

What does the mask show? What does it hide?

What contradictions are apparent in stanza 3?

1. **guile.** Secretiveness; sneakiness
2. **myriad.** Large number; of a varied nature
3. **vile.** Offensive

Responding to the Selection

Imagine that you are the speaker in the poem. Write an entry in your journal explaining the kinds of emotions you hide when wearing the mask.

Reviewing the Selection

1. What "grins and lies"?

2. What is paid "to human guile"?

3. What does the speaker suggest is not counted by the world?

4. From what kind of souls do the cries mentioned in the poem arise?

5. Who is the "we" mentioned in the poem? Who is the "them"?

6. What attitudes toward human duplicity does the speaker express?

7. Why does the speaker suggest "Nay, let them only see us, while/We wear the mask"?

8. Whom is the speaker addressing in the poem?

9. Who wears the mask? For what is the mask a metaphor in the poem?

10. What terrible consequence of discrimination does this poem relate? Why can't people expect the people whom they are discriminating against to be guileless and open about their feelings?

Understanding Literature (Questions for Discussion)

1. **Speaker.** The **speaker** is the person who speaks in or narrates a poem—the voice assumed by the writer. The speaker in this poem uses the pronoun *we,* not *I.* For and to whom do you think the speaker is speaking? How might your interpretation of the poem change if you decided that the speaker were speaking for the entire human race? Who, then, would be the "we"? Who would be the "them"?

2. **Rhyme.** **Rhyme** is the repetition of sounds at the ends of words. One type of rhyme is *end rhyme,* the use of rhyming words at the ends of lines. What is the end rhyme scheme of the poem?

Responding in Writing

Dialogue. Imagine a situation in which a person is hiding his or her true feelings. Write a dialogue between two people in which the second person tries to convince the first person to drop his or her mask and be open about his or her true feelings.

"I Am Alone"
by Cochise of the Apache

This for a very long time has been the home of my people; they came from the darkness, few in numbers and feeble. The country was held by a much stronger and more numerous people, and from their stone houses we were quickly driven. We were a hunting people, living on the animals that we could kill. We came to these mountains about us; no one lived here, and so we took them for our home and country. Here we grew from the first feeble band to be a great people, and covered the whole country as the clouds cover the mountains. Many people came to our country. First the Spanish, with their horses and their iron shirts, their long knives[1] and guns, great wonders to my simple people. We fought some, but they never tried to drive us from our homes in these mountains. After many years the Spanish soldiers were driven away and the Mexican ruled the land. With these little wars came, but we were now a strong people and we did not fear them. At last in my youth came the white man, your people. Under the counsels of my grandfather, who had for a very long time been the head of the Apaches, they were received with friendship. Soon their numbers increased and many passed through my country to the great waters of the setting sun.[2] Your soldiers came and their strong houses[3] were all through my country. I received favors from your people and did all that I could in return and we lived at peace. At last your soldiers did me a very great wrong, and I and my whole people went to war with them. At first we were successful and your soldiers were driven away and your people killed and we again possessed our land. Soon many soldiers came from the north and from the west, and my people were driven to the mountain hiding places; but these did not protect us, and soon my people were flying from one mountain to another, driven by the soldiers, even as the wind is now driving the clouds. I have fought long and as best I could against you. I have destroyed many of your people, but where I have destroyed one white man many have come in his place; but where an Indian has been killed, there has been none to come in his place, so that the great people that welcomed you with acts of kindness to this land are now but a feeble band that fly before your soldiers as the deer before the hunter, and must all perish if this war continues. I have come to you, not from any love for you or for your great father in Washington, or from any regard for his or your wishes, but as a conquered chief, to try to save alive the few people that still remain to me. I am the last of my family, a family that for very many years have been the leaders of this people, and on me depends their future, whether they shall utterly vanish from the land or that a small remnant remain for a few years to see the sun rise over these mountains, their home. I here pledge my word, a word that has never been broken, that if your great father will set aside a part of my own country, where I and my little band can live, we will remain at peace with your people forever. If from his abundance he will give food for my women and children, whose protectors his soldiers have killed, with blankets to cover their nakedness, I will receive them with gratitude. If not, I will do my best to feed and clothe them, in peace with the white man. I have spoken.

from *Life on the Mississippi*
by Mark Twain

When I was a boy, there was but one permanent ambition among my comrades in our village[4] on the west bank of the Mississippi River. That was, to be a steamboatman. We had transient ambitions of other sorts, but they were only transient.

When a circus came and went, it left us all burning to become clowns; the first Negro minstrel show that came to our section left us all suffering to try that kind of life; now and then we had a hope that if we lived and were good, God would permit us to be pirates. These ambitions faded out, each in its turn; but the ambition to be a steamboatman always remained.

Once a day a cheap, gaudy packet[5] arrived upward from St. Louis, and another downward form Keokuk.[6] Before these events, the day was glorious with expectancy; after them, the day was a dead and empty thing. Not only the boys, but the whole village, felt this. After all these years I can picture that old time to myself now, just as it was then: the white town drowsing in the sunshine of a summer's morning; the streets empty, or pretty nearly so; one or two clerks sitting in front of the Water Street stores, with their splint-bottomed chairs tilted back against the wall, chins on breasts, hats slouched over their faces, asleep—with shingle shavings enough around to show what broke them down; a sow and a litter of pigs loafing along the sidewalk, doing a good business in watermelon rinds and seeds; two or three lonely little freight piles scattered about the levee; a pile of skids[7] on the slope of the stone-paved wharf, and the

---

1. **horses . . . knives.** Spaniards introduced horses to the Americas. Metal armor and swords are referred to here.
2. **great . . . sun.** Pacific Ocean
3. **strong houses.** Forts
4. **our village.** Hannibal, Missouri
5. **packet.** Boat on a regular route
6. **Keokuk.** Town in southeastern Iowa
7. **skids.** Wooden platforms

fragrant town drunkard asleep in the shadow of them; two or three wood flats[1] at the head of the wharf, but nobody to listen to the peaceful lapping of the wavelets against them; the great Mississippi, the majestic, the magnificent Mississippi, rolling its mile-wide tide along, shining in the sun; the dense forest away on the other side; the point above the town, and the point below, bounding the river-glimpse and turning it into a sort of sea, and withal a very still and brilliant and lonely one. Presently a film of dark smoke appears above one of those remote points; instantly a Negro drayman,[2] famous for his quick eye and prodigious voice, lifts up the cry, "S-t-e-a-m-boat a-comin'!" and the scene changes! The town drunkard stirs, the clerks wake up, a furious clatter of drays follows, every house and store pours out a human contribution, and all in a twinkling the dead town is alive and moving. Drays, carts, men, boys, all go hurrying from many quarters to a common center, the wharf. Assembled there, the people fasten their eyes upon the coming boat as upon a wonder they are seeing for the first time. And the boat *is* rather a handsome sight, too. She is long and sharp and trim and pretty; she has two tall, fancy-topped chimneys, with a gilded device of some kind swung between them; a fanciful pilothouse, all glass and gingerbread, perched on top of the texas deck[3] behind them; the paddle-boxes are gorgeous with a picture or with gilded rays above the boat's name; the boiler, the hurricane deck, and the texas deck are fenced and ornamented with clean white railings; there is a flag gallantly flying from the jackstaff;[4] the furnace doors are open and the fires glaring bravely; the upper decks are black with passengers; the captain stands by the big bell, calm, imposing, the envy of all; great volumes of the blackest smoke are rolling and tumbling out of the chimneys—a husbanded grandeur created with a bit of pitch pine just before arriving at a town; the crew are grouped on the forecastle;[5] the broad stage is run far out over the port bow, and an envied deckhand stands picturesquely on the end of it with a coil of rope in his hand; the pent steam is screaming through the gauge cocks; the captain lifts his hand, a bell rings, the wheels stop; then they turn back, churning the water to foam, and the steamer is at rest. Then such a scramble as there is to get aboard, and to get ashore, and to take in freight and to discharge freight, all at one and the same time; and such a yelling and cursing as the mates facilitate it all with! Ten minutes later the steamer is under way again, with no flag on the jackstaff and no black smoke issuing from the chimneys. After ten more minutes the town is dead again, and the town drunkard asleep by the skids once more.

My father was a justice of the peace, and I supposed he possessed the power of life and death over all men and could hang anybody that offended him. This was distinction enough for me as a general thing; but the desire to be a steamboatman kept intruding, nevertheless. I first wanted to be a cabin boy, so that I could come out with a white apron on and shake a tablecloth over the side, where all my old comrades could see me; later I thought I would rather be the deckhand who stood on the end of the stage plank with the coil of rope in his hand, because he was particularly conspicuous. But these were only daydreams—they were too heavenly to be contemplated as real possibilities. By and by one of our boys went away. He was not heard of for a long time. At last he turned up as apprentice engineer or striker on a steamboat. This thing shook the bottom out of all my Sunday-school teachings. That boy had been notoriously worldly, and I just the reverse; yet he was exalted to this eminence, and I left in obscurity and misery. There was nothing generous about this fellow in his greatness. He would always manage to have a rusty bolt to scrub while his boat tarried at our town, and he would sit on the inside guard and scrub it, where we could all see him and envy him and loathe him. And whenever his boat was laid up he would come home and swell around the town in his blackest and greasiest clothes, so that nobody could help remembering that he was a steamboatman; and he used all sorts of steamboat technicalities in his talk, as if he were so used to them that he forgot common people could not understand them. He would speak of the labboard[6] side of a horse in an easy, natural way that would make one wish he was dead. And he was always talking about "St. Looey" like an old citizen; he would refer casually to occasions when he "was coming down Fourth Street," or when he was "passing by the Planter's House," or when there was a fire and he took a turn on the brakes of "the old Big Missouri"; and then he would go on and lie about how many towns the size of ours were burned down there that day. Two or three of the boys had long been persons of consideration among us because they had been to St. Louis once and had a vague general knowledge of its wonders, but the day of their glory was over now. They lapsed into a humble silence, and learned to disappear when the ruthless cub engineer approached. This fellow had money, too, and hair oil. Also an ignorant silver watch and a showy brass watch chain. He wore a leather belt and used no suspenders. If ever a youth was cordially admired and hated by his comrades, this one was. No girl could withstand his charms. He cut out every boy in the village. When his boat blew up at last, it diffused a tranquil contentment among us such as we had not known for months. But when he came home the next week, alive, renowned, and appeared in church all battered up and bandaged, a shining hero, stared at and wondered over by everybody, it seemed to us that the partiality of Providence for an undeserving reptile had reached a point where it was open to criticism.

---

1. **flats.** Flat-bottomed boats
2. **drayman.** Driver of a low cart called a dray
3. **texas deck.** Deck next to the officers' cabins
4. **jackstaff.** Rope running up and down a mast
5. **forecastle.** Front of the upper deck
6. **labboard.** Left side of a ship

This creature's career could produce but one result. and it speedily followed. Boy after boy managed to get on the river. The minister's son became an engineer. The doctor's and the postmaster's sons became mud clerks; the wholesale liquor dealer's son became a barkeeper on a boat; four sons of the chief merchant, and two sons of the county judge, became pilots. Pilot was the grandest position of all. The pilot, even in those days of trivial wages, had a princely salary—from a hundred and fifty to two hundred and fifty dollars a month, and no board to pay. Two months of his wages would pay a preacher's salary for a year. Now some of us were left disconsolate. We could not get on the river—at least our parents would not let us.

So by and by I ran away. I said I never would come home again till I was a pilot and could come in glory. But somehow I could not manage it. I went meekly aboard a few of the boats that lay packed together like sardines at the long St. Louis wharf, and very humbly inquired for the pilots, but got only a cold shoulder and short words from mates and clerks. I had to make the best of this sort of treatment for the time being, but I had comforting daydreams of a future when I should be a great and honored pilot, with plenty of money, and could kill some of these mates and clerks and pay for them.

"The Revolt of 'Mother'"
by Mary E. Wilkins Freeman

"Father!"

"What is it?"

"What are them men diggin' over there in the field for?"

There was a sudden dropping and enlarging of the lower part of the old man's face, as if some heavy weight had settled therein; he shut his mouth tight, and went on harnessing the great bay mare.[1] He hustled the collar on to her neck with a jerk.

"Father!"

The old man slapped the saddle upon the mare's back.

"Look here, father, I want to know what them men are diggin' over in the field for, an' I'm goin' to know."

"I wish you'd go into the house, mother, an' 'tend to your own affairs," the old man said then. He ran his words together, and his speech was almost as inarticulate as a growl.

But the woman understood; it was her most native tongue. "I ain't goin' into the house till you tell me what them men are doin' over there in the field," said she.

Then she stood waiting. She was a small woman, short and straight-waisted like a child in her brown cotton gown. Her forehead was mild and benevolent between the smooth curves of gray hair; there were meek downward lines about her nose and mouth; but her eyes, fixed upon the old man, looked as if the meekness had been the result of her own will, never of the will of another.

They were in the barn, standing before the wide open doors. The spring air, full of the smell of growing grass and unseen blossoms, came in their faces. The deep yard in front was littered with farm wagons and piles of wood; on the edges, close to the fence and the house, the grass was a vivid green, and there were some dandelions.

The old man glanced doggedly at his wife as he tightened the last buckles on the harness. She looked as immovable to him as one of the rocks in his pasture-land, bound to the earth with generations of blackberry vines. He slapped the reins over the horse, and started forth from the barn.

"Father!" said she.

The old man pulled up. "What is it?"

"I want to know what them men are diggin' over there in that field for."

"They're diggin' a cellar, I s'pose, if you've got to know."

"A cellar for what?"

"A barn."

"A barn? You ain't goin' to build a barn over there where we was goin' to have a house, father?"

The old man said not another word. He hurried the horse into the farm wagon, and clattered out of the yard, jouncing as sturdily on his seat as a boy.

The woman stood a moment looking after him, then she went out of the barn across a corner of the yard to the house. The house, standing at right angles with the great barn and a long reach of sheds and out-buildings, was infinitesimal compared with them. It was scarcely as commodious for people as the little boxes under the barn eaves were for doves.

A pretty girl's face, pink and delicate as a flower, was looking out of one of the house windows. She was watching three men who were digging over in the field which bounded the yard near the road line. She turned quietly when the woman entered.

"What are they digging for, mother?" said she. "Did he tell you?"

"They're diggin' for—a cellar for a new barn."

"Oh, mother, he ain't going to build another barn?"

"That's what he says."

A boy stood before the kitchen glass combing his hair. He combed slowly and painstakingly, arranging his brown hair in a smooth hillock over his forehead. He did not seem to pay any attention to the conversation.

"Sammy, did you know father was going to build a new barn?" asked the girl.

The boy combed assiduously.

"Sammy!"

He turned, and showed a face like his father's under his smooth crest of hair. "Yes, I s'pose I did," he said, reluctantly.

"How long have you known it?" asked his mother.

" 'Bout three months, I guess."

"Why didn't you tell of it?"

"Didn't think 'twould do no good."

"I don't see what father wants another barn for," said the

---

1. **bay mare.** Reddish-brown female horse

girl, in her sweet, slow voice. She turned again to the window, and stared out at the digging men in the field. Her tender, sweet face was full of a gentle distress. Her forehead was as bald and innocent as a baby's, with the light hair strained back from it in a row of curl-papers. She was quite large, but her soft curves did not look as if they covered muscles.

Her mother looked sternly at the boy. "Is he goin' to buy more cows?" said she.

The boy did not reply; he was tying his shoes.

"Sammy, I want you to tell me if he's goin' to buy more cows."

"I s'pose he is."

"How many?"

"Four, I guess."

His mother said nothing more. She went up into the pantry, and there was a clatter of dishes. The boy got his cap from a nail behind the door, took an old arithmetic from the shelf, and started for school. He was lightly built, but clumsy. He went out of the yard with a curious spring in his hips, that made his loose home-made jacket tilt up in the rear.

The girl went to the sink, and began to wash the dishes that were piled up there. Her mother came promptly out of the pantry, and shoved her aside. "You wipe 'em," said she; "I'll wash. There's a good many this mornin'."

The mother plunged her hands vigorously into the water, the girl wiped the plates slowly and dreamily. "Mother," said she, "don't you think it's too bad father's going to build that new barn, much as we need a decent house to live in?"

Her mother scrubbed a dish fiercely. "You ain't found out yet we're womenfolks, Nanny Penn," said she. "You ain't seen enough of men-folks yet to. One of these days you'll find it out, an' then you'll know that we know only what men-folks think we do, so far as any use of it goes, an' how we'd ought to reckon men-folks in with Providence, an' not complain of what they do any more than we do of the weather."

"I don't care; I don't believe George is anything like that, anyhow," said Nanny. Her delicate face flushed pink, her lips pouted softly, as if she were going to cry.

"You wait an' see. I guess George Eastman ain't no better than other men. You hadn't ought to judge father, though. He can't help it, 'cause he don't look at things jest the way we do. An' we've been pretty comfortable here, after all. The roof don't leak—ain't never but once—that's one thing. Father's kept it shingled right up."

"I do wish we had a parlor."

"I guess it won't hurt George Eastman any to come to see you in a nice clean kitchen. I guess a good many girls don't have as good a place as this. Nobody's ever heard me complain."

"I ain't complained either, mother."

"Well, I don't think you'd better, a good father an' a good home as you've got. S'pose your father made you go out an' work for your livin'? Lots of girls have to that ain't no stronger an' better able to than you be."

Sarah Penn washed the frying-pan with a conclusive air. She scrubbed the outside of it as faithfully as the inside. She was a masterly keeper of her box of a house. Her one living-room never seemed to have in it any of the dust which the friction of life with inanimate matter produces. She swept, and there seemed to be no dirt to go before the broom; she cleaned, and one could see no difference. She was like an artist so perfect that he has apparently no art. Today she got out a mixing bowl and a board, and rolled some pies, and there was no more flour upon her than upon her daughter who was doing finer work. Nanny was to be married in the fall, and she was sewing on some white cambric and embroidery. She sewed industriously while her mother cooked, her soft milk-white hands and wrists showed whiter than her delicate work.

"We must have the stove moved out in the shed before long," said Mrs. Penn. "Talk about not havin' things, it's been a real blessin' to be able to put a stove up in that shed in hot weather. Father did one good thing when he fixed that stove-pipe out there."

Sarah Penn's face as she rolled her pies had that expression of meek vigor which might have characterized one of the New Testament saints. She was making mince-pies. Her husband, Adoniram Penn, liked them better than any other kind. She baked twice a week. Adoniram often liked a piece of pie between meals. She hurried this morning. It had been later than usual when she began, and she wanted to have a pie baked for dinner. However deep a resentment she might be forced to hold against her husband, she would never fail in sedulous attention to his wants.

Nobility of character manifests itself at loop-holes when it is not provided with large doors. Sarah Penn's showed itself today in flaky dishes of pastry. So she made the pies faithfully, while across the table she could see, when she glanced up from her work, the sight that rankled in her patient and steadfast soul—the digging of the cellar of the new barn in the place where Adoniram forty years ago had promised her their new house should stand.

The pies were done for dinner. Adoniram and Sammy were home a few minutes after twelve o'clock. The dinner was eaten with serious haste. There was never much conversation at the table in the Penn family. Adoniram asked a blessing, and they ate promptly, then rose up and went about their work.

Sammy went back to school, taking soft sly lopes out of the yard like a rabbit. He wanted a game of marbles before school, and feared his father would give him some chores to do. Adoniram hastened to the door and called after him, but he was out of sight.

"I don't see what you let him go for, mother," said he. "I wanted him to help me unload that wood."

Adoniram went to work out in the yard unloading wood from the wagon. Sarah put away the dinner dishes, while Nanny took down her curl-papers and changed her dress. She was going down to the store to buy some more embroidery and thread.

When Nanny was gone, Mrs. Penn went to the door. "Father!" she called.

"Well, what is it!"

"I want to see you jest a minute, father."

"I can't leave this wood nohow. I've got to git it unloaded an' go for a load of gravel afore two o'clock. Sammy had ought to helped me. You hadn't ought to let him go to school so early."

"I want to see you jest a minute."

"I tell ye I can't, nohow, mother."

"Father, you come here." Sarah Penn stood in the door like a queen; she held her head as if it bore a crown; there was that patience which makes authority royal in her voice. Adoniram went.

Mrs. Penn led the way into the kitchen, and pointed to a chair. "Sit down, father," said she; "I've got somethin' I want to say to you."

He sat down heavily; his face was quite stolid, but he looked at her with restive eyes. "Well, what is it, mother?"

"I want to know what you're buildin' that new barn for, father?"

"I ain't got nothin' to say about it."

"It can't be you think you need another barn?"

"I tell ye I ain't got nothin' to say about it, mother; an' I ain't goin' to say nothin'."

"Be you goin' to buy more cows?"

Adoniram did not reply; he shut his mouth tight.

"I know you be, as well as I want to. Now, father, look here"—Sarah Penn had not sat down; she stood before her husband in the humble fashion of a Scripture woman[1]—"I'm goin' to talk real plain to you; I never have sence I married you, but I'm goin' to now. I ain't never complained, an' I ain't goin' to complain now, but I'm goin' to talk plain. You see this room here, father; you look at it well. You see there ain't no carpet on the floor, an' you see the paper is all dirty, an' droppin' off the walls. We ain't had no new paper on it for ten year, an' then I put it on myself, an' it didn't cost but ninepence a roll. You see this room, father; it's all the one I've had to work in an' eat in an' sit in sence we was married. There ain't another woman in the whole town whose husband ain't got half the means you have but what's got better. It's all the room Nanny's got to have her company in; an' there ain't one of her mates but what's got better, an' their fathers not so able as hers is. It's all the room she'll have to be married in. What would you have thought, father, if we had had our weddin' in a room no better than this? I was married in my mother's parlor, with a carpet on the floor, an' stuffed furniture, an' a mahogany cardtable. An' this is all the room my daughter will have to be married in. Look here, father!"

Sarah Penn went across the room as though it were a tragic stage. She flung open a door and disclosed a tiny bedroom, only large enough for a bed and bureau, with a path between. "There, father," said she—"there's all the room I've had to sleep in forty year. All my children were born there—the two that died, an' the two that's livin'. I was sick with a fever there."

She stepped to another door and opened it. It led into the small, ill-lighted pantry. "Here," said she, "is all the buttery[2] I've got—every place I've got for my dishes, to set away my victuals in, an' to keep my milk-pans in. Father, I've been takin' care of the milk of six cows in this place, an' now you're goin' to build a new barn, an' keep more cows, an' give me more to do in it."

She threw open another door. A narrow crooked flight of stairs wound upward from it. "There, father," said she, "I want you to look at the stairs that go up to them two unfinished chambers that are all the places our son an' daughter have had to sleep in all their lives. There ain't a prettier girl in town nor a more ladylike one than Nanny, an' that's the place she has to sleep in. It ain't so good as your horse's stall; it ain't so warm an' tight."

Sarah Penn went back and stood before her husband. "Now, father," said she, "I want to know if you think you're doin' right an' accordin' to what you profess. Here, when we was married, forty year ago, you promised me faithful that we should have a new house built in that lot over in the field before the year was out. You said you had money enough, an' you wouldn't ask me to live in no such place as this. It is forty year now, an' you've been makin' more money, an' I've been savin' of it for you ever since, an' you ain't built no house yet. You've built sheds an' cow-houses an' one new barn, an' now you're goin' to build another. Father, I want to know if you think it's right. You're lodgin' your dumb beasts better than you are your own flesh an' blood. I want to know if you think it's right."

"I ain't got nothin' to say."

"You can't say nothin' without ownin' it ain't right, father. An' there's another thing—I ain't complained; I've got along forty year, an' I s'pose I should forty more, if it wa'n't for that—if we don't have another house. Nanny she can't live with us after she's married. She'll have to go somewheres else to live away from us, an' it don't seem as if I could have it so, noways, father. She wa'n't ever strong. She's got considerable color, but there wa'n't never any backbone to her. I've always took the heft of everything off her, an' she ain't fit to keep house an' do everything herself. She'll be all worn out inside a year. Think of her doin' all the washin' an' ironin' an' bakin' with them soft white hands an' arms, an' sweepin'! I can't have it so, noways, father."

Mrs. Penn's face was burning; her mild eyes gleamed. She had pleaded her little cause like a Webster;[3] she had ranged from severity to pathos; but her opponent employed that obstinate silence which makes eloquence futile with mocking echoes. Adoniram arose clumsily.

"Father, ain't you got nothin' to say?" said Mrs. Penn.

"I've got to go off after that load of gravel. I can't stan' here talkin' all day."

---

1. **Scripture woman.** Biblical woman who is patient and obedient to her husband

2. **buttery.** Pantry

3. **Webster.** Daniel Webster (1782–1852), American diplomat and orator

"Father, won't you think it over, an' have a house built there instead of a barn?"

"I ain't got nothin' to say."

Adoniram shuffled out. Mrs. Penn went into her bedroom. When she came out, her eyes were red. She had a roll of unbleached cotton cloth. She spread it out on the kitchen table, and began cutting out some shirts for her husband. The men over in the field had a team to help them this afternoon; she could hear their halloos. She had a scanty pattern for the shirts; she had to plan and piece the sleeves.

Nanny came home with her embroidery, and sat down with her needlework. She had taken down her curl-papers, and there was a soft roll of fair hair like an aureole over her forehead; her face was as delicately fine and clear as porcelain. Suddenly she looked up, and the tender red flamed all over her face and neck. "Mother," said she.

"What say?"

"I've been thinking—I don't see how we're goin' to have any—wedding in this room. I'd be ashamed to have his folks come if we didn't have anybody else."

"Mebbe we can have some new paper before then; I can put it on. I guess you won't have no call to be ashamed of your belongin's."

"We might have the wedding in the new barn," said Nanny, with gentle pettishness. "Why, mother, what makes you look so?"

Mrs. Penn had started, and was staring at her with a curious expression. She turned again to her work, and spread out a pattern carefully on the cloth. "Nothin'," said she.

Presently Adoniram clattered out of the yard in his two-wheeled dump cart, standing as proudly upright as a Roman charioteer.[1] Mrs. Penn opened the door and stood there a minute looking out; the halloos of the men sounded louder.

It seemed to her all through the spring months that she heard nothing but the halloos and the noises of the saws and hammers. The new barn grew fast. It was a fine edifice for this little village. Men came on pleasant Sundays, in their meeting suits and clean shirt bosoms, and stood around it admiringly. Mrs. Penn did not speak of it, and Adoniram did not mention it to her, although sometimes, upon a return from inspecting it, he bore himself with injured dignity.

"It's a strange thing how your mother feels about the new barn," he said, confidentially, to Sammy one day.

Sammy only grunted after an odd fashion for a boy; he had learned it from his father.

The barn was all completed ready for use by the third week in July. Adoniram had planned to move his stock in on Wednesday; on Tuesday he received a letter which changed his plans. He came in with it early in the morning. "Sammy's been to the post-office," said he, "an' I've got a letter from Hiram." Hiram was Mrs. Penn's brother, who lived in Vermont.

"Well," said Mrs. Penn, "what does he say about the folks?"

"I guess they're all right. He says he thinks if I come up country right off there's a chance to buy jest the kind of horse I want." He stared reflectively out of the window at the new barn.

Mrs. Penn was making pies. She went on clapping the rolling-pin into the crust, although she was very pale, and her heart beat loudly.

"I dun' know but what I'd better go," said Adoniram. "I hate to go off jest now, right in the midst of hayin', but the ten-acre lot's cut, an' I guess Rufus an' the others can git along without me three or four days. I can't get a horse round here to suit me, nohow, an' I've got to have another for all the woodhaulin' in the fall. I told Hiram to watch out, an' if he got wind of a good horse to let me know. I guess I'd better go."

"I'll get out your clean shirt an' collar," said Mrs. Penn calmly.

She laid out Adoniram's Sunday suit and his clean clothes on the bed in the little bedroom. She got his shaving-water and razor ready. At last she buttoned on his collar and fastened his black cravat.[2]

Adoniram never wore his collar and cravat except on extra occasions. He held his head high, with a rasped dignity. When he was all ready, with his coat and hat brushed, and a lunch of pie and cheese in a paper bag, he hesitated on the threshold of the door. He looked at his wife, and his manner was defiantly apologetic. "*If* them cows come to-day, Sammy can drive 'em into the new barn," said he; "an' when they bring the hay up, they can pitch it in there."

"Well," replied Mrs. Penn.

Adoniram set his shaven face ahead and started. When he had cleared the door-step, he turned and looked back with a kind of nervous solemnity. "I shall be back by Saturday if nothin' happens," said he.

"Do be careful, father," returned his wife.

She stood in the door with Nanny at her elbow and watched him out of sight. Her eyes had a strange, doubtful expression in them; her peaceful forehead was contracted. She went in, and about her baking again. Nanny sat sewing. Her wedding-day was drawing nearer, and she was getting pale and thin with her steady sewing. Her mother kept glancing at her.

"Have you got that pain in your side this mornin'?" she asked.

"A little."

Mrs. Penn's face, as she worked, changed, her perplexed forehead smoothed, her eyes were steady, her lips firmly set. She formed a maxim for herself, although incoherently with her unlettered thoughts. "Unsolicited opportunities are the guide-posts of the Lord to the new roads of life," she repeated in effect, and she made up her mind to her course of action.

"S'posin' I *had* wrote to Hiram," she muttered once, when she was in the pantry—"s'posin' I had wrote, an' asked him if he knew of any horse? But I didn't, an' father's goin' wa'n't none of my doin'. It looks like a providence." Her voice rang out quite loud at the last.

"What you talkin' about, mother?" called Nanny.

---

1. **Roman charioteer.** Roman charioteers raced while standing on their vehicles.
2. **cravat.** Neckerchief or scarf; necktie

"Nothin'."

Mrs. Penn hurried her baking; at eleven o'clock it was all done. The load of hay from the west field came slowly down the cart track, and drew up at the new barn. Mrs. Penn ran out. "Stop!" she screamed—"stop!"

The men stopped and looked; Sammy upreared from the top of the load, and stared at his mother.

"Stop!" she cried out again. "Don't you put the hay in that barn; put it in the old one."

"Why, he said to put it in here," returned one of the haymakers, wonderingly. He was a young man, a neighbor's son, whom Adoniram hired by the year to help on the farm.

"Don't you put the hay in the new barn; there's room enough in the old one, ain't there?" said Mrs. Penn.

"Room enough," returned the hired man, in his thick, rustic tones. "Didn't need the new barn, nohow, far as room's concerned. Well, I s'pose he changed his mind." He took hold of the horses' bridles.

Mrs. Penn went back to the house. Soon the kitchen windows were darkened, and a fragrance like warm honey came into the room.

Nanny laid down her work. "I thought father wanted them to put the hay into the new barn?" she said, wonderingly.

"It's all right," replied her mother.

Sammy slid down from the load of hay, and came in to see if dinner was ready.

"I ain't goin' to get a regular dinner today, as long as father's gone," said his mother. "I've let the fire go out. You can have some bread an' milk an' pie. I thought we could get along." She set out some bowls of milk, some bread, and a pie on the kitchen table. "You'd better eat your dinner now," said she. "You might jest as well get through with it. I want you to help me afterward."

Nanny and Sammy stared at each other. There was something strange in their mother's manner. Mrs. Penn did not eat anything herself. She went into the pantry, and they heard her moving dishes while they ate. Presently she came out with a pile of plates. She got the clothes-basket out of the shed, and packed them in it. Nanny and Sammy watched. She brought out cups and saucers, and put them in with the plates.

"What you goin' to do, mother?" inquired Nanny, in a timid voice. A sense of something unusual made her tremble, as if it were a ghost. Sammy rolled his eyes over his pie.

"You'll see what I'm goin' to do," replied Mrs. Penn. "If you're through, Nanny, I want you to go up-stairs an' pack up your things; an' I want you, Sammy, to help me take down the bed in the bedroom."

"Oh, mother, what for?" gasped Nanny.

"You'll see."

During the next few hours a feat was performed by this simple, pious New England mother which was equal in its way to Wolfe's storming of the Heights of Abraham.[1] It took no more genius and audacity of bravery for Wolfe to cheer his wondering soldiers up those steep precipices, under the sleeping eyes of the enemy, than for Sarah Penn, at the head

of her children, to move all their little household goods into the new barn while her husband was away.

Nanny and Sammy followed their mother's instructions without a murmur; indeed, they were overawed. There is a certain uncanny and superhuman quality about all such purely original undertakings as their mother's was to them. Nanny went back and forth with her light loads, and Sammy tugged with sober energy.

At five o'clock in the afternoon the little house in which the Penns had lived for forty years had emptied itself into the new barn.

Every builder builds somewhat for unknown purposes, and is in a measure a prophet. The architect of Adoniram Penn's barn, while he designed it for the comfort of four-footed animals, had planned better than he knew for the comfort of humans. Sarah Penn saw at a glance its possibilities. Those great boxstalls, with quilts hung before them, would make better bedrooms than the one she had occupied for forty years, and there was a tight carriage-room. The harness room, with its chimney and shelves, would make a kitchen of her dreams. The great middle space would make a parlor, by-and-by, fit for a palace. Up stairs there was as much room as down. With partitions and windows, what a house would there be! Sarah looked at the row of stanchions[2] before the allotted space for cows, and reflected that she would have her front entry there.

At six o'clock the stove was up in the harness-room, the kettle was boiling, and the table set for tea. It looked almost as homelike as the abandoned house across the yard had ever done. The young hired man milked, and Sarah directed him calmly to bring the milk to the new barn. He came gaping, dropping little blots of foam from the brimming pails on the grass. Before the next morning he had spread the story of Adoniram Penn's wife moving into the new barn all over the little village. Men assembled in the store and talked it over, women with shawls over their heads scuttled into each other's houses before their work was done. Any deviation from the ordinary course of life in this quiet town was enough to stop all progress in it. Everybody paused to look at the staid independent figure on the side track. There was a difference of opinion with regard to her. Some held her to be insane; some, of lawless and rebellious spirit.

Friday the minister went to see her. It was in the forenoon, and she was at the barn door shelling peas for dinner. She looked up and returned his salutation with dignity, then she went on with her work. She did not invite him in. The saintly expression of her face remained fixed, but there was an angry flush over it.

The minister stood awkwardly before her, and talked. She handled the peas as if they were bullets. At last she looked up, and her eyes showed the spirit that her meek front had covered for a lifetime.

1. **Wolfe's . . . Heights of Abraham.** James Wolfe (1727–1759) was a British general who led the British forces against the French in the capturing of Quebec and died shortly after his victory on the Plains of Abraham.

2. **stanchions.** Restraining devices fitted loosely around the necks of cows to confine them to their stalls

"There ain't no use talkin', Mr. Hersey," said she. "I've thought it all over an' over, an' I believe I'm doin' what's right. I've made it the subject of prayer, an' it's betwixt me an' the Lord an' Adoniram. There ain't no call for nobody else to worry about it."

"Well, of course, if you have brought it to the Lord in prayer, and feel satisfied that you are doing right, Mrs. Penn," said the minister, helplessly. His thin gray-bearded face was pathetic. He was a sickly man; his youthful confidence had cooled; he had to scourge himself up to some of his pastoral duties as relentlessly as a Catholic ascetic, and then he was prostrated by the smart.

"I think it's right jest as much as I think it was right for our forefathers to come over from the old country 'cause they didn't have what belonged to 'em," said Mrs. Penn. She arose. The barn threshold might have been Plymouth Rock from her bearing. "I don't doubt you mean well, Mr. Hersey," said she, "but there are things people hadn't ought to interfere with. I've been a member of the church for over forty year. I've got my own mind an' my own feet, an' I'm goin' to think my own thoughts an' go my own ways, an' nobody but the Lord is goin' to dictate to me unless I've a mind to have him. Won't you come in an' set down? How is Mis' Hersey?"

"She is well, I thank you," replied the minister. He added some more perplexed apologetic remarks; then he retreated.

He could expound the intricacies of every character study in the Scriptures, he was competent to grasp the Pilgrim Fathers and all historical innovators, but Sarah Penn was beyond him. He could deal with primal cases, but parallel ones worsted him. But, after all, although it was aside from his province, he wondered more how Adoniram Penn would deal with his wife than how the Lord would. Everybody shared the wonder. When Adoniram's four new cows arrived, Sarah ordered three to be put in the old barn, the other in the house shed where the cooking-stove had stood. That added to the excitement. It was whispered that all four cows were domiciled in the house.

Towards sunset on Saturday, when Adoniram was expected home, there was a knot of men in the road near the new barn. The hired man had milked, but he still hung around the premises. Sarah Penn had supper all ready. There was brown-bread and baked beans and a custard pie; it was the supper that Adoniram loved on a Saturday night. She had on a clean calico, and she bore herself imperturbably. Nanny and Sammy kept close at her heels. Their eyes were large, and Nanny was full of nervous tremors. Still there was to them more pleasant excitement than anything else. An inborn confidence in their mother over their father asserted itself.

Sammy looked out of the harness-room window. "There he is," he announced, in an awed whisper. He and Nanny peeped around the casing. Mrs. Penn kept on about her work. The children watched Adoniram leave the new horse standing in the drive while he went to the house door. It was fastened. Then he went around to the shed. That door was seldom locked, even when the family was away. The thought how her father would be confronted by the cow

flashed upon Nanny. There was a hysterical sob in her throat. Adoniram emerged from the shed and stood looking about in a dazed fashion. His lips moved; he was saying something, but they could not hear what it was. The hired man was peeping around a corner of the old barn, but nobody saw him.

Adoniram took the new horse by the bridle and led him across the yard to the new barn. Nanny and Sammy slunk close to their mother. The barn doors rolled back, and there stood Adoniram, with the long mild face of the great Canadian farm horse looking over his shoulder.

Nanny kept behind her mother, but Sammy stepped suddenly forward, and stood in front of her.

Adoniram stared at the group. "What on airth you all down here for?" said he. "What's the matter over to the house?"

"We've come here to live, father," said Sammy. His shrill voice quavered out bravely.

"What"—Adoniram sniffed—"what is it smells like cookin?" said he. He stepped forward and looked in the open door of the harness-room. Then he turned to his wife. His old bristling face was pale and frightened. "What on airth does this mean, mother?" he gasped.

"You come in here, father," said Sarah. She led the way into the harness-room and shut the door. "Now, father," said she, "you needn't be scared. I ain't crazy. There ain't nothin' to be upset over. But we've come here to live, an' we're goin' to live here. We've got jest as good a right here as new horses an' cows. The house wa'n't fit for us to live in any longer, an' I made up my mind I wa'n't goin' to stay there. I've done my duty by you forty year, an' I'm goin' to do it now; but I'm goin' to live here. You've got to put in some windows and partitions; an' you'll have to buy some furniture."

"Why, mother!" the old man gasped.

"You'd better take your coat off an' get washed—there's the wash-basin—an' then we'll have supper."

"Why, mother!"

Sammy went past the window, leading the new horse to the old barn. The old man saw him, and shook his head speechlessly. He tried to take off his coat, but his arms seemed to lack the power. His wife helped him. She poured some water into the tin basin, and put in a piece of soap. She got the comb and brush, and smoothed his thin gray hair after he had washed. Then she put the beans, the hot bread, and tea on the table. Sammy came in, and the family drew up. Adoniram sat looking dazedly at his plate, and they waited.

"Ain't you goin' to ask a blessin', father?" said Sarah.

And the old man bent his head and mumbled.

All through the meal he stopped eating at intervals, and stared furtively at his wife; but he ate well. The home food tasted good to him, and his old frame was too sturdily healthy to be affected by his mind. But after supper he went out, and sat down on the step of the smaller door at the right of the barn, through which he had meant his Jerseys to pass in stately file, but which Sarah designed for her front house door, and he leaned his head on his hands.

After the supper dishes were cleared away and the milk-pans washed, Sarah went out to him. The twilight was deepening. There was a clear green glow in the sky. Before them stretched the smooth level of field; in the distance was a cluster of hay-stacks like the huts of a village; the air was very cool and calm and sweet. The landscape might have been an ideal one of peace.

Sarah bent over and touched her husband on one of his thin, sinewy shouders. "Father!"

The old man's shoulders heaved; he was weeping.

"Why, don't do so, father," said Sarah.

"I'll—put up the—partitions, an'—everything you—want, mother."

Sarah put her apron up to her face; she was overcome by her own triumph.

Adoniram was like a fortress whose walls had no active resistance, and went down the instant the right besieging tools were used. "Why, mother," he said, hoarsely, "I hadn't no idee you was so set on't as all this comes to."

from *The Age of Innocence*
by Edith Wharton

The immense accretion of flesh which had descended on her in middle life like a flood of lava on a doomed city had changed her from a plump active little woman with a neatly-turned foot and ankle into something as vast and august as a natural phenomenon. She had accepted this submergence as philosophically as all her other trials, and now, in extreme old age, was rewarded by presenting to her mirror an almost unwrinkled expanse of firm pink and white flesh, in the center of which the traces of a small face survived as if awaiting excavation. A flight of smooth double chins led down to the dizzy depths of a still-snowy bosom veiled in snowy muslins that were held in place by a miniature portrait of the late Mr. Mingott; and around and below, wave after wave of black silk surged away over the edges of a capacious arm-chair, with two tiny white hands poised like gulls on the surface of the billows.

"When I Heard the Learn'd Astronomer"
by Walt Whitman

> When I heard the learn'd astronomer,
> When the proofs, the figures, were ranged in
>   columns before me,
> When I was shown the charts and diagrams, to add,
>   divide, and measure them,
> When I sitting heard the astronomer where he
>   lectured with much applause in the lecture-room,
> 5 How soon unaccountable I became tired and sick,
> Till rising and gliding out I wander'd off by myself,
> In the mystical moist night-air, and from time to
>   time,
> Look'd up in perfect silence at the stars.

from *The Souls of Black Folk*
by W. E. B. Du Bois

Easily the most striking thing in the history of the American Negro since 1876[1] is the ascendancy of Mr. Booker T. Washington. It began at the time when war memories and ideals were rapidly passing; a day of astonishing commercial development was dawning; a sense of doubt and hesitation overtook the freedmen's sons,—then it was that his leading began. Mr. Washington came, with a simple definite program, at the psychological moment when the nation was a little ashamed of having bestowed so much sentiment on Negroes, and was concentrating its energies on Dollars. His program of industrial education, conciliation of the South, and submission and silence as to civil and political rights, was not wholly original; the Free Negroes from 1830 up to war-time had striven to build industrial schools, and the American Missionary Association had from the first taught various trades; and Price[2] and others had sought a way of honorable alliance with the best of the Southerners. But Mr. Washington first indissolubly linked these things; he put enthusiasm, unlimited energy, and perfect faith into this program, and changed it from a bypath into a veritable Way of Life. And the tale of the methods by which he did this is a fascinating study of human life.

It startled the nation to hear a Negro advocating such a program after many decades of bitter complaint; it startled and won the applause of the South, it interested and won the admiration of the North; and after a confused murmur of protest, it silenced if it did not convert the Negroes themselves.

To gain the sympathy and cooperation of the various elements comprising the white South was Mr. Washington's first task; and this, at the time Tuskegee[3] was founded, seemed, for a black man, well-nigh impossible. And yet ten years later it was done in the word spoken at Atlanta: "In all things purely social we can be as separate as the five fingers, and yet one as the hand in all things essential to mutual progress." This "Atlanta Compromise"[4] is by all odds the most notable thing in Mr. Washington's career. The South interpreted it in different ways: the radicals received it as a complete surrender of the demand for civil and political equality; the conservatives, as a generously conceived working basis for mutual understanding. So both approved it, and today its author is certainly the most distinguished Southerner since Jefferson Davis, and the one with the largest personal following.

---

1. **1876.** In 1876, Reconstruction ended, federal troops withdrew from the South, and African Americans lost political power.
2. **Price.** Thomas Frederick Price (1860–1919), editor, Roman Catholic priest, and founder of the American Missionary Association
3. **Tuskegee.** Tuskegee Institute, a vocational school for African Americans founded in 1881 by Booker T. Washington
4. **Atlanta Compromise.** Washington's speech at the Atlanta Exposition of 1895 essentially traded the political, civil, and social rights of African Americans for the promise of jobs and vocational-training schools.

Next to this achievement comes Mr. Washington's work in gaining place and consideration in the North. Others less shrewd and tactful had formerly essayed to sit on these two stools and had fallen between them, but as Mr. Washington knew the heart of the South from birth and training, so by singular insight he intuitively grasped the spirit of the age which was dominating the North. And so thoroughly did he learn the speech and thought of triumphant commercialism, and the ideals of material prosperity, that the picture of a lone black boy poring over a French grammar amid the weeds and dirt of a neglected home soon seemed to him the acme of absurdities.[1] One wonders what Socrates and St. Francis of Assisi[2] would say to this.

And yet this very singleness of vision and thorough oneness with his age is a mark of the successful man. It is as though Nature must needs make men narrow in order to give them force. So Mr. Washington's cult has gained unquestioning followers, his work has wonderfully prospered, his friends are legion, and his enemies are confounded. Today he stands as the one recognized spokesman of his ten million fellows, and one of the most notable figures in a nation of seventy millions. One hesitates, therefore, to criticize a life which, beginning with so little, has done so much. And yet the time is come when one may speak in all sincerity and utter courtesy of the mistakes and shortcomings of Mr. Washington's career, as well as of his triumphs, without being thought captious or envious, and without forgetting that it is easier to do ill than well in the world.

The criticism that has hitherto met Mr. Washington has not always been of this broad character. In the South especially has he had to walk warily to avoid the harshest judgments,—and naturally so, for he is dealing with the one subject of deepest sensitiveness to that section. Twice—once when at the Chicago celebration of the Spanish-American War he alluded to the color-prejudice that is "eating away the vitals of the South," and once when he dined with President Roosevelt[3]—has the resulting Southern criticism been violent enough to threaten seriously his popularity. In the North the feeling has several times forced itself into words, that Mr. Washington's counsels of submission overlooked certain elements of true manhood, and that his educational program was unnecessarily narrow. Usually, however, such criticism has not found open expression, although, too, the spiritual sons of the Abolitionists have not been prepared to acknowledge that the schools founded before Tuskegee, by men of broad ideals and self-sacrificing spirit, were wholly failures or worthy of ridicule. While, then, criticism has not failed to follow Mr. Washington, yet the prevailing public opinion of the land has been but too willing to deliver the solution of a wearisome problem into his hands, and say, "If that is all you and your race ask, take it."

Among his own people, however, Mr. Washington has encountered the strongest and most lasting opposition, amounting at times to bitterness, and even today continuing strong and insistent even though largely silenced in outward expression by the public opinion of the nation. Some of this opposition is, of course, mere envy; the disappointment of displaced demagogues and the spite of narrow minds. But aside from this, there is among educated and thoughtful colored men in all parts of the land a feeling of deep regret, sorrow, and apprehension at the wide currency and ascendancy which some of Mr. Washington's theories have gained. These same men admire his sincerity of purpose, and are willing to forgive much to honest endeavor which is doing something worth the doing. They cooperate with Mr. Washington as far as they conscientiously can; and, indeed, it is no ordinary tribute to this man's tact and power that, steering as he must between so many diverse interests and opinions, he so largely retains the respect of all.

But the hushing of the criticism of honest opponents is a dangerous thing. It leads some of the best of the critics to unfortunate silence and paralysis of effort, and others to burst into speech so passionately and intemperately as to lose listeners. Honest and earnest criticism from those whose interests are most nearly touched,—criticism of writers by readers, of government by those governed, of leaders by those led,—this is the soul of democracy and the safeguard of modern society. If the best of the American Negroes receive by outer pressure a leader whom they had not recognized before, manifestly there is here a certain palpable gain. Yet there is also irreparable loss,—a loss of that peculiarly valuable education which a group receives when by search and criticism it finds and commissions its own leaders. The way in which this is done is at once the most elementary and the nicest problem of social growth. History is but the record of such group leadership; and yet how infinitely changeful is its type and character! And of all types and kinds, what can be more instructive than the leadership of a group within a group?—that curious double movement where real progress may be negative and actual advance be relative retrogression. All this is the social student's inspiration and despair.

Now in the past the American Negro has had instructive experience in the choosing of group leaders, founding thus a peculiar dynasty which in the light of present conditions is worthwhile studying. When sticks and stones and beasts form the sole environment of a people, their attitude is largely one of determined opposition to and conquest of natural forces. But when to earth and brute is added an environment of men and ideas, then the attitude of the imprisoned group may take three main forms,—a feeling of revolt and revenge; an attempt to adjust all thought and action to the will of the greater group; or, finally, a determined effort at self-realization and self- development despite environing opinion. The influence of all of these attitudes at various times can be traced in

---

1. **acme of absurdities.** Refers to a passage in *Up From Slavery* in which Washington describes nonpractical knowledge as absurd
2. **Socrates and St. Francis of Assisi.** *Socrates*—(*circa* 470–399 BC), Greek philosopher; *St. Francis of Assisi*—(*circa* AD 1182–1226), founder of the Franciscan orders and leader of movements to reform the church
3. **he dined with President Roosevelt.** Theodore Roosevelt (1858–1919) asked Washington to dine with him in 1901, causing much controversy and criticism around the country.

the history of the American Negro, and in the evolution of his successive leaders.

Before 1750, while the fire of African freedom still burned in the veins of the slaves, there was in all leadership or attempted leadership but the one motive of revolt and revenge,—typified in the terrible Maroons, the Danish blacks, and Cato of Stono,[1] and veiling all the Americas in fear of insurrection. The liberalizing tendencies of the latter half of the eighteenth century brought, along with kindlier relations between black and white, thoughts of ultimate adjustment and assimilation. Such aspiration was especially voiced in the earnest songs of Phyllis, in the martyrdom of Attucks, the fighting of Salem and Poor, the intellectual accomplishments of Banneker and Derham, and the political demands of the Cuffes.[2]

Stern financial and social stress after the war cooled much of the previous humanitarian ardor. The disappointment and impatience of the Negroes at the persistence of slavery and serfdom voiced itself in two movements. The slaves in the South, aroused undoubtedly by vague rumors of the Haytian revolt, made three fierce attempts at insurrection,—in 1800 under Gabriel in Virginia, in 1822 under Vesey in Carolina, and in 1831 again in Virginia under the terrible Nat Turner.[3] In the Free States, on the other hand, a new and curious attempt at self-development was made. In Philadelphia and New York color prescription led to a withdrawal of Negro communicants from white churches and the formation of a peculiar socio-religious institution among the Negroes known as the African Church,—an organization still living and controlling in its various branches over a million of men.

Walker's[4] wild appeal against the trend of the times showed how the world was changing after the coming of the cotton-gin. By 1830, slavery seemed hopelessly fastened on the South, and the slaves thoroughly cowed into submission. The free Negroes of the North, inspired by the mulatto immigrants from the West Indies, began to change the basis of their demands; they recognized the slavery of slaves, but insisted that they themselves were freemen, and sought assimilation and amalgamation with the nation on the same terms with other men. Thus, Forten and Purvis of Philadelphia, Shad of Wilmington, Du Bois of New Haven, Barbadoes[5] of Boston, and others, strove singly and together as men, they said, not as slaves; as "people of color," not as "Negroes." The trend of the times, however, refused them recognition save in individual and exceptional cases, considered them as one with all the despised blacks, and they soon found themselves striving to keep even the rights they formerly had of voting and working and moving as freemen. Schemes of migration and colonization arose among them; but these they refused to entertain, and they eventually turned to the Abolition movement as a final refuge.

Here, led by Remond, Nell, Wells-Brown, and Douglass,[6] a new period of self-assertion and self-development dawned. To be sure, ultimate freedom and assimilation was the ideal before the leaders, but the assertion of the manhood rights of the Negro by himself was the main reliance, and John Brown's raid was the extreme of its logic. After the war and emancipation, the great form of Frederick Douglass, the greatest of American Negro leaders, still led the host. Self-assertion, especially in political lines, was the main program, and behind Douglass came Elliot, Bruce, and Langston, and the Reconstruction politicians, and, less conspicuous but of greater social significance Alexander Crummell and Bishop Daniel Payne.[7]

Then came the Revolution of 1876, the suppression of the Negro votes, the changing and shifting of ideals, and the seeking of new lights in the great night. Douglass, in his old age, still bravely stood for the ideals of his early manhood,—ultimate assimilation *through* self-assertion, and on no other terms. For a time Price arose as a new leader, destined, it

1. **Maroons . . . Stono.** *Maroons*—fugitive slaves or their descendants; *Danish blacks*—slaves in the Danish West Indies who revolted in 1733; *Cato of Stono*—leader of a slave revolt in South Carolina

2. **Phyllis . . . the Cuffes.** *Phillis Wheatley*—(*circa* 1753–1784), African-American poet; *Crispus Attucks*—(*circa* 1723–1770), slain leader of the Boston Massacre; *Peter Salem*—(d. 1816), African-American patriot who was killed in the battle of Bunker Hill; *Benjamin Banneker*—(1731–1800), African-American mathematician; *James Derham*—(1762–?), first recognized African-American physician; *Paul Cuffe*—(1759–1817), organizer of a movement to resettle African Americans in African colonies

3. **Gabriel . . . Turner.** *Gabriel*—(*circa* 1775–1800) conspired to attack Richmond, Virginia; *Denmark Vesey*—(*circa* 1767–1822) led an unsuccessful uprising in 1822; *Nat Turner*—(1800–1831) led the Southampton insurrection in 1831, in which one hundred slaves and sixty-one whites were killed.

4. **Walker's.** *David Walker*—(1785–1830) wrote an inflammatory antislavery pamphlet.

5. **Forten . . . Barbadoes.** *James Forten*—(1766–1842), African-American philanthropist and civic leader; *Robert Purvis*—(1810–1898), founder of the American Anti-Slavery Society and president of the Underground Railroad; *Abraham Shadd*—

African-American abolitionist and activist; *Alexander Du Bois*—(1803–1887), W. E. B. Du Bois's grandfather, helped form the Negro Episcopal Parish of St. Luke; *James G. Barbadoes*—attended the first National Negro Convention.

6. **Remond . . . Douglass.** *Charles Lenox Remond*—(1810–1873), African-American leader; *William Cooper Nell*—(1816–1874), first African American to acquire a governmental position (clerk in the post office), abolitionist, writer, and advocate for equal education; *William Wells Brown*—(*circa* 1816–1884), publisher of *Clotel*, the first novel and play by an African American; *Fredrick Douglass*—(1817–1895), African-American abolitionist and diplomat

7. **Elliot . . . Payne.** *Robert Brown Elliot*—(1842–1884), African-American South Carolina congressman in the United States House of Representatives; *Blanche K. Bruce*—(1841–1898), first African-American man to serve a full term in the United States Senate (1875–1881); *John Mercer Langston*—(1829–1897), African-American congressman, lawyer, diplomat, educator; *Alexander Crummell*—(1819–1898), clergyman of the protestant Episcopal Church, missionary in Liberia for twenty years and then in Washington, DC; *Daniel Alexander Payne*—(1811–1893), bishop of the African Methodist Episcopal Church and president of Wilberforce University (1863–1876)

seemed, not to give up, but to restate the old ideals in a form less repugnant to the white South. But he passed away in his prime. Then came the new leader. Nearly all the former ones had become leaders by the silent suffrage of their fellows, had sought to lead their own people alone, and were usually, save Douglass, little known outside their race. But Booker T. Washington arose as essentially the leader not of one race but of two,—a compromiser between the South, the North, and the Negro. Naturally the Negroes resented, at first bitterly, signs of compromise which surrendered their civil and political rights, even though this was to be exchanged for larger chances of economic development. The rich and dominating North, however, was not only weary of the race problem, but was investing largely in Southern enterprises, and welcomed any method of peaceful cooperation. Thus, by national opinion, the Negroes began to recognize Mr. Washington's leadership; and the voice of criticism was hushed.

Mr. Washington represents in Negro thought the old attitude of adjustment and submission; but adjustment at such a peculiar time as to make his program unique. This is an age of unusual economic development, and Mr. Washington's program naturally takes an economic cast, becoming a gospel of Work and Money to such an extent as apparently almost completely to overshadow the higher aims of life. Moreover, this is an age when the more advanced races are coming in closer contact with the less developed races, and the race-feeling is therefore intensified; and Mr. Washington's program practically accepts the alleged inferiority of the Negro races. Again, in our own land, the reaction from the sentiment of wartime has given impetus to race-prejudice against Negroes, and Mr. Washington withdraws many of the high demands of Negroes as men and American citizens. In other periods of intensified prejudice all the Negro's tendency to self-assertion has been called forth; at this period a policy of submission is advocated. In the history of nearly all other races and peoples the doctrine preached at such crises has been that manly self-respect is worth more than lands and houses, and that a people who voluntarily surrender such respect, or cease striving for it, are not worth civilizing.

In answer to this, it has been claimed that the Negro can survive only through submission. Mr. Washington distinctly asks that black people give up, at least for the present, three things,—

First, political power,

Second, insistence on civil rights,

Third, higher education of Negro youth,—
and concentrate all their energies on industrial education, the accumulation of wealth, and the conciliation of the South. This policy has been courageously and insistently advocated for over fifteen years, and has been triumphant for perhaps ten years. As a result of this tender of the palm-branch, what has been the return? In these years there have occurred:

1. The disfranchisement of the Negro.

2. The legal creation of a distinct status of civil inferiority for the Negro.

3. The steady withdrawal of aid from institutions for the higher training of the Negro.

These movements are not, to be sure, direct results of Mr. Washington's teachings; but his propaganda has, without a shadow of doubt, helped their speedier accomplishment. The question then comes: Is it possible, and probable, that nine millions of men can make effective progress in economic lines if they are deprived of political rights, made a servile caste, and allowed only the most meager chance for developing their exceptional men? If history and reason give any distinct answer to these questions, it is an emphatic *No*. And Mr. Washington thus faces the triple paradox of his career:

1. He is striving nobly to make Negro artisans businessmen and property-owners; but it is utterly impossible, under modern competitive methods, for workingmen and property-owners to defend their rights and exist without the right of suffrage.

2. He insists on thrift and self-respect, but at the same time counsels a silent submission to civic inferiority such as is bound to sap the manhood of any race in the long run.

3. He advocates common-school and industrial training, and depreciates institutions of higher learning; but neither the Negro common schools, nor Tuskegee itself, could remain open a day were it not for teachers trained in Negro colleges, or trained by their graduates.

This triple paradox in Mr. Washington's position is the object of criticism by two classes of colored Americans. One class is spiritually descended from Toussaint the Savior,[1] through Gabriel, Vesey, and Turner, and they represent the attitude of revolt and revenge; they hate the white South blindly and distrust the white race generally, and so far as they agree on definite action, think that the Negro's only hope lies in emigration beyond the borders of the United States. And yet, by the irony of fate, nothing has more effectually made this program seem hopeless than the recent course of the United States toward weaker and darker peoples in the West Indies, Hawaii, and the Philippines,—for where in the world may we go and be safe from lying and brute force?

The other class of Negroes who cannot agree with Mr. Washington has hitherto said little aloud. They deprecate the sight of scattered counsels, of internal disagreement; and especially they dislike making their just criticism of a useful and earnest man an excuse for a general discharge of venom from small-minded opponents. Nevertheless, the questions involved are so fundamental and serious that it is difficult to see how men like the Grimkes, Kelly Miller, J. W. E. Bowen,[2] and other representatives of this group, can much longer be silent. Such men feel in conscience bound to ask of this nation three things:

1. The right to vote.

2. Civic equality.

3. The education of youth according to ability.

---

1. **Toussaint the Savior.** Pierre-Dominique Toussaint (*circa* 1743–1803), Haitian general and liberator

2. **Grimkes . . . Bowen.** *Archibald Grimke*—(1849–1930) and *Francis Grimke*—(1850–1937), civic leaders concerned with African-American affairs; *Kelly Miller*—(1863–1939), dean of Howard University, lectured on African-American issues; *John Wesley Edward Bowen*—(1855–?), clergyman and educator

They acknowledge Mr. Washington's invaluable service in counselling patience and courtesy in such demands; they do not ask that ignorant black men vote when ignorant whites are debarred, or that any reasonable restrictions in the suffrage should not be applied; they know that the low social level of the mass of the race is responsible for much discrimination against it, but they also know, and the nation knows, that relentless color-prejudice is more often a cause than a result of the Negro's degradation; they seek the abatement of this relic of barbarism, and not its systematic encouragement and pampering by all agencies of social power from the Associated Press to the Church of Christ. They advocate, with Mr. Washington, a broad system of Negro common schools supplemented by thorough industrial training; but they are surprised that a man of Mr. Washington's insight cannot see that no such educational system ever has rested or can rest on any other basis than that of the well-equipped college and university, and they insist that there is a demand for a few such institutions throughout the South to train the best of the Negro youth as teachers, professional men, and leaders.

This group of men honor Mr. Washington for his attitude of conciliation toward the white South; they accept the "Atlanta Compromise" in its broadest interpretation; they recognize, with him, many signs of promise, many men of high purpose and fair judgment, in this section; they know that no easy task has been laid upon a region already tottering under heavy burdens. But, nevertheless, they insist that the way to truth and right lies in straightforward honesty, not in indiscriminate flattery; in praising those of the South who do well and criticizing uncompromisingly those who do ill; in taking advantage of the opportunities at hand and urging their fellows to do the same, but at the same time in remembering that only a firm adherence to their higher ideals and aspirations will ever keep those ideals within the realm of possibility. They do not expect that the free right to vote, to enjoy civic rights, and to be educated will come in a moment; they do not expect to see the bias and prejudices of years disappear at the blast of a trumpet; but they are absolutely certain that the way for a people to gain their reasonable rights is not by voluntarily throwing them away and insisting that they do not want them; that the way for a people to gain respect is not by continually belittling and ridiculing themselves that, on the contrary, Negroes must insist continually, in season and out of season, that voting is necessary to modern manhood, that color discrimination is barbarism, and that black boys need education as well as white boys.

In failing thus to state plainly and unequivocally the legitimate demands of their people, even at the cost of opposing an honored leader, the thinking classes of American Negroes would shirk a heavy responsibility,—a responsibility to themselves, a responsibility to the struggling masses, a responsibility to the darker races of men whose future depends so largely on this American experiment, but especially a responsibility to this nation,—this common Fatherland. It is wrong to encourage a man or a people in evil-doing, it is wrong to aid and abet a national crime simply because it is unpopular not to do so. The growing spirit of kindliness and reconciliation between the North and South after the fright-ful differences of a generation ago ought to be a source of deep congratulation to all, and especially to those whose mistreatment caused the war; but if that reconciliation is to be marked by the industrial slavery and civic death of those same black men, with permanent legislation into a position of inferiority, then those black men, if they are really men, are called upon by every consideration of patriotism and loyalty to oppose such a course by all civilized methods, even though such opposition involves disagreement with Mr. Booker T. Washington. We have no right to sit silently by while the inevitable seeds are sown for a harvest of disaster to our children black and white.

First, it is the duty of black men to judge the South discriminatingly. The present generation of Southerners are not responsible for the past, and they should not be blindly hated or blamed for it. Furthermore, to no class is the indiscriminate endorsement of the recent course of the South toward Negroes more nauseating than to the best thought of the South. The South is not "solid"; it is a land in the ferment of social change, wherein forces of all kinds are fighting for supremacy; and to praise the ill the South is today perpetrating is just as wrong as to condemn the good. Discriminating and broad-minded criticism is what the South needs,—needs it for the sake of her own white sons and daughters, and for the insurance of robust, healthy mental and moral development.

Today even the attitude of the Southern whites toward the blacks is not, as so many assume, in all cases the same; the ignorant Southerner hates the Negro, the workingmen fear his competition, the money-makers wish to use him as a laborer, some of the educated see a menace in his upward development, while others—usually the sons of the masters—wish to help him to rise. National opinion has enabled this last class to maintain the Negro common schools, and to protect the Negro partially in property, life, and limb. Through the pressure of the money-makers, the Negro is in danger of being reduced to semi-slavery, especially in the country districts; the workingmen, and those of the educated who fear the Negro, have united to disfranchise him, and some have urged his deportation; while the passions of the ignorant are easily aroused to lynch and abuse any black man. To praise this intricate whirl of thought and prejudice is nonsense; to inveigh indiscriminately against "the South" is unjust; but to use the same breath in praising Governor Aycock, exposing Senator Morgan, arguing with Mr. Thomas Nelson Page, and denouncing Senator Ben Tillman,[1] is not only sane, but the imperative duty of thinking black men.

It would be unjust to Mr. Washington not to acknowledge that in several instances he has opposed movements in the South which were unjust to the Negro; he sent memorials to

---

1. **Governor Aycock . . . Ben Tillman.** *Charles Brantley Aycock*— (1859–1905), governor of North Carolina; *Edwin Denison Morgan*—governor of New York (1859–1863) and United States senator; *Thomas Nelson Page*—(1853–1922), novelist who glamorized the southern plantation; *Benjamin Ryan Tillman*—(1847–1918), United States senator who presented the views of southern extremists

the Louisiana and Alabama constitutional conventions, he has spoken against lynching, and in other ways has openly or silently set his influence against sinister schemes and unfortunate happenings. Notwithstanding this, it is equally true to assert that on the whole the distinct impression left by Mr. Washington's propaganda is, first, that the South is justified in its present attitude toward the Negro because of the Negro's degradation; secondly, that the prime cause of the Negro's failure to rise more quickly is his wrong education in the past; and, thirdly, that his future rise depends primarily on his own efforts. Each of these propositions is a dangerous half-truth. The supplementary truths must never be lost sight of: first, slavery and race-prejudice are potent if not sufficient causes of the Negro's position; second, industrial and common-school training were necessarily slow in planting because they had to await the black teachers trained by higher institutions,—it being extremely doubtful if any essentially different development was possible, and certainly a Tuskegee was unthinkable before 1880; and, third, while it is a great truth to say that the Negro must strive and strive mightily to help himself, it is equally true that unless his striving be not simply seconded, but rather aroused and encouraged, by the initiative of the richer and wiser environing group, he cannot hope for great success.

In his failure to realize and impress this last point, Mr. Washington is especially to be criticized. His doctrine has tended to make the whites, North and South, shift the burden of the Negro problem to the Negro's shoulders and stand aside as critical and rather pessimistic spectators; when in fact the burden belongs to the nation, and the hands of none of us are clean if we bend not our energies to righting these great wrongs.

The South ought to be led, by candid and honest criticism, to assert her better self and do her full duty to the race she has cruelly wronged and is still wronging. The North—her co-partner in guilt—cannot salve her conscience by plastering it with gold. We cannot settle this problem by diplomacy and suaveness, by "policy" alone. If worse come to worst, can the moral fiber of this country survive the slow throttling and murder of nine millions of men?

The black men of America have a duty to perform, a duty stern and delicate,—a forward movement to oppose a part of the work of their greatest leader. So far as Mr. Washington preaches Thrift, Patience, and Industrial Training for the masses, we must hold up his hands and strive with him, rejoicing in his honors and glorying in the strength of this Joshua called of God and of man to lead the headless host. But so far as Mr. Washington apologizes for injustice, North or South, does not rightly value the privilege and duty of voting, belittles the emasculating effects of caste distinctions, and opposes the higher training and ambition of our brighter minds,—so far as he, the South or the Nation, does this,—we must unceasingly and firmly oppose them. By every civilized and peaceful method we must strive for the rights which the world accords to men, clinging unwaveringly to those great words which the sons of the Fathers would fain forget: "We hold these truths to be self-evident: That all men are created equal; that they are endowed by their Creator with certain inalienable rights; that among these are life, liberty, and the pursuit of happiness."

from *The Art of Fiction*
by Henry James

I remember an English novelist, a woman of genius, telling me that she was much commended for the impression she had managed to give in one of her tales of the nature and way of life of the French Protestant youth. She had been asked where she learned so much about this recondite[1] being, she had been congratulated on her peculiar opportunities. These opportunities consisted in her having once, in Paris, as she ascended a staircase, passed an open door where, in the household of a *pasteur*,[2] some of the young Protestants were seated at table round a finished meal. The glimpse made a picture; it lasted only a moment, but that moment was experience. She had got her direct personal impression, and she turned out her type. She knew what youth was, and what Protestantism, she also had the advantage of having seen what it was to be French, so that she converted these ideas into a concrete image and produced a reality. Above all, however, she was blessed with the faculty which when you give it an inch takes an ell,[3] and which for the artist is a much greater source of strength than any accident of residence or of place in the social scale.

The power to guess the unseen from the seen, to trace the implication of things, to judge the whole piece by the pattern, the condition of feeling life in general so completely that you are well on your way to knowing any particular corner of it— this cluster of gifts may also be said to constitute experience, and they occur in country and in town, and in the most differing stages of education. If experience consists of impressions, it may be said that impressions *are* experience, just as (have we not seen it?) they are the very air we breathe.

Therefore, if I should certainly say to a novice, "Write from experience and experience only," I should feel that this was rather a tantalizing monition[4] if I were not careful immediately to add, "Try to be one of the people on whom nothing is lost!"

---

1. **recondite.** Profound, extraordinary
2. **pasteur.** Minister
3. **ell.** Former unit of measure in England, equal to forty-five inches
4. **monition.** Warning

UNIT REVIEW

Frontiers

VOCABULARY FROM THE SELECTIONS

abeyance, 472
afflicted, 460
anathema, 428
append, 456
barbaric, 477
bellicose, 429
cavalcade, 428
cavort, 458
conjecture, 427, 456
contender, 473
contortion, 430
coquetry, 428
course, 444
creed, 472
demure, 442
dilapidated, 456
dilatory, 439
disposition, 473
dissuade, 430
equanimity, 429
esculent, 476
exhorter, 457

expatriated, 428
extemporize, 431
felonious, 431
fissure, 477
gallantly, 441
garrulous, 456
gravity, 441
guileless, 429
harbor, 472
hermitage, 441
impalpable, 473
importunity, 452
inaudibly, 441
infelicitous, 428
infidel, 476
interminable, 457
jag, 477
jocular, 430
linguist, 473
loiter, 477
ominous, 427
ornery, 458

ornithologist, 442
ostentatiously, 432
pinion, 445
ponderous, 445
precipitous, 429
predisposing, 427
premonition, 443
proffer, 441
quadruped, 476
querulous, 434
rebuke, 446
remonstrance, 429
shoal, 440
squalor, 441
suffice, 472
tumultuously, 452
vagabond, 460
vex, 446
vituperative, 433
vociferation, 432
wretched, 440

LITERARY TERMS

catalog, 479
conflict, 448
dialect, 461
dialogue, 470
elaboration, 479
essay, 462
frame tale, 462
free verse, 471, 479
irony, 454, 470

motif, 448
Naturalism, 468
oral tradition, 467
parallelism, 479
parody, 437
personification, 470
protagonist, 448
Psychological Realism, 423
Realism, 423

reversal, 454
rhyme, 482
Romanticism, 471
sentimentality, 437
speaker, 482
stereotype, 437
stock character, 437
symbol, 479
tall tale, 462

SYNTHESIS: QUESTIONS FOR WRITING, RESEARCH, OR DISCUSSION

GENRE STUDIES

1. **Short Story.** Review the definition of *point of view* in the Handbook of Literary Terms. Examine the point of view used in the short stories in the unit. Do any authors combine two points of view? to what effect?

THEMATIC STUDIES

2. **Frontiers.** The name of this unit is "Frontiers." For every geographical frontier there is an interior psychological frontier. Choose characters from three separate works and explain how each character crosses an interior frontier.

3. **Connection and Indifference.** Contrast the views of the world expressed in the poems of Crane and Whitman.

4. **Rite of Passage.** A rite-of-passage story chronicles moving from childhood to adulthood. Examine Sylvia in "A White Heron" and Tom and Piney in "The Outcasts of Poker Flat." What events mark their maturation?

HISTORICAL/BIOGRAPHICAL STUDIES

5. **Dialect.** Note the use of dialect in both the Harte and Twain selections. What does it tell you about the expansion of America? What else might this tell you about the social strata of the country? What might the impact of the dialect be on readers in other countries?

LANGUAGE LAB   PROOFREADING FOR COMMA ERRORS

When revising and proofreading, check for missing and misplaced commas.

COMMA USAGE	
MILD EXCLAMATION:	My, the prairie seems to stretch on forever.
PARTICIPIAL PHRASES:	Coming from the mountainous Northeast, I was quite surprised by the flatness of the land.
TWO PREPOSITIONAL PHRASES:	On the eve of our journey, I almost changed my mind.
ADVERB CLAUSE:	When I thought about the unknown dangers that lie ahead, I became uncertain about the journey.
PARENTHETICAL EXPRESSION:	I changed my mind, as you can see, when I thought about the lack of prospects in my hometown.
DIRECT ADDRESS:	Mother, I will write as soon as I am able.
WORDS IN A SERIES:	The heat, dust, and drudgery of the trail were sometimes unbearable.
PHRASES IN A SERIES:	We left Buffalo, reached Ohio a few days later, and arrived in Missouri by springtime.
CLAUSES IN A SERIES:	We had heard that the trip was long, that dangers were imminent, and that California was the land of promise.
TWO OR MORE ADJECTIVES:	The wagon train crawled like a long, white snake across the plain.
LONG INDEPENDENT CLAUSE:	The Oregon Trail opened the door to the "great migration," and thousands of people followed it to the Pacific.
SHORT CLAUSE:	The wagons rolled and the sky stretched endlessly.
RESTRICTIVE PHRASE OR CLAUSE:	The first thing that caught my eye was the buffalo.
NONRESTRICTIVE PHRASE OR CLAUSE:	The Oregon Trail, which opened in 1842, was eventually abandoned in 1870s.
APPOSITIVE OR APPOSITIVE PHRASE:	My father's ancestors, immigrants from Ireland, made the journey westward.

Exercise Avoiding Errors in Comma Usage

Rewrite the following sentences, adding commas as necessary.

1. First published in the *Overland Monthly* in 1869 "The Outcasts of Poker Flat" has become a classic of American literature.

2. Kate Chopin shocked turn-of-the-century critics with her depictions of women especially those in her novel *The Awakening.*

3. I sing a song of myself Walt Whitman.

4. Sarah Orne Jewett's father a doctor encouraged her to closely observe her environment.

5. In *The Souls of Black Folk* Du Bois proposes that a "veil" separates the races in America that education is crucial for young African Americans and that African Americans need to seek civil equality.

Can Fire in the Park. *Beauford Delaney, 1946. National Museum of American Art, Washington, DC/Art Resource, NY*

M ake it new.

—Ezra Pound

THE MODERN ERA (1900–1960)

A CENTURY OF CHANGE

WWI Troops in Gear. Courtesy of Archive/Welgos

When William Faulkner delivered his Nobel Prize acceptance address in 1950, he asked his audience to remember "the old verities and truths of the heart." He wanted to make the point that however much the world might change, some things, such as the human capacity for courage, compassion, sacrifice, honor, and pride, remain the same.

Like other artists living in the twentieth century, Faulkner had to come to grips with change, for at no other time had the basic conditions of life changed so rapidly and so completely. Think, for example, of the effects on everyday life of electric lights, mass merchandising, mass media such as television and the movies, transportation by automobiles and airplanes, and instant communication by telephone anywhere in the world. Or consider the effects of antibiotics and anesthesia, weapons of mass destruction, suburban housing and skyscrapers, labor unions, women in the work force, the population explosion and the concentration of people in cities, and the development of such political ideologies as Communism and Fascism. Take these things away now, and our lives would be scarcely recognizable, yet all these developments took place in a few decades.[1]

THE FIRST WORLD WAR

One of the defining events of the first half of the twentieth century was **World War I**. Before the war, the United States was isolationist, involved in its own concerns. Writing before the war tended to be traditional and regional, providing portraits of life in the many different milieus to be found throughout the country. **Edgar Lee Masters's** *Spoon River Anthology*, with

---

1. Some developments, such as the telephone, the concentration of people in cities, and the appearance of women in the work force, had their origins in the nineteenth century but did not become truly significant until the twentieth century.

its depictions of people from a small village in Illinois; **Edwin Arlington Robinson's** poems of life in New England; and **Jack London's** adventure tales of the great North country are examples of **regionalism.**

World War I began in 1914, but the United States delayed entering the conflict until 1917, primarily because Americans viewed the war as a European concern. The war changed the life and culture of the United States. The breakdown of traditional European society and the loss of ten million lives in Europe due to modern armaments led to a widespread belief among intellectuals and artists that the old order was passing away and that something altogether new would take its place.

Ernest Hemingway

THE LOST GENERATION

To some of the writers who fought or participated in the war, such as **John Dos Passos, Ernest Hemingway,** and **E. E. Cummings,** the old rhetoric of heroic and glorious combat seemed hollow. Many writers saw the emerging society as chaotic, destructive, and increasingly meaningless. Particularly after the war, they felt that traditional expressions of order or meaning no longer applied; they felt, in some way, that the real America had been lost or distorted, and they came to feel a sense of dislocation, or "alienation," a sense of being cut off from the past. One American writer living in Paris, **Gertrude Stein**, would label this group of postwar writers the **"lost generation."**

This sense of dislocation and alienation led writers of the lost generation to question many fundamental tenets of the American dream, including the idea immortalized in Benjamin Franklin's *Autobiography* and in nineteenth-century Horatio Alger stories that through hard work, industry, and self-reliance any American could grasp a piece of the dream. In an age dominated by massive social forces, individuals seemed increasingly dominated by their environs, dehumanized by the numbing and squalid work conditions of modern industry and by the living conditions of modern cities, which swelled with the ranks of poor immigrants.

▶1917. T. S. Eliot's *Prufrock and Other Observations* published and Edna St. Vincent Millay's *Renascence and Other Poems* published

▶1919. Sherwood Anderson publishes *Winesburg, Ohio*

▶1920. Sinclair Lewis's *Main Street* published

▶1923. Wallace Stevens's *Harmonium* and William Carlos Williams's *Spring and All* published

▶1925. Theodore Dreiser's *An American Tragedy,* F. Scott Fitzgerald's *The Great Gatsby,* and Ezra Pound's *The Cantos (I)* published

▶1926. Ernest Hemingway's *The Sun Also Rises* and Langston Hughes's *Weary Blues* published

1922. James Joyce publishes *Ulysses*

▶1922. T. S. Eliot's *The Wasteland* published

1930. Virginia Woolf's *A Room of One's Own*

▶1930. Katherine Ann Porter's *Flowering Judas*

▶1931. Henry Miller's *Tropic of Cancer* and Pearl Buck's *The Good Earth* published

▶1932. William Faulkner's *Light in August*

▶1933. Gertrude Stein's *The Autobiography of Alice B. Toklas*

▶1934. F. Scott Fitzgerald's *Tender Is the Night* published

| **1920** | **1925** | **1930** | **1935** |

▶1916. President Wilson reelected

▶1917. U.S. declares war on Germany

1917. Bolshevik revolution in Russia

1918. Armistice signed

1919. Versailles Peace Conference

▶1919. Prohibition begins

▶1920. Warren G. Harding elected president

1921. Southern Ireland gains dominion status

1922. Benito Mussolini heads fascist Italy

▶1923. President Harding dies; Calvin Coolidge succeeds

▶1924. President Coolidge reelected

▶1929. Stock market collapses; Great Depression begins

▶1928. Herbert Hoover elected president

▶1932. Franklin D. Roosevelt elected president

1933. Adolf Hitler becomes dictator of Germany

▶1934. Prohibition ends

Edith Wharton

The Jazz Age and the New York Literary Scene

Increasingly during the 1920s, the so-called **Jazz Age,** conflicts developed between older, conservative people and a materially prosperous but alienated younger generation. Young people demonstrated their rebelliousness by flaunting Prohibition, the law passed in 1919 that prohibited the manufacture or sale of alcohol, and by frequenting "speak-easies" or "juke joints" and listening to jazz music. This was the era of the flapper, the Charleston, goldfish-swallowing college students in raccoon coats, and the gangster.

Rebelliousness among young people also affected the literary scene in New York City. New York was a literary center, the home of a number of publishing houses, newspapers, and magazines. **Edith Wharton** chronicled the breakdown of the traditional ways of life of the wealthy citizens of old New York in such novels as *The Age of Innocence,* written in 1920. In the 1920s and 1930s, New York became a center for avant-garde, bohemian writers, artists, and intellectuals, many of whom lived and worked in the area of lower Manhattan known as Greenwich Village. Here **Eugene O'Neill's** plays were produced by the Greenwich Village Theatre and **Thomas Wolfe** wrote his most famous novel, *Look Homeward, Angel.* During the twenties, thirties, and forties, a group of New York writers and artists, including the humorists **Dorothy Parker** and **Robert Benchley** and the playwright **George S. Kaufman,** met regularly in the dining room of the Algonquin Hotel, forming what has become known as the **Algonquin Round Table.**

The Great Depression and Thirties Radicalism

In 1925, the chief chronicler of the Jazz Age, **F. Scott Fitzgerald,** produced a novel, *The Great Gatsby,* replete with disillusionment and ambivalence about the morality of the ideal "self-made man" in American society. After the financial collapse of 1929, which initiated the period known as the **Great Depression,** many other writers would take such moral and ethi-

LITERARY EVENTS

► = American Events

►1947. James Michener's *Tales of the South Pacific*

►1948. Truman Capote's *Other Voices, Other Rooms* published

►1949. Arthur Miller publishes *Death of a Salesman*

►1945. Tennessee Williams's *The Glass Menagerie* published

►1954. Wallace Stevens publishes *Collected Poems*

►1953. James Baldwin's *Go Tell It on the Mountain,* Karl Shapiro's *Poems, 1940–1953,* Theodore Roethke's *The Waking,* and Ralph Ellison's *Invisible Man* published

►1952. Ernest Hemingway publishes *The Old Man and the Sea*

►1951. J. D. Salinger's *The Catcher in the Rye* published

1940	1945	1950	1955	1960

HISTORICAL EVENTS

1936. World War II begins in Europe

►1941. Japanese attack Pearl Harbor; U.S. enters Word War II

►1942. Japanese Americans placed in internment camps

►1944. D-Day invasion; President Roosevelt reelected

►1945. President Roosevelt dies; Harry S Truman succeeds

1945. Atomic bombs dropped on Hiroshima and Nagasaki; World War II ends

►1948. President Truman elected

►1950. U.N. sends troops to South Korea

►1952. Dwight D. Eisenhower elected president

1953. Truce in Korea

►1954. Supreme Court rules racial segregation unconstitutional

►1955. Montgomery bus boycott

►1956. President Eisenhower reelected

cal questioning further, examining basic American ideals of individualism and free market capitalism. During the twenties and thirties, many American writers adopted socialist or communist ideals based on the theories of **Karl Marx**, the German political theorist who argued that the exploitation of workers would lead to the collapse of capitalism and to the establishment of states in which workers controlled the means of production. To many, the Great Depression, which put millions of Americans out of work, seemed proof that the unbridled capitalism of millionaire industrialists, such as **Andrew Carnegie**, **J. P. Morgan**, and **John D. Rockefeller**, offered little hope for the average worker. In the midst of the Great Depression, hunger, labor unrest in the cities, union organizing, and anarchist bombings seemed to indicate that the United States was headed toward a socialist revolution. That such a revolution did not occur can be attributed to later disillusionment with the totalitarian turn of the Russian communist state under Joseph Stalin, to cyclical economic recovery, and to President **Franklin D. Roosevelt's New Deal** policies, which provided Social Security, welfare, unemployment insurance, and federally funded jobs. In Oklahoma in the 1930s, severe droughts that caused the area to be known as the **Great Dust Bowl** added to the effects of the depression, leading to a great migration of workers to California. This story is eloquently told in **John**

Some of the many migrants from the Great Dust Bowl.

Steinbeck's novel *The Grapes of Wrath*. Other critics of American culture in the first half of the century included **Upton Sinclair**, whose book *The Jungle* offered a scathing exposé of the meatpacking industry; **Sinclair Lewis**, whose novels such as *Babbitt* and *Elmer Gantry* depicted the worst excesses of materialism—the hypocrisy and greed of small-town real estate dealers and showman preachers; and **Richard Wright**, whose *Native Son* told of discrimination against African Americans. Many American writers and intellectuals with socialist sympathies fought against fascism in the Spanish Civil War, in 1936–1937, only to turn from socialism on learning of Stalin's brutal purges of political opponents and his treaty with Germany's Adolph Hitler.

THE EXPATRIATES

For some, like Fitzgerald, Hemingway, **Ezra Pound**, **Edna St. Vincent Millay**, **T. S. Eliot**, and Gertrude Stein, the effort to find more authentic beliefs and forms of expression went beyond the United States. In the teens and twenties, a large number of important American writers were living in Paris and London, comprising an identifiable group of **expatriates** that often gathered in salons and cafes to exchange ideas about art, literature, and society. Some of these writers, such as Pound and Eliot, believed the U. S. to be inhospitable to high culture, reflecting a division between popular culture, with its westerns, romances, and adventure stories, and highbrow culture of the kind now referred to as Modernism.

MODERNISM IN AMERICAN LITERATURE

Modernism was an international literary and artistic movement characterized by a rejection of the artistic conventions of the past. As such, it was a response to the perceived

T. S. Eliot

breakdown of modern culture. This breakdown was reflected graphically in the Cubist paintings of **Pablo Picasso, Georges Braque,** and others, who rendered people, places, and objects as stylized, abstract collections of forms such as cubes. In literature, Modernism found expression in many experiments in form, including **free verse,** such as that of T. S. Eliot and E. E. Cummings, and **stream-of-consciousness** prose, such as the novels of **William Faulkner** that presented the unedited thoughts and impressions passing through characters' minds.[2] Stream-of-consciousness writing was one example of the **subjectivism** of Modernist literature, its tendency to treat reality not as absolute and orderly but as depending upon the point of view of the observer. Modernist works tended to be written in the first person, revealing an individual's momentary thoughts, feelings, or perceptions. Paradoxically, this rendering of subjective experience was often done by omitting conventional commentary about the subjective states of characters. The **Imagist** poetry of Ezra Pound, **Amy Lowell, William Carlos Williams, H. D. (Hilda Doolittle),** and others sought to present single moments of sense perception without reference to the emotions or opinions of the author, narrator, or speaker. Williams formulated this aesthetic in a famous phrase, "no ideas but in things." Modernist writing, including the work of Pound, Eliot, and **Wallace Stevens,** tended to be alienated, understated, ironic, impersonal, lacking in transitions between ideas, and full of odd juxtapositions and sophisticated references, or allusions. If Modernism had a credo, it was probably Ezra Pound's "make it new."

Eliot and Pound saw art as a way to order and give coherence to the decay they saw, but most Modernist writers were tentative about the meanings they discovered. **Irony** became a signature technique of Modernist literature, indicating a retreat from a new social vision into the cold comfort of a purely literary or imaginative order. That comfort was usually limited, and much of the writing of this group conveyed a sense of hopelessness.

CHANGES IN THE ROLES OF WOMEN

Although the twenties and thirties were years of turmoil and disillusionment for many, one bright spot was the expanded role of women in American society. In 1920, women won the right to vote. Increasingly, they were able to attain higher education and entered the world of work outside the home. Some of the male writers of the period targeted women's participation in the literary and artistic world as alienating and disorienting and engaged in what some scholars have called a "war of words." A mild example of this is Eliot's narrator in "The Love Song of J. Alfred Prufrock" who mocks these "new women" in the line "In the room, the women come and go, talking of Michelangelo." The women are portrayed as overcasual in their approach to serious art, treating it as small talk.

The increased role of women in the arts and literature is one of the most dramatic changes to occur during the twentieth century. Of course, the United States had already produced some great women writers, from Anne Bradstreet and Phillis Wheatley in the eighteenth century to Emily Dickinson, Sarah Jewett, and Kate Chopin in the nineteenth. However, the twentieth century has been the golden age of American women writers, including Edith Wharton, **Eudora Welty, Kay Boyle, Willa Cather, Katherine Anne Porter, Zora Neale**

---

2. While Faulkner was a Modernist in his radical experiments in form, he was a traditionalist in his upholding of older values and in his concentration on regional subject matter.

Hurston, Amy Lowell, **Marianne Moore**, Edna St. Vincent Millay, **Shirley Jackson**, Dorothy Parker, **Lillian Hellman, Gina Berriault, Elizabeth Bishop, May Swenson, Denise Levertov, Gwendolyn Brooks, Anne Sexton, Sylvia Plath, Lucille Clifton, Nikki Giovanni, Adrienne Rich, Tillie Olsen, Alice Walker, Louise Erdrich, Maxine Kumin, Lorraine Hansberry, Li-Young Lee, Amy Bloom, Joyce Carol Oates, Anne Tyler, Marsha Norman,** and **Beth Henley,** to name but a few.

ALTERNATIVE LITERARY RESPONSES: REGIONALISM AND THE HARLEM RENAISSANCE

Edna St. Vincent Millay

During the twenties and thirties, some writers responded to feelings of discontent and hopelessness by probing for sources of renewal in the United States itself. Though often using ideas and techniques of Modernism, they are distinguished from the Modernists in their use of traditional forms and in their expression of traditional values. Prominent among these writers were various postwar **regionalists**, who wrote an "American" literature about the local, rural areas in which they had settled. Sometimes these writers found strength and hope in their works, other times only what poet **Robert Frost** called "a momentary stay against confusion." Such regional writers included Frost, who wrote deceptively simple verses set in rural New England; **Sherwood Anderson,** who lived in New Orleans and wrote of the people of a mythical *Winesburg, Ohio;* Zora Neal Hurston, who wrote novels about the African-American experience in the rural South; and **John Crow Ransom,** a poet and critic associated with a movement to recapture traditional Southern values. The novels of William Faulkner, though Modernist in their experimentation with plot structure and point of view, were nonetheless traditional in their use of a regional setting (Faulkner's mythical Yoknapatawpha County, Mississippi) and in their espousal of the lost values of an older time.

Another important alternative to the attitude and approach of the expatriate Modernists was the politically committed work of the **Harlem Renaissance** in upper Manhattan in the late teens and twenties. The Harlem Renaissance involved not only an explosion of diversely creative work by black artists, writers, and performers, but also a new direction for literature as a force for creating community. African-American writing at the time was sometimes supported financially by the National Association for the Advancement of Colored People (NAACP), formed earlier in the century, and was part of an organized movement to give expression to the oppression African Americans experienced and to the cultural heritage and traditions they shared. The alienation of the Harlem Renaissance writers differed from that of their white counterparts: they were forced into a "double consciousness," as **W. E. B. Du Bois** had put it in 1903, of the self they knew and the "black" self-image society foisted on them. Alain Locke, in his 1925 book *The New Negro,* envisioned Harlem as a "race capital" where black culture, consciousness, and identity might find adequate social expression and stimulation and serve as a vital source for the future advancement of black people and "a new democracy in American culture." The social purpose behind this movement's literature influenced its choice of techniques and styles, as it sought to reach the entire community, not merely its most highly educated members. Important poets of the Harlem Renaissance include **Langston Hughes, Paul Laurence Dunbar, Countee Cullen, Claude McKay, Arna Bontemps,** and **Jean Toomer.**

WORLD WAR II

Robert Lowell

World War I was supposed to be the war to end all wars. Events at mid-century would show how wrong that notion was. The Great Depression of the 1930s was a worldwide phenomenon, and citizens of several countries in Europe reacted by placing their hopes in the hands of ultranationalist leaders—Francisco Franco in Spain, Benito Mussolini in Italy, and Adolph Hitler in Germany. Expounding mystical, pseudoscientific theories of "racial purity" and a belief that the so-called "Aryan race" was destined to rule the world, Hitler initiated a campaign to conquer Europe, beginning with an invasion of Poland. The United States was reluctant to enter the war, doing so only after Germany's ally, Japan, attacked the American naval base at Pearl Harbor, Hawaii. **World War II** lasted until 1945, when the United States dropped atomic bombs on the Japanese cities of Hiroshima and Nagasaki, and the Allied Forces of the United States, Britain, and France captured the German capital of Berlin. Only after the war did the full extent of the atrocities committed by Hilter's Nazis become known, when it was revealed that Germany had conducted a systematic campaign to exterminate millions of Jews, Gypsies, and others in death camps such as Auschwitz and Buchenwald.

POSTWAR LITERATURE: THE SECOND AMERICAN RENAISSANCE

The period following World War II is sometimes referred to as the Second American Renaissance (the first being the New England Renaissance of the nineteenth century). This was a period of relative prosperity in the United States, punctuated by the beginnings of the Cold War and social and political conservatism in most of the population. It was also a time of great literary creativity. The war itself gave rise to many fine literary works, including Ernest Hemingway's *For Whom the Bell Tolls,* **Norman Mailer's** *The Naked and the Dead,* and **James Jones's** *From Here to Eternity.* Many of the finest American writers of the early to mid-century period were at the height of their powers during this time, including Faulkner, Frost, Eliot, and Stevens. Other great writers who continued to produce superb work in the forties and fifties included John Steinbeck, Katherine Anne Porter, Marianne Moore, E. E. Cummings, William Carlos Williams, Lillian Hellman, and Eugene O'Neill. The postwar period saw a flowering of American drama in work by new dramatists such as **Arthur Miller, Tennessee Williams**, and **William Inge,** as well as new work by established dramatists such as Eugene O'Neill and Lillian Hellman. The period also saw the emergence of important new voices, including those of fiction writers **Robert Penn Warren, James Baldwin, Saul Bellow,** and **Bernard Malamud,** and those of poets Gwendolyn Brooks, **Robert Lowell, Theodore Roethke,** and **Randall Jarrell.**

Echoes:
The Modern Era

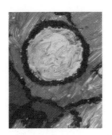

"Literature is news that STAYS news."
—Ezra Pound, from *The ABC of Reading*

"The critic . . . , if he is to justify his existence, should endeavor to discipline his personal prejudices and cranks . . . and compose his differences
with as many of his fellows as possible, in the common pursuit of true
judgment."
—T. S. Eliot, from "The Function of Criticism"

"She ran the whole gamut of emotions from A to B."
—Dorothy Parker, on a performance by an actress

"[L]ove and the imagination
        are of a piece"
—William Carlos Williams,
    coda to "Asphodel, That Greeny Flower"

". . . the old universal truths lacking which any story is ephemeral
and doomed—love and honor and pity and pride and compassion and
sacrifice."
—William Faulkner, from his Nobel Prize
    Acceptance Speech

"Writing free verse is like playing tennis with the net down."
—Robert Frost, from his Speech to the Milton Academy

"My soul has grown deep like the rivers."
—Langston Hughes, from "The Negro Speaks of Rivers"

from *Spoon River Anthology*
"Lucinda Matlock"
"Petit, the Poet"
by Edgar Lee Masters

ABOUT THE AUTHOR

Edgar Lee Masters (1868–1950) was born in Garnett, Kansas, but grew up in two small Illinois towns, Petersburg and Lewiston. Life in such small towns inspired his best-known work, *Spoon River Anthology* (1915). Masters briefly attended Knox College in Galesburg, Illinois; studied law in his father's office; and passed the bar. In 1891, he moved to Chicago, where he worked as a bill collector for the Edison Company until he was able to build a successful law practice. He later formed a law firm in which Clarence Darrow, the great criminal defense lawyer, was a partner. All the while, he was writing poems, having some published and many rejected. When an editor sent him a copy of *Selected Epigrams from the Greek Anthology,* Masters adapted the mode to his work. Harriet Monroe, editor of *Poetry: A Magazine of Verse,* discovered his work in this style and helped him get the work published as *Spoon River Anthology.* The book was an instant and undreamed of success. Masters gave up law and moved to New York City in the 1920s. His writing career included novels, plays, and biographies, but none of his other work ever achieved the recognition of *Spoon River Anthology.*

ABOUT THE SELECTIONS

  "Lucinda Matlock" and "Petit, the Poet" are from *Spoon River Anthology,* a collection of **epitaphs** (verse written to be inscribed on a tomb or to be read in commemoration of someone who has died). The speakers in these poems all address the reader from beyond the grave, telling about the lives that they lived. First serialized in the St. Louis *Mirror* in 1914–1915 under Masters's pseudonym, Webster Ford, these epitaphs tell stories reminiscent of the life stories of people whom Masters knew in Petersburg and Lewiston, Illinois, near the Spoon River. Many of the names that Masters used in his anthology can be found on tombstones in the Lewiston cemetery.

READER'S JOURNAL

Have you ever known someone who lived to be quite old? What attitude toward life did that person express? What advice did that person have? Write about the person in your journal. If you have not known an elderly person well, write about the kind of person you would like to be when you are quite old.

LANGUAGE SKILLS

Read the Language Arts Survey, 2.16, "Verbals: Participles," and 2.17, "Verbals: Gerunds." Then identify some verbs ending in *–ing* in the selection, and note whether each verb is a participle or a gerund.

FROM *SPOON RIVER ANTHOLOGY*

"Lucinda Matlock"

EDGAR LEE MASTERS

I went to the dances at Chandlerville,
And played snap-out[1] at Winchester.
One time we changed partners,
Driving home in the moonlight of middle June,
5 And then I found Davis.
We were married and lived together for seventy years,
Enjoying, working, raising the twelve children,
Eight of whom we lost
Ere[2] I had reached the age of sixty.
10 I spun, I wove, I kept the house, I nursed the sick,
I made the garden, and for holiday
Rambled over the fields where sang the larks,
And by Spoon River gathering many a shell,
And many a flower and medicinal weed—
15 Shouting to the wooded hills, singing to the green valleys.
At ninety-six I had lived enough, that is all,
And passed to a sweet repose.[3]
What is this I hear of sorrow and weariness,
Anger, discontent and drooping hopes?
20 Degenerate sons and daughters,
Life is too strong for you—
It takes life to love Life.

How many children did the speaker have? How many of her children were still living when the speaker turned sixty?

---

1. **snap-out.** Parlor game
2. **Ere.** Before
3. **repose.** Rest

Responding to the Selection

Imagine that you are Lucinda Matlock. Write a letter to your "degenerate sons and daughters," explaining to them your philosophy of life.

Reviewing the Selection

RECALLING

1. Whom does Lucinda marry?

2. What does Lucinda collect near Spoon River?

3. At what age does Lucinda decide that she "had lived enough"?

4. What does Lucinda call her sons and daughters?

INTERPRETING

5. What kind of life does Lucinda have with her husband?

6. Why does Lucinda have to collect medicinal herbs? What tragedies occurred in her life?

7. For what is "sweet repose" a euphemism?

8. Why is life "too strong" for her sons and daughters?

SYNTHESIZING

9. What qualities may have enabled Lucinda to live to be ninety-six?

10. What criticism does Lucinda have of the younger generation? Would she be sympathetic to what younger people consider to be the hardships in their lives? How would she react to people who complain all the time about how difficult their lives are? Why? Why does Lucinda believe that "It takes life to love Life"?

Understanding Literature (Questions for Discussion)

Tone. Tone is the emotional attitude toward the reader or toward the subject implied by a literary work. What tone, or emotional attitude, does Lucinda Matlock express toward weakness and sorrow? What attitude does she express toward life?

Responding in Writing

Epitaph. Think of someone who died within the last ten years. Gather some information about that person. Then write an epitaph to be inscribed on that person's grave. Have the speaker of the epitaph be the dead person, telling about his or her own life.

READER'S JOURNAL

Who is your favorite poet? What attracts you to his or her poetry? Which poems written by this person do you find particularly moving or expressive? Write about your favorite poet and his or her poetry in your journal. (If you do not yet have a favorite poet, look through this anthology until you find a poem that you really like and write about that poem.)

LANGUAGE SKILLS

Read the Language Arts Survey, 2.36, "The Functions of Sentences." Then identify the interrogative sentences in the selection and note what tone the question marks lend to each sentence.

FROM *SPOON RIVER ANTHOLOGY*

"Petit, the Poet"

EDGAR LEE MASTERS

Seeds in a dry pod, tick, tick, tick,
Tick, tick, tick, like mites[1] in a quarrel—
Faint iambics that the full breeze wakens—
But the pine tree makes a symphony thereof.
5   Triolets, villanelles, rondels, rondeaus,
Ballades by the score with the same old thought:
The snows and the roses of yesterday are vanished,
And what is love but a rose that fades?
Life all around me here in the village:
10   Tragedy, comedy, valor[2] and truth,
Courage, constancy, heroism, failure—
All in the loom, and oh what patterns!
Woodlands, meadows, streams and rivers—
Blind to all of it all my life long.
15   Triolets, villanelles, rondels, rondeaus,
Seeds in a dry pod, tick, tick, tick,
Tick, tick, tick, what little iambics,
While Homer and Whitman[3] roared in the pines? ■

To what does the speaker compare life in the village?

---

1. **mites.** Small insects
2. **valor.** Courage
3. **Homer and Whitman.** *Homer*—Ancient Greek poet; *Whitman*—Walt Whitman (1819–1892), American poet, one of the first to write in free verse

Responding to the Selection

Imagine that you are Petit, the poet. What do you admire about the poetry of Homer and Whitman? In your journal, write a letter to the two great poets, telling them what you think about their work.

Reviewing the Selection

RECALLING

1. To what three things does Petit compare his own poetry in lines 1–3?

2. In what different poetic forms did Petit write? What thoughts did his poems express?

INTERPRETING

▶▶ 3. Based on what Petit says about his poetry in lines 1–3, what characteristics would you say that it had?

▶▶ 4. What did Petit ignore as possible subjects for his poetry? What regrets does he have in this regard?

SYNTHESIZING

5. Petit compares the poetry that he wrote to seeds in a dry pod. Such seeds, of course, are not alive and will cause nothing to happen. To what does Petit compare the poetry of Homer and Whitman? In what ways does Petit wish that his verse had been different?

Understanding Literature (Questions for Discussion)

1. **Metaphor.** A **metaphor** is a figure of speech in which one thing is spoken or written about as if it were another. This figure of speech invites the reader to make a comparison between the two things, which can be analyzed into two parts: the *tenor* (or subject being described) and the *vehicle* (or object being used in the description). These two things can be compared because they share a particular quality. Consider the following metaphor from the selection: "While Homer and Whitman roared in the pines?" What is the tenor in this metaphor? What is the vehicle? What qualities do these two things share?

2. **Simile.** A type of metaphor, a **simile** is a comparison using *like* or *as*. Like any other metaphor, a simile can be analyzed into two parts, the *tenor* and the *vehicle*. Consider the following simile from the selection: "Seeds in a dry pod, tick, tick, tick,/Tick, tick, tick, like mites in a quarrel." What is the tenor of the simile? What is the vehicle? What quality do these two things share?

3. **Iamb and Iambic.** An **iamb** is a poetic foot made up of one weakly stressed syllable followed by one strongly stressed syllable, as in the word *afraid*. A line of poetry made up of iambs is said to be **iambic**. Petit describes his poetry as being made up of "faint iambics." With what should Petit have been concerned other than creating poems with regular rhythmical patterns?

Responding in Writing

Ballad. Write a ballad, a simple narrative poem in four-line stanzas that rhyme *abcb,* about someone who has a particular skill or talent, such as a poet, cabinetmaker, gardener, or singer. To what will you compare the person's talent or ability? Use metaphors in your ballad to invite the reader to make comparisons. Refer to the entry on *metaphor* in the Handbook of Literary Terms.

Language Lab

Clichés and Euphemisms. Read the Language Arts Survey, 2.152, "Clichés and Euphemisms." Then rewrite the following sentences, replacing the clichés and euphemisms.

1. Martin whispered to Yolanda, "Love is like a red, red rose."

2. The minister told Sasha that time heals all wounds.

3. Paula looked out the window and saw that it was raining cats and dogs.

4. After chopping a cord of firewood, Jason felt dog tired.

5. Deidre's mother was determined to look on the bright side of the situation.

Thinking Skills

Comparing and Contrasting. Read the Language Arts Survey, 4.8, "Comparing and Contrasting." Then, make two columns on a piece of paper, one headed *Petit* and the other headed *Homer and Whitman.* To the left of the columns, write *Compare* and then under that, write *Contrast.* Draw lines across your page starting under each of these two words. List the characteristics of each poet within the boxes of the chart you have created with these four headings.

PROJECT

Circle Poetry Reading. Select a poem from *Spoon River Anthology* for each person in the class. Then sit in a circle and take turns reading aloud the epitaphs. As you read, try to imagine yourself as the speaker of the poem. As you listen, try to draw conclusions about the speaker's character from what he or she has to say. Ask yourself, each time, What lesson did this person learn from his or her life?

"Mr. Flood's Party"
by Edwin Arlington Robinson

ABOUT THE AUTHOR

Edwin Arlington Robinson (1869–1935) was raised in the small town of Gardiner, Maine—a community he renamed "Tilbury Town" in some of his best poetry. A lonely child, Robinson's feelings of alienation followed him into maturity. He once wrote to a friend, "What strength I have is the result of tedious and almost intolerable isolation." Poor self-esteem plagued Robinson all of his life and was not eased when lack of funds forced him to drop out of Harvard. Then, depending on handouts to support himself as a poet, Robinson went into seclusion, feeling he had failed himself and his friends and family. In 1910, in spite of his pessimistic style, Robinson achieved critical acclaim with a fourth volume of poetry, *The Town Down the River.* His trilogy of long narrative poems based on the legends of King Arthur— *Merlin, Lancelot,* and *Tristram*—led to wider understanding of his work. During the 1920s, Robinson was a three-time winner of the Pulitzer Prize. Sometimes described as a "bridge" poet, Robinson's work reflects much of the traditional form of the nineteenth century, yet dwells on the problems of the inner self, which is more in keeping with twenti-eth-century styles.

ABOUT THE SELECTION

Psychological exploration of character is a central element in Robinson's longer narrative poems. In **"Mr. Flood's Party,"** the focus is on the character Eben Flood, an aging man who, in his loneliness, makes a party for one and engages in a dialogue with himself.

"Mr. Flood's Party"

EDWIN ARLINGTON ROBINSON

Old Eben Flood, climbing alone one night
Over the hill between the town below
And the forsaken upland hermitage[1]
That held as much as he should ever know
5   On earth again of home, paused warily.
The road was his with not a native near;
And Eben, having leisure, said aloud,
For no man else in Tilbury Town to hear:

"Well, Mr. Flood, we have the harvest moon
10   Again, and we may not have many more;
The bird is on the wing, the poet says.[2]
And you and I have said it here before.
Drink to the bird." He raised up to the light
The jug that he had gone so far to fill,
15   And answered huskily: "Well, Mr. Flood,
Since you propose it, I believe I will."

What time of year is it? What two signs tell you?

To whom is Eben Flood speaking?

---

1. **upland hermitage.** Retreat house on a hill; monastery
2. **The bird . . . the poet says.** Flood may be thinking of these lines from *The Rubáiyát* by Omar Khayyám: "Come, fill the Cup . . . . The bird of Time has but a little way/To fly—and Lo! the Bird is on the Wing." He might also be thinking, ironically, of these lines from Robert Browning's verse play *Pippa Passes:* "The lark's on the wing;/The snail's on the thorn:/God's in his heaven—/All's right with the world!"

Alone, as if enduring to the end
A valiant armor of scarred hopes outworn,
He stood there in the middle of the road
20 Like Roland's ghost winding a silent horn.[3]
Below him, in the town among the trees,
Where friends of other days had honored him,
A phantom salutation of the dead
Rang thinly till old Eben's eyes were dim.

25 Then, as a mother lays her sleeping child
Down tenderly, fearing it may awake,
He set the jug down slowly at his feet
With trembling care, knowing that most things break;
And only when assured that on firm earth
30 It stood, as the uncertain lives of men
Assuredly did not, he paced away,
And with his hand extended paused again:

"Well, Mr. Flood, we have not met like this
In a long time; and many a change has come
35 To both of us, I fear, since last it was
We had a drop together. Welcome home!"
Convivially returning with himself,
Again he raised the jug up to the light;
And with an acquiescent quaver said:
40 "Well, Mr Flood, if you insist, I might.

"Only a very little, Mr. Flood—
For auld lang syne.[4] No more, sir; that will do."
So, for the time, apparently it did,
And Eben evidently thought so too;

---

3. **Roland's . . . horn.** The line is an allusion to the
Christian martyr/soldier Roland, hero of the medieval
French epic poem *The Song of Roland*, who failed to blow
his horn to call Charlemagne and his troops to come to
his aid in battle.

4. **auld lang syne.** In Scottish dialect, these words
mean, literally, "old long since." The phrase is from a
song about remembered friendship by Robert Burns, the
national poet of Scotland. This song is traditionally sung
in English-speaking countries on New Year's Day.

WORDS FOR
EVERYDAY USE:

con • viv • i • al • ly (kən viv´ē əl lē) *adv.*, festively
ac • qui • es • cent (ak´wē es´ənt) *adj.*, without protest

45   For soon amid the silver loneliness
     Of night he lifted up his voice and sang,
     Secure, with only two moons listening,
     Until the whole harmonious landscape rang—

     "For auld lang syne." The weary throat gave out;
50   The last word wavered, and the song was done.
     He raised again the jug regretfully
     And shook his head, and was again alone.
     There was not much that was ahead of him,
     And there was nothing in the town below—
55   Where strangers would have shut the many doors
     That many friends had opened long ago.

What double meaning does this line have?

Responding to the Selection

How did you feel toward Flood after reading the poem? What makes this poem both funny and sad?

Reviewing the Selection

RECALLING

1. Where is Flood going and at what time? To whom does Flood speak?

2. What line from a poem does Flood quote in stanza 2?

3. What does Flood know about "most things"?

4. With whom does Flood hold a party? What song does he sing? Whom does he welcome home?

INTERPRETING

5. Why is he talking to himself? In what sense does he have leisure?

6. What does Flood not expect to have many more of? What, in addition to the bird, is "on the wing"?

7. How does Flood feel about life?

8. Under what circumstances do people normally sing "Auld Lang Syne"? What do the words *auld lang syne* mean? Why is this a sad situation?

SYNTHESIZING

9. What circumstances in the poem cause the reader or listener to feel empathy for Flood?

10. Why does Flood engage in a dialogue with himself and sing "Auld Lang Syne"?

Understanding Literature (Questions for Discussion)

1. **Simile. A simile** is a comparison using *like* or *as*. A type of metaphor, a simile can be analyzed into two parts, the *tenor* (or subject being described) and the *vehicle* (or object being used in the description). The two parts of a simile can be compared because they share some particular quality. Consider the following lines from the poem: "Alone, as if enduring to the end/A valiant armor of scarred hopes outworn,/He stood there in the middle of the road/Like Roland's ghost winding a silent horn." Identify and analyze the parts of each of the two similes contained within these lines. In the medieval French poem *The Song of Roland,* Roland is a warrior who has a horn for the purpose of summoning the aid of other warriors. What causes Flood to look like Roland? What makes the comparison of Flood with a young medieval warrior hero ironic?

2. **Allusion.** An **allusion** is a rhetorical technique in which reference is made to a person, event, object, or work from history or literature. This poem makes an allusion to Robert Burns's song "Auld Lang Syne," the opening lines of which read as follows:

    > Should auld acquaintance be forgot
    >   And never brought to mind?
    > Should auld acquaintance be forgot
    >   And days of auld lang syne.

    How do these lines from the song by Burns relate to Flood's experience on the hill?

Responding in Writing

Toast. Imagine that you are Flood standing on the hill, looking down at Tilbury Town. Write a toast, from Flood's point of view, in honor of the many friends who, long ago, had opened "the many doors" to you.

Language Lab

Expanding Sentences. Read the Language Arts Survey, 2.46–2.50, on expanding sentences. Then expand each of the following sentences by adding modifiers, prepositional phrases, appositives, predicates, or subordinate clauses.

1. Eben Flood walked to the top of the hill.

2. He looked down at Tilbury Town.

3. The harvest moon overhead symbolized not only the decline of the year but also the decline of Flood's life.

4. Flood drank a toast.

5. He remembered his friends.

"Grass"
by Carl Sandburg

ABOUT THE AUTHOR

Carl Sandburg (1878–1967) was born in Galesburg, Illinois, the son of an immigrant Swedish blacksmith. He is often considered the poet of America's common people. During his life he was a populist, journalist, folk singer, poet, and biographer. Sandburg left school after the eighth grade and held a variety of jobs until he was twenty, when he enlisted as a volunteer in the Spanish-American War. When he came home, he attended Lombard College in Illinois but left in 1902 without graduating. His poems were first published in 1904, the year he began his journalism career at the Galesburg newspaper. In 1914, some of his poems were published in the magazine *Poetry*, and two years later, his first book of verse was published. During these years he held a variety of political jobs and wrote editorials for the *Milwaukee Leader* and other newspapers. He wrote for the *Chicago Daily News* from 1922 to 1930. Sandburg collected and wrote songs as well as poems and as a young man had traveled the United States reading his work and singing his songs to the accompaniment of a guitar. After World War II, he took his readings to the college campus circuit. He was awarded two Pulitzer Prizes, one for his *Complete Poems* (1950), and the other for his biography *Abraham Lincoln: The War Years* (1939). In later years, Sandburg enjoyed extraordinary acclaim. Several schools in Illinois were named for him, and he was awarded the Presidential Medal of Freedom in 1964. Sandburg wrote several children's stories. In addition to these and his books of biography, his works include *Chicago Poems* (1914), *Cornhuskers* (1918), *Smoke and Steel* (1920), *Slabs of the Sunburnt West* (1922), and *The People, Yes* (1936). Sandburg also compiled collections of folk songs, most notably *The American Songbag* (1927).

ABOUT THE SELECTION

Although he participated in the Spanish-American War, Sandburg hated warfare. The following simple poem, **"Grass,"** is one of the most eloquent antiwar poems ever written, all the more so because of its simplicity. The poem **alludes**, or refers, to several battlefields—Austerlitz and Waterloo from the Napoleonic Wars, Gettysburg from the American Civil War, and Ypres and Verdun from World War I.

READER'S JOURNAL

Why do people visit old battlefields? Why are battlefields often set aside for future generations to visit? What kinds of feelings do people have when they visit old battlefields? Write about these questions in your journal.

LANGUAGE SKILLS

Read the Language Arts Survey, 2.121, on the capitalization of place names. Then, as you read the poem, copy the capitalized place names that you find.

"*Grass*"

CARL SANDBURG

What work does the grass do?

Pile the bodies high at Austerlitz and Waterloo.[1]
Shovel them under and let me work—
        I am the grass; I cover all.

    And pile them high at Gettysburg[2]
5   And pile them high at Ypres and Verdun.[3]
Shovel them under and let me work.
Two years, ten years; and passengers ask the conductor:
        What place is this?
        Where are we now?

10   I am the grass.
        Let me work. ■

---

1. **Austerlitz and Waterloo.** Northern European battle sites in the Napoleonic Wars
2. **Gettysburg.** Civil War battlefield in southern Pennsylvania where Confederate soldiers fought and lost
3. **Ypres and Verdun.** World War I battle sites in northern France where French soldiers fought and lost

Responding to the Selection

In this poem the grass covers over places of death, hiding the horrors of war. Do you think the grass is hiding human atrocities or is it part of a healing process? Discuss your opinion with your classmates.

Reviewing the Selection

RECALLING

1. Who is speaking in this poem? What is the speaker saying?

2. What do the passengers ask the conductor? When?

INTERPRETING

3. What work does the grass do?

4. What change occurs on the battlefields, over time, as a result of the work of the grass?

SYNTHESIZING

5. It is often said about soldiers and the battles in which they fight that they will be remembered forever. Does the speaker of this poem agree? Why, or why not? What indication does this poem give that soldiers' deaths are a terrible waste? Do you agree with the attitude toward soldiers and battles expressed by the speaker of this poem? Why, or why not?

Understanding Literature (Questions for Discussion)

1. **Personification. Personification** is a figure of speech in which an idea, animal, or thing is described as if it were a person. What is personified in this poem? What does that personified thing have to say? What is the work that it performs?

2. **Parallelism. Parallelism** is a rhetorical technique in which a writer emphasizes the equal value or weight of two or more ideas by expressing them in the same grammatical form. Identify instances of parallelism in this poem.

Responding in Writing

1. **Free Verse Poem. Free verse** is poetry that avoids use of regular rhyme, rhythm, meter, or division into stanzas. Write a free verse poem that expresses your feelings about an important issue facing people today.

2. **Slogan.** Many famous battles have been commemorated by slogans such as "Remember the Alamo." A slogan is simply a brief, catchy statement. Choose a cause that you feel strongly about and write a slogan to support that cause.

"Mending Wall"
"Home Burial"
by Robert Frost

ABOUT THE AUTHOR

Robert Frost (1874–1963) was without question the most popular American poet of the twentieth century. He was born in San Francisco and lived there until the age of eleven, when his father died. After that, Frost and his mother moved to New England. Frost graduated at the top of his high school class, sharing the position of valedictorian with Elinor White, whom he later married. At the age of seventeen, he published his first poem. After marrying Elinor, he continued to hold miscellaneous jobs and to write poetry, briefly going to Harvard as a special student before settling as a teacher at Pinkerton Academy in 1906. In 1912, Frost took his family to England, and it was there that his poetry first found a major audience with the publication of *A Boy's Will* (1913) and *North of Boston* (1914). Frost returned to the United States and began to achieve financial stability from the sale of his books. He taught and lectured at various colleges, including Dartmouth, Amherst, and Harvard. He was awarded Pulitzer Prizes in 1924, 1931, 1937, and 1943 and received honorary degrees from many universities. In 1961, he was invited to read a poem at the inauguration of John F. Kennedy, thirty-fifth president of the United States. Frost's many popular works, most of which deal with New England subject matter, include *Mountain Interval* (1916), *New Hampshire* (1923), *West-Running Brook* (1928), *A Way Out* (1929), *A Witness Tree* (1942), and *In the Clearing* (1962).

ABOUT THE SELECTIONS

Robert Frost had a rare talent that enabled him to produce poetry simple and clear enough to appeal to a large audience and yet intellectually rich enough to appeal to sophisticated literary critics. Frost wrote often of the nature and people of his adopted home of New England. He wrote in the language of ordinary speech and didn't care for modern free verse, which he likened to "playing tennis without a net." Instead, he wrote in conventional forms, including **blank verse** made up of unrhymed iambic pentameter lines, as in **"Mending Wall"** and **"Home Burial."** (An iambic pentameter line has ten alternating weakly stressed and strongly stressed syllables.) Many of Frost's finest poems such as "Home Burial" and "The Death of the Hired Man," in the Selections for Additional Reading on page 602, are **dramatic monologues** or **dramatic dialogues.** Such poems present a dramatic interaction in which one or two people speak.

"Mending Wall"

ROBERT FROST

Something there is that doesn't love a wall,
That sends the frozen-ground-swell[1] under it,
And spills the upper boulders in the sun,
And makes gaps even two can pass abreast.
5   The work of hunters is another thing:
I have come after them and made repair
Where they have left not one stone on a stone,
But they would have the rabbit out of hiding,
To please the yelping dogs. The gaps I mean,
10   No one has seen them made or heard them made,
But spring mending-time we find them there.
I let my neighbor know beyond the hill;
And on a day we meet to walk the line
And set the wall between us once again.
15   We keep the wall between us as we go.
To each the boulders that have fallen to each.
And some are loaves and some so nearly balls
We have to use a spell to make them balance:
"Stay where you are until our backs are turned!"
20   We wear our fingers rough with handling them.
Oh, just another kind of outdoor game.
One on a side. It comes to little more;
There where it is we do not need the wall:
He is all pine and I am apple orchard.
25   My apple trees will never get across

What do the speaker and his neighbor do together?

---

1. **frozen-ground-swell.** Winter ground heaves

And eat the cones under his pines, I tell him.
He only says, "Good fences make good neighbors."
Spring is the mischief in me, and I wonder
If I could put a notion in his head:
30   "*Why* do they make good neighbors? Isn't it
Where there are cows? But here there are no cows.
Before I built a wall I'd ask to know
What I was walling in or walling out,
And to whom I was like to give offense.
35   Something there is that doesn't love a wall,
That wants it down." I could say "Elves" to him,
But it's not elves exactly, and I'd rather
He said it for himself. I see him there
Bringing a stone grasped firmly by the top
40   In each hand, like an old-stone savage armed.
He moves in darkness as it seems to me,
Not of woods only and the shade of trees.
He will not go behind his father's saying,
And he likes having thought of it so well
45   He says again, "Good fences make good neighbors." ∎

Responding to the Selection

Imagine that you are the speaker in the poem, mending the stone wall with your neighbor. Are you understanding of his position regarding the existence of the wall? Write an entry in your journal expressing your feelings about your neighbor and about the wall.

Reviewing the Selection

RECALLING

1. What is the wall like in the spring?

2. Why does the speaker contact his neighbor? What do they do together?

3. What does the speaker tell his neighbor as they repair the wall? What quote does the speaker's neighbor repeat?

4. What would the speaker like to know before he builds a wall?

INTERPRETING

5. What forces act to tear down the wall?

6. How does the neighbor look to the speaker? What reveals that the speaker doesn't totally trust his neighbor?

7. Why might the neighbor want to have a wall where one is not absolutely necessary? What does the neighbor's desire for a wall tell you about him?

8. Who is being "walled out" in this poem? by whom?

SYNTHESIZING

9. The speaker says, "Something there is that doesn't love a wall." What doesn't?

10. Which person in this poem is more thoughtful and reflective, the speaker or the neighbor? Explain.

Understanding Literature (Questions for Discussion)

1. **Symbol.** A **symbol** is a thing that stands for or represents both itself and something else. For example, a rose is a traditional symbol of love or beauty. What does the wall in this poem symbolize? Why does the speaker question the value of walls?

2. **Character.** A **character** is a figure who participates in the action of a literary work. What sort of person is the neighbor in this poem? What does he look like? How does he respond when the speaker suggests that perhaps a wall is not necessary here? What does this response reveal about the neighbor? Why might the speaker actually want to have a wall between himself and such a person?

3. **Pun.** A **pun** is a play on words. The speaker says, "Before I built a wall I'd ask to know . . . to whom I was like to give offense." What two meanings might be suggested by the word *offense?* What pun might be found in the sound of the word?

Responding in Writing

Dialogue and Debate. Create two characters, one who believes the stone wall should be torn down and one who doesn't. Write a dialogue between the two characters in which they debate the value of the wall.

"Home Burial"[1]

ROBERT FROST

He saw her from the bottom of the stairs
Before she saw him. She was starting down,
Looking back over her shoulder at some fear.
She took a doubtful step and then undid it
5   To raise herself and look again. He spoke
Advancing toward her: "What is it you see
From up there always—for I want to know."
She turned and sank upon her skirts at that,
And her face changed from terrified to dull.
10   He said to gain time: "What is it you see,"
Mounting[2] until she <u>cowered</u> under him.
"I will find out now—you must tell me, dear."
She, in her place, refused him any help
With the least stiffening of her neck and silence.
15   She let him look, sure that he wouldn't see,
Blind creature; and awhile he didn't see.
But at last he murmured, "Oh," and again, "Oh."

"What is it—what?" she said.

---

1. **Home Burial.** Reference to the custom of keeping a
family cemetery on one's property
2. **Mounting.** Climbing

WORDS FOR
EVERYDAY USE:
    cow • er (kou´ər) vi., crouch or shrink back in fear

"Just that I see."

20   "You don't," she challenged. "Tell me what it is."

"The wonder is I didn't see at once.
I never noticed it from here before.
I must be wonted to it[3]—that's the reason.
The little graveyard where my people are!
25   So small the window frames the whole of it.
Not so much larger than a bedroom, is it?
There are three stones of slate and one of marble,
Broad-shouldered little slabs there in the sunlight
On the sidehill. We haven't to mind *those*.
30   But I understand: it is not the stones,
But the child's mound—"

"Don't, don't, don't, don't," she cried.

She withdrew shrinking from beneath his arm
That rested on the banister, and slid downstairs;
35   And turned on him with such a daunting[4] look,
He said twice over before he knew himself:
"Can't a man speak of his own child he's lost?"

"Not you!—Oh, where's my hat? Oh, I don't need it!
I must get out of here. I must get air.—
40   I don't know rightly whether any man can."

"Amy! Don't go to someone else this time.
Listen to me. I won't come down the stairs."
He sat and fixed his chin between his fists.
"There's something I should like to ask you, dear."

45   "You don't know how to ask it."
"Help me, then."

Her fingers moved the latch for all reply.

"My words are nearly always an offense.
I don't know how to speak of anything
50   So as to please you. But I might be taught
I should suppose. I can't say I see how.

---

3. **wonted to it.** Used to it
4. **daunting.** Challenging

What does the speaker see?

Does the speaker think he and his wife should agree to not speak about some things? Why, or why not?

A man must partly give up being a man
With womenfolk. We could have some arrangement
By which I'd bind myself to keep hands off
55   Anything special you're a-mind to name.
Though I don't like such things twixt those that love.
Two that don't love can't live together without them.
But two that do can't live together with them."
She moved the latch a little. "Don't—don't go.
60   Don't carry it to someone else this time.
Tell me about it if it's something human.
Let me into your grief. I'm not so much
Unlike other folks as your standing there
Apart would make me out. Give me my chance.
65   I do think, though, you overdo it a little.
What was it brought you up to think it the thing
To take your mother-loss of a first child
So inconsolably—in the face of love.
You'd think his memory might be satisfied—"

70   "There you go sneering now!"

                        "I'm not, I'm not!
You make me angry. I'll come down to you.
God, what a woman! And it's come to this,
A man can't speak of his own child that's dead."

75   "You can't because you don't know how to speak.
If you had any feelings, you that dug
With your own hand—how could you?—his little grave;
I saw you from that very window there,
Making the gravel leap and leap in air,
80   Leap up, like that, like that, and land so lightly
And roll back down the mound beside the hole.
I thought, Who is that man? I didn't know you.
And I crept down the stairs and up the stairs
To look again, and still your spade kept lifting.
85   Then you came in. I heard your rumbling voice
Out in the kitchen, and I don't know why,
But I went near to see with my own eyes.
You could sit there with the stains on your shoes
Of the fresh earth from your own baby's grave
90   And talk about your everyday concerns.
You had stood the spade up against the wall
Outside there in the entry, for I saw it."

"I shall laugh the worst laugh I ever laughed.
I'm cursed. God, if I don't believe I'm cursed."

Why does the speaker feel bitter?

95   "I can repeat the very words you were saying:
        'Three foggy mornings and one rainy day
        Will rot the best birch fence a man can build.'
        Think of it, talk like that at such a time!
        What had how long it takes a birch to rot
100   To do with what was in the darkened parlor?
        You *couldn't* care! The nearest friends can go
        With anyone to death, comes so far short
        They might as well not try to go at all.
        No, from the time when one is sick to death,
105   One is alone, and he dies more alone.
        Friends make pretense of following to the grave,
        But before one is in it, their minds are turned
        And making the best of their way back to life
        And living people, and things they understand.
110   But the world's evil. I won't have grief so
        If I can change it. Oh, I won't, I won't!"

Why does Amy think friends might as well not go?

        "There, you have said it all and you feel better.
        You won't go now. You're crying. Close the door.
        The heart's gone out of it: why keep it up?
115   Amy! There's someone coming down the road!"

        "*You*—oh, you think the talk is all. I must go—
        Somewhere out of this house. How can I make you—"

Where does the speaker think his wife is going? Why?

        "If—you—do!" She was opening the door wider.
        "Where do you mean to go? First tell me that.
120   I'll follow and bring you back by force. I *will!*—" ■

Responding to the Selection

Imagine that you are either the wife or husband in this poem. Why would you be unable to understand your spouse's way of expressing his or her grief? What comfort or consolation would you seek from your spouse? Write an entry in your journal expressing your feelings about the death of your child.

Reviewing the Selection

1. What does he see "Before she saw him"?

2. What kind of "creature" does the wife think her husband is?

3. What are the husband's words "nearly always" to his wife?

4. What does the wife "carry to someone else"?

5. How might the wife's actions have been different if she had seen her husband watching her?

6. Why does the wife challenge the husband to tell her what he sees?

7. With what does the husband ask for his wife's help?

8. What is the husband's defense against his grief?

9. What is the husband desperately trying to avoid?

10. What differences exist in how the husband and wife express their grief about the death of their infant son? How has the death of their child ruptured their marriage?

Understanding Literature (Questions for Discussion)

1. **Metaphor.** A **metaphor** is a figure of speech in which one thing is spoken or written about as if it were another. Consider the following lines in the poem: "I can repeat the very words you were saying:/'Three foggy mornings and one rainy day/Will rot the best birch fence a man can build.'" How are these lines an expression of the man's sense of loss? Does his wife understand that they are such an expression? What does she think that they mean? What has happened to the communication between this man and woman? If you were a therapist attempting to help this couple to deal with the death of their child, what advice would you give each person about communicating effectively with the other?

2. **Diction and Tone.** **Diction,** when applied to writing, refers to word choice. Much of a writer's style or voice is determined by his or her diction, the types of words that are chosen, whether formal or informal, simple or complex, contemporary or archaic, ordinary or unusual, standard or dialectical. **Tone** is the emotional attitude toward the reader or toward the subject implied by a literary work. Consider the following lines from the poem: "I saw you from that very window there,/Making the gravel leap and leap in air,/Leap up, like that, like that, and land so lightly/And roll back down the mound beside the hole." How would you describe the diction in these lines? How does the diction match with the character of the wife? What tone or emotional attitude toward the husband does the wife express in these lines? What effect do the repetitions within these lines have on the tone?

Responding in Writing

Critical Analysis. The two characters in this poem have very different ways of responding to grief and consequently fail to understand one another. Write a critical analysis contrasting the ways in which these characters deal with their grief and explaining why they do not understand one another.

Language Lab

Building Sentences. Read the Language Arts Survey, 2.36, "The Functions of Sentences." Then, decide what the function is of each of the following sentences from the selection. Write the classification of each sentence.

1. He saw her from the bottom of the stairs/Before she saw him.
2. "Tell me what it is."
3. "Can't a man speak of his own child he's lost?"
4. "I don't know how to speak of anything/So as to please you."
5. "There you go sneering now!"

Speaking and Listening Skills

Nonverbal Communication. Read the Language Arts Survey, 3.3, "Elements of Nonverbal Communication." Then, describe how each emotion listed below might be communicated through eye contact, facial expressions, gestures, body language, or proximity.

1. loneliness
2. grief
3. frustration
4. alienation

PROJECT

Dramatic Skit. Collaborate with one other student to write a dramatic scene based on this poem. In your scene, portray the characters of the husband and wife (and the failed communication between them) as they are portrayed in the poem. Write two parts and have one person play the husband and the other play the wife. Rehearse your skit and present it to the rest of the class.

"The Snow Man"
"Anecdote of the Jar"
"Thirteen Ways of Looking at a Blackbird"
by Wallace Stevens

ABOUT THE AUTHOR

Wallace Stevens (1879–1955) was born and raised in Reading, Pennsylvania. His day-to-day life was conventional to a fault. After spending three years at Harvard, he went to work for the *New York Herald Tribune,* but not liking this work, he left and went to the New York Law School. He was admitted to the bar in 1904 and maintained a private law practice until 1908, when he joined the legal staff of an insurance company. In 1916, he joined the Hartford Accident and Indemnity Company and moved to Hartford, Connecticut. In 1934, he was made a vice president of the company, a position he held until his death. Few of his colleagues knew that he wrote poetry. Five years before his death, he told a reporter, "It gives a man character as a poet to have this daily contact with a job." Stevens began writing poetry in high school and had some of his poetry published in the *Harvard Advocate.* His debut in a larger arena began, however, with the publication of some of his work in the magazine *Poetry* in 1914. *Harmonium,* his first volume, was published in 1923. While he lived in New York, Stevens was briefly involved in literary circles, but he dropped out of these after moving to Hartford. Unlike other poets of the time, he was not interested in political and social causes, so although he maintained an active correspondence with some literary figures like William Carlos Williams and Marianne Moore, his work as a poet did not drive the course of his life. His *Collected Poems* (1954) won a Pulitzer Prize and the National Book Award. Among his other works are *Ideas of Order* (1935), *The Man with the Blue Guitar* (1937), *Parts of a World* (1942), and *The Auroras of Autumn* (1950).

ABOUT THE SELECTIONS

These three selections were published in Stevens's first book of poems, *Harmonium,* which includes some of his finest work. The poems, while very different in subject matter, all treat a common theme, found in much of Stevens's poetry: the nature of perception and its relationship to the imagination. The first poem, **"The Snow Man,"** deals with what is known as the pathetic fallacy, the tendency of people to interpret nature in human ways and attribute to it human feelings and motivations. The second, **"Anecdote of the Jar,"** shows how even the simplest of human actions tends to bring order and form into the world. (The artist's job is, of course, to give order, shape, and meaning to things.) The third, **"Thirteen Ways of Looking at a Blackbird,"** shows how the same object of perception, in this case a blackbird, can yield different meanings, depending on the attitude and imagination of the perceiver.

"The Snow Man"

WALLACE STEVENS

One must have a mind of winter
To regard the frost and the boughs
Of the pine-trees crusted with snow;

5   And have been cold a long time
To behold the junipers shagged with ice,
The spruces rough in the distant glitter

Of the January sun; and not to think
Of any misery in the sound of the wind,
In the sound of a few leaves,

10   Which is the sound of the land
Full of the same wind
That is blowing in the same bare place

For the listener, who listens in the snow,
And, nothing himself, beholds
15   Nothing that is not there and the nothing that is. ■

What must one have in order to observe winter and not think of misery "in the sound of the wind"?

What is the "sound of the land"?

Responding to the Selection

Imagine that you are experiencing the scene described in the opening lines of this poem: the frost, the boughs of pine trees crusted with snow, the junipers shagged with ice, the distant January sun, and the sounds of the wind and the few leaves. How would this scene make you feel? How do you differ from the snowman?

Reviewing the Selection

RECALLING

1. What time of year does this poem describe? What details are used in the description of the poem's setting?

2. What kind of mind does the speaker say a person must have not to think that there is misery in the sound of the wind and the leaves?

INTERPRETING

3. How do the details of the setting of this poem make you feel?

4. What characteristics would a "mind of winter" have? (Hint: Think about the characteristics of winter—the coldness, the numbness, the lack of life. What would a mind that is like winter be like?)

SYNTHESIZING

5. What does the poem say that the snowman is? What does the snowman behold? How do people differ from the snowman? What comment is the speaker making about the differences between people and objects in nature?

Understanding Literature (Questions for Discussion)

Pathetic Fallacy. The **pathetic fallacy** is the tendency of people to attribute human emotions and motivations to things in nature. Consider this small poem:

Other People's Sorrow

In its extremity,
on the farthest hill,
the willow weeps
alone.

—Robin Lamb

In this poem, a willow tree is imagined as being in some extremity, as weeping, and as being alone. The title of the poem invites the reader to compare the isolation of the willow to the isolation of a person who is feeling sorrow. How does Stevens's depiction of the snowman differ from Lamb's depiction of the willow? What do people sometimes see in nature that is not there, according to "The Snow Man"? In what sense is there "nothing" in nature until it is perceived by a human being?

"Anecdote of the Jar"

WALLACE STEVENS

I placed a jar in Tennessee,[1]
And round it was, upon a hill.
It made the slovenly wilderness
Surround that hill.

5   The wilderness rose up to it,
And sprawled around, no longer wild.
The jar was round upon the ground
And tall and of a port in air.

It took dominion everywhere.
10   The jar was gray and bare.
It did not give of bird or bush,
Like nothing else in Tennessee. ∎

What effect does the jar have on the wilderness?

---

1. **Tennessee.** The speaker is not describing the real Tennessee but rather an imagined wilderness, what Tennessee was like before human beings came there. The actual Tennessee has not been a complete wilderness for a long, long time. Even the name *Tennessee* comes from that of a large Cherokee settlement, Tenasi, that existed before the coming of Europeans to North America.

Responding to the Selection

How does the wild, natural place described in the poem differ after a jar is placed there? How does a completely untouched natural place differ from one that shows the impact of humans? What does this difference tell you about human beings?

Reviewing the Selection

RECALLING

1. What makes the "slovenly wilderness/Surround that hill"?

2. What shape and color is the jar?

INTERPRETING

3. How does the jar make the wilderness "no longer wild"?

4. In what way is the jar like "nothing else in Tennessee"?

SYNTHESIZING

5. What relationship between the jar and the landscape is described in the poem? What effect does the speaker perceive the jar to have upon the landscape?

Understanding Literature (Questions for Discussion)

Anecdote. An **anecdote** is a brief story, usually with a specific point or moral. The title of the selection identifies the subject of the poem as an anecdote about the jar. Does the selection contain a moral? What is the specific point of the selection? What does the poem tell us about the effects of human activity, about human nature, and about human perceptions?

Responding in Writing

Myth. Imagine that civilization has collapsed and that a few human beings are left. A couple hundred years later, one of the surviving human beings finds the jar placed on a hill in a wilderness area in Tennessee. Imagine that you are the human being who finds the jar. Write a brief myth that explains the presence of the jar and the purpose that it serves or once served. Let your imagination go to create a really fantastic story around this lowly object. Refer to the discussion of *myth* in the Handbook of Literary Terms.

READER'S JOURNAL

What thoughts and feelings do you associate with blackbirds? Why do you think Alfred Hitchcock used blackbirds in his film about birds that turn malevolent and attack people? Freewrite about blackbirds in your journal. Share your freewriting with classmates, and discuss their thoughts and feelings.

LANGUAGE SKILLS

Read the Language Arts Survey, 2.138 and 2.139, "Using Context Clues I and II." Then identify some words in the selection that are unfamiliar to you and use context clues to decipher their meanings.

"Thirteen Ways of Looking at a Blackbird"

WALLACE STEVENS

I

Among twenty snowy mountains,
The only moving thing
Was the eye of the blackbird.

II

I was of three minds,
5   Like a tree
In which there are three blackbirds.

III

The blackbird whirled in the autumn winds.
It was a small part of the <u>pantomime</u>.

IV

A man and a woman
10   Are one.
A man and a woman and a blackbird
Are one.

V

I do not know which to prefer,
The beauty of <u>inflections</u>

What was the "only moving thing"?

WORDS FOR EVERYDAY USE:

pan • to • mime (pan´tə mīm´) *n.*, gesture without speech
in • flec • tion (in flek´shən) *n.*, change in pitch or tone of voice

15   Or the beauty of innuendoes,[1]
          The blackbird whistling
          Or just after.

VI

          Icicles filled the long window
          With barbaric[2] glass.
20   The shadow of the blackbird
          Crossed it, to and fro.
          The mood
          Traced in the shadow
          An indecipherable cause.

VII

25   O thin men of Haddam,[3]
          Why do you imagine golden birds?
          Do you not see how the blackbird
          Walks around the feet
          Of the women about you?

VIII

What does the speaker know?

30   I know noble accents
          And lucid, inescapable rhythms;
          But I know, too,
          That the blackbird is involved
          In what I know.

IX

35   When the blackbird flew out of sight,
          It marked the edge
          Of one of many circles.

X

          At the sight of blackbirds
          Flying in a green light,
40   Even the bawds of euphony
          Would cry out sharply.

XI

          He rode over Connecticut
          In a glass coach.

---

1. **innuendoes.** Hints
2. **barbaric.** Wild
3. **Haddam.** Town in Connecticut

WORDS FOR EVERYDAY USE:

in • de • ci • pher • a • ble (in´dē sī´fər ə bəl) *adj.,* illegible
lu • cid (lo͞o´sid) *adj.,* easily understood
eu • pho • ny (yo͞o´fə nē) *n.,* pleasing effect to the ear

Mother Moon, Sister Crow. Gillian Gatto, 1981.

Once, a fear pierced him,
In that he mistook
The shadow of his equipage[4]
For blackbirds.

XII

The river is moving.
The blackbird must be flying.

XIII

It was evening all afternoon.
It was snowing
And it was going to snow.
The blackbird sat
In the cedar-limbs.

45

50

Why did it seem like "evening all afternoon"?

---

4. **equipage.** Refers to his coach

Responding to the Selection

Which of the "Thirteen Ways of Looking at a Blackbird" do you find most interesting? Why?

Reviewing the Selection

1. In stanza 1, what does the speaker see "Among twenty snowy mountains"?
   ▶▶ What kind of eyesight would a person need to be able to see the eye of a blackbird move "Among twenty snowy mountains"? In what way is the perceptive power of the imagination greater than the perceptive power of the senses?

2. In stanza 2, to what does the speaker compare three blackbirds?
   ▶▶ In what circumstance might a person be "of three minds"?

3. In stanza 3, what does the blackbird do in the autumn winds?
   ▶▶ What is "the pantomime" referred to in stanza 3? In what way does nature sometimes seem to be acting out in the autumn?

4. In stanza 4, what groups of things are described as being "one"?
   ▶▶ In what circumstances are a man and a woman often spoken of as being "one"? Some critics have suggested that stanza 4 is a kind of joke in which the speaker demonstrates the absurdity of thinking of two people as one. If that reading of the stanza is accepted, why does the speaker say that "A man and a woman and a blackbird /Are one"? Suppose that the stanza is not a joke but is meant to be taken seriously. How might a man and a woman become one by sharing a moment of experiences, such as looking at a blackbird?

5. In stanza 5, what two aspects of human speech does the speaker of the poem compare to a blackbird whistling and "just after"?
   ▶▶ What is an inflection? What is an innuendo? What do these things have in common with a blackbird whistling and "just after"?

6. In stanza 6, what scene is described?
   ▶▶ What mood, or feeling, does that scene create? Why might the speaker consider a natural world that would create such a mood "indecipherable"?

7. In stanza 7, what do the men of Haddam look like? What do they imagine? What question does the speaker put to them?
   ▶ What might the "golden birds" represent? How do you feel when you think of blackbirds walking around people's feet? How does nature violate people's ambitions or wishes?

8. In stanza 8, what does the speaker know?
   ▶▶ A poet is someone who has command of "noble accents/And lucid, inescapable

rhythms." However, such a person does not come by these on his or her own. What role does nature play in teaching a poet his or her trade?

9. In stanza 9, what does the speaker think of when he sees the blackbird fly out of sight?
   ▶▶ The point at which the blackbird disappears from sight marks the limits of the speaker's physical perception. What might lie beyond those limits in other "circles"? What might one perceive through one's imagination or intuition that cannot be directly perceived by the senses? In what way is imagination or intuition dependent on the senses, so that in a sense the limits of imagination include, or encircle, the actual or concrete?

10. In stanza 10, what would cry out "At the sight of blackbirds/Flying in a green light"?
    ▶▶ Is green light natural? How would you feel if you saw a bunch of blackbirds flying in a green light? What is euphony? What is a bawd? Imagine a poet who normally writes only euphonious, pleasant-sounding verse. What kinds of subjects would force such a poet if he is to do justice to the subject, to "cry out sharply"?

11. In stanza 11, what does the man ride in? What causes him to feel fear?
    ▶▶ In the story of Cinderella, a fairy godmother creates for the central character a fancy coach and glass slippers. In what sense is being wealthy and privileged like magic? In what sense is wealth and privilege precarious, like riding in a glass coach? In what circumstance might the objects owned by a wealthy, privileged person, such as a fancy coach, take on a terrifying aspect to that person?

12. In stanza 12, what is moving? What must be flying?
    ▶▶ The ancient Greek philosopher Heraclitus wrote that "You can never step into the same river twice." What similar statement about the nature of the world is made by the speaker in stanza 12?

13. In stanza 13, what does the afternoon look like? What is happening? What is going to happen?
    ▶▶ What two things in this stanza are unchanging? How do you think the speaker feels? In what sense are both the speaker and the blackbird "waiting it out"? Picture the scene in the stanza in your mind. What would make the blackbird stand out in stark relief, thus intensifying the impression of the bird's stoic immobility?

SYNTHESIZING

14. Choose two stanzas from the poem that you especially like. What does the speaker think about as a result of observing the blackbird in these two stanzas?

15. With what is the number thirteen commonly associated? What sorts of feelings are associated in this poem with blackbirds? In which stanzas do blackbirds seem frightening? In which stanzas does the speaker seem to be attracted to or fascinated by blackbirds?

Understanding Literature (Questions for Discussion)

1. **Image and Imagery.** An **image** is a word or phrase that names something that can be seen, heard, touched, tasted, or smelled. The images in a literary work are referred to, collectively, as the work's **imagery.** What primary image is used throughout the poem? How does the winter setting in many of the poem's parts contribute to the poem's imagery?

2. **Abstract and Concrete.** An **abstract** word or phrase is one that refers to something that cannot be directly perceived by the senses. *Freedom, power,* and *dignity* are examples of abstract terms. A **concrete** word or phrase is one that describes something that can be directly perceived by one or more of the five senses. Examples of concrete terms include *rainbow, lark,* and *scorpion.* Consider stanza 5 in the selection:

   I do not know which to prefer,
   The beauty of inflections
   Or the beauty of innuendoes,
   The blackbird whistling
   Or just after.

   What abstract terms are used in this stanza? What concrete terms are used to provide examples of the abstract terms?

Responding in Writing

1. **Journal Entry.** How many ways can you look at something? Choose a concrete thing, such as an oak tree, a tulip, a pumpkin, a crow, a snake, a cat, a beach, a motorcycle, an earthmover, the moon, a child's doll, or a pair of sneakers. Then, in your journal, brainstorm a list of different ways of thinking about or looking at that object.

2. **Caption.** Write five captions for a photograph you've selected from a newspaper or magazine. Have each caption represent a different perspective in which to look at and understand the photograph.

Language Lab

Base Words and Prefixes. Read the Language Arts Survey, 2.140, "Base Words and Prefixes." Then, on your own paper, underline the base word once and the prefix twice in each of the following words from "Thirteen Ways of Looking at a Blackbird." Next write the meaning of each word, consulting this text or a dictionary as necessary.

1. inflections   2. innuendoes   3. indecipherable   4. inescapable

PREREADING

"This Is Just to Say"
"The Red Wheelbarrow"
"The Dance"
by William Carlos Williams

ABOUT THE AUTHOR

William Carlos Williams (1883–1963) was born in Rutherford, New Jersey. After graduating from high school, he began studying to become a dentist, but he soon switched to medicine. In college he met and became friends with Ezra Pound, who would become one of the most influential American literary figures, and Hilda Doolittle, who later achieved fame as the poet and novelist, H. D. These relationships fed his interest in literature and poetry and changed his career plans even as he was completing his medical internship in New York City and doing postgraduate study in Leipzig, Germany. In 1912, Williams married and settled in Rutherford, where he began his medical practice. Specializing in pediatrics, Williams delivered thousands of babies, made house calls, and gained a reputation as a dedicated, old-fashioned doctor. He lived and practiced medicine in Rutherford for the rest of his life. It was an occupation that supported his poetry and his other writing. He was active in local politics and helped found several small magazines. In the 1930s and 1940s, he occasionally supported leftist causes, which later resulted in his not receiving the post of consultant in poetry at the Library of Congress. A heart attack in 1948 and a series of strokes later caused him to cede his medical practice to one of his two sons, and by 1961 he had stopped writing because of his health. Williams was awarded the Pulitzer Prize in 1962 for *Pictures from Breughel,* the Bollingen Prize in 1953, and the National Book Award in 1950, among other honors. His other works include *Spring and All* (1923), *The Edge of the Knife* (1932), *The Wedge* (1944), and an epic poem with a city as its hero, *Paterson* (1946–1958).

ABOUT THE SELECTIONS

A map of Williams's lifelong journey in pursuit of the American idiom can be read in these three poems that span from 1923 to 1944. **"The Red Wheelbarrow,"** one of Williams's earlier poems, reflects the impact of **Imagism,** a movement that championed the use of free verse and concise images, or word pictures. In 1924, Williams rejected free verse and began his experimentation with controlled measure, eventually developing his signature "variable feet," or, as Williams called them, "loose verses." Williams said, "The iamb is not the normal measure of American speech. The foot has to be expanded or contracted in terms of actual speech. The key to modern poetry is measure, which must reflect the flux of modern life." The rhythm of speech that can be heard in **"This Is Just to Say,"** which Williams published in 1934, is further refined and experimented with in **"The Dance,"** which Williams published ten years later.

"This Is Just to Say"

WILLIAM CARLOS WILLIAMS

What has the speaker done?

I have eaten
the plums
that were in
the icebox[1]

5   and which
you were probably
saving
for breakfast

What does the speaker ask of the owner of the plums?

Forgive me
10   they were delicious
so sweet
and so cold ∎

---

1. **icebox.** Refrigerator

Responding to the Selection

Imagine that you are the recipient of the poem, which you have found on the kitchen table, explaining why your plums are missing from the icebox. Would you forgive the speaker of the poem, as he asks? Why, or why not? Write an entry in your journal expressing your response to the poem.

Reviewing the Selection

RECALLING

1. What has the speaker eaten?

2. How does the speaker say that the plums tasted?

INTERPRETING

3. Why does the speaker ask for forgiveness?

4. Whom is the speaker addressing in the poem?

SYNTHESIZING

5. What connotation does the title, "This Is Just to Say," lend to the poem?

Understanding Literature (Questions for Discussion)

1. **Speaker and Tone.** The **speaker** is the character who speaks in a poem—the voice assumed by the writer. **Tone** is the emotional attitude toward the reader or toward the subject implied by a literary work. What can be inferred about the speaker from what he says and how he says it? What emotional attitude does the speaker have toward the person he is addressing? What emotional attitude does the speaker have toward the plums?

2. **Rhythm and Meter. Rhythm** is the pattern of beats or stresses in a line of verse or prose. The **meter** of a poem is its rhythmical pattern. Scan the poem, including the title, and identify the types of rhythmical units, or feet, that make up the poem.

Responding in Writing

1. **Poem.** Write a poem in which the speaker addresses someone he or she knows, telling that person about an ordinary event in the day. Use rhythm and meter to reflect the speech pattern appropriate to the speaker and what he or she is saying.

2. **Personal Note.** Write a personal note in response to the speaker in "This Is Just to Say." In your note, explain what you were saving the plums for and why you do or do not forgive the speaker.

READER'S JOURNAL

Think of an image from your personal experience that you find particularly striking, one that stuck with you after the original experience. What emotional impact did the image have upon you? Write about the experience in your journal.

LANGUAGE SKILLS

Read the Language Arts Survey, 2.24, "Prepositions." Then identify the prepositions in the poem and note what prepositional phrases they introduce.

"The Red Wheelbarrow"

WILLIAM CARLOS WILLIAMS

> so much depends
> upon
>
> a red wheel
> barrow
>
> 5   glazed with rain
> water
>
> beside the white
> chickens   ■

Responding to the Selection

Imagine that you are the speaker who sees the red wheelbarrow. Write an entry in your journal explaining why "so much depends upon" the image of the red wheelbarrow.

Reviewing the Selection

1. With what is the red wheelbarrow glazed?

2. Beside what do the white chickens stand?

▶▶ 3. What colors are part of the image? What happens to your perception when those colors are placed beside each other?

▶▶ 4. How does the presence of the rainwater emphasize the momentariness of the image?

5. How does the phrase "so much depends/upon" intensify the image of the red wheelbarrow?

Understanding Literature (Questions for Discussion)

1. **Image and Imagery.** An **image** is a word or phrase that names something that can be seen, heard, touched, tasted, or smelled. The images in a literary work are referred to, collectively, as the work's **imagery.** Where might one see a red wheelbarrow and white chickens? To what kind of world does the imagery in the poem belong? Why does it matter to the speaker "how" the imagery is seen?

2. **Speaker and Effect.** The **speaker** is the character who speaks in a poem—the voice assumed by the writer. The **effect** of a literary work is the general impression or emotional impact that it achieves. With what kind of eye does the speaker see the image? What effect, or general impression, does the poem create upon the reader?

Responding in Writing

1. **Free Verse Poem.** Write a very brief free verse poem in which the speaker describes, from his or her vantage point, an ordinary, yet momentary, image seen through a window of a house or of a moving vehicle.

2. **Caption.** Write a caption, in which context is established, to accompany a photograph of each of the following objects: a blue shoe, a yellow notebook, a green lamp, and a black telephone.

READER'S JOURNAL

How can words create a sense of movement? What is different about the rhythm of the words *careen* and *lollipop?* In your journal, write a word or phrase that creates a sense of each of the following rhythms: lumbering, dreamy, smooth, choppy, rapid, uneven, sudden, and soaring.

LANGUAGE SKILLS

Read the Language Arts Survey, 2.16, "Verbals: Participles" and 2.17, "Verbals: Gerunds." Then identify some verbals in the poem and note which are participles and which are gerunds.

"The Dance"

WILLIAM CARLOS WILLIAMS

In Brueghel's great picture, The Kermess,[1]
the dancers go round, they go round and
around, the squeal and the blare and the
tweedle of bagpipes, a bugle and fiddles
5   tipping their bellies (round as the thick-
sided glasses whose wash they impound)[2]
their hips and their bellies off balance
to turn them. Kicking and rolling about
the Fair Grounds, swinging their butts, those
10   shanks[3] must be sound to bear up under such
rollicking measures, prance as they dance
in Brueghel's great picture, The Kermess. ∎

---

1. **Brueghel's . . . The Kermess.** Refers to *The Wedding Dance* by Flemish painter Pieter Brueghel the Elder (*circa* 1525–1569)
2. **wash they impound.** Beverage they drink
3. **shanks.** Upper legs.

Responding to the Selection

Imagine that you are one of the dancers going "round and around" in the poem. Write an entry in your journal describing what kind of music you were dancing to and what emotions you experienced while dancing.

Reviewing the Selection

RECALLING

1. What do the dancers do "In Brueghel's great picture"?

2. What instruments are making the music?

INTERPRETING

3. What actions on the part of the dancers suggest celebration and enjoyment?

4. What sounds of the instruments support "the rollicking measures" they create?

SYNTHESIZING

5. As the dancers "go round" in the great picture, how does the poem "go round" on the page?

Understanding Literature (Questions for Discussion)

1. **Repetition. Repetition** is the use, again, of a sound, word, phrase, sentence, or other element. What sounds are repeated in the poem? What words and phrases are repeated? What is the purpose of the repetitions?

2. **Run-on Line and Rhythm.** A **run-on line** is a line of verse in which the sense or the grammatical structure does not end with the end of the line, but rather is continued on one or more subsequent lines. **Rhythm** is the pattern of beats or stresses in a line of verse or prose. What effect do the run-on lines have upon the rhythm of "The Dance"?

Responding in Writing

1. **Critical Interpretation.** Write a critical interpretation that analyzes how the content of "The Dance" is reflected in the meter, or rhythm, of the poem. Use examples of scanned lines from the poem to support your interpretation. Refer to *meter* in the Handbook of Literary Terms.

2. **Descriptive Paragraph.** Write a descriptive paragraph about a work of art that you find interesting. In the paragraph, tell what you see when you look at the work of art, describing as clearly as possible what is happening in that work.

Language Lab

Titles of Artworks. Read the Language Arts Survey, 2.128, "Titles of Artworks." Then rewrite the following sentences, correcting the capitalization errors in each one.

1. Dated 1565, *the corn harvester* is one of five remaining panels representing months of the year.

2. Other paintings in Brueghel's cycle include *hunters in the snow, return of the herd, the gloomy day,* and *haymaking.*

3. *haymaking* is housed in the National Gallery in Prague.

4. In *the return of the herd,* cattle are shown leaving the pastures of summer.

5. *the gloomy day* depicts a cold, stormy day—probably in February.

Research Skills

Bibliography Cards. Read the Language Arts Survey, 4.29, "Bibliographies and Bibliography Cards." Then, on the topic of William Carlos Williams, write one bibliography card for each bibliography entry form listed below.

1. a book with one author

2. a book with an editor but no single author

3. a poem, short story, essay, or chapter in a collection of works by one author

4. an introduction, preface, foreword, or afterword written by someone other than the author(s) of a work

5. an article in an encyclopedia, dictionary, or other alphabetically organized reference work

PROJECT

Art History. Form small groups of three or four students to research the life and art of the sixteenth-century Flemish painter Pieter Brueghel the Elder. Assign to each group one of the following topics: biography, paintings, style, social and historical context, and works of other sixteenth-century Flemish painters. After completing the research, have each group present their findings to the rest of the class.

"Patterns"

by Amy Lowell

ABOUT THE AUTHOR

Amy Lowell (1874–1925) was born in Brookline, Massachusetts, into one of the state's wealthiest families, whose members had played prominent roles in public life since the American Revolution. Their status was immortalized in the 1910 doggerel, "And this is good old Boston,/The home of the bean and the cod,/Where the Lowells talk to the Cabots,/And the Cabots talk only to God." The Lowell men attended Harvard and then went on to run or found businesses or major institutions. The Lowell women raised children and had roles in the social and philanthropic life of Boston. Amy Lowell understood the importance of being a Lowell, but temperamentally she was miscast for the role assigned her by gender. She wanted an independent life, which fortunately she had the money to achieve. Lowell's desire to contribute to public life found its outlet beginning at the age of thirty-eight, when she launched her public literary career with the publication of her poetry in *A Dome of Many-Coloured Glass*. She soon adopted the Imagist style, becoming its chief spokesperson. The Imagists sought to create poems free of "authorial intervention," that presented precisely observed sensory experiences and left to the reader the interpretation of those experiences. Lowell greatly admired the poet John Keats and wrote a massive two-volume biography of him during the 1920s. She was awarded the Pulitzer Prize in poetry posthumously in 1926 for *What's O'Clock* (1925). Her other works include *Sword Blades and Poppy Seed* (1914); *Men, Women, and Ghosts* (1916); *Can Grande's Castle* (1918); *Pictures of the Floating World* (1919); and *Legends* (1921).

ABOUT THE SELECTION

"**Patterns,**" from *The Collected Poems of Amy Lowell*, presents a poetic counterpoint, the news of death against a backdrop of beauty. Without preaching, the poem becomes a compelling antiwar statement. As an Imagist, Lowell sought to break from the tyranny of form; this poem portrays war as a devastating form.

READER'S JOURNAL

Have you ever looked forward to a special event only to have it canceled? Have you ever received bad news on a beautiful day? In your journal, write about how you felt on these occasions.

LANGUAGE SKILLS

Read the Language Arts Survey, 2.24, "Prepositions." Then identify some prepositions in the selection and note how each preposition relates a noun or pronoun to some other word in the sentence in which it appears.

"Patterns"

AMY LOWELL

To what does the speaker compare herself?

I walk down the garden-paths,
And all the daffodils
Are blowing, and the bright blue squills.
I walk down the patterned garden-paths
5   In my stiff, brocaded[1] gown.
With my powdered hair and jeweled fan,
I too am a rare
Pattern. As I wander down
The garden-paths.
10   My dress is richly figured,[2]
And the train[3]
Makes a pink and silver stain
On the gravel, and the thrift
Of the borders.

What are some elements of the "current fashion"?

15   Just a plate of current fashion,
Tripping by in high-heeled, ribboned shoes.
Not a softness anywhere about me,
Only whalebone[4] and brocade.
And I sink on a seat in the shade

What conflict is occurring?

20   Of a lime-tree. For my passion
Wars against the stiff brocade.
The daffodils and squills
Flutter in the breeze
As they please.

---

1. **brocaded.** Embroidered
2. **figured.** Patterned
3. **train.** Trailing fabric on a gown
4. **whalebone.** Used as base for corsets

25   And I weep;
          For the lime-tree is in blossom
          And one small flower had dropped upon my bosom.

          And the plashing of waterdrops
          In the marble fountain
30   Comes down the garden-paths.
          The dripping never stops.
          Underneath my stiffened gown
          Is the softness of a woman bathing in a marble basin,[5]
          A basin in the midst of hedges grown
35   So thick, she cannot see her lover hiding,
          But she guesses he is near,
          And the sliding of the water
          Seems the stroking of a dear
          Hand upon her.
40   What is Summer in a fine brocaded gown!
          I should like to see it lying in a heap upon the ground.
          All the pink and silver crumpled up on the ground.

          I would be the pink and silver as I ran along the paths,
          And he would stumble after,
45   Bewildered by my laughter.
          I should see the sun flashing from his sword hilt[6] and the buckles on his shoes.
          I would choose
          To lead him in a maze along the patterned paths,
          A bright and laughing maze for my heavy-booted lover.
50   Till he caught me in the shade,
          And the buttons of his waistcoat bruised my body as he clasped me
          Aching, melting, unafraid.
          With the shadows of the leaves and the sundrops,
          And the plopping of the waterdrops,
55   All about us in the open afternoon—
          I am very like to swoon
          With the weight of this brocade,
          For the sun sifts through the shade.
          Underneath the fallen blossom
60   In my bosom,
          Is a letter I have hid.
          It was brought to me this morning by a rider from the Duke.[7]

What feeling does the speaker convey?

What does the speaker have hidden?

---

5. **basin.** Sink
6. **hilt.** Handle
7. **the Duke.** John Churchill, Duke of Marlborough
(1650–1722), military commander in the War of Spanish
Succession (1701–1714)

A Shoreham Garden. Samuel Palmer, circa 1829. Courtesy of the Trustees of the Victoria & Albert Museum

What news does the speaker receive?

"Madam, we regret to inform you that Lord Hartwell
Died in action Thursday se'nnight."[8]
65   As I read it in the white, morning sunlight,
The letters squirmed like snakes.
"Any answer, Madam," said my footman.
"No," I told him.
"See that the messenger takes some refreshment.
70   No, no answer."
And I walked into the garden,
Up and down the patterned paths,
In my stiff, correct brocade.
The blue and yellow flowers stood up proudly in the sun,

—————————————

8. **se'nnight.** Seven days and nights

75   Each one.
          I stood upright too,
          Held rigid to the pattern
          By the stiffness of my gown.
          Up and down I walked,
80   Up and down.

          In a month he would have been my husband.
          In a month, here, underneath this lime,
          We would have broke the pattern;
          He for me, and I for him,
85   He as Colonel, I as Lady,
          On this shady seat.
          He had a whim
          That sunlight carried blessing.
          And I answered, "It shall be as you have said."
90   Now he is dead.

          In Summer and in Winter I shall walk
          Up and down
          The patterned garden-paths
          In my stiff, brocaded gown.
95   The squills and daffodils
          Will give place to pillared roses, and to asters, and to snow.
          I shall go
          Up and down,
          In my gown.
100   Gorgeously arrayed,
          Boned and stayed.
          And the softness of my body will be guarded from embrace
          By each button, hook, and lace.
          For the man who should loose me is dead,
105   Fighting with the Duke in Flanders,
          In a pattern called a war.
          Christ! What are patterns for?

Who was Lord Hartwell?

What happened to Lord Hartwell?

Responding to the Selection

Imagine that you are the speaker, wearing a stiff, brocaded gown, walking along a garden path, and you receive bad news. What occasions were you anticipating? What memories leap to mind?

Reviewing the Selection

1. In what season does the poem take place?

2. What does not exist "anywhere about" the speaker?

3. What does the speaker recall about softness?

4. What does the speaker carry hidden in her bosom?

5. What were the speaker and Lord Hartwell planning?

6. What irony occurs because of the choice of season? What other ironies can you find?

7. What can the flowers in the garden do that the speaker cannot?

8. Why does the speaker wish to see her gown "lying in a heap upon the ground"?

9. In what figurative way is the message in the letter also hidden in the speaker's bosom?

10. What does the speaker mean when she says, "We would have broke the pattern"?

11. Although many beautiful things are described in the poem, **foreshadowing**, or the act of presenting materials that hint at later events, of the crisis occurs. Find examples of this foreshadowing throughout the poem.

Understanding Literature (Questions for Discussion)

1. **Rhyme and Repetition. Rhyme** is the repetition of sounds at the ends of words. Types of rhyme include *end rhyme* (the use of rhyming words at the ends of lines), *internal rhyme* (the use of rhyming words within lines), *exact rhyme* (in which the rhyming words end with the same sound or sounds), and *slant rhyme* (in which the rhyming sounds are similar but not identical). **Repetition** is the use, again, of a sound, word, phrase, sentence, or other element. Consider the following line from the poem: "And the plopping of the waterdrops." What kinds of rhyme are used in that line? What repetition of that line occurs in the poem? What effect is created by the repetition and slight alteration of the internal rhymes?

2. **Theme.** A **theme** is a central idea in a literary work. What themes are central to the selection? What is the speaker's attitude toward these ideas?

Responding in Writing

Essay. Write an essay that discusses in what ways war may be described as a pattern.

Language Lab

Prepositional Phrases. Read the Language Arts Survey, 2.47, "Adding Prepositional Phrases." Then expand each of the sentences below by adding a prepositional phrase.

1. The gardener knelt slowly.
2. Daffodils, tulips, and irises bloomed.
3. The rains washed the garden path.
4. The fountain had been carved from marble.
5. She enjoyed the sound of the water splashing.

Thinking Skills

Comparing and Contrasting. Read the Language Arts Survey, 4.8, "Comparing and Contrasting." Then, make two columns on a piece of paper, one headed "Patterns of Joy" and the other headed "Patterns of Sorrow." To the left of the columns, write *Comparison* and then under that *Contrast*. Draw lines across your page starting under each of these two words. List the characteristics of the patterns of joy and sorrow as described in the poem within the boxes of the chart that you have created with these four headings.

PROJECT

Patterns and Forms. Form small groups of three or four students. As a group, research various patterns and forms in different art media, such as textiles, ceramics, photographs, and so on, which have been inspired by or evoke a form or pattern in nature. For example, the form of a Japanese fan echoes the form of a gingko leaf. Have each group create three or four pairs of natural/artificial forms or patterns on a standard-size sheet of paper. Then, as a class, collect all of the pairs of patterns and forms in a book to display in your classroom.

"In a Station of the Metro"
by Ezra Pound

ABOUT THE AUTHOR

Ezra Pound (1885–1972) was born in Idaho but grew up in the East. The study of Latin in high school inspired him to become a poet. After graduating from Hamilton College in 1905 and receiving a master's degree from the University of Pennsylvania in 1906, he received a fellowship to go to France, Italy, and Spain to work on a dissertation. When he returned to the United States, he taught briefly at Wabash College in Indiana. He soon became an expatriate living in London, Paris, and Italy. He made his living teaching and reviewing. He also edited the magazines *Poetry* and *The Little Review.* Pound founded and defined Imagism, the literary movement that sought to present in poetry recreations of sensory experiences, without commentary about the emotional content or meaning of those experiences. Pound's influence on other writers was profound, especially in his call for a type of poetry that was harder, clearer, and nearer the bone and in his embracing of free verse.

Pound became obsessed with monetary reform and came to believe that Italian Fascist dictator Benito Mussolini embodied the ideal leader. By 1940, he had begun to give radio talks from Rome, denouncing American society, President Roosevelt, and the Jewish people. He continued the broadcasts when World War II began. He was indicted for treason, then arrested when United States soldiers entered Italy. After being held for weeks at a prison camp near Pisa, he was brought to trial but was declared insane and hospitalized. His winning of the Library of Congress's newly established Bollingen Prize for poetry in 1948 created a public furor. During his early years, Pound was generous with many other writers, including H. D. (Hilda Doolittle), T. S. Eliot, James Joyce, William Carlos Williams, Robert Frost, Ernest Hemingway, and Marianne Moore, helping them to refine their work and to find publication. Many of those writers rallied around him when he was charged with treason and imprisoned. The efforts of a committee of writers succeeded in winning Pound's release, and he returned to Italy, where he died at the age of eighty-seven. Pound began working on his long series of avant-garde poems, the *Cantos,* in 1915 and continued working on them throughout his imprisonment. He had produced more than one hundred by the time of his death. His other works include *Des Imagistes* (1915), *Hugh Selwyn Mauberly* (1920), *Make It New* (1934), *The ABC of Reading* (1934), *Polite Essays* (1937), and *Literary Essays* (1954).

ABOUT THE SELECTION

Pound said that one day, as he emerged from a train in the Paris subway, he suddenly saw "a beautiful face, and then another and another." He wrote the poem to convey that experience. Pound's original version of **"In a Station of the Metro"** was thirty lines long; his 1916 version of the poem, distilled into two lines, exemplifies the characteristic for which Pound's poetry is most noted, its imagery.

READER'S JOURNAL

Have you ever been startled or dazzled by an image of something? What did you see? What kind of emotional response did the image evoke? Write in your journal about the image and the emotional impact it created.

LANGUAGE SKILLS

Read the Language Arts Survey, 2.32, "Using Precise Nouns." Then identify the precise nouns in the selection and note what effect they have on the poem.

"In a Station of the Metro"[1]

EZRA POUND

The <u>apparition</u> of these faces in the crowd;
Petals on a wet, black bough. ■

---

1. **In a Station of the Metro.** In a Paris subway station

WORDS FOR EVERYDAY USE:
ap • pa • ri • tion (ap´ər rish´ən) *n.*, ghostly appearance of a person or thing

Responding to the Selection

Imagine that you are the speaker of this poem, standing in a station of the Paris subway. Write in your journal about what you saw in the Metro, explaining what effect the image had on you.

Reviewing the Selection

RECALLING

1. What does the speaker see "in the crowd"?

2. How does the speaker describe the bough?

INTERPRETING

▶▶ 3. What connotation does the word *apparition* have?

▶▶ 4. To what is the speaker comparing "these faces"?

SYNTHESIZING

5. What attitude toward "The apparition of these faces" does the speaker express?

Understanding Literature (Questions for Discussion)

1. **Image and Imagery.** An **image** is a word or phrase that names something that can be seen, heard, touched, tasted, or smelled. The images in a literary work are referred to, collectively, as the work's **imagery.** What two images are central to the poem? What effect, or emotional impact, is created by the poem's imagery?

2. **Metaphor.** A **metaphor** is a figure of speech in which one thing is spoken or written about as if it were another. This figure of speech invites the reader to make a comparison between the two things, which can be analyzed into two parts: the tenor (or subject being described) and the vehicle (or object being used in the description). These two things can be compared because they share a particular quality. "In a Station of the Metro" is a metaphor. What is the tenor of the metaphor? the vehicle? What quality do these two things share?

Responding in Writing

Haiku. A **haiku** is a traditional Japanese three-line poem containing five syllables in the first line, seven in the second, and five again in the third. A haiku presents a picture, or image, in order to arouse in the reader a specific emotional response. Write a haiku that presents an image of something you have suddenly witnessed, such as a bird landing on a rooftop, a father bending down to pick up his child, or a cat stretching awake from a nap.

"Poetry"
by Marianne Moore

ABOUT THE AUTHOR

Marianne Moore (1887–1972) was born in Kirkwood, Missouri. Moore graduated from Bryn Mawr College in 1909, traveled with her mother in England and France in 1911, and taught at the U.S. Indian School in Carlisle from 1911 to 1915. Her poems were first published in England beginning in 1915, and in 1921, two of her friends conspired to have a collection of them, *Poems* (1921), published there. Moore and her mother moved to New York City in 1916 and lived together until her mother died. Her brother, a Presbyterian minister, had a parish in Brooklyn, New York, and she had a close relationship with him her entire life. In New York, she made her living as a teacher and as a librarian. The poet, who often made animals the subject of her musings, was a frequent visitor to the Bronx Zoo. She was also a lifelong Dodger fan and was once invited to throw out the first ball of the season. Her *Observations* won the Dial Award in 1924, and in 1925, she began work as an editor of *Dial* and continued to do so until it disbanded in 1929. During her career, Moore wrote many essays of poetry criticism. She received the Bollingen Award, the National Book Award, and the Pulitzer Prize. Her *Collected Poems* appeared in 1951.

ABOUT THE SELECTION

Moore was often called a "poet's poet" because of her complex and subtle use of poetic technique. In using the entire stanza, rather than the word, line, image, or clause, as the unit of the poem, **"Poetry"** is characteristic of Moore's verse. The poem is also characteristic in its use of a catalog of particulars to define a general term, such as *poetry.*

READERS' JOURNAL
   Have you ever made lists of things you like or dislike? understand or do not understand? What particular things did you include on your lists? In your journal, write a list of characteristics that, for you, define the general term *poetry*.

LANGUAGE SKILLS
   Read the Language Arts Survey, 2.32, "Using Precise Nouns." Then identify some precise nouns in the selection and note how they are used to define the abstract noun *poetry*.

"*Poetry*"

MARIANNE MOORE

What does the speaker dislike?

I, too, dislike it: there are things that are important beyond all
      this fiddle.[1]
Reading it, however, with a perfect contempt for it, one
      discovers in
5   it after all, a place for the genuine

What real things can poetry describe?

    Hands that can grasp, eyes
      that can <u>dilate</u>, hair that can rise
        if it must, these things are important not because a

high-sounding interpretation can be put upon them but because
10   they are
useful. When they become so derivative[2] as to become
      unintelligible,
the same thing may be said for all of us, that we
      do not admire what
15   we cannot understand: the bat
      holding on upside down or in quest of something to

eat, elephants pushing, a wild horse taking a roll, a tireless wolf
      under

---

1. **fiddle.** Nonsense
2. **derivative.** Imitative

WORDS FOR EVERYDAY USE:
    di • late (dī´lāt) *vi.*, become larger or wider

20   a tree, the immovable[3] critic twitching his skin like a horse
                that feels a flea, the base-
      ball fan, the statistician[4]—
         nor is it <u>valid</u>
            to discriminate against "business documents and

      school-books"; all these phenomena are important. One must
                make a distinction
25   however: when dragged into <u>prominence</u> by half poets the
              result is not poetry,
       nor till the poets among us can be
          "literalists of
          the imagination"[5]—above
          <u>insolence</u> and <u>triviality</u> and can present

30   for inspection, "imaginary gardens with real toads in them," shall
               we have
      it. In the meantime, if you demand on the one hand,
      the raw material[6] of poetry in
          all its rawness and
35   that which is on the other hand
           genuine, then you are interested in poetry.   ■

What does poetry combine with imagination?

---

3. **immovable.** Stubborn
4. **statistician.** Expert in statistics
5. **"literalists of the imagination."** Term from W. B.
Yeats's *Ideas of Good and Evil*
6. **raw material.** Basic ingredients

Responding to the Selection

Imagine that you are the reader or listener who is included as sharing the speaker's dislike of poetry: "I, too, dislike it." Why does the speaker assume that you, too, dislike it? Write a letter to the speaker, explaining why you do or do not dislike poetry.

WORDS FOR EVERYDAY USE:

val • id (val´id) *adj.,* sound; just
prom • i • nence (prom´ə nəns) *n.,* conspicuousness
in • so • lence (in´sə ləns) *n.,* disrespectfulness
triv • i • al •i • ty (triv´ē al´i tē) *n.,* something insignificant

Reviewing the Selection

1. To what does "all this fiddle" refer?

2. What do we not admire?

3. About what must one "make a distinction"?

4. According to the speaker, what should "the poets among us" be?

5. What quality do "Hands that can grasp" and "eyes that can dilate" have in common?

6. Of what is the phrase "elephants pushing" an example?

7. What is the speaker's attitude toward what the half poets create?

8. What will the reader or listener prove by placing demands on poetry?

9. What is the difference between a half poet and a poet? What, according to the speaker, do the poets need to do?

10. According to the speaker, what demands should the reader or listener make on poetry?

Understanding Literature (Questions for Discussion)

1. **Stanza.** A **stanza** is a recurring pattern of grouped lines in a poem. Some types of stanzas include the couplet, triplet, quatrain, and quintain. What two types of stanzas are used in the selection?

2. **Abstract and Concrete.** An **abstract** word or phrase is one that refers to something that cannot be directly perceived by the senses. *Truth, love, force, theory,* and *sadness* are examples of abstract terms. A **concrete** word or phrase is one that describes something that can be directly perceived by one or more of the five senses. *Book, pool, light,* and *car* are examples of concrete terms. Identify one abstract word used in the poem and the concrete words or phrases that describe it.

Responding in Writing

Comparison-Contrast Paragraph. In Moore's 1967 revision of "Poetry," she altered the first lines of the poem to read, "I, too, dislike it./Reading it, however, with a perfect contempt/for it, one discovers in/it, after all, a place for the genuine." Write a brief essay in which you compare and contrast the opening lines of the 1923 version of "Poetry," as it appears in this text, with the opening lines of the 1967 revision.

"The Love Song of J. Alfred Prufrock"
by T. S. Eliot

ABOUT THE AUTHOR

T(homas) S(tearns) Eliot (1888–1965) was born in St. Louis, Missouri. He attended Milton Academy and Harvard University. In 1910, the year in which he earned his master's degree, he wrote one of his most famous poems, "The Love Song of J. Alfred Prufrock," a poem that was for its day radically experimental. During the pre-World War I period, Eliot attended the Sorbonne in Paris and studied Asian languages and religion. In 1915, following the outbreak of war, he moved to Oxford. A disappointment to his family, he supplemented his allowance by working as a bank teller. At the end of a difficult marriage to Vivian Haigh-Wood, Eliot received intensive psychiatric treatment for depression. Then, with the help of another expatriate poet, Ezra Pound, he published "Prufrock" and caught the attention of the literary world. In 1922, Eliot published an even more challenging poem, "The Waste Land"— a questioning of the moral bankruptcy of the interwar period poised against what Eliot saw as the superior values of the past. In 1928, shortly after embracing British citizenship, Eliot became a member of the Church of England. He married Valerie Fletcher in 1957. In addition to his invaluable poetic achievements, Eliot made successful contributions to other literary forms, including plays and literary criticism. In 1948, he was awarded the Nobel Prize for literature. *The Complete Poems and Plays of T. S. Eliot* was published in 1969.

ABOUT THE SELECTION

Eliot wrote **"The Love Song of J. Alfred Prufrock"** in 1910–1911 while a graduate student at Harvard. The poem, a dramatic monologue, presents the "conversation with himself" of J. Alfred Prufrock, a middle-aged man who hesitates to speak directly to the woman he loves. First published in *Poetry* magazine in 1915, the poem was later collected in *Prufrock and Other Observations and Poems*. In many ways, this poem is typical of Eliot's work, which is **elliptical**, leaving out nonessential details, and highly **allusive**, making reference to people, events, objects, or works from history or literature.

READER'S JOURNAL

Have you ever hesitated to tell someone how you feel about him or her? Why did you hesitate? What held you back? What would you have said if you had been able to speak frankly? Write about the experience in your journal.

LANGUAGE SKILLS

Read the Language Arts Survey, 2.36, "The Functions of Sentences." Then identify some interrogative sentences in the selection and note what the questions reveal about the speaker.

"The Love Song of J. Alfred Prufrock"

T. S. ELIOT

S'io credessi che mia risposta fosse
a persona che mai tornasse al mondo,
questa fiamma staria senza più scosse.
Ma per ciò che giammai di questo fondo
non tornò vivo alcun, s'i'odo il vero,
senza tema d'infamia ti rispondo.[1]

Let us go then, you and I,
When the evening is spread out against the sky
Like a patient <u>etherised</u> upon a table;
Let us go, through certain half-deserted streets,
5   The muttering retreats
Of restless nights in one-night cheap hotels
And sawdust restaurants with oyster-shells:
Streets that follow like a <u>tedious</u> argument
Of <u>insidious</u> intent
10   To lead you to an overwhelming question . . .

---

1. **S'io . . . rispondo.** Epigraph from Dante's *Inferno*, Canto XXVII, lines 61–66. The speaker is one of the damned telling of his torment: "If I believed that my response would be/to somebody who would ever return to the world,/this flame would be without more movement./But since nobody has returned from this depth alive,/if I hear the truth,/without fear of infamy, I answer you."

WORDS FOR EVERYDAY USE:
e • ther • ise (ē´ thə rīz´) *vt.*, render groggy or numb
te • di • ous (tē´dē əs) *adj.*, long and tiresome
in • sid • i • ous (in sid´ē əs) *adj.*, deceitful

Oh, do not ask, "What is it?"
Let us go and make our visit.
In the room the women come and go
Talking of Michelangelo.[2]

15 The yellow fog that rubs its back upon the window-panes,
    The yellow smoke that rubs its muzzle on the window-panes,
    Licked its tongue into the corners of the evening,
    <u>Lingered</u> upon the pools that stand in drains,
    Let fall upon its back the soot that falls from chimneys,
20 Slipped by the terrace, made a sudden leap,
    And seeing that it was a soft October night,
    Curled once about the house, and fell asleep.

    And indeed there will be time
    For the yellow smoke that slides along the street
25 Rubbing its back upon the window-panes;
    There will be time, there will be time
    To prepare a face to meet the faces that you meet;
    There will be time to murder and create,
    And time for all the works and days of hands
30 That lift and drop a question on your plate;
    Time for you and time for me,
    And time yet for a hundred indecisions,
    And for a hundred visions and revisions,
    Before the taking of a toast and tea.

35 In the room the women come and go
    Talking of Michelangelo.

    And indeed there will be time
    To wonder, "Do I dare?" and, "Do I dare?"
    Time to turn back and descend the stair,
40 With a bald spot in the middle of my hair—
    (They will say: "How his hair is growing thin!")
    My morning coat, my collar mounting firmly to the chin,
    My necktie rich and modest, but <u>asserted</u> by a simple pin—
    (They will say: "But how his arms and legs are thin!")
45 Do I dare

*What curls
around the house
and falls asleep?
What does the
color suggest?*

*Why might the
speaker "turn
back and descend
the stair"?*

---

2. **Michelangelo.** (1475–1564) Italian sculptor, painter,
architect, and poet

Disturb the universe?
In a minute there is time
For decisions and revisions which a minute will reverse.

50 For I have known them all already, known them all—
Have known the evenings, mornings, afternoons,
I have measured out my life with coffee spoons;
I know the voices dying with a dying fall
Beneath the music from a farther room.
        So how should I presume?

55 And I have known the eyes already, known them all—
The eyes that fix you in a formulated phrase,
And when I am formulated, sprawling on a pin,
When I am pinned and wriggling on the wall,
Then how should I begin
60 To spit out all the butt-ends of my days and ways?
        And how should I presume?

And I have known the arms already, known them all—
Arms that are braceleted and white and bare
(But in the lamplight, downed with light brown hair!)
65 Is it perfume from a dress
That makes me so digress?
Arms that lie along a table, or wrap about a shawl.
        And should I then presume?
        And how should I begin?

◆   ◆   ◆

70 Shall I say, I have gone at dusk through narrow streets
And watched the smoke that rises from the pipes
Of lonely men in shirt-sleeves, leaning out of windows? . . .

I should have been a pair of ragged claws
Scuttling across the floors of silent seas.

◆   ◆   ◆

75 And the afternoon, the evening, sleeps so peacefully!
Smoothed by long fingers,
Asleep . . . tired . . . or it malingers,

Does the speaker believe his life has been bold or fast-paced? Explain.

In what way does Prufrock describe himself?

WORDS FOR EVERYDAY USE:

pre • sume (pri zōōm´) *vi.*, dare; venture; take upon oneself

for • mu • lat • ed (fôr´myə lāt´əd) *part.*, systematical; precise

di • gress (di greś) *vi.*, deviate from the main topic in speaking or writing

ma • lin • ger (mə ling´gər) *vi.*, pretend illness

Stretched on the floor, here beside you and me.
Should I, after tea and cakes and ices,
80 Have the strength to force the moment to its crisis?
But though I have wept and fasted, wept and prayed,
Though I have seen my head (grown slightly bald) brought in
    upon a platter,
I am no prophet[3]—and here's no great matter;
I have seen the moment of my greatness flicker,
85 And I have seen the eternal Footman hold my coat, and snicker,
And in short, I was afraid.

And would it have been worth it, after all,
After the cups, the marmalade, the tea,
Among the porcelain, among some talk of you and me,
90 Would it have been worth while,
To have bitten off the matter with a smile,
To have squeezed the universe into a ball
To roll it towards some overwhelming question,
To say: "I am Lazarus,[4] come from the dead,
95 Come back to tell you all, I shall tell you all"—
If one, settling a pillow by her head,
        Should say: "That is not what I meant at all.
        That is not it, at all."

And would it have been worth it, after all,
100 Would it have been worth while,
After the sunsets and the dooryards and the sprinkled streets,
After the novels, after the teacups, after the skirts that trail along
    the floor—
And this, and so much more?—
105 It is impossible to say just what I mean!
But as if a magic lantern threw the nerves in patterns on a screen:
Would it have been worth while
If one, settling a pillow or throwing off a shawl,
And turning toward the window, should say:
110   "That is not it at all,
        That is not what I meant, at all."

♦   ♦   ♦

No! I am not Prince Hamlet, nor was meant to be;
Am an attendant lord, one that will do

---

3. **I am no prophet.** The head of the prophet John the
Baptist was brought to Princess Salome on a platter.
4. **Lazarus.** In John 11:1–44, Lazarus is resurrected.

Does the speaker believe he is a hero, a main character, or a minor character? Explain.

To swell a progress,[5] start a scene or two,
115 Advise the prince; no doubt, an easy tool,
Deferential, glad to be of use,
Politic, cautious, and meticulous;
Full of high sentence,[6] but a bit obtuse;
At times, indeed, almost ridiculous—
120 Almost, at times, the Fool.

I grow old . . . I grow old . . .
I shall wear the bottoms of my trousers rolled.

Shall I part my hair behind? Do I dare to eat a peach?
I shall wear white flannel trousers, and walk upon the beach.
125 I have heard the mermaids singing, each to each.

I do not think that they will sing to me.

I have seen them riding seaward on the waves
Combing the white hair of the waves blown back
When the wind blows the water white and black.

130 We have lingered in the chambers of the sea
By sea-girls wreathed with seaweed red and brown
Till human voices wake us, and we drown.   ∎

_____

5. **progress.** Procession
6. **sentence.** Opinions

Responding to the Selection

Imagine that you are J. Alfred Prufrock, the speaker who hesitates to declare his love. What causes you to hesitate? What would you say to the person you love if you could speak freely?

WORDS FOR
EVERYDAY USE:

def • er • en • tial (def´ə ren´shəl) *adj.,* respectful
ob • tuse (əb toos´) *adj.,* slow to understand or perceive; insensitive

Reviewing the Selection

1. What request does the speaker make in stanza 1 of the poem?

2. For how many indecisions, visions, and revisions will there be time "Before the taking of a toast and tea"?

3. What kind of moment has the speaker seen "flicker"?

4. What is impossible for the speaker to say?

5. What is the speaker's attitude toward himself?

6. What details in stanza 3 emphasize the difficulty the speaker has in committing himself to word or action?

7. Who is the "eternal Footman"? Of what is the speaker afraid?

8. Why does the speaker not think that the mermaids "will sing to me"? What happens when Prufrock begins to picture himself in a romantic scene? In what sense does reality intrude upon his daydreams? In what sense do human voices wake him, causing him to feel that he is drowning?

9. What are the causes of Prufrock's hesitation? What attitude does the speaker express toward himself and his hesitation?

10. What relationship between time and love is described in this poem?

Understanding Literature (Questions for Discussion)

1. **Dramatic Monologue.** A **dramatic monologue** is a poem that presents the speech of a single character in a dramatic situation. The speech is one side of an imagined conversation. In what dramatic situation is J. Alfred Prufrock? Does the reader have empathy for Prufrock's situation? Why, or why not?

2. **Allusion.** An **allusion** is a figure of speech in which a reference is made to a person, event, object, or work from history or literature. One of the allusions in the poem is to the poem "To His Coy Mistress," by Andrew Marvell, a seventeenth-century English writer. In Marvell's poem, the speaker appeals to the woman he loves for urgent action because there is not enough time to waste on pretenses such as coyness: "Had we but world enough, and time,/This coyness, Lady, were no crime." How do Prufrock's attitudes toward time and action differ from the attitudes of Marvell's speaker?

3. **Free Verse. Free verse** is poetry that avoids use of regular rhyme, rhythm, meter, or division into stanzas. Eliot controlled his free verse, however, with the precise use and variation of rhyme and meter. What rhyme pattern is used in stanza 1 of the poem? Of what poetic form is stanza 1 a variation?

Responding in Writing

Parody. A **parody** is a literary work that imitates another work for humorous, often satirical, purposes. Imitating one stanza from the poem, write a parody on the topic of hesitation.

Language Lab

Replacing Linking Verbs with Action Verbs. Read the Language Arts Survey, 2.34, "Replacing Linking Verbs with Action Verbs." Then, revise each of the following sentences, using action verbs in place of linking verbs.

1. Eliot's "The Love Song of J. Alfred Prufrock" is melancholy.
2. Prufrock is a man with many worries, including concerns about his baldness.
3. Prufrock's hesitations are sources of frustration for the reader.
4. Prufrock is, at times, the Fool.

Thinking Skills

Generalizing. Read the Language Arts Survey, 4.11, "Generalizing." Then, for each sentence below, decide whether the generalization is or is not supported by the poem.

1. Prufrock fears death.
2. Prufrock's youth is slipping away.
3. If Prufrock had been younger, he would not have hesitated to speak directly.
4. Prufrock is a man of action.
5. The mermaids will not sing to Prufrock because he is not intelligent.

PROJECT

Find the Allusion. In small groups, research the following allusions in the poem:

Epigram	Canto 27, lines 61–66, of the *Inferno,* book one of *The Divine Comedy,* by the Italian poet Dante Alighieri
Line 14	Michelangelo Buonoroti, Italian Renaissance painter
Line 23	Andrew Marvell's poem "To His Coy Mistress"
Line 29	"Works and Days," the title of a poem by the ancient Greek poet Hesiod
Line 52	Act I, scene i, line 4, of Shakespeare's play *Twelfth Night*
Line 82	The Bible, Mark 6:12–20 and Matthew 14:3–11
Line 94	The Bible, John 11:1–44

"Bells for John Whiteside's Daughter"
by John Crowe Ransom

ABOUT THE AUTHOR

John Crowe Ransom (1888–1974) was born in Pulaski, Tennessee; received an A.B. from Vanderbilt University in 1909; and as a Rhodes Scholar took a B.A. at Christ Church, Oxford, in 1913. After serving as a lieutenant in the Army during World War I, Ransom returned to Vanderbilt and joined the English faculty. In 1937, to the surprise of many, he left to teach poetry at Kenyon College in Ohio, where he also founded the *Kenyon Review.* He served as its editor until retiring in 1959. His three books of poems were published between 1919 and 1927. After that, his interest shifted to criticism, until later in his life when he began rewriting some of his early poems. Ransom helped to found the school of literary thought known as the New Criticism, which emphasized close readings of texts themselves without reference to their authors' biographies or to the historical circumstances that produced them. Ransom believed that science, technology, industrialization, and urbanization were destructive forces that dominated culture in the North. That belief informed his poetry and criticism and was expressed in *I'll Take My Stand* (1930), a collection of essays by Southerners. He once described himself as "something like this: In manners, aristocratic; in religion, ritualistic; in art, traditional." The 1963 edition of his *Selected Poems* won the Library of Congress's Bollingen Prize for Poetry; the 1969 edition received the National Book Award. His other works include *Poems about God* (1919), *Chills and Fever* (1924), *Two Gentlemen in Bonds* (1927), *The World's Body* (1938), and *The New Criticism* (1941).

ABOUT THE SELECTION

Ransom's small body of poems is characterized by irony, wit, and learning, but also by understatement, sincerity, and gracefulness of expression. These characteristics can all be found in **"Bells for John Whiteside's Daughter,"** about the death of a child.

READER'S JOURNAL

Have you ever attended a wake, funeral, or memorial service for someone who has died? What was the person like when he or she was alive? What did he or she enjoy doing? Write about your memories of that person in your journal.

LANGUAGE SKILLS

Read the Language Arts Survey, 2.147, "Formal and Informal English," and 2.149, "Tone and Voice." Then identify some formal and informal words in the poem and note what tone the choice of words lends to each stanza.

"Bells for John Whiteside's Daughter"

JOHN CROWE RANSOM

There was such speed in her little body,
And such lightness in her footfall,
It is no wonder her brown study[1]
Astonishes us all.

5   Her wars were bruited[2] in our high window.
We looked among orchard trees and beyond,
Where she took arms against her shadow,
Or <u>harried</u> unto the pond

The lazy geese, like a snow cloud
10   Dripping their snow on the green grass,
Tricking and stopping, sleepy and proud,
Who cried in goose, Alas,

Who cries "Alas"?

---

1. **study.** Serious thoughts
2. **bruited.** Rumored about

WORDS FOR EVERYDAY USE:

har • ry (har´ē´) *vt.*, push along; hurry forcefully

For the tireless heart within the little
Lady with rod that made them rise
15   From their noon apple-dreams and scuttle
Goose-fashion under the skies!

But now go the bells, and we are ready,
In one house we are sternly stopped
To say we are <u>vexed</u> at her brown study,
20   Lying so primly propped.   ■

What service do the bells announce?

Responding to the Selection

Imagine that you are the speaker in the poem attending the funeral of John Whiteside's daughter. How do you remember her? What was the young girl like when she was alive? Write an entry in your journal expressing your feelings about the death of this girl.

Reviewing the Selection

RECALLING

1. How does the speaker describe the footfall of John Whiteside's daughter?

2. Against what does the young girl take arms in stanza 2?

3. What are the lazy geese like?

4. What can be heard in the opening line of the last stanza? Where are the people? In what position is John Whiteside's daughter lying?

INTERPRETING

▶▶ 5. Why is the speaker astonished by the girl's "brown study"?

▶▶ 6. What actions on the part of the young girl showed her vitality and imagination?

▶▶ 7. With what feelings toward the dead girl does the speaker endow the geese?

▶▶ 8. Why are the bells ringing? For what are the people ready? What has "sternly stopped" them? Why are they "vexed"?

WORDS FOR EVERYDAY USE: **vex** (veks) *vt.*, irritate; annoy

9. What kind of child was John Whiteside's daughter? How does the speaker characterize her?

10. What are the speaker's feelings toward John Whiteside's daughter? What are the speaker's feelings about her death?

Understanding Literature (Questions for Discussion)

1. **Diction. Diction,** when applied to writing, refers to word choice. Ransom's poetry is noted for its surprising and unusual mix of diction. For example, in the line "Who cried in goose, Alas," the phrase "in goose" is childlike and fun, even more so when placed next to the formal cry "Alas." Identify another example of surprising or unusual diction, or word choice, in the poem and analyze what effect the word choice creates.

2. **Rhyme. Rhyme** is the repetition of sounds at the ends of words. *End rhyme,* the use of rhyming words at the ends of lines, is one type of rhyme. Two other types of rhyme include *exact rhyme* (in which the rhyming words end with the same sound or sounds) and *slant rhyme* (in which the rhyming sounds are similar but not identical). Analyze the end rhymes in the poem, identifying each word pair as an exact or slant rhyme. Which of the word pairs has the strongest exact rhyme? What emotional impact is created by that word pair?

3. **Understatement. Understatement** is an ironic expression in which something of importance is spoken of as though it were not important. Treating an important, emotionally laden subject in an offhand manner serves, paradoxically, to underscore its importance. In this poem, the speaker does not wail or weep. Instead, he uses subdued, understated language, describing death as a "brown study"; the people gathered about the body as being "astonished," "ready," "stopped," and "vexed"; and the body of the girl as being "primly propped." What effect does such understatement have when used on a subject such as this?

Responding in Writing

Elegy. An elegy is a piece of writing that remembers and praises someone who has died. Consider the following lines from the poem:

> There was such speed in her little body,
> And such lightness in her footfall,
> It is no wonder her brown study
> Astonishes us all.

These lines express how alive the young girl was and how the vitality of her life, when seen in contrast to her death, causes astonishment. Write an elegy, in prose or in verse, about the death of a child or a pet. In your poem, portray the character of the child or pet through his or her behavior and actions.

"Ars Poetica"
by Archibald MacLeish

ABOUT THE AUTHOR

Archibald MacLeish (1892–1982), born in Glencoe, Illinois, graduated from Yale in 1915 and earned his LL.D. from Harvard in 1919. He practiced law in Boston from 1920 to 1923 and lived in France from 1923 to 1928. MacLeish's military experience in World War I and his return to the United States during the Great Depression shaped and forged his intellectual interests and work. As his social awareness grew, it was reflected in his writing. MacLeish was Librarian of Congress (1939–1944), Assistant Secretary of State (1944–1945), Boylston Professor at Harvard (1949–1962), and a lecturer at Amherst College (1963–1967). A prolific writer, he was awarded three Pulitzers, two for poetry (*Conquistador* in 1933 and *Collected Poems, 1917–1952* in 1953) and one for drama (*J. B.* in 1958). The play *J. B.* treated the biblical story of Job in a modern setting and idiom. MacLeish's other works include *New Found Land* (1930), *Public Speech* (1936), *The Fall of the City* (1937), *Songs for Eve* (1954), *The Wild Old Wicked Man* (1968), and *Herakles* (1967).

ABOUT THE SELECTION

In a sense, a blade of grass or a cloud in the sky doesn't mean anything. It simply is. It exists. In **"Ars Poetica,"** the title of which means "The Art of Poetry" in Latin, MacLeish argues that a poem is like a blade of grass or a cloud in that respect. In his words, "A poem should not mean/But be." This idea was a central one to the New Criticism, which was a method of literary criticism that became popular in the 1930s and 1940s. This idea was also central to the Imagist movement of the early 1900s.

"Ars Poetica"

ARCHIBALD MACLEISH

To what two items does the speaker compare a poem?

A poem should be <u>palpable</u> and mute
As a globed fruit,

Dumb
As old medallions[1] to the thumb,

5   Silent as the sleeve-worn stone
Of casement ledges where the moss has grown—

A poem should be wordless
As the flight of birds.

A poem should be motionless in time
10   As the moon climbs,

Leaving, as the moon releases
Twig by twig the night-entangled trees,

Leaving, as the moon behind the winter leaves,
Memory by memory the mind—

---

1. **medallions.** Medals

WORDS FOR EVERYDAY USE: **pal • pa • ble** (pal′pə bəl) *adj.,* easily perceived; obvious; clear

15   A poem should be motionless in time
      As the moon climbs.

      A poem should be equal to:
      Not true.

      For all the history of grief
20   An empty doorway and a maple leaf.

      For love
      The leaning grasses and two lights above the sea—

      A poem should not mean
      But be.

■

How might a
poem depict love?

Responding to the Selection

Imagine that you are a photographer who has been asked to provide a concrete image as a striking metaphor for the art of poetry. In your journal, brainstorm a list of possible images, noting your thoughts beside each one.

Reviewing the Selection

1. What does it mean to be palpable? What, according to the speaker, should be "palpable and mute"?

2. According to the speaker, what should be "Dumb" and "wordless/As the flight of birds"?

3. According to the speaker, what should be "motionless in time"?

4. How might a poem express a "history of grief"? How might it express love?

5. Have you ever read or heard language that was so vivid that it made you feel as though you were actually experiencing the thing being described? In what sense should a poem be "palpable"?

6. When language is vivid and concrete, people forget that they are hearing or reading words and simply pay attention to the images that the words create in their minds. In what sense can a poem, which is made of words, be "Dumb" and "wordless"?

7. Is the moon actually motionless in the sky? What gives it the appearance of stillness despite its movement? How might a really good poem lead a reader or listener from part to part without that person being aware of its progression?

8. Near the end of the poem, the speaker gives examples of how concrete images might be used in place of abstract concepts such as grief and love. What concrete images does the speaker suggest to communicate each meaning? What do these images have in common with grief and love?

9. What kind of poetry do you think the speaker of this poem might prefer? Why?

10. The speaker ends the poem with the line "A poem should not mean/But be." In what other lines of the poem does the word *be* occur? Consider the following phrases from the poem:

    "all the history of grief"

    "An empty doorway and a maple leaf"

    Which of these lines "means" in the speaker's sense? Which line, in the speaker's sense, simply "is"?

Understanding Literature (Questions for Discussion)

1. **Simile.** A **simile** is a comparison using *like* or *as*. A simile can be analyzed into two parts, the *tenor* (or subject being described) and the *vehicle* (or object being used in the description). These two parts can be compared because they share some particular quality. Identify the tenor and the vehicle in the following simile in the first stanza of the poem: "A poem should be palpable and mute/As a globed fruit." What qualities do the tenor and vehicle share? Analyze another simile in the selection.

2. **Paradox.** A **paradox** is a contradictory statement, idea, or event. Consider the lines "A poem should be wordless/As the flight of birds." What paradox exists in that stanza? How can the paradox be resolved into a coherent, noncontradictory idea?

Responding in Writing

Imagist Poem. Choose a subject that is especially vivid in your imagination. Make a list of words that describe how the subject looks, sounds, tastes, feels, or smells. Then write a few lines that create a vivid picture of the subject. Keep all abstract statements of emotion out of your poem. For examples of Imagist poems, see Ezra Pound's "In a Station of the Metro," on page 560, and Amy Lowell's "Wind and Silver," on page 604 in Selections for Additional Reading. Refer to the Language Arts Survey, 1.10, "Recalling"; 1.11, "Observing"; 1.18, "Sensory Detail Charts"; and 2.4, "Concrete and Abstract Nouns." See also sections 2.32–2.35 on using precise, vivid, colorful nouns, verbs, and modifiers.

Language Lab

Concrete and Abstract Nouns. Read the Language Arts Survey, 2.4, "Concrete and Abstract Nouns." Then, for each of the abstract nouns listed below, write a definition using a simile that has as its vehicle a concrete noun.

EXAMPLE: fear   Fear is the sudden trembling of a bough.

  1. love   2. honor   3. cowardice   4. evil   5. purity

Research Skills

Using Searching Tools. Read the Language Arts Survey, 4.21, "Using Searching Tools." Then, use your library's computerized catalog to search for and provide a source of information about each of the following items.

1. *Poetry and the Age*
2. MacLeish, Archibald
3. modern American poetry
4. "Ars Poetica"
5. Marianne Moore
6. *The Well-Wrought Urn*
7. *The Verbal Icon*
8. Imagism
9. The New Criticism
10. *Seven Types of Ambiguity*

"somewhere i have never travelled,gladly beyond"
by E. E. Cummings

ABOUT THE AUTHOR

E(dward) E(stlin) Cummings (1894–1962) was born in Cambridge, Massachusetts. His father was a Congregationalist minister and a Harvard faculty member. Cummings graduated from Harvard in 1915 and earned an M.A. in 1916. When the United States entered World War I, Cummings joined the ambulance corps in France but was imprisoned by the French for his outspoken letters home. *The Enormous Room* (1922) is his prose account of the experience. Intervention by his father in the form of a letter to President Woodrow Wilson freed him, and Cummings found the experience of being made a prisoner by one's own side outrageous, yet funny. After the war, he made a life primarily in Greenwich Village in New York City, working full time as a poet and painter. Prizes, royalties, commissions, and a small allowance from his mother supported his independence. Cummings's work is known for its radical innovations in punctuation, capitalization, spelling, and grammar. Some of his poems seem literally to explode into fragments across the page, for he often arranged letters, words, and phrases in unique ways to make a visual as well as a verbal impact. In keeping with his innovative style, Cummings often had his name printed in all lowercase letters: *e. e. cummings*. His works include four volumes of well-received poetry in the 1920s and a book of collected poems toward the end of the 1930s. During the 1950s, he lectured and read on the college campus circuit. He received a special citation from the National Book Award Committee in 1955 and the Bollingen Prize for poetry at Yale in 1957. In 1950, he was honored with a fellowship from the Academy of American Poets for "great achievement" over a period of years.

ABOUT THE SELECTION

Following the prolific first decade of his work, Cummings published in 1931 the volume of verse *w[viva]* which included "**somewhere i have never travelled,gladly beyond.**" When Cummings wrote the selection, he was stretching to the limits his capacity for experimentation with poetic form. Seeking to catch the aliveness of the moment, Cummings manipulated typography, imagery, structure, diction, punctuation, grammar, syntax, rhyme, meter, and verse form.

READER'S JOURNAL

Have you ever looked deeply into the eyes of someone else? What did you see? How did your feelings for the person affect what you saw at that moment? Write about the experience in your journal.

LANGUAGE SKILLS

Read the Language Arts Survey, 2.93, "End Marks"; 2.94–2.96, "Commas I, II, and III"; and 2.98, "Colons." Then identify some commas and colons in the selection and note how Cummings experiments with their use.

"somewhere i have never travelled,gladly beyond"

E. E. CUMMINGS

somewhere i have never travelled,gladly beyond
any experience,your eyes have their silence:
in your most frail gesture are things which enclose me,
or which i cannot touch because they are too near

5   your slightest look easily will unclose me
though i have closed myself as fingers,
you open always petal by petal myself as Spring opens
(touching skilfully,mysteriously)her first rose

or if your wish be to close me,i and
10   my life will shut very beautifully,suddenly,
as when the heart of this flower imagines
the snow carefully everywhere descending;

nothing which we are to perceive in this world equals
the power of your intense fragility:whose texture
15   compels me with the colour of its countries,
rendering death and forever with each breathing

(i do not know what it is about you that closes
and opens; only something in me understands
the voice of your eyes is deeper than all roses)
20   nobody,not even the rain,has such small hands   ■

Where are things that enclose the speaker?

What has so much power over the speaker?

Responding to the Selection

How does the speaker feel about the person he or she is addressing? Have you ever felt this way about somebody? Explore these feelings in your journal and then discuss them with your classmates.

Reviewing the Selection

RECALLING

1. What does the speaker say "your eyes" have?

2. What will easily "unclose" the speaker, even if he has closed himself like fingers?

3. What equals "the power of your intense fragility"?

4. What does the speaker understand about "the voice of your eyes"?

INTERPRETING

5. Where has the speaker not traveled? What is gladly beyond any experience? What does it mean for eyes to "have their silence"? Is there a part of the self that others usually do not reach?

6. In the metaphor "you open always petal by petal," to what does the speaker compare the person addressed in the poem? To what does he compare himself? What does it usually mean when people speak of "opening up" to others?

7. What "compels" the speaker "with the colour of its countries"? What does the use of the word "countries" suggest about the vast, unexplored nature of the other person's personality?

8. What effect does rain have on roses? What effect does the person being addressed have on the speaker? What small gestures on the part of that person affect the speaker deeply?

SYNTHESIZING

9. Think of the various things to which the speaker compares the person being addressed: Spring opening a rose, snow descending and causing a rose to close, and the small hands of the rain. Then think of the descriptions of the person's frail gestures, slightest look, and intense fragility. What power does the person being addressed have over the speaker? What is ironic or paradoxical about this power?

10. What things mentioned in the poem are mysterious, not fully understandable or known, and thus "beyond experience"?

Understanding Literature (Questions for Discussion)

1. **Syntax and Inversion. Syntax** is the pattern of arrangement of words in a statement. Cummings begins the poem with two modifying phrases, delaying until the middle of the second line the appearance of the noun that is modified—*eyes*. An **inversion** is a poetic technique in which the normal order of words is altered. How are the words in the first two lines inverted? How would the first two lines read if Cummings had followed the usual order of words in a sentence, placing the subject first?

2. **Repetition and Rhyme. Repetition** is the use, again, of a sound, word, phrase, sentence, or other element. **Rhyme** is the repetition of sounds at the ends of words. Types of rhyme include *end rhyme* (the use of rhyming words at the ends of lines), *internal rhyme* (the use of rhyming words within lines), *exact rhyme* (in which the rhyming words end with the same sound or sounds), and *slant rhyme* (in which the rhyming sounds are similar but not identical). What repetition of the words *open* and *close* occurs in this poem? What types of rhyme are used in the various repetitions of these words? What effect is enacted by the various repetitions and rhymes of the words *open* and *close*?

Responding in Writing

Love Letter. Imagine that you are the person whom the speaker addresses in this poem. Write him or her a letter expressing your feelings of love. Refer to the material in the Language Arts Survey, 5.2, "The Form of a Personal Letter."

"Yet Do I Marvel"
by Countee Cullen

ABOUT THE AUTHOR

Countee Cullen (1903–1946) was born Countee Leroy Porter in New York City. In 1918, he was adopted by Reverend Frederick Cullen, a Methodist minister. He attended New York public schools, graduated Phi Beta Kappa with a B.A. from New York University in 1925, and took an M.A. at Harvard in 1926. He married twice. His first marriage to Yolande Du Bois, daughter of W. E. B. Du Bois, black educator and sociologist, lasted two years. Like many African Americans of his time, Cullen shaped the expression of his talents in reaction to racism in the society in which he lived. Recalling an incident in 1930 when he was barred from eating in a restaurant at the New York Central terminal in Buffalo, New York, he later said, "There may have been many things in my life that have hurt me, and I find that the surest relief from these hurts is in writing. Most things I write, I do for the sheer love of the music in them. Somehow or other, however, I find my poetry of itself treating of the Negro, of his joys and his sorrows, mostly of the latter, and of the heights and the depths of emotion which I feel as a Negro." From 1926 to 1928, Cullen was assistant editor of *Opportunity: Journal of Negro Life,* the magazine of the National Urban League, where he wrote "The Dark Tower," a column of reflections and literary criticism. He taught French at Frederick Douglass Junior High School in New York City from 1934 to 1945 and wrote and published children's stories. Cullen was proud of being African American, of his "ebony muse," but not surprisingly, he was bitter about the African-American experience in America. He is best known for his poems about racial issues, but was criticized by his contemporaries for the mildness of his attacks on racial injustice. Cullen was a middle-class New Yorker who wanted to be a traditional poet, and his ideas about poetry were counter to those of other writers of the Harlem Renaissance. Among other awards and honors, Cullen received a Guggenheim Fellowship in 1929 to complete *The Black Christ and Other Poems* (1929). His works include *Color* (poetry, 1925), *Caroling Dusk: An Anthology of Verse by Negro Poets* (1927), *Copper Sun* (1927), *The Ballad of the Brown Girl* (1928), *One Way to Heaven* (novel, 1932), and *On These I Stand* (1947).

ABOUT THE SELECTION

"Yet Do I Marvel" appeared in *On These I Stand,* the collection considered to include Cullen's best poetry. The final lines of the selection are among the most famous of all produced by the poets of the Harlem Renaissance.

"Yet Do I Marvel"

COUNTEE CULLEN

I doubt not God is good, well-meaning,
    kind,
And did He stoop to quibble could tell why
The little buried mole continues blind,
Why flesh that mirrors Him must some day die,

5   Make plain the reason tortured Tantalus[1]
Is baited by the fickle fruit, declare
If merely brute <u>caprice</u> dooms Sisyphus[2]
To struggle up a never-ending stair.
Inscrutable[3] His ways are, and immune

10   To catechism[4] by a mind too strewn
With petty cares to slightly understand
What awful brain compels His awful hand.
Yet do I marvel at this curious thing:
To make a poet black, and bid him sing! ∎

What kind of God does the speaker envision?

What does the speaker say about understanding the motivations of God?

---

1. **Tantalus.** King in Greek mythology who was doomed in Hades to stand in water that receded from him when he was thirsty and under branches of fruit that he could not reach when hungry
2. **Sisyphus.** King whose doom in Hades was to roll a heavy stone uphill only to have it always roll down again
3. **Inscrutable.** That cannot be easily understood
4. **catechism.** Close questioning; religious debate or discussion

WORDS FOR EVERYDAY USE:
ca • price (kə prēs´) *n.*, whim, change in way of thinking

Responding to the Selection

Review lines 9–12 of the poem. What explanation does the speaker offer for the existence of cruelty, pain, death, and injustice in the world? Do you agree with this explanation? Why, or why not?

Reviewing the Selection

RECALLING

1. What negative aspects of the world does the speaker mention in lines 3–8?

2. What comparison does the speaker make between the mind of God and the mind of a human?

INTERPRETING

▶▶ 3. What does the speaker not doubt, despite the existence of pain?

▶▶ 4. How does the speaker respond to the old argument that a just God would not allow pain or injustice to continue?

SYNTHESIZING

5. At what does the speaker marvel? What paradox does the speaker seem to see in "this curious thing"? How does this curiosity relate to the speaker's comments about God?

Understanding Literature (Questions for Discussion)

1. **Sonnet.** A **sonnet** is a fourteen-line poem that follows one of a number of different rhyme schemes. Like the **English, Elizabethan,** or **Shakespearean sonnet,** the selection can be divided into four parts: three **quatrains,** or four-line stanzas, and a final **couplet,** or two-line stanza. A Shakespearean sonnet usually has the rhyme scheme *abab cdcd efef gg.* What is the rhyme scheme of the selection? How does the selection's rhyme scheme vary slightly from that of a Shakespearean sonnet? Another way of viewing the organization of this sonnet is as an **octave,** or group of eight lines, followed by a **sestet,** or group of six lines. What question is raised in the octave of this sonnet? How is that question answered in the sestet? What comment does the speaker make in the concluding couplet, or pair of rhymed lines?

2. **Allusion.** An **allusion** is a figure of speech in which a reference is made to a person, event, object, or work from history or literature. Cullen alludes, or refers, to the Greek myths of Tantalus and Sisyphus. In the former myth, the gods condemned Tantalus to spend eternity in the underworld, poised between water below him and food above him. Whenever he moved to get the food or water, it receded from him, leaving him eternally thirsty and hungry. In the latter myth, the gods condemned Sisyphus to spend eternity in the underworld pushing a rock to the top of a hill only to have it roll back down so that his task could never be complete. What purpose is served by the allusions to these two myths? Of what kinds of experiences are the myths examples?

"The Tropics in New York"
by Claude McKay

ABOUT THE AUTHOR

Claude McKay (1890–1948), who also wrote under the pseudonym Eli Edwards, was born in Jamaica, in the West Indies, to poor farm workers. He was educated by his brother and by an Englishman who was a specialist in Jamaican folklore. His first two collections of poems, written in native dialect, were published in England in 1912. These collections earned him prize money that helped him to emigrate to the United States that year. He studied at Booker T. Washington's Tuskeegee Institute and at Kansas State College. He moved to Harlem in 1914, worked at odd jobs, and pursued his writing. He moved to England for a time, where his poems were published regularly, then returned to the United States in the early 1920s, where he took a job as editor of the radical newspapers *The Liberator* and *The Masses*. He was a prominent figure in the Harlem Renaissance, and the racial prejudice he witnessed and experienced helped to radicalize him. He left America to live in Europe but returned after the publication of his award-winning novel *Home to Harlem* (1928), one of the first bestsellers by an African-American writer. By the 1940s, he had repudiated his earlier radicalism and become a naturalized citizen. His poem "If We Must Die," written as a response to the Harlem race riots of 1919, was nevertheless embraced as a rallying cry by the majority white culture during World War II. Its stirring sentiments were admired by Winston Churchill, who read it to the British people. In the United States, the poem was entered into the Congressional Record. Some critics consider the poem to be a major impetus behind the Civil Rights movement that began after the war. One critic called it, "at once a shout of defiance and a proclamation of the unbreakable spirit and courage of the oppressed black American." In 1942, McKay joined the Catholic Church and for the last five years of his life lived in Chicago doing research for the National Catholic Youth Organization. His works include *Songs of Jamaica* (poetry, 1912), *Harlem Shadows* (poetry, 1922), *Banjo* (1929), *Banana Bottom* (1933), *Gingertown* (short stories, 1932), *A Long Way from Home* (autobiography, 1937), and *Harlem: Negro Metropolis* (sociological study, 1940).

ABOUT THE SELECTION

After moving to the United States from Jamaica in 1912, McKay started again to write. Perhaps reflective of McKay's own experience, the speaker in **"The Tropics in New York,"** noting with realistic detail the fruits in a grocer's window, is reminded of his former life in the tropics and longs for its old and familiar ways.

"The Tropics in New York"

CLAUDE MCKAY

Bananas ripe and green, and ginger-root,
    Cocoa in pods and alligator pears,
And tangerines and mangoes and grapefruit,
    Fit for the highest prize at parish fairs,

5   Set in the window, bringing memories
    Of fruit-trees laden by low-singing rills,
And dewy dawns, and mystical blue skies
    In benediction[1] over nun-like hills.

My eyes grew dim, and I could no more gaze;
10   A wave of longing through my body swept,
And, hungry for the old, familiar ways,
    I turned aside and bowed my head and wept. ∎

What does the speaker see in the window? What memories do these things bring?

For what did the speaker grow hungry? Why did the fruit have such an effect on him?

---

1. **benediction.** Blessing

Responding to the Selection

Imagine that you are the speaker standing outside the grocer's window, looking at the tropical fruits. Why does the image of those fruits suddenly fill you with longing? Write a letter to a friend in Jamaica, expressing to him or her your feelings of homesickness for the old and familiar ways.

Reviewing the Selection

RECALLING

1. What fruits are "fit for the highest prize at parish fairs"?

2. What sweeps through the speaker's body?

INTERPRETING

3. What images recall the past for the speaker? What effect, or emotional impact, do the images create?

4. How does the speaker feel toward "the old, familiar ways"?

SYNTHESIZING

5. What role does hunger have in the poem? What connotations and denotations of hunger are used in the poem?

Understanding Literature (Questions for Discussion)

1. **Meter and Rhyme.** The **meter** of a poem is its rhythmical pattern. A poem is made up of rhythmical units, called *feet*. Types of feet include iambic, trochaic, anapestic, dactylic, and spondaic. (For definitions of these terms, see the entry on *meter* in the Handbook of Literary Terms.) **Rhyme** is the repetition of sounds at the ends of words. One type of rhyme, **end rhyme**, is the use of rhyming words at the ends of lines. Scan the poem. What is the poem's meter? What is its rhyme scheme?

2. **Tone.** Tone is the emotional attitude toward the reader or toward the subject implied by a literary work. How do the different meanings of hunger cause the tone of the poem to shift in each stanza?

Responding in Writing

Greeting Card. Create a greeting card for the speaker of the poem, who is a long way from home. In your card, write a message that expresses your wishes and concerns for the speaker.

"The Negro Speaks of Rivers"
by Langston Hughes

ABOUT THE AUTHOR

Langston Hughes (1902–1967) was born in Joplin, Missouri, and lived for most of his childhood in Lawrence, Kansas, with his maternal grandmother, whose first husband had been one of the African-Americans killed in John Brown's raid on the arsenal at Harpers Ferry. Hughes was thirteen when she died, at which time he went to live with his mother. He graduated from high school in Cleveland, Ohio, and then spent more than a year with his father in Mexico. It was there that he wrote the poem "The Negro Speaks of Rivers," which would later gain him recognition as a writer. Hughes studied for a year at Columbia University, leaving in 1920. For the next several years, he traveled, taking whatever jobs he found, wherever he found himself. During this peripatetic period, he continued to write. His work began to be published in important African-American periodicals like *Opportunity* and *The Crises.* He accepted a scholarship from Lincoln University in Pennsylvania and graduated in 1929. While there, he wrote his first novel, *Not without Laughter* (1930). His political activism in the 1930s later resulted in his being called to testify before the House Un-American Activities Committee in 1953 and listed as a security risk by the FBI until 1959. Awards and honors recognizing his work include Rosenwald and Guggenheim fellowships and a grant from the American Academy of Arts and Letters. Hughes was a prolific, versatile writer and is especially well known for his famous fictional character Jesse B. Semple, or "Simple." His works include *The Weary Blues* (1926), *The Negro Artist and the Racial Mountain* (essay, 1926), *The Ways of White Folks* (stories, 1934), *Shakespeare in Harlem* (1942), *Simple Speaks His Mind* (1950), *First Book of Negroes* (anthology, 1952), *First Book of Jazz* (anthology, 1955), *Simple Stakes a Claim* (1957), *First Book of Negro Folklore* (anthology, 1958).

ABOUT THE SELECTION

Before graduating from Lincoln University in Pennsylvania, Hughes had published his first collection of verse, *The Weary Blues*. Included in that 1926 collection was **"The Negro Speaks of Rivers."** During the 1920s, while writing these poems, Hughes worked to unite the elements of blues with formal poetry.

READER'S JOURNAL

With what object in the natural world do you most strongly identify? Choose one object and write about it in your journal, telling why you are attracted to it and what it means to you.

LANGUAGE SKILLS

Read the Language Arts Survey, 2.43–2.45, on compound, complex, and compound-complex sentences. Then identify two sentences in the selection that build on the simple sentence "I've known rivers." Note how the other sentences expand on the original simple sentence.

"The Negro Speaks of Rivers"

LANGSTON HUGHES

I've known rivers:
I've known rivers ancient as the world and older than the
    flow of human blood in human veins.

My soul has grown deep like the rivers.

5   I bathed in the Euphrates when dawns were young.
I built my hut near the Congo and it lulled me to sleep.
I looked upon the Nile[1] and raised the pyramids above it.
I heard the singing of the Mississippi when Abe Lincoln
    went down to New Orleans, and I've seen its muddy
10   bosom turn all golden in the sunset.

I've known rivers:
Ancient, dusky rivers.

My soul has grown deep like the rivers.

What is significant about the rivers?

To what aspect of the rivers does the speaker compare his soul?

---

1. **Euphrates . . . Nile.** *Euphrates*—river that flows through Turkey, Syria, and Iraq; *Congo*—river in central Africa; *Nile*—river in north east Africa

Responding to the Selection

Imagine that you are the speaker in the poem. For whom do you speak? What is the purpose of your message? Discuss what it means to grow deep like a river.

Reviewing the Selection

1. What has the speaker known?

2. What phrases does the speaker use in lines 2 and 3 to describe the rivers?

3. What specific rivers does the speaker mention in the poem?

4. What has happened to the speaker's soul?

▶▶ 5. Who is the speaker in this poem?

▶▶ 6. The speaker associates himself with rivers "ancient as the world" and "older than the flow of human blood in human veins." What is the speaker saying about the age and experience of the Negro race?

▶▶ 7. What accomplishments and experiences are associated with each of the rivers in the poem?

▶▶ 8. What has caused the speaker's soul to deepen?

9. Is this a poem about an individual or about a group? Explain.

10. What overall emotion is expressed by this poem? Explain.

Understanding Literature (Questions for Discussion)

1. **Simile.** A **simile** is a comparison using *like* or *as.* A type of metaphor, a simile can be analyzed into two parts, the *tenor* (or subject being described), and the *vehicle* (or object being used in the description). The two parts can be compared because they share a particular quality. Consider the following simile in the selection: "My soul has grown deep like the rivers." What is the tenor? What is the vehicle? What quality do the two parts share? Identify and analyze another simile from the selection.

2. **Refrain and Effect.** A **refrain** is a line or group of lines repeated in a poem or song. The **effect** of a literary work is the general impression or emotional impact that it achieves. What refrains are used in the poem? What effect do these refrains lend to the overall emotional impact of the poem?

Responding in Writing

1. **Lyric Poem.** A **lyric poem** is a highly musical verse that expresses the emotions of a speaker. Write a lyric poem about a speaker's deep identity with a place. In your poem, use repetition and tone to express the feelings of the speaker.

2. **Family History.** Write a page of your family history. Begin by identifying a particular place where your family has lived for a long time, frequently visited, or gathered together.

Language Lab

Achieving Parallelism. Read the Language Arts Survey, 2.57, "Achieving Parallelism." Then revise the sentences below by correcting the faulty parallelism.

1. Langston Hughes attended high school in Cleveland and to publish fiction and poetry in his high school magazine.
2. For more than twenty years, Hughes wrote for the *Chicago Defender,* in which he introduced the character "Simple" and to make him the heart of his column.
3. Hughes said I've known rivers and his soul has grown deep like the rivers.
4. In 1932, the year Hughes lived and was working in the former Soviet Union, he wrote his most radical poetry.
5. Hughes published dozens of books of fiction, nonfiction, and poetry and to translate books by Lorca, Mistral, Guillen, and Roumain.

Research Skills

Using Reference Works. Read the Language Arts Survey, 4.23, "Using Reference Works." Then, for each subject in the following list, identify the type of reference work in which you can find out what you need to know.

1. location of the Congo River
2. history of the Nile River
3. news story about the most recent Mississippi River flood
4. quotations about rivers
5. name of the river with which the Euphrates unites

PROJECT

Oral History. Visit someone at a community for retired or elderly people, or seek out an elderly person in your own family. (Before visiting a facility, such as a retirement community, contact the administrative personnel to obtain permission for your visit.) Interview that person to prepare an oral history of his or her life in some specific place. If possible, tape record and transcribe the stories that the person tells you. If you do not have access to a tape recorder, take detailed notes during the interview, and then write up your notes in the form of a brief report. Share those stories in written form with your classmates.

"A Black Man Talks of Reaping"
by Arna Bontemps

ABOUT THE AUTHOR

Arna (Wendell) Bontemps (1902–1973) was born in Alexandria, Louisiana. His father was a brick mason and his mother a teacher. Arna was the nickname given him by his grandmother. He had a comfortable childhood, although his family relocated from Louisiana to Los Angeles after some racial harassment of his father. In 1923, Bontemps graduated from Pacific Union College. In 1943, he earned an M.A. from the University of Chicago. He married Alberta Johnson in 1926, and they had six children. A teacher, librarian, anthologist, poet, author of novels, plays, biographies, and children's fiction, Bontemps dealt in his work almost exclusively with black life and culture. Active in writers' organizations and in the American Library Association, he also served as a member of the Metropolitan Nashville Board of Education. He worked as a high school teacher and principal, as well as a freelance writer, before he was Librarian of Fisk University from 1943 to 1965. He also taught at the University of Chicago and Yale University. His writing identified him with the Harlem Renaissance. His correspondence with long-time friend and collaborator Langston Hughes was published in 1979. Much of his work, in all genres, reflects his attempts to reconcile his respect for the richness of African-American folk culture with his repudiation of negative ethnic stereotypes. His works for adults include *God Sends Sunday* (1931); *St. Louis Woman* (1946), a dramatization written with Countee Cullen; *Black Thunder* (1935); *Drums at Dusk* (1939); *Story of the Negro* (1948); *One Hundred Years of Negro Freedom* (1961); and *Popo and Fifina: Children of Haiti* (1932), written with Langston Hughes. His works for children include *Sam Patch* (1951), written with Jack Conroy, and *Famous Negro Athletes* (1964). Among the many awards and honors he received in recognition for his work were a Newbery Honor (for outstanding children's book, 1949), *The Crisis* magazine's poetry prize (1926), the Alexander Pushkin Poetry Prize (1926 and 1927), the short story prize of the journal *Opportunity* (1932), Julius Rosenwald fellowships (1938–1939, 1942–1943), a Guggenheim Fellowship for creative writing (1949–1950), and a Jane Addams Children's Book Award (1956).

ABOUT THE SELECTION

In his novels and poetry, Bontemps portrayed the lives and struggles of African Americans, a theme that can be seen in his poem **"A Black Man Talks of Reaping."** The speaker in the poem, in the process of telling about his experiences sowing and reaping, also reveals the disappointments, fears, and concerns of being human.

"A Black Man Talks of Reaping"

ARNA BONTEMPS

I have sown[1] beside all waters in my day.
I planted deep, within my heart the fear
that wind or fowl would take the grain away.
I planted safe against this stark, lean year.

5   I scattered seed enough to plant the land
in rows from Canada to Mexico
but for my reaping only what the hand
can hold at once is all that I can show.

Yet what I sowed and what the orchard yields
10   my brother's sons are gathering stalk and root:
small wonder then my children glean[2] in fields
they have not sown, and feed on bitter fruit. ∎

How has the speaker done this year?

How does the speaker estimate his labors?

---

1. **sown.** Planted
2. **glean.** Pick up tiny pieces or crumbs.

Responding to the Selection

Imagine that you are the speaker in the poem, who has seen his children "glean in fields/they have not sown, and feed on bitter fruit." What emotions would arise from watching your children eat what others have left behind in the fields? Write an entry in your journal expressing your feelings about the situation.

Reviewing the Selection

RECALLING

1. What kind of year is it?

2. How much seed has the speaker sown?

INTERPRETING

3. Why does the speaker plant the seeds "deep"?

4. Why do the speaker's children "feed on bitter fruit"?

SYNTHESIZING

5. Who reaps the benefits of the labor in this poem?

Understanding Literature (Questions for Discussion)

1. **Rhyme. Rhyme** is the repetition of sounds at the ends of words. One type of rhyme, *end rhyme,* is the use of rhyming words at the ends of lines. What is the end-rhyme scheme in this poem?

2. **Speaker.** The **speaker** is the character who speaks in a poem—the voice assumed by the writer. The speaker in this poem is identified in the title by his race. What is the speaker's view of reaping? How might his view of reaping be different from that of a white man?

"Miniver Cheevy"
by Edwin Arlington Robinson

Miniver Cheevy, child of scorn,
    Grew lean while he assailed the seasons;
He wept that he was ever born,
    And he had reasons.

5 Miniver loved the days of old
    When swords were bright and steeds
    were prancing;
The vision of a warrior bold
    Would set him dancing.

Miniver sighed for what was not,
10   And dreamed, and rested from his labors;
He dreamed of Thebes[1] and Camelot,[2]
    And Priam's[3] neighbors.

Miniver mourned the ripe renown
    That made so many a name so fragrant;
15 He mourned Romance, now on the town,
    And Art, a vagrant.

Miniver loved the Medici,[4]
    Albeit he had never seen one;
He would have sinned incessantly
20   Could he have been one.

Miniver cursed the commonplace
    And eyed a khaki suit with loathing;
He missed the medieval[5] grace
    Of iron clothing.

25 Miniver scorned the gold he sought,
    But sore annoyed was he without it;
Miniver thought, and thought, and thought,
    And thought about it.

Miniver Cheevy, born too late,
30   Scratched his head and kept on thinking;
Miniver coughed, and called it fate,
    And kept on drinking.

---

1. **Thebes.** Ancient Greek city
2. **Camelot.** Mythical kingdom of Arthur and
Guinevere (in southwestern England, Cornwall)
3. **Priam.** King of Troy (ancient Greek city)
4. **Medici.** Wealthy family in Renaissance Italy who
supported artists, especially in the city of Florence

"Richard Cory"
by Edwin Arlington Robinson

Whenever Richard Cory went down town,
We people on the pavement looked at him:
He was a gentleman from sole to crown,
Clean favored, and imperially slim.

5 And he was always quietly arrayed,
And he was always human when he talked;
But still he fluttered pulses when he said,
"Good-morning," and he glittered when he walked.

And he was rich—yes, richer than a king—
10 And admirably schooled in every grace:
In fine, we thought that he was everything
To make us wish that we were in his place.

So on we worked, and waited for the light,
And went without the meat, and cursed the bread;
15 And Richard Cory, one calm summer night,
Went home and put a bullet through his head.

"The Flower-Fed Buffaloes"
by Vachel Lindsay

The flower-fed buffaloes of the spring
In the days of long ago,
Ranged[6] where the locomotives sing
And the prairie flowers lie low:—
5 The tossing, blooming, perfumed grass
Is swept away by the wheat,
Wheels and wheels and wheels spin by
In the spring that still is sweet.
But the flower-fed buffaloes of the spring
10 Left us, long ago.
They gore[7] no more, they bellow no more,
They trundle around the hills no more:—
With the Blackfeet, lying low,
With the Pawnees,[8] lying low,
15 Lying low.

---

5. **medieval.** Of the Middle Ages
6. **Ranged.** Roamed, feeding on the prairie grass
7. **gore.** Attack with their horns
8. **Blackfeet . . . Pawnees.** Refers to two Native American
peoples of the western United States

"The Death of the Hired Man"
by Robert Frost

Mary sat musing on the lamp-flame at the table,
Waiting for Warren. When she heard his step,
She ran on tiptoe down the darkened passage
To meet him in the doorway with the news
5 And put him on his guard. "Silas is back."
She pushed him outward with her through the door
And shut it after her. "Be kind," she said.
She took the market things from Warren's arms
And set them on the porch, them drew him down
10 To sit beside her on the wooden steps.

"When was I ever anything but kind to him?
But I'll not have the fellow back," he said.
"I told him so last haying,[1] didn't I?
If he left then, I said, that ended it.
15 What good is he? Who else will harbor him
At his age for the little he can do?
What help he is there's no depending on.
Off he goes always when I need him most.
He thinks he ought to earn a little pay,
20 Enough at least to buy tobacco with,
So he won't have to beg and be beholden.[2]
'All right,' I say, 'I can't afford to pay
Any fixed wages, though I wish I could.'
'Someone else can.' 'Then someone else will have to.'
25 I shouldn't mind his bettering himself
If that was what it was. You can be certain,
When he begins like that, there's someone at him
Trying to coax him off with pocket money—
In haying time, when any help is scarce.
30 In winter he comes back to us. I'm done."

"Sh! not so loud: he'll hear you," Mary said.

"I want him to: he'll have to soon or late."

"He's worn out. He's asleep beside the stove.
When I came up from Rowe's I found him here,
35 Huddled against the barn-door fast asleep,
A miserable sight, and frightening, too—
You needn't smile—I didn't recognize him—
I wasn't looking for him—and he's changed.
Wait till you see."

40   "Where did you say he'd been?"

"He didn't say. I dragged him to the house,

1. **haying.** Harvest, gathering of hay
2. **beholden.** Indebted to anyone

And gave him tea and tried to make him smoke.
I tried to make him talk about his travels.
Nothing would do: he just kept nodding off."

45 "What did he say? Did he say anything?"

"But little."

          "Anything? Mary, confess
He said he'd come to ditch the meadow for me."

"Warren!"

50   "But did he? I just want to know."

"Of course he did. What would you have him say?
Surely you wouldn't grudge the poor old man
Some humble way to save his self-respect.
He added, if you really care to know,
55 He meant to clear the upper pasture, too.
That sounds like something you have heard before?
Warren, I wish you could have heard the way
He jumbled everything. I stopped to look
Two or three times—he made me feel so queer—
60 To see if he was talking in his sleep.
He ran on Harold Wilson—you remember—
The boy you had in haying four years since.
He's finished school, and teaching in his college.
Silas declares you'll have to get him back.
65 He says they two will make a team for work:
Between them they will lay this farm as smooth!
The way he mixed that in with other things.
He thinks young Wilson a likely lad, though daft
On education—you know how they fought
70 All through July under the blazing sun,
Silas up on the cart to build the load,
Harold along beside to pitch it on."

"Yes, I took care to keep well out of earshot."

"Well, those days trouble Silas like a dream.
75 You wouldn't think they would. How some things
     linger!
Harold's young college-boy's assurance piqued him.
After so many years he still keeps finding
Good arguments he sees he might have used.
I sympathize. I know just how it feels
80 To think of the right thing to say too late.
Harold's associated in his mind with Latin.
He asked me what I thought of Harold's saying
He studied Latin, like the violin,
Because he liked it—that an argument!

85 He said he couldn't make the boy believe
He could find water with a hazel prong—
Which showed how much good school had ever
   done him.
He wanted to go over that. But most of all
He thinks if he could have another chance
90 To teach him how to build a load of hay—"

"I know, that's Silas' one accomplishment.
He bundles every forkful in its place,
And tags and numbers it for future reference,
So he can find and easily dislodge it
95 In the unloading. Silas does that well.
He takes it out in bunches like big birds' nests.
You never see him standing on the hay
He's trying to lift, straining to lift himself."

"He thinks if he could teach him that he'd be
100 Some good perhaps to someone in the world.
He hates to see a boy the fool of books.
Poor Silas, so concerned for other folk,
And nothing to look backward to with pride,
And nothing to look forward to with hope,
105 So now and never any different."
Part of a moon was falling down the west,
Dragging the whole sky with it to the hills.
Its light poured softly in her lap. She saw it
And spread her apron to it. She put out her hand
110 Among the harplike morning-glory strings,
Taut with the dew from garden bed to eaves,
As if she played unheard some tenderness
That wrought on him beside her in the night.
"Warren," she said, "he has come home to die:
115 You needn't be afraid he'll leave you this time."

"Home," he mocked gently.

    "Yes, what else but home?
It all depends on what you mean by home.
Of course he's nothing to us, any more
120 Than was the hound that came a stranger to us
Out of the woods, worn out upon the trail."
"Home is the place where, when you have to go there,
They have to take you in."

        "I should have called it
125 Something you somehow haven't to deserve."

Warren leaned out and took a step or two,
Picked up a little stick, and brought it back
And broke it in his hand and tossed it by.
"Silas has better claim on us you think

130 Than on his brother? Thirteen little miles
As the road winds would bring him to his door.
Silas has walked that far no doubt today.
Why doesn't he go there? His brother's rich,
A somebody—director in the bank."

135 "He never told us that."

    "We know it though."

"I think his brother ought to help, of course.
I'll see to that if there is need. He ought of right
To take him in, and might be willing to—
140 He may be better than appearances.
But have some pity on Silas. Do you think
If he had any pride in claiming kin
Or anything he looked for from his brother,
He'd keep so still about him all this time?"

145 "I wonder what's between them."

    "I can tell you.
Silas is what he is—we wouldn't mind him—
But just the kind that kinsfolk can't abide.
He never did a thing so very bad.
150 He don't know why he isn't quite as good
As anybody. Worthless though he is,
He won't be made ashamed to please his brother."

"*I* can't think Si ever hurt anyone."

"No, but he hurt my heart the way he lay
155 And rolled his old head on that sharp-edged
   chair-back.
He wouldn't let me put him on the lounge.
You must go in and see what you can do.
I made the bed up for him there tonight.
You'll be surprised at him—how much he's broken.
160 His working days are done; I'm sure of it."

"I'd not be in a hurry to say that."

"I haven't been. Go, look, see for yourself.
But, Warren, please remember how it is:
He's come to help you ditch the meadow.
165 He has a plan. You mustn't laugh at him.
He may not speak of it, and then he may.
I'll sit and see if that small sailing cloud
Will hit or miss the moon."

    It hit the moon.
170 Then there were three there, making a dim row,
The moon, the little silver cloud, and she.

Warren returned—too soon, it seemed to her,
Slipped to her side, caught up her hand and waited.

"Warren?" she questioned.

175   "Dead," was all he answered.

"An Old Man's Winter Night"
by Robert Frost

All out-of-doors looked darkly in at him
Through the thin frost, almost in separate stars,
That gathers on the pane in empty rooms.
What kept his eyes from giving back the gaze
5   Was the lamp tilted near them in his hand.
What kept him from remembering what it was
That brought him to that creaking room was age.
He stood with barrels round him—at a loss.
And having scared the cellar under him
10   In clomping here, he scared it once again
In clomping off—and scared the outer night,
Which has its sounds, familiar, like the roar
Of trees and crack of branches, common things,
But nothing so like beating on a box.
15   A light he was to no one but himself
Where now he sat, concerned with he knew what,
A quiet light, and then not even that.
He consigned[1] to the moon—such as she was,
So late-arising—to the broken moon,
20   As better than the sun in any case
For such a charge, his snow upon the roof,
His icicles along the wall to keep;
And slept. The log that shifted with a jolt
Once in the stove, disturbed him and he shifted,
25   And eased his heavy breathing, but still slept.
One aged man—one man—can't keep a house,
A farm, a countryside, or if he can,
It's thus he does it of a winter night.

"Disillusionment of Ten O'Clock"
by Wallace Stevens

The houses are haunted
By white night-gowns.
None are green,
Or purple with green rings,
5   Or green with yellow rings,

Or yellow with blue rings.
None of them are strange,
With socks of lace
And beaded ceintures.[2]
10   People are not going
To dream of baboons and periwinkles.[3]
Only, here and there, an old sailor,
Drunk and asleep in his boots,
Catches tigers
15   In red weather.

"Wind and Silver"
by Amy Lowell

Greatly shining,
The Autumn moon floats in the thin sky;
And the fish-ponds shake their backs and flash their
    dragon scales
As she passes over them.

"A Lover"
by Amy Lowell

If I could catch the green lantern of the firefly
I could see to write you a letter.

"The River-Merchant's Wife: A Letter"[4]
by Ezra Pound

While my hair was still cut straight across my
    forehead
I played about the front gate, pulling flowers.
You came by on bamboo stilts, playing horse,
You walked about my seat, playing with blue plums.
5   And we went on living in the village of Chōkan:
Two small people, without dislike or suspicion.

At fourteen I married My Lord you.
I never laughed, being bashful.
Lowering my head, I looked at the wall.
10   Called to, a thousand times, I never looked back.

At fifteen I stopped scowling,
I desired my dust to be mingled with yours
Forever and forever and forever.
Why should I climb the look out?

---

1. **consigned.** Put in care of
2. **ceintures.** Sashes; belts
3. **periwinkles.** Tiny, pale blue-violet sea snails

4. **"The River-Merchant's Wife: A Letter."** Pound's version of a translation of the eighth-century Chinese epic by poet Li Po (Rihaku in Japanese)

15 At sixteen you departed,
You went into far Ku-tō-en, by the river of swirling
        eddies,
And you have been gone five months.
The monkeys make sorrowful noise overhead.

You dragged your feet when you went out.
20 By the gate now, the moss is grown, the different
        mosses,
Too deep to clear them away!
The leaves fall early this autumn, in wind.
The paired butterflies are already yellow with August
Over the grass in the West garden;
25 They hurt me. I grow older.
If you are coming down through the narrows of the
        river Kiang,
Please let me know beforehand,
And I will come out to meet you
        As far as Chō-fū-Sa.

By Rihaku

"Euclid Alone Has Looked on Beauty Bare"
by Edna St. Vincent Millay

Euclid alone has looked on Beauty bare.
Let all who prate of Beauty hold their peace,
And lay them prone upon the earth and cease
To ponder on themselves, the while they stare
5 At nothing, intricately drawn nowhere
In shapes of shifting lineage; let geese
Gabble and hiss, but heroes seek release
From dusty bondage into luminous air.
O blinding hour, O holy, terrible day,
10 When first the shaft into his vision shone
Of light anatomized! Euclid alone
Has looked on Beauty bare. Fortunate they
Who, though once only and then but far away,
Have heard her massive sandal set on stone.

"anyone lived in a pretty how town"
by E. E. Cummings

anyone lived in a pretty how town
(with up so floating many bells down)
spring summer autumn winter
he sang his didn't he danced his did

5 Women and men(both little and small)
cared for anyone not at all

they sowed their isn't they reaped their same
sun moon stars rain

children guessed(but only a few
10 and down they forgot as up they grew
autumn winter spring summer)
that noone loved him more by more

when by now and tree by leaf
she laughed his joy she cried his grief
15 bird by snow and stir by still
anyone's any was all to her

someones married their everyones
laughed their cryings and did their dance
(sleep wake hope and then)they
20 said their nevers they slept their dream

stars rain sun moon
(and only the snow can begin to explain
how children are apt to forget to remember
with up so floating many bells down)

25 one day anyone died i guess
(and noone stooped to kiss his face)
busy folk buried them side by side
little by little and was by was

all by all and deep by deep
30 and more by more they dream their sleep
noone and anyone earth by april
wish by spirit and if by yes.

Women and men(both dong and ding)
summer autumn winter spring
35 reaped their sowing and went their came
sun moon stars rain

"Any Human to Another"
by Countee Cullen

The ills I sorrow at
Not me alone
Like an arrow,
Pierce to the marrow,
5 Through the fat
And past the bone.

Your grief and mine
Must intertwine
Like sea and river,
10 Be fused and mingle,

Diverse yet single,
Forever and forever.

Let no man be so proud
And confident,
15 To think he is allowed
A little tent
Pitched in a meadow
Of sun and shadow
All his little own.

20 Joy may be shy, unique,
Friendly to a few,
Sorrow never scorned to speak
To any who
Were false or true.

25 Your every grief
Like a blade
Shining and unsheathed
Must strike me down.
Of bitter aloes[1] wreathed,
30 My sorrow must be laid
On your head like a crown.

"Storm Ending"
by Jean Toomer

Thunder blossoms gorgeously above our heads,
Great, hollow, bell-like flowers,
Rumbling in the wind,
Stretching clappers to strike our ears . . .
5 Full-lipped flowers
Bitten by the sun
Bleeding rain
Dripping rain like golden honey—
And the sweet earth flying from the thunder.

"For the Union Dead"
by Robert Lowell

"Relinquunt Omnia Servare Rem Publicam."[2]

The old South Boston Aquarium stands
in a Sahara of snow now. Its broken windows are
    boarded.
The bronze weathervane cod has lost half its scales.
The airy tanks are dry.

5 Once my nose crawled like a snail on the glass;
my hand tingled
to burst the bubbles drifting from the noses of the
    cowed, compliant fish.

My hand draws back. I often sigh still
10 for the dark downward and vegetating kingdom
of the fish and reptile. One morning last March,
I pressed against the new barbed and galvanized

fence on the Boston Common. Behind their cage,
yellow dinosaur steamshovels were grunting
15 as they cropped up tons of mush and grass
to gouge their underworld garage.

Parking spaces luxuriate like civic
sandpiles in the heart of Boston.
A girdle of orange, Puritan-pumpkin colored girders
20 braces the tingling Statehouse,

shaking over the excavations, as it faces Colonel Shaw[3]
and his bell-cheeked Negro infantry
on St. Gauden's shaking Civil War relief,
propped by a plank splint against the garage's
    earthquake.

25 Two months after marching through Boston,
half the regiment was dead;
at the dedication
William James[4] could almost hear the bronze
    Negroes breathe.

Their monument sticks like a fishbone
30 in the city's throat.
Its Colonel is as lean
as a compass-needle.

He has an angry wrenlike vigilance,
a greyhound's gentle tautness;
35 he seems to wince at pleasure,
and suffocate for privacy.

He is out of bounds now. He rejoices in man's lovely,
peculiar power to choose life and die—
when he leads his black soldiers to death,
40 he cannot bend his back.

---

1. **aloes.** Succulent plant known for its medicinal quality
2. **Relinquunt . . . Publicam.** They leave all behind to serve the republic. (Latin)

3. **Colonel Shaw.** Commanding officer of the African-American regiment from Massachusetts in the Civil War
4. **William James.** Harvard philosopher (1842–1910)

On a thousand small town New England greens,
the old white churches hold their air
of sparse, sincere rebellion; frayed flags
quilt the graveyards of the Grand Army of the
       Republic.[1]

45 The stone statues of the abstract Union Soldier
grow slimmer and younger each year—
wasp-waisted, they doze over muskets
and muse through their sideburns . . .

Shaw's father wanted no monument
50 except the ditch,
where his son's body was thrown[2]
and lost with his "niggers."

The ditch is nearer.
There are no statues for the last war here;
55 on Boylston Street, a commercial photograph
shows Hiroshima boiling

over a Mosler Safe,[3] the "Rock of Ages"
that survived the blast. Space is nearer.
When I crouch to my television set,
60 the drained faces of Negro school-children rise like
       balloons.

Colonel Shaw
is riding on his bubble,
he waits
for the blessed break.

65 The Aquarium is gone. Everywhere,
giant finned cars nose forward like fish;
a savage servility
slides by on grease.

"The Geranium"
by Theodore Roethke

When I put her out, once, by the garbage pail,
She looked so limp and bedraggled,
So foolish and trusting, like a sick poodle,
Or a wizened aster[4] in late September,
5 I brought her back in again

For a new routine—
Vitamins, water, and whatever
Sustenance seemed sensible
At the time: she'd lived
10 So long on gin, bobbie pins, half-smoked cigars, dead
       beer,
Her shriveled petals falling
On the faded carpet, the stale
Steak grease stuck to her fuzzy leaves.
(Dried-out, she creaked like a tulip.)

15 The things she endured!—
The dumb dames shrieking half the night
Or the two of us, alone, both seedy,
Me breathing booze at her,
She leaning out of her pot toward the window.

20 Near the end, she seemed almost to hear me—
And that was scary—
So when that snuffling cretin[5] of a maid
Threw her, pot and all, into the trash-can,
I said nothing.

25 But I sacked the presumptuous hag the next week,
I was that lonely.

"The Death of the Ball Turret Gunner"
by Randall Jarrell

From my mother's sleep I fell into the State,
And I hunched in its belly till my wet fur froze.
Six miles from earth, loosed from its dream of life,
I woke to black flak[6] and the nightmare fighters.
When I died they washed me out of the turret with a
       hose.

---

1. **Grand Army of the Republic.** Union Army
2. **thrown.** Tossed after the battle of Fort Wagner
3. **Hiroshima . . . Safe.** The speaker is describing an
advertisement for a safe that shows an atom bomb blowing up
Hiroshima, Japan.
4. **wizened aster.** Aged flower
5. **cretin.** Speaker means someone lacking intelligence;
brain damaged person
6. **black flak.** Antiaircraft bullet shells

UNIT REVIEW

Modern Poetry

VOCABULARY FROM THE SELECTIONS

acquiescent, 518
apparition, 561
assert, 569
caprice, 589
convivially, 518
cower, 528
deferential, 572
digress, 570

dilate, 564
etherise, 568
euphony, 540
formulated, 570
harry, 576
indecipherable, 540
inflection, 539
insidious, 568

insolence, 565
linger, 569
lucid, 540
malinger, 570
obtuse, 572
palpable, 580
pantomime, 539
presume, 570

prominence, 565
tedious, 568
triviality, 565
valid, 565
vex, 577

LITERARY TERMS

abstract, 544, 566
allusion, 520, 573, 590
anecdote, 538
blank verse, 524
character, 527
concrete, 544, 566
diction, 532, 578
dramatic monologue, 573
effect, 549, 596
epitaph, 510
free verse, 573
iamb, 514
iambic, 514

image, 544, 549, 562
imagery, 544, 549, 562
inversion, 587
metaphor, 514, 532, 562
meter, 547, 593
paradox, 583
parallelism, 523
pathetic fallacy, 536
personification, 523
pun, 527
refrain, 596
repetition, 551, 558, 587
rhyme, 558, 578, 587,

593, 600
rhythm, 547, 551
run-on line, 551
simile, 514, 520, 583, 596
sonnet, 590
speaker, 547, 549, 600
stanza, 566
symbol, 527
syntax, 587
theme, 559
tone, 512, 532, 547, 593
understatement, 578

GENRE STUDIES

1. **Imagist Poetry.** Poetry is a concentrated form of writing, and Imagist poetry is extremely concentrated, presenting single moments of sense perception without reference to the emotions or opinions of the author, narrator, or speaker. Select three Imagist poems from this unit and discuss the subject and message conveyed.

THEMATIC STUDIES

2. **Alienation.** Two world wars and a society rapidly changing yielded feelings of alienation and anxiety. Select three poems, one Imagist, one narrative, and one Modernist, that deal with the theme of alienation. Explore the differences and similarities in the treatment of this theme in the poems you select.

3. **Poetry.** Three poems in this unit—"Petit, the Poet," "Poetry," and "Ars Poetica"— are about poetry. What statements do the poets make in these poems? In what ways do these poems themselves reveal the changing face of poetry?

HISTORICAL/BIOGRAPHICAL STUDIES

4. **Harlem Renaissance.** In much the same way words were important in the American Revolution, the art that flourished in Harlem in the 1920s and 1930s gave voice to the African-American struggle. Look at the selections in the unit from this period and discuss the statements of identity.

LANGUAGE LAB   PROOFREADING FOR OTHER PUNCTUATION ERRORS

When proofreading your writing, check carefully for correct use of semicolons, colons, dashes, hyphens, apostrophes, quotation marks, parentheses, brackets, and ellipses.

LANGUAGE ARTS SURVEY

For additional help, see the Language Arts Survey, 2.97–2.106.

COMMON PUNCTUATION ERRORS

Semicolons. A **semicolon** is used in the following situations: between closely related independent clauses that are not joined by *and, but, for, nor, or, so,* or *yet;* between independent clauses joined by a conjunctive adverb or transitional expression that is followed by a comma; and between linked independent clauses or items in a list if the clauses or items already contain commas.

EXAMPLES: Sandburg depicts scenes from the Midwest; his verse duplicates the cadences of Midwestern speech.

Many people associate Sandburg with Chicago; however, the poet lived in several cities across the country during his lifetime.

"Chicago" immortalizes the city's noisy, bustling freight yards; hardworking, down-trodden citizens; and legendary spirit.

Colons. A **colon** introduces a long statement or quotation or a list of items.

EXAMPLE: Stock the icebox with the following: plums, milk, cheese, and grapes.

Dashes. A **dash** is used to show an abrupt break in thought or to replace an expression such as *in other words, that is,* or *namely.*

EXAMPLE: Do you remember who wrote "The Love Song"—oh, I remember now!

Hyphens. A **hyphen** is used to link words in a compound adjective, adverb, or noun.

EXAMPLES: flower-fed buffaloes, well-known book, self-knowledge

Apostrophes. An **apostrophe** is used to form the possessive of nouns and some pronouns. See the Language Arts Survey, 2.102, for complete rules about using apostrophes.

SINGULAR WITH ADDED *S:*   Mr. Flood's party, Whiteside's daughter, winter's cold

SINGULAR WITHOUT ADDED *S:*   goodness' sake

PLURAL ENDING WITH *S:*   tropics' heat, bells' ringing, buffaloes' pelts

PLURAL ENDING WITHOUT *S:*   women's conversation, geese's honking, mice's nests

Underlining and Italics. Italics are a type of slanted printing used to show emphasis. (**Underlining** is used when italics are not available.) Some words that receive italics are works of art, books, plays, films, television programs, periodicals, and long musical compositions. Words used as words, letters used as letters, and words from foreign languages also receive italics.

EXAMPLES: *Spoon River Anthology,* O'Keeffe's *New York Night, Consumer Reports, et tu Brute*

Quotation Marks. Quotation marks are used for a variety of purposes.

DIRECT QUOTATION: "Welcome home!" Mr. Flood cries.

DIRECT WITH PERIOD: Mr. Flood wears "valiant armor of scarred hopes outworn."

DIRECT WITH COMMA: "Drink to the bird," said Mr. Flood.

DIRECT WITH SEMICOLON: Mr. Flood drinks "for auld lang syne"; he seems weary of the world.

TITLES OF SHORT WORKS: "Mr. Flood's Party"

> **Ellipses. Ellipsis points** indicate an omission in quoted material or a pause in a written passage.
>
> EXAMPLE: "I don't think the professor knows what he's talking . . . oh, hello, Professor Alexander," the student finished sheepishly.

EXERCISE   Proofreading Sentences for Punctuation Errors

Proofread the following sentences for correct punctuation.

EXAMPLE: Critics do not agree on which poet began the Harlem Renaissance both Langston Hughes and Claude McKay have been credited with starting the literary movement.

Critics do not agree on which poet began the Harlem Renaissance; both Langston Hughes and Claude McKay have been credited with starting the literary movement.

For additional help, see the Language Arts Survey, 2.97–2.106.

1. The peasants in Breughel's "Kermess" are enjoying a great celebration.

2. J. Alfred Prufrock asks the question Do I dare?

3. Langston Hughes The Negro Speaks of Rivers—dedicated to W. E. B. Du Bois—was one of the first poems of the Harlem Renaissance.

4. Many people associate lawyer poet Wallace Stevens with early twentieth century poetry.

5. Pound's In a Station of the Metro reminds me of Monet's Gare Saint-Lazare.

6. How many ways can one look at a blackbird . . . oh, thirteen.

7. Please fill the wheelbarrow with the following items a bag of peat, seed packets, a trowel, and gardening gloves.

8. The owner of the apple orchard sees no need for the wall however he keeps his opinion from his neighbor.

9. Edgar Lee Masters "Spoon River Anthology" is based on the names taken from tombstones.

10. The note on the refrigerator reads Forgive me for eating the plums they were delicious.

Nighthawks. Edward Hopper, 1942. American, 1882–1967. Oil on Canvas, 84.1 × 152.4 cm. The Art Institute of Chicago, Friends of American Art Collection, 1942.51

A ll good books are alike in that they are truer than if they had really happened.

—Ernest Hemingway

"To Build a Fire"
by Jack London

ABOUT THE AUTHOR

Jack London (1876–1916) was born in San Francisco. He supported himself and helped support his family from the time he was fourteen. By the time he was eighteen, he had worked in a cannery, as an oyster pirate, seaman, jute-mill worker, and coal shoveler. While still a teenager, he tramped halfway across the continent with the "army of the unemployed" in its "March on Washington," then struck out on his own for the Northeast. After spending thirty days in jail for vagrancy, London decided it was time to improve his life. He returned to California, entered the state university, and took English classes. He soon left, disenchanted with his fellow students, the professors, and the formal educational system. Within a few months, the twenty-one-year-old was on his way to the gold rush in the Klondike. The only nuggets he found, however, were the experiences he later wove into his stories.

London, who had been a voracious reader from about the age of ten, had been writing stories for some years. By the time he returned to Oakland from the Klondike, he was determined to make a living as a writer. He won a local writing contest, which was followed by numerous rejections and then a string of small sales. His break came when the *Atlantic Monthly* paid $120 for his story "The Odyssey of the North." London often said he disliked his profession and that he wrote to make money, but he was a master storyteller who turned out a prodigious amount of work during his career. His two most famous works, *The Call of the Wild* (1903) and *The Sea-Wolf* (1904), were written before he was thirty. Among his other works are *The People of the Abyss* (1903), *War of the Classes* (1905), *White Fang* (1906), *The Iron Heel* (1908), and *Martin Eden* (autobiographical novel, 1909).

ABOUT THE SELECTION

Published in 1908, **"To Build a Fire"** is one of the twenty-eight stories included in London's Northland Saga. In addition to the twenty-eight stories, the Northland Saga comprises four novels, one play, and six nonfiction pieces, all of which serve as examples of **Naturalistic** fiction, a style of fiction that viewed actions and events as resulting from biological or natural forces or from forces in the environment.

One of hundreds of thousands of people who joined the Klondike Gold Rush in 1887, Jack London had firsthand experience surviving a winter in the Yukon, a territory in northwest Canada and the setting of "To Build a Fire."

"To Build a Fire"

JACK LONDON

Day had broken cold and gray, exceedingly cold and gray, when the man turned aside from the main Yukon[1] trail and climbed the high earth-bank, where a dim and little-traveled trail led eastward through the fat spruce timberland. It was a steep bank, and he paused for breath at the top, excusing the act to himself by looking at his watch. It was nine o'clock. There was no sun nor hint of sun, though there was not a cloud in the sky. It was a clear day, and yet there seemed an intangible <u>pall</u> over the face of things, a subtle gloom that made the day dark, and that was due to the absence of sun. This fact did not worry the man. He was used to the lack of sun. It had been days since he had seen the sun, and he knew that a few more days must pass before that cheerful orb, due south, would just peep above the skyline and dip immediately from view.

The man flung a look back along the way he had come. The Yukon lay a mile wide and hidden under three feet of ice. On top of this ice were as many feet of snow. It was all pure white, rolling in gentle <u>undulations</u> where the ice jams of the freeze-up had formed. North and south, as far as his eye could see, it was unbroken white, save for a dark hairline that curved and twisted from around the spruce-covered island to the south, and that curved and twisted away into the north, where it disappeared behind another spruce-covered island. This dark hairline was the trail—the main trail—that led south five hundred miles to the Chilcoot Pass, Dyea,[2] and salt water; and that led

What is the day like? Why does it have this atmosphere?

---

1. **Yukon.** Territory and river in northwest Canada
2. **Chilcoot Pass, Dyea.** *Chilcoot Pass*—mountain pass leading to the Klondike; *Dyea*—once a town in Alaska that marked the beginning of the Yukon trail

---

WORDS FOR
EVERYDAY USE:

pall (pôl) *n.*, covering that obscures or cloaks gloomily

un • du • la • tion (un′dyo͞o lā′shən) *n.*, wave, curve

north seventy miles to Dawson, and still on to the north a thousand miles to Nulato,[3] and finally to St. Michael on Bering Sea, a thousand miles and half a thousand more.

But all this—the mysterious, far-reaching hairline trail, the absence of sun from the sky, the tremendous cold, and the strangeness and weirdness of it all—made no impression on the man. It was not because he was long used to it. He was a newcomer in the land, a *chechaquo*,[4] and this was his first winter. The trouble with him was that he was without imagination. He was quick and alert in the things of life, but only in the things, and not in the significances. Fifty degrees below zero meant eighty-odd degrees of frost. Such fact impressed him as being cold and uncomfortable, and that was all. It did not lead him to meditate upon his frailty as a creature of temperature, and upon man's frailty in general, able only to live within certain narrow limits of heat and cold; and from there on it did not lead him to the <u>conjectural</u> field of immortality and man's place in the universe. Fifty degrees below zero stood for a bite of frost that hurt and that must be guarded against by the use of mittens, earflaps, warm moccasins, and thick socks. Fifty degrees below zero was to him just precisely fifty degrees below zero. That there should be anything more to it than that was a thought that never entered his head.

As he turned to go on, he spat speculatively. There was a sharp, explosive crackle that startled him. He spat again. And again, in the air, before it could fall to the snow, the spittle crackled. He knew that at fifty below spittle crackled on the snow, but this spittle had crackled in the air. Undoubtedly it was colder than fifty below—how much colder he did not know. But the temperature did not matter. He was bound for the old claim on the left fork of Henderson Creek, where the boys were already. They had come over across the divide from the Indian Creek country, while he had come the roundabout way to take a look at the possibilities of getting out logs in the spring from the islands in the Yukon. He would be in to camp by six o'clock: a bit after dark, it was true, but the boys would be there, a fire would be going, and a hot supper would be ready. As for lunch, he pressed his hand against the protruding bundle under his jacket. It was also under his shirt, wrapped up in a handkerchief and lying against the naked skin. It was the only way to keep the biscuits from freezing. He smiled agreeably to himself as he thought of those biscuits, each cut open and sopped in bacon grease, and each enclosing a generous slice of fried bacon.

He plunged in among the big spruce trees. The trail was faint. A foot of snow had fallen since the last sled had passed over, and he was glad he was without a sled, traveling light. In fact, he carried nothing but the lunch wrapped in the handkerchief. He was surprised, however, at the cold. It certainly was cold, he concluded, as he rubbed his numb nose and cheekbones with his mittened hand. He was a warm-whiskered man, but the hair on his face did not protect the high cheekbones

3. **Dawson . . . Nulato.** Gold-mining towns in the Yukon
4. **chechaquo.** Newcomer

WORDS FOR EVERYDAY USE: con • jec • tur • al (kən jek´chər əl) *adj.,* based on guesses

and the eager nose that thrust itself aggressively into the frosty air.

At the man's heels trotted a dog, a big native husky, the proper wolf dog, gray-coated and without any visible or temperamental difference from its brother, the wild wolf. The animal was depressed by the tremendous cold. It knew that it was no time for traveling. Its instinct told it a truer tale than was told to the man by the man's judgment. In reality, it was not merely colder than fifty below zero: it was colder than sixty below, than seventy below. It was seventy-five below zero. Since the freezing point is thirty-two above zero, it meant that one hundred and seven degrees of frost obtained. The dog did not know anything about thermometers. Possibly in its brain there was no sharp consciousness of a condition of very cold such as was in the man's brain. But the brute had its instinct. It experienced a vague but menacing <u>apprehension</u> that subdued it and made it slink along at the man's heels, and that made it question eagerly every unwonted movement of the man as if expecting him to go into camp or to seek shelter somewhere and build a fire. The dog had learned fire, and it wanted fire, or else to burrow under the snow and cuddle its warmth away from the air.

The frozen moisture of its breathing had settled on its fur in a fine powder of frost, and especially were its jowls, muzzle, and eyelashes whitened by its crystalled breath. The man's red beard and mustache were likewise frosted, but more solidly, the deposit taking the form of ice and increasing with every warm, moist breath he exhaled. Also, the man was chewing tobacco, and the muzzle of ice held his lips so rigidly that he was unable to clear his chin when he expelled the juice. The result was that a crystal beard of the color and solidity of amber was increasing its length on his chin. If he fell down it would shatter itself, like glass, into brittle fragments. But he did not mind the appendage. It was the penalty all tobacco chewers paid in that country, and he had been out before in two cold snaps. They had not been so cold as this, he knew, but by the spirit thermometer[5] at Sixty Mile he knew they had been registered at fifty below and at fifty-five.

He held on through the level stretch of woods for several miles, crossed a wide flat, and dropped down a bank to the frozen bed of a small stream. This was Henderson Creek, and he knew he was ten miles from the forks. He looked at his watch. It was ten o'clock. He was making four miles an hour, and he calculated that he would arrive at the forks at half past twelve. He decided to celebrate that event by eating his lunch there.

The dog dropped in again at his heels, with a tail drooping discouragement, as the man swung along the creek bed. The furrow of the old sled trail was plainly visible, but a dozen inches of snow covered the marks of the last runners. In a month no man had come up or down that silent creek. The man held steadily on. He was not much given to thinking, and just then particularly he had nothing to think about save that he would eat lunch at the forks

In what way is the dog more advanced than the man?

---

5. **spirit thermometer.** Thermometer that uses alcohol instead of mercury because of the lower freezing point of alcohol

WORDS FOR EVERYDAY USE: ap • pre • hen • sion (ap´rē hen´shən) n., anxiety, dread

What danger does the man know?

and that at six o'clock he would be in camp with the boys. There was nobody to talk to; and, had there been, speech would have been impossible because of the ice-muzzle on his mouth. So he continued monotonously to chew tobacco and to increase the length of his amber beard.

Once in a while the thought <u>reiterated</u> itself that it was very cold and that he had never experienced such cold. As he walked along he rubbed his cheekbones and nose with the back of his mittened hand. He did this automatically, now and again changing hands. But rub as he would, the instant he stopped his cheekbones went numb, and the following instant the end of his nose went numb. He was sure to frost his cheeks; he knew that, and experienced a pang of regret that he had not devised a nose strap of the sort Bud wore in cold snaps. Such a strap passed across the cheeks, as well, and saved them. But it didn't matter much, after all. What were frosted cheeks? A bit painful, that was all: they were never serious.

Empty as the man's mind was of thoughts, he was keenly observant, and he noticed the changes in the creek, the curves and bends and timber jams, and always he sharply noted where he placed his feet. Once, coming around a bend, he shied abruptly, like a startled horse, curved away from the place where he had been walking, and retreated several paces back along the trail. The creek he knew was frozen clear to the bottom—no creek could contain water in that arctic winter— but he knew also that there were springs that bubbled out from the hillsides and ran along under the snow and on top the ice of the creek. He knew that the coldest snaps never froze these springs, and he knew likewise their danger. They were traps. They hid pools of water under the snow that might be three inches deep, or three feet. Sometimes a skin of ice half an inch thick covered them, and in turn was covered by the snow. Sometimes there were alternate layers of water and ice skin, so that when one broke through he kept on breaking through for a while, some- times wetting himself to the waist.

That was why he had shied in such panic. He had felt the give under his feet and heard the crackle of a snow-hidden ice skin. And to get his feet wet in such a temperature meant trouble and danger. At the very least it meant delay, for he would be forced to stop and build a fire, and under its protection to bare his feet while he dried his socks and moccasins. He stood and studied the creek bed and its banks, and decided that the flow of water came from the right. He reflected awhile, rubbing his nose and cheeks, then skirted to the left, stepping gingerly and testing the footing for each step. Once clear of the danger, he took a fresh chew of tobacco and swung along at his four-mile gait.

In the course of the next two hours he came upon several similar traps. Usually the snow above the hidden pools had a sunken, candied appearance that advertised the danger. Once again, however, he had a close call; and once, suspecting danger, he compelled the dog to go on in front. The dog did not want to go. It hung back until the man shoved it forward, and then it went quickly across the white, unbroken surface. Suddenly it broke through, floun-

WORDS FOR EVERYDAY USE: re • it • er • ate (rē it´ə rāt´) *vt.,* repeat

dered to one side, and got away to firmer footing. It had wet its forefeet and legs, and almost immediately the water that clung to it turned to ice. It made quick efforts to lick the ice off its legs, then dropped down in the snow and began to bite out the ice that had formed between the toes. This was a matter of instinct. To permit the ice to remain would mean sore feet. It did not know this. It merely obeyed the mysterious prompting that arose from the deep crypts of its being. But the man knew, having achieved a judgment on the subject, and he removed the mitten from his right hand and helped tear out the ice particles. He did not expose his fingers more than a minute, and was astonished at the swift numbness that smote them. It certainly was cold. He pulled on the mitten hastily, and beat the hand savagely across his chest.

At twelve o'clock the day was at its brightest. Yet the sun was too far south on its winter journey to clear the horizon. The bulge of the earth intervened between it and Henderson Creek, where the man walked under a clear sky at noon and cast no shadow. At half-past twelve, to the minute, he arrived at the forks of the creek. He was pleased at the speed he had made. If he kept it up, he would certainly be with the boys by six. He unbuttoned his jacket and shirt and drew forth his lunch. The action consumed no more than a quarter of a minute, yet in that brief moment the numbness laid hold of the exposed fingers. He did not put the mitten on, but, instead, struck the fingers a dozen sharp smashes against his leg. Then he sat down on a snowcovered log to eat. The sting that followed upon the striking of his fingers against his leg ceased so quickly that he was startled. He had had no chance to take a bite of biscuit. He struck the fingers repeatedly and returned them to the mitten, baring the other hand for the purpose of eating. He tried to take a mouthful. but the ice muzzle prevented. He had forgotten to build a fire and thaw out. He chuckled at his foolishness, and as he chuckled he noted the numbness creeping into the exposed fingers. Also, he noted that the stinging which had first come to his toes when he sat down was already passing away. He wondered whether the toes were warm or numb. He moved them inside the moccasins and decided that they were numb.

He pulled the mitten on hurriedly and stood up. He was a bit frightened. He stamped up and down until the stinging returned into the feet. It certainly was cold, was his thought. That man from Sulphur Creek had spoken the truth when telling how cold it sometimes got in the country. And he had laughed at him at the time! That showed one must not be too sure of things. There was no mistake about it, it was cold. He strode up and down, stamping his feet and threshing his arms, until reassured by the returning warmth. Then he got out matches and proceeded to make a fire. From the undergrowth, where high water of the previous spring had lodged a supply of seasoned twigs, he got his firewood. Working carefully from a small beginning, he soon had a roaring fire, over which he thawed the ice from his face and in the protection of which he ate his biscuits. For the moment the cold of space was

What is the man starting to feel? Whom had he met? What had he been told?

WORDS FOR EVERYDAY USE: **thresh** (thresh) *vt.*, thrash, toss about

outwitted. The dog took satisfaction in the fire, stretching out close enough for warmth and far enough away to escape being singed.

When the man had finished, he filled his pipe and took his comfortable time over a smoke. Then he pulled on his mittens, settled the earflaps of his cap firmly about his ears, and took the creek trail up the left fork. The dog was disappointed and yearned back toward the fire. This man did not know cold. Possibly all the generations of his ancestry had been ignorant of cold, of real cold, of cold one hundred and seven degrees below freezing point. But the dog knew; all its ancestry knew, and it had inherited the knowledge. And it knew that it was not good to walk abroad in such fearful cold. It was the time to lie snug in a hole in the snow and wait for a curtain of cloud to be drawn across the face of outer space whence this cold came. On the other hand, there was no keen intimacy between the dog and the man. The one was the toil slave of the other, and the only caresses it had ever received were the caresses of the whiplash and of harsh and menacing throat sounds that threatened the whiplash. So the dog made no effort to communicate its apprehension to the man. It was not concerned in the welfare of the man; it was for its own sake that it yearned back toward the fire. But the man whistled, and spoke to it with the sound of whiplashes, and the dog swung in at the man's heels and followed after.

The man took a chew of tobacco and proceeded to start a new amber beard. Also, his moist breath quickly powdered with white his mustache, eyebrows, and lashes. There did not seem to be so many springs on the left fork of the Henderson, and for half an hour the man saw no signs of any. And then it happened. At a place where there were no signs, where the soft, unbroken snow seemed to advertise solidity beneath, the man broke through. It was not deep. He wet himself halfway to the knees before he floundered out to the firm crust.

What does the dog think should happen?

What happens unexpectedly?

He was angry, and cursed his luck aloud. He had hoped to get into camp with the boys at six o'clock, and this would delay him an hour, for he would have to build a fire and dry out his footgear. This was imperative at that low temperature—he knew that much; and he turned aside to the bank, which he climbed. On top, tangled in the underbrush about the trunks of several small spruce trees, was a high-water deposit of dry firewood—sticks and twigs, principally, but also larger portions of seasoned branches and fine, dry, last year's grasses. He threw down several large pieces on top of the snow. This served for a foundation and prevented the young flame from drowning itself in the snow it otherwise would melt. The flame he got by touching a match to a small shred of birch bark that he took from his pocket. This burned even more readily than paper. Placing it on the foundation. he fed the young flame with wisps of dry grass and with the tiniest dry twigs.

He worked slowly and carefully, keenly aware of his danger. Gradually, as the flame grew stronger, he increased the size of the twigs with which he fed it. He squatted in the snow, pulling the twigs out from their entanglement in the brush and feeding directly to the flame. He knew there must be no failure. When it is seventy-five below zero, a man must not fail in his first attempt to build a fire—that is, if his feet are wet. If his feet are dry, and he fails, he can run along the trail for half a mile and restore his circulation. But the circulation of wet and freezing feet cannot be restored by running when it is seventy-five below. No matter how fast one runs, the wet feet will freeze the harder.

All this the man knew. The old-timer on Sulphur Creek had told him about it the previous fall, and now he was appreciating the advice. Already all sensation had gone out of his feet. To build the fire he had been forced to remove his mittens, and the fingers had quickly gone numb. His pace of four miles an hour had kept his heart pumping blood to the surface of his body and to all the extremities. But the instant he stopped, the action of the pump eased down. The cold of space smote the unprotected tip of the planet, and he, being on that unprotected tip, received the full force of the blow. The blood of his body recoiled before it. The blood was alive, like the dog, and like the dog it wanted to hide away and cover itself up from the fearful cold. So long as he walked four miles an hour, he pumped that blood, willy-nilly, to the surface; but now it ebbed away and sank down into the recesses of his body. The extremities were the first to feel its absence. His wet feet froze the faster, and his exposed fingers numbed the faster, though they had not yet begun to freeze. Nose and cheeks were already freezing, while the skin of all his body chilled as it lost its blood.

But he was safe. Toes and nose and cheeks would be only touched by the frost, for the fire was beginning to burn with strength. He was feeding it with twigs the size of his finger. In another minute he would be able to feed it with branches the size of his wrist, and then he could remove his wet foot-gear, and, while it dried, he could keep his naked feet warm by the fire, rubbing them at first, of course, with snow. The fire was a success. He was safe. He remembered the

What does the man see as the negative consequences of his accident?

To what is the man's blood compared? In what way are they similar?

WORDS FOR EVERYDAY USE:

im • per • a • tive (im per´ə tiv) *adj.,* absolutely necessary

ebb (eb) *vi.,* flow back, recede

advice of the old-timer on Sulphur Creek, and smiled. The old-timer had been very serious in laying down the law that no man must travel alone in the Klondike after fifty below. Well, here he was; he had had the accident; he was alone; and he had saved himself. Those old-timers were rather womanish, some of them, he thought. All a man had to do was to keep his head, and he was all right. Any man who was a man could travel alone. But it was surprising, the rapidity with which his cheeks and nose were freezing. And he had not thought his fingers could go lifeless in so short a time. Lifeless they were, for he could scarcely make them move together to grip a twig, and they seemed remote from his body and from him. When he touched a twig, he had to look and see whether or not he had hold of it. The wires were pretty well down between him and his finger ends.

What does the fire symbolize in such cold?

All of which counted for little. There was the fire, snapping and crackling and promising life with every dancing flame. He started to untie his moccasins. They were coated with ice; the thick German socks were like sheaths of iron halfway to the knees; and the moccasin strings were like rods of steel all twisted and knotted as by some <u>conflagration</u>. For a moment he tugged with his numb fingers, then, realizing the folly of it, he drew his sheath-knife.

What terrible mistake does the man make?

But before he could cut the strings, it happened. It was his own fault or, rather, his mistake. He should not have built the fire under the spruce tree. He should have built it in the open. But it had been easier to pull the twigs from the brush and drop them directly on the fire. Now the tree under which he had done this carried a weight of snow on its boughs. No wind had blown for weeks, and each bough was fully freighted. Each time he had pulled a twig he had communicated a slight <u>agitation</u> to the tree—an imperceptible agitation, so far as he was concerned, but an agitation sufficient to bring about the disaster. High up in the tree one bough capsized its load of snow. This fell on the boughs beneath, capsizing them. This process continued, spreading out and involving the whole tree. It grew like an avalanche, and it descended without warning upon the man and the fire, and the fire was blotted out! Where it had burned was a mantle of fresh and disordered snow.

The man was shocked. It was as though he had just heard his own sentence of death. For a moment he sat and stared at the spot where the fire had been. Then he grew very calm. Perhaps the old-timer on Sulphur Creek was right. If he had only had a trail mate he would have been in no danger now. The trail mate could have built the fire. Well, it was up to him to build the fire over again, and this second time there must be no failure. Even if he succeeded, he would most likely lose some toes. His feet must be badly frozen by now, and there would be some time before the second fire was ready.

Such were his thoughts, but he did not sit and think them. He was busy all the time they were passing through his mind. He made a new foundation for a fire, this time in the open, where no treacherous tree could blot it out. Next, he gathered dry grasses and tiny twigs from the high-water flotsam.[6] He could not bring

_____

6. **flotsam.** Odds and ends washed up by the water

WORDS FOR EVERYDAY USE:

con • fla • gra • tion (kän´flə grā´shən) n., destructive fire

ag • i • ta • tion (aj´ə tā´shən) n., violent motion or disturbance

his fingers together to pull them out, but he was able to gather them by the handful. In this way he got many rotten twigs and bits of green moss that were undesirable, but it was the best he could do. He worked methodically, even collecting an armful of the larger branches to be used later when the fire gathered strength. And all the while the dog sat and watched him, a certain yearning wistfulness in its eyes, for it looked upon him as the fire provider, and the fire was slow in coming.

When all was ready, the man reached in his pocket for a second piece of birch bark. He knew the bark was there, and, though he could not feel it with his fingers, he could hear its crisp rustling as he fumbled for it. Try as he would, he could not clutch hold of it. And all the time, in his consciousness, was the knowledge that each instant his feet were freezing. This thought tended to put him in a panic, but he fought against it and kept calm. He pulled on his mittens with his teeth, and threshed his arms back and forth, beating his hands with all his might against his sides. He did this sitting down, and he stood up to do it; and all the while the dog sat in the snow, its wolf brush of a tail curled around warmly over its forefeet, its sharp wolf ears pricked forward intently as it watched the man. And the man, as he beat and threshed with his arms and hands, felt a great surge of envy as he regarded the creature that was warm and secure in its natural covering.

After a time he was aware of the first faraway signals of sensation in his beaten fingers. The faint tingling grew stronger till it evolved into a stinging ache that was excruciating, but which the man hailed with satisfaction. He stripped the mitten from his right hand and fetched forth the birch bark. The exposed fingers were quickly going numb again. Next he brought out his bunch of sulphur matches. But the tremendous cold had already driven the life out of his fingers. In his effort to separate one match from the others, the whole bunch fell in the snow. He tried to pick it out of the snow, but failed. The dead fingers could neither touch nor clutch. He was very careful. He drove the thought of his freezing feet, and nose, and cheeks, out of his mind, devoting his whole soul to the matches. He watched, using the sense of vision in place of that of touch, and when he saw his fingers on each side the bunch, he closed them—that is, he willed to close them, for the wires were down, and the fingers did not obey. He pulled the mitten on the right hand, and beat it fiercely against his knee. Then, with both mittened hands, he scooped the bunch of matches, along with much snow, into his lap. Yet he was no better off.

After some manipulation he managed to get the bunch between the heels of his mittened hands. In this fashion he carried it to his mouth. The ice crackled and snapped when by a violent effort he opened his mouth. He drew the lower jaw in, curled the upper lip out of the way, and scraped the bunch with his upper teeth in order to separate a match. He succeeded in getting one, which he dropped on his lap. He was no better off. He could not pick it up. Then he devised a way. He picked it up in his teeth and scratched it on his leg. Twenty times he scratched before he succeeded in lighting it. As it flamed he held it with his teeth to the birch bark. But the burning brimstone went up his nostrils and into his lungs, causing him to cough spasmodically. The match fell into the snow and went out.

The old-timer on Sulphur Creek was right, he thought in the moment of controlled despair that ensued: after fifty below, a man should travel with a partner. He beat his hands, but failed in exciting any sensation. Suddenly he bared both hands, removing the mittens with his

What does the man feel is happening? What is his reaction?

What advice did the man fail to heed?

teeth. He caught the whole bunch between the heels of his hands. His arm muscles not being frozen enabled him to press the hand heels tightly against the matches. Then he scratched the bunch along his leg. It flared into flame, seventy sulphur matches at once! There was no wind to blow them out. He kept his head to one side to escape the strangling fumes, and held the blazing bunch to the birch bark. As he so held it, he became aware of sensation in his hand. His flesh was burning. He could smell it. Deep down below the surface he could feel it. The sensation developed into pain that grew acute. And still he endured it, holding the flame of the matches clumsily to the bark that would not light readily because his own burning hands were in the way, absorbing most of the flame.

What plan does the man devise?

At last, when he could endure no more, he jerked his hands apart. The blazing matches fell sizzling into the snow, but the birch bark was alight. He began laying dry grasses and the tiniest twigs on the flame. He could not pick and choose, for he had to lift the fuel between the heels of his hands. Small pieces of rotten wood and green moss clung to the twigs, and he bit them off as well as he could with his teeth. He cherished the flame carefully and awkwardly. It meant life, and it must not perish. The withdrawal of blood from the surface of his body now made him begin to shiver, and he grew more awkward. A large piece of green moss fell squarely on the little fire. He tried to poke it out with his fingers, but his shivering frame made him poke too far, and he disrupted the <u>nucleus</u> of the little fire, the burning grasses and tiny twigs separating and scat-

tering. He tried to poke them together again, but in spite of the tenseness of the effort, his shivering got away with him, and the twigs were hopelessly scattered. Each twig gushed a puff of smoke and went out. The fire provider had failed. As he looked <u>apathetically</u> about him, his eyes chanced on the dog, sitting across the ruins of the fire from him, in the snow, making restless, hunching movements, slightly lifting one forefoot and then the other, shifting its weight back and forth on them with wistful eagerness.

The sight of the dog put a wild idea into his head. He remembered the tale of the man, caught in a blizzard, who killed a steer and crawled inside the carcass, and so was saved. He would kill the dog and bury his hands in the warm body until the numbness went out of them. Then he could build another fire. He spoke to the dog, calling it to him; but in his voice was a strange note of fear that frightened the animal, who had never known the man to speak in such way before. Something was the matter, and its suspicious nature sensed danger—it knew not what danger, but somewhere, somehow, in its brain arose an apprehension of the man. It flattened its ears down at the sound of the man's voice, and its restless, hunching movements and the liftings and shiftings of its forefeet became more pronounced; but it would not come to the man. He got on his hand and knees and crawled toward the dog. This unusual posture again excited suspicion, and the animal sidled mincingly away.

The man sat up in the snow for a moment and struggled for calmness. Then he pulled on his mittens, by means of his teeth, and got upon his feet. He glanced

---

Words for Everyday Use:

nu • cle • us (nōō′klē əs) *n.*, core, central part

ap • a • thet • i • cal • ly (ap′ə thet′ə kə lē) *adv.*, without emotion

down at first in order to assure himself that he was really standing up, for the absence of sensation in his feet left him unrelated to the earth. His erect position in itself started to drive the webs of suspicion from the dog's mind; and when he spoke peremptorily, with the sound of whiplashes in his voice, the dog rendered its customary allegiance and came to him. As it came within reaching distance, the man lost his control. His arms flashed out to the dog, and he experienced genuine surprise when he discovered that his hands could not clutch, that there was neither bend nor feeling in the fingers. He had forgotten for the moment that they were frozen and that they were freezing more and more. All this happened quickly, and before the animal could get away, he encircled its body with his arms. He sat down in the snow, and in this fashion held the dog, while it snarled and whined and struggled.

But it was all he could do, hold its body encircled in his arms and sit there. He realized that he could not kill the dog. There was no way to do it. With his helpless hands he could neither draw nor hold his sheath-knife nor throttle the animal. He released it, and it plunged wildly away, with tail between its legs, and still snarling. It halted forty feet away and surveyed him curiously, with ears sharply pricked forward. The man looked down at his hands in order to locate them, and found them hanging on the ends of his arms. It struck him as curious that one should have to use his eyes in order to find out where his hands were. He began threshing his arms back and forth, beating the mittened hands against his sides. He

did this for five minutes, violently, and his heart pumped enough blood up to the surface to put a stop to his shivering. But no sensation was aroused in the hands. He had an impression that they hung like weights on the ends of his arms, but when he tried to run the impression down, he could not find it.

A certain fear of death, dull and oppressive, came to him. This fear quickly became poignant as he realized that it was no longer a mere matter of freezing his fingers and toes, or of losing his hands and feet, but that it was a matter of life and death with the chances against him. This threw him into a panic, and he turned and ran up the creekbed along the old, dim trail. The dog joined in behind and kept up with him. He ran blindly, without intention, in fear such as he had never known in his life. Slowly, as he plowed and floundered through the snow, he began to see things again—the banks of the creek, the old timber jams, the leafless aspens, and the sky. The running made him feel better. He did not shiver. Maybe, if he ran on, his feet would thaw out: and, anyway, if he ran far enough, he would reach camp and the boys. Without doubt he would lose some fingers and toes and some of his face; but the boys would take care of him, and save the rest of him when he got there. And at the same time there was another thought in his mind that said he would never get to the camp and the boys; that it was too many miles away, that the freezing had too great a start on him, and that he would soon be stiff and dead. This thought he kept in the background and refused to consider. Sometimes it pushed itself forward and demanded to be heard,

What does the man begin to realize?

How does the plan proceed?

What thoughts fight in his mind?

WORDS FOR EVERYDAY USE:

per • emp • to • ri • ly (pər emp´tə ri lē) adv., commandingly

poign • ant (poin´yənt) adj., sharp; painful

but he thrust it back and strove to think of other things.

It struck him as curious that he could run at all on feet so frozen that he could not feel them when they struck the earth and took the weight of his body. He seemed to himself to skim along above the surface, and to have no connection with the earth. Somewhere he had once seen a winged Mercury,[7] and he wondered if Mercury felt as he felt when skimming over the earth.

His theory of running until he reached camp and the boys had one flaw in it: he lacked the endurance. Several times he stumbled, and finally he tottered, crumpled up, and fell. When he tried to rise, he failed. He must sit and rest, he decided, and next time he would merely walk and keep on going. As he sat and regained his breath, he noted that he was feeling quite warm and comfortable. He was not shivering, and it even seemed that a warm glow had come to his chest and trunk. And yet, when he touched his nose or cheeks, there was no sensation. Running would not thaw them out. Nor would it thaw out his hands and feet. Then the thought came to him that the frozen portions of his body must be extending. He tried to keep this thought down, to forget it, to think of something else; he was aware of the panicky feeling that it caused, and he was afraid of the panic. But the thought asserted itself, and persisted, until it produced a vision of his body totally frozen. This was too much, and he made another wild run along the trail. Once he slowed down to a walk, but the thought of the freezing extending itself made him run again.

What are the man's final thoughts?

And all the time the dog ran with him, at his heels. When he fell down a second time, it curled its tail over its forefeet and sat in front of him, facing him, curiously eager and intent. The warmth and security of the animal angered him, and he cursed it till it flattened down its ears appeasingly. This time the shivering came more quickly upon the man. He was losing in his battle with the frost. It was creeping into his body from all sides. The thought of it drove him on, but he ran no more than a hundred feet, when he staggered and pitched headlong. It was his last panic. When he had recovered his breath and control, he sat up and entertained in his mind the conception of meeting death with dignity. However, the conception did not come to him in such terms. His idea of it was that he had been making a fool of himself, running around like a chicken with its head cut off—such was the simile that occurred to him. Well, he was bound to freeze anyway, and he might as well take it decently. With this new-found peace of mind came the first glimmerings of drowsiness. A good idea, he thought, to sleep off to death. It was like taking an anaesthetic. Freezing was not so bad as people thought. There were lots worse ways to die.

He pictured the boys finding his body next day. Suddenly he found himself with them, coming along the trail and looking for himself. And, still with them, he came around a turn in the trail and found himself lying in the snow. He did not belong with himself any more, for even then he was out of himself; standing with the boys and looking at himself in the snow. It certainly was cold, was his thought. When he got back to the States he could tell the folks what real cold was. He drifted on from this to a vision of the old-timer on Sulphur Creek. He could see him quite clearly, warm and comfortable, and smoking a pipe.

"You were right, old hoss; you were right," the man mumbled to the old-timer of Sulphur Creek.

---

7. **Mercury.** In Roman mythology, Mercury, the messenger of the gods, is depicted with winged feet.

Then the man drowsed off into what seemed to him the most comfortable and satisfying sleep he had ever known. The dog sat facing him and waiting. The brief day drew to a close in a long, slow twilight. There were no signs of a fire to be made, and, besides, never in the dog's experience had it known a man to sit like that in the snow and make no fire. As the twilight drew on, its eager yearning for the fire mastered it, and with a great lifting and shifting of forefeet, it whined softly, then flattened its ears down in anticipation of being chidden[8] by the man. But the man remained silent. Later, the dog whined loudly. And still later it crept close to the man and caught the scent of death. This made the animal bristle and back away. A little longer it delayed, howling under the stars that leaped and danced and shone brightly in the cold sky. Then it turned and trotted up the trail in the direction of the camp it knew, where were the other food providers and fire providers. ∎

_____

8. **chidden.** Scolded

Responding to the Selection

Imagine that you are one of the people waiting at camp for the return of the solitary traveler. What concerns do you have for his safety? Why do you think he is late in returning to camp? What is probably the greatest threat to his survival?

Reviewing the Selection

RECALLING

1. What signals warn the man that it is much colder than he estimated?

2. What quality does the newcomer lack?

3. What advice, given by an old-timer on Sulphur Creek, does the newcomer ignore?

4. Against what does the man lose his battle?

INTERPRETING

5. What responses does the man have toward the cold? What does he think about to motivate himself to continue?

6. Why might the man's inexperience in this region make him slow to realize his own danger?

7. What would following the old-timer's advice have accomplished?

8. Why does the man think about the old-timer from Sulphur Creek? What is happening to the man's mind? What evidence do you have for your interpretation?

9. What does the man's conviction that "Fifty degrees below zero was to him just precisely fifty degrees below zero" tell you about his personality? What does it tell you about his understanding of nature? How does the man's relationship with nature differ from the dog's?

10. What is probably the reason that the author does not name the main character? Is the character unique, or does he possess traits common to all human beings? If so, what are those traits?

Understanding Literature (Questions for Discussion)

1. **Setting.** The **setting** of a literary work is the time and place in which it occurs, together with all the details used to create a sense of a particular time and place. What details are particularly effective in creating the Yukon setting? What details are particularly effective in creating a vivid sense of the cold temperatures?

2. **Conflict, Plot, and Catastrophe.** A **conflict** is a struggle between two forces in a literary work. A **plot** involves the introduction, development, and eventual resolution of a conflict. One side of the central conflict in a story or drama is usually taken by the main character. That character may struggle against another character, against the forces of nature, against society, against fate, or against some element within himself or herself. What is the external conflict, or outside force, against which the main character struggles? One of the elements of plot is the **catastrophe**, the event that marks the ultimate tragic fall of the central character. Often this event is the character's death. What causes the main character's downfall? Is his death inevitable? Why, or why not?

Responding in Writing

1. **Descriptive Paragraph.** London's description of the Yukon is made vivid and real through its use of sensory detail. Write a descriptive paragraph that portrays a real or imaginary setting. In your paragraph, make use of sensory details—words and phrases that describe how things look, sound, smell, taste, and feel—to evoke a vivid setting. Reveal characteristics of the setting through the use of elements such as landscape, buildings, furniture, clothing, the weather, or the season.

2. **Documentation.** In the selection, London describes all the steps in the process of building a fire in the wilderness. Think of a skill or activity with which you are familiar and write a set of guidelines documenting the procedure. (You may wish to refer to the Language Arts Survey, 5.7, "Technical Writing.") To get started, familiarize yourself with the procedure you will be documenting. Then, break the task into a series of short, simple steps, listing each step in the proper sequence. In your documentation of the procedure, use simple and precise language, written in the form of second-person imperative.

Language Lab

Base Words and Suffixes. Read the Language Arts Survey, 2.140, "Base Words and Prefixes," and 2.141, "Suffixes." Then underline the base word once and the suffix twice in each of the following words from "To Build a Fire." Next look up each suffix in a dictionary and write two additional words that end with the same suffix.

1. uncomfortable
2. solidity
3. eastward
4. numbness
5. sensation

Test-taking Skills

Synonyms and Antonyms. Read the Language Arts Survey, 4.44, "Synonym and Antonym Questions." Then, write the letter of the word that is most nearly opposite in meaning to the word in capital letters.

1. IMAGINATION
   a. invention   b. improvisation   c. unadorned   d. foolishness   e. whimsy

2. INSTINCT
   a. intuition   b. reason   c. knowledge   d. observation   e. perception

3. FACT
   a. falsehood   b. certainty   c. truth   d. reality   e. phenomenon

4. FRAILTY
   a. weakness   b. flaw   c. vigor   d. fault   e. fit

5. ALLEGIANCE
   a. devotion   b. disobedience   c. loyalty   d. duty   e. homage

PROJECT

Camping Trip. Plan an imaginary camping trip with your classmates. Working in small groups, choose an area of the world you would like to explore. Make lists of all the equipment and supplies you think you will need. Try to brainstorm difficulties you might encounter on your trip. Then, research your area of the world in an encyclopedia or in outdoor recreation magazines to see if there are any possible difficulties in this region you may have overlooked and for which you should be better prepared.

"A Wagner Matinee"
by Willa Cather

ABOUT THE AUTHOR

Willa Cather (1873–1947) was born in Virginia. When she was ten her family moved to Nebraska, where her father was a frontier farmer and owner of a farm loan and mortgage business. Cather graduated from the University of Nebraska in 1895. She began writing in college, working for the *Nebraska Journal* reviewing books, plays, and music.

In the late 1890s and early 1900s, she lived in Pittsburgh, Pennsylvania, and worked as a newspaper and magazine writer and editor before teaching high school English and Latin. In 1906, she moved to New York City and joined *McClure's* magazine, first as a contributing editor from 1906 to 1908 and then as managing editor from 1908 to 1912.

Her early work about the Nebraska prairie and its pioneers made her famous. She is also remembered for her powerful female figures, who are often unconventional, like Cather herself.

Her first novel, *Alexander's Bridge* (1912), was published when she was thirty-nine. Her other works include the poetry of *April Twilights* (1903), the short stories in *The Troll Garden* (1912), and the novels *O Pioneers!* (1913), *The Song of the Lark* (1915), *My Antonia* (1918), *A Lost Lady* (1923), *The Professor's House* (1925), and *Death Comes for the Archbishop* (1926).

Cather was awarded the Pulitzer Prize for the novel *One of Ours* (1922) and the Howells Medal from the American Academy and Institute of Arts and Letters in 1930 for *Death Comes for the Archbishop.*

ABOUT THE SELECTION

In **"A Wagner Matinee,"** Cather juxtaposes the pioneer world of Red Willow, Nebraska, and the musical world of Boston. Cather's method of writing from firsthand experience, particularly about growing up in Red Cloud, Nebraska, is well known and typical of her work. Music was one of Cather's passionate interests. In "A Wagner Matinee," she created the character of Aunt Georgiana, a woman who studied music at the Boston Conservatory. A martyr in the eyes of her nephew, Aunt Georgiana "inexplicably" gives up her musical life for a life on the silent Nebraska frontier.

READER'S JOURNAL

Have you ever had a strong emotional response to a piece of music? What was the music? What emotions did you experience while listening to the music? Why do you think you responded so strongly to that particular piece of music? Write about the experience in your journal.

LANGUAGE SKILLS

Read the Language Arts Survey, 2.46, "Adding Modifiers." Then identify some simple, compound, complex, and complex-compound sentences in the selection that have been expanded with modifiers.

"A Wagner Matinee"

WILLA CATHER

I received one morning a letter, written in pale ink on glassy, blue-lined note-paper, and bearing the postmark of a little Nebraska village. This communication, worn and rubbed, looking as if it had been carried for some days in a coat pocket that was none too clean, was from my Uncle Howard, and informed me that his wife had been left a small legacy[1] by a bachelor relative, and that it would be necessary for her to go to Boston to attend to the settling of the estate. He requested me to meet her at the station and render her whatever services might be necessary. On examining the date indicated as that of her arrival, I found it to be no later than tomorrow. He had characteristically delayed writing until, had I been away from home for a day, I must have missed my aunt altogether.

The name of my Aunt Georgiana opened before me a gulf of recollection so wide and deep that, as the letter dropped from my hand, I felt suddenly a stranger to all the present conditions of my existence, wholly ill at ease and out of place amid the familiar surroundings of my study. I became, in short, the gangling farmer-boy my aunt had known, scourged with chilblains[2] and bashfulness, my hands cracked and sore from the corn husking. I sat again before her parlor organ, fumbling the scale with my stiff, red fingers, while she, beside me, made canvas mittens for the huskers.

The next morning, after preparing my landlady for a visitor, I set out for the station. When the train arrived I had some difficulty in finding my aunt. She was the last of the passengers to alight, and it was not until I got her into the carriage that she seemed really to recognize me. She had come all the way in a day coach; her

Who wrote the letter to the narrator? Who is coming to visit? When is the visitor coming? What is the narrator asked to do?

1. **legacy.** Inheritance
2. **scourged with chilblains.** Tormented by blisters on hands and feet

WORDS FOR EVERYDAY USE:
ren • der (ren´dər) *vt.*, give, hand over, deliver, or present

linen duster[3] had become black with soot and her black bonnet grey with dust during the journey. When we arrived at my boarding-house the landlady put her to bed at once, and I did not see her again until the next morning.

Whatever shock Mrs. Springer experienced at my aunt's appearance, she considerately concealed. As for myself, I saw my aunt's battered figure with that feeling of awe and respect with which we behold explorers who have left their ears and fingers north of Franz-Joseph-Land, or their health somewhere along the Upper Congo.[4] My Aunt Georgiana had been a music teacher at the Boston Conservatory, somewhere back in the latter sixties.[5] One summer, while visiting in the little village among the Green Mountains where her ancestors had dwelt for generations, she had kindled the callow fancy of my uncle, Howard Carpenter, then an idle, shiftless boy of twenty-one. When she returned to her duties in Boston, Howard followed her, and the upshot of this infatuation was that she eloped with him, eluding the reproaches of her family and the criticism of her friends by going with him to the Nebraska frontier.[6] Carpenter, who, of course, had no money, took up a homestead in Red Willow County, fifty miles from the railroad. There they had measured off their land themselves, driving across the prairie in a wagon, to the wheel of which they had tied a red cotton handkerchief, and counting its revolutions. They built a dug-out in the red hillside, one of those cave dwellings whose inmates so often reverted to primitive conditions. Their water they got from the lagoons where the

How did Aunt Georgiana help the narrator with his studies? What did she teach the narrator? What musical instrument did they have?

How was the land measured? What did Georgiana and Howard build? Where did they get their water?

buffalo drank, and their slender stock of provisions[7] was always at the mercy of bands of roving Indians. For thirty years my aunt had not been farther than fifty miles from the homestead.

I owed to this woman most of the good that ever came my way in my boyhood, and had a reverential affection for her. During the years when I was riding herd for my uncle, my aunt, after cooking the three meals—the first of which was ready at six o'clock in the morning—and putting the six children to bed, would often stand until midnight at her ironing board, with me at the kitchen table beside her, hearing me recite Latin declensions and conjugations, gently shaking me when my drowsy head sank down over a page of irregular verbs. It was to her, at her ironing or mending, that I read my first Shakespeare, and her old textbook on mythology was the first that ever came into my empty hands. She taught me my scales and exercises[8] on the little parlor organ which her husband had bought her after fifteen years during which she had not so much as seen a musical instrument. She would sit beside me by the hour, darning and counting, while I struggled with the "Joyous Farmer." She seldom talked to me about music, and I understood why. Once when I had been doggedly beating out some easy

---

3. **duster.** Lightweight coat
4. **north of Franz-Joseph-Land . . . Congo.** *Franz-Joseph-Land*—group of tiny islands in the Arctic Ocean; *Congo*—river in central Africa
5. **sixties.** 1860s
6. **Nebraska frontier.** Western border of Nebraska; uncharted territory
7. **provisions.** Supplies
8. **scales and exercises.** Musical scales and practice pieces

---

WORDS FOR EVERYDAY USE:

in • fat • u • a • tion (in fach′oo a′shən) *n.*, foolish or shallow love or affection

re • vert (ri vʉrt′) *vi.*, return to a former practice, opinion, state, or subject

rev • er • en • tial (rev′ə ren′shal) *adj.*, showing a feeling of deep respect, love, and awe

passages from an old score of *Euryanthe* I had found among her music books, she came up to me and, putting her hands over my eyes, gently drew my head back upon her shoulder, saying <u>tremulously</u>, "Don't love it so well, Clark, or it may be taken from you."

When my aunt appeared on the morning after her arrival in Boston, she was still in a semi-somnambulant[9] state. She seemed not to realize that she was in the city where she had spent her youth, the place longed for hungrily half a lifetime. She had been so wretchedly train-sick throughout the journey that she had no recollection of anything but her discomfort, and, to all intents and purposes, there were but a few hours of nightmare between the farm in Red Willow County and my study on Newbury Street. I had planned a little pleasure for her that afternoon, to repay her for some of the glorious moments she had given me when we used to milk together in the straw-thatched cowshed and she, because I was more than usually tired, or because her husband had spoken sharply to me, would tell me of the splendid performance of the *Huguenots* she had seen in Paris, in her youth.

At two o'clock the Symphony Orchestra was to give a Wagner[10] program, and I intended to take my aunt; though, as I conversed with her, I grew doubtful about her enjoyment of it. I suggested our visiting the Conservatory and the Common[11] before lunch, but she seemed altogether too timid to wish to venture out. She questioned me absently about various changes in the city, but she was chiefly concerned that she had forgotten to leave instructions about feeding half-skimmed milk to a certain weakling calf, "old Maggie's calf, you know, Clark," she explained, evidently having forgotten how long I had been away. She was further troubled because she had neglected to tell her daughter about the freshly-opened kit of mackerel[12] in the cellar, which would spoil if it were not used directly.

I asked her whether she had ever heard any of the Wagnerian operas, and found that she had not, though she was perfectly familiar with their <u>respective</u> situations, and had once possessed the piano score of *The Flying Dutchman*. I began to think it would be best to get her back to Red Willow County without waking her, and regretted having suggested the concert.

From the time we entered the concert hall, however, she was a trifle less passive and inert, and for the first time seemed to perceive her surroundings. I had felt some trepidation lest she might become aware of her queer, country clothes, or might experience some painful embarrassment at stepping suddenly into the world to which she had been dead for a quarter of a century. But, again, I found how superficially I had judged her. She sat looking about her with eyes as impersonal, almost as stony, as those with which the granite Rameses[13] in a museum watches the froth and fret that ebbs and flows about his pedestal. I have seen this same aloofness in

Why did Aunt Georgiana tell the narrator not to love the music so well?

How does Aunt Georgiana react to being in the concert hall? About what is the narrator concerned?

What "little pleasure" does the narrator plan for the afternoon?

9. **semi-somnambulant.** Like one who is sleepwalking
10. **Wagner.** Richard Wagner (1813–1883), German composer
11. **the Common.** Boston Common, park in a historic section of Boston
12. **kit of mackerel.** Container of pickled fish
13. **Rameses.** Name of a number of Egyptian kings who ruled from *circa* 1315 BC to *circa* 1090 BC

WORDS FOR EVERYDAY USE:

trem • u • lous • ly (trem´yōo ləs lē) *adv.,* in a trembling or quivering manner; fearfully, timidly

re • spec • tive (ri spek´tiv) *adj.,* as relates individually to each of two or more persons or things

old miners who drift into the Brown hotel at Denver, their pockets full of bullion, their linen soiled, their haggard faces unshaven; standing in the thronged corridors as solitary as though they were still in a frozen camp on the Yukon.

The matinee audience was made up chiefly of women. One lost the contour of faces and figures, indeed any effect of line whatever, and there was only the color of bodices past counting, the shimmer of fabrics soft and firm, silky and sheer; red, mauve, pink, blue, lilac, purple, ecru, rose, yellow, cream, and white, all the colors that an impressionist[14] finds in a sunlit landscape, with here and there the dead shadow of a frock coat. My Aunt Georgiana regarded them as though they had been so many daubs of tube-paint on a palette.

When the musicians came out and took their places, she gave a little stir of anticipation, and looked with quickening interest down over the rail at that invariable grouping, perhaps the first wholly familiar thing that had greeted her eye since she had left old Maggie and her weakling calf. I could feel how all those details sank into her soul, for I had not forgotten how they had sunk into mine when I came fresh from ploughing forever and forever between green aisles of corn, where, as in a treadmill, one might walk from daybreak to dusk without perceiving a shadow of change. The clean profiles of the musicians, the gloss of their linen, the dull black of their coats, the beloved shapes of the instruments, the patches of yellow light on the smooth, varnished bellies of the cellos and the bass viols in the rear, the restless, wind-tossed forest of fiddle necks and bows—I recalled how, in the first orchestra I ever heard, those long bow-strokes seemed to draw the heart out of me, as a conjurer's stick[15] reels out yards of paper ribbon from a hat.

The first number was the *Tannhauser overture*. When the horns drew out the first strain of the Pilgrim's chorus, Aunt Georgiana clutched my coat sleeve. Then it was I first realized that for her this broke a silence of thirty years. With the battle between the two motives, with the frenzy of the Venusberg theme and its ripping of strings, there came to me an overwhelming sense of the waste and wear we are so powerless to combat; and I saw again the tall, naked house on the prairie, black and grim as a wooden fortress; the black pond where I had learned to swim, its margin pitted with sun-dried cattle tracks; the rain gullied clay banks about the naked house, the four dwarf ash seedlings where the dishcloths were always hung to dry before the kitchen door. The world there was the flat world of the ancients; to the east, a cornfield that stretched to daybreak; to the west, a corral that reached to sunset; between, the conquests of peace, dearer-bought than those of war.

The overture closed, my aunt released my coat sleeve, but she said nothing. She sat staring dully at the orchestra. What, I wondered, did she get from it? She had been a good pianist in her day, I knew, and her musical education had been broader than that of most music teachers of a quarter of a century ago. She had often told me

Who comprises the matinee audience? How are they dressed?

How does Aunt Georgiana react to the music? What awareness comes to the narrator?

14. **impressionist.** Painter, writer, or composer who seeks to render impressions and moods in which the chief aim is to capture a momentary glimpse of a subject
15. **conjurer's stick.** Magician's wand

WORDS FOR EVERYDAY USE:

o • ver • ture (o´vǝr chǝr) *n.,* musical introduction to an opera or other large musical work; independent orchestral composition of varying form

First Row Orchestra. Edward Hopper, 1951. Hirshhorn Museum and Sculpture Garden, Smithsonian Institution, Gift of the Joseph H. Hirshhorn Foundation, 1966

Photograph by Lee Stalsworth

of Mozart's operas and Meyerbeer's and I could remember hearing her sing, years ago, certain melodies of Verdi. When I had fallen ill with a fever in her house, she used to sit by my cot in the evening—when the cool, night wind blew in through the faded mosquito netting tacked over the window and I lay watching a certain bright star that burned red above the cornfield—and sing "Home to our mountains, O, let us return!" in a way fit to break the heart of a Vermont boy near dead of homesickness already.

I watched her closely through the <u>prelude</u> to *Tristan and Isolde*, trying vainly to conjecture what that seething turmoil of strings and winds might mean to her, but she sat mutely staring at the violin bows that drove obliquely downward, like the pelting streaks of rain in a summer shower. Had this music any message for her? Had she enough left to at all comprehend this power which had kindled the world since she had left it? I was in a fever of curiosity, but Aunt Georgiana sat silent upon her peak in Darien.[16] She preserved this utter <u>immobility</u> throughout the number from *The Flying Dutchman*, though her fingers worked mechanically upon her black dress, as if, of themselves,

What did Aunt Georgiana do when the narrator was sick? What effect did her action have on the narrator?

---

16. **peak in Darien.** Mountain in Panama (formerly called the Isthmus of Darien) where Cortés was said to have looked westward at the Pacific Ocean, a new discovery for Europeans

WORDS FOR EVERYDAY USE:

pre • lude (prel´yo͞od) *n.,* first movement of an opera; introduction

im • mo • bil • i • ty (im´mo bil´i tē) *n.,* state of being fixed or unmovable

they were recalling the piano score they had once played. Poor hands! They had been stretched and twisted into mere tentacles to hold and lift and knead with—on one of them a thin, worn band that had once been a wedding ring. As I pressed and gently quieted one of those groping hands, I remembered with quivering eyelids their services for me in other days.

Soon after the tenor began the "Prize Song," I heard a quick drawn breath and turned to my aunt. Her eyes were closed, but the tears were glistening on her cheeks, and I think, in a moment more, they were in my eyes as well. It never really died, then—the soul which can suffer so <u>excruciatingly</u> and so <u>interminably</u>; it withers to the outward eye only; like that strange moss which can lie on a dusty shelf half a century and yet, if placed in water, grows green again. She wept so throughout the development and elaboration of the melody.

During the intermission before the second half, I questioned my aunt and found that the "Prize Song" was not new to her. Some years before there had drifted to the farm in Red Willow County a young German, a tramp cow-puncher, who had sung in the chorus at Bayreuth[17] when he was a boy, along with the other peasant boys and girls. Of a Sunday morning he used to sit on his gingham-sheeted bed in the hands' bedroom which opened off the kitchen, cleaning the leather of his boots and saddle, singing the "Prize Song," while my aunt went about her work in the kitchen. She had hovered over him until

How does the tenor's solo affect Aunt Georgiana? the narrator? What insight into the human soul does the narrator have?

How does Aunt Georgiana know the "Prize Song"? Who used to sing it? What became of the singer?

she had prevailed upon him to join the country church, though his sole fitness for this step, in so far as I could gather, lay in his boyish face and his possession of this divine melody. Shortly afterward, he had gone to town on the Fourth of July, been drunk for several days, lost his money at a faro[18] table, ridden a saddled Texas steer on a bet, and disappeared with a fractured collar-bone. All this my aunt told me huskily, wanderingly, as though she were talking in the weak lapses of illness.

"Well, we have come to better things than the old *Trovatore* at any rate, Aunt Georgie?" I queried, with a well meant effort at <u>jocularity</u>.

Her lip quivered and she hastily put her handkerchief up to her mouth. From behind it she murmured, "And you have been hearing this ever since you left me, Clark?" Her question was the gentlest and saddest of <u>reproaches</u>.

The second half of the program consisted of four numbers from the *Ring*, and closed with Siegfried's funeral march. My aunt wept quietly, but almost continuously, as a shallow vessel overflows in a rain-storm. From time to time her dim eyes looked up at the lights, burning softly under their dull glass globes.

The deluge of sound poured on and on; I never knew what she found in the shining current of it; I never knew how far it bore her, or past what happy islands. From the trembling of her face I could well believe

---

17. **Bayreuth.** Site of international music festivals in Germany
18. **faro.** Gambling game

WORDS FOR EVERYDAY USE:	**ex • cru • ci • at • ing • ly** (eks krōō´shē āt´iŋ lē) *adv.*, in a painful or agonizing manner	**joc • u • lar • i • ty** (jäk´yōō lar´ə tē) *n.*, humor, joking
	in • ter • mi • na • bly (in tʉr´mi nə blē) *adv.*, endlessly; in a manner that seems to last forever	**re • proach** (ri prōch´) *n.*, blaming or reproving; rebuke

that before the last number she had been carried out where the myriad graves are, into the grey, nameless burying grounds of the sea; or into some world of death vaster yet, where, from the beginning of the world, hope has lain down with hope and dream with dream and, renouncing, slept.

The concert was over; the people filed out of the hall chattering and laughing, glad to relax and find the living level again, but my kinswoman made no effort to rise. The harpist slipped the green felt cover over his instrument; the flute-players shook the water from their mouthpieces; the men of the orchestra went out one by one, leaving the stage to the chairs and music stands, empty as a winter cornfield.

I spoke to my aunt. She burst into tears and sobbed pleadingly. "I don't want to go, Clark, I don't want to go!"

I understood. For her, just outside the concert hall, lay the black pond with the cattle-tracked bluffs; the tall, unpainted house, with weather-curled boards, naked as a tower; the crook-backed ash seedlings where the dishcloths hung to dry; the gaunt, moulting[19] turkeys picking up refuse about the kitchen door. ∎

---

19. **moulting.** Shedding feathers

Where does the narrator believe the music transports Aunt Georgiana?

Why does Aunt Georgiana want to stay in the concert hall?

Responding to the Selection

Imagine that you are Aunt Georgiana listening to the music in the concert hall. How do you feel listening to music you have not heard in many years? Do you regret removing yourself from the world of music?

Reviewing the Selection

RECALLING

1. What is the reason for Aunt Georgiana's visit to Boston?

2. After eloping, how does Aunt Georgiana "elude the reproaches of her family"?

3. What job does the narrator perform for his uncle on the farm?

4. What pleasure does the narrator plan for his aunt?

INTERPRETING

5. Why does the name "Aunt Georgiana" open before the narrator "a gulf of recollection so wide and deep"?

6. What facts emphasize the hardship of Aunt Georgiana's life on the Nebraska frontier?

7. What actions on the part of Aunt Georgiana emphasize that the narrator owes to her "most of the good" that came his way in boyhood?

8. Why doesn't Aunt Georgiana want to leave the concert hall?

9. Why does Aunt Georgiana warn the narrator "Don't love it so well, Clark, or it may be taken from you"? What relationship does the warning have to the aunt's own experience?

10. What kind of relationship between music and the human soul is described in this story? What evidence in the selection supports your analysis?

Understanding Literature (Questions for Discussion)

1. **Narrator and Point of View.** A **narrator** is one who tells a story. In this story, written in first-person **point of view,** the narrator is limited in his knowledge. As a character, however, the narrator is aware of his limitations and acknowledges his superficial judgment of Aunt Georgiana. In what ways does the narrator misjudge or underestimate his aunt? How does this affect the point of view of the narrator? Do you find him reliable? How does the narrator regard his uncle? What evidence supports your interpretation?

2. **Simile.** A **simile** is a comparison using *like* or *as.* A type of metaphor, a simile can be analyzed into two parts, the *tenor* (or subject being described) and the *vehicle* (or object being used in the description). Consider the simile in the following sentence from the selection: "It never really died, then—the soul which can suffer so excruciatingly and so interminably; it withers to the outward eye only; like that strange moss which can lie on a dusty shelf half a century and yet, if placed in water, grows green again." What is the tenor in the simile? the vehicle? What quality do the two parts of the simile share?

Responding in Writing

1. **Descriptive Paragraph.** In order to portray the vast and silent landscape of the prairie, Cather used sensory details—words and phrases that describe how things look, sound, smell, taste, and feel. For example, consider the following descriptive passage from the selection: ". . . and I saw again the tall, naked house on the prairie, black and grim as a wooden fortress; the black pond where I had learned to swim, its margin pitted with sun-dried cattle tracks. . . ." Write a descriptive paragraph that portrays a scene of a real or imaginary place. Use sensory details in your descriptive paragraph, emphasizing one of the senses, as Cather emphasized the sense of sight in her descriptive passages.

2. **Personal Letter.** Imagine that you are Aunt Georgiana in this story. Write a letter to your nephew, thanking him for taking you to the Wagner matinee, explaining what music used to mean in your life and why you sacrificed it. Try to explain to your nephew what two worlds battled for your heart. Refer to the Language Arts Survey, 5.2, "The Form of a Personal Letter."

Language Lab

Dangling and Misplaced Modifiers. Read the Language Arts Survey, 2.63, "Correcting Dangling or Misplaced Modifiers." Then, on your own paper, correct each of the following sentences so that its meaning is clear.

1. Carefully folded in half, he removed the rare and valuable letter from the envelope.

2. Searching for her lost necklace, the office was turned upside down.

3. To keep from feeling homesick, the cow herd occupied most of the young boy's time.

4. The young woman moved to the silent and faraway plains who wished to avoid her family's reproach.

5. Before moving to the Nebraska frontier, Boston had been Georgiana's home while studying music at the conservatory.

Vocabulary Skills

Base Words and Suffixes. Read the Language Arts Survey, 2.140, "Base Words and Prefixes," and 2.141, "Suffixes." On your own paper, underline the base word once and the suffix twice in each of the following words from "A Wagner Matinee." Next, look up each suffix in a dictionary and write two additional words that end with the same suffix.

1. reverential

2. mythology

3. martyrdom

4. glistening

5. immobility

PROJECT

Music History. As a class, do research on some or all of the following composers mentioned in the selection: Carl Maria von Weber, Giacomo Meyerbeer, Wolfgang Amadeus Mozart, Giuseppi Verdi, and Wilhelm Richard Wagner. Divide the class into small groups and assign one composer to each group. Research the life and works of these composers. Then present the results of your research in class, combining oral reporting with pictures from books and musical recordings.

"The Jilting of Granny Weatherall"
by Katherine Anne Porter

ABOUT THE AUTHOR

Katherine Anne Porter (1890–1980) was born Callie Porter in Indian Creek, Texas. Her mother died when she was about two, and her father moved the family to live with his mother, where their grandmother raised them in a house that Porter recalled as "full of books" and extreme poverty. When Porter was eleven her grandmother died; when she was sixteen she married so she could leave home. It was a short union, and by 1916 she began her writing career as a reporter. She worked for newspapers in Dallas and Fort Worth, Texas, and Denver, Colorado.

She moved to Greenwich Village in New York City in 1918 and then spent the years between 1918 and 1924 living mainly in Mexico, freelancing and becoming involved in revolutionary politics. "Maria Conception," her first fiction story, was written while she was in Mexico. Published in *Century* magazine in 1922, it won her critical acclaim.

Porter lived a life filled with travel, activity, many jobs, and four marriages. She was a self-supporting woman with expensive tastes, so even though she considered herself a "serious writer" she didn't want to give up lucrative freelance offers, which had the effect of limiting her literary production. In 1931, Porter used a Guggenheim Fellowship to return to Mexico for several years. In the 1950s she lectured, and was a writer-in-residence at college campuses. *Collected Stories* (1965) received a National Book Award, the Pulitzer Prize, and the Gold Medal for fiction of the National Institute of Arts and Letters.

Among her other works are *Flowering Judas* (1929), *Noon Wine* (1937), *Pale Horse, Pale Rider* (1939), *The Leaning Tower* (1944), and her only novel, *Ship of Fools,* begun in 1931, but not published until 1962. *Ship of Fools* was made into a film and brought her a great deal of money.

ABOUT THE SELECTION

Like all of the other short stories published in the 1930 collection *Flowering Judas,* **"The Jilting of Granny Weatherall"** was first published in a magazine. While Porter's earliest audience was quite small, comprising mostly writers who read obscure magazines, it was nonetheless enthusiastic for her perfection of style and the short story form.

"The Jilting of Granny Weatherall"

KATHERINE ANNE PORTER

She flicked her wrist neatly out of Doctor Harry's pudgy careful fingers and pulled the sheet up to her chin. The brat ought to be in knee breeches. Doctoring around the country with spectacles on his nose! "Get along now, take your schoolbooks and go. There's nothing wrong with me."

Doctor Harry spread a warm paw like a cushion on her forehead where the forked green vein danced and made her eyelids twitch. "Now, now, be a good girl, and we'll have you up in no time."

"That's no way to speak to a woman nearly eighty years old just because she's down. I'd have you respect your elders, young man."

"Well, Missy, excuse me," Doctor Harry patted her cheek. "But I've got to warn you, haven't I? You're a marvel, but you must be careful or you're going to be good and sorry."

"Don't tell me what I'm going to be. I'm on my feet now, morally speaking. It's Cornelia. I had to go to bed to get rid of her."

Her bones felt loose, and floated around in her skin, and Doctor Harry floated like a balloon around the foot of the bed. He floated and pulled down his waistcoat and swung his glasses on a cord. "Well, stay where you are, it certainly can't hurt you."

"Get along and doctor your sick," said Granny Weatherall. "Leave a well woman alone. I'll call for you when I want you. . . . Where were you forty years ago when I pulled through milk leg[1] and double pneumonia? You weren't even born. Don't let Cornelia lead you on," she shouted, because Doctor Harry appeared to float up to the ceiling and out. "I pay my own bills, and I don't throw my money away on nonsense!"

She meant to wave good-bye, but it was too much trouble. Her eyes closed of themselves, it was like a dark curtain drawn around the bed. The pillow rose and floated under her, pleasant as a hammock in a light wind. She listened to the leaves rustling outside the window. No, somebody was swishing newspapers: no, Cornelia and Doctor Harry were whispering together. She leaped broad awake, thinking they whispered in her ear.

How old is Granny Weatherall? Approximately how old is Doctor Harry?

---

1. **milk leg.** Painful swelling of the leg

Q What does Granny Weatherall need to do tomorrow?

Q What had she done twenty years ago?

"She was never like this, *never* like this!" "Well, what can we expect?" "Yes, eighty years old. . . ."

Well, and what if she was? She still had ears. It was like Cornelia to whisper around doors. She always kept things secret in such a public way. She was always being tactful and kind. Cornelia was dutiful: that was the trouble with her. Dutiful and good: "So good and dutiful," said Granny, "that I'd like to spank her." She saw herself spanking Cornelia and making a fine job of it.

"What'd you say, Mother?"

Granny felt her face tying up in hard knots.

"Can't a body think, I'd like to know?"

"I thought you might want something."

"I do. I want a lot of things. First off, go away and don't whisper."

She lay and drowsed, hoping in her sleep that the children would keep out and let her rest a minute. It had been a long day. Not that she was tired. It was always pleasant to snatch a minute now and then. There was always so much to be done, let me see: tomorrow.

Tomorrow was far away and there was nothing to trouble about. Things were finished somehow when the time came: thank God there was always a little margin over for peace: then a person could spread out the plan of life and tuck in the edges orderly. It was good to have everything clean and folded away, with the hair brushes and tonic bottles sitting straight on the white embroidered linen: the day started without fuss and the pantry shelves laid out with rows of jelly glasses and brown jugs and white stonechina jars with blue whirligigs and words painted on them: cof-

fee, tea, sugar, ginger, cinnamon. allspice: and the bronze clock with the lion on top nicely dusted off. The dust that lion could collect in twenty-four hours! The box in the attic with all those letters tied up, well, she'd have to go through that tomorrow. All those letters George's letters and John's letters and her letters to them both—lying around for the children to find afterwards made her uneasy. Yes, that would be tomorrow's business. No use to let them know how silly she had been once.

While she was <u>rummaging</u> around she found death in her mind and it felt clammy and unfamiliar. She had spent so much time preparing for death there was no need for bringing it up again. Let it take care of itself now. When she was sixty she had felt very old, finished, and went around making farewell trips to see her children and grandchildren, with a secret in her mind: This is the very last of your mother, children! Then she made her will and came down with a long fever. That was all just a notion like a lot of other things, but it was lucky too, for she had once for all got over the idea of dying for a long time. Now she couldn't be worried. She hoped she had better sense now. Her father had lived to be one hundred and two years old and had drunk a noggin of strong hot toddy on his last birthday. He told the reporters it was his daily habit, and he owed his long life to that. He had made quite a scandal and was very pleased about it. She believed she'd just plague Cornelia a little.

"Cornelia! Cornelia!" No footsteps, but a sudden hand on her cheek. "Bless you, where have you been?"

WORDS FOR EVERYDAY USE: **rum • mage** (rum´ij) *vt.,* search through thoroughly; ransack

"Here, mother."

"Well, Cornelia, I want a noggin of hot toddy."

"Are you cold, darling?"

"I'm chilly, Cornelia. Lying in bed stops the circulation. I must have told you that a thousand times."

Well, she could just hear Cornelia telling her husband that Mother was getting a little childish and they'd have to humor her. The thing that most annoyed her was that Cornelia thought she was deaf, dumb, and blind. Little hasty glances and tiny gestures tossed around her and over her head saying, "Don't cross her, let her have her way, she's eighty years old," and she sitting there as if she lived in a thin glass cage. Sometimes Granny almost made up her mind to pack up and move back to her own house where nobody could remind her every minute that she was old. Wait, wait, Cornelia, till your own children whisper behind your back!

In her day she had kept a better house and had got more work done. She wasn't too old yet for Lydia to be driving eighty miles for advice when one of the children jumped the track, and Jimmy still dropped in and talked things over: "Now, Mammy, you've a good business head, I want to know what you think of this? . . ." Old. Cornelia couldn't change the furniture around without asking. Little things, little things! They had been so sweet when they were little. Granny wished the old days were back again with the children young and everything to be done over. It had been a hard pull, but not too much for her. When she thought of all the food she had cooked, and all the clothes she had cut and sewed, and all the gardens she had made— well, the children showed it. There they were, made out of her, and they couldn't get away from that. Sometimes she wanted to see John again and point to them and

Photo courtesy of Digital Stock Corp.

say, Well, I didn't do so badly, did I? But that would have to wait. That was for tomorrow. She used to think of him as a man, but now all the children were older than their father, and he would be a child beside her if she saw him now. It seemed strange and there was something wrong in the idea. Why, he couldn't possibly recognize her. She had fenced in a hundred acres once, digging the post holes herself and clamping the wires with just a negro boy to help. That changed a woman. John would be looking for a young woman with the peaked Spanish comb in her hair and the painted fan. Digging post holes changed a woman. Riding country roads in the winter when women had their babies was another thing: sitting up nights with sick horses and sick children and hardly ever losing one. John, I hardly ever lost one of them! John would see that in a

What does Cornelia do that bothers her mother?

Who is John? What does Granny Weatherall want him to know?

What kinds of things has Granny done?

minute, that would be something he could understand, she wouldn't have to explain anything!

It made her feel like rolling up her sleeves and putting the whole place to rights again. No matter if Cornelia was determined to be everywhere at once, there were a great many things left undone on this place. She would start tomorrow and do them. It was good to be strong enough for everything, even if all you made melted and changed and slipped under your hands, so that by the time you finished you almost forgot what you were working for. What was it I set out to do? she asked herself intently, but she could not remember. A fog rose over the valley, she saw it marching across the creek swallowing the trees and moving up the hill like an army of ghosts. Soon it would be at the near edge of the orchard, and then it was time to go in and light the lamps. Come in, children, don't stay out in the night air.

Lighting the lamps had been beautiful. The children huddled up to her and breathed like little calves waiting at the bars in the twilight. Their eyes followed the match and watched the flame rise and settle in a blue curve, then they moved away from her. The lamp was lit, they didn't have to be scared and hang on to mother any more. Never, never, never more. God, for all my life I thank Thee. Without Thee, my God, I could never have done it. Hail Mary, full of grace.

I want you to pick all the fruit this year and see that nothing is wasted. There's always someone who can use it. Don't let good things rot for want of using. You waste life when you waste good food. Don't let things get lost. It's bitter to lose things. Now, don't let me get to thinking, not when I am tired and taking a little nap before supper. . . .

The pillow rose about her shoulders and pressed against her heart and the memory was being squeezed out of it: oh, push down the pillow, somebody: it would smother her if she tried to hold it. Such a fresh breeze blowing and such a green day with no threats in it. But he had not come, just the same. What does a woman do when she has put on the white veil and set out the white cake for a man and he doesn't come? She tried to remember. No, I swear he never harmed me but in that. He never harmed me but in that . . . and what if he did? There was the day, the day, but a whirl of dark, smoke rose and covered it, crept up and over into the bright field where everything was planted so carefully in orderly rows. That was hell, she knew hell when she saw it. For sixty years she had prayed against remembering him and against losing her soul in the deep pit of hell, and now the two things were mingled in one and the thought of him was a smoky cloud from hell that moved and crept in her head when she had just got rid of Doctor Harry and was trying to rest a minute. Wounded vanity, Ellen, said a sharp voice in the top of her mind. Don't let your wounded vanity get the upper hand of you. Plenty of girls get jilted. You were jilted, weren't you? Then stand up to it. Her eyelids wavered and let in streamers of blue-gray light like tissue paper over her eyes. She must get up and pull the shades down or she'd never sleep.

Words for Everyday Use:

jilt (jilt) *vt.*, reject; cast off

She was in bed again and the shades were not down. How could that happen? Better turn over, hide from the light, sleeping in the light gave you nightmares. "Mother, how do you feel now?" and a stinging wetness on her forehead. But I don't like having my face washed in cold water!

Hapsy? George? Lydia? Jimmy? No, Cornelia, and her features were swollen and full of little puddles. "They're coming, darling, they'll all be here soon." Go wash your face, child, you look funny.

Instead of obeying, Cornelia knelt down and put her head on the pillow. She seemed to be talking but there was no sound. "Well, are you tongue-tied? Whose birthday is it? Are you going to give a party?"

Cornelia's mouth moved urgently in strange shapes. "Don't do that, you bother me, daughter."

"Oh, no, Mother. Oh, no. . . ."

Nonsense. It was strange about children. They disputed your every word. "No what, Cornelia?"

"Here's Doctor Harry."

"I won't see that boy again. He just left five minutes ago."

"That was this morning, Mother. It's night now. Here's the nurse."

"This is Doctor Harry, Mrs. Weatherall. I never saw you look so young and happy!"

"Ah, I'll never be young again—but I'd be happy if they'd let me lie in peace and get rested."

She thought she spoke up loudly, but no one answered. A warm weight on her forehead, a warm bracelet on her wrist, and a breeze went on whispering, trying to tell her something. A shuffle of leaves in the everlasting hand of God, He blew on them and they danced and rattled. "Mother, don't mind, we're going to give you a little hypodermic."[2] "Look here, daughter, how do ants get in this bed? I saw sugar ants yesterday." Did you send for Hapsy too?

It was Hapsy she really wanted. She had to go a long way back through a great many rooms to find Hapsy standing with a baby on her arm. She seemed to herself to be Hapsy also, and the baby on Hapsy's arm was Hapsy and himself and herself, all at once, and there was no surprise in the meeting. Then Hapsy melted from within and turned flimsy as gray gauze and the baby was a gauzy shadow, and Hapsy came up close and said, "I thought you'd never come," and looked at her very searchingly and said, "You haven't changed a bit!" They leaned forward to kiss, when Cornelia began whispering from a long way off. "Oh, is there anything you want to tell me? Is there anything I can do for you?"

Yes, she had changed her mind after sixty years and she would like to see George. I want you to find George. Find him and be sure to tell him I forgot him. I want him to know I had my husband just the same and my children and my house like any other woman. A good house too and a good husband that I loved and fine children out of him. Better than I hoped for even. Tell him I was given back everything he took away and more. Oh, no, oh, God, no, there was something else besides the house and the man and the children. Oh, surely they were not all? What was it? Something not given back. . . . Her breath crowded down under her ribs and grew into a monstrous frightening shape with cutting edges; it bored up into her head, and the agony was unbelievable: Yes, John, get the Doctor now, no more talk, my time has come.

When this one was born it should be the last. The last. It should have been born first, for it was the one she had truly wanted. Everything came in good time. Nothing left out, left over. She was

Who is Hapsy? What are Granny Weatherall's feelings for her? What happened to her?

Has Granny Weatherall's life been complete?

---

2. **hypodermic.** Injection

strong, in three days she would be as well as ever. Better. A woman needed milk in her to have her full health.

"Mother, do you hear me?"

"I've been telling you—"

"Mother, Father Connolly's here."

"I went to Holy Communion only last week. Tell him I'm not so sinful as all that."

"Father just wants to speak to you."

He could speak as much as he pleased. It was like him to drop in and inquire about her soul as if it were a teething baby, and then stay on for a cup of tea and a round of cards and gossip. He always had a funny story of some sort, usually about an Irishman who made his little mistakes and confessed them, and the point lay in some absurd thing he would blurt out in the confessional showing his struggles between native piety and original sin. Granny felt easy about her soul. Cornelia, where are your manners? Give Father Connolly a chair. She had her secret comfortable understanding with a few favorite saints who cleared a straight road to God for her. All as surely signed and sealed as the papers for the new Forty Acres. Forever . . . heirs and assigns[3] forever. Since the day the wedding cake was not cut, but thrown out and wasted. The whole bottom dropped out of the world, and there she was blind and sweating with nothing under her feet and the walls falling away. His hand had caught her under the breast, she had not fallen, there was the freshly polished floor with the green rug on it, just as before. He had cursed like a sailor's parrot and said, "I'll kill him for you." Don't lay a hand on him, for my sake leave something to God. "Now, Ellen, you must believe what I tell you. . . ."

So there was nothing, nothing to worry about any more, except sometimes in the night one of the children screamed in a nightmare, and they both hustled out

Who came to her aid on the day she was jilted?

shaking and hunting for the matches and calling, "There, wait a minute, here we are!" John, get the doctor now. Hapsy's time has come. But there was Hapsy standing by the bed in a white cap. "Cornelia. tell Hapsy to take off her cap. I can't see her plain."

Her eyes opened very wide and the room stood out like a picture she had seen somewhere. Dark colors with the shadows rising towards the ceiling in long angles. The tall black dresser gleamed with nothing on it but John's picture, enlarged from a little one, with John's eyes very black when they should have been blue. You never saw him, so how do you know how he looked? But the man insisted the copy was perfect, it was very rich and handsome. For a picture, yes, but it's not my husband. The table by the bed had a linen cover and a candle and a crucifix. The light was blue from Cornelia's silk lampshades. No sort of light at all, just frippery. You had to live forty years with kerosene lamps to appreciate honest electricity. She felt very strong and she saw Doctor Harry with a rosy nimbus around him.

"You look like a saint, Doctor Harry, and I vow that's as near as you'll ever come to it."

"She's saying something."

"I heard you, Cornelia. What's all this carrying on?"

"Father Connolly's saying—"

Cornelia's voice staggered and bumped like a cart in a bad road. It rounded corners and turned back again and arrived nowhere. Granny stepped up in the cart very lightly and reached for the reins, but a man sat beside her and she knew him by his hands, driving the cart. She did not look in his face, for she knew without seeing, but looked instead down the road where the

---

3. **assigns.** People to whom property is transferred

trees leaned over and bowed to each other and a thousand birds were singing a Mass. She felt like singing too, but she put her hand in the bosom of her dress and pulled out a rosary, and Father Connolly murmured Latin in a very solemn voice and tickled her feet.[4] My God, will you stop that nonsense? I'm a married woman. What if he did run away and leave me to face the priest by myself? I found another a whole world better. I wouldn't have exchanged my husband for anybody except St. Michael himself, and you may tell him that for me with a thank you in the bargain.

Light flashed on her closed eyelids, and a deep roaring shook her. Cornelia, is that lightning? I hear thunder. There's going to be a storm. Close all the windows. Call the children in. "Mother, here we are, all of us." "Is that you, Hapsy?" "Oh, no, I'm Lydia. We drove as fast as we could." Their faces drifted above her, drifted away. The rosary fell out of her hands and Lydia put it back. Jimmy tried to help, their hands fumbled together, and Granny closed two fingers around Jimmy's thumb. Beads wouldn't do, it must be something alive. She was so amazed her thoughts ran round and round. So, my dear Lord, this is my death and I wasn't even thinking about it. My children have come to see me die. But I can't, it's not time. Oh, I always hated surprises. I wanted to give Cornelia the amethyst set—Cornelia, you're to have the amethyst set, but Hapsy's to wear it when she wants, and, Doctor Harry, do shut up. Nobody sent for you. Oh, my dear Lord, do wait a minute. I meant to do something about the Forty Acres, Jimmy doesn't need

it and Lydia will later on, with that worthless husband of hers. I meant to finish the altar cloth and send six bottles of wine to Sister Borgia for her dyspepsia. I want to send six bottles of wine to Sister Borgia, Father Connolly, now don't let me forget .

Cornelia's voice made short turns and tilted over and crashed. "Oh, Mother, oh, Mother, oh Mother. . . ."

"I'm not going, Cornelia. I'm taken by surprise. I can't go."

You'll see Hapsy again. What about her? "I thought you'd never come." Granny made a long journey outward, looking for Hapsy. What if I don't find her? What then? Her heart sank down and down, there was no bottom to death, she couldn't come to the end of it. The blue light from Cornelia's lampshade drew into a tiny point in the center of her brain, it flickered and winked like an eye, quietly it fluttered and <u>dwindled</u>. Granny lay curled down within herself, amazed and watchful, staring at the point of light that was herself: her body was now only a deeper mass of shadow in an endless darkness and this darkness would curl around the light and swallow it up. God, give a sign!

For the second time there was no sign. Again no bridegroom and the priest in the house. She could not remember any other sorrow because this grief wiped them all away. Oh, no, there's nothing more cruel than this—I'll never forgive it. She stretched herself with a deep breath and blew out the light. ■

---

4. **murmured . . . feet.** Administered the last rites, a sacrament for a person close to death

WORDS FOR EVERYDAY USE: **dwin •dle** (dwin′dəl) *vt.*, languish; fade

Responding to the Selection

Imagine that you are Granny Weatherall remembering George, the bridegroom who jilted her on their wedding day. After sixty years, how would you feel about him? Would you be able to forgive him? Why, or why not? What would you want him to know about your life? Write a letter to George in your journal expressing your feelings about his action years ago.

Reviewing the Selection

RECALLING

1. What explanation for being in bed does Granny Weatherall give to the doctor?

2. How had Granny Weatherall prepared herself for death when she was sixty years old?

3. What does Granny Weatherall remember most about her wedding day?

4. What does Granny Weatherall realize at the end of the story?

INTERPRETING

5. What traits might describe Granny Weatherall before she became ill?

6. Why doesn't Granny Weatherall worry now about death?

7. Why does Granny Weatherall mingle the thought of the bridegroom with the thought of losing her soul in hell?

8. What will Granny Weatherall never forgive?

SYNTHESIZING

9. How is Granny Weatherall's name appropriate for her character?

10. How is Granny Weatherall jilted a second time?

Understanding Literature (Questions for Discussion)

1. **Irony.** **Irony** is a difference between appearance and reality. In **irony of situation**, one of the types of irony, an event occurs that violates the expectations of the characters, the reader, or the audience. What are two major examples of irony of situation in this short story? How are the expectations of Granny Weatherall violated in each case?

2. **Simile.** A **simile** is a comparison using like or as. A type of metaphor, a simile can be analyzed into two parts, the *tenor* (or object being described) and the *vehicle* (or object being used in the description). In the simile from the selection "Her eyes closed of themselves, it was like a dark curtain drawn around the bed," the tenor is "eyes closed"

and the vehicle is "dark curtain." They can be compared because they share some quality, in this case, darkness. Identify another simile from the selection, analyzing the two parts and noting what quality they share.

3. **Stream-of-Consciousness Writing. Stream-of-consciousness writing** is literary work that attempts to render the flow of feelings, thoughts, and impressions within the minds of characters. Identify a passage in the selection that uses stream-of-consciousness writing to reveal the feelings, thoughts, or impressions within Granny Weatherall's mind. What effect is created in the passage by this type of writing?

Responding in Writing

1. **Dialogue.** Write an imaginary dialogue between Granny Weatherall and George, the bridegroom who jilted her on their wedding day, who meet again after death. Have them discuss what happened on their wedding day, including an explanation from George for his behavior.

2. **Obituary.** Write an obituary for Granny Weatherall, including more than simply important facts noted about her life in the selection. Try to include details that will communicate to your readers what was unique or characteristic about Granny Weatherall.

Language Lab

Precise Nouns. Read the Language Arts Survey, 2.32, "Using Precise Nouns." Then revise each of the sentences below by replacing the vague nouns with precise nouns.

1. The toys on the floor reminded her of the children.

2. Every fall, she lined the shelves with jars of food and spices.

3. Illnesses plagued the children throughout the horrible winter.

4. After finishing the evening chores, she came into the house and fixed dinner.

5. Years ago, the jilted bride was left behind with the promising vestiges of the day.

Speaking and Listening Skills

Nonverbal Communication. Read the Language Arts Survey, 3.3, "Elements of Nonverbal Communication." Then describe how each emotion listed below might be communicated through eye contact, facial expressions, gestures, body language, or proximity.

1. bewilderment
2. shock
3. determination
4. surprise
5. sorrow

"A Clean, Well-Lighted Place"
by Ernest Hemingway

ABOUT THE AUTHOR

Ernest Hemingway (1899–1961) was born and raised in Oak Park, Illinois, one of six children. His father was a successful doctor, his mother a music teacher. Hemingway began his writing career as a reporter at the *Kansas City Star* after high school. When World War I broke out and an eye problem prevented him from joining the United States army, he served as an ambulance driver and infantry soldier with the Italian army.

After the war he returned to Europe as a journalist and also began his serious writing career. There he was part of the large community of expatriate artists and writers—Gertrude Stein, Sherwood Anderson, Ezra Pound, and F. Scott Fitzgerald among others.

He was seriously injured in a 1953 plane crash in Africa and never fully recovered his mental health or productivity. He committed suicide in 1961 in Idaho after years of suffering from despair and paranoia.

Hemingway won a Pulitzer Prize in 1953 for *The Old Man and the Sea* (1952) and a Nobel Prize for literature in 1954. He was a prolific writer whose works include *The Sun Also Rises* (1926), *A Farewell to Arms* (1929), *The Snows of Kilimanjaro* (1936), *To Have and Have Not* (1937), *The Fifth Column* (play, 1938), *For Whom the Bell Tolls* (1940), *A Moveable Feast* (posthumously in 1964), and *Islands in the Stream* (posthumously in 1970).

ABOUT THE SELECTION

Between 1923 and 1933, Hemingway wrote all of his major short stories, including **"A Clean, Well-Lighted Place,"** which was published in the 1933 collection *Winner Take Nothing*. Five years later, *The Fifth Column* and the *First Forty-Nine Stories,* which compiled three collections—*In Our Time, Men Without Women,* and *Winner Take Nothing*—established Hemingway as one of the most admired writers of short fiction. Written with Hemingway's characteristic spare prose, "A Clean, Well-Lighted Place" unfolds primarily through dialogue. In the selection, two waiters at a Spanish café discuss one of their regular clients, an elderly man who likes to sit late at night at a table on the café terrace. A careful listener, Hemingway vitalized the writing of dialogue by stripping the verbal exchange to the essentials, producing the illusion of actual speech.

READER'S JOURNAL

Have you ever felt lonely? Do you have a special place you like to go when you are feeling this way? What comfort does this special place offer you? Write about the place in your journal.

SPEAKING AND LISTENING SKILLS

Read the Language Arts Survey, 3.4, "Active Listening." Then identify some of the word repetitions in the dialogue between the two waiters that signal feedback or understanding. Identify those places in the dialogue where you think a statement is misunderstood.

"A Clean, Well-Lighted Place"

ERNEST HEMINGWAY

It was late and every one had left the café except an old man who sat in the shadow the leaves of the tree made against the electric light. In the day time the street was dusty, but at night the dew settled the dust and the old man liked to sit late because he was deaf and now at night it was quiet and he felt the difference. The two waiters inside the café knew that the old man was a little drunk, and while he was a good client they knew that if he became too drunk he would leave without paying, so they kept watch on him.

"Last week he tried to commit suicide," one waiter said.

"Why?"

"He was in despair."

"What about?"

"Nothing."

"How do you know it was nothing?"

"He has plenty of money."

They sat together at a table that was close against the wall near the door of the café and looked at the terrace where the tables were all empty except where the old man sat in the shadow of the leaves of the tree that moved slightly in the wind. A girl and a soldier went by in the street. The street light shone on the brass number on his collar. The girl wore no head covering and hurried beside him.

"The guard will pick him up," one waiter said.

"What does it matter if he gets what he's after?"

"He had better get off the street now. The guard will get him. They went by five minutes ago."

The old man sitting in the shadow rapped on his saucer with his glass. The younger waiter went over to him.

"What do you want?"

The old man looked at him. "Another brandy," he said.

"You'll be drunk," the waiter said. The old man looked at him. The waiter went away.

"He'll stay all night," he said to his colleague. "I'm sleepy now. I never get into bed before three o'clock. He should have killed himself last week."

The waiter took the brandy bottle and another saucer from the counter inside the

What does the waiter think caused the man's despair?

café and marched out to the old man's table. He put down the saucer and poured the glass full of brandy.

What does the waiter say to the old man? Why?

"You should have killed yourself last week," he said to the deaf man. The old man motioned with his finger. "A little more," he said. The waiter poured on into the glass so that the brandy slopped over and ran down the stem into the top saucer of the pile. "Thank you," the old man said. The waiter took the bottle back inside the café. He sat down at the table with his colleague again.

"He's drunk now," he said.

"He's drunk every night."

"What did he want to kill himself for?"

"How should I know."

"How did he do it?"

How did the old man attempt suicide? Who rescued him? Why?

"He hung himself with a rope."

"Who cut him down?"

"His niece."

"Why did they do it?"

"Fear for his soul."

"How much money has he got?"

"He's got plenty."

"He must be eighty years old."

"Anyway I should say he was eighty."

"I wish he would go home. I never get to bed before three o'clock. What kind of hour is that to go to bed?"

"He stays up because he likes it."

On what do the two waiters agree?

"He's lonely. I'm not lonely. I have a wife waiting in bed for me."

"He had a wife once too."

"A wife would be no good to him now."

"You can't tell. He might be better with a wife."

"His niece looks after him."

"I know. You said she cut him down."

"I wouldn't want to be that old. An old man is a nasty thing."

"Not always. This old man is clean. He drinks without spilling. Even now, drunk. Look at him."

"I don't want to look at him. I wish he would go home. He has no regard for those who must work."

The old man looked from his glass across the square, then over at the waiters.

"Another brandy," he said, pointing to his glass. The waiter who was in a hurry came over.

"Finished," he said, speaking with that omission of syntax stupid people employ when talking to drunken people or foreigners. "No more tonight. Close now."

"Another," said the old man.

"No. Finished." The waiter wiped the edge of the table with a towel and shook his head.

The old man stood up, slowly counted the saucers, took a leather coin purse from his pocket and paid for the drinks, leaving half a peseta[1] tip.

The waiter watched him go down the street, a very old man walking unsteadily but with dignity.

"Why didn't you let him stay and drink?" the unhurried waiter asked. They were putting up the shutters. "It is not half past two."

"I want to go home to bed."

"What is an hour?"

"More to me than to him."

"An hour is the same."

"You talk like an old man yourself. He can buy a bottle and drink at home."

"It's not the same."

"No, it is not," agreed the waiter with a wife. He did not wish to be unjust. He was only in a hurry.

"And you? You have no fear of going home before your usual hour?"

"Are you trying to insult me?"

"No, hombre,[2] only to make a joke."

"No," the waiter who was in a hurry said, rising from pulling down the metal

1. **peseta.** Spanish currency
2. **hombre.** Man

Moulin de la Galette. *Pierre-Auguste Renoir*

shutters. "I have confidence. I am all confidence."

"You have youth, confidence, and a job," the older waiter said. "You have everything."

"And what do you lack?"

"Everything but work."

"You have everything I have."

"No. I have never had confidence and I am not young."

"Come on. Stop talking nonsense and lock up."

"I am of those who like to stay late at the café," the older waiter said. "With all those who do not want to go to bed. With all those who need a light for the night."

"I want to go home and into bed."

"We are of two different kinds," the older waiter said. He was now dressed to go home. "It is not only a question of youth and confidence although those things are very beautiful. Each night I am reluctant to close up because there may be some one who needs the café."

"Hombre, there are bodegas[3] open all night long."

"You do not understand. This is a clean and pleasant café. It is well lighted. The light is very good and also, now, there are shadows of the leaves."

"Good night," said the younger waiter.

"Good night," the other said. Turning off the electric light he continued the conversation with himself. It is the light of course but it is necessary that the place be clean and pleasant. You do not want music. Certainly you do not want music. Nor can you stand before a bar with dignity although that is all that is provided for these hours. What did he fear? It was not fear or dread. It was a nothing that he knew too well. It was all a nothing and a man was nothing too. It was only that and light was all it needed and a certain cleanness and order. Some lived in it and never felt it but he knew it all was nada[4] y pues nada y nada y pues nada. Our nada who art in nada, nada be thy name thy kingdom nada thy will be nada in nada as it is in nada. Give us this nada our daily nada

3. **bodegas.** Bars; taverns
4. **nada.** Nothing

How would you describe the older waiter's outlook on life?

With whom does the older waiter sympathize?

and nada us our nada as we nada our nadas and nada us not into nada but deliver us from nada; pues nada. Hail nothing full of nothing, nothing is with thee.[5] He smiled and stood before a bar with a shining steam pressure coffee machine.

"What's yours?" asked the barman.

"Nada."

"Otro loco mas,"[6] said the barman and turned away.

"A little cup," said the waiter.

The barman poured it for him.

"The light is very bright and pleasant but the bar is unpolished," the waiter said.

The barman looked at him but did not answer. It was too late at night for conversation.

"You want another copita?"[7] the barman asked.

"No, thank you," said the waiter and went out. He disliked bars and bodegas. A clean, well-lighted café was a very different thing. Now, without thinking further, he would go home to his room. He would lie in the bed and finally, with daylight, he would go to sleep. After all, he said to himself, it is probably only insomnia. Many must have it. ∎

---

5. **Our nada . . . thee.** The waiter is replacing words in two common prayers with *nada* or *nothing*.

6. **Otro loco mas.** Another crazy one

7. **copita.** Cup

Responding to the Selection

Imagine that you are one of the waiters watching the elderly man sit at the café table. Would you empathize with the man's loneliness? Would you patiently wait for him, or would you hurry him to leave in order to close the café?

Reviewing the Selection

RECALLING

1. What does one waiter tell the other the old man tried to do last week?

2. What reason does the younger waiter give for not letting the old man stay in the café?

3. What does the older waiter think he lacks?

4. What does the older waiter think is probably the reason he cannot sleep?

INTERPRETING

▶▶ 5. What attitudes toward the old man and his situation does the younger waiter express when stating the old man's despair was over "nothing"?

▶▶ 6. Why does the younger waiter tell the older waiter "You talk like an old man yourself"?

▶▶ 7. Why is the older waiter reluctant to close the café?

▶▶ 8. What is "a nothing" that the older waiter knows "too well"?

9. What is the importance of a clean, well-lighted place to the older waiter and the elderly client?

10. What is probably the reason that the older waiter empathizes with the elderly client? What do the two men have in common?

Understanding Literature (Questions for Discussion)

1. **Characterization and Dialogue. Characterization** is the use of literary techniques to create a character. In the selection, portrayal of a character's behavior, which presents the actions and speech of the character, is the technique primarily used. **Dialogue** is conversation involving two or more people or characters. In the selection, the older waiter states to the other waiter, "We are of two different kinds." How does the dialogue between the two men support the older waiter's assessment? What "two different kinds" are the two waiters?

2. **Internal Monologue.** An **internal monologue** presents the private sensations, thoughts, and emotions of a character. In the following passage from the selection, the reader is allowed to step inside the mind of the older waiter and overhear his private thoughts: "It is the light of course but it is necessary that the place be clean and pleasant. . . . What did he fear? It was not fear or dread. It was a nothing that he knew too well. It was all a nothing and a man was nothing too. It was only that and light was all it needed and a certain cleanness and order. . . . Our nada who art in nada, nada be thy name thy kingdom nada. . . ." What is revealed about the waiter's internal state? Why does the waiter substitute the Spanish word *nada*, which means "nothing," for words in the Lord's Prayer?

Responding in Writing

1. **Character Sketch.** Imagine you are sitting in a café people watching. Write a brief sketch about a person you see. What details do you notice about his or her appearance and dress? What is he or she doing? What do you hear the person say? Choose a few telling details about this character for your sketch.

2. **Dialogue.** Imagine that your character meets a person you know or another character you have invented. Write a dialogue between the two characters, portraying their attitudes, emotions, concerns, and so on, through their speech. After writing a first draft of the dialogue, listen carefully to how people speak and listen to each other. What kinds of words do they repeat? Do they speak in complete sentences? How do they indicate understanding or misunderstanding in their communication? Now revise your draft, working to make the dialogue seem like actual speech between the two characters.

"The Devil and Daniel Webster"
by Stephen Vincent Benét

It's a story they tell in the border country, where Massachusetts joins Vermont and New Hampshire.

Yes, Dan'l Webster's dead—or, at least, they buried him. But every time there's a thunderstorm around Marshfield, they say you can hear his rolling voice in the hollows of the sky. And they say that if you go to his grave and speak loud and clear, "Dan'l Webster—Dan'l Webster!" the ground'll begin to shiver and the trees begin to shake. And after a while you'll hear a deep voice saying, "Neighbor, how stands the Union?" Then you better answer the Union stands as she stood, rock-bottomed and copper-sheathed, one and indivisible, or he's liable to rear right out of the ground. At least, that's what I was told when I was a youngster.

You see, for a while, he was the biggest man in the country. He never got to be President, but he was the biggest man. There were thousands that trusted in him right next to God Almighty, and they told stories about him and all the things that belonged to him that were the stories of patriarchs and such. They said, when he stood up to speak, stars and stripes came right out of the sky, and once he spoke against a river and made it sink into the ground. They said, when he walked the woods with his fishing rod, Killall, the trout would jump out of the streams right into his pockets, for they knew it was no use putting up a fight against him; and, when he argued a case, he could turn on the harps of the blessed and the shaking of the earth underground. That was the kind of man he was, and his big farm up at Marshfield was suitable to him. The chickens he raised were all white meat down through the drumsticks, the cows were tended like children, and the big ram he called Goliath had horns with a curl like a morning-glory vine and could butt through an iron door. But Dan'l wasn't one of your gentlemen farmers; he knew all the ways of the land, and he'd be up by candlelight to see that the chores got done. A man with a mouth like a mastiff, a brow like a mountain and eyes like burning anthracite—that was Dan'l Webster in his prime. And the biggest case he argued never got written down in the books, for he argued it against the devil, nip and tuck and no holds barred. And this is the way I used to hear it told.

There was a man named Jabez Stone, lived at Cross Corners, New Hampshire. He wasn't a bad man to start with, but he was an unlucky man. If he planted corn, he got borers; if he planted potatoes, he got blight. He had good-enough land, but it didn't prosper him; he had a decent wife and children, but the more children he had, the less there was to feed them. If stones cropped up in his neighbor's field, boulders boiled up in his; if he had a horse with the spavins, he'd trade it for one with the staggers and give something extra. There's some folks bound to be like that, apparently. But one day Jabez Stone got sick of the whole business.

He'd been plowing that morning and he'd just broke the plowshare on a rock that he could have sworn hadn't been there yesterday. And, as he stood looking at the plowshare, the off horse began to cough—that ropy kind of cough that means sickness and horse doctors. There were two children down with the measles, his wife was ailing, and he had a whitlow[1] on his thumb. It was about the last straw for Jabez Stone. "I vow," he said, and he looked around him kind of desperate, "I vow it's enough to make a man want to sell his soul to the devil! And I would, too, for two cents!"

Then he felt a kind of queerness come over him at having said what he'd said; though, naturally, being a New Hampshireman, he wouldn't take it back. But, all the same, when it got to be evening and, as far as he could see, no notice had been taken, he felt relieved in his mind, for he was a religious man. But notice is always taken, sooner or later, just like the Good Book says. And, sure enough, next day, about suppertime, a soft-spoken, dark-dressed stranger drove up in a handsome buggy and asked for Jabez Stone.

Well, Jabez told his family it was a lawyer, come to see him about a legacy. But he knew who it was. He didn't like the looks of the stranger, nor the way he smiled with his teeth. They were white teeth, and plentiful—some say they were filed to a point, but I wouldn't vouch for that. And he didn't like it when the dog took one look at the stranger and ran away howling, with his tail between his legs. But having passed the word, more or less, he stuck to it, and they went out behind the barn and made their bargain. Jabez Stone had to prick his finger to sign, and the stranger lent him a silver pin. The wound healed clean, but it left a little white scar.

After that, all of a sudden, things began to pick up and prosper for Jabez Stone. His cows got fat and his horses sleek, his crops were the envy of the neighborhood, and

---

1. **whitlow.** Painful abscess

lightning might strike all over the valley, but it wouldn't strike his barn. Pretty soon he was one of the prosperous people of the county; they asked him to stand for selectman, and he stood for it; there began to be talk of running him for state senate. All in all, you might say the Stone family was as happy and contented as cats in a dairy. And so they were, except for Jabez Stone.

He'd been contented enough the first few years. It's a great thing when bad luck turns; it drives most other things out of your head. True, every now and then, especially in rainy weather, the little white scar on his finger would give him a twinge. And once a year, punctual as clockwork, the stranger with the handsome buggy would come driving by. But the sixth year the stranger lighted, and, after that, his peace was over for Jabez Stone.

The stranger came up through the lower field, switching his boots with a cane—they were handsome black boots, but Jabez Stone never liked the look of them, particularly the toes. And, after he'd passed the time of day, he said, "Well, Mr. Stone, you're a hummer! It's a very pretty property you've got here, Mr. Stone."

"Well, some might favor it and others might not," said Jabez Stone, for he was a New Hampshireman.

"Oh, no need to decry your industry!" said the stranger, very easy, showing his teeth in a smile. "After all, we know what's been done, and it's been according to contract and specifications. So when—ahem—the mortgage falls due next year, you shouldn't have any regrets."

"Speaking of that mortgage, mister," said Jabez Stone, and he looked around for help to the earth and the sky, "I'm beginning to have one or two doubts about it."

"Doubts?" said the stranger not quite so pleasantly.

"Why, yes," said Jabez Stone. "This being the U.S.A. and me always having been a religious man." He cleared his throat and got bolder. "Yes, sir," he said, "I'm beginning to have considerable doubts as to that mortgage holding in court."

"There's courts and courts," said the stranger, clicking his teeth. "Still, we might as well have a look at the original document." And he hauled out a big black pocketbook, full of papers. "Sherwin, Slater, Stevens, Stone," he muttered. "'I, Jabez Stone, for a term of seven years—' Oh, it's quite in order, I think."

But Jabez Stone wasn't listening, for he saw something else flutter out of the black pocketbook. It was something that looked like a moth, but it wasn't a moth. And as Jabez Stone stared at it, it seemed to speak to him in a small sort of piping voice, terrible small and thin, but terrible human. "Neighbor Stone!" It squeaked. "Neighbor Stone! Help me! For God's sake, help me!"

But before Jabez Stone could stir hand or foot, the stranger whipped out a big bandanna handkerchief,

caught the creature in it, just like a butterfly, and started tying up the ends of the bandanna.

"Sorry for the interruption," he said. "As I was saying—"

But Jabez Stone was shaking all over like a scared horse.

"That's Miser Stevens' voice!" he said in a croak. "And you've got him in your handkerchief!"

The stranger looked a little embarrassed.

"Yes, I really should have transferred him to the collecting box," he said with a simper, "but there were some rather unusual specimens there and I don't want them crowded. Well, well, these little contretemps[1] will occur."

"I don't know what you mean by contertan," said Jabez Stone, "but that was Miser Stevens' voice! And he ain't dead! You can't tell me he is! He was just as spry and mean as a woodchuck Tuesday!"

"In the midst of life . . ." said the stranger, kind of pious. "Listen!" Then a bell began to toll in the valley and Jabez Stone listened, with the sweat running down his face. For he knew it was tolled for Miser Stevens and that he was dead.

"These long-standing accounts," said the stranger with a sigh; "one really hates to close them. But business is business."

He still had the bandanna in his hand, and Jabez Stone felt sick as he saw the cloth struggle and flutter.

"Are they all as small as that?" he asked hoarsely.

"Small?" said the stranger. "Oh, I see what you mean. Why, they vary." He measured Jabez Stone with his eyes, and his teeth showed. "Don't worry, Mr. Stone," he said. "You'll go with a very good grade. I wouldn't trust you outside the collecting box. Now, a man like Dan'l Webster, of course—well, we'd have to build a special box for him, and even at that, I imagine the wing spread would astonish you. He'd certainly be a prize. I wish we could see our way clear to him. But, in your case, as I was saying—"

"Put that handkerchief away!" said Jabez Stone, and he began to beg and to pray. But the best he could get at the end was a three years' extension, with conditions.

But till you make a bargain like that, you've got no idea of how fast four years can run. By the last months of those years Jabez Stone's known all over the state and there's talk of running him for governor—and it's dust and ashes in his mouth. For every day, when he gets up, he thinks, "There's one more night gone," and every night, when he lies down, he thinks of the black pocketbook and the soul of Miser Stevens, and it makes him sick at heart. Till, finally, he can't bear it any longer, and, in the last days of the last year, he hitches up his horse and drives off to seek Dan'l Webster. For Dan'l was born in New Hampshire,

---

1. **contretemps.** Awkward occurrence

only a few miles from Cross Corners, and it's well known that he has a particular soft spot for old neighbors.

It was early in the morning when he got to Marshfield, but Dan'l was up already, talking Latin to the farm hands and wrestling with the ram, Goliath, and trying out a new trotter and working up speeches to make against John C. Calhoun. But when he heard a New Hampshireman had come to see him, he dropped everything else he was doing, for that was Dan'l's way. He gave Jabez Stone a breakfast that five men couldn't eat, went into the living history of every man and woman in Cross Corners, and finally asked him how he could serve him.

Jabez Stone allowed that it was a kind of mortgage case.

"Well, I haven't pleaded a mortgage case in a long time, and I don't generally plead now, except before the Supreme Court," said Dan'l, "but if I can, I'll help you."

"Then I've got hope for the first time in ten years," said Jabez Stone and told him the details.

Dan'l walked up and down as he listened, hands behind his back, now and then asking a question, now and then plunging his eyes at the floor, as if they'd bore through it like gimlets. When Jabez Stone had finished, Dan'l puffed out his cheeks and blew. Then he turned to Jabez Stone and a smile broke over his face like the sunrise over Monadnock.[1]

"You've certainly given yourself the devil's own row to hoe, Neighbor Stone," he said, "but I'll take your case."

"You'll take it?" said Jabez Stone, hardly daring to believe.

"Yes," said Dan'l Webster. "I've got about seventy-five other things to do and the Missouri Compromise[2] to straighten out, but I'll take your case. For if two New Hampshiremen aren't a match for the devil, we might as well give the country back to the Indians."

Then he shook Jabez Stone by the hand and said, "Did you come down here in a hurry?"

"Well, I admit I made time," said Jabez Stone.

"You'll go back faster," said Dan'l Webster, and he told 'em to hitch up Constitution and Constellation to the carriage. They were matched grays with one white forefoot, and they stepped like greased lightning.

Well, I won't describe how excited and pleased the whole Stone family was to have the great Dan'l Webster for a guest, when they finally got there. Jabez Stone had lost his hat on the way, blown off when they overtook a wind, but he didn't take much account of that. But after supper he sent the family off to bed, for he had most particular business with Mr. Webster. Mrs. Stone wanted him to sit in the front parlor, but Dan'l Webster knew front parlors and said he preferred the kitchen. So it was

there they sat, waiting for the stranger, with a jug on the table between them and a bright fire on the hearth—the stranger being scheduled to show up on the stroke of midnight, according to specification.

Well, most men wouldn't have asked for better company than Dan'l Webster and a jug. But with every tick of the clock Jabez Stone got sadder and sadder. His eyes roved round, and though he sampled the jug you could see he couldn't taste it. Finally, on the stroke of 11:30 he reached over and grabbed Dan'l Webster by the arm.

"Mr. Webster, Mr. Webster!" he said, and his voice was shaking with fear and a desperate courage. "For God's sake, Mr. Webster, harness your horses and get away from this place while you can!"

"You've brought me a long way, neighbor, to tell me you don't like my company," said Dan'l Webster, quite peaceable, pulling at the jug.

"Miserable wretch that I am!" groaned Jabez Stone. "I've brought you a devilish way, and now I see my folly. Let him take me if he wills. I don't hanker after it, I must say, but I can stand it. But you're the Union's stay and New Hampshire's pride! He mustn't get you, Mr. Webster! He mustn't get you!"

Dan'l Webster looked at the distracted man, all gray and shaking in the firelight, and laid a hand on his shoulder.

"I'm obliged to you, Neighbor Stone," he said gently. "It's kindly thought of. But there's a jug on the table and a case in hand. And I never left a jug or a case half finished in my life."

And just at that moment there was a sharp rap on the door.

"Ah," said Dan'l Webster very coolly, "I thought your clock was a trifle slow, Neighbor Stone." He stepped to the door and opened it. "Come in!" he said.

The stranger came in—very dark and tall he looked in the firelight. He was carrying a box under his arm—a black japanned box with little air holes in the lid. At the sight of the box Jabez Stone gave a low cry and shrank into a corner of the room.

"Mr. Webster, I presume," said the stranger, very polite, but with his eyes glowing like a fox's deep in the woods.

"Attorney of record for Jabez Stone," said Dan'l Webster, but his eyes were glowing too. "Might I ask your name?"

---

1. **Monadnock.** Mountain in New Hampshire
2. **Missouri Compromise.** Bill passed in 1820 that allowed slavery in Missouri but not anywhere else west of the Mississippi

"I've gone by a good many," said the stranger carelessly. "Perhaps Scratch will do for the evening. I'm often called that in these regions."

Then he sat down at the table and poured himself a drink from the jug. The liquor was cold in the jug, but it came steaming into the glass.

"And now," said the stranger, smiling and showing his teeth, "I shall call upon you, as a law-abiding citizen, to assist me in taking possession of my property."

Well, with that the argument began—and it went hot and heavy. At first Jabez Stone had a flicker of hope, but when he saw Dan'l Webster being forced back at point after point, he just sat scrunched in his corner, with his eyes on that japanned box. For there wasn't any doubt as to the deed or the signature—that was the worst of it. Dan'l Webster twisted and turned and thumped his fist on the table, but he couldn't get away from that. He offered to compromise the case; the stranger wouldn't hear of it. He pointed out the property had increased in value, and state senators ought to be worth more; the stranger stuck to the letter of the law. He was a great lawyer, Dan'l Webster, but we know who's the King of Lawyers, as the Good Book tells us, and it seemed as if, for the first time, Dan'l Webster had met his match.

Finally, the stranger yawned a little. "Your spirited efforts on behalf of your client do you credit, Mr. Webster," he said, "but if you have no more arguments to adduce, I'm rather pressed for time . . ." and Jabez Stone shuddered.

Dan'l Webster's brow looked dark as a thundercloud.

"Pressed or not, you shall not have this man!" he thundered. "Mr. Stone is an American citizen, and no American citizen may be forced into the service of a foreign prince. We fought England for that in '12 and we'll fight all hell for it again!"

"Foreign?" said the stranger. "And who calls me a foreigner?"

"Well, I never yet heard of the dev—of your claiming American citizenship," said Dan'l Webster with surprise.

"And who with better right?" said the stranger with one of his terrible smiles. "When the first wrong was done to the first Indian, I was there. When the first slaver put out for the Congo, I stood on her deck. Am I not in your books and stories and beliefs, from the first settlements on? Am I not spoken of still in every church in New England? 'Tis true the North claims me for a Southerner and the South for a Northerner, but I am neither. I am merely an honest American like yourself—and of the best descent— for, to tell the truth, Mr. Webster, though I don't like to boast of it, my name is older in this country than yours."

"Aha!" said Dan'l Webster with the veins standing out in his forehead. "Then I stand on the Constitution! I demand a trial for my client!"

"The case is hardly one for an ordinary court," said the stranger, his eyes flickering. "And, indeed, the lateness of the hour—"

"Let it be any court you choose, so it is an American judge and an American jury!" said Dan'l Webster in his pride. "Let it be the quick or the dead; I'll abide the issue!"

"You have said it," said the stranger, and pointed his finger at the door. And with that, and all of a sudden, there was a rushing of wind outside and a noise of footsteps. They came, clear and distinct, through the night. And yet they were not like the footsteps of living men.

"In God's name, who comes by so late?" cried Jabez Stone in an ague of fear.

"The jury Mr. Webster demands," said the stranger, sipping at his boiling glass. "You must pardon the rough appearance of one or two; they will have come a long way."

And with that the fire burned blue and the door blew open and twelve men entered, one by one.

If Jabez Stone had been sick with terror before, he was blind with terror now. For there was Walter Butler, the loyalist, who spread fire and horror through the Mohawk Valley in the times of the Revolution; and there was Simon Girty, the renegade, who saw white men burned at the stake and whooped with the Indians to see them burn. His eyes were green, like a catamount's, and the stains on his hunting shirt did not come from the blood of the deer. King Philip was there, wild and proud as he had been in life, with the great gash in his head that gave him his death wound, and cruel Governor Dale, who broke men on the wheel. There was Morton of Merry Mount, who so vexed the Plymouth Colony, with his flushed, loose, handsome face and his hate of the godly. There was Teach, the bloody pirate, with his black beard curling on his breast. The Reverend John Smeet, with his strangler's hands and his Geneva gown, walked as daintily as he had to the gallows. The red print of the rope was still around his neck, but he carried a perfumed handkerchief in one hand. One and all, they came into the room with the fires of hell still upon them, and the stranger named their names and their deeds as they came, till the tale of twelve was told. Yet the stranger had told the truth—they had all played a part in America.

"Are you satisfied with the jury, Mr. Webster?" said the stranger mockingly, when they had taken their places.

The sweat stood upon Dan'l Webster's brow, but his voice was clear.

"Quite satisfied," he said. "Though I miss General Arnold[1] from the company."

"Benedict Arnold is engaged upon other business," said the stranger with a glower. "Ah, you asked for a justice, I believe."

He pointed his finger once more, and a tall man, soberly clad in Puritan garb, with the burning gaze of the fanatic, stalked into the room and took his judge's place.

"Justice Hathorne is a jurist of experience," said the stranger. "He presided at certain witch trials once held in Salem. There were others who repented of the business later, but not he."

"Repent of such notable wonders and undertakings?" said the stern old justice. "Nay, hang them—hang them all!" And he muttered to himself in a way that struck ice into the soul of Jabez Stone.

Then the trial began, and, as you might expect, it didn't look anyways good for the defense. And Jabez Stone didn't make much of a witness in his own behalf. He took one look at Simon Girty and screeched, and they had to put him back in his corner in a kind of swoon.

It didn't halt the trial though; the trial went on, as trials do. Dan'l Webster had faced some hard juries and hanging judges in his time, but this was the hardest he'd ever faced, and he knew it. They sat there with a kind of glitter in their eyes, and the stranger's smooth voice went on and on. Every time he'd raise an objection, it'd be "Objection sustained," but whenever Dan'l objected, it'd be "Objection denied." Well, you couldn't expect fair play from a fellow like this Mr. Scratch.

It got to Dan'l in the end, and he began to heat, like iron in the forge. When he got up to speak he was going to flay that stranger with every trick known to the law, and the judge and jury too. He didn't care if it was contempt of court or what would happen to him for it. He didn't care any more what happened to Jabez Stone. He just got madder and madder, thinking of what he'd say. And yet, curiously enough, the more he thought about it, the less he was able to arrange his speech in his mind.

Till, finally, it was time for him to get up on his feet, and he did so, all ready to bust out with lightnings and denunciations. But before he started he looked over the judge and jury for a moment, such being his custom. And he noticed the glitter in their eyes was twice as strong as before, and they all leaned forward. Like hounds just before they get the fox, they looked, and the blue mist of evil in the room thickened as he watched them. Then he saw what he'd been about to do, and he wiped his forehead, as a man might who's just escaped falling into a pit in the dark.

For it was him they'd come for, not only Jabez Stone. He read it in the glitter of their eyes and in the way the stranger hid his mouth with one hand. And if he fought them with their own weapons, he'd fall into their power; he knew that, though he couldn't have told you how. It was his own anger and horror that burned in their eyes; and he'd have to wipe that out or the case was lost. He stood there for a moment, his black eyes burning like anthracite. And then he began to speak.

He started off in a low voice, though you could hear every word. They say he could call on the harps of the blessed when he chose. And this was just as simple and easy as a man could talk. But he didn't start out by condemning or reviling. He was talking about the things that make a country a country and a man a man.

And he began with the simple things that everybody's known and felt—the freshness of a fine morning when you're young, and the taste of food when you're hungry, and the new day that's every day when you're a child. He took them up and he turned them in his hands. They were good things for any man. But without freedom they sickened. And when he talked of those enslaved, and the sorrows of slavery, his voice got like a big bell. He talked of the early days of America and the men who had made those days. It wasn't a spread-eagle speech, but he made you see it. He admitted all the wrong that had ever been done. But he showed how, out of the wrong and the right, the suffering and the starvations, something new had come. And everybody had played a part in it, even the traitors.

Then he turned to Jabez Stone and showed him as he was—an ordinary man who'd had hard luck and wanted to change it. And, because he'd wanted to change it, now he was going to be punished for all eternity. And yet there was good in Jabez Stone, and he showed that good. He was hard and mean, in some ways, but he was a man. There was sadness in being a man, but it was a proud thing too. And he showed what the pride of it was till you couldn't help feeling it. Yes, even in hell, if a man was a man, you'd know it. And he wasn't pleading for any one person any more, though his voice rang like an organ. He was telling the story and the failures and the endless journey of mankind. They got tricked and trapped and bamboozled, but it was a great journey. And no demon that was ever foaled could know the inwardness of it—it took a man to do that.

The fire began to die on the hearth and the wind before morning to blow. The light was getting gray in

---

1. **General Arnold.** Benedict Arnold, notorious American traitor

the room when Dan'l Webster finished. And his words came back at the end to New Hampshire ground, and the one spot of land that each man loves and clings to. He painted a picture of that, and to each one of that jury he spoke of things long forgotten. For his voice could search the heart, and that was his gift and his strength. And to one his voice was like the forest and its secrecy, and to another like the sea and the storms of the sea; and one heard the cry of his lost nation in it, and another saw a little harmless scene he hadn't remembered for years. But each saw something. And when Dan'l Webster finished he didn't know whether or not he'd saved Jabez Stone. But he knew he'd done a miracle. For the glitter was gone from the eyes of judge and jury, and, for the moment, they were men again, and knew they were men.

"The defense rests," said Dan'l Webster and stood there like a mountain. His ears were still ringing with his speech, and he didn't hear anything else till he heard Judge Hathorne say, "The jury will retire to consider its verdict."

Walter Butler rose in his place and his face had a dark, gay pride on it.

"The jury has considered its verdict," he said and looked the stranger full in the eye. "We find for the defendant, Jabez Stone."

With that, the smile left the stranger's face, but Walter Butler did not flinch.

"Perhaps 'tis not strictly in accordance with the evidence," he said, "but even the damned may salute the eloquence of Mr. Webster."

With that, the long crow of a rooster split the gray morning sky, and judge and jury were gone from the room like a puff of smoke and as if they had never been there. The stranger returned to Dan'l Webster, smiling wryly.

"Major Butler was always a bold man," he said. "I had not thought him quite so bold. Nevertheless, my congratulations, as between two gentlemen."

"I'll have that paper first, if you please," said Dan'l Webster, and he took it and tore it into four pieces. It was queerly warm to the touch. "And now," he said, "I'll have you!" and his hand came down like a bear trap on the stranger's arm. For he knew that once you bested anybody like Mr. Scratch in fair fight, his power on you was gone. And he could see that Mr. Scratch knew it too.

The stranger twisted and wriggled, but he couldn't get out of that grip. "Come, come, Mr. Webster," he said, smiling palely. "This sort of thing is ridic—ouch!—is ridiculous. If you're worried about the costs of the case, naturally, I'd be glad to pay—"

"And so you shall!" said Dan'l Webster, shaking him till his teeth rattled. "For you'll sit right down at that table and draw up a document, promising never to bother Jabez Stone nor his heirs or assigns nor any other New Hampshireman till doomsday! For any hades we want to raise in this state, we can raise ourselves, without assistance from strangers."

"Ouch!" said the stranger. "Ouch! Well, they never did run very big to the barrel, but—ouch!—I agree!"

So he sat down and drew up the document. But Dan'l Webster kept his hand on his coat collar all the time.

"And now may I go?" said the stranger, quite humble, when Dan'l'd seen the document's in proper and legal form.

"Go?" said Dan'l, giving him another shake. "I'm still trying to figure out what I'll do with you. For you've settled the costs of the case, but you haven't settled with me. I think I'll take you back to Marshfield," he said, kind of reflective. "I've got a ram there named Goliath that can butt through an iron door. I'd kind of like to turn you loose in his field and see what he'd do."

Well, with that the stranger began to beg and to plead. And he begged and he pled so humble that finally Dan'l, who was naturally kindhearted, agreed to let him go. The stranger seemed terrible grateful for that and said, just to show they were friends, he'd tell Dan'l's fortune before leaving. So Dan'l agreed to that, though he didn't take much stock in fortunetellers ordinarily. But, naturally, the stranger was a little different.

Well, he pried and he peered at the lines in Dan'l's hands. And he told him one thing and another that was quite remarkable. But they were all in the past.

"Yes, all that's true, and it happened," said Dan'l Webster. "But what's to come in the future?"

The stranger grinned, kind of happily, and shook his head.

"The future's not as you think it," he said. "It's dark. You have a great ambition, Mr. Webster."

"I have," said Dan'l firmly, for everybody knew he wanted to be President.

"It seems almost within your grasp," said the stranger, "but you will not attain it. Lesser men will be made President and you will be passed over."

"And, if I am, I'll still be Daniel Webster," said Dan'l. "Say on."

"You have two strong sons," said the stranger, shaking his head. "You look to found a line. But each will die in war and neither reach greatness."

"Live or die, they are still my sons," said Dan'l Webster. "Say on."

"You have made great speeches," said the stranger. "You will make more."

"Ah," said Dan'l Webster.

"But the last great speech you make will turn many of your own against you," said the stranger. "They will call you Ichabod; they will call you by other names. Even in New England some will say you have turned your coat and sold your country, and their voices will be loud against you till you die."

"So it is an honest speech, it does not matter what men say," said Dan'l Webster. Then he looked at the stranger and their glances locked.

"One question," he said. "I have fought for the Union all my life. Will I see that fight won against those who would tear it apart?"

"Not while you live," said the stranger grimly, "but it will be won. And after you are dead, there are thousands who will fight for your cause, because of words that you spoke."

"Why, then, you long-barreled, slab-sided, lantern-jawed, fortune-telling note shaver," said Dan'l Webster with a great roar of laughter, "be off with you to your own place before I put my mark on you! For, by the thirteen original colonies, I'd go to the Pit itself to save the Union!"

And with that he drew back his foot for a kick that would have stunned a horse. It was only the tip of his shoe that caught the stranger, but he went flying out of the door with his collecting box under his arm.

"And now," said Dan'l Webster, seeing Jabez Stone beginning to rouse from his swoon, "let's see what's left in the jug, for it's dry work talking all night. I hope there's pie for breakfast, Neighbor Stone."

But they say that whenever the devil comes near Marshfield, even now, he gives it a wide berth. And he hasn't been seen in the state of New Hampshire from that day to this.

I'm not talking about Massachusetts or Vermont.

from *Winesburg, Ohio*
by Sherwood Anderson

THE BOOK OF THE GROTESQUE

The writer, an old man with a white mustache, had some difficulty in getting into bed. The windows of the house in which he lived were high and he wanted to look at the trees when he awoke in the morning. A carpenter came to fix the bed so that it would be on a level with the window.

Quite a fuss was made about the matter. The carpenter, who had been a soldier in the Civil War, came into the writer's room and sat down to talk of building a platform for the purpose of raising the bed. The writer had cigars lying about and the carpenter smoked.

For a time the two men talked of the raising of the bed and then they talked of other things. The soldier got on the subject of the war. The writer, in fact, led him to that subject. The carpenter had once been a prisoner in Andersonville prison and had lost a brother. The brother had died of starvation, and whenever the carpenter got upon that subject he cried. He, like the old writer, had a white mustache, and when he cried he puckered up his lips and the mustache bobbed up and down. The weeping old man with the cigar in his mouth was ludicrous. The plan the writer had for the raising of his bed was forgotten and later the carpenter did it in his own way and the writer, who was past sixty, had to help himself with a chair when he went to bed at night.

In his bed the writer rolled over on his side and lay quite still. For years he had been beset with notions concerning his heart. He was a hard smoker and his heart fluttered. The idea had got into his mind that he would some time die unexpectedly and always when he got into bed he thought of that. It did not alarm him. The effect in fact was quite a special thing and not easily explained. It made him more alive, there in bed, than at any other time. Perfectly still he lay and his body was old and not of much use any more, but something inside him was altogether young. He was like a pregnant woman, only that the thing inside him was not a baby but a youth. No, it wasn't a youth, it was a woman, young, and wearing a coat of mail like a knight. It is absurd, you see, to try to tell what was inside the old writer as he lay on his high bed and listened to the fluttering of his heart. The thing to get at is what the writer, or the young thing within the writer, was thinking about.

The old writer, like all of the people in the world, had got, during his long life, a great many notions in his head. He had once been quite handsome and a number of women had been in love with him. And then, of course, he had known people, many people, known them in a peculiarly intimate way that was different from the way in which you and I know people. At least that is what the writer thought and the thought pleased him. Why quarrel with an old man concerning his thoughts?

In the bed the writer had a dream that was not a dream. As he grew somewhat sleepy but was still conscious, figures began to appear before his eyes. He imagined the young indescribable thing within himself was driving a long procession of figures before his eyes.

You see the interest in all this lies in the figures that went before the eyes of the writer. They were all grotesques. All of the men and women the writer had ever known had become grotesques.

The grotesques were not all horrible. Some were amusing, some almost beautiful, and one, a woman all drawn out of shape, hurt the old man by her grotesqueness. When she passed he made a noise like a small dog whimpering. Had you come into the room you might have supposed the old man had unpleasant dreams or perhaps indigestion.

For an hour the procession of grotesques passed before the eyes of the old man, and then, although it was a painful thing to do, he crept out of bed and began to write. Some one of the grotesques had made a deep impression on his mind and he wanted to describe it.

At his desk the writer worked for an hour. In the end he wrote a book which he called "The Book of the Grotesque." It was never published, but I saw it once and it made an indelible impression on my mind. The book had one central thought that is very strange and has always remained with me. By remembering it I have been able to understand many people and things that I was never able to understand before. The thought was involved but a simple statement of it would be something like this:

That in the beginning when the world was young there were a great many thoughts but no such thing as a truth. Man made the truths himself and each truth was a composite of a great many vague thoughts. All about in the world were the truths and they were all beautiful.

The old man had listed hundreds of the truths in his book. I will not try to tell you of all of them. There was the truth of virginity and the truth of passion, the truth of wealth and of poverty, of thrift and of profligacy, of carelessness and abandon. Hundreds and hundreds were the truths and they were all beautiful.

And then the people came along. Each as he appeared snatched up one of the truths and some who were quite strong snatched up a dozen of them.

It was the truths that made the people grotesques. The old man had quite an elaborate theory concerning the matter. It was his notion that the moment one of the people took one of the truths to himself, called it his truth, and tried to live his life by it, he became a grotesque and the truth he embraced became a falsehood.

You can see for yourself how the old man, who had spent all of his life writing and was filled with words, would write hundreds of pages concerning this matter. The subject would become so big in his mind that he himself would be in danger of becoming a grotesque. He didn't, I suppose, for the same reason that he never published the book. It was the young thing inside him that saved the old man.

Concerning the old carpenter who fixed the bed for the writer, I only mentioned him because he, like many of what are called very common people, became the nearest thing to what is understandable and lovable of all the grotesques in the writer's book.

from *The Grapes of Wrath*[1]
by John Steinbeck

The spring is beautiful in California. Valleys in which the fruit blossoms are fragrant pink and white waters in a shallow sea. Then the first tendrils of the grapes, swelling from the old gnarled vines, cascade down to cover the trunks. The full green hills are round and soft as breasts. And on the level vegetable lands are the mile-long rows of pale green lettuce and the spindly little cauliflowers, the gray-green unearthly artichoke plants.

And then the leaves break out on the trees, and the petals drop from the fruit trees and carpet the earth with pink and white. The centers of the blossoms swell and grow and color: cherries and apples, peaches and pears, figs which close the flower in the fruit. All California quickens with produce, and the fruit grows heavy, and the limbs bend gradually under the fruit so that little crutches must be placed under them to support the weight.

Behind the fruitfulness are men of understanding and knowledge and skill, men who experiment with seed, endlessly developing the techniques for greater crops of plants whose roots will resist the million enemies of the earth: the molds, the insects, the rusts, the blights. These men work carefully and endlessly to perfect the seed, the roots. And there are the men of chemistry who spray the trees against pests, who sulphur the grapes, who cut out disease and rots, mildews and sicknesses. Doctors of preventive medicine, men at the borders who look for fruit

---

1. **Grapes of Wrath.** From the first stanza of Julia Ward Howe's "Battle Hymn of the Republic:"

Mine eyes have seen the glory of the coming of the
   Lord;
He is trampling out the vintage where the
   grapes of wrath are stored. . . .

Howe's battle hymn refers to the Civil War. The battle in Steinbeck's *The Grapes of Wrath* is being fought by poverty-stricken migrant workers during the Great Depression of the United States. Another source for the title is the Bible, where it is written in the Revelation of St. John that the "wine of wrath" is forced upon people by a "Babylon." In the Bible, Babylon is an ancient city-state that is described as being wicked. In *The Grapes of Wrath*, Steinbeck is comparing the mistreatment of the migrant workers to the mistreatment of the citizens of ancient Babylon. He seems to suggest that the wrath of the migrant workers will cause the fall of their own wicked Babylon.

flies, for Japanese beetle, men who quarantine the sick trees and root them out and burn them, men of knowledge. The men who graft the young trees, the little vines, are the cleverest of all, for theirs is a surgeon's job, as tender and delicate; and these men must have surgeons' hands and surgeons' hearts to slit the bark, to place the grafts, to bind the wounds and cover them from the air. These are great men.

Along the rows, the cultivators move, tearing the spring grass and turning it under to make a fertile earth, breaking the ground to hold the water up near the surface, ridging the ground in little pools for the irrigation, destroying the weed roots that may drink the water away from the trees.

And all the time the fruit swells and the flowers break out in long clusters on the vines. And in the growing year the warmth grows and the leaves turn dark green. The prunes lengthen like little green bird's eggs, and the limbs sag down against the crutches under the weight. And the hard little pears take shape, and the beginning of the fuzz comes out on the peaches. Grape blossoms shed their tiny petals and the hard little beads become green buttons, and the buttons grow heavy. The men who work in the fields, the owners of the little orchards, watch and calculate. The year is heavy with produce. And men are proud, for of their knowledge they can make the year heavy. They have transformed the world with their knowledge. The short, lean wheat has been made big and productive. Little sour apples have grown large and sweet, and that old grape that grew among the trees and fed the birds its tiny fruit has mothered a thousand varieties, red and black, green and pale pink, purple and yellow; and each variety with its own flavor. The men who work in the experimental farms have made new fruits: nectarines and forty kinds of plums, walnuts with paper shells. And always they work, selecting, grafting, changing, driving themselves, driving the earth to produce.

And first the cherries ripen. Cent and a half a pound. Hell, we can't pick 'em for that. Black cherries and red cherries, full and sweet, and the birds eat half of each cherry and the yellowjackets buzz into the holes the birds made. And on the ground the seeds drop and dry with black shreds hanging from them.

The purple prunes soften and sweeten. My God, we can't pick them and dry and sulphur them. We can't pay wages, no matter what wages. And the purple prunes carpet the ground. And first the skins wrinkle a little and swarms of flies come to feast, and the valley is filled with the odor of sweet decay. The meat turns dark and the crop shrivels on the ground.

And the pears grow yellow and soft. Five dollars a ton.

Five dollars for forty fifty-pound boxes; trees pruned and sprayed, orchards cultivated—pick the fruit, put it in boxes, load the trucks, deliver the fruit to the cannery—forty boxes for five dollars. We can't do it. And the yellow fruit falls heavily to the ground and splashes on the ground. The yellowjackets dig into the soft meat, and there is a smell of ferment and rot.

Then the grapes—we can't make good wine. People can't buy good wine. Rip the grapes from the vines, good grapes, rotten grapes, wasp-stung grapes. Press stems, press dirt and rot.

But there's mildew and formic acid in the vats.

Add sulphur and tannic acid.

The smell from the ferment is not the rich odor of wine, but the smell of decay and chemicals.

Oh, well. It has alcohol in it, anyway. They can get drunk.

The little farmers watched debt creep up on them like the tide. They sprayed the trees and sold no crop, they pruned and grafted and could not pick the crop. And the men of knowledge have worked, have considered, and the fruit is rotting on the ground, and the decaying mash in the wine vats is poisoning the air. And taste the wine—no grape flavor at all, just sulphur and tannic acid and alcohol.

This little orchard will be a part of a great holding next year, for the debt will have choked the owner.

This vineyard will belong to the bank. Only the great owners can survive, for they own the canneries too. And four pears peeled and cut in half, cooked and canned, still cost fifteen cents. And the canned pears do not spoil. They will last for years.

The decay spreads over the State, and the sweet smell is a great sorrow on the land. Men who can graft the trees and make the seed fertile and big can find no way to let the hungry people eat their produce. Men who have created new fruits in the world cannot create a system whereby their fruits may be eaten. And the failure hangs over the State like a great sorrow.

The works of the roots of the vines, of the trees, must be destroyed to keep up the price, and this is the saddest, bitterest thing of all. Carloads of oranges dumped on the ground. The people came for miles to take the fruit, but this could not be. How would they buy oranges at twenty cents a dozen if they could drive out and pick them up? And men with hoses squirt kerosene on the oranges, and they are angry at the crime, angry at the people who have come to take the fruit. A million people hungry, needing the fruit—and kerosene sprayed over the golden mountains.

And the smell of rot fills the country.

Burn coffee for fuel in the ships. Burn corn to keep warm, it makes a hot fire. Dump potatoes in the rivers and place guards along the banks to keep the hungry people from fishing them out. Slaughter the pigs and bury them, and let the putrescence drip down into the earth.

There is a crime here that goes beyond denunciation. There is a sorrow here that weeping cannot symbolize. There is a failure here that topples all our success. The fertile earth, the straight tree rows, the sturdy trunks, and the ripe fruit. And children dying of pellagra must die because a profit cannot be taken from an orange. And coroners must fill in the certificates—died of malnutrition—because the food must rot, must be forced to rot.

The people come with nets to fish for potatoes in the river, and the guards hold them back; they come in rattling cars to get the dumped oranges, but the kerosene is sprayed. And they stand still and watch the potatoes float by, listen to the screaming pigs being killed in a ditch and covered with quicklime, watch the mountains of oranges slop down to a putrefying ooze; and in the eyes of the hungry there is a growing wrath. In the souls of the people the grapes of wrath are filling and growing heavy, growing heavy for the vintage.

from *Invisible Man*
by Ralph Ellison

When I reached the door of Mr. Emerson's office it occurred to me that perhaps I should have waited until the business of the day was under way, but I disregarded the idea and went ahead. My being early would be, I hoped, an indication of both how badly I wanted work, and how promptly I would perform any assignment given me. Besides, wasn't there a saying that the first person of the day to enter a business would get a bargain? Or was that said only of Jewish business? I removed the letter from my brief case. Was Emerson a Christian or a Jewish name?

Beyond the door it was like a museum. I had entered a large reception room decorated with cool tropical colors. One wall was almost covered by a huge colored map, from which narrow red silk ribbons stretched tautly from each division of the map to a series of ebony pedestals, upon which sat glass specimen jars containing natural products of the various countries. It was an importing firm. I looked around the room, amazed. There were paintings, bronzes, tapestries, all beautifully arranged. I was dazzled and so taken aback that I almost dropped my brief case when I heard a voice say, "And what would

your business be?"

I saw the figure out of a collar ad: ruddy face with blond hair faultlessly in place, a tropical weave suit draped handsomely from his broad shoulders, his eyes gray and nervous behind clear-framed glasses.

I explained my appointment. "Oh, yes," he said. "May I see the letter, please?"

I handed it over, noticing the gold links in the soft white cuffs as he extended his hand. Glancing at the envelope he looked back at me with a strange interest in his eyes and said, "Have a seat, please. I'll be with you in a moment."

I watched him leave noiselessly, moving with a long hip-swinging stride that caused me to frown. I went over and took a teakwood chair with cushions of emerald-green silk, sitting stiffly with my brief case across my knees. He must have been sitting there when I came in, for on a table that held a beautiful dwarf tree I saw smoke rising from a cigarette in a jade ash tray. An open book, something called *Totem and Taboo*, lay beside it. I looked across to a lighted case of Chinese design which held delicate-looking statues of horses and birds, small vases and bowls, each set upon a carved wooden base. The room was quiet as a tomb—until suddenly there was a savage beating of wings and I looked toward the window to see an eruption of color, as though a gale had whipped up a bundle of brightly colored rags. It was an aviary of tropical birds set near one of the broad windows, through which, as the clapping of wings settled down, I could see two ships plying[1] far out upon the greenish bay below. A large bird began a song, drawing my eyes to the throbbing of its bright blue, red and yellow throat. It was startling and I watched the surge and flutter of the birds as their colors flared for an instant like an unfurled oriental fan. I wanted to go and stand near the cage for a better view, but decided against it. It might seem unbusinesslike. I observed the room from the chair.

These folks are the Kings of the Earth! I thought, hearing the bird make an ugly noise. There was nothing like this at the college museum—or anywhere else that I had ever been. I recalled only a few cracked relics from slavery times: an iron pot, an ancient bell, a set of ankle-irons and links of chain, a primitive loom, a spinning wheel, a gourd for drinking, an ugly ebony African god that seemed to sneer (presented to the school by some traveling millionaire), a leather whip with copper brads,[2] a branding iron with the double letter . . . Though I had seen them very seldom, they were vivid in my

---

1. **plying.** Sailing regularly back and forth
2. **brads.** Wire nails of uniform thickness with small heads

mind. They had not been pleasant and whenever I had visited the room I avoided the glass case in which they rested, preferring instead to look at photographs of the early days after the Civil War, the times close to those blind Barbee[1] had described. And I had not looked even at these too often.

I tried to relax; the chair was beautiful but hard. Where had the man gone? Had he shown any antagonism when he saw me? I was annoyed that I had failed to see him first. One had to watch such details. Suddenly there came a harsh cry from the cage, and once more I saw a mad flashing as though the birds had burst into spontaneous flame, fluttering and beating their wings maliciously against the bamboo bars, only to settle down just as suddenly when the door opened and the blond man stood beckoning, his hand upon the knob. I went over, tense inside me. Had I been accepted or rejected?

There was a question in his eyes. "Come in, please," he said.

"Thank you," I said, waiting to follow him.

"*Please*," he said with a slight smile.

I moved ahead of him, sounding the tone of his words for a sign.

"I want to ask you a few questions," he said, waving my letter at two chairs.

"Yes, sir?" I said.

"Tell me, what is it that you're trying to accomplish?" he said.

"I want a job, sir, so that I can earn enough money to return to college in the fall."

"To your old school?"

"Yes, sir."

"I see." For a moment he studied me silently. "When do you expect to graduate?"

"Next year, sir. I've completed my junior classes . . ."

"Oh, you have? That's very good. And how old are you?"

"Almost twenty, sir."

"A junior at nineteen? You *are* a good student."

"Thank you, sir," I said, beginning to enjoy the interview.

"Were you an athlete?" he asked.

"No, sir . . ."

"You have the build," he said, looking me up and down. "You'd probably make an excellent runner, a sprinter."

"I've never tried, sir."

"And I suppose it's silly even to ask what you think of your Alma Mater?"[2] he said.

"I think it's one of the best in the world," I said, hearing my voice surge with deep feeling.

"I know, I know," he said, with a swift displeasure that surprised me.

I became alert again as he mumbled something incomprehensible about "nostalgia for Harvard yard."

"But what if you were offered an opportunity to finish your work at some other college," he said, his eyes widening behind his glasses. His smile had returned.

"*Another* college?" I asked, my mind beginning to whirl.

"Why, yes, say some school in New England . . ."

I looked at him speechlessly. Did he mean Harvard? Was this good or bad. Where was it leading? "I don't know, sir," I said cautiously. "I've never thought about it. I've only a year more, and, well, I know everyone at my old school and they know me . . ."

I came to a confused halt, seeing him look at me with a sigh of resignation. What was on his mind? Perhaps I had been too frank about returning to the college, maybe he was against our having a higher education . . . But hell, he's only a secretary . . . Or *is* he?

"I understand," he said calmly. "It was presumptuous of me to even suggest another school. I guess one's college is really a kind of mother and father . . . a sacred matter."

"Yes, sir. That's it," I said in hurried agreement.

His eyes narrowed. "But now I must ask you an embarrassing question. Do you mind?"

"Why, no, sir," I said nervously.

"I don't like to ask this, but it's quite necessary . . ." He leaned forward with a pained frown. "Tell me, did you *read* the letter which you brought to Mr. Emerson? This," he said, taking the letter from the table.

"Why, no, sir! It wasn't addressed to me, so naturally I wouldn't think of opening it . . ."

"Of course not, I know you wouldn't," he said, fluttering his hand and sitting erect. "I'm sorry and you must dismiss it, like one of those annoying personal questions you find so often nowadays on supposedly impersonal forms."

I didn't believe him. "But was it opened, sir? Someone might have gone into my things . . ."

"Oh, no, nothing like that. Please forget the question . . . And tell me, please, what are your plans after graduation?"

"I'm not sure, sir. I'd like to be asked to remain at the college as a teacher, or as a member of the administrative staff. And . . . Well . . ."

"Yes? And what else?"

---

1. **Barbee.** The character Homer A. Barbee appeared earlier in the novel and gave a speech at the narrator's college about the period after the Emancipation during which the narrator's college was founded.

2. **Alma Mater.** College or school that one attended

"Well—er, I guess I'd really like to become Dr. Bledsoe's[1] assistant . . ."

"Oh, I see," he said, sitting back and forming his mouth into a thin-lipped circle. "You're very ambitious."

"I guess I am, sir. But I'm willing to work hard."

"Ambition is a wonderful force," he said, "but sometimes it can be blinding . . . On the other hand, it can make you successful—like my father . . ." A new edge came into his voice and he frowned and looked down at his hands, which were trembling. "The only trouble with ambition is that it sometimes blinds one to realities . . . Tell me, how many of these letters do you have?"

"I had about seven, sir," I replied, confused by his new turn. "They're—"

"*Seven!*" He was suddenly angry.

"Yes, sir, that was all he gave me . . ."

"And how many of these gentlemen have you succeeded in seeing, may I ask?"

A sinking feeling came over me. "I haven't seen any of them personally, sir."

"And this is your last letter?"

"Yes, sir, it is, but I expect to hear from the others . . . They said—"

"Of course you will, and from all seven. They're all loyal Americans."

There was unmistakable irony in his voice now, and I didn't know what to say.

"Seven," he repeated mysteriously. "Oh, don't let me upset you," he said with an elegant gesture of self-disgust. "I had a difficult session with my analyst last evening and the slightest thing is apt to set me off. Like an alarm clock without control— Say!" he said, slapping his palms against his thighs. "What on earth does that mean?" Suddenly he was in a state. One side of his face had begun to twitch and swell.

I watched him light a cigarette, thinking, What on earth is this all about?

"Some things are just too unjust for words," he said, expelling a plume of smoke, "and too ambiguous for either speech or ideas. By the way, have you ever been to the Club Calamus?"

"I don't think I've ever heard of it, sir," I said.

"You haven't? It's very well known. Many of my Harlem friends go there. It's a rendezvous for writers, artists and all kinds of celebrities. There's nothing like it in the city, and by some strange twist it has a truly continental flavor."

"I've never been to a night club, sir. I'll have to go there to see what it's like after I've started earning some money," I said, hoping to bring the conversation back to the problem of jobs.

He looked at me with a jerk of his head, his face beginning to twitch again.

"I suppose I've been evading the issue again—as always. Look," he burst out impulsively. "Do you believe that two people, two strangers who have never seen one another before can speak with utter frankness and sincerity?"

"Sir?"

"Oh, damn! What I mean is, do you believe it possible for us, the two of us, to throw off the mask of custom and manners that insulate man from man, and converse in naked honesty and frankness?"

"I don't know what you mean exactly, sir," I said.

"Are you sure?"

"I . . ."

"Of course, of course. If I could only speak plainly! I'm confusing you. Such frankness just isn't possible because all our motives are impure. Forget what I just said. I'll try to put it this way—and remember this, please . . ."

My head spun. He was addressing me, leaning forward confidentially, as though he'd known me for years, and I remembered something my grandfather had said long ago: *Don't let no white man tell you his business, 'cause after he tells you he's liable to git shame he tole it to you and then he'll hate you. Fact is, he was hating you all the time . . .*

". . . I want to try to reveal a part of reality that is most important to you—but I warn you, it's going to hurt. No, let me finish," he said, touching my knee lightly and quickly removing his hand as I shifted my position.

"What I want to do is done very seldom, and, to be honest, it wouldn't happen now if I hadn't sustained a series of impossible frustrations. You see—well, I'm a thwarted . . . Oh, damn, there I go again, thinking only of myself . . . We're both frustrated, understand? Both of us, and I want to help you . . ."

"You mean you'll let me see Mr. Emerson?"

He frowned. "Please don't seem so happy about it, and don't leap to conclusions. I want to help, but there is a tyranny involved . . ."

"A *tyranny?*" My lungs tightened.

"Yes. That's a way of putting it. Because to help you I must disillusion you . . ."

"Oh, I don't think I mind, sir. Once I see Mr. Emerson, it'll be up to me. All I want to do is speak to him."

"*Speak* to him," he said, getting quickly to his feet and mashing his cigarette into the tray with shaking fingers. "No one speaks *to* him. *He* does the speaking—" Suddenly he broke off. "On second thought, perhaps you'd better leave me your address and I'll mail you Mr. Emerson's reply in the morning. He's really a very busy man."

---

1. **Dr. Bledsoe.** President of the college which the narrator has been asked to leave. Bledsoe has, however, provided the narrator with letters of "introduction" to help him find a job.

His whole manner had changed.

"But you said . . ." I stood up, completely confused. Was he having fun with me? "Couldn't you let me talk to him for just five minutes?" I pleaded. "I'm sure I can convince him that I'm worthy of a job. And if there's someone who has tampered with my letter, I'll prove my identity . . . Dr. Bledsoe would—"

"Identity! My God! Who has any identity any more anyway? It isn't so perfectly simple. Look," he said with an anguished gesture. "Will you trust me?"

"Why, yes, sir, I trust you."

He leaned forward. "Look," he said, his face working violently, "I was trying to tell you that I know many things about you—not you personally, but fellows like you. Not much, either, but still more than the average. With us it's still Jim and Huck Finn.[1] A number of my friends are jazz musicians, and I've been around. I know the conditions under which you live— Why go back, fellow? There is so much you could do here where there is more freedom. You won't find what you're looking for when you return anyway; because so much is involved that you can't possibly know. Please don't misunderstand me; I don't say all this to impress you. Or to give myself some kind of sadistic catharsis. Truly, I don't. But I do know this world you're trying to contact—all its virtues and all its unspeakables— Ha, yes, unspeakables. I'm afraid my father considers me one of the unspeakables . . . I'm Huckleberry, you see . . ."

He laughed drily as I tried to make sense of his ramblings. *Huckleberry?* Why did he keep talking about that kid's story? I was puzzled and annoyed that he could talk to me this way because he stood between me and a job, the campus . . .

"But I only want a job, sir," I said. "I only want to make enough money to return to my studies."

"Of course, but surely you suspect there is more to it than that. Aren't you curious about what lies behind the face of things?"

"Yes, sir, but I'm mainly interested in a job."

"Of course," he said, "but life isn't that simple . . ."

"But I'm not bothered about all the other things, whatever they are, sir. They're not for me to interfere with and I'll be satisfied to go back to college and remain there as long as they'll allow me to."

"But I want to help you do what is best," he said. "What's *best*, mind you. Do you wish to do what's best for yourself?"

"Why, yes, sir. I suppose I do . . ."

"Then forget about returning to the college. Go somewhere else . . ."

"You mean leave?"

"Yes, forget it . . ."

"But you said that you would help me!"

"I did and I am—"

"But what about seeing Mr. Emerson?"

"Oh, God! Don't you see that it's best that you do *not* see him?"

Suddenly I could not breathe. Then I was standing, gripping my brief case. "What have you got against me?" I blurted. "What did I ever do to you? You never intended to let me see him. Even though I presented my letter of introduction. Why? Why? I'd never endanger *your* job—"

"No, no, no! Of course not," he cried, getting to his feet. "You've misunderstood me. You mustn't do that! God, there's too much misunderstanding. Please don't think I'm trying to prevent you from seeing my—from seeing Mr. Emerson out of prejudice . . ."

"Yes, sir, I do," I said angrily. "I was sent here by a friend of his. You read the letter, but still you refuse to let me see him, and now you're trying to get me to leave college. What kind of man are you, anyway? What have you got against me? You, a northern white man!"

He looked pained. "I've done it badly," he said, "but you must believe that I am trying to advise you what is best for you." He snatched off his glasses.

"But *I* know what's best for me," I said. "Or at least Dr. Bledsoe does, and if I can't see Mr. Emerson today, just tell me when I can and I'll be here . . ."

He bit his lips and shut his eyes, shaking his head from side to side as though fighting back a scream. "I'm sorry, really sorry that I started all of this," he said, suddenly calm. "It was foolish of me to try to advise you, but please, you mustn't believe that I'm against you . . . or your race. I'm your friend. Some of the finest people I know are Neg—Well, you see, Mr. Emerson is my father."

"Your father!"

"My father, yes, though I would have preferred it otherwise. But he is, and I could arrange for you to see him. But to be utterly frank, I'm incapable of such cynicism. It would do you no good."

"But I'd like to take my chances, Mr. Emerson, sir . . . This is very important to me. My whole career depends upon it."

"But you *have* no chance," he said.

"But Dr. Bledsoe sent me here," I said, growing more excited. "I must have a chance . . ."

"Dr. Bledsoe," he said with distaste. "He's like my . . . he ought to be horsewhipped! Here," he said, sweeping up the letter and thrusting it crackling toward me. I took it, looking into his eyes that burned back at me.

---

1. **Jim and Huck Finn.** Characters in the novel *The Adventures of Huckleberry Finn*, by Mark Twain

"Go on, read it," he cried excitedly. "Go on!"

"But I wasn't asking for this," I said.

"Read it!"

My dear Mr. Emerson:

The bearer of this letter is a former student of ours (I say *former* because he shall never, under any circumstances, be enrolled as a student here again) who has been expelled for a most serious defection from our strictest rules of deportment.

Due, however, to circumstances the nature of which I shall explain to you in person on the occasion of the next meeting of the board, it is to the best interests of the college that this young man have no knowledge of the finality of his expulsion. For it is indeed his hope to return here to his classes in the fall. However, it is to the best interests of the great work which we are dedicated to perform, that he continue undisturbed in these vain hopes while remaining as far as possible from our midst.

This case represents, my dear Mr. Emerson, one of the rare, delicate instances in which one for whom we held great expectations has gone grievously astray, and who in his fall threatens to upset certain delicate relationships between certain interested individuals and the school. Thus, while the bearer is no longer a member of our scholastic family, it is highly important that his severance with the college be executed as painlessly as possible. I beg of you, sir, to help him continue in the direction of that promise which, like the horizon, recedes ever brightly and distantly beyond the hopeful traveler.

Respectfully, I am your
humble servant,

A. Hebert Bledsoe

I raised my head. Twenty-five years seemed to have lapsed between his handing me the letter and my grasping its message. I could not believe it, tried to read it again. I could not believe it, yet I had a feeling that it all had happened before. I rubbed my eyes, and they felt sandy as though all the fluids had suddenly dried.

"I'm sorry," he said. "I'm terribly sorry."

"What did I do? I always tried to do the right thing . . ."

"*That* you must tell me," he said. "To what does he refer?"

"I don't know, I don't know . . ."

"But you must have done *something*."

"I took a man for a drive, showed him into the Golden Day[1] to help him when he became ill . . . I don't know . . ."

I told him falteringly of the visit to Trueblood's[2] and the trip to the Golden Day and of my expulsion, watching his mobile face reflecting his reaction to each detail.

"It's little enough," he said when I had finished. "I don't understand the man. He is very complicated."

"I only wanted to return and help," I said.

"You'll never return. You can't return now," he said. "Don't you see? I'm terribly sorry and yet I'm glad that I gave in to the impulse to speak to you. Forget it; though that's advice which I've been unable to accept myself, it's still good advice. There is no point in blinding yourself to the truth. Don't blind yourself . . ."

I got up, dazed, and started toward the door. He came behind me into the reception room where the birds flamed in the cage, their squawks like screams in a nightmare.

He stammered guiltily, "Please, I must ask you never to mention this conversation to anyone."

"No," I said.

"I wouldn't mind, but my father would consider my revelation the most extreme treason . . . You're free of him now. I'm still his prisoner. You have been freed, don't you understand? I've still my battle." He seemed near tears.

"I won't," I said. "No one would believe me. I can't myself. There must be some mistake. There must be . . ."

I opened the door.

"Look, fellow," he said. "This evening I'm having a party at the Calamus. Would you like to join my guests? It might help you—"

"No, thank you, sir. I'll be all right."

"Perhaps you'd like to be my valet?"

I looked at him. "No, thank you, sir," I said.

"Please," he said. "I really want to help. Look, I happen to know of a possible job at Liberty Paints. My father has sent several fellows there . . . You should try—"

I shut the door.

The elevator dropped me like a shot and I went out and walked along the street. The sun was very bright now and the people along the walk seemed far away. I stopped before a gray wall where high above me the headstones of a church graveyard arose like the tops of buildings. Across the street in the shade of an awning a shoeshine boy was dancing for pennies. I went on to the corner and got on a bus and went automatically to the rear. In the seat in front of me a dark man in a panama hat kept whistling a tune between his teeth.

---

1. **Golden Day.** Tavern
2. **Trueblood's.** Farm of a local African American near the narrator's college

My mind flew in circles, to Bledsoe, Emerson and back again. There was no sense to be made of it. It was a joke. Hell, it couldn't be a joke. Yes, it is a joke . . . Suddenly the bus jerked to a stop and I heard myself humming the same tune that the man ahead was whistling, and the words came back:

> O well they picked poor Robin clean
> O well they picked poor Robin clean
> Well they tied poor Robin to a stump
> Lawd, they picked all the feathers round
>   from Robin's rump
> Well they picked poor Robin clean.

Then I was on my feet, hurrying to the door, hearing the thin, tissue-paper-against-the-teeth-of-a-comb whistle following me outside at the next stop. I stood trembling at the curb, watching and half expecting to see the man leap from the door to follow me, whistling the old forgotten jingle about a bare-rumped robin. My mind seized upon the tune. I took the subway and it still droned through my mind after I had reached my room at Men's House and lay across the bed. What was the who-what-when-why-where of poor old Robin? What had he done and who had tied him and why had they plucked him and why had we sung of his fate? It was for a laugh, for a laugh, all the kids had laughed and laughed, and the droll tuba player of the old Elk's band had rendered it solo on his helical horn; with comical flourishes and doleful phrasing, "*Boo boo boo booooo,* Poor Robin clean"—a mock funeral dirge . . . But who was Robin and for what had he been hurt and humiliated?

Suddenly I lay shaking with anger. It was no good. I thought of young Emerson. What if he'd lied out of some ulterior motive of his own? Everyone seemed to have some plan for me, and beneath that some more secret plan. What was young Emerson's plan—and why should it have included me? Who was I anyway? I tossed fitfully. Perhaps it was a test of my good will and faith—But that's a lie, I thought. It's a lie and you know it's a lie. I had seen the letter and it had practically ordered me killed. By slow degrees . . .

"My dear Mr. Emerson," I said aloud. "The Robin bearing this letter is a former student. Please hope him to death, and keep him running. Your most humble and obedient servant, A. H. Bledsoe . . ."

Sure, that's the way it was, I thought, a short, concise verbal *coup de grace,*[1] straight to the nape of the neck. And Emerson would write in reply? Sure: "Dear Bled, have met Robin and shaved tail. Signed, Emerson."

I sat on the bed and laughed. They'd sent me to the rookery, all right. I laughed and felt numb and weak, knowing that soon the pain would come and that no matter what happened to me I'd never be the same. I felt numb and I was laughing. When I stopped, gasping for breath, I decided that I would go back and kill Bledsoe. Yes, I thought, I owe it to the race and to myself. I'll kill him.

And the boldness of the idea and the anger behind it made me move with decision. I had to have a job and I took what I hoped was the quickest means. I called the plant young Emerson had mentioned, and it worked. I was told to report the following morning. It happened so quickly and with such ease that for a moment I felt turned around. Had they planned it this way? But no, they wouldn't catch me again. This time *I* had made the move.

I could hardly get to sleep for dreaming of revenge.

from *Their Eyes Were Watching God*
by Zora Neale Hurston

It was a spring afternoon in West Florida. Janie had spent most of the day under a blossoming pear tree in the back-yard. She had been spending every minute that she could steal from her chores under that tree for the last three days. That was to say, ever since the first tiny bloom had opened. It had called her to come and gaze on a mystery. From barren brown stems to glistening leaf-buds; from the leaf-buds to snowy virginity of bloom. It stirred her tremendously. How? Why? It was like a flute song forgotten in another existence and remembered again. What? How? Why? This singing she heard that had nothing to do with her ears. The rose of the world was breathing out smell. It followed her through all her waking moments and caressed her in her sleep. It connected itself with other vaguely felt matters that had struck her outside observation and buried themselves in her flesh. Now they emerged and quested about her consciousness.

She was stretched on her back beneath the pear tree soaking in the alto chant of the visiting bees, the gold of the sun and the panting breath of the breeze when the inaudible voice of it all came to her. She saw a dust-bearing bee sink into the sanctum of a bloom; the thousand sister-calyxes arch to meet the love embrace and the ecstatic shiver of the tree from root to tiniest branch creaming in every blossom and frothing with delight. So this was a marriage! She had been summoned to behold a revelation. Then Janie felt a pain remorseless sweet that left her limp and languid.

---

1. **coup de grace.** Death blow

After a while she got up from where she was and went over the little garden field entire. She was seeking confirmation of the voice and vision, and everywhere she found and acknowledged answers. A personal answer for all other creations except herself. She felt an answer seeking her, but where? When? How? She found herself at the kitchen door and stumbled inside. In the air of the room were flies tumbling and singing, marrying and giving in marriage. When she reached the narrow hallway she was reminded that her grandmother was home with a sick headache. She was lying across the bed asleep so Janie tipped on out of the front door. Oh to be a pear tree—*any* tree in bloom! With kissing bees singing of the beginning of the world! She was sixteen. She had glossy leaves and bursting buds and she wanted to struggle with life but it seemed to elude her. Where were the singing bees for her? Nothing on the place nor in her grandma's house answered her. She searched as much of the world as she could from the top of the front steps and then went on down to the front gate and leaned over to gaze up and down the road. Looking, waiting, breathing short with impatience. Waiting for the world to be made.

Through pollinated air she saw a glorious being coming up the road. In her former blindness she had known him as shiftless Johnny Taylor, tall and lean. That was before the golden dust of pollen had beglamored his rags and her eyes.

In the last stages of Nanny's sleep, she dreamed of voices. Voices far-off but persistent, and gradually coming nearer. Janie's voice. Janie talking in whispery snatches with a male voice she couldn't quite place. That brought her wide awake. She bolted upright and peered out of the window and saw Johnny Taylor lacerating her Janie with a kiss.

"Janie!"

The old woman's voice was so lacking in command and reproof, so full of crumbling dissolution,—that Janie half believed that Nanny had not seen her. So she extended herself outside of her dream and went inside of the house. That was the end of her childhood.

from *The Great Gatsby*
by F. Scott Fitzgerald

About half way between West Egg and New York the motor-road hastily joins the railroad and runs beside it for a quarter of a mile so as to shrink away from a certain desolate area of land. This is a valley of ashes—a fantastic farm where ashes grow like wheat into ridges and hills and grotesque gardens, where ashes take the form of houses and chimneys and rising smoke and finally, with a transcendent effort, of men who move dimly and already crumbling through the powdery air. Occasionally a line of grey cars crawls along an invisible track, gives out a ghastly creak and comes to rest, and immediately the ash-grey men swarm up with leaden spades and stir up an impenetrable cloud which screens their obscure operations from your sight.

But above the grey land and the spasms of bleak dust which drift endlessly over it, you perceive, after a moment, the eyes of Doctor T. J. Eckleburg. The eyes of Doctor T. J. Eckleburg are blue and gigantic—their retinas[1] are one yard high. They look out of no face but, instead, from a pair of enormous yellow spectacles which pass over a nonexistent nose. Evidently some wild wag[2] of an oculist[3] set them there to fatten his practice in the borough of Queens and then sank down himself into eternal blindness or forgot them and moved away. But his eyes, dimmed a little by many paintless days under sun and rain, brood on over the solemn dumping ground.

The valley of ashes is bounded on one side by a small foul river, and when the drawbridge is up to let barges through, the passengers on waiting trains can stare at the dismal scene for as long as half an hour. There is always a halt there of at least a minute and it was because of this that I first met Tom Buchanan's mistress.

from *Tell Me How Long the Train's Been Gone*
by James Baldwin

My brother, Caleb, was seventeen when I was ten. We were very good friends. In fact, he was my best friend and, for a very long time, my only friend.

I do not mean to say that he was always nice to me. I got on his nerves a lot, and he resented having to take me around with him and be responsible for me when there were so many other things he wanted to be doing. Therefore, his hand was often up against the side of my head, and my tears caused him to be punished many times. But I knew, somehow, anyway, that when he was being punished for my tears, he was not being punished for anything he had done to me; he was being punished because that was the way we lived; and his punishment, oddly, helped unite us. More oddly still, even as his great hand caused my head to stammer and dropped a

---

1. **retinas.** Innermost coat lining the interior of the eyeballs
2. **wag.** Comical or humorous person
3. **oculist.** Early term for ophthalmologist or eye doctor

flame-colored curtain before my eyes, I understood that he was not striking *me*. His hand leapt out because he could not help it, and I received the blow because I was there. And it happened, sometimes, before I could even catch my breath to howl, that the hand that had struck me grabbed me and held me, and it was difficult indeed to know which of us was weeping. He was striking, striking out, striking out, striking out; the hand asked me to forgive him. I felt his bewilderment through the membrane of my own. I also felt that he was trying to teach me something. And I had, God knows, no other teachers.

For our father—how shall I describe our father?—was a ruined Barbados[1] peasant, exiled in a Harlem[2] which he loathed, where he never saw the sun or sky he remembered, where life took place neither indoors nor without, and where there was no joy. By which I mean no joy that he remembered. Had he been able to bring with him any of the joy he had felt on that far-off island, then the air of the sea and the impulse to dancing would sometimes have transfigured our dreadful rooms. Our lives might have been very different.

But no, he brought with him from Barbados only black rum and blacker pride and magic incantations, which neither healed nor saved.

He did not understand the people among whom he found himself; they had no coherence, no stature and no pride. He came from a race which had been flourishing at the very dawn of the world—a race greater and nobler than Rome or Judea, mightier than Egypt—he came from a race of kings, kings who had never been taken in battle, kings who had never been slaves. He spoke to us of tribes and empires, battles, victories, and monarchs of whom we had never heard—they were not mentioned in our textbooks—and invested us with glories in which we felt more awkward than in the secondhand shoes we wore. In the stifling room of his pretensions and expectations, we stumbled wretchedly about, stubbing our toes, as it were, on rubies, scraping our shins on golden caskets, bringing down, with a childish cry, the splendid purple tapestry on which, in pounding gold and scarlet, our destinies and our inheritance were figured. It could scarcely have been other-wise, since a child's major attention has to be concentrated on how to fit into a world which, with every passing hour, reveals itself as merciless.

If our father was of royal blood and we were royal children, our father was certainly the only person in the world who knew it. The landlord did not know it; our father never mentioned royal blood to *him*. When we were late with our rent, which was often, the landlord threatened, in terms no commoner had ever used before a king, to put us in the streets. He complained that our shiftlessness, which he did not hesitate to consider an attribute of the race, had forced him, an old man with a weak heart, to climb all these stairs to plead with us to give him the money we owed him. And this was the last time; he wanted to make sure we understood that this was the last time.

Our father was younger than the landlord, leaner, stronger, and bigger. With one blow, he could have brought the landlord to his knees. And we knew how much he hated the man. For days on end, in the wintertime, we huddled around the gas stove in the kitchen, because the landlord gave us no heat. When windows were broken, the landlord took his time about fixing them; the wind made the cardboard we stuffed in the windows rattle all night long; and when snow came, the weight of the snow forced the cardboard inward and onto the floor. Whenever the apartment received a fresh coat of paint, we bought the paint and did the painting ourselves; we killed the rats. A great chunk of the kitchen ceiling fell one winter, narrowly missing our mother.

We all hated the landlord with a perfectly exquisite hatred, and we would have been happy to see our proud father kill him. We would have been glad to help. But our father did nothing of the sort. He stood before the landlord, looking unutterably weary. He made excuses. He apologized. He swore that it would never happen again. (We knew that it *would* happen again.) He begged for time. The landlord would finally go down the stairs, letting us and all the neighbors know how good-hearted he was, and our father would walk into the kitchen and pour himself a glass of rum.

But we knew that our father would never have allowed any black man to speak to him as the landlord did, as policemen did, as storekeepers and welfare workers and pawnbrokers did. No, not for a moment. He would have thrown him out of the house. He would certainly have made a black man know that he was not the descendant of slaves! He had made them know it so often that he had almost no friends among them, and if we had followed his impossible lead, we would have had no friends, either. It was scarcely worthwhile being the descendant of kings if the kings were black and no one had ever heard of them.

And it was because of our father, perhaps, that Caleb and I clung to each other, in spite of the great difference in our ages; or, in another way, it may have been

---

1. **Barbados.** Island in the British West Indies
2. **Harlem.** Section of New York City

precisely the difference in our ages that made the clinging possible. I don't know. It is really not the kind of thing anyone can ever know. I think it may be easier to love the really helpless younger brother, because he cannot enter into competition with one on one's own ground, or on any ground at all, and can never question one's role or jeopardize one's authority. In my own case, certainly, it did not occur to me to compete with Caleb, and I could not have questioned his role or his authority, because I needed both. He was my touchstone,[1] my model and my only guide.

Anyway, our father, dreaming bitterly of Barbados, despised and mocked by his neighbors and all but ignored by his sons, held down his unspeakable factory job, spread his black gospel in bars on the weekends, and drank his rum. I do not know if he loved our mother. I think he did.

They had had five children—only Caleb and I, the first and the last, were left. We were both dark, like our father; but two of the three dead girls had been fair, like our mother.

She came from New Orleans. Her hair was not like ours. It was black, but softer and finer. The color of her skin reminded me of the color of bananas. Her skin was as bright as that, and contained that kind of promise, and she had tiny freckles around her nose and a small black mole just above her upper lip. It was the mole, I don't know why, which made her beautiful. Without it, her face might have been merely sweet, merely pretty. But the mole was funny. It had the effect of making one realize that our mother liked funny things, liked to laugh. The mole made one look at her eyes—large, extraordinary dark eyes, eyes which seemed always to be amused by something, eyes which looked straight out, seeming to see everything, seeming to be afraid of nothing. She was a soft, round, plump woman. She liked nice clothes and dangling jewelry, which she mostly didn't have, and she liked to cook for large numbers of people, and she loved our father.

She knew him—knew him through and through. I am not being coy or colloquial but bluntly and sadly matter-of-fact when I say that I will now never know what she saw in him. What she saw was certainly not for many eyes; what she saw got him through his working week and his Sunday rest; what she saw saved him. She saw that he was a man. For her, perhaps, he was a great man. I think, though, that for our mother any man was great who aspired to become a man: this meant that our father was very rare and precious. I used to wonder how she took it, how she bore it—his rages, his tears, his cowardice.

On Saturday nights he was almost always evil, drunk, and maudlin. He came home from work in the early afternoon and gave our mother some money. It was never enough, of course, but she never protested, at least not as far as I know. Then she would go out shopping. I would usually go with her, for Caleb would almost always be out somewhere, and our mother didn't like the idea of leaving me alone in the house. And this was probably, after all, the best possible arrangement. People who disliked our father were sure (for that very reason) to like our mother; and people who felt that Caleb was growing to be too much like his father could feel that I, after all, might turn out like my mother. Besides, it is not, as a general rule, easy to hate a small child. One runs the risk of looking ridiculous, especially if the child is with his mother.

And especially if that mother is Mrs. Proudhammer. Mrs. Proudhammer knew very well what people thought of Mr. Proudhammer. She knew, too, exactly how much she owed in each store she entered, how much she was going to be able to pay, and what she had to buy. She entered with a smile, ready.

"Evening. Let me have some of them red beans there."

"Evening. You know you folks been running up quite a little bill here."

"I'm going to give you something on it right now. I need some cornmeal and flour and some rice."

"You know, I got my bills to meet, too, Mrs. Proudhammer."

"Didn't I just tell you I was going to pay? I want some cornflakes, too, and some milk." Such merchandise as she could reach, she had already placed on the counter.

"When do you think you're going to be able to pay this bill? All of it, I mean."

"You know I'm going to pay it just as soon as I can. How much does it all come to? Give me that end you got there of that chocolate cake." The chocolate cake was for Caleb and me. "Well, now you put this against the bill." Imperiously, as though it were the most natural thing in the world, she put two or three dollars on the counter.

"You lucky I'm softhearted, Mrs. Proudhammer. "

"Things sure don't cost this much downtown—you think I don't know it? Here." And she paid him for what she had bought. "Thank you. You been mighty kind."

And we left the store. I often felt that in order to help her, I should have filled my pockets with merchandise while she was talking. But I never did, not only because the store was often crowded or because I was afraid of being caught by the storekeeper, but because I was afraid of humiliating her.

---

1. **touchstone.** Test of genuineness or value

When we had to do "heavy" shopping, we went marketing under the bridge at Park Avenue—Caleb, our mother, and I; and sometimes, but rarely, our father came with us. The most usual reason for heavy shopping was that some relatives of our mother's, or old friends of both our mother's and our father's, were coming to visit. We were certainly not going to let them go away hungry—not even if it meant, as it often did mean, spending more than we had. In spite of what I have been suggesting about our father's temperament, and no matter how difficult he may sometimes have been with us, he was much too proud to offend any guest of his; on the contrary, his impulse was to make them feel that his home was theirs; and besides, he was lonely, lonely for his past, lonely for those faces which had borne witness to that past. Therefore, he would sometimes pretend that our mother did not know how to shop, and our father would come with us under the bridge, in order to teach her.

There he would be then, uncharacteristically, in shirt sleeves, which made him look rather boyish; and as our mother showed no desire to take shopping lessons from him, he turned his attention to Caleb and me. He would pick up a fish, opening the gills and holding it close to his nose. "You see that? That fish looks fresh, don't it? Well, that fish ain't as fresh as I am, and I *been* out of the water. They done doctored that fish. Come on." And we would walk away, a little embarrassed but, on the whole, rather pleased that our father was so smart.

Meantime, our mother was getting the marketing done. She was very happy on days like this, because our father was happy. He was happy, odd as his expression of it may sound, to be out with his wife and his two sons. If we had been on the island that had been witness to his birth, instead of the unspeakable island of Manhattan, he felt that it would not have been so hard for us all to trust and love each other. He sensed, and I think he was right, that on that other, never to be recovered island, his sons would have looked on him very differently, and he would have looked very differently on his sons. Life would have been hard there, too; we would have fought there, too, and more or less blindly suffered and more or less blindly died. But we would not have been (or so it was to seem to all of us forever) so wickedly menaced by the mere fact of our relationship, would not have been so frightened of entering into the central, most beautiful and valuable facts of our lives. We would have been laughing and cursing and tussling in the water, instead of stammering under the bridge; we would have known less about vanished African kingdoms and more about each other. Or, not at all impossibly, more about both.

If it was summer, we bought a watermelon, which either Caleb or our father carried home, fighting with each other for this privilege. They looked very like each other on those days—both big, both black, both laughing.

Caleb always looked absolutely helpless when he laughed. He laughed with all his body, perhaps touching his shoulder against yours, or putting his head on your chest for a moment, and then careening off you, halfway across the room or down the block. I will always hear his laughter. He was always happy on such days, too. Caleb certainly needed his father. Such days, however, were rare—one of the reasons, probably, that I remember them now.

Eventually, we all climbed the stairs into that hovel which, at such moments, was our castle. One very nearly felt the drawbridge rising behind us as our father locked the door.

The bathtub could not yet be filled with cold water and the melon placed in the tub, because this was Saturday, and, come evening, we all had to bathe. The melon was covered with a blanket and placed on the fire escape. Then we unloaded what we had bought, rather impressed by our opulence, though our father was always, by this time, appalled by the money we had spent. I was always sadly aware that there would be nothing left of all this once tomorrow had come and gone and that most of it, after all, was not for us, but for others.

Our mother was calculating the pennies she would need all week—carfare for our father and for Caleb, who went to a high school out of our neighborhood; money for the life insurance; money for milk for me at school; money for light and gas; money put away, if possible, toward the rent. She knew just about what our father had left in *his* pockets and was counting on him to give me the money I would shortly be demanding to go to the movies. Caleb had a part-time job after school and already had his movie money. Anyway, unless he was in a very good mood or needed me for something, he would not be anxious to go to the movies with me.

Our mother never insisted that Caleb tell her where he was going, nor did she question him as to how he spent the money he made. She was afraid of hearing him lie, and she did not want to risk forcing him to lie. She was operating on the assumption that he was sensible and had been raised to be honorable and that he, now more than ever, needed his privacy.

But she was very firm with him, nevertheless. "I do not want to see you rolling in here at three in the morning, Caleb. I want you here in time to eat, and you know you got to take your bath."

"Yes, indeed, ma'am. Why can't I take my bath in the morning?"

"Don't you start being funny. You know you ain't going to get up in time to take no bath in the morning."

"Don't nobody want you messing around in that bathroom all morning long, man," said our father. "You just git back in the house like your ma's telling you."

"Besides," I said, "you never wash out the tub. "

Caleb looked at me in mock surprise and from a great height, allowing his chin and his lids simultaneously to drop and swiveling his head away from me.

"I see," he said, "that everyone in this family is ganging up on me. All right, Leo. I was planning to take you to the show with me, but now I've changed my mind."

"I'm sorry," I said quickly. "I take it back."

"You take *what* back?"

"What I said—about you not washing out the tub."

"Ain't no need to take it back," our father said stubbornly. "It's true. A man don't take back nothing that's true."

"So *you* say," Caleb said, with a hint of a sneer. But before anyone could possibly react to this, he picked me up, scowling into my face, which he held just above his own. "You take it back?"

"Leo ain't going to take it back," our father said.

Now I was in trouble. Caleb watched me, a small grin on his face. "You take it back?"

"Stop teasing that child, and put him down," our mother said. "The trouble ain't that Caleb don't wash out the tub—he just don't wash it out very clean."

"I never knew him to wash it out," our father said, "unless I was standing behind him."

"Well, ain't neither one of you much good around the house," our mother said.

Caleb laughed and set me down. "You didn't take it back," he said.

I said nothing.

"I guess I'm just going to have to go on without you."

Still, I said nothing.

"You going to have that child to crying in a minute," our mother said. "If you going to take him, go on and take him. Don't do him like that."

Caleb laughed again. "I'm going to take him. The way he got them eyes all ready to water, I'd better take him somewhere." We walked toward the door. "But you got to make up *your* mind," he said to me, "to say what *you* think is right. . . ."

UNIT REVIEW

Modern Fiction

VOCABULARY FROM THE SELECTIONS

agitation, 622
apathetically, 624
apprehension, 617
conflagration, 622
conjectural, 616
dwindle, 647
ebb, 621
excruciatingly, 636

immobility, 635
imperative, 621
infatuation, 632
interminably, 636
jilt, 644
jocularity, 636
nucleus, 624
overture, 634

pall, 615
peremptorily, 625
poignant, 625
prelude, 635
reiterate, 618
render, 631
reproach, 636
respective, 633

reverential, 632
revert, 632
rummage, 642
thresh, 619
tremulously, 633
undulation, 615

LITERARY TERMS

catastrohe, 628
characterization,
    655
conflict, 628

dialogue, 655
internal
    monologue, 655
irony, 648

narrator, 638
plot, 628
point of view, 638
setting, 628

simile, 638, 648
stream-of-
    consciousness
    writing, 649

SYNTHESIS: QUESTIONS FOR WRITING, RESEARCH, OR DISCUSSION

GENRE STUDIES

1. **Short Story.** According to Poe's definition, the short story must achieve creation of one dominant impression. How does portrayal of the cold in London's "To Build a Fire" and of the night in Hemingway's "A Clean, Well-Lighted Place" meet this requirement?

THEMATIC STUDIES

2. **Loss.** Both Ellen Weatherall and Georgiana Carpenter feel a "shock of recognition." They have both led lives filled with hard work and caring for family but acknowledge emptiness. What do both regret?

HISTORICAL/BIOGRAPHICAL STUDIES

3. **Roles of Women.** Review the comments in the introduction on page 502 about changes in the roles of women. In some ways the two female characters in the Porter and Cather stories bridge two eras. What eras are they? What do the authors seem to be saying about women?

LANGUAGE LAB PROOFREADING FOR CAPITALIZATION ERRORS

Proper nouns are always capitalized. The following chart shows other cases when capitalization is required.

CAPITALIZE	EXAMPLES
Awards	Pulitzer Prize, Nobel Prize in literature
Brand and Trade Names	Rollerblade skates, Band-Aid bandages
Buildings and Structures	Tate Gallery, Great Pyramid of Khufu
Days, Months, Years, and Holidays	Monday, September, Labor Day
Directions and Regions	The West, Pacific Rim
Events and Periods	Civil War, Gilded Age
Family Relationships (unmodified)	Mother, Aunt June
First Words	Read the story for tomorrow's class.
Letters	from A to Z, middle C
Personal Names	Jack London, Willa Cather
Place Names	Harlem, New York City, U.S.A.
Pronoun *I*	I wish I had read "The Bear."
Titles of Art, Literary, and Musical Works	"To Build a Fire," Copland's *Billy the Kid*

LANGUAGE ARTS SURVEY

For additional help, see the Language Arts Survey, 2.107–2.133.

Exercise A Correcting Capitalization Errors

In each of the following sentences decide if the underlined words should be capitalized or not. Write each word correctly along with the rule it follows.

1. The <u>south</u> has produced many great writers, such as <u>flannery o'Connor</u> and <u>william faulkner</u>.

2. Hurston's <u>*their eyes were watching god*</u> takes place in <u>florida</u>.

3. Katherine Anne Porter won a <u>pulitzer prize</u> in 1965.

4. Ernest Hemingway worked as a <u>Reporter</u> in <u>spain</u> during the <u>spanish civil war</u>.

5. You can use my <u>zippo</u> lighter to light the fire.

6. F. Scott Fitzgerald, a celebrated writer of the <u>jazz age</u>, experienced severe financial problems during the <u>depression</u>.

7. <u>unless</u> someone explains it to me, there's no way <u>i</u> will understand this Faulkner <u>Story</u>.

8. In *Invisible Man,* <u>brother jack</u> leads a revolutionary group called the <u>brother-hood.</u>

9. Next <u>sunday</u> the <u>chicago public library</u> will host a reading of Willa Cather's writing.

10. Eudora Welty is one of my favorite <u>Twentieth-Century</u> writers.

Exercise B Proofreading for Capitalization Errors

In the paragraph that follows correct any errors in capitalization.

LANGUAGE ARTS SURVEY

For additional help, see the Language Arts Survey, 2.107–2.133.

Although she was born in virginia, Willa cather is most often associated with nebraska, which became her home when she was Nine. The young Cather was graduated from the university of nebraska, worked as a Magazine Editor and english teacher in pittsburgh, and then moved to new york city to work as an editor for *mcClure's* magazine. However, when she began writing, her thoughts turned to her childhood in the midwest. many of Cather's most memorable novels, including *O pioneers!* and *My Antonia,* are set during Nebraska's frontier days. In these Novels, cather explores the myths of pioneer life in Nineteenth-Century America. The central characters of *O Pioneers!* are an immigrant family from sweden, and the title character of *My Antonia* is an immigrant woman from czechoslovakia. In *One of ours,* which was awarded the pulitzer prize, Cather intermingles scenes of Nebraska with world war I battle scenes. After her mother's death in 1931, Cather returned to her Home State for a brief family visit; it was to be her last one. Cather worked and lived out the rest of her life in her park avenue apartment in new york and in an Autumn retreat in new hampshire.

New York Movie. Edward Hopper, 1939. The Museum of Modern Art, New York, Given *anonymously*

am the opposite of the stage musician.
He gives you illusion that has the
appearance of truth. I give you truth in
the pleasant disguise of illusion.

—Tennessee Williams

The Glass Menagerie
by Tennessee Williams

ABOUT THE AUTHOR

Tennessee Williams (1911–1983) was the pen name of one of America's finest dramatists. Born Thomas Lanier Williams, he grew up in Mississippi and St. Louis. Williams began writing early, publishing his first short story at the age of fourteen. He attended the University of Washington and the University of Iowa and then worked at various jobs in Chicago, St. Louis, New Orleans, and California. In 1939, his *American Blues,* a collection of short plays, was produced in New York to enthusiastic reviews. However, his next play, *Battle of Angels,* later rewritten and retitled *Orpheus Descending,* failed when it was produced in Boston. *The Glass Menagerie,* produced in 1944 and a tremendous success, was followed by *A Streetcar Named Desire* (1947), *Summer and Smoke* (1948), *Camino Real* (1953), *Cat on a Hot Tin Roof* (1955), *Suddenly Last Summer* (1958), *Sweet Bird of Youth* (1959), and *The Night of the Iguana* (1962). Williams also wrote the novella *The Roman Spring of Mrs. Stone* (1950) and his *Memoirs* (1975). Williams's plays often deal with troubled, emotionally intense social misfits and are often set in the post-Civil War, or antebellum, South. Because of the intensity of emotion in these plays and because of their powerfully evocative settings, they are often referred to as examples of **Southern Gothic.** Williams was also a pioneering American Expressionist. **Expressionism** was an artistic movement of the early and mid-twentieth century that sought to express emotions by exaggerating the artistic medium itself. Expressionist painters tended to use heavy strokes of the brush or palette knife and vivid, intense colors. Expressionist dramatists often exaggerated the elements of spectacle and the literary techniques in their works, using lighting, sound, properties, and elements of the stage set for symbolic purposes.

ABOUT THE SELECTION

The closest companion of Williams's youth, his sister Rose, provided the model for the central character in the play that was to be his first major success, **The Glass Menagerie.** This largely autobiographical play, originally called *The Gentleman Caller,* deals with a socially isolated young woman, Laura, whose intense fragility is symbolized by her collection of glass figurines. Laura's nickname, "Blue Roses," recalls the name of Williams's sister, Rose, and evokes numerous connotations: oddness and rarity (because blue roses do not actually occur in nature), fragility and weakness (because of the association of the color blue with the blue veins that show so clearly against the white skin of a sickly, anemic person), and sadness (because of the use of the word *blues* to describe a melancholic or depressed state). Such strong symbolism is characteristic of Williams's work and that of other Expressionist writers. The character Tom in the play, a young writer, is something of a self-portrait, and critics have often expressed the idea that Williams wrote the play because of the guilt that he felt for abandoning his sister Rose, who ended up in a mental institution. Williams's sister, like Laura, collected glass figures, and this remembered detail became an evocative image in his work. Williams wrote of his fascination with his sister's glass collection, "They were mostly little glass animals. By poetic association they came to represent, in my memory, all the softest emotions that belong to recollection of things past. They stood for all the small and tender things that relieve the austere pattern of life and make it endurable to the sensitive."

First staged in Chicago in 1944, *The Glass Menagerie* was an immediate success, opening in New York the following year. Since that time the play has been produced many times on Broadway and by theater companies throughout the world. Several film versions of the play have been produced, one in 1950 starring Jane Wyman and Arthur Kennedy, one in 1973 starring Katherine Hepburn and Sam Waterston, and one in 1987 starring Joanne Woodward and John Malkovich. The last of these versions was directed by Paul Newman.

READER'S JOURNAL

Psychologists often speak of extroverts and introverts. An extrovert is someone who takes naturally to social situations. An introvert has a more introspective personality. Are you an extrovert, an introvert, or somewhere in between? Write about this question in your journal.

LANGUAGE SKILLS

Read the Language Arts Survey, 2.61, "Correcting Sentence Fragments." Plays consist of dialogue and stage directions. In dialogue, as in ordinary speech, people often use sentence fragments. As you read this play, copy onto a sheet of paper five examples of sentence fragments spoken by the characters.

The Glass Menagerie

TENNESSEE WILLIAMS

CAST OF CHARACTERS

AMANDA WINGFIELD
LAURA WINGFIELD

TOM WINGFIELD
JIM O'CONNOR

ACT ONE, SCENE 1

The Wingfield apartment is in the rear of the building, one of those vast hive-like conglomerations of cellular living-units that flower as warty growths in overcrowded urban centers of lower middle-class population and are symptomatic of the impulse of this largest and fundamentally enslaved section of American society to avoid fluidity and differentiation and to exist and function as one interfused mass of automatism. The apartment faces an alley and is entered by a fire-escape, a structure whose name is a touch of accidental poetic truth, for all of these huge buildings are always burning with the slow and implacable fires of human desperation. The fire-escape is included in the set—that is, the landing of it and steps descending from it. (Note that the stage L. alley may be entirely omitted, since it is never used except for TOM's first entrance, which can take place stage R.) The scene is memory and is therefore nonrealistic. Memory takes a lot of poetic license. It omits some details, others are exaggerated, according to the emotional value of the articles it touches, for memory is seated predominantly in the heart. The interior is therefore rather dim and poetic. (CUE #1. As soon as the house lights dim, dance-hall music

What does the author say about memory?

WORDS FOR EVERYDAY USE:

con • glom • er • a • tion (kən gläm´ər ā´shən) *n.*, collection or mixture

symp • to • mat • ic (simp´tə mat´ik) *adj.*, indicative; that constitutes a condition

in • ter • fused (in tər fyōōzd´) *part.*, combined, blended

im • pla • ca • ble (im plā´kə bəl) *adj.*, that cannot be appeased or pacified

heard on-stage R. *Old popular music of, say 1915–1920 period. This continues until* TOM *is at fire-escape landing, having lighted cigarette, and begins speaking.)*

AT RISE: *At the rise of the house curtain, the audience is faced with the dark, grim rear wall of the Wingfield tenement. (The stage set proper is screened out by a gauze curtain, which suggests the front part, outside, of the building.) This building, which runs parallel to the footlights, is flanked on both sides by dark, narrow alleys which run into murky canyons of tangled clotheslines, garbage cans and the sinister lattice-work of neighboring fire-escapes. (The alleys are actually in darkness, and the objects just mentioned are not visible.) It is up and down these side alleys that exterior entrances and exits are made, during the play. At the end of* TOM's *opening commentary, the dark tenement wall slowly reveals (by means of a transparency) the interior of the ground-floor Wingfield apartment. (Gauze curtain, which suggests front part of building, rises on the interior set.) Downstage is the living-room, which also serves as a sleeping room for* LAURA, *the day-bed unfolding to make her bed. Just above this is a small stool or table on which is a telephone. Up-stage,* C., *and divided by a wide arch or second proscenium[1] with transparent faded portieres (or second curtain, "second curtain" is actually the inner gauze curtain between the living-room and the dining-room, which is up-stage of it), is the dining-room. In an old-fashioned whatnot in the living-room are seen scores of transparent glass animals. A blown-up photograph of the father hangs on the wall of the living-room, facing the audience, to the* L. *of the archway. It is the face of a very handsome young man in a doughboy's[2] First World War*

cap. *He is gallantly smiling,* ineluctably *smiling, as if to say, "I will be smiling forever." (Note that all that is essential in connection with dance-hall is that the window be shown lighting lower part of alley. It is not necessary to show any considerable part of dance-hall.) The audience hears and sees the opening scene in the dining-room through both the transparent fourth wall (this is the gauze curtain which suggests outside of building) of the building and the transparent gauze portieres of the dining-room arch. It is during this revealing scene that the fourth wall slowly ascends, out of sight. This transparent exterior wall is not brought down again until the very end of the play, during* TOM's *final speech. The narrator is an undisguised convention of the play. He takes whatever license with dramatic convention as is convenient to his purposes.*

TOM *enters, dressed as a merchant sailor, from alley, stage* L. *(i.e., stage* R. *if* L. *alley is omitted), and strolls across the front of the stage to the fire-escape. (*TOM *may lean against grillwork of this as he lights cigarette.) There he stops and lights a cigarette. He addresses the audience.*

TOM.   I have tricks in my pocket—I have things up my sleeve—but I am the opposite of the stage magician. He gives you illusion that has the appearance of truth. I give you truth in the pleasant disguise of illusion. I take you back to an alley in St. Louis. The time that quaint period when the huge middle class of America was matriculating from a school for the blind. Their eyes had failed them,

What does Tom, the narrator, say about the nature of truth and illusion in this play?

---

1. **proscenium.** Plane, including the arch and the curtain, separating the stage proper from the audience
2. **doughboy's.** Belonging to a World War I United States infantryman

WORDS FOR EVERYDAY USE:

in • e • luc • ta • bly (in´ē luk´tə blē) *adv.*, in an inescapable or unavoidable manner

ma • tric • u • late (mə trik´yo͞o lāt´) *vt.*, enroll

or they had failed their eyes, and so they were having their fingers pressed forcibly down on the fiery Braille alphabet of a dissolving economy.—In Spain there was revolution.—Here there was only shouting and confusion and labor disturbances, sometimes violent, in otherwise peaceful cities such as Cleveland—Chicago—Detroit. . . . That is the social background of this play. . . . The play is memory. (MUSIC CUE #2.) Being a memory play, it is dimly lighted, it is sentimental, it is not realistic.—In memory everything seems to happen to music.—That explains the fiddle in the wings. I am the narrator of the play, and also a character in it. The other characters in the play are my mother, Amanda, my sister, Laura, and a gentleman caller who appears in the final scenes. He is the most realistic character in the play, being an <u>emissary</u> from a world that we were somehow set apart from.—But having a poet's weakness for symbols, I am using this character as a symbol—as the long-delayed but always expected something that we live for.—There is a fifth character who doesn't appear other than in a photograph hanging on the wall. When you see the picture of this grinning gentleman, please remember this is our father who left us a long time ago. He was a telephone man who fell in love with long distance—so he gave up his job with the telephone company and skipped the light fantastic out of town. . . . The last we heard of him was a picture postcard from the Pacific coast of Mexico, containing a message of two words—"Hello—Good-bye!" and no address.

(LIGHTS UP IN DINING-ROOM. TOM *exits* R. *He goes off downstage, takes off his sailor overcoat and skull-fitting knitted cap and remains off-stage by dining-room* R. *door for his entrance cue.* AMANDA's *voice becomes audible through the portieres—i.e., gauze curtains separating dining-room and living-room.* AMANDA *and* LAURA *are seated at a drop-leaf table.* AMANDA *is sitting in* C. *chair and* LAURA *in* L. *chair. Eating is indicated by gestures without food or utensils.* AMANDA *faces the audience. The interior of the dining-room has lit up softly and through the scrim[3]—gauze curtains—we see* AMANDA *and* LAURA *seated at the table in the upstage area.*)

AMANDA.   You know, Laura, I had the funniest experience in church last Sunday. The church was crowded except for one pew way down front and in that was just one little woman. I smiled very sweetly at her and said, "Excuse me, would you mind if I shared this pew?" "I certainly would," she said, "this space is rented." Do you know that is the first time that I ever knew that the Lord rented space. (*Dining-room gauze curtains open automatically.*) These Northern Episcopalians! I can understand the Southern Episcopalians, but these Northern ones, no. (TOM *enters dining-room* R., *slips over to table and sits in chair* R.) Honey, don't push your food with your fingers. If you have to push your food with something, the thing to use is a crust of bread. You must chew your food. Animals have secretions in their stomachs which enable them to digest their food without <u>mastication</u>, but human beings must chew their food before they swallow it down, and chew, chew. Oh, eat leisurely. Eat leisurely.

---

3. **scrim.** Hanging of light cloth as a semitransparent curtain in a theatrical production

WORDS FOR EVERYDAY USE:

em • is • sar • y (em´i ser´ē) *n.*, person or agent sent on a mission

mas • ti • ca • tion (mas´ti kā´shən) *n.*, chewing

A well-cooked meal has many delicate flavors that have to be held in the mouth for appreciation, not just gulped down. Oh, chew, chew—chew! *(At this point the scrim curtain—if the director decides to use it—the one suggesting exterior wall, rises here and does not come down again until just before the end of the play.)* Don't you want to give your salivary glands a chance to function?

TOM. Mother, I haven't enjoyed one bite of my dinner because of your constant directions on how to eat it. It's you that makes me hurry through my meals with your hawk-like attention to every bite I take. It's disgusting—all this discussion of animal's secretion—salivary glands—mastication! *(Comes down to armchair in living-room R., lights cigarette.)*

AMANDA. Temperament like a Metropolitan star! You're not excused from this table.

TOM. I'm getting a cigarette.

AMANDA. You smoke too much.

LAURA *(Rising)*. Mother, I'll bring in the coffee.

AMANDA. No, no, no, no. You sit down. I'm going to be the servant today and you're going to be the lady.

LAURA. I'm already up.

AMANDA. Resume your seat. Resume your seat. You keep yourself fresh and pretty for the gentlemen callers. *(LAURA sits.)*

LAURA. I'm not expecting any gentlemen callers.

AMANDA *(Who has been gathering dishes from table and loading them on tray)*. Well, the nice thing about them is they come when they're least expected. Why, I remember one Sunday afternoon in Blue Mountain when your mother was a girl . . .

(Goes out for coffee, U. R.)

TOM. I know what's coming now! *(LAURA rises.)*

LAURA. Yes. But let her tell it. *(Crosses to L. of day-bed, sits.)*

TOM. Again?

LAURA. She loves to tell it.

AMANDA *(Entering from R. in dining-room and coming down into living-room with tray and coffee)*. I remember one Sunday afternoon in Blue Mountain when your mother was a girl she received—seventeen—gentlemen callers! *(AMANDA crosses to TOM at armchair R., gives him coffee, and crosses C. LAURA comes to her, takes cup, resumes her place on L. of day-bed. AMANDA puts tray on small table R. of day-bed, sits R. on day-bed. Inner curtain closes, light dims out.)* Why sometimes there weren't chairs enough to accommodate them all and we had to send the servant over to the parish house to fetch the folding chairs.

TOM. How did you entertain all those gentlemen callers? *(TOM finally sits in armchair R.)*

AMANDA. I happened to understand the art of conversation!

TOM. I bet you could talk!

AMANDA. Well, I could. All the girls in my day could, I tell you.

TOM. Yes?

What event in her life does Amanda enjoy remembering?

Why does Amanda tell Laura to remain seated? How does Laura feel about her mother's expectations?

WORDS FOR EVERYDAY USE:

re • sume (ri zo͞om´) vt., take, get, or occupy again

AMANDA. They knew how to entertain their gentlemen callers. It wasn't enough for a girl to be possessed of a pretty face and a graceful figure—although I wasn't slighted in either respect. She also needed to have a nimble wit and a tongue to meet all occasions.

TOM. What did you talk about?

AMANDA. Why, we'd talk about things of importance going on in the world! Never anything common or coarse or vulgar. My callers were gentlemen—all! Some of the most <u>prominent</u> men on the Mississippi Delta—planters and sons of planters! There was young Champ Laughlin. (MUSIC CUE #3.) He later became Vice-President of the Delta Planters' Bank. And Hadley Stevenson; he was drowned in Moon Lake.—My goodness, he certainly left his widow well provided for—a hundred and fifty thousand dollars in government bonds. And the Cutrere Brothers—Wesley and Bates. Bates was one of my own bright particular beaus! But he got in a quarrel with that wild Wainwright boy and they shot it out on the floor of Moon Lake Casino. Bates was shot through the stomach. He died in the ambulance on his way to Memphis. He certainly left his widow well provided for, too—eight or ten thousand acres, no less. He never loved that woman; she just caught him on the rebound. My picture was found on him the night he died. Oh and that boy, that boy that every girl in the Delta was setting her cap for! That beautiful (MUSIC FADES OUT.) brilliant young Fitzhugh boy from Greene County!

TOM. What did he leave his widow?

AMANDA. He never married! What's the matter with you—you talk as though all my old admirers had turned up their toes to the daisies!

TOM. Isn't this the first you've mentioned that still survives?

AMANDA. He made an awful lot of money. He went North to Wall Street and made a fortune. He had the Midas touch—everything that boy touched just turned to gold! (Gets up.) And I could have been Mrs. J. Duncan Fitzhugh—mind you! (Crosses L. C.) But—what did I do?—I just went out of my way and picked your father! (Looks at picture on L. wall. Goes to small table R. of day-bed for tray.)

LAURA (Rises from day-bed). Mother, let me clear the table.

AMANDA (Crossing L. for LAURA's cup, then crossing R. for TOM's). No, dear, you go in front and study your typewriter chart. Or practice your shorthand a little. Stay fresh and pretty! It's almost time for our gentlemen callers to start arriving. How many do you suppose we're going to entertain this afternoon? (TOM opens curtains between dining-room and living-room for her. These close behind her, and she exits into kitchen R. TOM stands U. C. in living-room.)

LAURA (To AMANDA, off-stage). I don't believe we're going to receive any, Mother.

AMANDA (Off-stage). Not any? Not one? Why, you must be joking! Not one gentleman caller? What's the matter? Has there been a flood or a tornado?

LAURA (Crossing to typing table). It isn't a flood. It's not a tornado, Mother. I'm just

What does Amanda regret?

What reason does Amanda give for the lack of gentlemen callers? What does Laura see as the reason? How do you think her mother's joking and prodding might make Laura feel?

WORDS FOR EVERYDAY USE: **prom • i • nent** (präm´ə nənt) *adj.*, widely and favorably known

not popular like you were in Blue Mountain. Mother's afraid that I'm going to be an old maid. (MUSIC CUE #4.) *(Lights dim out.* TOM *exits* U. C. *in blackout.* LAURA *crosses to* menagerie R.)*

Responding to the Selection

How do you feel about Amanda Wingfield after reading the first scene of the play? In what sense does she live in a dream world? Why might her children sometimes find her talk irritating?

Reviewing the Selection

RECALLING

1. What does the narrator, Tom, say a stage magician does?

2. What memory from her past does Amanda relate? What question does she pose to Laura?

INTERPRETING

3. How does Tom differ from a stage magician?

4. About what is Amanda nostalgic? What does she want for her daughter?

SYNTHESIZING

5. Whom does Amanda expect to be calling? Why does she ask Laura to study her typewriter chart and to practice her shorthand? What does Amanda want for her daughter?

Understanding Literature (Questions for Discussion)

1. **Stage Directions. Stage directions** are notes included in a play in addition to the dialogue for the purpose of describing how something should be performed on stage. Sometimes writers also include information about the economic, political, or cultural background of the play. Reread the stage directions at the opening of this play, before the entrance of the narrator. What is the social class of the people who live in the "overcrowded urban centers" described in those stage directions? What "poetic truth" is expressed by the term *fire-escape?*

WORDS FOR EVERYDAY USE:

me • nag • er • ie (mə naj´ər ē) *n.,* collection of wild or strange animals kept in enclosures for exhibition

2. **Expressionism. Expressionism** is the name given to a twentieth-century movement in literature and art that reacted against Realism in favor of an exaggeration of the elements of the artistic medium itself. In the stage directions at the beginning of this play, we are told that the "scene is memory." Whose emotional recollections will be viewed by the audience? What elements of the setting, as described in the opening stage directions, are unrealistic and calculated to create emotional responses in the audience? What is special about the play's lighting and use of sound effects?

3. **Character.** A **character** is someone who figures in the action of a literary work. Amanda, the mother of Laura and Tom, is nostalgic about her Southern upbringing. What statements made by her show that she remembers the South as a special, cultivated, refined place where life was more decorous and elegant? What statements and actions on her part show that she wants the same kind of life for her children? What suggestions are there in scene 1 that Amanda's ideas are unrealistic, that she is clinging to a past that has disappeared?

4. **Metaphor.** A **metaphor** is a figure of speech in which something is spoken or written about as if it were another. The figure of speech invites the reader to make a comparison between the two things. Tom, the narrator, says that at the time in which the play is set, "the huge middle class of America was matriculating from a school for the blind. Their eyes had failed them, or they had failed their eyes, and so they were having their fingers pressed forcibly down on the fiery Braille alphabet of a dissolving economy." What is Tom saying about life just before the Great Depression? What does Tom compare to the Braille alphabet? What might people be reading or learning as a result of the economic depression?

ACT ONE, SCENE 2

Scene is the same. Lights dim up on living-room.

LAURA *discovered by menagerie, polishing glass. Crosses to phonograph, plays record. She times this business so as to put needle on record as* MUSIC CUE #4 *ends. Enter* AMANDA *down alley* R. *Rattles key in lock.* LAURA *crosses guiltily to typewriter and types. (Small typewriter table with typewriter on it is still on stage in living-room* L.*)* AMANDA *comes into room* R. *closing door. Crosses to armchair, putting hat, purse and gloves on it. Something has happened to* AMANDA. *It is written in her face: a look that is grim and hopeless and a lit-* tle absurd. *She has on one of those cheap or imitation velvety-looking cloth coats with imitation fur collar. Her hat is five or six years old, one of those dreadful cloche[4] hats that were worn in the late twenties and she is clasping an enormous black patent-leather pocketbook with nickel clasps and initials. This is her full-dress outfit, the one she usually wears to the* D.A.R.[5] *She purses her lips, opens her eyes very wide, rolls them upward and shakes her head. Seeing her mother's expression,* LAURA *touches her lips with a nervous gesture.*

LAURA. Hello, Mother, I was just . . .

---

4. **cloche.** Close-fitting, bell-shaped hat
5. **D.A.R.** Daughters of the American Revolution, a civic organization

AMANDA. I know. You were just practicing your typing, I suppose. *(Behind chair* R.*)*

LAURA. Yes.

AMANDA. Deception, deception, deception!

LAURA *(Shakily).* How was the D.A.R. meeting, Mother?

AMANDA *(Crosses to* LAURA*).* D.A.R. meeting!

LAURA. Didn't you go to the D.A.R. meeting, Mother?

AMANDA *(Faintly, almost inaudibly).* No, I didn't go to any D.A.R. meeting. *(Then more forcibly.)* I didn't have the strength—I didn't have the courage. I just wanted to find a hole in the ground and crawl in it and stay there the rest of my entire life.

(Tears type charts, throws them on floor.)

LAURA *(Faintly).* Why did you do that, Mother?

AMANDA *(Sits on* R. *end of day-bed).* Why? Why? How old are you, Laura?

LAURA. Mother, you know my age.

AMANDA. I was under the impression that you were an adult, but evidently I was very much mistaken.

(She stares at LAURA.*)*

LAURA. Please don't stare at me, Mother! *(*AMANDA *closes her eyes and lowers her head. Pause.)*

AMANDA. What are we going to do? What is going to become of us? What is the future? *(Pause.)*

LAURA. Has something happened, Mother? Mother, has something happened?

AMANDA. I'll be all right in a minute. I'm just bewildered—by life . . .

LAURA. Mother, I wish that you would tell me what's happened!

AMANDA. I went to the D.A.R. this afternoon, as you know; I was to be <u>inducted</u> as an officer. I stopped off at Rubicam's Business College to tell them about your cold and to ask how you were progressing down there.

LAURA. Oh . . .

AMANDA. Yes, oh—oh—oh. I went straight to your typing instructor and introduced myself as your mother. She didn't even know who you were. Wingfield, she said? We don't have any such scholar enrolled in this school. I assured her she did. I said my daughter Laura's been coming to classes since early January. "Well, I don't know," she said, "unless you mean that terribly shy little girl who dropped out of school after a few days' attendance?" "No," I said, "I don't mean that one. I mean my daughter, Laura, who's been coming here every single day for the past six weeks!" "Excuse me," she said. And she took down the attendance book and there was your name, unmistakable, printed, and all the dates you'd been absent. I still told her she was wrong. I still said, "No, there must have been some mistake! There must have been some mix-up in the records!" "No," she said, "I remember her perfectly now. She was so shy and her hands trembled so that her fingers couldn't touch the right keys! When we gave a speed-test—she just broke down completely—was sick at the stomach and had to be carried to the washroom! After that she never came back. We telephoned the house every single day and never got any answer." *(Rises*

How does Amanda say she feels? What effect does she hope to produce in Laura?

Why is Amanda angry with her daughter?

In what way does Laura's former teacher describe her?

WORDS FOR EVERYDAY USE: **in • duct** (in dukt´) *vt.,* place in official position

Q How has Laura been spending her time?

from day-bed, crosses R. C.*)* That was while I was working all day long down at that department store, I suppose, demonstrating those—(*With hands indicates brassiere.*) Oh! I felt so weak I couldn't stand up! (*Sits in armchair.*) I had to sit down while they got me a glass of water! (LAURA *crosses up to phonograph.*) Fifty dollars' tuition. I don't care about the money so much, but all my hopes for any kind of future for you—gone up the spout, just gone up the spout like that. (LAURA *winds phonograph up.*) Oh, don't do that, Laura!—Don't play that victrola![6]

LAURA.   Oh! (*Stops phonograph, crosses to typing table, sits.*)

AMANDA.   What have you been doing every day when you've gone out of the house pretending that you were going to business college?

LAURA.   I've just been going out walking.

AMANDA.   That's not true!

LAURA.   Yes, it is, Mother, I just went walking.

Q What does Amanda say they can't do now that Laura has failed at business school?

AMANDA.   Walking? Walking? In winter? Deliberately courting pneumonia in that light coat? Where did you walk to, Laura?

LAURA.   All sorts of places—mostly in the park.

AMANDA.   Even after you'd started catching that cold?

LAURA.   It was the lesser of two evils, Mother. I couldn't go back. I threw up on the floor!

Q What sort of future does Amanda envision?

AMANDA.   From half-past seven till after five every day you mean to tell me you walked around in the park, because you wanted to make me think that you were still going to Rubicam's Business College?

LAURA.   Oh, Mother, it wasn't as bad as it sounds. I went inside places to get warmed up.

AMANDA.   Inside where?

LAURA.   I went in the art museum and the bird-houses at the Zoo. I visited the penguins every day! Sometimes I did without lunch and went to the movies. Lately I've been spending most of my afternoons in the Jewelbox, that big glass house where they raise the tropical flowers.

AMANDA.   You did all that to deceive me, just for deception! Why? Why? Why? Why?

LAURA.   Mother, when you're disappointed, you get that awful suffering look on your face, like the picture of Jesus' mother in the Museum! (*Rises.*)

AMANDA.   Hush!

LAURA   (*Crosses* R. *to menagerie*). I couldn't face it. I couldn't. (MUSIC CUE #5.)

AMANDA   (*Rising from day-bed*). So what are we going to do now, honey, the rest of our lives? Just sit down in this house and watch the parades go by? Amuse ourselves with the glass menagerie? Eternally play those worn-out records your father left us as a painful reminder of him? (*Slams phonograph lid.*) We can't have a business career. (END MUSIC CUE #5.) No, we can't do that—that just gives us indigestion. (*Around* R. *day-bed.*) What is there left for us now but dependency all our lives? I tell you, Laura, I know so well what happens to unmarried women who aren't prepared to occupy a position in life. (*Crosses* L., *sits on day-bed.*) I've seen such pitiful cases in the South—barely tolerated spinsters living on some brother's wife or a sister's husband—tucked away in some mousetrap of a room—encouraged by one in-law to go on and visit the next in-law—little birdlike women—without any nest—eating the crust of humility all their lives! Is

---

6. **victrola.** Record player

that the future that we've mapped out for ourselves? I swear I don't see any other alternative. And I don't think that's a very pleasant alternative. Of course—some girls *do* marry. My goodness, Laura, haven't you ever liked some boy?

LAURA. Yes, Mother, I liked one once.

AMANDA. You did?

LAURA. I came across his picture a while ago.

AMANDA. He gave you his picture too? *(Rises from day-bed, crosses to chair R.)*

LAURA. No, it's in the year-book.

AMANDA *(Sits in armchair)*. Oh—a high-school boy.

LAURA. Yes. His name was Jim. *(Kneeling on floor, gets year-book from under menagerie.)* Here he is in "The Pirates of Penzance."

AMANDA *(Absently)*. The what?

LAURA. The operetta the senior class put on. He had a wonderful voice. We sat across the aisle from each other Mondays, Wednesdays and Fridays in the auditorium. Here he is with a silver cup for debating! See his grin?

AMANDA. So he had a grin, too! *(Looks at picture of father on wall behind phonograph. Hands year-book back.)*

LAURA. He used to call me—Blue Roses.

AMANDA. Blue Roses? What did he call you a silly name like that for?

LAURA *(Still kneeling)*. When I had that attack of pleurosis[7]—he asked me what was the matter when I came back. I said pleurosis—he thought that I said "Blue Roses." So that's what he always called me after that. Whenever he saw me, he'd holler, "Hello, Blue Roses!" I didn't care for the girl that he went out with. Emily Meisenbach. Oh, Emily was the best-dressed girl at Soldan. But she never struck me as being sincere . . . I read in a newspaper once that they were engaged. *(Puts year-book back on a shelf of glass menagerie.)* That's a long time ago—they're probably married by now.

AMANDA. That's all right, honey, that's all right. It doesn't matter. Little girls who aren't cut out for business careers sometimes end up married to very nice young men. And I'm just going to see that you do that, too!

LAURA. But, Mother—

AMANDA. What is it now?

LAURA. I'm—crippled!

AMANDA. Don't say that word! *(Rises, crosses to C. Turns to LAURA.)* How many times have I told you never to say that word! You're not crippled, you've just got a slight defect. *(LAURA rises.)* If you lived in the days when I was a girl and they had long graceful skirts sweeping the ground, it might have been considered an asset. When you've got a slight disadvantage like that, you've just got to <u>cultivate</u> something else to take its place. You have to cultivate charm—or vivacity—or *charm!* *(Spotlight on photograph. Then dim out.)* That's the only thing your father had plenty of—charm! *(AMANDA sits on day-bed. LAURA crosses to armchair and sits.)* (MUSIC CUE #6.) *(Blackout.)*

---

7. **pleurosis.** Inflammation of the lungs

What does Amanda ask Laura? Why does she ask her this?

What does Amanda set as her goal?

WORDS FOR EVERYDAY USE:
cul • ti • vate (kul´tə vāt) *vt.*, acquire and develop

Responding to the Selection

What is the difference between nervousness and fear? Which do you think Laura experienced when at the business college? Why might some people be prone to strong emotions in situations that would not upset another individual? In what way can sensitivity be both a special gift and a painful affliction?

Reviewing the Selection

RECALLING

1. What does Amanda discover when she stops by the business school? Why is she distraught?

2. According to Amanda, what alternative to going to business college does a young woman have?

INTERPRETING

3. What happened to Laura when she went to the business college? Why did she drop out? What does she spend her days doing? What did Jim call her, and how did he come up with this name? What do all of these details tell you about Laura's personality and character?

4. What does Amanda fear? What circumstance is she in because of the departure of her husband? What does she want for Laura? When she realizes that Laura will not attend business school, what alternative plan does she immediately devise?

SYNTHESIZING

5. Why doesn't Laura enthusiastically embrace Amanda's plan for her? How would you describe Laura's physical condition? her psychological condition? Why is the latter more significant than the former?

Understanding Literature (Questions for Discussion)

Irony. Irony is a difference between appearance and reality. At the end of this scene, Amanda mentions the portrait of the father that hangs in the room. What became of this man? What makes it ironic that Amanda should pin her hopes on Laura's having a gentleman caller and then immediately think of her husband's picture? What does this sequence of events suggest about the fulfillment of Amanda's hopes?

SCENE: *The same. Lights up again but only on* R. *alley and fire-escape landing, rest of the stage dark. (Typewriter table and typewriter have been taken offstage.) Enter* TOM, *again wearing merchant sailor overcoat and knitted-cap, in alley* R. *As* MUSIC CUE #6 *ends,* TOM *begins to speak.*

TOM *(Leans against grill of fire-escape, smoking).* After the <u>fiasco</u> at Rubicam's Business College, the idea of getting a gentleman caller for my sister Laura began to play a more and more important part in my mother's calculations. It became an obsession. Like some archetype[8] of the universal unconscious, the image of the gentleman caller haunted our small apartment. An evening at home rarely passed without some allusion to this image, this spectre, this hope. . . . And even when he wasn't mentioned, his presence hung in my mother's preoccupied look and in my sister's frightened, apologetic manner. It hung like a sentence passed upon the Wingfields! But my mother was a woman of action as well as words. (MUSIC CUE #7.) She began to take logical steps in the planned direction. Late that winter and in the early spring—realizing that extra money would be needed to properly feather the nest and plume the bird—she began a vigorous campaign on the telephone, roping in subscribers to one of those magazines for matrons called "The Homemaker's Companion," the type of journal that features the serialized <u>sublimations</u> of ladies of letters who think in terms of delicate cup-like breasts, slim, tapering waists, rich creamy thighs, eyes like wood-smoke in autumn, fingers that soothe and caress like soft, soft strains of music. Bodies as powerful as Etruscan[9] sculpture. *(He exits down* R. *into wings. Light in alley* R. *is blacked out, and a head-spot falls on* AMANDA, *at phone in living-room.* MUSIC CUE #7 *ends as* TOM *stops speaking.)*

AMANDA. Ida Scott? *(During this speech* TOM *enters dining-room* U. R. *unseen by audience, not wearing overcoat or hat. There is an unlighted reading lamp on table. Sits* C. *of dining-room table with writing materials.)* This is Amanda Wingfield. We missed you at the D.A.R. last Monday. Oh, first I want to know how's your sinus condition? You're just a Christian martyr. That's what you are. You're just a Christian martyr. Well, I was just going through my little red book, and I saw that your subscription to the "Companion" is about to expire just when that wonderful new serial by Bessie Mae Harper is starting. It's the first thing she's written since "Honeymoon for Three." Now, that was unusual, wasn't it? Why, Ida, this one is even lovelier. It's all about the horsey set on Long Island and a debutante is thrown from her horse while taking him over the jumps at the—regatta. Her spine—her spine is injured. That's what the horse did—he stepped on her. Now, there is only one surgeon in the entire world that can keep her from being completely paralyzed, and that's the man she's engaged to be married to and he's tall and he's blond and he's handsome. That's unusual, too, huh? Oh, he's not perfect. Of course he has a weakness. He has the

---

8. **archetype.** Original pattern; prototype
9. **Etruscan.** Of a culture that flourished on the Italian peninsula before the Romans

What does Tom say about his mother's plan? How does it change his mother and sister? Does he see this plan as realistic?

WORDS FOR EVERYDAY USE:

fi • as • co (fē as´ko) *n.,* complete failure

sub • li • ma • tion (sub´lə ma´shən) *n.,* expression of socially or personally unacceptable impulses in constructive, acceptable forms

most terrible weakness in the entire world. He just drinks too much. What? Oh, no, Honey, don't let them burn. You go take a look in the oven and I'll hold on . . . Why, that woman! Do you know what she did? She hung up on me. *(Dining-room and living-room lights dim in. Reading lamp lights up at same time.)*

What does Tom enjoy doing? In what way does this activity and his mother's personality conflict?

LAURA. Oh, Mother, Mother, Tom's trying to write. *(Rises from armchair where she was left at curtain of previous scene, goes to curtain between dining-room and living-room, which is already open.)*

AMANDA. Oh! So he is. So he is. *(Crosses from phone, goes to dining-room and up to Tom.)*

TOM *(At table)*. Now what are you up to?

AMANDA. I'm trying to save your eyesight. *(Business with lamp.)* You've only got one pair of eyes and you've got to take care of them. Oh, I know that Milton was blind, but that's not what made him a genius.

TOM. Mother, will you please go away and let me finish my writing?

AMANDA *(Squares his shoulders)*. Why can't you sit up straight? So your shoulders don't stick through like sparrows' wings?

TOM. Mother, please go busy yourself with something else. I'm trying to write.

AMANDA *(Business with Tom)*. Now, I've seen a medical chart, and I know what that position does to your internal organs. You sit up and I'll show you. Your stomach presses against your lungs, and your lungs press against your heart, and that poor little heart gets discouraged because it hasn't got any room left to go on beating for you.

TOM. What in hell! . . . *(Inner curtains between living-room and dining-room close. Lights dim down in dining-room. LAURA crosses, stands C. of curtains in living-room listening to following scene between TOM and AMANDA.)*

AMANDA. Don't you talk to me like that—

TOM. —am I supposed to do?

AMANDA. What's the matter with you? Have you gone out of your senses?

TOM. Yes, I have. You've driven me out of them.

AMANDA. What is the matter with you lately, you big—big—idiot?

TOM. Look, Mother—I haven't got a thing, not a single thing left in this house that I can call my own.

AMANDA. Lower your voice!

TOM. Yesterday you confiscated my books! You had the nerve to——

AMANDA. I did. I took that horrible novel back to the library—that awful book by that insane Mr. Lawrence.[10] I cannot control the output of a diseased mind or people who <u>cater</u> to them, but I won't allow such filth in my house. No, no, no, no, no!

TOM. House, house! Who pays the rent on the house, who makes a slave of himself to—!

AMANDA. Don't you dare talk to me like

---

10. **Mr. Lawrence.** D. H. Lawrence (1858–1930) was a poet and novelist whose writings were considered outrageous by some of his contemporaries.

WORDS FOR EVERYDAY USE: **ca • ter** (kāt´ər) *vi.*, take special pains in seeking to gratify another's needs or desires

that! *(LAURA crosses D. L. to back of armchair.)*

TOM. No, *I* mustn't say anything! I've just got to keep quiet and let you do all the talking.

AMANDA. Let me tell you something!

TOM. I don't want to hear any more.

AMANDA. You will hear more—*(LAURA crosses to phonograph.)*

TOM *(Crossing through curtains between dining-room and living-room. Goes up stage of door R. where, in a dark spot, there is supposedly a closet).* Well, I'm not going to listen. I'm going out. *(Gets out coat.)*

AMANDA *(Coming through curtains into living-room, stands C.).* You are going to listen to me, Tom Wingfield. I'm tired of your impudence.—And another thing— I'm right at the end of my patience!

TOM *(Putting overcoat on back of armchair and crossing back to AMANDA).* What do you think I'm at the end of, Mother? Aren't I supposed to have any patience to reach the end of? I know, I know. It seems unimportant to you, what I'm *doing*—what I'm trying to do—having a difference between them! You don't think that.

AMANDA. I think you're doing things that you're ashamed of, and that's why you act like this. *(TOM crosses to day-bed and sits.)* I don't believe that you go every night to the movies. Nobody goes to the movies night after night. Nobody in their right minds goes to the movies as often as you pretend to. People don't go to the movies at nearly midnight and movies don't let out at two A.M. Come in stumbling, muttering to yourself like a maniac. You get three hours' sleep and then go to work. Oh, I can picture the way you're doing down there. Moping, doping, because you're in no condition.

TOM. That's true—that's very, very true. I'm in no condition!

AMANDA. How dare you jeopardize your job? Jeopardize our security? How do you think we'd manage—? *(Sits armchair R.)*

TOM. Look, Mother, do you think I'm *crazy* about the *warehouse?* You think I'm in love with the Continental Shoemakers? You think I want to spend fifty-five years of my life down there in that—*celotex interior!* with *fluorescent tubes?!* Honest to God, I'd rather somebody picked up a crow-bar and battered out my brains— than go back mornings! But I *go!* Sure, every time you come in yelling that bloody *Rise and Shine!* Rise and shine!! I think how lucky dead people are. But I get up. *(Rises from day-bed.)* I *go!* For sixty-five dollars a month I give up all that I dream of doing and being *ever!* And you say that is all I think of. Oh, God! Why, Mother, if self is all I ever thought of, Mother, *I'd* be where *he* is—*GONE!* *(Crosses to get overcoat on back of armchair.)* As far as the system of transportation reaches! *(AMANDA rises, crosses to him and grabs his arm.)* Please don't grab at me, Mother!

AMANDA *(Following him).* I'm not grabbing at you. I want to know where you're going now.

TOM *(Taking overcoat and starts crossing to door R.)* I'm going to the movies!

AMANDA *(Crosses C.).* I don't believe that lie!

TOM *(Crosses back to AMANDA).* No? Well, you're right. For once in your life you're right. I'm not going to the movies. I'm going to opium dens! Yes, Mother, opium dens, dens of vice and criminals' hang-outs, Mother. I've joined the Hogan gang. I'm a hired assassin, I carry a tommy-gun in a violin case! I run a string of cathouses in the valley! They call me

How does Tom feel about his job? Why does he continue doing it? What has "doing the right thing" made him give up?

What happens to the glass menagerie?

Killer, Killer Wingfield, I'm really leading a double life. By day I'm a simple, honest warehouse worker, but at night I'm a dynamic <u>czar</u> of the underworld. Why, I go to gambling casinos and spin away a fortune on the roulette table! I wear a patch over one eye and a false moustache, sometimes I wear green whiskers. On those occasions they call me—El Diablo![11] Oh, I could tell you things to make you sleepless! My enemies plan to dynamite this place some night! Some night they're going to blow us all sky-high. And will I be glad! Will I be happy! And so will you be. You'll go up— up—over Blue Mountain on a broomstick! With seventeen gentlemen callers. You ugly babbling old witch! *(He goes through a series of violent, clumsy movements, seizing his overcoat, lunging to* R. *door, pulling it fiercely open. The women watch him,* <u>aghast</u>. *His arm catches in the sleeve of the coat as he struggles*

What feelings for his sister are revealed by Tom's actions?

to pull it on. For a moment he is <u>pinioned</u> *by the bulky garment. With an outraged groan he tears the coat off again, splitting the shoulder of it, and hurls it across the room. It strikes against the shelf of* LAURA's *glass collection, there is a tinkle of shattering glass.* LAURA *cries out as if wounded.)*

LAURA. My glass!—menagerie . . . *(She covers her face and turns away.* MUSIC CUE #8 *through to end of scene.)*

AMANDA *(In an awful voice).* I'll never speak to you again as long as you live unless you apologize to me! *(*AMANDA *exits through living-room curtains.* TOM *is left with* LAURA. *He stares at her stupidly for a moment. Then he crosses to shelf holding glass menagerie. Drops awkwardly on his knees to collect fallen glass, glancing at* LAURA *as if he would speak, but couldn't. Blackout.* TOM, AMANDA, *and* LAURA *exit in blackout.)*

---

11. **El Diablo.** Spanish for "the devil"

Responding to the Selection

How do you feel about Tom's outburst? Do you sympathize with him? What is difficult about conflict between one's personal desires and one's duties?

WORDS FOR EVERYDAY USE:

czar (zar) *n.*, emperor

a • ghast (ə gast´) *adj.*, feeling great horror or dismay

pin • ion (pin´yən) *vt.*, disable or impede

Reviewing the Selection

1. What does Tom do for a living? What is his role in the financial stability of the family? About what do Tom and Amanda argue?

2. What happens at the end of the scene to Laura's menagerie?

3. What does Tom want to do with himself? What does he fear will happen if he continues working at Continental Shoemakers?

4. As a result of his argument with his mother, Tom acts in a way that hurts Laura. What does Tom want to do with his life? How would doing that also harm Laura?

5. Tom and his mother want very different things in life, but in a sense they are quite similar, for they both are passionate dreamers. Of what does each person dream? In what ways do their dreams conflict with one another?

Understanding Literature (Questions for Discussion)

1. **Archetype.** An **archetype** is an inherited, often unconscious ancestral memory or motif that recurs throughout history and literature. The notion of the archetype derives from the psychology of Carl Jung, who wrote of archetypes as making up humanity's "collective unconscious." Tom says that "Like some archetype of the universal unconscious, the image of the gentleman caller haunted our small apartment." Why is Amanda so insistent on Laura's having gentlemen callers? How does Laura respond to the idea? How is the idea of the gentleman caller related to the picture of the absent father, the one that is always smiling?

2. **Conflict.** A **conflict** is a struggle between two forces in a literary work. What struggle does Tom face? What family circumstances make it very difficult for him to pursue his own dreams? What options does Tom have? Why do none of these options seem particularly attractive?

3. **Symbol.** A **symbol** is a thing that stands for or represents both itself and something else. Of what is the glass menagerie in this play a symbol? With whom is the menagerie associated? What similarities do the menagerie and this person have? How might Tom's actions affect his sister, Laura? What symbolic significance does the breaking of the menagerie have?

ACT ONE, SCENE 4

The interior is dark. Faint light in alley R. *A deep-voiced bell in a church is tolling the hour of five as the scene commences.*

TOM *appears at the top of* R. *alley. After each solemn boom of the bell in the tower he shakes a little toy noisemaker or rattle as if to express the tiny spasm of man in contrast to the sustained power and dignity of the Almighty. This and the unsteadiness of his advance make it evident that he has been drinking. As he climbs the few steps to the fire-escape landing light steals up inside.* LAURA *appears in night-dress, entering living-room from* L. *door of dining-room, observing* TOM's *empty bed (day-bed) in the living-room.* TOM *fishes in his pockets for door-key, removing a* motley *assortment of articles in the search, including a perfect shower of movie-ticket stubs and an empty bottle. At last he finds the key, but just as he is about to insert it, it slips from his fingers. He strikes a match and crouches below the door.*

TOM (*Bitterly*). One crack—and it falls through! (LAURA *opens door* R.)

LAURA. Tom! Tom, what are you doing?

TOM. Looking for a door-key.

LAURA. Where have you been all this time?

TOM. I have been to the movies.

LAURA. All this time at the movies?

TOM. There was a very long program. There was a Garbo picture and a Mickey Mouse and a travelogue and a newsreel[12] and a preview of coming attractions. And there was an organ solo and a collection for the milk-fund—simultaneously—

which ended up in a terrible fight between a fat lady and an usher!

LAURA (*Innocently*). Did you have to stay through everything?

TOM. Of course! And, oh, I forgot! There was a big stage show! The head-liner on this stage show was Malvolio the Magician. He performed wonderful tricks, many of them, such as pouring water back and forth between pitchers. First it turned to wine and then it turned to beer and then it turned to whiskey. I know it was whiskey it finally turned into because he needed somebody to come up out of the audience to help him, and I came up—both shows! It was Kentucky Straight Bourbon. A very generous fellow, he gave souvenirs. (*He pulls from his back pocket a shimmering rainbow-colored scarf.*) He gave me this. This is his magic scarf. You can have it, Laura. You wave it over a canary cage and you get a bowl of gold-fish. You wave it over the gold-fish bowl and they fly away canaries. . . . But the wonderfullest trick of all was the coffin trick. We nailed him into a coffin and he got out of the coffin without removing one nail. (*They enter.*) There is a trick that would come in handy for me—get me out of this 2 by 4 situation! (*Flops onto day-bed and starts removing shoes.*)

LAURA. Tom—shhh!

TOM. What're you shushing me for?

LAURA. You'll wake up Mother.

---

12. **travelogue and a newsreel.** *Travelogue*—film about a foreign place; *newsreel*—short motion picture of recent news events; both were formerly shown as part of the program in movie theaters.

What does Tom give Laura? Why does he give this to her?

To what trick does Tom compare his desire to get out of his situation?

WORDS FOR EVERYDAY USE: **mot • ley** (mät´lē) *adj.*, composed of many different elements

Tom. Goody goody! Pay'er back for all those "Rise an' Shines." *(Lies down groaning.)* You know it don't take much intelligence to get yourself into a nailed-up coffin, Laura. But who in hell ever got himself out of one without removing one nail? *(As if in answer, the father's grinning photograph lights up.* Laura *exits up* L. *Lights fade except for blue glow in dining-room. Pause after lights fade, then clock chimes six times. This is followed by the alarm clock. Dim in fore-stage.)*

Responding to the Selection

How do you think Laura was affected by her brother's strange behavior in this scene?

Reviewing the Selection

RECALLING

1. According to Tom, what was "the wonderfullest trick of all" performed by Malvolio the Magician?

2. What lights up at the end of this scene?

INTERPRETING

3. Why is Tom so impressed by the magic trick of escaping from a coffin without removing a nail? What similarities are there between the trick and what Tom would have to do to get himself out of his current situation?

4. What is Tom thinking about doing? How would doing that make him like his father?

SYNTHESIZING

5. In what ways is Tom already preparing to escape in this scene? In what ways is he distancing himself from his present life?

Understanding Literature (Questions for Discussion)

Symbol. A **symbol** is a thing that stands for or represents both itself and something else. Writers use two types of symbols—conventional, and personal or idiosyncratic. What does the coffin of which Tom speaks symbolize for him? What "trick" does Tom want to be able to perform? What "nails" would he have to remove in order to perform this trick? Why does Tom think that it would take magic for him to be able to do that?

Scene is the same. Immediately following. The churchbell is heard striking six. At the sixth stroke the alarm clock goes off in AMANDA's *room off* R. *of dining-room and after a few moments we hear her calling, "Rise and shine! Rise and shine!* LAURA, *go tell your brother to rise and shine!"*

TOM *(Sitting up slowly in day-bed)*. I'll rise—but I won't shine. *(The light increases.)*

AMANDA *(Offstage)*. Laura, tell your brother his coffee is ready. *(*LAURA, *fully dressed, a cape over her shoulders, slips into living-room.* TOM *is still in bed, covered with blanket, having taken off only shoes and coat.)*

LAURA. Tom!—It's nearly seven. Don't make Mother nervous. *(He stares at her stupidly. Beseechingly.)* Tom, speak to Mother this morning. Make up with her, apologize, speak to her!

TOM *(Putting on shoes)*. She won't to me. It's her that started not speaking.

LAURA. If you just say you're sorry she'll start speaking.

TOM. Her not speaking—is that such a tragedy?

LAURA. Please—please!

AMANDA *(Calling offstage* R. *from kitchen)*. Laura, are you going to do what I asked you to do, or do I have to get dressed and go out myself?

LAURA. Going, going—soon as I get on my coat! *(She rises and crosses to door* R.*)* Butter and what else?

(To AMANDA.*)*

AMANDA *(Offstage)*. Just butter. Tell them to charge it.

LAURA. Mother, they make such faces when I do that.

AMANDA *(Offstage)*. Sticks and stones can break our bones, but the expression on Mr. Garfinkel's face won't harm us! Tell your brother his coffee is getting cold.

LAURA *(At door* R.*)*. Do what I asked you, will you, will you, Tom? *(He looks sullenly away.)*

AMANDA. Laura, go now or just don't go at all!

LAURA *(Rushing out* R.*)* Going—going! *(A second later she cries out. Falls on fire-escape landing.* TOM *springs up and crosses to door* R. AMANDA *rushes anxiously in from dining-room, puts dishes on dining-room table.* TOM *opens door* R.*)*

TOM. Laura?

LAURA. I'm all right. I slipped, but I'm all right. *(Goes up* R. *alley, out of sight.)*

AMANDA *(On fire-escape)*. I tell you if anybody falls down and breaks a leg on those fire-escape steps, the landlord ought to be sued for every cent he——*(Sees* TOM.*)* Who are you? *(Leaves fire-escape landing, crosses to dining-room and returns with bowls, coffee cup, cream, etc. Puts them on small table* R. *of day-bed, crosses to armchair, sits. Counts 3.* MUSIC CUE #9. *As* TOM *reenters* R., listlessly *for his coffee, she turns her back to him, as she sits in armchair. The light on her face with its aged but childish*

What do Tom and Amanda do when Laura falls? What feelings are revealed by their actions?

WORDS FOR EVERYDAY USE:

list • less • ly (list´lis lē) *adv.*, in a disinterested manner

features is cruelly sharp, satirical as a Daumier print.[13] TOM *glances* <u>sheepishly</u> *but sullenly at her averted figure and sits on day-bed next to the food. The coffee is scalding hot, he sips it and gasps and spits it back in the cup. At his gasp,* AMANDA *catches her breath and half turns. Then catches herself and turns away.* TOM *blows on his coffee, glancing side-wise at his mother. She clears her throat.* TOM *clears his. He starts to rise. Sinks back down again, scratches his head, clears his throat again.* AMANDA *coughs.* TOM *raises his cup in both hands to blow on it, his eyes staring over the rim of it at his mother for several moments. Then he slowly sets the cup down and awkwardly and hesitantly rises from day-bed.)*

TOM *(Hoarsely).* I'm sorry, Mother. I'm sorry for all those things I said. I didn't mean it. I apologize.

AMANDA *(Sobbingly).* My devotion has made me a witch and so I make myself hateful to my children!

TOM. No, you don't.

AMANDA. I worry so much, I don't sleep, it makes me nervous!

TOM *(Gently).* I understand that.

AMANDA. You know I've had to put up a solitary battle all these years. But you're my right hand bower! Now don't fail me. Don't fall down.

TOM *(Gently).* I try, Mother.

AMANDA *(With great enthusiasm).* That's all right! You just keep on trying and you're bound to succeed. Why, you're—you're just full of natural <u>endowments</u>! Both my children are—they're very pre-cious children and I've got an awful lot to be thankful for; you just must promise me one thing.

(MUSIC CUE #9 stops.)

TOM. What is it, Mother?

AMANDA. Promise me you're never going to become a drunkard!

TOM. I promise, Mother. I won't ever become a drunkard!

AMANDA. That's what frightened me so, that you'd be drinking! Eat a bowl of Purina.

TOM. Just coffee, Mother.

AMANDA. Shredded Wheat Biscuit?

TOM. No, no, Mother, just coffee.

AMANDA. You can't put in a day's work on an empty stomach. You've got ten minutes—don't gulp! Drinking too-hot liquids makes cancer of the stomach. . . . Put cream in.

TOM. No, thank you.

AMANDA. To cool it.

TOM. No! No, thank you, I want it black.

AMANDA. I know, but it's not good for you. We have to do all that we can to build ourselves up. In these trying times we live in, all that we have to cling to is—each other. . . . That's why it's so important to—Tom, I—I sent out your sister so I could discuss something with you. If you hadn't spoken I would have spoken to you. *(Sits down.)*

---

13. **Daumier print.** Lithograph by Honoré Daumier (1808–1879), artist famed for his caricatures and satires

What has Amanda's life been like? Why does she depend on her son?

WORDS FOR EVERYDAY USE:

sheep • ish • ly (shēp ish lē) *adv.,* in an embarrassed manner

en • dow • ment (en dow'mənt) *n.,* gift of nature; inherent talent

Why is Laura upset?

TOM *(Gently)*. What is it, Mother, that you want to discuss?

AMANDA. Laura! *(TOM puts his cup down slowly.* MUSIC CUE #10.*)*

TOM. Oh.—Laura . . .

AMANDA *(Touching his sleeve)*. You know how Laura is. So quiet but—still water runs deep! She notices things and I think she—broods about them. *(TOM looks up.)* A few days ago I came in and she was crying.

TOM. What about?

AMANDA. You.

TOM. Me?

AMANDA. She has an idea that you're not happy here.

*(*MUSIC CUE #10 *stops.)*

TOM. What gave her that idea?

AMANDA. What gives her any idea? However, you do act strangely. *(TOM slaps cup down on small table.)* I—I'm not criticizing, understand that! I know your ambitions do not lie in the warehouse, that like everybody in the whole wide world—you've had to—make sacrifices, but—Tom—Tom—life's not easy, it calls for—Spartan endurance! There's so many things in my heart that I cannot describe to you! I've never told you but I—loved your father . . .

TOM *(Gently)*. I know that, Mother.

AMANDA. And you—when I see you taking after his ways! Staying out late—and—well, you had been drinking the night you were in that—terrifying condi-

What is hard for Amanda to admit?

tion! Laura says that you hate the apartment and that you go out nights to get away from it! Is that true, Tom?

TOM. No. You say there's so much in your heart that you can't describe to me. That's true of me, too. There's so much in my heart that I can't describe to you! So let's respect each other's—

AMANDA. But why—why, Tom—are you always so restless? Where do you go to, nights?

TOM. I—go to the movies.

AMANDA. Why do you go to the movies so much, Tom?

TOM. I go to the movies because—I like adventure. Adventure is something I don't have much of at work, so I go to the movies.

AMANDA. But, Tom, you go to the movies entirely too much!

TOM. I like a lot of adventure. *(AMANDA looks baffled, then hurt. As the familiar inquisition resumes he becomes hard and impatient again.* AMANDA *slips back into her querulous attitude toward him.)*

AMANDA. Most young men find adventure in their careers.

TOM. Then most young men are not employed in a warehouse.

AMANDA. The world is full of young men employed in warehouses and offices and factories.

TOM. Do all of them find adventure in their careers?

AMANDA. They do or they do without it!

WORDS FOR EVERYDAY USE:

Spar • tan (spart´'n) *adj.*, like the Spartans; warlike, stoical, or disciplined

in • qui • si • tion (in´qwə zish ´ən) *n.*, severe or intensive questioning

quer • u • lous (kwer´yōo ləs) *adj.*, full of complaint; peevish

Not everybody has a craze for adventure.

TOM. Man is by instinct a lover, a hunter, a fighter, and none of those instincts are given much play at the warehouse!

AMANDA. Man is by instinct! Don't quote instinct to me! Instinct is something that people have got away from! It belongs to animals! Christian adults don't want it!

TOM. What do Christian adults want, then, Mother?

AMANDA. Superior things! Things of the mind and the spirit! Only animals have to satisfy instincts! Surely your aims are somewhat higher than theirs! Than monkeys—pigs——

TOM. I reckon they're not.

AMANDA. You're joking. However, that isn't what I wanted to discuss.

TOM *(Rising)*. I haven't much time.

AMANDA *(Pushing his shoulders)*. Sit down.

TOM. You want me to punch in red at the warehouse, Mother?

AMANDA. You have five minutes. I want to talk about Laura.

TOM. All right! What about Laura?

AMANDA. We have to be making some plans and provisions for her. She's older than you, two years, and nothing has happened. She just drifts along doing nothing. It frightens me terribly how she just drifts along.

TOM. I guess she's the type that people call home girls.

AMANDA. There's no such type, and if there is, it's a pity! That is unless the home is hers, with a husband!

TOM. What?

AMANDA *(Crossing* D. R. *to armchair)*. Oh, I can see the handwriting on the wall as plain as I see the nose in front of my face! It's terrifying! More and more you remind me of your father! He was out all *(Sits in armchair)* hours without explanation!—Then left! Good-bye! And me with the bag to hold. I saw that letter you got from the Merchant Marine. I know what you're dreaming of. I'm not standing here blindfolded. Very well, then. Then do it! But not till there's somebody to take your place.

TOM. What do you mean?

AMANDA. I mean that as soon as Laura has got somebody to take care of her, married, a home of her own, independent— why, then you'll be free to go wherever you please, *(Rises, crosses to* TOM.*)* on land, on sea, whichever way the wind blows you! But until that time you've got to look out for your sister. *(Crosses* R. *behind armchair.)* I don't say me because I'm old and don't matter! I say for your sister because she's young and dependent. I put her in business college—a dismal failure! Frightened her so it made her sick at the stomach! I took her over to the Young People's League at the church. Another fiasco. She spoke to nobody, nobody spoke to her. *(Sits armchair.)* Now all she does is fool with those pieces of glass and play those worn-out records. What kind of a life is that for a girl to lead?

TOM. What can I do about it?

Under what circumstances does Amanda say Tom can free himself from the responsibility of supporting his family?

WORDS FOR EVERYDAY USE: **dis • mal** (diz´məl) *adj.,* causing gloom or misery

AMANDA. Overcome selfishness! Self, self, self is all that you ever think of! *(TOM springs up and crosses R. to get his coat and put it on. It is ugly and bulky. He pulls on a cap with earmuffs.)* Where is your muffler? Put your wool muffler on! *(He snatches it angrily from the hook and tosses it around his neck and pulls both ends tight.)* Tom! I haven't said what I had in mind to ask you.

TOM. I'm too late to——

AMANDA *(Catching his arm—very importunately. Then shyly).* Down at the warehouse, aren't there some—nice young men?

TOM. No!

AMANDA. There must be—some . . .

TOM. Mother——*(Gesture.)*

What does Amanda ask Tom to do?

AMANDA. Find out one that's clean-living—doesn't drink and—ask him out for sister!

TOM. What?

AMANDA. For sister! To meet! Get acquainted!

TOM *(Stamping to door R.).* Oh, my go-osh!

AMANDA. Will you? *(He opens door. Imploringly.)* Will you? *(He starts out.)* Will you? Will you, dear? *(TOM exits up alley R. AMANDA is on fire-escape landing.)*

TOM *(Calling back).* Yes!

AMANDA *(Re-entering R. and crossing to phone. MUSIC CUE #11).* Ella Cartwright? Ella, this is Amanda Wingfield. First, first, how's that kidney trouble? Oh, it has? It has come back? Well, you're just a Christian martyr, you're just a Christian martyr. I was noticing in my little red book that your subscription to the "Companion" has run out just when that wonderful new serial by Bessie Mae Harper was starting. It's all about the horsey set on Long Island. Oh, you have? You have read it? Well, how do you think it turns out? Oh, no. Bessie Mae Harper never lets you down. Oh, of course, we have to have complications. You have to have complications—oh, you can't have a story without them—but Bessie Mae Harper always leaves you with such an uplift——What's the matter, Ella? You sound so mad. Oh, because it's seven o'clock in the morning. Oh, Ella, I forgot that you never got up until nine. I forgot that anybody in the world was allowed to sleep as late as that. I can't say any more than I'm sorry, can I? Oh, you will? You're going to take that subscription from me anyhow? Well, bless you, Ella, bless you, bless you, bless you. *(MUSIC CUE #11 faces into MUSIC CUE #11-A, dance music, and continues into next scene. Dim out lights. MUSIC CUE #11-A.)*

Responding to the Selection

Have you ever known someone as talkative and persistent as Amanda? Why do such people tend to get their way? Why is it frustrating to talk to such a person?

WORDS FOR EVERYDAY USE:

im • por • tu • nate • ly (im pôr´chōō nit lē) *adv.,* in an annoyingly urgent or persistent manner

im • plor • ing • ly (im pôr´iŋ le) *adv.,* in a beseeching manner

Reviewing the Selection

RECALLING

1. What does Tom's mother say when she wakes him up in the morning?

2. How is Amanda acting toward Tom at the beginning of this scene? Why?

3. Amanda is afraid that Tom is becoming like someone else. Who is that person?

4. What does Amanda want Tom to delay doing? What specific request does she make of him at the end of the scene?

INTERPRETING

5. How does Tom feel about getting up in the morning and going to work at the warehouse? Why might Tom find his mother's way of waking him up particularly annoying, given the feelings that he has?

6. At the beginning of the scene, we learn that Amanda has decided not to speak to Tom. What happens in the rest of the scene? In what way is such behavior typical of Amanda?

7. What similarities does Amanda see between Tom and her husband? Of what is she afraid?

8. What is Amanda's plan for her family? Why does she need Tom in order to carry out that plan?

SYNTHESIZING

9. Why does Tom go to the movies? What does he want out of life? Where does Amanda suggest that he might find that? Why doesn't Tom agree?

10. What philosophical differences do Amanda and Tom have in their views of human beings? Why is Amanda horrified at Tom's discussion of instincts?

Understanding Literature (Questions for Discussion)

Cliché. A **cliché** is a tired or hackneyed expression such as *quiet as a mouse* or *couch potato.* Identify some of the many clichés with which Amanda's speech is peppered. What does Amanda's use of clichés reveal about her? How does her language differ from that of Tom? of Laura?

ACT ONE, SCENE 6

SCENE: *The same.—Only* R. *alley lighted, with dim light.*

TOM (*Enters down* R. *and stands as before, leaning against grillwork, with cigarette, wearing merchant sailor coat and cap*). Across the alley was the Paradise Dance Hall. Evenings in spring they'd open all the doors and windows and the music would come outside. Sometimes they'd turn out all the lights except for a large glass sphere that hung from the ceiling. It would turn slowly about and filter the dusk with delicate rainbow colors. Then the orchestra would play a waltz or a tango, something that had a slow and sensuous rhythm. The young couples would come outside, to the relative privacy of the alley. You could see them kissing behind ashpits and telephone poles. This was the compensation for lives that passed like mine, without change or adventure. Changes and adventure, however, were <u>imminent</u> this year. They were waiting around the corner for all these dancing kids. Suspended in the mist over Berchtesgaden,[14] caught in the folds of Chamberlain's umbrella. In Spain there was Guernica![15] Here there was only hot swing music and liquor, dance halls, bars, and movies, and sex that hung in the gloom like a chandelier and flooded the world with brief, deceptive rainbows. . . . While these unsuspecting kids danced to "Dear One, The World Is Waiting for the Sunrise." All the world was really waiting for <u>bombardments</u>. (MUSIC #11-A *stops. Dim in dining-room: faint glow.* AMANDA *is seen in dining-room.*)

AMANDA. Tom, where are you?

TOM (*Standing as before*). I came out to smoke. (*Exit* R. *into the wings, where he again changes coats and leaves hat.*)

AMANDA (TOM *re-enters and stands on fire-escape landing, smoking. He opens door for* AMANDA, *who sits on hassock on landing*). Oh, you smoke too much. A pack a day at fifteen cents a pack. How much would that be in a month? Thirty times fifteen? It wouldn't be very much. Well, it would be enough to help towards a night-school course in accounting at the Washington U! Wouldn't that be lovely?

TOM. I'd rather smoke.

AMANDA. I know! That's the tragedy of you. This fire-escape landing is a poor excuse for the porch we used to have. What are you looking at?

TOM. The moon.

AMANDA. Is there a moon this evening?

TOM. It's rising over Garfinkel's Delicatessen.

AMANDA. Oh! So it is! Such a little silver slipper of a moon. Have you made a wish on it?

TOM. Um-mm.

AMANDA. What did you wish?

TOM. That's a secret.

AMANDA. All right, I won't tell you what I wished, either. I can keep a secret, too. I can be just as mysterious as you.

TOM. I bet I can guess what you wished.

AMANDA. Why, is my head transparent?

---

14. **Berchtesgaden.** Town in southern Germany that was destroyed by an Allied air attack in 1945
15. **Guernica.** City in northern Spain that was heavily bombed by the Germans in 1937

WORDS FOR EVERYDAY USE:

im • mi • nent (imʹə nənt) *adj.,* likely to happen without delay

bom • bard • ment (bäm bardʹmənt) *n.,* attack by bombs

TOM. You're not a sphinx.

AMANDA. No, I don't have secrets. I'll tell you what I wished for on the moon. Success and happiness for my precious children. I wish for that whenever there's a moon, and when there isn't a moon, I wish for it, too.

TOM. I thought perhaps you wished for a gentleman caller.

AMANDA. Why do you say that?

TOM. Don't you remember asking me to fetch one?

AMANDA. I remember suggesting that it would be nice for your sister if you brought home some nice young man from the warehouse. I think that I've made that suggestion more than once.

TOM. Yes, you have made it repeatedly.

AMANDA. Well?

TOM. We are going to have one.

AMANDA. *What?*

TOM. A gentleman caller!

AMANDA. You mean you have asked some nice young man to come over? *(Rising from stool, facing* TOM.*)*

TOM. I've asked him to dinner.

AMANDA. You really did?

TOM. I did.

AMANDA. And did he accept?

TOM. He did!

AMANDA. He did?

TOM. He did.

AMANDA. Well, isn't that lovely!

TOM. I thought that you would be pleased.

AMANDA. It's definite, then?

TOM. Oh, very definite.

AMANDA. How soon?

TOM. Pretty soon.

AMANDA. How soon?

TOM. Quite soon.

AMANDA. How soon?

TOM. Very, very soon.

AMANDA. Every time I want to know anything you start going on like that.

TOM. What do you want to know?

AMANDA. Go ahead and guess. Go ahead and guess.

TOM. All right, I'll guess. You want to know when the gentleman caller's coming—he's coming tomorrow.

AMANDA. Tomorrow? Oh, no, I can't do anything about tomorrow. I can't do anything about tomorrow.

TOM. Why not?

AMANDA. That doesn't give me any time.

TOM. Time for what?

AMANDA. Time for preparations. Oh, you should have phoned me the minute you asked him—the minute he accepted!

TOM. You don't have to make any fuss.

AMANDA. Of course I have to make a fuss! I can't have a man coming into a place that's all sloppy. It's got to be thrown together properly. I certainly have to do some fast thinking by tomorrow night, too.

TOM. I don't see why you have to think at all.

AMANDA. That's because you just don't know. *(Enter living-room, crosses to* C. *Dim in living-room.)* You just don't know, that's all. We can't have a gentleman caller coming into a pig-sty ! Now, let's see. Oh, I've got those three pieces of wedding silver left. I'll polish that up. I wonder how that

What does Amanda wish for her children?

How does Amanda feel about Tom's news? In what way does her speech betray this emotion?

old lace tablecloth is holding up all these years? We can't wear anything. We haven't got it. We haven't got anything to wear. We haven't got it. (*Goes back to door* R.)

TOM. Mother! This boy is no one to make a fuss over.

Why is Amanda so excited about this gentleman caller?

AMANDA (*Crossing to* C.). I don't know how you can say that when this is the first gentleman caller your little sister's ever had! I think it's pathetic that that little girl has never had a single gentleman caller! Come on inside! Come on inside!

TOM. What for?

AMANDA. I want to ask you a few things.

TOM (*From doorway* R.). If you're going to make a fuss, I'll call the whole thing off. I'll call the boy up and tell him not to come.

AMANDA. No! You mustn't ever do that. People hate broken engagements. They have no place to go. Come on inside. Come on inside. Will you come inside when I ask you to come inside? Sit down. (*TOM comes into living-room.*)

TOM. Any particular place you want me to sit?

AMANDA. Oh! Sit anywhere. (*TOM sits armchair* R.) Look! What am I going to do about that? (*Looking at day-bed.*) Did you ever see anything look so sad? I know, I'll get a bright piece of cretonne.[16] That won't cost much. And I made payments on a floor lamp. So I'll have that sent out! And I can put a bright cover on the chair. I wish I had time to paper the walls. What's his name?

TOM. His name is O'Connor.

AMANDA. O'Connor—he's Irish and tomorrow's Friday—that means fish. Well, that's all right, I'll make a salmon loaf and some mayonnaise dressing for it. Where did you meet him? (*Crosses to day-bed and sits.*)

TOM. At the warehouse, of course. Where else would I meet him?

AMANDA. Well, I don't know. Does he drink?

TOM. What made you ask me that?

AMANDA. Because your father did.

TOM. Now, don't get started on that!

AMANDA. He drinks, then.

TOM. No, not that I know of.

AMANDA. You have to find out. There's nothing I want less for my daughter than a man who drinks.

TOM. Aren't you being a little bit pre-mature? After all, poor Mr. O'Connor hasn't even appeared on the scene yet.

AMANDA. But he will tomorrow. To meet your sister. And what do I know about his character? (*Rises and crosses to* TOM *who is still in armchair, smooths his hair.*)

TOM (*Submitting grimly*). Now what are you up to?

AMANDA. I always did hate that cowlick. I never could understand why it won't sit down by itself.

---

16. **cretonne.** Heavy, printed cotton used for slipcovers

WORDS FOR EVERYDAY USE: pre • ma • ture (prē′mə to͞or′) *adj.*, too early

TOM. Mother, I want to tell you something and I mean it sincerely right straight from my heart. There's a lot of boys who meet girls which they don't marry!

AMANDA. You know you always had me worried because you could never stick to a subject. *(Crosses to day-bed.)* What I want to know is what's his position at the warehouse?

TOM. He's a shipping clerk.

AMANDA. Oh! Shipping clerk! Well, that's fairly important. That's where you'd be if you had more get-up. How much does he earn? *(Sits on day-bed.)*

TOM. I have no way of knowing that for sure. I judge his salary to be approximately eighty-five dollars a month.

AMANDA. Eighty-five dollars? Well, that's not princely.

TOM. It's twenty dollars more than I make.

AMANDA. I know that. Oh, how well I know that! How well I know that! Eighty-five dollars a month. No. It can't be done. A family man can never get by on eighty-five dollars a month.

TOM. Mother, Mr. O'Connor is not a family man.

AMANDA. Well, he might be some time in the future, mightn't he?

TOM. Oh, I see . . . Plans and provisions.

AMANDA. You are the only young man that I know of who ignores the fact that the future becomes the present, the present the past, and the past turns into everlasting regret if you don't plan for it.

TOM. I will think that over and see what I can make of it!

AMANDA. Don't be <u>supercilious</u> with your mother! Tell me some more about this—What do you call him? Mr. O'Connor, Mr. O'Connor. He must have another name besides Mr.——?

TOM. His full name is James D. O'Connor. The D. is for Delaney.

AMANDA. Delaney? Irish on both sides and he doesn't drink?

TOM *(Rises from armchair).* Shall I call him up and ask him? *(Starts toward phone.)*

AMANDA *(Crossing to phone).* No!

TOM. I'll call him up and tell him you want to know if he drinks. *(Picks up phone.)*

AMANDA *(Taking phone away from him).* No, you can't do that. You have to be <u>discreet</u> about that subject. When I was a girl in Blue Mountain if it was (TOM *sits on* R. *of day-bed*) suspected that a young man was drinking and any girl was receiving his attentions—if any girl *was* receiving his attentions, she'd go to the minister of his church and ask about his character—or her father, if her father was living, then it was his duty to go to the minister of his church and ask about his character, and that's how young girls in Blue Mountain were kept from making tragic mistakes. *(Picture dims in and out.)*

TOM. How come you made such a tragic one?

AMANDA. Oh, I don't know how he did it, but that face fooled everybody. All he had to do was grin and the world was bewitched. *(Behind day-bed, crosses to arm-*

What does Tom try to tell his mother?

Does Amanda listen? What does she do instead?

Why does Amanda say you have to plan for the future?

WORDS FOR EVERYDAY USE:

su • per • cil • i • ous (sōō´pər sil´ē əs) *adj.*, disdainful, contemptuous

dis • creet (di skrēt´) *adj.*, careful about what one says and does

chair.) I don't know of anything more tragic than a young girl just putting herself at the mercy of a handsome appearance, and I hope Mr. O'Connor is not too good-looking.

TOM. As a matter of fact he isn't. His face is covered with freckles and he has a very large nose.

AMANDA. He's not right-down homely?

TOM. No. I wouldn't say right-down—homely—medium homely, I'd say.

AMANDA. Well, if a girl had any sense she'd look for character in a man anyhow.

TOM. That's what I've always said, Mother.

AMANDA. You've always said it—you've always said it! How could you've always said it when you never even thought about it?

TOM. Aw, don't be so suspicious of me.

What warning does Tom give about Laura?

AMANDA. I am. I'm suspicious of every word that comes out of your mouth, when you talk to me, but I want to know about this young man. Is he up and coming?

TOM. Yes. I really do think he goes in for self-improvement.

AMANDA. What makes you think it?

TOM. He goes to night school.

AMANDA. Well, what does he do there at night school?

TOM. He's studying radio engineering and public speaking.

AMANDA. Oh! Public speaking! Oh, that shows, that shows that he intends to be an executive some day—and radio engineering. Well, that's coming . . . huh?

TOM. I think it's here.

AMANDA. Well, those are all very illuminating facts. *(Crosses to back of armchair.)* Facts that every mother should know about any young man calling on her daughter, seriously or not.

TOM. Just one little warning, Mother. I didn't tell him anything about Laura. I didn't let on we had dark <u>ulterior</u> motives. I just said, "How about coming home to dinner some time?" and he said, "Fine," and that was the whole conversation.

AMANDA. I bet it was, too. I tell you, sometimes you can be as eloquent as an oyster. However, when he sees how pretty and sweet that child is, he's going to be, well, he's going to be very glad he was asked over here to have some dinner. *(Sits in armchair.)*

TOM. Mother, just one thing. You won't expect too much of Laura, will you?

AMANDA. I don't know what you mean. *(*TOM *crosses slowly to* AMANDA. *He stands for a moment, looking at her. Then—)*

TOM. Well, Laura seems all those things to you and me because she's ours and we love her. We don't even notice she's crippled any more.

AMANDA. Don't use that word.

TOM. Mother, you have to face the facts; she is, and that's not all.

AMANDA. What do you mean "that's not all"? *(*TOM *kneels by her chair.)*

WORDS FOR EVERYDAY USE: ul • te • ri • or (ul tir´ē ər) *adj.*, further; more remote; undisclosed; concealed

TOM. Mother—you know that Laura is very different from other girls.

AMANDA. Yes, I do know that, and I think that difference is all in her favor, too.

TOM. Not quite all—in the eyes of others—strangers—she's terribly shy. She lives in a world of her own and those things make her seem a little peculiar to people outside the house.

AMANDA. Don't use that word peculiar.

TOM. You have to face the facts.—She is.

AMANDA. I don't know in what way she's peculiar. (MUSIC CUE #12, *till curtain.* TOM *pauses a moment for music, then—*)

TOM. Mother, Laura lives in a world of little glass animals. She plays old phonograph records—and—that's about all——(TOM *rises slowly, goes quietly out the door* R., *leaving it open, and exits slowly up the alley.* AMANDA *rises, goes on to fire-escape landing* R., *looks at moon.*)

AMANDA. Laura! Laura! (LAURA *answers from kitchen* R.)

LAURA. Yes, Mother.

AMANDA. Let those dishes go and come in front! (LAURA *appears with dish towel. Gaily.*) Laura, come here and make a wish on the moon!

LAURA (*Entering from kitchen* R. *and comes down to fire-escape landing*). Moon—moon?

AMANDA. A little silver slipper of a moon. Look over your left shoulder, Laura, and make a wish! (LAURA *looks faintly puzzled as if called out of sleep.* AMANDA *seizes her shoulders and turns her at an angle on the fire-escape landing.*) Now! Now, darling, wish!

LAURA. What shall I wish for, Mother?

AMANDA (*Her voice trembling and her eyes suddenly filling with tears*). Happiness! And just a little bit of good fortune! (*The stage dims out.*)

Who views Laura's predicament and character more honestly? Who views her with blind devotion?

CURTAIN
End of Act One

Responding to the Selection

What emotions is Amanda feeling at the end of the scene? Is anticipating the success of one's endeavors sometimes more exciting than the success itself? Do you find it strange that Amanda is more excited than Laura?

Reviewing the Selection

1. What news does Tom give his mother at the beginning of the scene?

2. What questions does Amanda ask about Jim O'Connor?

▶▶ 3. Why is Amanda excited about Tom's news?

▶▶ 4. What do Amanda's questions about Jim O'Connor reveal about her plans for him? What makes it funny that she is making such plans at this time?

5. Amanda accuses Tom of ignoring "the fact that the future becomes the present, the present the past, and the past . . . everlasting regret if you don't plan for it." In your own words, what is the warning that Amanda gives Tom here?

Understanding Literature (Questions for Discussion)

1. **Symbol.** A **symbol** is a thing that stands for or represents both itself and something else. Explain the symbolic significance of the following elements of act one:
   a. the fire-escape
   b. the gauze curtains
   c. the gentleman caller
   d. the glass menagerie
   e. the name "Blue Roses"
   f. the father's picture
   g. Tom's breaking the glass menagerie
   h. the difficulty that Tom has in getting on his coat
   i. Laura's tripping and falling on her way out to Garfinkle's Delicatessen
   j. Tom's trying unsuccessfully to use a key to open the door
   k. the coffin trick performed by Malvolio the Magician

2. **Character.** A **character** is a person who figures in the action of a literary work. Amanda, Tom, and Laura are all dreamers. Amanda and Tom are alike in that they have dreams for the future. What are those dreams? What does Laura spend all of her time doing? How does Laura's dreaminess differ from Amanda's and Tom's?

3. **Setting.** The **setting** of a literary work is the time and place in which it occurs, together with all the details used to create a sense of a particular time and place. Writers create a setting by various means. In drama, the setting is often revealed by the stage set and the costumes, though it may be revealed through what the characters say about their environs. In its widest sense, setting includes the general social, political, moral, and psychological conditions in which characters find themselves. In part, *The Glass Menagerie* is a play about people's dreams for the future. In keeping with the play's subject, the play takes place in Tom's memory, and the setting itself has a dreamlike quality. What aspects of the setting are dreamlike? Laura herself may be read as a symbol of people's wishes or dreams. She is entirely out of touch with reality, incapable of acting in the world, and extremely fragile. In what sense are dreams also fragile? From what realities are the characters in the play escaping? What must Tom do if he is to confront reality and realize his dreams, rather than simply continuing to escape by going to the movies?

Responding in Writing

Dream Analysis. Throughout the centuries, people have been fascinated by dreams and their interpretation. In the past, many people believed that dreams provided clues about what was going to happen in the future. The father of psychoanalysis, Sigmund Freud, believed that dreams were wish fulfillments in which people's unexpressed desires were expressed symbolically. For example, a person who wanted to change his or her life might dream of rising out of a pool of water, a symbolic rebirth. Today, one popular theory or explanation of dreams is that they are an attempt of the sleeping person's mind to sort out, store, and catalog recent events. Another popular theory is that when a person dreams, stored memories, feelings, and thoughts simply appear at random, and some executive part of the mind tries to piece these random impressions together in a logical way by connecting them and giving them a narrative structure. This theory explains why dreams often seem so sensible when a person is dreaming and yet seem illogical when one is awake and thinking back on the dream.

Choose a dream you have had and write a paragraph interpreting it. Report the dream in detail and then explain what you think the dream might mean, using any combination of the theories about dreaming discussed above.

READER'S JOURNAL

What does being successful mean to you? Does it mean finding a good job and making a great deal of money? Does it mean finding fulfillment in work? in a creative life? in friends and family? Freewrite in your journal about the meaning of success.

READING SKILLS

Read the Language Arts Survey, 4.18, "Reading Actively." Then, based on what you have read in act one, predict what will happen in act two of the play when Laura's gentleman caller comes.

ACT TWO, SCENE 7

SCENE: *The same.*

Inner curtains closed between dining-room and living-room. Interiors of both rooms are dark as at beginning of play. TOM *has on the same jacket and cap as at first. Same dance-hall music as* CUE #1, *fading as* TOM *begins.*

TOM *(Discovered leaning against grill on fire-escape landing, as before, and smoking).* And so the following evening I brought Jim home to dinner. I had known Jim slightly in high school. In high school, Jim was a hero. He had tremendous Irish good nature and vitality with the scrubbed and polished look of white chinaware. He seemed to move in a continual spotlight. He was a star in basketball, captain of the debating club, president of the senior class and the glee club, and he sang the male lead in the annual light opera. He was forever running or bounding, never just walking. He seemed always just at the point of defeating the law of gravity. He was shooting with such <u>velocity</u> through his adolescence that you would just logically expect him to arrive at nothing short of the White House by the time he was thirty. But Jim apparently ran into more <u>interference</u> after his graduation from high school because his speed had definitely slowed. And so, at this particular time in our lives he was holding a job that wasn't much better than mine. He was the only one at the warehouse with whom I was on friendly terms. I was valuable to Jim as someone who could remember his former glory, who had seen him win basketball games and the silver cup in debating. He knew of my secret practice of retiring to a cabinet of the washroom to work on poems whenever business was slack in the warehouse. He called me Shakespeare. And while the other boys in the warehouse regarded me with suspicious hostility, Jim took a humorous attitude toward me. Gradually his attitude began to affect the other boys and their hostility wore off. And so, after a time they began to smile at me too, as people smile at some oddly fashioned dog that

What happened to Jim after high school?

What was Jim like in high school? What did people expect of him?

WORDS FOR EVERYDAY USE:

ve • loc • i • ty (və läs´ə tē) *n.,* quickness or rapidity of motion or action

in • ter • fer • ence (in´ter fir´ens) *n.,* something that comes into collision or opposition

trots across their path at some distance. I knew that Jim and Laura had known each other in high school because I had heard my sister Laura speak admiringly of Jim's voice. I didn't know if Jim would remember her or not. Because in high school Laura had been as <u>unobtrusive</u> as Jim had been astonishing. And, if he did remember Laura, it was not as my sister, for when I asked him home to dinner, he smiled and said, "You know, a funny thing, Shakespeare, I never thought of you as having folks!" Well, he was about to discover that I did . . . (MUSIC CUE #13. TOM *exits* R. *Interior living-room lights dim in.* AMANDA *is sitting on small table* R. *of day-bed sewing on hem on* LAURA'*s dress.* LAURA *stands facing the door* R. AMANDA *has worked like a Turk in preparation for the gentleman caller. The results are astonishing. The new floor lamp with its rose-silk shade is in place,* R. *of living-room next to wall, a colored paper lantern conceals the broken light fixture in the ceiling, chintz[1] covers are on chairs and sofa, a pair of new sofa pillows make their initial appearance.* LAURA *stands in the middle of room with lifted arms while* AMANDA *crouches before her, adjusting the hem of the new dress,* <u>devout</u> *and ritualistic. The dress is colored and designed by memory. The arrangement of* LAURA'*s hair is changed; it is softer and more becoming. A fragile, unearthly prettiness has come out in* LAURA; *she is like a piece of translucent glass touched by light, given a momentary radiance, not actual, not lasting.* AMANDA, *still seated, is sewing* LAURA'*s dress.* LAURA *is standing* R. *of* AMANDA.)

AMANDA. Why are you trembling so, Laura?

LAURA. Mother, you've made me so nervous!

AMANDA. Why, how have I made you nervous?

LAURA. By all this fuss! You make it seem so important.

AMANDA. I don't understand you at all, honey. Every time I try to do anything for you that's the least bit different you just seem to set yourself against it. Now take a look at yourself. (LAURA *starts for door* R.) No, wait! Wait just a minute—I forgot something. (*Picks two powder puffs from day-bed.*)

LAURA. What is it?

AMANDA. A couple of improvements. (*Business with powder puffs.*) When I was a girl we had round little lacy things like that and we called them "Gay Deceivers."

LAURA. I won't wear them!

AMANDA. Of course you'll wear them.

LAURA. Why should I?

AMANDA. Well, to tell you the truth, honey, you're just a little bit flat-chested.

LAURA. You make it seem like we were setting a trap.

AMANDA. We are. All pretty girls are a trap and men expect them to be traps. Now look at yourself in that glass. (LAURA *crosses* R. *Looks at mirror, invisible to audience, which is in darkness up* R. *of* R. *door.*) See? You look just like an angel on a postcard. Isn't that lovely? Now you just wait. I'm going to dress myself up. You're going

---

1. **chintz.** Cotton cloth printed in color with flower designs or other patterns

To what does Laura object? What does her mother say in response about the relationship between men and women? Do you agree with Amanda's statement? Why, or why not?

to be astonished at your mother's appearance. (END OF MUSIC CUE. *End of music cue leads into dance music, which then leads in* MUSIC CUE #14, *a few lines below, at stage direction.* AMANDA *exits through curtains upstage off* L. *in dining-room.* LAURA *looks in mirror for a moment. Removes "Gay Deceivers," hides them under mattress of day-bed. Sits on small table* R. *of day-bed for a moment, goes out to fire-escape landing, listens to dance music, until* AMANDA'S *entrance.* AMANDA, *off.*) I found an old dress in the trunk. But what do you know? I had to do a lot to it but it broke my heart when I had to let it out. Now, Laura, just look at your mother. Oh, no! Laura, come look at me now! (*Enters dining-room* L. *door. Comes down through living-room curtain to living-room* C. MUSIC CUE. #14.)

LAURA   (*Re-enters from fire-escape landing. Sits on* L. *arm of armchair*). Oh, Mother, how lovely! (AMANDA *wears a girlish frock. She carries a bunch of jonquils.*)

AMANDA   (*Standing* C., *holding flowers*). It used to be. It used to be. It had a lot of flowers on it, but they got awful tired so I had to take them all off. I led the cotillion[2] in this dress years ago. I won the cakewalk[3] twice at Sunset Hill, and I wore it to the Governor's ball in Jackson. You should have seen your mother. You should have seen your mother how she just <u>sashayed</u> around (*Crossing around* L. *of day-bed back to* C.) the ballroom, just like that. I had it on the day I met your father. I had malaria fever, too. The change of climate from East Tennessee to the Delta—weakened my resistance. Not enough to be dangerous, just enough to make me restless and giddy. Oh, it was lovely. Invitations poured in from all over. My mother said, "You can't go any place because you have a fever. You have to stay in bed." I said I wouldn't and I took quinine[4] and kept on going and going. Dances every evening and long rides in the country in the afternoon and picnics. That country—that country—so lovely—so lovely in May, all lacy with dogwood and simply flooded with jonquils. My mother said, "You can't bring any more jonquils in this house." I said, "I will," and I kept on bringing them in anyhow. Whenever I saw them I said, "Wait a minute, I see jonquils," and I'd make my gentlemen callers get out of the carriage and help me gather some. To tell you the truth, Laura, it got to be a kind of a joke. "Look out," they'd say, "here comes that girl and we'll have to spend the afternoon picking jonquils." My mother said, "You can't bring any more jonquils in the house, there aren't any more vases to hold them." "That's quite all right," I said, "I can hold some myself." Malaria fever, your father and jonquils. (AMANDA *puts jonquils in* LAURA's *lap and goes out on to fire-escape landing.* MUSIC CUE #14 *stops. Thunder heard.*) I hope they get here before it starts to rain. I gave your brother a little extra change so he and Mr. O'Connor could take the service car home. (LAURA *puts flowers on armchair* R., *and crosses to door* R.)

LAURA.   Mother!

AMANDA.   What's the matter now? (*Re-entering room.*)

What three things are united in Amanda's memory? In what way are her associations bitterly humorous?

Of what does Amanda's dress remind her? Why might she always think back to this time?

---

2. **cotillion.** Formal ball, especially one at which debutants are presented

3. **cakewalk.** Elaborate, strutting dance

4. **quinine.** Bitter medicine used to treat malaria

WORDS FOR EVERYDAY USE: **sa • shay** (sa shā´) *vi.*, move or walk in such a way as to attract attention

LAURA. What did you say his name was?

AMANDA. O'Connor. Why?

LAURA. What is his first name?

AMANDA (*Crosses to armchair* R.). I don't remember—Oh, yes, I do too—it was—Jim! (*Picks up flowers.*)

LAURA. Oh, Mother, not Jim O'Connor!

AMANDA. Yes, that was it, it was Jim! I've never known a Jim that wasn't nice. (*Crosses* L., *behind day-bed, puts flowers in vase.*)

LAURA. Are you sure his name was Jim O'Connor?

AMANDA. Why, sure I'm sure. Why?

LAURA. Is he the one that Tom used to know in high school?

AMANDA. He didn't say so. I think he just got to know him—(*Sits on day-bed.*) at the warehouse.

LAURA. There was a Jim O'Connor we both knew in high school. If that is the one that Tom is bringing home to dinner——Oh, Mother, you'd have to excuse me, I wouldn't come to the table!

AMANDA. What's this now? What sort of silly talk is this?

LAURA. You asked me once if I'd ever liked a boy. Don't you remember I showed you this boy's picture?

AMANDA. You mean the boy in the year-book?

LAURA. Yes, that boy.

AMANDA. Laura, Laura, were you in love with that boy?

LAURA (*Crosses to* R. *of armchair*). I don't know, Mother. All I know is that I couldn't sit at the table if it was him.

AMANDA (*Rises, crosses* L. *and works up* L. *of day-bed*). It won't be him! It isn't the least bit likely. But whether it is or not, you will come to the table—you will not be excused.

LAURA. I'll have to be, Mother.

AMANDA (*Behind day-bed*). I don't intend to humor your silliness, Laura, I've had too much from you and your brother, both. So just sit down and compose yourself till they come. Tom has forgotten his key, so you'll *have* to let them in when they arrive.

LAURA. Oh, Mother—*you* answer the door! (*Sits chair* R.)

AMANDA. How can I when I haven't even finished making the mayonnaise dressing for the salmon?

LAURA. Oh, Mother, please answer the door, don't make me do it! (*Thunder heard off-stage.*)

AMANDA. Honey, do be reasonable! What's all this fuss about—just one gentleman caller—that's all—just one! (*Exits through living-room curtains.* TOM *and* JIM *enter alley* R., *climb fire-escape steps to landing and wait outside of closed door. Hearing them approach,* LAURA *rises with a panicky gesture. She retreats to living-room curtains. The doorbell rings.* LAURA *catches her breath and touches her throat. More thunder heard off-stage.*)

AMANDA (*Off-stage*). Laura, sweetheart, the door!

LAURA. Mother, please, you go to the door! (*Starts for door* R., *then back.*)

AMANDA (*Off-stage, in a fierce whisper*). What is the matter with you, you silly thing? (*Enters through living-room curtains, and stands by day-bed.*)

LAURA. Please you answer it, please.

AMANDA. Why have you chosen this moment to lose your mind? You go to that door.

Why can't Laura sit at the table with Jim O'Connor?

Does Amanda understand why Laura is afraid? What words does she use to describe her daughter's behavior?

LAURA. I can't.

AMANDA. Why can't you?

LAURA. Because I'm sick. (*Crosses to* L. *end of day-bed and sits.*)

AMANDA. You're sick! Am I sick? You and your brother have me puzzled to death. You can never act like normal children. Will you give me one good reason why you should be afraid to open a door? You go to that door. Laura Wingfield, you march straight to that door!

LAURA (*Crosses to door* R.). Yes, Mother.

AMANDA (*Stopping* LAURA). I've got to put courage in you, honey, for living. (*Exits through living-room curtains, and exits* R. *into kitchen.* LAURA *opens door.* TOM *and* JIM *enter.* LAURA *remains hidden in hall behind door.*)

TOM. Laura—(LAURA *crosses* C.) this is Jim. Jim, this is my sister Laura.

JIM. I didn't know that Shakespeare had a sister! How are you, Laura?

LAURA (*Retreating stiff and trembling. Shakes hands*). How—how do you do?

JIM. Well, I'm okay! Your hand's *cold,* Laura! (TOM *puts hats on phone table.*)

LAURA. Yes, well—I've been playing the victrola. . . .

JIM. Must have been playing classical music on it. You ought to play a little hot swing music to warm you up. (LAURA *crosses to phonograph.* TOM *crosses up to* LAURA. LAURA *starts phonograph—looks at* JIM. *Exits through living-room curtains and goes off* L.)

JIM. What's the matter?

TOM. Oh—Laura? Laura is—is terribly shy. (*Crosses and sits on day-bed.*)

JIM (*Crosses down* C.). Shy, huh? Do you know it's unusual to meet a shy girl nowa-

days? I don't believe you ever mentioned you had a sister?

TOM. Well, now you know I have one. You want a piece of the paper?

JIM (*Crosses to* TOM). Uh-huh.

TOM. Comics?

JIM. Comics? Sports! (*Takes paper. Crosses, sits chair* R.) I see that Dizzy Dean is on his bad behavior.

TOM (*Starts to door* R. *Goes out*). Really?

JIM. Yeah. Where are *you* going? (*As* TOM *reaches steps* R. *of fire-escape landing.*)

TOM (*Calling from fire-escape landing*). Out on the terrace to smoke.

JIM (*Rises, leaving newspaper in arm-chair, goes over to turn off victrola. Crosses* R. *Exits to fire-escape landing*). You know, Shakespeare—I'm going to sell you a bill of goods!

TOM. What goods?

JIM. A course I'm taking.

TOM. What course?

JIM. A course in public speaking! You know you and me, we're not the warehouse type.

TOM. Thanks—that's good news. What has public speaking got to do with it?

JIM. It fits you for—executive positions!

TOM. Oh.

JIM. I tell you it's done a helluva lot for me.

TOM. In what respect?

JIM. In all respects. Ask yourself: what's the difference between you and me and the guys in the office down front? Brains?—No!—Ability?—No! Then what? Primarily, it amounts to just one single thing——

TOM. What is that one thing?

What reason does Amanda say she has for forcing Laura to open the door?

Does Tom seem willing to take part in bringing Jim together with his sister?

JIM. Social <u>poise</u>! The ability to square up to somebody and hold your own on any social level!

AMANDA *(Off-stage).* Tom?

TOM. Yes, Mother?

AMANDA. Is that you and Mr. O'Connor?

TOM. Yes, Mother.

AMANDA. Make yourselves comfortable.

TOM. We will.

AMANDA. Ask Mr. O'Connor if he would like to wash his hands?

JIM. No, thanks, ma'am—I took care of that down at the warehouse. Tom?

TOM. Huh?

JIM. Mr. Mendoza was speaking to me about you.

TOM. Favorably?

JIM. What do you think?

TOM. Well——

JIM. You're going to be out of a job if you don't wake up.

TOM. I'm waking up——

JIM. Yeah, but you show no signs.

TOM. The signs are interior. I'm just about to make a change. I'm right at the point of committing myself to a future that doesn't include the warehouse or Mr. Mendoza, or even a night school course in public speaking.

JIM. Now what are you gassing[5] about?

TOM. I'm tired of the movies.

JIM. The movies!

TOM. Yes, movies! Look at them. *(He waves his hands.)* All of those glamorous people—having adventures—hogging it all, gobbling the whole thing up! You know what happens? People go to the *movies* instead of *moving.* Hollywood characters are supposed to have all the adventures for everybody in America, while everybody in America sits in a dark room and watches them having it! Yes, until there's a war. That's when adventure becomes available to the masses! Everyone's dish, not only Gable's![6] Then the people in the dark room come out of the dark room to have some adventures themselves—goody—goody! It's our turn now to go to the South Sea Island—to make a safari—to be exotic, far off! . . . But I'm not patient. I don't want to wait till then. I'm tired of the movies and I'm about to move!

JIM *(Incredulously).* Move?

TOM. Yes.

JIM. When?

TOM. Soon!

JIM. Where? Where?

TOM. I'm starting to boil inside. I know I seem dreamy, but inside—well, I'm boiling! Whenever I pick up a shoe I shudder a little, thinking how short life is and what I am doing!—Whatever that means, I know it doesn't mean shoes—except as something to wear on a traveler's feet! *(Gets card from inside coat pocket.)* Look!

JIM. What?

TOM. I'm a member.

What quality does Jim value? Which characters have this quality? Which characters lack it?

What does Tom see as the problem with movies?

---

5. **gassing.** Talking in an idle or boastful way

6. **Gable's.** Clark Gable (1901–1960), leading star in Hollywood films who often played a rough, adventurous, romantic hero

WORDS FOR EVERYDAY USE:

poise (poiz) *n.,* ease and dignity of manner

in • cred • u • lous • ly (in krej´oo ləs lē) *adv.,* in a doubting or skeptical manner

What has Tom joined? Where has he acquired the money?

JIM *(Reading).* The Union of Merchant Seamen.

TOM. I paid my dues this month, instead of the electric light bill.

JIM. You'll regret it when they turn off the lights.

TOM. I won't be here.

JIM. Yeah, but how about your mother?

To whom does Tom feel that he is similar? What desire makes the two similar?

TOM. I'm like my father. See how he grins? And he's been absent going on sixteen years.

JIM. You're just talking, you drip. How does your mother feel about it?

TOM. Sh! Here comes Mother! Mother's not acquainted with my plans!

AMANDA *(Off-stage).* Tom!

TOM. Yes, Mother?

AMANDA *(Off-stage).* Where are you all?

TOM. On the terrace, Mother.

In what way does Amanda appear before Jim and Tom? Why do the two men react differently to her presence?

AMANDA *(Enters through living-room curtain and stands* C.*).* Why don't you come in? *(They start inside. She advances to them. TOM is distinctly shocked at her appearance. Even JIM blinks a little. He is making his first contact with girlish Southern vivacity and in spite of the night-school course in public speaking is somewhat thrown off the beam[7] by the unexpected outlay of social charm. Certain responses are attempted by JIM but are swept aside by AMANDA's gay laughter and chatter. TOM is embarrassed but after the first shock JIM reacts very warmly. Grins and chuckles, is altogether won over. TOM and JIM come in, leaving door open.)*

TOM. Mother, you look so pretty.

AMANDA. You know, that's the first compliment you ever paid me. I wish you'd look pleasant when you're about to say something pleasant, so I could expect it. Mr. O'Connor? *(JIM crosses to AMANDA.)*

JIM. How do you do?

AMANDA. Well, well, well, so this is Mr. O'Connor? Introduction's entirely unnecessary. I've heard so much about you from my boy. I finally said to him, "Tom, good gracious, why don't you bring this paragon to supper finally? I'd like to meet this nice young man at the warehouse! Instead of just hearing you sing his praises so much?" I don't know why my son is so stand-offish—that's not Southern behavior. Let's sit down. *(TOM closes door, crosses* U. R.*, stands. JIM and AMANDA sit on day-bed, JIM, R., AMANDA L.)* Let's sit down, and I think we could stand a little more air in here. Tom, leave the door open. I felt a nice fresh breeze a moment ago. Where has it gone to? Mmmm, so warm already! And not quite summer, even. We're going to burn up when summer really gets started. However, we're having—we're having a very light supper. I think light things are better fo'—for this time of year. The same as light clothes are. Light clothes and light food are what warm weather calls fo'. You know our blood get so thick during th' winter—it takes a while fo' us to adjust ourselves—when the season changes. . . . It's come so quick this year. I wasn't prepared. All of a sudden—Heavens! Already summer!—I ran to the trunk an'—pulled out this light dress—terribly old!

---

7. **off the beam.** Off-balance or in the wrong direction

WORDS FOR EVERYDAY USE:

vi • vac • i • ty (vī vas´ə tē) *n.*, liveliness of spirit; animation

par • a • gon (par´ə gän´) *n.*, model or pattern of perfection or excellence

Historical almost! But feels so good—so good and cool, why, y' know——

TOM. Mother, how about our supper?

AMANDA *(Rises, crosses* R. *to* TOM). Honey, you go ask sister if supper is ready! You know that sister is in full charge of supper. Tell her you hungry boys are waiting for it. (*TOM exits through curtains and off* L. *AMANDA turns to* JIM.) Have you met Laura?

JIM. Well, she came to the door.

AMANDA. She let you in?

JIM. Yes, ma'am.

AMANDA *(Crossing to armchair and sitting).* She's very pretty.

JIM. Oh, yes ma'am.

AMANDA. It's rare for a girl as sweet an' pretty as Laura to be domestic! But Laura is, thank heavens, not only pretty but also very domestic. I'm not at all. I never was a bit. I never could make a thing but angel-food cake. Well, in the South we had so many servants. Gone, gone, gone. All <u>vestige</u> of gracious living! Gone completely! I wasn't prepared for what the future brought me. All of my gentlemen callers were sons of planters and so of course I assumed that I would be married to one and raise my family on a large piece of land with plenty of servants. But man proposes—and woman accepts the proposal!—To vary that old, old saying a little bit—I married no planter! I married a man who worked for the telephone company!—That gallantly smiling gentleman over there! *(Points to picture.)* A telephone man who—fell in love with long-distance!—Now he travels and I don't even know where!—But what am I going on for about my—<u>tribulations</u>? Tell me yours—I hope you don't have any! Tom?

TOM *(Re-enters through living-room curtains from off* L.). Yes, Mother.

AMANDA. What about that supper?

TOM. Why, supper is on the table. (*Inner curtains between living-room and dining-room open. Lights dim up in dining-room, dim out in living-room.*)

AMANDA. Oh, so it is. *(Rises, crosses up to table* C. *in dining-room and chair* C.) How lovely. Where is Laura?

TOM *(Going to chair* L. *and standing).* Laura is not feeling too well and thinks maybe she'd better not come to the table.

AMANDA. Laura!

LAURA *(Off-stage. Faintly).* Yes, Mother? (*TOM gestures re:* JIM.)

AMANDA. Mr. O'Connor. (*JIM crosses up* L. *to table and to chair* L. *and stands.*)

JIM. Thank you, ma'am.

AMANDA. Laura, we can't say grace till you come to the table.

LAURA *(Enters* U. L., *obviously quite faint, lips trembling, eyes wide and staring. Moves unsteadily toward dining-room table).* Oh, Mother, I'm so sorry. (*TOM catches her as she feels faint. He takes her to day-bed in living-room.*)

AMANDA *(As* LAURA *lies down).* Why, Laura, you are sick, darling! Laura—rest on the sofa. Well! *(To* JIM.) Standing over the hot stove made her ill!—I told her that it was just too warm this evening, but—— *(To* TOM.) Is Laura all right now?

What happens when Laura comes to the table? Why might she apologize to her mother and not the others?

WORDS FOR EVERYDAY USE:

ves • tige (ves´tij) *n.,* trace, mark, or sign of something that once existed but has passed away

trib • u • la • tion (trib´yoo lā´shən) *n.,* great misery or distress

TOM. She's better, Mother. *(Sits chair* L. *in dining-room. Thunder off-stage.)*

AMANDA *(Returning to dining-room and sitting at table, as* JIM *does)*. My goodness, I suppose we're going to have a little rain! Tom, you say grace.

TOM. What?

AMANDA. What do we generally do before we have something to eat? We say grace, don't we?

TOM. For these and all Thy mercies— God's Holy Name be praised. *(Lights dim out.* MUSIC CUE #15.*)*

Responding to the Selection

How do Tom and Jim differ in their goals, their dreams for the future? Which believes in the "American Dream" of material success? Which has a different sort of dream, and what is it? Consider the philosophies of the two young men. Which is more attractive to you? With which do you most agree? Why?

Reviewing the Selection

RECALLING

1. Why doesn't Laura want to come to the table when she learns who the gentleman caller will be?

2. What is Jim's nickname for Tom?

3. What course is Jim taking in night school? Why?

4. What plan does Tom have? What did he pay instead of the electric bill?

INTERPRETING

5. How does Laura feel toward Jim? How do you know?

6. What attitude does Jim have toward Tom's writing? What comment is the playwright making about the role of the artist in a society driven by material success?

7. Why is Jim studying public speaking? What does he hope to do? Why is Tom not interested in taking such a course?

8. According to Tom, what do people in America do instead of living their own lives and having their own adventures? What has Tom decided to do?

SYNTHESIZING

9. Is Jim O'Connor the sort of person whom Amanda would want to have as a suitor for Laura? Why, or why not?

10. Do you believe that Amanda's hopes for Jim and Laura are realistic? Why, or why not? In what ways are Jim and Laura different? Explain.

ACT TWO, SCENE 8

SCENE: *The same. A half-hour later. Dinner is coming to an end in dining-room.*

AMANDA, TOM *and* JIM *sitting at table as at end of last scene. Lights dim up in both rooms, and* MUSIC CUE #15 *ends.*

AMANDA *(Laughing, as* JIM *laughs too).* You know, Mr. O'Connor, I haven't had such a pleasant evening in a very long time.

JIM *(Rises).* Well, Mrs. Wingfield, let me give you a toast. Here's to the old South.

AMANDA. The old South. *(Blackout in both rooms.)*

JIM. Hey, Mr. Light Bulb!

AMANDA. Where was Moses when the lights went out? Do you know the answer to that one, Mr. O'Connor?

JIM. No, ma'am, what's the answer to that one?

AMANDA. Well, I heard one answer, but it wasn't very nice. I thought you might know another one.

JIM. No, ma'am.

AMANDA. It's lucky I put those candles on the table. I just put them on for orna-mentation, but it's nice when they prove useful, too.

JIM. Yes, ma'am.

AMANDA. Now, if one of you gentlemen can provide me with a match we can have some illumination.

JIM *(Lighting candles. Dim in glow for candles).* I can, ma'am.

AMANDA. Thank you.

JIM *(Crosses back to* R. *of dining-room table).* Not at all, ma'am.

AMANDA. I guess it must be a burnt-out fuse. Mr. O'Connor, do you know anything about a burnt-out fuse?

JIM. I know a little about them, ma'am, but where's the fuse box?

AMANDA. Must you know that, too? Well it's in the kitchen. *(*JIM *exits* R. *into kitchen.)* Be careful. It's dark. Don't stumble over anything. *(Sound of crash off-stage.)* Oh, my goodness, wouldn't it be awful if we lost him! Are you all right, Mr. O'Connor?

JIM *(Off-stage).* Yes, ma'am, I'm all right.

AMANDA. You know, electricity is a very mysterious thing. The whole universe is mysterious to me. Wasn't it Benjamin Franklin who tied a key to a kite? I'd like to have seen that—he might have looked mighty silly. Some people say that science clears up all the mysteries for us. In my opinion they just keep on adding more. Haven't you found it yet?

JIM *(Re-enters* R.*).* Yes, ma'am. I found it all right, but them fuses look okay to me. *(Sits as before.)*

AMANDA. Tom.

TOM. Yes, Mother?

AMANDA. That light bill I gave you several days ago. The one I got the notice about?

TOM. Oh—yeah. You mean last month's bill?

AMANDA. You didn't neglect it by any chance?

By the end of the dinner, how do Amanda and Jim get along? Why might they get along so well?

What happens to the lights? Why?

WORDS FOR EVERYDAY USE: **or • na • men • ta • tion** (ôr′na men tā′shen) *n.,* decoration

TOM. Well, I——

AMANDA. You did! I might have known it!

JIM. Oh, maybe Shakespeare wrote a poem on that light bill, Mrs. Wingfield?

AMANDA. Maybe he did, too. I might have known better than to trust him with it! There's such a high price for negligence in this world today.

JIM. Maybe the poem will win a ten-dollar prize.

AMANDA. We'll just have to spend the rest of the evening in the nineteenth century, before Mr. Edison[8] found that Mazda lamp!

JIM. Candle-light is my favorite kind of light.

AMANDA. That shows you're romantic! But that's no excuse for Tom. However, I think it was very nice of them to let us finish our dinner before they plunged us into everlasting darkness. Tom, as a penalty for your carelessness you can help me with the dishes.

JIM (*Rising.* TOM *rises*). Can I be of some help, ma'am?

AMANDA (*Rising*). Oh, no, I couldn't allow that.

JIM. Well, I ought to be good for *something*.

AMANDA. What did I hear?

JIM. I just said, "I ought to be good for something."

What does Amanda suggest that Jim do?

AMANDA. That's what I thought you said. Well, Laura's all by her lonesome out front. Maybe you'd like to keep her company. I can give you this lovely old candelabrum[9] for light. (JIM *takes candles.*) It used to be on the altar at the Church of the Heavenly Rest, but it was melted a little out of shape when the church burnt down. The church was struck by lightning one spring, and Gypsy Jones who was holding a revival meeting in the village, said that the church was struck by lightning because the Episcopalians had started to have card parties right in the church.

JIM. Is that so, ma'am?

AMANDA. I never say anything that isn't so.

JIM. I beg your pardon.

AMANDA (*Pouring wine into glass—hands it to* JIM). I'd like Laura to have a little dandelion wine. Do you think you can hold them both?

JIM. I can try, ma'am.

AMANDA (*Exits* U. R. *into kitchen*). Now, Tom, you get into your apron.

TOM. Yes, Mother. (*Follows* AMANDA. JIM *looks around, puts wine-glass down, takes swig from wine decanter, replaces it with thud, takes wine-glass—enters living-room. Inner curtains close as dining-room dims out.* LAURA *sits up nervously as* JIM *enters. Her speech at first is low and breathless from the almost intolerable strain of being alone with a stranger. In her speeches in this scene, before* JIM's *warmth overcomes her paralyzing shyness,* LAURA's *voice is thin and breathless as though she has just run up a steep flight of stairs.*)

---

8. **Mr. Edison.** American inventor of the incandescent lamp
9. **candelabrum.** Large, branched candleholder

WORDS FOR EVERYDAY USE: in • tol • er • a • ble (in täl´ər ə bəl) *adj.,* too severe, painful, or cruel to be endured

JIM (*Entering holding candelabra with lighted candles in one hand and glass of wine in other, and stands*). How are you feeling now? Any better? (*JIM's attitude is gently humorous. In playing this scene it should be stressed that while the incident is apparently unimportant, it is to LAURA the climax of her secret life.*)

LAURA. Yes, thank you.

JIM (*Gives her glass of wine*). Oh, here, this is for you. It's a little dandelion wine.

LAURA. Thank you.

JIM (*Crosses C.*). Well, drink it—but don't get drunk. (*He laughs heartily.*) Say, where'll I put the candles?

LAURA. Oh, anywhere . . .

JIM. Oh, how about right here on the floor? You got any objections?

LAURA. No.

JIM. I'll spread a newspaper under it to catch the drippings. (*Gets newspaper from armchair. Puts candelabra down on floor C.*) I like to sit on the floor. (*Sits on floor.*) Mind if I do?

LAURA. Oh, no.

JIM. Would you give me a pillow?

LAURA. What?

JIM. A pillow!

LAURA. Oh . . . (*Puts wine-glass on telephone table, hands him pillow, sits L. on day-bed.*)

JIM. How about you? Don't you like to sit on the floor?

LAURA. Oh, yes.

JIM. Well, why don't you?

LAURA. I—will.

JIM. Take a pillow! (*Throws pillow as she sits on floor.*) I can't see you sitting way over there. (*Sits on floor again.*)

LAURA. I can—see you.

JIM. Yeah, but that's not fair. I'm right here in the <u>limelight</u>. (*LAURA moves a little closer to him.*) Good! Now I can see you! Are you comfortable?

LAURA. Yes. Thank you.

JIM. So am I. I'm comfortable as a cow! Say, would you care for a piece of chewing-gum? (*Offers gum.*)

LAURA. No, thank you.

JIM. I think that I will indulge. (*Musingly unwraps it and holds it up.*) Gee, think of the fortune made by the guy that invented the first piece of chewing gum! It's amazing, huh? Do you know that the Wrigley Building is one of the sights of Chicago?—I saw it summer before last at the Century of Progress.[10] Did you take in the Century of Progress?

LAURA. No, I didn't.

JIM. Well, it was a wonderful <u>exposition</u>, believe me. You know what impressed me most? The Hall of Science. Gives you an idea of what the future will be like in America. Oh, it's more wonderful than the present time is! Say, your brother tells me you're shy. Is that right, Laura?

LAURA. I—don't know.

JIM. I judge you to be an old-fashioned type of girl. Oh, I think that's a wonderful type to be. I hope you don't think I'm being too personal—do you?

---

10. **Century of Progress.** World's Fair held in Chicago in 1933

What do Laura's brief responses reveal about her feelings? Is she comfortable? overwhelmed? nervous? annoyed?

What description of Laura does Jim suggest? How does he feel about such a girl?

WORDS FOR EVERYDAY USE:

lime • light (līm līt´) *n.*, prominent or conspicuous position, as if under a spotlight

ex • po • si • tion (eks´pə zish´ən) *n.*, large, public exhibition or show, often international in scope

LAURA. Mr. O'Connor?

JIM. Huh?

LAURA. I believe I *will* take a piece of gum, if you don't mind. (JIM *peels gum— gets on knees, hands it to* LAURA. *She breaks off a tiny piece.* JIM *looks at what remains, puts it in his mouth, and sits again.*) Mr. O'Connor, have you—kept up with your singing?

JIM. Singing? Me?

LAURA. Yes. I remember what a beautiful voice you had.

JIM. You heard me sing?

LAURA. Oh, yes! Very often. . . . I— don't suppose—you remember me—at all?

JIM (*Smiling doubtfully*). You know, as a matter of fact I did have an idea I'd seen you before. Do you know it seemed almost like I was about to remember your name. But the name I was about to remember—wasn't a name! So I stopped myself before I said it.

LAURA. Wasn't it—Blue Roses?

JIM (*Grinning*). Blue Roses! Oh, my gosh, yes—Blue Roses! You know, I didn't connect you with high school somehow or other. But that's where it was, it was high school. Gosh, I didn't even know you were Shakespeare's sister! Gee, I'm sorry.

LAURA. I didn't expect you to.—You barely knew me!

JIM. But, we did have a speaking acquaintance.

LAURA. Yes, we—spoke to each other.

JIM. Say, didn't we have a class in something together?

LAURA. Yes, we did.

JIM. What class was that?

LAURA. It was—singing—chorus!

JIM. Aw!

LAURA. I sat across the aisle from you in the auditorium Mondays, Wednesdays, and Fridays.

JIM. Oh, yeah! I remember now—you're the one who always came in late.

LAURA. Yes, it was so hard for me, getting upstairs. I had that brace on my leg then—it clumped so loud!

JIM. I never heard any clumping.

LAURA (*Wincing at recollection*). To me it sounded like—thunder!

JIM. I never even noticed.

LAURA. Everybody was seated before I came in. I had to walk in front of all those people. My seat was in the back row. I had to go clumping up the aisle with everyone watching!

JIM. Oh, gee, you shouldn't have been self conscious.

LAURA. I know, but I was. It was always such a relief when the singing started.

JIM. I remember now. And I used to call you Blue Roses. How did I ever get started calling you a name like that?

LAURA. I was out of school a little while with pleurosis. When I came back you asked me what was the matter. I said I had pleurosis and you thought I said Blue Roses. So that's what you always called me after that!

JIM. I hope you didn't mind?

What made high school hard for Laura? Did other people notice this difficulty?

What shared memory establishes a connection between Laura and Jim?

WORDS FOR EVERYDAY USE: wince (wins) *vi.,* Shrink or draw back slightly, usually with a grimace, as in pain, embarrassment, or alarm

LAURA. Oh, no—I liked it. You see, I wasn't acquainted with many—people . . .

JIM. Yeah. I remember you sort of stuck by yourself.

LAURA. I never did have much luck at making friends.

JIM. Well, I don't see why you wouldn't.

LAURA. Well, I started out badly.

JIM. You mean being——?

LAURA. Well, yes, it—sort of—stood between me . . .

JIM. You shouldn't have let it!

LAURA. I know, but it did, and I——

JIM. You mean you were shy with people!

LAURA. I tried not to be but never could——

JIM. Overcome it?

LAURA. No, I—never could!

JIM. Yeah. I guess being shy is something you have to work out of kind of gradually.

LAURA. Yes—I guess it——

JIM. Takes time!

LAURA. Yes . . .

JIM. Say, you know something, Laura? *(Rises to sit on day-bed* R.*)* People are not so dreadful when you know them. That's what you have to remember! And everybody has problems, not just you but practically everybody has problems. You think of yourself as being the only one who is disappointed. But just look around you and what do you see—a lot of people just as disappointed as you are. You take me, for instance. Boy, when I left high school I thought I'd be a lot further along at this time than I am now. Say, you remember that wonderful write-up I had in "The Torch"?

LAURA. Yes, I do! *(She gets year-book from under pillow* L. *of day-bed.)*

JIM. Said I was bound to succeed in anything I went into! Holy Jeez! "The Torch"! *(She opens book, shows it to him and sits next to him on day-bed.)*

LAURA. Here you are in "The Pirates of Penzance"!

JIM. "The Pirates"! "Oh, better far to live and die under the brave black flag I fly!" I sang the lead in that operetta.

LAURA. So beautifully!

JIM. Aw . . .

LAURA. Yes, yes—beautifully—beautifully!

JIM. You heard me then, huh?

LAURA. I heard you all three times!

JIM. No!

LAURA. Yes.

JIM. You mean all three performances?

LAURA. Yes!

JIM. What for?

LAURA. I—wanted to ask you to—autograph my program. *(Takes program from book.)*

JIM. Why didn't you ask me?

LAURA. You were always surrounded by your own friends so much that I never had a chance.

JIM. Aw, you should have just come right up and said, "Here is my——"

LAURA. Well, I—thought you might think I was——

JIM. Thought I might think you was—what?

LAURA. Oh——

JIM *(With reflective* relish*)*. Oh! Yeah, I was beleaguered by females in those days.

On what period in their lives—past, present, or future—do Laura and Jim seem to be focused? Do they have the same feelings about this period? Why might Jim be focused on it? Laura?

In what way is Jim disappointed?

WORDS FOR EVERYDAY USE:

rel • ish (rel´ish) *n.*, pleasure; enjoyment

be • lea • guer (bē lē´gər) *vt.*, besiege by encircling

LAURA. You were terribly popular!

JIM. Yeah . . .

LAURA. You had such a—friendly way——

JIM. Oh, I was spoiled in high school.

LAURA. Everybody liked you!

JIM. Including you?

LAURA. I—why, yes, I—I did, too. . . .

JIM. Give me that program, Laura. *(She does so, and he signs it.)* There you are—better later than never!

LAURA. My—what a—surprise!

JIM. My signature's not worth very much right now. But maybe some day—it will increase in value! You know, being disappointed is one thing and being discouraged is something else. Well, I may be disappointed but I am not discouraged. Say, you finished high school?

LAURA. I made bad grades in my final examinations.

JIM. You mean you dropped out?

LAURA *(Rises).* I didn't go back. *(Crosses R. to menagerie.* JIM *lights cigarette still sitting on day-bed.* LAURA *puts year-book under menagerie. Rises, picks up unicorn[11]—small glass object—her back to* JIM. *When she touches unicorn,* MUSIC CUE #16-A.) How is Emily Meisenbach getting along?

JIM. That kraut-head!

LAURA. Why do you call her that?

JIM. Because that's what she was.

LAURA. You're not still—going with her?

JIM. Oh, I never even see her.

LAURA. It said in the Personal section that you were—engaged!

JIM. Uh-huh. I know, but I wasn't impressed by that—propaganda!

LAURA. It wasn't the truth?

JIM. It was only true in Emily's optimistic opinion!

LAURA. Oh . . . *(Turns* R. *of* JIM. JIM *lights a cigarette and leans* <u>indolently</u> *back on his elbows, smiling at* LAURA *with a warmth and charm which lights her inwardly with altar candles. She remains by the glass menagerie table and turns in her hands a piece of glass to cover her tumult.* CUT MUSIC CUE #16-A.)

JIM. What have you done since high school? Huh?

LAURA. What?

JIM. I said what have you done since high school?

LAURA. Nothing much.

JIM. You must have been doing something all this time.

LAURA. Yes.

JIM. Well, then, such as what?

LAURA. I took a business course at business college . . .

JIM. You did? How did that work out?

LAURA *(Turns back to* JIM). Well, not very—well . . . I had to drop out, it gave me—indigestion. . . .

JIM *(Laughs gently).* What are you doing now?

LAURA. I don't do anything—much. . . . Oh, please don't think I sit around doing nothing! My glass collection takes a good

---

11. **unicorn.** According to legend, the mythical unicorn could only be tamed by a young, unmarried woman.

WORDS FOR EVERYDAY USE: **in • do • lent • ly** (inˊdə lənt lē) *adv.,* lazily

deal of time. Glass is something you have to take good care of.

JIM. What did you say—about glass?

LAURA *(She clears her throat and turns away again, acutely shy).* Collection, I said—I have one.

JIM *(Puts out cigarette. Abruptly).* Say! You know what I judge to be the trouble with you? *(Rises from day-bed and crosses R.)* Inferiority complex! You know what that is? That's what they call it when a fellow low-rates himself! Oh, I understand it because I had it, too. Uh-huh! Only my case was not as aggravated as yours seems to be. I had it until I took up public speaking and developed my voice, and learned that I had an aptitude for science. Do you know that until that time I never thought of myself as being outstanding in any way whatsoever!

LAURA. Oh, my!

JIM. Now I've never made a regular study of it—*(Sits armchair R.)* mind you, but I have a friend who says I can analyze people better than doctors that make a profession of it. I don't claim that's necessarily true, but I can sure guess a person's psychology. Excuse me, Laura. *(Takes out gum.)* I always take it out when the flavor is gone. I'll just wrap it in a piece of paper. *(Tears a piece of paper off the newspaper under candelabrum, wraps gum in it, crosses to day-bed, looks to see if LAURA is watching. She isn't. Crosses around day-bed.)* I know how it is when you get it stuck on a shoe. *(Throws gum under day-bed, crosses around L. of day-bed. Crosses R. to LAURA.)* Yep—that's what I judge to be your principal trouble. A lack of confidence in yourself as a person.

Now I'm basing that fact on a number of your remarks and on certain observations I've made. For instance, that clumping you thought was so awful in high school. You say that you dreaded to go upstairs? You see what you did? You dropped out of school, you gave up an education all because of a little clump, which as far as I can see is practically non-existent! Oh, a little physical defect is all you have. It's hardly noticeable even! Magnified a thousand times by your imagination! You know what my strong advice to you is? You've got to think of yourself as *superior* in some way! *(Crosses L. to small table R. of day-bed. Sits. LAURA sits in armchair.)*

LAURA. In what way would I think?

JIM. Why, man alive, Laura! Look around you a little and what do you see? A world full of common people! All of 'em born and all of 'em going to die! Now, which of them has one-tenth of your strong points! Or mine! Or anybody else's for that matter? You see, everybody excels in some one thing. Well—some in many! You take me, for instance. My interest happens to lie in electrodynamics.[12] I'm taking a course in radio engineering at night school, on top of a fairly responsible job at the warehouse. I'm taking that course *and* studying public speaking.

LAURA. Ohhhh. My!

JIM. Because I believe in the future of television! I want to be ready to go right up along with it. *(Rises, crosses R.)* I'm planning to get in on the ground floor. Oh, I've already made the right connections.

---

12. **electrodynamics.** Branch of physics dealing with electric currents and magnetic forces

What problem does Jim say that he and Laura share? Do you believe his assessment of Laura? of himself?

What does Jim really think about himself?

What does Jim do with his gum? What does this action reveal about him?

WORDS FOR EVERYDAY USE:

a • cute • ly (ə kyoot′lē) *adv.*, sharply, painfully, or severely

ap • ti • tude (ap′tə tood′) *n.*, natural tendency or inclination

All that remains now is for the industry itself to get under way—full steam! You know, *knowledge*—ZSZZppp! *Money*—Zzzzzzpp! *POWER*! Wham! That's the cycle democracy is built on! *(Pause.)* I guess you think I think a lot of myself!

LAURA. No—o-o-o, I don't.

JIM *(Kneels at armchair* R.*).* Well, now how about you? Isn't there some one thing that you take more interest in than anything else?

LAURA. Oh—yes . . .

JIM. Well, then, such as what?

LAURA. Well, I do—as I said—have my—glass collection . . . (MUSIC CUE #16-A.)

JIM. Oh, you do. What kind of glass is it?

LAURA *(Takes glass ornament off shelf.).* Little articles of it, ornaments mostly. Most of them are little animals made out of glass, the tiniest little animals in the world. Mother calls them the glass menagerie! Here's an example of one, if you'd like to see it! This is one of the oldest, it's nearly thirteen. *(Hands it to* JIM.*)* Oh, be careful—if you breathe, it breaks! (THE BELL SOLO SHOULD BEGIN HERE. *This is last part of* CUE #16-A *and should play to end of record.)*

JIM. I'd better not take it. I'm pretty clumsy with things.

LAURA. Go on, I trust you with him! *(*JIM *takes horse.)* There—you're holding him gently! Hold him over the light, he loves the light! *(*JIM *holds horse up to light.)* See how the light shines through him?

JIM. It sure does shine!

LAURA. I shouldn't be partial, but he is my favorite one.

JIM. Say, what kind of a thing is this one supposed to be?

LAURA. Haven't you noticed the single horn on his forehead?

JIM. Oh, a unicorn, huh?

LAURA. Mmmm-hmmmmm!

JIM. Unicorns, aren't they extinct in the modern world?

LAURA. I know!

JIM. Poor little fellow must feel kind of lonesome.

LAURA. Well, if he does he doesn't complain about it. He stays on a shelf with some horses that don't have horns and they all seem to get along nicely together.

JIM. They do. Say, where will I put him?

LAURA. Put him on the table. *(*JIM *crosses to small table* R. *of day-bed, puts unicorn on it.)* They all like a change of scenery once in a while!

JIM *(*C.*, facing upstage, stretching arms).* They do. (MUSIC CUE #16-B: *Dance Music.)* Hey! Look how big my shadow is when I stretch.

LAURA *(Crossing to* L. *of day-bed).* Oh, oh, yes—it stretched across the ceiling!

JIM *(Crosses to door* R.*, exits, leaving door open, and stands on fire-escape landing. Sings to music. [Popular record of day for dance-hall.] When* JIM *opens door, music swells).* It's stopped raining. Where does the music come from?

LAURA. From the Paradise Dance Hall across the alley.

JIM *(Re-entering room, closing door* R.*, crosses to* LAURA*).* How about cutting the rug[13] a little, Miss Wingfield? Or is your program filled up? Let me take a look at it. *(Crosses back* C. *Music, in dance hall, goes into a waltz. Business here with imaginary*

---

13. **cutting the rug.** Dancing

Does Laura talk about her glass animals as if they were objects or companions?

Why does Laura give Jim the glass unicorn to hold? How does she feel about the unicorn?

dance-program card.) Oh, say! Every dance is taken! I'll just scratch some of them out. Ahhhh, a waltz! *(Crosses to* LAURA.*)*

LAURA. I—can't dance!

JIM. There you go with that inferiority stuff!

LAURA. I've never danced in my life!

JIM. Come on, try!

LAURA. Oh, but I'd step on you!

JIM. Well, I'm not made out of glass.

LAURA. How—how do we start?

JIM. You hold your arms out a little.

LAURA. Like this?

JIM. A little bit higher. *(Takes* LAURA *in arms.)* That's right. Now don't tighten up, that's the principal thing about it—just relax.

LAURA. It's hard not to.

JIM. Okay.

LAURA. I'm afraid you can't budge me.

JIM *(Dances around* L. *of day-bed slowly).* What do you bet I can't?

LAURA. Goodness, yes, you can!

JIM. Let yourself go, now, Laura, just let yourself go.

LAURA. I'm——

JIM. Come on!

LAURA. Trying!

JIM. Not so stiff now—easy does it!

LAURA. I know, but I'm——!

JIM. Come on! Loosen your backbone a little! *(When they get to up-stage corner of day-bed—so that the audience will not see him lift her—*JIM's *arm tightens around her waist and he swings her around* C. *with her feet off floor about 3 complete turns before they hit the small table* R. *of day-bed. Music swells as* JIM *lifts her.)* There we go! *(*JIM *knocks glass horse off table.* MUSIC FADES.*)*

LAURA. Oh, it doesn't matter——

JIM *(Picks horse up).* We knocked the little glass horse over.

LAURA. Yes.

JIM *(Hands unicorn to* LAURA*).* Is he broken?

LAURA. Now he's just like all the other horses.

JIM. You mean he lost his——?

LAURA. He's lost his horn. It doesn't matter. Maybe it's a blessing in disguise.

JIM. Gee, I bet you'll never forgive me. I bet that was your favorite piece of glass.

LAURA. Oh, I don't have favorites— *(Pause)* much. It's no tragedy. Glass breaks so easily. No matter how careful you are. The traffic jars the shelves and things fall off them.

JIM. Still I'm awfully sorry that I was the cause of it.

LAURA. I'll just imagine he had an operation. The horn was removed to make him feel less—freakish! *(Crosses* L., *sits on small table.)* Now he will feel more at home with the other horses, the ones who don't have horns. . . .

JIM *(Sits on arm of armchair* R., *faces* LAURA*).* I'm glad to see that you have a sense of humor. You know—you're—different than anybody else I know? (MUSIC CUE #17.) Do you mind me telling you that? I mean it. You make me feel sort of—I don't know how to say it! I'm usually pretty good at expressing things, but—this is something I don't know how to say! Did anybody ever tell you that you were pretty? *(Rises, crosses to* LAURA.*)* Well, you are! And in a different way from anyone else. And all the nicer because of the difference. Oh, boy, I wish that you were my sister. I'd teach you to have confidence in yourself. Being different is nothing to

What happens to the unicorn? What does Laura say about her favorite piece being broken? How do you think she really feels?

What does Laura imagine the horn made the unicorn feel? Is this a feeling with which she is familiar?

What does Jim say about Laura? Why is she special?

What does Jim say that hurts Laura? Has he misled her in any way?

What does Laura give Jim? Why does she give this to him? Is this an appropriate gesture? Why, or why not?

Given what has occurred, in what way is Amanda's song ironic?

be ashamed of. Because other people aren't such wonderful people. They're a hundred times one thousand. You're one times one! They walk all over the earth. You just stay here. They're as common as—weeds, but—you, well you're—*Blue Roses!*

LAURA. But blue is—wrong for—roses . . .

JIM. It's right for you!—You're pretty!

LAURA. In what respect am I pretty?

JIM. In all respects—your eyes—your hair. Your hands are pretty! You think I'm saying this because I'm invited to dinner and have to be nice. Oh, I could do that! I could say lots of things without being sincere. But I'm talking to you sincerely. I happened to notice you had this inferiority complex that keeps you from feeling comfortable with people. Somebody ought to build your confidence up—way up! and make you proud instead of shy and turning away and—blushing——(JIM *lifts* LAURA *up on small table on "way up."*) Somebody ought to—(*Lifts her down.*) somebody ought to kiss you, Laura! *(They kiss.* JIM *releases her and turns slowly away, crossing a little* D. R. *Then, quietly, to himself:* As JIM *turns away,* MUSIC ENDS.*)* Gee, I shouldn't have done that—that was way off the beam. (*Gives way* D. R. *Turns to* LAURA. LAURA *sits on small table.*) Would you care for a cigarette? You don't smoke, do you? How about a mint? Peppermint—Life-Saver? My pocket's a regular drug-store. . . . Laura, you know, if I had a sister like you, I'd do the same thing as Tom. I'd bring fellows home to meet you. Maybe I shouldn't be saying this. That may not have been the idea in having me over. But what if it was? There's nothing wrong with that.—The only trouble is that in my case—I'm not in a position to——I can't ask for your number and say

I'll phone. I can't call up next week end—ask for a date. I thought I had better explain the situation in case you—misunderstood and I hurt your feelings . . .

LAURA. (*Faintly*). You—won't—call again?

JIM. (*Crossing to* R. *of day-bed, and sitting*). No, I can't. You see, I've—got strings on me. Laura, I've—been going steady! I go out all the time with a girl named Betty. Oh, she's a nice quiet home girl like you, and Catholic and Irish, and in a great many ways we—get along fine. I met her last summer on a moonlight boat trip up the river to Alton, on the *Majestic*. Well—right away from the start it was—love! Oh, boy, being in love has made a new man of me! The power of love is pretty tremendous! Love is something that—changes the whole world. It happened that Betty's aunt took sick and she got a wire and had to go to Centralia. So naturally when Tom asked me to dinner—naturally I accepted the invitation, not knowing—I mean—not knowing. I wish that you would—say something. (LAURA *gives* JIM *unicorn.*) What are you doing that for? You mean you want me to have him? What for?

LAURA. A—souvenir. (*She crosses* R. *to menagerie.* JIM *rises.*)

AMANDA (*Off-stage*). I'm coming, children. (*She enters into dining-room from kitchen* R.) I thought you'd like some liquid refreshment. (*Puts tray on small table. Lifts a glass.*) Mr. O'Connor, have you heard that song about lemonade? It's "Lemonade, lemonade, Made in the shade and stirred with a spade—And then it's good enough for any old maid!"

JIM. No, ma'am, I never heard it.

AMANDA. Why are you so serious, honey? (*To* LAURA.)

JIM. Well, we were having a serious conversation.

AMANDA. I don't understand modern young people. When I was a girl I was gay about everything.

JIM. You haven't changed a bit, Mrs. Wingfield.

AMANDA. I suppose it's the gaiety of the occasion that has rejuvenated me. Well, here's to the gaiety of the occasion! *(Spills lemonade on dress.)* Oooo! I baptized myself. *(Puts glass on small table R. of day-bed.)* I found some cherries in the kitchen, and I put one in each glass.

JIM. You shouldn't have gone to all that trouble, ma'am.

AMANDA. It was no trouble at all. Didn't you hear us cutting up[14] in the kitchen? I was so outdone with Tom for not bringing you over sooner, but now you've found your way I want you to come all the time—not just once in a while—but all the time. Oh, I think I'll go back in that kitchen. *(Starts to exit U. C.)*

JIM. Oh, no, ma'am, please don't go, ma'am. As a matter of fact, I've got to be going.

AMANDA. Oh, Mr. O'Connor, it's only the shank of the evening![15] (JIM *and* AMANDA *stand* U. C.)

JIM. Well, you know how it is.

AMANDA. You mean you're a young working man and have to keep working-men's hours?

JIM. Yes, ma'am.

AMANDA. Well, we'll let you off early this time, but only on the condition that you stay later next time, much later—— What's the best night for you? Saturday?

JIM. Well, as a matter of fact, I have a couple of time-clocks to punch, Mrs. Wingfield, one in the morning and another one at night!

AMANDA. Oh, isn't that nice, you're so ambitious! You work at night, too?

JIM. No, ma'am, not work but—Betty!

AMANDA *(Crosses* L. *below day-bed).* Betty? Who's Betty?

JIM. Oh, just a girl. The girl I go steady with!

AMANDA. You mean it's serious? *(Crosses* D. L.)

JIM. Oh, yes, ma'am. We're going to be married the second Sunday in June.

AMANDA *(Sits on day-bed).* Tom didn't say anything at all about your going to be married?

JIM. Well, the cat's not out of the bag at the warehouse yet. *(Picks up hat from telephone table.)* You know how they are. They call you Romeo and stuff like that.—It's been a wonderful evening, Mrs. Wingfield. I guess this is what they mean by Southern hospitality.

AMANDA. It was nothing. Nothing at all.

JIM. I hope it don't seem like I'm rushing off. But I promised Betty I'd pick her up at the Wabash depot an' by the time I get my jalopy[16] down there her train'll be in. Some women are pretty upset if you keep them waiting.

AMANDA. Yes, I know all about the tyranny of women! Well, good-bye, Mr. O'Connor. (AMANDA *puts out hand.* JIM *takes it.*) I wish you happiness—and good fortune. You wish him that, too, don't you, Laura?

LAURA. Yes, I do, Mother.

---

14. **cutting up.** Clowning, joking
15. **shank of the evening.** Early part of the evening
16. **jalopy.** Old, ramshackle car

What is Amanda's response when Jim thanks her for her hospitality? Why is this comment appropriate given the evening's outcome?

Q What does Amanda say about Tom?

JIM (*Crosses* L. *to* LAURA). Good-bye, Laura. I'll always treasure that souvenir. And don't you forget the good advice I gave you. So long, Shakespeare! (*Up* C.) Thanks, again, ladies.—Good night! (*He grins and ducks <u>jauntily</u> out* R.)

AMANDA (*Faintly*). Well, well, well. Things have a way of turning out so badly——(LAURA *crosses to phonograph, puts on record.*) I don't believe that I would play the victrola. Well, well—well, our gentleman caller was engaged to be married! Tom!

TOM (*Off*). Yes, Mother?

AMANDA. Come out here. I want to tell you something very funny.

TOM (*Entering through* R. *kitchen door to dining-room and into living-room, through curtains,* D. C.). Has the gentleman caller gotten away already?

AMANDA. The gentleman caller made a very early departure. That was a nice joke you played on us, too!

TOM. How do you mean?

AMANDA. You didn't mention that he was engaged to be married.

TOM. Jim? Engaged?

AMANDA. That's what he just informed us.

TOM. I'll be jiggered! I didn't know.

AMANDA. That seems very peculiar.

TOM. What's peculiar about it?

AMANDA. Didn't you tell me he was your best friend down at the warehouse?

TOM. He is, but how did I know?

AMANDA. It seems very peculiar you didn't know your best friend was engaged to be married!

Q Why is Amanda angry with Tom? Is she more angry with the expense incurred or in the sad situation of both mother and daughter?

TOM. The warehouse is the place where I work, not where I know things about people!

AMANDA. You don't know things anywhere! You live in a dream; you manufacture illusions! (TOM *starts for* R. *door.*) Where are you going? Where are you going? Where are you going?

TOM. I'm going to the movies.

AMANDA (*Rises, crosses up to* TOM). That's right, now that you've had us make such fools of ourselves. The effort, the preparations, all the expense! The new floor lamp, the rug, the clothes for Laura! All for what? To entertain some other girl's fiancé! Go to the movies, go! Don't think about us, a mother deserted, an unmarried sister who's crippled and has no job! Don't let anything interfere with your selfish pleasure! Just go, go, go—to the movies!

TOM. All right, I will, and the more you shout at me about my selfish pleasures, the quicker I'll go, and I won't go to the movies either. (*Gets hat from phone table, slams door* R., *and exits up alley* R.)

AMANDA (*Crosses up to fire-escape landing, yelling*). Go, then! Then go to the moon—you selfish dreamer! (MUSIC CUE #18. INTERIOR LIGHT *dims out. Re-enters living-room, slamming* R. *door.* TOM's *closing speech is timed with the interior <u>pantomime</u>. The interior scene is played as though viewed through soundproof glass, behind outer scrim curtain.* AMANDA, *standing, appears to be making a comforting speech to* LAURA *who is huddled on* R. *side of day-bed. Now that we cannot hear the mother's speech, her silliness is gone and she has dignity and tragic beauty.* LAURA's *hair*

WORDS FOR EVERYDAY USE:

jaun • ti • ly (jônt′ə lē) *adv.,* in a confident, carefree manner

pan • to • mime (pan′tə mīm) *n.,* dramatic presentation without words

hides her face until at the end of the speech she lifts it to smile at her mother. AMANDA'*s gestures are slow and graceful, almost dance-like, as she comforts her daughter.* TOM, *who has meantime put on, as before, the jacket and cap, enters down* R. *from off-stage, and again comes to fire-escape landing, stands as he speaks. Meantime lights are upon* AMANDA *and* LAURA, *but are dim.)*

TOM. I didn't go to the moon. I went much farther. For time is the longest distance between two places. . . . I left Saint Louis. I descended these steps of this fire-escape for the last time and followed, from then on, in my father's footsteps, attempting to find in motion what was lost in space. . . . I travelled around a great deal. The cities swept about me like dead leaves, leaves that were brightly colored but torn away from the branches. I would have stopped, but I was pursued by something. It always came upon me unawares, taking me altogether by surprise. Perhaps it was a familiar bit of music. Perhaps it was only a piece of transparent glass. . . . Perhaps I am walking along a street at night, in some strange city, before I have found companions, and I pass the lighted window of a shop where perfume is sold. The window is filled with pieces of colored glass, tiny transparent bottles in delicate colors, like bits of a shattered rainbow. Then all at once my sister touches my shoulder. I turn around and look into her eyes. . . . Oh, Laura, Laura, I tried to leave you behind me, but I am more faithful than I intended to be! I reach for a cigarette, I cross the street, I run into a movie or a bar. I buy a drink, I speak to the nearest stranger—anything that can blow your candles out!—for nowadays the world is lit by lightning! Blow out your candles, Laura . . . (LAURA *blows out candles still burning in candelabrum and the whole interior is blacked out.)* And so—good-bye! *(Exits up alley* R. *Music continues to the end.)* ∎

What does Tom say about his sister? What image does he use to describe her?

CURTAIN

END OF PLAY

Responding to the Selection

If you had been Tom, would you have left? Why, or why not?

Reviewing the Selection

1. What happens to the lights in the apartment? Why?

2. What does Amanda ask Jim to do while she and Tom take care of the dishes?

3. What source of illumination is used by Jim and Laura during their scene together?

4. What figurine does Laura show to Jim? What is special about this figurine? What does Jim reveal about himself after kissing Laura and dancing with her? What happens to the figurine?

5. How does being plunged into darkness affect the final scene of the play? What situation is thereby created for Jim and Laura? What might this darkness represent?

6. Why does Amanda want to leave Jim and Laura alone together? In what sense is this "apparently unimportant" event the climax of Laura's "secret life"?

7. What is special about the candelabrum? With whom is the candelabrum associated? How is this candelabrum related to Tom's comments at the very end of the play?

8. With whom is the figurine associated? What do this person and the figurine have in common? How is the breaking of the figurine related to the breaking of Laura's heart and of her dreams?

9. What is an inferiority complex? Who, according to Jim, has one? What advice does Jim give about overcoming an inferiority complex? Does his advice seem realistic to you? Why, or why not?

10. Why does Tom leave? Years afterward, how does he feel about leaving? What continues to haunt him?

Understanding Literature (Questions for Discussion)

1. **Theme.** A **theme** is a central idea in a literary work. Jim, who is taking night classes and who wishes to become an executive, epitomizes those people who aspire to a dream of material success. What sort of person is Jim? Would you describe him as optimistic or pessimistic? What indications does the play give that Jim is shallow and egotistical? Jim says, "You know, *knowledge*—ZSZZppp! *Money*—Zzzzzzpp! *POWER!* Wham! That's the cycle democracy is built on!" Do you agree with him? Why, or why not? What has happened to the old, gracious way of life that Amanda remembers? At

the end of the play, Tom says, "I speak to the nearest stranger—anything that can blow your [Laura's] candles out!—for nowadays the world is lit by lightning!" How is Tom's phrase "lit by lightning" related to Jim's statements about television and electricity? Is someone like Laura suited to life in the modern world? Why not? What commentary is Williams making about modern urban life by drawing this comparison?

2. A **symbol** is a thing that stands for or represents both itself and something else. Explain the symbolic significance of the following elements of act 2:

   a. Amanda's jonquils

   b. the movies

   c. the partially melted candelabrum

   d. the glass unicorn

   e. Jim's giant shadow

   f. the bits of colored glass that Tom sees in shop windows

   g. the candles referred to by Tom at the end of the play

   h. the lightning that now lights the world, referred to by Tom at the end of the play

Responding in Writing

1. **Diary Entry.** According to the sociologist Erik Erickson, young people go through a stage that can be called an identity crisis in which they attempt to break away from childhood and establish their own adult identities. This period in a person's life is often characterized by turmoil and uncertainty and sometimes involves conflicts with parents. In this play, Tom experiences an identity crisis and decides to break away for good. Write a diary entry from the point of view of Tom explaining how he views himself and why he feels he must break away in order to be the person that he wants to be.

2. **Critical Analysis.** Write a critical analysis on one of the following topics related to the play:

   a. What view of artists and their relationship to the culture around them is presented in *The Glass Menagerie?* What aspects of the character Tom are in direct conflict with the values of the society in which he lives? Why might a person who has the values and experiences that Tom has be driven to write?

   b. How do the dreams of the various characters in this play differ? What dreams do Tom, Amanda, and Jim have? Which of these dreams is presented most sympathetically in the play? Which are treated unsympathetically?

   c. How does Williams use symbolism in the play to characterize Laura? What symbols are related to her, and what do these symbols mean?

d. What commentary on modern urban life is made by this play? How is the modern world contrasted with the world that Amanda remembers? What role does the artist, Tom, play in offering a critique of that world?

e. What is Expressionism? What elements of *The Glass Menagerie* make it an Expressionist play?

f. What is the central conflict in *The Glass Menagerie?* How is that conflict introduced, developed, and resolved? What remains unresolved at the end of the play?

PROJECTS

1. **Acting.** With other students in your class, stage a scene from *The Glass Menagerie* for other students in the class.

2. **Film Criticism.** Find a film version of *The Glass Menagerie* at a video store or at a library and view it with your class. After the viewing, discuss the film. Consider these questions:

   a. Is the film version true to the play? What differences, if any, exist in the film version and in the script that you have read? Do these differences make the play better or worse? Why?

   b. Which are the best performances in the film? Which are the worst? Why?

   c. What aspects of the play are emphasized in the film?

   d. Does the film live up to the playwright's expressed intention of creating a "memory play"? Do its scenes have the dreamlike quality described in the playwright's stage directions? If so, how are these effects achieved? If not, what might the director and set designers have done to give the film such a quality?

UNIT REVIEW

Modern Drama

VOCABULARY FROM THE SELECTION

acutely, 731
aghast, 698
aptitude, 731
beleaguer, 729
bombardment, 708
cater, 696
conglomeration, 684
cultivate, 693
czar, 698
devout, 717
discreet, 711
dismal, 705
emissary, 686
endowment, 703

exposition, 727
fiasco, 695
imminent, 708
implacable, 684
imploringly, 706
importunately, 706
incredulously, 721
indolently, 730
induct, 691
ineluctably, 685
inquisition, 704
interference, 716
interfused, 684
intolerable, 726
jauntily, 736

limelight, 727
listlessly, 702
mastication, 686
matriculate, 685
menagerie, 689
motley, 700
ornamentation, 725
pantomime, 736
paragon, 722
pinion, 698
poise, 721
premature, 710
prominent, 688
querulous, 704
relish, 729

resume, 687
sashay, 718
sheepishly, 703
Spartan, 704
sublimation, 695
supercilious, 711
symptomatic, 684
tribulation, 723
ulterior, 712
unobtrusive, 717
velocity, 716
vestige, 723
vivacity, 722
wince, 728

LITERARY TERMS

archetype, 699
character, 690, 714
cliché, 707
conflict, 699

Expressionism, 682, 690
irony, 694
metaphor, 690
setting, 715

Southern Gothic, 682
stage directions, 689
symbol, 699, 701, 714, 739
theme, 738

SYNTHESIS: QUESTIONS FOR WRITING, RESEARCH, OR DISCUSSION

1. In *The Glass Menagerie,* each character in the Wingfield family faces a struggle. Identify each character's conflict and whether it is primarily internal or external. In what ways does each character face the challenge of balancing personal desires with familial responsibilities?

2. *The Glass Menagerie* is an example of Expressionist drama. In such drama, literary and dramatic elements such as the set design and symbolism are often heightened or exaggerated. What elements of this setting are exaggerated and unrealistic? Why? What symbolism does Williams use and for what purposes?

LANGUAGE LAB   PROOFREADING FOR SPELLING ERRORS

After checking for other errors in your writing, you should read it carefully for errors in spelling. If you come across any words that you are not completely sure about, check them in a dictionary.

LANGUAGE ARTS SURVEY

For additional help, see the Language Arts Survey, 2.134–2.136.

COMMON SPELLING ERRORS

Forming Plurals

Add *es* to nouns ending in *o* preceded by a consonant and to nouns ending in *s, x, z, ch,* or *sh.*

    EXAMPLES: *potatoes, vetoes, tomatoes, dresses, boxes, splashes*

Add *s* to most musical terms ending in *o.*

    EXAMPLES: *solos, concertos, pianos*

Add *s* to nouns ending in *y* preceded by a vowel.

    EXAMPLES: *Mondays, keys, boys, turkeys*

In nouns ending in *y* preceded by a consonant, change the *y* to *i* and add *es.*

    EXAMPLES: *theories, stories, flies*

Remember irregular plurals of certain words.

    EXAMPLES: *oxen, feet, men, mice*

Form the plural of a compound noun consisting of a noun and a modifier by making the noun component plural.

    EXAMPLES: *mothers-in-law, attorneys-at-law*

Adding Prefixes

A **prefix** is a letter or a group of letters added to the beginning of a word to change its meaning. When adding a prefix to a word, do not change the word itself.

    EXAMPLES: super + highway = superhighway
                      re + crystallize = recrystallize
                      un + founded = unfounded

Adding Suffixes

A **suffix** is a letter or group of letters added to the end of a word to change its meaning. The spelling of most words is not changed when the suffix *-ness* or *-ly* is added.

    EXAMPLES: high + ness = highness
                      high + ly = highly

If a word has more than one syllable and ends in *y,* change the *y* to *i* before adding *-ly* or *-ness.*

    EXAMPLES: easy + ly = easily
                      easy + ness = easiness

In most cases of words ending in a final silent *e,* drop the *e* when adding a suffix beginning with a vowel, and keep the *e* when adding a suffix beginning with a consonant.

    EXAMPLES: live + able = liva**ble**
                      strange + er = strang**er**
                      hate + ful = hate**ful**
                      taste + less = tast**eless**

Exercise A Using Spelling Rules

In the following sentences, make all the italicized words plural, and add prefixes or suffixes to the underlined words. Use the spelling rules and refer to a dictionary if you are unsure of the correct spelling.

1. Of the many <u>wonder</u> (ful) *play* that Thornton Wilder wrote, he is most <u>fame</u> (ous) for one.

2. Wilder won <u>great</u> (ly) deserved Pulitzer *Prize* for <u>imagine</u> (ative) writing.

3. The stage *direction* indicate that the set should be decorated <u>sparing</u> (ly), without any <u>scene</u> (ry).

4. The play offers a lighting designer many *opportunity* to use <u>experiment</u> (al) lighting methods.

5. Emily speaks <u>moving</u> (ly) of her *memory* of the man and woman whom she knew in the town.

Exercise B Proofreading for Spelling Errors

Read the following paragraph carefully and correct any spelling errors you find. If you are uncertain about any words, refer to a dictionary.

Thornton Wilder had an inter-national education, experiencing the dramatickally different societys of China and the United States during his youth. He had many literary success' during his lifetime; one of his noveles and two of his playes won Pulitzer Prizes'. He also enjoyed remarkble success as a creative writing instructer at the University of Chicago, engaging his students' with his fascinateing lecturs. As he did with *Our Town,* Wilder structured his play *The Skin of Our Teeth* loosly, allowing the characters to speak directlee to the audience. The play addresses morality through satireic and humorrous elements, using many of the unnusual theatriccal technique's that made *Our Town* so succesful.

Incantation. Charles Sheeler, 1946. Oil on canvas, 61.0 x 50.8 (24 x 20).
The Brooklyn Museum, 49.67. John B. and Ella C. Woodward Memorial Funds

An essayist is a lucky person who has found
a way to discourse without being interrupted.

—Charles Poore

"Newsreel LXVIII"
from *The Big Money*,
the third volume in the trilogy *U.S.A.*
by John Dos Passos

ABOUT THE AUTHOR

John Dos Passos (1896–1970) was born in Chicago and educated at Harvard University. After graduating from college, he went to Europe and served in World War I as an ambulance driver and a medic. His wartime experiences provided the basis of *One Man's Initiation: 1917* (1919) and *Three Soldiers* (1921). His first great novel, *Manhattan Transfer* (1925), was written using the technique that would become Dos Passos's trademark and his major contribution to the form of the novel. In *Manhattan Transfer* and in his three-volume *U.S.A.* (1938), Dos Passos attempted to create epic portraits of American life by telling many interrelated or parallel stories. *U.S.A.*, which consisted of *The 42nd Parallel, 1919,* and *The Big Money*, was Dos Passos's major contribution to Modernism, the twentieth-century artistic movement characterized by experiments in form, impersonality, and extensive use of allusion. In the three *U.S.A.* volumes, Dos Passos included not only stories of many characters' lives but also biographies of famous Americans such as Andrew Carnegie, personal commentaries called "The Camera Eye," and collages of materials from popular culture that he called "newsreels." The total effect was to create an overall portrait of the country in the early part of this century. In addition to his novels, Dos Passos wrote poetry, history, biographies of famous Americans, and autobiographical works.

ABOUT THE SELECTION

The Big Money is the third volume in John Dos Passos's *U.S.A.* trilogy. As an experiment in providing context for the stories in the volume, Dos Passos created a new fictional form, the newsreel, modeled on the newsreels that, prior to the introduction of television, were shown before films in movie houses. Dos Passos's newsreels were collages, reminiscent of the work of such Modernist painters as Picasso and Braque. They contained bits and pieces of the popular culture of the day, including headlines, advertising slogans, jingles, bits of popular song, common sayings of the time, and excerpts from conversations and speeches. "**Newsreel LXVIII**" focuses on issues related to the Great Depression of the 1930s, a time when millions of Americans were without work and facing severe economic hardship. At the time, strong and sometimes violent conflicts arose between those who felt that government should help and those who felt that it should not.

READER'S JOURNAL

People today are deluged with information, much of it trivial. Carry a notebook with you for a day. Jot down an assortment of words that you encounter—headlines, lyrics of songs, phrases from cereal boxes, announcements over the school P. A. system, slogans from billboards, phrases from television or the movies, and so on. Then, compare your list with lists made by your classmates. What do these lists tell you about the culture in which you live? What are its preoccupations? its values? its goals? Write about these questions in your journal.

READING SKILLS

"Newsreel LXVIII" is a challenging text without traditional narrative structure. As such, it may require careful and repeated readings. Refer to the Language Arts Survey, 4.16, "Reading Rates," and 4.18, "Reading Actively," for suggestions on how to approach the text.

FROM *THE BIG MONEY*

"Newsreel LXVIII"

JOHN DOS PASSOS

WALL STREET STUNNED

*This is not Thirtyeight, but it's old
    Ninetyseven
You must put her in Center on time*[1]

MARKET SURE TO RECOVER FROM SLUMP

DECLINE IN CONTRACTS

POLICE TURN MACHINE GUNS ON
COLORADO MINE STRIKERS KILL 5 WOUND 40

sympathizers appeared on the scene just as thousands of office workers were pouring out of the buildings at the lunch hour. As they raised their <u>placard</u> high and started an <u>indefinite</u> march from one side to the other, they were jeered and hooted not only by the office workers but also by workmen on a building under construction

NEW METHODS OF SELLING SEEN

RESCUE CREWS TRY TO UPEND
ILL-FATED CRAFT
WHILE WAITING FOR <u>PONTOONS</u>

*He looked 'round an' said to his black greasy
    fireman
Jus' shovel in a little more coal
And when we cross that White Oak Moun-
    tain
You can watch your Ninety-seven roll*

I find your column interesting and need advice. I have saved four thousand dollars

---

1. **This is not . . . on time.** The allusion is to the "old Ninetyseven" train, which was wrecked and became a subject for popular railroad ballads. One recording of such a railroad ballad sold over a million copies in the 1920s and was one of the earliest pop singles.

Who jeers and hoots at the sympathizers?

WORDS FOR EVERYDAY USE:

plac • ard (plak´ärd) *n.,* notice for display in a public place; sign

in • def • i • nite (in def´ə nit) *adj.,* having no exact limits

pon • toon (pän tōōn´) *n.,* flat-bottomed boat; floating object used for support

which I want to invest for a better income.
Do you think I might buy stocks?

POLICE KILLER FLICKS CIGARETTE AS HE
GOES TREMBLING TO DOOM

PLAY AGENCIES IN RING OF SLAVE GIRL
MARTS

MAKER OF LOVE <u>DISBARRED</u> AS LAWYER

Oh the right wing clothesmakers
And the Socialist fakers
They make by the workers . . .
Double cross

They preach Social-ism
But practice Fasc-ism
To keep capitalism
By the boss[2]

MOSCOW CONGRESS OUSTS OPPOSITION

It's a mighty rough road from Lynchburg to
Danville
An' a line on a three mile grade
It was on that grade he lost his average
An' you see what a jump he made

MILL THUGS IN MURDER RAID

here is the most dangerous example of
how at the decisive moment the bourgeois
<u>ideology</u> liquidates class <u>solidarity</u> and
turns a friend of the workingclass of yesterday into a most miserable <u>propagandist</u>
for imperialism[3] today

RED[4] PICKETS FINED FOR PROTEST HERE

We leave our home in the morning
We kiss our children goodbye

OFFICIALS STILL HOPE FOR
RESCUE OF MEN

He was goin' downgrade makin' ninety
miles an hour

What two
opinions of
economics are
juxtaposed?

When his whistle broke into a scream
He was found in the wreck with his hand on
the throttle
An' was scalded to death with the steam

RADICALS FIGHT WITH CHAIRS
AT UNITY MEETING

PATROLMEN PROTECT REDS

U.S. CHAMBER OF COMMERCE
URGES CONFIDENCE

REAL VALUES UNHARMED

While we slave for the bosses
Our children scream an' cry
But when we draw our money
Our grocery bills to pay

PRESIDENT SEES PROSPERITY NEAR

Not a cent to spend for clothing
Not a cent to lay away

STEAMROLLER IN ACTION
AGAINST MILITANTS

MINERS BATTLE SCABS[5]

But we cannot buy for our children
Our wages are too low
Now listen to me you workers
Both you women and men
Let us win for them the victory
I'm sure it ain't no sin

---

2. **Oh the . . . By the boss.** Socialist labor-union
protest song that is interspersed throughout the work
3. **imperialism.** Policy or practice of seeking to domi-
nate the economic or political affairs of underdeveloped
areas or weaker countries
4. **red.** Political radical or reactionary, especially a communist
5. **scab.** Derogatory term for a worker who refuses to
join a union, or who works for lower wages or under different conditions than those accepted by the union; worker
who refuses to strike, or who takes the place of a striking
worker

WORDS FOR
EVERYDAY USE:

dis • bar (dis bär´) *vt.*, deprive (a lawyer) of the
right to practice law
i • de • ol • o • gy (ī´dē äl´ə gē) *n.*, doctrine,
opinion, or way of thinking

sol • i • dar • i • ty (säl´ə dar´ə tē) *n.*, combination or agreement of all elements or individuals
prop • a • gan • dist (präp´ə gan´dist) *n.*, one
who spreads ideas for a particular cause

the President declared it was impossible to view the increased advantages for the many without smiling at those who a short time ago expressed so much fear lest our country might come under the control of a few individuals of great wealth.

HAPPY CROWDS THRONG CEREMONY

on a tiny island nestling like a green jewel in the lake that mirrors the singing tower, the President today participated in the dedication of a bird sanctuary and its pealing carillon, fulfilling the dream of an immigrant boy

The Camera Eye (51)

at the head of the valley in the dark of the hills on the broken floor of a lurched-over[7] cabin a man halfsits halflies propped up by an old woman two wrinkled girls that might be young   chunks of coal flare in the hearth flicker in his face white and sagging as dough   blacken the cavedin mouth the taut throat the belly swelled enormous with the wound he got working on the minetipple[8]

the barefoot girl brings him a tincup of water   the woman wipes sweat off his streaming face with a dirty denim sleeve the firelight flares in his eyes stretched big with fever in the women's scared eyes and in the blanched faces of the foreigners

without help in the valley hemmed by dark strike-silent hills the man will die (my father died we know what it is like to see a man die) the women will lay him out on the rickety cot the miners will bury him

in the jail it's light too hot the steamheat hisses we talk through the greenpainted iron bars to a tall white mustachioed old man some smiling miners in shirtsleeves a boy   faces white from mining have already the tallowy look of jailfaces

foreigners what can we say to the dead? foreigners what can we say to the jailed? the representative of the political party talks fast through the bars join up with us and no other union we'll send you tobacco candy solidarity our lawyers will write briefs speakers will shout your names at meetings they'll carry your names on cardboard on picketlines   the men in jail shrug their shoulders smile thinly our eyes look in their eyes through the bars

what can I say?   (in another continent I have seen the faces looking out through the barred basement windows behind the ragged sentry's boots I have seen before day the straggling footsore prisoners herded through the streets limping between bayonets   heard the volley

I have seen the dead lying out in those distant deeper valleys)   what can we say to the jailed?

in the law's office we stand against the wall the law is a big man with eyes angry in a big pumpkinface   who sits and stares at us meddling foreigners through the door the deputies crane with their guns   they stand guard at the mines

What does the party representative say the party will do for the prisoners?

How does the imagery in this passage, or "clip," compare with the imagery in the rest of the newsreel? Explain.

Who is "the law"?

---

6. **carillon . . . singing tower.** *Carillon*—set of stationary bells, each producing one tone of the chromatic scale; *singing tower*—the Spring Tower erected in Florida; President Calvin Coolidge spoke at the dedication of the tower in 1929.

7. **lurchedover.** Dos Passos has run the words *lurched* and *over* together. The selection contains several more run-together words.

8. **minetipple.** Equipment that tips cars in a coal mine to unload the coal

---

they blockade the miners' soup-kitchens they've cut off the road up the valley   the hiredmen with guns stand ready to shoot (they have made us foreigners in the land where we were born they are the conquering army that has filtered into the country unnoticed they have taken the hilltops by stealth they levy toll they stand at the minehead   they stand at the polls   they stand by when the bailiffs carry the furniture of the family evicted from the city tenement out on the sidewalk they are there when the bankers foreclose[9] on a farm they are ambushed and ready to shoot down the strikers marching behind the flag up the switchback road to the mine   those that the guns spare they jail)

the law stares across the desk out of

angry eyes his face reddens in splotches like a gobbler's neck with the strut of the power of submachine guns sawedoffshotguns teargas and vomitinggas the power that can feed you or leave you to starve

sits easy at his desk his back is covered he feels strong behind him he feels the prosecutingattorney the judge an owner himself the political boss the minesuperintendent the board of directors   the president of the utility the manipulator of the holdingcompany

    he lifts his hand towards the telephone
    the deputies crowd in the door
    we have only words against   ■

---

9. **foreclose.** Deprive a mortgagor of the right to redeem a mortgage through a legal procedure in which satisfaction may be obtained from the proceeds of a forced sale of the property

What powers does "the law" have? Who supports "the law"?

Responding to the Selection

Do you enjoy literary works that employ nontraditional structures? Did you find "Newsreel LXVIII" interesting? Why, or why not? Which parts were easy to understand? Which were not so easy? Why?

Reviewing the Selection

RECALLING

1. How were sympathizers greeted as they started a march outside an office building?

2. What events led to the death of the train operator?

3. What did the workers say they wanted for their families?

4. What issues are raised throughout "Newsreel LXVIII"?

INTERPRETING

5. Why was there tension between people who were protesting conditions and others who tolerated them?

6. How did the train operator's death symbolize what was happening at the time to other American workers?

7. Why couldn't workers buy what their families needed?

8. What conflict in American society did Dos Passos present in "Newsreel LXVIII"?

9. How do the many elements in "Newsreel LXVIII" contribute to the selection's overall point?

10. What makes the newsreel structure suitable for presenting a portrait of life at a particular time and in a particular place?

Understanding Literature (Questions for Discussion)

Collage. In literature, a **collage** is a work that incorporates or brings together an odd assortment of materials, such as allusions, quotations, bits of song, dialogue, foreign words, mythical or folkloric elements, headlines, and pictures or other graphic devices. John Dos Passos used collage as a way to capture a moment of history. List the kinds of materials that make up the collage that is "Newsreel LXVIII."

Responding in Writing

A Moment in Your Life. Using the collage approach, create an impression of a particular time in your life. Pick any time you like and incorporate as many different types of materials as you wish. Try to follow the approach used in "Newsreel LXVIII." Do research in the library to gather materials for your collage. Try to use as wide a variety of materials as possible. Refer to the Language Arts Survey, 4.20–4.28, for information on possible sources of information.

Language Lab

Apostrophes. Read the Language Arts Survey, 2.102, "Apostrophes." Then rewrite the sentences below to correct errors in the use of apostrophes.

1. John Dos Passos *U.S.A.* depicts a moment in Americas history.

2. In each of his newsreel's, Dos Passos was able to capture a moment, including it's vivid contradictions.

3. Dos Passoss vision was molded by his wartime experiences and by the Great Depression.

4. Were fortunate to have been born after the Great Depression, arent we?

5. Todays society is no less troubled, despite it's many advances.

"The Night the Bed Fell"
by James Thurber

ABOUT THE AUTHOR

James Thurber (1894–1961), born in Columbus, Ohio, lost an eye in a childhood accident and had impaired vision in his other eye. He attended Ohio State University from 1913 to 1918 but never graduated. He then spent sixteen months in Paris writing and deciphering coded messages for the army. Returning to Columbus, he became a reporter, and in 1922 began his first marriage, which lasted twelve years. In 1925, Thurber went to France as a freelance writer for English-language papers in Paris and Nice, but returned to the United States a year later and moved to New York City. He soon joined *The New Yorker* magazine, where he was managing editor from 1927 to 1933. He shared an office with E. B. White, who had an enormous influence on his writing style, helping to make it direct and clear. White also discovered Thurber's ability to draw; soon his cartoons became as well known and loved as his essays. His story "The Secret Life of Walter Mitty," which first appeared in *New Yorker* in 1939, is considered an American classic. Thurber had a happy second marriage, but the last twenty years of his life were filled with serious health problems, including a series of small strokes and failing vision. Toward the end of his life, he wrote stories for children. Collections of his works include *The Owl in the Attic* (1931), *The Seal in the Bedroom* (1932), *My Life and Hard Times* (1933), *The Middle-aged Man on the Flying Trapeze* (1935), *Fables of Our Time* (1940), *The Thurber Carnival* (1945), and *The Thurber Album* (1952).

ABOUT THE SELECTION

"**The Night the Bed Fell**" is a fine example of a personal essay, using an informal, first-person voice to recount a particular experience in the writer's life. A comedy of errors, the essay describes a night in James Thurber's childhood when confusion and chaos overtook the household. Thurber's father, asleep in the attic, is believed to be trapped under his fallen bed. In the scramble to rescue him, no one notices Thurber, the narrator, who actually is trapped under his overturned bed. A collection of odd relatives people the story, from Briggs Beall, who must be awakened every hour for fear that he will stop breathing while he sleeps, to Aunt Gracie Shoaf, who every night throws shoes at imaginary burglars. While Thurber is said to have based his story on a real event, he did embellish it significantly. A matter-of-fact tone mixed with exaggeration lends the piece its humor. "The Night the Bed Fell" is just one of many personal reminiscences James Thurber captured in his writing.

"The Night the Bed Fell"

JAMES THURBER

I suppose that the high-water mark[1] of my youth in Columbus, Ohio, was the night the bed fell on my father. It makes a better recitation (unless, as some friends of mine have said, one has heard it five or six times) than it does a piece of writing, for it is almost necessary to throw furniture around, shake doors, and bark like a dog, to lend the proper atmosphere and <u>verisimilitude</u> to what is admittedly a somewhat incredible tale. Still, it did take place.

It happened, then, that my father had decided to sleep in the attic one night, to be away where he could think. My mother opposed the notion strongly because, she said, the old wooden bed up there was unsafe; it was wobbly and the heavy headboard would crash down on father's head in case the bed fell, and kill him. There was no <u>dissuading</u> him, however, and at a quarter past ten he closed the attic door behind him and went up the narrow twisting stairs. We later heard <u>ominous</u> creakings as he crawled into bed. Grandfather, who usually slept in the attic bed when he was with us, had disappeared some days before. (On these occasions he was usually gone six or eight days and returned growling and out of temper, with the news that the federal Union was run by a passel[2] of blockheads and that the Army of the Potomac[3] didn't have any more chance than a fiddler's bitch.)

We had visiting us at this time a nervous first cousin of mine named Briggs Beall, who believed that he was likely to cease breathing when he was asleep. It was his feeling that if he were not awakened every

Why did Thurber's father sleep in the attic?

Who is Briggs Beall? Of what is he afraid?

---

1. **high-water mark.** Culminating point, highest point
2. **passel.** Group or collection, especially a fairly large one
3. **Army of the Potomac.** One of the main armies of the Union Forces in the Civil War; led by General George B. McClellan

hour during the night, he might die of suffocation. He had been accustomed to setting an alarm clock to ring at intervals until morning, but I persuaded him to abandon this. He slept in my room and I told him that I was such a light sleeper that if anybody quit breathing in the same room with me, I would wake instantly. He tested me the first night—which I had suspected he would—by holding his breath after my regular breathing had convinced him I was asleep. I was not asleep, however, and called to him. This seemed to <u>allay</u> his fears a little, but he took the precaution of putting a glass of spirits of camphor[4] on a little table at the head of his bed. In case I didn't arouse him until he was almost gone, he said, he would sniff the camphor, a powerful reviver. Briggs was not the only member of his family who had his crotchets.[5] Old Aunt Melissa Beall (who could whistle like a man, with two fingers in her mouth) suffered under the <u>premonition</u> that she was destined to die on South High Street, because she had been born on South High Street and married on South High Street. Then there was Aunt Sarah Shoaf, who never went to bed at night without the fear that a burglar was going to get in and blow chloroform[6] under her door through a tube. To avert this calamity—for she was in greater dread of anesthetics than of losing her household goods—she always piled her money, silverware, and other valuables in a neat stack just outside her bedroom, with a note reading: "This is all I have. Please take it and do not use your chloroform, as this is all I have." Aunt Gracie Shoaf also had a burglar phobia,

How did Beall test Thurber?

What did Aunt Sarah do to avoid being chloroformed?

but she met it with more <u>fortitude</u>. She was confident that burglars had been getting into her house every night for forty years. The fact that she never missed anything was to her no proof to the contrary. She always claimed that she scared them off before they could take anything, by throwing shoes down the hallway. When she went to bed she piled, where she could get at them handily, all the shoes there were about her house. Five minutes after she had turned off the light, she would sit up in bed and say "Hark!" Her husband, who had learned to ignore the whole situation as long ago as 1903, would either be sound asleep or pretend to be sound asleep. In either case he would not respond to her tugging and pulling, so that presently she would arise, tiptoe to the door, open it slightly and heave a shoe down the hall in one direction, and its mate down the hall in the other direction. Some nights she threw them all, some nights only a couple of pair.

But I am straying from the remarkable incidents that took place during the night that the bed fell on father. By midnight we were all in bed. The layout of the rooms and the disposition of their occupants is important to an understanding of what later occurred. In the front room upstairs (just under father's attic bedroom) were my mother and my brother Herman, who sometimes sang in his sleep, usually

---

4. **spirits of camphor.** Solution with a strong characteristic odor, derived from the wood of the camphor tree; in medicine used as an irritant and stimulant

5. **crotchets.** Peculiar whims or stubborn notions

6. **chloroform.** Toxic, carcinogenic, colorless liquid used as a solvent, fumigant, and formerly, as a general anesthetic

---

WORDS FOR EVERYDAY USE:

al • lay (a lā´) vt., put to rest; quiet, calm
prem • o • ni • tion (prēm´ə nish ən) n., warning; feeling that something bad will happen

for • ti • tude (fort ´ə tōōd) n., strength to bear misfortune or pain

"Marching Through Georgia" or "Onward, Christian Soldiers." Briggs Beall and myself were in a room adjoining this one. My brother Roy was in a room across the hall from ours. Our bull terrier, Rex, slept in the hall.

My bed was an army cot, one of those affairs which are made wide enough to sleep on comfortably only by putting up, flat with the middle section, the two sides which ordinarily hang down like the sideboards of a drop-leaf table. When these sides are up, it is <u>perilous</u> to roll too far toward the edge, for then the cot is likely to tip completely over, bringing the whole bed down on top of one, with a tremendous banging crash. This, in fact, is precisely what happened, about two o'clock in the morning. (It was my mother who, in recalling the scene later, first referred to it as "the night the bed fell on your father.")

Always a deep sleeper, slow to arouse (I had lied to Briggs), I was at first unconscious of what had happened when the iron cot rolled me onto the floor and toppled over on me. It left me still warmly bundled up and unhurt, for the bed rested above me like a canopy. Hence I did not wake up, only reached the edge of consciousness and went back. The <u>racket</u>, however, instantly awakened my mother, in the next room, who came to the immediate conclusion that her worst dread was realized: the big wooden bed upstairs had fallen on father. She therefore screamed, "Let's go to your poor father!" It was this shout, rather than the noise of my cot falling, that awakened Herman, in the same room with her. He thought that

mother had become, for no apparent reason, hysterical. "You're all right, Mamma!" he shouted, trying to calm her. They exchanged shout for shout for perhaps ten seconds: "Let's go to your poor father!" and "You're all right!" That woke up Briggs. By this time I was conscious of what was going on, in a vague way, but did not yet realize that I was under my bed instead of on it. Briggs, awakening in the midst of loud shouts of fear and apprehension, came to the quick conclusion that he was suffocating and that we were all trying to "bring him out." With a low moan, he grasped the glass of camphor at the head of his bed and instead of sniffing it poured it over himself. The room reeked of camphor. "Ugf, ahfg," choked Briggs, like a drowning man, for he had almost succeeded in stopping his breath under the <u>deluge</u> of pungent spirits. He leaped out of bed and groped toward the open window, but he came up against one that was closed. With his hand, he beat out the glass, and I could hear it crash and tinkle on the alleyway below. It was at this <u>juncture</u> that I, in trying to get up, had the uncanny sensation of feeling my bed above me! Foggy with sleep, I now suspected, in my turn, that the whole uproar was being made in a frantic endeavor to <u>extricate</u> me from what must be an unheard-of and perilous situation. "Get me out of this!" I bawled. "Get me out!" I think I had the nightmarish belief that I was entombed in a mine. "Gugh," gasped Briggs, floundering in his camphor.

By this time my mother, still shouting, pursued by Herman, still shouting, was trying to open the door to the attic, in

On what kind of bed did the author sleep? What happened to it?

What happened when the author tried to stand up? What did he think had happened?

WORDS FOR EVERYDAY USE:

per • il • ous (per´ə ləs) *adj.,* dangerous
rack • et (rak´it) *n.,* noisy confusion; uproar
del • uge (del´yo͞oj) *n.,* overwhelming floodlike rush

junc • ture (junk´chər) *n.,* point in time
ex • tri • cate (eks´tri kāt) *vt.,* release or disentangle

order to go up and get my father's body out of the wreckage. The door was stuck, however, and wouldn't yield. Her frantic pulls on it only added to the general banging and confusion. Roy and the dog were now up, the one shouting questions, the other barking.

Father, farthest away and soundest sleeper of all, had by this time been awakened by the battering on the attic door. He decided that the house was on fire. "I'm coming, I'm coming!" he wailed in a slow, sleepy voice—it took him many minutes to regain full consciousness. My mother, still believing he was caught under the bed, detected in his "I'm coming!" the mournful, resigned note of one who is preparing to meet his Maker. "He's dying!" she shouted.

"I'm all right!" Briggs yelled to reassure her. "I'm all right!" He still believed that it was his own closeness to death that was

Why did Thurber's mother think his father was dying?

worrying mother. I found at last the light switch in my room, unlocked the door, and Briggs and I joined the others at the attic door. The dog, who never did like Briggs, jumped for him—assuming that he was the <u>culprit</u> in whatever was going on—and Roy had to throw Rex and hold him. We could hear father crawling out of bed upstairs. Roy pulled the attic door open, with a mighty jerk, and father came down the stairs, sleepy and irritable but safe and sound. My mother began to weep when she saw him. Rex began to howl. "What in the name of God is going on here?" asked father.

The situation was finally put together like a gigantic jig-saw puzzle. Father caught a cold from prowling around in his bare feet but there were no other bad results. "I'm glad," said mother, who always looked on the bright side of things, "that your grandfather wasn't here." ■

Responding to the Selection

Do you enjoy reading personal memoirs? How do they offer insight into people's emotions, behavior, and motivations? Did you find "The Night the Bed Fell" funny? Why, or why not?

WORDS FOR EVERYDAY USE: cul • prit (kul′prit) *n.*, guilty person

Reviewing the Selection

1. Where was Thurber's father on the night the bed fell? How does Thurber's mother feel about his location?

2. Who is visiting at Thurber's house on the night in question? What odd behavior has he displayed during the earlier part of his visit?

3. Who and where are the other members of the household?

4. Why can't the family reach Thurber's father to insure his safety?

▶▶ 5. How does his location contribute to the confusion of the night?

▶▶ 6. What does Thurber think of his roommate's behavior? How does he respond to it?

▶▶ 7. What event first triggered the confusion of the night? Which family member initiated it? What events followed?

▶▶ 8. How does Thurber's father react to the chaos? How does the description of his behavior suggest Thurber's own view of his family?

9. What do you think is suggested by the stories about Thurber's odd relatives?

10. Why do you think Thurber chose to poke fun at his own family?

Understanding Literature (Questions for Discussion)

1. **Anecdote.** An **anecdote** is a brief story, usually with a specific point or moral. With an anecdote, a writer can support a persuasive argument or, as in the case of "The Night the Bed Fell," show a character's behavior. Find one or two anecdotes within the selection. How do they contribute to James Thurber's description of his family and the characters it contains?

2. **Farce.** A **farce** is a type of comedy that depends heavily on so-called low humor and on improbable, exaggerated, extreme situations or characters. "The Night the Bed Fell" contains many elements of farce. What elements of farce can you identify in the selection?

Responding in Writing

1. **Press Release.** In a press release, the important facts or points related to an event are presented to the media in a brief form. Suppose you had to tell a newspaper or television reporter about the events in "The Night the Bed Fell." Try your hand at writing a press release that includes only the most essential information while still capturing the humorous tone of the night.

2. **Family History.** "The Night the Bed Fell" is based on an actual event, and presumably real people, from James Thurber's family history. Think about your family. Identify some eccentric or interesting characters. Write a brief family history portraying an incident involving these characters.

Language Lab

Editing for Correct Use of Parentheses. Read the Language Arts Survey, 2.101, "Parentheses and Brackets." Then rewrite the sentences below using parentheses correctly.

1. James Thurber was affiliated for many years with *The New Yorker* (a literary magazine based in New York.

2. He became skilled at writing casuals (,brief works that appear to have been very quickly, or casually, written.)

3. E. B. White (Who also worked for *The New Yorker*), became Thurber's friend during this period.

4. Thurber's classic short story "The Secret Life of Walter Mitty"—which now appears as an entry in many dictionaries) first appeared in *The New Yorker*

5. His cartoons (,for White had earlier discovered this additional Thurber talent,) became popular as well.

Thinking Skills

Remembering and Visualizing. One way to experience a work of literature is to visualize its events and characters. Seeing them in your mind, as if through a camera's eye, makes these people and events more immediate. Recall and visualize a favorite section of "The Night the Bed Fell." Describe what you see and how you respond to it. Before beginning, you may want to read the Language Arts Survey, 4.5, "Remembering and Visualizing."

Letter to *The Amherst Student*
by Robert Frost

ABOUT THE AUTHOR

See the biography of **Robert Frost** on page 524.

ABOUT THE SELECTION

After the success of his first few volumes of poetry, Robert Frost became a renowned public figure, one of the few poets in this century to make a living writing verse. He taught at several colleges, including Amherst College, in Massachusetts, and was much in demand as a visiting teacher, lecturer, and artist in residence. The following letter from Frost appeared in *The Amherst Student,* a college newspaper, on March 25, 1935, and was written in response to the paper's congratulating him on reaching his sixtieth birthday. Frost took the occasion of this response to provide some words of wisdom, his message to the young people of the Modern Age.

READER'S JOURNAL

Do you think that life today is better or worse than it was in the past? Read the Language Arts Survey, 1.22, "Pro and Con Charts." Then write one of these sentences at the top of a piece of paper: "Life is better today than it was in the past" or "Life is worse today than it was in the past." Draw a line down the middle of the page and label the columns thus created *Pro* and *Con*. Then list reasons for and against the position listed at the top of the page.

THINKING SKILLS

Read the Language Arts Survey, 4.11, "Generalizing," and 4.14, "Avoiding Faulty Arguments." Then, as you read the selection, think about why it is an overgeneralization to say that "These are terrible times" or "This is the most difficult age so far in the history of humankind."

Letter to The Amherst Student

ROBERT FROST

It is very, very kind of the *Student* to be showing sympathy with me for my age. But sixty is only a pretty good age. It is not advanced enough. The great thing is to be advanced. Now ninety would be really well along and something to be given credit for.

But speaking of ages, you will often hear it said that the age of the world we live in is particularly bad. I am impatient of such talk. We have no way of knowing that this age is one of the worst in the world's history. Arnold[1] claimed the honor for the age before this. Wordsworth[2] claimed it for the last but one. And so on back through literature. I say they claimed the honor for their ages. They claimed it rather for themselves. It is immodest of a man to think of himself as going down before the worst forces ever <u>mobilized</u> by God.

All ages of the world are bad—a great deal worse anyway than Heaven. If they weren't the world might just as well be Heaven at once and have it over with. One can safely say after from six to thirty thousand years of experience that the evident design is a situation here in which it will always be about equally hard to save your soul. Whatever progress may be taken to mean, it can't mean making the world any easier a place in which to save your soul—or if you dislike hearing your soul mentioned in open meeting, say your decency, your <u>integrity</u>.

Of what talk is Frost impatient?

---

1. **Arnold.** Matthew Arnold (1822–1888) was one of the foremost poets and critics of the Victorian Age in England.
2. **Wordsworth.** William Wordsworth (1770–1850) was one of the leading poets of the Romantic Movement in England.

WORDS FOR EVERYDAY USE:

mo • bi • lize (mō´bə līz´) *vi.*, become organized and ready, as for war

in • teg • ri • ty (in teg´rə tē) *n.*, uprightness, honesty, and sincerity

Ages may vary a little. One may be a little worse than another. But it is not possible to get outside the age you are in to judge it exactly. Indeed it is as dangerous to try to get outside of anything as large as an age as it would be to engorge a donkey. Witness the many who in the attempt have suffered a dilation from which the tissues and the muscles of the mind have never been able to recover natural shape. They can't pick up anything delicate or small any more. They can't use a pen. They have to use a typewriter. And they gape in agony. They can write huge shapeless novels, huge gobs of raw sincerity bellowing with pain and that's all that they can write.

Fortunately we don't need to know how bad the age is. There is something we can always be doing without reference to how good or bad the age is. There is at least so much good in the world that it admits of form and the making of form. And not only admits of it, but calls for it. We people are thrust forward out of the suggestions of form in the rolling clouds of nature. In us nature reaches its height of form and through us exceeds itself. When in doubt there is always form for us to go on with. Anyone who has achieved the least form to be sure of it, is lost to the larger excruciations. I think it must stroke faith the right way. The artist [,] the poet [,] might be expected to be the most aware of such assurance. But it is really everybody's sanity to feel it and live by it. Fortunately, too, no forms are more engrossing [,] gratifying, comforting, staying than those lesser ones we throw off, like vortex rings of smoke, all our individual enterprise and needing nobody's co-operation; a basket, a letter, a garden, a room, an idea, a picture, a poem. For these we haven't to get a team together before we can play.

The background in hugeness and confusion shading away from where we stand into black and utter chaos; and against the background any small man-made figure of order and concentration. What pleasanter than that this should be so? Unless we are novelists or economists we don't worry about this confusion; we look out on [it] with an instrument or tackle it to reduce it. It is partly because we are afraid it might prove too much for us and our blend of democratic-republican-socialist-communist-anarchist party. But it is more because we like it, we were born to it, born used to it and have practical reasons for wanting it there. To me any little form I assert upon it is velvet,[3] as the saying is, and to be considered for how much more it is than nothing. If I were a Platonist[4] I should have to consider it, I suppose, for how much less it is than everything. ∎

According to Frost, is it possible to judge the age one is in?

What are the results of trying to judge something as large as an age?

According to Frost, why do most people not worry about the confusion in the world?

In what ways might nature reach its height through humanity? exceed itself through humanity?

---

3. **is velvet.** Literally, like velvet cloth, soft and comfortable; figuratively, a luxury, something that brings comfort

4. **Platonist.** A follower of Plato, the ancient Greek philosopher who believed that things in the world were but reflections or imitations of pure forms that existed in the transcendent realm of ideas. Plato didn't think much of art, which he considered an imitation of nature and thus, to him, an imitation of an imitation of ideal form.

WORDS FOR EVERYDAY USE:

en • gorge (en gôrj´) vt., devour greedily
di • la • tion (dī lā´shən) n., widening, expansion

ex • cru • ci • a • tion (ex cru´cī ā´shən) n., torment
vor • tex (vôr´ teks´) n. pl. swirling mass

Responding to the Selection

Frost says that "no forms are more engrossing, gratifying, comforting, staying than those lesser ones we throw off, like vortex rings of smoke, all our individual enterprise and needing nobody's co-operation: a basket, a letter, a garden, a room, an idea, a picture, a poem." What individual activities, like these, do you enjoy? Why is it fulfilling to bring a little form, a little order into the world by creating something on one's own? What did Frost want his readers, the students at Amherst, to do instead of worrying about how good or bad the age they lived in was?

Reviewing the Selection

RECALLING

1. What was the occasion that prompted Frost to write this letter to *The Amherst Student*?

2. With what sort of talk was Frost impatient?

3. What did Frost think of novelists who try in their works to capture a picture of the entire age?

4. According to Frost, where do people come from, and what do they find gratifying, comforting, and staying?

INTERPRETING

5. What did Frost think of turning sixty years old?

6. Why was Frost impatient with talk about how bad the age was?

7. What are the consequences, according to Frost, of an artist's trying to step outside his or her age and consider it as a whole?

8. What do baskets, letters, gardens, rooms, ideas, pictures, and poems have in common? Why is creating such things important?

SYNTHESIZING

9. What advice would Frost give to people for dealing with the "hugeness and confusion" of life?

10. Of what larger human propensity or inclination does Frost consider writing poetry to be one example? In an essay, Frost once described the writing of poetry as "a momentary stay against confusion." How can writing a poem, weaving a basket, planting a garden, or decorating a room help to make the world more sensible, comprehensible, meaningful? What does Frost think people should do instead of worry about large questions about the nature of the age in which they live?

Understanding Literature (Questions for Discussion)

1. **Essay.** An **essay** is a brief piece of nonfictional prose that treats a single subject and advances a single thesis, or main idea. What is the main idea of Frost's Letter to *The Amherst Student*?

2. **Modernism. Modernism** was a twentieth-century artistic movement characterized by a rejection of traditional forms and much experimentation. Some poets and other writers of the twentieth century rejected Modernism as a retreat from the central purpose of art, which they believed to be giving clear, sensible form to experience. Robert Frost was one such poet. He claimed, for example, that "Writing free verse is like playing tennis with the net down." Do you agree with Frost? Do you prefer traditional, representational art or the abstract, experimental work characteristic of much of the twentieth century? Do you prefer traditional verse that employs regular patterns of meter, rhyme, and stanza form, or do you prefer free verse, which rejects all these elements of form as too limiting or constraining? Why?

Responding in Writing

Comparison-and-Contrast Essay on Representational and Abstract Art. Choose one piece of traditional, representational art from this text, such as the Grant Wood painting on page 416, and one piece of modern abstract art, such as the Jackson Pollock on page 744. Write a brief essay in which you define representational and abstract art and discuss the two pieces you have chosen as examples of the two styles. Compare and contrast the two pieces and explain which you prefer and why.

PROJECT

Artistic Movements of the Twentieth Century. Using art history books, encyclopedias, dictionaries of art, and other reference works, identify and provide examples of the following movements and styles in twentieth-century art. Work with other students to prepare a poster describing each movement or style and providing an example of it. Examples can be photocopied from art books or found on postcards or posters available in art supply shops, frame shops, museum stores, and bookstores.

Abstract Expressionism	Impressionism
Dada, or Dadaism	Minimalism
Expressionism	Proletarian Art
Fauvism	Surrealism
Futurism	Trompe d'Oeil

Nobel Prize Acceptance Speech
by William Faulkner

ABOUT THE AUTHOR

William Faulkner (1897–1962) was born in New Albany, Mississippi, to a prominent Southern family and spent most of his life in Oxford, Mississippi. He dropped out of high school and, except for one year as a student at the University of Mississippi, had no further formal education. His first novel, *Soldier's Pay* (1926), published through the help of Sherwood Anderson, earned him an advance of two hundred dollars each on his next two novels. Recalling those events, he is reported to have said, "I liked that money," and to have noted that Anderson "worked only in the morning," which seemed to him "a mighty easy way to earn money." Whether or not it was easy, Faulkner spent most of his adult life earning his living as a writer. Most of his many novels are set in a mythical Yoknapatawpha County, Mississippi, and tell stories related to the decline of traditional Southern ways of life. Long, sonorous sentences with abundant details are one of the hallmarks of Faulkner's style. He also experimented considerably with **point of view**, telling the stories in some of his novels from the points of view of several different characters, including that of a mentally handicapped man in *The Sound and the Fury* (1929) and those of a mentally deficient poor white family in *As I Lay Dying* (1930). Much of Faulkner's fiction employed a **stream-of-consciousness** mode, presenting characters' random thoughts, feelings, and impressions in **interior monologues**. In addition to his novels, Faulkner wrote screenplays, the most notable of which are his adaptations of Ernest Hemingway's *To Have and Have Not* and Raymond Chandler's *The Big Sleep*. Faulkner's work was recognized with a Nobel Prize for literature and two Pulitzer Prizes, among other awards and honors. Other works by Faulkner include *The Marble Faun* (poetry, 1924), *Mosquitoes* (1927), *Sartoris* (1929), *Sanctuary* (1931), *Light in August* (1932), *Absalom, Absalom!* (1936), *Go Down, Moses* (1942), and *Intruder in the Dust* (1948).

ABOUT THE SELECTION

Faulkner received the Nobel Prize for literature in 1950 for his novel *As I Lay Dying*. The brief address that he delivered on accepting the prize presents a noble view of the role to be played by imaginative literature in the modern age.

READER'S JOURNAL

What roles can literature play in people's lives, besides simply providing entertainment? Write about this question in your journal.

LANGUAGE SKILLS

Read the Language Arts Survey, 2.4, "Concrete and Abstract Nouns." Then, as you read the selection, make a list of the abstract nouns that Faulkner uses to describe human qualities or characteristics.

Nobel Prize Acceptance Speech

WILLIAM FAULKNER

I feel that this award was not made to me as a man, but to my work—a life's work in the agony and sweat of the human spirit, not for glory and least of all for profit, but to create out of the materials of the human spirit something which did not exist before. So this award is only mine in trust.[1] It will not be difficult to find a dedication for the money part of it <u>commensurate</u> with the purpose and significance of its origin. But I would like to do the same with the acclaim too, by using this moment as a pinnacle from which I might be listened to by the young men and women already dedicated to the same anguish and <u>travail</u>, among whom is already that one who will some day stand here where I am standing.

Our tragedy today is a general and universal physical fear so long sustained by now that we can even bear it. There are no longer problems of the spirit. There is only the question: When will I be blown up? Because of this, the young man or woman writing today has forgotten the problems of the human heart in conflict with itself which alone can make good writing because only that is worth writing about, worth the agony and the sweat.

He must learn them again. He must teach himself that the basest of all things is to be afraid; and, teaching himself that, forget it forever, leaving no room in his workshop for anything but the old <u>verities</u> and truths of the heart, the old universal truths lacking which any story is <u>ephemeral</u> and doomed—love and honor and pity and pride and compassion and sacrifice. Until he does so, he labors under a curse. He writes not of love but of lust, of defeats in which nobody loses anything of value, of victories without hope and,

What have young writers forgotten today?

What is "the basest of all things"?

---

1. **in trust**. In another's care

WORDS FOR
EVERYDAY USE:

com • men • su • rate (kə men´shoor it) *adj.*, equal in measure or size, proportionate
trav • ail (trə vāl) *n.*, very hard work, toil

ver • i • ty (ver´ə tē) *n.*, principle or belief taken to be fundamentally and permanently true
e • phem • er • al (e fem´ər əl) *adj.*, short-lived, transitory

worst of all, without pity or compassion. His griefs grieve on no universal bones, leaving no scars. He writes not of the heart but of the glands.

Until he relearns these things, he will write as though he stood among and watched the end of man. I decline to accept the end of man. It is easy enough to say that man is immortal simply because he will <u>endure</u>: that when the last ding-dong of doom has clanged and faded from the last worthless rock hanging tideless in the last red and dying evening, that even then there will still be one more sound: that of his puny inexhaustible voice, still talking. I refuse to accept this. I believe that man will not merely endure: he will <u>prevail</u>. He is immortal, not because he alone among creatures has an inexhaustible voice, but because he has a soul, a spirit capable of compassion and sacrifice and endurance. The poet's, the writer's, duty is to write about these things. It is his privilege to help man endure by lifting his heart, by reminding him of the courage and honor and hope and pride and compassion and pity and sacrifice which have been the glory of his past. The poet's voice need not merely be the record of man, it can be one of the props, the pillars to help him endure and prevail. ■

Responding to the Selection

Speaking at the height of the cold war, a few years after the end of World War II and the dropping of atomic bombs on Hiroshima and Nagasaki, Faulkner said, "There are no longer problems of the spirit. There is only the question: When will I be blown up?" Do you feel that the world is more or less dangerous today than it was when Faulkner gave his address in 1950? Why do you think Faulkner wanted his listeners not to live in fear but rather to remember the "old verities and truths of the heart"?

WORDS FOR EVERYDAY USE:

en • dure (en door´) *vi.* continue in existence, last, remain

pre • vail (prē vāl) *vi.* gain advantage or mastery, be victorious, triumph

Reviewing the Selection

RECALLING

1. Faulkner said that he felt that the Nobel Prize was given not to him as a man but to what?

2. According to the first sentence of the address, what did Faulkner attempt to do in his fiction?

3. According to Faulkner, what is the "general and universal physical fear" with which people in the modern age live?

4. According to Faulkner, what elements must any story have if it is not to be ephemeral and doomed?

INTERPRETING

5. A carpenter works in wood. A blacksmith works in metal. In what, according to the first sentence of Faulkner's address, does a writer work? What human characteristic, according to Faulkner, gives rise to writing and to the immortality of humankind?

6. Why did Faulkner say that the award was "only [his] in trust"? To whom does he address his comments? What does he want to communicate to these people?

7. According to Faulkner, what have young writers today forgotten? Why?

8. According to Faulkner, why must a story deal with "the old verities and truths of the heart"?

SYNTHESIZING

9. Despite the possibility of universal annihilation created by the advent of nuclear weapons, Faulkner remained optimistic about the human capacity not only to endure but to prevail. Why? What reason does he give for his optimism?

10. What, according to Faulkner, is a writer's duty? What can writers do to be "the props, the pillars to help [human beings] endure and prevail"?

Understanding Literature (Questions for Discussion)

1. **Aim.** A writer's **aim** is the primary purpose that his or her work is meant to achieve. What do you think Faulkner wanted to achieve in his Nobel Prize acceptance speech? What was his purpose, or aim?

2. **Alliteration. Alliteration** is the repetition of initial consonant sounds. Faulkner's writing makes frequent use of alliteration. Find three examples in the selection.

3. **Antithesis. Antithesis** is a rhetorical technique in which opposing ideas are presented in balanced grammatical forms, as in the sentence "To err is human, to forgive divine." Find three examples of antithesis in the selection.

4. **Onomatopoeia. Onomatopoeia** is the use of words that sound like what they name or describe. Examples of onomatopoeia include the words *murmur* and *buzz*. What examples of onomatopoeia can you find in the selection?

5. **Parallelism. Parallelism** is a rhetorical technique in which a writer emphasizes the equal value or weight of two or more ideas by expressing them in the same grammatical form. Find examples of parallelism in Faulkner's speech that involve using the coordinating conjunction *and* and the relative pronoun *that*.

Responding in Writing

Biographical Sketch. According to Faulkner, "the glory" of our past has been our capacity for "courage and honor and hope and pride and compassion and pity and sacrifice." Think of someone you know who has at some time demonstrated one of these virtues. Write a brief narrative in which you describe what that person did and why you consider his or her actions virtuous.

Language Lab

Colorful Adjectives. Read the Language Arts Survey, 2.19, "Adjectives and Articles," and 2.35, "Using Colorful Modifiers." Then identify all the adjectives, along with the nouns that they modify, in the following sentence from Faulkner's speech:

> "It is easy enough to say that man is immortal simply because he will endure: that when the last dingdong of doom has clanged and faded from the last worthless rock hanging tideless in the last red and dying evening, that even then there will still be one more sound: that of his puny inexhaustible voice, still talking."

PROJECT

Themes in Literature. Faulkner said that it was the poet's and writer's duty to write about the human spirit's capacity for compassion, sacrifice, endurance, courage, honor, hope, pride, and pity. Work with other students to find short works of literature that illustrate each of these themes. Hold a reading of these works, following each reading with a discussion of the virtue that the work illustrates.

"Walden"
by E. B. White

ABOUT THE AUTHOR

E. B. White (1899–1985) was born in Mount Vernon, New York and as he explained, ". . . was a busy writer long before [he] went into long pants." He studied English at Cornell University and was editor-in-chief of the *Cornell Daily Sun.* After graduating in 1921, White worked for newspapers and an advertising agency before becoming a regular contributor to *The New Yorker* in 1927. His witty essays in the "Notes and Comment" column helped shape the magazine's early success. In 1929 he published a book of poetry, *The Lady is Cold*, and *Is Sex Necessary?*, a collection of humorous essays by White and his colleague, James Thurber. In 1938 White and his wife, Katharine Angell, an editor for *The New Yorker,* moved to a farm in Maine where White later received his inspiration to write the children's stories, *Stuart Little, Charlotte's Web*, and *The Trumpet of the Swan.* He wrote the "One Man's Meat" column for *Harper's* and contributed often to *The New Yorker.* White also continued to publish essay and poetry collections as well as a revision of William Strunk, Jr.'s *The Elements of Style.* In 1978, E. B. White received a Pulitzer Prize Committee special citation in recognition of his life's work.

ABOUT THE SELECTION

In this satirical essay, E. B. White responds to Henry David Thoreau's important Transcendental work, *Walden*, which was written by Thoreau from the journals he kept during his stay on Walden Pond between 1845 and 1847. Thoreau's work focused on many ideas, but a central point was that people need considerably fewer material comforts than they think they do to live a full life. Thoreau also felt that he, and others, could learn and experience the truly essential realities and requirements of life by observing nature. As E. B. White visits Concord, Massachusetts, site of Walden Pond, he questions the validity of Thoreau's ideas in today's world.

READER'S JOURNAL

Think about a recent visit you made to a place you knew through literature or another source. Describe the ideas and expectations you had before reaching your destination. How did the visit confirm or unseat your initial assumptions?

THINKING SKILLS

"Walden" contains many elements of a comparison-contrast essay. Read the Language Arts Survey, 4.8, "Comparing and Contrasting." Then list two similarities and two differences between E. B. White's experience of Walden today and his view of Thoreau's Walden.

"Walden"

E. B. WHITE

June 1939

Miss Nims, take a letter[1] to Henry David Thoreau. Dear Henry: I thought of you the other afternoon as I was approaching Concord doing fifty on Route 62. That is a high speed at which to hold a philosopher in one's mind, but in this century we are a <u>nimble</u> bunch.

On one of the lawns in the outskirts of the village a woman was cutting the grass with a motorized lawn mower. What made me think of you was that the machine had rather got away from her, although she was <u>game</u> enough, and in the brief glimpse I had of the scene it appeared to me that the lawn was mowing the lady. She kept a tight grip on the handles, which throbbed violently with every explosion of the one-cylinder motor, and as she <u>sheered</u> around bushes and lurched along at a reluctant trot behind her <u>impetuous</u> servant, she looked like a puppy who had grabbed something that

was too much for him. Concord hasn't changed much, Henry: the farm <u>implements</u> and the animals still have the upper hand.

I may as well admit that I was journeying to Concord with the deliberate intention of visiting your woods; for although I have never knelt at the grave of a philosopher nor placed wreaths on moldy poets, and have often gone a mile out of my way to avoid some place of historical interest, I have always wanted to see Walden Pond. The account which you left of your <u>sojourn</u> there is, you will be amused to learn, a document of increasing <u>pertinence</u>; each year it seems to gain a little headway, as the world loses ground. We may all be transcendental[2] yet,

---

1. **take a letter.** Write down the letter dictated
2. **transcendental.** Refers to the Transcendental movement in New England in the nineteenth century. The philosophical ideas of Ralph Waldo Emerson and Henry David Thoreau were based on a search for reality through spiritual intuition.

Why was White journeying to Concord? What does he say to Thoreau about Walden?

WORDS FOR EVERYDAY USE:

nim • ble (nim´ bəl) *adj.,* mentally quick
game (gām) *adj.,* having spirit or enthusiasm
sheer (shir) *vi.,* turn sharply aside from a course
im • pet • u • ous (im pech´ ōō əs) *adj.,* rushing with force or violence
im • ple • ment (im´plə mənt) *n.,* tool
so • journ (sō´ jʉrn) *n.,* brief visit
per • ti • nence (pʉr´tə nəns) *n.,* relevance

whether we like it or not. As our common complexities increase, any tale of individual simplicity (and yours is the best written and the cockiest) acquires a new fascination; as our goods <u>accumulate,</u> but not our well-being, your report of an existence without material adornment takes on a certain awkward credibility.

My purpose in going to Walden Pond, like yours, was not to live cheaply or to live dearly there, but to transact some private business with the fewest obstacles. Approaching Concord, doing forty, doing forty-five, doing fifty, the steering wheel held snug in my palms, the highway held grimly in my vision, the crown of the road now serving me (on the righthand curves), now defeating me (on the lefthand curves), I began to rouse myself from the <u>stupefaction</u> which a day's motor journey induces. It was a delicious evening, Henry, when the whole body is one sense, and imbibes delight through every pore, if I may coin a phrase. Fields were richly brown where the harrow,[3] drawn by the stripped Ford, had lately sunk its teeth; pastures were green; and overhead the sky had that same everlasting great look which you will find on page 144 of the Oxford pocket edition:[4] I could feel the road entering me, through tire, wheel, spring, and cushion: shall I not have intelligence with earth too? Am I not partly leaves and vegetable mold myself?—a man of infinite horsepower, yet partly leaves.

Stay with me on 62 and it will take you into Concord. As I say, it was a delicious evening. The snake had come forth to die in a bloody S on the highway, the wheel upon its head, its bowels flat now and exposed. The turtle had come up too to cross the road and die in the attempt, its hard shell smashed under the rubber blow, its intestinal yearning (for the other side of the road) forever squashed. There was a sign by the wayside which announced that the road had a "cotton surface." You wouldn't know what that is, but neither, for that matter, did I. There is a <u>cryptic</u> ingredient in many of our modern improvements—we are awed and pleased without knowing quite what we are enjoying. It is something to be traveling on a road with a cotton surface.

The civilization round Concord today is an odd <u>distillation</u> of city, village, farm, and manor. The houses, yards, fields look not quite suburban, not quite rural. Under the bronze beech and the blue spruce of the departed baron grazes the milch[5] goat of the heirs. Under the porte-cochère[6] stands the reconditioned station wagon; under the grape arbor sit the puppies for sale. But why do men degenerate ever? What makes families run out?

It was June and everywhere June was publishing her <u>immemorial</u> stanza; in the lilacs, in the syringa,[7] in the freshly edged paths and the sweetness of moist beloved gardens, and the little wire wickets that preserve the tulips' front. Farmers were already moving the fruits of their toil into their yards, arranging the rhubarb, the

What is cryptic about modern improvements? What point is White making about modern improvements?

---

3. **harrow.** Frame with spikes drawn by a horse or tractor and used for breaking up and leveling plowed ground

4. **Oxford pocket edition.** Edition of Thoreau's *Walden* published by the Oxford University Press

5. **milch.** Milk-giving

6. **porte-cochère.** Covered driveway

7. **syringa.** Shrub or tree with large clusters of small white flowers

WORDS FOR EVERYDAY USE:

ac • cu • mu • late (ə kyōōm´ yōō lāt´) *vi.*, pile up over time
stu • pe • fac • tion (stōō´pə fak´ shən) *n.*, state of dullness or lethargy
cryp • tic (krip´tik) *adj.*, having a hidden meaning; baffling
dis • til • la • tion (dis´tə lā´ shən) *n.*, something separated out into parts
im • me • mo • ri • al (im´me môr´ ē əl) *adj.*, something too old to be remembered

asparagus, the strictly fresh eggs on the painted stands under the little shed roofs with the patent shingles. And though it was almost a hundred years since you had taken your ax and started cutting out your home on Walden Pond, I was interested to observe that the philosophical spirit was still alive in Massachusetts: in the center of a vacant lot some boys were assembling the framework of a rude shelter, their whole mind and skill concentrated in the rather <u>inauspicious</u> helter-skeleton of studs and rafters. They too were escaping from town, to live naturally, in a rich blend of savagery and philosophy.

That evening, after supper at the inn, I strolled out into the twilight to dream my shapeless transcendental dreams and see that the car was locked up for the night (first open the right front door, then reach over, straining, and pull up the handles of the left rear and the left front till you hear the click, then the handle of the right rear, then shut the right front but open it again, remembering that the key is still in the ignition switch, remove the key, shut the right front again with a bang, push the tiny keyhole cover to one side, insert key, turn, and withdraw). It is what we all do, Henry. It is called locking the car. It is said to confuse thieves and keep them from making off with the laprobe. Four doors to lock behind one robe. The driver himself never uses a laprobe, the free movement of his legs being vital to the operation of the vehicle; so that when he locks the car it is a pure and unselfish act. I have in my life gained very little essential heat from laprobes, yet I have ever been at pains to lock them up.

The evening was full of sounds, some of which would have stirred your memory. The robins still love the elms of New England villages at sundown. There is enough of the thrush in them to make song inevitable at the end of day, and enough of the tramp to make them hang round the dwelling of men. A robin, like many another American, dearly loves a white house with green blinds. Concord is still full of them.

Your fellow-townsmen were stirring abroad—not many afoot, most of them in their cars; and the sound which they made in Concord at evening was a rustling and a whispering. The sound lacks <u>steadfastness</u> and is wholly unlike that of a train. A train, as you know who lived so near the Fitchburg line, whistles once or twice sadly and is gone, trailing a memory in smoke, soothing to ear and mind. Automobiles, skirting a village green, are like flies that have gained the inner ear—they buzz, cease, pause, start, shift, stop, halt, brake, and the whole effect is a nervous polytone[8] curiously disturbing.

As I wandered along, the toc toc of ping pong balls drifted from an attic window. In front of the Reuben Brown house a Buick was drawn up. At the wheel, motionless, his hat upon his head, a man sat, listening to Amos and Andy[9] on the radio (it is a drama of many scenes and without an end). The deep voice of Andrew Brown, emerging from the car, although it originated more than two hundred miles away, was unstrained by

---

8. **polytone.** Variety of sounds
9. **Amos and Andy.** Radio show popular in the 1930's and 1940's

WORDS FOR EVERYDAY USE:

in • aus • pi • cious (in´ô spish´əs) *adj.*, unfavorable, unlucky
stead • fast • ness (sted´fast´nes) *n.*, quality of being firm, fixed, or settled

What does White say is still alive? What observation causes him to say this? Is White serious or satiric here?

What sounds does White describe? In what way do the two sounds differ?

Walden Pond

distance. When you used to sit on the shore of your pond on Sunday morning, listening to the church bells of Acton and Concord, you were aware of the excellent filter of the intervening atmosphere. Science has attended to that, and sound now maintains its intensity without regard for distance. Properly sponsored, it goes on forever.

A fire engine, out for a trial spin, roared past Emerson's house, hot with readiness for public duty. Over the barn roofs the martins dipped and chittered. A swarthy daughter of an asparagus grower, in culottes,[10] shirt, and bandanna, pedaled past on her bicycle. It was indeed a delicious evening, and I returned to the inn (I believe it was your house once) to rock with the old ladies on the concrete veranda.

Next morning early I started afoot for Walden, out Main Street and down Thoreau, past the depot and the Minuteman Chevrolet Company. The morning was fresh, and in a bean field along the way I flushed an agriculturalist, quietly studying his beans. Thoreau Street soon joined Number 126, an artery of the State. We number our highways nowadays, our speed being so great we can remember little of their quality or character and are lucky to remember their number. (Men have an indistinct notion that if they keep up this activity long enough all will at length ride somewhere, in next to no time.) Your pond is on 126.

I knew I must be nearing your woodland retreat when the Golden Pheasant lunchroom came into view—Sealtest ice cream, toasted sandwiches, hot frankfurters, waffles, tonics, and lunches. Were I the proprietor, I should add rice, Indian meal, and molasses—just for old time's sake. The Pheasant, incidentally, is for sale: a chance for some nature lover who wishes to set himself up beside a pond in the

---

10. **culottes.** Trousers that resemble a skirt

Concord atmosphere and live deliberately, fronting only the essential facts of life on Number 126. Beyond the Pheasant was a place called Walden Breezes, an oasis whose porch pillars were made of old green shutters sawed into lengths. On the porch was a distorting mirror, to give the traveler a comical image of himself, who had miraculously learned to gaze in an ordinary glass without smiling. Behind the Breezes, in a sun-parched clearing, dwelt your philosophical descendants in their trailers, each trailer the size of your hut, but all grouped together for the sake of <u>congeniality</u>. Trailer people leave the city, as you did, to discover solitude and in any weather, at any hour of the day or night, to improve the nick of time; but they soon collect in villages and get bogged deeper in the mud than ever. The camp behind Walden Breezes was just rousing itself to the morning. The ground was packed hard under the heel, and the sun came through the clearing to bake the soil and enlarge the wry smell of cramped house-keeping. Cushman's bakery truck had stopped to deliver an early basket of rolls. A camp dog, seeing me in the road, barked petulantly. A man emerged from one of the trailers and set forth with a bucket to draw water, from some forest tap.

Leaving the highway I turned off into the woods toward the pond, which was apparent through the foliage. The floor of the forest was strewn with dried old oak leaves and *Transcripts*.[11] From beneath the flattened popcorn wrapper (*granum explosum*) peeped the frail violet. I followed a footpath and descended to the water's edge. The pond lay clear and blue in the morning light, as you have seen it so many times. In the shallows, a man's waterlogged shirt <u>undulated</u> gently. A few flies came out to greet me and convoy me to your cove, past the No Bathing signs on which the fellows and the girls had scrawled their names. I felt strangely excited suddenly to be snooping around your premises, tiptoeing along watchfully, as though not to tread by mistake upon the <u>intervening</u> century. Before I got to the cove I heard something which seemed to me quite wonderful: I heard your frog, a full, clear *troonk*, guiding me, still hoarse and solemn, bridging the years as the robins had bridged them in the sweetness of the village evening. But he soon quit, and I came on a couple of young boys throwing stones at him.

Your front yard is marked by a bronze tablet set in a stone. Four small granite posts, a few feet away, show where the house was. On top of the tablet was a pair of faded blue bathing trunks with a white stripe. Back of it is a pile of stones, a sort of cairn, left by your visitors as a tribute I suppose. It is a rather ugly little heap of stones, Henry. In fact the hillside itself seems faded, browbeaten; a few tall skinny pines, bare of lower limbs, a smattering of young maples in suitable green, some birches and oaks, and a number of trees felled by the last big wind. It was from the bole of one of these fallen pines, torn up by the roots, that I extracted the stone which I added to the cairn—a sentimental act in which I was interrupted by a small terrier from a nearby picnic group, who confronted me and wanted to know about the stone.

---

11. **Transcripts.** *The Evening Transcripts*, a Boston newspaper that is no longer published

What comparison is made between trailer people and Thoreau? What is the experience of the trailer people actually like?

Thoreau believed that he could learn a lot about life by observing nature. What natural items does White observe? What signs of humans does he observe?

WORDS FOR EVERYDAY USE:

con • ge • ni • al • i • ty (kən jē´nē al´ə tē) *n.,* friendliness

un • du • late (un´dyōō lāt) *vi.,* move in waves

in • ter • ven • ing (in tər vēn´ing) *part.,* coming or lying between

I sat down for a while on one of the posts of your house to listen to the bluebottles and the dragonflies. The invaded glade sprawled shabby and mean at my feet, but the flies were tuned to the old vibration. There were the remains of a fire in your ruins, but I doubt that it was yours; also two beer bottles trodden in the soil and become part of the earth. A young oak had taken root in your house, and two or three ferns, unrolling like the ticklers at a banquet. The only other furnishings were a DuBarry pattern sheet, a page torn from a picture magazine, and some crusts in wax paper.

Before I quit I walked clear round the pond and found the place where you used to sit on the northeast side to get the sun in the fall, and the beach where you got sand for scrubbing your floor. On the eastern side of the pond, where the highway borders it, the State has built dressing rooms for swimmers, a float with diving towers, drinking fountains of porcelain, and rowboats for hire. The pond is in fact a State Preserve, and carries a twenty-dollar fine for picking wild flowers, a decree signed in all solemnity by your fellow citizens Walter C. Wardwell, Erson B. Barlow, and Nathaniel I. Bowditch. There was a smell of creosote where they had been building a wide wooden stairway to the road and the parking area. Swimmers and boaters were arriving; bodies plunged vigorously into the water and emerged wet and beautiful in the bright air. As I left, a boatload of town boys were splashing about in mid-pond, kidding and fooling, the young fellows singing at the tops of their lungs in a chorus:

Amer-ica, Amer-ica, God shed his grace
on thee,
  And crown thy good with brotherhood
  From sea to shi-ning sea!

I walked back to town along the railroad, following your custom. The rails were expanding noisily in the hot sun, and on the slope of the roadbed the wild grape and the blackberry sent up their creepers to the track.

The expense of my brief sojourn in Concord was:

Canvas shoes	$1.95	
Baseball bat	.25	} gifts to
Left-handed fielder's glove	1.25	} take back to a boy
Hotel and meals	4.25	
In all	$7.70	

As you see, this amount was almost what you spent for food and eight months. I cannot defend the shoes or the expenditure for shelter and food: they reveal a meanness and grossness in my nature, which you would find contemptible. The baseball equipment, however, is the kind of impediment with which you were never on even terms. You must remember that the house where you practiced the sort of economy which I respect was haunted only by mice and squirrels. You never had to cope with a shortstop. ■

What changes have taken place at Walden Pond? What do you think Thoreau would think of these changes?

Responding to the Selection

Do you enjoy reading literary criticism, in which one writer analyzes or responds to another writer's work? Why, or why not? What emotions do you feel when you read satire? How does it make the writer's ideas harder or easier to understand?

Reviewing the Selection

1. To whom is E. B. White's essay addressed? To what journey does the writer refer?

2. What description of the civilization around Concord does White give?

3. What does White enjoy about Concord? What elements does he enthusiastically describe?

4. When White finally reaches Walden Pond, what does he find? What natural element links him briefly to Thoreau's Walden?

▶▶ 5. Why is the location relevant to White's essay?

▶▶ 6. In what ways does White suggest the town has changed since Thoreau's time?

▶▶ 7. How do machines work throughout "Walden" to symbolize the contrast between White's Walden and Thoreau's Walden?

▶▶ 8. How have the sounds of Walden Pond changed and stayed the same since Thoreau's time?

9. Why do you think E. B. White traveled to Concord? How do his reasons compare to Thoreau's long-ago quest for what he called the "essential facts of life"?

10. How do White's descriptions of Concord and Walden suggest his feelings about Thoreau's ideas?

Understanding Literature (Questions for Discussion)

1. **Simile.** A **simile** is a comparison using *like* or *as,* as in "she blossomed like a rose." Find at least one example of a simile in "Walden." In what ways are the things being compared similar?

2. **Tone. Tone** is emotional attitude toward the reader or toward the subject implied by a literary work. Tone ranges from humor, sadness, and anger to sarcasm, seriousness, and friendlines. Describe the tone of E. B. White's "Walden."

UNIT REVIEW

Modern Nonfiction

VOCABULARY FROM THE SELECTIONS

accumulate, 771	ephemeral, 765	intervening, 774	racket, 755
allay, 754	excruciation, 761	juncture, 755	rickety, 749
commensurate, 765	extricate, 755	meddling, 749	sheer, 770
congeniality, 774	fortitude, 754	mobilize, 760	sojurn, 770
cryptic, 771	game, 770	nimble, 770	solidarity, 748
culprit, 756	hem, 749	ominous, 753	steadfastness, 772
deluge, 755	ideology, 748	perilous, 755	stupefaction, 771
dilation, 761	immemorial, 771	pertinence, 770	tallowy, 749
disbar, 748	impetuous, 770	placard, 747	travail, 765
dissuade, 753	implement, 770	pontoon, 747	undulate, 774
distillation, 771	inauspicious, 772	premonition, 754	verisimilitude, 753
endure, 766	indefinite, 747	prevail, 766	verity, 765
engorge, 761	integrity, 760	propagandist, 748	vortex, 761

LITERARY TERMS

aim, 767	collage, 751	onomatopoeia, 768
alliteration, 767	essay, 763	parallelism, 768
anecdote, 757	farce, 757	simile, 776
antithesis, 768	Modernism, 763	tone, 776

▶ SYNTHESIS: QUESTIONS FOR WRITING, RESEARCH, OR DISCUSSION

1. **Mass Media.** Modern mass media have made it possible for people to reach enormous audiences. What elements of mass media are reflected in John Dos Passos's "Newsreel LXVIII"?

2. **Purpose or Aim.** A writer's purpose, or aim, is the goal that he or she wishes to accomplish. What is the major purpose of each of the selections in this unit? How does each writer achieve his purpose?

LANGUAGE LAB   VOCABULARY DEVELOPMENT

Most times when you encounter a new word, you can check the meaning in a dictionary. However, when a dictionary is not available, you can use the following strategies to help you deduce the meaning.

LANGUAGE ARTS SURVEY

For additional help, see the Language Arts Survey, 2.138–2.139.

USING CONTEXT CLUES

Restatement. In a **restatement** the author reveals the meaning of a word by using different words to express the same idea in another sentence.

EXAMPLE: Dos Passos's newsreels were *collages* of news headlines, song lyrics, and catch phrases. He used these *pieced-together fragments of diverse ideas* to comment on society.

Apposition. Apposition is the use of a word or phrase that is specifically intended to clarify or modify an unknown word.

EXAMPLE: Thurber uses *hyperbole,* or *extreme exaggeration,* when he says he's such a light sleeper that he will wake up if someone in the room stops breathing.

Examples. Sometimes **examples** are included within the sentence to reveal a word's meaning.

EXAMPLE: Black Elk speaks of such *mystical* experiences as *visions* and *prophecies.*

Comparison. Comparison allows a reader to deduce a word's meaning by comparing it to familiar meanings.

EXAMPLE: There was no way to *dissuade* my father. Once he made up his mind, my mother couldn't *talk him out of* his decision. No amount of *reasoning or pleading* could make him reverse himself.

Contrast. Contrast allows a reader to deduce a word's meaning by contrasting it to familiar meanings.

EXAMPLE: Lewis Thomas's *lucid* prose makes his scientific essays intriguing and enjoyable. His essays are a refreshing change from the *difficult* and sometimes *incomprehensible* writings of most scientists.

PREFIXES AND SUFFIXES

Prefixes and Base Words. Some words are formed by adding a **prefix** to a **base word**. If the word is unfamiliar, you can deduce its meaning by looking at the meaning of these parts. The following are some common prefixes and their meanings.

Suffixes. Suffixes are added to the end of words. The following are some common suffixes and their meanings.

Prefix	Meaning	Suffix	Meaning
il–	"not"	–ible, –ic	"capable of, able to be"
pre–	"before"		
post–	"after"	–ly	"having nature of"
un–	"not"	–ness	"in the manner of"

LANGUAGE ARTS SURVEY

For additional help, see the Language Arts Survey, 2.138–2.139.

Exercise A Using Context Clues

Write the meaning of the italicized word in each sentence that follows. Then write the type of context clue you used to deduce the meaning.

1. Faulkner is known for his *monolithic* sentences. A reader might read for several pages before encountering a period.

2. E. B. White declared that essayists must always be *veracious* because readers can instantly detect deceit or half-truths.

3. I would describe my literary tastes as *eclectic.* Rather than limit myself to nonfiction, I enjoy various types of literature.

4. Some feminist scholars have criticized the *patriarchal,* or male-centered, elements of Faulkner's writing.

5. *Black Elk Speaks* is not the only *ethnographic* autobiography. In *Black Hawk, An Autobiography* (1833), Black Hawk's recollections of his Sauk culture are systematically recorded.

LANGUAGE ARTS SURVEY

For additional help, see the Language Arts Survey, 2.140–2.141.

Exercise B Using Prefixes and Suffixes

Identify the prefixes and suffixes in the italicized words in the following sentences. Then write a definition for each word. If necessary, use a dictionary to check the meaning of a particular prefix or suffix.

1. After the cot turned over, Thurber appeared to be in a state of *unconsciousness.*

2. Lewis Thomas has an *optimistic* attitude toward science.

3. The disturbing events leading to World War II prompted Dos Passos to adopt a *utopian* viewpoint in his writing.

4. Some scientific writing is nearly *unintelligible* to the layperson.

5. Thousands listened *raptly* to Kennedy's speech.

Photograph by Lee Stalsworth

Number 3, 1949: TIGER. *Jackson Pollock, 1949. Hirshhorn Museum and Sculpture Garden, Smithsonian Institution. Gift of Joseph H. Hirshhorn, 1972*

write of one life only. My own. If my story is true, I trust it will resonate with significance for other lives.

—Richard Rodriguez

CONTEMPORARY LITERATURE
(1960–PRESENT)

PRELUDE TO THE SIXTIES

John F. Kennedy

The events that would shake the United States in the 1960s had their roots in the Cold War Era of the 1940s and 1950s. The Korean War, fought against North Korea and its ally Communist China, led the United States to commit itself to defense against Communism in other parts of Southeast Asia, thus laying the groundwork for war in Vietnam. Throughout the late forties and the fifties, tensions escalated between the United States and the Communist "Eastern Bloc," especially after such events as the detonation of an atomic bomb by the Soviet Union in 1949 and the Soviet repression of an uprising in Hungary in 1956. In 1957, the Soviet Union launched the first orbital satellite, Sputnik, raising fears that the United States was falling behind technologically and initiating the Space Race that would result in the landing of United States astronauts on the moon in 1969.

Domestically, the 1950s were a time of prosperity characterized by rising employment, movement of workers into suburban housing developments, the building of an unprecedented system of interstate highways, the growth of the television industry, political and social conservatism, and rapidly rising birth rates (the so-called "baby boom" of the late fifties and early sixties).

THE TURBULENT SIXTIES

When **John F. Kennedy** defeated **Richard Nixon** in 1960, becoming the youngest man ever to hold the office of president, it seemed to many that a new age had dawned. Kennedy, a committed cold warrior, supported a covert operation to invade **Fidel Castro's**

LITERARY EVENTS

► = American Events

►1964. Saul Bellow's *The Zog* published
►1963. Sylvia Plath's *The Bell Jar* published
►1962. Rachel Carson's *Silent Spring* published
►1961. Joseph Heller's *Catch 22* published
►1960. John Updike's *Rabbit, Run* and Anne Sexton's *To Bedlam and Half Way Back* published

1967. Gabriel García Márquez's *One Hundred Years of Solitude* published
►1966. Katherine Anne Porter's *Collected Short Stories* published
►1965. *The Autobiography of Malcolm X* published

1970. John Fowles's *The French Lieutenant's Woman* published

1960 — **1965** — **1970**

HISTORICAL EVENTS

►1960. John F. Kennedy elected president
►1961. United States severs relations with Cuba; Bay of Pigs invasion fails; Berlin wall erected
►1962. Cuban missile crisis
►1963. President Kennedy assassinated; Lyndon B. Johnson sworn in as president; Martin Luther King, Jr., delivers his "I have a dream" speech
►1964. President Johnson reelected

►1965. Vietnam War begins; Malcolm X is killed
►1967. Thurgood Marshall becomes first African-American Supreme Court justice
►1968. Robert F. Kennedy assassinated
►1968. Martin Luther King, Jr. assassinated
►1969. Neil Armstrong walks on the moon

Cuba, the Bay of Pigs Invasion. The invasion failed and further increased tensions with the Soviets, leading in 1962 to the Cuban Missile Crisis, in which Kennedy warned the Soviets to remove newly installed nuclear missiles from Cuba or face war. The threat of nuclear war seemed, for a few days, all too real. Thereafter, the Soviet Union, Great Britain, and the United States negotiated the first of many treaties related to limitations on the testing and use of nuclear arms. However, the arms race continued unabated, with each side following a policy of "mutually assured destruction" to prevent the other from making a first strike.

In the 1950s, race relations had become a central issue in the United States following the 1954 decision in which the Supreme Court ruled separate but unequal schools unconstitutional. This ruling was followed in 1955 by a successful boycott, led by the **Reverend Martin Luther King, Jr.,** of segregated buses in Montgomery, Alabama. Kennedy supported the Civil Rights movement, sending federal troops in 1962 and 1963 to ensure enrollment of African-American students in two Southern universities. Late in 1963, the popular President Kennedy was assassinated in Dallas, Texas. This act and the subsequent assassinations of Martin Luther King, Jr. and Robert Kennedy left the United States reeling.

Kennedy's successor, Lyndon Johnson, carried on his predecessor's civil rights policies, pressing for the passage of the Civil Rights Act of 1964, which protected against discrimination in accommodations and employment and tied federal funding of education to desegregation of schools. The Voting Rights Act of 1965, followed protecting against discrimination at the polls. In spite of these measures, major race riots occurred in several American cities in 1965, 1967, and 1968.

After defeating Barry Goldwater in the presidential election of 1964, Johnson initiated a legislative program designed to build what he called the "Great Society," using his considerable political skills to push through a series of social welfare measures, including bills related to housing, health care for the elderly, and education. The political life of the United States since the Johnson Era has been dominated by debates over such legislation, with conservatives supporting greater defense spending and less spending on domestic programs and liberals supporting less spending on defense and greater spending on domestic programs.

Reverend Martin Luther King, Jr.

▶1983. Jamaica Kincaid's *At the Bottom of the River*, Neil Simon's *Brighton Beach Memoirs,* and David Mamet's *Glengarry Glen Ross* published

▶1978. John Cheever's *Falconer* published

▶1989. Amy Tan's *The Joy Luck Club* published

▶1971. John Gardner's *Grendel* published

▶1980. Anne Tyler's *Morgan's Passing* and Walker Percy's *The Second Coming* published

▶1987. Toni Morrison's *Beloved* published

▶1976. Alex Haley's *Roots* and Alice Walker's *Meridian* published

▶1985. Garrison Keillor's *Lake Wobegone Days* published

1975	1980	1985

▶1972. Watergate affair; Nixon reelected

▶1980. Ronald Reagan elected president

▶1987. Soviet leader Mikhail Gorbachev and Reagan sign disarmament treaty

▶1973. Vietnam War ends

▶1981. Iran releases United States hostages

▶1974. Nixon resigns; Gerald Ford becomes president

▶1983. Terrorists bomb United States Embassy at Beirut

▶1976. Jimmy Carter elected president

▶1984. Reagan reelected

▶1988. George Bush elected president

▶1979. Iran takes United States citizens hostage

Despite his political accomplishments, Johnson was to have a troubled administration because of involvement in a widely unpopular war in the Southeast Asian country of Vietnam. In 1964, an attack on United States ships led to the Gulf of Tonkin Resolution, committing the country to a "police action," commonly referred to as the Vietnam War, that proved to be extremely divisive, fomenting antiwar demonstrations throughout the United States. These demonstrations were part of a larger "counterculture" rebellion among American youth who, relatively prosperous themselves due to their parents' material gains during the fifties, challenged the war and traditional "materialistic" values. The extreme styles of dress and speech that characterized the so-called "Hippie Movement" soon passed into oblivion, along with the more radical politics of the period. However, the resurgence of feminism that occurred as part of the youth movement had a more lasting influence, leading to an expanded role for women in American society.

THE SEVENTIES AND EIGHTIES

Following the turbulent Democratic National Convention in Chicago in 1968, Richard Nixon, a Republican from California, was elected by a landslide. The Nixon Administration pursued a policy of détente, or improved relations, with the Soviet Union, negotiating the first of a series of Strategic Arms Limitation Treaties (SALT) with the Soviets. Relations with China also improved following President Nixon's visit there in 1972. In 1973, after the signing of a peace treaty, the United States withdrew from Vietnam. Then, in 1974, following charges of a coverup of improprieties during the 1972 election campaign, including a break-in at the Watergate hotel in Washington, DC, President Nixon resigned, to be succeeded by Gerald Ford.

The Ford Administration faced difficult economic problems, not the least of which was an oil embargo during the Yom Kippur War that caused fuel prices to soar. Ford lost the 1976 election campaign to Jimmy Carter of Georgia. The Carter Administration followed a policy of promoting human rights around the world and succeeded in bringing Israel and Egypt, traditional enemies in the Middle East, to the negotiating table. However, domestic economic troubles, coupled with the administration's inability to deal with the Iran Hostage Crisis, in which Islamic fundamentalists in Tehran, Iran, took over the American Embassy and held its

LITERARY
EVENTS

► = American Events

1990	**1995**

1990. Germany reunited; Iraq invades Kuwait; and Nelson Mandela released from South African prison

►1992. Bill Clinton elected president

HISTORICAL
EVENTS

1991. Serbo-Croatian war begins in Yugoslavia

►1991. United States Desert Storm attack on Iraq

Space Shuttle Challenger.
National Aeronautics and
Space Administration. (NASA)

occupants hostage, led to Carter's defeat by Ronald Reagan in 1980. During his two terms in office, Reagan, an extremely popular president, increased defense spending considerably, which greatly boosted the country's budget deficit but helped to hasten the collapse of the Soviet Union. That collapse occurred during the administration of George Bush, Reagan's vice-president and successor. Despite fairly high standings in the polls at the end of the Gulf War with Iraq, Bush was defeated for reelection by Bill Clinton of Arkansas.

AMERICAN LITERATURE AND THE CONTEMPORARY ERA

The end of the 1950s and beginning of the 1960s saw the emergence in California of the Beatnik Movement. Centered in San Francisco, this avant-garde literary movement, whose leading lights included the novelist Jack Kerouac and the poets Lawrence Ferlinghetti and Allen Ginsberg, drew heavily on Existentialist thought. **Existentialism** was a twentieth-century philosophical movement that posited the absurd freedom of the individual to create meaning in a world that was itself devoid of meaning. Ridiculed in the popular media, the beatniks nonetheless represented another variation on the theme of American individualism.

The 1960s were a time of radical experimentation in all the arts in the United States, including literature. Boundaries between literature, painting, sculpture, music, and dance broke down in the development of "Happenings," spontaneous expressions of creative freedom that were precursors of the performance art of the 1970s and 1980s. Emerging during this period were a number of experimental literary forms, including found poems, made up primarily or exclusively of bits of language collected from the culture at large, from billboards,

Nikki Giovanni

graffiti, subway posters, and other such materials. Concrete poems, designed to appeal to the eye, also enjoyed a vogue during this time. Many poets of the period, notably **Robert Lowell, Anne Sexton, Sylvia Plath**, and **John Berryman,** wrote what is known as confessional poetry, extremely personal verse that described intimate, often troubled or troubling experiences. During the political agitation of the sixties and early seventies, a number of antiwar poets emerged, including **Robert Bly** and **Denise Levertov,** and many African-American poets, such as **LeRoi Jones, Nikki Giovanni, Gwendolyn Brooks,** and **Mari Evans,** produced compelling work related to problems of race and discrimination. The sixties and seventies were also times of experimentation in fictional forms, which reached new heights of zaniness and dark comic invention in the works of **John Barth, J. D. Salinger, Kurt Vonnegut, Thomas Pynchon, Richard Brautigan, Philip Roth, John Updike, John Fowles, Ursula K. Le Guin, E. L. Doctorow, John Irving, Walker Percy,** and **Joyce Carol Oates.**

In the period from the mid-seventies to the nineties, the audience for poetry and short stories in the United States dwindled considerably, while nonfiction and novels in many genres—romances, science fiction, detective stories, mysteries, and the like—remained extremely popular. Despite this trend, the United States continued to produce many fine young poets and writers of short fiction who found their chief outlets in small literary magazines. Perhaps the most significant of all developments in recent years in American literature has been the appearance of a large number of superb women writers of novels and short fiction, including **Alice Walker, Anne Tyler, Alice Hoffman, Amy Bloom,** and **Ellen Gilchrist.** Excellent dramatists of the contemporary era include **Beth Henley, August Wilson, Lanford Wilson, Lorainne Hansberry, Marsha Norman, David Mamet, Sam Shepard,** and **Christopher Durang.** Recent nonfiction writers of note include the essayists **Joan Didion, Stephen Jay Gould, Lewis Thomas, Annie Dillard,** and **Diane Ackerman.**

Echoes:

The Contemporary Era

"I have a dream . . . that my four little children will one day live in a nation where they will not be judged by the color of their skin but by the content of their character."

—Martin Luther King, Jr.

"The first problem for all of us, men and women, is not to learn, but to unlearn."

—Gloria Steinem, "A New Egalitarian Life Style"
The New York Times
August 26, 1971

"And so, my fellow Americans, ask not what your country can do for you; ask what you can do for your country."

—John F. Kennedy

"Yes Celie, she say. Everything want to be loved. Us sing and dance, make faces and give flower bouquets, trying to be loved. You ever notice that trees do everything to git attention we do, except walk?"

—Alice Walker, from *The Color Purple*

"Auto Wreck"
by Karl Shapiro

ABOUT THE AUTHOR

Karl Shapiro (1913–) was born in Baltimore, Maryland, the grandson of Russian Jewish immigrants. He attended the University of Virginia and Johns Hopkins University. During World War II, while serving in the United States Army in the South Pacific, he wrote and published his first successful poetry collection, *V-Letter and Other Poems* (1944), for which he received a Pulitzer Prize. As a poet, editor of poetry journals, and critic, Shapiro developed strong ideas about what poetry should be. He embodied his opinions in his own poems, which were raw expressions of sensations. Shapiro believed in using common, everyday language in poetry and was highly critical of the intellectual poetry of the Modernists Ezra Pound and T. S. Eliot, praising instead poets of the people such as Walt Whitman and William Carlos Williams. His later poetry, which included *Poems of a Jew* (1957) and *The Bourgeois Poet* (1964), explores his own past. Critical works by Shapiro include his *Essay on Rime* (1945); a verse commentary on modern poetry, *Beyond Criticism* (1953); and *In Defense of Ignorance* (1960). Shapiro has served as editor of the influential literary magazines *Poetry* and *Prairie Schooner* and has taught at many universities around the United States, including the University of Nebraska, the University of Illinois, and the University of California at Davis.

ABOUT THE SELECTION

The automobile has been a major force in shaping twentieth-century life. Cars have changed the American landscape, given people unprecedented mobility, created millions of jobs, and threatened environmental quality. The poet T. S. Eliot even claimed that the rhythms of the internal combustion engine affected the rhythms of modern poetry. In **"Auto Wreck,"** Karl Shapiro details an all too frequent experience made commonplace by the presence of the automobile in the modern world.

READER'S JOURNAL

Why do automobile accidents draw onlookers? What do people find so fascinating about such tragedies? What questions are raised by the seemingly arbitrary and absurd nature of such accidents? Freewrite about these questions in your journal.

LANGUAGE SKILLS

Read the Language Arts Survey, 2.19, "Adjectives and Articles"; 2.16, "Verbals: Participles"; and 2.35, "Using Colorful Modifiers." Then, as you read the selection, make a list of the precise adjectives and participles used by the author to make his poem vivid and memorable.

"Auto Wreck"

KARL SHAPIRO

Its quick soft silver bell beating, beating,
And down the dark one ruby flare
Pulsing out red light like an artery,
The ambulance at top speed floating down
5   Past beacons and illuminated clocks
Wings in a heavy curve, dips down,
And brakes speed, entering the crowd.
The doors leap open, emptying light;
Stretchers are laid out, the mangled lifted
10   And stowed into the little hospital.
Then the bell, breaking the hush, tolls once,
And the ambulance with its terrible cargo
Rocking, slightly rocking, moves away,
As the doors, an afterthought, are closed.

15   We are <u>deranged</u>, walking among the cops
Who sweep glass and are large and <u>composed</u>.
One is still making notes under the light.
One with a bucket douches ponds of blood
Into the street and gutter.

How do the spectators feel? the police?

WORDS FOR
EVERYDAY USE:

de • ranged (dē rānj´d) *adj.,* disordered; upset; insane

com • posed (kəm pōzd´) *adj.,* calm, tranquil

Steering Wheel. David Hockney, October 1982. Photographic Collage, 30 × 36. © David Hockney

20   One hangs lanterns on the wrecks that cling,
      Empty husks of locusts,[1] to iron poles.

      Our throats were tight as tourniquets,[2]
      Our feet were bound with splints, but now,
      Like <u>convalescents</u> intimate and <u>gauche</u>,
25   We speak through sickly smiles and warn
      With the stubborn saw of common sense,
      The grim joke and the <u>banal</u> resolution.
      The traffic moves around with care,

      1. **locusts.** Large grasshoppers
      2. **tourniquets.** Devices used to stop the flow of blood

WORDS FOR
EVERYDAY USE:

con • va • les • cent (kän´ və les´ ənt) *n.*, person recovering from an illness
gauche (gōsh) *adj.*, tactless; lacking social grace
ba • nal (bā´ nəl) *adj.*, commonplace; trite

But we remain, touching a wound
30 That opens to our richest horror.
Already old, the question Who shall die?
Becomes unspoken Who is innocent?

For death in war is done by hands;
Suicide has cause and stillbirth, logic;
35 And cancer, simple as a flower, blooms.
But this invites the <u>occult</u> mind,
Cancels our physics with a sneer,
And spatters all we knew of dénouement[3]
Across the <u>expedient</u> and wicked stones. ■

---

3. **dénouement.** Revelation or outcome

Responding to the Selection

What details in the poem are particularly striking emotionally? How do the people viewing the scene respond? What questions does the accident raise in their minds? Discuss these questions with your classmates.

WORDS FOR EVERYDAY USE:

oc • cult (ə kult´) *adj.*, mysterious; hidden

ex • pe • di • ent (ek spē´dē ənt) *adj.*, convenient

Reviewing the Selection

1. To what does the speaker compare the red light of the ambulance?

2. What words does the speaker use to describe the contents of the ambulance?

3. What do the police do after the ambulance speeds away?

4. What words characterize the statements made by the onlookers after the ambulance leaves?

5. What do the ambulance and its red light foreshadow?

6. What mood is created by the descriptions in stanzas 1 and 2? In what sense are the onlookers' throats "tight as tourniquets" and their feet "bound with splints"?

7. How do the descriptions of the police and of the onlookers differ? Why might these people react differently to the scene?

8. What might be the reason for the types of statements the onlookers make? What difficult questions are the onlookers confronting?

9. According to the speaker, how does death in an auto accident differ from death by other causes?

10. People generally expect the events in their lives to be significant or meaningful. In what sense does an auto accident violate this expectation?

Understanding Literature (Questions for Discussion)

1. **Existentialism. Existentialism** is a twentieth-century philosophy that postulates the absurdity and meaninglessness of life. Existentialist philosophers such as Albert Camus and Jean-Paul Sartre argued that existence, or being, emerges out of nothingness without any essential, or defining, nature. As described in the poem, what is absurd or meaningless about an auto accident? What decides who will die and who will not? In what sense do auto accidents defy attempts to explain them, to make sense of them, to describe them in terms of purpose or cause?

2. **Metaphor.** A **metaphor** is a figure of speech in which one thing is spoken or written about as if it were another. This figure of speech invites the reader to make a comparison between the two things. What in the poem is compared to a bird? to the pulsing of blood from an artery? to the empty husks of locusts? to being bound with tourniquets or splints? to convalescents? to a wound?

"Those Winter Sundays"
by Robert Hayden

ABOUT THE AUTHOR

Robert Hayden (1913–1980) grew up in a poor neighborhood of Detroit, Michigan, a place to which he would return in poems collected in *Elegies for Paradise Valley* (1978). He attended Wayne State University and received a master's degree from the University of Michigan, where he was professor of English from 1968 until his death in 1980. From 1946 to 1968, he taught at Fisk University in Tennessee. Hayden built upon his experiences and on the heritage of African Americans to write poetry that spoke for different groups of people throughout history. He made connections to the universal from the experiences and voice of the individual, be it the gypsy, the slave, or the slave trader. His poem "Middle Passage" uses the technique of collage, pioneered by writers such as John Dos Passos, T. S. Eliot, and William Carlos Williams, to evoke the many voices associated with the slave ships that brought African Americans to the New World. Hayden was a versatile writer, trying various poetic forms and styles to express universal emotions. His collections include *Heart-Shape in the Dust* (1940), *The Lion and the Archer* (1948), and *A Ballad of Remembrance* (1962), which contains the poem "Those Winter Sundays." He received the Grand Prize for Poetry at the First World Festival for Negro Arts in 1966 for *A Ballad of Remembrance.* In 1976, Hayden was appointed poetry consultant to the Library of Congress in Washington, DC.

ABOUT THE SELECTION

  "**Those Winter Sundays**" recalls a single, recurring event from the speaker's childhood and draws from it a moving generalization about the nature of love. The poem thus demonstrates how writers can arrive at and justify conclusions by presenting even minor events in concrete detail. The poem is remarkable for its simplicity, beauty, and precision of language.

READER'S JOURNAL

Think of some small service that someone once did for you that demonstrated their love or concern. Write about this person and what he or she did for you in your journal.

THINKING SKILLS

Read the Language Arts Survey, 4.11, "Generalizing." Then, as you read the poem, think about what conclusions you can draw from it about the speaker's father and about the nature of love.

"Those Winter Sundays"

ROBERT HAYDEN

Sundays too my father got up early
and put his clothes on in the blueblack cold,
then with cracked hands that ached
from labor in the weekday weather made
5   <u>banked</u> fires blaze. No one ever thanked him.

I'd wake and hear the cold splintering, breaking.
When the rooms were warm, he'd call,
and slowly I would rise and dress,
fearing the <u>chronic</u> angers of that house,

10   Speaking indifferently to him,
who had driven out the cold
and polished my good shoes as well.
What did I know, what did I know
of love's <u>austere</u> and lonely offices? ∎

What reaction did the father get for making the fire?

What other task did the father do for the speaker? What didn't the speaker realize about the father's actions?

WORDS FOR EVERYDAY USE:

banked (baŋkd) *part.,* arranged to continue burning slowly
chron • ic (krän´ ik) *adj.,* constant; perpetual

aus • tere (o stir´) *adj.,* plain; without luxury or ornamentation

Responding to the Selection

What makes the father's actions especially admirable? How did the speaker feel about those actions when he was a child? How does the speaker feel as an adult looking back on those actions? In what ways has the speaker changed since his childhood? Discuss these questions with your classmates.

Reviewing the Selection

RECALLING

1. What did the speaker's father do on Sunday mornings?

2. How did the hands of the speaker's father look?

3. When would the speaker's father call him to get up?

4. What did the speaker fear, and how did he speak to his father?

INTERPRETING

5. What did the speaker's father do on weekdays? Why does the speaker use the word *too* in line 1 of the poem?

6. What changed the appearance of the speaker's father's hands?

7. What did the speaker's father want to spare his child?

8. Was the speaker's household always happy? Was his relationship with his father always a warm one? How do you know?

SYNTHESIZING

9. What other deed did the speaker's father do for him on those winter mornings? Why did the father do these deeds, even though he did not receive thanks for them?

10. What has the speaker learned about love since his childhood? What does he now recognize that he did not recognize before? What makes love's offices, or duties, sometimes austere and lonely?

Understanding Literature (Questions for Discussion)

1. **Assonance. Assonance** is the repetition of vowel sounds in stressed syllables that end with different consonant sounds. An example is the repetition of the long *o* sound in the words *clothes* and *cold* in line 2 of the poem. Find two other examples of assonance in the poem.

2. **Consonance. Consonance** is the repetition of a consonant sound preceded by a different vowel sound. An example in the poem is the repetition of the final consonant sounds in the words *cracked* and *ached*. Find one other example of consonance in the poem.

3. **Alliteration. Alliteration** is the repetition of initial consonant sounds, as in the words *babbling brook.* Identify six examples of alliteration in this poem.

4. **Repetition. Repetition** is the use, again, of a word, phrase, or other element in a work. Find one example of repetition in the poem. What does this repetition indicate about the emotion with which the line is spoken?

Responding in Writing

Lyric Poem. Review your Reader's Journal entry on the small service performed because of someone's love or concern for you. Write a list of images or sensory details connected with this event. Think about what physical details best characterize the person who performed the service. Did you understand what this act meant at the time? Has it developed a richer meaning for you now? After you have jotted down your ideas, select the most powerful phrases and images as building blocks for your poem. You may either select a rhyme scheme and meter that you feel comfortable using or you may write free verse.

"A Story That Could Be True"
by William Stafford

ABOUT THE AUTHOR

William Stafford (1914–1993) was born in Hutchinson, Kansas. He attended the University of Kansas and began a long-term teaching position at Oregon's Lewis and Clark College in 1948. Stafford's poetry explores the difficult choices faced by people all over the world. For example, how can the delicate relationship between nature and humanity be preserved? His simple, poignant verses reflect his reverence for nature and the need to protect the outdoors from urban expansion and technological greed. Like Robert Lowell and Anne Sexton, Stafford often writes what can be called confessional poetry, laying bare private, deep, intimate experiences. Stafford's lifelong horror of war led him to register as a conscientious objector during World War II. His personal account of that experience, *Down In My Heart,* was published in 1947. Although he submitted poems to literary journals as a young man, his first collection of poetry, *West of Your City,* was not published until 1960. His poetry collection *Traveling Through the Dark* won the National Book Award in 1962. Other collections of Stafford's sensitive, moving verse include *The Rescued Year* (1966); *Allegiances* (1970); *Someday, Maybe* (1973); and *Stories That Could Be True* (1977).

ABOUT THE SELECTION

As its title indicates, **"A Story That Could Be True"** invites the reader to consider something that could be true of any reader of the poem, something that is nonetheless exotic and wonderful. Like much imaginative literature, the poem begins by posing a "What if" question and ends with an intriguing answer.

READER'S JOURNAL

In your journal, write ten interesting questions beginning with the words *What if.* Save these questions as possible ideas for future writing.

THINKING SKILLS

Read the Language Arts Survey, 4.13, "Making Hypotheses." Then, as you read the selection, pose these questions to yourself: With what hypothesis does the selection begin? What conclusions does the speaker draw based on this hypothesis?

"A Story That Could Be True"

WILLIAM STAFFORD

Why might no one know "your" name?

If you were exchanged in the cradle and
your real mother died
without ever telling the story
then no one knows your name,
5   and somewhere in the world
your father is lost and needs you
but you are far away.

He can never find
how true you are, how ready.
10   When the great wind comes
and the robberies of the rain
you stand on the corner shivering.
The people who go by—
you wonder at their calm.

15   They miss the whisper that runs
any day in your mind,
"Who are you really, wanderer?"—
and the answer you have to give
no matter how dark and cold
20   the world around you is:
"Maybe I'm a king."   ■

Responding to the Selection

What parts of the poem indicate that the "you" referred to by the speaker is not a famous, well-known person? What other parts of the poem show that the speaker recognizes himself to be someone special? Discuss with your classmates what really determines who a person is and what he or she might become.

Reviewing the Selection

RECALLING

1. To whom is this poem addressed?

2. What hypothetical situation does the speaker ask the reader to consider in lines 1–3? What would be true, given that situation, of "your name"?

3. What would be true of "your" father?

4. Given that situation, what would "you" wonder at, and what would other people miss?

INTERPRETING

5. About whom was this poem written?

6. What does the phrase "no one knows your name" suggest about how well people know one another's true, inner selves?

7. What does the father in the poem not know about "you"? What does the speaker of the poem suggest is true about "you"?

8. Do you ever feel like a wanderer, like someone out of place whose true qualities are not recognized? Explain.

SYNTHESIZING

9. What parts of the poem suggest that "you" sometimes do not find the world to be a warm, hospitable place?

10. What can "you" reasonably believe even if the world is sometimes dark and cold?

Understanding Literature (Questions for Discussion)

Irony. Irony is a difference between appearance and reality. This poem makes the ironic point that even when people feel out of place and different, even when they experience the world as cold and dark, they remain unique, they have unrecognized potentials, in fact, they could be royalty. Note that what is true of the "you" in the poem is also true of all those other people, the ones that go by and cause "you" to "wonder at their calm." Given this observation, what makes the poem doubly ironic?

Responding in Writing

A Story That Could Be True. Think of something wildly improbable that could, nonetheless, be true. Some famous examples of such "stories that could be true" include the idea that someone was switched at birth, the idea that some famous person from the past didn't really die but is still living an obscure life somewhere on the planet, and the idea that the last hour didn't really happen but was really part of a dream that you are having while lying in bed at night. With a group of classmates, brainstorm a list of such "stories that could be true" but probably aren't. Choose one of these ideas and develop it into a paragraph, an essay, a poem, or a story of your own.

PROJECT

Let Us Now Praise Nonfamous People. Long ago, the poet Thomas Gray, in his "Elegy Written in a Country Churchyard," pointed out that fame isn't all it is cracked up to be, for "the paths of glory lead but to the grave." In "A Story That Could Be True," William Stafford reminds us that everyone, whether famous or not, has greatness inside. Choose someone you know well but who is not well known in the outside world and prepare some work to celebrate his or her greatness. Your work can be a thank-you letter, a poem, or song of praise, an illustration or drawing, an interpretive dance, or any other work that demonstrates or celebrates the special qualities of the person you have chosen.

POETRY

"House Guest"
by Elizabeth Bishop

ABOUT THE AUTHOR

Elizabeth Bishop (1911–1979) was born in Worcester, Massachusetts, but, on the death of her father just eight months after her birth, Bishop's mother took her to live with her maternal grandparents in Nova Scotia, Canada. When she was five years old, her mother was permanently institutionalized, and Bishop became the pawn of warring family members, eventually being returned to Worcester by her paternal grandparents. Those early traumatic experiences left Bishop with a series of stress-related illnesses and an emotionally restrained personality that was later to characterize her poetry. While attending Vassar College in the early 1930s, Bishop became an ardent admirer of poet Marianne Moore and abandoned thoughts of medical school for the greater attraction of travel. She finally settled in Brazil for sixteen years. On her return to the United States, Bishop taught at Harvard from 1970 to 1977. Inspired by such events as the exile of her youth and her life as an expatriate in Brazil, Bishop's poetry is known for its meticulous detail and understated style. Her many honors include the 1956 Pulitzer Prize for the combined collection *Poems: North and South—A Cold Spring* and the 1969 National Book Award for *Complete Poems*.

ABOUT THE SELECTION

Some people's personalities challenge us, raising basic, uncomfortable questions. Elizabeth Bishop's **"House Guest"** presents a portrait of such a person. Bishop creates this portrait through precise description, vivid images, and bits of dialogue.

"House Guest"

ELIZABETH BISHOP

Who is visiting the speaker? What is the visitor like?

The sad seamstress
who stays with us this month
is small and thin and bitter.
No one can cheer her up.
5   Give her a dress, a drink,
roast chicken, or fried fish—
it's all the same to her.

She sits and watches TV.
No, she watches zigzags.
10   "Can you adjust the TV?"
"No," she says. No hope.
She watches on and on,
without hope, without air.[1]

Her own clothes give us pause,
15   but she's not a poor orphan.
She has a father, a mother,
and all that, and she's earning
quite well, and we're stuffing
her with fattening foods.

20   We invite her to use the binoculars.
We say, "Come see the jets!"

---

1. **without air.** Without spirit

We say, "Come see the baby!"
Or the knife grinder who cleverly
plays the National Anthem[2]
25   on his wheel so shrilly.
Nothing helps.

She speaks: "I need a little
money to buy buttons."
She seems to think it's useless
30   to ask. Heavens, buy buttons,
if they'll do any good,
the biggest in the world—
by the dozen, by the gross![3]
Buy yourself an ice cream,
35   a comic book, a car!

Her face is closed as a nut,
closed as a careful snail
or a thousand-year-old seed.
Does she dream of marriage?
40   Of getting rich? Her sewing
is decidedly <u>mediocre</u>.

Please! Take our money! Smile!
What on earth have we done?
What has everyone done
45   and when did it all begin?
Then one day she confides
that she wanted to be a nun[4]
and her family opposed her.

Perhaps we should let her go,
50   or deliver her straight off
to the nearest convent—and wasn't
her month up last week, anyway?

What does the visitor ask for? What is her attitude toward her request? What is the speaker's response?

What personal secret does the visitor share? What light does this shed on her life?

---

2. **National Anthem.** "The Star Spangled Banner" by Francis Scott Key (1779–1843)
3. **gross.** Twelve dozen
4. **nun.** Religious woman who takes vows of obedience to the Roman Catholic Church

WORDS FOR EVERYDAY USE:

me • di • o • cre (mē´dē ō´ kər) adj., average; not very good

Can it be that we nourish
one of the Fates[5] in our bosoms?
55   Clotho,[6] sewing our lives
with a bony little foot
on a borrowed sewing machine,
and our fates will be like hers,
and our hems crooked forever?   ■

What fear does
the speaker raise
at the end of the
poem?

---

5. **Fates.** In Greek and Roman mythology, Clotho,
Lachesis, and Atropos, the three goddesses who control
human destiny and life
6. **Clotho.** Spinner of the thread of human life

Responding to the Selection

How would being around someone like the seamstress make you feel? What advice
might you have for her? Discuss these questions with your classmates.

Reviewing the Selection

RECALLING

1. Who has come to stay at the speaker's
house, and what adjectives are used in
the first three lines to describe her?

2. How does the seamstress spend her
spare time?

3. In what ways do the people in the
house try to cheer up the seamstress?

4. What questions does the seamstress
raise in the mind of the speaker?

INTERPRETING

5. How would you describe the
seamstress's attitude toward life?

6. What is unusual about the way in
which the seamstress watches
television? about her clothing? about
the way in which she asks for money
for buttons? What do these things
reveal about her?

7. How does the seamstress respond to
attempts to cheer her up?

8. What lines in the poem indicate that
the speaker is uncomfortable about the
presence of the seamstress and would
like to see her out of the house?

9. Why is the seamstress so unhappy?

10. What uncomfortable question does the seamstress raise for the speaker about dreams in general?

Understanding Literature (Questions for Discussion)

1. **Tone. Tone** is the emotional attitude toward the reader or toward the subject implied by a literary work. What is the tone of the speaker's comments in stanza 5? Why does the speaker take this tone?

2. **Allusion.** An **allusion** is a rhetorical technique in which reference is made to a person, event, object, or work from history or literature. In Greek mythology, the Fates were three goddesses, often pictured as extremely ancient sisters, who controlled the destinies of human beings. Clotho, the spinner, spun the thread of human fate; Lachesis, the allotter, spooled it out; and Atropos cut it, thus deciding when a person would die. To which of these sisters does the speaker allude in the final stanza of the poem? Why is this choice of allusions particularly appropriate? What fears about her own fate does the seamstress raise in the speaker? Why does the seamstress make the speaker think of Clotho?

3. **Pun.** A **pun** is a play on words, one that wittily exploits a double meaning. What pun exists in the name *Clotho*, applied to the seamstress?

POETRY

"The Secret"
by Denise Levertov

ABOUT THE AUTHOR

Denise Levertov (1923–   ) draws from many rich traditions to create her unique, visionary poetry, including the Welsh mysticism of her mother's ancestry and the Russian Hasidic Judaism of her father's. Born in Essex, England, Levertov was schooled at home. During the London blitz of World War II, she served as a nurse. She became a poet at a very early age, publishing her first collection, *The Double Image,* in 1946. In 1947, she moved to the United States. There she developed her distinctive voice, finding, in poem after poem, the magic and mystery just behind the banal and ordinary. Influences on Levertov's style include the poet H. D. (Hilda Doolittle) and, later, William Carlos Williams, whom she credits with helping her to find a voice as an American poet. During the 1960s, she translated, with Edward Dimock, Jr., *In Praise of Krishna: Songs from the Bengali* and became involved in the antiwar movement. *Relearning the Alphabet* appeared in 1970 and contains some of her best verse, including the magnificent "A Tree Telling of Orpheus." Other collections of her poetry include *Here and Now* (1957), *Overland to the Islands* (1958), *Candles in Babylon* (1982), and *Breathing the Water* (1987). Levertov has taught at Drew University, Vassar College, and Stanford University.

ABOUT THE SELECTION

  "The Secret" is from Levertov's collection *O Taste and See,* published in 1964. The title poem of that collection encourages people to taste and see "all that lives/to the imagination's tongue." Levertov wants us not simply to exist from day to day but to live our lives fully, intensely, engaged with the wonders of the world around us. Such enthusiasm for life, active engagement in the world coupled with imagination, constitutes a secret worth remembering.

READER'S JOURNAL

What do you think is "the secret of life"? Can you even begin to answer such a question? If so, write about your answer in your journal. If not, write in your journal about why you find the question difficult to answer.

LANGUAGE SKILLS

Read the Language Arts Survey, 2.29, "Interjections." Then, as you read the poem, find one interjection and explain how it is used to emphasize the poem's main idea.

"The Secret"

DENISE LEVERTOV

Two girls discover
the secret of life
in a sudden line of
poetry.

5   I who don't know the
secret wrote
the line. They
told me

(through a third person)
10   they had found it
but not what it was,
not even

what line it was. No doubt
by now, more than a week
15   later, they have forgotten
the secret,

What does the word sudden *suggest here?*

the line, the name of
the poem. I love them
for finding what
20   I can't find,

and for loving me
for the line I wrote,
and for forgetting it
so that

25   a thousand times, till death
finds them, they may
discover it again, in other
lines,

in other
30   happenings. And for
wanting to know it,
for

assuming there is
such a secret, yes,
35   for that
most of all.   ■

What qualities do the two girls have?

Responding to the Selection

What is the secret to which the title of this poem refers? How can having lots of little enthusiasms that change from day to day or from week to week help a person to live a happy, healthy, productive life?

Reviewing the Selection

RECALLING

1. What do the two girls discover in a line of poetry? Who wrote the line? What does the speaker think most likely happened "more than a week/later"?

2. Why does the speaker love these girls?

INTERPRETING

3. Does the speaker of this poem think that she knows the secret of life? Why is she so sure that, a week later, the girls have forgotten the line?

4. Why does the speaker love the fact that the girls have forgotten the line? What does the speaker's loving this fact reveal about her?

SYNTHESIZING

5. Why might it be important for people to assume that "there is/such a secret"? Why is it also important for people to "discover it again, in other/lines,/in other/happenings"?

Understanding Literature (Questions for Discussion)

Free Verse. Free verse, or **vers libre,** is poetry that avoids use of regular rhyme, rhythm, meter, or division into stanzas. Notice that this poem is written in complete sentences. How many sentences make up the poem? Notice also that the breaks between lines and stanzas often occur in the middles of sentences. A poet writing free verse can decide where to break a line or stanza not based on the number of beats, or stresses, in the line but rather based on what he or she wants to emphasize. The materials before and after breaks receive the greatest emphasis. Consider, for example, the breaks between stanzas 8 and 9. What two points are emphasized by breaking the sentence in this particular place?

"The Starry Night"
by Anne Sexton

ABOUT THE AUTHOR

Anne Sexton (1928–1974) made a significant contribution to American poetry though she did not begin writing until she was twenty-eight years old. Sexton was born in Newton, Massachusetts, and attended boarding school and Garland Junior College before marrying Alfred Sexton II in 1948. Sexton gave birth to two daughters, Linda and Joyce. Sexton began writing in 1956 after attending a class taught by Robert Lowell at Boston University. In her work, Sexton presented painful memories and experiences in extremely personal poetry of a kind referred to by critics as confessional. Sexton's first collection, *To Bedlam and Part Way Back* (1959), described her stay in a mental institution and her recovery from an emotional breakdown. In 1967, Sexton received the Pulitzer Prize for her collection *Live or Die.* Sexton's shockingly personal poems brought her literary fame but received mixed reactions from critics. Her *Transformations* (1971) is a collection of frightening, macabre retellings of fairy tales by the Brothers Grimm. Unfortunately, she was plagued by depression and tragically ended her life on October 4, 1974. Two volumes of her poetry and a collection of her personal letters were published after her death by her daughter Linda.

ABOUT THE SELECTION

"**The Starry Night**" comes from Sexton's collection *All My Pretty Ones* (1962). The title of the collection comes from a statement made by MacDuff, in Shakespeare's tragedy *Macbeth,* after hearing of the deaths of his wife and children. The title of the poem refers to a famous painting by Vincent van Gogh. Van Gogh, like Sexton, suffered from depression, which was intensified by a crisis of religious faith. The epigraph at the beginning of Sexton's poem comes from one of the remarkable letters that van Gogh wrote to his brother Theo.

"The Starry Night"

ANNE SEXTON

> That does not keep me from having a terrible
> need of—shall I say the word—religion.
> Then I go out at night to paint the stars.
> —Vincent van Gogh[1]
> in a letter to his brother

The town does not exist
except where one black-haired tree slips
up like a drowned woman into the hot sky.
The town is silent. The night boils with eleven stars.
5   Oh starry starry night! This is how
I want to die.

It moves. They are all alive.
Even the moon bulges in its orange irons
to push children, like a god, from its eye.
10   The old unseen serpent swallows up the stars.
Oh starry starry night! This is how
I want to die:

into that rushing beast of the night,
sucked up by that great dragon, to split
15   from my life with no flag,
no belly,
no cry.

To what is the tree compared?

What is the "rushing beast"?

---

1. **Vincent van Gogh.** (1853–1890) Dutch artist, first of the great modern Expressionist painters. This letter was written while he was painting "Starry Night on the Rhône."

Responding to the Selection

Look at the reproduction of van Gogh's painting *The Starry Night* on page 813. Do you feel that Sexton captured the feeling of the painting in her poem? Why, or why not?

Reviewing the Selection

1. What "does not exist"?

2. What is the "one black-haired tree" like?

3. What does the speaker see in the sky? What is the moon like? What is it doing? What is happening to the stars?

4. What does the speaker address directly in the last two lines of stanza 2? What does she say to this thing?

5. What view overpowers and blots out the town?

6. What is the town's response to the "drowned woman" who "slips . . . into the hot sky"? What might the speaker be suggesting about the relationship between the woman and the town?

7. What emotion do you think the speaker feels looking at this sky? What is the sky like?

8. What is "the old unseen serpent"? What is being swallowed up? What is being born? How does the second stanza portray birth and death? In what sense are all things eventually swallowed up by night?

9. Assuming that the flag mentioned in the last lines of the poem is a flag of surrender, with what attitude does the speaker want to go into her death? What does she want that death to be like?

10. The poet Dylan Thomas wrote to his dying father, "Do not go gentle into that good night." In what ways is the sentiment expressed in Sexton's poem similar? In what ways is it different?

Understanding Literature (Questions for Discussion)

1. **Allusion.** An **allusion** is a figure of speech in which reference is made to a person, event, object, or work from history or literature. To what work is this entire poem an allusion? What thoughts and emotions does this work create in the speaker? Do you feel that the speaker caught the essence of the painting in her interpretation of it?

2. **Epigraph.** An **epigraph** is a quotation placed at the beginning of a literary work to help establish the work's theme. In the epigraph to this poem, van Gogh implies that painting the stars is for him a religious experience. What mythic elements are found in Sexton's poem?

3. **Rhyme. Rhyme** is the repetition of sounds at the ends of words. What end rhyme ties together the stanzas of the poem? What lines contain end rhymes? What are the rhyming words at the ends of these lines?

4. **Confessional Poetry. Confessional poetry** is verse that presents extremely personal ideas, feelings, or experiences. Often confessional poetry has the quality of a diary entry or of an overheard interior monologue, but equally often it is highly artificial, employing much personal symbolism. What personal experience does this poem relate? With what extremely personal subject does it deal?

Responding in Writing

Allusion Piece. Try to capture the essence of a particular painting, photograph, sculpture, or song in a poem or short essay of your own. What about your chosen piece do you find fascinating? Freewrite about your subject before you begin.

The Starry Night. Vincent van Gogh, 1889. Oil on canvas, 29" x 36^{1}/4" (73.7 x 92.1 cm). The Museum of Modern Art, NY. Acquired through the Lillie P. Bliss Bequest

POETRY

"Winter Poem"
by Nikki Giovanni

ABOUT THE AUTHOR

Nikki (Yolande Cornelia) Giovanni (1943–   ) grew up in Cincinnati, Ohio, but returned often to her birthplace in Knoxville, Tennessee, to visit her grandmother. She attended Nashville's Fisk University in the mid-1960s. Entering college as a self-described conservative, Giovanni soon switched to activism in the African-American Civil Rights movement and was a college organizer for the Student Non-Violent Coordinating Committee (SNCC). By 1970, Giovanni had a son, was teaching at Rutgers University, and had already published three books of poetry—*Black Feeling, Black Talk; Black Judgment;* and *Re: Creation.* Though hailed as a leading figure of the new African-American poetry between 1968 and 1971, motherhood shifted her priorities. In 1975 she said, "To protect [my son] Tommy there is no question I would give my life. I just cannot imagine living without him. But I can live without the revolution." Her later publications are more personal and more concentrated on the African-American family. Some of her most popular poems, including *Spin a Soft Black Song* (1971) and *Ego Tripping* (1973), were written for children. Giovanni has received dozens of honorary degrees and literary awards and is much sought after as a lecturer and reader of her own works. *A Dialogue* (1972) and *A Poetic Equation* (1974) are transcripts of talks between Giovanni and her fellow authors James Baldwin and Alice Walker.

ABOUT THE SELECTION

  "Winter Poem" demonstrates why Nikki Giovanni has become such a widely read, beloved poet. It shows her ability to transform an ordinary event, through imagination, into a miracle.

READER'S JOURNAL

The American poet E. E. Cummings once wrote that "children guessed (but only a few/and down they forgot as up they grew/autumn winter spring summer)." Have your attitudes toward play changed since your childhood? How might retaining playful, childlike qualities help people to be happier and more productive as adults? Write about these questions in your journal.

THINKING SKILLS

Read the Language Arts Survey, 4.5, "Remembering and Visualizing." Then, as you read the following poem, visualize the scene remembered by the speaker in the poem, part by part. Outline the sequence of events of the poem in your journal.

"Winter Poem"

Nikki Giovanni

once a snowflake fell
on my brow and i loved
it so much and i kissed
it and it was happy and called its cousins
5   and brothers and a web
of snow <u>engulfed</u> me then
i reached to love them all
and i squeezed them and they became
a spring rain and i stood perfectly
10   still and was a flower   ■

WORDS FOR
EVERYDAY USE:
    en • gulf (en gulf´) *vt.,* swallow up; overwhelm

Responding to the Selection

What feelings does this poem create in you? Describe an experience you have had that created a similar feeling.

Reviewing the Selection

RECALLING

1. What fell and where? What did the speaker do in response?

2. In what was the speaker engulfed? What happened when the speaker squeezed the flakes?

INTERPRETING

▶▶ 3. What emotion was created in the speaker by the event that occurs in the first line?

▶▶ 4. What action do you imagine the speaker performing when she says, "i squeezed them"? Why does the speaker squeeze the flakes?

SYNTHESIZING

5. Spring is a time of beginnings, when the world blossoms. In what sense do the events described in this poem cause the speaker to blossom? What emotion is conveyed by the speaker's standing "perfectly still"?

Understanding Literature (Questions for Discussion)

1. **Personification. Personification** is a figure of speech in which an idea, animal, or thing is described as if it were a person. What things are personified in this poem? In what sense is the event described at the end of the poem the opposite of personification? What does the event at the end of the poem tell you about the speaker's feelings about her connection to the natural world?

2. **Symbol.** A **symbol** is a thing that stands for or represents both itself and something else. For example, a rose is a traditional symbol of beauty. What do flowers and spring rain traditionally symbolize?

Responding in Writing

Dialogue Poem. Think of an imaginative game that is often played by children, and create a cluster chart to come up with details related to the game. Refer to the Language Arts Survey, 1.17, "Clustering." Then create two children to be characters in a dialogue. Write a brief free verse poem that captures the dialogue of your two characters playing an imaginative game. Try to capture in your characters' voices the actual sound of the speech of children. Refer to the Language Arts Survey, 2.147, "Formal and Informal English"; 2.148, "Register"; and 2.149, "Tone and Voice."

Language Lab

Capitalization. Review the Language Arts Survey, 2.107–2.133, on capitalization rules. What capitalization rules are broken in Nikki Giovanni's "Winter Poem"? Why might poets choose to bend the rules of capitalization? Discuss this question with your classmates.

PROJECT

Social Science/Psychology: The Play of Children. With other students in your class, research current thought about the nature and function of play in children. Refer to child development textbooks, books on parenting, and encyclopedias. Then hold a full-class discussion of the following topic: "Play Is Children's Work." Consider such issues as the role that play performs in socialization with peers, in learning to talk, and in learning about the adult world.

Selected Poems
by James Worley

ABOUT THE AUTHOR

James Worley (1921–   ) was born in the Miner's Hospital in Welch, West Virginia, in the heart of coal-mining country. He attended Emory University and Atlanta University, then served in the United States Army in World War II, spending nineteen months in combat. He was among the United States soldiers who liberated the Nazi concentration camp at Dachau. After the war, he attended Columbia University on the G.I. Bill. There he was privileged to have as teachers some of the leading thinkers of his day, including Mark Van Doran, Lionel Trilling, Margaret Mead, and W. Y. Tyndall. After receiving his M.A. from Columbia, Worley taught high school English in Virginia, Tennessee, and New York. For twenty-four years he served on the English Department staff of Columbus East High School, in Columbus, Indiana. Throughout this time, he published his poetry widely in newspapers and magazines, including *The Christian Science Monitor,* the *Western Humanities Review,* the *New York Herald Tribune,* and *Prairie Schooner.* His poetry, similar to Emily Dickinson's in its wonderful economy of language and flashes of insight, appears in two collections, *Cold Comfort* and *Colder Comfort.* Worley lives in Columbus, Indiana, with his wife and his many cats.

ABOUT THE SELECTIONS

The poet and critic Randall Jarrell once wrote that when taking up the collected works of a fine poet, one has the sense of being in the presence not of a book but of a life. This is especially true of the poems of James Worley. In these poems one finds hundreds of moments captured as if in a snapshot, exquisitely rendered in precise, often playfully punning language. In "The Figure a Poem Makes," Robert Frost wrote that "it is but a trick poem and no poem at all if the best of it was thought of first and saved for the last." Worley's poems meet Frost's criteria: they begin with delight in some small observation and then skate through imagination and reflection into wisdom.

READER'S JOURNAL

Why do people keep pets? What functions do pets serve in people's lives? What do pets teach their owners? What do different kinds of pets reveal about those owners? Freewrite about these questions in your journal.

LANGUAGE SKILLS

Read the Language Arts Survey, 2.153, "Connotation and Denotation." Then, as you read the following poems, pick three words that are particularly rich in connotations, or associations, and describe the connotations of these words in your journal.

Selected Poems

JAMES WORLEY

"PETS"

Living, they are <u>surrogates</u> for our sadness,
but at their times of sudden ice,
when dawn doesn't and noon nevers and night is,
they go without apology or regret
and leave all grief to us.

"TO WALDEN WHEREVER"

My eyes mist
as I remember Walden the tomcat
who leapt upon the small dog's back
and off again—whist!—
just because it was spring.
Walden wherever, leap and leap and
leap!

"SWANS TRAPPED IN A WINTER STREAM"

Betrayed by water, then <u>crucified</u> by ice,
their beaks now soldered shut with frozen blood,
they suffer silent the foxes gliding out.

WORDS FOR EVERYDAY USE:

sur • ro • gate (sʉr´ə git) *n.*, substitute
cru • ci • fy (krōō´sə fī´) *vt.*, torment; be cruel to

"The Readiness is All"

That moon there quite above the woods
botched its first attempts at verse tonight
(a branch evaded, an insistent twig was <u>spurned</u>,
a trunk hid what another might have etched)
but wait—there's <u>cadenced</u> foliage to come—
and go—and come most delicately again:
see the cirrus?[1] quick! a sonnet sails.

---

1. **cirrus.** Wispy clouds

Words for Everyday Use:

spurn (spʉrn) *vt.*, reject
ca • denced (kād´'nst) *adj.*, measured; rhythmic

"At Vespers"

Its bells a-meow, a dusk-cuff round its neck,
the church crouched like a great iron-throated cat
godawful in the plangent[2] gloom,
where belfry bats, black beyond confession,
wove a net of night,
and cattle at their evening gate lowed long their discontent.

"In Re: Notification of Wives and Mothers"

If first she sits, so much the better;
but do not touch the woman
even if she trembles terribly:
what she is hearing no touch can <u>quell</u>,
no presence <u>mitigate</u>:
leave the letter and go away.

"Adlai Stevenson"[3]

(JULY, 14, 1965)

On a day when Mars first had its mystery forced
and the Bastille[4] fell again in the few freed minds,
by an exercise of taste (on Grosvenor Street)
a man of grace graced England with his death.
At home both man and grace went still ungrasped:
a president cocked his head from side to side
to find the cameras he'd been told would watch
and said some "right" things at the unwitting land.   ■

---

2. **plangent.** Loud, mournful sounding
3. **Adlai Stevenson.** (1900–1965) Delegate to the United Nations, governor of Illinois, and presidential candidate
4. **Bastille.** State prison in Paris, France, that was destroyed on July 14, 1789, during the French Revolution

Responding to the Selection

Choose one of these poems that you particularly like and write a letter to the poet explaining what you like about it.

WORDS FOR
EVERYDAY USE:
quell (kwel) *vt.*, end
mit • i • gate (mit´ə gāt´) *vt.*, make less severe or painful

Reviewing the Selection

RECALLING

1. According to the speaker in "Pets," what function is served by pets while they are alive?

2. What did the tomcat Walden do?

3. What "betrayed" and "crucified" the swans?

4. In "The Readiness is All," what is compared to the moon? What does the speaker want the person being addressed to see?

5. What is compared to a cat in "At Vespers"? How are the bats described, and what do they do?

6. Who is being addressed by the speaker in "In Re: Notification of Wives and Mothers"? What advice does the speaker give?

7. Who was the "man of grace" who died on July 14, 1965? What else happened on that day? What was the response, at home, to this man's death?

INTERPRETING

8. What ends with the death of a pet? What can people no longer do with their emotions?

9. Why do you think the speaker's "eyes mist" when he remembers Walden? What characteristic in humans and in animals does the speaker admire?

10. Why do the swans "suffer silent"? An old myth has it that the swan, silent throughout its life, trumpets at the time of its death. What happens, instead, in "Swans Trapped in a Winter Stream"? In what sense does the poem speak for those creatures that cannot speak for themselves? What aspect of nature does this poem describe?

11. Why are the twigs and the cirrus clouds necessary to make the view of the moon really interesting in "The Readiness is All"? Why is some sort of complication, conflict, or tension necessary to the production of a great work of literature?

12. What details in "At Vespers" create an ominous mood?

13. Why does the speaker in "In Re: Notification of Wives and Mothers" advise the person being addressed to "leave the letter and go away"? Why would any words that were said be hollow at such a time?

14. Of what does the cocking of the head from side to side in "Adlai Stevenson" remind you? What is literally being described? What aspects of the description show that the remarks made to the cameras are insincere?

15. Several of these poems deal with death or with responses to death. What differing responses to death are treated in these poems? What recurring themes can you find in them?

Understanding Literature (Questions for Discussion)

1. **Modernism. Modernism** was a twentieth-century artistic movement characterized by a rejection of traditional forms and much experimentation. One common device in Modernist poetry that can be found in the poetry of Walt Whitman, who strongly influenced the Modernists, is the intentional use of words in ways that violate traditional grammatical expectations. The word *never,* for example, is usually an adverb, a word that modifies a verb, an adjective, or another adverb. As what part of speech is the word *never* used in "Pets"? What state is described by the line "when dawn doesn't and noon nevers and night is"? What does it mean to say that "dawn doesn't and noon nevers"?

2. **Alliteration. Alliteration** is the repetition of initial consonant sounds. Find two examples of alliteration in "Swans Trapped in a Winter Stream." Find five examples in "At Vespers." Find two examples in "In Re: Notification of Wives and Mothers." Find three examples in "Adlai Stevenson."

3. **Objective Correlative.** An **objective correlative** is a group of images that together create a particular emotion in a reader. What emotion, or mood, is created by the images in "At Vespers"? What details in the poem contribute to the creation of this mood?

4. **Metaphor.** A **metaphor** is a figure of speech in which one thing is spoken or written about as if it were another. The figure of speech invites the reader to make a comparison between two things. Explain the metaphors in the following lines from these poems:

"their beaks now soldered shut"
"cadenced foliage"
"a sonnet sails"
"Its bells a-meow"
"a dusk-cuff round its neck"
"belfry bats, black beyond confession"
"a net of night"
"the Bastille fell again in the few freed minds"
"cocked his head from side to side"

POETRY

"To Black Women"
by Gwendolyn Brooks

ABOUT THE AUTHOR

Gwendolyn Brooks (1917–) was born in Topeka, Kansas, and raised in the "Bronzeville" section of Chicago, Illinois. She attended Englewood High School and Wilson Junior College. Brooks began writing poetry at age seven and published her earliest work in the *Chicago Defender.* Her first book of poetry, *A Street in Bronzeville,* appeared in 1945. In 1950, Brooks received the Pulitzer Prize for her second book of poetry, *Annie Allen* (1949), becoming the first African American to receive this prestigious award. Brooks's first two books of poetry and her novel *Maude Martha* (1953) all draw upon her experiences growing up in the Chicago inner city. Other works by Brooks include *The Bean Eaters* (1960), a collection of poetry; *Bronzeville Boys and Girls* (1956), a children's book; and *Report from Part One* (1972), an autobiographical work. In 1969, Brooks was named poet laureate of the State of Illinois. In 1985, she was appointed Poetry Consultant to the Library of Congress, the first African-American woman to hold that position. Her *Winnie* (1988) is a book of poetry inspired by the South African leader Winnie Mandela, wife of Nelson Mandela, the anti-apartheid activist who became president of South Africa's first black majority government.

ABOUT THE SELECTION

The Civil Rights Movement of the late 1950s and 1960s made enormous strides toward achieving equality of rights for African Americans in the United States. An important part of that movement was the call by activists such as Eldridge Cleaver, Malcolm X, and others for Black Pride—pride in the traditions, history, and culture of the African-American people. Gwendolyn Brooks has for many years been an important voice for Black Pride, and especially for pride among African-American women, reminding the world of her sisters' struggles, triumphs, and potential in poems such as **"To Black Women."**

"To Black Women"

GWENDOLYN BROOKS

Sisters,
where there is cold silence—
no hallelujahs, no hurrahs at all, no handshakes,
no neon red or blue, no smiling faces—
5   prevail.
Prevail across the editors[1] of the world!
who are obsessed, self-honeying and self-crowned
in the seduced arena.

     It has been a
10 hard trudge, with fainting, bandaging and death.
There have been startling confrontations.
There have been tramplings. Tramplings
of monarchs[2] and of other men.

What do "sisters" face? What does the speaker tell them to do?

Why has it been a hard trudge?

---

1. **editors.** Those who revise and make corrections in written statements of thought
2. **monarchs.** Kings, queens; rulers of nations, who have absolute authority

WORDS FOR EVERYDAY USE: pre • vail (prē vāl´) *vi.,* triumph; be common
ob • sessed (əb sest´) *part.,* greatly preoccupied or troubled

Gemini Etching. *Lout Mills, 1969.*
Evans-Tibbs collection Washington, DC.

What remains in the people addressed in the poem? What do they continue to do? Why does the speaker feel these things are important?

15   But there remain large countries in your eyes.
      Shrewd sun.
      The civil balance.
      The listening secrets.

      And you create and train your flowers still. ∎

Responding to the Selection

Read the Language Arts Survey, 1.23, "Analysis Charts." Then, make an analysis chart with four heads, one for each of the four stanzas of this poem. (The last stanza consists of a single line.) On your chart, list the topic and main idea of each stanza.

Reviewing the Selection

RECALLING

1. To whom is this poem addressed? What does the speaker tell these people to do in line 5?

2. What adjectives does the speaker use to describe "the editors of the world"?

3. What sorts of trials or struggles are mentioned in stanza 3?

4. What can be found in the "sisters'" eyes?

INTERPRETING

5. What conditions listed in stanza 1 would make life difficult for the people mentioned in line 1?

6. Editors are people who make decisions about what ideas and writings will be published or broadcast. Does the speaker believe that the "editors of the world" pay proper attention to the voices of her "sisters"? Why, or why not?

7. To what might the "It" at the beginning of line 9 refer?

8. Which line in stanza 3 suggests that the "sisters" have large, unexplored potentials? that they are intelligent and warm? that they help others to achieve harmony and community? that they pay attention to other people and therefore know many things that others do not know?

SYNTHESIZING

9. If the statements made in stanza 3 are true, why should "the editors of the world" pay more attention to what the "sisters" have to say?

10. The verb *train* means "to guide the growth of." What might be the "flowers" that the "sisters" create and train?

Understanding Literature (Questions for Discussion)

1. **Parallelism. Parallelism** is a rhetorical technique in which a writer emphasizes the equal value or weight of two or more ideas by expressing them in the same grammatical form, as in Abraham Lincoln's reference in The Gettysburg Address to "government of the people, by the people, for the people." Find four examples of parallelism in this poem.

2. **Internal Rhyme. Internal rhyme** is the use of rhyming words within lines. What word at the beginning of stanza 3 rhymes with what word in the final line?

Language Lab

Base Words and Prefixes. Read the Language Arts Survey, 2.140, "Base Words and Prefixes," and 2.142, "Greek and Latin Roots." The word monarch comes from *mono,* meaning "one," and *arch,* meaning "to rule." Use a dictionary to find the meanings of the following words that use the prefix *mono* and the root *arch.*

1. monopoly
2. monotone
3. monochromatic
4. monogamy
5. monologue
6. monotheism
7. archangel
8. archbishop
9. archenemy
10. matriarch

PROJECT

A Celebration of African-American Women Poets. Work with students in your class to plan a celebration of the work of the many great women poets of African descent in the American literary tradition. Divide into small groups and assign one poet from the following list to each group.

Brooks, Gwendolyn
Clifton, Lucille
Dove, Rita
Evans, Mari
Giovanni, Nikki
Harper, Frances

Sanchez, Sonia
Shange, Ntozake
Walker, Alice
Walker, Margaret
Wheatley, Phillis

Inaugural Address
by John F. Kennedy

ABOUT THE AUTHOR

John F. Kennedy (1917–1963), thirty-fifth president of the United States, was born in Brookline, Massachusetts, to a family already very familiar with politics. Kennedy earned his undergraduate degree at Harvard University in 1940. That same year, his senior thesis, *Why England Slept,* was published. It examined Britain's reaction to the rise of the Nazi Party in Germany. From 1941 to 1945, Kennedy served in World War II as a torpedo boat commander and was honored for his bravery. His political career began when he returned home to Massachusetts. In 1946, he was elected to the United States House of Representatives and, in 1952, to the United States Senate. During his eight years as a senator, Kennedy married Jacqueline Bouvier and wrote the 1956 Pulitzer Prize winner *Profiles in Courage*, a book that examined the brave and moral actions of eight politicians. In 1960, he was elected president of the United States, the youngest person and the first Catholic to achieve that office. In 1962, President Kennedy faced a serious nuclear confrontation with what was then the Soviet Union in an episode known as the Cuban Missile Crisis. He also created the Peace Corps and was a supporter of civil rights legislation. Kennedy was assassinated on November 22, 1963, in Dallas, Texas.

ABOUT THE SELECTION

When John F. Kennedy was elected president of the United States, he took over the office from Dwight Eisenhower, who had been a much-decorated general in World War II. At the time of Kennedy's election, the nation was essentially peaceful and prosperous. Tensions existed, however, between the United States and the Communist-run Soviet Union—allies during World War II but later competitors for global influence.

In his **inaugural address**, Kennedy spoke of this turning point for his country and set the goals of his presidency. He also sought to establish himself as a forceful leader, a special challenge for him as the youngest man ever elected president. This speech is considered one of Kennedy's most inspiring, incorporating both literary techniques such as repetition and unifying cultural references.

Inaugural Address

JOHN F. KENNEDY

What are the characteristics of the new American generation?

We observe today not a victory of party but a celebration of freedom—symbolizing an end as well as a beginning—signifying renewal as well as change. For I have sworn before you and Almighty God the same solemn oath our forebears[1] prescribed nearly a century and three-quarters ago.

The world is very different now. For man holds in his mortal hands the power to abolish all forms of human poverty and all forms of human life. And yet the same revolutionary beliefs for which our forebears fought are still at issue around the globe—the belief that the rights of man come not from the generosity of the state but from the hands of God.

We dare not forget today that we are the heirs of that first revolution. Let the word go forth from this time and place, to friend and foe alike, that the torch has been passed to a new generation of Americans—born in this century, <u>tempered</u> by war,

disciplined by a hard and bitter peace, proud of our ancient heritage—and unwilling to witness or permit the slow undoing of those human rights to which this nation has always been committed, and to which we are committed today at home and around the world.

Let every nation know, whether it wishes us well or ill, that we shall pay any price, bear any burden, meet any hardship, support any friend, oppose any foe to assure the survival and the success of liberty.

This much we pledge—and more.

To those old allies whose cultural and spiritual origins we share, we pledge the loyalty of faithful friends. United, there is little we cannot do in a host of cooperative <u>ventures</u>. Divided, there is little we can do—for we dare not meet a powerful challenge at odds and split <u>asunder</u>.

---

1. **forebears.** Ancestors

To those new states whom we welcome to the ranks of the free, we pledge our word that one form of colonial control shall not have passed away merely to be replaced by a far more iron tyranny. We shall not always expect to find them supporting our view. But we shall always hope to find them strongly supporting their own freedom—and to remember that, in the past, those who foolishly sought power by riding the back of the tiger ended up inside.

To those people in the huts and villages of half the globe struggling to break the bonds of mass misery, we pledge our best efforts to help them help themselves, for whatever period is required—not because the Communists may be doing it, not because we seek their votes, but because it is right. If a free society cannot help the many who are poor, it cannot save the few who are rich.

To our sister republics south of our border, we offer a special pledge—to convert our good words into good deeds—in a new alliance for progress—to assist free men and free governments in casting off the chains of poverty. But this peaceful revolution of hope cannot become the prey of hostile powers. Let all our neighbors know that we shall join with them to oppose aggression or <u>subversion</u> anywhere in the Americas. And let every other power know that this hemisphere intends to remain the master of its own house.

To that world assembly of <u>sovereign</u> states, the United Nations, our last best hope in an age where the instruments of war have far outpaced the instruments of peace, we renew our pledge of support—to prevent it from becoming merely a forum for invective—to strengthen its shield of the new and the weak—and to enlarge the area in which its writ may run.

Finally, to those nations who would make themselves our adversary, we offer not a pledge but a request—that both sides begin anew the quest for peace before the dark powers of destruction unleashed by science engulf all humanity in planned or accidental self-destruction. We dare not tempt them with weakness. For only when our arms are sufficient beyond doubt can we be certain beyond doubt that they will never be employed.

But neither can two great and powerful groups of nations take comfort from our present course—both sides overburdened by the cost of modern weapons, both rightly alarmed by the steady spread of the deadly atom, yet both racing to alter that uncertain balance of terror that stays the hand of mankind's final war.

So let us begin anew—remembering on both sides that <u>civility</u> is not a sign of weakness, and sincerity is always subject to proof. Let us never negotiate out of fear. But let us never fear to negotiate.

Let both sides explore what problems unite us instead of <u>belaboring</u> those problems which divide us.

Let both sides, for the first time, formulate serious and precise proposals for the inspection and control of arms—and bring the absolute power to destroy other nations under the absolute control of all nations.

Let both sides seek to <u>invoke</u> the wonders of science instead of its terrors. Together let us explore the stars, conquer the deserts, <u>eradicate</u> disease, tap the

WORDS FOR EVERYDAY USE:

sub • ver • sion (səb ver´zhən) *n.*, systematic attempt to overthrow a government
sov • er • eign (säv´ərn) *adj.*, independent
ci • vil • i • ty (sə vil´ə tē) *n.* politeness
be • la • bor (bē lā´bər) *vt.*, spend too much time or effort on
in • voke (in vōk´) *vt.*, call on for blessing, help, or inspiration
e • rad • i • cate (ē rad´i kāt´) *vt.*, get rid of; wipe out; destroy

ocean depths, and encourage the arts and commerce.

Let both sides unite to heed in all corners of the earth the command of Isaiah—to "undo the heavy burdens . . . [and] let the oppressed go free."[2]

And if a beachhead[3] of cooperation may push back the jungle of suspicion, let both sides join in creating a new endeavor, not a new balance of power but a new world of law, where the strong are just and the weak secure and the peace preserved.

All this will not be finished in the first 100 days. Nor will it be finished in the first 1,000 days, nor in the life of this administration, nor even perhaps in our lifetime on this planet. But let us begin.

In your hands, my fellow citizens, more than mine, will rest the final success or failure of our course. Since this country was founded, each generation of Americans has been summoned to give testimony to its national loyalty. The graves of young Americans who answered the call to service surround the globe.

Now the trumpet summons us again—not as a call to bear arms, though arms we need—not as a call to battle, though embattled we are—but a call to bear the burden of a long twilight struggle, year in and year out, "rejoicing in hope, patient in tribulation"[4]—a struggle against the common enemies of man: tyranny, poverty, disease, and war itself.

Can we forge against these enemies a grand and global alliance, North and South, East and West, that can assure a more fruitful life for all mankind? Will you join in that historic effort?

In the long history of the world, only a few generations have been granted the role of defending freedom in its hour of maximum danger. I do not shrink from this responsibility—I welcome it. I do not believe that any of us would exchange places with any other people or any other generation. The energy, the faith, the devotion which we bring to this endeavor will light our country and all who serve it—and the glow from that fire can truly light the world.   ∎

---

2. **undo . . . free.** Isaiah 58:6
3. **beachhead.** Position gained as a secure starting point for an action
4. **rejoicing . . . tribulation.** Romans 12:12

Responding to the Selection

How do you think Kennedy felt about becoming president? How would you feel about undertaking such an important job, on which the lives of millions depended? Can you imagine ever seeking such a position? Why, or why not?

Reviewing the Selection

1. How does Kennedy compare the world at the time of his address to the world facing the founders of the United States?

2. What does Kennedy pledge to the nations of South and Central America? To whom is he also speaking?

3. To what emotion does Kennedy link negotiation? What issue is at highest stake in the negotiations he discusses?

4. In what way does Kennedy feel his generation is uniquely situated?

5. To what important change does Kennedy refer?

6. Why might Kennedy's pledge be particularly important?

7. How does Kennedy suggest the two sides approach negotiation? What benefits for humanity might arise from his plans?

8. What challenges and privileges does the unique situation of Kennedy's generation create?

9. Why do you think Kennedy included several references to God and the Bible? How might these references engage listeners?

10. What unifying concept runs through Kennedy's speech? How does he build his ideas around this concept?

Understanding Literature (Questions for Discussion)

1. **Anaphora. Anaphora** is any word or phrase that repeats or refers to something that precedes or follows it. For example, the phrase "Let both sides" is repeated at the beginning of several paragraphs in Kennedy's speech. How does this anaphora emphasize Kennedy's ideas? Find two other examples of anaphora in the inaugural address.

2. **Parallelism. Parallelism** is a rhetorical technique in which a writer emphasizes the equal weight of two or more ideas by presenting them in the same grammatical form. Look at the opening phrase of Kennedy's speech. What is similar about the grammatical structure of the phrases "victory of party" and "celebration of freedom"? What does Kennedy suggest about the two ideas? How does he link them?

"Everyday Use"
by Alice Walker

ABOUT THE AUTHOR

Alice Walker (1944–   ) was raised in a sharecropping family in Eatonton, Georgia, and educated at Atlanta's Spelman College and then at Sarah Lawrence. In 1964, Walker visited Africa, and then took part in the voter registration drive in Mississippi in 1966. She tapped these experiences for her first book of poetry, *Once,* which explores her roots and the African-American struggle for civil rights. Her first novel, *Meridian,* also dealt with civil rights and was later hailed as a sensitive portrayal of the movement. Walker was married to civil rights lawyer Mel Leventhal from 1967 to 1976 and has one daughter. Her works reached a wider audience when her 1983 novel *The Color Purple* won the Pulitzer Prize for fiction and was turned into a successful movie. A central theme in Walker's writing is her belief that "not enough credit has been given to the black woman who has been oppressed beyond recognition."

ABOUT THE SELECTION

Like many of Alice Walker's writings, the story **"Everyday Use"** explores the idea of African-American heritage. In a conflict between a woman and her sister and mother, two different interpretations of heritage are explored.

"Everyday Use"

ALICE WALKER

for your grandmama

I will wait for her in the yard that Maggie and I made so clean and wavy yesterday afternoon. A yard like this is more comfortable than most people know. It is not just a yard. It is like an extended living room. When the hard clay is swept clean as a floor and the fine sand around the edges lined with tiny, irregular grooves, anyone can come and sit and look up into the elm tree and wait for the breezes that never come inside the house.

Maggie will be nervous until after her sister goes: she will stand hopelessly in corners, <u>homely</u> and ashamed of the burn scars down her arms and legs, eying her sister with a mixture of envy and awe. She thinks her sister has held life always in the palm of one hand, that "no" is a word the world never learned to say to her.

You've no doubt seen those TV shows where the child who has "made it" is confronted, as a surprise, by her own mother and father, tottering in weakly from backstage.[1] (A pleasant surprise, of course: What would they do if parent and child came on the show only to curse out and insult each other?) On TV mother and child embrace and smile into each other's faces. Sometimes the mother and father weep, the child wraps them in her arms and leans across the table to tell how she would not have made it without their help. I have seen these programs.

Sometimes I dream a dream in which Dee and I are suddenly brought together on a TV program of this sort. Out of a dark and soft-seated limousine I am <u>ushered</u> into a bright room filled with many people. There I meet a smiling, gray, sporty man like Johnny Carson[2] who

How does Maggie feel toward her sister?

---

1. **TV shows . . . backstage.** Refers to *This Is Your Life*, a television show in which celebrities were surprised by a group of family and friends.
2. **Johnny Carson.** Host of a television show

WORDS FOR EVERYDAY USE:
home • ly (hōmʹlē) *adj.,* simple, plain
ush • er (ushʹər) *vt.,* escort, conduct

To what does the speaker compare Maggie?

How does the speaker describe herself in real life? How does she visualize herself appearing on TV?

What happened to the other house? What happened to Maggie? How did Dee appear to feel about the house?

shakes my hand and tells me what a fine girl I have. Then we are on the stage and Dee is embracing me with tears in her eyes. She pins on my dress a large orchid, even though she has told me once that she thinks orchids are tacky flowers.

In real life I am a large, big-boned woman with rough, man-working hands. In the winter I wear flannel nightgowns to bed and overalls during the day. I can kill and clean a hog as mercilessly as a man. My fat keeps me hot in zero weather. I can work outside all day, breaking ice to get water for washing; I can eat pork liver cooked over the open fire minutes after it comes steaming from the hog. One winter I knocked a bull calf straight in the brain between the eyes with a sledge hammer and had the meat hung up to chill before nightfall. But of course all this does not show on television. I am the way my daughter would want me to be: a hundred pounds lighter, my skin like an uncooked barley pancake. My hair glistens in the hot bright lights. Johnny Carson has much to do to keep up with my quick and witty tongue.

But that is a mistake. I know even before I wake up. Who ever knew a Johnson with a quick tongue? Who can even imagine me looking a strange white man in the eye? It seems to me I have talked to them always with one foot raised in flight, with my head turned in whichever way is farthest from them. Dee, though. She would always look anyone in the eye. Hesitation was no part of her nature.

"How do I look, Mama?" Maggie says, showing just enough of her thin body enveloped in pink skirt and red blouse for me to know she's there, almost hidden by the door.

"Come out into the yard," I say.

Have you ever seen a lame animal, perhaps a dog run over by some careless person rich enough to own a car, sidle up to someone who is ignorant enough to be kind to him? That is the way my Maggie walks. She has been like this, chin on chest, eyes on ground, feet in shuffle, ever since the fire that burned the other house to the ground.

Dee is lighter than Maggie, with nicer hair and a fuller figure. She's a woman now, though sometimes I forget. How long ago was it that the other house burned? Ten, twelve years? Sometimes I can still hear the flames and feel Maggie's arms sticking to me, her hair smoking and her dress falling off her in little black papery flakes. Her eyes seemed stretched open, blazed open by the flames reflected in them. And Dee. I see her standing off under the sweet gum tree she used to dig gum out of; a look of concentration on her face as she watched the last dingy gray board of the house fall in toward the red-hot brick chimney. Why don't you do a dance around the ashes? I'd wanted to ask her. She had hated the house that much.

I used to think she hated Maggie, too. But that was before we raised the money, the church and me, to send her to Augusta[3] to school. She used to read to us without pity; forcing words, lies, other folks' habits, whole lives upon us two, sitting trapped and ignorant underneath her voice. She washed us in a river of make-believe, burned us with a lot of knowledge we didn't necessarily need to know. Pressed us to her with the serious way she read, to shove us away at just the moment, like dimwits, we seemed about to understand.

Dee wanted nice things. A yellow organdy[4] dress to wear to her graduation from high school; black pumps to match a green suit she'd made from an old suit

---

3. **Augusta.** City in Georgia where Paine College is located

4. **organdy.** Sheer cotton fabric

somebody gave me. She was determined to stare down any disaster in her efforts. Her eyelids would not flicker for minutes at a time. Often I fought off the temptation to shake her. At sixteen she had a style of her own: and knew what style was.

I never had an education myself. After second grade the school was closed down. Don't ask me why: in 1927 colored asked fewer questions than they do now. Sometimes Maggie reads to me. She stumbles along good-naturedly but can't see well. She knows she is not bright. Like good looks and money, quickness passed her by. She will marry John Thomas (who has mossy teeth in an earnest face) and then I'll be free to sit here and I guess just sing church songs to myself. Although I never was a good singer. Never could carry a tune. I was always better at a man's job. I used to love to milk till I was hooked in the side[5] in '49. Cows are soothing and slow and don't bother you, unless you try to milk them the wrong way.

I have deliberately turned my back on the house. It is three rooms, just like the one that burned, except the roof is tin; they don't make shingle roofs any more. There are no real windows, just some holes cut in the sides, like the portholes in a ship, but not round and not square, with rawhide holding the shutters up on the outside. This house is in a pasture, too, like the other one. No doubt when Dee sees it she will want to tear it down. She wrote me once that no matter where we "choose" to live, she will manage to come see us. But she will never bring her friends. Maggie and I thought about this

and Maggie asked me, "Mama, when did Dee ever *have* any friends?"

She had a few. <u>Furtive</u> boys in pink shirts hanging about on washday after school. Nervous girls who never laughed. Impressed with her they worshiped the well-turned phrase, the cute shape, the <u>scalding</u> humor that erupted like bubbles in lye.[6] She read to them.

When she was courting Jimmy T she didn't have much time to pay to us, but turned all her faultfinding power on him. He *flew* to marry a cheap city girl from a family of ignorant flashy people. She hardly had time to <u>recompose</u> herself.

When she comes I will meet—but there they are!

Maggie attempts to make a dash for the house, in her shuffling way, but I stay her with my hand. "Come back here," I say. And she stops and tries to dig a well in the sand with her toe.

It is hard to see them clearly through the strong sun. But even the first glimpse of leg out of the car tells me it is Dee. Her feet were always neat-looking, as if God himself had shaped them with a certain style. From the other side of the car comes a short, stocky man. Hair is all over his head a foot long and hanging from his chin like a kinky mule tail. I hear Maggie suck in her breath. "Uhnnnh," is what it sounds like. Like when you see the wriggling end of a snake just in front of your foot on the road. "Uhnnnh."

Dee next. A dress down to the ground, in this hot weather. A dress so loud it hurts

In what way does the speaker characterize Dee's humor?

5. **hooked in the side.** Kicked by a cow
6. **lye.** Alkaline substance used to make soap

WORDS FOR EVERYDAY USE:

fur • tive (fur´tiv) *adj.,* sneaky; stealthy

scald • ing (skôld´iŋ) *part.,* burning; injuring

re • com • pose (rē´kəm pōz´) *vt.,* restore calmness of mind

my eyes. There are yellows and oranges enough to throw back the light of the sun. I feel my whole face warming from the heat waves it throws out. Earrings gold, too, and hanging down to her shoulders. Bracelets dangling and making noises when she moves her arm up to shake the folds of the dress out of her armpits. The dress is loose and flows, and as she walks closer, I like it. I hear Maggie go "Uhnnnh" again. It is her sister's hair. It stands straight up like the wool on a sheep. It is black as night and around the edges are two long pigtails that rope about like small lizards disappearing behind her ears.

What reason does Dee cite for changing her name to Wangero?

"Wa-su-zo-Tean-o!"[7] she says, coming on in that gliding way the dress makes her move. The short stocky fellow with the hair to his navel is all grinning and he follows up with "Asalamalakim,[8] my mother and sister!" He moves to hug Maggie but she falls back, right up against the back of my chair. I feel her trembling there and when I look up I see the perspiration falling off her chin.

"Don't get up," says Dee. Since I am stout it takes something of a push. You can see me trying to move a second or two before I make it. She turns, showing white heels through her sandals, and goes back to the car. Out she peeks next with a Polaroid. She stoops down quickly and lines up picture after picture of me sitting there in front of the house with Maggie cowering behind me. She never takes a shot without making sure the house is included. When a cow comes nibbling around the edge of the yard she snaps it and me and Maggie *and* the house. Then she puts the Polaroid in the back seat of the car, and comes up and kisses me on the forehead.

Why might Dee want to include the house in all the photographs?

Meanwhile Asalamalakim is going through motions with Maggie's hand. Maggie's hand is as limp as a fish, and

probably as cold, despite the sweat, and she keeps trying to pull it back. It looks like Asalamalakim wants to shake hands but wants to do it fancy. Or maybe he don't know how people shake hands. Anyhow, he soon gives up on Maggie.

"Well," I say. "Dee."

"No, Mama," she says. "Not 'Dee,' Wangero Leewanika Kemanjo!"

"What happened to 'Dee'?" I wanted to know.

"She's dead," Wangero said. "I couldn't bear it any longer, being named after the people who oppress me."

"You know as well as me you was named after your aunt Dicie," I said. Dicie is my sister. She named Dee. We called her "Big Dee" after Dee was born.

"But who was she named after?" asked Wangero.

"I guess after Grandma Dee," I said.

"And who was *she* named after?" asked Wangero.

"Her mother," I said, and saw Wangero was getting tired. "That's about as far back as I can trace it," I said. Though, in fact, I probably could have carried it back beyond the Civil War through the branches.

"Well," said Asalamalakim, "there you are."

"Uhnnnh," I heard Maggie say.

"There I was not," I said, "before 'Dicie' cropped up in our family, so why should I try to trace it that far back?"

He just stood there grinning, looking down on me like somebody inspecting a Model A car.[9] Every once in a while he and Wangero sent eye signals over my head.

"How do you pronounce this name?" I asked.

---

7. **Wa-su-zo-Tean-o.** African dialect greeting
8. **Asalamalakim.** Muslim greeting
9. **Model A car.** Very old type of car

"You don't have to call me by it if you don't want to," said Wangero.

"Why shouldn't I?" I asked. "If that's what you want us to call you, we'll call you."

"I know it might sound awkward at first," said Wangero.

"I'll get used to it," I said. "Ream it out again."

Well, soon we got the name out of the way. Asalamalakim had a name twice as long and three times as hard. After I tripped over it two or three times he told me to just call him Hakim-a-barber. I wanted to ask him was he a barber, but I didn't really think he was so I didn't ask.

"You must belong to those beef-cattle peoples down the road," I said. They said "Asalamalakim" when they met you, too, but they didn't shake hands. Always too busy: feeding the cattle, fixing the fences, putting up salt-lick shelters,[10] throwing down hay. When the white folks poisoned some of the herd the men stayed up all night with rifles in their hands. I walked a mile and a half just to see the sight.

Hakim-a-barber said, "I accept some of their <u>doctrines</u>, but farming and raising cattle is not my style." (They didn't tell me, and I didn't ask, whether Wangero (Dee) had really gone and married him.)

We sat down to eat and right away he said he didn't eat collards[11] and pork was unclean. Wangero, though, went on through the chitlins and corn bread, the greens and everything else. She talked a blue streak over the sweet potatoes. Everything delighted her. Even the fact

---

10. **salt-lick shelters.** Places where cows are kept out of the heat by being given salt to lick
11. **collards.** Leafy vegetable

that we still used the benches her daddy made for the table when we couldn't afford to buy chairs.

"Oh, Mama!" she cried. Then turned to Hakim-a-barber. "I never knew how lovely these benches are. You can feel the rump prints," she said, running her hands underneath her and along the bench. Then she gave a sigh and her hand closed over Grandma Dee's butter dish. "That's it!" she said. "I knew there was something I wanted to ask you if I could have." She jumped up from the table and went over in the corner where the churn stood, the milk in it clabber[12] by now. She looked at the churn and looked at it.

"This churn top is what I need," she said. "Didn't Uncle Buddy whittle it out of a tree you all used to have?"

"Yes," I said.

"Uh huh," she said happily. "And I want the dasher, too."

"Uncle Buddy whittle that, too?" asked the barber.

Dee (Wangero) looked up at me.

"Aunt Dee's first husband whittled the dash," said Maggie so low you almost couldn't hear her. "His name was Henry, but they called him Stash."

"Maggie's brain is like an elephant's," Wangero said, laughing. "I can use the churn top as a centerpiece for the alcove table," she said, sliding a plate over the churn, "and I'll think of something artistic to do with the dasher."

When she finished wrapping the dasher the handle stuck out. I took it for a moment in my hands. You didn't even have to look close to see where hands pushing the dasher up and down to make

For what is Dee going to use the churn top? the dasher? For what were the speaker and Maggie using them?

butter had left a kind of sink in the wood. In fact, there were a lot of small sinks; you could see where thumbs and fingers had sunk into the wood. It was beautiful light yellow wood, from a tree that grew in the yard where Big Dee and Stash had lived.

After dinner Dee (Wangero) went to the trunk at the foot of my bed and started <u>rifling</u> through it. Maggie hung back in the kitchen over the dishpan. Out came Wangero with two quilts. They had been pieced by Grandma Dee and then Big Dee and me had hung them on the quilt frames on the front porch and quilted them. One was in the Lone Star pattern. The other was Walk Around the Mountain. In both of them were scraps of dresses Grandma Dee had worn fifty and more years ago. Bits and pieces of Grandpa Jarrell's Paisley shirts. And one teeny faded blue piece, about the size of a penny matchbox, that was from Great Grandpa Ezra's uniform that he wore in the Civil War.

"Mama," Wangero said sweet as a bird. "Can I have these old quilts?"

I heard something fall in the kitchen, and a minute later the kitchen door slammed.

"Why don't you take one or two of the others?" I asked. "These old things was just done by me and Big Dee from some tops your grandma pieced before she died."

"No," said Wangero. "I don't want those. They are stitched around the borders by machine."

"That'll make them last better," I said.

---

12. **clabber.** Sour milk

WORDS FOR EVERYDAY USE:

al • cove (al´kōv´) n., recessed section, nook
ri • fle (rīf´əl) vt., shuffle, move quickly through

"That's not the point," said Wangero. "These are all pieces of dresses Grandma used to wear. She did all this stitching by hand. Imagine!" She held the quilts securely in her arms, stroking them.

"Some of the pieces, like those lavender ones, come from old clothes her mother handed down to her," I said, moving up to touch the quilts. Dee (Wangero) moved back just enough so that I couldn't reach the quilts. They already belonged to her.

"Imagine!" she breathed again, clutching them closely to her bosom.

"The truth is," I said, "I promised to give them quilts to Maggie, for when she marries John Thomas."

She gasped like a bee had stung her.

"Maggie can't appreciate these quilts!" she said. "She'd probably be backward enough to put them to everyday use."

"I reckon she would," I said. "God knows I been saving 'em for long enough with nobody using 'em. I hope she will!" I didn't want to bring up how I had offered Dee (Wangero) a quilt when she went away to college. Then she had told me they were old-fashioned, out of style.

"But they're *priceless!*" she was saying now, furiously; for she has a temper. "Maggie would put them on the bed and in five years they'd be in rags. Less than that!"

"She can always make some more," I said. "Maggie knows how to quilt."

Dee (Wangero) looked at me with hatred. "You just will not understand. The point is these quilts, *these* quilts!"

"Well," I said, stumped. "What would *you* do with them?"

"Hang them," she said. As if that was the only thing you *could* do with quilts.

Maggie by now was standing in the door. I could almost hear the sound her feet made as they scraped over each other.

"She can have them, Mama," she said, like somebody used to never winning anything, or having anything reserved for her. "I can 'member Grandma Dee without the quilts."

I looked at her hard. She had filled her bottom lip with checkerberry snuff and it gave her face a kind of dopey, <u>hangdog</u> look. It was Grandma Dee and Big Dee who taught her how to quilt herself. She stood there with her scarred hands hidden in the folds of her skirt. She looked at her sister with something like fear but she wasn't mad at her. This was Maggie's portion. This was the way she knew God to work.

When I looked at her like that something hit me in the top of my head and ran down to the soles of my feet. Just like when I'm in church and the spirit of God touches me and I get happy and shout. I did something I never had done before: hugged Maggie to me, then dragged her on into the room, snatched the quilts out of Miss Wangero's hands and dumped them into Maggie's lap. Maggie just sat there on my bed with her mouth open.

"Take one or two of the others," I said to Dee.

But she turned without a word and went out to Hakim-a-barber.

"You just don't understand," she said, as Maggie and I came out to the car.

"What don't I understand?" I wanted to know.

What does the speaker do? To whom does she give the quilts?

WORDS FOR EVERYDAY USE: hang • dog (haŋ´dôg´) *adj.*, ashamed and cringing

"Your <u>heritage</u>," she said. And then she turned to Maggie, kissed her, and said, "You ought to try to make something of yourself, too, Maggie. It's really a new day for us. But from the way you and Mama still live you'd never know it."

She put on some sunglasses that hid every-thing above the tip of her nose and her chin.

Maggie smiled; maybe at the sunglasses. But a real smile, not scared. After we watched the car dust settle I asked Maggie to bring me a dip of snuff. And then the two of us sat there just enjoying, until it was time to go in the house and go to bed. ■

Responding to the Selection

Who valued the quilts more, Dee or Maggie? With whom do you agree about the use of the quilts? Do you think it is important to preserve historic and family heirlooms, or do you think they are better honored by being put to "everyday use"?

Reviewing the Selection

RECALLING

1. What does the mother dream?

2. To what does the mother compare Maggie?

3. What is Dee wearing? What greeting does she give? To what has she changed her name?

4. What things does Dee ask her mother to give her while she is at the house?

INTERPRETING

5. What does the mother's dream reveal about how she would like her life to be like? What does it reveal about the reality of her life?

6. In what ways are Maggie and Dee different in both personality and appearance?

7. What did Dee think of life with her mother and Maggie? For what reasons did she make changes in her life?

8. Why does Dee want several items from the house? Why does she think they are significant? What meaning do the items have for Maggie and her mother?

WORDS FOR EVERYDAY USE: **her • it • age** (her´ i tij´) *n.*, cultural traditions handed down by ancestors

9. Dee says that her mother does not understand her heritage. Does Dee understand her heritage? Do Maggie and the mother understand? Explain.

10. What does Dee suggest Maggie and their mother do with their lives? What kind of life does she think they should lead? What kind of life do you think Maggie and the mother want? What do they think of Dee's life?

Understanding Literature (Questions for Discussion)

1. **Point of View. Point of view** is the vantage point from which a story is told. This story is told from a first-person point of view, in which the narrator uses words such as *I* and *we*. What information do we learn from the narrator? What information is she unable to tell us? What might we know if the story were told by an omniscient narrator, one who knows all things including the minds of others, or from the point of view of Dee?

2. **Plot.** A **plot** is a series of events related to a central conflict, or struggle. Review the parts of a plot in the Handbook of Literary Terms. Then identify the inciting incident, climax, crisis, and resolution of the plot of "Everyday Use."

Responding in Writing

Family History. Maggie knows many family stories and the histories of many items created by her family. Write about a story from your own family. It may be one that has been told to you, or it may be something that has happened during your lifetime that you wish to share with future generations of your family. Try to write the story as you would orally tell it. You may wish to share the story with a classmate or another person in your family to get a feel for telling it.

"I Stand Here Ironing"
by Tillie Olsen

ABOUT THE AUTHOR

Tillie Olsen (1913–   ) was born in Nebraska to parents who escaped from Russia during the political repression of 1905. Olsen dropped out of high school and worked at various jobs while raising her children. "My great colleges were the worlds of work, motherhood, struggle, and literature," she says of herself. When still in her teens, she began writing a novel, *Yonnondio,* a chapter of which was published in the prestigious *Partisan Review* in 1934. Work, union activities, and, above all, duties as a mother consumed her time for many years; however, when her youngest child enrolled in school, she began writing again in earnest, assisted by a writing fellowship received in 1956 and a Ford grant received in 1959. The title story of her collection *Tell Me a Riddle* won the O. Henry Award in 1961, one of many awards she has received for her works. *Yonnondio: From the Thirties,* the story of a family struggling through the Great Depression, was finally completed for publication in 1974. Her collection of essays and lectures, *Silences* (1978), champions writers whose voices have been silenced because of their class or gender.

ABOUT THE SELECTION

"**I Stand Here Ironing**" shows characteristics common to much of the great short fiction produced in the United States in the past few decades. This fiction is often written in the first person, employing a narrator who tells his or her own story, and often deals with significant issues involving relationships with others. The first-person narrators so common in contemporary fiction tend to relate intense, private experiences, but they do so in what has come to be known as a **Minimalist** style marked by concreteness, compression of language, the inclusion of no more details than are absolutely necessary to advance the story, and avoidance of direct statements of the narrator's feelings. As you read this story, notice how the details speak for themselves, revealing clearly the narrator's pain, pride, defensiveness, and other emotions by letting the narrator's tone and the details of the story speak for themselves. Also note that the basic situation to which the narrator responds is given only in the barest of outlines, providing just enough background information to let the reader infer what is going on.

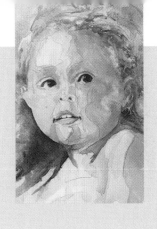

"I Stand Here Ironing"

TILLIE OLSEN

I stand here ironing, and what you asked me moves tormented back and forth with the iron.

"I wish you could manage the time to come in and talk with me about your daughter. I'm sure you can help me understand her. She's a youngster who needs help and whom I'm deeply interested in helping."

"Who needs help." Even if I came, what good would it do? You think because I am her mother I have a key, or that in some way you could use me as a key? She has lived for nineteen years. There is all that life that has happened outside of me, beyond me.

And when is there time to remember, to sift, to weigh, to estimate, to total? I will start and there will be an interruption and I will have to gather it all together again. Or I will become engulfed with all I did or did not do, with what should have been and what cannot be helped.

She was a beautiful baby. The first and only one of our five that was beautiful at birth. You do not guess how new and uneasy her tenancy in her now-loveliness. You did not know her all those years she was thought homely, or see her poring over her baby pictures, making me tell her over and over how beautiful she had been—and would be, I would tell her—and was now, to the seeing eye. But the seeing eyes were few or nonexistent. Including mine.

I nursed her. They feel that's important nowadays. I nursed all the children, but with her, with all the fierce rigidity of first motherhood, I did like the books then said. Though her cries battered me to trembling and my breasts ached with swollenness, I waited till the clock decreed.

Why do I put that first? I do not even know if it matters, or if it explains anything.

What does the speaker believe will happen if she tries to remember her daughter's life?

WORDS FOR EVERYDAY USE:

en • gulf (en gulf´) *vt.,* overwhelm
ten • an • cy (ten´ən sē) *n.,* occupation of something by right

ri • gid • i • ty (ri jid´ə tē) *n.,* state of being inflexible
de • cree (dē krē´) *vt.,* order

She was a beautiful baby. She blew shining bubbles of sound. She loved motion, loved light, loved color and music and textures. She would lie on the floor in her blue overalls, patting the surface so hard in ecstasy her hands and feet would blur. She was a miracle to me, but when she was eight months old, I had to leave her daytimes with the woman downstairs, to whom she was no miracle at all, for I worked or looked for work and for Emily's father, who "could no longer endure" (he wrote in his goodbye note) "sharing want with us."

I was nineteen. It was the pre-relief, pre-WPA world of the depression.[1] I would start running as soon as I got off the streetcar, running up the stairs, the place smelling sour, and awake or asleep to startle awake, when she saw me, she would break into a clogged weeping that could not be comforted, a weeping I can yet hear.

After a while I found a job hashing[2] at night so I could be with her days, and it was better. But it came to where I had to bring her to his family and leave her.

It took a long time to raise the money for her fare back. Then she got chicken pox, and I had to wait longer. When she finally came, I hardly knew her, walking quick and nervous like her father, looking like her father, thin, and dressed in a <u>shoddy</u> red that yellowed her skin and glared at the pockmarks. All the baby loveliness gone.

She was two. Old enough for nursery school they said, and I did not know then what I know now—the fatigue of the long day, and the <u>lacerations</u> of group life in the nurseries that are only parking places for children.

Except that it would have made no difference if I had known. It was the only place there was. It was the only way we could be together, the only way I could hold a job.

And even without knowing, I knew. I knew the teacher was evil because all these years it has curdled into my memory, the little boy hunched in the corner, her rasp, "Why aren't you outside, because Alvin hits you? That's no reason, go out, scaredy." I knew Emily hated it even if she did not clutch and <u>implore</u> "Don't go, Mommy" like the other children, mornings.

She always had a reason why we should stay home. Momma, you look sick. Momma, I feel sick. Momma, the teachers aren't there today, they're sick. Momma, there was a fire there last night. Momma, it's a holiday today, no school, they told me.

But never a direct protest, never rebellion. I think of our others in their three-, four-year-oldness—the explosions, the tempers, the <u>denunciations</u>, the demands—and I feel suddenly ill. I put the iron down. What in me demanded that goodness in her? And what was the cost, the cost to her of such goodness?

The old man living in the back once said in his gentle way: "You should smile at Emily more when you look at her." What

What changes have occurred in Emily when she returns?

---

1. **pre-relief . . . depression.** The WPA (Works Progress Administration) was one of several relief programs instituted by the government during the Great Depression to help the poor and unemployed.
2. **hashing.** Serving hash (chopped mixture of meat and vegetables) in a diner

WORDS FOR EVERYDAY USE:	**shod • dy** (shäd´ē) *adj.*, poorly made; cheap, inferior **lac • er • a • tion** (las´ər ā´shən) *n.*, wound; distress	**im • plore** (im plôr´) *vt.*, beg **de • nun • ci • a • tion** (dē nun´sē ā´shən) *n.*, criticism; speaking against

was in my face when I looked at her? I loved her. There were all the acts of love.

It was only with the others I remembered what he said, and it was the face of joy, and not of care or tightness or worry I turned to them—too late for Emily. She does not smile easily, let alone almost always as her brothers and sisters do. Her face is closed and somber, but when she wants, how fluid. You must have seen it in her pantomimes;[3] you spoke of her rare gift for comedy on the stage that rouses a laughter out of the audience so dear they applaud and applaud and do not want to let her go.

Where does it come from, that comedy? There was none of it in her when she came back to me that second time, after I had had to send her away again. She had a new daddy now to learn to love, and I think perhaps it was a better time.

Except when we left her alone nights, telling ourselves she was old enough.

"Can't you go some other time, Mommy, like tomorrow?" she would ask. "Will it be just a little while you'll be gone? Do you promise?"

The time we came back, the front door open, the clock on the floor in the hall. She rigid awake. "It wasn't just a little while. I didn't cry. Three times I called you, just three times, and then I ran downstairs to open the door so you could come faster. The clock talked loud. I threw it away; it scared me when it talked."

She said the clock talked loud again that night when I went to the hospital to have Susan. She was <u>delirious</u> with the fever that comes before red measles, but she was fully conscious all the week I was gone and the week after we were home, when she could not come near the new baby or me.

She did not get well. She stayed skeleton thin, not wanting to eat, and night after night she had nightmares. She would call for me, and I would rouse from exhaustion to sleepily call back, "You're all right, darling—go to sleep—it's just a dream," and if she still called, in a sterner voice, "now go to sleep Emily, there's nothing to hurt you." Twice, only twice, when I had to get up for Susan anyhow, I went in to sit with her.

Now, when it is too late (as if she would let me hold and comfort her like I do the others), I get up and go to her at once at her moan or restless stirring. "Are you awake, Emily? Can I get you something?" And the answer is always the same: "No, I'm all right, go back to sleep, Mother."

They persuaded me at the clinic to send her away to a convalescent home[4] in the country where "she can have the kind of food and care you can't manage for her, and you'll be free to concentrate on the new baby." They still send children to that place. I see pictures on the society page of sleek young women planning affairs to raise money for it, or dancing at the affairs, or decorating Easter eggs or filling Christmas stockings for the children.

They never have a picture of the children, so I do not know if the girls still wear those gigantic red bows and the

What does Emily not do easily?

---

3. **pantomimes.** Acting without words, using only actions and gestures

4. **convalescent home.** Place where one can recover from illness and regain strength and health

---

WORDS FOR EVERYDAY USE: de • lir • i • ous (di lir´ē əs) *adj.,* hallucinating; restless and confused

Illustration © Rodney Busch

How does the description of the surroundings of the convalescent home differ from the description of the children's lives there?

ravaged looks on the every other Sunday when parents can come to visit "unless otherwise notified"— as we were notified the first six weeks.

Oh, it is a handsome place, green lawns and tall trees and fluted flower beds. High up on the balconies of each cottage the children stand, the girls in their red bows and white dresses, the boys in white suits and giant red ties. The parents stand below shrieking up to be heard and the children shriek down to be heard, and between them the invisible wall "Not to Be Contaminated by Parental Germs or Physical Affection."

There was a tiny girl who always stood hand in hand with Emily. Her parents never came. One visit she was gone. "They moved her to Rose Cottage," Emily shouted in explanation. "They don't like you to love anybody here."

She wrote once a week, the labored writing of a seven-year-old. "I am fine. How is the baby. If I write my leter nicly I will have a star. Love." There never was a star. We wrote every other day, letters she could never hold or keep but only hear read—once. "We simply do not have room for children to keep any personal possessions," they patiently explained when we pieced one Sunday's shrieking together to plead how much it would mean to Emily, who loved so to keep things, to be allowed to keep her letters and cards.

Each visit she looked frailer. "She isn't eating," they told us. (They had runny eggs for breakfast or mush with lumps, Emily said later; I'd hold it in my mouth and not swallow. Nothing ever tasted good, just when they had chicken.)

It took us eight months to get her

WORDS FOR EVERYDAY USE: rav • aged (rav´ijd) *part.,* ruined; devastated

released home, and only the fact that she gained back so little of her seven lost pounds convinced the social worker.

I used to try to hold and love her after she came back, but her body would stay stiff, and after a while she'd push away. She ate little. Food sickened her, and I think much of life too. Oh, she had physical lightness and brightness, twinkling by on skates, bouncing like a ball up and down, up and down, over the jump rope, skimming over the hill; but these were momentary.

She fretted about her appearance, thin and dark and foreign-looking at a time when every little girl was supposed to look or thought she should look a chubby blonde replica of Shirley Temple.[5] The doorbell sometimes rang for her, but no one seemed to come and play in the house or be a best friend. Maybe because we moved so much.

There was a boy she loved painfully through two school semesters. Months later she told me how she had taken pennies from my purse to buy him candy. "Licorice was his favorite and I brought him some every day, but he still liked Jennifer better'n me. Why, Mommy?" The kind of question for which there is no answer.

School was a worry to her. She was not glib or quick in a world where glibness and quickness were easily confused with ability to learn. To her overworked and exasperated teachers she was an overconscientious "slow learner" who kept trying to catch up and was absent entirely too often.

I let her be absent, though sometimes the illness was imaginary. How different from my now-strictness about attendance with the others. I wasn't working. We had a new baby, I was home anyhow. Sometimes, after Susan grew old enough, I would keep her home from school, too, to have them all together.

Mostly Emily had asthma, and her breathing, harsh and labored, would fill the house with a curiously tranquil sound. I would bring the two old dresser mirrors and her boxes of collections to her bed. She would select beads and single earrings, bottle tops and shells, dried flowers and pebbles, old postcards and scraps, all sorts of oddments; then she and Susan would play Kingdom, setting up landscapes and furniture, peopling them with action.

Those were the only times of peaceful companionship between her and Susan. I have edged away from it, that poisonous feeling between them, that terrible balancing of hurts and needs I had to do between the two, and did so badly, those earlier years.

Oh, there are conflicts between the others too, each one human, needing, demanding, hurting, taking—but only between Emily and Susan, no, Emily toward Susan, that corroding resentment. It seems so obvious on the surface, yet it is not obvious. Susan, the second child, Susan, golden- and curly-haired and chubby, quick and articulate and assured, everything in appearance and manner Emily was not. Susan, not able to resist Emily's precious things, losing or sometimes clumsily breaking them; Susan

What sickened Emily? What words are used to describe her actions?

How did Emily feel toward Susan? In what ways were they different?

---

5. **Shirley Temple.** (1928–   ), famous child actress of the 1930s

---

WORDS FOR EVERYDAY USE:

rep • li • ca (rep´li kə) n., copy
glib (glib) adj., able to speak in a smooth, easy manner

cor • rod • ing (kə rōd´iŋ) part., wearing away; causing deterioration
ar • tic • u • late (är tik´yŏō lit) adj., able to express oneself easily and clearly

telling jokes and riddles to company for applause, while Emily sat silent (to say to me later: that was *my* riddle, Mother, I told it to Susan); Susan, who for all the five years' difference of age was just a year behind Emily in developing physically.

I am glad for that slow physical development that widened the difference between her and her contemporaries, though she suffered over it. She was too vulnerable for that terrible world of youthful competition, of <u>preening</u> and parading, of constant measuring of yourself against every other, of envy, "If I had that copper hair," "If I had that skin . . . ." She tormented herself enough about not looking like the others, there was enough of the unsureness, the having to be conscious of words before you speak, the constant caring—what are they thinking of me?—without having it all magnified by the merciless physical drives.

Ronnie is calling. He is wet and I change him. It is rare there is such a cry now. That time of motherhood is almost behind me when the ear is not one's own but must always be racked and listening for the child cry, the child call. We sit for a while and I hold him, looking out over the city spread in charcoal with its soft aisles of light. "*Shoogily*," he breathes and curls closer. I carry him back to bed, asleep. *Shoogily*. A funny word, a family word, inherited from Emily, invented by her to say: *comfort.*

In this and other ways she leaves her seal, I say aloud. And startle at my saying it. What do I mean? What did I start to gather together, to try and make <u>coherent</u>? I was at the terrible, growing years. War

Why is the speaker glad for Emily's slow physical development?

What special family word did Emily invent? What does it mean?

What does the speaker suggest Emily do? What does Emily do?

years. I do not remember them well. I was working, there were four smaller ones now, there was not time for her. She had to help be a mother, and housekeeper, and shopper. She had to set her seal. Mornings of crisis and near hysteria trying to get lunches packed, hair combed, coats and shoes found, everyone to school or child care on time, the baby ready for transportation. And always the paper scribbled on by a smaller one, the book looked at by Susan then mislaid, the homework not done. Running out to that huge school where she was one, she was lost, she was a drop; suffering over her unpreparedness, stammering and unsure in her classes.

There was so little time left at night after the kids were bedded down. She would struggle over books, always eating (it was in those years she developed her enormous appetite that is legendary in our family), and I would be ironing, or preparing food for the next day, or writing V-mail[6] to Bill, or tending the baby. Sometimes, to make me laugh, or out of her despair, she would imitate happenings or types at school.

I think I said once: "Why don't you do something like this in the school amateur shows?" One morning she phoned me at work, hardly understandable through the weeping: "Mother, I did it. I won, I won; they gave me first prize; they clapped and clapped and wouldn't let me go."

---

6. **V-Mail.** Mail to or from the armed forces in World War II, reduced to microfilm to save shipping space

WORDS FOR
EVERYDAY USE:
    preen (prēn´) vi., dress up in a fussy, vain way
    co • her • ent (kō hir´ənt) adj., logically connected; making sense

Now suddenly she was Somebody, and as imprisoned in her difference as she had been in her <u>anonymity</u>.

She began to be asked to perform at other high schools, even in colleges, then at city and statewide affairs. The first one we went to, I only recognized her that first moment when thin, shy, she almost drowned herself into the curtains. Then: Was this Emily? the control, the command, the convulsing and deadly clowning, the spell, then the roaring, stamping audience, unwilling to let this rare and precious laughter out of their lives.

Afterward: You ought to do something about her with a gift like that—but without money or knowing how, what does one do? We have left it all to her, and the gift has as often <u>eddied</u> inside, clogged and clotted, as been used and growing.

She is coming. She runs up the stairs two at a time with her light, graceful step, and I know she is happy tonight. Whatever it was that occasioned your call did not happen today.

"Aren't you ever going to finish the ironing, Mother? Whistler[7] painted his mother in a rocker. I'd have to paint mine standing over an ironing board." This is one of her <u>communicative</u> nights, and she tells me everything and nothing as she fixes herself a plate of food out of the icebox.

She is so lovely. Why did you want me to come in at all? Why were you concerned? She will find her way.

She starts up the stairs to bed. "Don't get *me* up with the rest in the morning," "But I thought you were having midterms." "Oh, those," she comes back in, kisses me, and says quite lightly, "in a couple of years when we'll be atom-dead, they won't matter a bit."

She has said it before. She *believes it*. But because I have been <u>dredging</u> the past, and all that compounds a human being is so heavy and meaningful in me, I cannot endure it tonight.

I will never total it all. I will never come in to say: She was a child seldom smiled at. Her father left me before she was a year old. I had to work away from her her first six years when there was work, or I sent her home and to his relatives. There were years she had care she hated. She was dark and thin and foreign-looking in a world where the <u>prestige</u> went to blondness and curly hair and dimples; she was slow where glibness was prized. She was a child of anxious, not proud, love. We were poor and could not afford for her the soil of easy growth. I was a young mother, I was a distracted mother. There were the other children pushing up, demanding. Her younger sister seemed all that she was not. There were years she did not let me touch her. She kept too much in herself; her life has been such she had to keep too much in herself. My wisdom came too late. She has much to her and probably little will come of it. She is a child of her age, of depression, of war, of fear.

Let her be. So all that is in her will not bloom—but in how many does it? There is still enough left to live by. Only help her to know—help make it so there is cause for her to know—that she is more than this dress on the ironing board, helpless before the iron. ∎

----

7. **Whistler.** James Abbot McNeil Whistler (1834–1903), American painter in England, best known for the portrait of his mother in a rocking chair

How might being "Somebody" imprison a person? being anonymous?

What does Emily believe about the future?

How does the speaker know Emily is happy?

What does the speaker seem to be saying about people fulfilling their potential?

WORDS FOR EVERYDAY USE:

an • o • nym • i • ty (an´ə nim´ə tē) *n.,* condition of having no special or distinguishing qualities

ed • dy (ed´ē) *n.,* move with a circular motion against the main current

com • mu • ni • ca • tive (kə myoo´ni kāt´iv) *adj.,* talkative; giving information readily

dredge (drej) *vt.,* dig up (in search of something)

pres • tige (pres tēzh´) *n.,* reputation; power to impress

Responding to the Selection

What parts of Emily's childhood were painful? In what way has Emily managed to become successful despite the pain of her childhood? Emily's mother says, "My wisdom came too late. She has much to her and probably little will come of it." To what wisdom is she referring? What has she learned? Given the second half of her statement, what has she not learned?

Reviewing the Selection

RECALLING

1. What is the mother doing throughout the story? What request sets her to thinking about her daughter?

2. What is the mother's initial response to the request made of her?

3. What circumstances in the mother's life made Emily's young life difficult? What circumstances isolated Emily from others?

4. What talent did Emily discover that she had?

INTERPRETING

5. Who do you think might have made the request to Emily's mother? What kind of problem do you think Emily might have?

6. Why does the mother feel incapable of helping her daughter? How do you feel about the mother's attitude in this respect? Do you agree with her, or do you think that the mother's attitude is a continuation of the problem that the daughter has? Explain.

7. What economic conditions contributed to making young Emily's life difficult, and in what ways?

8. Why might Emily have developed this particular talent? What perspective does isolation give that a comedic actor might exploit?

SYNTHESIZING

9. The mother says of Emily, "So all that is in her will not bloom—but in how many does it? There is still enough left to live by." To what has the mother resigned herself? What do you think of this philosophy of life? Why might it be important that people around Emily want to see all that is in her bloom? How might they help to make that happen?

10. The mother in this story asks the unnamed person who has contacted her to "help [Emily] to know . . . that she is more than this dress on the ironing board, helpless before the iron." In what sense is the mother like the dress on the ironing board? In what ways does she feel helpless? What circumstances have contributed to making her feel that way?

Understanding Literature (Questions for Discussion)

1. **Theme.** A **theme** is a central idea in a literary work. What attitude does the mother in this story have about helping her daughter? What circumstances in the mother's life have led her to develop this attitude? What points do you think the author of the story wanted to make about the effects of poverty, youth, and abandonment on poor, young, single mothers?

2. **Tone. Tone** is the emotional attitude toward the reader or the subject implied by a literary work. What is the mother's tone throughout this story? How does that tone differ from the tone of the daughter in the concluding scene? The narrator in this story talks about her daughter, but the story is really not about the daughter; it is about the narrator herself. Why does this narrator feel so burdened, so helpless, so unable to take control and effect change in the world around her? In what sense does the mother herself feel "helpless before the iron"?

Responding in Writing

Professional Letter. Imagine that you are a school counselor and that you have received a letter from Emily's mother that reads as follows:

> *Let her be. So all that is in her will not bloom—but in how many does it? There is still enough left to live by. Only help her to know—help make it so there is cause for her to know—that she is more than this dress on the ironing board, helpless before the iron.*

How would you respond to the mother? Write a letter addressed to the mother, stating your response. Follow proper business letter form as described in the Language Arts Survey, 5.3, "The Form of a Business Letter."

Language Lab

Writing Grammatical Sentences. "I Stand Here Ironing" is told from a first-person point of view. It presents an interior monologue—the thoughts, associations, and impressions that float through the mind of the central character. To render the narrator's stream-of-consciousness realistically, Tillie Olsen has occasionally scrambled the grammar of her sentences. Rewrite each of the following sentences from the story using more conventional grammar.

1. You do not guess how new and uneasy her tenancy in her now-loveliness.

2. I would start running as soon as I got off the streetcar, running up the stairs, the place smelling sour, and awake or asleep to startle awake, when she saw me, she would break into a clogged weeping that could not be comforted, a weeping I can yet hear.

3. But it came to where I had to bring her to his family and leave her.

4. "Why aren't you outside, because Alvin hits you? That's no reason, go out, scaredy."

5. Oh, there are conflicts between the others too, each one human, needing, demanding, hurting, taking—but only between Emily and Susan, no, Emily toward Susan, that corroding resentment.

"For the Last Wolverine"[1]
by James Dickey

They will soon be down

To one, but he still will be
For a little while   still will be stopping

The flakes in the air with a look,
5 Surrounding himself with the silence
Of whitening snarls. Let him eat
The last red meal of the condemned

To extinction, tearing the guts

From an elk. Yet that is not enough
10 For me. I would have him eat

The heart, and, from it, have an idea
Stream into his gnawing head
That he no longer has a thing
To lose, and so can walk

15 Out into the open, in the full

Pale of the sub-Arctic sun
Where a single spruce tree is dying

Higher and higher. Let him climb it
With all his meanness and strength.
20 Lord, we have come to the end
Of this kind of vision of heaven,

As the sky breaks open

Its fans around him and shimmers
And into its northern gates he rises

25 Snarling   complete   in the joy of a weasel
With an elk's horned heart in his stomach
Looking straight into the eternal

Blue, where he hauls his kind. I would have it all

My way: at the top of that tree I place

30 The New World's last eagle

Hunched in mangy feathers   giving

Up on the theory of flight.
Dear God of the wildness of poetry, let them mate
To the death in the rotten branches,
35 Let the tree sway and burst into flame

And mingle them, crackling with feathers,

In crownfire. Let something come
Of it   something gigantic   legendary

Rise beyond reason over hills
40 Of ice   SCREAMING   that it cannot die,
That it has come back, this time
On wings, and will spare no earthly thing:

That it will hover, made purely of northern

Lights, at dusk   and fall
45 On men building roads: will perch

On the moose's horn like a falcon
Riding into battle   into holy war against
Screaming railroad crews: will pull
Whole traplines like fibres from the snow

50 In the long-jawed night of fur trappers.

But, small, filthy, unwinged,
You will soon be crouching

Alone, with maybe some dim racial notion
Of being the last, but none of how much
55 Your unnoticed going will mean:

How much the timid poem needs

The mindless explosion of your rage,

The glutton's internal fire   the elk's
Heart in the belly, sprouting wings,

60 The pact of the "blind swallowing
Thing," with himself, to eat

---

1. **Wolverine.** Fur-bearing animal related to the weasel and mink

The world, and not to be driven off it
Until it is gone, even if it takes

Forever. I take you as you are

65 And make of you what I will,
Skunk-bear, carcajou,[1] bloodthirsty

Non-survivor.
                   Lord, let me die   but not die
Out.

"A Story"
by Li-Young Lee

Sad is the man who is asked for a story
and can't come up with one.

His five-year-old son waits in his lap.
Not the same story, Baba. A new one.
5 The man rubs his chin, scratches his ear.

In a room full of books in a world
of stories, he can recall
not one, and soon, he thinks, the boy
will give up on his father.

10 Already the man lives far ahead, he sees
the day this boy will go. Don't go!
Hear the alligator story! The angel story once more!
You love the spider story. You laugh at the spider.
Let me tell it!

15 But the boy is packing his shirts,
he is looking for his keys. *Are you a god,*
the man screams, *that I sit mute before you?*
Am I a god that I should never disappoint?

But the boy is here. *Please, Baba, a story?*
20 It is an emotional rather than logical equation,
an earthly rather than heavenly one,
which posits that a boy's supplications
and a father's love add up to silence.

"The Lesson of Walls"
by Alberto Ríos

Florencio built a wall and told no one why.
He was stubborn this way about things.
Too beautiful to be described by the ill-educated

tax assessor in this small but honorable town,
5 it was entered in no book and so did not exist
in that way that other walls are known.
Florencio stood behind his invisible wall
and so quite reasonably was invisible himself
and could do for the first time whatever he chose.
10 People came from the big cities on Sunday noons
to see this thing that did not by its nature exist
and Florencio, Florencio as he had always wanted
since the early days of his troublesome schooling,
made his five ugly faces at the faces of the people,
15 inverting his eyelids and pushing to the side his nose
so as to look like the devil that children imagine,
and he made sounds with his mouth to his pleasure.
But through the years finally he grew
bored of his invisible fame, and his mouth, or
    entirely
20 his face, became tired, so that it rested,
let its weight fall, and it rolled over onto itself
in its leisure making Florencio wrinkled and heavy.
One morning he took a workman's hammer to his
    wall.
People saw him again, and he found himself
25 drawing up his face, as one might pull up
a stomach in front of a favorite aunt.
He was young again, and unhappy, and happy.
This business of the invisible,
of a thing too beautiful for the weak
30 recreations of words and of penmanship,
had taught Florencio who was a young fine horse of
    a boy
again, why a man builds a common wall
ugly, two bricks uneven, why he lets the paint chip.

"Traveling Through the Dark"
by William Stafford

Traveling through the dark I found a deer
dead on the edge of the Wilson River road.
It is usually best to roll them into the canyon:
that road is narrow; to swerve might make more
    dead.

5 By glow of the tail-light I stumbled back of the car
and stood by the heap, a doe, a recent killing;
she had stiffened already, almost cold.
I dragged her off; she was large in the belly.

---

1. **Skunk-bear, carcajou.** Other names for the wolverine

My fingers touching her side brought me the
    reason—
10 her side was warm; her fawn lay there waiting,
    alive, still, never to be born.
    Beside that mountain road I hesitated.

    The car aimed ahead its lowered parking lights;
    under the hood purred the steady engine.
15 I stood in the glare of the warm exhaust turning red;
    around our group I could hear the wilderness listen.

    I thought hard for all of us—my only swerving—,
    then pushed her over the edge into the river.

"Song of Solomon"
by Amy Bloom

Kate stood in front of the mirror trying on dresses. She could almost get into her black suit, but that couldn't be right for the New Year and it was almost eighty outside. She put on a yellow sleeveless dress with a white linen blazer and white sandals. Too summery but not bizarre. Do they wear hats? In church, women wear hats. Do Jewish women wear hats? Kate stared into the mirror, sweating in her slip, milk starting to come through her nursing pads.

Not now, she thought. If I nurse the baby, I'll be late for the ceremony—no, the services. Be calm, you must nurse the baby, Dr. Sheldon would want you to nurse the baby, you can tell him that you were almost late because you had to nurse Sarah and he'll smile. Kate relaxed, thinking of his smile, like a cool cloth on her cheek.

Okay, we're all right. Kate took off her yellow dress, laid it out, and called to Sarah, who was just starting to make her little sucking noises, "It's okay, Mommy's coming, everything's okay." On her way to the baby's room, she grabbed a towel and looked on the top shelf of the closet for her white cartwheel straw hat. God did love her. He knew she had to get to the temple. The hat was there, and it was unblemished and unbent.

Kate looked at Sarah and felt the milk slide under her bra, down her rib cage. "Here we are, little duck. Mommy's baby. Dr. Sheldon's perfect girl." She picked Sarah up and changed her, watching herself move smoothly and competently, like a Pampers commercial. Sarah didn't wiggle, just knotted her toes in Kate's long blond hair. She plunked down in the rocking chair with Sarah and nursed her, wincing for a second as that ruthless, sweet mouth clamped down on her nipple. She watched Sarah and she watched the clock.

"Okay, Sarah beans, ten on one, ten on the other, and then we're out of here. Going to temple. Going out today, Miss Sarah." While Sarah took a short break between breasts, Kate grabbed a clean blue dress from the laundry basket and put Sarah into it.

We're almost there, Kate thought. Come on, plan ahead. Plan it so you don't screw up. Okay, she finishes nursing, I burp her, on the towel. I put her in her crib while I get dressed, my shoes are not in my closet, they're still in the hall closet. Okay, we're walking down the hall—no, the diaper bag. The diaper bag is in Sarah's room and it's already packed, with another dress. Good girl, Kate. Okay, we have a fed baby, a diaper bag, a dressed mother. The hat, the hat is still in the closet, you don't put it on until you get there and you can see what they wear.

Make-up. You put your make-up in your purse, your white purse sitting on the hall bench, ready to roll. All you need is a little lip gloss and some cover-up for your raccoon eyes. You're all right. He doesn't care for make-up. Remember, in the hospital, sitting on your bed, he said that he didn't care for makeup and that you didn't need it anyway.

Kate closed her eyes, to remember better what he said, his saying it, to feel the weight of his body at the end of the bed, her bare feet almost touching his hip.

The whole seventy-two hours in the hospital Kate's body was never dry. She was damp and awake for every sunrise, her wet nightgown twisted up around her waist. Blood, milk, and sweat streamed over and through her. The night nurse had told her to get up and walk, but she was terrified that when she stood up her organs would just fall out, the cut muscles and tissue crumbling away like rotted newspaper.

"I promise you, you start walking now, when all the other ladies are home taking Percoset you'll be pushing Miss Sarah around the block. I'll take that catheter out now, too."

She saw the nurse's smooth, thick hands flick back the heavy hem of her nightgown, and she shut her eyes when she felt the slight emptying tug.

"All right, let's roll."

Let's roll, Kate thought, and stood up, wanting her voice to match the nurse's light bounce. Let's roll on out of here. She could hear the crowds cheering in her head as she walked down the hall; the i.v. rack skittering alongside her, the nurse's hand gently pulling on her good arm. She felt the shimmery heat of his presence before she really saw him, his back to her, talking to the nurses at the coffee station. They were barricaded behind twin coffeepots, personalized mugs, wide open doughnut boxes.

Kate shook off her nurse and strolled, with great effort, toward the coffee station.

"Wonderful. You're walking already, isn't that wonderful?" Dr. Sheldon turned to the nurses, who smiled politely; they didn't care if she walked or not, and Kate didn't care about them either. If she didn't say something, he'd be gone, and she was too tired to stand around waiting for the right moment.

"Could I speak to you?" The sweat slid from her underarms right down to her feet, wetting the paper slippers they'd given her.

"Of course. I'll save your nurse a trip, even if your quality of care suffers a little."

The nurses all smiled; he was a corny old guy, but nice. He practically lived in the maternity ward. His patient, the new mother, looked like she was about to pass out, and Kate's nurse went to grab a cup of coffee before the inevitable call.

He put his hand around her bicep, and Kate could feel the blood rushing from her arm to her cheeks.

"The nurses like you," she said, looking at the passing room numbers so he couldn't see her face.

"Yes? I like them. It's hard work, they're terribly understaffed. First there weren't enough nurses because they were paid so badly. Now there aren't enough nurses because it costs the hospitals too much to keep a full shift."

Kate smiled. Even though her back ached and she could picture each of her twenty stitches clearly, lighting a hot, narrow torch across her belly, she beamed. He gripped her arm a little tighter, and as her face went white and the walls around Dr. Sheldon began to spin, she smiled again and he smiled back before he called the nurse.

Sarah had stopped sucking a little sooner than usual, and Kate was so grateful she sang to her all the way through burping. Everything went smoothly; little Sarah, stoned from nursing, was completely content to lie in her crib and murmur to the world. Kate dressed like a surgeon prepping, precise and careful in every movement. She checked her watch again. Twenty-five minutes to get to the temple. She had driven there yesterday and timed it; it was only fifteen minutes away. Five minutes to find a parking space, five minutes to get Sarah out of her NASA-designed carseat and into her Snugli. Forget the Snugli, in a summer dress and a blazer you can't carry a baby in a blue corduroy Snugli. Okay, no Snugli. I carry her in my arms, wrapped in a yellow and blue blanket, to show off her eyes and her hair. Fine.

Kate moved through all of her steps, locked the front door, and got into the car, strapping Sarah in with the blanket tucked around her, supporting her soft boneless neck.

"We're rolling now. Off we go, into the wild blue yonder, flying high into the sky . . ." Sarah had fallen into one of her instant naps, from which she would emerge charming and alert but not yet hungry. Perfect for seeing Dr. Sheldon.

Kate didn't even look pregnant until her sixth month. The other women in the library began to talk to her a little, to tell her things. They had left her alone all summer, feeling that whether her silence was due to a bad attitude, problems at home, or painful shyness, she was too much trouble. Pregnant and single and willing to take anyone's advice, Kate was not too much trouble. "Go to Dr. Sheldon," they said over lunch in the back room. "He's the best." Especially for the weird, the dispossessed, the single mothers, the ones who wished they were, the ones who needed to talk at two in the morning, not just about their babies. And when Kate met Dr. Sheldon and he didn't purse his lips when she said she had only met the father once and hoped she never would again, she knew that she and the baby were in the right place. When he helped her out of her chair, she felt ethereally beautiful and as delicate as baby's breath, her ankles and heartburn forgotten.

She drove up to the synagogue and was appalled to see millions of cars. It looked like an airport terminal, women and children piling out of backseats, all the women wearing hats. Kate laid her hand happily on the white hat next to her, perfect for her blond hair. He'd like it. She could tell he liked her hair from the way he commented on Sarah's duck fuzz. "Not much now," he said the night he sat so close to her, "but she'll have your curls by the time she's one." The men were pulling away from the entrance, craning their necks to find parking spaces. They weren't wearing hats, of course, just those little beanies—what were they called? She could ask Dr. Sheldon. Unless he'd be offended by her ignorance, rather than charmed by her interest? Please let him find me charming, and my daughter irresistible.

She was damp and rumpled by the time she found a spot behind the A&P. She scooped up Sarah like she was going for a touchdown and trotted toward the temple, hugely domed and out of scale between a sandwich shop and a dry cleaners. A block away, Kate slowed down, licked her lips, and smoothed the front of her dress with her free hand. Please.

He was standing on the sidewalk talking to some other men, but alone. No wife. She would put one of those St.

Jude ads in the paper, the kind that said, "Thank you for helping me. Now I need you more than ever." She shifted Sarah to her left shoulder, lined up her purse and the diaper bag on her right shoulder, and smiled the way her mother had always wanted her to.

"Why, Dr. Sheldon."

"Ms. Tillinghast. What a surprise, what a pleasure. I didn't know we belonged to the same shul."

Kate thought quickly, circling the strange word. "I've never been here before, actually, but I've wanted to come for a long time. I hope nobody will mind the baby, my regular sitter couldn't make it." Kate smiled self-deprecatingly, showing that she knew some people didn't like babies and would consider her careless for having brought Sarah. But Dr. Sheldon wouldn't think so, which was why she had told Joan not to come today.

"No, of course not. Who could object to this angel, this proof of God's goodness?"

As he bent his head toward Sarah to kiss the back of her round moist head, Kate felt so happy she thought her heart would break through her chest and fly around the temple, like a dove released.

They squinted at each other in the September light, smiling and wondering what the other person saw. Dr. Sheldon thought Kate saw a pallid, overweight man sweating in an old navy blue suit, black-rimmed glasses sliding halfway down his big nose and wild gray curls floating around his bald spot. She didn't; she saw God. Kate thought he saw a slightly crazy woman, wild with exhaustion and loneliness, but he didn't see that. He saw that her dark blue eyes lit up when they rested on his face and that her hand lay tenderly, unconsciously, on his sleeve, like a lily. He saw that their house would have white flowers and bright plastic toys on the floor. He would not be alone.

"People are starting to go in," he said.

"Oh." She sounded wounded, which alarmed him. Had he offended her? Maybe she didn't want to sit with him.

Dr. Sheldon shuffled backward, to show that he hadn't meant to intrude, and Kate's eyes filled with tears. How could he be leaving now, now that they were together?

Sarah thrust one pink foot through her blanket, and they both looked at it, flexing in the air. Dr. Sheldon reached out for her, and she pressed his hand to her hip as they carried Sarah up the temple stairs.

UNIT REVIEW

Contemporary Literature

SYNTHESIS: QUESTIONS FOR WRITING, RESEARCH, OR DISCUSSION

GENRE STUDIES

1. **Poetry.** Figures of speech, especially simile and metaphor, are the tools of the poet. Refer to the Handbook of Literary Terms for definitions of figures of speech. Then, select two poems and analyze the figures of speech.

THEMATIC STUDIES

2. **Symbols.** In "Everyday Use" and "I Stand Here Ironing" domestic items represent abstract ideas. What are the items and what do they represent? In "Everyday Use," for Dee the concept changes. Discuss both concepts and what Walker tells us about this character.

3. **Despair.** Select two poems that present views of despair. Compare their treatment of the theme and the ultimate effect on the reader.

4. **Advice Column.** Tillie Olsen, Gwendolyn Brooks, and to some extent, William Stafford and Elizabeth Bishop offer advice in their work. Analyze the message they send. Do they present views of those who succeed or fail to follow good advice?

5. **Love.** Several poems in this unit are about love, though not romantic love. Discuss the theme of love and the relationships in three poems from this unit.

6. **Artistic Expression.** Select one of the illustrations in the unit. Discuss how the theme and mood of the art are related to the theme and mood of the writing. Create or describe your artistic expression of this piece of writing.

HISTORICAL/BIOGRAPHICAL STUDIES

7. **Anti-Cultural Poetry.** Karl Shapiro advocated a move away from the complex, demanding style of T. S. Eliot and Ezra Pound toward the simple, straightforward style of Walt Whitman and Carl Sandburg. Which poems in the unit are most like the "poetry for the common person" of Whitman and Sandburg? in what ways?

LANGUAGE LAB VARIETIES OF ENGLISH

Formal English is used in writing papers, some magazine articles and nonfiction books, and some literary works. It is spoken at public ceremonies and in official speeches. Check your writing to be sure it is free of informal English, clichés, euphemisms, and connotations that might make your writing unclear or inappropriate. The following chart describes these varieties of English.

VARIETIES OF ENGLISH

Informal English. Informal English allows grammatical constructions that would not be acceptable in formal English. Informal English also includes **colloquialisms**, which are words and phrases that speakers of a language use naturally in conversation, and **slang**, a form of speech made up of coined words, words whose meanings have been changed for no known reason, and words used facetiously.

EXAMPLES: Where are you going *to?*
I'm going to *catch* that new *flick.*
Hey, can I *tag* along?

Clichés and Euphemisms. A **cliché** is an expression that has been used so often it has become colorless and uninteresting. A **euphemism** is an inoffensive term that substitutes for one considered offensive.

CLICHÉS: green with envy, stick out like a sore thumb
EUPHEMISM: passed away (for "died")

Denotations and Connotations. A **denotation** of a word is its dictionary definition. A **connotation** of a word is all the associations that it has in addition to its literal meaning.

EXAMPLES: disease, pestilence, plague
conversation, talk, discussion, chat

LANGUAGE ARTS SURVEY

For additional help, see the Language Arts Survey, 2.147, 2.152, and 2.153.

Exercise A Recognizing Varieties of English

Rewrite the following sentences, eliminating any instances of informal English, clichés, euphemisms, or inappropriate connotations.

EXAMPLE: The two cars slammed into each other.
The two cars hit each other with great force.

1. The traveler finds a deer taking an eternal rest at the roadside.

2. Hey, did you check out Alice Walker's lastest book?

3. Dee was mad as a wet hen when her mother gave the quilts to Maggie.

4. The host is sick and tired of the seamstress hanging around the house all the time.

5. Gwendolyn Brooks's poetry really knocks my socks off.

6. Although the pressure was on, she stayed cool as a cucumber.

7. Where is the powder room?

8. In July even a shady place gets hot as an oven.

9. Emily found that being in the spotlight was just her cup of tea.

10. The speaker doesn't realize what a swell guy his old man is in "Those Winter Sundays."

Exercise B Using Formal English

Rewrite the following paragraph, eliminating any instances of informal English, clichés, euphemisms, or inappropriate connotations.

LANGUAGE ARTS SURVEY

For additional help, see the Language Arts Survey, 2.147, 2.152, and 2.153.

American poetry since 1960 comes in lots of different forms and is mostly a response to Modernism. Most contemporary poets have a much more autobiographical focus than their predecessors, drawing from really strong personal feelings of being cut off from people and not being sure about things. Although some poets, such as Donald Hall, still use old-fashioned poetic forms, most poets scribble away in free verse. The Black Mountain Poets, a movement that lists Denise Levertov on its roll call, attempt to escape suffocating poetic forms. Confessional poets, most notably Sylvia Plath and Anne Sexton, spill their guts about such problems feeling blue. Of course, few of the greatest contemporary poets can be pigeonholed into a single category.

LANGUAGE ARTS
SURVEY

ESSENTIAL SKILLS:
Writing

INTRODUCTION TO WRITING

For writers of all ages and abilities, writing can sometimes seem a daunting task. The key to writing with confidence and pleasure, though, is simple: just keep writing as much as you can, as often as you can. Like any other skill, writing will improve with practice. Reading will also improve your writing, for reading can expose you to the full range and power of the written word.

1.1 THE PROCESS OF WRITING

Any writing task is much more manageable if you think of it as a process. Each person's writing process is a little different. Some people prefer to get everything down on paper quickly in rough form. Then they rewrite many times to "boil down" and refine what they have written. Other people work slowly and carefully, refining their thoughts and words as they go. For the purpose of instruction, the writing process is often divided into six stages:

SIX STAGES IN THE PROCESS OF WRITING	
1. Prewriting	Choose a topic, audience, purpose, and form. Then gather ideas and organize these in a reasonable way.
2. Drafting	Get your ideas down on paper in rough form without worrying about perfecting spelling, grammar, usage, and mechanics.
3. Peer and Self-Evaluation	Study your draft by yourself or with one or more of your peers to find ways to improve it.
4. Revising	Revise your draft to improve its content, organization, and style.
5. Proofreading	Check your revised draft for errors in spelling, grammar, usage, and mechanics (including punctuation and capitalization). Then prepare a final copy in an appropriate manuscript form and proofread again.
6. Publishing and Presenting	Share your work with an audience.

► ► ► A C T I V I T Y **1.1**

Take a few moments to reflect on your past experiences as a writer. In your journal or on a sheet of paper, answer the following questions.

1. Do you usually enjoy writing? What positive and negative experiences have you had as a writer? What do you think are your strengths and weaknesses as a writer?

2. Is there a certain kind of writing that you most enjoy doing? (Consult the list of Forms of Writing on pages 876–878.) Do you like to write stories, persuasive essays, reports, or poems? What do you enjoy about this kind of writing? At what kind of writing would you like to improve?

3. Many writers find they can work more easily when they use certain tools. What sort of writing materials do you prefer? Do you generally use a pencil or a pen? Does it have to be a particular kind? Do you prefer to write on lined or unlined paper? in a notebook or on loose sheets? on a typewriter or a computer?

4. In your previous writing experiences, how much time did you generally spend on prewriting? What types of prewriting activities did you do? Which activities were generally most helpful to you?

5. Describe your approach to writing. Do you like to produce a very rough draft and then revise it heavily, or do you like to work slowly, refining the material as you go?

6. Which of the six stages of the writing process gives you the most trouble?

7. When other people read or listen to your writing, how do you feel? How might other people, such as your classmates and teacher, help you become a better writer?

1.2 KEEPING A WRITER'S JOURNAL

Keeping a **writer's journal** can help you capture ideas that you may want to use later in your writing. You can keep your journal in a spiral notebook, a loose-leaf binder, a composition book, a scrapbook, or a bound "blank book" of the kind sold in bookstores and stationery stores. Keeping your journal separate from your other notebooks will help you remember its special purpose. No matter where you store your ideas, you'll get more out of your journal if you write an entry in it every day. The following ideas will help get you started.

IDEAS FOR JOURNAL ENTRIES	
The Journal as Diary	Record the observations and experiences from your daily life. Explore your feelings about people and events.
The Journal as Commonplace Book	Record interesting phrases or ideas that you hear from others or that you encounter in your reading.
The Journal as Writer's Lab	Record your ideas for pieces of writing to do in the future. Do freewriting on subjects of interest to you. Try out different kinds of writing, such as monologues, dialogues, song lyrics, concrete poetry, and riddles.

CONTINUED

The Journal as Planner	Write about what you want to do over the next week, month, year, or ten years. Explore your goals and dreams. Think on paper about how to meet your goals. Make lists of activities to help yourself grow.
The Journal as Reader Response Forum	Record your reactions to works that you read for class and on your own. Talk back to the authors, take issue with them, expand on what they say, and explore their ideas

►►► A C T I V I T Y 1.2

Start a journal. During the first week, write at least one daily entry of each type described. Add a date to each entry. Be sure to write your name and address somewhere on your journal in case it gets lost.

1.3 KEEPING A WRITER'S PORTFOLIO

Your teacher may ask you to keep a **writer's portfolio** in which you store your drafts and finished pieces of writing. A portfolio allows you and your teacher to review past work and evaluate your progress.

The portfolio you keep may be a comprehensive or a selected portfolio. A **comprehensive portfolio** contains all the writing that you do for your class along with evaluation forms for that writing. A **selected portfolio** contains the pieces of writing that you think are your best. The pieces that you choose for a selected portfolio should demonstrate the various skills you have developed in your class as well as the various types of writing you have done (such as informative, persuasive, and creative writing).

For each piece of writing you place in your portfolio, attach any earlier notes or drafts. Your teacher can then refer to these to see how each piece of writing developed. Also include any completed evaluation forms that your teacher requests.

If you are keeping a selected portfolio, hang on to the pieces that you decide not to include. Store them in a safe place, so they will be available for you or your teacher to review later.

At different times, you and your teacher will evaluate your portfolio. You will probably each evaluate the portfolio separately and then have a meeting, or **student-teacher conference**, to discuss your work and to set goals for your writing in the future.

►►► A C T I V I T Y 1.3

Following your teacher's instructions, start a writer's portfolio. You can include in this portfolio past pieces of writing that you felt were especially successful. You could also include your answers to the Activity questions that follow Language Arts Survey, 1.1, "The Process of Writing."

1.4 USING COMPUTERS FOR WRITING

A computer cannot make you a good writer, but it can make some of the mechanical tasks of writing much easier. A computer is especially helpful during the revising and proofreading stages of the writing process.

Computer Hardware

Hardware refers to the physical components, or machinery, of the computer. The most important part of this machinery is the **central processing unit**, or **CPU**. The CPU carries out the instructions given by the computer user. Connected to the CPU, or sometimes in the same case with it, are various **peripherals**, devices for storing, inputting, and outputting information, or **data**.

COMMON COMPUTER PERIPHERALS	
Storage Devices	• **Floppy diskettes**, or **floppies**, are small, flat media used to store and to transport limited amounts of data, such as individual computer files and programs. • **Hard drives** store large amounts of data on revolving disks. A hard drive can be **internal** (located inside the case with the CPU) or **external** (housed in a separate case and connected to the CPU by a cable). • **Removable media**, like hard drives, store large amounts of data. However, unlike hard drives, they can be inserted and ejected, like floppy disks. Common removable media include CD/ROMs, optical disks, and DAT tapes.
Input Devices	• **Keyboards**, the most common of all input devices, allow you to type numbers, alphabetic characters, and special computer commands. • **Mice** and **trackballs** are devices that are used to point to and select items on a computer monitor. • **Digitizing tablets** allow you to write in longhand and to draw directly onto the computer screen. • **Scanners** allow you to turn pictures or words into computer files that can then be edited or otherwise manipulated. • **Voice recognition devices** allow you to speak commands to the computer. Some will even transcribe, or write, your speech into a computer file that can then be edited.
Output Devices	• **Monitors** are the most common output devices. A monitor is a screen, similar to the ones on televisions, that shows you the work that you are doing on the computer. • **Printers** are machines that create **hard copies**, or printed paper, of the work that you have done on the computer. • **Modems** are devices for communicating, over telephone lines, with other computers.

Computer Software

Software is the set of instructions for making a computer do particular tasks. A specific piece of software is called a program, and the people who create software are called **programmers**. The chart below describes common software used by writers.

SOFTWARE FOR WRITERS

Operating System	An **operating system**, or **OS**, is a program that tells the computer how to do general tasks—how to create, save, and store files; what to do when specific commands are given; how to print files, and so on.
Application Software	An **application program** enables the user to accomplish a particular kind of task. Common application programs include the following:

- **Word-processing programs** allow you to key in words. Most such programs also allow you to revise your writing, to check its spelling, to add special formatting such as boldface or italic letters, and to save and print your work. Many of these programs also allow you to consult a built-in dictionary and/or thesaurus and to check your grammar, usage, capitalization, and punctuation.
- **Page-layout programs** allow you to put your writing into columns and boxes and to add graphic elements such as lines, borders, photographs, and illustrations. Such programs are used to produce newsletters, posters, flyers, newspapers, magazines, and books.
- **Graphics programs** allow you to create illustrations and to edit photographs.
- **Telecommunications programs** allow you to use a **modem** to connect over telephone lines to other computers, to **on-line information services**, or to **computer networks** such as the **Internet**.

Other types of programs often used by writers include ones for creating outlines, graphs, charts, indexes, and bibliographies.

Applications of Computers to Writing

A computer, like a typewriter, enables you to put words down on a page, but a computer has other capabilities as well. Equipped with the appropriate applications software, a computer allows you to

- revise your writing easily, simply by moving words, sentences, or paragraphs;
- format your writing in special ways (by adding bold or italic, by specifying a particular style of lettering, by automating functions such as paragraph, page, and line breaks, and so on);
- perform editing functions (such as checking spelling, punctuation, and grammar) automatically;
- look up definitions, synonyms, and antonyms;
- print multiple copies of your work;
- add photographs and illustrations to your work;
- use computer-accessed information sources such as on-line information services and CD/ROM encyclopedias.

Although the computer offers numerous advantages over the typewriter, many writers prefer to use a typewriter or to write with a pen or pencil. The choice of writing tool is a personal one. Of course, it also depends on the availability of machines and instruction on how to use them. Many schools have **writing labs** where computers are available to students. In addition, computers are sometimes available in school and public libraries.

PREWRITING: DEVELOPING A PLAN FOR WRITING

Experienced writers spend some time prewriting, or planning, what they will write. Prewriting is something like drawing a map before you set off on a trip; the plan you develop becomes your guide when you begin to write. By collecting your thoughts on paper in some form, you have a chance to "see" your ideas. Then you can react to them, manipulate them, and build on them before you settle down to write.

Good writing sometimes does occur spontaneously. However, if you make a plan before you write, your writing is likely to go more smoothly and be more enjoyable. The elements of a good writing plan are described in the following chart.

ELEMENTS OF A WRITING PLAN	
Topic	The specific subject that you will be writing about
Purpose	The aim, or goal, that you want the piece of writing to accomplish: to express yourself, to create a literary work, to inform, or to persuade
Audience	The person or persons who will read or hear your work
Form	The specific type of writing that you will be doing (for example, a press release or a short story)
Mode	The method of presentation of the ideas in a piece of writing. Common modes, often combined in actual pieces of writing, include narration, dialogue, description, and various kinds of exposition, such as analysis or comparison and contrast.

▶ ▶ ▶ A C T I V I T Y **1.4b**

On a page of your journal, develop a plan for a piece of writing that you would like to do sometime in the future. Briefly describe the topic, purpose, audience, form, and mode of the piece. Refer to sections 1.5–1.8 of the Language Arts Survey for information to help you complete this activity.

1.5 CHOOSING AND FOCUSING A TOPIC

Choosing a Topic

Ideas for writing can come from anywhere—from memories, research, conversations, observations. They come simply from your awareness of the world around you. Even so, most writers find it difficult to come up with good ideas for writing. The following suggestions can help you find an interesting and engaging topic.

TIPS FOR DISCOVERING WRITING TOPICS

Mine Your Journal	Make a habit of jotting down ideas for writing in your journal. Pretty soon, you will have a store of good ideas to draw from.
Draw on Your Experience	Think about experiences that you have had in the past, from early childhood on. People, places, and events from personal experience make excellent topics for writing. Making a time line of your life might help to jog your memory.
Consult Reference Works and Other Media	Browsing through reference works, looking through the shelves in a library, paging through magazines or newspapers, exploring the contents of informational CD/ROMs—all can help you to find topics worth writing about.
Do Some Freewriting	One interesting way to come up with a writing idea is simply to put your pen to paper and start writing about whatever pops into your mind, without stopping to think about spelling, grammar, usage, and mechanics. Don't force yourself to stick to one subject. Freewriting is one situation in which it's actually good to let your mind wander! Write for five to ten minutes. Then look over your freewriting for topic ideas.
Talk to People	Other people can be excellent resources for writing ideas. Draw on the experiences of the people around you. Ask them about subjects of interest to you and to them.

► ► ► **A C T I V I T Y**

Select a separate part of your journal to list possible writing topics. Using the techniques described, come up with a list of at least ten topics. Continue to add to your list as other ideas occur to you. Then, when you have writing assignments in the future, refer to your list for possible ideas.

Focusing a Topic

One technique for coming up with topics is to start with a general topic and then think about more specific, or narrower, topics that are related it. Here is an example:

General topic: the American Revolution

Focused topic 1: what a soldier's life was like

Focused topic 2: Thomas Jefferson's role

Focused topic 3: popular patriotic tunes

During prewriting, check the focus of your topic to make sure that you can cover it in sufficient detail. Generally the shorter the piece of writing that you plan to do, the more focused the topic should be. For example, in a few paragraphs you would not be able to provide much detail about a topic as broad as the American Revolution. However, if you were writing about just one aspect of it, such as the life of a typical soldier, you could include more detail. By the same token, you might begin with the idea of writing about several patriotic tunes but decide during prewriting to focus on just one tune so you can treat that topic in greater depth.

TECHNIQUES FOR FOCUSING TOPICS	
Analyze the Topic	Break the topic down into its parts. Then think about how the parts relate to one another.
Do a Tree Diagram	Write the topic at the top of a page. Then break it into parts, and break those parts into parts.
Ask Questions	Write questions about the topic beginning with the words *who*, *what, where, when, why,* and *how.* Decide which answers to these questions are most important for your piece.

Other techniques for focusing topics include freewriting and clustering. (See the Language Arts Survey, 1.12, "Freewriting," and 1.17, "Clustering.")

► ► ► A C T I V I T Y 1.5

Choose a general topic from the list below. Using one of the techniques described, come up with three specific, focused topics that are related to it:

General topics:	freedom	singing	astronomy
	religion	boredom	being a teenager

1.6 CHOOSING A PURPOSE OR AIM

Although a topic is a starting point for writing, you really can't move forward until you know your purpose in writing about that topic. The **purpose,** or **aim,** of a piece of writing is the goal that the writer wants to achieve. It is the writer's reason for writing. The study of purpose in writing and speaking is called **rhetoric.**

Teachers of rhetoric, going back to the ancient Greeks, have worked out various systems for classifying types of writing and speech. One useful classification scheme, described in the chart that follows, is based on the writer's purpose.

THE CLASSIFICATION OF WRITING AND SPEECH BY PURPOSE OR AIM			
Type	**Focus is on . . .**	**Purpose is to . . .**	**Examples**
Expressive Writing	the sender (the writer or speaker)	express the feelings of the writer or speaker	journal entry, credo
Informative Writing	the subject	provide information about the subject	accident reports, book report
			CONTINUED

Persuasive Writing	the recipient (the reader or listener)	move the reader or listener to adopt a point of view or to act in a particular way	campaign speech, public service ad
Literary Writing	the signs or symbols used to communicate the message	create a work of art	lyric poem, short story

This classification scheme also takes into account the fact that writing is a form of communication. **Communication** is the act of sending and receiving **messages**. Each time a message is sent, four elements are involved: the **sender** of the message, the **recipient** of the message, the **subject** of the message, and the **code** (the signs or symbols) used to communicate the message. This model of communication is often pictured as a **communication triangle**. Notice that each classification, or type of writing, in this scheme stresses one part of the communication triangle.

The Communication Triangle

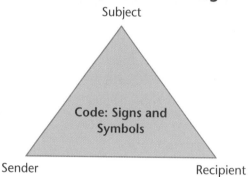

Subject

Code: Signs and Symbols

Sender   Recipient

Limitations of Classification Systems

A classification scheme is helpful for thinking about and discussing writing and speech. In reality, however, a single piece of writing often has more than one purpose. Take, for example, the *Declaration of Independence,* which was drafted by Thomas Jefferson (see page 172). The primary purpose of this document is to *inform* its readers that the thirteen American colonies have decided to separate from England and become a sovereign nation. It describes recent events that led Americans to claim their independence, and it gives reasons for the decision. The document, however, is also *persuasive.* It seeks to persuade readers of the validity of the American claim to independence. The writing is also *literary* in that the language is elegant and memorable and was carefully selected for its effect upon the reader.

Purpose and the Writing Process

Thinking about purpose can help you decide what tasks to focus on. If you have decided that your main purpose is to persuade the reader to take a certain action—for example, to use negotiation rather than violence to resolve disputes—you will need to find arguments to support your position. You might also make lists of words and phrases that will appeal to your readers emotionally. If your purpose is to inform, you will probably need to gather facts.

Purpose is also an important consideration during revision. As you reread your draft to evaluate it, ask yourself, "Have I accomplished my purpose?" If the answer is no, think about how you could change the piece to accomplish your goal.

▶ ▶ ▶ **ACTIVITIES 1.6**

A. Identify the primary purpose of each of type of writing in the following list.

1. a statement on an anti-littering poster

2. instructions for playing a board game

3. a poem about the first day of spring

4. a magazine article about surfing

B. For each of the following communications situations, identify the sender, the recipient, the subject, and the code (signs or symbols) used.

1. A mayor addresses a local community group to inform them about construction plans for a new water-treatment plant.

2. A student describes her personal goals in a written statement on a college application.

3. A hiker on a mountaintop uses a small mirror that reflects the sunlight to signal to another hiker below that he has arrived at the summit.

4. A computer sends a document that has been converted into digital code to another computer via a modem, which transmits information over regular telephone lines.

1.7 CHOOSING AND ANALYZING AN AUDIENCE

All those who read or hear what a writer has written, the receivers of the message, are collectively known as the **audience.** Experienced writers write with a specific audience in mind. They tailor their text so it is appropriate and interesting to those they expect to read it. Often you may not know exactly who your audience will be, but thinking about a specific audience can assist the writing process. Knowing your audience can help you

• focus your writing;

• select details, examples, or arguments that your reader will find interesting or convincing;

• decide what information to include or to leave out;

• determine how formal or informal and how complex or simple your language should be.

QUESTIONS TO ASK ABOUT YOUR AUDIENCE

How much does my audience already know about the subject? How much background information do I have to provide to make my writing understandable to this audience? Does the audience know enough about the subject to make it possible for me to write technically or to use jargon?

What interests, wishes, or goals does my audience have? How can I relate what I am writing to those interests, wishes, and goals?

How old and how well educated is my audience? How complex or sophisticated should my writing be?

Which would be more effective and appropriate for my audience, formal or informal language?

▶ ▶ ▶ ACTIVITY 1.7

Rewrite each of the following passages for the audience indicated in parentheses. Discuss with your classmates the kinds of changes you introduced to make the piece appropriate for its new audience.

1. From a science text: "To ward off 'predatory' herbivores, many plants produce chemicals that render them unpalatable." (Rewrite as an explanation for fourth graders.)

2. From a sports story in a magazine: The score was 30-love when underdog Regina McIntyre aced three serves in a row to tie the score at 30-all. (Rewrite for someone from another country who knows nothing about tennis.)

3. From a newspaper article: Cleanup teams working along the Scioto River gathered 654 pounds of trash including paper and plastic, cans and bottles, thirty-four old tires, and a dilapidated couch. (Rewrite as part of a paragraph designed to persuade people to volunteer in a riverbank cleanup project.)

4. From a television weather report: The sun set today at 7:49, and the sunset was quite beautiful, I might add. (Rewrite as a description in a letter to a friend; assume that you viewed the sunset.)

1.8 CHOOSING A FORM

The form you choose for your writing will be influenced by the nature of your topic, your purpose, and your audience, as well as your personal and creative inclinations. The following chart lists some forms you can use in the writing you do for class and on your own.

Obviously, a single topic can be treated in many different forms, but some forms are more suited to certain topics than others. A good way to become familiar with the possibilities and limitations of forms of writing is to try your hand at transforming one form into another.

FORMS OF WRITING

Abstract	Biography	Cinquain
Acceptance speech	Birth announcement	Classified ad
Ad copy	Blank verse	Comeback speech
Address to a jury	Book review	Comedy
Adventure	Brief	Comic strip
Advice column	Brochure	Community calendar
Afterword	Bulletin board	Concrete poem
Agenda	Business letter	Constitution
Allegory	Business proposal	Constructive speech
Annals	Bylaws	Consumer report
Annotation	Campaign speech	Contract
Annual report	Captions	Court decision
Apology	Cartoon	Credo
Appeal	Cause-and-effect essay	Critical analysis
Autobiography	Chant	Curriculum
Ballad	Character sketch	Daydream
Ballet	Charter	Debate
Bibliography	Cheer	Detective story
Billboard	Children's story	Dialogue

CONTINUED

Diary
Diatribe
Dictionary entry
Directions
Docudrama
Dramatic narrative
Dream analysis
Dream report
Editorial
Elegy
Encyclopedia article
Epic
Epic poem
Epilogue
Epistolary fiction
Epitaph
Essay
Eulogy
Experiment
Explication
Exposé
Fable
Fabliaux
Family history
Fantasy
Filmstrip
Flyer
Foreword
Fortune cookie insert
Found poem
Free verse
Gothic tale
Graduation speech
Graffiti
Grant application
Greeting card
Haiku
Headline
History
Horoscope
Human interest story
Informative essay
Instructions
Insult
Interview questions
Introduction
Invitation
Itinerary
Jingle
Joke
Journal entry

Keynote address
Lament
Law (statute)
Learning log
Letter of complaint
Letter to the editor
Libretto
Limerick
Love letter
Lyric poem
Magazine article
Manifesto
Manual
Memorandum
Memorial plaque
Menu
Minutes
Monologue
Monument inscription
Movie review
Mystery
Myth
Narrative poem
Nature guide
News story
Nomination speech
Nonsense rhyme
Novel
Novella
Nursery rhyme
Obituary
One-act play
Oracle
Ottava rima
Packaging copy
Parable
Paragraph
Paraphrase
Parody
Party platform
Pastoral
Persuasive essay
Petition
Play
Police/Accident
   report
Political advertisement
Prediction
Preface
Press release
Proclamation

Profile
Prologue
Proposal
Prose poem
Protocol
Public service announcement
Quatrain
Radio play
Radio spot
Rap
Reader's theater production
Rebuttal
Recipes
Recommendation
Referendum question
Research report
Resignation
Restaurant review
Résumé
Riddle
Roast
Romance
Sales letter
Schedule
Science fiction
Screenplay
Sermon
Short short story
Short story
Sign
Situation comedy
Slide show
Slogan
Song lyric
Sonnet (Petrarchan,
   Elizabethan, or
   Spenserian)
Specifications
Spell
Sports story
Storyboard
Stream-of-consciousness
   fiction
Summary
Summation
Survey
Sutra
Tall tale
Tanka
Technical writing
Terza rima

CONTINUED

Test	Tragedy	Vows
Thank-you note	Translation	Want ad
Theater review	Treaty	Wanted poster
Toast	TV spot	Warrant
Tour guide	Villanelle	Wish list

► ► ► **A C T I V I T Y 1.8**

Choose one of the rewriting exercises that follow and experiment with it in your journal. Refer to the Handbook of Literary Terms if you need more information about a particular form of writing.

1. Choose a short or long passage from a science textbook. Rewrite the passage as a poem.

2. Rewrite the lyrics to a popular song about relationships as an advice column.

3. Convert a scene from a play into a narrative passage; that is, describe what takes place in the scene and omit all the dialogue.

4. Choose a paragraph or two from an encyclopedia article about an interesting, faraway place. Rewrite the passage as an excerpt from a travel guide.

1.9 MODES OF WRITING

A piece of writing can also be classified by **mode.** A mode is a way of presenting ideas, information, and details. The following chart lists some of the most common modes.

COMMON MODES OF WRITING		
Mode	**Explanation**	**Forms in Which This Mode Dominates**
Narration	Presents events, usually in chronological order	Short story News report Process/How-to writing
Dialogue	Presents the speech of characters	Drama Dramatic poem Docudrama
Description	Uses images to present a portrait in words	Imagist poem Tour guide
Exposition	Presents information	(See below)

Most forms of writing combine several different modes, but one is usually dominant. For example, in drama the primary mode is dialogue. In a news report, narration is the primary mode. Short stories and novels usually use several modes. The writer will use narration to present events in sequence, description to flesh out the setting and characters, dialogue to show characters interacting, and exposition to comment on what is happening in the story.

Exposition is the mode writers use when they want to clarify or explain something. There are many, many types of exposition. Among the most common types of exposition are analysis, comparison and contrast, classification, and cause-and-effect analysis.

In an **analysis,** the writer breaks a subject down into parts and then shows how the parts are related to each other and to the whole. An analysis of a speech might break it down into the introduction, body, and conclusion. An analysis of a short story might break it down into setting, characters, plot, and theme.

A writer using **comparison and contrast** points out similarities and differences between one or more subjects. For example, a writer might compare and contrast the careers of two early-American patriots or two poems about the same subject.

An exposition based on **classification** divides some group of things into smaller groups of things that have one or more features in common. An author discussing modern American fiction might group writers from different regions of the country, such as the South, the Northeast, and the Great Plains.

In a **cause-and-effect** analysis the writer describes events that led to or resulted from certain other events. For instance, a writer might use this form of exposition to explain how the westward movement of settlers affected the lives of Indians in North America, or how social reformers of the late 1800s influenced labor laws and practices.

▶ ▶ ▶ A C T I V I T Y **1.9**

Write a short passage about each topic in the mode indicated.

1. an activity in physical education class (narration)

2. a minor car accident (dialogue)

3. a day outdoors in March (description)

4. friendship (exposition)

PREWRITING: EXPLORING IDEAS ON YOUR OWN

Once you have settled on a particular topic, purpose, and form for a piece of writing, you are ready to begin exploring ideas and gathering information. This stage may involve reading and research, holding conversations, making notes to yourself, drawing charts, asking questions, and any other kind of activity that helps you collect your thoughts and gather useful details for writing. Some of the most common activities that writers use to explore ideas and prepare for writing are described in the following sections.

1.10 RECALLING

Students sometimes think that they must be experts before they can write about a topic in a serious or meaningful way. The fact is, you *are* an expert—on the subject of your own life. Experiences from your life, past and present, can be turned into excellent writing. The key is **recalling,** or remembering, these experiences vividly. The suggestions in the chart that follows can help you use recalling to generate topics and ideas for writing:

USING RECALL TO GATHER WRITING IDEAS

1. Choose some time in your life that you want to think about. It might be early childhood, for example, when you were first learning about the world around you. It might be the time when you started going to a new school or working at a new part-time job.

CONTINUED

---

2. Make a time line of events that occurred during that period. (See the Language Arts Survey, 1.19, for more information on making time lines.)

3. Make a list of questions, problems, opinions, wishes, dreams, or goals that you had during that time.

4. List important things that you learned during that time. How did you grow or change? What brought about this growth or change?

5. Make a list of the important people in your life at that time. What was interesting or engaging or unusual about each of these people? How did they look , dress, talk, and behave? What ideas, opinions, attitudes, and habits did they have? What did you learn from them? How did they act toward you and you toward them? Why?

6. Make a list of specific places that you associate with that time in your life. Close your eyes and try to imagine one of these places. Think about what it looked like. What sights, sounds, smells, or tastes come to mind when you think of this place? How did the place make you feel?

7. If you wish to do a piece of imaginative writing, think of past experiences as raw materials to be reshaped and transformed. Choose aspects of your past experience and ask yourself questions about them. Begin your questions with the words "What if . . ."

What if my family had moved to a foreign country when I was young?

What if I discovered that I had a twin whom I had never met before?

What if someone like my mother or father had lived during the Civil War?

When you have decided on a particular person, place, thing, or event from your past to write about, try to recall as many details about it as you can. Use a graphic device such as a cluster diagram, sensory detail chart, or time line to generate specific details to use in your writing. For information about these devices, see the Language Arts Survey, 1.17–1.24.

▶ ▶ ▶ A C T I V I T I E S 1.10

A. In your journal, make a chart with three columns, one for each year you've spent in high school. In each column, list two or three experiences that stand out in your mind. Consider experiences related to school, family, work, or other aspects of your life.

B Choose one experience from your chart and do a cluster diagram or freewrite about this experience.

C. Write two or three "what if" questions based on past experiences that you might use in a piece of imaginative writing. (See the examples in item 7 of the chart above.)

1.11 OBSERVING

Good writers are people who look closely at life. They notice details in everyday events—the way passengers sway on a city bus, the shape of clouds and autumn leaves, the sound of a basketball whamping the spring pavement. They also record interesting observations in their journals so they won't forget them. Later, they can browse and study these, like snapshots in a scrapbook, for possible use in their writing. Writers are especially alert for the **telling detail**, one that implies a great deal. For example, in a newsroom the nonstop clatter of keys at dozens of computers could suggest the industry and determination of the reporters to meet their deadlines.

One way to make sure that your observations of an event or situation are thorough is to use the questions that news reporters use when they gather information: *who? what? where? when? why?* and *how?* These questions are especially helpful when you are gathering information at a live event, such as a meeting or performance. Jot down answers to these questions in brief form as you view the event. Also record details of sight, sound, touch, taste, and smell. (See section 1.18, "Sensory Details Charts.")

► ► ► **A C T I V I T I E S   1.11**

A. Take a seat in a place where plenty of activity is going on, such as a restaurant, shopping mall, or city park. Closely observe the scene, using all of your senses, and make notes of your observations. Afterward, use your details to make a sensory details chart.

B. Describe the physical appearance of a friend or relative you know well. Include in your description details about the person's features, facial expressions, clothing, posture, movements, voice, way of talking, and so on. Try to choose details that tell your readers something about the person's personality.

C. Make observations at a live event, such as a track meet, pep rally, concert, or play rehearsal. Before observing, jot down the headings *who? what? where? when? why?* and *how?* on a sheet of paper, leaving space for notes. Then take notes under each heading while observing the event.

1.12 FREEWRITING

Another way to come up with ideas and details for writing is freewriting. When you freewrite, you write quickly and freely, about a particular subject or about no subject at all. The point is to keep writing, letting your mind roam where it will. Don't stop to organize or judge or revise what you have already written; just try to generate as much material as you can. Generally, you should attempt to write for several minutes without stopping. If you find yourself getting stuck, try repeating the last few words you wrote until something else comes into your head. Here's a portion of what one student wrote during a three-minute freewriting session:

> Hmmmm. What in the world should I write about? write about. write about. Well, there's always the weather. It's a really nice April day today. Sunny, warm enough to take off your sweater. The daffodils are still around. Looking kind of tired though. Some of the blossoms look like soggy bits of crepe paper. Lots of rain the last two days. Now you can smell the earth warming up again. warming up. warming up. Warming up for track is a lot more fun now. Wonder if I'll break my personal record in the 200-meter this year. Or maybe I'll try the 400-meter. Coach thinks I have the staying power for a longer race. My best friend Jill runs in the 400-meter. She's really good. Might feel funny, though, to compete against your best friend. What if I did better? Or what if I did worse? Hey, that might even make a good story idea, only I would use two other people as the characters. I mean, how do you balance friendship and competition? There's got to be a way to blend them. There would have to be a race, of course, in the story. Funny to be thinking about a story now—maybe this freewriting actually works . . .
>
> —Keiko Weber

You can use freewriting to come up with topics for writing, as in the preceding example. You can also use it to explore a particular topic. A focused freewrite is like a regular freewrite, except that you begin with a topic and keep bringing yourself back to that topic whenever your mind wanders somewhere else.

A. Do a ten-minute freewrite. Write about anything that comes into your mind, and try to keep your pen or pencil moving throughout the period. At the end of ten minutes, look over what you have written and circle two or three ideas that might serve as writing topics in the future.

B. Choose one of the following topics. Do a five-minute focused freewrite about the topic in your journal.

competition	using computers	Saturdays
homework	popular music	language
preparing for college	clothing	abstract art
swimming	neighborhood safety	things that fly

1.13 QUESTIONING

An excellent way to gather ideas or focus a writing topic is to ask questions. Many writers approach questioning by asking the so-called **reporting questions:** *who? what? where? when? why?* and *how?* This approach is especially useful when collecting information about an event for a news story or review or planning a narrative such as a short story or narrative poem.

When you're doing expressive or literary writing, questions that begin with *what if* can be useful. Asking *what if* questions can get your creative juices flowing and lead you down some surprising and interesting paths. Here are a few examples:

EXAMPLES *What if* you were designing a city from scratch? How would it be organized? Where would people live and work? Where would businesses, shops, and recreational facilities be located? What transportation systems would be used?

What if Thomas Paine were somehow transported into the present? How would he react to current politics? What causes would he support? How would he be regarded by the public? by the media? by politicians?

What if the next president was a woman or an African American?

What if the United States officially became a bilingual nation?

▶ ▶ ▶ ACTIVITIES 1.13

A. Choose one of the following topics. In your journal, write questions about the topic beginning with *who, what, where, when, why,* and *how.*

B. Choose three topics from the list above and write *"What if . . . ?"* questions about them.

baseball	job training	pets	space travel
elections	Africa	television	the American Civil War
tourism	English	the ocean	car racing
fashion	tornadoes	pollution	elephants

1.14 ANALYZING

Analyzing is a technique you can use to gather and sort information about a topic. In analyzing, you break down a thing into its parts and then think about how the parts are related. An **analysis chart** lists and describes the parts and explains how each part is related to the whole.

ANALYSIS OF EMERSON'S "CONCORD HYMN" (PAGE 317)		
Part	**Description**	**Relationship of Part to Whole**
Stanza 1 (lines 1–4)	The speaker describes where he is and what happened there (in battle, farmers "fired the shot" that sparked the American Revolutionary War)	Establishes the setting of the poem and states the significant event that took place there.
Stanza 2 (lines 5–8)	The speaker notes that those who fought are long gone, as is the bridge they fought by.	Gives additional information about the site and the people who made it significant.
Stanza 3 (lines 9–12)	The speaker states that a memorial to those who fought is being raised today, and he explains the purpose of the memorial (to restore the memory of the event in people's minds, now and in the future).	Describes the present occasion and its connection to the past and the future.
Stanza 4 (lines 13–16)	The speaker remembers why the heroic soldiers fought (to "leave their children free") and asks the spirit that guided them to preserve the memorial through time.	Restates the significance of the past event and underscores the connection between the past, the present, and the future.

▶ ▶ ▶ **A C T I V I T I E S 1.14**

A. Choose a poem from Unit 5, 6, 7, or 8. Do an analysis chart for the poem, following the preceding model.

B. Analyze a work of art created by you or another student. First, decide how you will break the work down into parts (for example, subject matter, style, materials used, and impact on the viewer). Then describe and explain each part in an analysis chart.

C. Choose an activity that you are familiar with, such as practicing a musical instrument, cleaning your bedroom, tuning an engine, or preparing a certain food. Create an analysis chart to describe that process.

1.15 IMAGINING

When you think about things not as they actually are but as they might be, you are **imagining.** The faculty of imagination is what enables writers to create new settings, themes, characters, and plots.

The sources of the imagination have long been regarded as a mystery. The ancient Greeks pointed to the **Muses** as the source of creative inspiration. The Muses were the nine daughters of Memory and the king of the gods, Zeus. An artist engaged in creative work, the Greeks believed, was filled by the spirit of one of the Muses. Each Muse was the guiding light for a different art form such as lyric poetry, tragedy, comedy, history, and dance.

The creative process remains quite mysterious. Inspiration doesn't always occur when you need it most. However, some simple techniques, called **heuristics**, can help a writer come up with new, creative ideas. Some examples are given in the following chart.

HEURISTICS FOR IMAGINING

1. Ask questions beginning with the words *what if.* (Example: What if humans evolved in such a way that either a man or a woman could bear children?)

2. Combine previously existing things in a new way. (Example: Create a plot for a story that involves the Internet, a world-wide computer network, and two characters from hostile families who are similar to Romeo and Juliet.)

3. Magnify something, making it bigger or more significant than it is now. (Example: Coyotes, which have spread to the fringes of many urban areas, move into cities in large numbers and cause new problems.)

4. Simplify something to make it more manageable to write about. (Example: In a story, name two related minor characters after human qualities, such as Charity and Mercy, and let the single quality define each character.)

5. Make a drawing, sketch, or diagram of the thing. (Example: Draw a diagram that shows the different social classes of a society on another planet where a story takes place.)

6. Start with something as it is and change it systematically. (Example: Write a children's story about a family that is like your family except that they live in the 1880s instead of the 1990s, in a sod house instead of an apartment, in Nebraska instead of Indiana, and so on.)

7. Project a trend into the future. (Example: Write a poem about a "colorblind" society—that is, one where full racial equality has been achieved.)

8. Work against type. (Example: Write a poem about a seventy-year-old person who loves skydiving.)

► ► ► A C T I V I T Y 1.15

Select a heuristics technique from the chart and use it to come up with an idea for a piece of imaginative writing.

1.16 ROLE PLAYING

Role playing is acting out an imagined situation with others. Each person takes the role of a different character. Role playing can help you generate ideas for writing and is especially useful when you are developing characters for a story or exploring different points of view for a piece of persuasive writing. You might consider tape recording or videotaping the role-playing session for closer study later. Alternatively, you might have someone watch the role playing and take notes on it.

> ▶ ▶ ▶ A C T I V I T I E S **1.16**
>
> **A.** Work with a partner to role play one of the following situations, or one you come up with on your own:
>
> - a guidance counselor and a student talking about the student's plans after high school
> - two teachers sharing positive or negative classroom experiences with each other
> - two friends talking about plagiarizing: one is astonished to discover that the other has plagiarized material for a report
> - a discussion between two neighbors about the damage that one neighbor's dog did to the other neighbor's garden
>
> **B.** Use the preceding role plays as source material to write a scene for a play.

1.17 CLUSTERING

A **cluster chart** is one way to gather and relate ideas and details for a piece of writing. To begin a cluster chart, write your topic in the middle of a sheet of paper and circle it. Then, in the space around the circle, jot down ideas that are related to your topic, circling each item and connecting related items with lines. Continue in this manner until you have a web of associated ideas. This technique can help you group related details and also discover connections between ideas that you may not have noticed before.

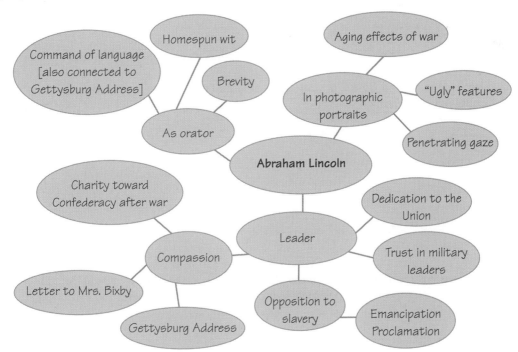

1.18 SENSORY DETAIL CHARTS

When you are planning a piece of descriptive writing, a **sensory detail chart** is a useful tool for gathering details. Begin by listing your subject at the top of a page. Beneath the subject, make five columns with headings for the five senses: sight, hearing, touch, taste, and smell. Then, under each heading, list details about your subject.

Sample Sensory Detail Chart

OWLING HIKE				
Sight	Hearing	Touch	Taste	Smell
crescent moon	guide whispering	cold hands without gloves	lip balm	dry leaves
beams from flashlights	horselike whinny (screech owl)			
owl taking off from oak tree	hoo-hoo, hoo-hoo (barred owl)			
dim outlines of trees				

1.19 TIME LINES

A **time line** is often useful when you are planning a piece of narrative writing. Draw a straight line on a piece of paper and divide it into equal units of time. Then add key events at the appropriate points on the time line. Examples of time lines can be found in the unit introductions throughout this textbook.

1.20 FLOWCHARTS

A **flowchart** shows a series of events. If you are writing an expository piece that deals with a process or sequence of events, making a flowchart can help you gather and organize information. In this type of chart, a circle around a step means "continue to the next step," a triangle means "make a decision," and a square means stop.

Sample Flowchart

❶ Pour water on suction cups of rack

❷ Center rack on top of car

❸ Does car have gutters above windows?

❹ If yes, attach and tighten gutter straps

❺ Strap kayak to rack

❻ Stop

❼ If no, strap kayak to rack

❽ Tie ends of kayak to front and rear bumpers with rope

❾ Stop

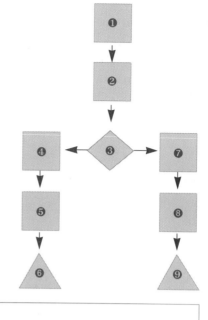

▶ ▶ ▶ A C T I V I T Y 1.20

Create a flow chart to describe a process that you go through often.

1.21 STORY MAPS

A **story map** is a chart that shows the elements of a short story. You can use a story map to lay out the basic elements of a story you are planning. While story maps take different forms, most include notes about the mood, conflict, plot, major characters, and theme.

Sample Story Map

Setting and Mood

Time _1990s_

Place _a large city_

Mood _optimistic_

Major characters

Phil Whisner (a middle-class teenager)

Jerry Spate (a middle-aged homeless man)

Conflict ___✓___ internal _____ external

Teenager must confront his ignorance and wariness of homeless persons.

Plot

Inciting incident _Phil begins a conversation with Jerry, who has approached him seeking a handout._

Climax _Jerry invites Phil to visit his "home" in a subway tunnel._

Resolution _Phil discovers that he shares a common interest in art with Jerry, who makes sculptures with found objects._

Themes _Each person is an individual worthy of respect._

This story map gives only a brief description of the major elements. Some story maps go into great detail, describing elements of the setting, traits of the characters, and the specific events in the plot.

▶ ▶ ▶ A C T I V I T Y 1.21

Create a story map for a story that you have read.

1.22 Pro and Con Charts

A **pro and con chart** lists arguments or evidence for and against a particular point of view or course of action. This type of chart is helpful when you are planning a piece of persuasive writing or trying to make a decision. List the proposition at the top of the chart. This could be a statement of fact, a policy, or a personal value. Under the proposition, create two columns, one labeled *Pro* and the other *Con.* Then list the appropriate arguments in each column.

Sample Pro and Con Chart

Proposition: A new outerbelt should be built around our town.	
Pro	**Con**
—will help solve traffic problems in the center of town	—will draw business away from downtown area, leaving empty storefronts
—will draw new companies (that need good transportation network) to the area, improving employment	—will require sacrifice of farmland and other private property

> ▶ ▶ ▶ A C T I V I T Y **1.22**
>
> Create a pro and con chart about an important decision faced by students.

1.23 Analysis Charts

An **analysis chart** breaks down a thing into its parts and then shows how the parts are related to the whole and to each other. See the sample chart in the Language Arts Survey, 1.14, "Analyzing."

> ▶ ▶ ▶ A C T I V I T Y **1.23**
>
> Create an analysis chart to show the elements of a city.

1.24 Venn Diagrams

A **Venn diagram** allows you to show the similarities and differences between two things. Use this type of diagram when you plan a piece of writing that involves comparison and contrast. To create a Venn diagram, draw two overlapping circles. Label each with the name of one of your subjects. Note the similarities of the two subjects in the space where the circles overlap. Note differences outside the overlapping space.

Sample Venn Diagram

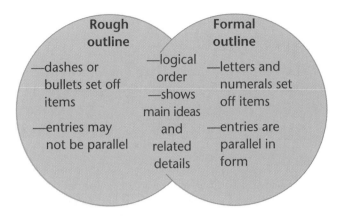

Rough outline
—dashes or bullets set off items

—entries may not be parallel

—logical order
—shows main ideas and related details

Formal outline
—letters and numerals set off items

—entries are parallel in form

► ► ► A C T I V I T Y **1.24**

Choose a graphic device from sections 1.17 through 1.24. Use it to develop an idea for a piece of writing.

PREWRITING: USING OUTSIDE SOURCES

1.25 BRAINSTORMING

Brainstorming is the process of thinking of as many different ideas as you can within a limited period of time. The process is akin to freewriting or to improvisation in acting. You can brainstorm alone, but the process works best in a group. Brainstorming can be used to solve a problem or plan a creative project. Keep things loose and spontaneous, and do not reject or judge any idea that is offered. Encourage everyone to contribute ideas. The more different the ideas are, the better. Once you have generated a large number of ideas, you can go back and evaluate them.

► ► ► A C T I V I T Y **1.25**

In a small group, pick a subject about which you can brainstorm for ten minutes. For example, you might brainstorm ideas for a story about a main character who has a physical disability. Have one person record ideas on a chalkboard or flip chart. Be sure to give everyone a chance to speak.

1.26 DISCUSSION

Discussion is another idea-generating technique that involves other people. In a discussion, participants often have specific roles as they focus their conversation on a specific topic. The **group leader** introduces the topic, asks questions, encourages responses, mediates between group members, and generally keeps the discussion on track. The **participants** in the discussion share their thoughts, listen attentively to others, and build on others' comments. All discussion members should speak calmly and politely. Sometimes the group appoints a **secretary** to record the ideas that are discussed.

▶ ▶ ▶ **A C T I V I T Y 1.26**

Get together with four other students to hold a discussion about planning a literary celebration for Martin Luther King, Jr., Day. Choose names out of a hat to designate a group leader and a secretary.

1.27 INTERVIEWING

Conducting an **interview** is another way to gather information and ideas for writing. The person you interview will probably be someone who has an extensive understanding of your subject. Newspaper articles, for example, frequently include information obtained from experts through interviews. When you interview, remember these tips:

- Get permission from the interviewee to print his or her statements.
- Ask questions that start with the words *who, what, when, where, why,* and *how.*
- Write down the interviewee's most important statements word-for-word, so you can quote some of them in your writing.
- Get the correct spelling of the interviewee's name, so that you can properly attribute the information you gather to its source.

▶ ▶ ▶ **A C T I V I T Y 1.27**

Think of a person you know who is well informed about a subject that interests you, and conduct an interview with that person. For example, if you are interested in horseback riding and know someone who has taken riding lessons for several years, you could interview that person. Use a notepad or tape recorder to record your interview. Then write a brief article that includes a quotation from your expert.

1.28 USING PRINT SOURCES

For certain kinds of writing projects, you will need to gather information about your subject from print sources. These are likely to include books, magazines, newspapers, brochures, and reference works. To locate books, use your library's card catalog or online catalog. For magazines, consult the *Readers' Guide to Periodical Literature.* To find newspaper articles, use the print, microfilm, or microfiche indexes to newspapers.

▶ ▶ ▶ **A C T I V I T Y 1.28**

Choose a subject that interests you and that has been covered in magazines and newspapers in the past few years. At the library, find three different kinds of print sources of information about your subject. Briefly identify each source by author and title. In addition, for books list the publisher and date; for magazines and newspapers list the publication name and date.

1.29 USING NONPRINT SOURCES

The number of nonprint sources of information is growing rapidly. Explore these sources as well as you gather ideas and information for writing. Nonprint sources include radio and television programs, films, videos, slides, photographic prints, filmstrips, audiocassette tapes, and CD/ROM discs as well as computer services, networks, and bulletin boards. Many nonprint sources are available in libraries. For specific information about accessing information via computer, talk to a resource person at your school or library.

► ► ► A C T I V I T Y **1.29**

Locate at least three nonprint sources offering information about one of the subjects that follow or another that you would like to explore. List the sources that you found and write a brief description of the content of each source.

the Olympics   birdwatching   acid rain   folk music

PREWRITING: ORGANIZING YOUR IDEAS

1.30 REVISING YOUR WRITING PLAN

After you have collected information for a piece of writing, review your writing plan. Are you still satisfied with the topic, purpose, audience, and form you have chosen? Do you know what mode or modes of writing you will be using? You may decide to change certain parts of your plan as a result of your research and other preparation. For example, while doing research for an informative piece about state fair livestock competitions, you might become interested in the debate about whether huge cash prizes encourage cheating in the show ring. You might then decide to focus on this narrower topic. This change in topic, in turn, might lead you to change your purpose, from informative to persuasive.

► ► ► A C T I V I T Y **1.30**

Choose a subject that you find interesting and make plans for two very different pieces of writing related to that subject. For each piece of writing, list a topic, purpose, audience, form, and primary mode.

1.31 IDENTIFYING MAIN IDEAS AND SUPPORTING DETAILS

Once you have gathered information for a piece of writing, read through your notes to select the main ideas that you will present. Then look for details to support these main ideas. For a short piece of writing, such as a paragraph, you will need to identify one main idea and several supporting details. For a longer piece of writing, you might begin by writing a **thesis statement** that presents the major idea that you want to express. Then select several main ideas related to the thesis statement and details to support them.

> ► ► ► **A C T I V I T Y 1.31**
>
> Choose one of the following subjects for a persuasive paragraph.
> - How television influences young people
> - All-boy or all-girl high schools
> - Conflict-resolution programs that use peer mediators
>
> Write a topic sentence to express a main idea about the subject. Then write three sentences that support the main idea.

1.32 MAKING A ROUGH OUTLINE

Outlines are useful for sorting and organizing main ideas and details. In a **rough outline**, or **informal outline**, main ideas are listed in some logical order and supporting details are grouped under each main idea. Dashes or bullets precede each supporting detail. Here is a rough outline for a composition about nineteenth-century whaling in New England:

Importance of whale oil

—Source of illumination in lamps
—Used in soap-making and lubrication
—Whalebone used in corsets

Hunting the whale

—Lookout on mast spots whales
—Six-man crews in small boats pursue whale
—Harpooned whale drags boat along until it tires
—Boat tows dead animal back to ship

Processing the whale

—Whale is lashed to side of ship
—Crew carves hulk into pieces
—Pieces are boiled to yield oil
—Oil is stored in barrels below deck

> ► ► ► **A C T I V I T Y 1.32**
>
> Make a rough outline for a composition on a topic from American history.

1.33 MAKING A FORMAL OUTLINE

In a **formal outline**, the writer uses Roman numerals, letters, and numbers to identify headings and subheadings. The entries at each level should be parallel in grammatical structure and begin with capital letters. A formal outline may be one of two types. A **topic outline** uses words, phrases, or clauses in the entries. A **sentence outline** uses complete sentences. The following sample is from a topic outline:

Plantations in the Old South

  I. Cotton
    A. Entire South
    B. Labor-intensive harvesting
      1. Picking from August to January

   2. Slave labor
   3. Long sacks tied to waist
C. Horse-powered gins

II. Sugar
   A. Mainly southeastern Louisiana
   B. Sugar cane stalks slashed with machete-type knives
   C. Mills for grinding and boiling cane

►►► **A C T I V I T Y 1.33**

Choose a subject related to wildlife or the environment. Create a sentence outline for a paper on that subject.

1.34 ORGANIZING IDEAS

Outlines provide a way to put ideas and information into some logical order before writing. The chart that follows shows some common methods for organizing ideas for writing.

METHODS FOR ORGANIZING IDEAS	
Chronological Order	Events are organized in order of their occurrence, often from first to last. Ideas are connected by transitional words and phrases that indicate time or sequence, such as *first, second, finally, next, then, afterward,* and *before.*
Spatial Order	Subjects are organized according to their their positions or locations, often from top to bottom, left to right, front to back, clockwise, or the reverse of any of these. Ideas are connected by transitional words and phrases that indicate position or location, such as *beside, in the middle, next, to the right, on top,* and *in front.*
Degree Order	Ideas are presented in order of degree from most to least or vice versa. For example, they might be presented from most important to least important. Ideas are connected by transitional words and phrases that indicate degree, such as *more, less, most, least, most important,* and *least promising.*
Comparison and Contrast Order	Details about two subjects are presented, in one of two ways. In the first method, the characteristics of one subject are presented, followed by the characteristics of a second subject. In the second method, both subjects are compared and contrasted with regard to one characteristic, then with regard to a second characteristic, and so on. Ideas are connected by transitional words and phrases that indicate similarities or differences, such as *likewise, similarly, in contrast, a different kind,* and *another difference.*
Cause-and-Effect Order	One or more causes are presented followed by one or more effects, or one or more effects are presented followed by one or more causes. Ideas are connected by transitional words and phrases that indicate cause and effect, such as *one cause, another effect, as a result, consequently,* and *therefore.*

CONTINUED

Classification Order	Subjects are divided into groups, or classes. These groups are then presented, one-by-one, in some reasonable order. Ideas are connected by transitional words and phrases that indicate class membership or the method by which the writer has organized the classes, such as *another group, the first type, one kind,* and *other sorts.*
Part-by-Part Order	Ideas are presented according to no *overall* organizational pattern. However, each idea is connected logically to the one that precedes it and/or to the one that follows it. After chronological order, this is the most common method for organizing ideas in writing. Ideas are connected by any transitional word or phrase that indicates the relationship or connection between the ideas.

► ► ► A C T I V I T Y **1.34**

Choose an appropriate method for organizing ideas for each piece of writing listed. Then briefly explain why you think the method you chose is appropriate.

1. a composition about the works of two humorous writers
2. a paper about life in a Puritan colony in New England
3. a description of a flower garden
4. a composition explaining Lincoln's reasons for issuing the Emancipation Proclamation
5. a paragraph analyzing the wildlife in a particular forest

DRAFTING: APPROACHES TO WRITING A DRAFT

1.35 Writing a Discovery Draft

Drafting is the stage where you begin to impose a particular form on your prewriting material. There are several approaches you can take to drafting. Some writers begin by writing a **discovery draft**. In a discovery draft, the writer tries to get all of his or her ideas down on paper quickly, without worrying much about matters such as organization, style, grammar, spelling, and mechanics. This type of draft is generally quite rough. It furnishes raw material that the writer then shapes and polishes in extensive revisions.

► ► ► A C T I V I T Y **1.35**

Choose one of the following topics and take a few minutes to think about what you want to say on the subject. Then write a discovery draft for a paragraph about the topic. As you write, strive to put all of your ideas on paper without going back to revise and polish those ideas.

- a movie that had a strong effect on you
- a place where you feel comfortable
- a celebration or holiday that you enjoy

1.36 Writing a Careful Draft

Some writers prefer to work slowly and carefully through the first draft. As they write, they reread sentences and paragraphs, revising and polishing them before continuing. Such a **careful**

draft usually unfolds more easily when it is based on a thorough outline. The choice of whether to create a careful draft, by writing slowly and revising as you go, or a discovery, which is written quickly and then revised in subsequent drafts, is up to the writer. Either approach can produce excellent writing.

> ► ► ► **A C T I V I T Y 1.36**
>
> Select a topic from the list in the Activity for section 1.35, and write a careful draft of a paragraph on that subject. To begin, outline your paragraph, listing the main idea and three or four supporting details. Next, draft the topic sentence and revise it until it reads just the way you want it to. Draft the next sentence; reread it and revise it as needed. Continue in this manner until you have completed your paragraph.

1.37 THE PREWRITING, DRAFTING, AND REVISING CYCLE

Writing sometimes occurs in neat stages—first prewriting, then drafting, and then revising. More frequently, however, writers shift back and forth between these activities. For example, in the middle of writing your draft, you might realize that you haven't really thought through one of the arguments you want to present. You might need to return to a prewriting activity such as role playing to clarify your position. Then you would go back and revise the new material before continuing with the rest of the draft. The steps in the writing process are flexible and can be adapted to meet specific problems that arise as you write.

DRAFTING: PARAGRAPHS

1.38 PARAGRAPHS WITH TOPIC SENTENCES

A paragraph frequently contains a **topic sentence**, which presents the main idea of the paragraph. This topic sentence can occur at the beginning, in the middle, or at the end of the paragraph. Most paragraphs also contain two or more sentences that illustrate, give examples of, or elaborate on the topic sentence. The **supporting sentences** often begin with transitions that relate them to the other sentences or to the topic sentence. The paragraph may also end with a **clincher sentence**, which restates the main idea of the paragraph. These parts of a paragraph are identified in the following sample.

Topic Sentence	John Muir was a key figure in the national parks movement. The son of a Wisconsin farmer, he studied natural science and philosophy and read the great naturalists. From a young age, Muir felt a sense of fulfillment and exhilaration in the presence of nature. In the 1860s, he traveled throughout the majestic Sierra Nevada, becoming intimately familiar with it. He urged others to experience the power and splendor of wilderness, which he saw as a precious resource of the human spirit. Wilderness, however, needed protection
Supporting Sentences	from those who would plunder it, especially lumberers, who had been eating away at centuries-old redwood groves in California. Muir believed that federal government control was needed to preserve California's forests. In the early 1890s, he organized the Sierra Club, wrote articles, and personally lobbied President Theodore Roosevelt to help preserve the Sierra Nevada. The persuasive Muir was successful. The state-controlled redwood forests came
Clincher Sentence	under federal protection as a national park. Muir's efforts fueled the conservation movement which helped to create sixteen national parks by 1916.

Write a paragraph about one of the following topics or one of your own. Lead off your paragraph with a topic sentence. Then write three sentences that present details related to the topic sentence. Close with a clincher sentence that wraps up the paragraph.

- a person who has contributed to your school or community
- a book, story, or poem you would recommend to others

1.39 Paragraphs without Topic Sentences

Not every paragraph contains a topic sentence. In some cases, the main idea of the paragraph is not stated directly but implied. In other cases, the paragraph serves simply as a transition between sections of a composition. Probably the most common kind of paragraph with a topic sentence is a narrative paragraph that presents a sequence of events but does not include a sentence summarizing the events. The following paragraph is an example:

> The sign at the top of the trail read "Steep Descent." Miranda plunged both ski poles into the snow as she took off. The wooded trail was straight at first, and she picked up speed. Luckily the first turn was wide and well banked. Miranda made a slight snowplow to slow her speed as she rounded it. Then came a twisty section. She leaned inward slightly ahead of each turn. Finally, the trail flattened out, and she coasted to a stop to catch her breath.

► ► ► A C T I V I T Y 1.39

Write a narrative paragraph about a procedure or activity, such as performing a lab experiment, demonstrating a skill in sports, or preparing a certain food. Organize your paragraph in chronological order, and do not include a topic sentence.

1.40 Elaboration: Types of Supporting Details

In a typical paragraph, the main idea is stated in a topic sentence. Other sentences in the paragraph elaborate on the main idea. The kinds of supporting details used to **elaboration** include **sensory details, facts and statistics, illustrations and examples, anecdotes,** and **quotations.** In the sample paragraph in section 1.38, the author uses illustrations and examples to expand on the main topic.

► ► ► A C T I V I T Y 1.40

For each topic sentence, write at least two supporting sentences that contain details of the type specified.

1. The weekly farmer's market is always a delight to the senses. (sensory details)
2. Cramming for a test has several drawbacks. (examples)
3. Even when you fail at something, you can learn a valuable lesson. (anecdote)
4. Smoking is hazardous to your health in a number of ways. (facts and statistics)

DRAFTING: COMPOSITIONS

1.41 WRITING A THESIS STATEMENT AND TOPIC SENTENCES

A **thesis statement** expresses the main idea of a composition and usually occurs in the first paragraph. The remainder of the paragraph introduces the composition as a whole, using one of many techniques for writing introductions. (See section 1.42, "Organizing a Composition.") Your thesis statement should be brief and to the point. Readers should be able to tell from your thesis statement whether the composition is primarily expressive, informative, or persuasive.

Once you have written a thesis statement, you may wish to write the **topic sentences** for each paragraph. These sentences should express the major ideas that support your thesis. Approaching drafting in this way will help to ensure the unity and coherence of your composition. (See section 1.43, "Self-evaluation.") Once you have the basic framework of a thesis statement and related topic sentences, you can write the rest of your introduction, supporting sentences for the body paragraphs, and your conclusion.

> ► ► ► A C T I V I T Y **1.41**
>
> Develop a focused topic from one of the general topics in the following list. Write a thesis statement for an informative or persuasive composition about the focused topic. Then write three topic sentences for body paragraphs to support the thesis statement.
>
> an organization in your community   cultural traditions
> graduating from high school   the effects of technology

1.42 ORGANIZING A COMPOSITION

Every composition should have three parts: an introduction, a body, and a conclusion.

Introduction. The purpose of the introduction is to capture the reader's attention and present the main idea of the composition. To draw readers in to your composition, you can do the following:

- Describe a scene
- State an opinion
- Pose a question
- Present a fascinating fact
- Offer a quotation
- Tell an anecdote
- Give a summary
- Use an allusion
- Provide background information
- Paraphrase a statement or idea

Body. The body of the composition includes several paragraphs that support the thesis statement. Generally, each paragraph has a topic sentence that expresses one main idea related to the thesis. The rest of the sentences in each paragraph elaborate on the main idea.

Conclusion. The conclusion should wrap up the composition and give the reader a sense that your presentation is complete. In writing your conclusion, you might want to use any of the following techniques:

- Make a generalization
- Pose a question
- Restate the thesis
- Make a prediction
- Issue a call to action
- Summarize the main ideas
- Imagine the future
- Present a resolution
- Present the last event

A. Find an essay in a magazine, textbook, or essay collection that has an introduction that you especially like. Bring the selection to class and read the introduction aloud in a small group of students. Before or after your reading, explain what technique the writer used to interest the reader and what the piece is about.

B. Repeat the preceding activity, but this time look for an interesting conclusion. Before reading each conclusion, briefly describe the content and purpose of the piece as background for your listeners.

REVISING: APPROACHES TO REVISION

1.43 SELF-EVALUATION

When your draft is finished, read it through to **evaluate**, or judge, the effectiveness of the piece at this point. Many writers recommend waiting a couple of days before reading it for **self-evaluation**. Waiting allows you to look at your work more objectively. The purpose of the self-evaluation is to make any needed changes that will improve the content, organization, and style of the piece.

A good method for doing a self-evaluation is to read the composition three times. On the first reading, look particularly at the content of the piece. Second, read for organization and coherence. Third, check the voice and style. You can use the questions in the checklists that follow to guide you in evaluating your draft.

REVISION CHECKLIST: CONTENT AND UNITY

1. Does the writing achieve its purpose?
2. Are the main ideas related to the thesis statement?
3. Are the main ideas clearly stated and supported by details?

REVISION CHECKLIST: ORGANIZATION AND COHERENCE

1. Are the ideas arranged in a logical order?
2. Do transitions connect ideas to one another both within and between paragraphs?

REVISION CHECKLIST: VOICE AND STYLE

1. Is the voice—the tone, word choice, and perspective of the writing—authentic? Is it consistent?
2. Is the level of language appropriate to the audience and purpose?
3. Is the mood appropriate to the purpose and form of the writing?

Making improvements in a draft usually involves adding, deleting, replacing, and moving material. (See section 1.45, "Four Types of Revision.") When you have made your revisions, read through the piece aloud to spot and adjust any awkward passages.

> ▶ ▶ ▶ A C T I V I T Y 1.43

Choose a piece of writing that you have already done. Revise your work using the three checklists provided.

1.44 PEER EVALUATION

Peer evaluation is a type of evaluation in which another person reads your writing and gives you suggestions for improving it. Both the writer and the evaluator have specific roles in this process. The guidelines that follow will help you get the most out of a peer evaluation.

For the evaluator

- Focus on matters of revision. Evaluate content, organization, and style. Ignore proofreading matters, such as spelling, punctuation, and mechanics, which can be dealt with later.

- Be positive. Let the writer know what he or she has done right. Discuss weak spots by pointing out what the writer would gain by making a certain change.

- Be specific. Give the writer concrete ideas for improving the piece. For example, if you think that organizing the piece in chronological order rather than in spatial order makes more sense, suggest how the writer could rearrange the content of the piece to fit this pattern.

- Be tactful. Use constructive language and a pleasant tone of voice. Word your comments so the writer knows you are critiquing the writing, not the writer.

For the writer

- Tell your evaluator what aspect of the composition worries you. Here are some examples:

    —Should I move the quotation in the conclusion to the introduction? (organization)

    —Do you think my vocabulary level is suited to this audience? (style)

    —Did you find my arguments persuasive? (content)

- Accept the evaluator's comments politely. If you are confused by a particular comment, ask the evaluator to clarify it. Avoid taking criticism of your writing personally.

> ▶ ▶ ▶ A C T I V I T Y 1.44

Choose a writing assignment that all members of the class have done. Trade drafts with another student, then take turns offering comments on each other's work.

1.45 FOUR TYPES OF REVISION

The four basic processes used in revising what you have written are **adding, deleting, replacing**, and **moving**. These processes can be applied to words, phrases, sentences, and entire paragraphs. For example, as you revise a paragraph, you might add transition words to help the sentences flow more smoothly. You might delete a detail that does not relate to the main idea. You might replace a paraphrase with a quotation, and you might move a passage that is out of sequence to its correct place.

Revise the following paragraph to improve its unity, organization, and style. Add, delete, replace, or move material as needed.

There is nothing wrong with having a litter of kittens or puppies in the house as long as each of these pets finds a home and proper care. Too many of these animals become unwanted pets. They are discarded. They may end up abandoned along a country road or some such thing. All pet owners should know about the importance of spaying or neutering their pets. Spaying and neutering is part of responsible pet ownership. According to the American Society for the Prevention of Cruelty to Animals, out of every 100 dogs and cats born, only 10 find permanent, loving homes. Some folks think spaying and neutering is too darned expensive, but consider the cost of not doing it. One unspayed female dog and her descendants can produce over 4,000 puppies in just seven generations! This creates a terrible overpopulation problem. It creates starving and unhealthy animals roaming everywhere. An unspayed female cat and her offspring can produce even more individuals.

1.46 MARKING A MANUSCRIPT

To mark revisions on a draft, use the standard proofreading symbols shown in the following chart. Using these symbols saves space on your draft and makes it easier to read when you are ready to make a clean copy.

SYMBOL AND EXAMPLE	MEANING OF SYMBOL
The very first time	Delete this material.
french toast	Capitalize this letter.
the vice-President	Lowercase this letter.
cat's cradle	Insert something that is missing. Write the missing letter(s) or punctuation above the line.
George	Replace this letter or word.
housse	Take out this letter and close up space.
book keeper	Close up space.
gebril	Change the order of these letters.
All the horses king's	Move this word to where the arrow points.
end. "Watch out," she yelled.	Begin a new paragraph.
Love conquers all	Put a period here.
Welcome friends.	Put a comma here.
Get the stopwatch	Put a space here.
Dear Madam	Put a colon here.
She walked he rode.	Put a semicolon here.
	CONTINUED

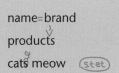

name=brand	Put a hyphen here.
products	Put an apostrophe here.
cats meow (stet)	Ignore the correction.

PROOFREADING AND PUBLISHING

1.47 PROOFREADING CHECKLIST

After making a clean copy of your revised draft, proofread it for errors in spelling, grammar, usage, and mechanics. Use the following proofreading checklist.

PROOFREADING CHECKLIST	
Spelling	• Are all words, including names, spelled correctly?
Grammar	• Does each verb agree in number with its subject? • Are verb tenses consistent and correct? • Are irregular verbs formed correctly? • Is the referent of each pronoun clear? • Does every pronoun agree with its antecedent? • Are subject and object forms of pronouns used correctly? • Are there any sentence fragments or run-on sentences? • Have double negatives been avoided?
Usage	• Have frequently confused words, such as *affect* and *effect*, been used correctly?
Mechanics	• Does every sentence end with an end mark? • Are commas, semicolons, hyphens, and dashes used correctly? • Do all proper nouns and proper adjectives begin with capital letters? • Has proper manuscript form been used?

▶ ▶ ▶ A C T I V I T Y 1.47

Using the Proofreading Checklist, correct the following paragraph for spelling, grammar, usage, and mechanics errors. Use a dictionary as needed to check spelling.

The gutenberg elegies, by Sven Birkerts, is a very interesting book. His topic is "the fate of reading in an electronic age." Birkerts believes, that the world of reading will be transformed as much by computers as it was by Gutenberg's invention of the printing press. His view somewhat is bleak, however. He fears that people will be preoccupied with organizing data rather than discovering truth. He also points out that books have a Magical influence on our lives. They provide a placce for escape and dreaming.They teach us about what it means to be human. All bok lovers will share the authors concerns.

1.48 PREPARING YOUR MANUSCRIPT

When you have proofread your draft, you are ready to prepare the final manuscript. Follow the guidelines given by your teacher. The following guidelines, however, are typical:

Guidelines for preparing your manuscript:

1. Type, word process, or write neatly in blue or black ink.
2. Double-space your paper. In other words, leave one blank line between every line of type.
3. Use one side of the paper.
4. Leave one-inch margins on all sides of the text.
5. Indent the first line of each paragraph.
6. In the upper right-hand corner, put your name, class, and date. On every page after the first, include the page number in this heading as follows:

    > Gloria Ramirez
    > English 12
    > May 6, 1999
    > p. 2

7. Make a cover sheet containing the title of the work, your name, the date, and the class.

After preparing a final manuscript based on these guidelines, proofread it one last time for errors introduced in the typing, word processing, or handwriting.

1.49 PUBLISHING OR PRESENTING YOUR WORK

Some writing is done just for oneself. Journal writing usually falls into that category. However, most writing is meant to be shared with others. There are many, many ways in which to share your work. Here are several ways in which you can publish your writing or present it to others:

*   Find a local publication that will accept such work (a school literary magazine, a school newspaper, or a community newspaper are possibilities).
*   Submit the work to a regional or national publication. Check a reference work such as *Writer's Market* to find information on types of manuscripts accepted, manuscript form, methods and amounts of payment, and so on.
*   Enter the work in a contest. Your teacher may be able to tell you about writing contests for students. You can also find out about such contests by looking for announcements in writer's magazines and literary magazines.
*   Read your work aloud to classmates, friends, or family members.
*   Obtain permission to read your work aloud over the school's public address system.
*   Work with other students to prepare a publication—a brochure, literary magazine, anthology, or newspaper.
*   Prepare a poster or bulletin board, perhaps in collaboration with other students, to display your writing.
*   Make your own book by typing or word processing the pages and binding them together in some way. Another possibility is to copy your work into a blank book.
*   Hold a recital of student writing as a class or school-wide project.

- Share your writing with other students in a small writer's group that meets periodically to discuss one or two students' recent work. (Members of the group should receive the work to be discussed beforehand so they can read it and make notes on it.)

- If the work is dramatic in nature, work with other students to present a performance of it, either as straight drama or as reader's theater. If the work is poetry, fiction, or nonfiction, work with others to present it as an oral interpretation. (One possibility is to pair with another student, exchange pieces, and then coach one another in oral interpretations of the pieces.)

ESSENTIAL SKILLS:
Language

GRAMMAR HANDBOOK

INTRODUCTION TO GRAMMAR

2.1 THE GRAMMAR YOU ALREADY KNOW

Grammar is something you know, even if you have never studied it. Inside the head of every person is a sophisticated device that works, all by itself, to learn how to put words and phrases together grammatically. Even if you don't know an adverb from an aardvark, you know, if you are a speaker of English, that

the little leaf-eating bug

is grammatical and that

the bug little leaf-eating

is not. You can tell that one string of words is grammatical and the other isn't because you have learned, unconsciously, many thousands of rules governing how words can be put together and how they can't.

When you study a grammar textbook, therefore, what you are really learning is not the grammar of the language—for the most part, that's something you already know. What you are learning is terminology for describing what you know so that you can use that terminology when discussing language. Incidentally, as you study textbook grammar, you will also learn a few rules that you never quite learned unconsciously. Remember, however, that most of the grammar is already inside your head. Learning to describe that grammar can therefore be viewed as learning more about yourself and your amazing unconscious abilities.

2.2 THE USES OF GRAMMAR

Why study grammar? After all, no amount of grammar study can match the value of hands-on reading and writing. Grammar is useful, however. It gives you a way to speak about and understand your own writing and that of others. Contrast the following examples:

He had been contemptuous of those who wrecked. You did not have to like it because you understood it. He could beat anything, he thought, because no thing could hurt him if he did not care.

—Ernest Hemingway, "The Snows of Kilimanjaro"

He seemed to see it entire with a child's complete divination before he ever laid eyes on either—the doomed wilderness whose edges were being constantly and punily gnawed at by men with axes and plows who feared it because it was wilderness, men myriad and nameless even to one another in the land where the old bear had earned a name, through which ran not even a mortal animal but an anachronism, indomitable and invincible, out of an old dead time, a phantom, epitome and apotheosis of the old wild life at which the puny humans swarmed and hacked in a fury of abhorrence and fear, like pygmies about the ankles of a drowsing elephant: the old bear solitary, indomitable and alone, widowered, childless, and absolved of mortality—old Priam reft of his old wife and having outlived all his sons.

—William Falkner, "The Bear"

If you had to describe the difference between these two passages, you would find it useful to have precise grammatical terms at your command. The first passage by Faulkner is one long, complex sentence containing many parts—numerous prepositional phrases, appositions, clauses, and Faulkner's characteristic vivid modifiers (*myriad, nameless, indomitable, invincible, wild, puny, drowsing, solitary,* and so on). In contrast, the second passage is characterized by short sentences containing few modifiers or embedded clauses or phrases. You may *sense* the differences in these two styles of writing instinctively, but grammar gives you a way to *understand* and *communicate* those differences.

THE PARTS OF SPEECH

2.3 COMMON AND PROPER NOUNS

A **noun** is a word used to refer to a person, place, thing, or idea.

NOUNS	David Robinson, Mexico, tree, honesty

A **common noun** is a name that belongs to (is *common* to) all the persons, places, or things in a group. A **proper noun** refers to a *particular* person, place, or thing and begins with a capital letter.

COMMON NOUNS	star, beach, river
PROPER NOUNS	Malibu Beach, Spoon River

2.4 CONCRETE AND ABSTRACT NOUNS

A **concrete noun** refers to an object that you can perceive by hearing, seeing, smelling, tasting, or touching. An **abstract noun** names a quality, characteristic, or idea.

CONCRETE	scream, onions, chocolate, asphalt
ABSTRACT	meanness, sincerity, patience

2.5 COMPOUND AND COLLECTIVE NOUNS

A **compound noun** is made up of two or more words used together as a single noun. A **collective noun** refers to a group of similar things.

COMPOUND NOUNS	basketball, houseboat, stoplight, torchbearer
COLLECTIVE NOUNS	litter, Celtics, senators, faculty, cast

2.6 PERSONAL PRONOUNS

A **pronoun** is a word used as a substitute for a noun. The word a pronoun stands for is called an **antecedent** or **referent**. In the following example, *student* is the antecedent of the pronoun *he*.

PRONOUN AND ANTECEDENT	Was the **student** bored? **He** may just have been tired.

A **personal pronoun** is a pronoun that substitutes for the name of a person or thing. The personal pronouns are *I, me, my, mine, we, us, our, ours, you, your, yours, he, him, his, she, her, hers, it, its, they, them, their,* and *theirs.*

PERSONAL PRONOUNS	**They** were convinced it would not be on the test.
	Our only hope was a multiple-choice test.

2.7 REFLEXIVE AND INTENSIVE PRONOUNS

A **reflexive pronoun** is a pronoun used to show that an action is done to or reflects upon someone or something. An **intensive pronoun** is a pronoun used to emphasize a noun or pronoun already given. The reflexive and intensive pronouns are *myself, ourselves, yourself, yourselves, himself, herself, itself,* and *themselves.*

REFLEXIVE PRONOUN	After final exams, he rewarded **himself** with a new CD player.
INTENSIVE PRONOUN	I **myself** would never have agreed to it in the first place.

2.8 DEMONSTRATIVE PRONOUNS

A **demonstrative pronoun** is a pronoun used to point out a particular person, place, or thing. The demonstrative pronouns are *this, that, these,* and *those.*

DEMONSTRATIVE PRONOUNS	**This** too shall pass.
	That was the last time we saw each other.

2.9 INDEFINITE PRONOUNS

An **indefinite** pronoun is a pronoun that points out a person, place, or thing, but not a particular one. Some of the most common indefinite pronouns are *some, someone, somebody, something, any, anyone, anybody, anything, everyone, everybody, everything, other, another, either, neither, all, many, few, each, both, one, none, nobody,* and *nothing.*

INDEFINITE PRONOUNS	**Nothing** she can say will change my mind.
	Someone had better explain this to me right now.

2.10 INTERROGATIVE PRONOUNS

An **interrogative pronoun** is a pronoun used in asking a question. The interrogative questions are *who, whose, what, whom,* and *which.*

INTERROGATIVE PRONOUNS	**Whose** magazine is this?
	Which one of you is responsible for this mess?

2.11 RELATIVE PRONOUNS

A **relative pronoun** is a pronoun that connects a group of words with an antecedent. The relative pronouns are *that, which, who, whom,* and *whose.*

RELATIVE PRONOUNS	The mansion **that** Gatsby owned was on Long Island.
	The uncle **who** left them the money had been a stockbroker.

2.12 ACTION VERBS

A **verb** is a word that expresses action or a state of being. An **action verb** expresses physical or mental activity.

ACTION VERBS	skate, worry, scream, fly, lurch

2.13 LINKING VERBS

A **linking verb** connects a noun with another noun, pronoun, or adjective that describes it or identifies it. Most linking verbs are forms of the verb *to be.* They include *am, are, is, was,* and *been.* Other words that can be used as linking verbs include *seem, sound, look, stay, feel, remain* and *become.*

LINKING VERBS	The Caribbean **is** the vacationer's paradise.
	Their latest song **will become** a hit.

2.14 AUXILIARY VERBS

An **auxiliary verb** is a verb that helps to make some form of another verb. Common auxiliary verbs are *can, could, may, might, must, shall, should, will, would,* and forms of the verbs *to be, to have,* and *to do.*

AUXILIARY VERBS	**must** persist, **shall** fight, **will** become, **may** leave
	We **would** win more games if we played less selfishly.

2.15 Transitive and Intransitive Verbs

The **direct object** of a verb is a noun or pronoun that names the person or thing upon which the verb acts. Verbs that must have direct objects are **transitive verbs**. Verbs that do not need direct objects are **intransitive verbs**. Some verbs are both transitive and intransitive.

TRANSITIVE VERB   He **named** the band after his favorite city.
INTRANSITIVE VERB   The storm **ended** abruptly, and we resumed our picnic.

2.16 Verbals: Participles

A **participle** is a form of a verb that can be used as an adjective. (See the Language Arts Survey, 2.19, for the definition of an adjective.)

PARTICIPLES   The **broken** glass was everywhere.
Seeing an opening in the traffic, he stepped on the gas.

2.17 Verbals: Gerunds

A **gerund** is a form of a verb ending in *–ing* that is used as a noun. Be careful not to confuse gerunds with participles, verbal adjectives that end in *–ing*.

GERUNDS   The German philosopher Martin Heidegger stressed **becoming** over **being**.

2.18 Verbals: Infinitives

An **infinitive** is a form of a verb that can be used as a noun, an adjective, or an adverb. Most infinitives begin with *to*. (See the Language Arts Survey, 2.19 and 2.22, for more information about adjectives and adverbs.)

INFINITIVES   I have taken pains **to show** you how this works.
I did not intend **to offend** anyone.
To offend intentionally is unacceptable in this school.

2.19 Adjectives and Articles

An **adjective** is a word used to modify a noun or pronoun. *To modify* means to change the meaning of something. Adjectives change the meaning of nouns or pronouns by answering the questions *What kind? Which one?* or *How many?*

ADJECTIVES   **inferior** writer, **last** resort, **third** loss

The adjectives *a, an,* and *the* are called **articles**. *A* and *an* are **indefinite articles** because they refer indefinitely to any one of a group. *The* is the **definite article** because it refers to a definite person, place, thing, or idea.

ARTICLES   **a** disappointment, **an** orange, **the** films of Scorsese

2.20 PROPER ADJECTIVES

A **proper adjective** is an adjective formed from a proper noun.

PROPER ADJECTIVES   **American** humor, **British** invasion, **Nirvanaesque** sound

2.21 PREDICATE ADJECTIVES

Every sentence is made up of two parts, a **subject** and a **predicate**. The subject is what or whom the sentence is about. The predicate tells something about the subject's actions or condition.

SUBJECT   **Eddie Vedder** may soon retire.
PREDICATE   Michael Stipe is **environmentally conscious**.

A **predicate adjective** is an adjective that follows a linking verb and modifies the subject of a verb.

PREDICATE ADJECTIVES   That play was **humorless**.
In his prime, Michael Jordan was **unstoppable**.

2.22 ADVERBS

An **adverb** is a word used to modify a verb, an adjective, or another adverb.

ADVERBS   She **briskly** reviewed the novel before the test.
He closed the door **quietly**, but they still heard him come in.
There is nothing left for me to do, he thought **despairingly**.

2.23 ADJECTIVE OR ADVERB?

If you know a word is either an adjective or adverb but are not sure which it is, look at the word it modifies. Adjectives modify nouns and pronouns. Adverbs modify verbs, adjectives, and adverbs.

ADJECTIVES   **bald** eagle, **lame** excuse, **awesome** performance
ADVERBS   Her fingers ran up and down the frets **effortlessly**.

Many, but not all words with –ly endings are adverbs. Generally speaking, if you take the –ly ending off a word and are left with a noun, the –ly word is an adjective. If you are left with an adjective, the –ly word is an adverb.

ADJECTIVES   quarterly, neighborly, deathly, stately
ADVERBS   lamely, hopelessly, anxiously, maniacally, senselessly, brilliantly

2.24 PREPOSITIONS

A **preposition** is used to show how a noun or a pronoun, its **object**, is related to some other word in the sentence. Common prepositions are *after, among, at, behind, beside, off, through, until, upon,* and *with.* A preposition introduces a **prepositional phrase**. The following examples show prepositional phrases in sentences.

PREPOSITIONAL PHRASES	They had hoped to stay on the camping trip **until** the day before school started.
	He had been seen **in** the audience.
	She had hidden the book **behind** the planter.

2.25 COORDINATING CONJUNCTIONS

A **conjunction** is a word used to join words or groups of words. A **coordinating conjunction** connects words or groups of words that are used in the same way—nouns with nouns, verbs with verbs, and so on. Thus a coordinating conjunction *coordinates,* or orders the relationship between, two words or groups of words. The main coordinating conjunctions are *and, but, for, nor, or, so,* and *yet.*

COORDINATING CONJUNCTIONS	Stevens **and** Williams were poets.
	We drove into town **but** the shops were all closed.
	You can have the compact disc **or** the laserdisc, but not both.

2.26 CORRELATIVE CONJUNCTIONS

A **correlative conjunction** is a pair of conjunctions that joins words or groups of words that are used in the same way. Some common correlative conjunctions are *both . . . and; either . . . or; neither . . . nor; not only . . . but also;* and *whether . . . or.*

CORRELATIVE CONJUNCTIONS	William Carlos Williams was **both** a poet **and** a physician.
	I was **neither** prepared **nor** motivated.

2.27 SUBORDINATING CONJUNCTIONS

A **clause** is a group of words with its own subject and verb.

CLAUSES	**The world is a very small place.**
	Life is a long song.
	Ernest Hemingway, **who went to high school in Oak Park, Illinois,** won the Nobel Prize for literature.

A **subordinate clause** is a clause that cannot stand by itself as a complete sentence. It depends on another clause and adds information about that clause. A **subordinating conjunction** connects a subordinate clause to another clause. Some common subordinating conjunctions are *after, as, as well as, because, if, in order that, provided, since, so that, than, that, though, unless, when,* and *why.*

SUBORDINATING CONJUNCTIONS	**Since** I joined the team, I have not had much time to study.
	Although he had been saving for a long time, he still could not afford a new car.

2.28 CONJUNCTIVE ADVERBS

A **conjunctive adverb** is a conjunction that both introduces and modifies a clause. Some conjunctive adverbs are *accordingly, furthermore,* and *moreover.*

CONJUNCTIVE ADVERBS	They were not good musicians; **moreover,** they did not have good equipment or a sellable image.
	In the last year, he had caused two car accidents; **accordingly,** his parents revoked his driving privileges indefinitely.

2.29 INTERJECTIONS

An **interjection** is a word used to express emotion. It stands apart from the rest of a sentence. Common interjections are *ah, oh, say, well,* and *wow.*

INTERJECTIONS	**Gee,** do you think Mom and Dad will be mad at me, Wally?
	Well, do the best you can.

2.30 WORDS AS OTHER PARTS OF SPEECH I

Words often serve as more than one part of speech. A noun, for instance, can become an adjective when it is used to modify another noun.

NOUNS AS ADJECTIVES	**speed** trap, **speech** therapy, **performance** artist

Sometimes pronouns can be used as adjectives. Such pronouns show who possesses something and are called *possessive pronouns.*

PRONOUNS AS ADJECTIVES	**my** genius, **your** ignorance, **their** stupidity

2.31 WORDS AS OTHER PARTS OF SPEECH II

A word that is commonly used as a preposition may also be used as an adverb. In such cases, you can tell that such a word is being used as an adverb because it will not have a **prepositional object.** A prepositional object is the noun or pronoun that ends the prepositional phrase.

PREPOSITION	He had never seen a grunge band **before** the Nirvana concert.
ADVERB	He had never seen a grunge band **before.**

Not only can other parts of speech serve as adjectives and adverbs, but nearly any word can serve as a noun or verb if necessary.

ESSENTIAL SKILLS: LANGUAGE

INTERJECTION AS NOUN	He was pleased by the number of **okays** he heard after his speech.
INTERJECTION AS VERB	We were **wowed** by the originality of her lyrics.

USING THE PARTS OF SPEECH IN WRITING

2.32 USING PRECISE NOUNS

When you are writing, choose nouns that tell your reader precisely what you mean. If you use precise nouns, rather than nouns with a vague or general meaning, your writing will be more effective. Avoid using an adjective and a noun, as in *expensive house,* when using a single precise noun, such as *mansion,* will do.

VAGUE	The landscape was stunning.
PRECISE	The green, sunny hills and broad, towering oak trees were stunning.

Note the use of precise nouns in this passage from Whitman's "There Was a Child Went Forth":

PRECISE NOUNS	**Shadows, aureola** and **mist**, the light falling on the roofs and **gables** of white or brown two miles off,
	The **schooner** near by sleepily dropping down the tide, the little boat slack-towed astern,
	The hurrying tumbling **waves**, quick-broken **crests**, slapping,
	The **strata** of colored clouds, the long bar of **maroon-tint** away solitary by itself, the spread of **purity** it lies motionless in,
	The horizon's **edge**, the flying **sea-crow**, the fragrance of salt **marsh** and shore **mud**

2.33 USING VIVID VERBS

Like precise nouns, vivid verbs create a picture in the reader's mind. Instead of using a vague, general verb like *walk,* a writer can produce a concrete picture by using a vivid verb such as *hobble, stroll, meander, saunter, march, tramp, pace, stride, trudge, trek, hoof,* or *hike.* Instead of using an adverb and a verb, as in *ran quickly,* a writer can use a single precise verb such as *sprinted.*

DULL	He **left** the party without saying any goodbyes.
VIVID	He **slipped out** of the party without saying any goodbyes.

Note the vivid verbs Emily Dickinson uses to describe children's activity:

> They storm the Earth and stun the Air
> A Mob of solid Bliss

2.34 REPLACING LINKING VERBS WITH ACTION VERBS

To give color to your writing, avoid using linking verbs, especially forms of the verb *to be (am, are, is, was,* and so on). Instead, use action verbs. Using action verbs will force you to restructure your sentences for greater impact.

LINKING	Jodie Foster **gave** an overwhelming performance.
ACTION	Jodie Foster's performance **overwhelmed** us.

Note how Dickinson uses the action verb "beheads" instead of the more common "covers" or "wilts":

> Apparently with no surprise
> To any happy Flower
> The Frost **beheads** it at its play—
> In accidental power—

2.35 USING COLORFUL MODIFIERS

A **modifier** is a word that modifies—that is, changes or explains—the meaning of another word. Adjectives and adverbs are modifiers. Rather than use trite or vague modifiers in your writing, search out adjectives and adverbs that add freshness and meaning. Notice the modifiers Wallace Stevens chose for his poem "Sunday Morning":

COLORFUL MODIFIERS	. . . Neither the **golden** underground, nor isle **melodious**, where spirits gat them home, Nor **visionary** south, nor **cloudy** palm . . .
	. . . The **silken** weavings of our afternoons And pick the strings of our **insipid** lutes!

By using precise nouns, vivid action verbs, and colorful modifiers, you can turn bland prose into dynamic reading.

DULL	We went to the park to look at the flowers.
COLORFUL	We strolled to Wilson Park to enjoy the blooming tulips.

BUILDING SENTENCES

2.36 THE FUNCTIONS OF SENTENCES

Sentences are classified according to their functions. They may be **declarative**, **imperative**, **interrogative**, or **exclamatory**. A **declarative sentence** makes a statement and is followed by a period.

DECLARATIVE SENTENCES	David Letterman is losing his hair. John Lennon once allegedly did a guest recording appearance under the pseudonym Winston O. Boogie.

An **imperative sentence** gives a command or makes a request. It usually ends with a period but may end with an exclamation point.

IMPERATIVE SENTENCES	Take out the garbage! Get a life!

An **interrogative sentence** asks a question. It ends with a question mark.

INTERROGATIVE SENTENCES	Why don't you take out the garbage? May I have the car Saturday night?

An **exclamatory sentence** expresses a strong feeling about something. It ends with an exclamation point.

EXCLAMATORY SENTENCES	I'm not taking the garbage out! She started dating his best friend the next day! There was a car accident right on our front lawn!

2.37 SUBSTANTIVES

A **substantive** is a noun or any other word or group of words that is used as a noun. If a word is used as a subject, direct object, indirect object, object of a preposition, predicate nominative, or objective complement, then it is a substantive. The following are some examples of substantives used as **subjects,** words that name the thing that does the action of the verb.

SUBSTANTIVES

NOUN	**Shakespeare** wrote *King Lear.*
PRONOUN	**He** made the whole team do an extra ten laps.
INFINITIVE	**To teach** us discipline was his motive.
GERUND	**Coaching** was his life's passion.
CLAUSE	**That he loved coaching** was obvious.

2.38 SIMPLE SENTENCES: SUB + V

The most basic sentence is one that combines a **substantive** and a verb in the form SUB + V. A substantive is anything used as a noun—a noun, pronoun, gerund, infinitive, or noun clause.

NOUN	The **convict** escaped.
PRONOUN	**We** lost the game.
GERUND	**Dieting** is popular.
INFINITIVE	**To worry** would be a waste of time.
NOUN CLAUSE	**What to do after school lets out** is never a problem.

2.39 SIMPLE SENTENCES: SUB + AV + SUB

You can build the next kind of basic sentence by adding another substantive as the direct object of an action verb, producing a sentence with the form SUB + AV + SUB. In the following examples, the direct object is boldfaced.

EXAMPLES The fireworks impressed **everyone**.
To study exhausts **me**.
Thinking generates **results**.
They motivated the **school**.

2.40 SIMPLE SENTENCES: SUB + LV + SUB OR ADJ

Imagine you had a linking verb in your simple sentence instead of an action verb. Your sentence would then follow the pattern SUB + LV + SUB. The second substantive would be a **predicate nominative**, which is a word or group of words that follows a linking verb and refers to the same person or thing as the subject of the verb. In the following examples, the predicate nominative is boldfaced.

EXAMPLES Clinton is a consummate **politician**.
We are **members**.
Studying is **suffering**.
To work is **to sacrifice**.

Now imagine you made the element after the verb a predicate adjective. (See the Language Arts Survey, 2.21, for the definition of a predicate adjective.) Then the sentence pattern would be SUB + LV + ADJ. In the following examples, the predicate adjective is boldfaced.

EXAMPLES Kennedy was **charismatic**.
They felt **fortunate**.
Writing seems **difficult**.
To argue would be **ridiculous**.

2.41 SIMPLE SENTENCES: SUB + AV + SUB + SUB

Another type of simple sentence can be formed by following the pattern substantive + action verb + substantive + substantive (SUB + AV + SUB + SUB). One of the substantives after the action verb will be a direct object. The other may be an **indirect object**. An indirect object is a noun or pronoun that comes between an action verb and a direct object. It shows *to whom* or *to what* or *for whom* or *for what* the action of the verb is done. In the following examples, the indirect object is boldfaced.

EXAMPLES The student offered **the teacher** his excuse.
He gave **the president** his regards.
Exercise gave **them** a new attitude.
To wait earns **you** nothing.

Instead of an indirect object, however, one of the elements may be an **objective complement**. An objective complement is a word or group of words that helps complete the meaning of an action verb by identifying or modifying the direct object. The words *to be* may be inferred as appearing before the objective complement. In the following examples, the objective complement is boldfaced.

The team elected Scottie **captain**.
Clinton made Reich his **labor secretary**.

2.42 INDEPENDENT CLAUSES

An **independent clause** expresses a complete thought and can stand by itself as a sentence. All the examples in the Language Arts Survey, 2.38 through 2.41, are also examples of independent clauses.

2.43 COMPOUND SENTENCES

You can expand on a sentence that has only one independent clause by adding another independent clause. You will then have a **compound sentence**—one formed of two or more independent clauses but no subordinate clauses. (See the Language Arts Survey, 2.27, for the definition of a subordinate clause.) Related independent clauses can be joined by a semicolon; by a coordinating conjunction such as *and, or, for, nor, but, so,* or *yet* and a comma; or by a semicolon followed by a conjunctive adverb such as *however* or *therefore* and a comma.

COMPOUND SENTENCES   The tree shook; the birds chirped.
I failed the math test; however, the teacher will be giving a make-up exam.
Home improvements can be costly, but in the long run they pay off.

2.44 COMPLEX SENTENCES

You can also expand a sentence that has only one independent clause by adding a subordinate clause. You will then have a **complex sentence**—one formed of an independent clause and at least one subordinate clause. In the following examples, the subordinate clauses are boldfaced.

COMPLEX SENTENCES   She finally finished the paper, **which was on Mark Twain.**
Dickens wrote novels **that deal with social issues.**

2.45 COMPOUND-COMPLEX SENTENCES

If you combine a compound sentence and a complex sentence, you will have a **compound-complex** sentence. This kind of sentence must have two or more independent clauses and at least one subordinate clause. In the following examples the subordinate clauses are boldfaced.

COMPOUND-COMPLEX SENTENCES   **Although they are extremely long,** Dickens's novels are often humorous, and I enjoy reading them.
The movie ended abruptly, and people left the theater confused **when they realized it was really over.**

EXPANDING SENTENCES

2.46 ADDING MODIFIERS

Simple, compound, complex, and compound-complex sentences can be expanded by adding modifiers such as adjectives and adverbs.

BASIC SENTENCE	The class ended.
SENTENCE WITH ADDED MODIFIERS	The **literature** class ended **suddenly**.
BASIC SENTENCE	The tree shook, which made it brush against the house.
SENTENCE WITH ADDED MODIFIERS	The tree shook **violently**, which made it brush against the house **threateningly**.
BASIC SENTENCE	The rock star retired and applied to law school when his money ran out.
SENTENCE WITH ADDED MODIFIERS	The **teenage** rock star retired and applied **reluctantly** to law school when his money ran out.

2.47 ADDING PREPOSITIONAL PHRASES

Adding a prepositional phrase is another way to expand sentences. The prepositional phrase you add can be an **adjectival phrase** or an **adverbial phrase**. An adjectival phrase modifies a noun or pronoun. An adverbial phrase modifies a verb, an adjective, or an adverb. The following examples are from the Language Arts Survey, 2.46, with added prepositional phrases.

WITH ADDED PREPOSITIONAL PHRASES	The literature class **for advanced students** ended suddenly.
	The tree **with the hanging limb** shook violently in the storm, which made it brush against the house threateningly.
	The teenage rock star **with the solar system tattoos** retired and applied reluctantly to law school **in his hometown** when his money ran out.

Note that expanding sentences can cause problems instead of adding interest and variety. The third sentence above is bloated and should be trimmed down.

2.48 ADDING APPOSITIVES AND APPOSITIVE PHRASES

Still another way to expand sentences is to add an **appositive** or an **appositive phrase**. An appositive is a noun or pronoun placed beside another noun or pronoun to identify or explain it. An appositive phrase is the appositive and its modifiers. The modifiers can be adjectives or adverbs.

BASIC SENTENCE	William Butler Yeats wrote poetry.
WITH APPOSITIVES	William Butler Yeats, a **playwright** and **essayist**, wrote poetry.
WITH APPOSITIVE PHRASES	William Butler Yeats, a **symbolist playwright** and **visionary essayist**, wrote poetry.

2.49 ADDING PREDICATES

A **predicate** is a main verb and any auxiliary verbs, together with any words, phrases, or clauses that modify or complement the verb. You can expand sentences by adding predicates.

BASIC SENTENCE	Orson Welles directed movies.
WITH ADDED PREDICATE	Orson Welles directed movies **and performed in television commercials.**

2.50 ADDING SUBORDINATE CLAUSES

Subordinate clauses may also be used to expand the meaning of a sentence.

BASIC SENTENCE	*Raging Bull* and *Goodfellas* are Martin Scorsese's best films.
WITH SUBORDINATE CLAUSES	*Raging Bull*, **which chronicles the violent life of a boxer,** and *Goodfellas*, **which demythologizes organized crime,** are Martin Scorsese's best films.

COMBINING SENTENCES

2.51 COMBINING SENTENCES USING SINGLE WORDS

Often you can combine two sentences that deal with the same topic to make your writing briefer and more effective. Rather than repeat information, you take the vital information from one sentence and insert it in the other, either in its original form or slightly altered.

GIVEN SENTENCES	Tom left the play. He did it noisily.
COMBINED SENTENCE	Tom left the play **noisily**.
GIVEN SENTENCES	Angela called Rayanne on the phone. She called her repeatedly.
COMBINED SENTENCE	Angela called Rayanne on the phone **repeatedly**.
GIVEN SENTENCES	The school punished the students. They were tardy.
COMBINED SENTENCE	The school punished the **tardy** students.

2.52 COMBINING SENTENCES USING PHRASES

A second way to combine two sentences that deal with the same topic is to take a prepositional phrase or a participial phrase from one sentence and move it into the other.

GIVEN SENTENCES	He wanted a retest. He wanted it on the second part.
COMBINED SENTENCE	He wanted a retest **on the second part**.
GIVEN SENTENCES	Anthony was arguing for gun control. He said it would reduce violent crime.
COMBINED SENTENCE	Anthony, **arguing for gun control,** said it would reduce violent crime.

Sometimes you may need to change a part of the sentence into a prepositional phrase or change a verb into a participle before you can insert the idea into another sentence.

GIVEN SENTENCES	Bishop sometimes created an abstract poetry. She used unusual images.
COMBINED SENTENCE	Bishop sometimes created a highly abstract poetry **with unusual images**.
GIVEN SENTENCES	He ran around the track energetically. He tried to decide what his next paper would be about.
COMBINED SENTENCE	**Running around the track energetically,** he tried to decide what his next paper would be about.

2.53 COMBINING SENTENCES USING CLAUSES

A third way to combine two sentences that have the same topic is to make one the independent clause and the other the subordinate clause in a combined sentence.

GIVEN SENTENCES	That movie was exciting. That movie was too long.
COMBINED SENTENCE	**Though it was exciting,** that movie was too long.
GIVEN SENTENCES	I love English class. We often watch movies or plays.
COMBINED SENTENCE	I love English class **when we watch movies or plays**.

EDITING SENTENCES

2.54 VARYING SENTENCE OPENINGS

Many of the examples in this handbook begin with a subject for the sake of simplicity. When you are writing, however, you will find that *always* beginning with a subject makes for a dull style. You can make your writing more varied and interesting by beginning sentences with adjectives, adverbs, participles—just about any part of speech—as well as with phrases and clauses. You may have to reword your sentences slightly as you vary the sentence openings.

GIVEN SENTENCE	Life is easy for those with money.
EDITED SENTENCE	**For those with money,** life is easy.
GIVEN SENTENCE	The newsanchor excused herself, coughing heavily.
EDITED SENTENCE	**Coughing heavily,** the newsanchor excused herself.
GIVEN SENTENCE	The parents agreed that summer was a time for their children to learn the value of work.
EDITED SENTENCE	**Summer,** the parents agreed, was a time for their children to learn the value of work.

2.55 VARYING SENTENCE LENGTH AND STRUCTURE

Repeated sentences of the same length and structure soon become monotonous. Use a variety of simple, compound, complex, and compound-complex sentences in your writing.

PASSAGE WITH SIMPLE SENTENCES

There was music from my neighbor's house through the summer nights. In his blue gardens men and girls came and went. They were like moths among the whisperings and the champagne and the stars. At high tide in the afternoon I watched his guests diving from the tower of his raft. I watched them taking the sun on the hot sand of his beach. Meanwhile, his two motor-boats slit the waters of the Sound, drawing aqua-planes over the cataracts of foam. On week-ends, his Rolls-Royce became an omnibus. It bore parties to and from the city between nine in the morning and long past midnight. His station wagon scampered like a brisk yellow bug to meet all trains.

PASSAGE WITH VARIED SENTENCE LENGTH AND STRUCTURE

There was music from my neighbor's house through the summer nights. In his blue gardens men and girls came and went like moths among the whisperings and the champagne and the stars. At high tide in the afternoon I watched his guests diving from the tower of his raft, or taking the sun on the hot sand of his beach while his two motorboats slit the waters of the Sound, drawing aquaplanes over the cataracts of foam. On week-ends, his Rolls-Royce became an omnibus, bearing parties to and from the city between nine in the morning and long past midnight, while his station wagon scampered like a brisk yellow bug to meet all trains.

—F. Scott Fitzgerald, *The Great Gatsby*, chapter 3

2.56 USING THE ACTIVE VOICE

A verb is in the **active voice** when the subject of the verb performs the action. It is in the **passive voice** when the subject of the verb receives the action.

ACTIVE   Students **flooded** the school with requests.
PASSIVE   The school **was flooded** with requests.

A common characteristic of poor writing is overuse of the passive voice. Keep your verbs in the active voice unless you have a good reason for using the passive voice. In the examples that follow, note how the active verbs make the writing more natural, interesting, and concise.

WITH PASSIVE VERBS   One week after graduation, Anthony was accosted by his younger brother. He was given a letter by his brother. It was a notice to appear in court. The request was from the Clerk of the Court. A jury summons was enclosed; Anthony had been ordered by the court to appear in one month. He was upset by the letter because he knew his summer vacation in Canada might be interrupted by jury duty.

WITH ACTIVE VERBS   One week after graduation, Anthony's brother accosted him and gave him a letter. It was a notice from the Clerk of the Court summoning Anthony to appear for jury duty in one month. Anthony found this upsetting, since he knew it might interrupt his vacation in Canada.

2.57 ACHIEVING PARALLELISM

A sentence has **parallelism** when it uses the same grammatical forms to express ideas of equal, or parallel, importance. When you edit your sentences during revision, check to be sure that your parallelism is not faulty.

FAULTY	The teacher told me to think better and having more focus.
PARALLEL	The teacher told me to think better and **to have more focus**.
FAULTY	Being too late for the bus and to get something to eat, I decided to walk through the mall.
PARALLEL	Being too late for the bus and **wanting to get something to eat**, I decided to walk through the mall.
FAULTY	Clinton said, "I will not run for public office again, so he will have more time to spend with his family."
PARALLEL	Clinton said, "I will not run for public office again, so **I** will have more time to spend with **my** family."

2.58 DELETING REPEATED OR UNNECESSARY IDEAS

When you edit your writing, check carefully for repeated or unnecessary ideas.

SENTENCE WITH REPETITION	They moved the boat **down the river** and began fishing **down the river**.
CORRECTED SENTENCE	They moved the boat down the river and began fishing.
SENTENCE WITH UNNECESSARY IDEA	She was always happiest on **Christmas Day, the twenty-fifth of December**.
CORRECTED SENTENCE	She was always happiest on Christmas Day.

2.59 REDUCING WORDINESS

When you write, use only as many words as you need to express your meaning. While editing, remove words that do not contribute to your meaning and replace complicated or unclear words with ones that are simple and clear.

WORDY	With regard to summer employment, I have not been successful in securing a position that will provide a source of income.
DIRECT	I haven't found a paying job for the summer.
WORDY	With respect to house refuse materials, he has not yet executed the plan to fully collect and consolidate all transferable disposables into one location outside.
DIRECT	He hasn't taken the garbage out.

Look for ways to reduce the length of your sentences by replacing a clause with a phrase that conveys the same meaning. In some cases, you can even replace a lengthy phrase with a single word.

WORDY	Elizabeth, **who was a three-time champion**, was favored to win.
DIRECT	Elizabeth, **a three-time champion**, was favored to win.
WORDY	Most young people believe they are **going to live forever**.
DIRECT	Most young people believe they are **immortal**.

2.60 Correcting Sentence Strings

Sentence strings are formed of several sentences strung together with conjunctions. Edit sentence strings by breaking them up into separate sentences and subordinate clauses. In the examples that follow, the first passage is a sentence string; the second is a passage broken up into separate sentences and clauses.

STRINGY	All night there were coaches in my broken sleep, going to wrong places instead of to London, and having in the traces, now dogs, now cats, now pigs, now men—never horses, and fantastic failures of journeys occupied me until the day dawned and the birds were singing, and then, I got up and partly dressed, and sat at the window to take a last look out, and in taking it fell asleep.
REVISED	All night there were coaches in my broken sleep, going to wrong places instead of to London, and having in the traces, now dogs, now cats, now pigs, now men—never horses. Fantastic failures of journeys occupied me until the day dawned and the birds were singing. Then, I got up and partly dressed, and sat at the window to take a last look out, and in taking it fell asleep.

—Charles Dickens, *Great Expectations,* chapter 19

2.61 Correcting Sentence Fragments

A **sentence** should express a complete thought and contain both a subject and a verb. A **sentence fragment** is a phrase or clause that does not express a complete thought but has been punctuated as though it did. You can correct a sentence fragment by changing its punctuation or structure so that it expresses a complete thought.

FRAGMENTED	I was confident of success. **Being a master of deception.**
CORRECTED	I was confident of success, being a master of deception.
FRAGMENTED	Each of them was given three detentions. **Which they deserved.**
CORRECTED	Each of them was given three detentions, which they deserved.

In sentences in which the subject will be understood by the reader, the subject can be left unexpressed. Such sentences are not sentence fragments.

SENTENCE WITH IMPLIED, UNEXPRESSED SUBJECT	[You] Remember to bring an umbrella.

2.62 CORRECTING RUN-ONS

A **run-on** is formed of two or more sentences that have been run together as if they were one complete thought. Edit a run-on by making it into two sentences, by adding a comma and a coordinating conjunction, or by adding a semicolon.

RUN-ONS	I drove the car to the garage my sister picked it up later.
TWO SENTENCES	I drove the car to the garage. My sister picked it up later.
COORDINATED CLAUSES	I drove the car to the garage, and my sister picked it up later.

2.63 CORRECTING DANGLING OR MISPLACED MODIFIERS

A **dangling modifier** is a modifying phrase or clause that seems to modify a word it is not intended to modify. Sometimes this error occurs because the modifier is too far from the word it is supposed to modify. It is then called a **misplaced modifier**. You can edit dangling and misplaced modifiers by adding a word for the phrase or clause to modify or by rewording the sentence.

DANGLING	Reading Foucault, the purpose of prisons became clear.
WORDS ADDED	Reading Foucault, I came to understand the purpose of prisons.
DANGLING	Waiting for the light to change, the car she drove was revving.
REWORDED	Waiting for the light to change, she revved the car she was driving.
MISPLACED	The principal questioned my motives at the end of the meeting.
REWORDED	At the end of the meeting, the principal questioned my motives.
MISPLACED	The owner of the building had the student who was tired of the noise from the stereo evicted.
REWORDED	The owner of the building, who was tired of the noise from the stereo, had the student evicted.

2.64 INVERTING SENTENCES FOR EMPHASIS

When editing your writing, look for opportunities to add emphasis and clarify your meaning. One way to add emphasis is to **invert** a sentence—to change the usual order of its parts.

REGULAR ORDER	I cannot take all the credit for the ghastly performance.
INVERTED ORDER	For this ghastly performance I cannot take all the credit.
REGULAR ORDER	Shakespeare's play ends with dead bodies strewn all over the stage.
INVERTED ORDER	With dead bodies strewn all over the stage, Shakespeare's play ends.

EDITING FOR ERRORS IN VERB TENSE

2.65 IMPROPER SHIFTS IN VERB TENSE

When the verbs in a sentence or group of sentences shift from past to present or from present to past without reason, the reader may not be able to follow the intended meaning. Correct the shift by using consistent tenses for all verbs.

WITH TENSE SHIFT	We were all tired from the drive but **are** still looking forward to dinner.
CORRECTED	We were all tired from the drive but **were** still looking forward to dinner.

2.66 IRREGULAR VERBS I

Every verb has four **principal parts**: the **base form**, the **present participle**, the **past**, and the **past participle**. All the other verb forms can be made from these parts. As you can see from the table below, the present participle is formed by adding *–ing* to the base form (sometimes dropping an *e*), and the past and past participle are formed by adding *–d* or *–ed* (or sometimes *–t*) to the base form.

BASE FORM	PRESENT PARTICIPLE	PAST	PAST PARTICIPLE
believe	[is] believing	believed	[have] believed
obey	[is] obeying	obeyed	[have] obeyed
serve	[is] serving	served	[have] served

Some verbs, however, form the past and past participle in some other way than by adding *–d* or *–ed* (or sometimes *–t*) to the base form. These verbs are called *irregular verbs*. English has dozens of them. The table below shows just a few examples. If you are in doubt about whether a verb is irregular, look it up in the dictionary; if it is irregular, you will find its principal parts listed.

BASE FORM	PRESENT PARTICIPLE	PAST	PAST PARTICIPLE
do	[is] doing	did	[have] done
fly	[is] flying	flew	[have] flown
know	[is] knowing	knew	[have] known
eat	[is] eating	ate	[have] eaten
break	[is] breaking	broke	[have] broken

2.67 IRREGULAR VERBS II

When using irregular verbs in the so-called perfect tenses (with *has* or *have*), make sure you do not use the past form instead of the past participle.

NONSTANDARD PARTICIPLE	**I have knew** him since I was in junior high.
STANDARD PARTICIPLE	**I have known** him since I was in junior high.

Another error to watch for is using the past participle form without a helping verb or mistaking the past participle for the past.

NONSTANDARD PARTICIPLE	**I flown** this plane dozens of times.
STANDARD PARTICIPLE	**I have flown** this plane dozens of times.
NONSTANDARD PARTICIPLE	**I done** all I could with that bike.
STANDARD PARTICIPLE	**I did** all I could with that bike.

Finally, do not add *–d* or *–ed* or *–t* to the past form of an irregular verb.

NONSTANDARD	I ated an apple.
STANDARD	I ate an apple.

2.68 SPLIT INFINITIVES

In English, the infinitive often takes the form of two words, *to* and the base. In their discussion of this form, the first English grammarians—influenced by their knowledge of Latin in which the infinitive is a single word—decreed that the infinitive should never be "split" in English. Under this rule, adverbs and other sentence components should not stand between *to* and the base form. However, the normal sentence rhythms of English, and the demands of sense, often call for an infinitive to be split.

STRAINED WORD ORDER	Finally, I would like **to discuss briefly** my proposal for a shorter school year.
NATURAL WORD ORDER	Finally, I would like **to briefly discuss** my proposal for a shorter school year.
STRAINED WORD ORDER	They hoped to find a way **to refute quickly** their opponents' claims.
NATURAL WORD ORDER	They hoped to find a way **to quickly refute** their opponents' claims.
EXAMPLES	**To freely express** themselves without fear of government reprisals . . .
	To truly believe in themselves they . . .

In using the infinitive, keep *to* and the base form together where possible, but do not hesitate to separate them where the rhythm or sense of the sentence requires it. (Note that a phrase such as *to be proudly aware* is not a split infinitive; it is an infinitive of the verb *to be* followed by a predicate nominative modified by an adverb.)

Although the rule that infinitives should not be split was based on Latin rather than English, it has been widely accepted. You should be aware that some people may find fault with the use of a split infinitive even in cases where such a use is required by sound and sense. (For more information on the use of split infinitives, see the entry on split infinitives in Fowler's *Modern English Usage.*)

2.69 VOICE AND MOOD

Shifts in **voice** from active to passive can be as confusing as shifts in tense. Check your sentences to be sure voice is consistent. Rewrite and change subjects as necessary.

WITH VOICE SHIFT	Although **she admitted** leaving early, **a reason was not given** by her.
CORRECTED	Although she admitted leaving early, she gave no reason.

In addition to watching for voice shifts, check to be sure your verbs are in the appropriate **mood.** Mood is a characteristic that shows the way in which a verb is used. Each verb has three moods: **indicative**, **imperative**, and **subjunctive.**

Use a verb in the *indicative mood* to express a fact, an opinion, or a question.

INDICATIVE MOOD	For long bike rides, most professionals **carry** two water bottles.
	Roosevelt **believed** that the country was at a crossroads.
	Didn't Shakespeare **own** shares in the Globe Theater?

Use the *imperative mood* to express a direct command or request.

IMPERATIVE MOOD	**Get** a clue!
	Please **leave** this room.

Use the *subjunctive mood* in the present to express a suggestion or a necessity.

SUBJUNCTIVE MOOD	Shakespeare suggests through one of his characters that we **be** neither borrowers nor lenders.
	It is essential that we **conserve** resources.

Use the *past subjunctive* to express a wish or a condition that is not true (contrary to fact).

PAST SUBJUNCTIVE	He wished they **were** young again.
	If the responsible parties **were** here, I would give them a piece of my mind.

Notice that the singular of most verbs in the subjunctive looks like a plural of a verb in the indicative.

INDICATIVE PLURAL	They **were** upset at the decision.
SUBJUNCTIVE SINGULAR	If I **were** really mad, I would cancel my membership.

EDITING FOR ERRORS IN SUBJECT/VERB AGREEMENT

2.70 AGREEMENT OF SUBJECT AND VERB

A word that refers to one person or thing is said to be **singular in number.** A word that refers to more than one person or thing is said to be **plural in number.** Most nouns that end in *s* are plural, but most verbs that refer to the present and end in *s* are singular.

SINGULAR NOUNS	book, faucet, car, scone
PLURAL NOUNS	books, faucets, cars, scones
SINGULAR VERBS	entangles, aggravates, extinguishes, heightens
PLURAL VERBS	entangle, aggravate, extinguish, heighten

Each verb in a sentence should be singular if its subject is singular and plural if its subject is plural. In other words, a verb must **agree in number** with its subject.

EXAMPLES   **It bothers** me all the time.
            The **poems heighten** our awareness of time.

The pronouns *I* and *you,* though singular, almost always take forms that look plural. The only exceptions are the forms *I am* and *I was.*

EXAMPLES   **I believe** the car industry will continue to rebound.
            You sense my uneasiness.

2.71 AGREEMENT WITH COMPOUND SUBJECTS

A **compound subject** is formed of two or more nouns or pronouns that are joined by a conjunction and have the same verb. A compound subject joined by the conjunction *and* usually takes a plural verb.

EXAMPLE   **Salt** and **acid rain are** hard on a car's body.

A compound subject in which the subjects are joined by the conjunction *and* takes a singular verb if the compound subject really names only one person or thing.

EXAMPLE   His **work** and **love is** writing

A compound subject formed of two singular subjects joined by the conjunctions *or* or *nor* takes a singular verb.

EXAMPLES   Neither **Streep** nor **Foster is** usually guilty of underpreparing.
            Either **poetry** or **drama is** appropriate for public performance.

A compound subject formed of a singular subject and a plural subject joined by the conjunctions *or* or *nor* takes a verb that agrees in number with the subject nearer the verb.

EXAMPLES   Either **Kim** or the backup **vocalists are** responsible for the recording.
            Either the backup **vocalists** or **Kim is** responsible for the recording.

2.72 AGREEMENT WITH INDEFINITE PRONOUNS

These indefinite pronouns are singular and take a singular verb: *anybody, anyone, anything, each, either, everybody, everyone, everything, neither, nobody, no one, nothing, one, somebody, someone,* and *something.*

EXAMPLES   **Nobody wants** to take the exam on Friday.
            Everybody enjoys some kind of music.

These indefinite pronouns are plural and take a plural verb: *both, few, many,* and *several.*

> EXAMPLES   **Both** of these choices **are** unacceptable.
> **Several** new students **are** on the honor roll.

The following indefinite pronouns can be singular or plural: *all, any, most, none,* and *some.*

> EXAMPLES   **All** of the cookies **were saved.** (*All* is plural.)
> **All** of the pie **was eaten.** (*All* is singular.)

2.73 AGREEMENT IN INVERTED SENTENCES

When you invert sentences for emphasis, make sure you maintain agreement in number between subject and verb.

> EXAMPLES   For those ghastly performances **he takes** full credit.
> The last straw **she took.**

2.74 AGREEMENT WITH *DOESN'T* AND *DON'T*

The contraction *doesn't* (from *does not*) is third-person singular and should be used only with a third-person singular subject. The contraction *don't* (from *do not*) should be used with all other subjects.

> EXAMPLES   **She doesn't** want material things.
> **They don't** understand the procedure.
> **I don't** find the subject boring.

2.75 OTHER PROBLEMS IN SUBJECT/VERB AGREEMENT

When a sentence begins with *here, there, when,* or *where,* often the subject follows the verb. In editing your writing, use extra care to check that the subject and verb of such sentences agree in number. Remember that the contractions *here's, there's, when's,* and *where's* contain a singular verb (*is*) and should only be used with a singular subject.

> EXAMPLES   Here's the team.
> There is one more exam being given.
> When's the test?
> When are the band members joining us?
> Where's the rub?

Also check to be sure a verb in a sentence with a predicate nominative agrees in number with the subject and not with the predicate nominative.

> EXAMPLES   Essays are the hardest part of school.
> The hardest part of school is essays.

A collective noun takes a singular verb when the noun refers to the group as a unit, and it takes a plural verb when it refers to the members of the group as individuals.

AS SINGULAR   The team runs laps every day.
AS PLURAL   The team joke among themselves behind the coach's back.

While editing your work, check for nouns that are plural in form but singular in meaning. They should take singular verbs.

EXAMPLES   cryogenics, slacks, measles

The title of a creative work such as a book or song takes a singular verb, as does a group of words used as a unit.

EXAMPLES   *Aphorisms* **has** been on the bestseller list for two weeks.
            Sidney and Austen **is** the smallest firm in Chicago.

An expression stating an amount is singular and takes a singular verb when the amount is considered as one unit. It is plural and takes a plural verb when the amount is considered as something with many parts.

AS SINGULAR   Three eggs is a high-cholesterol breakfast.
AS PLURAL   Three eggs were found splattered across the windshield.

A fraction or a percentage is singular when it refers to a singular word and plural when it refers to a plural word.

AS SINGULAR   One-fourth of the text was footnotes.
AS PLURAL   One-fourth of all the pages were footnotes.
AS SINGULAR   Over 60 percent of the nation is hopeful about the economy.
AS PLURAL   Over 60 percent of all citizens are hopeful about the economy.

Expressions of measurement, such as area, length, volume, and weight, are usually singular.

EXAMPLE   **Two quarts** is a lot of milk to drink in one sitting.

EDITING FOR ERRORS IN PRONOUN USAGE

2.76 PRONOUN CASE I

Case is the form that a noun or a pronoun takes to indicate its use in a sentence. English nouns and pronouns have three cases: **nominative, objective,** and **possessive.** The nominative case is used for the subject of a verb or for a predicate nominative. The objective case is used for a direct object, an indirect object, or the object of a preposition. The possessive case is used to show possession. The form of the nominative and objective cases of nouns is the same, and most nouns form possessives by adding an apostrophe and an s to the singular and an apostrophe only to the plural. But many pronouns have different forms to show nominative, objective, and possessive cases.

PERSONAL PRONOUNS		
SINGULAR		
Nominative Case (for subjects or predicate nominatives)	**Objective Case** (for direct objects, indirect objects, and objects of prepositions)	**Possessive Case** (to show possession)
I	me	my, mine
you	you	your, yours
he, she, it	him, her, it	his, her, hers, its
PLURAL		
we	us	our, ours
you	you	your, yours
they	them	their, theirs

To determine which form of the pronoun to use when writing a sentence, first decide whether the pronoun is used as a subject, predicate nominative, as some kind of object, or as a possessive. Doing so will tell you what case the pronoun should be.

SUBJECT	**He** is no longer working for that company.
PREDICATE NOMINATIVE	It is **she** you should be blaming.
DIRECT OBJECT	The cold weather depressed **her.**
INDIRECT OBJECT	The nurse brought **me** the book.
OBJECT OF PREPOSITION	I brought three boxes for **you** and **me**.

Remember that in standard English, prepositions *always* take an object in the objective case. The phrase *between you and I* is nonstandard English.

2.77 PRONOUN CASE II

Use the possessive pronouns *mine, yours, his, hers, its, ours,* and *theirs* just as you use the pronouns in the nominative and objective cases.

AS SUBJECT	**Theirs** is a complicated relationship
AS PREDICATE NOMINATIVE	This book is **yours**.
DIRECT OBJECT	He ticketed **ours**.
INDIRECT OBJECT	The officer gave **ours** the ticket.
OBJECT OF PREPOSITION	The most-improved-house award went to **theirs**.

Use the possessive pronouns *my, your, his, her, its, our,* and *their* as adjectives before nouns.

EXAMPLE	**His** indignation allowed him to escape criticisms.

As you edit your writing, check the case of nouns and pronouns before a gerund. They should always be in the possessive case.

WITH GERUND   **Her calling for help** saved his life.

Do not confuse the gerund and the present participle (see the Language Arts Survey, 2.17). Compare the example above with the following example, in which no possessive is required before the participle:

WITH PARTICIPLE   We watched her **painting** the ceiling.

2.78 *Who* and *Whom*

The pronoun *who* is referred to as an **interrogative pronoun** when it is used to form a question. When it is used to introduce a **subordinate clause**, it is referred to as a **relative pronoun**. In both cases, the nominative is *who,* the objective is *whom,* and the possessive is *whose.* As you edit your writing, check these pronouns to see if the form of the pronoun you have used is appropriate for its use in the sentence or subordinate clause in which it appears.

SUBJECT	**Who** asked that question?
SUBJECT	The student **who** came in late had no admit slip.
DIRECT OBJECT	**Whom** did you say you were calling?
DIRECT OBJECT	The teacher **whom** you saw driving toward the mall has recently retired.
OBJECT OF PREPOSITION	**To whom** did you wish to address your complaint?
OBJECT OF PREPOSITION	We do not care **from whom** you were sent; you are not welcome here.

In spoken English, *whom* is gradually being replaced by *who.* In some formal speech, however, and in all writing of standard English except dialogue, the form *whom* should still be used where grammatically correct.

2.79 Pronouns with Appositives

When a pronoun is used with an appositive, its form matches its use in the sentence.

SUBJECT	**I, Claudius,** am emperor of Rome.
PREDICATE NOMINATIVE	The burned-out wrecks in this photo are **we students** after exam week.
INDIRECT OBJECT	Give **us expert hostage negotiators** a chance.
OBJECT OF PREPOSITION	The blame for the revolt fell upon **us peasants.**

2.80 Pronouns as Appositives

When a pronoun is itself used as an appositive, it should be in the same case as the word to which it refers.

PRONOUN IN APPOSITION TO SUBJECT	Two consummate rhymers, Skelton and **he**, wrote about the death of a sparrow.
PRONOUN IN APPOSITION TO THE OBJECT OF A PREPOSITION	Praising Yeats, T. S. Eliot gave the title of great poet only to Dante, Shakespeare, and **him**.

2.81 PRONOUNS IN COMPARISONS

The ends of sentences that compare people or things are often left unexpressed. Pronouns in such sentences should be in the same case as they would have been if the sentence had been completed.

EXAMPLES	Sting knew that there were pop stars wealthier than **he** [was].
	His success as a performer meant as much to his father as [it did to] **him**.

2.82 AGREEMENT OF PRONOUNS AND ANTECEDENTS

Check the pronouns in your writing to be sure they agree in **number, person,** and **gender** with their antecedents. (For a discussion of number, see the Language Arts Survey, 2.70.) Person is the form a word takes to indicate the person speaking (the *first person,* corresponding to *I* or *we*), the person spoken to (the *second person,* corresponding to *you*), or the person spoken of or about (the *third person,* corresponding to *he, she, it,* or *they*). Gender is the form a word takes to indicate whether it is *masculine, feminine,* or *neuter* (neither masculine nor feminine).

INCORRECT NUMBER	The **individual** who is cautious and reserved should know **they** cannot avoid all risk in life.
CORRECT NUMBER	**Individuals** who are cautious and reserved should know **they** cannot avoid all risk in life.
INCORRECT GENDER	Elizabeth Bishop lived much of her adult life in South America, though **he** had been born in the United States.
CORRECT GENDER	Elizabeth Bishop lived much of her adult life in South America, though **she** had been born in the United States.

2.83 REFERENCE OF PRONOUNS TO ANTECEDENTS I

As you edit, check each pronoun to be sure that it refers clearly to its antecedent.

CLEAR REFERENCE	**Emily** could not stop for death; **she** had appointments through the end of the month.
CLEAR REFERENCES	The **leaves** were scattered across **the lawn; they** gave **it** a new look.

Weak reference occurs when a pronoun refers to an antecedent that has not been expressed. If you find a weak reference while editing your writing, either change the pronoun into a noun or give the pronoun a clear antecedent.

WEAK REFERENCE	In the postgame locker-room meeting, **it** was discussed very briefly.
PRONOUN CHANGED TO NOUN	In the postgame locker-room meeting, **the game** was discussed very briefly.
WEAK REFERENCE	The teacher had a reputation for coming to a room full of students and mispronouncing **them** all.
PRONOUN GIVEN CLEAR ANTECEDENT	The teacher had a reputation for coming to a room full of students and mispronouncing **the names** of **them** all.

Ambiguous reference occurs when a pronoun can refer to either of two antecedents. Clarify ambiguous references by rewording the sentence or by replacing the pronouns with a noun.

| AMBIGUOUS | Tom suggested his father supplement **his** income. |
| CLEAR | Tom suggested his father supplement **Tom's** income. |

2.84 REFERENCE OF PRONOUNS TO ANTECEDENTS II

An **indefinite reference** occurs when the pronouns *you, it,* or *they* have no reference to a specific person or thing. Edit out an indefinite reference by rewording the sentence to explain to whom or what the pronoun refers, or by eliminating the pronoun altogether.

INDEFINITE REFERENCE	In convenience stores **they** don't allow skating.
PRONOUN ELIMINATED	**Convenience stores** don't allow skating.
INDEFINITE REFERENCE	In some rural areas **they** depend on government price supports for grain and soybeans.
PRONOUN ELIMINATED	In some rural areas **farmers** depend on government price supports for grain and soybeans.

A **general reference** occurs when a pronoun refers to a general idea implied in the previous clause, rather than to a specific antecedent. Edit general references by replacing the pronoun with a noun or by rewording the sentence.

GENERAL REFERENCE	He clearly stated his opposition to gun control during his announcement he would run for the Senate, **which** worried some voters.
SENTENCE REWORDED	**His clear opposition to gun control,** stated during his announcement he would run for the Senate, worried some voters.
GENERAL REFERENCE	The team had lost six in a row, **which** angered some of the players.
PRONOUN REPLACED AND SENTENCES REWORDED	**The team's six-game losing streak** angered some of the players.

EDITING FOR ERRORS IN MODIFIER USAGE

2.85 MODIFIERS WITH ACTION AND LINKING VERBS

When you wish to modify the subject of a linking verb, use an adjective. When you wish to modify an action verb, use an adverb.

| LINKING VERB AND ADJECTIVE | It **is cold** outside, and some people are staying indoors. |
| ACTION VERB AND ADVERB | He **drove carefully** after hearing of the accident. |

Check whether your use of an adjective or adverb is correct by temporarily replacing the verb you have written with the verb *seem*. If the sentence still makes some kind of sense, the original verb is a linking verb and should take an adjective. If the substitution of *seem* produces nonsense, the original verb is an action verb and should take an adverb. You can see how this works by substituting *seem* in each of the examples given above.

| SUBSTITUTION MAKES SENSE | It **seems cold** outside, and some people are staying indoors. |
| SUBSTITUTION MAKES NO SENSE | He **seemed carefully** after hearing of the accident. |

2.86 COMPARISON OF ADJECTIVES AND ADVERBS

Comparison refers to the change in the form of a modifier to show an increase or a decrease in the quality expressed by the modifier. Each modifier has three forms of comparison: **positive**, **comparative**, and **superlative**. Most one-syllable modifiers and some two-syllable modifiers form the comparative and superlative degrees by adding *–er* and *–est*. Other two-syllable modifiers, and all modifiers of more than two syllables, use *more* and *most* to form these degrees.

	POSITIVE	COMPARATIVE	SUPERLATIVE
ADJECTIVES	dumb	dumber	dumbest
	tall	taller	tallest
	perilous	more perilous	most perilous
	enigmatic	more enigmatic	most enigmatic
ADVERBS	easily	more easily	most easily
	happily	more happily	most happily
	sonorously	more sonorously	most sonorously

To show a decrease in the quality of any modifier, form the comparative and superlative degrees by using *less* and *least*.

| EXAMPLES | angry, less angry, least angry |
| | frivolously, less frivolously, least frivolous |

Some modifiers form their comparative and superlative degrees irregularly. Check the dictionary if you are unsure about the comparison of a modifier.

| EXAMPLES | some, more, most | bad, worse, worst |

Use the comparative degree when comparing two things. Use the superlative degree when comparing more than two things.

| COMPARATIVE | Of the novels *Bleak House* and *Little Dorrit,* there has been much debate over which is the **more important** contribution to English literature. |
| SUPERLATIVE | China is the **most populous** of the world's nations. |

2.87 ILLOGICAL AND DOUBLE COMPARISONS

As you edit your writing, check sentences for **illogical comparison.** Such comparison occurs when one member of a group is compared with the group of which it is a part. Clarify illogical comparison by including the word *other* or *else* in the sentence.

ILLOGICAL	Eliot wrote poems more than bankers in England.
LOGICAL	Eliot wrote poems more than other bankers in England.

Another problem to check for is **double comparison.** This occurs when two comparative forms or two superlative forms are used to modify the same word. Correct double comparison by editing out one of the comparative or superlative forms.

DOUBLE COMPARISON	Let's not put language into the contract that is even **more redundanter** than what we have already.
SINGLE COMPARISON	Let's not put language into the contract that is even **more redundant** than what we have already.

2.88 DOUBLE NEGATIVES

In English a **double negative** is a nonstandard construction in which two negative words are used instead of one. Check your writing to be sure you have not used a negative word such as *no, none, not* (and its contraction, *–n't*), *nothing, barely, hardly,* or *scarcely* with any other negative word. If you find a double negative, change it by deleting one of the negative words.

DOUBLE NEGATIVE	He who does not know himself **cannot hardly** know the world.
SINGLE NEGATIVE	He who does not know himself **cannot** know the world.
SINGLE NEGATIVE	He who does not know himself **can hardly** know the world.
DOUBLE NEGATIVE	Like most writers, Coleridge did**n't** make **no** money.
SINGLE NEGATIVE	Like most writers, Coleridge made **no** money.

2.89 OTHER PROBLEMS WITH MODIFIERS

The demonstrative pronouns *this* and *these* are used to refer to things near the speaker. The pronouns *that* and *those* refer to objects at some distance. Thus you might say, "This apple in my hand is poisonous" if you were referring to an apple you were actually holding, but if you were pointing at an apple in a picture of yourself, you might say, "That apple in my hand is poisonous." The two pairs of pronouns are often used to distinguish between objects or sets of objects.

EXAMPLE	This scar is almost invisible; that one is unsightly.

Check your writing to see that your use of *this* and *these,* and *that* and *those* makes sense.

NONSENSICAL	Those blisters on my face are worse than these blisters on your face.
SENSIBLE	These blisters on my face are worse than those blisters on your face.

The pronoun *them* is a personal pronoun in standard English and should not be substituted for the demonstrative pronoun *those.*

NONSTANDARD	**Them** mice are annoying.
STANDARD	**Those** mice are annoying.

Modifiers that often give writers trouble are *bad* and *badly.* Check instances of these words in your writing to make sure you have used *bad* as an adjective and *badly* as an adverb. Only the adjective should follow a linking verb such as *feel, hear, see, smell,* or *taste.*

NONSTANDARD	The food tasted **badly,** and I had to excuse myself from the table.
STANDARD	The food tasted **bad,** and I had to excuse myself from the table.

Similarly distinguish between *good* and *well. Good* is an adjective and should not be used to modify an action verb. *Well,* however, can be used either as an adverb meaning "capably" or "in a satisfactory way," or as an adjective meaning "healthy" or "of a satisfactory condition."

NONSTANDARD	Henry James wrote complex sentences **good.**
STANDARD	Henry James wrote complex sentences **well.**
STANDARD	Henry James wrote **good** complex sentences.
STANDARD	His aging car did not run **well.**
STANDARD	Though they had been through surgery, his knees worked **well.**

USAGE HANDBOOK

2.90 USAGE PROBLEMS I

Sections 2.90–2.92 explain some common problems to watch for as you edit your writing.

adapt, adopt. *Adapt* means "to make something fit a specific use or situation by modifying"; *adopt* means to "take something and make it in some sense one's own."

EXAMPLES	He was a great one-on-one player, but he **adapted** to the team concept.
	After already having three children, they **adopted** three more.

affect, effect. If you wish to use a verb meaning "have an effect on," use *affect.* If you wish to use a noun meaning "the result of an action," use *effect.*

VERB	In one of Chopin's short stories, the news of her husband's death **affects** a woman strangely.
NOUN	The news of her husband's death had a strange **effect** on her.

As a verb, *effect* means to bring something about despite obstacles.

EXAMPLE	They **effected** an agreement between the two nations.

2.91 Usage Problems II

imply, infer. Most writers accept the following meanings for these words: *imply* means "to express indirectly rather than openly"; *infer* means "to arrive at a conclusion by reasoning from evidence." Although this distinction between *imply* and *infer* has not always been observed, it is a useful one.

EXAMPLES   Her absence **implied** that she did not think it was a very important event.
He **inferred** from her absence that she had better things to do.

like, as, as if. Although *like* is frequently used to introduce subordinate clauses in informal English, it is considered a preposition, not a conjunction. Do not use it in place of *as* or *as if* in your writing.

INFORMAL   It looks **like** it might rain
FORMAL   It looks **as if** it might rain
FORMAL   Houses look **like** snow from a distance.

literally. Most writers limit their use of *literally* to the sense "actually" and avoid using it in the sense "not actually, but in effect, or for all practical purposes." This distinction, though sometimes ignored, is worth observing.

CLEAR   She **literally** fell to the floor when I told her what I had won.
CONFUSING   She **literally** went off the deep end when I came home late.

2.92 Usage Problems III

of. The preposition *of* should not be used in place of *have* after verbs such as *could, should, would, might, must,* and *ought.*

NONSTANDARD   They should **of** at least called to say they could not come.
STANDARD   They should **have** at least called to say they could not come.
STANDARD   They should**'ve** at least called to say they could not come.

Avoid *off of.*

NONSTANDARD   The apple fell **off of** William's head.
STANDARD   The apple fell **off** William's head.

then, than. Use *than* as a conjunction in comparisons. Use *then* as an adverb that tells when something occurred.

EXAMPLES   Symbols are more important **than** images.
First find the symbols, **then** the images.

PROOFREADING FOR ERRORS IN END MARKS AND COMMAS

2.93 END MARKS

An **end mark** signals the end of a sentence. It also shows the purpose of the sentence.

A declarative sentence ends with a **period.** If a declarative sentence already has a period at the end because an abbreviation occurs there, no other end mark is needed. If a declarative sentence ends with a quotation, place the period inside the quotation marks.

DECLARATIVE	His most interesting worker was Bartleby.
WITH ABBREVIATION AT END	He had worked for three years at Winston and Barnes, Inc.
WITH QUOTATION AT END	One day Bartleby responded to a job request by saying "I prefer not to."

A question ends with a **question mark.** Indirect questions, however, do not require a question mark. If a question ends with an abbreviation, add a question mark after the final period. If a question is quoted, the question mark appears inside the closing quotation marks; if a question contains a quotation, the question mark appears outside the closing quotation marks. Polite questions often end with a period instead of a question mark.

DIRECT QUESTION	Who took my collection of poems?
ENDING IN ABBREVIATION	Who expected him to end up with a Ph.D.?
INDIRECT QUESTION	They asked where we lived.
QUOTED QUESTION	They asked, "Where do you live?"
QUESTION INCLUDING QUOTATION	Did she say "I like Ezra Pound's poetry"?
POLITE QUESTION	Will you please take out a blank sheet of paper.

An exclamation ends with an **exclamation point.** If an exclamation is quoted, the exclamation point appears inside the closing quotation marks; if an exclamation contains a quotation, the exclamation point appears outside the closing quotation marks. An imperative sentence may end with a period instead of an exclamation point.

EXCLAMATION	Now! Take out a sheet of paper now!
QUOTED EXCLAMATION	Edward reflected, "Pound's Cantos are impenetrable!"
EXCLAMATION CONTAINING QUOTE	I can't believe Edward said "I am dropping this course"!
IMPERATIVE SENTENCE	Let us all recite the Pisan Cantos together.

2.94 COMMAS I

As you proofread your writing, check to see that you have used commas after certain introductory elements. Such elements include mild exclamations such as *yes, no, oh,* and *well;* participial phrases; two or more prepositional phrases; and adverb clauses.

MILD EXCLAMATION	**Well,** take your time while you're at it.
PARTICIPIAL PHRASE	**Believing the library to be closed,** he decided to stop and visit a friend.
TWO PREPOSITIONAL PHRASES	**Out of the game for a fairly short time,** Jordan hoped to easily regain his old form.
ADVERB CLAUSE	**While waiting for his friends at the mall,** he suddenly remembered his term paper was due the next day.

A comma is also used to set off an element that interrupts a sentence, such as a parenthetical expression or a word used in direct address.

PARENTHETICAL EXPRESSION	Rebecca planned, **despite her misgivings,** to go with Cody to the dance.
DIRECT ADDRESS	**Hilary,** have you seen our health insurance policy anywhere?

2.95 COMMAS II

A **serial comma** is a comma used to separate items in a series, whether the items are words, phrases, or clauses. Some writers omit the last comma when *and, or,* or *nor* joins the last two items in a series, but this construction sometimes makes a sentence unclear.

WORDS	**Fans, players, and owners** all had their share of frustration during the baseball strike.
PHRASES	He has constrained our fellow citizens taken captive on the high seas, **to bear arms against their country, to become the executioners of their friends and brethren, or to fall themselves by their hands.**
	—Thomas Jefferson, "Declaration of Independence"
OR	He has **plundered our seas, ravaged our coasts, burnt our towns, and destroyed the lives of our people.**
	—Thomas Jefferson, "Declaration of Independence"
CLAUSES	Twain's novel is proof **that humor can be used for quite serious purposes, that race and politics can be part of good literature, and that first-person narration can be effective with younger characters.**

Some paired words may be considered a single item.

PAIRED WORDS	Recognizing that we had lost our luggage, they offered us dry clothes, **food and drink,** and shelter.

If all the items in a series are joined by *and, or,* or *nor,* do not separate them with commas.

EXAMPLE	The team **attacked and defended and contested relentlessly,** until their opponents were exhausted.

Two or more adjectives preceding a noun are separated by commas.

> EXAMPLE   He had a **cold, weary, humorless expression** on his face that made us all very uncomfortable.

Use a comma before *and, but, for, nor, or, so,* and *yet* when they join two independent clauses. The comma may be omitted before *and, but, nor,* and *or* if the clauses are very short and the resulting sentence is still clear in meaning.

> LONG CLAUSE   My eyes were the greenest of things blue, and hers were the bluest of things gray.
> SHORT CLAUSE   Clarissa sighed but Franz did not hear.

Do not use a comma between two parts of a compound verb or compound predicate.

> EXAMPLE   Alvin bought a burger and ate it.

2.96 Commas III

A **nonrestrictive** participial phrase or clause is one that does not restrict or limit the meaning of the substantive to which it refers. You can test a phrase or clause when proofreading your writing by seeing if the main meaning of the sentence is lost if you omit the phrase or clause. If the phrase or clause is indeed nonrestrictive, make sure it is set off by commas.

> RESTRICTIVE   The play we attended is the one **that has been sold out for the last two months**.
> NONRESTRICTIVE   I have tickets for *Fences*, **which has been sold out for the last two months**.

Appositives and appositive phrases can be either restrictive or nonrestrictive.

> RESTRICTIVE   The movie directed by Quentin Tarantino was criticized for having too much violence.
> NONRESTRICTIVE   *Pulp Fiction*, **a movie directed by Quentin Tarantino**, was criticized for having too much violence.

PROOFREADING FOR OTHER PUNCTUATION ERRORS

2.97 Semicolons

A **semicolon** is used as punctuation between clauses in several situations. Use a semicolon between closely related independent clauses that are not joined by *and, but, for, nor, or, so,* or *yet.*

EXAMPLE   Mr. Heard, the chair of the Chemistry Department, refused to hear the petition; he sent the students out of his office without further discussion.

Use a semicolon between independent clauses joined by a conjunctive adverb or transitional expression that is followed by a comma.

EXAMPLE   Mr. Heard, the chair of the Chemistry Department, refused to postpone the test; however, he invited the students to stay and discuss the material covered on it.

Use a semicolon between linked independent clauses or items in a list if the clauses or items already contain commas.

EXAMPLES   He entered the mayoral race, though his family was against it; he invested his own money in advertising for it, though he had little to spare; and he campaigned around the clock, though he was in poor health.
The car was loaded: it had the latest audio system, with six speakers and a CD player; it had advanced handling features, including double-wishbone suspension; and it had many luxury features, including power door locks and windows.

2.98 COLONS

A **colon** introduces a long statement or quotation or a list of items.

QUOTATION   Faulkner had simple advice for those who would be writers: read everything you can get your hands on to see how other writers do it.
LIST   In the last twenty years, three state governors have gone on to become president: Jimmy Carter, Ronald Reagan, and Bill Clinton.

2.99 DASHES

A **dash** is used to show an abrupt break in thought.

EXAMPLE   Everyone had been late for the rehearsal—again.

Sometimes the dash serves in place of an expression such as *in other words, that is,* or *namely.*

EXAMPLE   He had been given clear instructions—to take no prisoners.

2.100 HYPHENS

A **hyphen** is used to link words in a compound adjective, adverb, or noun.

EXAMPLES   cross-reference, lily-livered, full-blown war, ill-conceived prank, self-absorbed junior, self-congratulatory senior, pseudo-intellectual, card-carrying member

If you have questions about whether you should hyphenate a particular compound word, look it up in the dictionary. If the dictionary offers no information, consider whether the hyphen is needed to make the meaning of the sentence clear.

UNCLEAR	The new homeowners decided to use plants as living room dividers.
CLEAR	The new homeowners decided to use plants as living-room dividers.

2.101 PARENTHESES AND BRACKETS

Parentheses are used to enclose an aside or information that is less important than the main information offered in a sentence.

EXAMPLES	If you happen to be near the Art Institute **(which some think is the best of its kind)**, you should stop in to see the Hockney exhibit.
	When I get the inclination to memorize **(and that's not often)**, I usually reach for a book of poetry.

Brackets are used to enclose a writer's corrections or comments in someone else's quoted material, and as parentheses within parentheses.

QUOTED MATERIAL	Stevens writes, "The squirming facts exceed squamous **[scaly]** mind."
PARENTHESES WITHIN PARENTHESES	The story "Carried Away" (in Alice Munro, *Open Secrets* **[New York: Knopf, 1994]**) uses flashback and an epistolary format to create one of the great short stories of the decade.

2.102 APOSTROPHES

An **apostrophe** is used to form the possessive of nouns and some—but not all—pronouns. To form the possessive of a singular noun, add an apostrophe and an *s*. If the noun already ends in an *s* sound, has two or more syllables, and would be hard to pronounce with an additional *s*, add only an apostrophe. These rules apply also to hyphenated words, names of organizations, and indefinite pronouns.

WITH ADDED *S*	Hamlet's ghost, Harvard's Business School, sister-in-law's family, Emily's privacy, Keats's odes, everyone's business
WITHOUT ADDED *S*	fairness' sake, Summersons', Aeschelus' play

To form the possessive of a plural noun, add only an apostrophe if the plural form ends in *s*. If the plural form ends in some other letter, add an apostrophe and an *s*.

ENDING WITH *S*	three weeks' vacation, twenty dollars' worth
ENDING WITHOUT *S*	men's hairstyles, children's habits

While proofreading, check to see that you have not used an apostrophe to form the plural of a noun. Note also that the possessive pronouns, including *yours, ours, hers,* and *its,* do not have an apostrophe.

INCORRECT PLURAL	The state will ticket all **vehicle's** without license plates.
CORRECT PLURAL	The state will ticket all **vehicles** without license plates.
INCORRECT POSSESSIVE	The novel's greatest strength was **it's** brevity.
CORRECT POSSESSIVE	The novel's greatest strength was **its** brevity.

To show joint possession by all people in a group, add 's (or an apostrophe only) to the last word. To show individual possession of similar items by each member of a group, add 's (or an apostrophe only) to each noun in the group.

JOINT POSSESSION	They revoked Whitman, Thoreau, and **Hawthorne's** lease.
INDIVIDUAL POSSESSION	They removed **Whitman's, Thoreau's,** and **Hawthorne's** manuscripts.

Use an apostrophe to form the possessive of words that refer to time or that indicate amounts in dollars or cents.

EXAMPLES	a week's reprieve on the exam, a long night's journey into day, a dollar's worth of gas for free

2.103 UNDERLINING AND ITALICS

Italics are a type of slanted printing used to show emphasis. (**Underlining** is used instead of italics in handwritten documents or in forms of printing in which italics are not available.) The following examples show the categories of words that should receive italics (underlining) for emphasis.

WORKS OF ART	Hopper's *Nighthawks at the Diner,* Picasso's *The Three Musicians,* Brueghel's *The Fall of Icarus*
BOOKS, PLAYS	O'Neill's *Mourning Becomes Electra,* Hemingway's *A Farewell to Arms*
FILMS, TELEVISION PROGRAMS, PERIODICALS	*Critical Inquiry, The New England Journal of Medicine, Forrest Gump, 60 Minutes*
AIRCRAFT, SHIPS, SPACECRAFT, TRAINS	*Commodore, Robert E. Lee, Apollo, Discovery*

Italicize the titles of long musical compositions unless they are merely the names of musical forms such as *fantasy, symphony, concerto, sonata,* and *nocturne.* The titles of short pieces such as songs should be placed in quotation marks.

SHORT MUSICAL COMPOSITION	"You're So Vain"
LONG MUSICAL COMPOSITION	Gorecki's *Symphony no. 3*

As you proofread your writing, check for words used as words, letters used as letters, and words from foreign languages. These should all be in italics (or underlined).

EXAMPLES	The letter *x* is sometimes pronounced as a *z.*
	The word *friend* is often used loosely.
	I enjoyed being thought of as a *bête noire* until I learned it referred to someone who is especially disliked.

2.104 QUOTATION MARKS I

Quotation marks are used to enclose a **direct quotation,** or a person's exact words. They are not used to enclose an **indirect quotation,** which is a reworded version of a person's words. Commas and periods that follow a quotation should be placed inside closing quotation marks; colons and semicolons should be placed outside. Do not, however, use a period to separate a direct quotation from the rest of a sentence.

When writing **dialogue,** a conversation between speakers, begin a new paragraph each time the speaker changes and enclose each speaker's words in quotation marks. When an indication of the speaker, such as *she said,* divides a sentence into two parts, the second part begins with a small letter.

2.105 QUOTATION MARKS II

Quotation marks are also used to enclose titles of short works.

PARTS OF BOOKS	"The Colonial Period"
SONGS	"Corduroy"
SHORT POEMS	"The Love Song of J. Alfred Prufrock"
STORIES	"Hills Like White Elephants"
ESSAYS, ARTICLES	Hawthorne's "Concept of Evil"

Single quotation marks are used to enclose a quotation within a quotation.

EXAMPLE	The boy's father said, "When that coach says 'be more aggressive,' do what he tells you."

2.106 ELLIPSIS

Ellipsis points are used to indicate an omission in quoted material. Use three ellipsis points (with a space before the first point) if the quoted material that precedes the omission is not a complete sentence; if it is a complete sentence, keep the end mark and add the ellipsis points.

INCOMPLETE SENTENCE BEFORE OMISSION	Franklin admits his failings openly: "In truth I found . . . I never arrived at the Perfection I had been so ambitious of obtaining, but fell far short of it."
COMPLETE SENTENCE BEFORE OMISSION	"Life is a series of surprises. . . . I can know that truth is divine and helpful, but how it shall help me, I can have no guess."

Ellipsis points are also used in much the same way to show a pause in a written passage.

EXAMPLE	"Take this reward . . . oh never mind," said the aging miser.

PROOFREADING FOR ERRORS IN CAPITALIZATION

2.107 ASTRONOMICAL TERMS

Capitalize the names of astronomical bodies.

PLANETS	Neptune, Jupiter, Venus
STARS	Elnath, North Star (Polaris)
CONSTELLATIONS	Taurus, Little Dipper, Centaurus

2.108 AWARDS

Capitalize the names of awards and prizes. Some words that go with prize names are not capitalized, however.

EXAMPLES   National Book Award, O. Henry Prize, Grammy Award, Nobel Prize in
literature

2.109 BRAND AND TRADE NAMES

Capitalize the brand names and trademarks of products made by businesses. The dictionary may indicate if a name is trademarked. Do not capitalize the noun following a trade name that indicates what type of product it is.

EXAMPLES   Guess shirts, Kleenex facial tissues, Gatorade

2.110 BUILDINGS AND STRUCTURES

Capitalize the names of important or widely recognized buildings and other structures or monuments. Capitalize the noun following a building, structure, or monument name that indicates its type.

EXAMPLES   the Lincoln Memorial, Fenway Park, Sears Tower, the Roman Coliseum,
Westminster Abbey

Contrast the absence of capitalization in the following example of a building that is not widely known:

EXAMPLE   The covered bridge is very shaky.

2.111 Days, Months, Years, and Holidays

Capitalize the names of days, months, and holidays.

DAYS OF THE WEEK	Wednesday, Friday
MONTHS	August, March, June
HOLIDAYS	Christmas, Independence Day

Do not capitalize references to decades or centuries.

EXAMPLES	the twenties, the twelfth century

2.112 Directions and Regions

Capitalize the names of commonly recognized geographical regions.

EXAMPLES	the Mississippi Delta, the Caribbean, the Great Plains

Do not capitalize words such as *east, west, north,* and *south* when they are used only to indicate direction.

EXAMPLES	Move that sensor two miles west of the riverbed.
	She flew east every fall.

The adjectives *eastern, western, northern,* and *southern* are not capitalized when they are used as temporary designations.

TEMPORARY	south central Los Angeles, upper east side
STANDARD	Eastern cultures, Southern Hemisphere

2.113 Events and Periods

Capitalize historical events, special events, and recognized periods of time.

HISTORICAL EVENTS	Haymarket Riots, Cuban Missile Crisis, March on Washington
HISTORICAL PERIODS	Progressive Era, Renaissance
SPECIAL EVENTS	World Series, Canadian Shakespeare Festival

2.114 Family Relationships

Capitalize the names of family relationships used as titles unless they are preceded by a modifier.

MODIFIED	your great aunt, my youngest sister, Tom's father
NOT MODIFIED	Say, Mom, do you need any help with those groceries?

If the name of a family relationship precedes a proper name, capitalize it even if it is modified.

EXAMPLES   boisterous **Auntie Mame**, belligerent **Uncle Henry**

2.115 FIRST WORDS

Capitalize the first word in a sentence.

EXAMPLES   **Under** the bridge lies a long lost poem of mine.
Her explanation was completely unacceptable.

2.116 INTERJECTIONS

Do not capitalize an interjection such as *oh* unless it begins a sentence or stands alone. Do, however, capitalize the word *O*, which is technically not an interjection but a **vocative**—a word used to call someone.

EXAMPLES   **Oh**, why not try again?
This deserves a celebration . . . **oh**, never mind.
O Stella, why won't you come to the window?
Tell me, **O** great one, the secret of eternal life.

2.117 LETTERS

Capitalize letters used as grades, as musical tones, or as a designation for a person, thing, or location.

EXAMPLES   Krakow always gets an **A** in English.
We just bought a new recording of Mozart's Serenade in **D** major.
If **A** is greater than **B**, and **B** is less than **C**, is **A** greater than **C**?
How much force will be required to move this one-pound weight from point **A** to point **B**?

2.118 ORGANIZATIONS AND INSTITUTIONS

Capitalize the names of organizations and institutions, whether they are public, private, athletic, business, or government bodies.

PUBLIC	State University of New York, Major League Players Association
PRIVATE	Chicago Lyric Opera
ATHLETIC	Orlando Magic, Boston Red Sox
BUSINESS	Apple Computer, Sun Microsystems
GOVERNMENT	Circuit Court, Federal Aviation Administration

2.119 OUTLINES

Capitalize the first word of each entry in an outline. Most of the index letters that identify parts of the outline are also capitalized. The following example is the first part of an outline for a report on Matthew Arnold; observe that lowercase letters are used as index letters after the Arabic numeral level.

Title: Matthew Arnold as Poet

Thesis statement: Matthew Arnold found less and less impetus to write poetry as he grew older.

I. Background and early life
   A. Family
      1. Mother
      2. Father
      3. Siblings
   B. Education
      1. Rugby School
      2. Oxford University
         a. Newdigate Prize
         b. Second-class honors

II. Employment
   A. Private secretary
   B. School inspector

2.120 PERSONAL NAMES

Capitalize the names of persons and titles of address such as *Mr., Mrs., Ms., Miss, Madame,* or *Monsieur* when used in addressing a person or before a name.

EXAMPLES   Elizabeth Bishop, Georgia Yeats, Dr. Shorthair, Mr. Potter

Check a reference book if you are unsure about the capitalization of *de la, du, van, von,* and other parts of names. Sometimes the part of a name that follows *Mc–* or *Mac–* is capitalized and sometimes it is not.

EXAMPLES   Charles de Gaulle, William McKinley, Douglas MacArthur, Alexander Mackenzie

2.121 PLACE NAMES

Capitalize the names of places, including terms such as *lake, mountain, river,* or *valley,* if it is used as part of a name.

BODIES OF WATER	Lake Michigan, Mississippi River, Yangtze River
CITIES AND TOWNS	Leeds, Austen, Durham, Seattle
COUNTIES	Fulton County, Dupage County

CONTINUED

COUNTRIES	Paraguay, Guatemala, Canada
ISLANDS	Grenada, St. Thomas
MOUNTAINS	Mount Everest, Pikes Peak, Mount Whitney
STATES	Rhode Island, Oregon
STREETS AND HIGHWAYS	Fifth Avenue, State Street, Highway 61

Do not capitalize generic terms for places without specific modifiers.

EXAMPLES   We drove to **the park** for a walk.
The cat stared at us for a moment and then darted into **the forest**.

2.122 POETRY

The first word in each line of a poem was capitalized in English until recent times.

EXAMPLE   A noiseless patient spider,
I mark'd where on a little promontory it stood isolated,
Mark'd how to explore the vacant vast surrounding,
It launched forth filament, filament, filament, out of itself,
Ever unreeling them, ever tirelessly speeding them.
—Walt Whitman

Most writers in this century, however, have broken with this tradition.

EXAMPLE   so much depends
upon

a red wheel
barrow

glazed with rain
water

beside the white
chickens
—William Carlos Williams

2.123 PROPER NOUNS AND ADJECTIVES

Capitalize proper nouns and adjectives.

EXAMPLES   Francis, Franciscan priest
Canada, Canadian water

2.124 QUOTATIONS

Capitalize the first word of a sentence in a direct quotation even if it begins within the sentence where it is quoted.

EXAMPLE   Thoreau wrote, "At a certain season of our life we are accustomed to consider every spot as the possible site of a house."

Do not capitalize a quoted fragment that completes the sense of part of the sentence outside the quotation marks.

EXAMPLE   Poe claimed that to be effective a story must not "exceed in length what might be perused in an hour."

2.125 SACRED BEINGS AND WRITINGS

Capitalize references to sacred beings or persons, including God, gods, prophets, apostles, and saints. Some adjectives traditionally linked to such beings and persons are sometimes capitalized as well.

EXAMPLE   Son of God, the Prophet, Allah, Jesus, Buddha, Mohammed

Capitalize the names of sacred writings and parts of such writings.

EXAMPLES   Book of Psalms, Quran, Old Testament, the Talmud, the Bible

2.126 SCHOOL SUBJECTS, COURSES, GRADES, AND YEARS

Capitalize a school subject when it is also the name of a language or when it is followed by a number indicating that it is the name of a specific course.

EXAMPLES   Calculus II, Chinese, computer studies, English

Expressions such as *tenth grade, twelfth grade, sophomore, junior,* or expressions such as *freshman year, junior year,* are not capitalized unless they are part of the title of an official program.

EXAMPLES   Senior Honors Program, sophomore English

2.127 THE PRONOUN *I*

Capitalize the pronoun *I* wherever it appears, except in quoted material where the pronoun is lowercased in the original.

EXAMPLE   for life's not a paragraph
            And death i think is no parenthesis
                                    —e. e. cummings

2.128 TITLES OF ARTWORKS

Apply **title capitalization** to titles of works of art. In title capitalization, the following are capitalized: the first word, the last word, all nouns, pronouns, adjectives, verbs, adverbs, and subordinating conjunctions. Articles *(a, an, the)* are written lowercased unless they are the first or last word. Some writers also capitalize any preposition over five letters long.

EXAMPLES   Hopper's *Nighthawks at the Diner,* Vermeer's *Young Woman with a Jug,* Van Gogh's
            The Public Gardens in Arles

2.129 TITLES OF LITERARY WORKS

Apply title capitalization to titles of literary works.

EXAMPLES   Yeats's "Sailing to Byzantium," Thoreau's *Civil Disobedience,* Fitzgerald's *The
            Beautiful and the Damned*

2.130 TITLES OF MUSICAL WORKS

Apply title capitalization to titles of musical works.

EXAMPLES   "All Apologies," Mozart's Serenade in D Major, "The Man Who Fell to Earth"

2.131 TITLES OF PERSONS AND OCCUPATIONS

Capitalize official titles of persons when they immediately precede a person's name or when they are used instead of a name in direct address.

EXAMPLES   President Dwight Eisenhower, Prince Philip, Sir Laurence Olivier, Reverend King;
            Captain, the enemy vessels have surrounded us!

Do not capitalize references to occupations.

EXAMPLES   the banker, the broker, the lawyer, the doctor, the teacher

2.132 UNITS OF TIME

Do not capitalize units of time such as the words *second, minute, hour, day, year, decade, century,* or the names of the seasons.

> EXAMPLES We missed the flight by ten minutes, and our weekend was ruined.
> In the summer we travel north; in the winter we don't travel.

2.133 VEHICLES

Capitalize the names of vehicles only if they are trade names.

> EXAMPLES Acura, Triumph, Volvo, Hyundai, van, wagon, sports, coupe, rickshaw

SPELLING HANDBOOK

2.134 PROOFREADING FOR SPELLING ERRORS

After you have checked your writing for other problems, read it through for spelling errors. Even if you have confidence in your spelling, you may make a mistake in keyboarding your work or writing it out by hand. Of course, the difficulty in detecting errors is that you will tend to see the words as you meant to write them, rather than as they really stand on the page. Professional proofreaders have a helpful technique: they read the text backward word by word. If you come across a word that causes the slightest doubt, check it in the dictionary.

2.135 USING SPELLING RULES I

Many spelling problems arise from a common operation: forming plurals. Form the plurals of most nouns by simply adding *s.*

> EXAMPLES fools, trees, friends, fees

Some nouns ending in *o* preceded by a consonant have plurals ending in *es,* as do nouns ending in *s, x, z, ch,* or *sh.*

> EXAMPLES heroes, tomatoes
> crashes, mixes, bushes, foxes

Form the plurals of most musical terms ending in *o* by adding *s.*

> EXAMPLES The duos on the pianos were not coordinated in those concertos.

Form the plurals of nouns ending in *y* preceded by a vowel by adding *s*. (The **vowels** are the letters *a, e, i, o, u*. Sometimes the letter *y* also represents a vowel sound.)

> EXAMPLES   The candidate's pl**oys** to distract us with dec**oys** were orchestrated by attorn**eys**.

Form the plurals of nouns ending in *y* preceded by a consonant by changing the *y* to *i* and adding *es*. (The **consonants** are all the letters that are not vowels.)

> EXAMPLES   Several new theo**ries** about government were tested in the eigh**ties**.

The plurals of some nouns are irregular.

> EXAMPLES   Do more **women** than **men** have problems with their **teeth**?

Form the plural of a compound noun consisting of a noun and a modifier by making the main noun component plural.

> EXAMPLES   The brother**s**-in-law showed interest in becoming sergeant**s**-at-arms for the organization.

2.136 USING SPELLING RULES II

Another operation that causes spelling errors is adding **prefixes** or **suffixes** to a word. A prefix is a letter or a group of letters added to the beginning of a word to change its meaning. When adding a prefix to a word, do not change the word itself.

> EXAMPLES   pre + amble = **pre**amble
> dis + concert = **dis**concert
> un + reliable = **un**reliable

A **suffix** is a letter or group of letters added to the end of a word to change its meaning. The spelling of most words is not changed when the suffix *–ness* or *–ly* is added.

> EXAMPLES   sad + ness = sad**ness**
> sad + ly = sad**ly**

In the case of many words of more than one syllable ending in *y*, however, change the *y* to *i* before adding *–ly* or *ness*.

> EXAMPLES   happy + ly = happ**ily**
> happy + ness = happ**iness**

In most cases of words ending in a final silent *e*, drop the *e* when adding a suffix beginning with a vowel, and keep the *e* when adding a suffix beginning with a consonant.

VOCABULARY DEVELOPMENT

2.137 MAKING A PLAN FOR VOCABULARY DEVELOPMENT

You can increase your **vocabulary**—the words you have at your command that empower you in communicating with others—by taking a few simple steps. When you encounter a new word, whether in reading, in speaking with others, in class, or outside school altogether, write it down in a list in your journal. Check the meaning in a dictionary and jot that down, too. Then review your vocabulary list from time to time. This procedure will vastly increase the chances that you will recall the new words you encounter.

2.138 USING CONTEXT CLUES I

Although a dictionary is the best resource to check when you encounter a new word, sometimes a dictionary is not at hand. Even if a dictionary is available, you may prefer not to break the stream of your thought by consulting it. At times like these, you can often deduce the meaning of a word from context clues.

One type of context clue to look for is **restatement.** The author may tell you the meaning of a word you do not know by using different words to express the same idea in another sentence. Consider the following example.

EXAMPLE   During political campaigns, candidates often offer **nostrums** for our most serious problems. Special interest groups weigh in with donations to insure that their causes will not be singled out for reform, and the politicians respond by offering vague but **popular solutions that have no track record.**

The reader will notice here from the restatement that *nostrum* means "a favored but untested remedy for problems or evils."

A second and related type of context clue is **apposition.** Look for a word or phrase that is specifically intended to clarify or modify the word you do not know.

EXAMPLE   The book was really a **melange, or mixture,** of styles.

A third related type of context clue is the use of **examples.**

EXAMPLE   The Nixon presidency, **despite its accomplishments**, had its **nadir** during the Watergate scandal; the Reagan presidency had its during the Iran-Contra affair.

Here the context shows that *nadir* is a "low point."

2.139 Using Context Clues II

Another context clue is the use of **comparison.** Imagine a reader does not know the meaning of the word *kumquat.* The comparison in the following passage will allow him or her to deduce the meaning from the context.

> EXAMPLE   Two kumquats sat on the counter. I couldn't decide whether to have one. I thought first about having an apple, but we had none. Then I decided to have a pear, but the only one left was rotten. I was saving the bananas for baking. Finally, I decided to eat something sweeter—a large slice of watermelon.

Comparison indicates that a *kumquat* is some kind of fruit.

Contrast is a similar type of context clue. Contrast here suggests that watermelon is sweeter than a kumquat.

2.140 Base Words and Prefixes

Building vocabulary is easier if you know the building blocks of words. Many words are formed by adding **prefixes** to a **base.** For example, imagine you come across the word *counter-revolution* and are unfamiliar with it. You do, however, recognize the **base word,** *revolution.* And you know from words such as *counterclockwise* and *countermeasure* that the prefix *counter–* means "against" or "contrary to." You can then quickly deduce that a counterrevolution is a movement in opposition to a revolution. The following table gives further examples.

PREFIX	MEANING	EXAMPLE	MEANING
anti–	"against"	antiformalist	against formalism
bi–	"two"	bipolar	having two poles
re–	"again"	reassign	assign again
co–	"together, joint"	coauthor	joint author

2.141 Suffixes

Like prefixes, **suffixes** can provide valuable clues to words you do not know. The following table lists a few examples.

SUFFIX	MEANING	EXAMPLE	MEANING
–ment	"action"	atonement	act of atoning
–al	"act or process"	retrieval	act of retrieving
–y	"quality"	honesty	quality of being honest
–ship	"office, rank"	professorship	rank of professor

2.142 Greek and Latin Roots

Although English is primarily a Germanic language, its vocabulary is in large part based on ancient Greek and Latin. Some Greek and Latin words came to English by way of other languages such as French; others were borrowed directly from Greek and Latin sources by scientists, researchers, and writers, who have always looked to Greek and Latin for components to build new words. The word *telephone,* for instance, comes from the Greek root *tele–,* meaning "far away," and *phone,* meaning "voice."

The following table shows some words with **Greek and Latin roots.** Notice that the words formed from Latin roots are more common, though the words formed from Greek roots are nearly identical in meaning.

FROM GREEK	FROM LATIN	MEANING OF GREEK AND LATIN ROOTS
dys-trophy	mal-nutrition	"bad-nourishment"
hypo-thesis	sup-position	"under-put"
peri-phrasis	circum-locution	"around-say"
sym-pathy	com-passion	"with-feel"
dia-phanous	trans-parent	"through-show"
mono-morphic	uni-form	"one-form"
poly-glottal	multi-lingual	"many-tongued"

2.143 WORD ORIGINS I

Knowing how speakers of English form words can help you recognize new words when you see them. **Names of people and places** are a common source of new words. The following table gives several examples.

WORD	ORIGIN
Spartan	From Sparta, Greece, a city-state known for its "austerity" and "frugality" in the service of military prowess. Today the word means "rigorously self-disciplined or self-restrained."
Machiavellian	From the name of an Italian political writer who wrote a famous book, *The Prince,* in 1513 that described the maneuvers of a calculating and morally unscrupulous ruler. The word now means "characterized by expediency, deceit, and cunning."

Another source of new words are **acronyms,** or words formed from the first letter or letters of each of the major parts of a compound term.

EXAMPLES   radar, from "**ra**dio **d**etecting **and r**anging"; pixel, from "**pic**ture **el**ement"; smog, from **sm**oke and f**og**

Many words are simply **borrowed** from other languages.

EXAMPLES   **ensemble** (French), **sonata** (Italian), **arroyo** (Spanish), **delicatessen** (German), **sauna** (Finnish), **honcho** (Japanese), **yacht** (Dutch), **luau** (Hawaiian), **tomato** (Nahuatl), **potato** (Taino)

2.144 WORD ORIGINS II

New words are also formed by shortening longer words. The word *phone,* short for *telephone,* is one such **clipped form.**

EXAMPLES   **memo** (from *memorandum,* "something that should be remembered"), **limo** (from *limousine*), **cab** (from *cabriolet,* "light carriage"), **bus** (from *omnibus*), **piano** (from *pianoforte*), **stereo** (from *stereophonic receiver*)

New words are often **coined,** or deliberately created to fill a need.

EXAMPLES   **spin doctor,** from the expression "to put a positive spin on something." The term now means an official whose job it is to interpret news in a way that furthers the ends of the group with which he or she is associated.
boom box, a term applied to a portable stereo because of its shape and its ability to project a high volume of sound

Brand names are often taken into the language, even though their owners may struggle to protect their exclusive status.

EXAMPLES   Kleenex, Band-Aid, Xerox

2.145 WORDS FROM OTHER CURRICULAR AREAS I

As you study other subjects besides English, be alert for colorful words that have extended meanings that might be of use in your writing. Keep a list of these words in your journal. The table below gives a few examples of words of this type, as well as sample sentences showing how these words might be used in the study of English.

SUBJECT	WORDS
Arts and Humanities	Many contemporary novels have a **metaphysical** component. Some of the fiction of the Vietnam War is **surrealistic** in its portrayal of events. Ginsberg calls to Whitman in the supermarket in a kind of **hortatory**.
Mathematics	The critic remains **obtuse** about Stevens's "Sunday Morning." It is true that Stevens makes his point **obliquely**; but that is part of his point about perception in the poem. Stevens **divides** our attention between the woman and the poet.

2.146 WORDS FROM OTHER CURRICULAR AREAS II

More examples of words from other curricular areas are shown in the table below.

SUBJECT	WORDS
Social Studies	Eliot was **at war** with himself when he wrote *The Wasteland*. Some critics have an **impoverished** view of modern poetry.
Science	The poem's contrary tendencies reach an **equilibrium** by the end. Near the end of the play, Laertes **explodes** in anger. Until that point in the play, she had been living in an emotional **vacuum**, without any way to grow.
Technical Preparatory	In the first staging of the play, the audience was **charged** with enthusiasm by the final curtain. Yeats's poetry was sometimes **fueled** by political concerns.

VARIETIES OF ENGLISH

2.147 FORMAL AND INFORMAL ENGLISH

Formal English is the kind of English used in writing papers, some magazine articles and nonfiction books, and some literary works. It is spoken at public ceremonies and in official speeches. **Informal English** is the kind of English used in personal notes and letters, in most newspaper and magazine articles, in some nonfiction and fiction books, and in some short stories and plays. It is spoken in everyday conversation.

How do you decide whether to use formal or informal English? You will naturally tend to use informal English, so all you need to bear in mind are those situations (just described) in which formal English may be expected instead.

How do you distinguish formal from informal English? First, informal English allows grammatical constructions that would not be acceptable in formal English. Many of these constructions are described in the Grammar Handbook (where they are labeled "nonstandard"). Second, informal English is enlivened by **colloquialisms**. These are the words and phrases that speakers of a language use naturally in conversation.

> EXAMPLES That test just **blew me away!**
> He **went off on me** for being late.
> She asked me if I wanted to **hang out with** them.

Third, informal English is often salted with **slang**, a form of speech made up of coined words, words whose meaning has been changed for no known reason, and words used facetiously.

> EXAMPLES That's a nice new **ride** you're driving. (car)
> That coach must hate me because he never gives me any **clock**. (playing time)

Informal grammatical constructions, colloquialisms, and slang sometimes have a place even in writing that is otherwise formal. Literary works, for example, may rely on these devices to make dialogue colorful and realistic.

2.148 REGISTER

To understand the concept of **register,** imagine that all the different kinds of usage in a language—both formal and informal—form one large set. A register is a subset of language usage that is used in a particular relationship between people. In talking to a friend, for example, you speak in a register that is casual, warm, and open. In speaking to a little child, you speak in a register that is nonthreatening and simple to understand. In speaking to an official such as a police officer or a government clerk, you speak in a register that is polite but firm—the same register they should use with you. The words you choose, the grammar you employ to say those words, and your tone of voice will change depending on the register in which you are speaking.

Another way to understand register is to think of the meaning of the musical term. In music, *register* means the range of notes a singer or instrument is capable of producing. Your speaking and writing, however, are not limited to one range of usage. You can use any part of a broad scale of usage from a grunt to a complex and formal declaration of your thought.

One hallmark of people who adapt to society is their ability to choose and use the appropriate register for whatever situation they are in. They do not offend strangers by being too familiar or puzzle their friends by being too formal. The same is true of written language. When you write, use language that is appropriate for the context and for your intended reader. Your personal journal will be in a different register from a term paper, and a story you write for a child will be in a different register from a short story you write for your English class.

2.149 TONE AND VOICE

Tone is the quality of a work that shows the attitude of the person writing or supposedly writing it. Compare the dark and foreboding tone of "The Raven" introduced in the first line, "Once upon a midnight dreary, while I pondered weak and weary," and continued throughout the poem to the joyous celebratory tone of "The Rhodora."

In any writing you do, you can adopt a tone appropriate for the message you wish to convey. Your **diction,** or choice of words, determines much of your tone. For instance, when writing a letter to a government official protesting a new regulation, do you want to say, "Your new regulation is utterly unacceptable to the honest citizens of this state," or "The new regulation is unpopular among many of your constituents"? The tone you convey will depend on your choice.

Voice is the quality of a work that tells you that one person in particular wrote it—not several, and not just anyone. Voice is one feature that makes a work unique. The voice of a work can be difficult to define; it may have to do with the way a writer views people, events, objects, ideas, the passage of time, even life itself. If this treatment of the subject is consistent throughout, despite variations in tone, register, point of view, and so forth, then the writer has **established a voice,** a sense of individuality, in the work.

In your own writing, you should strive to develop your own voice, not to imitate the voices of others. What that voice is, and how it compares to those of others, are matters no one can decide for you. "To thine own self be true," says Polonius in Shakespeare's *Hamlet,* "and thou canst not then be false to any man." He might well have been speaking about literary voice. Be true to your own voice, and your experience will speak directly to the experience of others.

2.150 DIALECTS OF ENGLISH

Dialects are varieties of a language. Dialects fall into one of two main classes: dialects based on **social differences** (for example, upper class, middle class, and lower class) and dialects based on **regional differences** (in the United States the major regional dialects are northern, southern, midland, and western).

All dialects are equally capable of expressing thought, which is what language is for. Therefore, no dialect is *better* than any other dialect. Some dialects are accepted by social classes that hold power; their dialect is generally considered the **standard** form of a language, and other dialects are considered **nonstandard**. But *standard* does not mean "correct" or "better than others." Knowledge of the standard dialect is useful because it is widely understood, and because in many situations, speaking or writing in the standard dialect will ensure that people focus on *what* you say rather than *how* you say it. They will understand your meaning, without being distracted by your use of an unfamiliar dialect.

2.151 JARGON AND GOBBLEDYGOOK

Jargon is the specialized vocabulary used by members of a profession. It tends to be incomprehensible to people outside the profession. A plumber may speak of a "hubless fitting" or a "street elbow" (kinds of pipe). A computer programmer may talk of "ram cache" (part of computer memory) or a "shell" (a type of operating software for computers).

Jargon is useful to writers who want to lend authenticity to their description of situations in which jargon would naturally be used. For instance, a novel about fighter pilots on an aircraft carrier would probably be full of aviation jargon. A scriptwriter developing a science fiction film would be sure to work in futuristic jargon about warps in space, energy shields, and tractor beams.

Gobbledygook is unclear, wordy jargon used by bureaucrats or government officials. For instance, instead of saying, "raise taxes," a bureaucrat might say "proactively maximize voluntary revenue income." In requesting six billion dollars for a kind of paper handkerchief for the armed services, a military planner might call the product a "disposable fiber wipeage utensil."

The most famous literary examples of gobbledygook occur in the novel *Nineteen Eighty-four,* by the English writer George Orwell. Gobbledygook is there raised to a standard of its own; called *doublespeak,* it is the officially approved form of communication between the government and the people.

2.152 CLICHÉS AND EUPHEMISMS

A **cliché** is an expression that has been used so often it has become colorless and uninteresting. The use of clichés makes writing dull.

EXAMPLES   tried and true
happy as a clam
busy as a bee
white as a ghost
ax to grind

A **euphemism** (from the Greek verb meaning "to speak with good words") is an inoffensive term that substitutes for one considered offensive.

EXAMPLES   the company let her go (for "the company fired her")
conflict (for "war")

2.153 CONNOTATION AND DENOTATION

A **denotation** of a word is its dictionary definition. A **connotation** of a word is all the associations that it has in addition to its literal meaning. For example, the denotations of *mud* and *muck* are identical; but *muck* carries a connotation of moral filthiness that makes it a much stronger word than *mud*. Contrast the denotations and connotations of the following examples.

EXAMPLES   bald-headed, hairless, tonsured, smooth-topped
fat, hefty, corpulent, rotund, overweight, wide-bodied

Writers should be aware of the connotations as well as the denotations of the words they use. You would be remiss to say, "The honcho jabbered for eons about his pet proposition," when what you meant was "The president spoke for a long time about the proposal he favored."

ESSENTIAL SKILLS:
Speaking and Listening

3.1 A COMMUNICATION MODEL

Sometimes when we communicate with others, our message is conveyed just as we intended. Other times, communication breaks down or becomes unclear. To see how communication works, or doesn't work, it is helpful to consider a model.

In any act of communication, there is a **sender** and a **recipient** of a **message**. The sender **encodes** the message using **symbols,** and the recipient **decodes** the message and provides **feedback.** The message is sent along a particular **channel.** Among humans the channel of communication is often speech, but people use many different channels to communicate, such as hand gestures, facial expressions, body movement, and music. The following chart shows an application of this model.

COMMUNICATION MODEL	
Sender	You
Message	"Do you want to go to the game Saturday night?"
Symbols Used	Words in the English language
Channel	Speech
Recipient	Your friend
Feedback	"Sure, I haven't missed a game yet."

For communication to be successful, the encoding must be correct, the channel must be clear, and the decoding must be correct. For example, if your friend couldn't hear you because a large truck was passing by, the communication would be incomplete. You might adjust to this situation by repeating your question in a louder voice. This basic communication system is one you use every day and modify frequently when communication problems arise.

> ► ► ► **ACTIVITY 3.1**
>
> 1. Identify the sender, the message, the channel, and the recipient in each communication situation.
>
>   a. Two drivers have had a minor car accident. While they wait for the police, one person uses hand signals to direct traffic around the two cars.
>
>   b. A blind student gets on an elevator and places her fingertips on the braille "numbers" next to the elevator buttons. She pushes the button for her floor.
>
>   *CONTINUED*

2. Explain what adjustment you would make to successfully communicate in each of the following situations.

  a. You have just had two wisdom teeth taken out. Your mouth is swollen and the anesthetic has not yet worn off. You say to a friend, "Ah con tah ery ell." Your friend gives you a puzzled look.

  b. From across a crowded room Angie asks, "Where's Tyrone?" You answer, "He's in the doorway." Angie responds, "He's in Norway?"

3. What feedback might you give in each communication example? In each case, what does the feedback tell the sender of the message?

  a. You are at a rock concert and really enjoying the music.

  b. A friend is telling you about a problem.

  c. Someone pays you a compliment.

  d. A newspaper publishes an editorial with which you strongly disagree.

3.2 ELEMENTS OF VERBAL COMMUNICATION

In **verbal communication**, also called oral communication, messages are conveyed using words and other sounds uttered by speakers. In **nonverbal communication**, channels other than spoken words or sounds are used. The following chart describes the most important elements of verbal communication:

ELEMENTS OF VERBAL COMMUNICATION

ELEMENT	DESCRIPTION	GUIDELINES FOR SPEAKERS
Volume	The loudness or softness of the voice	Speak loudly enough to be heard, but not so loudly as to make your audience uncomfortable.
Pitch, or Intonation	The highness or lowness of the voice	Vary your pitch to give your expressions a musical quality and to communicate meaning (for example, a rising pitch at the end of a sentence indicates a question). Avoid using a single pitch, or **monotone**.
Enunciation	The clearness with which syllables are spoken	Slightly exaggerate the clearness of your syllables to ensure that you are understood. Do not drop or clip the ends of words or sentences.
Pace	The speed with which something is said	Do not speak too slowly or too quickly.
Stress	The emphasis given to syllables, words, or phrases	Use stress to emphasize important ideas. Vary stress along with pitch to avoid monotony.
Tone	The emotional quality of the speech	Suit the tone to the message. Vary the tone appropriately throughout the communication.

In everyday speech, people use the elements of verbal communication without thinking much about them. In more formal situations, such as speaking to an audience, controlling how you use these elements can greatly enhance your communication. When speaking in front of a group, follow these guidelines:

USING ELEMENTS OF VERBAL COMMUNICATION IN PUBLIC SPEAKING

1. Make sure that you can be heard and understood by using an appropriate volume and pace.
2. Suit your volume, pitch, pace, stress, and tone to your message.
3. Vary all the verbal elements of your speech to make the presentation more lively, colorful, and interesting.
4. Slightly heighten or exaggerate each of the verbal elements of your speech over the level that you would use in ordinary conversation.

▶ ▶ ▶ **ACTIVITY 3.2**

Choose a poem from this textbook to read aloud to your classmates. Make a copy of the poem and mark it to show the following:

- Places where you will increase or decrease your volume

- Places where you will increase or decrease your pace

- Words or phrases you will emphasize using volume, pitch, or stress

- Words or phrases that you might have trouble enunciating and will want to give special attention to when practicing

- Changes in tone or emotion through the piece

Take time to practice reading the selection aloud following the notes that you have made.

3.3 ELEMENTS OF NONVERBAL COMMUNICATION

Nearly every face-to-face message is accompanied by nonverbal communication. When you ask a question, you may raise your eyebrows. When you listen to someone, you may nod your head. When a friend tells you something in confidence, you may lean closer. Much nonverbal communication is unconscious. When speaking in public, however, you will want to consciously use nonverbal communication to enhance your message. The following chart offers some guidelines for using the elements of nonverbal communication.

ELEMENTS OF NONVERBAL COMMUNICATION

ELEMENT	DESCRIPTION	GUIDELINES FOR SPEAKERS
Eye contact	Looking your audience in the eye	Maintain eye contact to keep your audience engaged in what you are saying.
Facial expressions	Displays of emotion using the face (e.g., smiles, scowls, frowns, etc.)	Match your facial expressions to your message.
Body language	Positions of the body that have meaning to an audience	Match your body language to your message. Maintain good posture.
Gestures	Meaningful motions of the hands and arms	Use gestures sparingly to emphasize points. Match gestures to your message.
Proximity	Distance from the audience	Maintain a comfortable distance, not too close for comfort, but not so far away as to hamper communication.

► ► ► A C T I V I T Y 3.3

Go back to the poem that you selected for Section 3.2. Mark the poem to show how you will use appropriate facial expressions, gestures, and body language to make your reading more interesting to the audience.

3.4 ACTIVE LISTENING

Think about a pitcher and a catcher in baseball. One sends the ball and the other receives it, but both are active participants in the exchange. It's the same with a speaker and a listener. For complete communication to occur, the listener must participate fully in the process. Here are some suggestions for listening actively:

- **Mentally process what you hear.** Listen for main ideas and supporting details. Summarize, predict, question, and interpret as you listen.

- **Take notes.** Jot down especially interesting ideas or details. If you are listening to a lecture, you may want to take notes in outline form.

- **Ask questions and give other feedback.** Maintain eye contact. Use gestures, facial expression, and body language to give feedback to the speaker. In conversation, you might show that you have understood the speaker by saying "uh-huh" or "I see." If you are confused by something the speaker said, pause and rephrase it to check your understanding. Ask questions if you need to, but wait till the speaker has finished a whole thought.

3.5 INTERPERSONAL COMMUNICATION

Communication between individuals is called **interpersonal communication.** This type of communication can be quite formal, as in a job interview, or very informal, as in a telephone chat with a friend. Individuals use interpersonal communication to:

- **Transmit information**

- **Establish relationships**

- **Maintain relationships**

- **Confirm their identity**

- **Form personal bonds**

You can use both verbal and nonverbal techniques to improve your interpersonal communication. Here are some examples:

- Make eye contact and stand in a relaxed way.

- Provide feedback by asking questions or reflecting back what the speaker said. For example:

> SPEAKER   Whew! We met the deadline, but I'm so tired I can barely move.
> LISTENER   Sounds like you've been working really hard. Maybe you should give yourself a reward.

- Think before you speak. Thinking first makes communication clearer and more efficient. It also shows respect for your listener.

- Keep strong emotions under control. If you begin to feel angry, for example, pause and take a deep breath before continuing the conversation. If you don't think you can get your anger under control, ask to resume the conversation later.

3.6 DISCUSSION

A discussion is an exchange of ideas and information among a group of people. Discussions range widely in their degree of formality, from congressional committee meetings to after-school conversations with friends. In formal and semiformal discussions, the participants often assume roles and the discussion is structured in some way.

DISCUSSION	
Roles	• **Group leader or chairperson.** Keeps the discussion on track when people begin to digress or veer away from the subject, asks questions when the discussion starts to flag, makes sure everyone participates
	• **Secretary.** Takes notes or records what is said and later prepares a description (**minutes**) of the discussion
	• **Participants.** Take part in the discussion, listen attentively to others, provide feedback
Process	• **Discussion question.** States the goal or main idea of the discussion and is usually put forward by the group leader. In a formal discussion, the discussion question is called a **proposition.**
	• **Agenda.** A step-by-step plan for the discussion, usually written and distributed at the beginning of the discussion by the group leader or secretary

▶ ▶ ▶ ACTIVITY 3.6

Assume that a committee from the junior class is meeting to discuss what to do with the money that is in its treasury at the end of the year. Write an agenda for a meeting at which you will discuss possible plans for the money.

3.7 PUBLIC SPEAKING

The prospect of speaking in public makes many people nervous. Even famous people have this common fear. Speaking in public, however, need not be a grueling experience. Preparation can help you to feel more comfortable about speaking. Remember that nervousness is a form of energy. If you can convert this energy into enthusiasm about your subject, speaking in front of others will seem much easier.

Types of Speeches. There are three main types of speeches. An **impromptu speech** is spontaneous; it is given without any preparation. A **memorized speech** is one that is written out before the occasion and then recited almost word for word to the audience. An impromptu speech can seem unfocused; on the other hand, a memorized speech may not engage the audience completely. For these reasons, most professional speakers prefer to deliver an **extemporaneous speech.** In this type of speech, the speaker refers to concise, carefully organized notes while giving the speech. The extemporaneous speech thus combines the liveliness of the impromptu speech with the careful preparation of the memorized speech.

Writing a Speech. A well-prepared speech has a beginning, a middle, and an end. The **beginning,** or **introduction,** should spark the audience's interest and present your main topic or idea. The **middle,** or **body,** should elaborate on the main idea. The **end,** or **conclusion,** should cap off the speech in a memorable way and give the audience a sense of completion. For more information on writing introductions and conclusions, see the Language Arts Survey, 1.42, "Organizing a Composition."

Preparing an Extemporaneous Speech. The chart below gives the basic procedure for preparing an extemporaneous speech:

STEPS IN PREPARING AN EXTEMPORANEOUS SPEECH

1. Do prewriting.
2. Do research.
3. Prepare note cards.
4. Make a plan for using verbal and nonverbal elements of communication in your speech.
5. Rehearse with your note cards, using a tape recorder, a video recorder, a mirror, or a practice audience.
6. Deliver your speech, attending to both verbal and nonverbal elements of the delivery.

> ► ► ► **ACTIVITY 3.7**
>
> Prepare an extemporaneous speech for one of the following situations of for an occasion of your choice. Complete steps 1 through 5 in the foregoing list.
>
> - A thank-you speech to a local community group that awarded you a $500 college scholarship, in which you discuss your plans for college and after
>
> - A speech at a school Earth Day celebration about one way in which people can care for the environment
>
> - A speech to accompany a slide presentation about your neighborhood to a group of friends

3.8 ORAL INTERPRETATION

An **oral interpretation** is a dramatic reading of a literary work or group of works. In this type of presentation, the speaker vividly conveys the particular feeling or sense of the work. The art of oral presentation is an ancient one. Before the dawn of writing, stories and poems were presented orally in front of other people and transmitted from generation to generation in this way.

To prepare an oral presentation, follow these steps:

1. **Choose a cutting.** The cutting may be a single piece, a selection from a single piece, or several short, related pieces on a single topic.

2. **Write the introduction and any needed transitions.** The introduction should present the overall topic or theme of the presentation. The transitions should introduce and connect the different readings. Be sure to include the author and title of each selection.

3. **Plan your use of verbal and nonverbal elements.** Decide how you will use volume, pitch, stress, tone, gestures, facial expressions, and body language to present the work effectively. However, avoid movement. Movement is a characteristic of drama rather than oral interpretation. If there are different voices (for different characters), be sure to distinguish them.

4. **Rehearse.** Practice in front of an audience or a mirror. Alternatively, you can make an audiotape or videotape of your presentation to review and critique.

► ► ► **A C T I V I T Y   3.8**

Select three short pieces or portions of pieces in this text for an oral interpretation. All cuttings should be from a particular period of American literature (Units 2–8). Copy the cuttings onto notebook paper. Then write an introduction and transitions. In the introduction, present your topic or theme in a way that will capture the attention of your listeners. In each transition, state the title and author of the selection and briefly relate the selection to the overall topic or theme. Combine the introduction, the cuttings, and the transitions to make a script. Mark the script to show variations in volume, pitch, pace, stress, tone, gestures, facial expressions, and body language. Memorize your script and rehearse your presentation. Then present it to your classmates.

ESSENTIAL SKILLS:
Study and Research

THINKING SKILLS

Although every human being is capable of thinking, most people do not take time to cultivate and improve their thinking skills. The effort, however, can be rewarding. By learning how to use a number of essential thinking strategies, you can learn more, solve problems more easily, and make decisions more effectively.

4.1 STRATEGIES FOR PROBLEM SOLVING I

All problem solving involves four steps.

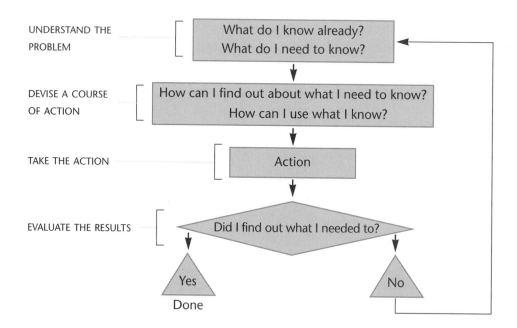

UNDERSTAND THE PROBLEM — What do I know already? What do I need to know?

DEVISE A COURSE OF ACTION — How can I find out about what I need to know? How can I use what I know?

TAKE THE ACTION — Action

EVALUATE THE RESULTS — Did I find out what I needed to?

Yes — Done

No

You can use many strategies within this **general problem-solving framework**. An **algorithm** is a step-by-step procedure that leads to a definite solution. A math formula is an example of an algorithm. Other strategies, called **heuristics**, do not lead to a specific solution but help you explore a problem: for example, asking "what if" questions to explore the problem of homelessness or using feedback from a listener to improve your oral presentation skills. A **rule of thumb** is a guideline or principle that is roughly accurate and based on common sense. To solve a complex problem, you will need to use more than one strategy. Try to stay flexible, and remember that using a good strategy does not guarantee that you will solve a specific problem.

Trial and error. In this problem-solving strategy, you make a guess and see if it works. Trial and error can be useful when only a few possible solutions seem likely. You can also use this strategy when there are many possibilities and you need to become familiar with the problem in order to find a more systematic strategy. Generally, though, other problem-solving methods will be more fruitful and efficient.

Representing the situation. When you are working on a complex or confusing problem, making a visual or physical **representation** of the problem may help. You might draw a diagram or a picture or construct a model. This technique often helps you to see how different parts of a problem are related. The communications triangle in the Language Arts Survey, 1.6, "Choosing a Purpose or Aim," on page 874 is an example of a visual representation. Try to be creative and flexible: using even a good strategy does not guarantee that you will solve a given problem.

4.2 STRATEGIES FOR PROBLEM SOLVING II

Means-end analysis. An **end** is a goal, and **means** are the tools and methods used to achieve the goal. To use means-end analysis, you compare what you know about the current situation and what you know about the situation that will exist when the goal has been reached. Then you think of ways to reduce the differences between the two situations.

Divide and conquer. Sometimes the best way to tackle a complex problem is to divide it into parts and then solve each part in a logical sequence. If a particular part is still difficult to solve, you can divide it into more parts.

PROBLEM	You want to ensure passage of the school tax levy so your high school will not have to switch to a "pay to play" policy for school athletics and other extracurricular activities.
SOLUTION STRATEGY	Break the goal down into parts: the levy needs the support of voters who are (1) parents, (2) nonparents, and (3) senior citizens. Then for each group, such as parents, decide (1a) what message will work best, and (1b) what techniques will work best to get the message across.

Work backward. This strategy involves thinking about a cause-and-effect chain of events, only backward. Describe in detail the final situation you want to achieve. Then think about what would have to happen to have that situation come about. Continue working backward until you get to a situation that you know how to create.

4.3 STRATEGIES FOR DECISION MAKING

When making a decision, you must often compare outcomes or weigh several factors. Making a chart like one of those that follow can help you evaluate your options.

Pros and cons. Make a list of your options. For each option, list the reasons for choosing it (the *pros*) and the drawbacks of choosing it (the *cons*). Then compare the lists.

PROS AND CONS OF PLANTING DIFFERENT TREES			
	White Pine	**Apple**	**Maple**
Pros	green year round no leaf cleanup in fall	spring blossoms fruit for eating and cooking	shade beautiful fall color
Cons	no bright fall color	picking up rotten apples extra maintenance (pruning, spraying)	raking leaves in fall

Criteria analysis. On the left side of the chart, list the results you want to achieve. Across the top, list your options. Assign points from 1 to 5 to each option based on how well it will achieve each result you have listed. Then add up the points in each column and choose the option with the highest total.

CRITERIA ANALYSIS: CHOOSING A ROUTE FOR BICYCLE TRIP			
	Route A	**Route B**	**Route C**
1. Interesting sights	4	3	3
2. Good-quality roads	2	3	1
3. Terrain not too hilly	3	2	1
4. Plenty of camping places	2	3	3
	11	11	8

4.4 MEMORIZING

Remembering involves two steps: storing the information in your mind and being able to retrieve it when you need it. Because the memory function has these two aspects, it has sometimes been compared to a filing system. For example, if you want to save an important document, such as a letter of recommendation from a teacher, you wouldn't just toss it into a large drawer with other papers. To be sure you can find it later, you might put it in a folder labeled "Recommendations" or "Letters: Recommendations," and then place the folder in alphabetical order with other folders. By thinking about why you are saving the letter, you can save it in a way that makes it easier to find later. Your mind works in a similar way. If you take time to understand an idea or a piece of information and relate it to things you already know, you will be able to "file" it in a logical place in your mind and to retrieve it more easily later.

Mnemonics. An association that aids memorizing is called a **mnemonic.** To use a mnemonic, you combine new information that you need to remember with information you already know very well or can remember very easily. For example, many children learn the alphabet by associating it with an easy-to-remember tune. Mnemonics are commonly based on either words or images.

	MNEMONICS		
Name of Strategy	**Strategy**	**Information to be Learned**	**Information Easy to Remember**
Embellished Letter	Form an acronym using the first letters of the information to be remembered.	Items in a series, e.g., the colors of the spectrum (<u>r</u>ed, <u>o</u>range, <u>y</u>ellow, <u>g</u>reen, <u>b</u>lue, <u>i</u>ndigo, <u>v</u>iolet)	Roy G. Biv
Method of Loci	Imagine a place you know well (a baseball diamond, etc.). Form an image of each object to be remembered in a particular spot in that place.	Items in a series, e.g., the first ten presidents (Washington, Adams, Jefferson, Adams, Madison, Monroe, Jackson, Van Buren, Harrison, Tyler)	Washington is pitcher, Adams is catcher, Jefferson at first base, etc.
Key Word	Form an image of the items doing something to or with each other.	Associations, e.g., a server at a restaurant must remember that the man in the blue shirt ordered chicken with baked potato.	Bizarre images, e.g., a man is terrified (chicken) of a potato.

Repetition. Generally, simply repeating information over and over is not a good way to remember it. A better approach is to become familiar with the information in a variety of ways. However, repetition, has an effect on remembering. The more often you use a piece of information or work with an idea, the more likely you are to remember it. For example, to remember the content of the Gettysburg Address, you might write a paraphrase of the address, present it as an oral interpretation, and discuss its importance in American history with other students.

4.5 REMEMBERING AND VISUALIZING

Think back to your last birthday. Can you see and feel the event in your mind? Close your eyes and try.

Visualizing a place, person, event, or object can help you write about it and describe it accurately and vividly. As you visualize, you can use various thinking skills to help you remember details. If you are trying to remember your birthday, you might think about the events of the day in the order in which they occurred. If you are trying to visualize your twin cousins, you might think about the ways in which they are different and similar.

4.6 OBSERVING

Both purpose and point of view can affect how you observe a situation. Consider two observers of a high school basketball game. One is a college coach prospecting for new talent. Another is a sociologist studying the behavior of crowds. The two observers will come away from the game with very different information. Before you observe any situation, think about what kinds of details you need to accomplish your purpose. Then, when you are observing, focus your attention on the relevant details.

Sometimes when you observe, you will be gathering evidence to test a hypothesis. (See the Language Arts Survey, 4.13, "Making Hypotheses.") In such situations, you need to avoid making prejudgments. If you have a bias or strong expectation about what you will see, you may be blind to evidence that goes against your expectation.

4.7 CLASSIFYING

When you put items or ideas into categories, you are **classifying.** Items in the same category share one or more characteristics. For example, Ralph Waldo Emerson and Henry David Thoreau are classified as Transcendentalists because their writings express ideas characteristic of Transcendentalism (e.g., nature as a source of eternal truths, the presence of spirit in nature).

Developing a classification scheme is an excellent way to organize a piece of informative or persuasive writing. Remember that categories often overlap. Some items may have features that allow them to be classified in more than one of the categories you have selected. The following chart gives some guidelines for using categories when you think about literature.

GUIDELINES FOR USING CLASSIFICATION	
Guideline	**Example**
Define categories precisely.	When classifying poems based on use of rhyme, you might define a rhymed poem as one that "has a distinct pattern of rhyme throughout" (rather than one that "has some rhyme").
Choose categories that fit your purpose.	If your purpose is to analyze an author's style, you might classify his or her works using the categories *essays, letters, speeches,* and *poems,* and then show how style is related to the form of writing.
Ignore characteristics unrelated to the categories chosen.	When classifying short stories based on theme, you would ignore characteristics related to setting, mood, plot, and so on.
Use parallel (nonoverlapping) categories.	When classifying poems from the Harlem Renaissance, you might use the categories "poems about childhood" and "poems about work" (rather than "poems about childhood" and "poems about the black experience").

4.8 COMPARING AND CONTRASTING

Both comparing and contrasting involve analyzing two things at the same time. When **comparing**, you describe similarities between two things. When **contrasting**, you describe their differences. When you compare two things, you place them in the same category. When you contrast them, you place them in separate categories.

When you compare and contrast, you will often be contrasting items that are similar in some important way. For example, in the novel *Huckleberry Finn,* Huck and Jim are both runaways, but they are different in that Huck is a runaway child and Jim is a runaway slave. Thus, while they possess a common characteristic, they possess it in different ways. As characters, they belong in the same category but in different **subcategories.** In literature, characters, often exhibit shared features, but they exhibit these features in different ways. Such differences are often well worth exploring.

In your literature class, you will probably be asked to compare and contrast the subject matter, techniques, and themes used in different works and by different authors. Remember to discuss both points of similarity and points of difference. (See also the Language Arts Survey, 1.18, "Sensory Detail Charts;" and 1.34, "Organizing Ideas," for tips on organizing a "compare and contrast" essay.)

4.9 ESTIMATING AND QUANTIFYING

In a persuasive essay or speech, you need to support your points with facts. Frequently, the facts you need are numbers, or **quantities.** For example, if you claim that smoking is a significant cause of lung cancer, you ought to **quantify** your claim by stating **how many** smokers develop lung cancer. The number you need may be available in reference works. (See the Language Arts Survey, 4.23, "Using Reference Works.") If not, you may be able to come up with an **estimate,** or approximate quantity, based on a combination of research, general knowledge, and common-sense reasoning. Sometimes you may only be able to estimate a **range** within which the actual number probably falls.

UNQUANTIFIED:	Cigarette smoking causes lung cancer.
QUANTIFIED:	Cigarette smoking is responsible for 87 percent of lung cancer cases and accounts for 30 percent of all cancer deaths.
ESTIMATED:	Almost a third of all lung cancer deaths can be attributed to cigarette smoking.

4.10 ANALYZING

Analyzing is the process of breaking something down into logical parts and then examining the parts individually to see how they are related. Since the idea of "parts" can be understood in many different ways, there are many ways to analyze a particular thing. For instance, if you were to analyze a city, you might analyze it in terms of population groups (by age, sex, ethnic background, and so on), infrastructure systems (roads, bridges, sewage and water lines), sources of employment (businesses, industries, government offices, schools and colleges), government departments (administration, taxation, development, and so on), or individual neighborhoods.

You can analyze a work of literature in many ways. With a play, you might analyze different acts or different scenes within an act. With an essay, you might analyze the introduction, the body, and the conclusion, or the individual arguments presented. With a poem, you might analyze such figures of speech as metaphor, simile, and personification. (For other ideas on analyzing written works, see the Language Arts Survey, 1.14, "Analyzing;" and 1.34, "Organizing Ideas.")

4.11 GENERALIZING

Generalizing is making a broad claim based on some particular observations. Generalizations are frequently false because they make a claim that is not justified by the available information. Perhaps you have observed squirrels in a city park nearly every day on your way to school and have seen only gray squirrels there. From this experience, you might make the generalization "All squirrels are gray." However, there are red and albino squirrels. Thus, a broad generalization based on a limited number of observations may be very flimsy. A generalization that is qualified, or more restricted in scope, however, is less likely to be false. For example, you could truthfully generalize from your observations, "All the squirrels I have ever seen in the park are gray."

A generalization based on reasoning, not merely observation, is likely to be true. Say that at the zoo you observe an unfamiliar animal that has fur and is suckling its young and you conclude that the animal is a mammal. Your conclusion is not based on numerous observations of these animals; you have seen only one. It is based on knowing the scientific concept of *mammal*—an animal that has skin covered with hair and that nourishes its young with milk from its own body. Making a generalization about a particular situation based on reasoning, rather than mere observation, is called **induction**.

4.12 DEDUCING

Deducing, or inferring, is the process of drawing a logical conclusion from certain facts, which are called **premises.** When the conclusion follows from, or is forced by, the premises, the deduction is **valid,** as in the following:

PREMISES: (1) The members of the 1787 Constitutional Convention are called the Founding Fathers of the United States.
(2) Thomas Jefferson was a member of the 1787 Convention.
CONCLUSION: Thomas Jefferson was a Founding Father of the United States.

If, from the same premises, you had concluded "Thomas Jefferson was a man of many talents," that conclusion would be **invalid.** Although this statement is true, it is not true *because* the premises stated above are true. Valid deductions are said to preserve truth; if the premises are true, then the conclusion is always true.

A deduction is commonly expressed in the form of a **conditional,** or "If . . . , then . . ." statement. A conditional says that *if* something is true, *then* something else must be true: If a person was a member of the 1787 Constitutional Convention, then that person was a Founding Father of the United States. In a conditional, the part of the statement following the *if* is called the **antecedent,** and the part following *then* is called the **consequent.**

You can draw certain kinds of conclusions, or inferences, from conditional statements. First, if the antecedent in a conditional is true, you can conclude that the consequent is true:

EXAMPLE   If it rains today, I cannot play softball.
           It rained today. (antecedent is true)
           Therefore, I did not play softball today. (consequent is also true)

Second, you can draw a conclusion when the consequent is false: if the consequent is false, then the antecedent is also false.

EXAMPLE   If it rains today, I cannot play softball.
           I played softball today. (consequent is false)
           Therefore, it did not rain. (antecedent is also false)

You cannot make a valid inference, however, when the antecedent is false or the consequent is true. (See the Language Arts Survey, 4.14, "Avoiding Faulty Arguments.")

4.13 MAKING HYPOTHESES

A **hypothesis** is an educated guess about a cause or an effect. When you observe something and then suggest an explanation for it, your explanation is a hypothesis. A prediction based on a theory is also a hypothesis. A hypothesis must always be tested against experience. You can test a hypothesis by performing actual experiments, by examining numerous relevant examples, or by conducting a **thought experiment**, asking "What if" questions. (See the Language Arts Survey, 1.13, "Questioning: 'What if' Questions.")

Remember that a single counterexample is enough to disprove a hypothesis, and you cannot prove a hypothesis by gathering a large number of examples (see the Language Arts Survey, 4.11, "Generalizing"). The examples lend support for the hypothesis but they do not guarantee its truthfulness. Thus, hypotheses are continually modified as new evidence is discovered.

4.14 AVOIDING FAULTY ARGUMENTS

When you are writing a persuasive piece of writing or evaluating the writing of others, be alert for faulty arguments or errors in logical reasoning. Many of these errors are based on **logical fallacies.** A writer commits a fallacy when he or she makes an **invalid** inference, one that is not justified by the facts at hand.

Errors in reasoning can result from incorrect information, lack of information, carelessness, or other problems. It is often hard to tell when a mistake in thinking is due to faulty logic or some other factor.

False analogy. An argument by analogy claims that if two things are alike in some way, then they must be alike in another way.

EXAMPLE   "The president is the captain of the ship of state. People in government should
           obey his orders."
ANALYSIS   This analogy creates a striking image, but there are many ways in which the
           president is not like the captain of a ship. For example, the power of the
           president is checked and balanced by the powers of the legislative and judi-
           cial branches of government.

Although analogies are useful for stimulating discussion and help us see things in new and interesting ways, arguments based on analogy do not prove what they state.

Circularity. A circular argument assumes the truth of what it is trying to prove. This type of argument is sometimes called **question-begging.** In a circular argument, the premises and the conclusion often state the same thing, only in different words.

EXAMPLE	"Joe Montana was king among football players because he was the greatest and he excelled beyond all other players."
ANALYSIS	The "reasons" the speaker gives for the proposition are other ways of stating that Montana was the best.

Post hoc (ergo) propter hoc. In a cause-and-effect sequence, the effect always follows the cause. A speaker who commits the *post hoc* fallacy assumes that because one event followed another it must have been caused by that event. However, not every sequence of events involves cause and effect.

EXAMPLE	"Under Mayor Lashutka's administration, the streets are in much better condition. This winter there were hardly any potholes."
ANALYSIS	This argument confuses sequence with consequence. The streets might be in better condition, not because of the mayor's actions, but because the winter was unusually mild and dry, without the freezing and thawing that damages road surfaces. Many politicians are fond of the *post hoc* argument.

Fallacies of denying the antecedent and of affirming the consequent. A conditional states that *if* something (the antecedent) is true, *then* something else (the consequent) must be true. As shown in the Language Arts Survey, 4.12, "Deducing," you can draw a valid conclusion from a conditional when the antecedent is true or when the consequent is false. If the antecedent is false, however, nothing is implied about the consequent.

EXAMPLE	"If it rains today, then I cannot play softball. It did not rain today. Did I play softball?"
ANALYSIS	Maybe yes, maybe no. The proposition makes "raining" a condition of "not playing softball"; it does not establish a conditional for "not raining." You cannot draw a conclusion when the antecedent is denied.

In addition, if the consequent is true, nothing is implied about the antecedent.

EXAMPLE	"If it rains today, then I will not play softball. I did not play softball. Did it rain today or not?"
ANALYSIS	Again, you cannot draw a conclusion because raining is not the only possible cause of not playing softball. Too much homework, a sprained ankle, or a lack of other players could also prevent you from playing softball.

Fallacies of composition and decomposition. If a whole has a certain quality, it does not follow that each part of that whole has that quality on its own. To assume that it does is to commit the fallacy of decomposition.

EXAMPLE	"Switzerland is a pacifist country; it does not take arms against other countries. Therefore, each person in Switzerland is a pacifist."
ANALYSIS	Many people in Switzerland may agree with the country's pacifist stance, but others may not. The characteristic of the whole does not necessarily apply to each person who makes up the whole.

Likewise, it is fallacious to argue that because some parts have a certain quality, then the whole must also have that quality. This is the fallacy of composition.

EXAMPLE	"The first chapter of this book is very exciting. Therefore, the whole book must be very exciting."
ANALYSIS	Generally, some parts of a book are more exciting than others. The author may have made the first chapter especially exciting as a way to draw readers into the story.

Non sequitur. A *non sequitur* is a conclusion that simply does not follow from the reasons given and may have nothing to do with them.

EXAMPLE	"Abraham Lincoln was a master of rhetoric because he came from a very humble background."
ANALYSIS	To support the claim that Lincoln was a master of rhetoric, the writer would have to furnish evidence relating to the use of language in writing or speaking. The fact that Lincoln grew up in a small log cabin of the American frontier is not relevant to the writer's claim.

Ad hominem. The phrase *ad hominem* means "to the person." An ad hominem argument attacks or defends a person instead of the point under discussion. The truth of what people say, however, is not determined by their background, political affiliation, or social ties. It is determined by the validity of their arguments.

EXAMPLE	"There's no reason to support this new welfare reform law. Only Democrats are in favor of it, and we all know that Democrats can't solve social problems."
ANALYSIS	This statement does not address the merits or deficiencies of the new law. It simply attacks those who support it.

False dichotomy. To set up a false dichotomy is to assume that there are only two sides to an issue. This type of argument is also known as an "either/or" argument.

EXAMPLE	"If you're not a Christian, then you must be an atheist."
ANALYSIS	A Christian is a person who believes in the teachings of Jesus. An atheist is someone who does not believe in the existence of a deity. There are, however, many examples of non-Christians who believe in a deity, such as Muslims, Buddhists, and Jews.

Hasty generalization. A generalization, or universal claim, that is based on only a few examples or unrepresentative samples is faulty (see Language Arts Survey, 4.11, "Generalizing").

EXAMPLE   "Three Canadian men were recently charged with planting a bomb at the metropolitan airport. Therefore, all Canadians should be considered dangerous."

ANALYSIS   This claim is based on a sample that is infinitesimally small (Canada has some 28 million people). Furthermore, the men have only been charged with, not convicted of, a crime.

Equivocation. To equivocate is to shift the meaning of an ambiguous term in the middle of an argument. Equivocation creates the appearance of a logical connection between the reasons and the conclusion where, in fact, there is no logical connection. Like other logical fallacies, equivocation may be intentional or unintentional.

EXAMPLE   "By his many past actions Senator Samuelson has shown his patriotism, his affection and high regard for his own country. Now, however, he is criticizing our country's foreign policy. This lack of patriotism makes him unworthy of reelection."

ANALYSIS   The passage equivocates on the word *patriotism*. In the first sentence, it is defined as "affection and high regard for one's country." In the second passage, the term includes the idea of never criticizing one's country. Because of this shift of meaning, it is difficult to accept the speaker's conclusion as logical.

Vague terms. In all kinds of speaking situations, from everyday conversation to public debates, people often do not use precise language. They may not clarify what they mean by terms such as *good, large, harmful,* or *morally wrong.* Such imprecise language hinders communication and can lead to misunderstandings. It can also slow decision making and keep people from getting to the heart of difficult issues.

EXAMPLE   "I believe in family values."

ANALYSIS   What does this speaker believe in? It's hard to say. The term "family values" is extremely vague. It can mean many different things to different people, in part because families are so different. Would the "family values" of a Buddhist be the same as those of a Catholic? What specific values, or principles, does the speaker have in mind—obedience to one's parents? reverence for one's ancestors? equal sharing of childcare responsibilities by both parents? To be clear, the speaker should be more specific about what he or she means.

4.15   UNDERSTANDING PROPAGANDA TECHNIQUES

Messages and materials created with the aim of stirring up support for (or opposition to) a particular cause are known as **propaganda.** Writers of propaganda materials frequently employ faulty arguments, such as those described in the preceding section. In addition, they try to influence readers and listeners by appealing to the emotions rather than logic. Becoming aware of the common techniques used in these materials can help you avoid being manipulated by propaganda appeals.

Bandwagon. Human beings have a basic need to feel included. **Bandwagon appeals** exploit this need by trying to make people worry about being different from others or being left out of the crowd.

EXAMPLE "If you don't take a cruise of the Caribbean on the *Grand Regina,* you'll be missing out on the time of your life. Don't be left out of the fun!"

ANALYSIS Is this statement really true? Are you being left out of the fun by not taking the cruise? Are there other ways you could have fun?

Transfer. The propaganda technique of **transfer** works on the principle of association. Two different things are linked together to make a positive (or negative) impression on the receiver of the message. For example, a television commercial for a particular cat food may show a cat doing amusing tricks. A billboard may show an attractive model wearing a certain brand of jeans. A political poster may show the candidate in front of a large American flag. In each example, the message-maker's intention is for the good qualities of one thing (the cat, the model, the flag) to "rub off on," or transfer to, another thing (the cat food, the jeans, the politician). Messages based on transfer, of course, do not appeal to your powers of reasoning.

False testimonial. A testimonial is a statement endorsing a person, product, or idea. Advertisers and politicians often solicit testimonials from experts as well as celebrities. Unpaid testimonials may be worth listening to, provided the person giving the testimonial has the appropriate expertise.

EXAMPLE A veterinarian, whose real name is given, appears on a television commercial to recommend a particular dog food.

ANALYSIS Although a veterinarian may be knowledgeable enough about dog nutrition to make a trustworthy endorsement, the vet was almost surely paid to take part in the commercial. Thus, his opinion may not be objective.

Loaded words. Different words can refer to the same thing but carry radically different connotations. (See the Language Arts Survey, 2.153, "Connotation and Denotation.") A word may have strongly positive, strongly negative, or relatively neutral connotation. Using words with strong connotations can be a way to sway opinion without offering reasons.

EXAMPLE "It's time to transfer responsibility for welfare from the federal government to the states."
"Congress is dumping the welfare program on the states without channeling funds to the states to carry out the programs."

ANALYSIS The word choices in each statement reflect different points of view. The first speaker views the shifting of welfare programs to the states positively and thus uses the phrase *transfer responsibility.* The second speaker describes the same action using the word *dumping,* a word with a negative connotation.

Character assassination. This is a form of *ad hominem* argument that tries to persuade by attacking the character of one's opponent.

EXAMPLE   "Ms. Velasquez, a mother of three children, was divorced after five years of marriage. Anyone who can't keep a family together doesn't belong on the school board."

ANALYSIS   Ms. Velasquez may be very well qualified to serve on the school board. The speaker, however, has not addressed her relevant qualifications but only attacked her character.

Bias charges. The charge of bias is a form of *ad hominem* argument that attacks a speaker's neutrality on an issue. A person who has something to gain from the outcome of a decision has a motive for distorting information in his or her favor. However, a person may have a personal stake in an issue and still be objective. If you suspect that a person is biased, use extra care in examining his or her arguments to make sure they are logical.

EXAMPLE   "Congressman Doody of Texas is only in favor of this legislation because it will give a big tax break to Texas ranchers."

ANALYSIS   The congressman represents a state that will benefit significantly from the legislation, so he may indeed be biased. The possibility of bias does not mean his arguments on the issue should be ignored, but they should be scrutinized.

READING SKILLS

4.16 READING RATES

The purpose you have for reading something affects how you read it. You may read slowly and carefully in many situations and use skimming or scanning in others.

READING RATES		
Technique	**Purpose**	**Tips**
Scanning	Finding specific information quickly	Look for key words; look at chapter and part headings.
Skimming	Getting a general idea of the content of a piece	Ask questions; look at introductions; look at chapter and part headings.
Slow and careful reading	Learning and enjoyment	Read actively.

Scanning

When you are looking through written material to locate some particular piece of information, you use the quick-reading technique of **scanning.** For example, you might scan the newspaper to find out whether your city council voted to approve a curbside recycling program at a recent meeting. You would turn to the section on city news, and then glance quickly over the headlines on each page until you saw the words "city council" or "recycling." Once you located the article, you would then begin reading carefully to gather the information.

You use scanning frequently during research, whenever you consult a reference work or look up something in the index of a book. In your classes, you have probably also scanned reading selections to find answers to questions or quotations and other support for your opinions. When you scan, you should pick out just a few key words to look for; this will help you find the desired information faster.

Skimming

When you read by **skimming,** you glance quickly through a piece of writing to get a general idea of it. When doing research, skimming can help you determine which books and articles will be most useful or interesting. Skimming is also a good way to preview assigned reading selections or review them before taking a test or writing an essay.

Your skimming will be more effective if you keep the following questions in mind:

- What is this piece of writing about?
- What does the author say about it?
- What evidence or support is given?

When you skim, read the title and any headings and subheadings within the piece first. This step should answer the first question. Then, read the first few paragraphs until you have a satisfactory answer to the second question. To find an answer to the third question, read the first and last paragraphs of each section. Also, glance at any material that is set off from the main text, such as boxed paragraphs or other special features.

Slow and Careful Reading

When you read for learning or for pleasure, you will read slowly and carefully to get the most out of what you are reading. When reading in this thorough way, you will read every word and look up any words you do not know in a dictionary. You will also take time to reread sentences or passages that you found especially striking or that seemed unclear the first time through.

Slow and careful reading allows you to reflect on your reading as you go. You may pose questions, evaluate evidence, or imagine yourself in the place of a character or the author. In these ways and many more, you become engaged in what you are reading. (See the Language Arts Survey, 4.18, "Reading Actively.")

4.17 PREVIEWING YOUR READING

If you take a few moments to preview your reading, you will read more efficiently. The previewing steps described can help get you thinking about what you are about to read.

	PREVIEWING ACTIVITIES
1. **Read** the title.	**Ask:** What is the piece about? What seems to be the author's attitude toward it?
2. **Skim** the first paragraph(s).	**Ask:** What is the main point of the piece?
3. **Skim** the last paragraph(s) (but not if the piece to be read is work of literature).	**Ask:** What is the author's conclusion?
4. **Read** the headings.	**Ask:** What are the main points?
5. **Summarize** and **plan** your reading.	**Ask:** Do all the parts seem to fit together? Do I have any unresolved questions?

4.18 READING ACTIVELY

When you read actively, you respond mentally to what you are reading. Thinking about what you are reading can increase your enjoyment of reading as well as your comprehension.

Responding to Your Reading

One good active-reading technique is to keep your journal close by and record your reactions to what you are reading (see the Language Arts Survey, 1.2, "Keeping a Writer's Journal"). After a section or paragraph you might pause to ask yourself questions like these:

- "Do I agree with what the author (or character) just said?"
- "This last section makes me feel especially happy (or sad). What in particular makes me feel this way?"

You can note and evaluate your responses as you read, or you might prefer to wait until after you finish reading to record your thoughts and feelings.

Questioning

Questions have a way of commanding a listener's attention more than statements. If you pose questions to yourself as you read, your mind will be more alert to the content and meaning of what you are reading. You can use *who, what, where, when, why,* and *how* questions, as shown in the chart that follows. In this book, you can also use the Guided Reading questions and the Responding to the Selection questions to assist your reading.

TYPES OF READER RESPONSE QUESTIONS	
Who?	• Questions about characters or persons in the text • Questions about the author
What?	• Questions about objects and events
Where?	• Questions about location
When?	• Questions about sequence • Questions about time period

CONTINUED

Why?	• Questions about motivation
	• Questions about reasoning and evidence
How?	• Questions about possibilities
	• Questions about actions

Predicting

Trying to guess what will happen next, and why, is an excellent way to become involved in your reading. The impulse to predict is a natural part of reading, and predictions can be a useful starting point for a discussion when you are reading a selection with others.

Summarizing

To **summarize** is to simplify a piece of writing into a briefer statement of main points. Summarizing can help you understand what you have read by forcing you to focus on the most important points. When you summarize ideas in your own words, you are more likely to remember and understand them. Just remember not to go beyond the ideas that are actually in the piece.

Identifying Main Ideas

You can often locate the main idea in a piece of nonfiction writing in the introduction; look for a thesis statement. In a single paragraph, the main idea will frequently be stated in a topic sentence. Sometimes, though, you will have to infer the main idea because it is not stated directly. When you are reading difficult material, pausing briefly after each paragraph to restate the main idea in your own words can increase your understanding.

Identifying Relationships

Another technique that can improve your understanding of what you read is to notice words and phrases that reveal how the piece is organized. For example, words such as *first, second,* and *finally* are clues that the ideas are being presented in chronological or degree order. In addition, writers often use phrases or explicit statements to call attention to relationships between people, things, or ideas.

Making Inferences

When you **make an inference,** you put together pieces of information to draw a conclusion that is not explicitly stated. In a work of fiction, an author may describe a character's personality directly. More often, though, the author shows what the character is like through the character's actions and words. The reader must then infer the character's traits from these details.

Making inferences is an essential skill in reading nonfiction. An author may present certain evidence but leave the intended conclusion unstated. In other cases, such as a persuasive piece, an author may be unaware of certain inferences that can be drawn from the evidence given. As a critical reader, you might spot such overlooked inferences and use them to show flaws in the author's reasoning.

4.19 READING CHARTS AND GRAPHS

Charts and graphs are handy ways to present ideas and information in a compact, visual form. Readers use the title, headings, labels, and notes on the chart or graph to understand the information it contains.

Pie charts. A **pie chart** is a circle divided into pie-shaped sections that represent portions of some whole thing. It shows how different amounts compare to each other and to the whole.

EXAMPLE: The whole pie represents the crop production in a particular state. The pie is divided into four sections. Each section represents a different crop harvested: corn, soybeans, wheat, and all others. Each section is also labeled, in thousands of bushels as well as the percentage of the whole represented by that amount. The pie chart quickly shows that corn represents more than half the total crop production of the state, and that more than twice as much corn as soybeans was produced.

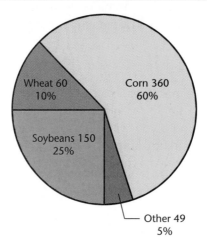

Bar graphs. A **bar graph** shows absolute amounts of something by representing the amounts as parallel bars of different lengths. A bar graph allows you to quickly compare relative quantities. However, you cannot tell from a bar graph how those quantities are related to some whole amount. Be sure to read all the labels on a bar graph carefully so you know exactly what quantities are represented.

EXAMPLE: The following graph shows the number of fiction and nonfiction books read by students in four different English classes in one year. Each class's totals are grouped together, so you can readily make comparisons within and between classes.

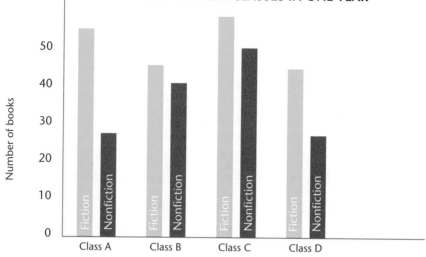

**FICTION AND NONFICTION BOOKS READ
BY FOUR ENGLISH CLASSES IN ONE YEAR**

Sometimes designers use unusual "bars" to make bar graphs more interesting visually. These design changes can misrepresent the relative sizes of the bars and give a misleading impression. Be sure to read the graph labels and related text carefully before drawing a conclusion.

Line graphs. A **line graph** shows how the amount of one thing changes in relation to some other thing over time. The line connecting the amounts shows that the change is a continuous process.

RESEARCH SKILLS

When you conduct **research,** you are looking for ideas and information. The spark for your research could be a question you want to answer, a hypothesis you want to test, or a certain subject or idea you want to better understand. As you explore various sources of information, you will find not only part of the answer to your question but also leads to additional sources of information that will assist your investigation.

Different kinds of library materials require slightly different researching techniques. The ones you will use most frequently are described in the following sections.

4.20 THE CLASSIFICATION OF LIBRARY MATERIALS

Each book in a library has a unique identification number, or **call number,** that is printed on the **spine,** or edge of the book. This number is used to classify the book; it also helps the library keep track of the book as it is used.

There are two common systems for classifying library books. The **Dewey Decimal System** is used in most school and public libraries. The **Library of Congress Classification System** (known as the LC system) is used in most college libraries.

In either system, the first part of the call number categorizes the book by its subject. Books on the same subject are conveniently grouped together on the library shelves in call number order. As you can see from the following charts, the subjects used in each system are very general. Each classification system has a way to narrow down the book's subject by using a specific number for each different subtopic. For example, in the Dewey Decimal System the book *Arctic Dreams* by Barry Lopez might have the call number 508.98 / Lo. This book is in the 500s, the general category that includes science. Within that class the number 508 shows that the book is a work of literature about natural history. The additional numbers after the decimal indicate that the book is about the natural history of the Arctic region.

THE DEWEY DECIMAL SYSTEM	
Call Numbers	**Subjects[1]**
000–099	Reference and General Works
100–199	Philosophy, Psychology
200–299	Religion
300–399	Social Studies
400–499	Language
500–599	Science, Mathematics
600–699	Technology
700–799	Arts
800–899	Literature
900–999	History, Geography, Biography[2]

1. The Dewey system does not number fiction. Works of fiction are arranged alphabetically by author.
2. Biographies (920s) are arranged alphabetically by subject.

In the LC system, the call number begins with one or two letters that identify the general subject area. The numbers after the letters identify the more precise topic within the overall area. For example, the Lopez book might have the call number QH84.1 / L67 /1986. The Q shows that the book is in the general category that includes science. The letter pair QH identifies the subject more specifically as natural history, and the number after QH specifies the geographic area that the author is writing about.

The second part of the call number distinguishes individual books on the same subject. In the Dewey system, the first one to three letters of the author's last name may be added on a second line; notice the *Lo* in the Dewey number above. In the LC system, the second part of the number usually includes a letter (the author's last initial) and number that uniquely identifies the author. This second element falls after a decimal point. An LC call number may also include a date of publication.

THE LIBRARY OF CONGRESS SYSTEM

Call Letters	Subjects
A	Reference and General Works
B–BJ	Philosophy, Psychology
BK–BX	Religion
C–DF	History
G	Geography, Autobiography, Recreation
H	Social Sciences
J	Political Science
K	Law
L	Education
M	Music
N	Fine Arts
P	Language, Literature
Q	Science, Mathematics
R	Medicine
S	Agriculture
T	Technology
U	Military Science
V	Naval Science
Z	Bibliography, Library Science

Locating materials in the library. In addition to books, library collections contain many other types of materials including magazines, newspapers, audio and video recordings, microfilm and microfiche, and government documents. Each type of material is typically stored in a separate part of the library and has its own classification system. For example, back issues of newspapers stored on microfilm have their own index and numbering system, and the microfilm materials and equipment may be located in the periodicals department or a separate microfilm section. Government documents are shelved in one location and also have their own numbering system.

If you know the call number of a book or the subject classification number you want, you can generally go directly to the bookshelves, or **stacks,** to obtain the book. Use the signs at the ends of the rows to locate the section of call numbers that you need. Then scan the call numbers on the spines of the books to find the right shelf. In a large library you may need to consult a map or sign showing where different call number areas are located. Look for these signs at assistance desks or near elevators and room entrances.

Some libraries, such as large city libraries or historical societies, have closed rather than open stacks. If you want to obtain a book, you write its call number on a request slip and give it to a librarian, who will retrieve the book for you.

4.21 USING SEARCHING TOOLS

The library's **catalog** lists of all the books in the library. If your library has a computerized catalog, you will need to learn how to use your library's particular system. Usually you will find a sign or flyer near the computer that explains how to use the system. In addition, the computer keys may be labeled to assist you.

Author info.	Lopez, Barry Holstun, 1945-
Title	Arctic dreams: Imagination and Desire in a Northern Landscape
Date of pub.	1986
Publisher	Charles Scribner's Sons
LC Call no.	QH84.1 L67 1986
ISBN no.	ISBN 0-684-18578-4
No. of pages	xxix, 464 p.
Page size, cover material	23 cm., pap
Copyright info.	c1986 Barry Lopez
Index info.	Includes index
Supplementary sections	xvi, 222 p.: maps: 24 cm.
Subject	Natural history—Arctic regions

With most computerized catalogs, you have a choice of searching by author, title, subject, or key words. The following chart gives you some hints for doing each type of search. Capitalization does not matter when you type your entry. You should, however, double-check your spelling, because the computer cannot compensate for spelling errors.

COMPUTERIZED CATALOG SEARCHES

Search by . . .	Example	Hints
author	gould, stephen j	Type last name first. Type as much of the name as you know.
title	mismeasure of man	Omit articles such as *a, an,* or *the* at the beginning of titles.
subject	intelligence tests; ability—testing	Use the list of subjects provided by the library.
key words	darwin; intelligence; craniology	Use related topics if you can't find anything in your subject.

Author and title searches are generally straightforward. Subject searches, on the other hand, require extra thought. It is important to make sure that the subject heading you use is one that the computer recognizes. For example, if you look up "South Sea Islands" and find nothing, it is likely that the library uses different wording for this subject, such as "Pacific Islands." Sometimes the system will respond with a message telling you how to reword your heading or with a list of related subject headings.

Many libraries use the list of subjects published by the Library of Congress, but others use different lists. Your best bet is to look up a particular subject before doing your search to see what wording the library uses. **Cross-references** in the list will help you find the right subject headings to use. For example, after typing in the search heading: "South Sea Islands," you might find "*See* Pacific Islands."

Once you locate a list of books that match your subject search, you can "page" through the list of titles and call up a screen of detailed information for each title that interests you. This screen provides such information as the number of pages in the book and the subject headings that are used to classify the book. This screen may also tell you if the book is checked out. If you find books that seem to be exactly what you are looking for, jot down the subject headings listed on the screen and use those in new searches. For each book you want, write down the call number and then head for the stacks. (See the Language Arts Survey, 4.20, "The Classification of Library Materials: Locating Materials in the Library.")

Interlibrary Loan. Many libraries are part of a larger library network. In these libraries, the computerized catalog lists all the books owned by several libraries. The catalog will tell you which library has the volume you want. If the book is in a different library, you can request it. In some libraries, you do this by typing a particular command on the computer and entering your library card number; in other libraries, you fill out a request slip and give it to a librarian. The book is then shipped to your library. Depending on whether the book is checked out by someone else, you may wait a few days or several weeks for the book.

4.22 USING THE CARD CATALOG

A **card catalog,** like a computerized catalog, contains brief information about each book in the library. In this type of catalog, the information is typed on paper cards, and the cards are arranged alphabetically in drawers. For each book there is a **title card,** one **author card** for each author, and at least one **subject card.** All of these cards show the book's title, author, and call number. Thus, you can search for a book by author, title, or subject. (See the Language Arts Survey, 4.21, "Using Searching Tools.")

Once you have located the books you want, write down the call number of each book and then go to the shelves. (See the Language Arts Survey, 4.20, "The Classification of Library Materials: Locating Materials in the Library.") If you cannot find a particular book you need in the card catalog, ask the librarian if your library can obtain books from another library through an interlibrary loan.

Some libraries are in the process of changing from card catalogs to computerized catalogs. To be thorough in your search, you may need to search in the computer system for newer books and in the card catalog for older books.

AN AUTHOR CARD

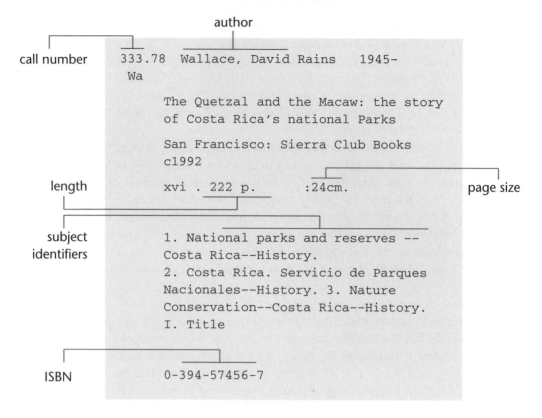

call number — 333.78 Wa

author — Wallace, David Rains   1945-

The Quetzal and the Macaw: the story
of Costa Rica's national Parks

San Francisco: Sierra Club Books
c1992

length — xvi . 222 p.   :24cm. — page size

subject identifiers —
1. National parks and reserves --
Costa Rica--History.
2. Costa Rica. Servicio de Parques
Nacionales--History. 3. Nature
Conservation--Costa Rica--History.
I. Title

ISBN — 0-394-57456-7

A TITLE CARD

333.78   The Quetzal and the Macaw: the story
Wa   of Costa Rica's national parks

          Wallace, David Rains, 1945-.

          The Quetzal and the Macaw: the story
          of Costa Rica's national parks.

          San Francisco: Sierra Club Books,
          1992

          xvi. 222 p: maps:24cm.

          1. National Parks and reserves--
          Costa Rica--History.
          2. Costa Rica. Servicio de Parques
          Nacionales--History. 3. Nature
          conservation--Costa Rica--History.
          I. Title

          0-394-57456-7

A SUBJECT CARD

```
        NATIONAL PARKS AND RESERVES--COSTA RICA--
                        HISTORY

  333.78  Wallace, David Rains, 1945-
    Wa.

            The Quetzal and the Macaw: the story
            of Costa Rica's national parks

            San Francisco: Sierra Club Books,1992

            xvi. 222 p.: maps: 24cm.



            1. National parks and reserves--Costa
            Rica--History.  2.  Costa  Rica.
            Servicio de Parques Nacionales--
            History. 3. Nature conservation--
            Costa Rica--History. I. Title.


            0-394-57456-7
```

4.23 USING REFERENCE WORKS

If you've ever browsed through the reference section of a library, you have some idea of the fabulous array of reference books that are published. **Reference works** are compilations of knowledge organized for easy access. No matter what question you have, the chances are good that a reference book can help satisfy your curiosity. Some reference works, such as the library catalog and **indexes**, list sources of information. Other reference works, such as encyclopedias, atlases, and almanacs, contain the actual information that may answer your question. In most libraries, current reference works cannot be checked out.

Almanacs and **Yearbooks.** An **almanac** is a densely packed collection of facts and statistics of all sorts, often presented in list form. The information in an almanac covers many different fields such as economics, education, crime, postal information, elections, natural disasters, and sports. Do you want to find out the year when President Woodrow Wilson was born? the Oscar-winning pictures for last year? the capital of Bosnia Herzgovina? An almanac is often the quickest way to answer such factual questions. Use the index to locate information in an almanac.

Most almanacs are published annually and include a summary of major events from the previous year. A more detailed overview of the year's events can be found in a **yearbook,** which is published separately. Some encyclopedia publishers produce yearbooks, which are shelved with the encyclopedias.

Atlases. An **atlas** is a collection of maps, but every atlas has a specific focus and typically includes other information as well. The maps in some atlases show natural features, such as rivers, lakes, and mountain ranges. Others show political features, such as countries and cities. Still others show more specialized kinds of geographic information, such as climate, population, natural resources, or transportation routes. A **historical atlas** features maps of places as they were in the past; such maps can help you locate and trace historical events. To locate a specific item on a map, use the **gazetteer,** an index that lists every feature on each map.

Encyclopedias. An encyclopedia is intended to be a survey of knowledge. **General encyclopedias,** such as *Grolier's, Britannica,* and *World Book,* contain information on topics from all branches of knowledge. **Specialized encyclopedias,** such as *The Encyclopedia of World War II,* contain articles about a particular branch of knowledge.

The different topics in an encyclopedia are treated in **articles,** which are arranged alphabetically by topic. Sometimes you will look up a topic in an encyclopedia and not find an article about it. In such cases, a different word or phrase was probably used to identify the topic. Look in the index to determine which headings to use for your topic. The index of a multivolume encyclopedia is found in one or two separate volumes.

When you begin to research a topic, the relevant article in the encyclopedia will give you a concise overview of the subject. However, since an encyclopedia article is a survey, it may not contain the specific information you need. For more detailed information, you will need to delve into books, magazine articles, and other sources. The sources of information listed at the end of the encyclopedia article can be a good starting point.

Indexes. An **index** lists articles or other published works according to their subject. Indexes help you locate possible sources of information about your topic.

An index covers a limited number of publications, usually of a certain type. For example, *The Readers' Guide to Periodical Literature* is a comprehensive index to articles in a large number of popular weekly, monthly, and quarterly magazines and journals. Other indexes list only newspapers. Some periodicals, such as the *New York Times* and *National Geographic,* publish their own indexes, listing articles in past issues. Most indexes are published in sequential volumes that are issued yearly, monthly, or every few months. Some indexes, including the *New York Times Index,* are available on microfilm.

Periodicals. A **periodical** is a publication that is issued at regular intervals, such as weekly, monthly, or quarterly. Magazines, newspapers, and professional journals are all examples of periodicals. Because they are published frequently, periodicals are excellent sources of up-to-date information. However, they are also published quickly; therefore, the information in periodicals is sometimes less reliable than similar information found in books.

You can usually find current issues of periodicals in a library reading room. Recent issues may be stored beneath or behind the current issues or on shelves in the periodicals section. Older issues may be stored as bound volumes in open or closed stacks, or copied onto microfilm or microfiche. Generally, older issues will be kept only for periodicals containing information of lasting interest.

Other reference works. In addition to the works previously described, most libraries have a range of basic reference works, including collections of biographies (for example, *Dictionary of American Biography, Contemporary Authors, Who's Who*), quotations (for example, *Bartlett's Familiar Quotations*), and book reviews (for example, *Book Review Digest*). Your library may also have specialized dictionaries, telephone and business directories, law books, college catalogs, and many other kinds of materials.

4.24 USING DICTIONARIES

Dictionaries provide the spelling and definition of words, but they also provide other kinds of information about each word.

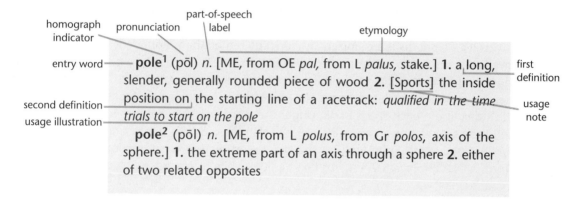

Directly after the entry word the **pronunciation** is given, usually in parentheses. A complete key to pronunciation symbols is given in the Table of Contents. In some dictionaries, a simplified key is also provided at the bottom of each page.

The abbreviation of the **part of speech** commonly follows the pronunciation. (See the Language Arts Survey, 2.3–2.31, "The Parts of Speech.") In the example, the letter *n* shows that the word is used as a noun. If a word can be used as more than one part of speech, the definitions will be grouped by part of speech; for example, all noun meanings might precede all verb meanings.

The **etymology** is the history of a word. In the first entry, the word *pole* can be traced back through Middle English (ME) and Old English (OE) to the Latin word *palus* which means "stake." Sometimes two words that are spelled exactly alike have different etymologies. Such words are called **homographs** and are always listed as separate entries. A number superscript before or after the word indicates that the word is a homograph.

Each **definition**, or meaning of the word, is numbered. The first definition is the most common meaning.

Usage notes, such as "slang" or "colloquial," describe any nonstandard usages. Sometimes an entry includes an illustration of how the word is used. In the second definition of *pole*[1], the **usage note** is in square brackets and the **usage illustration** appears in italics after the colon.

4.25 USING THESAURUSES

When writers find themselves at a loss for the right word, they often turn to a thesaurus. A **thesaurus** is a reference book that groups words with similar meanings. The entries lists synonyms and related words, as well as antonyms. You can use a thesaurus to find fresh words and more precise words to use in your writing. If you become a frequent user of a thesaurus, as well as the dictionary, you will become more aware of the different shades of meaning that similar words can have. This knowledge will add richness to your writing.

Thesauruses are of two types. A dictionary-type thesaurus is organized alphabetically. However, it does not contain as many entries as a dictionary. If a particular word is not listed, try looking up a word with a similar meaning. In lengthy entries, words that share a particular shade of meaning may be grouped together under a subheading. Antonyms are listed at the end of the entry. You may also find cross-references to entries for related words.

Roget's Thesaurus is organized by concept rather than alphabetically. Pierre Roget invented a system to categorize all existence and ideas. He used his categories as headings and grouped words with similar or related meanings under each heading. He also created an index of related words. To use *Roget's Thesaurus,* you look up your word in the index at the back of the book. Under the word are listed a number of related words and their essential meanings. Choose the related word with the meaning that is closest to what you want. Then look up the numbered section or subsection given after the word. Although *Roget's Thesaurus* takes a little while to master, many writers prefer this thesaurus.

4.26 COMPUTER-ASSISTED RESEARCH

On-line Research

Many different sources of information are available via computer. Users access these on-line sources by subscribing to individual services such as CompuServe, Nexis, America Online, and Eworld. Through such services you can obtain current news, refer to on-line encyclopedias, look at government documents, receive homework and study assistance, and use various research databases. You may also be able to use the service to connect to the Internet, an electronic network that links you to universities, libraries, businesses, government agencies, and individuals around the world. Your school may also be connected to a special education network, such as TENET (Texas Education Network). If your school and library have access to some on-line services, take some time to find out what resources are available to students.

CD/ROM and Other Computer Media

A large and growing number of databases, indexes, reference works, and other educational materials are available on CD/ROM. For example, many public libraries have a comprehensive periodicals index on CD/ROM, similar to the *Reader's Guide,* that is updated regularly. In some cases the CDs are changed only by the librarians; in other situations, you may be able to select from a collection of CDs and insert them in the computer yourself.

4.27 OTHER SOURCES OF INFORMATION

Vertical files. Many libraries collect and store useful information of various kinds in vertical file cabinets. The folders in these files contain miscellaneous materials such as brochures, local newspaper clippings, maps, posters, and photographs. The files are usually arranged alphabetically, but the materials are uncataloged. Depending on your topic, you may want to check these files for relevant materials.

Organizations and associations. For some research projects you may need to obtain information from organized groups. Local businesses and business associations; religious, political, and community organizations; and professional societies are usually eager to provide information on topics of interest to them. Keep in mind, though, that such groups often take a particular stand on an issue or have a particular point of view. Since their materials may be biased, you will need to read them carefully. (See the Language Arts Survey, 4.15, "Understanding Propaganda Techniques.")

Community institutions such as colleges, museums, historical societies, art galleries, orchestras, and other performing arts groups can also be good sources of ideas and information on certain topics.

You can find information about many kinds of organizations in the *Encyclopedia of Associations*. If you need to contact local groups, check the telephone book for names and addresses.

Experts. You may be able to find someone in your own community who is knowledgeable about your topic. This person might be a working professional with a specialized education—such as a college professor, doctor, engineer, or lawyer—or someone who has acquired their expertise simply through experience, such as a business owner, weekend woodworker, or Little League coach. Many of these people are eager to share their knowledge and experience with others.

If you don't know anyone who is an expert on your topic, ask your teachers, parents, friends, and relatives if they know of anyone who might help you. You can either ask your contact to arrange an interview, or arrange one yourself by calling the person directly. (See the Language Arts Survey, 1.27, "Interviewing.") You can also check the phone book or library resources to locate experts.

Before speaking to your expert for the first time, remember that you are asking a favor. When you call, be specific about why you are contacting the person and how you would like the person to help you. Then prepare for the interview, so you can obtain the information you need without wasting the interviewee's time. A maximum time limit on the interview of fifteen to twenty minutes is a good guideline.

4.28 EVALUATING SOURCES

When researching a project, you won't be able to read everything that has been written on your topic. Because you must be selective about your sources, you will need to evaluate each one carefully. A source must not only contain the information you need, but also be accurate. Ideally, a source will be

- **Unbiased.** An author who has something to gain personally from what people think about a subject may distort or omit certain facts. Possible signs of author bias are using loaded words, overlooking obvious counterarguments, and being associated with a particular organization, especially one that is politically active.

- **Authoritative.** When a source is reliable and trustworthy, it is considered authoritative. An authoritative author is one who is highly respected by others in the same field. An authoritative publication is one that has a reputation for being responsible and precise in presenting information.
- **Timely.** Depending on the subject, a current source or a less-than-current source may be reliable. In fields such as medicine or computer science, knowledge is expanding rapidly, and books can go out of date very fast. In a field such as mythology or art, however, a book that is ten years old may be acceptable. If you are doing historical research, you might seek out older works deliberately. Your teacher or librarian can help you decide how current your sources need to be.
- **Available.** If a source seems excellent but will not be available in the time you need it, you may have to rely on other sources instead. If you want to use a book that is not immediately available, find out from your librarian how long you can expect to wait.
- **At the appropriate level.** A source must present the information you need at a level you can understand. Materials written for much younger readers may be uninformative or even misleading. On the other hand, books written for an expert audience may presume knowledge that you do not have, and thus be too difficult to use.

4.29 BIBLIOGRAPHIES AND BIBLIOGRAPHY CARDS

Bibliographies. A **bibliography** is a list of sources on a particular topic. When you write a research paper, your teacher will ask you to include one of the following types of bibliography.

TYPES OF BIBLIOGRAPHY	
Complete Bibliography	A comprehensive list of works on your topic
Works Cited *or* **References**	A list of all the works referred to or quoted in your paper
Works Consulted	A list of every work you learned from in your research, even if you did not directly use or cite these works in your paper

The chart on pages 999–1002 gives examples of proper bibliographic form for many different types of materials.

When you are preparing your bibliography, first arrange your bibliography cards (see page 1003) in alphabetical order. Type or copy the information from each card onto your paper. Follow the correct form for each type of entry, as shown in the chart. Set up your pages and type the bibliography as described in the chart on page 1003.

FORMS FOR BIBLIOGRAPHY ENTRIES

A. A book with one author

Freidel, Frank. <u>Franklin D. Roosevelt: A Rendezvous with
  Destiny</u>. Boston: Little, Brown, 1990.

B. A book with two authors

Note that only the first author's name is inverted.

Laycock, George, and Ellen Laycock. <u>The Ohio Valley: Your Guide
  to America's Heartland</u>. Garden City, NY: Doubleday, 1983.

C. A book with three authors

Note that only the first author's name is inverted.

Alred, Gerald, Walter Oliu, and Charles Brusaw. <u>The
  Professional Writer: A Guide for Advanced Technical Writing</u>.
  New York: St. Martin's, 1992.

D. A book with four or more authors

The abbreviation *et al.* means "and others." Use *et al.* (and others) instead of listing all
the authors.

Carlson, Arthur E., et al. <u>Essentials of Accounting</u>. 6th ed.
  Cincinnati, OH: South-Western, 1991.

E. A book with no author given

<u>Pictures of Ideas: Learning Through Visual Comparison and
  Analogy</u>. Dickson, Australia: Curriculum Development Centre,
  1980.

F. A book with an editor, but no single author

Wiggington, Eliot ed. <u>The Foxfire Books</u>. Garden City, NY:
  Anchor/Doubleday, 1972.

G. A book with two or three editors

Driscoll, Mark, and Jere Confrey, eds. <u>Teaching Mathematics:
  Strategies That Work</u>. Portsmouth, NH: Heinemann, 1986.

H. A book with four or more editors

The abbreviation *et al.* means "and others." Use *et al.* instead of listing all the editors.

Covington, Paula H., et al. <u>Latin America and the Caribbean: A
  Critical Guide to Research Sources</u>. New York: Greenwood
  Press, 1992.

I. A book with an author and a translator

Dostoevsky, Fyodor. <u>The Brothers Karamazov</u>. Trans. Constance
  Garnett. New York: Modern Library, 1950.

J. A second or later edition of a book

Kennedy, X. J. <u>An Introduction to Poetry</u>. 2nd ed. Boston:
  Little, Brown, 1971.

K. A book or monograph that is part of a series

McNeil, W. K., ed. <u>Southern Folk Ballads</u>. American Folklore
   Series. Little Rock, AR: August House, 1987.

L. A multivolume work

If you use only one volume of a multivolume work, cite only that volume; otherwise
cite only the entire work.

James, D. Clayton. <u>The Years of MacArthur</u>. Vol. 3. Boston:
   Houghton Mifflin, 1985.

James, D. Clayton. <u>The Years of MacArthur</u>. 3 vols. Boston:
   Houghton Mifflin, 1970-1985.

**M. A titled volume with its own title that is part of a multivolume work with a
different title**

Smith, Page. <u>A New Age Begins</u>. Vol. 1, <u>A People's History of
   the American Revolution</u>. New York: Penguin Books, 1976.

N. A republished book or literary work available in several editions

Give the original publication date after the title. Then give complete information, for
the edition that you have used.

Austen, Jane. <u>Sense and Sensibility</u>. 1811. New York: Oxford
   University Press, 1990.

O. A government publication

U.S. Commission on Civil Rights. <u>Accommodating the Spectrum of
   Individual Abilities</u>. Washington, DC: GPO, 1983.

Parts of Books

A. A poem, short story, essay, or chapter in a collection of works by one author

Helprin, Mark. "A Vermont Tale." <u>Ellis Island and Other Stories</u>.
   New York: Laurel, 1981. 84-104.

B. A poem, short story, essay, or chapter in a collection of works by several authors

Dickinson, Emily. "There's a certain slant of light." <u>Master
   Poems of the English Language</u>. Ed. Oscar Williams. New York:
   Washington Square Press, 1967. 783.

C. A novel or play in a collection under one cover

Shakespeare, William. <u>Henry VIII</u>. <u>King John and Henry VIII</u>. Ed.
   David Bevington. New York: Bantam Books, 1988. 179-295.

**D. An introduction, preface, foreword, or afterword written by the author(s)
of a work**

Altick, Richard. Introduction. <u>The Scholar Adventurers</u>. New
   York: Free Press, 1966.

**E. An introduction, preface, foreword, or afterword written by someone other
than the author(s) of a work**

Keillor, Garrison. Foreword. <u>The Sheep Book</u>. By Ron Parker. New
   York: Ballantine Books, 1983.

F. A reprint of a previously published article or essay

Give complete information for the original publication, followed by "Rpt. in" and complete information for the collection.

```
Toth, Susan Allen. "Free to Just Be." Family Life (Mar./Apr.)
    1994. Rpt. in Utne Reader (July/Aug. 1994): 128-130.
```

Magazines, Encyclopedias, Reports, Newspapers, and Newsletters

A. An article in a quarterly or monthly magazine

```
Hill, Mary. "Medieval Dyeing." Spin-Off. Fall 1989: 66-69.
```

B. An article in a weekly magazine

```
Lodge, Sally. "The School Book Club Wars." Publishers Weekly,
    27 July 1990: 118-126.
```

C. A magazine article with no author given

```
"Cameras." Consumers Digest, Nov./Dec. 1993:90+.
```

D. An article in a daily newspaper

```
Hong, Sun. "China Spurs German Trade." China Daily, 25 April
    1995:5.
```

E. An editorial in a newspaper

```
"Talking Straight about Taxes." Editorial. Plain Dealer, 26
    April 1995: 10B.
```

F. An article or story in a journal

Give the volume number, the year, and the page number(s) after the title of the journal.

```
Miller, Allan, and Dorita Coen. "The Case for Music in the
    Schools." Choral Journal, 35.7 (1995): 9-11.
```

G. An article in an encyclopedia, dictionary, or other alphabetically organized reference work

Give the title of the article, the title of the work, and the year.

```
"Ida Bell Wells-Barnett." Black Women in America: An Historical
    Encyclopedia. Ed. Darlene Clark Hine. Brooklyn, NY: Carlson,
    1993.
```

H. A review

```
Slung, Michele. "Hairballs and Havoc." Rev. of James Herriot's
    Cat Stories. By James Herriot. New York: St. Martin's Press,
    1994. New York Times Book Review, 11 Sept. 1994: 12.
```

I. A report for a pamphlet

Same as for a book.

Media and Other Sources

A. An interview that you have conducted
Jacques, Brian. Personal interview. 3 March 1995.

B. A letter that you have received
Giovanni, Nikki. Letter to the author. 10 November 1994.

C. A fax or e-mail communication
Same as for a letter.

D. A thesis or dissertation
Debois, Hayward. "Archaeological Remains in Mammoth Cave, Kentucky." Thesis. University of Kentucky, 1991.

E. A film
The Conversation. Writ., prod., dir. Francis Ford Coppola. 113 min. Paramount Pictures, 1974.

F. A work of visual art
Klee, Paul. The Idea of Firs. Solomon R. Guggenheim Museum, New York.

G. A television or radio program
Give the episode name; the names of the episode's writer, director, producer, or actors; the series or program title; and any information that you wish to include about the series's writer, director, or producer. Then give the network, station call letters, city, and date.
"Ambos Nogales." Writ. Marty Rochlin. SoundPrint. PBS. WOSU-AM News 820, Columbus, 6 May 1995.

H. A musical composition
Weill, Kurt. The Three-Penny Opera.

I. An audio recording (LP, compact disc, audio-cassette tape)
O'Brien, Tim and Molly. Remember Me (CD). Dunham, NC: Sugar Hill Records, 1992.

J. A lecture, speech, or address
Give the name of the speaker and the name of the speech. If there is no title, give the kind of speech—e.g. lecture, introduction, address. Then give the event, place, and date.
Abraham, Ronald. Keynote address. Tree-planting ceremony. Mount Vernon, OH. 30 April 1995.

MANUSCRIPT FORM FOR BIBLIOGRAPHIES

1. Begin on a new page.

2. Indent one inch from both side margins, one and one-half inches on the left side and one inch on the right side if the report is to be bound.

3. Place your last name and the page number, flush right, half-an-inch from the top of the paper.

4. Drop down another one-half-inch and insert the title "Works Consulted" or "Works Cited." Use uppercase and lowercase letters, and do not underscore.

5. Begin each entry at the left margin. Single space within each entry. Indent run-over lines five spaces from the left margin.

6. Double space between the title and the first entry and between each entry.

Bibliography cards. For each source that you might use, you should prepare a 3" x 5" card giving complete bibliographical information. Having each source on an individual card will make it easy to organize and prepare your list of sources when you are done writing. (See the Language Arts Survey, 4.33, "Documenting Sources in a Report.") The cards can also help you find the source again later if you need it. Follow the proper form for the type of material when preparing your cards. A sample bibliography card is shown following the chart.

INFORMATION TO INCLUDE ON A BIBLIOGRAPHY CARD

Author(s)	Write the complete name(s) of all author(s), editor(s), and translator(s).
Title	Write the complete title, including any subtitle and any series title. If the piece is an article or chapter in a periodical or book, write • the title of the particular piece; • the beginning and ending page numbers; and • the title of the larger work.
Edition	Note "2nd edition," "revised edition," etc.
Publisher	Write exactly as it appears on the title page.
Place and date of publication	For periodicals, write the date as well as the issue and volume numbers. For republished works, write both the original publication date and the date of your edition.
Location and call number	Note where you found the book. If it is in a library collection, write the call number.
Card number	Give each bibliography card that you prepare a number. Write that number in the top right-hand corner of the card and circle it. When you take notes from the source, include this number on each note card so that you will be able to identify the source of the note later.

①

Lopez, Barry. <u>Arctic Dreams: Imagination</u>
<u>and Desire in a Northern Landscape</u>.
        New York: Charles Scribner's Sons,
        1986.

QH   Ferguson Public Library
84.1
L67

4.30 PARAPHRASING AND SUMMARIZING

Quoting. A **quotation** is a phrase, statement, or passage borrowed word for word from someone else. To show that the words are not your own, place quotation marks before and after the quoted sentences or words. (See the Language Arts Survey, 2.104 and 2.105, "Quotation Marks I and II," and 2.124, "Quotations.") Generally, you should use quotations in your writing when you need to prove that someone made a specific statement or when the unique wording of the quotation is essential to a point you are trying to make. Do not use quotations simply as a replacement for writing about a topic in your own words. Whenever you quote someone else, be sure to check the accuracy of the quote and provide an appropriate citation. (See the Language Arts Survey, 4.33, "Documenting Sources in a Report.")

Paraphrasing. A **paraphrase** is a restatement of someone else's ideas in your own words. Many of the notes you take may be paraphrases. However, it is generally safer to quote directly in your notes and then paraphrase as you draft your piece. This practice can help you avoid quoting a source without realizing it.

Remember that if you paraphrase someone else's ideas, you are still obliged to give credit to the source of those ideas. (See the language Arts Survey, 4.33, "Documenting Sources in a Report.") In this way, you acknowledge that you are borrowing the ideas.

Summarizing. When you summarize a piece of writing, you condense and simplify it into a brief statement of the main points. Most details are omitted. A one-sentence summary of a

Gettysburg Address
President Lincoln mourns the Union and Confederate soldiers who died at Gettysburg and places their sacrifice in the larger context of preserving the Union.

piece of writing will include very few details, as in the following example:

A summary should be written entirely in your own words and should present only what the author said. Be careful not to incorporate your own ideas or opinions when you write a summary.

Outlining. Outlining is a good way to summarize nonfiction reading. (See the Language Arts Survey, 1.32 and 1.33, on outlining.) An **outline** includes the main points of a piece of writing and the most important details about each main point. Minor or trivial details are omitted. When making an outline, you may wish to paraphrase the headings in the piece and to use your paraphrases as headings in your outline. After each heading, you can note the main points made in the section.

4.31 INFORMAL NOTE-TAKING

When you are gathering information for personal use only, you can take **informal notes.** Informal note-taking is appropriate during class, when reading homework, or taking reporter's notes at a live event. Informal note-taking is similar to outlining. (See the Language Arts Survey, 1.32, "Making a Rough Outline.") The main ideas become headings in your notes, and related details are written under each heading. If you are taking notes at a live event, you will also want to record the date, time, place, speaker or performer, and so on. Using phrases and abbreviations in your notes will allow you to take notes more efficiently.

EXAMPLE OF INFORMAL NOTES

SOURCE MATERIAL "Immigrants to the United States came for many reasons: to escape poverty, unemployment, and crowded living conditions and to escape religious and political persecution."

NOTE Reasons for immig. to U.S.
—poverty, unemploy., overpop.
—relig., and polit. persecution

When you are through taking notes, it's a good idea to read over them. If you spot any illegible or confusing phrases or abbreviations, write them out so they will make sense when you review your notes later.

4.32 FORMAL NOTE-TAKING

When you may need to quote or document your sources, you will need to take **formal notes.** Research for a paper or debate, for example, requires formal note-taking. Use 4" x 6" index cards and record a single quotation, paraphrase, or summary on each card, as shown in the following:

SAMPLE NOTE CARD

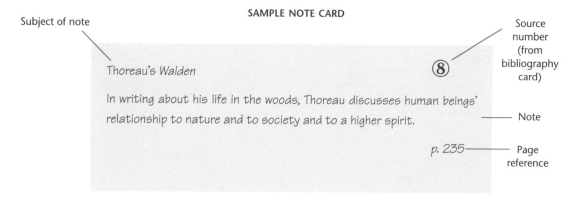

Subject of note

Thoreau's Walden   ⑧

In writing about his life in the woods, Thoreau discusses human beings' relationship to nature and to society and to a higher spirit.

p. 235

Source number (from bibliography card)

Note

Page reference

PREPARING NOTE CARDS

1. Identify the source at the top right corner of the card. (Use the source numbers from your bibliography cards.)
2. Identify the subject or topic of the note on the top line of the card. (This will make it easier to organize the cards later.)
3. Use a separate card for each fact or quotation. (This will make it easier to organize the cards later.)
4. Write the page number or numbers after the note.

Observe the guidelines that follow when making each type of formal note.

FORMAL NOTE-TAKING

Type of Note	When to Use	What to Watch for
Quotation	When the exact wording of a primary source is important to your topic; or When you are providing a definition; or When the wording of a secondary source is particularly elegant, pithy, concise, amusing, etc.	Be sure you exactly copy spelling, capitalization, punctuation, and numbers. Place quotation marks around all direct quotations. Record, when appropriate, explanatory background information about the speaker or the context of a quotation.
Paraphrase	Most of the time	Bear in mind your main purpose, and note only points that are related to your topic. Place quotation marks around any quoted words or phrases.
Summary	When the point in which you are interested does not require the detail of a paraphrase	Reread the source after writing your summary to be sure that you have not altered the meaning.

4.33 DOCUMENTING SOURCES IN A REPORT

Documentation. Always let your readers know when you are using the words or ideas of others by **documenting** your sources. A note that tells the source of an idea or statement is called a **citation** or a **reference.**

Any writer who presents the words or ideas of someone else as if they were the writer's own is guilty of **plagiarism.** Plagiarizing may be intentional or unintentional; in either case, the writer has used others' words or ideas without giving them credit. Plagiarism is a form of stealing. This offense is seriously punished in most schools, often with a failing grade for the project, or worse. Outside of school, those who plagiarize may be charged with violating copyright law and sued by those from whom they have stolen.

Documenting your sources helps to prevent plagiarizing, but it is important for other reasons as well.

- **Accuracy.** Properly documenting facts and opinions helps readers to judge their accuracy and reliability. Your writing will be more convincing and authoritative if you tell readers the exact source of your information.
- **Courtesy to Reader.** Knowing the source for an idea or fact allows readers to go to the source on their own for further information.
- **Scholarship.** Furnishing documentation shows honesty as well as respect for the contributions to knowledge made by others.

Parenthetical documentation. The most widely used method for citing sources is **parenthetical documentation.** In this method, the writer places a brief note identifying the source immediately after the borrowed material. This type of note is called a **parenthetical citation,** and the act of placing such a note is called **citing a source.**

A parenthetical citation has two parts. The first part briefly identifies the source. This identification should clearly correspond to the entry as it appears in your list of "Works Cited" or "Works Consulted" (see the following examples). For example, if the entry begins with a title, the citation often includes the first word or two of the title. The second part of the citation gives the specific page number or place in the source where the information can be found. If the source is named in the text, omit the source in the citation and give only the page number.

SAMPLE PARENTHETICAL CITATIONS

A. For works listed by title, use an abbreviated title.

Sample bibliographic entry

"Ida Bell Wells-Barnett." <u>Black Women in America: An Historical Encyclopedia</u>. Ed. Darlene Clark Hine. Brooklyn, NY: Carlson, 1983.

Sample citation

. . . Wells, orphaned at the age of sixteen, became the caretaker of her younger brothers and sisters . . .("Ida" 1242)

B. For works listed by author or editor, use the author's or editor's last name.

Sample bibliographic entry

Mettger, Zak. <u>Reconstruction: American After the Civil War</u>. New York: Lodestar, 1994.

CONTINUED

Sample citation

. . . Many female teachers who set up schools for freed slaves were persecuted by white vigilantes (Mettger 32–33). . .

C. When the listed name or title is stated in the text, cite only the page number.

. . . Mettger notes that Southern churches acted as schoolhouses (34). . . .

D. For works of multiple volumes, use a colon after the volume number.

Sample bibliographic entry

"Man in the Moon." <u>Funk and Wagnalls Standard Dictionary of Folklore, Mythology and Legend</u>, 2 vols. Ed. Maria Leach. New York: Funk and Wagnalls, 1950.

Sample citation

"Probably all North American Indians . . .have some explanation for the dark patches of the moon." ("Man" 2:672).

E. For works quoted in secondary sources, use the abbreviation "qtd. in."

Sample bibliographic entry

Lloyd, Pamela. <u>How Writers Write</u>. Portsmouth, NH: Heinemann, 1987.

Sample citation

. . . Sue Townsend notes, "My characters are all the people I've ever observed or met." (qtd. in Lloyd 73). . . .

F. For classic works that are available in various editions, give the page number from the edition you are using, followed by a semicolon; then identify the section of the work to help people with other editions find the reference.

Sample citation

. . . At the opening of Hardy's <u>Tess of the D'Urbervilles</u>, Tess's father learns that his ancestors were once nobility (18:ch.1). . . .

G. For classic works of poetry or drama you may omit the page reference completely and cite the section and line numbers.

Sample citation

. . . Wordsworth describes the soothing effects of solitude in nature (<u>Prelude</u> 4.354–369). . . .

pt.	part
bk.	book
ch.	chapter
sec.	section
sc.	scene
par.	paragraph

4.34 FOOTNOTES AND ENDNOTES

Footnoting and endnoting are less widely used than parenthetical documentation. You may encounter these two systems of documentation in your research.

Footnotes. Citations that are placed at the bottom of the page rather than within the text in parentheses are called **footnotes.** With this system, a superscript number or other symbol is placed in the text at the appropriate point, and a matching number or symbol identifies the footnote. Footnotes may be used for purposes other than documentation. They may supply additional information that is useful or interesting but not important enough to be placed in the text. For example, the numbered footnotes in the literature selections of this book define obscure words and provide background information.

Endnotes. Many books have **endnotes** instead of footnotes. Endnotes are exactly like footnotes, but they are gathered at the end of a book, chapter, or article. Some authors or publishers prefer endnotes because they are less distracting to the reader than footnotes and they make it easier to lay out the pages of the book.

TEST-TAKING SKILLS

OBJECTIVE TESTS

4.35 STRATEGIES FOR TAKING OBJECTIVE TESTS

The tests you take in your classes, like other tests that life offers, challenge you to do and be your best. Most athletes, for example, willingly enter into challenging situations. These situations test their skills and allow them to excel to new levels. In the same way, when you prepare for and take a classroom test, you can actually increase your knowledge and understanding. Tests not only assess learning; they stimulate it.

To do your very best on a classroom test, you need to study and get involved with the material presented by your teacher. When you read your text or other books, read carefully. During class discussions, listen actively and take thorough notes. It's also important to stay healthy, so you will be alert to the information and ideas you encounter.

Many of the tests you take will be objective tests containing multiple-choice, true/false, and short-answer questions. The suggestions in the following chart and the subsequent sections can help you do your best when taking objective tests.

STRATEGIES FOR TAKING OBJECTIVE TESTS

Before the Test
- Get ample sleep the night before the test.
- Eat a nutritious breakfast.
- Study over as long a period of time as possible.
- Review frequently.
- Try to predict questions that may be on the test, and make sure you can answer them.
- Bring *extra* pencils, erasers, and any other required materials.

During the Test
- Determine how much time is allowed for each question. If a question takes too long, guess and/or come back to it if you have time.
- *Read each question carefully.*
- Work quickly but do not rush.
- Write legibly.
- Review all your work before submitting it.

4.36 TRUE/FALSE QUESTIONS

A true/false question is really a statement; your task is to decide whether the statement is true or false. If you do not know the answer to a true/false question, guess.

Because true/false tests are strongly influenced by guessing, you have a 50/50 chance of guessing correctly on each question. Their results may not accurately reflect a person's knowledge. If you are given a true/false test, keep an eye out for these possible traps:

Negatives and double negatives. The word *not* completely changes the meaning of a sentence. To evaluate a sentence that contains a negative, see if its opposite makes sense or is plausible. If it does, the original must be false.

Quantifiers and qualifiers. Look for words such as *all, sometimes, never, many, some,* and *few.* Since few statements are true without exception, statements containing absolute words such as *all* or *never* are more likely to be false. Statements with qualifiers such as *some* or *few* are more likely to be true.

Excess information. In a true/false question, the more information a statement contains, the more likely it is to be false. Only one part of the statement needs to be false to make the entire statement false.

4.37 MULTIPLE-CHOICE QUESTIONS

In a multiple-choice item, a question is presented and you must select the correct or best answer from a list of choices. Sometimes the "question" is an incomplete statement and you must complete the statement correctly from the list of choices. If you read a question and know the answer immediately, look for it in the choices. Otherwise, read through each answer to rule out incorrect or inappropriate choices.

> **EXAMPLE** The "Gettysburg Address" and "Concord Hymn" are two works that pay honor to
> a. the foresight of the founding fathers.
> b. the sacrifice of soldiers killed in battle.
> c. the contributions of African Americans.
> d. the ideals of the transcendentalists.

4.38 SHORT-ANSWER QUESTIONS

Short-answer questions are answered with a word, a phrase, or a sentence. They frequently occur in quizzes and in class discussions. Your teachers may require that responses to short-answer questions be complete sentences.

> **EXAMPLE** What incident gave rise to Walt Whitman's poem, "When Lilacs Last in the Dooryard Bloom'd"?
> **The poem was a response to the assassination of President Abraham Lincoln.**

STANDARDIZED TESTS

4.39 STRATEGIES FOR TAKING STANDARDIZED TESTS

As a high school student, you may encounter standardized tests at several points in your school career. States and school districts use such tests to assess achievement. In addition, students planning to go to college take standardized tests in order to apply for admission and scholarships.

SOME STANDARDIZED TESTS	
Common Abbreviation	**Test**
PSAT/NMSQT	Pre-Scholastic Aptitude Test/National Merit Scholarship Qualifying Test
ACT	American College Testing Program
MAT	Miller Analogies Test
SAT	Scholastic Aptitude Test
ACH	College Board Achievement Tests

Standardized tests are made up of multiple-choice questions. You answer the questions on special sheets that can then be read and graded by a computer. To show your answer, you fill in a bubble. Be sure to use the type of pencil or pen specified by the test monitor and to fill in the bubble *completely* and *neatly*.

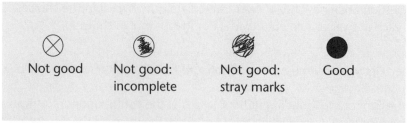

Not good Not good: incomplete Not good: stray marks Good

As you choose answers on a standardized test, keep these points in mind. If you don't know the answer, try to rule out some choices and then guess from the ones that remain. If you are worried about time, you can skip a difficult question and come back to it later (look for a blank space on your answer sheet). You should, however, try to fill in a bubble for each question, since an unanswered question is automatically incorrect. Remember, too, that you can only go back to questions within the current section of the test. Always follow the instructions of the test monitor.

4.40 ANALOGY QUESTIONS

An analogy question asks you to detect the relationship between a given pair of words and then recognize a similar relationship between another pair of words.

> EXAMPLE WIND : AIR
> (A) sound : instrument   (C) sky : atmosphere   (E) heat : furnace
> (B) current : water   (D) breath : lungs

Before answering an analogy question, read and evaluate *all* of the answers. If two or more answers seem correct, choose the *best* answer. Make sure you focus on the *relationship* between the two words in the example. Do not be thrown off by irrelevant connections between individual words in the example and words in the choices.

4.41 SENTENCE-COMPLETION QUESTIONS

A sentence-completion question presents a sentence in which one or two words are missing. You must discover the relationship between the parts of the sentence, and then choose the word or words that best complete the sentence.

To answer a sentence-completion question you must try *all* of the choices to see which pair of words work *best* in the sentence. You can usually rule out one or two answers right away because they do not fit the structure or the context of the sentence.

> EXAMPLE The senator_____ the new bill; he said it would have _____ effects on the environment.
> (A) praised . . . mixed   (C) invented . . . interesting
> (B) denounced . . . unfavorable   (D) rejected . . . positive
> (E) ignored . . . incredible

4.42 GRAMMAR, USAGE, AND MECHANICS QUESTIONS

Grammar, usage, and mechanics questions present a sentence or paragraph with underlined and labeled words or passages for you to evaluate.

An **error-identification question** asks you to identify the part of the sentence that contains an error. You do not have to identify the type of error.

> Choose the letter that corresponds to any error in the sentence.
>
> "The Notorious Jumping Frog of Calaveras County" is among
>   A
>
> Twain's most famous short storys. No error.
>   B   C   D   E
>
> (A) (B) (C) (D) (E)

An **error-correction question** asks you to choose a word or passage to replace the erroneous part of the sentence.

> Select the letter of the word or words that should replace the underlined word.
>
> By the time people arrive for the picnic, Marcus mows the lawn.
>
> (A) had mowed   (C) has mowed   (E) had been mowing
> (B) will have mowed   (D) will mow

ANSWERING ERROR-IDENTIFICATION AND ERROR-CORRECTION QUESTIONS

1. Ignore the underlining and proofread the sentence or paragraph carefully.
   - Proofread for errors in grammar, usage, and mechanics.
   - Look especially for agreement—in tense, person, number, and mood.
2. If you do not find the error, look specifically at the underlined passages.
3. Read the whole sentence through before settling on your answer.

For information about grammar, usage, and mechanics refer to the Language Arts Survey, 2.1–2.153, "Essential Skills: Language." Completing your reading and writing assignments conscientiously will also help you prepare for these kinds of questions.

4.43 READING COMPREHENSION QUESTIONS

Reading comprehension questions require you to read a short piece of writing and then answer several questions about it. Some questions may address the content of the passage. Others may ask you to make an inference or draw a conclusion from the text. To select the correct answer, try all the choices. Make your selection based on the passage itself, rather than other knowledge or opinions.

STEPS IN ANSWERING READING COMPREHENSION QUESTIONS

1. Read all the questions quickly.
2. Read the passage.
3. Reread the first question carefully.
4. Reread the passage while bearing in mind the first question.
5. Answer the first question.
6. Continue with each subsequent question in the same manner.

4.44 SYNONYM AND ANTONYM QUESTIONS

A synonym and antonym question presents a word and asks you to select a word that has the same meaning (for a synonym) or the opposite meaning (for an antonym). If none of the answers seem exactly correct, select the *best* answer.

EXAMPLE   Write the letter of the word that is most nearly the *same* in meaning to the word in capital letters.
1. SVELT
(A) sour   (B) soft   (C) swollen   (D) sleek   (E) severe

To answer this type of question, try all of the choices to see which one works best. Often both synonyms and antonyms are included among the answers, so you should have the instructions clearly in mind to avoid accidentally choosing the wrong type of word. Also, don't choose an answer just because it (1) looks like or sounds like the given word, (2) has the same root, prefix, or suffix as the given word, or (3) is a long or unfamiliar word.

STRATEGIES FOR TAKING ESSAY TESTS

4.45 ANALYZING AN ESSAY QUESTION

The first step in writing a good answer to an essay question is to make sure you understand the question. Read through the entire question. Then underline the key words that show what type of response is expected; if this is not possible, jot down the key words on your own paper. Many questions have more than one part, so check to see if more than one type of response is requested. By taking a few moments to analyze the question, you will know what tasks you must accomplish in the time available. The following chart identifies several common types of essay questions. The numbers in parentheses refer to the related sections of the Language Arts Survey.

UNDERSTANDING AN ESSAY QUESTION	
Type of Essay Question	**Tasks of Essay**
analyze (1.14, 1.33, 4.11)	break into parts and describe the parts and their relationships
compare; compare and contrast (1.33, 4.8)	identify and describe similarities and differences
describe; explain (1.33, 4.6)	tell the steps in a process; identify causes and effects
define; describe; identify (4.7)	classify and tell the features of
interpret (4.13)	tell the meaning and significance of
summarize (4.30)	retell very briefly, stating only the main points
argue; prove; show (4.12)	tell and evaluate reasons for believing a statement

4.46 ORGANIZING AN ANSWER TO AN ESSAY QUESTION

Although you will probably not have time to go through the entire writing process, you should allow time for planning, drafting, and reviewing. If you take a moment to sketch out a plan and then pace yourself as you write, you should be able to complete your essay in the time available.

The planning stage is critical to your success. Begin by making a brief outline of the main points you want to make. Keep the tasks of the question in mind as you plan. Then add notes to support each point, such as examples and any quotations that fit your purpose.

When you begin drafting, work carefully to write a clear introduction that states your main points and leads logically into the body of your essay. Refer to the introduction as you write the body of the essay to help yourself stay on track.

If you find yourself running out of time, try to state your remaining main points, even if you cannot elaborate on them, and add a conclusion. Rounding out your essay in this way gives your reader a better idea of what you know and understand than if you abruptly break off before the end.

4.47 REVIEWING AN ANSWER TO AN ESSAY QUESTION

Take as much time as you can to review and polish your essay. If you revise as you go, make sure you don't use up all your time editing an incomplete essay. The following chart offers some guidelines for reviewing essay questions.

QUESTIONS FOR REVIEWING AN ANSWER TO AN ESSAY QUESTION

- Does the essay answer all parts of the question?
- Does the introduction state clearly the main point of the essay?
- Is the conclusion consistent with the main point?
- Does the essay cover all the points in your outline?
- Are there any points that could be made more strongly or clearly?
- Is every word in the essay easily legible?
- Is the essay free of errors in grammar, usage, and mechanics?

ESSENTIAL SKILLS:
Applied English/Tech Prep

LETTERS AND FORMS

Writing letters is one of the most practical kinds of writing you will ever do. You can use letters to develop and maintain friendships, to obtain information, to solve problems with individuals or businesses, to express appreciation, to speak out on social issues, and to impress future employers. Whenever you write a letter, you'll want to make sure that your writing reflects your purpose, has a voice and style appropriate for your reader, and conveys your message clearly.

Becoming familiar with the conventions of letter writing will help you achieve positive results with your letters. Following these conventions is especially important when writing letters to individuals or groups who don't know you personally.

5.1 FILLING OUT FORMS AND APPLICATIONS

Because forms are such an efficient tool for obtaining information, you can expect to encounter them in many day-to-day situations, such as registering for courses, visiting the doctor or dentist, doing business at the bank, and, of course, applying for employment. When you fill out a form or application, you should provide all of the information requested. At the same time, you should strive to make a positive impression on those who will read and evaluate the information you give.

Guidelines for completing forms:
- If possible, obtain an extra copy of the form or application.
- Gather any information you will need to complete the form.
- Read all the directions before you begin to enter your data.
- Be neat. Type or print your responses legibly, in pencil or ink, as directed. Avoid smudges or cross-outs.
- Write "N.A." or "not applicable," rather than leave a space blank, if a section of the form or application does not apply to you.
- Proofread. When you've completed the form, check your spelling, grammar, and punctuation, and review the information you've provided.
- If the form is messy or inaccurate, discard it and complete the extra form or application if you have one.
- When you've completed the form to your satisfaction, submit it to the appropriate person, or mail it to the correct address.

Application for Employment
City Services Department

Position Desired: <u>Groundskeeping Assistant</u>

Personal Data

Applicant's Name: <u>Alvarez   Hector   M.</u>
                       Last name   First Name   Middle Initial

Address: <u>9818 Pontius Avenue   Santee   CA   92071</u>
                 Street   City   State   Zip

Phone: <u>(619) 555-7643</u>

Previous Work Experience

(List last two positions held, beginning with the most recent.)

Employer: <u>Santee Public Library   200 James St.</u>
                 Name   Address

Phone: <u>(619) 555-9818</u>

Employment Period: <u>1/95–present</u>

Job Title: <u>Library Assistant</u>

Hours Worked: <u>4:00–6:00, Monday–Friday</u>

Salary: <u>$5.50/hr.</u>

Description: <u>Shelve books; assist at book return desk</u>

Reason for Leaving: <u>N.A.</u>

Employer: <u>Shawn's Lawn Care Service   927 West High Street</u>
                 Name   Address

Phone: <u>(619) 555-1918</u>

Employment Period: <u>June–August 1995</u>

Job Title: <u>Mower/trimmer</u>

Hours Worked: <u>Flexible, about 20 hrs./wk.</u>

Salary: <u>$5.00/hr.</u>

Description: <u>Mowed and trimmed lawns of all sizes; cleaned and maintained equip.</u>

Reason for Leaving: <u>Returned to school after summer vacation</u>

CONTINUED

Education

(List last school attended.)

Santee High School	Santee CA 92071	9/93–	College Prep	N.A.
School Name	Address	Dates Attended	Field of Study	Date Graduated

References

Name: Mr. Shawn Dudgeon

Relationship to
Job Applicant: Owner, Shawn's Lawn Care Service   Years Acquainted: 1

Address: 22096 Montgomery Rd., Santee CA   Phone: (619) 555-1177

Name: Mrs. Nadia Nijinski

Relationship to
Job Applicant: Director, Milton Public Library   Years Acquainted: 1

Address: 200 James St., Santee CA   Phone: (619) 555-1918

Signature: *Hector M Alvarez*   Date: 4/30/96

5.2 THE FORM OF A PERSONAL LETTER

In an age when phones can follow us anywhere, communicating with distant friends and family by letter is far less common than it once was. Still, most people are delighted when a personal letter appears in the mail box. Unlike a phone call, a letter can be saved and enjoyed more than once. In addition, comments made in a letter tend to carry more weight than spontaneous comments. The reader knows that the writer sat down to compose the letter and took time to express his or her thoughts with care.

You can use personal letters to stay in touch with friends and relatives. You can also use them to say thank you for a gift or kindness, to congratulate others on their achievements, and to extend invitations. A personal letter may be semiformal or quite informal depending on the writer's relationship with the person who will receive the letter. It will typically include the following parts:

1. a **return address**, including the writer's address and the date the letter was composed;
2. a **salutation**, or greeting, followed by a comma;
3. the **body**, or text, of the letter;
4. an appropriate **closing**, followed by a comma;
5. a **signature**; and
6. an optional **postscript**, preceded by the abbreviation "P.S."

SAMPLE THANK-YOU LETTER

❶
35889 Blanchard Road
Indianapolis, IN 46240
May 12, 1996

❷ Dear Grandad,

❸   I just want to thank you for the wonderful week at your cabin. I can't seem to keep myself from daydreaming about the Smokies—the popsicle-colored rhododendrons, the sunsets over the peaks, the soaring hawks—and your blueberry pancakes!
    I especially enjoyed our early morning hike up Bald Mountain. The views in all directions were amazing. It would be fun to make the same trip in the fall or winter (hint, hint). Hope to see you soon.

❹   Love,

❺   *Lyonel*

❻   P.S.—In a separate package I'm sending you one of the sketches I made from the front porch of the cabin.

5.3 THE FORM OF A BUSINESS LETTER

When you write a personal letter, you can usually expect the recipient to respond positively to the letter and to you. A business letter, however, is frequently addressed to someone who has never met you or does not know you very well. The recipient often has only the letter on which to form an impression of you. Therefore, a more formal tone is appropriate. Following the widely accepted format for a business letter will also help to ensure that your letter makes a positive impression.

A business letter includes a **heading, salutation, body, closing,** and **signature,** just as in a personal letter. In addition, an **inside address** is used. The inside address is placed below the heading and above the salutation. It includes the name and title of the person to whom you are writing, the name of the company or organization, and its address. (See the letter on page 1022.) If you do not know the name of a person at an organization, you can use a department name instead. Occasionally, a business letter will include a **postscript.**

Make sure the salutation and closing of a business letter are respectful and formal. The most common salutation begins with the word "Dear" followed by the courtesy or professional title used in the inside address, such as "Ms.," "Mr.," "Dr.," "Miss," or "Mrs." If you are not writing to a specific person, use a salutation such as "Ladies and Gentlemen" or "Dear Sir or Madam." Complete the salutation with a colon.

In a business letter, you should avoid using creative closings. There are a number of acceptable closings, such as "Sincerely," "Yours truly," "Very truly yours," or "Respectfully yours." Capitalize only the first word of the closing and end the closing with a comma. Add your signature below the closing, in either blue or black ink. Your full name should be typed below your signature.

Business letters commonly take one of two forms. In **block form** (see page 1022), all the elements of the letter—the heading, inside address, salutation, body, closing, and signature—are aligned at the left margin. Paragraphs are not indented. In **modified block form** (see page 1022), the heading and closing appear on the right side of the page, just left of center and aligned with each other. Paragraphs are indented, usually five spaces in from the left margin.

In the body of your letter, word your message in a way that is clear and courteous. Use standard English, and avoid using slang or pet expressions, as you might in a personal letter. To make sure your letter is well organized, outline your main points before you begin to write. Then when you draft, strive to get your message across without wasting any words. Finally, proofread your letter carefully. Using correct grammar, punctuation, and spelling is essential if you want your reader to respond favorably to your letter.

Guidelines for Writing a Business Letter

- Outline your letter's main points before you begin the writing process.
- Type your letter, if at all possible, and use clean $8^{1}/_{2}$" × 11" white or off-white paper. Type on one side of the paper only.
- Select a standard business-letter format, either block form or modified block form.
- Use single-spacing, leaving a blank line between paragraphs.
- Select a standard salutation and closing.
- Stick to the subject, keeping the letter brief and informative.
- Be neat. A sloppy appearance may make your letter less effective.
- Check your grammar, usage, punctuation, capitalization, and spelling.
- Reread your letter. Have you conveyed your main points clearly and effectively? Don't make your reader guess at your intentions.

5.4   Types of Business Letters I

You will have many opportunities to compose business letters. For example, you might want to obtain information from a college or organization, request a refund from a company for a faulty product, tell an author why you admire a certain book, or state an opinion to your representative in Congress.

In any of these situations, you make a phone call, but a letter is often more effective. People generally pay more attention to written communications than they do to verbal ones. In addition, writing a letter allows you to save a copy of it as a record of your action. The copy could be an electronic one (if you typed your letter on a computer) or a photocopy. For example, if you are sending letters to several colleges to obtain admissions information, having copies of the letters allows you to keep track of your correspondence.

850 Bethel Road
Racine, WI 53404
November 30, 1996

Kenyon College
Office of Admissions
Gambier, OH 43022

Ladies and Gentlemen:

At a recent college fair at James Madison High School, I met Charlie Otting, an alumnus of Kenyon College who lives in the Racine area. His glowing comments about Kenyon made me think that this is a school I would like to know more about.

I think I would like the small-college atmosphere at Kenyon as well as the rural setting, since I come from a small town. Kenyon's high academic standards are also attractive to me, as is its commitment to high-quality teaching. I might be interested in studying biology or English.

I would appreciate receiving an information packet from you as well as information about how to apply for financial aid. I look forward to hearing from you soon.

Sincerely,

Rohini Pragasam

Rohini Pragasam

5.5 TYPES OF BUSINESS LETTERS II

Some of the most important business letters you will write are those you address to potential employers. These letters will strongly influence which jobs you are hired for and thus the course of your career.

When you apply for a position, you will typically submit both a **résumé** and a letter of application, also called a **cover letter.** Your résumé presents a summary of your work experience and education. Your cover letter highlights specific accomplishments from your résumé and suggests how your unique mix of skills and abilities qualifies you for the position.

The information in your résumé and cover letter must be truthful and accurate, but you should shed a positive light on your experience. Don't be shy about emphasizing your strengths. Your résumé should be fairly specific in describing your background, but it's best to word it in a way that allows you to use it in various situations. You can use your cover letter to address specific qualifications for a particular job.

Guidelines for composing a cover letter:

- Limit your cover letter to a single page.
- State your interest in obtaining a position within the organization, indicating the type of position (or specific job opening) for which you'd like to be considered.
- If you are applying for a specific position, describe how you learned of the job's availability.
- Briefly describe your qualifications.
- Refer to your résumé, enclosed with your letter.
- Mention your interest in scheduling an interview and where and when you may be reached (typically by telephone) to make arrangements.
- Thank the reader for considering your application.

SAMPLE COVER LETTER

212 Hart Road
Centralia, IA 52009
May 15, 1996

Mr. Lynn Brannon
Director
Agriculture Broadcasting Network
4656 Lane Avenue
Dubuque, IA 52001

Dear Mr. Brannon:

Recently I spoke with an officer of the Dubuque County Farm Bureau, Ced Clinton, who told me that you may be looking for a summer intern to work as an office assistant at ABN. I am very eager to get involved with an agriculture-related organization and would like to be considered for the position, if it becomes available.

I have been a member of Future Farmers of America at Centralia High School for the past two years and have just been elected president of the local chapter. This summer I will be attending a National FFA Leadership Conference in Washington, DC. My plans after graduation in 1996 are to attend a four-year college and eventually join an agricultural business or organization.

I also have a strong interest in journalism. As a junior, I edit news articles for the school paper, *The Bee,* and contribute a monthly column about farm subjects of interest to teenagers. As a writer and editor, I have strong word skills and am familiar with word processing software.

If you would be interested in talking to me about my background and qualifications, please call me at 555–6636 any weekday after 4 p.m. Thank you for your interest.

Sincerely,

Donna McCreary

Donna McCreary
Enclosure: résumé

The information in a résumé may be organized in many different ways. Before you select an arrangement and style, take a look at some sample résumés in books at the library. Your guidance counselor also may have samples that you can study. Choose a style that looks neat and businesslike. Most résumés list the applicant's **objective,** or career goal, **work experience, education, extracurricular activities, skills,** and **references.**

The information in your résumé should fit on a single page and be typed on high-quality paper. Printed copies should also be on high-quality paper, preferably of the same type that you used for your cover letter. Make sure the printed copies are clean and easy to read.

SAMPLE RÉSUMÉ

Donna McCreary
212 Hart Road
Centralia, IA 52009
(319) 555–6636

Objective:

To obtain an entry-level job related to agriculture.

Work Experience:

10/95–present   Check-out clerk, Quality Farm and Fleet, Dubuque, IA 52001

Handle customer purchases at check-out including returns and discounts. Named "Employee of the Month," March 1995

Summer 1995   Member, Junior Fair Board, Dubuque County Fair
Assist in planning and scheduling fair activities for youth, including livestock competitions, equine events, and 4-H displays

Education:

Centralia High School, Class of '97, College Preparatory program
Grade-point average: 3.4

Extracurricular Activities:
President, Future Farmers of America, Centralia Chapter
Secretary, Students Against Drunk Driving
Statistician for the varsity wrestling team

References:

Mr. Ced Clinton
President, Dubuque County Farm Bureau
3468 Amity Road, Dubuque, IA
(319) 555–9571

Ms. Debbie Armfeldt
Supervisor, Quality Farm and Fleet
460 Rockton Avenue, Dubuque, IA
(319) 555–8398

WRITING ON THE JOB

The ability to communicate clearly in writing is essential not just in the communications professions, such as journalism and publishing, but in almost every job. At work, you might use your writing skills to prepare instructions for others to use, evaluate a procedure, or summarize a conference with a coworker or client. If you know how to organize your thoughts and communicate them clearly on paper, you will have a big advantage in the workplace.

5.6 WRITING MEMORANDA

Employees within organizations frequently communicate using the interoffice **memorandum,** or **memo.** A memo may be sent to just one person, to a group of people, or to everyone working for an organization. The type of information communicated by memo varies. For example, a personnel officer might send a memo to all employees explaining a new benefit. A department manager might outline an assignment for someone in a memo. A secretary might send the boss a memo requesting a certain vacation time.

Memos are generally short, just a few sentences or paragraphs, but in some cases a longer memo is appropriate. A memo should be clear and to the point. It should also be free of errors, both factual and grammatical. Therefore, it's a good idea to review and proofread all memos before sending them.

In many organizations employees compose and type memos at computer workstations at their desks. Then, instead of distributing paper copies of the memo, they send the message over a computer network via electronic mail, or e-mail, to the desired recipients. In organizations that do not use computers extensively, employees may type their memos on standard forms. In the top area of a standard memo, after the letter "c:" (for "copies to") the sender usually lists the names of all recipients of the memo.

Memos range in tone from formal to informal. If you are conveying work-related information, the tone will be formal to semiformal. If the recipient knows you well or the purpose of the memo is social (such as announcing an office party), the tone will probably be more informal.

SAMPLE MEMO

MEMORANDUM

TO: Marketing Staff
FROM: Maria Kelly
DATE: June 30, 1995
SUBJECT: Tricia's going-away party
c: Ann Leonardo, president

As we all sadly know, Tricia Martin's last day will be Friday, July 3. However, we won't let her go without a proper send-off. At 4:00 on Friday, we will cut a cake and enjoy some punch in Tricia's honor and wish her well in her new job. The festivities will be in the large conference room on the second floor.

—Maria

5.7 TECHNICAL WRITING

Technical writing is writing that tells the reader how to use certain equipment or execute certain tasks. Companies that produce complex equipment, such as computers or machines used in medical analysis, hire technical writers to produce the documentation that accompanies these products. This documentation is essential for using the equipment successfully. Consumers, as well as specialists such as automotive mechanics, engineers, pilots, and lab workers, rely on technical materials for instruction and training.

Regardless of what job you may have in the future, knowing the basic principles of technical writing can help you in your work. For example, most employees are at some time asked to explain a procedure or complex process in writing so that others can learn it. Understanding the characteristics of good technical writing can help you prepare clear and useful instructions.

Guidelines for documenting technical procedures:

- First, make sure you are very familiar with the procedure you'll be documenting.
- Break the task into a series of short, simple steps.
- Warn the reader of any potentially hazardous steps or materials.
- List any tools or equipment needed to complete the process.
- List each step in the proper sequence.
- Use the second person imperative. Write "Press the enter key," not "The user should press the enter key."
- Keep your vocabulary simple, avoiding unexplained technical jargon.
- If appropriate, incorporate pictures and diagrams.
- Don't leave out any steps or include unnecessary steps.
- Proofread your instructions to make sure they are easy to follow and unambiguous.
- Ask someone who isn't familiar with the operation to follow the directions you have written. If necessary, adjust your instructions based on his or her experience.

Writing about a technical procedure is a good test of how well you understand what you are trying to explain. Indeed, after you have written about the process, you will probably understand it much better. The ultimate test of your documentation, however, is to give it to someone else and see if your instructions lead to successful results.

5.8 WRITING PROMOTIONAL AND PUBLIC RELATIONS COPY

Like technical writing, public relations (PR) writing is a profession unto itself. The job of PR writers is to promote a particular product, organization, or cause through the messages they compose. They must know how to seize readers' attention and persuade them to feel positive about the thing they are promoting. PR writers must have excellent writing skills, but they must also have an in-depth understanding of both the product and the audience they are trying to appeal to. This understanding allows them to predict how people will respond to their messages. By studying the basic principles of good promotional writing, you can make your own persuasive writing more effective.

Promotional writers produce many kinds of materials including ads for radio, television, and newspapers; news and feature articles; press releases; scripts for audiovisual presentations; direct-mail materials; speeches for political candidates; and copy for annual reports. They work for private companies as well as government and community organizations.

Research and planning are essential for good public relations writing. Although the purpose of promotional writing is to persuade, the content of the writing must reflect the actual merits of the product. Messages that distort the truth can backfire, creating negative rather than positive feelings in the audience. At the top of a press release, you list the date on which the information can be released to the public, the name and phone number of the person to contact with questions about the release, and the name of the city in which the announcement is being made. At the bottom of a press release, write the word *end* surrounded by dashes.

SAMPLE PRESS RELEASE

For immediate release
June 1, 1996

Contact:
Trish Howley
(614) 555-1032

Columbus:
The Thurber House summer picnic series, a regular program of outdoor readings by authors, begins June 19. This year's lineup includes five distinguished writers of poetry and fiction: Peter Meindl (June 19), Sue Miller (July 3), P. F. Kluge (July 17), Julia Kastner (July 31), and David Citino (August 14).

The Wednesday-evening readings are held on the west lawn of the Thurber House, 77 Jefferson Avenue (indoors in inclement weather), just off the Broad Street exit from Interstate 71. Admission is $3. Box picnic dinners, catered by Moveable Feast, may be reserved in advance for $7. Doors open at 6:30. Readings begin at 7:30.

The Thurber House is a boyhood home of writer and cartoonist James Thurber. As a nonprofit learning center, Thurber House sponsors public readings, writing workshops, and literary conferences, as well as the Thurber House writer-in-residence program.

—END—

Handbook of
Literary Terms

abridgment   An **abridgment** is a shortened version of a work. When doing an abridgment, an editor attempts to preserve the most significant elements of the original. See also *abstract, bowdlerize,* and *paraphrase.*

abstract   1. *n.* An **abstract,** *précis,* or **summary** is a brief account of the main ideas or arguments presented in a work. A well-made abstract presents those ideas or arguments in the same order as in the original. Writing an abstract is an excellent way to commit to memory the major ideas of a nonfiction work such as an essay or a chapter in a textbook. See *paraphrase.* 2. *adj.* An **abstract** word or phrase is one that refers to something that cannot be directly perceived by the senses. *Liberty, justice, hope, courage,* and *loyalty* are examples of abstract terms. The opposite of *abstract* in this sense is *concrete.* See *concrete.*

absurd   See *literature of the absurd.*

accent   See *stress.*

acronym   An **acronym** is a word created from the first, or initial, letters of a series of words. Examples of acronyms include *scuba,* from the words *self-contained underwater breathing apparatus,* and *SADD,* from the phrase *students against drunk driving.*

acrostic   An **acrostic** is a poem organized so that the first or last letters of each line form a word, a phrase, or a regular sequence of letters of the alphabet.

act   An **act** is a major division of a drama. The dramas of ancient Rome were generally divided into five acts, as were the plays of Shakespeare and other dramatists of the Elizabethan Age. In modern times, plays are most often divided into three acts, and short plays called "one-acts" are quite common. Tennessee Williams's "The Glass Menagerie" is a two-act play.

action   The **action** is the sequence of events that actually occur in a literary work, as opposed to those that occur off-scene or that precede or follow the events in the work itself. A common literary technique, inherited from the classical *epic,* is to begin a work *in medias res,* in the middle of the action, and to fill in the background details later through flashbacks. This technique is often used in modern fiction, as in Ambrose Bierce's "Occurrence at Owl Creek Bridge." See *flashback.*

actor   An **actor** is one who performs the role of a character in a play. The term is now used both for male and female performers.

adage   See *proverb.*

adaptation   An **adaptation** is a rewriting of a literary work in another form. A film adaptation of Edith Wharton's *The Age of Innocence,* directed by Martin Scorsese, appeared in 1993.

aesthetics   **Aesthetics** is the philosophical study of beauty. *Aesthetic principles* are guidelines established for the making and judging of works of art. From age to age, accepted aesthetic principles have differed, and these differences have dramatically influenced the nature of works of art produced in those ages.

The ancient Greek philosopher Aristotle propounded an aesthetic of *mimesis,* or *imitation,* believing that the proper function of art was to provide an accurate portrayal of life, an idea perhaps best expressed in Shakespeare's description of dramatic art as "a mirror held up to nature." In sharp contrast to such an aesthetic is the idea, derived from the Greek philosopher Plato, that the function of art is to rise above ordinary nature and to embody ideal, or *sublime,* forms of a kind not found in this material world of the ordinary and transient.

In England and the United States, the dominant aesthetics have been the Neoclassical, dating from the eighteenth century; the Romantic, dating from the nineteenth century; and the Realistic and Naturalistic, dating from the late nineteenth and early twentieth centuries.

The Neoclassical aesthetic, typified by the works of Phillis Wheatley and Benjamin Franklin, values order, rationality, and artifice. The Romantic aesthetic, typified by the works of Edgar Allan Poe, values wildness, emotion, imagination, and nature. The Realistic aesthetic, typified by the works of Edith Wharton, Ernest Hemingway, and John Steinbeck, harkens back to Aristotle and values imitation, but imitation of a modern kind—of the depths as well as the heights of human experience. The Naturalistic aesthetic, like the Realistic, views the purpose of art as the accurate imitation of life, but it also attempts to show how all things, including human actions, thoughts, and feelings, are caused, or determined, by circumstances. Superb Naturalist writers include Stephen Crane and Theodore Dreiser.

The critic I. A. Richards claimed that a radical shift away from an aesthetic based on beauty to one based on interest occurred in the twentieth century. While beauty, however defined, remains the guiding principle of artistic judgment in lowbrow circles—as for example, in popular judgments made about sentimental novels and verses—interest has emerged as the primary standard by which professional critics today judge works of art. See *Naturalism, Neoclassicism, Realism,* and *Romanticism.*

affective fallacy   The **affective fallacy** is the evaluation of works of art based not on their artistic merit but rather on their emotional effects on the reader, viewer, or listener. A person who holds a didactic or utilitarian view of the function of art would not consider this approach a fallacy. See *didacticism* and *Utilitarianism.*

afterword   An **afterword** is a statement made at the end of a work, often an analysis, a summary, or a celebration of the preceding work. See *epilogue.*

Age of Reason   See *Enlightenment* and *Neoclassicism.*

aim   A writer's **aim** is the primary purpose that his or her work is meant to achieve. One commonly used method of classifying writing by aim, proposed by James Kinneavey in *A Theory of Discourse,* describes four major aims: to express oneself (expressive writing), to persuade (persuasive writing), to inform (informative writing), and to create a work of literary art (literary writing).

alexandrine   An **alexandrine,** or **iambic hexameter,** is a verse with six iambic feet. See *meter.*

allegory   An **allegory** is a work in which each element *symbolizes,* or represents, something else. Spirituals such as "Go Down, Moses" are often allegorical. "Go Down, Moses" is on one level about the captivity of the Israelites in Egypt but on another level can be read as being about the captivity of African Americans during the era of slavery. The fiction of Nathaniel Hawthorne, in which characters, objects, and events often represent moral qualities or circumstances, is highly allegorical. In one sense, all literature can be viewed as allegorical in that individual characters, objects, places, and actions are types representing others of their kind. See *concrete universal* and *extended metaphor.*

alliteration   **Alliteration** is the repetition of initial consonant sounds. Some writers use the term as well to describe repeated initial vowel sounds. The following line from Henry Wadsworth Longfellow's "The Village Blacksmith" contains two examples of alliteration:

the repetition of the *h* sound in *He* and *hears* and the repetition of the *p* sound in *parson, pray,* and *preach:* "**H**e **h**ears the **p**arson **p**ray and **p**reach."

allusion An **allusion** is a rhetorical technique in which reference is made to a person, event, object, or work from history or literature. In *Walden,* Henry David Thoreau makes allusions to many sources, including the *New England Primer,* the Bible, and Virgil's *Aeneid.* The alphabet rhymes in the *New England Primer* make many allusions to the Bible.

ambiguity An **ambiguity** is a statement that has a double meaning or a meaning that cannot be clearly resolved. In English, the word *cleave* is oddly ambiguous, for it can mean either "to cling together" or "to cut apart." Many literary *figures of speech,* including *metaphors, similes, personifications,* and *symbols,* are examples of intentional ambiguity, speaking of one thing when another is intended. In Poe's "The Pit and the Pendulum," after several struggles and victories with his "shackles," the prisoner exclaims "Free!—and in the grasp of the Inquisition!" He has staved off immediate doom but is still held prisoner. Poe thus examines the ambiguity or shades of meaning of a state like freedom.

amplification See *elaboration.*

anagram An **anagram** is a word or a phrase created by rearranging the letters of another word or phrase.

analogy An **analogy** is a comparison of two things that are alike in some respects but different in others. In an analogy, the comparison is direct, not implied. A *simile* is a type of analogy. See *simile.*

analysis **Analysis** is a thinking strategy in which one divides a subject into parts and then examines the relationships among the parts and between individual parts and the whole. An analysis of a short story, for example, might consist of a division of the work into such parts as the exposition, the rising action, the climax, the resolution, and the dénouement, along with an examination of the role played by each of these parts in advancing the plot. An analysis of a line of poetry might consist of a careful

examination of its rhythm, its figures of speech, its images, and its meaning or meanings.

anapest An **anapest** is a poetic foot containing two weakly stressed syllables followed by one strongly stressed syllable, as in the word *wolverine.* A line of poetry made up of anapests is said to be *anapestic.*

anaphora An **anaphora,** as that term is used by linguists, is any word or phrase that repeats or refers to something that precedes or follows it. Consider, for example, the opening line of the Tewa "Song of Sky Loom":

O our Mother the Earth, O our Father
  the Sky,

In this line, *the Earth* and *the Sky* are both examples of anaphora because they refer back to, or rename, the Mother and Father. The simplest form of anaphora is repetition of a word or phrase, as in the repetition of the word *nevermore* in Poe's "The Raven."

anecdote An **anecdote** is a brief story, usually with a specific point or moral. See *exemplum.*

antagonist See *character.*

antihero An **antihero** is a central character who lacks all the qualities traditionally associated with heroes. An antihero may be lacking in beauty, courage, grace, intelligence, or moral scruples. Antiheroes are common figures in modern fiction and drama.

antithesis **Antithesis** is a rhetorical technique in which words, phrases, or ideas are strongly contrasted, often by means of a repetition of grammatical structure.

aphorism An **aphorism** is a short saying or pointed statement. Examples of aphorisms include "Little strokes fell great oaks" and "Don't count your chickens before they hatch," both from Franklin's *Poor Richard's Almanac.* An aphorism that gains currency and is passed from generation to generation is called a *proverb* or *adage.* See *proverb.*

apology An **apology** is a literary defense. Emily Dickinson's "This is my letter the World" can be read as an apology.

apostrophe An **apostrophe** is a rhetorical technique in which an object or person is directly addressed. In "Song of the Sky Loom," the earth and the sky are addressed in the opening line.

apposition   An **apposition** is a grammatical form in which a thing is renamed, in different words, in a word, phrase, or clause. The title of Frederick Douglass's autobiography contains an example: *Frederick Douglass, an American Slave.*

archaic language   **Archaic language** consists of old or obsolete words or phrases such as *smote* for *hit.*

archetype   An **archetype** is an inherited, often unconscious ancestral memory or motif that recurs throughout history and literature. The notion of the archetype derives from the psychology of Carl Jung, who wrote of archetypes as making up humanity's "collective unconscious." The term is often used, more generally, to refer to any element that recurs throughout the literature of the world. Thus the story of the journey, in which someone sets out on a path, experiences adventures, and emerges wiser, may be considered archetypal, for it is found in all cultures and in all times. See *motif.*

argument   1. An **argument** is a summary, in prose, of the plot or meaning of a poem or drama.   2. In nonfiction writing, an **argument** is the case for accepting or rejecting a proposition or course of action.

argumentation   **Argumentation,** one of the modes of writing, presents reasons or arguments for accepting a position or for adopting a course of action. See *mode.*

art for art's sake   **Art for art's sake** was the rallying cry of a group of nineteenth-century writers who believed that art should serve the ends of beauty and beauty alone, rather than some political, social, religious, or moral purpose. Champions of art for art's sake included Edgar Allan Poe and British writers Walter Pater, Oscar Wilde, and Andrew Lang.

article   An **article** is a brief work of nonfiction on a specific topic. The term *article* is typically used of encyclopedia entries and short nonfiction works that appear in newspapers and popular magazines. The term is sometimes used as a synonym of *essay,* though the latter term often connotes a more serious, important, or lasting work. See *essay.*

aside   An **aside** is a statement made by a character in a play, intended to be heard by the audience but not by other characters on the stage.

assonance   **Assonance** is the repetition of vowel sounds in stressed syllables that end with different consonant sounds. An example is the repetition of the short *i* sound in this line from Robert Frost's "Birches":

> I like to think some boy's been swinging them.

atmosphere   See *mood.*

autobiography   An **autobiography** is the story of a person's life, written by that person. *The Autobiography of Benjamin Franklin* is a famous American autobiography. *Narrative of the Life of Frederick Douglass* is another well-known autobiography. Some editors and critics distinguish between *autobiographies,* which focus on personal experiences, and *memoirs,* which focus on public events, though the terms are often used interchangeably.

background information   See *flashback, plot,* and *setting.*

ballad   A **ballad** is a simple narrative poem in four-line stanzas, usually meant to be sung and usually rhyming *abcb. Folk ballads,* composed orally and passed by word of mouth from generation to generation, have enjoyed enormous popularity throughout history, from the Middle Ages to the present. Examples of popular American ballads include "The Ballad of Casey Jones" and "Bonny Barbara Allan." *Literary ballads* are ones written in imitation of folk ballads. The folk ballad stanza usually alternates between lines of four and three feet. Common techniques used in ballads include repeated lines, or *refrains,* and *incremental repetition,* the repetition of lines with slight, often cumulative, changes throughout the poem. See *refrain.*

bibliography   A **bibliography** is a list of works on a given subject or of works consulted by an author. See *List of Works Cited.*

Bildungsroman   A *Bildungsroman* is a novel that tells the story of the growth or development of a person from youth to adulthood. A fine American example is Betty Smith's *A Tree Grows in Brooklyn.*

biographical criticism   See *criticism.*

biography   A **biography** is the story of a person's life, told by someone other than that person. Carl Sandburg wrote a famous six-volume biography of Abraham Lincoln.

blank verse   **Blank verse** is unrhymed poetry written in iambic pentameter. An *iambic pentameter* line consists of five *feet*, each containing two syllables, the first weakly stressed and the second strongly stressed.

blend   A **blend,** or **portmanteau,** is a word created by joining together two previously existing words, such as *walrus,* from *whale* and *horse,* or *pixel,* from *picture* and *element.*

bowdlerize   To **bowdlerize** a piece of writing is to censor it by deleting material considered offensive. The term comes from the name of Thomas Bowdler, who published a "bowdlerized" edition of Shakespeare's works in the nineteenth century.

bucolic   A **bucolic** is a fanciful pastoral poem. See *pastoral poem.*

cacophony   **Cacophony** is harsh or unpleasant sound. Writers sometimes intentionally use cacophony for effect, as Randall Jarrell does to describe an airplane dogfight: "I woke to blackflak and the nightmare fighters."

cæsura   A **cæsura** is a major pause in a line of poetry, as in the following line from T. S. Eliot's "The Love Song of J. Alfred Prufrock":

Let us go then, || you and I,

Calvinism   **Calvinism** is a Protestant theology, based on the teachings of John Calvin, that stresses original sin, the inability of people to exercise free will, the preordination of events by God, and the choice (or election) by God of those who will be saved (the elect) and those who will be condemned. Puritanism was a Calvinist movement. See *Puritanism.*

canon   A **canon** is a group of literary works considered to be authentic or worthy. The term was originally used for Biblical books believed to be divinely inspired. It was later adapted to describe works that can be definitely assigned to a given author (as in *the canonical works of Mark Twain).* The term is also used to describe those works in a given literary tradition considered to be classics and thus worthy of inclusion in textbooks, in anthologies, and on the reading lists of courses in schools and universities. In the eighteenth century, there was much debate in France and England concerning whether the canon should include primarily modern or ancient works. In the twentieth century, debates over the canon often centered on the extent to which it should include works by non-male, non-European writers. Feminist critics, in particular, noted the tendency of editors and anthologists to include in their collections works by writers and to exclude works by female writers. See *feminist criticism* under the entry for *criticism.*

canto   A **canto** is a section or part of a long poem. The word comes from the Latin *cantus,* meaning "song." Ezra Pound's masterwork was a collection of poems called *The Cantos.*

caricature   In literature, a **caricature** is a piece of writing that exaggerates certain qualities of a character in order to satirize or ridicule that character or type. Washington Irving's Ichabod Crane in "The Legend of Sleepy Hollow" is an example of a caricature. See *satire.*

carmen figuratum   See *concrete poem.*

carpe diem   *Carpe diem* is a Latin term meaning "seize the day." The *carpe diem* theme urges people not to waste time but rather to enjoy themselves while they have a chance.

catalog   A **catalog** is a list of people or things. Many examples of catalogs can be found in Walt Whitman's "Song of Myself."

catastrophe   The **catastrophe** is a conclusion of a play, particularly of a tragedy, marked by the fall of the central character. In the catastrophe, the central conflict of the play is ended, or resolved. See *plot.*

catharsis   The ancient Greek philosopher Aristotle described tragedy as bringing about a

catharsis, or purging, of the emotions of fear and pity. Debate has raged around the proper interpretation of Aristotle's statement. Some critics take it to mean, simply, that at the end of a tragedy, in the catastrophe or resolution, the emotional equilibrium of the characters is restored. Others take it to mean that viewing a tragedy causes the audience to feel emotions of fear and pity, which are then released at the end of the play, leaving the viewer calm, wiser, and perhaps more thoughtful. This idea of the purgative or cathartic effect of viewing enacted displays of strong emotion is contradicted by psychological studies that suggest that people tend to imitate enacted feelings and behaviors that they witness. Much of the current debate over violence on television and in films centers on this question of whether enacted violence has a cathartic or an arousing effect on the viewer.

censorship **Censorship** is the act of examining works to see if they meet predetermined standards of political, social, or moral acceptability. Official censorship is aimed at works that will undermine authority or morals and has often in the past resulted in the suppression of works considered dangerous or licentious. Famous American novels that have been frequent targets of censorship include *The Adventures of Huckleberry Finn,* by Mark Twain, and *Catcher in the Rye,* by J. D. Salinger.

central conflict A **central conflict** is the primary struggle dealt with in the plot of a story or drama. See *conflict* and *plot.*

character A **character** is a person (or sometimes an animal) who figures in the action of a literary work. A *protagonist,* or *main character,* is the central figure in a literary work. An *antagonist* is a character who is pitted against a protagonist. *Major characters* are ones who play significant roles in a work. *Minor characters* are ones who play lesser roles. A *one-dimensional character, flat character,* or *caricature* is one who exhibits a single dominant quality, or *character trait.* A *three-dimensional, full,* or *rounded character* is one who exhibits the complexity of traits associated with actual human beings. A *static character* is one who does not change during the course of the action. A *dynamic character* is one who does change. A *stock character* is one found again and again in different literary works. Examples of stock characters include the gunslinging outlaw of western fiction and the mad scientist of science fiction.

characterization **Characterization** is the use of literary techniques to create a character. Writers use three major techniques to create characters: direct description, portrayal of characters' behavior, and representations of characters' internal states. When using direct description, the writer, through a speaker, a narrator, or another character, simply comments on the character, telling the reader about such matters as the character's appearance, habits, dress, background, personality, motivations, and so on. When using portrayal of a character's behavior, the writer presents the actions and speech of the character, allowing the reader to draw his or her own conclusions from what the character says or does. When using representations of internal states, the writer reveals directly the character's private thoughts and emotions, often by means of an *internal monologue.* See *character* and *internal monologue.*

chiasmus A **chiasmus** is a rhetorical technique in which the order of occurrence of words or phrases is reversed, as in the line "We can weather changes, but we can't change the weather." Benjamin Franklin uses a chiasmus in "Remarks Concerning the Natives of North America" when he writes, "we should find no people so rude, as to be without any rules of politeness; nor any so polite, as not to have some remains of rudeness."

chronicle A **chronicle** is a record of historical events. *The General History of Virginia,* by John Smith, is a chronicle of the early years of the Virginia colony from 1607 through 1609.

chronological order **Chronological order** is the arrangement of details in order of their occurrence. It is the primary method of organization used in narrative writing. It is also common in nonfiction writing that describes processes, events, and cause-and-effect relationships.

classic A **classic** is a work of literature that is widely believed to be one of the greatest creations within a given literary tradition. (Mark Twain defined a classic as "something that everybody wants to have read and nobody wants to read.") The question of just what works may be considered classic, and thus the question of what constitutes the *canon,* is a much-debated one. See *canon.*

Classical Era   The **Classical Era** is the period in European history that saw the flowering of the ancient Greek and Roman cultures. *Classical literature* is the literature of ancient Greece and Rome from the time of Homer and Hesiod to the fall of the Roman Empire in AD 410.

Classicism   **Classicism** is a collection of ideas about literature and art derived from study of works by Greeks and Romans of the *Classical Era.* Definitions of what constitutes the Classical style differ, but most would agree that the Classical aesthetic emphasizes authority, austerity, clarity, conservatism, decorum, imitation, moderation, order, reason, restraint, self-control, simplicity, tradition, and unity. Classicism is most often contrasted with *Romanticism.* See *Classical Era* and *Neoclassicism.*

cliché   A **cliché** is a tired or hackneyed expression such as *old as the hills* or *slow as molasses.* Most clichés originate as vivid, colorful expressions but lose their interest because of overuse. Careful writers and speakers avoid clichés, which are dull and signify lack of originality.

climax   The **climax** is the point of highest interest and suspense in a literary work. The term also is sometimes used to describe the *turning point* of the action in a story or play, the point at which the rising action ends and the falling action begins. See *crisis* and *plot.*

closed couplet   A **closed couplet** is a pair of rhyming lines that present a complete statement. The alphabet rhymes in the *New England Primer* are written in closed couplets, for example:

My *Book* and *Heart*
Shall never part.

closet drama   A **closet drama** is one that is meant to be read rather than acted. Tennessee Williams wrote two versions of *The Glass Menagerie,* one of them a closet drama and the other an acting version of the play.

coherence   **Coherence** is the logical arrangement and progression of ideas in a speech or piece of writing. Writers achieve coherence by presenting their ideas in a logical sequence and by using transitions to show how their ideas are connected to one another. See *transition.*

coined words   **Coined words** are ones that are intentionally created, often from the raw materials provided by already existing words and word parts. Examples of recently coined words include *yuppie* and *e-mail.*

collage   In literature, a **collage** is a work that incorporates or brings together an odd assortment of materials, such as allusions, quotations, bits of song, dialogue, foreign words, mythical or folkloric elements, headlines, and pictures or other graphic materials. Collage is an interesting way to present a portrait of a particular time. The "Newsreels" in John Dos Passos's *U. S. A.* trilogy of novels are collages. The technique is also used in much modern poetry, including Ezra Pound's *The Cantos.*

colloquialism   **Colloquialism** is the use of informal language. Modern poetry often makes use of colloquialism, as in Robert Frost's "The Death of the Hired Man" and "Home Burial."

comedy   Originally a literary work with a happy ending, a **comedy** is any lighthearted or humorous work, especially one prepared for the stage or the screen. Comedy is often contrasted with tragedy, in which the hero meets an unhappy fate. (It is perhaps only a slight exaggeration to say that comedies end with wedding bells and tragedies with funeral bells.) Comedies typically present less-than-exalted characters who display all-too-human limitations, foibles, faults, and misunderstandings. The typical progression of the action in a comedy is from initial order to a humorous misunderstanding or confusion and back to order again. Stock elements of comedy include mistaken identities, word play, satire, and exaggerated characters and events. See *tragedy.*

comic relief   Writers sometimes insert into a serious work of fiction or drama a humorous scene that is said to provide **comic relief** because it relieves the seriousness or emotional intensity felt by the audience. Paradoxically, a scene introduced for comic relief can sometimes, because of the contrast it provides, increase the perceived intensity or seriousness of the action around it.

commonplace book A **commonplace book** is a collection of quotations gleaned from various sources.

comparative literature **Comparative literature** is the study of relationships among works of literature written at different times, in different places, or in different languages. A study that showed influences of English *Romanticism* on American *Transcendentalism* would be an example.

complication The **complication** is the part of a plot in which the conflict is developed or built to its high point of intensity. See *plot.*

conceit A **conceit** is an elaborate or extremely fanciful analogy or metaphor. Oliver Wendell Holmes's comparison in "The Chambered Nautilus" of the development of the soul to the building of a nautilus shell is an example of a conceit.

concrete A **concrete** word or phrase is one that names or describes something that can be directly perceived by one or more of the five senses. *Buffalo, geranium, storm,* and *heron* are examples of concrete terms. See *abstract* and *concrete universal.*

concrete poem A **concrete poem** is one printed or written in a shape that suggests its subject matter. A concrete poem is also known as a *shape poem* or *carmen figuratum.*

concrete universal A **concrete universal** is a particular object, person, action, or event that provides an instance or example of a general type. Thus in writing about one lonely, isolated man in "Mr. Flood's Party," Edwin Arlington Robinson in a sense writes about all such men. In our time, literary taste tends toward the particular and concrete. In the *minimalist style* championed by writers such as Ezra Pound, T. S. Eliot, and Hilda Doolittle, direct statement of abstract ideas and emotions is avoided. Instead, images are presented as concrete examples meant to arouse abstract ideas and emotions in readers. So, for example, instead of saying, abstractly, "My life has not amounted to much; I'm cultured but have not been creative," Eliot writes, "I have measured out my life with coffee spoons." See *abstract, concrete, Neoclassicism,* and *objective correlative.*

confessional poetry **Confessional poetry** is verse that describes, sometimes with painful explicitness, the private or personal experiences of the writer. Contemporary American confessional poets include Sylvia Plath, Anne Sexton, Robert Lowell, and Allen Ginsberg.

conflict A **conflict** is a struggle between two forces in a literary work. A *plot* involves the introduction, development, and eventual resolution of a conflict. One side of the *central conflict* in a story or drama is usually taken by the *main character.* That character may struggle against another character, against the forces of nature, against society or social norms, against fate, or against some element within himself or herself. A struggle that takes place between a character and some outside force is called an *external conflict.* A struggle that takes place within a character is called an *internal conflict.* Melville's Captain Ahab experiences an external conflict with the white whale Moby-Dick and an internal conflict against the limits placed on human power. See *central conflict* and *plot.*

connotation A **connotation** is an emotional association or implication attached to an expression. For example, the word *inexpensive* has positive emotional associations, whereas the word *cheap* has negative ones, even though the two words both *denote,* or refer to, low cost. Good writers choose their words carefully in order to express appropriate connotations. See *denotation.*

consonance **Consonance** is the repetition of a consonant sound preceded by a different vowel sound, as in the words *roads* and *wood* in Robert Frost's line "Two r<u>oad</u>s diverged in a yellow w<u>ood</u>."

convention A **convention,** in a literary work, is an unrealistic element that is accepted by readers or viewers because the element is traditional. One of the conventions of fiction, for example, is that it uses the past tense to describe current or present action. Rhyme schemes and organization into stanzas are among the many commonly employed conventions of poetry. Violation of accepted conventions is one of the hallmarks of *avant garde* or *Modernist* literature. See *dramatic convention*.

conventional symbol   See *symbol*.

couplet   A **couplet** is a pair of rhyming lines that expresses a complete thought. These lines from Phillis Wheatley's "To S. M., a Young African Painter, on Seeing His Works" are an example:

> Cease, gentle muse! the solemn gloom
>   of night
> Now seals the fair creation from my
>   sight.

A pair of rhyming iambic pentameter lines, like these, is also known as a *heroic couplet*.

crisis   In the plot of a story or a drama, the **crisis** is that point in the development of the conflict at which a decisive event occurs that causes the main character's situation to become better or worse. See *plot*.

critic   A literary **critic** is a person who evaluates or interprets a work of literature. See *criticism*.

critical essay   A **critical essay** is a type of informative or persuasive writing that presents an argument in support of a particular interpretation or evaluation of a work of literature. A well-constructed critical essay presents a clear *thesis*, or main idea, supported by ample evidence from the work or works being considered.

criticism   **Criticism** is the act of evaluating or interpreting a work of art or the act of developing general guidelines or principles for such evaluation or interpretation. Over the centuries, many schools, or philosophies, of criticism have been developed. However, most readers and teachers are eclectic critics, drawing consciously or unconsciously upon various schools of critical thought. Common schools of criticism include the following:

Biographical criticism attempts to account for elements of literary works by relating them to events in the lives of their authors. A reading of Anne Bradstreet's poem "To My Dear and Loving Husband" as a reflection on her real-life relationship with Simon Bradstreet would be an example of biographical criticism.

Deconstructionist criticism calls into question the idea that a literary work has a particular interpretation by inviting the reader to reverse the binary, or two-part, relations that structure meaning in the work. For example, a deconstructionist analysis of *The Glass Menagerie* might invite the reader to reconsider the play's opposition of the artistic temperament as embodied in the character Tom and the materialistic temperament as embodied in the character Jim, arguing that the artist produces illusions and believes them to be truths, a process leading inevitably to subjectivism and isolation, whereas the materialist successfully operates in the world, finding or creating purpose and connection. Such a reading deconstructs the conventional reading of the play, which insists that Williams intended a critique of materialistic values. See *structuralist criticism*.

Didactic criticism evaluates works of art in terms of the moral, ethical, or political messages that they convey. Dismissal of a book as dangerous or obscene would be an example of didactic criticism.

Feminist criticism evaluates and interprets works of art with regard to their portrayal of or influence upon gender roles. Many feminist critics and scholars have been particularly concerned to rescue women writers from obscurity. Other critics have been concerned with pointing out gender bias in literary works, with analyzing variations in literary depictions of males and females, and with understanding the effects of literary works, activities, and movements on cultural norms related to gender. An example of feminist criticism would be an analysis of the determination and self-reliance of women characters in literature of the American frontier.

Formal criticism analyzes a work of literature in terms of its genre or type. An explanation of those characteristics of "Swing Low, Sweet Chariot" that make it a spiritual would be an example of formal criticism.

Freudian criticism draws upon the works of the founder of psychoanalysis, Sigmund

Freud, and generally views literary works or the parts thereof as expressions of unconscious desires, as wish fulfillments, or as neurotic sublimations of unresolved conflicts from childhood. An example of Freudian criticism would be the interpretation of the ancient Greek Œdipus myth, in which Œdipus unwittingly marries his mother, as an expression of the young male child's competition with his father for his mother's affection.

Historical criticism views the work of art as a product of the period in which it was produced. An example of historical criticism would be an analysis of the Puritan influence on Nathaniel Hawthorne's "Rappaccini's Daughter."

Jungian criticism explores the presence in works of art of *archetypes*—unconscious images, symbols, associations, or concepts presumed to be a common inheritance of all human beings. An analysis of symbols of rebirth in a number of myths or folk tales would be an example of Jungian criticism.

Marxist criticism, based upon the work of the German-born political philosopher Karl Marx, evaluates and interprets works of art with regard to the material economic forces that shape them or with regard to their origins in or depictions of struggle between the social classes. An example of Marxist criticism would be an explanation of the emergence of Realism in the novels of early twentieth-century American writers such as Theodore Dreiser and Sinclair Lewis in terms of increased awareness of the disparity between the classes, poor labor conditions, and urban discontent.

Mimetic criticism, which derives from the teachings of Aristotle, views works of art as imitations of nature or of the real world and evaluates them according to the accuracy of those portrayals. Insisting that a character is poorly drawn because he or she is unrealistic is an example of mimetic criticism.

The *New Criticism* championed in the early to mid-twentieth century by such critics as I. A. Richards and Cleanth Brooks insisted upon the interpretation and evaluation of literary works based on details found in the works themselves rather than on information gathered from outside the works. It disregarded such matters as the life of the author, the period in which the work was written, the literary movement that led to its production, and the emotional effect of the work upon the reader. The New Critics insisted on the importance of close analysis of literary texts and the irreducibility of those texts to generalizations or paraphrases.

Pragmatic or *rhetorical criticism* interprets or evaluates a work of art in terms of its effects on an audience. An example of rhetorical criticism would be a reading of Poe's "The Raven" that describes the various techniques used in the poem to evoke feelings of mystery, sorrow, and horror.

Reader-response criticism views the meaning of a text as resulting from a relationship between the text itself and the subjective experiences or consciousness of a reader. According to reader-response theory, a literary text has no meaning *per se.* It is, instead, an occasion for a participatory experience that the reader has. That experience may be meaningful or significant to the reader, but the meaning and significance of the experience will depend, in part, on what the reader brings to the text.

Romantic or *expressivist criticism* views a work of art as primarily an expression of the spirit, ideas, beliefs, values, or emotions of its creator. A reading of *Invisible Man* as expressive of the beliefs and emotions of Ralph Ellison would be an example of expressivist criticism.

Structuralist criticism analyzes works of literature and art in terms of binary, or two-part, relationships or structures. A structuralist analysis of Williams's *The Glass Menagerie,* for example, might view the characters as caught between dreams and realities, a rural Southern past and an urban Northern present, and so on.

Textual criticism analyzes the various existing manuscript and printed versions of a work to construct an original or definitive text for use by readers.

dactyl A **dactyl** is a poetic foot made up of a strongly stressed syllable followed by two weakly stressed syllables, as in the word *feverish.* A line of poetry made up of dactyls is said to be *dactylic.*

dead metaphor A **dead metaphor** is one that is so familiar that its original metaphorical meaning is rarely thought of when the expression is used. An example would be the word *nightfall,* which describes the coming of darkness as a falling object.

deconstructionist criticism   See *criticism.*

definition   A **definition** is an explanation of the meaning of a word or phrase. A dictionary definition typically consists of two parts: the *genus,* or class to which the thing belongs, and the *differentia,* or differences between the thing and other things of its class. Consider, for example, Ambrose Bierce's tongue-in-cheek definition of *love:* "A temporary insanity, curable by marriage." In this definition, "insanity" is the genus. The rest of the definition presents the differentia.

denotation   The **denotation** is the basic meaning or reference of an expression, excluding its emotional associations, or *connotations.* For example, the words *dirt* and *soil* share a single common denotation. However, *dirt* has negative connotations of uncleanliness, whereas *soil* does not. See *connotation.*

dénouement   See *plot.*

description   A **description,** one of the modes of writing, portrays a character, an object, or a scene. Descriptions make use of *sensory details*—words and phrases that describe how things look, sound, smell, taste, or feel. See *mode.*

dialect   A **dialect** is a version of a language spoken by the people of a particular place, time, or social group. Writers often use dialect, as in Mark Twain's "The Notorious Jumping Frog of Calaveras County," to give their works a realistic flavor. A *regional dialect* is one spoken in a particular place. A *social dialect* is one spoken by members of a particular social group or class.

dialogue   1. **Dialogue** is conversation involving two or more people or characters. Plays are made up of dialogue and stage directions. Fictional works are made up of dialogue, narration, and description. 2. **Dialogue** is also used to describe a type of literary composition in which characters debate or discuss an idea. Many of Plato's philosophical works were presented in the form of dialogues.

diary   A **diary** is a day-to-day record of a person's activities, experiences, thoughts, and feelings. Both Ralph Waldo Emerson and Henry David Thoreau kept diaries in which they experimented with thoughts and feelings they later reworked into speeches and essays.

diction   **Diction,** when applied to writing, refers to word choice. Much of a writer's *style* is determined by his or her diction, the types of words that he or she chooses. Diction can be formal or informal, simple or complex, contemporary or archaic, ordinary or unusual, foreign or native, standard or dialectical, euphemistic or blunt. See *style.*

didactic criticism   See *criticism.*

didactic poem   A **didactic poem** is a verse that has a primary purpose of teaching one or more lessons. James Russell Lowell's "Stanzas on Freedom" is an example. See *didacticism.*

didacticism   **Didacticism** is the use of works of art to convey moral, social, educational, or political messages. A didactic work is one in which the artistic values of the work are subordinated to the message or meaning. Henry Wadsworth Longfellow's "A Psalm of Life" is an example of a didactic poem.

dimeter   See *meter.*

dominant impression   See *effect.*

drama   A **drama** is a story told through characters played by actors. The script of a drama typically consists of characters' names, *dialogue* spoken by the characters, and *stage directions.* Because it is meant to be performed before an audience, drama can be distinguished from other forms of non-performance-based literary works by the central role played in it by the *spectacle*—the sensory presentation to the audience, which includes such elements as lighting, costumes, make-up, properties, set pieces, music, sound effects, and the movements and expressions of actors. Another important distinguishing feature of drama is that it is *collaborative.* The interpretation of the work depends not only upon the author and his or her audience but also upon the director, the actors, and others involved in mounting a production. Two major types of drama are *comedy* and *tragedy.* See *comedy, dialogue, spectacle, stage directions,* and *tragedy.*

dramatic convention   A **dramatic convention** is an unreal element in a drama that is accepted as realistic by the audience because it is traditional. Such conventions include the impersonation of characters by actors, the use of a curtain to open or close an act or a scene, the revelation of a character's thoughts through *asides* and *soliloquies,* and the removal of the so-called *fourth wall* at the front of the stage that allows the audience to see action taking place in an imagined interior. See *convention* and *suspension of disbelief.*

dramatic irony   See *irony.*

dramatic monologue   A **dramatic monologue** is a poem that presents the speech of a single character in a dramatic situation. The speech is one side of an imagined conversation. The British poet Robert Browning is often credited with the creation of the dramatic monologue. A modern example of a dramatic monologue is Edwin Arlington Robinson's "Mr. Flood's Party." See *soliloquy.*

dramatic poem   A **dramatic poem** is a verse that relies heavily on dramatic elements such as monologue or dialogue. Types of dramatic poetry include the *dramatic monologue* and the *soliloquy.*

dramatis personæ   *Dramatis personæ* are the characters in a literary work. The term is most often used for the characters in a drama.

dream record   A **dream record** is a *diary* or *journal* in which a writer records his or her dreams. See *diary* and *journal.*

dynamic character   See *character.*

dystopia   A **dystopia** is an imaginary horrible world, the opposite of a *utopia.* Dystopias are common in science fiction. Famous examples of dystopias include the societies described in Aldous Huxley's *Brave New World,* H. G. Wells's *The Time Machine,* George Orwell's *1984,* and Ray Bradbury's *Fahrenheit 451.* See *utopia.*

eclogue   An **eclogue** is a pastoral poem written in imitation of Greek works by Theocritus and Virgil. See *pastoral poem.*

editorial   An **editorial** is a short persuasive piece that appears in a newspaper, magazine, or other periodical.

effect   The **effect** of a literary work is the general impression or emotional impact that it achieves. Some writers and critics, notably Edgar Allan Poe, have insisted that a successful short story or poem is one in which each detail contributes to the overall effect, or *dominant impression,* produced by the piece.

elaboration   **Elaboration,** or **amplification,** is a writing technique in which a subject is introduced and then expanded upon by means of repetition with slight changes, the addition of details, or similar devices.

elegiac lyric   An **elegiac lyric** is a poem that expresses a speaker's feelings of loss. Emily Dickinson's "After great pain, a formal feeling comes—" and Edgar Allan Poe's "Annabel Lee" are examples.

elegy   An **elegy** is a long formal poem about death or loss. Walt Whitman's "When Lilacs Last in the Dooryard Bloom'd" and John Crowe Ransom's "Bells for John Whiteside's Daughter" are examples.

Elizabethan sonnet   See *sonnet.*

emphasis   **Emphasis** is importance placed on an element in a literary work. Writers achieve emphasis by various means, including repetition, elaboration, stress, restatement in other words, and placement in a strategic position at the beginning or end of a line or a sentence.

end rhyme   **End rhyme** is rhyme that occurs at the ends of lines of verse. See *rhyme.*

end-stopped line   An **end-stopped line** is a line of verse in which both the sense and the grammar are complete at the end of the line. The opposite of an end-stopped line is a *run-on line.* The following lines are end-stopped:

> Make me, O Lord, Thy Spinning Wheel
>   complete.
> Thy Holy Word my Distaff make for me.
>   —Edward Taylor, "Huswifery"

Excessive use of end-stopped lines gives verse an unnatural, halting quality. See *run-on line.*

English sonnet   See *sonnet.*

enjambment   See *run-on line.*

Enlightenment   The **Enlightenment** was an eighteenth-century philosophical movement characterized by belief in reason, the scientific method, and the perfectibility of people and society. Thinkers of the Enlightenment Era, or Age of Reason, believed that the universe was governed by discoverable, rational principles like the laws of physics discovered by Sir Isaac Newton. By extension, they believed that people could, through application of reason, discover truths relating to the conduct of life or of society. Leading thinkers of the Enlightenment included Diderot, Franklin, Gibbon, Hume, Jefferson, Kant, Montesquieu, Pope, Swift, and Voltaire. See *Neoclassicism.*

epic   An **epic** is a long story, often told in verse, involving heroes and gods. Grand in length and scope, an epic provides a portrait of an entire culture, of the legends, beliefs, values, laws, arts, and ways of life of a people. Famous epic poems include Homer's *Iliad* and *Odyssey,* Virgil's *Aeneid,* Dante's *The Divine Comedy,* the anonymous Old English *Beowulf,* and Milton's *Paradise Lost.*

epigram   An **epigram** is a short, often witty, saying. An example of an epigram is Benjamin Franklin's "Three may keep a secret, if two of them are dead."

epigraph   An **epigraph** is a quotation or motto used at the beginning of the whole or part of a literary work to help establish the work's theme. T. S. Eliot uses an epigraph from Dante's *Inferno* at the beginning of "The Love Song of J. Alfred Prufrock."

epilogue   An **epilogue** is a concluding section or statement, often one that comments on or draws conclusions from the work as a whole.

epiphany   When applied to literature, the term *epiphany* refers to a moment of sudden insight in which the essence, or nature, of a person, thing, or situation is revealed. The use of the term in this sense was introduced by James Joyce.

episode   An **episode** is a complete action within a literary work.

episodic structure   **Episodic structure** is the stringing together of loosely related incidents, or episodes. Mark Twain's *The Adventures of Huckleberry Finn* has an episodic structure.

epistle   An **epistle** is a letter, especially one that is highly formal. Letters in verse are sometimes called epistles.

epistolary fiction   **Epistolary fiction** is imaginative prose that tells a story through letters, or epistles. Samuel Richardson pioneered this form in his novels *Pamela* and *Clarissa,* written in the mid-1700s. Despite a slight decline in popularity, epistolary fiction is still written today. Richard Brautigan's *Trout Fishing in America* is a contemporary example of epistolary fiction.

epitaph   An **epitaph** is an inscription or verse written to be used on a tomb or written in commemoration of someone who has died. The epitaph on the grave of Benjamin Franklin, written by Franklin himself, reads as follows:

> The body of
> Benjamin Franklin, printer,
> (Like the cover of an old book,
> Its contents worn out,
> And stript of its lettering and gilding)
> Lies here, food for worms!
> Yet the work itself shall not be lost,
> For it will, as he believed, appear once more
> In a new
> And more beautiful edition,
> Corrected and amended
> By its Author!

epithet   An **epithet** is a word or phrase used to describe a characteristic of a person, place, or thing. Eliot's description of sea-girls as "wreathed with seaweed red and brown" is an example.

eponym   An **eponym** is a person or character from whose name a word or title is derived, or a name that has become synonymous with some general characteristic or idea. Julius Cæsar is the eponym of the medical term *Cesarean section.* England's Queen Victoria is the eponym of Victoria Falls. A reference to *Helen of Troy,* used in place of the more general term *beauty,* or a reference to *an Einstein,* in place of a more general term such as *a smart person,* would be an eponym.

essay An **essay** is a brief work of prose non-fiction. The original meaning of essay was "a trial or attempt," and the word retains some of this original force. An essay need not be a complete or exhaustive treatment of a subject but rather a tentative exploration of it. A good essay develops a single idea and is characterized by *unity* and *coherence*. See *coherence* and *unity.*

euphemism A **euphemism** is an indirect word or phrase used in place of a direct statement that might be considered too offensive. The phrase *the dearly departed,* used instead of *the dead person,* is a euphemism.

euphony **Euphony** is pleasing sound. Writers achieve euphony by various means, including repetitions of vowel and consonant sounds, rhyme, and parallelism. See *cacophony.*

Existentialism **Existentialism** is a twentieth-century philosophical school that postulates the essential absurdity and meaninglessness of life. Existentialist philosophers such as Albert Camus and Jean-Paul Sartre argued that existence, or being, emerges out of nothingness without any essential, or defining, nature. A human being simply finds himself or herself alive and aware without having any essential defining direction. Any choices that a person makes in order to define himself or herself are made freely and therefore absurdly—one may as well make one choice as another. Freedom of the will is therefore seen by the Existentialist as a terrific burden, one causing anguish to the thinking person, who longs for meaningfulness, not absurd choices. Another significant aspect of Existentialism is its insistence on the essential isolation of each individual consciousness and the consequent anguish of people looking for meaningful connection to others. Though many of the essential tenets of Existentialism have been discredited by contemporary philosophers, the school nonetheless exerted tremendous influence on mid-twentieth-century literature in Europe, Great Britain, and the United States. See *literature of the absurd* and *theater of the absurd.*

exposition **1. Exposition**, one of the modes of writing, presents factual information. See *mode.* **2.** In a plot, the **exposition** is that part of a narrative that provides background information, often about the characters, setting, or conflict. See *plot.*

Expressionism **Expressionism** is the name given to a twentieth-century movement in literature and art that reacted against Realism in favor of an exaggeration of the elements of the artistic medium itself in an attempt to express ideas or feelings. Tennessee Williams's *The Glass Menagerie,* with its unrealistic setting and its generous use of symbolism, is an example of Expressionism.

extended metaphor An **extended metaphor** is a point-by-point presentation of one thing as though it were another. The description is meant as an implied comparison, inviting the reader to associate the thing being described with something that is quite different from it. Dickinson's "Because I could not stop for Death—" is an extended metaphor, where Death is characterized as a carriage driver and the speaker of the poem as his passenger.

external conflict See *conflict.*

eye rhyme See *sight rhyme.*

fable A **fable** is a brief story with animal characters told to express a moral. Famous fables include those of Æsop and La Fontaine.

fairy tale A **fairy tale** is a story that deals with mischievous spirits and other supernatural occurrences, often in medieval settings. The name is generally applied to stories of the kinds collected by Charles Perrault in France and the Brothers Grimm in Germany or told by Hans Christian Andersen of Denmark. "Cinderella" and "The Little Mermaid" are famous examples.

falling action See *plot.*

fantasy A **fantasy** is a literary work that contains highly unrealistic elements. Stephen Vincent Benét's "The Devil and Daniel Webster" is a fantasy. Fantasy is often contrasted with *science fiction*, in which the unreal elements are given a scientific or pseudoscientific basis. See *science fiction.*

farce A **farce** is a type of comedy that depends heavily on so-called low humor and on improbable, exaggerated, extreme situations or characters.

feminist criticism   See *criticism.*

fiction   Fiction is prose writing about imagined events or characters. The primary forms of fiction are the *novel* and the *short story.*

figurative language   Figurative language is language that suggests something more than the literal meanings of the words might be taken to suggest. See *figures of speech.*

figures of speech   Figures of speech, or **tropes,** are expressions that have more than a literal meaning. Hyperbole, metaphor, metonymy, personification, simile, synaesthesia, synecdoche, and understatement are all figures of speech. See *hyperbole, metaphor, metonymy, personification, simile, synaesthesia, synecdoche,* and *understatement.*

first-person point of view   See *point of view.*

flashback   A **flashback** is a section of a literary work that presents an event or series of events that occurred earlier than the current time in the work. Writers use flashbacks for many purposes, but most notably to provide *background information,* or exposition. In popular melodramatic works, including modern romance fiction and detective stories, flashbacks are often used to end suspense by revealing key elements of the plot such as a character's true identity or the actual perpetrator of a crime. One common technique is to begin a work with a final event and then to tell the rest of the story as a flashback that explains how that event came about. Another common technique is to begin a story *in medias res* (in the middle of the action) and then to use a flashback to fill in the events that occurred before the opening of the story.

flash fiction   See *short short.*

flat character   See *character.*

foil   A **foil** is a character whose attributes, or characteristics, contrast with and therefore throw into relief the attributes of another character. In "The Legend of Sleepy Hollow," Brom Bones, "a burley, roaring, roystering blade," provides a foil for Ichabod Crane, who is char-acterized as a coward and described as "tall, but exceedingly lank."

folk ballad   See *ballad.*

folk song   A **folk song** is an anonymous song that is transmitted orally. Examples include the ballad "Bonny Barbara Allan," the sea chantey "Blow the Man Down," the children's song "Row, Row, Row Your Boat," the spiritual "Go Down, Moses," the railroad song "Casey Jones," and the cowboy song "The Streets of Laredo." The term *folk song* is sometimes used for works composed in imitation of true folk songs. Contemporary composers of songs in the folk tradition include Bob Dylan, Paul Simon, Joan Baez, and the Indigo Girls. See *ballad.*

folk tale   A **folk tale** is a brief story passed by word of mouth from generation to generation. Writers often make use of materials from folk tales, such as the little people who appear in Washington Irving's "The Legend of Rip Van Winkle." Famous collections of folk tales include the German *Märchen,* or fairy tales, collected by the Brothers Grimm; Yeats's collection of Irish stories, *Mythologies;* and Zora Neale Hurston's collection of African-American folk tales and other folklore materials, *Their Eyes Were Watching God.* See *fairy tale, folklore,* and *oral tradition.*

folklore   Folklore is a body of orally transmitted beliefs, customs, rituals, traditions, songs, verses, or stories. Folk tales, fables, fairy tales, tall tales, nursery rhymes, proverbs, legends, myths, parables, riddles, charms, spells, and ballads are all common kinds of folklore, though each of these can be found, as well, in literary forms made in imitation of works from the *oral tradition.*

foot   In a poem, a **foot** is a unit of rhythm consisting of strongly and weakly stressed syllables. See *meter* and *scansion.* Also see the specific types of feet: *anapest, dactyl, iamb, spondee,* and *trochee.*

foreshadowing   Foreshadowing is the act of presenting materials that hint at events to occur later in a story. In "Rappaccini's Daughter," when Guasconti first sees the figure of Rappaccini, the latter man's "demeanor was that of one walking among malignant influences, . . . which . . . would wreak upon him some terrible fatality." The events of the tale lead inexorably to the grim conclusion foreshadowed in that line.

foreword   See *preface.*

formal criticism   See *criticism.*

fourteener   See *meter.*

fourth wall   See *dramatic convention.*

frame tale   A **frame tale** is a story that itself provides a vehicle for the telling of other stories. The *Thousand and One Nights,* Boccaccio's *Decameron,* Chaucer's *The Canterbury Tales,* and Sherwood Anderson's *Winesburg, Ohio,* are frame tales.

free verse   **Free verse,** or *vers libre,* is poetry that avoids use of regular rhyme, rhythm, meter, or division into stanzas. Denise Levertov's "The Secret" and James Dickey's "For the Last Wolverine" are examples, though both poems make use of numerous regularities of rhythm. Much of the English and American poetry written in the twentieth century is in free verse.

Freudian criticism   See *criticism.*

full character   See *character.*

genre   A **genre** (zhän´rə) is one of the types or categories into which literary works are divided. Some terms used to name literary genres include *autobiography, biography, comedy, drama, epic, essay, lyric, narrative, novel, pastoral, poetry, short story,* and *tragedy.* Literary works are sometimes classified into genres based on subject matter. Such a classification might describe *detective stories, mysteries, adventure stories, romances, westerns,* and *science fiction* as different genres of fiction.

Gothic novel   A **Gothic novel,** or **Gothic romance,** is a long story containing elements of horror, suspense, mystery, and magic. Gothic novels often contain dark, brooding descriptions of settings and characters. Mary Shelley's *Frankenstein* and Daphne du Maurier's *Rebecca* are examples of the form. Gothic elements can also be found in the short stories of Nathaniel

Hawthorne and Edgar Allan Poe. See *Southern Gothic.*

Gothic romance   See *Gothic novel.*

haiku   A **haiku** is a traditional Japanese three-line poem containing five syllables in the first line, seven in the second, and five again in the third. A haiku presents a picture, or image, in order to arouse in the reader a specific emotional and/or spiritual state.

half rhyme   See *slant rhyme.*

heptameter   See *meter.*

Harlem Renaissance   The Harlem Renaissance was a period of intense creative activity among African-American writers and other artists living in Harlem in New York City during the 1920s. Major writers of the Harlem Renaissance included Arna Bontemps, Countee Cullen, Langston Hughes, Claude McKay, and Jean Toomer.

heroic couplet   See *couplet.*

heroic epic   A **heroic epic** is an epic that has a main purpose of telling the life story of a great hero. Examples of the heroic epic include Homer's *Iliad* and *Odyssey,* Virgil's *Aeneid,* and the Old English poem *Beowulf.* See *epic.*

hexameter   See *meter.*

high style   See *style.*

historical criticism   See *criticism.*

hymn   A **hymn** is a song or verse of praise, often religious. "Just a Closer Walk with Thee," by Red Foley, is a contemporary hymn.

hyperbole   A **hyperbole** (hī pʉr´bə lē) is an exaggeration made for rhetorical effect. Anne Bradstreet uses hyperbole when she writes,

> My love is such that rivers cannot quench,
> Nor ought but love from thee, give recompense.

iamb   An **iamb** is a poetic foot containing one weakly stressed syllable followed by one strongly stressed syllable, as in the words *afraid* and *release.* A line of poetry made up of iambs is said to be *iambic.*

iambic   See *iamb.*

image   An **image** is a word or phrase that names something that can be seen, heard, touched, tasted, or smelled. The images in a literary work are referred to, collectively, as the work's *imagery.*

imagery   See *image.*

Imagism   **Imagism** was a twentieth-century literary movement that championed short verse free of anything except images. Important Imagist writers included Amy Lowell, Ezra Pound, H. D. and William Carlos Williams.

inciting incident   See *plot.*

incremental repetition   See *ballad.*

in medias res   See *action* and *flashback.*

internal conflict   See *conflict.*

internal monologue   An **internal monologue** presents the private sensations, thoughts, and emotions of a character. The reader is allowed to step inside the character's mind and overhear what is going on there. Which characters' internal states can be revealed in a work of fiction depends on the *point of view* from which the work is told. See *point of view.*

introduction   See *preface.*

inversion   An **inversion** is a poetic technique in which the normal order of words in an utterance is altered. Robert Frost's "Whose woods these are, I think I know" is an inversion of the usual order of expression: "I think I know whose woods these are."

irony   **Irony** is a difference between appearance and reality. Types of irony include the following: *dramatic irony,* in which something is known by the reader or audience but unknown to the characters; *verbal irony,* in which a statement is made that implies its opposite; and *irony of situation,* in which an event occurs that violates the expectations of the characters, the reader, or the audience.

irony of situation   See *irony.*

journal   A **journal**, like a *diary,* is a day-to-day record of a person's activities, experiences, thoughts, and feelings. In contrast to *diary,* the word *journal* connotes an outward rather than an inward focus. However, the two terms are often used interchangeably. See *diary.*

limited point of view   See *narrator* and *point of view.*

List of Works Cited   A **List of Works Cited** is a type of bibliography that lists works used or referred to by an author. A standard feature of a research paper, the List of Works Cited appears at the end of the paper and is arranged in alphabetical order.

literature of the absurd   **Literature of the absurd** is literature influenced by Existentialist philosophy, which represents human life as meaningless or absurd because of the supposed lack of essential connection between human beings and the world around them. In brief, the existentialist philosophers, such as Albert Camus and Jean-Paul Sarte, believed that a person's conscious existence precedes, or comes before, any essential self-definition and that self-definition can occur only as a result of making an absurd, completely free choice to act, think, or believe in certain ways. The literature of the absurd emphasizes the meaninglessness of life and the isolation, or alienation, of individuals. Much of the literature of the absurd is filled with horrors, anguish, random events, and illogical or improbable occurrences. Modern practitioners of the literature of the absurd include the novelists Franz Kafka, Thomas Pynchon, and Kurt Vonnegut, Jr., and the playwrights Eugène Ionesco, Samuel Beckett, Edward Albee, and Harold Pinter. See *Existentialism* and *theater of the absurd.*

lyric poem   A **lyric poem** is a highly musical verse that expresses the emotions of a speaker. Edna St. Vincent Millay's "Sonnet XXX" and Ralph Waldo Emerson's "Brahma" are examples. Lyric poems are often contrasted with narrative poems, which have telling a story as their main purpose.

Magical Realism   **Magical Realism** is a kind of fiction that is for the most part realistic but that contains elements of fantasy. Bernard Malamud's "The Magic Barrel" is an example of Magical Realism.

main character   See *character.*

major character   See *character.*

Marxist criticism   See *criticism.*

metaphor   A **metaphor** is a figure of speech in which one thing is spoken or written about as if it were another. This figure of speech invites the reader to make a comparison between the two things. The two "things" involved are the writer's actual subject, the *tenor* of the metaphor, and another thing to which the subject is likened, the *vehicle* of the metaphor. When, in "'Hope' is the thing with feathers," Emily Dickinson writes that "'Hope' is the thing with feathers—/that perches in the soul—," she is using a metaphor.

Personifications and similes are types of metaphor. See *dead metaphor, mixed metaphor, personification,* and *simile.*

meter   The **meter** of a poem is its rhythmical pattern. English verse is generally described as being made up of rhythmical units called *feet,* as follows:

TYPE OF FOOT	STRESS PATTERN	EXAMPLE
iambic	⌣ /	insist
trochaic	/ ⌣	freedom
anapestic	⌣ ⌣ /	unimpressed
dactylic	/ ⌣ ⌣	feverish
spondaic	/ /	baseball

Some scholars also use the term *pyrrhic* to describe a foot with two weak stresses. Using this term, the word *unbelievable* might be described as consisting of two feet, an anapest followed by a pyrrhic:

⌣ ⌣ / | ⌣ ⌣
un be liev | a ble

Terms used to describe the number of feet in a line include the following:

monometer for a one-foot line

dimeter for a two-foot line

trimeter for a three-foot line

tetrameter for a four-foot line

pentameter for a five-foot line

hexameter, or *Alexandrine,* for a six-foot line

heptameter for a seven-foot line

octameter for an eight-foot line

A seven-foot line of iambic feet is called a *fourteener.*

A complete description of the meter of a line includes both the term for the type of foot that predominates in the line and the term for the number of feet in the line. The most common English meters are iambic tetrameter and iambic pentameter. The following are examples of each:

IAMBIC TETRAMETER:

⌣ /   ⌣   /   ⌣ /   ⌣ /
I would | your bloom | of youth | re pair

IAMBIC PENTAMETER:

⌣ /   ⌣ /   ⌣ /   ⌣ /
Now seals | the fair | cre a | tion from |

⌣ /
my sight.

metonymy   **Metonymy** is the naming of an object associated with a thing in place of the name of the thing itself. Speaking of *the White House* when one means *the administrative or executive branch of the United States government* is an example of metonymy.

middle style   See *style.*

mimetic criticism   See *criticism.*

minor character   See *character.*

mixed metaphor   A **mixed metaphor** is an expression or passage that conflates, or garbles together, two or more metaphors. An example of mixed metaphor would be the sentence "The chariot of the sun screamed across the sky," in which the sun is described, inconsistently, as both a chariot and as something that screams. See *metaphor.*

mode   A **mode** is a form of writing. One common classification system, based on content, divides types of writing into four modes: argumentation, description, exposition, and narration. See *argumentation, description, exposition,* and *narration.*

Modernism   **Modernism** was an artistic and literary movement of the early twentieth century that championed experimentation, technicality, primitivism, impersonalism, aestheticism, and intellectualism. Important Modernists included the poets Ezra Pound and T. S. Eliot, the painters

Pablo Picasso and Paul Klee, and the musicians Arnold Schönberg and Anton Webern.

monometer See *meter*.

mood **Mood,** or **atmosphere,** is the emotion created in the reader by part or all of a literary work. A writer creates a mood through judicious use of concrete details.

motif A **motif** is any element that recurs in one or more works of literature or art. Examples of common folk tale motifs found in oral traditions throughout the world include grateful animals or the grateful dead, three wishes, the trial or quest, and the magical metamorphosis, or transformation of one thing into another. Much can be revealed about a literary work by studying the motifs within it. In "Rappaccini's Daughter," Nathaniel Hawthorne uses the recurring motifs of deadliness and of beauty, both natural and unnatural, to explore Giovanni's attraction to Beatrice.

motivation A **motivation** is a force that moves a character to think, feel, or behave in a certain way. In Ambrose Bierce's "An Occurrence at Owl Creek Bridge," the main character is motivated by a desire to save his own life by escaping from his captors.

Muse In ancient Greek and Roman myth, the **Muses**—the nine daughters of Zeus and Mnemosyne, or Memory—were believed to provide the inspiration for the arts and sciences. Calliope was the Muse of epic poetry; Clio, the Muse of history; Erato, the Muse of lyrical poetry; Euterpe, the Muse of music; Melpomene, the Muse of tragedy; Polyhymnia, the Muse of sacred choral poetry; Terpischore, the Muse of choral dance and song; Thalia, the Muse of comedy; and Urania, the Muse of astronomy. The idea of the Muse has often been used by later writers to explain the vagaries and mysteries of literary inspiration. For example, Phillis Wheatley writes, "And may the muse inspire each future song!" in "To S. M., a Young African Painter, on Seeing His Works." The connection of the Muses with entertainments and the arts survives in our words *amusing* and *amusement*.

myth A **myth** is a story that explains objects or events in the natural world as resulting from the action of some supernatural force or entity, most often a god. Every early culture around the globe has produced its own myths. An example of a myth is the explanation of the sky as a piece of weaving in "Song of the Sky Loom."

narration **Narration,** one of the modes of writing, tells a story. The story is made up of occurrences, or events. See *mode*.

narrative poem A **narrative poem** is a verse that tells a story. Edwin Arlington Robinson's "Mr. Flood's Party" and Robert Frost's "Home Burial" are examples of narrative poems. See *ballad* and *epic*.

narrator A **narrator** is one who tells a story. In a drama, the narrator may be a character who introduces, concludes, or comments upon the action of the play. However, dramas typically do not have narrators. Works of fiction, on the other hand, always do, unless they consist entirely of dialogue without *tag lines,* in which case they become no longer fictions but *closet dramas,* ones meant to be read but not performed. The narrator in a work of fiction may be a central or minor character or simply someone who witnessed or heard about the events being related. Writers achieve a wide variety of ends by varying the characteristics of the narrator chosen for a particular work. Of primary importance is the choice of the narrator's *point of view.* Will the narrator be *omniscient,* knowing all things, including the internal workings of the minds of the characters in the story, or will the narrator be *limited* in his or her knowledge? Will the narrator participate in the action of the story or stand outside that action and comment on it? Will the narrator be reliable or unreliable? That is, will the reader be able to trust the narrator's statements? These are all questions that a writer must answer when developing a narrator. See *point of view* and *speaker*.

Naturalism **Naturalism** was a literary movement of the late nineteenth and early twentieth centuries that saw actions and events as resulting inevitably from biological or natural forces or from forces in the environment. Often these forces were beyond the comprehension or control of the characters subjected to them. Taken to its extreme, Naturalism views all events as mechanically determined by external forces, including the decisions made by people. Much of modern fiction, with its emphasis on social conditions leading to particular consequences for characters, is naturalistic in this sense. Great writers of fiction informed by the philosophy of Naturalism include Émile Zola, Stephen Crane, Jack London, and Theodore Dreiser.

near rhyme   See *slant rhyme.*

Neoclassicism   Neoclassicism is the term used to describe the revival during the English Enlightenment or Restoration Era of ideals of art and literature derived from the Greek and Roman classics. These ideals included respect for authority and tradition, austerity, clarity, conservatism, decorum, economy, grace, imitation of the natural order, harmony, moderation, proportion, reason, restraint, self-control, simplicity, tradition, wit, and unity. Neoclassical literature was witty and socially astute but tended toward excessive *didacticism* and an excessive distrust of invention and imagination. Popular forms of Neoclassical writing included the essay, the epistle, the satire, the parody, poems in rhymed couplets, and the earliest novels. As if in response to Pope's dictum that "The proper study of man is man," Neoclassical writers wrote primarily about social life and social interactions. Of all American writers, Benjamin Franklin perhaps best reflects the Neoclassical spirit of urbane rationality. Romanticism can be seen as a reaction against Neoclassical restraint. See *Classicism, didacticism,* and *Romanticism.*

New Criticism   See *criticism.*

nonfiction   Nonfiction is writing about real events. Essays, autobiographies, biographies, and news stories are all types of nonfiction. See *prose.*

nonsense verse   A **nonsense verse** is a kind of light verse that contains elements that are silly, absurd, or meaningless. Sometimes, as is the case with Lewis Carroll's "Jabberwocky," the apparent nonsense of the verse gives way to sense upon closer analysis. Carroll's poem turns out not to be nonsense at all, but rather an ingenious retelling, in a mock heroic ballad, of a stock folk tale story, that of a young person who sets off on a quest, slays a terrible beast, and returns home victorious. A purer example of nonsense can be found in the following lines of a famous nursery rhyme:

> As I was going up the stair,
> I met a man who wasn't there.
> He wasn't there again today.
> I wish, I wish he'd go away.

novel   A **novel** is a long work of prose fiction. Often novels have involved plots; many characters, both major and minor; and numerous settings. Among the first extended works of prose fiction in English were Aphra Behn's *Oroonoko,* written in 1688; John Bunyan's *Pilgrim's Progress,* completed in 1684; and Swift's *Gulliver's Travels,* written in 1726. Early novels of note include Defoe's *Robinson Crusoe,* Richardson's *Pamela* and *Clarissa,* Fielding's *Tom Jones,* and Sterne's *Tristram Shandy.* Nineteenth-century American novelists include Herman Melville, Mark Twain, and Stephen Crane. Some outstanding modern American novelists include Edith Wharton, Henry James, Ernest Hemingway, William Faulkner, Ralph Ellison, Alice Walker, and Anne Tyler.

novella   A **novella** is a short novel.

objective correlative   An **objective correlative** is a group of images that together create a particular emotion in the reader. The term was coined by T. S. Eliot. See *image.*

occasional verse   An **occasional verse** is one written to celebrate or commemorate some particular event. Ralph Waldo Emerson's "Concord Hymn," for example, was written for the dedication of a monument to soldiers who fought in the first battle of the Revolutionary War.

octameter   See *meter.*

octave   An **octave** is an eight-line stanza. A Petrarchan sonnet begins with an octave. See *meter* and *sonnet.*

off rhyme   See *slant rhyme.*

omniscient point of view   See *narrator* and *point of view.*

one-act   See *act*.

one-dimensional character   See *character*.

onomatopoeia   **Onomatopoeia** is the use of words or phrases that sound like the things to which they refer. Examples of onomatopoeia include words such as *buzz*, *click*, and *pop*. Poets and other writers often make use of onomatopoeia, as in Edgar Lee Masters's description of flat poetry in "Petit, the Poet":

> Seeds in a dry pod, tick, tick, tick,
> Tick, tick, tick, what little iambics

oral tradition   An **oral tradition** is a work, a motif, an idea, or a custom that is passed by word-of-mouth from generation to generation. Materials transmitted orally may be simplified in the retelling. They also may be sensationalized because of the tendency of retellers to add to or elaborate upon the materials that come down to them. Often, works in an oral tradition contain miraculous or magical elements. Common works found in the oral traditions of peoples around the world include *folk tales*, *fables*, *fairy tales*, *tall tales*, *nursery rhymes*, *proverbs*, *legends*, *myths*, *parables*, *riddles*, *charms*, *spells*, and *ballads*. The spiritual "Follow the Drinking Gourd" belongs to the African-American oral tradition. See *folklore*.

ottava rima   *Ottava rima* is a stanza form made up of eight iambic pentameter lines rhyming *abababcc*.

oxymoron   An **oxymoron** is a statement that contradicts itself. Words like *bittersweet*, *tragicomedy*, and *pianoforte* (literally, "soft-loud") are oxymorons that develop complex meanings from seemingly contradictory elements.

palindrome   A **palindrome** is a word, a phrase, or a sentence that reads the same backward as forward. Examples include the word *radar* and the sentence *Able was I ere I saw Elba*, which describes Napoleon's condition prior to his exile to the island of Elba.

parable   A **parable** is a very brief story told to teach a moral lesson. The most famous parables are those such as "The Parable of the Prodigal Son" told by Jesus in the Bible.

paradox   A **paradox** is a seemingly contradictory statement, idea, or event. All forms of *irony* involve paradox. An *oxymoron* is a paradoxical statement. Anne Bradstreet's line "That when we live no more, we may live ever" is paradoxical. Some paradoxes present unresolvable contradictory ideas. An example of such a paradox is the statement, "This sentence is a lie." If the sentence is true, then it is false; if it is false, then it is true. See *irony* and *oxymoron*.

parallelism   **Parallelism** is a rhetorical technique in which a writer emphasizes the equal value or weight of two or more ideas by expressing them in the same grammatical form. Thomas Jefferson used parallelism in the Declaration of Independence in his list of grievances against King George, starting each grievance with "He has . . . ."

paraphrase   A **paraphrase** is a rewriting of a passage in different words. A paraphrase is often distinguished from an *abstract* or *summary* as follows: a summary is shorter than the original, whereas a paraphrase may be as long as or longer than the original. One of the central ideas of the so-called New Criticism was that it is impossible to paraphrase a literary work precisely. Much of the content or meaning of a literary work lies in how it is expressed. Changing the expression therefore inevitably changes the meaning. See *abstract*.

parody   A **parody** is a literary work that imitates another work for humorous, often satirical, purposes. In the indented stanzas of "Do Not Weep, Maiden, for War is Kind," Stephen Crane subtly parodies hortatory patriotic speech.

pathetic fallacy   The **pathetic fallacy** is the tendency to attribute human emotions to nonhuman things, particularly to things in the natural world. The term was coined by the Victorian critic John Ruskin and has often been used to describe the excesses of sentimental verse.

pentameter   See *meter*.

periodical   A **periodical** is a newspaper, magazine, journal, newsletter, or other publication that is produced on a regular basis. *The Dial*, a periodical, was the chief organ of American Transcendentalism. *Poetry* magazine has been a leading force in shaping the course of modern American poetry.

persona A **persona** consists of the qualities of a person or character that are shown through speech or actions.

personal essay A **personal essay** is a short work of nonfictional prose on a single topic related to the life or interests of the writer. Personal essays are characterized by an intimate and informal style and tone. They often, but not always, are written in the first person. See *essay*.

personal symbol See *symbol*.

personification **Personification** is a figure of speech in which an idea, animal, or thing is described as if it were a person. The speaker in Edgar Allan Poe's "The Raven" uses personification when he addresses and questions the raven:

" . . . Tell this soul with sorrow laden if,
    within the distant Aidenn,
It shall clasp a sainted maiden whom the
    angels name Lenore—
Clasp a rare and radiant maiden whom the
    angels name Lenore.
                Quoth the raven, 'Nevermore.'"

Petrarchan sonnet See *sonnet*.

plagiarism **Plagiarism** is the act of using material gathered from another person or work without crediting the source of the material.

plot A **plot** is a series of events related to a central *conflict*, or struggle. A typical plot involves the introduction of a conflict, its development, and its eventual resolution. Terms used to describe elements of plot include the following:

- The **exposition,** or **introduction,** sets the tone or mood, introduces the characters and the setting, and provides necessary background information.

- The **inciting incident** is the event that introduces the central conflict.

- The **rising action,** or **complication,** develops the conflict to a high point of intensity.

- The **climax** is the high point of interest or suspense in the plot.

- The **crisis,** or **turning point,** often the same event as the climax, is the point in the plot where something decisive happens to determine the future course of events and the eventual working out of the conflict.

- The **falling action** is all of the events that follow the climax.

- The **resolution** is the point at which the central conflict is ended, or resolved.

- The **dénouement** is any material that follows the resolution and that ties up loose ends.

- The **catastrophe,** in tragedy, is the event that marks the ultimate tragic fall of the central character. Often this event is the character's death.

Plots rarely contain all these elements in precisely this order. Elements of exposition may be introduced at any time in the course of a work. A work may begin with a catastrophe and then use flashback to explain it. The exposition or dénouement or even the resolution may be missing. The inciting incident may occur before the beginning of the action actually described in the work. These are but a few of the many possible variations that plots can exhibit. See *conflict*.

poetic license **Poetic license** is the right claimed by writers to change elements of reality to suit the purposes of particular works that they create. Edgar Lee Master's use in his *Spoon River Anthology* of characters who rise from their graves and talk is an example of poetic license. Such things do not happen in reality, but they are accepted by readers willing to suspend disbelief in order to have imaginary experiences. See *suspension of disbelief*.

point of view **Point of view** is the vantage point from which a story is told. Stories are typically written from a *first-person point of view,* in which the narrator uses words such as *I* and *we,* or from a *third-person point of view,* in which the narrator uses words such as *he, she, it,* and *they* and avoids the use of *I* and *we.* In stories written from a first-person point of view, the narrator may be a participant or witness of the action. In stories told from a third-person point of view, the narrator generally stands outside the action. In some stories, the narrator's point of view is *limited.* In such stories, the narrator can reveal the private, internal thoughts of himself or herself or of a single character. In other stories, the narrator's point of view is *omniscient.* In such stories the narrator can reveal the private, internal thoughts of any character.

portmanteau   See *blend.*

poulter's measure   Poulter's measure is a metrical form that makes use of couplets containing alternating iambic hexameter and iambic heptameter lines.

pragmatic criticism   See *criticism.*

précis   See *abstract.*

preface   A **preface** is a statement made at the beginning of a literary work, often by way of introduction. The terms *foreword, preface,* and *introduction* are often used interchangeably.

prologue   A **prologue** is an introduction to a literary work, often one that sets the scene and introduces the conflict or the main characters. *The Glass Menagerie,* by Tennessee Williams, begins with a prologue by Tom Wingfield, the protagonist and narrator of the play.

proscenium stage   See *stage.*

prose   Prose is the broad term used to describe all writing that is not drama or poetry, including fiction and nonfiction. Types of prose writing include novels, short stories, essays, and news stories. Most biographies, autobiographies, and letters are written in prose. See *fiction.*

prose poem   A **prose poem** is a work of prose, usually a short work, that makes such extensive use of poetic language, such as figures of speech and words that echo their sense, that the line between prose and poetry, never a clear one, becomes blurred. Many passages from the work of William Faulkner have the quality of prose poetry.

prosody   Prosody, or **versification**, is the study of the structure of poetry. In particular, prosodists study meter, rhyme, rhythm, and stanza form. See *meter, rhyme, rhythm,* and *stanza.*

protagonist   See *character.*

proverb   A **proverb**, or **adage**, is a traditional saying, such as "You can lead a horse to water, but you can't make it drink" or the title of Shakespeare's play "All's Well That Ends Well."

psalm   A **psalm** is a lyrical hymn of praise, supplication, or thanksgiving. The Biblical hymn, attributed to David, that begins with the line "The Lord is my shepherd," is an example.

pseudonym   A **pseudonym** is a name assumed by a writer. For example, *Mark Twain* was the pseudonym of Samuel Clemens.

psychological fiction   Psychological fiction is fiction that emphasizes the interior, subjective experiences of its characters, and especially such fiction when it deals with emotional or mental disturbance or anguish. Kate Chopin's "The Story of an Hour" is an example.

pun   A **pun** is a play on words, one that wittily exploits a double meaning. In "Mending Wall," Frost uses a pun in the sentence "Before I built a wall I'd ask to know . . . to whom I was like to give offense." The sentence can also be read (or heard) as "to whom I was like to give a fence."

Puritanism   Puritanism was a Protestant religious movement that emerged in England in the 1500s and later spread to the colonies of New England. The Puritans objected to the wealth, power, authority, and elaborate ritual of the Catholic Church. They professed a desire to "purify" the Church of England by ridding it of Catholic practices. The Puritans are known for their austerity and acceptance of the basic principles of Calvinism, including the ideas of preordination and original sin. The Plymouth Colony in Massachusetts was founded by Separatist Puritans who came from England via Holland. Important British Puritan writers include John Bunyan and John Milton. Important American Puritan writers include Cotton Mather and Jonathan Edwards. See *Calvinism.*

purpose   See *aim.*

pyrrhic   See *meter.*

quatrain   A **quatrain** is a stanza containing four lines.

quintain A **quintain,** or **quintet,** is a stanza containing five lines.

quintet See *quintain.*

rap A **rap** is an improvised rhymed verse that is chanted or sung, often to a musical accompaniment.

reader-response criticism See *criticism.*

Realism **Realism** is the attempt to render in art an accurate portrayal of reality. The theory that the purpose of art is to imitate life is at least as old as Aristotle. The eighteenth-century development of the novel, with its attention to details of character, setting, and social life, can be thought of as a step toward increased Realism in writing. However, the term *Realism* is generally applied to literature of the late nineteenth century written in reaction to Romanticism and emphasizing details of ordinary life.

redundancy **Redundancy** is needless repetition. The phrase *firmly determined* is redundant because the word *determined* already implies firmness.

refrain A **refrain** is a line or group of lines repeated in a poem or song. Many ballads contain refrains.

regional dialect See *dialect.*

Renaissance The **Renaissance** was the period from the fourteenth to the early seventeenth century when Europe was making the transition from the medieval to the modern world. The word *renaissance* means "rebirth." The term refers to the rebirth of interest in ancient Greek and Latin writing that occurred during the period, a rebirth that is known as Humanism. The Renaissance was characterized by a lessening of reliance on authority, by a decline in feudalism and in the universal authority of the church, by increased nationalism, by increasingly active university and city life, by increased opportunities for individual economic attainment and freedom, and by increased belief in the value of this life in and of itself.

repetition **Repetition** is the use, again, of a sound, word, phrase, sentence, or other element.

resolution See *plot.*

reversal A **reversal** is a dramatic change in the direction of events in a drama or narrative, especially a change in the fortunes of the protagonist. See *plot.*

review A **review** is a written evaluation of a work of art, a performance, or a literary work, especially one that appears in a periodical or on a broadcast news program. Common subjects of reviews include books, films, art exhibitions, restaurants, and performances of all kinds, from rock concerts to ballets.

rhetoric **Rhetoric** is the study of ways in which speech and writing affect or influence audiences.

rhetorical criticism See *criticism.*

rhetorical question A **rhetorical question** is one asked for effect but not meant to be answered because the answer is clear from context. The questions "Are ye then truly free and brave?" and "are ye fit to be/mothers of the brave and free?" in Lowell's "Stanzas on Freedom" are rhetorical questions.

rhetorical technique A **rhetorical technique** is an extraordinary but literal use of language to achieve a particular effect on an audience. Common rhetorical techniques include *antithesis, apostrophe, catalog, chiasmus, parallelism, repetition,* and the *rhetorical question.*

rhyme **Rhyme** is the repetition of sounds at the ends of words. Types of rhyme include *end rhyme* (the use of rhyming words at the ends of lines), *internal rhyme* (the use of rhyming words within lines), *exact rhyme* (in which the rhyming words end with the same sound or sounds), and *slant rhyme* (in which the rhyming sounds are similar but not identical). An example of exact rhyme is the word pair *moon/June.* Examples of slant rhyme are the word pairs *rave/rove* and *rot/rock.* See *slant rhyme.*

rhythm **Rhythm** is the pattern of beats or stresses in a line of verse or prose. See *meter.*

riddle A **riddle** is a word game in which something is described in an unusual way and the reader or listener must figure out what that something is. Riddles are common in folklore and myth throughout the world.

rising action   See *plot*.

romance   **Romance** is a term used to refer to four types of literature: 1. medieval stories about the adventures and loves of knights; 2. novels and other fictions involving exotic locales and extraordinary or mysterious events and characters; 3. nonrealistic fictions in general; and 4. in popular modern usage, love stories of all kinds. The term originated in the Middle Ages. It was first used to describe stories believed to be based upon Latin originals (stories told by the Romans). It came to be used in Europe and England for stories in prose or poetry about knightly exploits. Because the later medieval romances were for the most part told in prose, the term came to be applied to prose fictions in general, and especially to those that were highly imaginative. In the nineteenth century, the term was commonly used to describe fictional works, such as the novels of Sir Walter Scott, that dealt with adventure in exotic locales. It was used by Nathaniel Hawthorne to describe stories like his *Blithedale Romance* and *House of the Seven Gables* because of their deviations from Realism. Today, the term is quite widely used to refer to love stories, especially popular, sentimental stories of the sort often turned into television movies.

Romantic criticism   See *criticism*.

Romanticism   **Romanticism** was a literary and artistic movement of the eighteenth and nineteenth centuries that placed value on emotion or imagination over reason, the individual over society, nature and wildness over human works, the country over the town, common people over aristocrats, and freedom over control or authority. Whittier's *Snow-Bound: A Winter Idyl* is Romantic in its celebration of the connection between people and nature. Much of Poe's poetry is Romantic in its intensity of emotion. Transcendentalism was a particularly American form of Romanticism. See *Transcendentalism*.

rounded character   See *character*.

run-on line   A **run-on line** is a line of verse in which the sense or the grammatical structure does not end with the end of the line but rather is continued on one or more subsequent lines. The following lines from Whittier's "Telling the Bees" form a single sentence:

> Then I said to myself, "My Mary weeps
>   For the dead today:
> Haply her blind old grandsire sleeps
>   The fret and the pain of his age away."

The act of continuing a statement beyond the end of a line is called *enjambment*. See *end-stopped line*.

satire   **Satire** is humorous writing or speech intended to point out errors, falsehoods, foibles, or failings. It is written for the purpose of reforming human behavior or human institutions. Edwin Arlington Robinson's "Miniver Cheevy," for example, satirizes those who reject modern times as debased.

scansion   **Scansion** is the art of analyzing poetry to determine its meter. See *meter*.

scene   A **scene** is a short section of a literary work that presents action that occurs in a single place or at a single time. Long divisions of dramas are often divided into scenes.

science fiction   **Science fiction** is highly imaginative fiction containing fantastic elements based on scientific principles, discoveries, or laws. It is similar to *fantasy* in that it deals with imaginary worlds but differs from fantasy in having a scientific basis. Often science fiction deals with the future, the distant past, or with worlds other than our own such as distant planets, parallel universes, and worlds under the ground or the sea. The genre allows writers to suspend or alter certain elements of reality in order to create fascinating and sometimes instructive alternatives. Important writers of science fiction include H. G. Wells, Jules Verne, Ray Bradbury, Arthur C. Clarke, Isaac Asimov, Ursula K. Le Guin, Robert Heinlein, and Kurt Vonnegut, Jr. See *fantasy*.

sensory detail   See *description*.

sentimentality   **Sentimentality** is an excessive expression of emotion. Much popular literature of the nineteenth and twentieth centuries is characterized by sentimentality.

septet   A **septet** is a stanza with seven lines.

sestet   A **sestet** is a stanza with six lines, such as the second part of a Petrarchan sonnet. See *meter* and *sonnet*.

set   A **set** is a collection of objects on a stage arranged in such a way as to create a scene.

setting   The **setting** of a literary work is the time and place in which it occurs, together with all the details used to create a sense of a particular time and place. Writers create setting by various means. In drama, the setting is often revealed by the stage *set* and the costumes, though it may be revealed through what the characters say about their environs. In fiction, setting is most often revealed by means of description of such elements as landscape, scenery, buildings, furniture, clothing, the weather, and the season. It can also be revealed by how characters talk and behave. In its widest sense, setting includes the general social, political, moral, and psychological conditions in which characters find themselves. See *set*.

Shakespearean sonnet   See *sonnet*.

shape poem   See *concrete poem*.

short short   A **short short,** or **flash fiction,** is an extremely brief short story. This recently recognized genre of the short story is currently enjoying considerable popularity among readers of literary magazines and short story collections published in the United States. Short shorts sometimes take the form of *anecdotes,* or retellings of single incidents. Alternatively, they may attempt to develop an entire plot within the compass of a few paragraphs. Many short shorts are highly poetic and may be considered prose poems. See *anecdote* and *prose poem*.

sight rhyme   A **sight rhyme,** or **eye rhyme,** is a pair of words, generally at the ends of lines of verse, that are spelled similarly but pronounced differently. These lines from Phillis Wheatley's "To S. M., a Young African Painter, on Seeing His Works" provide an example.

On what seraphic pinions shall we *move,*
And view the landscape in the realms *above?*

simile   A **simile** is a comparison using *like* or *as.* Henry Wadsworth Longfellow uses a simile when he describes a blacksmith, saying, "And the muscles of his brawny arms/Are strong as iron bands."

A simile is a type of *metaphor,* and like any other metaphor, can be analyzed into two parts, the *tenor* (or subject being described), and the *vehicle* (or object being used in the description). In Longfellow's simile, the tenor is *brawny arms* and the vehicle is *iron bands.* They can be compared because they share some quality, in this case, strength. See *metaphor*.

slang   **Slang** is extremely colloquial speech not suitable for formal occasions and usually associated with a particular group of people. An example of slang current among young people in the United States in the 1920s is "the bee's knees," for something uniquely attractive or wonderful. Among young people in the northeastern United States, the word *wicked* is now sometimes used as a slang term meaning "extremely," as in "That song is *wicked* good." Writers sometimes use slang in an attempt to render characters and setting vividly.

slant rhyme   A **slant rhyme, half rhyme, near rhyme,** or **off rhyme** is substitution of assonance or consonance for true rhyme. The pairs *world/boiled* and *bear/bore* are examples. See *assonance, consonance,* and *rhyme*.

social dialect   See *dialect*.

soliloquy   A **soliloquy** is a speech delivered by a lone character that reveals the speaker's thoughts and feelings. Tom's opening and closing speeches in *The Glass Menagerie* are soliloquies.

sonnet   A **sonnet** is a fourteen-line poem that follows one of a number of different rhyme schemes. The *English, Elizabethan,* or *Shakespearean sonnet* is divided into four parts: three *quatrains* and a final *couplet.* The rhyme scheme of such a sonnet is *abab cdcd efef gg.* "Sonnet XXX" by Edna St. Vincent Millay is an example of an English sonnet. The *Italian or Petrarchan sonnet* is divided into two parts: an *octave* and a *sestet.* The rhyme scheme of the octave is *abbaabba.* The rhyme scheme of the sestet can be *cdecde, cdcdcd,* or *cdedce.* Millay's sonnet "Euclid Alone Has Looked on Beauty Bare" is an Italian sonnet.

sonnet cycle   See *sonnet sequence.*

sonnet sequence   A **sonnet sequence** is a group of related sonnets. See *sonnet.*

source   A **source** is a work from which an author takes his or her materials.

Southern Gothic   **Southern Gothic** is writing containing elements of horror, suspense, mystery, or magic, produced in or set in the southern States. Tennessee Williams's work is often described as Southern Gothic.

speaker   The **speaker** is the character who speaks in, or narrates, a poem—the voice assumed by the writer. The speaker and the writer of a poem are not necessarily the same person. For example, T. S. Eliot takes on the voice of J. Alfred Prufrock in "The Love Song of J. Alfred Prufrock." In Carl Sandburg's "Grass," the grass is the speaker.

spectacle   In drama, the **spectacle** is all the elements that are presented to the senses of the audience, including the lights, setting, costumes, makeup, music, sound effects, and movements of the actors.

spondee   A **spondee** is a poetic foot containing two strongly stressed syllables, as in the words *compound* and *roughhouse.* Such a foot is said to be *spondaic.*

stage   A **stage** is any arena on which the action of a drama is performed. In the Middle Ages, stages often consisted of the beds of wagons, which were wheeled from place to place for performances. From the use of such wagons in innyards, the *thrust stage* developed. This was a platform that extended out into the audience and that was closed at the back. In front of the platform in the first English theaters, such as Shakespeare's Globe Theatre, was an open area, the pit, where common people stood. Around the pit were balconies in imitation of the balconies of inns.

The modern *proscenium stage* typically is closed on three sides and open at the front, as though the fourth wall had been removed. Sometimes contemporary plays are performed as *theater in the round,* with the audience seated on all sides of the playing area.

stage directions   **Stage directions** are notes included in a play in addition to the dialogue for the purpose of describing how something should be performed on stage. Stage directions describe setting, lighting, music, sound effects, entrances and exits, properties, and the movements of characters. They are usually printed in italics and enclosed in brackets or parentheses.

stanza   A **stanza** is a recurring pattern of grouped lines in a poem. The following are some types of stanza:

two-line stanza	couplet
three-line stanza	tercet or triplet
four-line stanza	quatrain
five-line stanza	quintain
six-line stanza	sestet
seven-line stanza	heptastich
eight-line stanza	octave

static character   See *character.*

stereotype   A **stereotype** is an uncritically accepted fixed or conventional idea, particularly such an idea held about whole groups of people. A *stereotypical,* or *stock,* character is one who does not deviate from conventional expectations of such a character. Examples of stereotypical characters include the merciless villain, the mad scientist, and the hard-boiled private eye. In his autobiography, Frederick Douglass disputes the stereotype of the contented singing slave because, in his experience, slave songs were a release of sorrow. See *character.*

stock character   See *character* and *stereotype.*

story   A **story,** or **narrative,** is writing or speech that relates a series of events. When these events are causally connected and related to a conflict, they make up a *plot.* See *plot.*

stream-of-consciousness writing   **Stream-of-consciousness writing** is literary work that attempts to render the flow of feelings, thoughts, and impressions within the minds of characters. Modern masters of stream-of-consciousness writing include Virginia Woolf, James Joyce, and William Faulkner. An example of stream-of-consciousness writing is the work of Katherine Anne Porter in "The Jilting of Granny Weatherall."

stress Stress, or **accent,** is the level of emphasis given to a syllable. In English *metrics,* the art of rhythm in written and spoken expression, syllables are generally described as being *strongly* or *weakly stressed,* in other words, *accented* or *unaccented.* A strongly stressed or accented syllable receives a strong emphasis. A weakly stressed or unaccented syllable receives a weak one. In the following line from Walt Whitman's "When Lilacs Last in the Dooryard Bloom'd," the strongly stressed or accented syllables are marked with a slash mark (/).

> /   /   /   /
> When lilacs last in the dooryard bloom'd

structuralist criticism See *criticism.*

style Style is the manner in which something is said or written. Traditionally, critics and scholars have referred to three levels of style: *high style,* for formal occasions or lofty subjects; *middle style,* for ordinary occasions or subjects; and *low style,* for extremely informal occasions or subjects. A writer's style depends upon many things, including his or her *diction* (the words that the writer chooses), selection of grammatical structures (simple versus complex sentences, for example), and preference for abstract or concrete words. Any recurring feature that distinguishes one writer's work from another can be said to be part of that writer's style. See *abstract* and *fiction.*

subplot A **subplot** is a subordinate story told in addition to the major story in a work of fiction. Often a subplot mirrors or provides a foil for the primary plot. See *plot* and *story.*

summary See *abstract.*

suspense Suspense is a feeling of expectation, anxiousness, or curiosity created by questions raised in the mind of a reader or viewer.

suspension of disbelief Suspension of disbelief is the phrase used by Coleridge in his *Biographia Literaria* to describe the act by which the reader willingly sets aside his or her skepticism in order to participate imaginatively in the work being read. In Stephen Vincent Bénet's "The Devil and Daniel Webster" the dead and damned return to earth to pass judgment on Jabez Stone. To enjoy the story, readers must suspend their disbelief in people rising from the dead. The willingness to suspend disbelief, to participate imaginatively in a story being read, is the most important attribute, beyond literacy, that a person can bring to the act of reading.

symbol A **symbol** is a thing that stands for or represents both itself and something else. Writers use two types of symbols—conventional, and personal or idiosyncratic. A *conventional symbol* is one with traditional, widely recognized associations. Such symbols include doves for peace; laurel wreaths for heroism or poetic excellence; the color green for jealousy; the color purple for royalty; the color red for anger; morning or spring for youth; winter, evening, or night for old age; wind for change or inspiration; rainbows for hope; roses for beauty; the moon for fickleness or inconstancy; roads or paths for the journey through life; woods or darkness for moral or spiritual confusion; thorns for troubles or pain; stars for unchangeableness or constancy; mirrors for vanity or introspection; snakes for evil or duplicity; and owls for wisdom. A *personal* or *idiosyncratic symbol* is one that assumes its secondary meaning because of the special use to which it is put by a writer. In "Song of Myself" Walt Whitman uses grass as a personal symbol for the beauty and value of simple, lowly things.

synaesthesia Synaesthesia is a figure of speech that combines in a single expression images related to two or more different senses. In Emily Dickinson's "I heard a Fly buzz—when I died—", the line "With Blue—uncertain stumbling Buzz—" contains an example of synaesthesia because "stumbling Buzz" is an image that appeals both to the senses of sight and of sound.

synecdoche   A **synecdoche** is a figure of speech in which the name of part of something is used in place of the name of the whole or *vice versa*. In the command "*All hands on deck!*" *hands* is a synecdoche in which a part (hands) is used to refer to a whole (people, sailors). Addressing a representative of the country of France as *France* would be a synecdoche in which a whole (France) is used to refer to a part (one French person).

syntax   **Syntax** is the pattern of arrangement of words in a statement. Abraham Lincoln's Gettysburg Address is often noted for its unusual syntax. Poets often vary the syntax of ordinary speech or experiment with unusual syntactic arrangements as in "anyone lived in a pretty how town/(with up so floating many bells down)," from E. E. Cummings's, "anyone lived in a pretty how town." See *inversion*.

tag line   A **tag line** is an expression in a work of fiction that indicates who is speaking and sometimes indicates the manner of speaking. Examples include the familiar *she said* as well as more elaborate expressions such as *Bernard muttered moodily*.

tall tale   A **tall tale** is a story, often light-hearted or humorous, that contains highly exaggerated, unrealistic elements. Mark Twain's "The Notorious Jumping Frog of Calaveras County" is an example.

tenor   See *metaphor*.

tercet   See *triplet*.

terza rima   **Terza rima** is a three-line stanza of the kind used in Dante's *Divine Comedy*, rhyming *aba, bcb, cdc, ded,* and so on.

tetrameter   See *meter*.

textual criticism   See *criticism*.

theater (playing area)   See *stage*.

theater in the round   See *stage*.

theater of the absurd   The **theater of the absurd** is a kind of twentieth-century drama that presents illogical, absurd, or unrealistic scenes, characters, events, or juxtapositions in an attempt to convey the essential meaning-lessness of human life, although playwrights have often used the form to convey significant moral messages. Practitioners of the theater of the absurd, which grew out of the philosophy of *Existentialism*, include Eugène Ionesco, Samuel Becket, Edward Albee, and Harold Pinter. See *Existentialism* and *literature of the absurd*.

theme   A **theme** is a central idea in a literary work. The value of each individual is the theme of Ralph Waldo Emerson's "The Rhodora."

thesis   A **thesis** is a main idea that is supported in a work of nonfictional prose.

third-person point of view   See *point of view*.

three-dimensional character   See *character*.

thrust stage   See *stage*.

tone   **Tone** is the emotional attitude toward the reader or toward the subject implied by a literary work. Examples of the different tones that a work may have include familiar, ironic, playful, sarcastic, serious, and sincere.

tragedy   A **tragedy** is a drama (or by extension any work of literature) that relates the fall of a person of high status. Tragedy tends to be serious. It celebrates the courage and dignity of a tragic hero in the face of inevitable doom. Sometimes that doom is made inevitable by a *tragic flaw* in the hero. In the twentieth century, writers have extended the definition of *tragedy* to cover works that deal with the fall of any sympathetic character, despite his or her status. Willie Loman in Arthur Miller's play *The Death of a Salesman* is such a character. His downfall is precipitated by his adherence to the mistaken belief that success in life is gained by being "well liked" by people of importance.

tragic flaw   A **tragic flaw** is a personal weakness that brings about the fall of a character in a tragedy. See *tragedy*.

Transcendentalism   As a variation of European Romanticism, Transcendentalism advocated a belief in spiritual, or transcendent, truths beyond sense perception and material existence. Placing oneself in natural environs would increase one's ability to attain transcendent thought. In contrast to the materialism valued by the Puritans and Benjamin Franklin, Transcendentalists exalted the spiritual and the individual. The group of Transcendental thinkers and writers gathered in Boston and Concord, Massachusetts, in the middle of the nineteenth century included Henry David Thoreau, Ralph Waldo Emerson, Bronson Alcott, Margaret Fuller, and W. H. Channing.

transition A **transition** is a word, phrase, sentence, or paragraph used to connect ideas and to show relationships between them. *However, therefore, in addition,* and *in contrast* are common transitions. Repeated nouns, synonyms, and pronouns can also serve as transitions. For more information on transitions, see the Language Arts Survey, 1.34, "Organizing Ideas"; 1.38, "Paragraphs with Topic Sentences"; and 1.39, "Paragraphs without Topic Sentences." See *coherence.*

translation **Translation** is the art of rendering speech or writing into another language.

trimeter See *meter.*

triplet A **triplet,** or **tercet,** is a stanza of three lines.

trochee A **trochee** is a poetic foot consisting of a strongly stressed syllable followed by a weakly stressed syllable, as in the word *winter.* A line of poetry made up of trochees is said to be *trochaic.*

trope See *figure of speech.*

turning point See *plot.*

understatement An **understatement** is an ironic expression in which something of importance is emphasized by being spoken of as though it were not important, as in the opening lines of "Sonnet XXX" by Edna St. Vincent Millay:

> Love is not all: it is not meat nor drink
> Nor slumber nor a roof against the rain

unity A work has **unity** when its various parts all contribute to creating an integrated whole. An essay with unity, for example, is one in which all the parts help to support the thesis statement, or main idea. See *essay.*

Utilitarianism **Utilitarianism** was a philosophical movement of the nineteenth century associated with Jeremy Bentham and John Stuart Mill in England and with Charles Peirce and William James in the United States. The primary guiding principle of Utilitarianism was that the truth of an idea or the rightness of an action should be judged not according to some abstract or ideal principle but rather according to its practical consequences. Another tenet of Utilitarianism was that moral and political decisions should be made as a result of considering what course of action would bring about "the greatest good [or happiness] for the greatest number" of people.

utopia A **utopia** is an imaginary, idealized world. The term comes from the title of Sir Thomas More's *Utopia,* which described what More believed to be an ideal society. More took the word from the Greek roots meaning "no-place." See *dystopia.*

vehicle See *metaphor.*

verbal irony See *irony.*

vernacular The **vernacular** is the speech of the common people. The term *vernacular* is often used to refer to dialogue or to writing in general that uses colloquial, dialectical, or slang expressions.

versification See *prosody.*

vers libre See *free verse.*

villanelle A **villanelle** is a complex and intricate nineteen-line French verse form. The rhyme scheme is *aba aba aba aba abaa.* The first line is repeated as lines 6, 12, and 18. The third line is repeated as lines 9, 15, and 19. The first and third lines appear as a rhymed couplet at the end of the poem.

Glossary

OF WORDS FOR EVERYDAY USE

ab • di • cate (ab´di kāt´) *vt.,* give up a right or a responsibility

a • bey • ance (ə bā´əns) *n.,* temporary suspension, as of an activity or function

ab • hor (ab hôr´) *vt.,* shrink from in disgust

ab • ject • ly (ab´jekt´ lē) *adv., miserably; in a manner that* suggests a lack of self-respect

ab • strac • tion (ab strak´shən) *n.,* mental withdrawal; absent-mindedness

a • byss (ə bis´) *n.,* bottomless hole

ac • cen • tu • a • tion (ak sen´cho͞o ā´ shən) *n.,* emphasis; clear pronunciation

ac • cliv • i • ty (ə kliv´ə tē) *n.,* upward slope

ac • cu • mu • late (ə kyo͞om´yo͞o lāt´) *vi.,* pile up over time

ac • qui • esce (ak´wē es´) *vi.,* agree without protest

ac • qui • es • cent (ak´wē es´ənt) *adj.,* without protest

a • cute • ly (ə kyoot´lē) *adv.,* sharply, painfully, or severely

ad • jure (ə jer´) *vt.,* urge; beg

ad • mon • ish (ad män´ish) *vt.,* caution against specific faults

af • fin • i • ty (ə fin´i tē) *n.,* close relationship; connection

af • flic • ted (ə flikt´ əd) *part.,* having a physical condition, usually painful or distressing

a • ghast (ə gast´) *adj.,* feeling great horror or dismay

ag • i • ta • tion (aj´ə tā´shən) *n.,* violent motion or disturbance

a • gue (a´gyo͞o) *n.,* fever with chills

al • cove (al´kōv´) *n.,* recessed section, nook

al • lay (a lā´) *vt.,* put to rest; quiet, calm

a • nal • o • gy (ə nal´ə jē) *n.,* similarity in some respects between things otherwise unlike

a • nath • e • ma (ə nath´ə mə) *n.,* curse

a • noint • ed (ə noint´əd) *part.,* rubbed with the oil from the meat

an • o • nym • i • ty (an´ə nim´ə tē) *n.,* condition of having no special or distinguishing qualities

ap • a • thet • i • cal • ly (ap´ə thet´ə kə lē) *adv.,* without emotion

ap • er • ture (ap´ər cher) *n.,* opening; hole

ap • pa • ra • tus (ap´ə rat´ əs) *n.,* materials and tools needed for a specific purpose

ap • pa • ri • tion (ap´ər rish´ən) *n.,* ghostly appearance of a person or thing

ap • pend (ə pend´) *vt.,* attach or affix

ap • pre • hen • sion (ap´rē hen´shən) *n.,* anxiety, dread

ap • ti • tude (ap´tə to͞od´) *n.,* natural tendency or inclination

ar • dent (ärd´ 'nt) *adj.*, intensely enthusiastic or devoted

ar • du • ous (är´jōō əs) *adj.*, difficult

ar • tic • u • late (är tik´yōō lit) *adj.*, able to express oneself easily and clearly

ar • tic • u • lat • ed (ar tik´yōō lāt´əd) *adj.*, made up of distinct syllables or words, as human speech

as • cet • ic (ə set´ik) *adj.*, self-denying; austere

as • cribe (ə skrīb´) *vt.*, assign; attribute

as • pect (as´pekt´) *n.*, appearance

as • pi • rat • ed (as´pə rāt´əd) *adj.*, articulated with a puff of breath before or after

as • pi • ra • tion (as´pə rā´shən) *n.*, strong ambition

as • sent (ə sent´) *n.*, agreement

as • sert (ə sûrt´) *vt.*, declare; affirm

as • suage (ə swāj´) *vt.*, lessen; calm; pacify

a • sun • der (ə sun´der´) *adv.*, apart or separate in direction or position

au • gust (ô gust´) *adj.*, magnificent; worthy of respect

aus • tere (o stir´) *adj.*, plain; without luxury or ornamentation

a • vail (ə vāl´) *vi.*, be of use or advantage

a • ver • sion (ə vɤr´zhən) *n.*, definite dislike

a • vert (ə vɤrt´) *vt.*, prevent

a • vid • i • ty (ə vid´ə tē) *n.*, eagerness; enthusiasm

a • vow (ə vou´) *vt.*, admit frankly

balm (bäm) *n.*, anything healing or soothing

balm • y (bäm´ē) *adj.*, soothing, mild, or pleasant

ba • nal (bā´nəl) *adj.*, commonplace; trite

bane • ful (bān´fəl) *adj.*, causing distress, death, or ruin

banked (baŋkd) *part.*, arranged to continue burning slowly

bar • bar • ic (bär ber´ik) *adj.*, wild, crude, and unrestrained

be • guil • ing (bē gīl´iŋ) *part.*, charming; leading by deception

be • la • bor (bē lā´bər) *vt.*, spend too much time or effort on

be • lea • guer (bē lē´gər) *vt.*, besiege by encircling

bel • li • cose (bel´i kōs) *adj.*, hostile, eager to fight

be • nig • ni • ty (bi nig´nə tē) *n.*, kindliness

blight (blīt) *n.*, anything that destroys or prevents growth

bom • bard • ment (bäm bard´mənt) *n.*, attack by bombs

brink (briŋk) *n.*, edge, especially at the top of a steep place

buf • fet (buf´it) *n.*, blow with the hand or fist

bur • nish (bɤr´nish) *vt.*, make shiny by rubbing

ca • dence (kād´ns) *n.*, rhythmic flow of sound or tone

ca • denced (kād´´nst) *adj.*, measured; rhythmic

ca • lam • i • ty (kə lam´ə tē) *n.*, deep trouble or misery

can • on • ize (kan´ən īz´) *vt.*, declare a deceased person a saint in formal church procedure

ca • price (kə prēs´) *n.*, whim, change in way of thinking

cat • a • lyst (kat´ə list) *n.*, something that stimulates or hastens a result

ca • ter (kāt´ər) *vi.*, take special pains in seeking to gratify another's needs or desires

cav • al • cade (kav´əl kād´) *n.*, procession (of horses)

ca • vort (kə vôrt´) *vi.*, leap about, prance

cen • ser (sen´sər) *n.*, container for burning incense

ces • sa • tion (se sā´shən) *n.*, ceasing or stopping

chron • ic (krän´ik) *adj.*, constant; perpetual

ci • vil • i • ty (sə vil´ə tē) *n.*, gentleness; a civilized manner

clod (kläd) *n.*, lump, such as lump of earth or clay

cog • ni • zance (käg´nə zəns) *n.*, knowledge

co • her • ent (kō hir´ənt) *adj.*, logically connected; making sense

com • men • da • tion (käm´ən dā´shən) *n.*, praise

com • men • su • rate (kə men´shoor it) *adj.*, equal in measure or size, proportionate

com • mu • ni • ca • tive (kə myōō´ni kāt´iv) *adj.*, talkative; giving information readily

com • mun • ion (kə myōōn´yən) *n.*, act of sharing thoughts and actions

com • pli • ance (kəm plī´əns) *n.*, act of giving in to wishes or demands

com • port (kəm pôrt´) *vi.*, agree; go along

com • posed (kəm pōzd´) *adj.*, calm, tranquil

con • ceit (kən sēt´) *n.*, idea, thought; personal opinion

con • ceiv • a • bly (kən sēv´ə blē) *adv.*, in a manner that can be understood or imagined

con • fed • er • a • cy (kən fed´ ər ə sē) *n.*, people or groups united for common purpose

con • fla • gra • tion (kän´flə grā´shən) *n.*, destructive fire

con • found (kən found´) *vt.*, confuse, bewilder

con • ge • ni • al • i • ty (kən jē´nē al´ə tē) *n.*, friendliness

con • glom • er • a • tion (kən gläm´ər ā´shən) *n.*, collection or mixture

con • jec • tur • al (kən jek´chər əl) *adj.*, based on guesses

con • jec • ture (kən jek´chər) *n.*, speculation; *vi.*, guess

con • junc • tion (kən juŋk´shən) *n.*, association; combination

con • jur • a • tion (kän´joo rā´shən) *n.*, magic; sorcery

con • jure (kun´jər) *vt.*, call

con • nois • seur (kän´ə sɤr´) *n.*, person who has expert knowledge in some field

con • se • crate (kan´si krāt´) *vt.*, make or declare sacred

con • so • la • tion (kän´sə lā´shən) *n.*, comfort

con • ster • na • tion (kän´stər nā´shən) *n.*, dismay; great fear con • sti • tu • tion (kän´stə too´shən) n., physical makeup of a person

con • sul • ta • tion (kän´səl tā´shən) n., meeting to discuss, decide, or plan something

con • tem • pla • tion (kän´ təm plā´shən) n., thoughtful inspection, study, or meditation

con • tend • er (kən ten´dər) n., one who strives or fights in competition

con • tor • tion (kən tôr´shən) n., twisting out of shape

con • triv • ance (kən trī´vəns) n., invention; ingenious plan

con • va • les • cent (kän´ və les´ ənt) n., person recovering from an illness

con • viv • i • al • ly (kən viv´ē əl lē) adv., festively

con • vo • lu • tion (kän´və loo´ shən) n., twist, coil, fold

con • vul • sion (kən vul´shən) n., sudden, violent disturbance

con • vul • sive (kən vul´siv) adj., marked by violent contractions or spasms

co • quet • ry (kō´kə trē) n., flirting

cor • di • al • i • ty (kôr´jē al´ə tē) n., warm, friendly act or remark

cor • rod • ing (kə rōd´iŋ) part., wearing away; causing deterioration

course (kôrs) vi., move swiftly; flow through

cow • er (kou´ər) vi., crouch or shrink back in fear

cra • ven (krā´vən) adj., very cowardly; n., coward

creed (krēd) n., statement of belief, principles, or opinions on any subject

cru • ci • fy (kroo´sə fī´) vt., torment; be cruel to

cryp • tic (krip´tik) adj., having a hidden meaning; baffling

cul • prit (kul´prit) n., guilty person

cul • ti • vate (kul´tə vāt) vt., acquire and develop

czar (zar) n., emperor

dal • ly (dal´ē) vi., waste time

de • cree (dē krē´) vt., order

def • er • en • tial (def´ə ren´shəl) adj., respectful

del • e • te • ri • ous (del´ə tir´ ē əs) adj., harmful to health or well-being

de • lib • er • a • tion (di lib´ər ā´shən) n., discussion; consideration of alternatives

de • lir • i • ous (di lir´ē əs) adj., hallucinating; restless and confused

del • uge (del´yooj) n., overwhelming floodlike rush

de • lu • so • ry (di loo´sə rē) adj., quality of seeming unreal

de • mean • or (di mēn´ər) n., way of behaving; manner

de • mure (di myoor´) adj., modest; shy

de • nun • ci • a • tion (dē nun´sē ā´shən) n., criticism; speaking against

de • pop • u • late (dē päp´yə lāt´) vt., reduce the population of, especially by violence or disease

de • port • ment (dē pôrt´mənt) n., manner of conducting or bearing oneself

de • praved (dē prāvd´) adj., morally bad; corrupt

de • ranged (dē rānjd´) adj., disordered; upset; insane

de • vout (di vout´) adj., showing reverence

dif • fuse (di fyoos´) vt., spread out; pour out

di • gress (di gres´) vi., deviate from the main topic in speaking or writing

di • lap • i • dat • ed (də lap´ə dāt´ id) adj., falling to pieces or into disrepair

di • late (dī´lāt) vi., become larger or wider

di • la • tion (dī lā´shən) n., widening, expansion

dil • a • to • ry (dil´ə tôr´ē) adj., causing delay

dil • i • gent • ly (dil´ə jənt lē) adv. painstakingly, industriously

dis • bar (dis bär´) vt., deprive (a lawyer) of the right to practice law

dis • cord • ant (dis kôrd´´nt) adj., disagreeing; conflicting

dis • creet (di skrēt´) adj., careful about what one says and does

dis • mal (diz´məl) adj., causing gloom or misery

dis • po • si • tion (dis´ pə zish´ ən) n., state of mind; general nature

dis • suade (di swād´) vt., talk out of

dis • til • la • tion (dis´tə lā´shən) n., something separated out into parts

di • ver • si • ty (də vʉr´sə tē) n., variety

doc • trine (däk´trin) n., teachings; beliefs

dole • ful (dōl´fəl) adj., full of or causing sorrow or sadness

dredge (drej) vt., dig up (in search of something)

du • ra • tion (doo rā´shən) n., continuance in time

dwin •dle (dwin´dəl) vt., languish; fade

ear • nest (ʉr´nist) adj., serious; intense

ebb (eb) vi., flow back, recede

eb • ul • li • tion (eb´ə lish´ ən) n., boiling or bubbling up

ed • dy (ed´ē) n., move with a circular motion against the main current

ee • rie (ir´ē) adj., mysterious; weird

ef • face (ə fās´) vt., erase, wipe out

ef • fec • tu • al (e fek´choo əl) adj., effective

ef • fi • ca • cious (ef´i kā´shəs) adj., producing or capable of producing the desired effect

e • late (ē lāt´) vt., raise the spirits of

e • lu • ci • date (ə loo´sə dāt´) vt., make clear

e • ma • ci • at • ed (ē mā´shē āt əd) part., abnormally thin

em • bra • sure (em brā´zhər) n., slanted opening in a wall that increases the firing angle of a gun

em • is • sar • y (em´i ser´ē) *n.*, person or agent sent on a mission

en • com • pass (en kum´pəs) *vt.*, surround

en • cum • brance (en kum´brəns) *n.*, hindrance

en • deav • or (en dev´ər) *n.*, effort, attempt

en • dow • ment (en dow´mənt) *n.*, gift of nature; inherent talent

en • dure (en door´) *vi.* continue in existence, last, remain

en • gorge (en gôrj´) *vt.*, devour greedily

en • gulf (en gulf´) *vt.*, overwhelm

en • sue (en soo) *vi.*, come afterward; follow immediately

en • treat (en trēt´) *vt.*, beg; implore; ask earnestly

en • treat • y (en trēt´ē) *n.*, earnest request

en • voy (än´voi) *n.*, messenger; agent

e • phem • er • al (e fem´ər əl) *adj.*, short-lived, transitory

e • qua • nim • i • ty (ek´wə nim´ ə tē) *n.*, evenness of mind or temper

e • rad • i • cate (ē rad´i kāt´) *vt.*, get rid of; wipe out; destroy

er • ro • ne • ous (ər rō´nē əs) *adj.*, mistaken, wrong

es • cu • lent (es´kyoo lənt) *adj.*, fit for food, edible

es • ti • ma • tion (es´ tə mā´ shən) *n.*, respect; value

e • the • re • al (ē thir´ē əl) *adj.*, not earthly; heavenly, celestial

e • ther • ise (ē´thə rīz´) *vt.*, render groggy or numb

eu • pho • ny (yoo´fə nē) *n.*, pleasing effect to the ear

e • vade (ē vād´) *vt.*, avoid or escape from by deceit or cleverness

ev • a • nes • cent (ev´ə nes´ənt) *adj.*, tending to fade; vanishing

e • vince (ē vins´) *vt.*, show plainly; indicate

ex • as • per • a • ting (eg zas´pər āt iŋ) *part.*, irritating, annoying

ex • cru • ci • at • ing • ly (eks kroo´shē āt´iŋ lē) *adv.*, in a painful or agonizing manner

ex • cru • ci • a • tion (ex kru´shē ā´shən) *n.*, torment

ex • hor • ter (eg zôrt´ər) *n.*, one who urges earnestly, by advice or warning

ex • pa • tri • at • ed (eks pā´trē āt´id) *part.*, driven from one's land

ex • pe • di • ent (ek spē´dē ənt) *adj.*, convenient

ex • po • si • tion (eks´pə zish´ən) *n.*, large, public exhibition or show, often international in scope

ex • tem • po • rize (eks tem´pə rīz´) *vt.*, contrive in a makeshift way to meet a pressing need

ex • trem • i • ty (ek strem´ə tē) *n.*, state of extreme necessity, danger, etc.

ex • tri • cate (eks´tri kāt) *vt.*, release or disentangle

feign (fān) *vt.*, make up, invent

fe • lo • ni • ous (fə lō´nē əs) *adj.*, of a criminal

fer • vor (fur´vər) *n.*, great warmth or emotion

fes • tooned (fes toond´) *part.*, adorned with curving decorations

fet • ter (fet´ər) *n.*, shackle or chain for the feet

fi • as • co (fē as´ko) *n.*, complete failure

fis • sure (fish´ər) *n.*, deep crack

flour • ish (flur´ish) *vi.*, grow vigorously; thrive; prosper

fluc • tu • ate (fluk´choo āt´) *vi.*, change or vary continuously

for • mal • ize (fôr´ mə līz´) *vt.*, give definite form to

for • mi • da • ble (fôr´mə də bəl) *adj.*, strikingly impressive

for • mu • lat • ed (fôr´myə lāt´əd) *part.*, systematical; precise

for • ti • tude (fort´ ə tood) *n.*, strength to bear misfortune or pain

fur • nish (fur´nish) *vt.*, supply or provide

fur • tive (fur´tiv) *adj.*, secretive, stealthy

gal • lant • ly (gal´ənt lē) *adv.*, politely, nobly

game (gām) *adj.*, having spirit or enthusiasm

gar • ru • lous (gar´ə ləs) *adj.*, talking much or too much

gauche (gōsh) *adj.*, tactless; lacking social grace

gaud • i • est (göd´ē əst) *adj.*, brightest and showiest, but lacking good taste

gaunt • let • ed (gônt´lit id) *adj.*, wearing a gauntlet, or glove; figuratively, combative

ges • tic • u • late (jes tik´yoo lat´) *vi.*, make gestures with hands or arms

ges • tic • u • lat • ing (jes tik´yoo lāt´iŋ) *part.*, making gestures

glib (glib) *adj.*, able to speak in a smooth, easy manner

glut • ton • y (glut´'n ē) *n.*, habit or act of eating too much

grav • i • ty (grav´i tē) *n.*, seriousness

guile • less (gīl´lis) *adj.*, without deceit

gulf (gulf) *n.*, wide, deep gap or separation

gull (gul) *vt.*, trick; dupe

hag • gard (hag´ərd) *adj.*, having a wasted or exhausted look

hang • dog (haŋ´dôg) *adj.*, ashamed and cringing

har • bor (här´bər) *vt.*, serve as, or provide, a place of protection

har • ry (har´ē) *vt.*, push along; hurry forcefully

heart • i • ly (härt´'l ē) *adv.*, in a friendly, sincere, way

hem (hem) *vt.*, encircle; surround

her • it • age (her´i tij´) *n.*, cultural traditions handed down by ancestors

her • mi • tage (hur´mi tij) *n.*, place where a person can live away from others

hoar • y (hôrʹē) *adj.,* having white or gray hair

home • ly (hōmʹlē) *adj.,* simple, plain

hy • poc • ri • sy (hi päkʹrə sē) *n.,* pretending to be what one is not, or to feel what one does not feel

i • de • ol • o • gy (ī´dē älʹə gē) *n.,* doctrine, opinion, or way of thinking

il • lu • mi • nate (i lo͞oʹmə nāt´) *vt.,* light up

im • bue (im byo͞o´) *vt.,* fill; saturate

im • me • mo • ri • al (imʹme môrʹē əl) *adj.,* something too old to be remembered

im • mi • nent (imʹə nənt) *adj.,* likely to happen without delay

im • mo • bil • i • ty (imʹmo bilʹi tē) *n.,* state of being fixed or unmovable

im • pal • pa • ble (im palʹpə bəl) *adj.,* that which cannot be felt by touching

im • par • ti • al • i • ty (im pärʹshē alʹi tē) *n.,* free of bias

im • pede (im pēd´) *vt.,* obstruct; hinder

im • pend (im pend´) *vi.,* be about to happen

im • per • a • tive (im perʹə tiv) *adj.,* absolutely necessary

im • per • cep • ti • ble (imʹpər sepʹtə bəl) *adj.,* not able to be detected by the senses or the mind

im • per • turb • a • ble (imʹpər tʉrʹbə bəl) *adj.,* that cannot be disconnected or disturbed

im • pet • u • ous (im pechʹo͞o əs) *adj.,* rushing with force or violence

im • pe • tus (imʹpə təs) *n.,* driving force behind an activity

im • pi • ous (imʹpē əs) *adj.,* lacking reverence for God

im • pla • ca • ble (im plāʹkə bəl) *adj.,* that cannot be appeased or pacified

im • ple • ment (imʹplə mənt) *n.,* tool

im • plore (im plôr´) *vt.,* beg

im • plor • ing • ly (im plôrʹiŋ lē) *adv.,* in a beseeching manner

im • por • tu • nate • ly (im pôrʹcho͞o nit lē) *adv.,* in an annoyingly urgent or persistent manner

im • por • tu • ni • ty (imʹpor to͞onʹi tē) *n.,* persistent demand

im • pre • ca • tion (imʹpri kāʹshən) *n.,* curse

in • a • ni • tion (inʹə nishʹən) *n.,* lack of strength due to lack of food

in • au • di • bly (in ôʹdə blē) *adv.,* not loudly enough to be heard

in • aus • pi • cious (inʹô spishʹəs) *adj.,* unfavorable, unlucky

in • can • ta • tion (inʹkan tāʹshən) *n.,* chanting of magical words; spell

in • cense (in sens´) *vt.,* make very angry

in • ces • sant (in sesʹənt) *adj.,* not ceasing or stopping

in • cred • u • lous • ly (in krejʹo͞o ləs lē) *adv.,* in a doubting or skeptical manner

in • de • ci • pher • a • ble (inʹdē sīʹfər ə bəl) *adj.,* illegible

in • def • i • nite (in defʹə nit) *adj.,* having no exact limits

in • de • ter • mi • nate (inʹdē tʉrʹmi´ nit) *adj.,* unspecific; unsettled

in • do • lent (inʹdə lənt) *adj.,* lazy or inactive

in • do • lent • ly (inʹdə lənt lē) *adv.,* lazily

in • duce (in do͞os) *vt.,* persuade; prevail on

in • duct (in dukt´) *vt.,* place in official position

in • dul • gence (in dulʹjəns) *n.,* favor or privilege

in • ef • fa • ble (in efʹə bəl) *adj.,* too overwhelming to be expressed in words; awesome

in • e • luc • ta • bly (inʹē lukʹtə blē) *adv.,* in an inescapable or unavoidable manner

in • es • ti • ma • ble (in esʹtə mə bəl) *adj.,* too great to be measured

in • ev • i • ta • ble (in evʹi tə bəl) *adj.,* that cannot be avoided or evaded

in • fat • u • a • tion (in fachʹo͞o āʹshən) *n.,* foolish or shallow love or affection

in • fe • lic • i • tous (in fə lisʹə təs) *adj.,* unfortunate, unsuitable

in • fest (in fest´) *vt.,* overrun or inhabit in large numbers

in • fi • del (inʹfə del´) *n.,* person who does not believe in a particular religion

in • flec • tion (in flekʹshən) *n.,* change in pitch or tone of voice

in • fring • ing (in frinjʹ iŋ) *part.,* violating; trespassing

in • gen • ious (in jēnʹyəs) *adj.,* having great mental ability

in • ge • nu • i • ty (inʹjə no͞oʹə tē) *n.,* cleverness

in • her • ent • ly (in hirʹ ənt lē) *adv.,* characteristically; naturally

in • hu • man (in hyo͞oʹmən) *adj.,* unfeeling; cruel; barbarous

in • qui • si • tion (inʹqwə zishʹən) *n.,* severe or intensive questioning

in • quis • i • to • ri • al (in kwizʹə tôrʹē əl) *adj.,* prying

in • sen • si • ble (in senʹsə bəl) *adj.,* lacking sensation; unaware

in • sid • i • ous (in sidʹē əs) *adj.,* deceitful; sly; crafty

in • sin • u • ate (in sinʹyo͞o āt´) *vt.,* introduce or work into gradually

in • so • lence (inʹsə ləns) *n.,* disrespectfulness

in • su • per • a • ble (in so͞oʹpər• ə bəl) *adj.,* insurmountable

in • sur • rec • tion (inʹsə rekʹshən) *n.,* uprising

in • teg • ri • ty (in tegʹrə tē) *n.,* uprightness, honesty, and sincerity

in • ter • fer • ence (inʹter firʹ ens) *n.,* something that comes into collision or opposition

in • ter • fused (in tər fyo͞ozd´) *part.,* combined, blended

in • ter • mi • na • ble (in tʉrʹmi nə bəl) *adj.,* without, or seemingly without, end

in • ter • mi • na • bly (in tʉrʹmi nə blē) *adv.*, endlessly; in a manner that seems to last forever

in • ter • ven • ing (in tər vēnʹing) *part.*, coming or lying between

in • tol • er • a • ble (in tälʹər ə bəl) *adj.*, too severe, painful, or cruel to be endured

in • vi • o • late (in vīʹə lit) *adj.*, sacred

in • voke (in vōkʹ) *vt.*, call on for blessing, help, or inspiration

ir • re • spec • tive (irʹri spekʹtiv) *adj.*, regardless

jag (jag) *n.*, sharp, toothlike projection

jaun • ti • ly (jôntʹə lē) *adv.*, in a confident, carefree manner

jilt (jilt) *vt.*, reject; cast off

joc • u • lar (jäkʹyoo lər) *adj.*, humorous

joc • u • lar • i • ty (jäkʹyoo larʹə tē) *n.*, humor, joking

junc • ture (junkʹchər) *n.*, point in time

lac • er • a • tion (lasʹər āʹshən) *n.*, wound; distress

lapse (laps) *n.*, gliding or passing away

lat • tice (latʹis) *n.*, shutter; openwork structure used as a screen

lax • ly (laksʹlē) *adv.*, loosely, not strictly

light (līt) *vi.*, fall or strike suddenly

lime • light (līmʹlītʹ) *n.*, prominent or conspicuous position, as if under a spotlight

lin • ger (liŋʹgər) *vi.*, remain or stay longer than usual

lin • guist (liŋʹgwist) *n.*, specialist in the science of language

list • less • ly (listʹlis lē) *adv.*, in a disinterested manner

loath (lōth) *adj.*, unwilling, reluctant

loath • some (lōthʹsəm) *adj.*, disgusting

lo • cu • tion (lō kyooʹshən) *n.*, word; phrase

loi • ter (loiʹtər) *vi.*, linger in an aimless way

loz • enge (läzʹənj) *n.*, diamond shape

lu • cid (looʹsid) *adj.*, easily understood

lu • di • crous (looʹdi krəs) *adj.*, absurd, ridiculous

lu • rid (loorʹid) *adj.*, vivid in a harsh or shocking way

mach • i • na • tion (mak ə nāʹshən) *n.*, clever plot or scheme

mag • na • nim • i • ty (magʹnə nimʹə tē) *n.*, state of being above pettiness

ma • lign (mə līnʹ) *adj.*, malicious, evil

ma • lig • nant (mə ligʹnənt) *adj.*, wishing evil

ma • lin • ger (mə liŋgər) *vi.*, pretend illness

man • i • fold (manʹə fōldʹ) *adv.*, in many forms or ways

mar • tial (märʹshəl) *adj.*, warlike; of the military

mas • ti • ca • tion (masʹti kāʹshən) *n.*, chewing

ma • tric • u • late (mə trikʹyoo lātʹ) *vt.*, enroll

mea • ger (mēʹgər) *adj.*, not rich or bountiful; inadequate

med • dling (medʹliŋ) *part.*, interfering; concerning oneself with other people's affairs without being asked

me • di • o • cre (mēʹdē ōʹkər) *adj.*, average; not very good

me • nag • er • ie (mə najʹər ē) *n.*, collection of wild or exotic animals

met • ri • cal (meʹtri kəl) *adj.*, related to the number of beats in each line of a verse or song

mien (mēn) *n.*, manner; appearance

mit • i • gate (mitʹə gātʹ) *vt.*, make less severe or painful

mo • bi • lize (mōʹbə līzʹ) *vi.*, become organized and ready, as for war

moi • e • ty (moi ə tē) *n.*, half

mol • li • fy (mälʹə fīʹ) *vt.*, soothe the temper of

mor • row (märʹō) *n.*, next day

mot • ley (mätʹlē) *adj.*, composed of many different elements

mu • ti • nous (myootʹʹn əs) *adj.*, inclined to revolt against authority

nat • u • ral • i • za • tion (nachʹər əl izʹā shən) *n.*, bestowal of the rights of citizenship

nim • ble (nimʹbəl) *adj.*, mentally quick

nu • cle • us (nooʹklē əs) *n.*, core, central part

nup • tial (nupʹshəl) *adj.*, concerning marriage or a wedding

ob • dur • ate (äbʹdoor it) *adj.*, unsympathetic; hardened

o • bei • sance (ō bāʹsəns) *n.*, gesture of respect

ob • lit • er • ate (ə blitʹər ātʹ) *vt.*, do away with entirely, leaving no trace

ob • sessed (əb sestʹ) *part.*, greatly preoccupied or troubled

ob • tuse (əb toosʹ) *adj.*, slow to understand or perceive; insensitive

oc • cult (ə kultʹ) *adj.*, mysterious; hidden

of • fen • sive (ə fenʹsiv) *adj.*, attacking; aggressive

om • i • nous (ämʹə nəs) *adj.*, threatening, sinister

op • pres • sion (ə prashʹən) *n.*, keeping down by cruel or unjust use of authority

op • u • lent (äpʹyoo lənt) *adj.*, very wealthy or rich

or • a • to • ry (ôrʹə tôrʹē) *n.*, art of public speaking

or • dain (ôr dānʹ) *vt.*, officially give someone the authority and duties of a minister, priest, or rabbi

or • di • nance (ôrdʹʹn əns) *n.*, regulation; direction, command

or • na • men • ta • tion (orʹna men tāʹshən) *n.*, decoration

or • ner • y (ôrʹnər ē) *adj.*, having an ugly or mean disposition

or • ni • thol • o • gist (ôrʹnə thälʹə jist) *n.*, one who studies birds

os • cil • la • tion (äs´ə lā´shən) *n.*, act of swinging back and forth

os • ten • ta • tious • ly (äs ten tā´shəs lē) *adv.*, so as to attract attention

o • ver • ture (o´vər chər) *n.*, musical introduction to an opera or other large musical work; independent orchestral composition of varying form

pall (pôl) *n.*, covering that obscures or cloaks gloomily

pal • pa • ble (pal´pə bəl) *adj.*, easily perceived; obvious; clear

pal • sied (pôl´zēd) *part.*, paralyzed

pal • try (pôl´trē) *adj.*, insignificant

pan • to • mime (pan´tə mīm) *n.*, dramatic presentation without words

par • a • gon (par´ə gän) *n.*, model or pattern of perfection or excellence

pa • tri • arch (pā´trē ärk´) *n.*, father, ruler; founder

pen • i • ten • tial • ly (pen´i ten´shəl lē) *adv.*, in a manner suggesting regret for wrongdoing

pen • sive (pen´siv) *adj.*, expressing deep thoughtfulness, often with some sadness

per • emp • to • ri • ly (pər emp´tə ri lē) *adv.*, commandingly

per • en • ni • al (pər en´ē əl) *adj.*, throughout the year; perpetual

per • il • ous (per´ə ləs) *adj.*, dangerous

per • se • vere (pʉr sə vir´) *vi.*, continue in spite of difficulty; persist

per • ti • nac • i • ty (pʉr´tə nas´ə tē) *n.*, stubborn persistence; obstinacy

per • ti • nence (pʉr´tə nəns) *n.*, relevance

phe • nom • e • non (fə näm´ə nən´) *n.*, extremely unusual or extraordinary thing or occurrence

pil • fer (pil´fər) *vt.*, steal

pin • ion (pin´yən) *n.*, part of a bird's wing; *vt.*, disable or impede

plac • ard (plak´ärd) *n.*, notice for display in a public place; sign

plume (plüm) *n.*, feather

poign • ant (poin´yənt) *adj.*, sharp; painful

poise (poiz) *n.*, ease and dignity of manner

pon • der • ous (pän´dər əs) *adj.*, very heavy

pon • toon (pän tōōn´) *n.*, flat-bottomed boat; floating object used for support

por • tal (pôrt´l) *n.*, doorway, gate, or entrance

por • ten • tous (pôr ten´təs) *adj.*, ominous; warning of evil

pos • ter • i • ty (päs ter´ə tē) *n.*, succeeding generations

pre • cip • i • tous (prē sip´ə təs) *adj.*, steep

pre • dis • pos • ing (prē dis pō´ziŋ) *part.*, giving previous tendency

pre • dom • i • nant • ly (prē däm´ə nənt lē) *adv.*, mostly; prevailingly

pre • dom • i • nate (prē däm´ə nāt´) *vi.*, have authority or influence over others

preen (prēn´) *vi.*, dress up in a fussy, vain way

pre • lude (prel´yōōd) *n.*, first movement of an opera; introduction

pre • ma • ture (prē´mə tōōr´) *adj.*, too early

prem • o • ni • tion (prēm´ə nish ən) *n.*, warning; feeling that something bad will happen

pres • tige (pres tēzh´) *n.*, reputation; power to impress

pre • sume (pri zōōm´) *vi.*, dare; venture; take upon oneself

pre • sump • tion (prē zump´shən) *n.*, overstepping of proper bounds or the taking of something for granted

pre • vail (prē vāl´) *vi.* gain advantage or mastery, be victorious, triumph

pri • me • val (prī mē´vəl) *adj.*, of the earliest times or ages

pro • fane (prō fān´) *adj.*, showing disrespect for sacred things

prof • fer (präf´ər) *vt.*, offer

pro • fu • sion (prō fyōō´zhən) *n.*, large number; abundance

prom • i • nence (präm´ə nəns) *n.*, conspicuousness

prom • i • nent (präm´ə nənt) *adj.*, widely and favorably known

prop • a • gan • dist (präp´ə gan´dist) *n.*, one who spreads ideas for a particular cause

pros • per • ous (präs´pər əs) *adj.*, conducive to success; favorable

pros • trate (präs´trāt´) *vt.*, bow down

pro • vi • sion • al (prō vizh´ə nəl) *adj.*, lasting for a short while, not permanent

pro • voke (prō vōk´) *vt.*, anger, irritate, annoy

pun • gent • ly (pun´jənt lē) *adv.*, sharply, strongly

quad • ru • ped (kwä´drōō ped´) *n.*, animal, especially a mammal, with four feet

quaff (kwäf) *vi.*, drink deeply

quell (kwel) *vt.*, end

quer • u • lous (kwer´yōō ləs) *adj.*, full of complaint; peevish

rack • et (rak´it) *n.*, noisy confusion; uproar

rap • tur • ous (rap´chər əs) *adj.* full of joy or pleasure

rav • aged (rav´ijd) *part.*, ruined; devastated

rav • e • nous • ly (rav´ə nəs lē) *adv.*, in a greedy or wildly hungry manner

re • buke (ri byōōk´) *vt.*, blame or scold in a sharp way

rec • om • pense (rek´əm pens´) *vt.*, repay; reward; *n.*, payment or reward

re • com • pose (rē´kəm pōz´) *vt.*, restore calmness of mind

rec • ti • tude (rek´tə tōōd´) *n.*, correctness

re • dress (rē´dres´) n., compensation

re • flec • tion (ri flek´shən) n., serious thought; contemplation

re • frain (ri frān´) vi., hold back; keep oneself from doing something

re • it • er • ate (rē it´ə rāt´) vt., repeat

re • lent • less (ri lent´lis) adj., harsh; pitiless

rel • ish (rel´ish) n., pleasure; enjoyment

rem • i • nis • cence (rem´ə nis´əns) n., memory or something remembered

re • mon • strance (ri män´ strəns) n., protest, objection

re • mon • strate (ri män´strāt´) vt., demonstrate

ren • der (ren´dər) vt., give, hand over, deliver, or present

rep • li • ca (rep´li kə) n., copy

re • proach (ri prōch´) n., blaming or reproving; rebuke

re • prove (ri proov´) vt., speak to in disapproval

re • pulse (ri puls´) vt., drive back

res • ig • na • tion (rez´ig nā´shən) n., submission, patient acceptance

res • o • lu • tion (rez´ə loo´ shən) n., determined state of mind; faithfulness to some person or idea

re • spec • tive (ri spek´tiv) adj., as relates individually to each of two or more persons or things

re • splend • ent (ri splen´dənt) adj., shining brightly

re • sume (ri zoom´) vt., take, get, or occupy again

rev • er • en • tial (rev´ə ren´shəl) adj., showing a feeling of deep respect, love, and awe

rev • er • ie (rev´ər ē) n., dreamy thinking

re • vert (ri vurt´) vi., return to a former practice, opinion, state, or subject

rib • and (rib´ənd) n., ribbon

rick • e • ty (rik´it ē) adj., weak in the joints; shaky

ri • fle (rī´fəl) vt., shuffle, move quickly through

ri • gid • i • ty (ri jid´ə tē) n., state of being inflexible

ruf • fi • an (ruf´ē an) adj., brutal; violent; lawless

ru • mi • nate (roo´mə nāt´) vt., turn over in one's mind

rum • mage (rum´ij) vt., search through thoroughly; ransack

sa • shay (sa shā´) vi., move or walk in such a way as to attract attention

sat • u • rat • ed (sach´ə rāt´ əd) adj., thoroughly soaked

scald • ing (skôld´iŋ) part., burning; injuring

score (skôr) n., set of twenty

sen • ti • nel (sen´ti nəl) n., person acting as a guard

sep • ul • cher (sep´əl kər) n., vault for burial

sheep • ish • ly (shēp ish lē) adv., in an embarrassed manner

sheer (shir) vi., turn sharply aside from a course

shoal (shōl) adj., shallow

shod • dy (shäd´ē) adj., poorly made; cheap, inferior

sin • ew • y (sin´yoo ē) adj., muscular; strong

so • journ (sō´ jurn) n., brief visit

so • lace (säl´is) vt., comfort, relieve

sol • i • dar • i • ty (säl´ə dar´ə tē) n., combination or agreement of all elements or individuals

soph • ist • ry (säf´is trē) n., unsound or misleading but clever, plausible, and subtle argument or reasoning

sot • tish (sät´ish) adj., foolish

sov • er • eign (säv´ərn) adj., independent; above or superior to all others

Spar • tan (spart´'n) adj., like the Spartans; warlike, stoical, or disciplined

spec • u • la • tive (spek´yoo lāt´ iv) adj., theoretical

spurn (spurn) vt., reject

squal • id (skwäl´id) adj., wretched, miserable

squal • or (skwäl´ər) n., filth and misery

stead • fast • ness (sted´fast´nes) n., quality of being firm, fixed, or settled

sto • lid • i • ty (stə lid´ə tē) n., display of little or no emotion

stu • pe • fac • tion (stoo´pə fak´shən) n., state of dullness or lethargy

sub • jec • tion (sub jek´shən) n., bringing under control or dominion

sub • ju • ga • tion (sub´jə gā´shen) n., takeover; enslavement

sub • li • ma • tion (sub´lə ma´shən) n., expression of socially or personally unacceptable impulses in constructive, acceptable forms

sub • lime (sə blīm´) adj., noble; majestic

sub • mis • sion (sub mish´ən) n., act of yielding; surrendering

sub • serve (səb surv´) vt., be useful or helpful; serve

sub • ver • sion (səb ver´zhən) n., systematic attempt to overthrow a government

suf • fer • ance (suf´ər əns) n., power to tolerate pain

suf • fice (sə fīs´) vi., be enough

sun • dry (sun´drē) adj., various; miscellaneous

su • per • cil • i • ous (soo´pər sil´ē əs) adj., disdainful, contemptuous

su • per • flu • ous (sə pur´floo əs) adj., excessive

su • per • vene (soo´pər vēn´) vi., happen unexpectedly

su • pine • ly (soo´pīn´lē) adv., passively

sur • cease (sur sēs´) n., respite; end

sur • mise (sər mīz´) n., conjecture; guess

sur • ro • gate (sur´ə git) n., substitute

symp • to • mat • ic (simp´tə mat´ik) adj., indicative; that constitutes a condition

tal • low • y (tal´ō ē) adj., fatty and pale

te • di • ous (tē′dē əs) *adj.,* long and tiresome

tem • per (tem′pər) *vt.,* toughen, as by rigors or trying experiences

tem • pest (tem′pəst) *n.,* violent storm

tem • po • ral (tem′pə rəl) *adj.,* lasting only for a time; temporary

ten • an • cy (ten′ən sē) *n.,* occupation of something by right

ten • ure (ten′yər) *n.,* right to hold a position permanently

ter • mi • nate (tur′mə nāt′) *vi.,* end, stop, cease

tes • ti • ly (tes′tə lē) *adv.,* in an irritable manner

thresh (thresh) *vt.,* thrash, toss about

tran • scend • ent (tran sen′dənt) *adj.,* beyond the limits of knowledge or experience

tran • si • ent (tran′sē ənt) *adj.,* not permanent; temporary

trans • mute (trans myōōt′) *vt.,* change from one form, species, or condition into another

trans • port (trans′pôrt) *n.,* strong emotion; rapture

trav • ail (trə vāl) *n.,* very hard work, toil

trem • u • lous • ly (trem′yōō ləs lē) *adv.,* in a trembling or quivering manner; fearfully, timidly

trep • i • da • tion (trep′ ə dā′ shən) *n.,* anxiety; nervousness

trib • u • la • tion (trib′yoo lā′shən) *n.,* great misery or distress

triv • i • al • i • ty (triv′ē al′i tē) *n.,* something insignificant

tu • mul • tu • ous • ly (tōō mul′ chōō əs lē) *adv.,* wildly

ul • te • ri • or (ul tir′ē ər) *adj.,* further; more remote; undisclosed; concealed

un • al • ien • a • ble (un āl′yən ə bəl) *adj.,* that which may not be taken away

un • daunt • ed (ən dônt′əd) *adj.,* resolute in the face of danger

un • du • late (un′dyōō lāt) *vi.,* move in waves

un • du • la • tion (un′dyōō lā′shən) *n.,* act of moving in waves

un • in • tel • li • gi • ble (un in tel′i jə bəl) *adj.,* that cannot be understood

un • ob • tru • sive (un əb trōō′siv) *adj.,* not calling attention to itself

un • to • ward (un tō′ərd) *adj.,* improper, unseemly; not favorable

un • wield • y (un wēl′dē) *adj.,* hard to manage

ush • er (ush′ər) *vt.,* escort, conduct

u • sur • pa • tion (yōō zər pā′ shən) *n.,* unlawful or violent taking of power

va • cu • i • ty (va kyōō′ə tē) *n.,* empty space, void, or vacuum

vag • a • bond (vag′ə bänd′) *n.,* wandering, idle, disreputable, or shiftless person

va • ga • ry (və ger′ē) *n.,* odd, whimsical, or freakish idea or notion

val • id (val′id) *adj.,* sound; just

ve • loc • i • ty (və läs′ə tē) *n.,* quickness or rapidity of motion or action

ven • er • a • ble (ven′ər ə bəl) *adj.,* worthy of respect by reason of age and dignity

venge • ance (ven′jəns) *n.,* revenge

ven • ture (ven′chər) *n.,* risky or dangerous undertaking; undertake the risk of

ver • dure (vur′jər) *n.,* green growing plants and trees

ver • i • si • mil • i • tude (vər′ si mil′ə tōōd′) *n.,* appearance of being true or real

ver • i • ty (vər′ə tē) *n.,* principle or belief taken to be fundamentally and permanently true

ver • min (vur′mən) *n.,* small animals regarded as pests

ves • ti • bule (ves′tə byōōl′) *n.,* hallway or small room at the entrance of a building

ves • tige (ves′tij) *n.,* trace, mark, or sign of something that once existed but has passed away

vex (veks) *vt.,* irritate; annoy

vi • and (vī′ənd) *n.,* article of food

vi • tu • per • a • tive (vī tōō′ pə rā′tiv) *adj.,* abusive; viciously fault-finding

vi • vac • i • ty (vī vas′ə tē) *n.,* liveliness of spirit; animation

vo • cif • er • a • tion (vō sif′ər ā′shən) *n.,* shouting

vol • a • tile (väl′ə təl) *adj.,* unstable; fleeting

vo • rac • i • ty (vô ras′ə tē) *n.,* greediness

vor • tex (vôr′ teks) *n. pl.* swirling mass

wince (wins) *vi.,* shrink or draw back slightly, usually with a grimace, as in pain, embarrassment, or alarm

wretch • ed (rech′id) *adj.,* miserable

writhe (rīth) *vt.,* make twisting movements

wrought (rôt) *alt. pp. of* work, worked; made

Index of Titles and Authors

Index of Skills

Reading and Literature

abstract, 170, 544, 566, 1028

acts, 45, 1028

aim, 112, 183, 767, 1029

alliteration, 16, 177, 310, 320, 344, 403, 767, 796, 823, 1029

allusion, 112, 169, 222, 250, 270, 373, 520, 567, 573, 590, 805, 812, 1030

ambiguity, 38, 1030

amplification, 250, 295, 1030

anaphora, 833, 1030

anecdote, 59, 538, 757, 1030

annotation, 112

antagonist, 24, 1030

antithesis, 17, 378, 768, 1030

aphorism, 145, 256, 270, 1030

apology, 327, 1030

apostrophe, 300, 305, 320, 1030

archetype, 699, 1031

argumentation, 164, 1031

aside, 44, 1031

assonance, 16, 164, 334, 795, 1031

atmosphere, 239, 1031

autobiography, 52, 145, 1031

background information, 41, 1031

ballad, 4, 1031

biography, 52, 256, 1032

blank verse, 295, 524, 1032

blocking, 45, 50

caricature, 24, 1032

catalog, 479, 1032

catastrophe, 628, 1032

character, 24, 47, 50, 527, 690, 714, 1033

character trait, 24

characterization, 24, 41, 655, 1033

chiasmus, 17, 150, 1033

chronological order, 108, 1033

cliché, 707, 1034

climax, 25, 38, 390, 1034

collage, 751, 1034

comedy, 42, 1034

complication, 25, 34, 1035

concrete, 544, 566, 1035

confessional poetry, 786, 813, 1035

conflict, 25, 448, 628, 699, 1035

consonance, 16, 796, 1035

couplet, 14, 112, 305, 590, 1036

crisis, 25, 1036

curriculum, 112

dénouement, 25, 39, 1038

dialect, 41, 461, 1038

dialogue, 44, 47, 50, 470, 655, 1038

diary, 52, 1038

diction, 532, 578, 1038

didacticism, 353, 1038

drama, 42, 44, 1038

dramatic dialogue, 524

dramatic monologue, 524, 573, 1039

dramatic poetry, 12, 1039

dynamic character, 24, 1039

effect, 123, 549, 596, 1039

elaboration, 250, 295, 479, 1039

elegiac lyric, 12, 1039

elegy, 578, 1039

elliptical, 567

emphasis, 123, 1039

end rhyme, 16, 593, 1039

Enlightenment, 157, 1040

epigraph, 813, 1040

essay, 256, 462, 763, 1041

euphony, 300, 1041

Existentialism, 785, 792, 1041

exposition, 25, 27, 1041

Expressionism, 682, 690, 1041

extended metaphor, 334, 1041

eye rhyme, 117, 331, 1041

falling action, 25, 1041

fantasy, 222, 1041

farce, 757, 1041

fiction, 22, 24, 25, 1042

figurative language, 41, 1042

figures of speech, 16, 1042

flashback, 389, 1042

flat character, 24

foot, 13, 14, 1042

frame tale, 462, 1043

free verse, 12, 403, 471, 479, 523, 573, 809,

1043

full character, 24, 1043

haiku, 562, 1043

heptastich, 15

heroic couplet, 169, 1043

history, 52

hymn, 86, 1043

hyperbole, 16, 117, 1043

iamb, 514, 1043

image, 16, 310, 544, 549, 562, 1044

imagery, 544, 549, 562, 1044

Imagism, 545, 1044

imagist poem, 12

inciting incident, 25, 27, 1044

internal conflict, 448, 1044

internal monologue, 655, 1044

internal rhyme, 16, 828

introduction, 25, 1044

inversion, 587, 1044

irony, 108, 334, 403, 454, 470, 648, 694, 800, 1044

journal, 52, 1044

legend, 4

letter, 52

lyric poetry, 12, 108, 596, 1044

major character, 24, 1045

metaphor, 16, 85, 256, 400, 514, 532, 562, 690, 792, 823, 1045

meter, 13, 16, 319, 327, 547, 593, 1045

metonymy, 17, 1045

minor character, 24, 33, 1045

Minimalist style, 844

Modernism, 763, 823, 1045

monologue, 44

mood, 25, 93, 239, 315, 1046

motif, 448, 1046

motivation, 24, 41, 1046

myth, 4, 85, 538, 1046

narrative poem, 12, 310, 1046

narrator, 638, 1046

Naturalism, 389, 400, 468, 614, 1046

Neoclassicism, 150, 1047

nonfiction, 52, 54, 1047

novel, 22, 1047

novella, 22, 1045

objective correlative, 16, 823, 1047

occasional verse, 353, 1047

octave, 15, 590, 1047

ode, 12

one-dimensional character, 24, 1048

onomatopoeia, 16, 250, 337, 768, 1048

oral tradition, 4, 467, 1048

oxymoron, 117, 1048

paradox, 583, 1048

parallelism, 17, 20, 85, 157, 177, 378, 403, 479, 523, 768, 828, 833, 1048

parody, 437, 574, 1048

pathetic fallacy, 536, 1048

persona, 144, 1049

personification, 17, 20, 327, 470, 523, 816, 1049

playwright, 44

plot, 25, 628, 843, 1049

point of view, 93, 238, 315, 334, 638, 843, 1049

properties, 45, 50

protagonist, 24, 448, 1050

proverb, 145, 1050

psychological fiction, 389, 400, 1050

pun, 527, 805, 1050

quatrain, 15, 590, 1050

quintain, 15, 1051

refrain, 8, 373, 596, 1051

repetition, 8, 17, 331, 551, 558, 587, 796, 1051

resolution, 25, 39, 1051

reversal, 454, 1051

rhetoric, 17, 873, 1051

rhetorical question, 17, 156, 164, 305, 1051

rhyme, 16, 323, 344, 482, 558, 578, 587, 593, 600, 813, 1051

rhyme scheme, 20

rhythm, 16, 547, 551, 1051

rising action, 25, 1052

romance, 239, 1052

Romantic poetry, 353

Romanticism, 323, 471, 1052

rounded character, 24, 1052

run-on line, 344, 551, 1052

scenes, 45, 1052

script, 44

sentimentality, 437, 1052

sestet, 15, 590, 1053

set, 45, 50, 1053

setting, 25, 628, 715, 1053

short short, 22

short story, 22

sight rhyme, 117, 331, 1053

simile, 17, 400, 514, 520, 583, 596, 638, 648, 776, 1053

slant rhyme, 16, 331, 1053
soliloquy, 44, 1053
sonnet, 12, 19, 590, 1053
sound effects, 45
Southern Gothic, 682, 1054
speaker, 482, 547, 549, 600, 1054
spectacle, 44, 45, 1054
speech, 81
special vocabulary, 59
spiritual, 4, 8, 361, 373
stage directions, 44, 46, 50, 689, 1054
stages, 42, 44, 45, 1054
stanza, 13, 300, 305, 334, 566, 1054
static character, 24, 1054
stereotype, 150, 369, 437, 1054
stock character, 24, 437, 1054
stream-of-consciousness writing, 323, 649,
    1054
style, 144, 1055
symbol, 20, 80, 222, 337, 479, 527, 699, 701,
    714, 739, 816, 1055
synaesthesia, 17, 336, 1055
synechdoche, 17, 1056
syntax, 378, 587, 1056
tall tale, 4, 462, 1056
tercet, 14, 1056
theme, 8, 20, 26, 34, 50, 256, 373, 400, 559,
    738, 853, 1056
three-dimensional character, 24, 1056
thesis, 369, 1056
tone, 86, 270, 315, 369, 512, 532, 547, 593,
    776, 805, 853, 1056
tragedy, 42, 1056
triplet, 14, 1057
tropes, 16, 1057
turning point, 25, 1057
understatement, 17, 578

Writing

abstract, 170
adding, 899
advice column, 256
agenda, 150
aim, 54, 365, 873
allusion piece, 813
analysis, 55, 879
analysis charts, 888
analyzing, 883

annotations, 112
audience, 81, 302, 871, 875
ballad, 515
billboard ad, 256
biographical sketch, 768
biography, 256
blues, 270
body, 897
brainstorming, 889
captions, 170, 544, 549
careful draft, 894
cartoon, 150
cause-and-effect analysis, 879
cause-and-effect order, 893
character sketch, 310, 448, 655
choosing a topic, 871
chronological order, 893
citation, 401
classification, 55, 873, 879
classification order, 894
clincher sentence, 895
clustering, 310, 885
collage, 751
comic strip, 344
communication triangle, 874
comparison and contrast, 55, 123, 467, 566,
    763, 879, 893
comparison-and-contrast order, 893
compositions, 897
computer hardware, 869
computer software, 869
computers and writing, 868
conclusion, 897
credo, 177
critical analysis, 533, 739
critical interpretation, 551
curriculum, 112
daydream, 390
debate, 527
degree order, 893
deleting, 899
description, 55, 337, 878
descriptive paragraph, 250, 551, 628, 638
dialogue, 55, 470, 482, 527, 649, 655, 878
dialogue poem, 817
diary entries, 223, 316, 454, 739
directions, 390
discovery draft, 894
discussion, 150, 889

reading actively, 172, 716, 747, 984
reading charts and graphs, 986
reading comprehension questions, 1014
reading rates, 253, 747, 982
reading skills, 982
reference to sources, 1007
reference works, 300, 345, 597, 993, 995
remembering, 390, 758, 815, 973
repetition, 973
representing the situation, 971
research skills, 987
responding to reading, 984
reviewing an answer to an essay question, 1016
scanning, 982, 983
searching tools, 305, 583, 990
sentence-completion questions, 1012
short-answer questions, 1011
skimming, 982, 983
slow and careful reading, 982, 983
source evaluation criteria, 997
standardized tests, 1011
subject card, 991
summarizing, 183, 257, 985, 1004, 1006
synonym questions, 629, 1014
test-taking skills, 1009
thesauruses, 811, 996
thought experiment, 977
title card, 991
transfer, 981
trial and error, 971
true/false questions, 1010
usage notes, 995
vague terms, 980
vertical files, 997
visualizing, 390, 758, 815, 973
work backward, 971
yearbooks, 993

Applied English/Tech Prep

applications, guidelines for completing, 1017
body, 1019
business letter, 183, 853, 1020, 1021, 1022
closing, 1019
cover letter, 1022, 1023
documenting technical procedures, 1026
forms, guidelines for completing, 1017
letter of request, 1022
letters and forms, 1017
memoranda, 170, 1025
personal letter, 328, 587, 638, 1019
postscript, 1019
press release, 1027
promotional writing, 1026
public relations writing, 1026
résumé, 1022, 1024
return address, 1019
salutation, 1019
signature, 1019
technical writing, 628, 1026

Index of Fine Art

Art Acknowledgments

Breezing Up (a Fair Wind). Winslow Homer, 1876. National Gallery of Art, Washington, DC (1943.13.1). Gift of the W. L. and May T. Mellon Foundation **cover**; In the Morning. Winslow Homer. Courtesy Corel Professional Photos. **2**; The Lord Is My Shepherd. Eastman Johnson. National Museum of American Art, Washington DC/Art Resource, NY **4, 5**; The Hilltop. Frank Weston Benson, Malden Public Library **11**; The Poor Man's Store. John Frederick Peto, 1885. Courtesy of Museum of Fine Arts, Boston. Gift of Maxim Karolik to the M. and M. Karolik Collection of American Paintings, 1815–1865 **22, 23**; The trial of two "witches" at Salem, Massachusetts, in 1692. Illustration by Howard Pyle. The Granger Collection, NY **42, 43**; Share Croppers. Robert Gwathmey, 1941. Courtesy of San Diego Museum of Art. Museum purchase with funds provided by Mrs. Leon D. Bonnet **53**; Folksinger. Charles White. Collection of Harry Belafonte. Courtesy Heritage Gallery, Los Angeles, CA **57**; Quaker Meeting. Courtesy of Museum of Fine Arts, Boston. Bequest of Maxim Karolik **66**; Buffalo Bull's Back Fat, head chief, Blood Tribe (Blackfoot). George Catlin, 1832. National Museum of American Art, Washington DC/Art Resource, NY **68**; A witch trial at Salem, Massachusetts, in 1692. The Granger Collection, NY **73**; Arrowheads. Collection of Bob and Helen Abraham. Photo by Don Welch **76**. Indians Building a Canoe. Helen Abraham **79**. Elk Foot of the Taos Tribe. Eanger Irving Couse, *circa* 1909. National Museum of American Art, Washington, DC/Art Resource, NY **83**; The Beginning of New England: after the painting by Clyde O. Deland. The Granger Collection, NY **103**; Elizabeth Freake and Baby Mary. Artist unknown, *circa* 1671–74. Worcester Art Museum, Worcester, MA. Gift of Mr. and Mrs. Albert W. Rice **115**; The Sermon. Gari Melchers, 1886. National Museum of American Art, Washington, DC/Art Resource, NY **119, 121**; Midnight Ride of Paul Revere. Grant Wood, 1931. The Metropolitan Museum of Art. Arthur Hoppock Hearn Fund, 1950. (50.117) **132, 139**; Portrait of Benjamin Franklin. Robert Feke, *circa* 1746. Harvard University, Portrait Collection. Bequest of Dr. John Collins Warren, 1856 **134**; Phillis Wheatley, Courtesy, Library of Congress Photo Duplication Service **138, 165**; The Twin, Wife of Bloody Hand. George Catlin, 1832. National Museum of American Art, Washington, DC/Art Resource, NY **147, 148**; Patrick Henry speaking against the Stamp Act in the Virginia House of Burgesses in 1765. Nineteenth-century colored engraving. The Granger Collection, NY **153, 154**; The Janitor Who Paints. Palmer Hayden, *circa* 1937. National Museum of American Art, Washington, DC/Art Resource **166, 168**; John Adams.

Gilbert Stuart, 1826. National Museum of American Art, Washington DC/Art Resource, NY **181**; Watson and the Shark. John Singleton Copley. Courtesy of Museum of Fine Arts, Boston. Gift of Mr. George von Lengerke Meyer **190, 197**; Washington Irving, Courtesy, Library of Congress Photo Duplication Service **194**; Nathaniel Hawthorne. Peabody Essex Museum **195, 198**; Carnival Evening. Henri Rousseau, 1886. Philadelphia Museum of Art, Louis E. Stern Collection **199, 207**; The Whale Fishery, The Sperm Whale in a Flurry. Lithograph by Currier & Ives. The Granger Collection, NY **242, 246**; Still Life with Copper Tankard. William M. Harnett, Courtesy Corel Professional Photos **288**; Among the Sierra Nevada Mountains, California. Albert Bierstadt, 1868. National Museum of American Art, Washington, DC/Art Resource, NY **291, 292**; Last Sale of Slaves on Courthouse Steps. T. Satterwhite Noble, 1860. Missouri Historical Society **302, 303**; Pat Lyon at the Forge. John Neagle, 1826–7. Courtesy of the Museum of Fine Arts, Boston. Herman and Zoe Oliver Sherman Fund, 1975 **308**; Stone City Iowa. Grant Wood. Joslyn Art Museum, Omaha, NE **312, 313**; Winter Sunday in Norway, Maine. Artist unknown, *circa* 1860. New York State Historical Association, Cooperstown, NY **332**; Illustration to Edgar Allan Poe's Le Corbeau (The Raven). Edouard Manet, 1875. Courtesy, Museum of Fine Arts, Boston **339, 341**; Rainy Day in Camp. Winslow Homer, 1871. The Metropolitan Museum of Art. Gift of Mrs. William F. Milton, 1923 (23.77.1) **356, 363**; Robert E. Lee, Courtesy, Library of Congress Photo Duplication Service **360**; Ulysses S. Grant, Courtesy, Library of Congress Photo Duplication Service **360, 361**; Young Soldier. Separate study of a soldier giving water to a wounded companion. Winslow Homer, 1861. Cooper-Hewitt, National Design Museum, Smithsonian Inst./Art Resource, NY. Photograph: Ken Pelka **381, 387**; American Gothic. Grant Wood, American, 1891–1942. Oil on beaverboard, 1930, 74.3 × 62.4 cm. Friends of the American Art Collection, 1930.934 **416**; Jesse James. Courtesy, Library of Congress Photo Duplication Service **419**; Four Young Ilte Indians. Popper photo/Archive photo **420**; Jack London. Courtesy, Library of Congress Photo Duplication Service **424**; Sarah Orne Jewett. Courtesy, Library of Congress Photo Duplication Service **438**; Louisiana Heron. Rodney Busch. Private collection **439, 443**; Walt Whitman. Courtesy, Library of Congress Photo Duplication Service **471**; Paul Laurence Dunbar. Courtesy, Library of Congress Photo Duplication Service **480**; Mask. Sargeant Claude Johnson. National Museum of American Art, Washington, DC/Art Resource **481**; Can Fire in the Park. Beauford Delaney, 1946.

National Museum of American Art, Washington, DC/Art Resource, NY **500** WWI Troops in Gear. Courtesy of Archive/Welgos **502**; Ernest Hemingway. Courtesy, Library of Congress Photo Duplication Service **503, 650**; Edith Wharton. Courtesy, Library of Congress Photo Duplication Service **504**; Courtesy, Library of Congress Photo Duplication Service **505**; Edna St. Vincent Millay. Courtesy, Library of Congress Photo Duplication Service **507**; Carl Sandburg. Courtesy, Library of Congress Photo Duplication Service **521**; Robert Frost. Courtesy, Library of Congress Photo Duplication Service **524**; Mother Moon, Sister Crow, 1981. Gillian Gatto **541**; A Shoreham Garden. Samuel Palmer, *circa* 1829. Courtesy of the Trustees of the Victoria & Albert Museum **556**; Langston Hughes. Courtesy, Library of Congress Photo Duplication Service **594**; Nighthawks. Edward Hopper, 1942. American, 1882–1967. Oil on Canvas, 84.1 x 152.4 cm. The Art Institute of Chicago, Friends of American Art Collection, 1942.51 **612**; Jack London. Courtesy, Library of Congress Photo Duplication Service **614**; First Row Orchestra. Edward Hopper, 1951. Hirshhorn Museum and Sculpture Garden, Smithsonian Institution, Gift of the Joseph H. Hirshhorn Foundation, 1966 **635**; Moulin de la Galette. Pierre-Auguste Renoir. Courtesy Corel Professional Photos **653**; New York Movie. Edward Hopper, 1939. The Museum of Modern Art, New York, Given anonymously **680**; Incantation. Charles Sheeler, 1946. Oil on canvas, 61.0 x 50.8 (24 x 20).The Brooklyn Museum, 49.67. John B. and Ella C. Woodward Memorial Funds **744**; Courtesy, Library of Congress Photo Duplication Service **747**; Number 3, 1949: TIGER. Jackson Pollock, 1949. Hirshhorn Museum and Sculpture Garden, Smithsonian Institution. Gift of Joseph H. Hirshhorn, 1972. **780**; John and Robert Kennedy. Courtesy, Library of Congress Photo Duplication Service **782**; Reverend Martin Luther King, Jr. Courtesy, Library of Congress Photo Duplication Service **783**; Space Shuttle Challenger. National Aeronautics and Space Administration. (NASA) **785**; Steering Wheel. David Hockney, October 1982. Photographic Collage, 30 x 36. © David Hockney. **790**; The Starry Night. Vincent van Gogh, 1889. Oil on canvas, 29" x 36^1/4" (73.7 x 92.1 cm). The Museum of Modern Art, NY. Acquired through the Lillie P. Bliss Bequest **813**; Gemini Etching. Lout Mills, 1969. Evans-Tibbs collection Washington, DC **826**; John F. Kennedy. Courtesy, Library of Congress Photo Duplication Service **829**

Additional Photo and Illustration Credits

Courtesy Digital Stock Corp.: 472, 476, 511, 535, 537, 564, 576, 580, 581, 589, 595, 599, 760, 864, 866, 904, 970, 1017 **Courtesy Corel Professional Photos:** 69, 71, 136, 137, 358, 418, 421, 423, 451, 517, 522, 528, 550, 568, 592, 615, 620, 641, 643, 684, 716, 753, 765, 794, 798, 802, 807, 815, 820, 830, 962 **Jena Busch:** 513, 546 **Rodney Busch:** 456, 561, 819, 845, 848, 854 **David Benoit:** 265, 770, 773 **Ed Parker:** 506, 567 **Helen Abraham:** 585 **Heath P. O'Leary:** 835, 839

Literary Acknowledgments *(continued from copyright page)*

Elizabeth Barnett
"Euclid Alone Has Looked On Beauty Bare" and Sonnet XXX of FATAL INTERVIEW by Edna St. Vincent Millay. From COLLECTED POEMS, HarperCollins. Copyright © 1923, 1931, 1951, 1958 by Edna St. Vincent Millay and Norma Millay Ellis. Reprinted by permission of Elizabeth Barnett, literary executor.

BOA Editions, Ltd.
LI-YOUNG LEE. "A Story" copyright © 1990, by Li-Young Lee. Reprinted from THE CITY IN WHICH I LOVE YOU, by Li-Young Lee, with the permission of BOA Editions, Ltd., 92 Park Ave., Brockport, NY 14420

Brandt & Brandt Literary Agents, Inc.
"The Devil and Daniel Webster" by Stephen Vincent Benet. From THE SELECTED WORKS OF STEPHEN VINCENT BENET. Copyright 1936 by The Curtis Publishing Company. Copyright renewed © 1964 by Thomas C. Benet, Stephanie B. Mahin, and Rachel Lewis Benet. Reprinted by permission of Brandt & Brandt Literary Agents, Inc.

Gwendolyn Brooks
"To Black Women," © 1991 by Gwendolyn Brooks. From BLACKS, 1991. Published by Third World Press, Chicago. Reprinted by permission of the author.

The Continuum Publishing Company
from *The Very Brief Relation of the Devastation of the Indies* by Bartolome de las Casas. Copyright © 1974.

David Campbell Publishers Ltd.
from "Letters from an American Farmer" by J. Hector St. Jean de Crèvecoeur. By permission of Everyman's Library, Campbell Publishers Ltd.

Elizabeth H. Dos Passos
"Newsreel LXVII," by John Dos Passos. From *The Big Money,* copyright by Elizabeth H. Dos Passos. Reprinted by permission of Elizabeth H. Dos Passos.

Farrar, Straus & Giroux, Inc.
"House Guest" from THE COMPLETE POEMS 1927–1979 by Elizabeth Bishop. Copyright ©1979, 1983 by Alice Helen Methfessel. Reprinted by permission of Farrar, Straus & Giroux, Inc. "The Death of the Ball Turret Gunner" from THE COMPLETE POEMS by Randall Jarrell. Copyright © 1969 by Mrs. Randall Jarrell. Reprinted by permission of Farrar, Straus & Giroux, Inc. "For the Union Dead" from FOR THE UNION DEAD by Robert Lowell. Copyright © 1960 by Robert Lowell. Copyright renewed ©1992 by Harriet Lowell, Sheridan Lowell, and Caroline Lowell. Reprinted by permission of Farrar, Straus & Giroux, Inc. "The Magic Barrel" from THE MAGIC BARREL by Bernard Malamud. Copyright © 1958 and renewed © 1986 by Bernard Malamud. Reprinted by permission of Farrar, Straus & Giroux, Inc.

Harcourt Brace & Company
"The Jilting of Granny Weatherall" from FLOWERING JUDAS AND OTHER STORIES, copyright 1930 and renewed 1958 by Katherine Anne Porter, reprinted by permission of Harcourt Brace & Company. "Grass" from CORNHUSKERS by Carl Sandburg, copyright 1918 by Holt, Rinehart and Winston, Inc. and renewed 1946 by Carl Sandburg, reprinted by permission of Harcourt Brace & Company. "Everyday Use" from IN LOVE AND TROUBLE: STORIES OF BLACK WOMEN © 1973 by Alice Walker. Reprinted by permission of Harcourt Brace and Company. Booker T. Washington, "Boyhood Days," from *Up from Slavery.* Used by permission of Harcourt Brace & Company.

Harold Ober Associates
"A Black Man Talks of Reaping" by Arna Bontemps. Reprinted by permission of Harold Ober Associates Incorporated. Copyright © 1963 by Arna Bontemps.

HarperCollins Publishers, Inc.
"SONG OF SOLOMON" from COME TO ME by AMY BLOOM. Copyright © 1993 by Amy Bloom. Reprinted by permission of HarperCollins Publishers, Inc. EXCERPT from THEIR EYES WERE WATCHING GOD by ZORA NEALE HURSTON. Copyright 1937 by Harper & Row, Publishers, Inc. Renewed 1965 by John C. Hurston and Joel Hurston. Reprinted by permission of HarperCollins Publishers, Inc. ALL PAGES from "WALDEN" FROM ONE MAN'S MEAT by E. B. WHITE. Copyright 1939 by E. B. White. Copyright renewed 1967 by E. B. White. Reprinted by permission of HarperCollins Publishers, Inc.

Harvard University Press
Letter from Abigail Adams to John Adams. Reprinted by permission of the publishers from THE ADAMS FAMILY CORRESPONDENCE edited by L.H. Butterfield et al, Cambridge, Mass.: The Belknap Press of Harvard University Press, Copyright © 1963 by the Massachusetts Historical Society. "Some Verses Upon the Burning of Our House" and "To My Dear and Loving Husband." Reprinted by permission of the publishers from THE WORKS OF ANNE BRADSTREET edited by Jeannine Hensley, Cambridge, Mass.: The Belknap Press of Harvard University Press, Copyright © 1967 by the President and Fellows of Harvard College. From THE POEMS OF EMILY DICKINSON: "After great pain a formal feeling comes," "Because I could not stop for Death," "'Hope' is the thing with feathers," "I heard a Fly buzz—when I died—," "I never saw a Moor," "The Soul selects her own Society," "If you were coming in the fall," "Much Madness is divinest Sense," "There's a certain Slant of light," and "This is my letter to the World," Reprinted by permission of the publishers and

1952, 1953, 1954, renewed © 1980 by Arthur Miller. Used by permission of Viking Penguin, a division of Penguin Books USA, Inc. Excerpt from *The Grapes of Wrath* by John Steinbeck. Copyright 1939 by John Steinbeck, renewed © 1969 by John Steinbeck. Used by permission of Viking Penguin, a division of Penguin Books USA, Inc.

Princeton University Press

Taylor, Edward; HUSWIFERY. © 1943 by Princeton University Press. Reprinted by permission of Princeton University Press.

Random House, Inc.

From INVISIBLE MAN by Ralph Ellison. Copyright 1947, 1948, 1952 by Ralph Ellison. Reprinted by permission of Random House, Inc. "Address upon Receiving the Nobel Prize for Literature" From ESSAYS SPEECHES & PUBLIC LETTERS by William Faulkner, edited by James B. Meriwether. Copyright © 1950 by William Faulkner. Copyright © 1965 by Random House, Inc. Reprinted by permission of Random House, Inc. From THE GLASS MENAGERIE by Tennessee Williams. Copyright © 1945 by Tennessee Williams and Edwina D. Williams. Reprinted by permission of Random House, Inc.

Alberto Ríos

"The Lesson of Walls" from *Five Indiscretions* (Sheep Meadow Press), © 1985 by Alberto Ríos. Reprinted by permission of author. All rights reserved.

Simon and Schuster, Inc.

"Miniver Cheevy" from THE TOWN DOWN THE RIVER by Edwin Arlington Robinson (New York: Charles Scribner's Sons, 1910) "Mr. Flood's Party" Reprinted with permission of Simon & Schuster, Inc. from COLLECTED POEMS OF EDWIN ARLINGTON ROBINSON. Copyright 1921 by Edwin Arlington Robinson, renewed 1949 by Ruth Nivison. "Richard Cory" from THE CHILDREN OF THE NIGHT by Edwin Arlington Robinson (New York: Charles Scribner's Sons, 1987) Reprinted with permission of Scribner, Division of Simon & Schuster, Inc., from THE GREAT GATSBY ("Authorized Text") by F. Scott Fitzgerald. Copyright 1925 Charles Scribner's Sons. Copyright renewed 1953 by Frances Scott Fitzgerald Lanahan. Copyright © 1991, 1992 by Eleanor Lanahan, Matthew J. Bruccoli, and Samuel J. Lanahan as Trustees u/a dated 7/3/75, Created by Frances Scott Fitzgerald Smith. "A Clean, Well-Lighted Place." Reprinted with permission of Scribner, an imprint of Simon & Schuster, Inc., from WINNER TAKE NOTHING by Ernest Hemingway. Copyright 1933 Charles Scribner's Sons. Copyright renewed © 1961 by Mary Hemingway. "Poetry" Reprinted with permission of Simon & Schuster, Inc. from COLLECTED POEMS OF MARIANNE MOORE. Copyright 1935 by Marianne

Moore, renewed 1963 by Marianne Moore and T. S. Eliot.
Reprinted with the permission of Scribner, an imprint of Simon & Schuster, Inc. from THE AGE OF INNOCENCE by Edith Wharton. Copyright 1920 D. Appleton and Company; copyright renewed 1948 William R. Tyler.

Sterling Lord Literistic, Inc.

Crisis, No.1, by Thomas Paine. From THE SELECTED WORK OF TOM PAINE, edited by Howard Fast. Reprinted by permission of Sterling Lord Literistic, Inc. Copyright © 1945 by Howard Fast.

Sunstone Press

"Song of the Sky Loom" This poem from SONGS OF THE TEWA by Joseph Spinden appears courtesy of Sunstone Press, Box 2321, Santa Fe, NM 87504-2321, USA.

Syracuse University Press

From "The Iroquois Constitution" from Arthur C. Parker, "The Constitution of the Five Nations" in *Parker on the Iroquois,* edited with an introduction by William N. Fenton. Syracuse, N.Y.: Syracuse University Press, 1968. By permission of the publisher.

University of North Carolina Press

"To S. M., a Young African Painter, on Seeing His Works" and "To the Right Honorable William, Earl of Dartmouth." Reprinted from THE POEMS OF PHILLIS WHEATLEY. Revised and enlarged edition. Edited by Julian D. Mason, Jr. Copyright © 1989 by the University of North Carolina Press. Used by permission of the publisher.

University Press of New England

James Dickey, "For the last Wolverine" from *Poems 1957–1967* © 1978 by James Dickey, Wesleyan University Press by permission of University Press of New England.

University Press of Virginia

"A Mystery of Heroism" from *The Complete Works of Stephen Crane, Volume 60,* edited by Fredson Bowers (Charlottesville: Virginia 1969) Used by permission of the University Press of Virginia.

Wieser and Wieser, Inc.

"Auto Wreck" by Karl Shapiro. Copyright © 1968 by Karl Shapiro and appears by arrangement with Weiser and Weiser, Inc. 118 East 25th Street, New York, NY 10010.

William Morrow & Company, Inc.

Text of "Winter Poem" from MY HOUSE by Nikki Giovanni. Copyright © 1972 by Nikki Giovanni. By permission of William Morrow and Company, Inc. Text pgs. 66–70 from BLUES PEOPLE by LeRoi Jones. Copyright © 1963 by LeRoi Jones. By permission of William Morrow and Company, Inc.

The Estate of William Stafford

"A Story That Could Be True" and "Traveling Though the Dark," by William Stafford. Copyright © 1978 William Stafford, from *Stories That Could Be True* (Harper & Row). Reprinted by permission of The Estate of William Stafford.

James Worley

Selected poems by James Worley reprinted by permission of the author.

Yale University Press

"Sinners in the Hands of an Angry God" by Jonathan Edwards from *Images Or Shadows of Divine Things* (The Works of Jonathan Edwards). By permission of Yale University Press.

Every effort has been made to trace the ownership of all copyrighted selections found in this book. Omissions brought to our attention will be corrected in subsequent editions.